International
Energy Agency

Secure • Sustainable • Together

World
Energy
Outlook
2014

INTERNATIONAL ENERGY AGENCY

The International Energy Agency (IEA), an autonomous agency, was established in November 1974. Its primary mandate was – and is – two-fold: to promote energy security amongst its member countries through collective response to physical disruptions in oil supply, and provide authoritative research and analysis on ways to ensure reliable, affordable and clean energy for its 29 member countries and beyond. The IEA carries out a comprehensive programme of energy co-operation among its member countries, each of which is obliged to hold oil stocks equivalent to 90 days of its net imports. The Agency's aims include the following objectives:

■ Secure member countries' access to reliable and ample supplies of all forms of energy; in particular, through maintaining effective emergency response capabilities in case of oil supply disruptions.

■ Promote sustainable energy policies that spur economic growth and environmental protection in a global context – particularly in terms of reducing greenhouse-gas emissions that contribute to climate change.

■ Improve transparency of international markets through collection and analysis of energy data.

■ Support global collaboration on energy technology to secure future energy supplies and mitigate their environmental impact, including through improved energy efficiency and development and deployment of low-carbon technologies.

■ Find solutions to global energy challenges through engagement and dialogue with non-member countries, industry, international organisations and other stakeholders.

IEA member countries:

Australia
Austria
Belgium
Canada
Czech Republic
Denmark
Estonia
Finland
France
Germany
Greece
Hungary
Ireland
Italy
Japan
Korea (Republic of)
Luxembourg
Netherlands
New Zealand
Norway
Poland
Portugal
Slovak Republic
Spain
Sweden
Switzerland
Turkey
United Kingdom
United States

International
Energy Agency
1974●2014

Secure ● Sustainable ● Together

The European Commission
also participates in
the work of the IEA.

Few propositions gain unanimity as readily as the case for rapidly developing sub-Saharan Africa's energy infrastructure; while few issues are so controversial between nations as the place nuclear power should take in future global energy supply.

Controversy and challenge, however, do not daunt Dr. Fatih Birol and his team as they bring objective information and projections to bear on energy issues, nor do they hesitate to draw out the implications of their findings. In this year's *World Energy Outlook*, they explore in depth the energy needs and possibilities of Africa and the situation and prospects for nuclear power. These are the themes of this year's special features, set alongside the comprehensive coverage of other fields and energy issues so familiar to our readers, with projections now extending to 2040.

Increasing access to modern forms of energy is crucial to unlocking faster economic and social development in Africa, specifically in sub-Saharan Africa. More than two-thirds of the population live without electricity, and many more rely on dangerous, inefficient forms of cooking. A better functioning energy sector is vital to ensuring that the citizens of Africa can fulfil their aspirations.

The share of nuclear power in global electricity generation peaked at 18% almost twenty years ago and has been in decline ever since. Its future prospects are now particularly uncertain in many parts of the world. But whatever happens – retreat, recovery or renaissance – nuclear power is and will remain an important part of energy policy as it inherently works on long timelines. Plants require extensive planning and construction time and, once built, operate for decades while producing radioactive waste that needs to be safely isolated for thousands of years.

The IEA has argued for many years that energy supply can be regarded as secure only if it is produced and delivered in a manner compatible with modern environmental expectations. But winning public acceptance today goes well beyond that; and social acceptance, in this broader sense, is a constant theme of the *WEO*. Advocates of particular energy solutions must convince a sceptical public that they have satisfactory answers to the full range of related social, environmental and safety issues. This is particularly true for nuclear power, where proponents and opponents alike need to convince their citizens of their answers to the challenges that may arise from its use or from its abandonment. Sub-Saharan African economies will not take off until entrepreneurs and investors are convinced that they can have confidence in the continuity of electricity supply and the integrity of the business environment. Those concerned about climate change must be assured that energy will be supplied by means which are compatible with international climate goals.

I trust that readers will find within this report analysis and insights that will help them make better energy choices. I also encourage those interested in diving further into any of the subjects covered in this *WEO* to also take a look at other IEA publications, such as our Medium-Term Reports and our Energy Technology Perspectives series – the *WEO* is a flagship publication of the IEA, which is complimented by many others that cover a broad range of topics and time horizons.

This publication is issued under my authority as Executive Director of the IEA.

Maria van der Hoeven
Executive Director
International Energy Agency

This study was prepared by the Directorate of Global Energy Economics of the International Energy Agency in co-operation with other directorates and offices of the Agency. It was designed and directed by **Fatih Birol**, Chief Economist of the IEA. **Laura Cozzi** co-ordinated the analysis of Africa, efficiency and overall demand modelling; **Amos Bromhead** co-ordinated the analysis of nuclear and fossil-fuel subsidies; **Tim Gould** co-ordinated the analysis of Africa, oil, natural gas and coal; **Marco Baroni** co-ordinated the analysis of power, renewables and nuclear; **Dan Dorner** co-ordinated the analysis of Africa; and **Timur Gül** co-ordinated the analysis of transport and demand modelling. Other colleagues in the Directorate of Global Energy Economics contributed to multiple aspects of the analysis and were instrumental in delivering the study: **Ali Al-Saffar** (Africa, oil); **Christian Besson** (oil, natural gas); **Alessandro Blasi** (natural gas, Africa); **Stéphanie Bouckaert** (Africa, buildings); **Ian Cronshaw** (coal, natural gas); **Capella Festa** (Africa, oil); **Matthew Frank** (nuclear, renewables); **Antoine Herzog** (nuclear); **Shigetoshi Ikeyama** (nuclear, policies); **Bartosz Jurga** (unconventional gas, oil); **Fabian Kęsicki** (efficiency, competitiveness); **Soo-Il Kim** (buildings, policies); **Hui Shan Koh** (fossil-fuel subsidies, nuclear); **Atsuhito Kurozumi** (assumptions, policies); **Bertrand Magné** (Africa, competitiveness); **Ugbizi Banbeshie Ogar** (Africa); **Paweł Olejarnik** (oil, natural gas, coal); **Kristine Petrosyan** (oil, Africa); **Stéphane Rouhier** (nuclear); **Nora Selmet** (energy access, fossil-fuel subsidies); **Daniele Sinopoli** (Africa, renewables); **Shigeru Suehiro** (Africa, industry); **Timur Topalgoekceli** (Africa, oil); **Johannes Trüby** (power, coal); **Kees Van Noort** (Africa, natural gas); **Brent Wanner** (Africa, power, renewables); **David Wilkinson** (power, renewables, nuclear); **Georgios Zazias** (fossil-fuel subsidies, Africa); **Shuwei Zhang** (transport, Africa). **Lucius Mayer-Tasch** and **Henri Dziomba** (Deutsche Gesellschaft für Internationale Zusammenarbeit [GIZ]), and **Almag Fira Pradana** (University College London) were also part of the *Outlook* team. **MaryRose Cleere, Teresa Coon and Sandra Mooney** provided essential support. More details about the team can be found at *www.worldenergyoutlook.org*.

Robert Priddle carried editorial responsibility.

The study also benefited from input provided by numerous IEA experts. In particular, Manuel Baritaud, Simon Bennett, Philippe Benoit, Pierre Boileau, Toril Bosoni, Adam Brown, Tyler Bryant, Pierpaolo Cazzola, Emmanouil Christinakis, Carlos Fernández Alvarez, Araceli Fernández Pales, Paolo Frankl, Rebecca Gaghen, Jean-François Gagné, Stephen Gallogly, Jean-Yves Garnier, Veronika Gyuricza, Antoine Halff, Harald Hecking, Wolf Heidug, Christina Hood, Didier Houssin, Juho Lipponen, Lorcan Lyons, Sean McCoy, Matthew Parry, Vida Rozite, Keisuke Sadamori, Misako Takahashi, Cecilia Tam, László Varró and Roman Wisznia. Thanks go to the IEA's Communication and Information Office for their help in producing the final report, and to Bertrand Sadin and Anne Mayne for graphics. Experts from the OECD and the Nuclear Energy Agency (NEA) also contributed to the report: Henri Paillere, Ronald Steenblik and Robert Vance. Debra Justus was the copy-editor.

François Lévêque (Mines ParisTech), Trevor Morgan (Menecon Consulting), Uğur Öcal (Ocal Energy Consulting), Hans-Holger Rogner (Royal Institute of Technology) and Jay Wagner (Plexus Energy) provided valuable input to the analysis.

The special focus on Africa benefited from collaboration with the following organisations: African Development Bank; African Union; CITAC Africa Ltd; GIZ; European Union Energy Initiative Partnership Dialogue Facility; Government of Germany; Government of Italy; Government of Norway; Government of the United Kingdom; Government of the United States; Milan Polytechnic, Department of Energy, Italy; Nigerian Central Bank; Nigerian National Petroleum Corporation; OECD Development Centre; Royal Institute of Technology, Division of Energy Systems Analysis (KTH-dESA), Sweden and their sponsors at the World Bank and the Swedish International Development Cooperation Agency (SIDA); Department of Energy, South Africa; and World Economic Forum.

The work could not have been achieved without the support and co-operation provided by many government bodies, organisations and companies worldwide, notably: Natural Resources Canada; CEZ; Climate Works Foundation; Ministry of Foreign Affairs, Denmark; Enel; Eni; Economic Research Institute for ASEAN and East Asia (ERIA); Directorate-General for the Environment, European Commission; Gestore dei Servizi Energetici (GSE); IEA Coal Industry Advisory Board; The Institute of Energy Economics, Japan; Ministry of Economy, Trade and Industry, Japan; Korea Energy Economics Institute; Michelin; Ministry of Economic Affairs, the Netherlands; Ministry of Foreign Affairs, Norway; Oak Ridge National Laboratory; Polish Geological Institute; Schlumberger; Schneider Electric; Shell; Statoil; Terna; Toshiba Corporation; Toyota Motor Corporation; Department of Energy and Climate Change, United Kingdom; Foreign and Commonwealth Office, United Kingdom; Department of Energy, United States; Vattenfall; and Westinghouse.

A number of workshops and meetings were organised to get essential input to this study. The participants offered valuable new insights, feedback and data for this analysis.

- World Energy Investment Outlook, Paris: 28 February 2014
- IEA Unconventional Gas Forum, Calgary: 25-26 March 2014
- The Future of Nuclear Power, Paris: 31 March 2014
- Africa Energy Outlook, Paris: 14-15 April 2014

Further details on these events are at *www.worldenergyoutlook.org/aboutweo/workshops* and *www.iea.org/ugforum*.

IEA Energy Business Council

Special thanks go to the companies that participated in the activities of the IEA Energy Business Council (EBC) during 2014, as these generated valuable inputs to this study. The EBC is the overarching body through which the IEA interacts with industry and brings together many of the world's largest companies involved in all aspects of the energy industry. Further details may be found at *www.iea.org/energybusinesscouncil*.

Peer reviewers

Many senior government officials and international experts provided input and reviewed preliminary drafts of the report. Their comments and suggestions were of great value. They include:

Emmanuel Ackom	UNEP DTU Partnership
Prasoon Agarwal	Global Green Growth Institute
Hamad Al Kaabi	Permanent Mission of the UAE to the International Atomic Energy Agency
Marco Annunziata	General Electric
Olivier Appert	French Institute of Petroleum
Marco Arcelli	Enel
Christopher Baker	Department of Climate Change and Energy Efficiency, Australia
Joachim Balke	European Commission
Andrew Barfour	Ministry for Energy and Petroleum, Ghana
Paul Baruya	IEA Clean Coal Centre
Georg Bäuml	Volkswagen
Nazim Bayraktar	Independent consultant
Chris Beaton	Global Subsidies Initiative
Carmen Becerril	Acciona Energia
H.E. Kamel Bennaceur	Minister of Industry, Energy and Mines, Tunisia
Raphaël Berger	AREVA
Paul Bertheau	Reiner Lemoine Institut
Ashok Bhargava	Asian Development Bank
Tomas Björnsson	Vattenfall
Kornelis Blok	Ecofys
Aad van Bohemen	Ministry of Economic Affairs, The Netherlands
Rina Bohle Zeller	Vestas
Nils Borg	European Council for an Energy Efficient Economy
Jean-Paul Bouttes	EDF
Keith Bowen	Eskom
Daniel Brady	Natural Resources Canada
Albert Bressand	Rijksuniversiteit Groningen and Columbia Center for Sustainable Investment
Nigel Bruce	World Health Organization
Mick Buffier	Glencore
Nick Butler	King's College London
Francisco Caballero-Sanz	European Commission
Ron Cameron	Nuclear consultant to UK government

Claudia Canevari	European Commission
Antonio de Castro	Petrobras
Peter Cattelaens	EU Energy Initiative Partnership Dialogue Facility
Bong Seok Choi	Korea Energy Economics Institute
Kieran Clarke	Global Subsidies Initiative
Elisabeth Clemens	Ministry of Foreign Affairs, Norway
Benedict Clements	International Monetary Fund
Emanuela Colombo	Milan Polytechnic, Department of Energy, Italy
John Corben	Schlumberger
Matthew Crozat	Department of Energy, United States
Pavel Cyrani	CEZ
Ralf Dickel	Energy Consultant
Giles Dickson	ALSTOM
Carmine Difiglio	Department of Energy, United States
Ryoji Doi	Ministry of Economy, Trade and Industry (METI), Japan
Jens Drillisch	KfW, Germany
Francois Durvye	Schlumberger
Adeline Duterque	GDF SUEZ
Luis Echavarri	Former Secretary General, OECD Nuclear Energy Agency
Hussein Elhag	African Energy Commission
Jonathan Elkind	Department of Energy, United States
Mosad Elmissiry	NEPAD
Mike Enskat	GIZ, Germany
Joseph Essandoh-Yeddu	Energy Commission, Ghana
Latsoucabé Fall	World Energy Council
Liwen Feng	China Energy Net Consulting
Nikki Fisher	Anglo American
Patrick Foo	Energy Market Authority, Singapore
John Foran	Natural Resources Canada
John Francis Kitonga	Ministry of Energy and Minerals, Tanzania
Peter Fraser	Ontario Energy Board, Canada
Antony Froggatt	Chatham House
Kenichiro Fujimoto	Nippon Steel & Sumitomo Metal Corporation
Francis Gatare	Government of Rwanda
Francesco Gattei	Eni
Adama Gaye	Newforce Africa
Elitsa Georgieva	CITAC Africa Limited
Dolf Gielen	International Renewable Energy Agency (IRENA)

Avi Gopstein	Department of State, United States
Andrii Gritsevskyi	International Atomic Energy Agency
Haruna Gujba	African Union
John Hamre	Center for Strategic and International Studies
Wenke Han	Energy Research Institute of NDRC, China
Ali Hasanbeigi	Lawrence Berkeley National Laboratory
Hergen Haye	Department of Energy and Climate Change, United Kingdom
Klas Heising	GIZ, Germany
James Henderson	Oxford Institute of Energy Studies
Andrew Herscowitz	Agency for International Development (Power Africa), United States
Masazumi Hirono	Japan Gas Association
Mark Howells	Royal Institute of Technology (KTH-dESA), Sweden
Tom Howes	European Commission
Noé van Hulst	Delegation of the Netherlands to the OECD
Elham Ibrahim	African Union
Robert Ichord	Department of State, United States
Anil Jain	Planning Commission, India
Kanya Williams James	Central Bank of Nigeria
Ivan Jaques	World Bank
James Jensen	Jensen Associates
Jan-Hein Jesse	Clingendael Institute
Marianne Kah	ConocoPhillips
Michio Kawamata	Mitsubishi Corporation
Daniel Ketoto	Office of the President, Kenya
Hisham Khatib	World Energy Council
Shinichi Kihara	Ministry of Economy, Trade and Industry (METI), Japan
Bongsuck Kim	KEPCO
Mike Kirst	Westinghouse EMEA
John Francis Kitonga	Ministry of Energy and Minerals, Tanzania
David Knapp	Energy Intelligence Group
Ron Knapp	International Aluminium Institute
Joerg Koehli	European Commission
Masami Kojima	World Bank
Joel Nana Kontchou	Schlumberger
Robert Kool	Europe NL Agency
Doug Koplow	Earth Track
Ken Koyama	Institute of Energy Economics, Japan

Sarah Ladislaw	Center for Strategic and International Studies
Richard Lavergne	Ministry of Ecology, Sustainable Development and Energy, France
Benoit Lebot	International Partnership for Energy Efficiency Cooperation
Steve Lennon	Eskom
Miroslaw Lewinski	Ministry of Economy, Poland
Yanfei Li	Economic Research Institute for ASEAN and East Asia (ERIA)
Wenge Liu	China Coal Information Institute
Xiaoli Liu	Energy Research Institute of NDRC, China
Peter Lyons	Department of Energy, United States
Joan MacNaughton	Energy Institute, London
Teresa Malyshev	The Charcoal Project
Claude Mandil	Former Executive Director, IEA
Elizabeth Marabwa	Department of Energy, South Africa
Luigi Marras	Ministry of Foreign Affairs, Italy
William Martin	Washington Policy & Analysis
Taketo Matsumoto	The Kansai Electric Power Company
Michael Mellish	Department of Energy, United States
Lawrence Metzroth	Independent consultant
Tatiana Mitrova	Energy Research Institute of the Russian Academy of Sciences
Vijay Modi	Columbia University, Earth Institute
Jacques Moulot	African Development Bank
Mark Muldowney	BNP Paribas
Steve Nadel	American Council for an Energy-Efficient Economy (ACEEE)
Itaru Nakamura	J-Power
Laura Nhancale	Ministry of Energy, Mozambique
Philippe Niyongabo	African Union
H.E. Fidel M. Meñe Nkogo	Deputy Minister of Mining, Industry and Energy, Equatorial Guinea
Koshi Noguchi	Toshiba of Europe
Petter Nore	Ministry of Foreign Affairs, Norway
Bright Okogu	Federal Ministry of Finance, Nigeria
Tim Okon	Nigerian National Petroleum Corporation
Rodolphe Olard	ING Group
Patrick Oliva	Michelin
Todd Onderdonk	ExxonMobil
Ciro Pagano	Eni
Monojeet Pal	African Development Bank
Marilena Petraglia	TERNA

Volkmar Pflug	Siemens
Christian Pichat	AREVA
Roberto Potí	Edison
David Powell	GE Hitachi
Ireneusz Pyc	Siemens
Pamela Quanrud	Department of State, United States
Pippo Ranci	Florence School of Regulation, European University Institute
Anil Razdan	Energy and Environment Foundation, India
Christhian Rengifo	UX Consulting Company
Gustav Resch	Vienna University of Technology, Austria
Brian Ricketts	EURACOAL
Agneta Rising	World Nuclear Association
Alex Rugamba	African Development Bank
Jeffrey Sachs	Earth Institute and United Nations
Jamal Saghir	World Bank
Kostis Sakellaris	European Commission
Yoshitaka Sato	The Japan Steel Works
Steve Sawyer	Global Wind Energy Council
Jules Schers	CIRED
Hans-Wilhelm Schiffer	Consultant and Advisor to the Executive Board of RWE
Sandro Schmidt	German Federal Institute for Geosciences and Natural Resources (BGR)
Hana-Muriel Setteboun	FK Group
Baoguo Shan	State Grid Energy Research Institute, China
Adnan Shihab-Eldin	Kuwait Foundation for the Advancement of Sciences
David Shropshire	International Atomic Energy Agency
Maria Sicilia Salvadores	Ministry of Industry, Energy and Tourism, Spain
Jonathan Sinton	World Bank
Christopher Snary	Department of Energy and Climate Change, United Kingdom
Yasunori Sota	Hitachi
James Steel	Department of Energy and Climate Change, United Kingdom
Jonathan Stern	Oxford Institute of Energy Studies
Even Stormoen	Ministry of Foreign Affairs, Norway
Ulrik Stridbaek	Dong Energy
Ørnulf Strøm	Ministry of Foreign Affairs, Norway
Dmitriy Sukhanov	Rosatom
Cartan Sumner	Peabody Energy
Glen Sweetnam	Department of Energy, United States

Minoru Takada	United Nations
Mika Takehara	Japan Oil, Gas and Metals National Corporation (JOGMEC)
Kuniharu Takemata	J-POWER
Nobuo Tanaka	Former Executive Director, IEA
Tom Tannion	Nuclear Electric Insurance
Wim Thomas	Shell
Philippine de T'serclaes	Schneider Electric
Sergey Tverdokhleb	Siberian Coal Energy Company (SUEK)
Jo Tyndall	Ministry of Foreign Affairs and Trade, New Zealand
Timothy E. Valentine	Oak Ridge National Lab
Frank Verrastro	Center for Strategic and International Studies
Damon Vis-Dunbar	Global Subsidies Initiative
Gerhard Wächter	European Commission
Kristin Wæringsaasen	Ministry of Foreign Affairs, Norway
Eirik Wærness	Statoil
H.E. Alhaji Mohammed Wakil	Minister of State for Power, Nigeria
Molly Walton	Center for Strategic and International Studies
Henry Wang	SABIC
Graham Weale	RWE
Rick Westerdale	Department of State, United States
Peter Westerheide	BASF
Marcus Wiemann	Alliance for Rural Electrification
Jacob Williams	Peabody Energy
Steve Winberg	Battelle
Peter Wooders	Global Subsidies Initiative
Sun Xiansheng	China National Petroleum Corporation (CNPC)
Xiaojie Xu	Chinese Academy of Sciences
Dadi Zhou	Energy Research Institute of NDRC, China
Florian Ziegler	KfW, Germany

The individuals and organisations that contributed to this study are not responsible for any opinions or judgments it contains. All errors and omissions are solely the responsibility of the IEA.

Comments and questions are welcome and should be addressed to:

Dr. Fatih Birol
Chief Economist
Director, Directorate of Global Energy Economics
International Energy Agency
9, rue de la Fédération
75739 Paris Cedex 15
France

Telephone: (33-1) 40 57 66 70
Email: weo@iea.org

More information about the *World Energy Outlook* is available at
www.worldenergyoutlook.org.

TABLE OF CONTENTS

PART A
**GLOBAL
ENERGY
TRENDS**

PART B
**OUTLOOK FOR
NUCLEAR POWER**

PART C
**AFRICA
ENERGY
OUTLOOK**

ANNEXES

A FRAMEWORK FOR OUR ENERGY FUTURE | 1

GLOBAL ENERGY TRENDS TO 2040 | 2

OIL MARKET OUTLOOK | 3

NATURAL GAS MARKET OUTLOOK | 4

COAL MARKET OUTLOOK | 5

POWER SECTOR OUTLOOK | 6

RENEWABLE ENERGY OUTLOOK | 7

ENERGY EFFICIENCY OUTLOOK | 8

FOSSIL-FUEL SUBSIDIES | 9

NUCLEAR POWER TODAY AND DECISIONS TO COME | 10

PROSPECTS FOR NUCLEAR POWER TO 2040 | 11

THE IMPLICATIONS OF NUCLEAR POWER | 12

ENERGY IN AFRICA TODAY | 13

OUTLOOK FOR AFRICAN ENERGY TO 2040 | 14

AFRICAN ENERGY ISSUES IN FOCUS | 15

BUILDING A PATH TO PROSPERITY | 16

ANNEXES

Foreword   3
Acknowledgements   5
Executive Summary   23

Part A: GLOBAL ENERGY TRENDS   31

1   A framework for our energy future   33
Scope of the report   34
Methodological approach   35
   Modelling framework   35
   Defining the scenarios   36
Main non-policy assumptions   39
   Economic growth   39
   Demographic trends   42
   Carbon-dioxide prices   44
   Technology   45
Energy supply costs and prices   47
   Oil prices   49
   Natural gas prices   50
   Coal prices   52

2   Global energy trends to 2040   53
Energy trends by scenario   54
Energy trends in the New Policies Scenario   56
   Demand   56
   Supply   74
   Inter-regional trade   80
   Energy investment   84
Energy-related CO_2 emissions   86
   Recent developments   86
   Emissions and climate impact in the New Policies Scenario   87
   450 Scenario   89

3   Oil market outlook   95
Global overview   96
Demand   98
   Regional trends   98
   Sectoral trends   101
   Trends by product   108
Production   110
   Resources and reserves   110
   Production prospects   114
Refining and trade   131
   Trade in crude oil and oil products   133

4 Natural gas market outlook 135

Global overview 136
Demand 137
  Regional trends 137
  Sectoral trends 143
Production 146
  Resources and reserves 146
  Gas production trends 146
Outlook for gas supply security 158
  Rising gas import needs 159
  A growing cast of gas suppliers 161
  Implications for the main importing regions 166

5 Coal market outlook 171

Overview 172
Demand 176
  Regional trends 176
Sectoral trends 179
Supply 181
  Reserves and resources 181
  Production 181
  Trade 183
  Pricing of internationally traded coal 185
  Costs and investment 189
Regional insights 191
  China 191
  United States 194
  India 197
  Europe 199

6 Power sector outlook 201

Context 202
Electricity demand 204
Electricity supply 208
  Overview 208
  Power generation capacity 208
  Power generation 215
  Investment 217
  Power generation costs 221
  Electricity-related carbon-dioxide emissions 225
Electricity prices 226
  Industry 227
  Residential 229
Regional focus 230
  United States 230

European Union   231

Japan   233

China   234

India   235

Middle East   236

7   **Renewable energy outlook**   239

Recent trends and policies   240

Outlook by scenario   241

Renewables outlook by sector in the New Policies Scenario   243

Global and regional trends   243

Sectoral trends   244

Power generation   246

Transport   251

Industry and buildings   254

Avoided CO_2 emissions   255

Renewables outlook by source in the New Policies Scenario   257

Bioenergy   257

Hydropower   259

Wind power   261

Solar photovoltaics   264

Other renewables   270

Economics of renewables   271

Investment   271

Subsidies   274

8   **Energy efficiency outlook**   279

Introduction   280

Current status of energy efficiency   280

Recent progress   280

Recent policy developments   282

Outlook for energy efficiency   285

Trends by fuel   287

Trends by sector   291

Energy efficiency and competitiveness   300

How energy efficiency affects international competitiveness   301

Scope for energy efficiency to cut costs in energy-intensive industries   302

Impact of improved energy efficiency on economic competitiveness   308

Broader benefits   310

Household spending on energy   310

Fossil-fuel import bills   311

CO_2 emissions   312

9   **Fossil-fuel subsidies**   313

Overview   314

Identifying the problem   315
    Defining fossil-fuel subsidies   315
    Forms of subsidy and why they exist   315
    Why reform is needed   317
Measuring their size   318
    Methodology   318
    Estimates of fossil-fuel subsidies in 2013   320
Impacts of fossil-fuel subsidies on clean energy technologies   324
    Low-carbon power generation   324
    Energy efficiency   326
Implementing reforms   328
    Recent policy developments   329
    Case studies of reform   329
    Guidelines on best practice   340

Part B: OUTLOOK FOR NUCLEAR POWER   **345**

10 Nuclear power today and decisions to come   347
Context   348
    Historical and current developments   348
    Reactor technology and designs   353
Policy framework   356
    Countries with existing programmes   358
    Potential newcomer countries   361
Economics and financing   362
    Economics of existing capacity   365
    Economics of new builds   366
    Financing   373
Facing public concerns   375
    Issues across the lifecycle of nuclear power   377
    Risk, perception and public opinion   381

11 Prospects for nuclear power to 2040   383
Introduction   384
New Policies Scenario   384
    Approach and key assumptions   384
    Nuclear power capacity and generation   386
    Investment needs and associated costs   391
    Regional trends   394
Low Nuclear Case   400
    Developments that could slow the expansion of nuclear power   400
    Assumptions   401
    Nuclear power capacity and generation   402
High Nuclear Case   403
    Assumptions   403
    Nuclear power capacity and generation   404

450 Scenario   405
Outlook for nuclear fuel   406

12   **The implications of nuclear power**   **411**
Introduction   412
Energy security   413
    Energy trade, self-sufficiency and diversity   414
National economic considerations   418
Environment   419
    CO_2 emissions   420
    High-level radioactive waste disposal   423
    Water   427
Policy priorities for nuclear power   427

Part C: AFRICA ENERGY OUTLOOK   **431**

13   **Energy in Africa today**   **433**
Context   434
    Economy   434
    Demography   438
    Business environment and infrastructure   439
    Governance   440
Access to modern energy   441
    Access to electricity   444
    Access to clean cooking facilities   448
Overview of energy demand   450
    Power sector   453
    End-use sectors   459
Overview of energy resources and supply   461
    Oil and natural gas   462
    Renewables   469
    Other   474
Energy trade   475
Energy affordability   478

14   **Outlook for African energy to 2040**   **483**
Projecting future developments   484
    Economic and population growth   484
    Policy environment   487
Overview of energy demand trends   490
Outlook for the power sector   493
    Electricity demand   493
    Electricity supply   495
    Electricity transmission and trade   500
Outlook for other energy-consuming sectors   500
    Residential   502

	Transport	503
	Productive uses	505
	Outlook for energy supply	507
	Oil	507
	Natural gas	512
	Coal	516
	Renewables	518
	International energy trade	524
	Crude oil	524
	Oil products	525
	Natural gas	526
	Coal	529
	Energy and the environment	530
	Energy-related CO_2 emissions	531
	Deforestation and forest degradation	532

15 African energy issues in focus — 535

Five features of Africa's energy outlook — 536
Electricity access: what is the path to power? — 536
Biomass: here to stay? — 545
Is oil the way forward for Nigeria? — 552
South Africa: will energy diversity deliver? — 560
Mozambique and Tanzania: how to get best value from gas? — 568

16 Building a path to prosperity — 575

Towards a better-functioning sub-Saharan energy sector — 576
Three keys to Africa's energy future — 579
Investment in the region's energy supply — 579
Making the most of Africa's resources — 589
Regional energy co-operation and integration — 593
An African Century Case — 595
Africa's energy choices in a global context — 598

ANNEXES — 601

Annex A. Tables for scenario projections — 603
Annex B. Policies and measures by scenario — 687
Annex C. Definitions — 699
Annex D. References — 711

An energy system under stress

The global energy system is in danger of falling short of the hopes and expectations placed upon it. Turmoil in parts of the Middle East – which remains the only large source of low-cost oil – has rarely been greater since the oil shocks in the 1970s. Conflict between Russia and Ukraine has reignited concerns about gas security. Nuclear power, which for some countries plays a strategic role in energy security (and which is examined in depth in this edition of the *World Energy Outlook* [*WEO-2014*]), faces an uncertain future. Electricity remains inaccessible to many people, including two out of every three people in sub-Saharan Africa (the regional focus in *WEO-2014*). The point of departure for the climate negotiations, due to reach a climax in 2015, is not encouraging: a continued rise in global greenhouse-gas emissions and stifling air pollution in many of the world's fast-growing cities.

Advances in technology and efficiency give some reasons for optimism, but sustained political efforts will be essential to change energy trends for the better. Signs of stress would be much more serious, were it not for improvements in efficiency and continuous efforts to innovate and reduce the cost of emerging energy technologies, such as solar photovoltaics (PV). But global energy trends are not easily changed and worries over the security and sustainability of energy supply will not resolve themselves. Actions from well-informed policy-makers, industry and other stakeholders are needed. *WEO-2014*, with projections and analysis extended to 2040 for the first time, provides insights that can help to ensure that the energy system is changed by design, rather than just by events.

Energy: the answer to – and the cause of – some urgent problems

Global energy demand is set to grow by 37% by 2040 in our central scenario, but the development path for a growing world population and economy is less energy-intensive than it used to be. In our central scenario, growth in global demand slows markedly, from above 2% per year over the last two decades to 1% per year after 2025; this is a result both of price and policy effects, and a structural shift in the global economy towards services and lighter industrial sectors. The global distribution of energy demand changes more dramatically, with energy use essentially flat in much of Europe, Japan, Korea and North America, and rising consumption concentrated in the rest of Asia (60% of the global total), Africa, the Middle East and Latin America. A landmark is reached in the early 2030s, when China becomes the largest oil-consuming country, crossing paths with the United States, where oil use falls back to levels not seen for decades. But, by this time, it is India, Southeast Asia, the Middle East and sub-Saharan Africa that take over as the engines of global energy demand growth.

By 2040, the world's energy supply mix divides into four almost-equal parts: oil, gas, coal and low-carbon sources. Resources are not a constraint over this period, but each of these four pillars faces a distinct set of challenges. Policy choices and market developments that bring the share of fossil fuels in primary energy demand down to just under three-quarters in 2040 are not enough to stem the rise in energy-related carbon dioxide (CO_2) emissions, which grow by one-fifth. This puts the world on a path consistent with a long-term global average temperature increase of 3.6 °C. The Intergovernmental Panel on Climate Change estimates that in order to limit this temperature increase to 2 °C – the internationally agreed goal to avert the most severe and widespread implications of climate change – the world cannot emit more than around 1 000 gigatonnes of CO_2 from 2014 onwards. This entire budget will be used up by 2040 in our central scenario. Since emissions are not going to drop suddenly to zero once this point is reached, it is clear that the 2 °C objective requires urgent action to steer the energy system on to a safer path. This will be the focus of a *WEO Special Report*, to be released in mid-2015 in advance of the critical UN climate talks in Paris.

Energy security concerns on the rise

The short-term picture of a well-supplied oil market should not disguise the challenges that lie ahead as reliance grows on a relatively small number of producers. Regional oil demand trends are quite distinct: for each barrel of oil no longer used in OECD countries, two barrels more are used in the non-OECD. Increased oil use for transport and petrochemicals drives demand higher, from 90 million barrels per day (mb/d) in 2013 to 104 mb/d in 2040, although high prices and new policy measures gradually constrain the pace of overall consumption growth, bringing it towards a plateau. Investment of some $900 billion per year in upstream oil and gas development is needed by the 2030s to meet projected demand, but there are many uncertainties over whether this investment will be forthcoming in time – especially once United States tight oil output levels off in the early 2020s and its total production eventually starts to fall back. The complexity and capital-intensity of developing Brazilian deepwater fields, the difficulty of replicating the US tight oil experience at scale outside North America, unresolved questions over the outlook for growth in Canadian oil sands output, the sanctions that restrict Russian access to technologies and capital markets and – above all – the political and security challenges in Iraq could all contribute to a shortfall in investment below the levels required. The situation in the Middle East is a major concern given steadily increasing reliance on this region for oil production growth, especially for Asian countries that are set to import two out of every three barrels of crude traded internationally by 2040.

Demand for natural gas grows by more than half, the fastest rate among the fossil fuels, and increasingly flexible global trade in liquefied natural gas (LNG) offers some protection against the risk of supply disruptions. The main regions that push global gas demand higher are China and the Middle East, but gas also becomes the leading fuel in the OECD energy mix by around 2030, helped by new regulations in the United States limiting power sector emissions. In contrast to oil, gas production increases almost everywhere (Europe is the main exception) and unconventional gas accounts for almost 60% of global supply growth. The key uncertainty – outside North America – is whether gas can be made available at prices that are attractive to consumers while still offering incentives for the necessary large capital-intensive investments in gas supply; this is an issue of domestic regulation in many of the emerging non-OECD markets, notably in India and across the Middle East, as well as a concern in international trade. Import needs are set to rise across much of Asia as well as in Europe, but concerns about the security of future gas supply are allayed in part by a growing cast of international gas suppliers, a near-tripling of global liquefaction sites and a rising share of LNG that can be re-directed in response to the short-term needs of increasingly interconnected regional markets.

While coal is abundant and its supply secure, its future use is constrained by measures to tackle pollution and reduce CO_2 emissions. Global coal demand grows by 15% to 2040, but almost two-thirds of the increase occurs over the next ten years. Chinese coal demand plateaus at just over 50% of global consumption, before falling back after 2030. Demand declines in the OECD, including the United States, where coal use for electricity generation plunges by more than one-third. India overtakes the United States as the world's second-biggest coal consumer before 2020, and soon after surpasses China as the largest importer. Current low coal prices have put pressure on producers worldwide to cut costs, but the shedding of high-cost capacity and demand growth are expected to support an increase in price sufficient to attract new investment. China, India, Indonesia and Australia alone account for over 70% of global coal output by 2040, underscoring Asia's importance in coal markets. Adoption of high-efficiency coal-fired generation technologies, and of carbon capture and storage in the longer term, can be a prudent strategy to ensure a smooth transition to a low carbon power system, while reducing the risk that capacity is idled before recovering its investment costs.

Prices and policies have to be right to get more efficiency into the mix

Energy efficiency is a critical tool to relieve pressure on energy supply and it can also mitigate in part the competitive impacts of price disparities between regions. A renewed policy focus on efficiency is taking hold in many countries and the transport sector is in the front line. With more than three-quarters of global car sales now subject to efficiency standards, oil transport demand is expected to rise by only one-quarter despite the number of cars and trucks on the world's roads more than doubling by 2040. New efficiency efforts have the effect of suppressing total oil demand growth by an estimated 23 mb/d in 2040 – more than current oil production of Saudi Arabia and Russia combined – and measures mainly in power generation and industry hold the growth in gas demand back by 940 billion cubic metres, more than current gas output in North America. Aside from reducing energy-import bills and environmental impacts, efficiency measures can also help in part to address the concern, felt in some import-dependent regions, that relatively high prices for natural gas and electricity put their energy-intensive industries at a competitive disadvantage. But regional energy price disparities are set to persist and North America, in particular, remains a relatively low-cost region through to 2040: the average amount spent on a unit of energy in the United States is expected even to fall below that of China in the 2020s.

Fossil-fuel subsidies totalled $550 billion in 2013 – more than four-times those to renewable energy – and are holding back investment in efficiency and renewables. In the Middle East, nearly 2 mb/d of crude oil and oil products are used to generate electricity when, in the absence of subsidies, the main renewable energy technologies would be competitive with oil-fired power plants. In Saudi Arabia, the additional upfront cost of a car twice as fuel-efficient as the current average would, at present, take about 16 years to recover through lower spending on fuel: this payback period would shrink to 3 years if gasoline were not subsidised. Reforming energy subsidies is not easy and there is no single formula for success. However, as our case studies of Egypt, Indonesia and Nigeria show, clarity over the objectives and timetable for reform, careful assessment of the effects and how they can (if necessary) be mitigated, and thorough consultation and good communication at all stages of the process are essential.

Power sector is leading the transformation of global energy

Electricity is the fastest-growing final form of energy, yet the power sector contributes more than any other to the reduction in the share of fossil fuels in the global energy mix. In total, some 7 200 gigawatts (GW) of capacity needs to be built to keep pace with increasing electricity demand while also replacing existing power plants due to retire by 2040 (around 40% of the current fleet). The strong growth of renewables in many countries raises their share in global power generation to one-third by 2040. Adequate price signals will be needed to ensure timely investments in the new thermal generation capacity, which is necessary, alongside investment in renewables, to maintain the reliability of electricity supply. This will require reforms to market design or electricity pricing in some cases. The shift towards more capital-intensive technologies and high fossil fuel prices lead to increasing average electricity supply costs and end-user prices in most countries in the world. However, end-use efficiency gains help reduce the proportion of household income spent on electricity.

Renewable energy technologies, a critical element of the low-carbon pillar of global energy supply, are rapidly gaining ground, helped by global subsidies amounting to $120 billion in 2013. With rapid cost reductions and continued support, renewables account for almost half of the increase in total electricity generation to 2040, while use of biofuels more than triples to 4.6 mb/d and the use of renewables for heat more than doubles. The share of renewables in power generation increases most in OECD countries, reaching 37%, and their growth is equivalent to the entire net increase in OECD electricity supply. However, generation from renewables grows more than twice as much in non-OECD countries, led by China, India, Latin America and Africa. Globally, wind power accounts for the largest share of growth in renewables-based generation (34%), followed by hydropower (30%) and solar technologies (18%). As the share of wind and solar PV in the world's power mix quadruples, their integration both from a technical and market perspective becomes more challenging, with wind reaching 20% of total electricity generation in the European Union and solar PV accounting for 37% of summer peak demand in Japan.

A complex set of elements in decision-making on nuclear power

Policies concerning nuclear power will remain an essential feature of national energy strategies, even in countries which are committed to phasing out the technology and that must provide for alternatives. Global nuclear power capacity increases by almost 60% in our central scenario, from 392 GW in 2013 to over 620 GW in 2040. However, its share of global electricity generation, which peaked almost two decades ago, rises by just one percentage point to 12%. This pattern of growth reflects the challenges facing all types of new thermal generation capacity in competitive power markets and the specific suite of other economic, technical and political challenges that nuclear power has to overcome. Growth is concentrated in markets where electricity is supplied at regulated prices, utilities have state backing or governments act to facilitate private investment. Of the growth in nuclear generation to 2040, China accounts for 45% while India, Korea and Russia collectively make up a further 30%. Generation increases by 16% in the United States, rebounds in Japan (although not to the levels prior to the accident at Fukushima Daiichi) and falls by 10% in the European Union.

Despite the challenges it currently faces, nuclear power has specific characteristics that underpin the commitment of some countries to maintain it as a future option. Nuclear plants can contribute to the reliability of the power system where they increase the diversity of power generation technologies in the system. For countries that import energy, it can reduce their dependence on foreign supplies and limit their exposure to fuel price movements in international markets. In a Low Nuclear Case – in which global capacity drops by 7% compared with today – indicators of energy security tend to deteriorate in countries that utilise nuclear power. For example, the share of energy demand met from domestic sources is reduced in Japan (by 13 percentage points), Korea (by six) and the European Union (by four) relative to our central scenario.

Nuclear power is one of the few options available at scale to reduce carbon-dioxide emissions while providing or displacing other forms of baseload generation. It has avoided the release of an estimated 56 gigatonnes of CO_2 since 1971, or almost two years of total global emissions at current rates. Annual emissions avoided in 2040 due to nuclear power (as a share of projected emissions at that time) reach almost 50% in Korea, 12% in Japan, 10% in the United States, 9% in the European Union and 8% in China. The average cost of avoiding emissions through new nuclear capacity depends on the mix and the costs of the fuels it displaces, and therefore ranges from very low levels to over $80/tonne.

Almost 200 reactors (of the 434 operational at the end of 2013) are retired in the period to 2040, with the vast majority in Europe, the United States, Russia and Japan; the challenge to replace the shortfall in generation is especially acute in Europe. Utilities need to start planning either to develop alternative capacity or to continue operating existing plants years in advance of nuclear plants reaching the end of their current licence periods. To facilitate this process, governments need to provide clarity on their approach to licence extensions and details of the regulatory steps involved well ahead of possible plant closures. We estimate the cost of decommissioning nuclear plants that are retired in the period to 2040 at more than $100 billion. Considerable uncertainties remain about these costs, reflecting the relatively limited experience to date in dismantling and decontaminating reactors and restoring sites for other uses. Regulators and utilities need to continue to ensure adequate funds are set aside to cover these future expenses.

Public concerns about nuclear power must be heard and addressed. Recent experience has shown how public views on nuclear power can quickly shift and play a determining role in its future in some markets. Safety is the dominant concern, particularly in relation to operating reactors, managing radioactive waste and preventing the proliferation of nuclear weapons. Confidence in the competence and independence of regulatory oversight is essential, especially as nuclear power spreads: in our central scenario, the number of economies operating reactors rises from 31 to 36 as newcomers outnumber those that phase out nuclear power. The cumulative total of spent nuclear fuel doubles to more than 700 thousand tonnes over the projection period, but, to date, no country has opened a permanent disposal facility to isolate the most long-lived and highly radioactive waste produced by commercial reactors. All countries that have ever produced radioactive waste should have an obligation to develop a solution for permanent disposal.

Power to shape the future in sub-Saharan Africa

Those who have no access to modern energy suffer from the most extreme form of energy insecurity. An estimated 620 million people in sub-Saharan Africa do not have access to electricity, and for those that do have it, supply is often insufficient, unreliable and among the most costly in the world. Around 730 million people in the region rely on solid biomass for cooking, which – when used indoors with inefficient cookstoves – causes air pollution that results in nearly 600 000 premature deaths in Africa each year. Sub-Saharan Africa accounts for 13% of the global population, but only 4% of global energy demand (more than half of which is solid biomass). The region is rich in energy resources, but they are largely undeveloped. Almost 30% of global oil and gas discoveries made over the last five years were in the region, and it is also endowed with huge renewable energy resources, especially solar and hydro, as well as wind and geothermal.

The sub-Saharan energy system is set to expand rapidly but, even so, many of the existing energy challenges will be only partly overcome. By 2040, the region's economy quadruples in size, the population nearly doubles and energy demand grows by around 80%. Power generation capacity quadruples and almost half of the growth in generation comes from renewables, which also increasingly provide the source of power for mini- and off-grid systems in rural areas. Overall, nearly one billion people gain access to electricity, but more than half a billion still remain without it in 2040. Output from Nigeria, Angola and a host of smaller producers means that sub-Saharan Africa remains an important centre of global oil supply – although an increasing share of output is consumed within the region. The region emerges also as an important player in gas, as development of the major east coast discoveries off Mozambique and Tanzania accompanies increased production in Nigeria and elsewhere.

Sub-Saharan Africa's energy sector can do more to support inclusive growth. In an "African Century Case", three actions in the energy sector – if accompanied by more general governance reforms – boost the sub-Saharan economy by a further 30% in 2040, delivering an extra decade's worth of growth in per-capita incomes:

- An upgraded power sector: additional investment that reduces power outages by half and achieves universal electricity access in urban areas.

- Deeper regional co-operation: expanding markets and unlocking a greater share of the continent's hydropower potential.

- Better management of energy resources and revenues: more efficiency and transparency in financing essential improvements to Africa's infrastructure.

A modern and integrated energy system allows for more efficient use of resources and brings energy to a greater share of the poorest parts of sub-Saharan Africa. Concerted action to improve the functioning of the energy sector is essential if the 21st is to become an African century.

GLOBAL ENERGY TRENDS

PREFACE

Part A of this *WEO* (Chapters 1-9) presents energy projections to 2040 and considers the implications for energy security, the economy and climate change. The main focus is on the New Policies Scenario – the central scenario in *WEO-2014*. However, two other scenarios are also presented – the Current Policies Scenario and the 450 Scenario.

Chapter 1 defines the scenarios and provides a detailed description of the policy and modelling assumptions underpinning each of them.

Chapter 2 summarises the projections for global energy trends and their implications for CO_2 emissions, investment needs and energy access. It also includes a detailed evaluation of the value and volume of trade in energy over the projection horizon.

Chapters 3-7 analyse the outlook for oil, natural gas, coal, power and renewables.

Chapter 8 examines recent trends and future prospects for energy efficiency and analyses the link between energy efficiency and economic and industrial competitiveness.

Chapter 9 provides an update on fossil-fuel subsidies, analyses their impact on clean energy investment and proposes some guiding principles for countries seeking to make reforms to energy pricing.

Chapter 1

A framework for our energy future
How do we project energy demand and supply?

Highlights

- The New Policies Scenario – the central scenario in *WEO-2014* – describes a pathway for energy markets based on the continuation of existing policies and measures as well as the implementation (albeit cautiously) of policy proposals, even if they are yet to be formally adopted. The Current Policies Scenario only takes account of policies that were enacted as of mid-2014. The 450 Scenario illustrates what it would take to achieve an energy trajectory consistent with limiting the long-term increase in average global temperature to 2 °C.

- The rate of GDP growth is a principal driver of energy demand. In *WEO-2014*, world GDP growth averages 3.4% per year over 2012-2040. Growth slows in almost all parts of the world during the projection period. The economies of sub-Saharan Africa (led by Nigeria at 6.4% per year) and non-OECD Asia (led by India at 6.0% per year) see the fastest growth. China's annual rate of GDP growth averages 5.0%, compared with an estimated 7.5% in 2013 and almost 10% over 2000-2012.

- The rate of population growth is a second key assumption. *WEO-2014* assumes world population expands from 7.0 billion in 2012 to 9.0 billion in 2040. Population growth averages 0.9% per year during the projection period but decelerates in line with the historical trend. The majority of growth occurs in Africa and non-OECD Asia. China's population peaks around 2030 and India becomes the world's most populous country around the same time. Populations increasingly concentrate in urban areas, whose growth accounts for all of the net increase in the global population over 2012-2040.

- Energy prices, which are derived from iterative runs of our World Energy Model, vary across the three scenarios, in part due to the strength of policies to address energy security and environmental challenges. In the New Policies Scenario, the average IEA crude oil import price edges upward from $106/barrel in 2013 to $112/barrel (in year-2013 dollars) in 2020 and $132/barrel in 2040. Natural gas prices rise in Europe and North America, but fall marginally in Japan, contributing to a narrowing of price differences across markets. The average OECD steam coal import price reaches just over $110/tonne in 2040. Assumptions for CO_2 prices also vary across the scenarios, both in terms of price levels and geographical coverage.

- Rates of technological development and deployment, and their impact on energy efficiency, vary by scenario. They take into account the current status of technologies and R&D, the potential for further improvements, the degree of policy support and other sector-specific factors, notably the rate of retirement and replacement of capital stock. No fundamental technological breakthrough is assumed.

Scope of the report

The *World Energy Outlook (WEO)* assesses the prospects for global energy markets and considers the implications for energy security, the economy and the environment. The aim is to provide policy-makers, industry and energy consumers with a rigorous quantitative framework to understand the drivers of future energy trends and to evaluate the impact of government policies designed to address energy-related challenges.

Based on an initial update of events since *WEO-2013*, this edition provides a full update of energy demand and supply projections by fuel, sector and region, as well as projections of international energy prices. It also gives an updated outlook for trends in energy efficiency, energy-related carbon-dioxide (CO_2) emissions, investment in energy supply infrastructure, and subsidies to fossil fuels and renewable energy sources. The projection period is extended by five years, to 2040.

Part A of this report (Chapters 2-9) details the results of our projections under three scenarios: the New Policies Scenario, the Current Policies Scenario and the 450 Scenario. As in previous editions, these scenarios use common assumptions on key drivers such as the rates of economic and population growth, but differ with respect to assumptions about future policies. Chapter 2 summarises the projections for global energy trends and their implications for CO_2 emissions, investment needs and energy access. Chapters 3-8 review the outlook for oil, natural gas, coal, power, renewables and energy efficiency (including its role in boosting international energy competitiveness, an issue first addressed in depth in last year's *WEO*). Chapter 9 sets out the results of our updated analysis of fossil-fuel subsidies.

The rest of *WEO-2014* focuses on two special topics:

■ *Outlook for Nuclear Power* (Part B, Chapters 10-12): Several uncertainties cloud the future for nuclear power, including the nature of government policy, public confidence issues, the availability of financing in liberalised markets, the competitiveness of nuclear power versus alternatives and the implications of the looming large-scale retirement of ageing plants. Part B assesses the outlook for nuclear power and its implications for global energy markets, energy security and climate change.

■ *Africa Energy Outlook* (Part C, Chapters 13-16): Part C analyses of the current status of the African energy sector and outlook, focusing on sub-Saharan Africa. It includes newly collected data and new projections at the regional and country levels. It reviews the prospects for improving access to modern energy services and for developing the region's huge energy resources in a way that contributes best to local economic and social well-being, but also to international energy markets.

Methodological approach

Modelling framework

The World Energy Model (WEM) is the principal tool for producing the energy projections in this report.[1] The model is a large-scale simulation model, designed to replicate how energy markets function. Developed over more than 20 years, it consists of three main modules covering final energy consumption (including industry, transport, buildings, agriculture and non-energy use), fossil fuel and bioenergy supply, and energy transformation (including power and heat generation, refinery and other transformation). The primary outputs from the model for each region are energy demand and supply by fuel, investment needs and CO_2 emissions.

The WEM is a very data-intensive model that covers the entire global energy system. The current version divides the world's energy demand into 30 regions, modelling 13 countries individually. Global oil and gas supply is modelled for 120 countries and regions; global coal supply is modelled for 31 countries and regions. Most of the data on energy demand, supply, and transformation, as well as energy prices, are obtained from IEA databases of energy and economic statistics.[2] These are supplemented by additional data from many external sources, including governments, international organisations, energy companies, consulting firms and financial institutions. These sources are indicated in the relevant sections of this document.

The WEM is constantly reviewed and updated to ensure that it provides an accurate representation of regional and global energy markets.[3] The latest improvements to the WEM include the following:

- For the *Africa Energy Outlook*, the number of separately modelled energy demand regions in Africa was increased from three to eight. The energy demand model now consists of two country models (Nigeria and South Africa) and six regional models (Mozambique and Tanzania, North Africa, Western Africa, Southern Africa, Central Africa and Eastern Africa). Africa's oil and gas supply is modelled for 43 countries and regions, and coal supply is modelled for Mozambique, South Africa and two aggregate regions.

- A new power sector module related to electricity access was added to enhance analysis of generation, capacity and investment in off-grid and mini-grid systems.

- The residential module in Africa has been improved with new data on energy use, costs and efficiency by end-uses and technologies, enhancing the analysis of clean cooking and electricity access.

---

1. A complete description of the WEM is available at *www.worldenergyoutlook.org/weomodel/*.

2. Many of these data are available at *www.iea.org/statistics*.

3. The development of the WEM benefits from expert review within and outside the IEA, including through IEA participation in a number of leading conferences for the energy modelling community.

- In the industry module, the modelling of petrochemical feedstock has been enhanced using detailed bottom-up estimation by product. Simulation of industry carbon capture and storage (CCS) deployment has been improved by introducing a detailed sector-by-sector cost analysis.

- The road-transport module has been enhanced to improve the representation of passenger light-duty vehicle sales and to improve projections of freight loads to reflect regionally specific drivers of economic growth.

- Investment cost assumptions along the entire energy supply chain on both the demand and supply sides have been updated through detailed surveys of industry and research bodies.[4]

Defining the scenarios

WEO-2014 continues the approach of using scenarios to prepare detailed quantitative projections of long-term energy trends. Three scenarios, differing in their assumptions about the evolution of government policies with respect to energy and the environment, are presented: the New Policies Scenario and the Current Policies Scenario, which were introduced in 2010, and the 450 Scenario, first presented in detail in 2008. Differences in government policies lead to divergent trends in energy markets, notably through the level of subsidies or prices, which affect learning and deployment. Details of the key policies and measures taken into account in each scenario can be found in Annex B.[5] For each scenario, we offer a set of internally consistent projections to 2040. None should be considered forecasts: the Current Policies Scenario and New Policies Scenario are indications of where we are heading unless things are changed; the 450 Scenario is an illustration of how radical change could be effected. The starting year for the projections is 2013, as reliable market data for all countries were available only up to 2012 at the time the modelling work was completed. However, where preliminary data for 2013 were available (which was often the case), they have been incorporated.

The **New Policies Scenario** is the central scenario of *WEO-2014*. It takes into account the policies and implementing measures affecting energy markets that had been adopted as of mid-2014, together with relevant policy proposals, even though specific measures needed to put them into effect have yet to be fully developed. These proposals include targets and programmes to support renewable energy, energy efficiency, and alternative fuels and vehicles, as well as commitments to reduce carbon emissions, reform energy subsidies and expand or phase out nuclear power. We make a case-by-case judgement (which is often cautious) of the extent to which policy proposals will be implemented. This is done in view of the many institutional, political and economic obstacles which exist, as well as, in some cases, a lack of detail in announced intentions and about how they will be implemented.

---

4. The new cost assumptions are available at *www.worldenergyoutlook.org/weomodel/investmentcosts*.

5. A policies and measures database, detailing policies addressing renewable energy, energy efficiency and climate change is available at *www.iea.org/policiesandmeasures*.

Box 1.1 ▷ **Notable developments in energy policy in selected regions**

In June 2014, the **United States** Environmental Protection Agency (EPA) proposed the Clean Power Plan, which aims to cut power sector emissions in 2030 by 30%, compared with 2005 levels, as well as to reduce soot and smog pollution by over 25%. States have the flexibility to propose their own individual plans or develop multi-state plans to meet the targets for power plants. Four "building blocks" are to be used: improved efficiency at coal-fired power plants; expanded utilisation of combined-cycle gas turbines; more nuclear and renewables; and improved end-use energy efficiency. We assume in the New Policies Scenario that the proposals are implemented as proposed.

In January 2014, the European Commission proposed a climate and energy policy framework for the **European Union** for 2030. Its centrepiece is a goal to reduce greenhouse-gas emissions by 40% below 1990 levels to keep the region on track to cut emissions by at least 80% by 2050. The target is to be met, in part, by increasing the share of renewables in total EU energy use to at least 27%. The targets are still subject to approval by the European Council and the European Parliament. The New Policies Scenario assumes cautious movement in the direction of these targets, strengthened by progressive implementation of the European Energy Security Strategy, released by the European Commission in May 2014.

In September 2013, the State Council in **China** announced an Action Plan for Prevention and Control of Air Pollution, with targets to control coal consumption and phase out heavily polluting vehicles. A speech by Chinese President Xi Jinping in June 2014 called for a "revolution" in energy consumption, energy supply, energy technology and energy governance, while the Chinese Premier announced a "war on pollution" in March 2014. These speeches are expected to set the tone for the 13th Five-Year Plan. As details of this plan are not yet known, it is not yet included in the New Policies Scenario.

Japan's new Strategic Energy Plan, approved by the government in April 2014 following an energy policy review in response to the Fukushima Daiichi nuclear accident provides for nuclear power to remain an important source of baseload electricity. As of September 2014, none of the country's 48 reactors was operating, but the new plan calls for them to be restarted once regulatory approvals have been obtained. Targets for the future energy mix are expected to be announced later, with the contribution of renewable energy expected to increase. In the New Policies Scenario, we assume that most idled nuclear plants steadily return to service after receiving regulatory approval.

In early 2014, **India** announced new vehicle fuel-economy standards of 4.8 litres per 100 kilometres (l/100 km) by 2021-2022 (a 15% improvement). Also in discussion are whether to subsidise the purchase of electric and hybrid vehicles and to increase the ethanol blending mandate. **Saudi Arabia** has announced fuel-economy labelling for new cars, fuel-economy standards of up to 5.4 l/100 km by 2019-2020 for imported vehicles (depending on the size), insulation standards for new buildings and tightened minimum energy performance standards for air conditioners. Elsewhere, **Dubai** has introduced building codes and **Qatar** has introduced efficiency standards for air conditioners.

Thus, the policies taken into account in the New Policies Scenario include a number of proposals that have been announced over the past year, but are not yet formally adopted (Box 1.1). Examples are regulations in the United States to cut greenhouse-gas emissions from power plants, the European Union's 2030 policy framework for climate and energy policies, and changes to energy subsidy schemes (for fossil fuels and renewables) in many countries.

The **Current Policies Scenario**, by contrast, takes into consideration only those policies and implementing measures that had been formally adopted as of mid-2014. In other words, it describes a business-as-usual future in which governments fail to follow through on policy proposals that have yet to be backed-up by legislation or other bases for implementation and do not introduce any other policies that affect the energy sector. The scenario is designed to offer a baseline picture of how global energy markets would evolve without any new policy intervention. It provides a series of points of reference against which the potential impact of new energy and environmental policies can be assessed.

The **450 Scenario** takes a different approach, adopting a specified outcome – the international goal to limit the rise in long-term average global temperature to two degrees Celsius (2 °C) – and illustrating how that might be achieved. The scenario assumes a set of policies that bring about a trajectory of greenhouse-gas emissions from the energy sector that is consistent with the goal (Box 1.2). In this scenario, the concentration of greenhouse gases in the atmosphere peaks by around the middle of this century, at a level above 450 parts per million (ppm), but not so high as to be likely to precipitate changes that make the 2 °C objective ultimately unattainable. The concentration of greenhouse gases stabilises after 2100 at around 450 ppm. The 450 Scenario is not given the same coverage in this *Outlook* as in previous editions for two main reasons: first, specific short-term opportunities for action in the energy sector to mitigate climate change and their potential results were covered in detail in recent *WEO* Special Reports (*Redrawing the Energy-Climate Map* [IEA, 2013a] and *World Energy Investment Outlook* [IEA, 2014a]); and second, another *WEO* Special Report on climate change will cover this in detail in 2015.[6] The results of the 450 Scenario are nonetheless included for reference purposes in many of the tables and figures throughout this report, as well in the detailed tables in Annex A.

As in previous *Outlooks*, we deliberately focus on the results of the New Policies Scenario to provide a clear picture of where currently planned policies would take us. Nonetheless, this scenario should not be interpreted as a forecast: even though it is likely that many governments around the world will take firm policy action to tackle energy-related problems, the policies that are actually put in place in the coming years may deviate markedly from those assumed in this scenario.

---

6. A *WEO* Special Report on Climate Change will be released in mid-2015. It will aim to inform international climate policy negotiations in the run-up to the critical meeting in Paris in November 2015, which will try to reach an agreement on policy action in the period after 2020.

Box 1.2 ▷ **A change in the way the 450 Scenario is built in *WEO-2014***

The 450 Scenario in this report differs in important ways from preceding versions. Concerted global policy action before 2020 is now unlikely, as this is the earliest date by which any agreement reached at COP-21 (the meeting of the Conference of the Parties to the UN Convention on Climate Change, which is due to take place in Paris 2015) could be expected to take effect. Near-term policy assumptions for the period to 2020 draw on measures that were outlined in the *WEO* Special Report *Redrawing the Energy-Climate Map,* which were welcomed and encouraged by energy ministers who attended the IEA 2013 Ministerial meeting (IEA, 2013a). Emissions reductions to 2020 come from four sets of measures that, taken together, have no net economic cost:

■ Targeted energy efficiency improvements in industry, buildings and transport.

■ Limits on the use and construction of inefficient coal-fired power plants.

■ Curbs on methane emissions in upstream oil and gas production.

■ The partial phase-out of fossil-fuels subsidies to end-users.

In the period after 2020, it is assumed that one of the main deficiencies of current climate policy is remedied: a CO_2 price is adopted in Organisation for Economic Co-operation and Development (OECD) countries and other major economies in the power generation and industry sectors, at a level high enough to make investment in low-carbon technologies attractive. It is implemented in OECD countries first and then progressively extended to other major economies. We assume that all fossil-fuel subsidies are removed in all regions except the Middle East (where some element of subsidisation is assumed to remain) by 2035 and that CO_2 pricing is extended to the transport sector everywhere, accelerating energy efficiency improvements. There is also a further extension and strengthening of minimum energy performance standards in the transport and buildings sectors.

Main non-policy assumptions

Economic growth

Economic activity is the principal driver of demand for each type of energy service. The projections in all three scenarios described in this *Outlook* are, therefore, highly sensitive to the underlying assumptions about the rate of growth of gross domestic product (GDP) in each region. Energy demand tends to grow in line with GDP, though typically at a lower rate – especially in the most advanced economies, where saturation effects curb income-driven increases in demand and a shift toward services occur (Figure 1.1). Over 1990-2012, for example, world primary energy demand increased by 0.6% each year on average for every percentage point of GDP growth (expressed in real purchasing power parity [PPP] terms). The income elasticity of demand, as this ratio is termed, has fluctuated over time: it averaged 0.5 in the 1990s, rose to 0.7 in the 2000s and fell back to 0.5 in the early 2010s (mainly as a result of structural changes in the economy and more efficient energy use).

Figure 1.1 ▷ Total primary energy demand and GDP in selected countries, 1971-2012

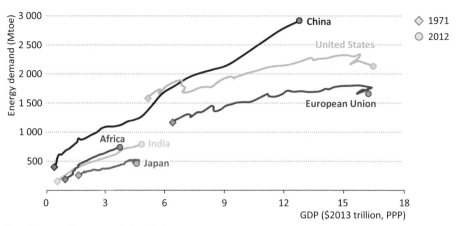

Note: Mtoe = million tonnes of oil equivalent.

There are considerable differences across regions in the amount of energy used per dollar of GDP (energy intensity) and trends over time. Leading emerging economies have remained on a broadly linear path, with the exception of China, which saw its energy use accelerate relative to GDP in the 2000s with the boom in energy-intensive manufacturing. In OECD countries, the link between GDP and energy use has weakened to some degree.

Near- to medium-term economic prospects are improving at a moderate and uneven pace. Economic activity expands at a relatively firm rate in the United States though growth in Europe continues to be slow. Despite experiencing weaker economic growth than previously forecast, emerging and developing economies are still expected to account for the bulk of future growth. According to the International Monetary Fund (IMF), world GDP expanded by an estimated 3.3% in 2013, down marginally from 3.4% in 2012, but growth rate is projected to rebound to 3.3% in 2014 and 3.8% in 2015 (IMF, 2014). There remain large downside risks to these projections: persistent geopolitical risks, renewed financial volatility in emerging markets and deflation in advanced economies (especially in Europe).

Our assumptions about trends in economic growth over the long term are little changed from last year.[7] In all three scenarios in this *Outlook*, world GDP is assumed to grow at an average annual rate of 3.4% over 2012-2040 (Table 1.1).[8] This means the global economy

---

7. GDP growth assumptions to 2020 are based on the April 2014 IMF forecasts, with some adjustments to reflect information from regional, national and other sources. Thereafter, they are based on our assessment of developments in the labour force, accumulation of capital stock (investment) and total factor productivity, supplemented by projections made by various economic forecasting bodies, including the OECD.

8. Across the scenarios presented in this *Outlook*, the policies that are assumed to be introduced and the energy price levels that prevail could be expected to lead to some variations in GDP. However, due to the uncertainty associated with estimating these effects and in order to more precisely identify the implications of different policy options on energy trends, the same level of GDP growth is assumed in each scenario.

is about two-and-a-half times the present level at the end of the projection period than in 2012. For the period to 2035 (the end point of our projections last year), the average overall rate of growth, at 3.5%, is almost the same as that assumed in last year's *Outlook* – though this disguises a downward revision to rates in the period to 2020 and a matching upward revision for the period thereafter. For the period as a whole, the biggest upward revision occurs in Africa, which is now assumed to grow by 4.7% over 2012-2040, reflecting an improved outlook for productivity and employment in sub-Saharan Africa.[9] The biggest downward revisions are in Russia and Brazil. Growth in the OECD is marginally slower.

Table 1.1 ▷ **Real GDP growth assumptions by region**

	Compound average annual growth rate				
	1990-2012	2012-2020	2020-2030	2030-2040	2012-2040
OECD	2.2%	2.2%	2.0%	1.7%	1.9%
Americas	2.6%	2.6%	2.2%	2.0%	2.2%
United States	2.5%	2.6%	2.0%	1.9%	2.1%
Europe	1.9%	1.7%	1.9%	1.6%	1.7%
Asia Oceania	1.9%	1.9%	1.8%	1.3%	1.7%
Japan	0.9%	1.1%	1.1%	0.8%	1.0%
Non-OECD	4.9%	5.3%	4.9%	3.7%	4.6%
E. Europe/Eurasia	0.8%	2.8%	3.5%	2.7%	3.0%
Russia	0.7%	2.2%	3.5%	2.5%	2.8%
Asia	7.5%	6.3%	5.4%	3.9%	5.1%
China	9.9%	6.9%	5.3%	3.2%	5.0%
India	6.5%	6.2%	6.6%	5.3%	6.0%
Southeast Asia	5.1%	5.3%	4.6%	3.9%	4.5%
Middle East	4.4%	3.7%	3.9%	3.3%	3.6%
Africa	4.0%	5.1%	4.8%	4.4%	4.7%
Sub-Saharan Africa	4.1%	5.5%	5.2%	4.9%	5.1%
Latin America	3.4%	3.1%	3.5%	3.0%	3.2%
Brazil	2.9%	2.9%	4.0%	3.3%	3.4%
World	3.3%	3.7%	3.6%	3.0%	3.4%
European Union	1.7%	1.6%	1.8%	1.5%	1.6%

Note: Calculated based on GDP expressed in year-2013 dollars in purchasing power parity terms.

Sources: IMF (2014); OECD (2014); Economist Intelligence Unit and World Bank databases; IEA databases and analysis.

With these changes, the economy of sub-Saharan Africa expands at the fastest rate, at 5.1% per year on average over the period 2012-2040. Alongside it is non-OECD Asia, where annual growth also averages 5.1% over the projection period, led by India (6.0%).

---

9. GDP growth rates in several African countries, most notably Nigeria, were also revised, as national administrations have updated assessments of their economies (see Chapter 13).

China's rate of economic growth averages 5.0%, compared with an estimated 7.5% in 2013 and an average of almost 10% over the period 2000-2012, as its economy matures and its population growth levels off. Rates of economic growth slow in almost all regions as economies mature and their population levels off.

Our projections do not take account of a major revision to PPP rates which has been made by the World Bank, since the IMF has not yet adjusted its GDP forecasts accordingly. When it does, the GDP of the emerging economies will rise relative to the rest of the world, boosting their weight in global GDP (Box 1.3). Since they generally grow faster than OECD countries, this boosts average growth rates for the world as a whole. This adjustment, which is due to be completed in October (and so will be too late to be incorporated in this year's *Outlook*), will be taken on board in next year's edition.

Box 1.3 ▷ Revised purchasing power parity data shakes up global economic rankings

In April 2014, the World Bank's International Comparison Program (ICP) released revised PPP data for 2011 – the first such revision for six years. PPPs allow comparison of real levels of expenditure between countries, just as conventional price indices allow comparison of real values over time, and are calculated by simultaneously comparing the prices of similar goods and services among a large number of countries. PPPs are published by the ICP only for a single benchmark year, although the OECD and Eurostat (the statistics agency of the European Commission) publish estimates for 47 countries on an annual basis. The IEA Energy Data Centre uses the revised indicators in its latest publications.

In October 2014, the IMF, whose forecasts we use for the medium term, released new historical figures and forecasts for GDP that have been adjusted using the new PPP factors. This will result in large upward revisions to GDP in most emerging economies – the opposite effect of the previous revision in 2008. For example, based on the IMF's new PPP rates, the GDP of Indonesia in 2013 is estimated to be 85% higher than what we use in this edition. The new figures also boost GDP in China (by 20%), India (by 34%) and the Middle East economies (by 59%). With the revision, China is set to become the world's largest economy in 2014, while the total GDP of non-OECD regions will have already surpassed that of the OECD in 2010 (in the previous estimate, this did not occur until 2017). The new figures from the IMF were published too late to be taken into account in this edition of the *WEO*, but will be reflected in future ones.

Demographic trends

The level of population is an important driver of both overall demand for energy services (through its impact on economic activity) and the mix of fuels to provide those services. The rates of population growth assumed in the *Outlook* for each region – the same for all three scenarios – are based on the most recent projections by the United Nations (UNPD, 2013).

World population is projected to grow by 0.9% per year on average, from an estimated 7.0 billion in mid-2012 (and 7.1 billion in 2013) to 9.0 billion in 2040. These projections are based on the "medium-variant" projection, which assumes a decline in fertility rates in those countries where large families are still prevalent and a slight increase in fertility rates in several countries which currently have fewer than two children per woman on average. The rate of population growth slows progressively over the projection period, in line with the long-term historical trend, from 1.0% per year in 2012-2025 to 0.8% in 2025-2040. The global population expanded by 1.6% per year from 1980 to 2012.

Table 1.2 ▷ Population assumptions by region

	Population growth*			Population (million)		Urbanisation	
	1990-2012	2012-25	2012-40	2012	2040	2012	2040
OECD	0.7%	0.5%	0.4%	1 258	1 403	80%	86%
Americas	1.1%	0.8%	0.7%	488	594	82%	87%
United States	1.0%	0.8%	0.7%	318	383	83%	88%
Europe	0.5%	0.3%	0.2%	566	604	75%	82%
Asia Oceania	0.4%	0.1%	0.0%	205	205	89%	94%
Japan	0.1%	-0.2%	-0.4%	128	115	92%	97%
Non-OECD	1.5%	1.1%	1.0%	5 783	7 601	47%	60%
E. Europe/Eurasia	0.0%	0.0%	-0.2%	341	326	63%	69%
Russia	-0.1%	-0.3%	-0.4%	144	127	74%	80%
Asia	1.3%	0.8%	0.6%	3 678	4 382	42%	58%
China	0.8%	0.4%	0.1%	1 358	1 416	52%	74%
India	1.6%	1.1%	0.8%	1 237	1 566	32%	46%
Southeast Asia	1.5%	1.0%	0.8%	608	760	45%	61%
Middle East	2.4%	1.7%	1.4%	213	313	68%	74%
Africa	2.5%	2.4%	2.2%	1 083	1 998	40%	52%
Sub-Saharan Africa	2.7%	2.5%	2.4%	914	1 771	37%	51%
Latin America	1.4%	1.0%	0.8%	468	581	79%	85%
Brazil	1.3%	0.7%	0.5%	199	229	85%	90%
World	1.3%	1.0%	0.9%	7 042	9 004	53%	64%
European Union	0.3%	0.1%	0.1%	507	516	74%	81%

* Compound average annual growth rates.

Sources: UN Population Division databases; IEA analysis.

Most of the projected increase in global population occurs in Africa and non-OECD Asia (Table 1.2). Africa experiences the fastest rate of growth over 2012-2040, at 2.2% per year, resulting in a near doubling of the continent's population. China's population peaks around 2030, at which time India becomes the world's most populous country. Overall, the population of non-OECD countries expands by 1.0% per year in the period to 2040, compared with growth of only 0.4% per year in OECD countries. The only major non-OECD country that sees a decline in population is Russia. In OECD countries, the United States contributes most of the increase; Europe's population increases slightly, while the population of OECD Asia Oceania is unchanged, with a decline in Japan. Populations increasingly concentrate in urban areas, whose growth accounts for all of the net increase in the global population over 2012-2040. This trend will have a significant impact on energy demand, particularly in Africa and non-OECD Asia, where modern energy services are more readily available in towns and cities than in rural areas.

Projections for per-capita income, which is closely correlated with energy demand, are derived from the assumptions for GDP and population. Average and median incomes rise in all regions, underpinning increased demand for goods and services and, therefore, demand for the energy needed to produce and operate the equipment and appliances used to provide those services. Globally, GDP per capita increases by 2.5% per year, from $12 100 in 2012 to just over $24 000 in 2040 (based on GDP in PPP terms). Per-capita incomes grow fastest in the emerging economies, though in 2040 these reach only one-third of the level in OECD countries.

Carbon-dioxide prices

The pricing of CO_2 emissions affects demand for energy by altering the relative costs of using different fuels. Regional and national carbon pricing initiatives – including cap-and-trade schemes and carbon taxes – are continuing to spread, with 20 now operating globally. Several trading programmes were launched in 2013 and 2014, including in Canada (the province of Quebec), China (the provinces of Guangdong and Hubei and the cities of Beijing, Shanghai, Shenzhen, Chongqing and Tianjin), Kazakhstan, and the United States (the state of California). Switzerland's scheme became mandatory. Some existing programmes have recently been extended, including in Europe: the EU Emission Trading System (ETS) – the world's largest – grew when Croatia joined the European Union. Chile's parliament passed a carbon tax in 2014, which is to take effect in 2017. Korea plans to launch a new trading scheme by 2015. South Africa, which had planned to do the same, has delayed the launch by one year. There has also been some movement against carbon pricing: Australia's new government repealed an existing mechanism that was to have entered into full operation in 2015 in response to concerns about higher electricity costs.

The extent of carbon pricing schemes and the level of CO_2 prices vary across the scenarios according to the assumed degree of policy intervention to curb growth in CO_2 emissions. It is assumed in each scenario that all existing carbon trading schemes and taxes are retained (with the exception of Australia's scheme in the Current Policies and New Policies Scenarios) and that the price of CO_2 rises throughout the projection period (Table 1.3). In the New Policies Scenario, the CO_2 price in Europe increases from less than $6/tonne in 2013 to $22/tonne (in year-2013 dollars) in 2020 and to $50/tonne in 2040.[10] Similar

---

10. CO_2 prices under the EU ETS fell from around €30/tonne in mid-2008 to less than €3/tonne in early 2013, but have recovered to average almost €6/tonne ($8/tonne) in 2014 (through September).

price levels are assumed from 2015 in Korea. In China, a national CO_2 price is introduced in the New Policies Scenario in 2020, rising from \$10/tonne initially to \$35/tonne by 2040. We also assume that from 2015 all investment decisions in the power sector in Canada, the United States and Japan include an implicit, or "shadow", carbon price that starts at \$13/tonne and rises to \$40/tonne in 2040. In the 450 Scenario, it is assumed that carbon pricing is eventually adopted in all OECD countries and that CO_2 prices in most of these markets reach \$140/tonne in 2040. Several major non-OECD countries are also assumed to put a price on carbon in the 450 Scenario, with prices rising to a slightly lower level in 2040 than in OECD countries.

Table 1.3 ▷ **CO_2 price assumptions in selected regions by scenario**
($2013 per tonne)

	Region	Sectors	2020	2030	2040
Current Policies Scenario	European Union	Power, industry and aviation	20	30	40
	Korea	Power and industry	20	30	40
New Policies Scenario	European Union	Power, industry and aviation	22	37	50
	Chile	Power	7	15	24
	Korea	Power and industry	22	37	50
	China	All	10	23	35
	South Africa	Power and industry	7	15	24
450 Scenario	United States and Canada	Power and industry	20	100	140
	European Union	Power, industry and aviation	22	100	140
	Japan	Power and industry	20	100	140
	Korea	Power and industry	22	100	140
	Australia and New Zealand	Power and industry	20	100	140
	China, Russia, Brazil and South Africa	Power and industry*	10	75	125

* All sectors in China.

Technology

The development and deployment of advanced energy technologies will have a major impact on the evolution of energy markets over the long term and on the achievement of socio-economic, energy security and environmental goals, not least those of limiting greenhouse-gas emissions. The projections are, therefore, sensitive to rates of technological development and how they affect energy efficiency, supply costs and fuel choice. The chosen assumptions vary by fuel, sector and technology, taking into account the current status of the technologies and the results of R&D programmes, the potential for further improvement, the degree of policy support and other sector-specific factors, notably the rate of retirement and replacement of capital stock (Table 1.4).

Table 1.4 ▷ **Recent developments and key conditions for faster deployment of clean energy technologies**

Technology	Recent developments	Key conditions for faster deployment
Renewable power	• Investment declined by 10% in 2013, reflecting technology cost reductions, policy uncertainty and revisions to support schemes in selected markets. • Wind investment declined by 30%, while that in solar photovoltaics rose by 3%, on account of investment in China and Japan (which together accounted for over half of annual global capacity additions).	• Minimise regulatory risks, including retroactive changes to subsidy schemes. • Promote renewables integration in mature markets and create frameworks to attract financing in developing markets. • Encourage increased RD&D spending in emerging technologies.
Nuclear power	• At the end of 2013, 76 gigawatts of nuclear capacity was under construction, of which about three-quarters was in non-OECD countries. • Ten projects began construction in 2013. • Almost 40 countries are considering developing their first plants; three are committed to phasing out nuclear power.	• Reductions in cost as investment moves from first-of-a-kind to number-of-a-kind reactor construction. • Addressing public concerns about safety, costs, proliferation and long-term waste disposal.
Carbon capture and storage (CCS)	• At the end of 2013, four large-scale demonstration projects and eight enhanced oil recovery projects using anthropogenic CO_2 were operating. • To comply with regulations proposed by the US EPA in 2014, new coal-fired power plants would need to be equipped with CCS within ten years.	• Scale up financial and policy commitments by governments to accelerate the transition from demonstration to deployment. • A commercial market for captured CO_2 for enhanced oil recovery.
Biofuels	• After a steep decline in 2012, investment increased by about 30% in 2013, as production capacity was expanded. • Two commercial-scale advanced biofuel production facilities opened in 2013 in the United States and Europe.	• Develop long-term policies to encourage investment in advanced biofuel projects. • Formulation and implementation of sustainability criteria and standards.
Hybrid and electric vehicles	• Hybrid vehicle sales reached 1.3 million in 2012, with 52% of sales in Japan and 39% in the United States. • Electric vehicle recharging infrastructure continued to expand rapidly in 2013.	• Improve the performance of batteries and significantly reduce their cost to enhance competitiveness versus conventional vehicles. • Expand policy measures and programmes to support manufacturers' confidence. • Continued expansion of charging infrastructure.
Energy efficiency	• Several new efficiency policies and measures in major energy consuming countries were introduced in 2013 and in the first half of 2014 (see Chapter 8).	• Policy action to remove the barriers obstructing the implementation of energy efficiency measures that are economically viable (see Chapter 8).

Source: IEA (2014b).

It is assumed in all three scenarios that energy technologies that are in use today or are approaching commercialisation achieve continued cost reductions as their wider deployment contributes to more efficient production. The rates of improvement vary by scenario, according to differences in the level of deployment, which is driven by the policies assumed, as well as by energy and CO_2 prices. Though possible, no technological breakthroughs are assumed to be made, as it cannot be known what they might involve, whether or when they might occur and how quickly they might be commercialised.

Energy supply costs and prices

Demand for an energy-related service is strongly influenced by the price for the service, which in turn reflects the relative costs of the fuels and technologies used to provide it. Other things being equal, an increase in the price of a fuel will depress demand for it, and vice versa; an increase in the price of a fuel has the opposite effect on supply. Higher energy costs will also cause a reduction in the energy intensity (relative to capital, labour and materials) in an economy. The price elasticities of demand and supply, i.e. the responsiveness of demand and supply to changes in price, vary across fuels and sectors and over time. Among other factors, they depend on the scope for substituting the fuel by another or adopting more efficient energy-using equipment, the need for the energy service, the pace of technological change, inventory, spare production capacity, lead times to build new production capacity, policies of resource-rich countries and the extent of energy resources.

In each scenario presented, international energy prices result from an iterative modelling exercise, underpinned by assumptions about the cost of supply of different fuels. First, the demand modules of the IEA's World Energy Model (WEM) are run under a given set of international prices, which determine prices to energy users in each region (taking account of any taxes, excise duties, CO_2 prices and subsidies). Once the resultant demand level is determined, the fossil-fuel supply modules of the WEM calculate the levels of production of oil, natural gas and coal that result from the given price levels, taking account of the costs of different supply options (including upstream taxes and royalties) and the constraints on the production rates of various types of resources.[11] In the event that the price for a fossil fuel is not sufficient to generate enough supply to cover the projected global demand, price levels are increased and a new level of demand and supply is established. This procedure is carried out repeatedly, with prices adjusting until demand and supply are in balance in each year of the projection period. End-user electricity prices are based on projected wholesale prices (either in regulated or competitive markets), network, retail and other costs, as

---

11. In the near to medium term, the fossil-fuel supply curves take into account our assessment of specific individual projects that are currently operating or have already been sanctioned, planned or announced. For the longer term, they are consistent with our top-down assessment of the costs of exploration and development of the world's oil, natural gas and coal resources and our judgements of the feasibility and rate of investment in different regions needed to turn these resources into production. Our cost assumptions incorporate the results of an extensive survey of energy companies, banks and other experts carried out this year as part of our special study of investment (Part B). A detailed discussion of oil-supply costs and their link to oil prices can be found at the end of Chapter 13 in *WEO-2013* (IEA, 2013b).

well as the costs of renewables subsidies that are passed on to consumers. Wholesale prices must be high enough to cover variable costs (including fuel and CO_2 costs) of all power plants and ensure that new power plants recover all their costs (including capital investment recovery, operation and maintenance, fuel and CO_2 costs).

The price paths vary across the three scenarios, in part due to differences in the strength of policies to address energy security and environmental challenges and their respective impacts on supply and demand (Table 1.5). In the Current Policies Scenario, policies adopted to reduce the use of fossil fuels are limited, so rising demand and supply costs combine to push prices up. Lower energy demand in the 450 Scenario means that limitations on the production rates of various types of resources are less significant and there is less need to produce fossil fuels from resources higher up the supply cost curve. As a result, international fossil fuel prices are lower than in the other two scenarios.[12]

Table 1.5 ▷ **Fossil-fuel import prices by scenario**

	2013	New Policies Scenario			Current Policies Scenario			450 Scenario		
		2020	2030	2040	2020	2030	2040	2020	2030	2040
Real terms (2013 prices)										
IEA crude oil imports ($/barrel)	106	112	123	132	116	139	155	105	102	100
Natural gas ($/MBtu)										
United States	3.7	5.5	6.6	8.2	5.5	6.8	8.5	5.1	5.9	6.1
Europe imports	10.6	11.1	12.1	12.7	11.5	13.2	14.0	10.5	10.0	9.2
Japan imports	16.2	14.4	14.6	15.3	15.0	16.3	17.3	13.6	12.6	12.0
OECD steam coal imports ($/tonne)	86	101	108	112	107	117	124	88	78	77
Nominal terms										
IEA crude oil imports ($/barrel)	106	131	181	244	136	205	286	123	151	185
Natural gas ($/MBtu)										
United States	3.7	6.4	9.7	15.2	6.4	10.0	15.7	6.0	8.7	11.4
Europe imports	10.6	13.0	17.9	23.5	13.5	19.5	25.9	12.3	14.7	17.0
Japan imports	16.2	16.9	21.6	28.3	17.6	23.9	31.9	15.9	18.6	22.2
OECD steam coal imports ($/tonne)	86	119	158	207	125	173	229	104	115	141

Notes: MBtu = million British thermal units. Gas prices are weighted averages expressed on a gross calorific-value basis. All prices are for bulk supplies exclusive of tax. The US price reflects the wholesale price prevailing on the domestic market. Nominal prices assume inflation of 2.3% per year from 2014.

---

12. In the 450 Scenario, the effect of lower international prices on final end-user prices is offset by increased taxes.

Our assumptions about subsidies also differ across the scenarios. In the New Policies Scenario, we assume subsidies to fossil fuel consumption are phased out in all net-energy importing countries within ten years at the latest. However, in net-energy exporting countries, we assume they are phased out only if specific policies to that end have been announced, in recognition of the difficulties these countries are likely to face in reforming domestic energy pricing (see Chapter 9). In the Current Policies Scenario, no change in subsidy rates is assumed, unless a formal reform programme is already in place. In the 450 Scenario, fossil-fuel subsidies are assumed to be removed in net-importing regions within a decade and in net-exporting regions by the end of the projection period.[13]

Oil prices

Oil prices near and above $100/barrel have been a regular feature of the global energy landscape since their rebound after the financial crisis. Support for prices at this level has stemmed from rapid demand growth in non-OECD countries, which has more than offset the aggregate decline in OECD countries. On the supply side, booming production of tight oil in the United States has been a key source of incremental growth, though the increase has been tempered by reduced production stemming from outages and turmoil in parts of the Middle East and North Africa. The extended period of high oil prices has triggered responses by consumers and producers alike. Oil demand in OECD countries has continued to decline from a peak in 2005; even in several major emerging economies, growth rates have slowed. Meanwhile, interest in developing resources that were previously considered too costly or too difficult to produce has increased. Current trends point to a slight easing of the global oil balance over the next few years, though geopolitical instability could continue to support high prices. In the mid-2020s, however, a tighter market could well emerge as non-OPEC output flattens and starts to fall back.

Figure 1.2 ▷ **Average IEA crude oil import price by scenario**

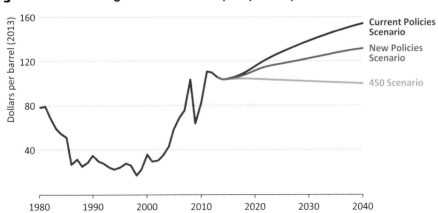

13. Except for the Middle East, where subsidisation rates are assumed to decline to a maximum of 20% toward the end of the projection period.

Oil prices in the scenarios vary according to the strength of policy action to limit demand growth. In the New Policies Scenario, the average IEA crude oil import price – a proxy for international oil prices – reaches $112/barrel (in year-2013 dollars) in 2020 and $132/barrel in 2040 (Figure 1.2). In nominal terms, prices more than double over the projection period to over $240/barrel. In the Current Policies Scenario, considerably higher oil prices are needed to balance supply with faster growth in demand: crude oil prices reach $155/barrel in 2040. In the 450 Scenario, oil prices are flat in the period to 2020 before falling demand – the result of decisive policy action – and a consequent reduction in the need for oil from costly fields in non-OPEC countries cause prices to drift down to around $100/barrel at the end of the projection period. These long-term oil price trajectories are illustrated in Figure 1.2 as smooth trend lines; in reality, prices will fluctuate in shorter time steps.

Natural gas prices

Natural gas price differentials across the main regional markets – North America, Asia Pacific and Europe – have partially narrowed since mid-2013 but nonetheless remain wide and well above historical levels. The regional spread in prices reflects differences in pricing mechanisms, limited arbitrage options, the high cost of transport between regions and local gas market conditions.

In North America, gas prices are determined by gas-to-gas competition at trading hubs. Shale gas production growth in North America has kept prices relatively low, though they increased temporarily in early 2014 as a result of higher demand from exceptionally cold weather. In Asia-Pacific, trade is dominated by long-term contracts in which gas prices are indexed to oil prices. The higher price that Asian importers continue to pay for imported natural gas reflects oil price levels, transportation distances, a premium that buyers have been obliged to pay for security of supply, the ability of regulated utility buyers to pass on their costs to consumers and the region's relatively tight market. In Europe's more competitive gas market, average import price levels have been moderated in recent years by the increasing reference to European hub prices in import contracts, notably across Northwest Europe (oil indexation remains the preferred pricing structure in the south of the continent). This has allowed prevailing gas market dynamics, with subdued demand and relatively ample supply, to feed through into European prices, although this has not been enough to prevent gas losing out to coal in European power generation.

Over the projection period to 2040, pricing mechanisms for internationally traded natural gas around the world are expected to become more flexible and sensitive to the underlying balance of gas supply and demand in each market. This comes about because of fewer restrictions in gas supply contracts on the destination or re-sale of the gas, and greater use of indices linked to the prices on gas trading hubs to determine the level and movement of prices, alongside or instead of traditional oil-based formulas. In Europe, the trend in this direction is already clear: in the Asia-Pacific region, this process is likely to take longer. With an increasing volume of gas – typically in the form of liquefied natural gas (LNG) – set to be available without commitment to a specific destination and free to seek the most advantageous sales price, the result is to create new linkages between regional markets and to narrow the price differences between them (Figure 1.3). There are, though, significant constraints on the emergence of a more globalised gas market, the main one being the capital intensity of gas infrastructure development and the consequently high cost – compared with other fuels – of moving gas between markets. This means that long-term contracting of gas to specific buyers, rather than sales on to competitive spot markets, is likely to remain essential for the bankability of most large-scale LNG and pipeline projects. And, even if LNG markets become more efficient and competitive, the significant costs of moving gas between markets limits the scope for a single global gas price to emerge.

Figure 1.3 ▷ **Natural gas price by region in the New Policies Scenario**

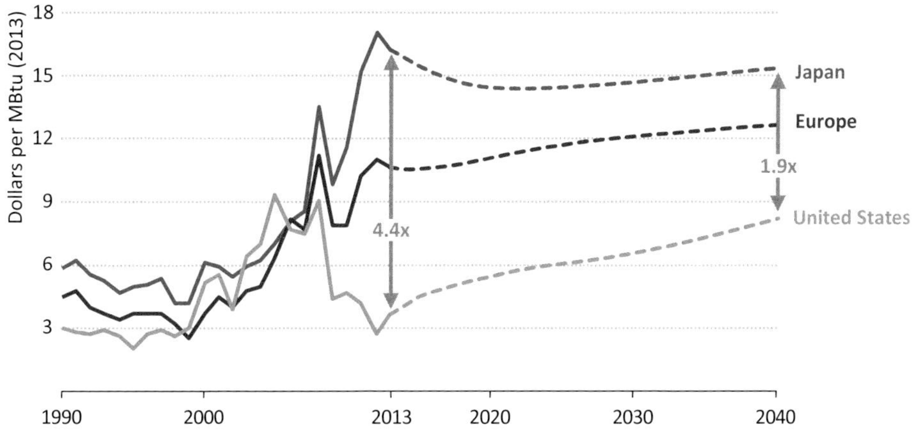

Notes: MBtu = million British thermal units. Average import prices are shown for Japan and Europe; the wholesale price is shown for the United States.

In the New Policies Scenario, gas prices in North America remain lower than in Europe or the Asia-Pacific region, thanks to the region's resurgent gas production outlook. These prices nonetheless are expected to rise over time, reaching $8.2/MBtu in 2040, as lower-cost resources are gradually depleted and the costs of production increase. Average import prices to Japan are expected to decline over the coming years as the exceptional need for additional gas to compensate for idled nuclear capacity starts to ease, but rise again in the longer term to reach $15.3/MBtu in 2040. This is the anticipated average price of LNG imported into the Asia-Pacific region, but it does not represent the natural gas price that is expected to prevail in China, the main emerging regional gas consumer. In addition to imported LNG, China has access also to imported pipeline gas from Turkmenistan and Russia, as well as substantial projected domestic gas production, which keeps the expected average domestic price to consumers in China closer to $10.9/MBtu in 2020 and $12.4/MBtu in 2040. This is closer, in practice, to the average price of imports into Europe, which reaches $12.7/MBtu by the end of our projection period.

Coal prices[14]

Steam and coking (or metallurgical) coal prices have experienced downward pressure in recent years. Australia, Colombia, Indonesia and South Africa have contributed to increased supply. At the same time, demand in the United States has weakened, because of strong competition from natural gas, and demand growth in China – by far the world's largest consumer and importer of coal – and other emerging markets has slowed. The average price of OECD steam coal imports in 2013, at $86 per tonne was two-thirds of the peak reached in 2008.

Figure 1.4 ▷ **Coal price relative to gas price by region in the New Policies Scenario** (in energy equivalent terms)

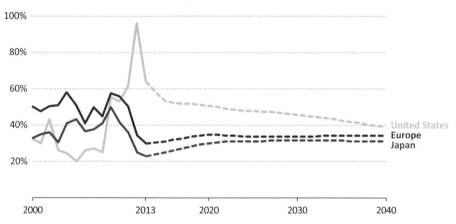

The outlook for steam coal prices depends on how well this fuel is able to compete against natural gas in power generation (Figure 1.4). Given the large difference in the carbon intensity of coal and gas (compared with gas, coal emits about twice as much CO_2 per unit of electricity generated), climate policies will have a major impact on inter-fuel competition. Steam coal prices, therefore, follow markedly different trajectories in the three scenarios presented. In the New Policies Scenario, the average OECD steam coal import price reaches just over $100/tonne (in year-2013 dollars) in 2020. It then increases very slowly, reaching a plateau of just over $110/tonne in the period 2035-2040 (though, in reality, prices will tend to fluctuate around a trend). In the Current Policies Scenario, prices increase more quickly, on stronger demand growth, while they fall in the 450 Scenario, as coal faces much more stringent measures to curb CO_2 emissions. Coking coal prices follow similar trends.

---

14. Chapter 5 features an analysis of how coal supply costs drive our price assumptions.

Chapter 2

Global energy trends to 2040
Change or be changed

Highlights

- In the New Policies Scenario, which takes account of existing and planned government policies, world primary energy demand increases by 37% between 2012 and 2040. Demand grew faster over previous decades; the slowdown in demand growth is mainly due to energy efficiency gains and structural changes in the global economy in favour of less energy-intensive activities.

- The share of fossil fuels in the primary energy mix falls through the *Outlook* period. In 2040, oil, natural gas and coal each account for roughly one-quarter of demand; low-carbon fuels (mainly renewable energy and nuclear power) make up the rest. Oil remains the single largest energy source, but renewables use grows fastest.

- Almost all of the growth in energy demand comes from non-OECD countries. Asia accounts for 60%, shifting the centre of gravity of energy markets decisively away from the Americas and Europe. China is the dominant force behind global demand growth for the next decade, accounting for more than one-third of the increase. But after 2025, India takes over as Chinese growth slows down noticeably.

- Energy use per capita in non-OECD countries rises strongly over the *Outlook* period, but, in 2040, is still well below the level that was reached in OECD countries in the early 1970s. Technological progress and improved energy efficiency, however, allow a higher level of demand for energy services to be satisfied per unit of energy. Nevertheless, increasing energy prices and changes to economic structure increase average spending on energy end-uses in non-OECD countries by close to 50%.

- World oil supply rises by 14 mb/d to 104 mb/d in 2040, but the trend hinges critically on timely investments in the Middle East, which becomes the major source of global supply growth once non-OPEC oil supply starts to fall back in the 2020s. All major regions, except Europe, contribute to the more than 50% rise in natural gas output.

- The re-ordering of energy trade flows towards Asian markets gathers pace, and the rising crude oil-import needs of China and India, from the Middle East and other regions, increases their vulnerability to the implications of a possible shortfall in investment or a disruption to oil supply. The share of natural gas in total inter-regional trade rises by one-quarter to more than 20% by 2040; concerns about gas security are eased by the increasing availability of LNG.

- In the run-up to the UN climate change summit in Paris in 2015, many governments have announced new measures to curb CO_2 emissions; but emissions still rise by 20% in the New Policies Scenario – consistent with a long-term global temperature increase of 3.6 °C. Increasing power sector decarbonisation through 2040 by about 25% would take the world half-way towards limiting the increase to 2 °C.

Energy trends by scenario

Despite the inevitable uncertainties, some key features of the evolution of global energy markets over the coming decades are already evident. These include the continuing persistent rise in demand for energy services that results from a growing world population and economy, and a continued shift in the centre of energy use to developing Asia and other emerging economies. But although some major contours are clear and the global energy system does not change direction easily (Box 2.1), this does not mean that its future direction is set in stone. Choices made by individual countries, responding to their unique local circumstances, can have far-reaching consequences for the global system, as with the rapid rise in unconventional oil and gas production in North America or the growing deployment of renewable technologies in many parts of the world. Choices can also be motivated by challenges that are globally shared, as in the case of climate change, or by reactions to other signs of stress in the system: for example, concerns over the security of gas supply to Europe or questions, prompted by the current turmoil in parts of the Middle East, over the outlook for oil supply. Market developments and individual and collective policy choices interact in complex ways: our analysis of their effect on energy trade and security, economic and social development, and the environment is introduced in this chapter and then taken up, in more detail, in the remainder of this *Outlook*.

Box 2.1 ▷ **Global energy use maintains its steady upward trajectory**

Comprehensive energy data for 2012 show a rise in global primary energy demand of 1.7%, a slightly slower rate of growth than the 1.9% seen in 2011. Coal use accounted for the largest share of this growth, with 40% of the total: renewables (26%), oil (25%) and natural gas (24%) also contributed, while the use of nuclear energy continued its decline since the accident at Fukushima Daiichi (-14%). Energy demand declined by 1.0% in OECD countries, a lower rate of reduction than in 2011 (-1.8%), as contractions in the European Union (-1.1%) and Japan (-2.1%) were lower than in the previous year, moderating the stronger decline in the United States (-2.4%). The lower rate of increase in overall global demand stems largely from much lower growth in China, at 5.1% in 2012, compared with 8.9% in 2011. Demand in India grew, by 4.8%, in Indonesia by 3.9% and Africa by 3.1% (where demand in North Africa rebounded from its decline in 2011).

Preliminary indications for 2013 show a continuing rise in global energy use, estimated at 1.9%, back to the same rate as in 2011. This figure hides markedly different trends across countries. In the OECD, preliminary data suggests that demand bounced back strongly in 2013, by an estimated 0.7%, after falling for two consecutive years. The main reason behind this is strong demand in the United States, partly the result of unusually cold winter weather. In non-OECD countries, the trend is in the opposite direction, with the rate of demand growth slowing further in 2013.

The three scenarios presented in this *Outlook* demonstrate, in particular, the impact of the policy choices made by governments: rates of growth in energy use and the types of fuels supplied are markedly different across those scenarios (see Chapter 1 for a detailed description of the policy assumptions underpinning each scenario). In our central scenario, the New Policies Scenario, which takes into account both existing and planned policies, world primary energy demand is projected to increase on average by 1.1% per year between 2012 and 2040, reaching almost 18 300 million tonnes of oil equivalent (Mtoe) – an increase of around 4 900 Mtoe, or 37% (Figure 2.1). Demand expands much more rapidly in the Current Policies Scenario, in which no new government policies are assumed, rising at an average rate of 1.5% per year to a level in 2040 that is 50% higher than in 2012. In the 450 Scenario, in which policies are assumed to be introduced to bring the world onto an energy trajectory that provides a 50% chance of constraining the long-term average global temperature increase to 2 degrees Celsius (°C), global energy demand grows on average by only 0.6% per year; in 2040, demand is 17% up on 2012. The gap in 2040 between demand in the different scenarios is substantial: taking the New Policies Scenario as the base, demand is 10% higher in the Current Policies Scenario and 15% lower in the 450 Scenario.

Figure 2.1 ▷ **World total primary energy demand by scenario**

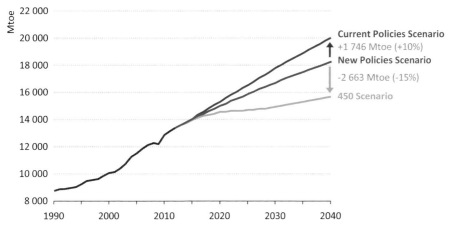

The share of fossil fuels in the overall primary fuel mix, which has remained broadly constant over the past three decades, falls in all three scenarios, though they remain dominant in 2040. Their share falls from 82% in 2012 to 80% in the Current Policies Scenario, to 74% in the New Policies Scenario and to below 60% in the 450 Scenario (Table 2.1). The range of outcomes is widest for coal and non-hydro renewable energy (excluding traditional use of solid biomass), as these energy sources are affected most by the evolution of environmental, energy security and climate policies worldwide. Coal demand rises by more than half between 2012 and 2040 in the Current Policies Scenario, but falls by one-third in the 450 Scenario. Trends in the use of modern renewable energy run in the opposite direction: use is highest in the 450 Scenario and lowest in the Current Policies Scenario. Of all the sources of energy, the variation across scenarios is smallest for hydropower, as its use is to a large degree determined by the extent of technically exploitable resources. Among final fuels, the outlook for electricity is the most constant, demand growing steadily in each scenario.

Table 2.1 ▷ **World primary energy demand by fuel and scenario** (Mtoe)

	2012	New Policies		Current Policies		450 Scenario	
	2012	2020	2040	2020	2040	2020	2040
Coal	3 879	4 211	4 448	4 457	5 860	3 920	2 590
Oil	4 194	4 487	4 761	4 584	5 337	4 363	3 242
Gas	2 844	3 182	4 418	3 215	4 742	3 104	3 462
Nuclear	642	845	1 210	838	1 005	859	1 677
Hydro	316	392	535	383	504	392	597
Bioenergy*	1 344	1 554	2 002	1 551	1 933	1 565	2 535
Other renewables	142	308	918	289	658	319	1 526
Total	13 361	14 978	18 293	15 317	20 039	14 521	15 629
Fossil fuel share	*82%*	*79%*	*74%*	*80%*	*80%*	*78%*	*59%*
*Non-OECD share**	*60%*	*63%*	*70%*	*63%*	*70%*	*63%*	*68%*

* Includes traditional and modern uses of biomass. ** Excludes international bunkers.

Energy trends in the New Policies Scenario

Demand

In our central scenario, the rate of growth in global primary energy demand slows noticeably over the coming decades, compared with the recent past. Demand grew by 2.1% per year on average over the two decades to 2012, but this drops to an average of 1.3% per year in the period from 2012 to 2025 and then falls further to 1.0% per year from 2025 to 2040. The projected slowdown in demand growth is mainly the result of energy efficiency gains and structural changes in the economy, which favour less energy-intensive activities. It also reflects a slower pace of economic and population growth in some non-OECD countries, as well as the effects over time of new efficiency policies that have only recently been adopted or are yet to be implemented. Some of these policies continue to affect demand over a period of many years, due to the slow turnover of energy-related equipment, appliances and buildings.

Global demand for every primary energy source increases between 2012 and 2040, but the rates of growth are markedly different (Table 2.2). The share of fossil fuels in the overall primary fuel mix, which has remained broadly constant over the past three decades, falls gradually through the *Outlook* period, though these fuels remain dominant in 2040, each of the three fuels accounting for roughly one-quarter of demand. Renewable energy sources and nuclear power together make up the remaining quarter (Figure 2.2), with the use of renewables growing faster than that of any other fuel.

Figure 2.2 ▷ Fuel shares in world primary energy demand in the
New Policies Scenario

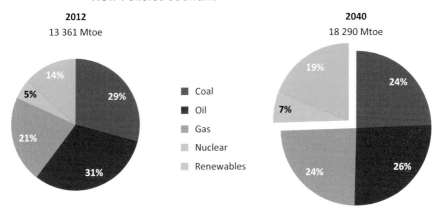

The trend towards greater use of the low-carbon fuels such as renewables and nuclear is most notable in OECD countries (Figure 2.3). Many of the leading economies see significant changes in their energy mix over the next two-and-a-half decades, resulting to some degree from major policy initiatives over the past few years. In many OECD countries, where total primary energy demand barely grows over the *Outlook* period, low-carbon fuels increasingly replace fossil fuels, in particular in the power sector. Growth in the use of low-carbon fuels in absolute terms is about twice as large in non-OECD countries, although it is exceeded by the growing use of fossil fuels, as countries use all possible means to satisfy the strong growth in demand for energy services.

Figure 2.3 ▷ Primary energy demand growth by region and fuel type in the
New Policies Scenario, 2012-2040

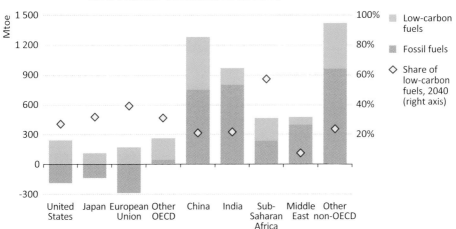

Table 2.2 ▷ **World primary energy demand by fuel in the New Policies Scenario** (Mtoe)

	1990	2012	2020	2025	2030	2035	2040	CAAGR* 2012-2040
Coal	2 231	3 879	4 211	4 293	4 342	4 392	4 448	0.5%
Oil	3 232	4 194	4 487	4 612	4 689	4 730	4 761	0.5%
Gas	1 668	2 844	3 182	3 487	3 797	4 112	4 418	1.6%
Nuclear	526	642	845	937	1 047	1 137	1 210	2.3%
Hydro	184	316	392	430	469	503	535	1.9%
Bioenergy**	905	1 344	1 554	1 675	1 796	1 911	2 002	1.4%
Other renewables	36	142	308	435	581	744	918	6.9%
Total	8 782	13 361	14 978	15 871	16 720	17 529	18 293	1.1%

*Compound average annual growth rate. ** Includes traditional and modern uses of biomass.

Outlook by fuel

Oil remains the single largest energy source throughout the projection period, though its share of total demand falls from 31% in 2012 to 26% in 2040 – just ahead of coal and natural gas. Demand growth slows gradually, from 0.9% per year until 2020 (in line with the growth trend of the past three years) to 0.3% per year in the 2030s. In volume terms, oil demand increases from 90 mb/d in 2013 to 104 mb/d in 2040.[1] High prices, technological advances and policies combine to drive energy efficiency improvements, switching to other fuels (including gas in transport) and conservation. These factors offset, to some degree, continuing growth in demand for transport and other oil-related services. Almost all of the net increase in oil demand comes from transport, industry and use of oil as a feedstock for petrochemicals. Oil consumption declines in other sectors, such as power generation, these other uses accounting for 20% of total oil demand in 2040, compared with 28% in 2013.

For each barrel of oil no longer used in OECD countries, two barrels more are used in the non-OECD. Among the OECD regions, US oil demand is reduced the most in absolute terms, resting stable through to about 2020 and then drifting lower as new vehicle efficiency standards take effect. Chinese oil demand continues to grow, China overtaking the United States as the world's largest consumer by around 2030; but demand growth decelerates markedly in the 2030s, with a slowdown in the country's population growth and then a modest absolute decline, a gradual reduction in economic growth and policy-driven efficiency improvements, in particular in transport. In volume terms, oil consumption rises more in the 2030s than in the 2020s only in India, Indonesia and Africa (Figure 2.4). A rapid growth in car ownership makes India and Nigeria the countries with the highest rates of oil demand growth over the projection period. Oil demand in India overtakes that of the European Union (EU) by the mid-2030s. The Middle East sees stronger absolute growth in oil demand than any region outside Asia, driven by the transport and petrochemicals sector and the assumed maintenance of widespread subsidies.

---

1. See Chapter 3 for the definition of oil demand used in the *World Energy Outlook*.

Figure 2.4 ▷ Incremental oil demand in selected non-OECD regions in the New Policies Scenario

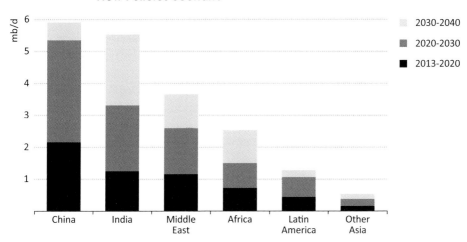

Coal demand is projected to continue to grow through the projection period, but at a much slower pace than over the past decade: demand expands on average by 1% per year in the period 2012-2020, but by only 0.3% per year in the 2020s and just 0.2% per year in the 2030s. In 2040, coal consumption, at almost 6 400 million tonnes of coal equivalent (Mtce), is still 15% up on the 2012 level of 5 540 Mtce, but its share of global demand dips from 29% to 24%. Coal has been the fastest-growing major fuel over the last decade, supplying nearly half of global incremental energy demand between 2002 and 2012; more than 85% of the increase came from China – now the world's biggest consumer, producer and importer. But growing concerns about the environmental impact of coal use and flagging gross domestic product (GDP) growth are set to temper coal demand growth in China. Coal use expands in most other non-OECD regions, notably Southeast Asia and India, which overtakes the United States to become the world's second-largest consumer by 2020 (though its demand remains about a third of China's even in 2040). By contrast, demand in almost all OECD regions continues to shrink: despite the current surge in coal use, EU demand falls by well over a half over the *Outlook* period (mostly after 2020 due to climate and local pollution policies), while US demand contracts by a third between 2012 and 2040.

Worldwide, coal use remains heavily concentrated in the power sector, where it remains the single largest energy source (though renewables as a whole overtake coal). Its share of total world power production nonetheless drops ten percentage points, to 31%, between 2012 and 2040. The use of coal in industry peaks during the projection period and then declines as it is substituted by natural gas and electricity. It also dwindles in the buildings sector. By contrast, coal inputs to coal-to-liquids plants grow strongly.

Global demand for natural gas is projected to grow faster than that for either of the two other fossil fuels and grows more, in absolute terms, than that for any other fuel between 2012 and 2040. It rises in an almost linear fashion from 3.4 trillion cubic metres (tcm) in

2012 to 5.4 tcm in 2040 – an increase of 57%, or 1.6% per year. Consumption of gas reaches the level of coal, in energy-equivalent terms, by around 2040. The share of gas in global primary energy demand edges up three percentage points to 24%. Non-OECD countries account for around four-fifths of the increase, led by China – which overtakes the EU in terms of gas demand by around 2035 – and the rest of developing Asia. Demand also grows strongly in the Middle East.

The more mature gas market in North America sees continued expansion, as measures to cut emissions in the United States power sector favour the use of gas over coal. Gas demand in Europe, though, struggles to retain a competitive foothold in the power mix, its use increasing largely on the back of retiring coal-fired and nuclear capacity. Russian demand grows at an even slower pace and our projection of gas consumption in Japan is lowered by the envisaged restart of the nuclear programme and the push for renewables and efficiency. In almost all regions, power generation is the largest user of gas and therefore the leading driver of increased gas use, although gas also starts to make inroads into road transport and more quality constrained marine bunkers.

Nuclear power generation increases by almost 90% over the *Outlook* period, to more than 4 600 terawatt-hours (TWh) in 2040 (see Part B). Installed capacity increases from 392 gigawatts (GW) in 2013 to 624 GW in 2040, with its share of electricity supply increasing only marginally from the current level of 11% to 12% (having peaked at 18% in 1996). The number of economies operating reactors rises from 31 to 36, as newcomers outnumber those that phase out nuclear power. Almost two-fifths of the existing nuclear fleet is retired in the period to 2040, involving the closure of almost 200 reactors. The projected level of capacity in 2040 involves a construction rate of new plants of 14 GW per year on average. This rate is slower than the peak rate in the 1980s, but significantly faster than the rate realised in the more recent past.

The use of renewable energy sources (excluding fuelwood and charcoal – a form of solid biomass) grows briskly through the projection period, driven by subsidies, technological advances (which are expected to reduce costs), projected high fossil-fuel prices and, in several cases, rising carbon-dioxide (CO_2) prices. The share of renewables in world primary energy demand reaches 15% in 2040, compared with 8% in 2012.[2] The power sector contributes most to this increase: the share of renewables in total generation increases from 21% in 2012 to 33% by 2040. Around half of this increase is due to solar and wind power, generation from the two sources together growing at a combined rate of almost 8% per year on average. Hydropower also expands, but at a more modest rate of 1.9% per year, as much of the resource's technical potential is already being exploited, and environmental and economic factors limit the exploitation of the undeveloped resources (mainly in non-OECD regions). The use of biofuels also expands substantially over the same period, from 1.3 million barrels per day (mb/d) to 4.6 mb/d, with an increasing contribution coming from advanced biofuels after 2020. By contrast, the use

---

2. The share of renewables was 13% in 2012 and reaches 19% in 2040 when including fuelwood and charcoal.

of fuelwood and charcoal for domestic heating and cooking, mainly in poor developing countries, declines. More than one-third of fuelwood and charcoal consumption is in sub-Saharan Africa, where its use peaks around 2030 and then starts to decline gradually.

Among the leading fuels used in final applications (after transformation of primary energy), electricity sees the biggest absolute increase and the fastest rate of growth in demand. Worldwide, electricity consumption nearly doubles between 2012 and 2040, growing at an annual average rate of 2.1%, and its share of final energy consumption climbs from 18% to 23% (Figure 2.5). As with all other fuels, the bulk of the increase occurs in non-OECD countries.

Box 2.2 ▷ Technology, diverging prices and fuel switching

Technological developments and shifting relative prices are increasing the scope for fuel switching in a range of end-uses and transformation activities, adding to the uncertainty surrounding the prospects for specific fuels and sectors. The last few years have seen some large falls in the cost of some types of renewables, notably solar photovoltaic (PV), which have brought them closer to being commercially viable and boosted their deployment where government incentives are in place. Further cost reductions and technological advances could lead to even higher levels of deployment and further transform the way the world meets its rapidly growing demand for electricity. Solar energy (photovoltaics and concentrating solar power) provides 4% of the world's electricity supply in 2040 in the New Policies Scenario, while wind power contributes 8%. Onshore wind power technology has already matured to the point where it is competitive in some locations well-endowed with wind resources, without the need for subsidy; strong cost reductions are expected for offshore wind as well over the *Outlook* period, but they still require subsidies in most regions in 2040.

Road transport is poised for a shift, in this case away from oil products, which dominate today: at 95%, oil product share of total energy use in that sector worldwide is barely lower than just before the first oil price crisis in 1973. The share of biofuels grows rapidly, thanks mainly to government support, usually in the form of blending mandates; it reaches 8% in 2040, almost triple the current share. This prospective rate of growth is uncertain, however, as policy support in the main consuming regions is waning. Natural gas, in compressed or liquefied form, is also set to play a bigger role in transport in countries where its price is low, notably North America, or where it enjoys government support, as in China. But the need for costly investment in refuelling infrastructure and modifying vehicles is likely to constrain demand in many cases. The prospects for electric vehicles (EVs) – plug-in hybrids and battery-electric vehicles – are also highly uncertain, as the breakthrough to fully commercial models has yet to come and consumers would have to adjust to the characteristics of the new vehicles. Our projections point to only modest growth in the EV fleet, but a breakthrough in battery and recharging technology could revolutionise road transport in the longer term.

Figure 2.5 ▷ **Fuel shares in global final energy consumption in the New Policies Scenario**

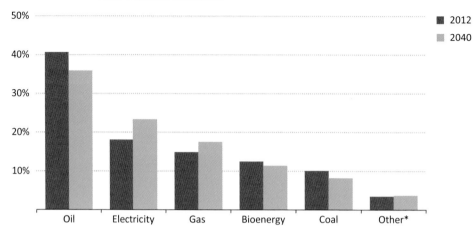

* Includes heat and renewables except bioenergy.

Outlook by region

A feature of the changing global energy map is the increasing predominance of non-OECD countries in global energy demand. Energy demand in non-OECD countries overtook that of OECD countries in 2005, and continues its rise over the *Outlook* period as a result of much faster rates of economic and population growth. In the New Policies Scenario, 97% of the growth in demand comes from non-OECD countries (excluding international bunkers), of which the developing Asian countries – led by China – account for 65% (Table 2.3). These trends shift the dynamics of global energy consumption decisively away from the Americas and Europe towards Asia and, to a lesser extent, the Middle East and Africa (Figure 2.6).

Regional trends in energy use over the first and second halves of the projection period vary markedly. In the period to 2025, China remains the dominant driving force behind the rise in global demand, accounting for more than one-third of the total increase (Figure 2.7). China overtook the United States to become the world's biggest energy consumer in 2009 and continues to pull away as the global leader in the medium term. By 2025, China makes up 24% of global energy demand against a share in 2012 of 22% and just 12% ten years earlier. The picture over the period 2025-2040 is very different, as economic growth in China slows down and population growth first levels off and then starts to decline slowly after 2030. By around the late 2020s, India takes over from China as the main source of global demand growth, as the Indian population exceeds that of China, while GDP per capita by the late 2020s reaches the level of China today and continues to grow rapidly thereafter.[3] By 2040, India's total energy use is fast approaching that of the United States, which remains the world's second-largest consumer. Other non-OECD regions also account for a bigger share of demand growth after 2025, increasingly diversifying global energy demand and leading to the emergence of multiple major demand centres.

3. Following the regional focus on sub-Saharan Africa in *WEO-2014*, India will be the focus region of the *World Energy Outlook* 2015.

Figure 2.6 ▷ Primary energy demand by region in the New Policies Scenario (Mtoe)

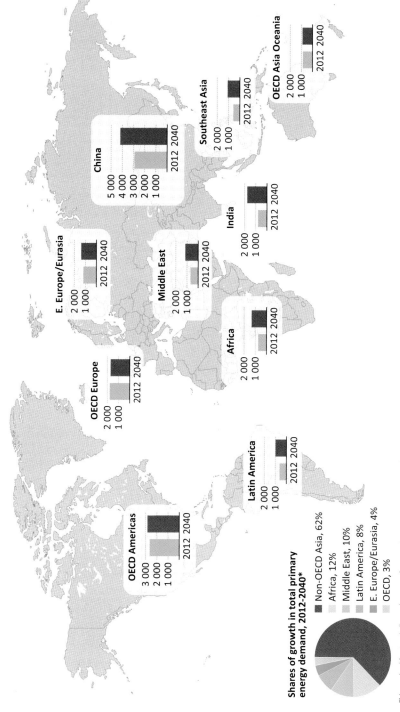

This map is without prejudice to the status of or sovereignty over any territory, to the delimitation of international frontiers and boundaries, and to the name of any territory, city or area. Note: Values in the pie chart do not sum to 100% due to rounding.

*Growth in primary demand excludes bunkers.

Table 2.3 ▷ World primary energy demand by region in the New Policies Scenario (Mtoe)

	1990	2012	2020	2025	2030	2035	2040	CAAGR* 2012-2040
OECD	4 522	5 251	5 436	5 423	5 392	5 399	5 413	0.1%
Americas	2 260	2 618	2 781	2 782	2 771	2 793	2 821	0.3%
United States	1 915	2 136	2 256	2 233	2 197	2 192	2 190	0.1%
Europe	1 630	1 769	1 762	1 738	1 717	1 704	1 697	-0.1%
Asia Oceania	631	864	893	903	905	903	895	0.1%
Japan	439	452	447	440	434	429	422	-0.2%
Non-OECD	4 059	7 760	9 151	10 031	10 883	11 656	12 371	1.7%
E. Europe/Eurasia	1 538	1 178	1 194	1 238	1 286	1 340	1 384	0.6%
Russia	880	741	730	748	770	798	819	0.4%
Asia	1 588	4 551	5 551	6 115	6 653	7 118	7 527	1.8%
China	879	2 909	3 512	3 802	4 019	4 145	4 185	1.3%
India	317	788	1 004	1 170	1 364	1 559	1 757	2.9%
Southeast Asia	233	577	708	784	870	967	1 084	2.3%
Middle East	211	680	800	899	992	1 070	1 153	1.9%
Africa	391	739	897	994	1 095	1 203	1 322	2.1%
Latin America	331	611	709	784	857	926	985	1.7%
Brazil	138	278	337	384	427	465	494	2.1%
World**	8 782	13 361	14 978	15 871	16 720	17 529	18 293	1.1%
European Union	1 642	1 641	1 615	1 582	1 552	1 534	1 523	-0.3%

* Compound average annual growth rate. ** Includes international marine and aviation bunkers (not included in regional totals).

Figure 2.7 ▷ Primary energy demand growth by selected region in the New Policies Scenario

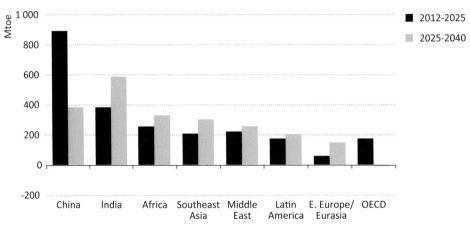

Despite the dominant role of non-OECD countries for global energy demand growth, on a per-capita basis, average levels of energy demand in non-OECD (at 1.3 tonnes of oil equivalent [toe] per capita in 2012) remain more than three-times below those in the OECD (4.2 toe). There is some degree of convergence in these indicators over the period to 2040, with the OECD figure falling slightly to 3.9 toe per capita and the non-OECD average rising slightly to 1.6 toe per capita. But, in practice, the trend in non-OECD countries is proceeding along a path quite distinct from the route followed earlier by the OECD, as technology advances and more efficient use of energy, triggered by higher prices and by energy efficiency policies in some countries, are changing the link between incomes and energy use. By 2040, average per-capita incomes in non-OECD countries are projected to reach a comparable level to that of OECD countries in 1971. Yet the energy use associated with similar per-capita incomes at these two points in time is quite different. Back in 1970, this level of per-capita income in OECD countries required more than twice the energy than that anticipated for non-OECD consumers in 2040 (Figure 2.8). The reason is that technological progress and increased energy efficiency allow in 2040 to satisfy a higher level of demand for energy services per unit of energy than in the 1970s.

Figure 2.8 ▷ **Energy demand and GDP per capita, and corresponding oil price in the New Policies Scenario**

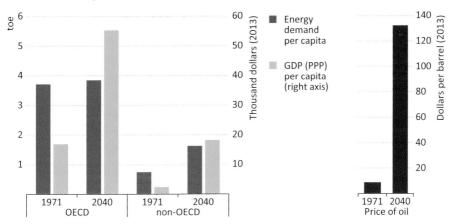

Note: PPP = purchasing power parity.

The United States is among the countries facing the most significant changes in its energy mix over the projection period. Demand peaks by around 2020 and is barely higher than today in 2040. But the fuel mix undergoes a very dramatic change: oil loses almost 10 percentage points to 27% and is overtaken by gas before 2030 as the dominant fuel in the energy mix. Oil use (in volumetric terms) drops by around 2030 to levels not seen for decades and continues its decline thereafter. Coal also loses market share and is overtaken by renewables in the 2030s. Those changes are a result of several policy initiatives and the boom in domestic production of shale gas. Recent policy efforts include a proposal by US Environmental Protection Agency (EPA) to reduce carbon emissions from the power sector by 30% in 2030, relative to 2005, and the announcement of the extension of fuel-economy standards for heavy-duty vehicles into the next decade. Other measures involve efficiency standards to reduce the average fuel consumption of road passenger vehicles and to improve the efficiency of appliances and lighting in the buildings sector, together with incentives for the use of efficient motors in the industry sector.

Similar changes are projected in the European Union, where the decline in primary energy demand until 2040 continues at much the same rate as over the past decade. Coal demand falls particularly fast (its share drops by about half to just 9% in 2040), while the share of renewables rises to more than one-quarter and natural gas demand also expands modestly. These trends are mainly driven by the power sector, where the share of renewable energies in electricity generation almost doubles to 46% in 2040, posing challenges to the design of power markets and threatening the adequacy of investment in thermal generation.[4] The projected changes are largely driven by policy efforts in Europe to decarbonise the power sector; existing goals to 2020 are assumed to be extended on the lines proposed in the 2030 framework for climate and energy, the objective being to reduce greenhouse-gas emissions by 40%, relative to 1990. They also take account of the provisions to promote energy security by reducing the energy intensity of the economy through energy efficiency.

In Japan, demand continues its slow decline with 2040 levels 7% lower than 2012. In contrast, electricity demand expands by 11% and nuclear power output is assumed to recover progressively over the period to 2020 to three-quarters of the level prevailing just before the Fukushima Daiichi accident, reducing the need to burn gas and oil for power. In the longer term, nuclear generation increases modestly (in line with the government's announcement that nuclear should continue to play an important role) though its share in total generation (21% in 2040) does not reach levels prior to the accident. The recent wave of investment in non-hydro renewables – particularly solar PV – slows over the *Outlook* period, but still boosts their share in total power generation by more than four-times over 2012 levels, to 22% in 2040 (Chapter 7).

Energy demand in Russia grows by 11%, but the fuel mix changes less than in the other major economies, primarily because the policy push is less pronounced. Gas remains far and away the leading source of energy, still meeting well over half of the country's energy needs in 2040. Oil demand plateaus and declines as of the mid-2020s, as vehicles become more efficient, resulting in a somewhat reduced market share for oil. The share of coal in the primary mix drops, offset by a rise in the share of nuclear power and non-hydro renewables, though their share remains modest.

The energy sector of China is confronted with a host of challenges, meeting an overall increase in energy demand of 44% by 2040, while dealing with rising energy security

---

4. See the *World Energy Investment Outlook*, published in June 2014, for a discussion of the European power sector (IEA, 2014): *www.worldenergyoutlook.org/investment*.

concerns and environmental pollution. In June 2014, the president called for a "revolution" in energy consumption, energy supply, energy technology and energy governance. The Action Plan for Air Pollution Prevention and Control, released by China's State Council in September 2013, is an important programme to curb coal consumption and increase non-fossil energy use. As a result, our projections point to a significant slowdown in the growth of coal use, with coal use peaking around 2030 and being just 7% above 2012 levels in 2040. The share of coal in the energy mix drops from two-thirds in 2012 to around half in 2040. As the engine of growth moves away from heavy industries, the power sector becomes increasingly important in setting the country's primary demand trends, accounting for almost 75% of primary demand growth, compared to less than 50% in the period 2000-2012. Electricity generation is set to double to 2040, with coal and non-hydro renewables accounting each for around 30% of growth. Despite efforts to improve energy efficiency in transport, oil demand in China continues to rise. But the rate of Chinese consumption growth slows noticeably over the projection period: 90% of the total increase in oil use occurs prior to 2030; thereafter, growth is minimal as vehicle fuel-economy policies take effect, industrial production slows and the population starts to slowly decline. Nonetheless, China overtakes the United States in the early 2030s as the largest oil-consuming country and is projected to use 15.7 mb/d of oil in 2040.

India energy demand more than doubles, as per-capita consumption increases and access to modern energy expands. The power sector has experienced financial difficulties in recent years and continues to struggle to secure adequate returns on investment, indicating the scale of the challenge.[5] In recognition of this problem, the Indian government is taking steps to improve the financial situation of utilities (see Chapter 6). In our projections, coal use for power continues to rise with booming electricity demand, leading to increasing reliance on coal imports, even though the share of coal in the fuel mix in generation and in the overall primary fuel mix falls, as gas plays an increasing role. India becomes the largest coal importer, with import needs in 2040 twice as large as China today. The use of oil also rises strongly as car ownership takes off, household incomes rise (boosting demand for modern cooking fuels) and business activity expands. India becomes the key centre of global oil demand growth after 2030, consolidating its position as the world's third-largest oil consumer after China and the United States. By contrast, the use of fuelwood and charcoal in India falls, its share of final fuel use plummeting from a quarter at present to below 10% by 2040, due to a shift to electricity and other modern forms of energy.

Energy demand in sub-Saharan Africa has been growing strongly over the past decade, but demand per capita is still among the lowest in the world today: at 0.6 toe, per-capita energy consumption is only one-third of the world average. About 620 million people in the region, or two-thirds of the entire population, lack access to electricity, and more than 700 million rely on the traditional use of solid biomass for cooking. Strong economic

---

5. See the *World Energy Investment Outlook* for a discussion of the Indian power sector (IEA, 2014): *www.worldenergyoutlook.org/investment*.

expansion, increasing urbanisation and a legacy of unmet demand mean that energy demand will increase at a rapid pace, almost doubling to around 1 000 Mtoe in 2040. However, there continue to be significant disparities within sub-Saharan Africa (the subject of an in-depth analysis in Part C), as more than half of energy demand growth occurs in Nigeria and the countries of Southern Africa. Overall, despite a large resource base and some improvements in the performance of its energy sector, energy supply still falls short of sub-Saharan Africa's needs in the New Policies Scenario: the region accounts for one-fifth of the global population in 2040 and yet only around one-twentieth of world energy demand. But there are ways in which stronger growth could be achieved (discussed in detail in Chapter 16): increased investment in the power sector to improve the reliability of supply, increased regional co-operation and a larger share of oil and gas revenues reinvested in infrastructure would allow Africa's energy sector to act as an engine for economic transformation and growth, lifting the combined GDP of sub-Saharan Africa 30% above the levels anticipated in the New Policies Scenario, an increase in regional output of some $2 trillion.

The Middle East is central to the long-term outlook for oil, not only as a supplier to global oil markets, but also because it becomes a major centre of oil demand over the *Outlook* period – the third-largest market after China and the United States. The prevalence of fossil-fuel consumption subsidies (see detailed analysis in Chapter 9) undermines efforts to improve energy efficiency in many countries in the region and mean that oil demand growth in the region is among the fastest in the world. Growth is strongest in the transport and petrochemicals sectors. Oil continues to be used on a large scale for power generation, an expensive way to generate electricity and a practice that is rare anywhere else in the world. The use of gas grows more strongly than that of oil, driven by the power and industry sectors. The use of non-hydro renewables expands at double-digit rates, their share of power generation reaching 14% by 2040.

Outlook by sector

More than half of the projected increase in global primary energy demand over the *Outlook* period comes from the power sector – the result of the continuing electrification of the world economy. Power generation already absorbs just under 40% of global primary energy and that share increases to 42% in 2040, demand for inputs to generation being dragged higher by steadily rising demand for electricity in all end-use and other transformation sectors (Figure 2.9), despite further improvements in the efficiency of energy conversion in power stations. The share of coal in power generation drops by ten percentage points to 31% in 2040, as the use of renewables (whose combined share overtakes coal in the early 2030s) and, to a lesser extent, natural gas gains ground.

Among the final sectors, demand is projected to grow fastest in industry, at 1.4% per year on average over the projection period, just ahead of transport and buildings (i.e. residential and commercial sectors). Almost 50% of the growth in industrial energy demand occurs in China and India, with the rest spread in almost equal parts across other emerging regions.

Among the OECD regions, only North America sees any significant increase in industrial energy use, thanks to relatively strong economic growth and the boost in competitiveness provided by relatively low energy prices there. In aggregate, OECD industrial energy demand increases slowly through to 2020, levelling off thereafter. Over the whole projection period, the OECD contributes just 2% to the global growth in industrial energy demand.

Figure 2.9 ▷ **World energy demand by selected sector in the New Policies Scenario**

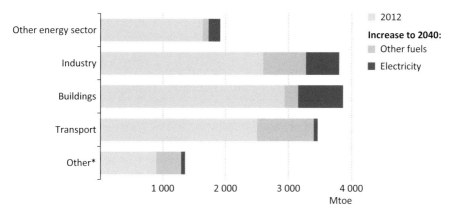

*Other includes agriculture and non-energy use.

The number of vehicles on the world's roads doubles between 2012 and 2040, but the increasingly widespread adoption of vehicle fuel-economy standards mitigates the impact on transport demand, which rises on average by 1.2% per year – a significantly slower pace than in recent decades (Chapters 3 and 8). Mexico, India and Saudi Arabia are among the countries that have announced adoption of vehicle fuel-economy standards over the past year. Airplanes and ships also become a lot more fuel efficient, offsetting part of the projected rise in demand for air travel and maritime freight. All of the growth in transport demand comes from non-OECD countries, notably China; it declines in the OECD, where efficiency gains more than outweigh a modest expansion of the vehicle fleet (Figure 2.10). Oil-based fuels continue to dominate transport energy demand, even though alternative fuels, in particular biofuels, take a gradually increasing share of the total. Of the transport fuels, diesel demand grows strongest and diesel overtakes gasoline as the dominant oil product in the transport sector by mid-2030s. The use of kerosene for aviation also grows strongly.

In the buildings sector, energy use grows at an average rate of 1.0% per year through the *Outlook* period, with about one-third of the growth coming from developing Asia and most of the rest from the Middle East, Africa and Latin America. Electricity accounts for most of the increase – mainly because of strong growth in demand for air-conditioning, computing facilities, refrigerators and other appliances such as mobile phones – and natural gas for most of the rest (mostly for water heating and cooking).

Figure 2.10 ▷ **Change in energy demand by sector and region in the New Policies Scenario, 2012-2040**

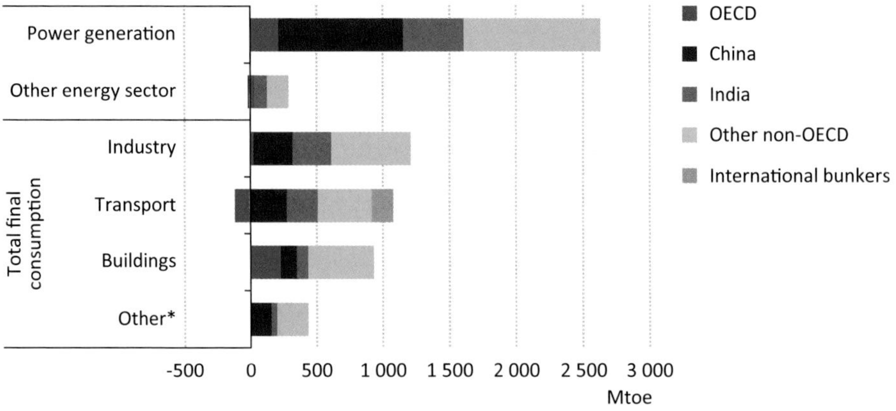

*Other includes agriculture and non-energy use. Note: Total final consumption includes electricity and heat generated by the power sector.

Box 2.3 ▷ Fossil-fuel transformation gets more complex

New ways of converting fossil fuels into higher value end-use products are set to play an increasingly important role in meeting global energy needs in the coming decades. Traditionally, the main fossil-fuel transformation pathways are oil refining and power generation. But things are becoming more complex. The high price of oil in recent years has stimulated investment in plants to convert natural gas and coal into liquid fuels that can either substitute for oil products or be blended into them. Coal-to-gas conversion is also gaining some ground, notably in China. Price differentials are expected to continue to boost this trend over the longer term, though the attraction of these processes is dimmed by their energy-intensive nature and the associated emissions.

Gas-to-liquids (GTL) production jumped in 2011 with the start-up of the 140 thousand barrels per day (kb/d) Pearl GTL plant in Qatar, taking global capacity to 215 kb/d. All existing plants use the Fischer-Tropsch (FT) process, producing mainly diesel, gasoline and lubricants. One other such plant, in Nigeria, produced its first liquids this year while two others are in the front-end engineering design phase in Uzbekistan and the United States. Some others are being considered, for example in Canada, Algeria and Russia. Together, they could bring global capacity to more than 400 kb/d by 2025. Beyond that, advances in small-scale production units may make it economically feasible to develop small, remote pockets of gas using GTL technology, permitting a more rapid growth. GTL output is projected to climb to more than 360 kb/d by 2025 and almost 1 mb/d by 2040 in the New Policies Scenario.

Technology to convert coal into oil products is developing rapidly. Coal-to-liquids (CTL), or coal liquefaction converts coal into diesel, gasoline and other oil products, and has been commercially used in South Africa since the 1950s, based on FT technology. Capacity there today stands at approximately 70 kb/d of transport fuels, meeting about 20% of the country's needs. The relatively low price of coal and energy security concerns are driving interest in CTL technology in China and other coal-producing countries, though there are question marks over the economics and the environmental implications – carbon emissions are high in the absence of capture and storage and the technology relies on large volumes of water. The first Chinese CTL plant using direct conversion technology, with a capacity of 30 kb/d, was commissioned at Ordos in 2009 and others are under development. In total, CTL production worldwide is projected to reach 450 kb/d in 2025 and 1.1 mb/d in 2040, with most of the capacity being built in Asia.

Coal is also likely to be used increasingly as a feedstock for producing a range of petrochemicals. China already has a large industry to convert coal to methanol – an intermediate product for the chemical industry and a blend-stock for transport-fuel – with capacity standing at around 45 million tonnes (Mt) today. The conversion of coal to olefins – producing ethylene and/or propylene, intermediate products for making plastics and other chemicals – via methanol in an integrated process is growing rapidly in China: capacity has jumped from zero to around 4 Mt/year in just the past few years and is expected to reach 16 Mt by the end of the current decade. As with CTL, further expansion is likely to be constrained by the technology's high carbon and water intensity. China is also planning to convert coal into synthetic gas (similar to conventional methane, but typically with more impurities) in order to reduce its dependence on gas imports. Two coal-to-gas (CTG) plants are already operational, providing about 3 bcm of natural gas, and there are plans by other companies for an additional 65 bcm of capacity. CTG output is projected to increase to over 50 bcm by 2040, accounting for 14% of China's total natural gas production.

Energy prices and energy spending

The final prices of energy paid by consumers, be they business or households, is a combination of international prices, the domestic costs of transformation and delivery, profit margins and prevalent tax regimes. Taking all end-user prices as a whole, weighted by consumption, can yield a measure of an economy's spending on a unit of energy. Such weighted average end-use spending has risen sharply over the past decade, particularly in OECD countries, closely mirroring international fuel price developments (Figure 2.11). It was on average more than 50% higher in 2012 than in 2000 in OECD countries. In non-OECD countries, spending rose by only 10% over the same period, partly because of subsidies. Today, the average spending per unit of energy is more than twice as high in OECD countries as that in non-OECD countries. Such differences spring from a variety of causes. Some of these, such as access to cheaper fossil resources, are here to stay. In the New Policies Scenario, the average spending on energy use in OECD countries in 2040 is still more than 50% higher than in non-OECD countries.

Figure 2.11 ▷ **Weighted average spending on energy end-use by region in the New Policies Scenario**

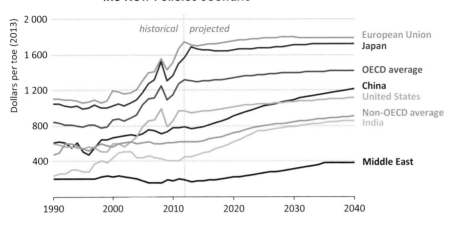

Increasing energy prices and rising energy spending are one reason for the new wave of energy efficiency policies adopted in recent years in many OECD countries. Their implementation helps to moderate the effect of increasing fuel prices in OECD countries: as final energy demand barely grows in the New Policies Scenario, the total spending on the use of energy across all end-use sectors remains, despite increasing energy prices, broadly constant until 2040 in the New Policies Scenario (Figure 2.12).

Figure 2.12 ▷ **Spending on energy end-use by selected region in the New Policies Scenario**

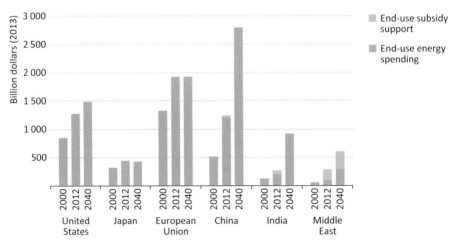

Note: Subsidy data are not available for the year 2000.

In non-OECD countries, however, the picture is very different. Demand for energy services is increasing rapidly, driven by population and economic growth, which means that the spending on the use of energy is set to rise considerably, moderated only by increased energy efficiency. The effect of rising energy demand on total energy spending is further augmented by structural shifts in the economy in many non-OECD countries. In China, for example, the gradual shift away from energy-intensive industries increases average spending per unit of energy in the industry sector, as energy prices paid for by energy-intensive industries are below the average of those of other industry sectors, in particular for electricity. Policies to displace coal in the industry sector by other, more expensive fuels further increase the average spending on energy. The strong increase in transport service demand in many non-OECD countries is another factor that contributes to higher spending on the use of energy in those countries.

Some countries are using subsidies to fossil fuels to shield their citizens from international fuel price developments. Adding in the cost of fossil-fuel subsidies, however, boosts the spending discussed above to much higher levels, in particular in the Middle East, and indicates the significance of subsidies as a burden on the overall economy. When the cost of fossil-fuel subsidies is included, the spending on energy use relative to GDP in the Middle East in 2040 is higher than in the other major energy-consuming regions.

Box 2.4 ▷ **Current status of energy access**

Worldwide 1.3 billion people – a population equivalent to that of the entire OECD – continue to live without access to electricity. This is equivalent to 18% of the global population and 22% of those living in developing countries (Table 2.4). Nearly 97% of those without access to electricity live in sub-Saharan Africa and developing Asia.[6] The latest estimate for sub-Saharan Africa has been revised up by 22 million, illustrating how rapid population growth can continue to outpace the rate of electrification in many countries and conceal the progress that has been made (see Chapter 13). In developing Asia, the general trend shows an improving picture, but the pace varies. The largest populations without electricity are in India, Nigeria, Ethiopia, Bangladesh, Democratic Republic of Congo (DR Congo) and Indonesia.

Nearly 2.7 billion people – almost 40% of the world population and about half of those living in developing countries – rely on the traditional use of solid biomass for cooking, an increase of 38 million compared with last year. Here, the issue is much more skewed towards developing Asia, which accounts for nearly 1.9 billion of the total. India, alone, has more than 800 million people using inefficient, polluting means for cooking – a greater number than in the whole of sub-Saharan Africa.

---

6. See Part C for an in-depth study of energy access in sub-Saharan Africa.

Table 2.4 ▷ Number of people without access to modern energy services by region, 2012 (million)[7]

	Without access to electricity		Traditional use of biomass for cooking*	
	Population	Share of population	Population	Share of population
Developing countries	1 283	24%	2 679	49%
Africa	622	57%	728	67%
Sub-Saharan Africa	621	68%	727	80%
Nigeria	93	55%	115	68%
Ethiopia	70	77%	87	95%
DR Congo	60	91%	61	93%
North Africa	1	1%	1	1%
Asia	620	17%	1 875	51%
India	304	25%	815	66%
Bangladesh	62	40%	138	89%
Indonesia	59	24%	105	42%
Pakistan	56	31%	112	62%
China	3	0%	448	33%
Latin America	23	5%	68	15%
Brazil	1	1%	12	6%
Middle East	18	8%	8	4%
World**	1 285	18%	2 679	38%

* Based on World Health Organization (WHO) and IEA databases. ** Includes OECD countries and Eastern Europe/Eurasia.

Note: The estimate for India's electrification rate is in line with those published in India's 12th Five-Year Plan. However, a number of recent sources have resulted in a range of electrification rates, particularly in rural areas, that could change the estimate of the total number of people without access to electricity in India significantly. The Five-Year Plan recognised the issue of discrepancies across sources, stating that it may be due to differences in questionnaire design and needed to be examined further. *WEO-2015* will include a special focus on energy developments in India, including the critical issue of energy access.

Supply

Resources

Remaining economically exploitable resources of fossil fuels and uranium worldwide are easily sufficient to meet the projected growth in demand through to 2040 in the New Policies Scenario (and the Current Policies Scenario, in which demand for each fossil fuel is higher). But whether these resources will actually be developed is far less certain, given uncertainties about the investment climate stemming from the confluence of geopolitical, economic and policy-related factors, and the impact of technological change. If it proves

---

7. For a complete country-by-country breakdown, see the *World Energy Outlook* electricity access database at: *www.worldenergyoutlook.org/resources/energydevelopment.*

that they are developed more slowly than we project, then market prices would be higher and production rates and demand correspondingly lower. Similarly, more concerted action to rein in the use of fossil fuels for environmental reasons than assumed here would reduce the pace at which resources would need to be extracted.

Remaining economically recoverable coal resources are particularly large, representing around 2 900 years of production at current rates (Figure 2.13), though less than 5% of these resources have as yet been proven (see Chapter 5). In the New Policies Scenario, only around 1% of these resources are produced between 2012 and 2040, though that is still well in excess of the amount that could be produced without overshooting the 2 °C climate target (unless a far higher proportion of the carbon released by burning coal or gas were captured and stored and/or much less oil and gas consumed than is projected). Natural gas reserves and resources, though much smaller in both energy terms and years of potential production, have grown in recent years, as a result of technological advances (which have made possible the exploitation of resources that were previously considered too difficult or expensive to recover) (see Chapter 4). Gas resources are now equal to more than 230 years of production at current rates, and reserves over 60 years. Oil resources show a smaller forward coverage: resources cover almost 190 years of current production and reserves more than 50 years. A significant proportion of oil resources are categorised as unconventional – mainly extra-heavy oil and bitumen (EHOB), tight oil and kerogen oil (see Chapter 3). Total remaining oil resources at end-2013 amounted to 6 trillion barrels.

Figure 2.13 ▷ **Lifetimes of fossil-fuel and uranium resources***

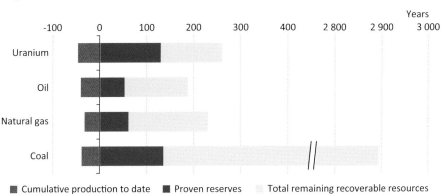

* Expressed as number of years of produced and remaining resources based on estimated production rates in 2013. For uranium, proven reserves include reasonably assured and inferred resources (see Chapter 11 for more details). Sources: BGR (2013); O&GJ (2013); USGS (2012a); USGS (2012b); BP (2014); NEA/IAEA (2014); IEA estimates and analysis.

Remaining uranium resources are also substantial: total identified resources would last more than 120 years at current rates of consumption. There are also large (in some cases, infinite) technically recoverable resources of renewable energy. With the exception of hydropower and bioenergy, only a small proportion is as yet economically exploitable, though the share will undoubtedly increase with continued progress in reducing the cost of emerging renewable technologies (see Chapter 7).

Production trends

Worldwide production of all types of modern energy increases over the projection period in the New Policies Scenario.[8] In line with demand, natural gas output sees the biggest increase in absolute terms. Most of the projected increase in total production occurs in non-OECD countries, as their demand grows fastest and their resources are generally larger (Figure 2.14). They account for over 80% of the global gross production growth between 2012 and 2040 for coal, almost 75% for oil and almost 80% for gas. OECD countries contribute a bigger share of the growth in renewables – 42%, excluding hydro and bioenergy.

Figure 2.14 ▷ **Change in energy production by region in the New Policies Scenario, 2012-2040**

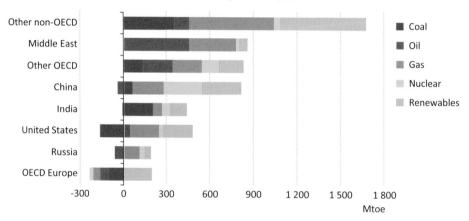

World oil production (i.e. net of processing gains) rises from 87 mb/d to 101 mb/d in 2040. Total production of conventional crude stays at around 68 mb/d until the early 2030s, before dipping to 66 mb/d by the end of the period, meaning that the task of meeting rising demand is left entirely to unconventional production and to natural gas liquids. The first half of the projection period is one in which non-OPEC production continues to rise, pushed higher in the main by developments in the Americas: deepwater projects in Brazil, oil sands in Canada and the continuing vitality of tight oil (and, to a lesser extent, deepwater) in the United States. However, in the 2020s, non-OPEC supply flattens and then starts to fall back, as a result of declines in conventional output in Russia, China and Kazakhstan and, eventually, a tailing off in US production. Projected output increases in Brazil and Canada

---

8. Globally, the supply of each source and form of energy balances demand in every year of the projection period. In the case of oil, supply equals production plus processing gains (volume increases in supply that occur during crude oil refining).

(as does global production of natural gas liquids, from a number of sources), but, with global consumption inching steadily higher, reliance for production growth increasingly shifts to the large resource-holders in the Middle East, raising questions – particularly in the light of the current turmoil in Iraq – about whether the necessary investment will be made in time to avert a period of tighter markets and higher prices (Spotlight).

Coal production worldwide is projected to climb from 5 670 Mtce in 2012 to almost 6 400 Mtce in 2040, with most of the growth coming from non-OECD countries in the period to 2025. Eight countries account for 90% of the global coal production, a share that barely changes over the projection period. China, India, Indonesia and Australia alone account for over 70% of global coal output by 2040, highlighting the importance of developments in Asian markets for coal demand, trade and pricing. As with coal demand, coal production trends differ sharply between OECD and non-OECD producers. All the leading OECD producers see large declines, with the exception of Australia, which becomes the largest OECD coal producer by around 2035, as it achieves continued strong growth in export markets. The United States remains one of the largest coal producers in the world, though it is the only major producing country that sees a decline in production, with output plummeting by more than a third, mainly due to lower domestic demand. Non-OECD coal production increases almost 900 Mtce, with India and Indonesia together accounting for 60% of the projected growth. With a near doubling of coal production, output in both India and Indonesia overtakes declining US production soon after 2030, making these countries the world's second- and third-largest coal producers. China sees the third-largest production increase among non-OECD countries, its production peaking around 2030, at levels around 10% higher than today, in line with a peak in domestic demand. At around 2 800 Mtce by 2040, China remains by far the world's largest coal producer and requires only 8% of its domestic demand to be covered by imports.

Global production of natural gas rises in a near-linear fashion through the *Outlook* period, from 3 480 bcm in 2013 to almost 5 400 bcm in 2040. Conventional sources continue to provide the bulk of production, but unconventional gas – primarily shale gas, and also coalbed methane and tight gas – plays an increasingly important role, its share in total gas output rising from 17% to 31%. Gas production increases in all major countries and regions of the world, with the exception of Europe, where the downward trend that started around the mid-2000s persists throughout the projection period. Gas resources are more than sufficient to meet this increase in demand, but the requirement for more than $11 trillion in investment along the gas supply chain (about 70% in the upstream and a further 30% in pipelines and liquefied natural gas [LNG] infrastructure) nonetheless represents a stern challenge, with the way that gas will be priced on domestic and international markets a key uncertainty. Within many non-OECD countries, including India and across the Middle East, and in some international negotiations, finding a price level and pricing mechanisms acceptable to consumers but nonetheless sufficient to incentivise large new investments in gas supply is proving challenging.

Are warning signs appearing on the horizon for oil production?

Although technologies and high prices are unlocking new types of resources, our *Outlook* for oil production rests heavily on the performance of a relatively small group of countries. In the period to 2025, non-OPEC countries are to the fore: tight oil (and, to some extent, deepwater) from the United States, oil sands in Canada and deepwater developments in Brazil all contribute to output growth, while Russia is able to combat the effects of decline at existing fields and to maintain production above 10 mb/d, at least until the 2030s. In the latter part of our projection period, Canada and Brazil continue to achieve growth in production, but others start to fall back, increasing the call on major resource-holding countries in the Middle East, notably Iraq, but also Saudi Arabia (Figure 2.15).

There are other countries with the resource base to join this select group. But it is too soon for the moment to confidently judge the impact of Mexico's energy reforms on long-term production growth. There are few signs yet of the resolution of Iran's negotiations with the international community that is a pre-condition to an eventual rise in output. Political uncertainty in Venezuela continues to forestall an increase in investment. Although resources are large, tight oil production is not expected to spread far enough and fast enough outside North America to act as the engine for long-term oil production growth. Thus, although supply developments in a number of countries could turn out more positively than we project, the task of bringing production up above 100 mb/d – and of sustaining upstream investment at an average of more than half a trillion dollars per year – rests, in our projections, on a fairly limited number of shoulders.

Investment at these levels should not be taken for granted. Brazil's deepwater pre-salt fields are large and prolific, but also highly complex and capital-intensive, factors that could lead to further delays in project implementation. Achieving a large expansion in Canadian production depends on new transportation capacity to bring it to market, obtaining the approval for which is proving far from straightforward. Some of Russia's upstream ambitions are being curtailed or pushed back because of the sanctions, imposed in response to events in Ukraine, that are now restricting access to Western capital markets and technology. Most important of all, the political, security and logistical challenges to growth in Iraqi output have been highlighted by renewed conflict in the north of the country: while this has not had any marked impact on production or export, it hardly encourages the large-scale commitments of capital that are needed for the next phase of Iraq's oil development. Given the long lead times for upstream projects, the consequences of a shortfall in investment may not be apparent for some time. But clouds are starting to form on the long-term horizon for oil supply, holding out the possibility of stormy conditions ahead.

Figure 2.15 ▷ Change in oil production relative to the level in 2013 in the New Policies Scenario (mb/d)

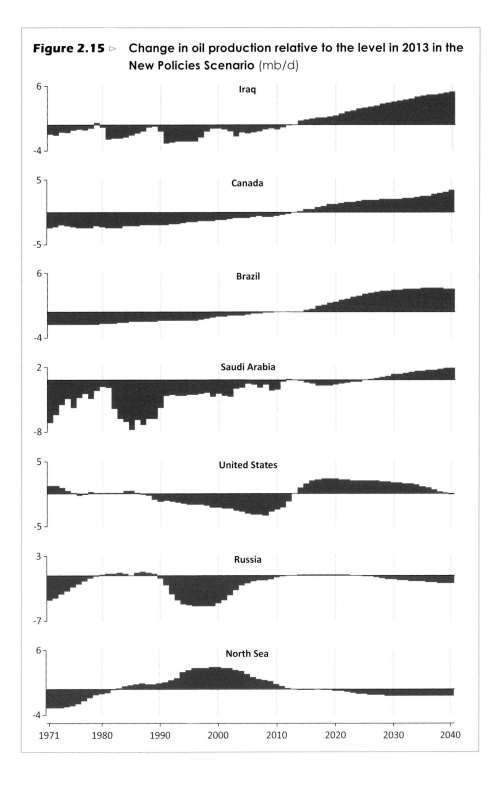

Nuclear power generation rises from a starting point of 2 461 TWh in 2012 to more than 4 600 TWh in 2040, its share of total electricity supply remaining fairly constant over the period. Trends at the global level, however, mask significant differences in the fortunes of nuclear power regionally. It fares best in markets where prices are regulated, utilities have state backing or where governments act to facilitate private investment. China alone accounts for 46% of incremental world nuclear generation to 2040, surpassing the United States as the largest producer just after 2030. India, Korea and Russia collectively account for a further 28% of the global increase. Nuclear generation rebounds in Japan, albeit not to the level just prior to the Fukushima Daiichi accident, and falls by 10% in the European Union.

Globally, the supply of renewable energies is not limited by the availability of resources; but the extent of use of renewables is constrained by geographical and economic factors and currently requires policy support in many regions. The use of renewables almost doubles between 2012 and 2040, supported by government policies, technological advances and higher fossil-fuel prices, which render renewables more competitive. The share of renewables in primary energy use has remained broadly constant at 13% over the past decade, but it rises sharply to 19% by 2040, driven by the growth in solar and wind energy which outpaces the growth of all other fuels. While supply of fuelwood and charcoal falls over the course of the projection period, the output of modern renewables expands substantially in all regions and sectors, with the biggest increases occurring in China, North America and Europe. China sees the largest expansion, more than six-fold, led by a further significant rise in wind power output. India also sees a significant expansion, with increasing expansion of wind and solar PV.

World electricity production rises steadily through the *Outlook* period, by around three-quarters between 2012 and 2040 to around 40 000 TWh, with non-OECD countries contributing more than four-fifths of the increase. Coal remains the leading source of power production, accounting for a third of the total – down from 41% in 2012. The share of oil drops from 5% to 1% (with the Middle East and parts of Africa being the regions where oil is still used for power generation by 2040), while that of natural gas increases by more than one percentage point, to 24%, and that of nuclear power to 12%. The share of hydro (16%) stays flat. By contrast, the share of non-hydro renewables in power production more than triples to 17%. These trends hide significant differences across countries and regions, largely according to the degree of economic maturity and policy push, and the local resource endowment. The share of renewables in electricity production grows more in OECD countries; the European Union reaches one of the highest shares, at 46% – almost double the current share. The use of coal remains more widespread in non-OECD countries, especially China and India.

Inter-regional trade

Inter-regional energy trade is set to take a gradually rising share of global energy supply. The patterns of trade are also changing, in line with the new geography of global production and consumption. This means a major shift in trade away from the Atlantic Basin – where the Americas are increasingly becoming a net provider of energy to the rest of the world

– and towards the Asia-Pacific region. The growing import markets of China, India and Southeast Asia, alongside the traditionally import-dependent markets of Japan and Korea, are set to absorb an increasing share of internationally traded fossil fuels from all parts of the world (Table 2.5).

Table 2.5 ▷ Energy net import/export shares* by fuel and region in the New Policies Scenario

	Oil		Gas		Coal		Bioenergy		Total	
	2012	2040	2012	2040	2012	2040	2012	2040	2012	2040
OECD	52%	22%	25%	18%	7%	21%	0%	3%	26%	9%
Americas	25%	19%	2%	6%	14%	15%	1%	1%	7%	10%
United States	47%	24%	6%	3%	14%	13%	1%	1%	16%	4%
Europe	71%	74%	47%	66%	46%	56%	1%	5%	42%	43%
Asia Oceania	92%	85%	70%	20%	3%	55%	1%	10%	52%	5%
Japan	99%	98%	97%	99%	100%	100%	6%	22%	94%	69%
Non-OECD	41%	21%	19%	11%	3%	4%	0%	1%	18%	7%
E.Europe/Eurasia	66%	58%	21%	33%	22%	27%	3%	9%	36%	35%
Russia	72%	69%	28%	36%	33%	44%	5%	10%	45%	44%
Asia	58%	82%	2%	32%	2%	11%	0%	0%	13%	26%
China	54%	77%	27%	39%	8%	8%	0%	1%	15%	22%
India	74%	92%	32%	46%	25%	39%	0%	2%	30%	45%
Southeast Asia	41%	76%	28%	1%	69%	30%	1%	4%	22%	7%
Middle East	75%	73%	25%	24%	77%	82%	4%	5%	62%	56%
Africa	64%	38%	44%	38%	30%	28%	0%	0%	37%	23%
Latin America	27%	42%	9%	7%	66%	56%	1%	7%	20%	25%
Brazil	7%	41%	40%	7%	80%	88%	1%	9%	11%	18%
World	50%	52%	21%	22%	18%	23%	0%	2%	25%	24%
European Union	85%	89%	66%	82%	42%	54%	1%	5%	51%	50%

* Net trade between main *WEO* regions, not including trade within regions. Shaded numbers indicate net imports.

Notes: Import shares for each fuel are calculated as net imports divided by primary demand. Export shares are calculated as net exports divided by production. Column "Total" additionally includes nuclear and other renewables. All values are calculated on an energy-equivalent basis.

Oil remains the most heavily traded fuel, both in volume terms and as a share of world production. As of 2013, the Asia-Pacific region imports around 18 mb/d of crude oil, roughly half of the total inter-regional trade in crude oil. By 2040, this import requirement rises to around 29 mb/d, two-thirds of the 44 mb/d total. The Middle East can satisfy only a part of this increase: squeezed by rising domestic demand and refinery runs, crude oil exports from the Middle East rise by more than 4 mb/d (to 22 mb/d in total). The share of the Asia-Pacific region in Middle East crude oil export flows goes up from an estimated 75% today to around 90% in 2040, but Asian importers also draw in supplies from a variety of other exporting countries and regions (a process that is helped by the concurrent reduction in North American import needs). This reorientation in global trade means that the share of Europe in Russia's crude oil exports, currently around 80%, falls to less than 60% in 2040, by which time more than half of Caspian crude oil exports also have Asian markets as their ultimate destination. Exports from Latin America, Africa and Canada are subject to the same dynamics: for example, over two-thirds of crude oil exported from Latin America heads for Asia in 2040, compared with just over one-third today. Alongside this importance in crude oil trade, Asia also accounts for an increasing share of global trade in oil products, as increases in projected refinery runs do not keep pace with rising demand.

This shift in international oil trade has implications for efforts to ensure security of oil supply. Any oil supply disruption to one market, if not contained and dealt with promptly, will have implications for other regions; but specific vulnerability to a possible physical shortage in supply and to high and volatile oil-import bills becomes increasingly concentrated in the major emerging oil-importing economies of Asia: China and India in particular. These countries, both with a high degree of current and projected dependency on oil imports from the Middle East, are already developing capacity to deal with the possibility of disruptions to supply, by building up oil stocks and creating other mechanisms for emergency preparedness. International co-operation in these areas is an increasingly important feature of strategies to ensure the integrity of long-term oil supply.

Figure 2.16 ▷ **World fossil-fuel production and trade* in the New Policies Scenario**

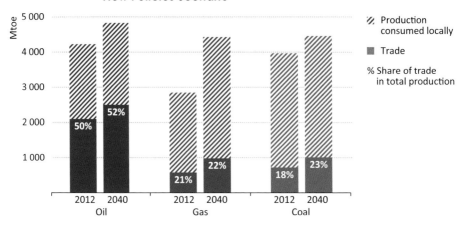

* Net trade between main *WEO* regions, not including trade within regions.

Concerns about the security of gas supply are also rising, at least in Europe, in light of the conflict in Ukraine. However, in this area – in contrast to oil – there are some more encouraging signs in the longer term outlook, despite the rising import needs in many countries. Among all fuels, natural gas sees, in energy terms, the biggest increase in trade (Figure 2.16), boosting its share of total inter-regional fossil-fuel trade from 17% in 2012 to 22% in 2040. LNG trade grows more quickly than pipeline trade, accounting for almost 60% of the increase. All the current gas-importing regions become even more dependent on imports, with the exception of Brazil and North America (rising production turns both countries from importers to exporters). The European Union remains the main destination for internationally traded gas, its imports rising by almost 50% to more than 450 bcm; but China's imports expand most in volumetric terms – by almost 200 bcm – making the country by far the largest single importing country (overtaking Japan before 2020). India also becomes a major importer (most of its gas needs today are met by local production).

Rising import needs are matched by a growing cast of producers and exporters. The main contributors to increased trade are Russia (both piped gas and LNG), the Caspian region (piped gas), Australia (LNG), the Middle East (both piped and LNG) and North and East Africa (largely via LNG). Several countries are expected to join the ranks of LNG-exporting nations in the next few years, including the United States, Canada, Mozambique and Tanzania. What is more, the LNG-led development of a more diverse, flexible and integrated system of international gas trade is set to provide a more robust way to mitigate the impact of shortfalls or disruptions to supply.

The geography of coal trade is set to shift markedly over the coming two-and-a-half decades. Import needs in China – the world's biggest importer today – are projected to peak by around 2020, while demand and imports in Europe, Korea and Japan fall back; by contrast, India's imports surge, overtaking those of China early in the next decade. Australia and Indonesia consolidate their position as the leading coal exporters, ahead of Colombia, Russia, South Africa and the United States.

The value of trade

The New Policies Scenario projections imply a significant increase in the overall value of global energy trade – the result of a rise in both volumes and international prices (Figure 2.17). Net spending on imports as a whole has risen sharply in the last few years, with the jump in prices and growth in demand: in 2012, energy-import bills in importing regions reached almost $2 trillion (in year-2013 dollars). But trends in energy-import bills in the main importing countries and regions diverge markedly. In 2012, it reached highs of $270 billion in China, $140 billion in India, and $280 billion in Japan, though spending fell back slightly to $530 billion in the European Union and $340 billion in the United States, in both cases mainly due to lower oil imports. Oil accounts for the bulk of the spending in all five countries/regions.

The level of spending on energy imports is projected to continue to rise substantially to reach $2.9 trillion in 2040, driven mostly by non-OECD countries where spending on energy imports nearly triples. This is mainly a result of surging demand, which outstrips indigenous production in many non-OECD countries; in China, oil and gas account for most of the increase, while coal is also an important contributor to the increase in India. Among the countries importing gas and coal, India is the only one where spending is higher for coal than for gas in 2040. Import bills remain at similar levels as in 2012 in the European Union, as falling oil and coal demand and, therefore, need for imports helps to offset the effect of rising gas imports and higher international fossil-fuel prices. In Japan and the United States, spending falls – heavily in the United States – thanks to lower oil demand and, in the US case, sustained production of oil and gas.

Figure 2.17 ▷ Value of net trade in fossil fuels in the New Policies Scenario

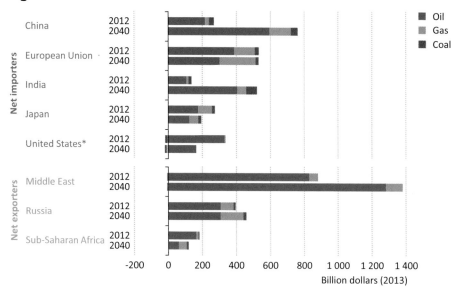

* The United States is a net coal exporter already and becomes a net gas exporter over the *Outlook* period.

Export earnings in the exporting countries grow, especially in the Middle East. OPEC oil revenues jump from $1.2 trillion in 2012 to $1.8 trillion in 2040 as a result of higher oil-export volumes and prices. Russia also sees a rise in export earnings, thanks to increased gas exports to Europe and to Asia, in particular China; Russian oil-export earnings increase until the mid-2020s and then drop with declining output, while the value of coal exports rises modestly.

Energy investment[9]

Over the period to 2040, the investment required each year in energy supply infrastructure in order to meet projected demand in the New Policies Scenario rises steadily to around $2 trillion per year (in year-2013 dollars), compared with just over $1.6 trillion in 2013. In cumulative terms, this amounts to over $51 trillion over the projection period (Figure 2.18). Fossil-fuel extraction, transport and oil refining make up $30 trillion, or almost 60%, of this total; $21 trillion, or about 40%, goes to the power sector, of which low-carbon technologies – renewables ($7.4 trillion) and nuclear ($1.5 trillion) – account for more than 40%, while $8.7 trillion is invested in transmission and distribution. Spending on energy efficiency,

---

9. Investment figures cover capital expenditure for the creation or refurbishment of assets, but do not reflect operating expenses. Energy efficiency investments cover the money spent by end-users on energy-consuming products, relative to a 2012 baseline. Prospects for global energy investment were analysed in the *World Energy Investment Outlook*, released in June 2014 and available for download at *www.worldenergyoutlook.org/investment*. The investment projections here are slightly different to those in that report, as underlying projections have been updated and extended to 2040.

which moderates energy supply investment needs, totals $14.5 trillion over 2014-2040, an average of more than $500 billion per year, bringing the overall global investment bill to about $66 trillion.

Less than half of the investment in energy supply goes to meet growth in demand; the larger share is required to offset declining production from existing oil and gas fields and to replace power plants and other assets that reach the end of their productive life before 2040. These declines and retirements set a major investment challenge for policy-makers and the industry, but they also represent a real opportunity to change the nature of the energy system by switching fuels or deploying more efficient technologies.

Nearly two-thirds of energy supply investment takes place in non-OECD countries, with the focus for investment moving beyond China to other parts of Asia, Africa and Latin America. But ageing infrastructure and climate policies also create large requirements across the OECD. The largest share of energy efficiency spending is in the European Union, China and North America.

Figure 2.18 ▷ Cumulative global energy supply investment by fuel and type in the New Policies Scenario, 2014-2040 ($2013 billion)

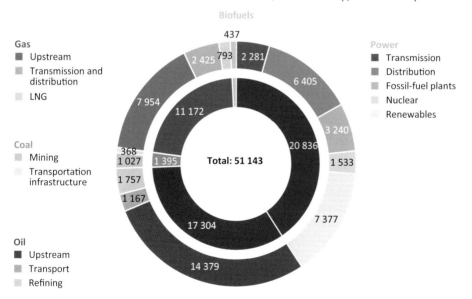

Decisions to commit capital to the energy sector are increasingly shaped by government policy measures and incentives, rather than by signals coming from competitive markets (IEA, 2014). In the oil sector, reliance on countries with more restrictive terms of access to their resources is set to grow, as output from North America flattens from around 2030 onwards. Geopolitical turmoil, as in Iraq, Libya and other parts of the Middle East and North Africa underlines the downside risks to long-term oil production, indicating that there is a significant risk that investment will fail to pick up in time, during the present decade, to avert a shortfall in supply after 2020. In the electricity sector, administrative signals or regulated rates of return have become by far the most important drivers for investment and have stimulated particularly strong growth in the use of renewable energies in many countries. A continued flow of investment is needed though to meet low-carbon power generation targets over the long-term, but also to ensure system adequacy in particular in power markets with an ageing fleet. Against this backdrop, mobilising private investors and capital will require a concerted effort to reduce political and regulatory uncertainties. Market reforms may be necessary to reassure investors about the adequacy of prospective financial returns in the future.

New types of investors in the energy sector are emerging, but the supply of long-term finance on suitable terms is still far from guaranteed. Much of the dynamism in energy markets is coming from smaller market players or new entrants; these players tend to rely on external sources of financing. Outside North America (where external financing is more readily available), there is a need to unlock new sources of finance, via the growth of bond, securitisation and equity markets and, potentially, by tapping into the large funds held by institutional investors, such as pension funds and insurers. This would help to diminish undue reliance on the relatively short maturity of loans available from the banking sector, which may be constrained by new capital adequacy requirements (the Basel III accord) in the wake of the financial crisis.

Energy-related CO_2 emissions[10]

Recent developments

The latest Assessment Report from the International Panel on Climate Change (IPCC) – the fifth in the series – reports that the global average temperature of land and ocean surface combined increased by 0.85 °C over the period 1880 to 2012, and that it is extremely likely that human influence has been the dominant cause of this observed warming since the mid-20th century (IPCC, 2014). The evidence of human influence has grown since the previous Assessment Report, which was released in 2008. Higher temperatures are expected to be associated, among other things, with an increase in the frequency and intensity of extreme weather events. In September 2014, the World Meteorological Organization reported that the concentration of CO_2 in the atmosphere reached 142% of the pre-industrial era and that radiative forcing – the warming effect on our climate – had increased by 34% since 1990, due to long-lived greenhouse gases, such as CO_2.[11]

International climate negotiations under the United Nations Framework Convention on Climate Change (UNFCCC) are moving into a critical phase. Countries have been invited to communicate their intended nationally determined contributions (INDCs) to the climate

---

10. A *WEO* Special Report on climate change will be released in mid-2015, as a follow-up analysis of the 2013 *Redrawing the Energy-Climate Map: World Energy Outlook Special Report*.

11. See *www.wmo.int/pages/mediacentre/press_releases/pr_1002_en.html*.

agreement in the first quarter of 2015.[12] The intention is to reach an agreement in Paris in December 2015 and to apply its terms from 2020: its first round of targets will set the course for the important decade from 2020 to 2030. In putting forward their contributions, countries with lower capacity to take action are expected to emphasise what can be achieved by unilateral action, but also to indicate their full potential, with assistance. For countries with high potential to reduce emissions quickly, but with low domestic capacity, the technology, finance and capacity building elements of the UNFCCC framework will be critical. To shift energy sector investment onto a low-carbon track, the 2015 agreement will need to send a strong signal to private and public energy investors that all major countries are committed to long-term decarbonisation.

Because the energy sector accounts for around two-thirds of all greenhouse-gas emissions, its opportunities and constraints need to be a strong influence on the climate negotiations and the sector will play a full part in effective implementation of the outcome. The point of departure is not very encouraging: global energy-related emissions of CO_2 – the leading greenhouse gas – reached 31.6 gigatonnes (Gt) in 2012. Compared with 2011, this is an increase of around 400 million tonnes (or 1.2%). Coal – the most carbon-intensive fuel – contributes 44% of total emissions, oil 36% and gas – the least emissions-intensive – the remaining 20%. CO_2 emissions fell in the United States (-4.1%) and the European Union (-1.2%), but all of the other major emitters contributed to the global emissions increase in 2012. CO_2 emissions increased by 3.1% in China and 6.8% in India; in both cases an increasing demand for coal in power generation was the primary cause. Emissions increased by 4.0% in the Middle East, 8% in Brazil (a result of several consecutive dry years that curtailed hydropower output) and 0.3% in Russia. Emissions also increased in Japan, at 3.4%, a result of the nuclear shutdown that lead to an increasing use of fossil fuels.

Emissions and climate impact in the New Policies Scenario

Many governments are in the process of formulating policies to address climate change, directly or indirectly, and a whole range of climate-relevant policy proposals has been formulated over the past year. These policies include additional measures to reduce air pollution from the use of coal and improve energy efficiency in China, a plan to cut power sector emissions and extend fuel-economy and emissions standards for heavy-duty vehicles in the United States, a proposed climate and energy package for 2030 in the European Union, and building codes and fuel-efficiency standards for passenger vehicles in India.

In the New Policies Scenario, all these and other measures announced by governments around the world have been taken into account. The sobering news is that they are not sufficient to reach the 2 °C target: CO_2 emissions increase to 38.0 Gt in 2040 – an increase of 6.4 Gt, or 20%, over 2012. Projected out to 2050 and beyond, and taking account of emissions of other greenhouse gases from all sources, this trend is consistent with an increase in the greenhouse-gas concentration in the atmosphere to over 700 parts per

---

12. INDCs may also cover climate change adaptation, finance, technology and capacity building, but this section considers mitigation only.

million of carbon-dioxide equivalent (ppm CO_2-eq) in 2100, leading, therefore, to a long-term global temperature increase of 3.6 °C, compared with pre-industrial levels. Additional emissions could result from irreversible changes (for example slowly melting permafrost), but those are not yet factored into models. It is possible that if they were factored in, it would drive temperatures beyond 3.6 °C even in the New Policies Scenario. With 4 °C warming, severe and widespread changes are expected in human and natural systems, including substantial species extinction and large risks to global and regional food security.

The IPCC estimates that to have a 50% chance of meeting the internationally agreed goal of limiting the temperature increase to 2 °C over and above pre-industrial levels to avert irreversible and catastrophic climate change, the world cannot emit more than a total of around 1 000 Gt of CO_2 from 2014 onwards. We are fast eating into this carbon budget: in the New Policies Scenario, the entire budget is used up by around 2040. Were this to happen, emissions would need to drop to zero immediately thereafter in order to stay within that budget. In other words, achieving the objective requires urgent action now to steer the energy system onto a lower emissions path (IEA, 2013).

In the New Policies Scenario, coal remains the principal source of global energy-related CO_2 emissions, though growth from this source levels off after 2020, as coal use flattens out and carbon capture and storage (CCS) starts to be deployed, albeit on a relatively limited scale before 2030 (Figure 2.19). By contrast, emissions from natural gas and oil continue to increase, with the strong rise in gas demand making this fuel the largest contributor to emissions growth over the *Outlook* period. But, even though gas consumption approaches that of coal in energy terms, the lower carbon content of gas means that emissions from this source are still more than one-third lower than those of coal in 2040.

Figure 2.19 ▷ Global fossil-fuel energy-related CO_2 emissions and total cumulative CO_2 emissions in the New Policies Scenario

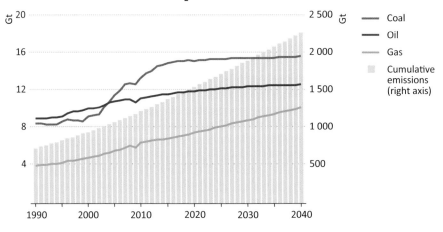

Emission trends diverge across regions, depending largely on the policies currently in place and in preparation to address climate change directly or indirectly. Growth in emissions

slows down gradually, but there are only a handful of regions in which emissions peak and then actually decline over the projection period. These include some of the largest emitters, in particular the United States (which sees emissions peak before 2020), China (peaking soon after 2030), and the European Union (for which emissions have already peaked). The recent policy initiatives in the United States (which, together with policies announced earlier, lower emissions by 1.3 Gt in 2040 compared with the Current Policies Scenario) and China (2.9 Gt savings in 2040) bear fruit, but they are not sufficient to offset the global growth. Moreover, despite these efforts, China remains the world's largest emitter by a wide margin until 2040 in the New Policies Scenario, and approaches the United States as the country with the largest historical emissions (Figure 2.20).

Figure 2.20 ▷ **Cumulative energy-related CO$_2$ emissions by region in the New Policies Scenario**

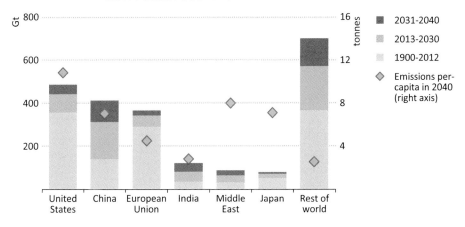

India overtakes the United States in terms of annual CO$_2$ emissions just before 2040, but its cumulative emissions and per-capita emissions remain low. US per-capita emissions, at 10.7 tonnes, are still almost four-times higher in 2040 than those of India (2.9 tonnes), and more than twice the global average (4.2 tonnes). Per-capita emissions in China (7.1 tonnes) and the Middle East (7.9 tonnes) in 2040 are higher than in most other regions.

450 Scenario

In the 450 Scenario, energy trends and the associated greenhouse-gas emissions trajectory are consistent with stabilisation of the concentration of those gases in the atmosphere at 450 ppm CO$_2$-eq and the international target of containment of the temperature increase to no more than 2 °C above pre-industrial levels. The reductions in emissions, relative to the New Policies Scenario, result from the assumption of much stronger government policies, including a set of measures that, if adopted together, do not harm economic growth, and that are adopted before 2020 – the year when a new international climate agreement, to be negotiated in Paris in 2015, is due to come into effect. These measures include energy efficiency, limits to the use and construction of inefficient coal power stations, minimising methane emissions from upstream oil and gas and accelerating the phase-out of fossil-fuel consumption subsidies (IEA, 2013) (Box 2.5). After 2020, further rapid action is needed fundamentally to reset the course of the energy sector. The policies adopted depend on national circumstances, and reflect the current policy framework, but also the long-term abatement potentials and costs of each region. Various policy instruments are used to achieve decarbonisation, including pricing carbon in the power sector for major regions (Chapter 1).

Box 2.5 ▷ **Reducing methane emissions from upstream oil and gas**

The reduction of CO_2 emissions is imperative to mitigating climate change, given their weight in overall greenhouse-gas emissions and their long lifetime in the atmosphere. But the reduction of short-lived climate pollutants, such as methane or black carbon, is an important complementary strategy to mitigate the rate of climate change in the short term.

Past work in the *WEO* series has analysed the impact of reducing methane emissions from the oil and gas sector, highlighting is as one of the four key measures to keep the door open to 2 °C (IEA, 2013). During upstream production, methane is released to the atmosphere through leaks, vents, incomplete combustion and operational upsets. A number of initiatives exist, at global as well as company level, to mitigate such emissions (the most recent being the Oil & Gas Methane Partnership launched in September 2014), but emissions were still in the order of 1 Gt CO_2-eq in 2013. In the New Policies Scenario, methane emissions from oil and gas production remain at similar levels until 2020 and then gradually rise to 1.1 Gt CO_2-eq in 2030 and to 1.2 Gt CO_2-eq in 2040, broadly following the trend of conventional crude oil production (with related associated gas) and assuming that new infrastructure leaks less than past equipment.

So far, announced policies for the reduction of methane emissions are largely confined to the United States. Several of the main obstacles remain, such as lack of measurement and the low value assigned to the gas. Successful and (cost) effective policies to reduce methane emissions from upstream oil and gas production must be informed by reliable measurements and could include policies to reduce flaring and regulations that encourage best practice standards. Their implementation in the 450 Scenario, which already has a lower output of oil and gas, helps reduce emissions to 0.9 Gt CO_2-eq in 2020, 0.3 Gt CO_2-eq in 2030 and 0.1 Gt CO_2-eq in 2040. The largest scope for reductions is in the Middle East, Russia and Africa.

In the 450 Scenario, energy-related emissions of CO_2 peak at 33.0 Gt before 2020 and then fall back to 25.4 Gt in 2030 and 19.3 Gt in 2040, which is almost 50% lower than in the New Policies Scenario (Figure 2.21). Already in 2020, CO_2 emissions are 1.7 Gt, or 5%, lower as a result of these four key policy measures. Owing to the sheer size of their economies, the three-biggest contributors to emissions reductions are China, at one-third of cumulative emissions savings, the United States (almost 15%) and India (about 10%). They are followed by the European Union (6%) and the Middle East (5%). Globally, per-capita emissions of CO_2 are cut by almost half, to 2.1 tonnes, in 2040.

Figure 2.21 ▷ **Reduction in energy-related CO_2 emissions in 450 Scenario relative to the New Policies Scenario**

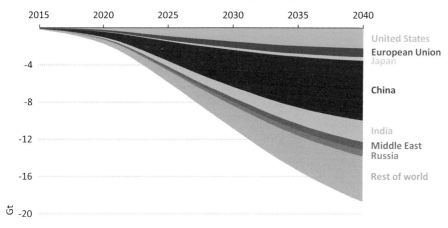

The power sector offers the largest possibility of additional abatement, despite already being the focus of much government action: new measures are needed, both in developed and developing countries, to further cut emissions in 2040, by more than 25% in total. Such increased emissions reductions in the power sector would deliver almost 110 Gt of cumulative CO_2 savings over the projection period and reduce the emissions gap between the two scenarios by around half (Figure 2.22).

Figure 2.22 ▷ **Cumulative CO_2 emissions reduction by sector and region in the 450 Scenario relative to the New Policies Scenario**

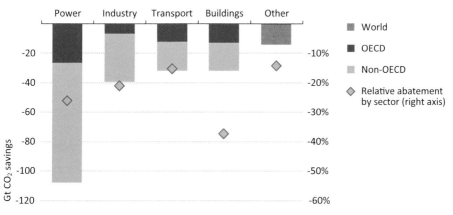

Stepping up efforts in industry, including through more stringent efficiency measures to reduce electricity consumption, would reduce the gap by an additional 17%. The transport sector is the second-largest source of CO_2 emissions today, accounting for 23% of global energy-related CO_2 emissions. As much of the global vehicle market is already covered by fuel-economy standards, the need for additional abatement from the transport sector is comparatively lower than for the power and industry sectors, at 16% of the total savings required in the 450 Scenario, relative to the New Policies Scenario. While the buildings sector contributes only 14% to the total savings in the 450 Scenario, the relative effort required is largest among all sectors, a reduction of 37%. Many of the impacts of the measures in the buildings sector will have long-lasting impacts beyond the projected time horizon, given the long asset lifetimes in this sector.

Figure 2.23 ▷ **Average annual capacity additions of low-carbon technologies by scenario and cumulative CO_2 savings in the power sector in the 450 Scenario relative to the New Policies Scenario**

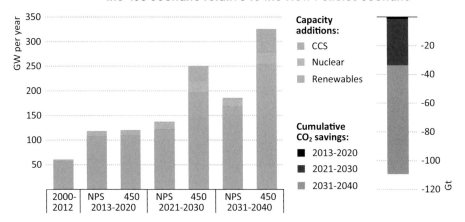

Note: NPS = New Policies Scenario; 450 = 450 Scenario.

The vast majority of emissions reductions in the 450 Scenario occur after 2030, accounting for around 70% of cumulative savings relative to the New Policies Scenario. This is largely a result of the long lead times required to build up low-carbon technologies in the market, underlining the urgency of action before 2030. In the power sector, almost every third GW of new capacity installed worldwide over the past decade was low-carbon (predominantly sourced from renewables), amounting to about 60 GW per year on average (Figure 2.23). Average annual low-carbon capacity additions double to around 120 GW by 2020, but a significantly larger effort is required after 2020. At 250 GW per year, average annual installations between 2021 and 2030 in the 450 Scenario are far higher than is achieved under planned policies (140 GW). This means that three out of four GW of new capacity added need to be low-carbon to achieve the necessary reductions after 2030. Beyond 2030, almost all new capacity installed is required to be low-carbon in the 450 Scenario.

Achieving the 2 °C goal will entail a substantial transformation in the ways we produce and consume energy, involving major improvements in energy efficiency and a switch to low-carbon energy sources and technologies. Around the world, many of the challenges are broadly similar, including the need to reduce the amount of energy required to produce a unit of GDP and to channel investment towards low-carbon technologies and energy efficiency (Table 2.6). The best ways to achieve these goals will differ across countries, something that will need to be accounted in structuring the global climate deal in 2015.

Table 2.6 ▷ **Energy- and climate-related indicators by Scenario**

	2012	New Policies 2020	New Policies 2030	New Policies 2040	450 Scenario 2020	450 Scenario 2030	450 Scenario 2040
Energy-related CO$_2$ emissions (Gt)							
World	31.6	34.2	36.3	38.0	32.5	25.4	19.3
United States	5.0	5.1	4.5	4.1	4.8	3.0	1.9
European Union	3.4	3.1	2.7	2.3	3.0	2.0	1.4
Japan	1.2	1.0	0.9	0.8	1.0	0.7	0.4
China	8.2	9.5	10.2	10.0	9.0	6.3	3.6
India	2.0	2.5	3.5	4.5	2.4	2.3	2.2
Energy intensity (toe/GDP in $2013 MER)							
World	0.18	0.16	0.13	0.11	0.16	0.12	0.09
United States	0.13	0.11	0.09	0.07	0.11	0.08	0.07
European Union	0.09	0.08	0.07	0.06	0.08	0.06	0.05
Japan	0.09	0.08	0.07	0.07	0.08	0.07	0.06
China	0.33	0.23	0.16	0.12	0.23	0.14	0.10
India	0.44	0.35	0.25	0.19	0.34	0.21	0.15
Carbon intensity (tCO$_2$/toe)							
World	2.4	2.3	2.2	2.1	2.2	1.7	1.2
United States	2.4	2.2	2.1	1.9	2.2	1.5	1.0
European Union	2.1	1.9	1.7	1.5	1.9	1.4	1.0
Japan	2.7	2.3	2.1	1.9	2.2	1.7	1.1
China	2.8	2.7	2.5	2.4	2.6	1.8	1.0
India	2.5	2.5	2.5	2.6	2.4	2.0	1.6
Clean energy investment* (billion $2013)							
World	355	709	987	1 238	881	1 814	2 411
United States	57	98	151	184	124	268	280
European Union	109	172	215	217	241	350	341
Japan	16	27	34	43	37	64	77
China	77	165	184	227	197	341	452
India	14	32	65	98	40	157	252
Energy-import bills (billion $2013)							
United States	325	205	142	147	197	111	35
European Union	531	522	542	531	477	377	269
Japan	278	218	207	198	198	145	101
China	271	409	653	761	373	481	374
India	137	216	357	521	198	243	265

* Notes: Clean energy in this table includes energy efficiency, renewables, nuclear, and CCS in the power and industry sectors. Energy efficiency investment is measured relative to a 2012 baseline efficiency level. MER = market exchange rate; tCO$_2$/toe = tonnes of carbon dioxide per tonne of oil equivalent.

Chapter 3

Oil market outlook
Calm before the storm?

Highlights

- Oil demand rises by 14 mb/d to reach 104 mb/d in 2040 in the New Policies Scenario. The pace of demand growth decreases markedly, from an annual average of 0.9% over the period to 2020 down to only 0.3% per year in the 2030s, moving towards a plateau in global oil consumption. Prices that reach $132 per barrel in 2040 (in real terms) and policy measures to improve energy efficiency and promote fuel switching constrain oil use. By 2040, nearly 75% of oil use is concentrated in just two sectors where substitution is most challenging: transport and petrochemicals.

- The net growth in oil demand comes entirely from non-OECD countries: for each barrel of oil eliminated from demand in OECD countries, two additional barrels of oil are consumed in the developing world. India and Nigeria are the countries with the highest rates of oil demand growth. China becomes the largest oil-consuming country in the early 2030s, but higher efficiency and lower rates of growth in industrial activity and in demand for mobility (as population numbers level off in the 2030s) mean that, by 2040, oil demand growth all but comes to a halt in China.

- Growth in the Americas, led by US tight oil, Canadian oil sands and Brazilian deepwater output, pushes non-OPEC production higher until the early-2020s. As US tight oil output flattens and then starts to fall back, Canadian oil sands emerge as the engine of North American supply. Despite a gradual spread of tight oil production to Argentina, Russia, China and elsewhere, non-OPEC supply falls back to 51 mb/d by 2040, slightly higher than today's levels but on a declining trend. Mexico offers some potential upside to the non-OPEC outlook following recent energy sector reforms.

- Meeting long-term demand depends increasingly on the large OPEC resource-holders in the Middle East. OPEC production increases by less than 1 mb/d over the remainder of this decade, but then needs to increase substantially in the 2020s (by more than 6 mb/d) and by almost as much again in the 2030s. Renewed turmoil in Iraq, Libya and other parts of the Middle East and North Africa has underlined the downside risks to oil production. The apparent breathing space provided by the rise in non-OPEC output over the next decade is in many respects illusory, given the long-lead times of new upstream projects. With a legacy of under-investment, Iranian production would take time to bounce back even if sanctions were removed.

- The global refining sector has to adjust to the new geography of oil demand and supply and the changing composition of feedstocks, a process that looks particularly difficult for Europe, which continues to have a large excess of refinery capacity over projected refinery runs. By 2040, two out of every three barrels of crude oil traded internationally are destined for Asia, up from less than half today, drawing into Asia a rising share of the available crude from the Middle East and beyond.

Global overview

Before the most recent decline, which took oil below $90 per barrel in October 2014, the relative stability of prices since 2011 – trading in a fairly narrow range around $100 per barrel – had provided few hints as to the underlying dynamism in the oil sector and to the uncertainties concerning its future.[1] On the supply side, there has been remarkable strength in oil production in the United States, which has surged above 10 million barrels per day (mb/d). Yet the impact of this increase (tight oil output in the United States has risen by 2 mb/d since 2010) has been partly offset by under-performance elsewhere in the world. Outages, both scheduled and unscheduled, project delays, and turmoil in parts of the Middle East and North Africa invite the question, examined below, about who can step up to support longer term growth once US production eventually levels off.

On the demand side, elevated price levels, government policies, technological advances and concerns about the environmental and financial cost of increasing oil use are stimulating changes in the nature and location of oil consumption. Demand in non-OECD countries is already higher than within the OECD, but across the board there is a gradual increase in the deployment of more efficient technologies and some signs of fuel switching, where possible. Oil remains central to the global energy economy – and retains its position as the largest single fuel in the global energy mix even out to 2040 – but these developments suggest that economic and population growth may not automatically push oil demand inexorably higher, as they have done in the past. How this plays out in practice is the subject of analysis in this chapter. In our scenarios, the key variable affecting the trajectory for oil production and use is whether – and how – government policies evolve (see Chapter 1).

Table 3.1 ▷ **Oil and liquids demand by region and scenario** (mb/d)

	1990	2013	New Policies 2020	New Policies 2040	Current Policies 2020	Current Policies 2040	450 Scenario 2020	450 Scenario 2040
OECD	38.9	41.5	40.2	31.3	40.9	35.7	39.5	21.5
Non-OECD	23.4	41.6	48.2	63.1	49.4	70.4	46.7	43.9
Bunkers*	3.9	7.0	7.6	9.5	7.7	10.4	7.3	6.5
World oil	66.1	90.1	96.0	103.9	98.0	116.6	93.4	71.9
Share of non-OECD	*35%*	*46%*	*50%*	*61%*	*50%*	*60%*	*50%*	*61%*
World biofuels**	0.1	1.3	2.2	4.6	1.8	3.6	2.1	8.7
World total liquids	66.3	91.4	98.1	108.5	99.8	120.2	95.5	80.7

* Includes international marine and aviation fuels. ** Expressed In energy-equivalent volumes of gasoline and diesel.

Note: More information on methodology and data issues (including an explanation of differences with the IEA *Medium-Term Oil Market Report*) is on the *WEO* website *www.worldenergyoutlook.org/weomodel/*.

---

1. The oil price is the average price for crude oil imports into IEA countries, used as a proxy for international oil prices.

In the Current Policies Scenario, the influence of population and economic growth – particularly in emerging economies – is constrained only by rising oil prices and government policies already in place today, so global oil demand rises relatively rapidly to reach almost 117 mb/d by 2040 (Table 3.1 and Figure 3.1). Conversely, the impact of policy action on efficiency and carbon dioxide (CO_2) emissions is much stronger in the 450 Scenario, leading to a peak in oil demand already by around 2020 and a subsequent decline in consumption to 72 mb/d by the end of the projection period. In the New Policies Scenario, our central scenario and the focus for analysis in this chapter, demand grows but at a steadily decreasing pace to just under 104 mb/d in 2040. Economic and population growth is increasingly offset by the dampening impact of greater efficiency and the deployment of alternative vehicle fuels and technologies, stimulated by policies in place as well as those that are under discussion.

Figure 3.1 ▷ **World oil demand and oil price by scenario**

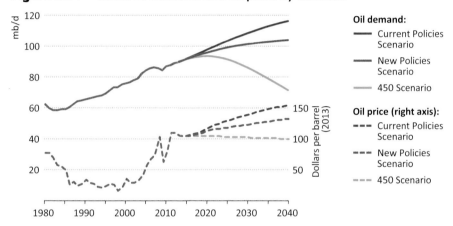

In 2013, the IEA crude oil import price remained at a level above $100 per barrel for the third consecutive year ($106 per barrel in year-2013 dollars). The oil price required to balance demand and supply out to 2040 differs markedly across the scenarios, according to how different forms of policy intervention affect the underlying market conditions. In the New Policies Scenario, it reaches $118/barrel in 2025 and $132/barrel in 2040 (in real terms). The price rises more quickly in the Current Policies Scenario, reaching $155/barrel in 2040, as higher prices are needed to keep supply in line with higher demand, because existing reserves are depleted faster and oil companies are forced to turn sooner to more costly new sources of oil. In the 450 Scenario, the oil price hovers around $105/barrel until 2020 and then gradually declines to $100/barrel in 2040, as policy action causes oil demand to fall steeply; the impact of lower international prices is not reflected in a rebound in consumption in this scenario, as governments are assumed to act to keep end-user prices in the transport sector at higher levels through taxation and, in some cases, the removal of subsidies.

Demand

Regional trends

Global oil demand grew at an average rate of 1.4% per year over the first decade of this century, but has since slowed considerably, to 1.0% per year, dampened by weak global economic growth, improved energy efficiency and persistently high international crude oil prices. Global oil demand reached 90.1 mb/d in 2013, and is projected to continue to rise at an average 0.9% per year until 2020 in the New Policies Scenario. Oil demand growth then slows to 0.5% per year until 2030 and then 0.3% until 2040, as fuel efficiency policy in the transport sector changes the vehicle stock and saturation effects become more widespread, in particular in OECD countries. By 2040, demand for oil reaches 104 mb/d and biofuels use boosts total liquid fuel demand to 108.5 mb/d (Table 3.2).

Table 3.2 ▷ Oil demand by region in the New Policies Scenario (mb/d)

								2013-2040	
	1990	2013	2020	2025	2030	2035	2040	Delta	CAAGR*
OECD	38.9	41.5	40.2	38.1	35.4	33.4	31.3	-10.2	-1.0%
Americas	19.4	21.9	22.2	21.2	19.7	18.6	17.6	-4.3	-0.8%
United States	16.0	17.5	17.8	16.8	15.4	14.4	13.4	-4.1	-1.0%
Europe	12.6	12.0	11.2	10.5	9.7	9.0	8.3	-3.7	-1.3%
Asia Oceania	6.9	7.7	6.8	6.4	6.0	5.7	5.4	-2.3	-1.3%
Japan	5.1	4.4	3.7	3.3	3.0	2.8	2.6	-1.8	-1.9%
Non-OECD	23.4	41.6	48.2	53.1	57.3	60.4	63.1	21.5	1.6%
E. Europe/Eurasia	9.3	4.9	5.1	5.2	5.2	5.3	5.2	0.3	0.2%
Russia	5.2	3.2	3.2	3.2	3.2	3.2	3.2	-0.0	0.0%
Asia	6.3	19.7	23.9	27.1	30.0	32.0	33.5	13.7	2.0%
China	2.4	9.8	12.0	13.9	15.1	15.6	15.7	5.9	1.8%
India	1.2	3.7	4.9	5.8	7.0	8.2	9.2	5.5	3.5%
Middle East	2.8	7.6	8.7	9.6	10.2	10.7	11.3	3.7	1.5%
Africa	1.9	3.6	4.3	4.7	5.1	5.6	6.2	2.5	2.0%
Latin America	3.1	5.7	6.1	6.5	6.8	6.9	7.0	1.3	0.7%
Brazil	1.2	2.5	2.7	3.0	3.3	3.5	3.5	1.1	1.3%
Bunkers**	3.9	7.0	7.6	8.1	8.6	9.0	9.5	2.6	1.2%
World oil	66.1	90.1	96.0	99.2	101.3	102.8	103.9	13.8	0.5%
European Union	12.4	11.0	10.1	9.4	8.5	7.8	7.2	-3.8	-1.6%
World biofuels ***	0.1	1.3	2.2	2.8	3.4	4.1	4.6	3.3	4.7%
World total liquids	66.3	91.4	98.1	102.0	104.8	107.0	108.5	17.1	0.6%

* Compound average annual growth rate. ** Includes international marine and aviation fuels.
*** Expressed in energy-equivalent volumes of gasoline and diesel.

The share of OECD countries in global oil use has decreased from about 60% in 2000 to around 45% today, as demand growth in emerging economies outpaced OECD demand growth. Indeed, OECD oil consumption has been in actual decline since 2005, and continues to shrink by an average of 1.0% per year over the *Outlook* period, such that, by 2040, OECD countries account for less than one-third of global oil use. This decline is pushed by a renewed focus on energy efficiency in the transport, industry and buildings sectors in almost all countries. The United States sees the largest fall in absolute terms, with oil use contracting by more than 4 mb/d: fuel-economy standards, both for passenger and for heavy-duty vehicles, exploits the large untapped potential for efficiency gains in this sector.[2]

Japan sees the most rapid rate of decline in oil consumption of all the regions and countries individually modelled in our World Energy Model (WEM). Between 2013 and 2040 it sheds 40% of its current oil demand, under the impetus of energy efficiency policy, saturation effects in transport and the rapid decline of oil use in the power sector following the temporary increase in the aftermath of the Fukushima Daiichi accident. Oil demand from the Japanese petrochemical industry declines, as 30% of its capacity is closed over the projection period, due to weak domestic demand and high feedstock prices. Projected demand in Korea falls by around 20%, or 0.4 mb/d, mostly due to lower petrochemical output, fuel substitution in buildings and increased transport efficiency. Demand also falls across most of the European continent, although some countries in Eastern and Southeast Europe, outside the European Union (EU), see an increase in consumption. Almost half of the total drop of 3.8 mb/d in EU demand to 2040 is in road transport, where the EU has been moving in recent years towards the adoption of a long-term strategy on mobility to 2050, which includes a shift towards rail and waterborne transport, creation of an EU-wide core network of transport corridors and a framework for urban road pricing, alongside policies oriented at improving the fuel-economy of vehicles and promoting alternative fuels.

For each barrel of oil that is eliminated from consumption in OECD countries, two additional barrels of oil are consumed in the developing world (Table 3.2). Oil consumption grows by more than 21 mb/d in non-OECD countries over the period to 2040, at an average rate of 1.6% per year. Two-thirds of this comes from developing Asia, with China (5.9 mb/d) and India (5.5 mb/d) adding almost equal parts to global oil demand growth. Although Saudi Arabia has announced the introduction of its first-ever vehicle fuel-economy standards, the Middle East as a whole emerges as an important centre of global oil demand growth, adding 3.7 mb/d to reach 11 mb/d in 2040. There is strong growth in demand from the Middle East transport and petrochemical sectors, where continuing fossil-fuel subsidies in the region (Iran and Saudi Arabia are the countries with the largest subsidies in the world today) impede the market uptake of fuel-efficient vehicles. Some countries with large fossil-fuel subsidies recognise the need to reduce them or are even beginning to do

---

2. These standards target the vehicle model years to 2025 in the case of passenger light-duty vehicles, and 2014 to 2018 for heavy-duty vehicles. In early 2014, the administration announced its intention to further develop the heavy-duty vehicle standards into the next decade.

so, including Iran, but often they face consumer resistance (see Chapter 9). Oil demand in Africa (subject to detailed analysis in Part C), has been revised upward, compared with previous *Outlooks*, and reaches 6 mb/d in 2040.

Figure 3.2 ▷ Growth in world oil demand by region in the New Policies Scenario

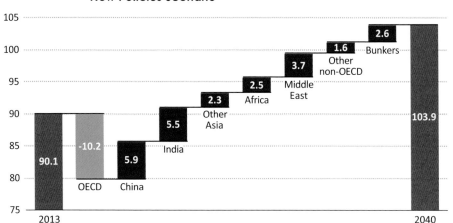

Nigeria and India, both of which currently subsidise oil consumption, are the countries among those modelled individually in the WEM that have the highest rates of demand growth to 2040: 3.5% per year. By 2040, oil demand in both countries is around 2.5 times today's levels, pushed up mainly by strong growth in transport (70% of the growth in India, and almost 60% in Nigeria) and in the residential sectors (10% of the growth in India, and almost 20% in Nigeria). On a per-capita basis, however, India still uses only half of the global average in 2040, and Nigeria just one-quarter. Oil demand in East Africa grows at a very high pace as well, at 3.9% per year, but generally oil use per capita in Africa remains at a very low level. The notable exception is South Africa, where consumption per capita exceeds the world average for the first time during the 2030s.

Non-OECD consumption growth occurs despite important measures already being taken in many countries to dampen this trend (see transport section). In China, where security of oil supply is an important strategic issue, a combination of transport policies – notably fuel-economy standards – and slowing growth in industrial production and population (the latter peaking in the 2030s) have a large impact on the growth rate of oil consumption in China. Ninety percent of the total increase in oil demand occurs prior to 2030, after which average growth is only 0.4% per year. The trend is more than enough for China to overtake the United States in the early 2030s as the largest oil-consuming country, but the implication is that a plateau in Chinese oil demand starts to come into view, even though it does not materialise before 2040 in the New Policies Scenario.

Sectoral trends

Projected global oil demand is increasingly concentrated in two sectors where substitution is most challenging, transport and petrochemicals (Table 3.3). By 2040, these sectors account, in volumetric terms, for almost three-quarters of total oil consumption, up from around two-thirds today. Oil use continues to fall back in power generation and in the residential and commercial sectors, while its use in industry (excluding petrochemicals) remains flat. By 2040, two-thirds of the remaining consumption of oil for power generation is in the Middle East, parts of Latin America and sub-Saharan Africa (see Part C). Oil use in buildings remains largely confined to the residential sector, with India and countries of sub-Saharan Africa the main sources of consumption, in the form of liquefied petroleum gas (LPG) or kerosene for cooking purposes. Oil demand is projected to remain steady in the agriculture sector, while it decreases in energy transformation, as a result of higher efficiency. The use of bitumen and lubricants increases by almost 30% due to the overall rise in economic activity.

Table 3.3 ▷ **Oil demand by sector in the New Policies Scenario** (mb/d)

								2013-2040	
	1990	2013	2020	2025	2030	2035	2040	Delta	CAAGR*
Total oil demand	66.1	90.1	96.0	99.2	101.3	102.8	103.9	13.8	0.5%
Power generation	7.0	5.8	4.4	3.6	3.0	2.7	2.5	-3.3	-3.1%
Transport	30.5	48.7	53.1	56.2	58.5	59.9	60.8	12.1	0.8%
Petrochemicals	6.3	11.1	13.6	14.7	15.4	16.1	16.8	5.6	1.5%
of which feedstocks	5.4	9.7	11.9	12.9	13.7	14.4	15.0	5.3	1.6%
Other industry	5.5	5.0	5.0	5.1	5.1	5.1	5.1	0.1	0.1%
Buildings	7.0	7.8	7.4	7.0	6.6	6.4	6.4	-1.5	-0.8%
Other**	9.8	11.7	12.4	12.7	12.7	12.6	12.4	0.7	0.2%

* Compound average annual growth rate. **Other includes agriculture, transformation, and other non-energy use (mainly bitumen and lubricants).

Note: The 2013 data show some marked differences with those for 2012 (published in *WEO-2013*) due to updates in volumetric conversion factors and reallocation of sectoral oil demand in some regions.

As a share of total consumption in each sector (i.e. considering all fuels) the share of oil is actually retreating everywhere – even in its strongholds of transport and petrochemicals. While oil still accounts for 85% of total transport demand in 2040, this is a lower share than today's 93%, as alternative fuels, such as natural gas, biofuels and electricity, gain ground. The deployment of alternative fuels is higher in OECD countries, where they account for more than 20% of total transport demand by the end of the projection period. In petrochemicals, the share of oil likewise declines, from 74% today to 71% in 2040, as the share of both coal and natural gas rises slightly. In other sectors, where oil has already been displaced to a large degree, its share of total demand continues to ebb.

Without the impact of fuel switching and efficiency gains, the increase in oil demand implied by our projections (e.g. from increased vehicle ownership and rising industrial activity) would result in an increase in consumption of 53 mb/d by 2040 (Figure 3.3). But this – purely theoretical – increase is moderated in practice by the switch to alternative fuels (a reduction of 17 mb/d) and adoption of more efficient technologies (a reduction of 23 mb/d): in the New Policies Scenario energy efficiency has a stronger impact on moderating oil demand growth than fuel switching in transport, while fuel switching plays a more important role in power generation and buildings.

Figure 3.3 ▷ **Impact of fuel switching and efficiency on the change in global oil demand by sector in the New Policies Scenario, 2013-2040**

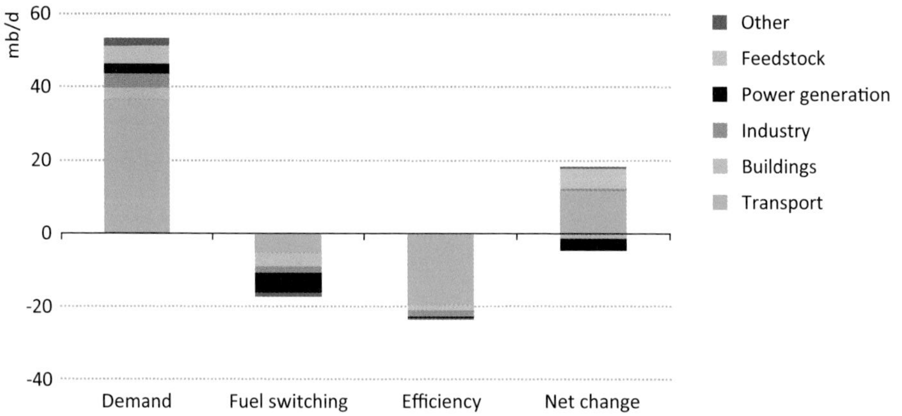

Note: This analysis uses a rolling decomposition technique on a sub-sector level to distinguish three effects: changes in the demand for energy services, such as mobility ("demand"), changes due to the switch from one fuel to another, e.g. from oil to gas in transport ("fuel switching"), and changes related to the use of more efficient equipment ("efficiency").

Transport

Around 2000, the transport sector crossed a threshold to account for more than half of total oil demand and it has not looked back. The projected share of the transport sector continues to increase from 55% today to more than 60% in 2040, despite increased fuel efficiency and the growth of alternative fuels. More than three-quarters of transport oil demand comes from road transport today, a share which is set to remain broadly unchanged until 2040. Although aviation is the fastest-growing of all transport sectors, road transport is set to account for over two-thirds of transport oil demand growth. The growth in oil demand for transport occurs almost exclusively in emerging and developing countries, transport oil demand in OECD countries declines across all sub-sectors, except aviation.

The main oil products used in transport today are gasoline (22 mb/d) and diesel (18 mb/d), but the balance between them is set to change, with diesel projected to overtake gasoline as the largest oil product in transport during the 2030s. The main reason for this reversal is that while gasoline is used almost exclusively in road transport, mostly for passenger and commercial light-duty vehicles (where fuel-economy standards have a large impact on demand), diesel predominates in the fast-growing road freight sector (where efficiency measures are less common) and it is also a more versatile fuel, used also in rail and navigation. Among the other fuels used in the transport sector, kerosene, at 5.5 mb/d, is used only in aviation, while heavy fuel oil, at 3.4 mb/d, is exclusively used in navigation.

Figure 3.4 ▷ **World transport oil demand change by main products and sub-sector in the New Policies Scenario, 2013-2040**

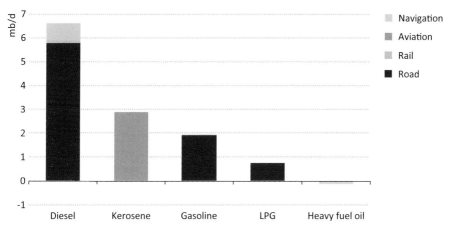

Over the *Outlook* period, demand for all oil products used for transport increases, with the exception of heavy fuel oil (Figure 3.4). Diesel growth is strongest in absolute terms because of strong growth in road freight transport, in particular in developing countries. Gasoline demand growth is underpinned by the increasing stock of passenger light-duty vehicles (PLDVs), which more than doubles to 1.9 billion vehicles in 2040 (although the influence of this growth on oil demand will also depend on the way that driving habits evolve, [Box 3.1]); but growth is held back by the growing application of fuel-economy standards. Over the course of the past year, additional fuel-economy standards for PLDVs have been adopted in Mexico, targeting the model years until 2016. In an attempt to reduce air pollution, China is reportedly planning to remove from the road more than 5 million cars that fail fuel standards. The Indian government also introduced fuel efficiency norms in early 2014, with a target fuel usage of 4.8 litres per 100 kilometres by 2021-22: possible subsidies for the purchase of electric cars and hybrid vehicles are under discussion. Saudi Arabia, too, is taking some first steps to curb oil demand growth from PLDVs through fuel-economy labels and standards for imported vehicles starting in 2015/2016, although the prevalence of fossil-fuel subsidies is likely to counteract these efforts.

Box 3.1 ▷ Vehicle occupancy: empty seats and extra barrels

For oil demand and vehicle emissions, what matters is not just how many vehicles are owned, but how they are used. People use cars for a variety of purposes, including travel to work, shopping and errands, and for social or recreational purposes. While the perceived attractiveness of cars is in decline in some countries (IEA, 2013a), leading to discussions of a possible peak in car use and, even, a possible reduction, there are many places in the world where people simply rely on the use of a personal vehicle due to the lack of other options.

One option to reduce car mileage is through ride-sharing. In the United States, vehicle occupancy per trip averaged 1.9 people per car in the late 1970s, a value that declined to 1.59 in the mid-1990s, boosting oil demand (US Department of Transportation, 2009). Vehicle occupancy has since risen again, to 1.67 people per car in 2009, partially thanks to efforts to support ride-sharing, e.g. car-pooling priority lanes. The use of modern telecommunications has helped to revitalise the concept of ride-sharing, with countless websites aiming to match spare car seats with potential passengers in return for a share of the fuel costs. With the advent of smart phones and mobile applications, the idea is gaining further traction: a French start-up, operating since 2006, attracted $100 million in venture capital in a recent fund-raising, indicating investors' expectations of strong growth in this sector.

Assessing the possible impact of trends in vehicle occupancy on long-term oil demand is a challenging task. Most of the examples and impacts thus far are concentrated in OECD markets; but the most interesting implications may be for those fast-growing emerging economies that are increasingly concerned about oil security and local pollution. In the New Policies Scenario, the average global vehicle occupancy drops from around 1.9 people per car today to 1.8 in 2040, because of an assumed decline in occupancy levels in non-OECD countries, following the historical trend. If more seats were occupied and global occupancy levels remained, on average, at today's levels, oil demand in 2040 would be lower by 1.5 mb/d.

After improvements in efficiency, the in-roads made by alternative fuels, such as natural gas, biofuels and electricity, are the next most important factor curbing transport oil demand growth. The largest effect comes from biofuels, the use of which more than triples in the New Policies Scenario and displaces 4.5 million barrels of gasoline, diesel and some kerosene by 2040 (see Chapter 7). The use of natural gas, too, increases, mainly in the United States, India and China. In the United States, low prices relative to oil incentivise the use of liquefied natural gas (LNG) in road freight transport (IEA, 2013a). In China, 2013 was the third consecutive year of strong increases in natural gas vehicle sales, both in the light-duty and heavy-duty segments. Globally, the use of natural gas in road transport displaces 2.8 million barrels of oil equivalent per day (mboe/d) by 2040. Sales of plug-in hybrids and electric vehicles increase to 5.7% of total PLDV sales in 2040, from less than 0.2% today, helped by subsidies in several countries: they displace almost 800 thousand barrels per day (kb/d) of gasoline in road transport by 2040. At this point, our projections do not anticipate any contribution from hydrogen fuel cell vehicles to oil demand reduction, even though Toyota recently announced the launch of a first commercial model for 2015.

In most cases, alternative fuels cannot compete, without support, with oil products in the passenger car segment (Figure 3.5). The reasons vary, depending on the fuel and region in question. While for electric vehicles and hydrogen fuel cell vehicles, the high upfront cost of the vehicle currently cannot be offset by lower running cost, this is generally less of an issue for natural gas vehicles, where the additional upfront investment is usually around $2 000 to $3 000. In the case of natural gas (and also for hydrogen and electric vehicles), the lack of refuelling infrastructure holds back wider market penetration. Policy support is therefore very important to the penetration of alternatives to gasoline-powered passenger vehicles. In addition, as with any emerging technology, the expansion of new vehicle types can be projected only on the basis of present knowledge of likely technology and cost evolutions, which are key determinants of the pace of market uptake, as all vehicles offer basically the same service, i.e. mobility. As in other fields, technology breakthroughs or a big fall in cost could lead to a more rapid uptake of new vehicle and fuel technologies: this is a market which, so far, has remained resistant to rapid change ever since the car was introduced.

Figure 3.5 ▷ **Discounted total annual costs of passenger light-duty vehicles in selected regions in the New Policies Scenario, 2020**

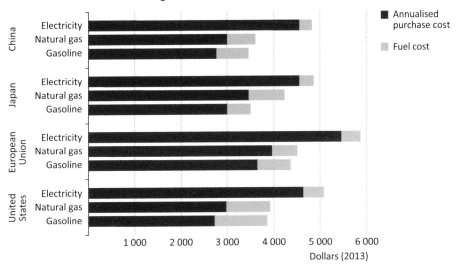

Notes: Assumes a common vehicle lifetime of 12 years and a discount rate of 8% for the purpose of comparison. The average annual mileage is assumed to be equal for each vehicle type and is 20 000 km in the United States, 15 000 km in the European Union and 10 000 km in Japan and China. Fuel prices exclude taxes but include the costs of the retail infrastructure for gas and electricity (from the World Energy Model).

Petrochemicals

After transport, petrochemicals is the sector that sees the highest growth in oil demand, consumption increasing by more than 5 mb/d to reach 15 mb/d in 2040, an annual growth rate of 1.6%. This is closely linked to the output of the most important petrochemical intermediary product, ethylene, where output grows by close to 2% per year, due to robust demand for resins, fibres and plastics as a relatively low-cost, versatile and resistant packaging material. However, oil use in this sector grows more slowly than over the past two decades (when annual growth was over 3%) as a consequence of saturation effects in developed countries, of coal gaining ground as a feedstock in China, and of the higher recycling rates that are anticipated in the future.

Figure 3.6 ▷ Global demand for petrochemical feedstock by oil product in the New Policies Scenario

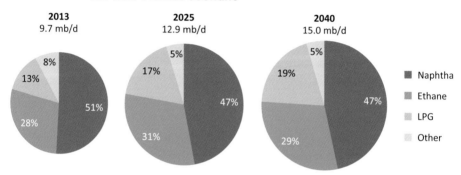

Most feedstock for petrochemical products originates from steam crackers or from refinery units (catalytic reforming and catalytic cracking). The most important oil-based feedstock is naphtha, which currently accounts for more than half of all inputs (Figure 3.6). While naphtha demand for petrochemicals grows by around 2 mb/d over the period to 2040, mainly because of higher consumption in Asia, the relative importance of naphtha declines. This a consequence of quickly growing demand for lighter feedstocks – LPG and ethane – particularly in North America and the Middle East.

Together with China and the Middle East, the United States sees the highest increase in oil consumption for petrochemicals to 2025. Thanks to a surge in natural gas liquids from wet gas plays, the United States is, at present, experiencing oversupply of ethane, which has driven down the price for this petrochemical raw material. Responding to the anticipated growth in ethane supply, chemical companies have announced plans for ten new steam crackers (almost all producing more than 1 million tonnes per year) and several capacity expansions at existing plants. In our projections, US ethylene production increases by about 9 million tonnes (Mt) to 2025 (an increase of almost 40% compared with today), levelling off in the later 2020s. Currently, the ethane price in the United States trades close to the natural gas price, as this represents a lower bound for ethane prices (ethane can be retained in the natural gas stream up to a certain limit). In the first nine months of 2014, the US ethane price of $5 per million British thermal units (MBtu) has compared to a price of $21/MBtu for naphtha in Europe (the principal petrochemical feedstock in that region), providing US crackers with healthy margins.

These large regional price differences for petrochemical feedstocks are set to result in an expansion of international trade. The possibility to import lower priced LPG from the United States has already prompted European flexible fuel crackers to switch from naphtha to LPG as a feedstock. As a consequence LPG exports from the United States have increased substantially and are expected to pick up further in the near future. There are currently no exports of ethane as – in contrast to LPG (but similar to LNG) – it needs to be refrigerated for transport and currently no suitable infrastructure exists. But, as of mid-2014, there are plans for four European crackers (one of them to be converted from naphtha to ethane) and for one cracker project in India to import ethane from the United States. Further ethane exports to Europe are possible but would be complicated by the need for significant changes to enable existing steam crackers to handle ethane instead of heavier feedstocks. Moreover, the price advantage of ethane would lessen if the balance of ethane supply and demand becomes tighter as a result of higher demand (as recently as 2012, US ethane prices were above $10/MBtu).

In the long term, the Middle East accounts in our projections for the largest increase in petrochemical oil demand, which more than doubles from 2013 to 3.3 mb/d in 2040. This development is helped both by the region's competitive position as the lowest cost producer of petrochemicals (largely due to cheap ethane) and by its geographical position of relative proximity to the large import markets in Asia. After the Middle East, China sees the second-largest rise in petrochemical oil demand of 1.6 mb/d to reach 2.8 mb/d in 2040, due to strong domestic demand and the desire to increase self-sufficiency in plastics production. However, oil demand growth in this sector in China is somewhat dampened by the use of coal as a (comparatively cheap) feedstock in coal-to-olefin (CTO) and methanol-to-olefin (MTO) plants.[3] China currently has an annual capacity to produce 6 Mt of ethylene and propylene from CTO/MTO plants and we project this to increase to about 20 Mt by 2025.[4]

Europe, Japan and Korea all see a decline in petrochemical production in the future as they are the highest cost producers, leading to a reduction of 0.6 mb/d in oil demand for these three regions. In OECD countries, lower refinery runs in the future mean that less naphtha is available for steam crackers, and the throughput in catalytic crackers (the main source of propylene) and catalytic reformers (the main source of aromatics) declines as gasoline production in these regions is scaled back, due to decreasing demand. The anticipated decline in propylene production from refineries is expected to be compensated for by the construction of propane dehydrogenation facilities that produce propylene from LPG, particularly in the United States and China.

---

3. These plants either produce methanol from coal or import it to produce olefins (mainly ethylene and propylene).

4. At present, China is the only country using methanol on a large scale to produce olefins, although a plant exists in Europe and plans have been announced in the United States for an MTO plant using natural gas as a feedstock.

Trends by product

The trends identified in the various demand sectors, with the increasing concentration of oil use in transport and in petrochemicals, are reflected in the outlook for the oil products that make up overall oil supply (Figure 3.7). Consumption of ethane and naphtha, both exclusively used in petrochemicals, grow from 2013 levels of 2.8 mb/d and 5.2 mb/d, respectively, to reach 4.4 mb/d and 7.2 mb/d in 2040. Ethane use growth is generally limited to regions with local supply (particularly North America and the Middle East), although we do project some exports from the United States to Europe and Asia. LPG increases its share as a petrochemical feedstock since it is cheaper than naphtha (as it comes from relatively low-cost natural gas liquids [NGLs] fractionation) and it is easier to transport in sea tankers than ethane. The transport sector is another area of growth for LPG – consumption doubles from 0.7 mb/d in 2013 – but its global use in other sectors (including industry, residential and services) is either flat or on a gradually declining trend. Overall, LPG demand grows from 7.4 mb/d in 2013 to 9.5 mb/d in 2040.

Figure 3.7 ▷ **World oil demand growth by product in the New Policies Scenario**

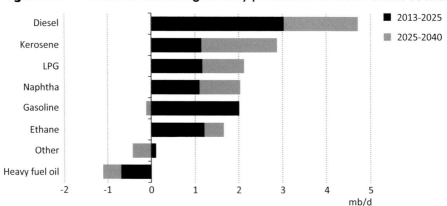

Gasoline, which is almost exclusively a road transport fuel, grows by almost 2 mb/d to 2040, but by the end of our projection period its global use is in decline. The cumulative impact of the passenger vehicle efficiency policies in many major economies and continued substitution by other transport fuels and products induces a peak in gasoline demand, at around 24.2 mb/d, in the early 2030s. Among the middle distillates, kerosene demand rises to 9.4 mb/d by 2040 (a higher overall volume growth than gasoline) thanks to the expansion in demand for aviation. The dominant fuel among the oil products, though, both in terms of current consumption and in terms of volume growth to 2040, is diesel: consumption rises by 4.7 mb/d to 30.4 mb/d in 2040. The increase in diesel use is even higher in the transport sector – rising by 6.6 mb/d – but this is offset in part by declining consumption elsewhere.

One significant shift in oil product consumption over the coming decades is the continued decline in global demand for residual fuel oil, as consumers switch both to other fuels (to natural gas, nuclear and renewables in the power sector; to natural gas or electricity in industry) and, in some cases, to other oil products. In domestic and international navigation, which currently account for 45% of fuel oil use, fuel oil consumption remains static in volume terms, which means that all of the increase in demand in this sector is picked up by diesel (and, to a smaller degree, by LNG) and the share of fuel oil in navigation fuel demand goes down from 75% to less than 60%. That this share does not decline further, despite tighter environmental standards for maritime shipping, is a result of refining economics and product price differentials (Box 3.2). Among the other oil products, use of refinery fuel increases in line with higher refinery runs and demand for products for non-energy use (asphalt, lubricants, solvents) likewise increases. There is, though, a decline in the direct burning of crude oil, from 1.4 mb/d in 2013 to 0.4 mb/d in 2040, which brings the overall consumption in this category slightly down.

Box 3.2 ▷ Marine bunkers: a sea change?

Although data for the sector are weak, of the estimated current 4 mb/d of global marine bunker fuel demand the predominant fuel is fuel oil (around 80%), with the remainder largely marine diesel. However, the prospect of stricter emissions controls, focusing initially on the sulphur content of fuels but possibly extending to other pollutants in the future, is expected to shift this balance over the *Outlook* period.[5]

The measures being introduced or contemplated for the maritime sector highlight a key disadvantage of the heavier components produced during the process of crude distillation. Sulphur molecules are disproportionately more attached to the heavier components of crude oil than to the lighter components. The sulphur content in residual fuels can, accordingly, be several times that of the original crude. For example, Russia's main export, Urals grade crude with 1.35% sulphur, will mostly produce residual fuels with 3.5% sulphur. By contrast, its atmospheric gasoil, coming straight from the distillation tower, can have 0.8% sulphur which, in the case of fuel for export to European markets, is then additionally hydrotreated to remove all but 0.001% of sulphur (or 10 parts per million, [ppm]), the allowed specification in the EU for road diesel fuels. Gasoil for heating purposes is allowed to have 50 ppm.

Residual fuels are the main component in marine bunkers, which have long had a very high-sulphur content. As sulphur content restrictions are introduced, the options for compliance include a switch to lower sulphur oil products, such as marine diesel, the adoption of "scrubber" technologies that remove bunker fuel gases before they are released to the atmosphere (allowing for continued use of higher sulphur fuels) or switching to a lower emissions fuel, such as LNG.

---

5. Key regulations include the introduction in coastal Emission Control Areas (ECA) of a 0.1% limit to the sulphur content of a ship's fuel as of 1 January 2015. ECAs currently include the North Sea, the Baltic Sea and coastal areas in North America and the US Caribbean Sea. Other areas are currently under discussion. The International Maritime Organization (IMO) also aims to restrict sulphur content in areas outside ECAs from the current limit of 3.5% to 0.5%, although the timing is as yet unclear: the application of the new fuel standard is scheduled for 2020, but could be pushed back to 2025.

None of these options is cost free. Low-sulphur bunker fuels cannot be produced at the scale required in the current refinery configuration and the hydrotreating process, used for diesel and gasoline, is expensive. Adopting or retrofitting scrubber technologies is not only a costly investment in itself, but (for retrofits) requires taking vessels out of service while the work is being done. Switching to LNG requires LNG-powered vessels and new refuelling infrastructure (see Chapter 4). This may point to a switch to marine gasoil, which, as a middle distillate fraction, is produced with lower sulphur content. However, middle distillates are already the fastest-growing market in the world, which is putting pressure on refiners. To fully replace fuel oil in navigation demand by 2030 would mean a further reduction in the consumption of residual fuels, by 3.4 mb/d, and the addition of a similar amount to demand for middle distillates. This would imply additional massive investments in the refining sector to reduce the fuel oil yields practically to zero and to produce diesel instead. The process of cracking fuel oil, however, yields not only diesel, but other by-products, i.e. a barrel of fuel oil would yield less than a barrel of diesel. In our view, this would result in the price spread between these two fuels increasing to the point at which either scrubbing or refinery fuel oil hydrotreating becomes economic. Thus, for now, we do not envisage a large-scale switch to marine gasoil in global bunkers demand.

Production

Resources and reserves

Even with the extension of our *Outlook* to 2040, remaining technically recoverable resources of oil are sufficient to meet anticipated demand in all the scenarios (Table 3.4). Estimates of remaining recoverable oil resources are at similar levels as discussed in detail in *World Energy Outlook-2013* (*WEO-2013*) (IEA 2013a, see also IEA 2013b), i.e. considerably higher than the 944 billion barrels of cumulative oil production required in the New Policies Scenario (and likewise for the 836 billion barrels and 995 billion barrels required in the 450 Scenario and Current Policies Scenario, respectively).

Although the range of overall resource estimates for conventional oil has not changed, the United States Geological Survey (USGS) has released some additional details over the last year – notably the split, for undiscovered oil, between onshore and offshore resources. To recall, the *WEO* resources database relies extensively on USGS data, which divides the overall conventional resource base for oil into three parts:

- Known oil, including both cumulative production and reserves in known reservoirs.
- Reserves growth, an estimate of how much oil may be produced from known reservoirs on top of the "known oil".
- Undiscovered oil, a basin-by-basin estimate of how much more oil may be found.

In the latter category, out of the mean value of around 565 billion barrels of undiscovered conventional crude oil resources, almost two-thirds (367 billion barrels) are estimated to lie offshore. For NGLs, of the mean value of 167 billion barrels of undiscovered resources, almost three-quarters (122 billion barrels) are offshore.

Table 3.4 ▷ **Remaining recoverable oil resources and proven reserves, end-2013** (billion barrels)

	Conventional resources		Unconventional resources			Total	
	Crude oil	NGLs	EHOB	Kerogen oil	Tight oil	Resources	Proven reserves
OECD	316	99	810	1 016	114	2 355	250
Americas	247	54	807	1 000	80	2 187	230
Europe	63	34	3	4	17	121	15
Asia Oceania	6	11	-	12	18	47	4
Non-OECD	1 923	377	1 068	57	230	3 655	1 449
E.Europe/Eurasia	342	83	552	20	78	1 074	136
Asia	110	29	3	4	56	202	45
Middle East	968	179	14	30	0	1 190	814
Africa	284	55	2	-	38	379	131
Latin America	219	32	497	3	57	809	323
World	2 239	476	1 879	1 073	344	6 010	1 699

Sources: IEA databases; OGJ (2013); BP (2014); BGR (2013); US EIA (2013).

Notes: Proven reserves (which are typically not broken down by conventional/unconventional) are usually defined as discovered volumes having a 90% probability that they can be extracted profitably. EHOB is extra-heavy oil and bitumen. The IEA databases do not include NGLs from unconventional reservoirs (i.e. associated with shale gas) outside the United States, because of the lack of comprehensive assessment: unconventional NGLs resources in the United States are included in conventional NGLs for simplicity.

The size and likely location of undiscovered conventional oil resources remains significant for the global oil outlook, even though – at nearly 1 700 billion barrels, including unconventional oil – today's proven reserves are already sufficient to meet projected consumption on their own. The explanation for this apparent paradox lies, in part, with the location of the world's proven reserves. The largest, lowest cost reserves are in Organization of Petroleum Exporting Countries (OPEC), many of which may limit their production rates (to balance supply and demand at an oil price that meets their financial requirements or to preserve resources for the longer term). This creates a market opportunity for others to produce and sell a large amount of oil, as well as continued incentives for companies to engage in exploration for, and appraisal of, new resources.

Our projections suggest that a distinct share of future conventional production is set to come from fields that are yet to be found: 16 mb/d by 2040 in the New Policies Scenario and 10 mb/d even in the 450 Scenario. The discoveries implied by our scenarios are not, though, excessive by comparison with historical rates of discovery (Figure 3.9). The role of discoveries in our scenarios is one reason why today's proven reserves should not be taken as accurate guide to the oil that is actually likely to be developed and produced over the coming decades. Another contributing factor is the importance to our projections of unconventional resources, for which data are not as broadly available as for conventional resources (Box 3.3).

Box 3.3 ▷ **What is the right burden of proof for unconventional oil and gas?**

Deposits of unconventional resources, such as tight oil, shale gas, Canadian oil sands or extra-heavy oil in the Venezuelan Orinoco Belt, tend to be spread over large geographical areas, with only a small amount of hydrocarbons recoverable per well. Their exploitation requires a large number of wells, each with a small "drainage area", i.e. the extent of rock feeding the production from the well. This large number of wells may be drilled over a long period of time: for example, in the Bakken tight oil play in North Dakota, it is thought that some 40 000 wells could be drilled over 20 years.

One result of these characteristics is that, under present classification systems, the reserves in unconventional deposits, whether 1P (proven) or 2P (proven + probable) are not representative of the extent of likely long-term production. Indeed, to be classified as reserves under the Petroleum Resources Management System (PRMS) classification, the hydrocarbons need to be ready to be produced by a "project" that is either approved (investment decision taken) or likely to be approved. As such, only the production from wells already likely to be approved for drilling can be counted as reserves; wells that might be drilled 20 years from now do not qualify.

Yet, it is quite likely that the locations that will be drilled in 20 years will produce hydrocarbons. Such resources are classified under PRMS as "contingent resources", 1C, 2C or 3C with geological likelihood of 90%, 50% or 10%. This situation is in contrast to many conventional oil and gas reservoirs, for which the reserves figure (even though it tends to grow with time, as some contingent resources move to the reserves category), gives a more representative indication of possible future production. Indeed in tight oil plays, proven reserves can even fluctuate from one year to the next, as drilling can be put on hold due to volatility in oil prices.

But the contingent resources category is a catch-all that encompasses all resources that are known to exist and to be technically recoverable but which are not sufficiently close to commercial exploitation to be classified as reserves. Some may be too expensive to produce under current or reasonably forecasted economic conditions, some may not have the required approvals to be produced, some may just be kept for future development by the entity having the rights to exploit them. This is why PRMS recommends assigning contingent resources to different sub-classes: development pending; development on hold or unclarified; and development not viable (Figure 3.8).[6]

Although, historically, companies have tended not to report contingent resource numbers, and, even less, the various sub-classes, there is a growing trend of such disclosure, spearheaded in particular by the Alberta Stock Exchange and the Calgary Society of Petroleum Evaluation Engineers, who provided guidance for such disclosures

---

6. PRMS is the most widely used classification system in the oil and gas industry, but broader internationally recognised systems, such as the United Nations Framework Classification for Fossil Energy and Mineral Reserves and Resources, provide analogous sub-classes, for example F2.1, F2.2 and F2.3.

in their Resources Other Than Reserves study. This trend is very welcome and should be encouraged, as it will enable energy analysts to put projections of future unconventional oil and gas production on a firmer footing.

Figure 3.8 ▷ **Schematic of the PRMS* classification**

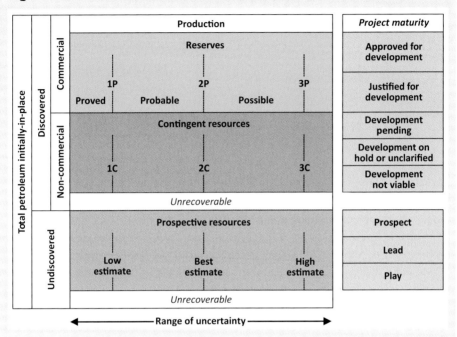

* PRMS: Petroleum Resources Management System.

More detailed disclosure of contingent resources would also be welcome for conventional reservoirs, for example to provide a better basis for a company's valuation or a better understanding of resources in OPEC countries. Indeed in countries with very large conventional resources, such as Saudi Arabia, Iraq or Iran, the situation is somewhat similar to that for unconventional oil: ample hydrocarbons are known to exist and to be economically recoverable that will not be produced for many years; under PRMS those amounts should properly be considered contingent resources, rather than reserves, and some of the reserves numbers given by such countries might be better classified as 1P + 1C (or even 2P + 2C).[7]

---

7. PRMS leaves quite a bit of freedom to the resource owner on what constitutes "near-commerciality" or "development decision", so a national oil company is, in principle, entitled to consider as near-commercial, (and therefore reserves), amounts that will be developed only in a number of years time.

Figure 3.9 ▷ **Volumes of global conventional oil discovered by decade versus discoveries required in the New Policies Scenario**

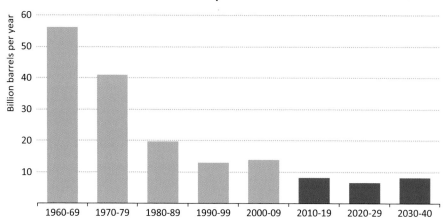

Production prospects[8]

Oil production, including crude oil, NGLs and unconventional oil, follows the same trajectory as demand in each of the three scenarios (Table 3.5); capacity in excess of production is not modelled in our WEM and therefore is implicitly assumed to remain unchanged. In the New Policies Scenario, oil supply (including processing gains) rises from 89 mb/d in 2013 to 104 mb/d in 2040, with all of the increase coming from NGLs and unconventional oil. Output of crude oil (excluding tight oil, which we classify as unconventional) in this scenario fluctuates between 68 mb/d and 66 mb/d over the *Outlook* period, finishing at the low end of this range.

Oil production to 2040 in the New Policies Scenario can usefully be divided into two periods, with the transition between them occurring in the 2020s (Figure 3.10). The first period is characterised by continued buoyancy in non-OPEC production: tight oil (and to some extent deepwater) from the United States, oil sands in Canada, deepwater developments in Brazil and rising output of NGLs from a variety of sources all push non-OPEC output up towards a high point of 56 mb/d in the early 2020s. But then non-OPEC supply flattens and falls back, due to declines in conventional output in Russia, China and, later, in Kazakhstan and, eventually, a tailing off in US production. With global consumption inching steadily higher, the onus for growth in supply then shifts. Canada and Brazil remain major contributors, but a steadily larger role is played by the major OPEC resource-holders, notably those in the Middle East. After remaining stable at just over 40%, the share of OPEC in global oil production starts rising again in the 2020s, reaching 49% by 2040.

---

8. For detail on the production outlook for Africa, refer to Part C.

Table 3.5 ▷ **Oil production and liquids supply by source and scenario** (mb/d)

	1990	2013	New Policies 2020	New Policies 2040	Current Policies 2020	Current Policies 2040	450 Scenario 2020	450 Scenario 2040
OPEC	23.9	36.8	37.3	49.5	37.8	54.8	36.4	33.1
Crude oil	21.9	30.0	29.1	36.4	29.5	40.8	28.6	23.9
Natural gas liquids	2.0	6.0	6.7	9.9	6.8	10.4	6.3	7.1
Unconventional	0.0	0.7	1.5	3.2	1.5	3.5	1.4	2.1
Non-OPEC	41.7	50.5	56.1	51.2	57.6	58.2	54.5	36.2
Crude oil	37.7	38.6	38.9	30.0	39.9	33.1	38.0	21.5
Natural gas liquids	3.6	6.4	7.9	8.3	8.0	9.1	7.6	6.2
Unconventional	0.4	5.4	9.3	13.0	9.7	16.0	9.0	8.6
World oil production	65.6	87.3	93.4	100.7	95.4	113.0	90.9	69.4
Crude oil	59.6	68.6	68.0	66.4	69.3	73.9	66.6	45.4
Natural gas liquids	5.6	12.5	14.6	18.2	14.9	19.5	13.8	13.3
Unconventional	0.4	6.1	10.8	16.2	11.2	19.6	10.4	10.7
Processing gains	*1.3*	*2.2*	*2.5*	*3.2*	*2.6*	*3.5*	*2.5*	*2.6*
World oil supply*	66.9	89.4	96.0	103.9	98.0	116.6	93.4	71.9
World biofuels supply**	0.1	1.3	2.2	4.6	1.8	3.6	2.1	8.7
World total liquids supply	67.0	90.8	98.1	108.5	99.8	120.2	95.5	80.7

* Differences between historical supply and demand volumes shown earlier in the chapter are due to changes in stocks.
** Expressed in energy-equivalent volumes of gasoline and diesel. The average energy to volume conversion factor is close to 7.8 barrels per tonne of oil equivalent throughout the projection period in the New Policies Scenario, reflecting the projected share of biodiesel versus ethanol.

Note: More information on methodology and data issues (including an explanation of differences with the IEA *Medium-Term Oil Market Report*) is on the *WEO* website *www.worldenergyoutlook.org/weomodel/*.

Figure 3.10 ▷ **Change in oil production by selected region in the New Policies Scenario**

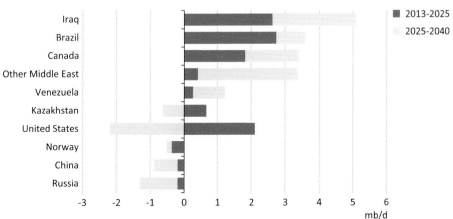

One source of uncertainty over the oil market outlook, underlined by the current turmoil in Iraq, is which countries might be ready to pick up the baton to meet long-term growth in oil demand, if anticipated production from any of the main sources in our projections falls short. One possible answer to this question is that the current upswing in non-OPEC supply will, in practice, be more durable than we project due, for instance, to higher output of tight oil from the United States and more rapid exploitation of tight oil worldwide (a question discussed in the next section), or to the availability of ample transportation capacity for higher production from Canada's oil sands, or to faster conventional development elsewhere (for example, in Mexico, where the current reforms could unlock a larger share of a very large resource base). Alternatively, the upside could come from countries like Iran or Venezuela, for which we currently have only modest expectations of growth, but which have huge remaining resources that could be developed more quickly if the political climate were to encourage an upswing in investment. But another distinct possibility is that a shortfall in investment and production would become manifest in tighter markets and higher prices (and consequently lower oil demand) – an outcome that we have examined in numerous recent analyses.[9]

A focus on production growth can present a misleading picture of the scale of the challenges facing the industry. Signs of strain affecting global oil supply can appear not just in countries that are aiming to increase output, but also in those that are attempting to maintain production at high levels. Russia, for example, faces a significant challenge to compensate for declines at its main production areas in Western Siberia and to keep production at around 10 mb/d. As examined in detail in the World Energy Investment Outlook (IEA, 2014a), by far the greater part of upstream investment over the coming decades is needed just to maintain production at today's levels. The requirement for total upstream oil and gas investment is estimated at $22.5 trillion over the period to 2040 (out of a total for the oil and gas sectors, including transportation and refining, of $29 trillion), with annual average upstream expenditure rising above $900 billion by the 2030s. Of this, 80% is required just to keep output at today's levels.

Conventional crude oil production from existing fields is set to fall by 58% by 2040, meaning that, by the end of the projection period, 38 mb/d of production has to come from conventional oil fields that are at present either awaiting development or, in some cases, awaiting discovery (Table 3.6). Because a significant part of the undiscovered oil is thought to be offshore, in particular in deepwater (defined in *WEO* as water depth greater than 400 metres), this explains why the share of deepwater in total production gradually increases from 7% in 2013 to 11% in 2040, reaching a level of almost 11 mb/d.

For many producers, extracting more oil from old reservoirs makes more and more sense compared to exploring for new oil fields in remote places. This is reflected in our projections in an increasing importance of enhanced oil recovery (EOR) technologies, such as CO_2 injection, chemical injection and, to a lesser extent, steam techniques, which gradually

9. See the Deferred Investment Case in *WEO-2011* (IEA, 2011), the Low Iraq Case in *WEO-2012* (IEA, 2012) or the Delayed Case in the *World Energy Investment Outlook* (IEA, 2014a).

gain in importance through the period, The contribution from EOR projects is projected to grow from 1.4 mb/d to 5.8 mb/d (Table 3.6), with large producers in the Middle East instrumental to this increase.[10]

Table 3.6 ▷ **World oil production by type in the New Policies Scenario** (mb/d)

	1990	2013	2020	2025	2030	2035	2040	2013-2040 Delta	2013-2040 CAAGR*
Conventional	65.2	81.1	82.6	83.8	84.1	84.2	84.6	3.4	0.2%
Crude oil	59.6	68.6	68.0	68.4	67.8	67.0	66.4	-2.3	-0.1%
Existing fields	58.6	67.3	52.8	43.0	35.1	29.1	22.9	-44.3	-3.9%
Yet to be developed	-	-	13.2	17.4	18.7	19.3	21.3	21.3	n.a.
Yet to be found	-	-	0.5	5.5	10.3	13.8	16.4	16.4	n.a.
Enhanced oil recovery	1.0	1.4	1.6	2.4	3.6	4.8	5.8	4.4	5.5%
Natural gas liquids	5.6	12.5	14.6	15.4	16.4	17.2	18.2	5.7	1.4%
Unconventional	0.4	6.1	10.8	12.6	14.3	15.6	16.2	10.0	3.6%
Tight oil	-	2.9	5.5	6.2	6.6	6.4	5.4	2.5	2.3%
Total	65.6	87.3	93.4	96.4	98.4	99.8	100.7	13.4	0.5%

* Compound average annual growth rate.

With conventional crude output below today's levels in 2040, rising production of unconventional oil (including tight oil) and NGLs accounts for all of the net growth in oil production. Decline rates for individual tight oil wells are higher than for conventional wells, implying a greater intensity of drilling to maintain overall production at a given level. This explains, in part, how difficult it is for tight oil to act as a continued engine of supply growth throughout the projection period. Instead, it is other sources of unconventional oil, notably extra-heavy oil, coal-to-liquids and gas-to-liquids projects, as well as NGLs, which see sustained increases over the period to 2040. In the case of unconventional oil, this is largely attributable to production from the oil sands in Canada and the Orinoco Belt in Venezuela, supplemented by smaller volumes of bitumen or extra-heavy oil from Russia and China.

The main additions to the supply of NGLs come from North America, the Middle East (where gas generally has a higher liquids content than in most other regions) and from a reduction in the flaring of associated gas in Nigeria, Russia and Iraq (associated gas, likewise, tends to be relatively rich in NGLs). Growth in oil production over the coming decades therefore tends to be either at the light end of the spectrum (tight oil, NGLs) or at the heavy end (extra-heavy oil). By 2040, conventional crude oil accounts for only 66% of total production, compared with 88% as recently as 2000. As discussed later in this chapter, this bifurcation of oil supply and the squeeze that it exerts on the share of conventional crude is one of the challenges facing the global refining sector (Figure 3.11).

---

10. Volumes recovered with enhanced oil recovery (EOR) technologies are included as a component of production from existing fields. WEO-2013 (IEA, 2013a) provides a detailed explanation of how we derive the contribution of EOR.

Figure 3.11 ▷ **Change in world oil production by type in the New Policies Scenario**

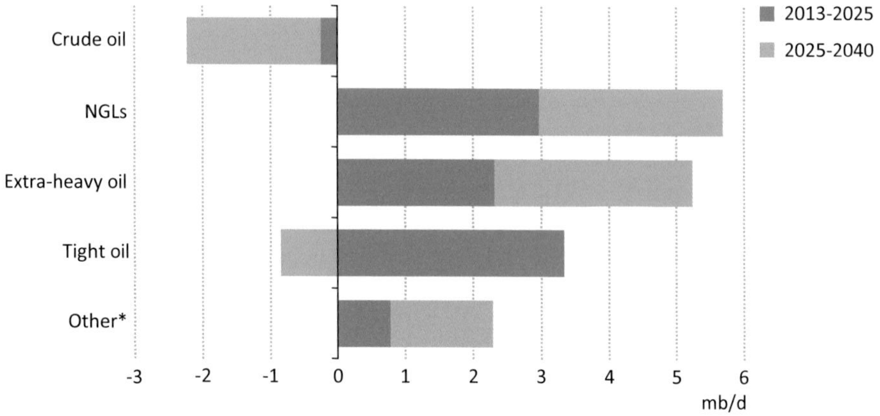

* Includes coal-to-liquids and gas-to-liquids projects, production of additives and of kerogen oil.

Update on tight oil developments

Tight oil production in the United States continues to race ahead, with the Bakken, the Eagle Ford (which have both now passed the 1 mb/d mark) and now the Permian plays setting production record after production record, complemented by soaring NGLs production from the Marcellus and Utica shale gas plays. This raises two fundamental questions for our oil outlook: how long is this surge in growth going to last in the United States; and will we see similar revolutions in other countries?

The future growth of tight oil in the United States is all a question of economics. With the steep decline rates for each well, the two determining variables are the cost of drilling and completing a well and the extent and value of the average amount of oil recovered from each well: the value of the latter needs to exceed the former. The industry has been very successful in reducing the cost per well, through optimisation of the process: small mobile rigs, batch drilling and completion on pads with multiple wells maximise equipment and crew utilisation, while increased knowledge of the geology allows optimisation of well length, well patterns and the number of hydraulic fracturing stages. In the most active plays, such as the Bakken and the Eagle Ford, this cost optimisation has probably reached its limit; in other plays it continues and, in some cases, a cost-effective set of practices has yet to be found (this is why, for example, the US Energy Information Administration [EIA] recently downgraded its estimate of recoverable resources in the Monterey shale in California: the oil is still there, but none of the standard practices has yet to yield economic recovery).

The amount of oil recovered per well is very much a function of geology: each play typically has "sweet spots", where recovery per well is high (often due to the presence of natural fractures in the rock, or to zones that are not as tight) and the rest of the target formation, where recovery is lower. This leads to the expectation that, as the sweet spots are depleted and drilling moves to less productive zones, the economics will start to deteriorate, leading to stabilisation and then a decrease in production. Further improvements in technology could well offset this effect: at present, oil recovery rates in shales often do not exceed a few percent of the oil originally in place; there is plenty of room for new technologies (pumping, injection of water or chemicals) to increase the recovery per well, even if, so far, none has proven effective. In addition, the value of the recovered oil is a function of the wellhead oil price; this is affected by international prices, but also by regional prices as in the United States (which are affected in turn by infrastructure constraints and the current ban on crude oil exports), by the need for and capacity of refineries to process the light crude that is being produced and by transportation costs, whether by pipeline or rail.

In our *Outlook*, we assume that, one way or another, wellhead prices will be strongly linked to international prices and that, while technology learning continues, there will be no technological breakthroughs on the supply side.[11] The result is that – with the current estimates of US recoverable resources – tight oil production in the United States is projected to level off in the 2020s and then to start a gradual decline, as it becomes less economically attractive, compared with other sources.

Current estimates of tight oil resources around the world are close to 350 billion barrels, and the United States represents only about 17% of the global resource base. If all resource-endowed regions were to proportionally reproduce the 4.5 mb/d production peak projected for the United States, the effect on oil markets would be extraordinary. It is often said that the system of the United States is uniquely supportive to tight oil production, due to the legal structure of mineral rights ownership, the existence of numerous small and innovative producing companies, easy access to capital, a well-developed upstream services industry and upstream expertise, and so on. But there are fundamental geological and geographical issues also at work. For tight oil to be attractive one needs:

- An oil-bearing sedimentary basin in which conventional reservoirs are largely depleted (tight oil is almost always more expensive to extract than conventional oil, so if there are conventional opportunities left, these will be favoured); this excludes for example most of the Middle East, where tight oil resources are likely to be large, but are currently largely unknown.

- A fairly large and easily accessible land mass. With the current state of production technology, tight oil production in offshore basins is simply too expensive. Similarly, onshore basins in remote, difficult to access locations are generally too expensive: tight oil requires drilling a large number of wells over a large geographical area; this is difficult in, for example, the middle of tropical forests or in harsh northern climates. In Western Siberia, for example, the very extensive Bazhenov shale is likely to be exploited only in the vicinity of existing conventional fields, where infrastructure is in place to facilitate the extensive drilling required.

---

11. Technology learning puts downward pressure on costs, offsetting in part the impact of resource depletion, i.e. the transition to more challenging resources over time. However, we do not model or assume any technological breakthroughs that might have a more dramatic impact on the productivity of wells.

- A relatively sparsely populated landscape, typically mostly agricultural. The nuisances linked to extensive drilling make public acceptance less likely in densely populated areas. In the United States, with the exception of the Barnett shale which extends close to the Dallas metropolis, most successful plays meet this criterion.

- Reasonable access to water. Desert areas, though not impossible (water from saline aquifers is usually available, or waterless hydraulic fracturing technologies can be used), usually entail additional costs that prejudice the economics.

With these factors in mind, what are the most other promising countries and regions for tight oil production? The first port of call is Canada, which benefits from many of the same advantages as the United States. Although development started later than south of the border, interest is growing with production of around 330 kb/d in 2013. This is expected to grow gradually to more than 700 kb/d in the mid-2020s, before falling back below 300 kb/d in 2040 (Figure 3.12). The growth rate is, to some extent, slowed by the competition for capital with oil sands projects and by the constraints on access to markets other than the United States. Mexico has good shale resources and the ongoing reform of the upstream sector could unleash tight oil production from the Burgos and other basins from 2025. For Mexico, we project over 400 kb/d in 2040.

Figure 3.12 ▷ **Tight oil production by country in the New Policies Scenario**

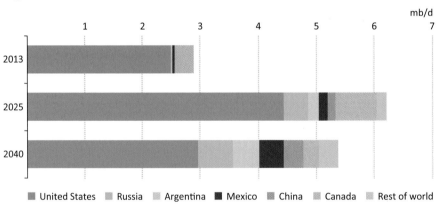

Argentina, an old hydrocarbon province with a well-developed oil and gas industry, has very promising shale formations, notably the Vaca Muerta. Both YPF and foreign companies are actively drilling the first wells, and tight oil production started in 2013. We project it will steadily grow to 200 kb/d in 2025 and 470 kb/d in 2040, though the recurring debt problems of the country could hinder investment. Elsewhere in Latin America, Colombia is thought to have sizeable resources in the Magdalena basin; it is still early days, with the regulatory framework being developed, but interest in both shale gas and tight oil is growing as conventional production approaches its peak. A first well drilled in the La Luna shale by Canacol reportedly tested at an initial rate of 590 barrels per day of oil, significant by shale standards.

Russia has good potential in the Bazhenov in Western Siberia, though we expect only a small part of this very extensive formation to be exploited. The Volga Ural region is possibly an even better candidate with a well-developed industrial base, accessible agricultural land and geography not unlike that of North Dakota. The results of the Statoil-Rosneft collaboration in the Domanik shale near Samara will be an important indicator. Overall we project tight oil production in Russia will grow to 500 kb/d in 2030 and 600 kb/d in 2040.

In China, the current focus is on shale gas. Tight oil is not yet a priority for the government, but it could become so if shale gas is confirmed to be a success. Indeed, resources are likely to be significant and China is one of the few countries likely to be able to reach a scale of operation comparable to that of the United States. Obstacles are population density and water scarcity. We project growth to 330 kb/d in 2040 in the New Policies Scenario. In other parts of Asia, Indonesia is likely to have tight oil resources and strong motivation to exploit them, as the level of conventional production has been on a steep decline for the last 20 years and is now only half of the peak level. Activity has yet to start, though, so we remain conservative in our projections through to 2040. India, with conventional oil production probably nearing its peak and rapidly growing demand, is interested to explore its tight oil resources, though it is too early to tell if this will lead to successful exploitation. Japan has started drilling for both shale gas and tight oil, but the resources are small and, while any domestic production is good news for the country, the impact on global markets will be marginal at best. Australia has a dynamic oil and gas industry which is beginning to show interest in shale gas and tight oil. Exploration has started and production could start in earnest in the next five years; it reaches 170 kb/d in 2040 in our projections.

Among OPEC countries, Algeria has tight oil resources, which are thought to be significant, and is expected to exploit them as a way of offsetting its dwindling conventional production. However, the decline in conventional production is not just due to resource depletion; it is also affected by above-ground barriers to investment (the regulatory regime and concerns about security). Those same barriers are likely to hamper tight oil production, which we project will reach only 110 kb/d in 2040. In other OPEC countries, the large remaining conventional resources remove any incentive to exploit tight oil and, indeed, even the potential resources are largely unknown at the moment.

Overall we expect North America to remain the dominant contributor to tight oil production for a long time, supplying 85% of global output in 2025 and 68% in 2040, (even though production is in steep decline by then). The sheer scale of the activity required for significant production cannot be attained quickly in other countries. The Bakken shale alone currently uses more than 150 drilling rigs, and the Eagle Ford around 300; each is an order of magnitude greater than the total number of rigs available in most other countries, with the exception of China and, to a lesser extent, Russia. In many countries, importing a new drilling rig or a new set of hydraulic fracturing equipment can take the best part of a year. To scale up to the intensity of large-scale production of tight oil will take considerable time.

Non-OPEC production

At a high point in the early 2020s, non-OPEC countries are projected to produce 56 mb/d of oil, almost 12 mb/d higher than in 2000 and 5.8 mb/d above the level of 2013. But, by 2040, non-OPEC production falls back to 51 mb/d, slightly higher than today's levels, but on a declining trend. Production growth over the period as a whole is concentrated in the Americas, thanks mainly to the United States, Canada and Brazil, although potentially supplemented by Mexico. In other parts of the world, the only non-OPEC region that sees growth in production is the Caspian, and expectations there have been revised downwards since *WEO-2013*, as some of the large-scale projects in Kazakhstan continue to experience significant delays. Europe, Russia, the rest of Asia and Africa all see a net decline in output. This geographical asymmetry is accompanied by a shift in the quality of the oil produced. Among the large producers, only Brazil and Kazakhstan achieve growth in conventional oil production (in both cases developing large but challenging deposits); in the United States and Canada, output growth is concentrated in tight oil and oil sands respectively, with NGLs generally increasing across the board. Non-OPEC countries account for 56% of the barrels produced over the projection period, but for around three-quarters of the estimated $14.5 trillion in cumulative investment in upstream oil, with North America alone (including Mexico) accounting for 30% of the global total.

Almost half of the present oil output in the United States comes from just two states, North Dakota and Texas, which are at the epicentre of the unconventional oil boom; this is supplemented by NGLs from gas developments in the Appalachian basin that are close to markets which are short of petroleum products. As described in the previous section, tight oil and to some extent deepwater resources in the Gulf of Mexico continue to push overall US production higher, surpassing the previous record for US output (11.3 mb/d in 1970) and setting a new high-water mark of 12.5 mb/d in the latter part of this decade. After a plateau above 12 mb/d until the late 2020s, production starts to fall back, as tight oil and NGLs join conventional oil production on a downward trend. By 2040, US production is around the 2013 level, some 2.5 mb/d below its peak.

Canadian production growth relies heavily on output from oil sands to achieve the anticipated increase from 4 mb/d in 2013 to 7.4 mb/d in 2040, the second-largest rise among non-OPEC countries, after Brazil. The main uncertainty over this projection is not related to the resource base, but rather to the transport capacity required to get the oil to market, bearing in mind the reduced import needs of the United States, Canada's traditional export market. Three main pipeline projects have been proposed to carry Canadian oil to international markets; all of them face regulatory and political hurdles. In June 2014, the Canadian pipeline operator Enbridge's Northern Gateway project, designed to transport just over half a million barrels a day of oil sands output west from Alberta to a port in British Columbia, was conditionally approved by the Canadian government.[12] Keystone XL,

---

12. This was followed shortly afterwards by a landmark Supreme Court ruling confirming the title of Tsilhqot'in First Nation over a territory in British Columbia, which covers a section of the proposed route. The ruling means that the project will additionally need to obtain the consent of the title-holder.

the pipeline proposed to take Canadian oil south to the refining hubs of the United States or to Gulf coast ports for export, saw no change in its status. Another project, proposed by the same operator, Transcanada, aims to move 1.1 mb/d of crude eastwards to feed both domestic refiners and export outlets through Atlantic ports. In the same direction, the operator of the existing 240 kb/d Line 9 pipeline, originally carrying imported crude oil from Montreal to a port on the Great Lakes, has successfully obtained regulatory approval for the reversal of the line to carry crude from both western Canada and the US tight oil plays to refineries in eastern Canada.

Despite its large resource base, until recently Mexico was not able to generate much excitement in its upstream industry. Pemex, the sole entity allowed to explore for and produce oil and gas in the country, in 2013 produced less hydrocarbons than ExxonMobil (3.7 mboe/d versus 4.2 mboe/d), while employing twice as many people (150 000 versus 75 000). The giant Eagle Ford unconventional play, which extends from Texas into Mexico, is extensively developed on the US side of the border, but activity drops abruptly south of the border; the same situation prevails in offshore developments in the Gulf of Mexico. This disparity is set to narrow with the implementation of the energy reforms launched in Mexico last year (Box 3.4).

Oil production in OECD Europe is expected to drop to 2.2 mb/d by 2040 compared with 3.3 mb/d today. This is despite efforts to increase recovery and develop new, smaller deposits in the North Sea, as well as more remote fields on both the United Kingdom and Norwegian sides. These bear fruit in the medium term, but are not sufficient to stem the underlying difficulties and rising costs of this mature producing area. We do not anticipate any significant unconventional oil production in Europe.

Russia's large resource base gives it scope to counteract falling output from its traditional production areas in Western Siberia by moving to even more remote regions in Eastern Siberia or offshore in the Arctic, or by tapping into tight oil formations. This will require continued improvements in operational efficiency, major capital investment (a cumulative $1 trillion over the period to 2040 for upstream oil), a more supportive fiscal and regulatory environment and the deployment of modern technologies. Partnerships with major international companies should help in all of these areas, although such arrangements are threatened if the current sanctions, imposed in response to events in Ukraine, remain in place for an extended time. The potential impact arises less on the technology side (although this is an issue for Arctic developments) and more from restricted access to capital. This presents downside risk to our projection that Russia will be able to maintain production at or above 10 mb/d until the 2030s, with output still at 9.7 mb/d in 2040. The development of offshore Arctic resources plays only a relatively limited role in the early years of this projection, until production ramps up from the early 2030s, reaching 250 kb/d by 2040. Tight oil (600 kb/d in 2040) and NGLs (an additional 0.8 mb/d by 2040, on top of today's 0.8 mb/d) both play a more significant role (Table 3.7).

Kazakhstan's battered flagship project, Kashagan, suffered another setback in late 2013, when leaks were discovered in the gas line to the shore and, subsequently, in oil lines too, meaning that production ceased almost as soon as it started (first oil had originally been scheduled for 2005). Given the need to complete investigations and perform necessary repairs, production is now not expected to resume until 2017. The continued problems with Kashagan are pushing the possibility of Phase II development – beyond the 300 kb/d foreseen for Phase I – further back into the 2020s. The Caspian Sea, with all the challenges associated with offshore production, plus wide seasonal variations in climate and difficult access, is set to remain an expensive place for oil production, even if the massive costs of Kashagan are not necessarily typical. Even so, on the back of Kashagan, expansion projects at Tengiz and Karachaganak, Kazakhstan remains the only non-OPEC producer outside the Americas with an identified potential to deliver a substantial increase in oil output. Although revised downwards since *WEO-2013*, production in Kazakhstan rises to 2.5 mb/d in the late 2020s, before tailing off to 1.8 mb/d in 2040.

Table 3.7 ▷ **Non-OPEC oil production in the New Policies Scenario** (mb/d)

	1990	2013	2020	2025	2030	2035	2040	2013-2040 Delta	2013-2040 CAAGR*
OECD	18.9	20.7	24.5	24.5	24.3	24.0	23.7	2.9	0.5%
Americas	13.9	17.0	20.6	21.2	21.3	21.0	20.7	3.7	0.7%
Canada	2.0	4.0	5.3	5.8	6.1	6.4	7.4	3.4	2.3%
Mexico	3.0	2.9	2.9	3.2	3.4	3.4	3.3	0.4	0.5%
United States	8.9	10.1	12.3	12.2	11.9	11.2	10.0	-0.1	0.0%
Europe	4.3	3.3	3.1	2.5	2.2	2.2	2.2	-1.1	-1.5%
Asia Oceania	0.7	0.5	0.8	0.8	0.8	0.8	0.8	0.3	1.7%
Non-OECD	22.7	29.8	31.6	31.6	30.5	29.0	27.5	-2.2	-0.3%
E. Europe/Eurasia	11.7	14.1	14.2	14.2	13.6	12.8	12.1	-2.0	-0.6%
Kazakhstan	0.5	1.7	2.0	2.4	2.5	2.1	1.8	0.0	0.1%
Russia	10.4	10.9	11.0	10.7	10.2	9.9	9.7	-1.3	-0.4%
Asia	6.0	7.9	7.6	6.9	6.4	6.1	5.8	-2.0	-1.1%
China	2.8	4.3	4.4	4.1	3.8	3.6	3.4	-0.9	-0.9%
India	0.7	0.9	0.8	0.7	0.7	0.7	0.7	-0.2	-1.0%
Middle East	1.3	1.3	1.3	1.3	1.4	1.2	1.0	-0.3	-1.1%
Africa	1.7	2.3	2.5	2.3	1.9	1.6	1.4	-0.9	-1.8%
Latin America	2.0	4.2	6.0	6.9	7.3	7.4	7.2	3.0	2.0%
Brazil	0.7	2.1	3.7	4.9	5.5	5.8	5.7	3.6	3.7%
Total non-OPEC	41.7	50.5	56.1	56.0	54.8	53.0	51.2	0.7	0.1%
Non-OPEC share	64%	58%	60%	58%	56%	53%	51%	-7%	n.a.
Conventional	41.3	45.0	46.8	45.3	42.9	40.2	38.2	-6.8	-0.6%
Crude oil	37.7	38.6	38.9	37.3	34.9	32.2	30.0	-8.6	-0.9%
Natural gas liquids	3.6	6.4	7.9	8.0	8.0	8.0	8.3	1.8	0.9%
Unconventional	0.4	5.4	9.3	10.7	11.9	12.8	13.0	7.5	3.3%
Canada oil sands	0.2	1.9	3.0	3.3	3.7	4.2	5.2	3.2	3.7%
Tight oil	-	2.9	5.5	6.2	6.5	6.3	5.3	2.4	2.3%
Coal-to-liquids	0.1	0.1	0.2	0.5	0.7	1.0	1.1	1.0	9.4%
Gas-to-liquids	0.0	0.0	0.0	0.1	0.3	0.5	0.5	0.5	10.3%

* Compound average annual growth rate.

Box 3.4 ▷ **Mexico – start of a new oil and gas era?**

In 2013, Mexico embarked on a major reform of its energy sector, focusing in particular on hydrocarbon exploration and production. Several constitutional changes and a new energy bill have opened the door to exploitation of hydrocarbon resources by foreign companies for the first time since 1938, introducing a prospect of competition for Pemex, the national oil company. The details of the new regime, including a decision on which fields will be reserved for Pemex, were finalised in August 2014. The result is expected to be a reversal of the gradual decline in Mexican oil production observed since 2004, when production was 3.8 mb/d (it has now dipped below 3 mb/d). The turnaround could start about 2017 (IEA, 2014b) with the aim to reach production of around 3.6 mb/d by 2027, the target stated in Mexico's National Energy Strategy.

Figure 3.13 ▷ **Oil production by type in Mexico in the New Policies Scenario**

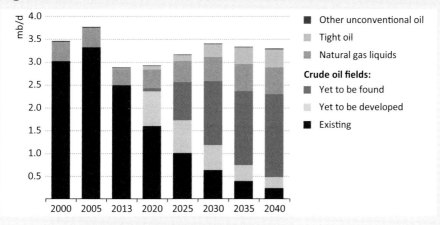

Resources are abundant, both in the offshore deepwater of the Gulf of Mexico, in the form of heavy oil on land, and tight oil in several parts of the country, not least in the Burgos Basin, where the Eagle Ford shale extends into Mexican territory. New developments have so far been hampered by the limited investment budget available to Pemex, inefficiencies and limited access to the latest technologies. Not only will the reform bring in much-needed capital and technology, but it will also let Pemex (which will remain the dominant player, but with a new status of state enterprise and a new tax regime) focus on optimising its operations. We project that the reforms will be effective, though more slowly than planned, with Mexican oil production reaching 3.4 mb/d by 2030 but declining slowly thereafter to 3.3 mb/d in 2040. If above-ground conditions are supportive, the ample resource base would allow for a larger contribution to global production after 2025, at a time when aggregate production from other non-OPEC countries is expected to level out and then decline. In this case, Mexico could play an important role in mitigating potential risks of reliance of production growth in the Middle East.

In Latin America, the outlook for Brazil is likewise slightly lower than envisaged in *WEO-2013*, due to some slippage in project timetables. The major investment already made in new pre-salt fields is starting to translate into production growth after two years of flat or declining output, but the technological and investment challenges are still formidable. The cumulative upstream capital expenditure associated with our oil projections to 2040 is almost $1.5 trillion (or an average of $53 billion per year), two-thirds of the figure for the whole of the Middle East ($2.2 trillion and an annual average of $80 billion). Brazil, together with Canada, is the major source of anticipated non-OPEC production growth over the coming years. Total output in Brazil is projected to reach 3.7 mb/d by 2020 and 5.7 mb/d by 2040. In Colombia, total output crossed the million barrel threshold in 2013, almost double the levels of mid-2000s. However, with increased instances of attacks on oil infrastructure, resulting in shutdowns, production so far in 2014 has been at lower levels. Colombian heavy crude is facing competition in the US market not only from growing US output, but also from Canadian bitumen shipments to the United States: the search for new markets in Asia will be aided by the construction of the Pacific Pipeline project, linking the Llanos production basin in eastern Colombia to the Pacific coast through the Andes, the construction of which is expected to start by 2020. Production edges up to 1.1 mb/d by 2016 before a gradual decline sets in. In Argentina, production is buoyed by rising tight oil production, as well as NGLs, and reaches 0.8 mb/d in 2040.

In the Asia-Pacific region, oil output in China and India, the world's fastest-growing refining centres, drops by 1.1 mb/d in total over the period to 2040. In China, significant volumes of tight oil and coal-to-liquids projects do not manage to offset fully the decline in conventional oil. Falling production is a common theme in other parts of the region: despite the ambitions of the Indonesian government to see oil production restored to around 1 mb/d (with chemical and steam EOR techniques playing an important role), we project a gradual decline from the second-half of this decade onwards, with output falling to 0.7 mb/d by 2040. In other Southeast Asian countries, which are emerging as a major new source of global oil consumption growth, oil production is likewise declining, both crude oil and NGLs. In the Middle East, the major non-OPEC producer, Oman, sees oil output flattening out at around 1 mb/d, thanks to EOR, before it drops to 0.7 by 2040.

OPEC production

Oil output from OPEC countries rises by a relatively modest 0.6 mb/d in aggregate over the period to 2020, compared with production of 37 mb/d in 2013 (this includes both crude and NGLs). However, production thereafter builds rapidly, 6.3 mb/d being added to the total in the 2020s and a further 5.9 mb/d in the 2030s, bringing combined output to 49.5 mb/d by the end of the projection period (Table 3.8). As events in Libya and Iraq have underlined, the risks to oil production in this region remain substantial and the anticipated rise in other parts of the world over the period to 2020 is no reassurance. Long-lead times for upstream projects mean that bringing production up from the early 2020s requires increased investment in the immediate future. If this investment is not made in time, because of an uncertain investment climate or because fiscal and demographic pressures lead to spending being diverted to other areas, then – as examined in the *World Energy Investment Outlook* (IEA, 2014a) – tighter and more volatile oil markets lie ahead.

The patterns of growth and the types of oil produced in OPEC countries differ considerably from those in non-OPEC countries. The relative abundance of accessible conventional resources means that the share of conventional crude oil remains high and the role of unconventional oil production is much more subdued. Venezuelan extra-heavy oil volumes do not reach half the level of projected Canadian output from the oil sands, despite a comparably large resource base. Tight oil and other unconventional oil is not produced at any scale, with the exception of an increase in anticipated gas-to-liquids output in Qatar. One area of commonality, though, is the increasing importance of NGLs, which contribute 20% to overall OPEC production in 2040 (similar to the 16% seen in non-OPEC countries).

Table 3.8 ▷ **OPEC oil production in the New Policies Scenario** (mb/d)

	1990	2013	2020	2025	2030	2035	2040	2013-2040 Delta	2013-2040 CAAGR*
Middle East	16.4	26.7	27.3	29.8	32.5	34.9	36.9	10.2	1.2%
Iran	3.1	3.3	3.8	4.1	4.3	4.5	4.7	1.4	1.3%
Iraq	2.0	3.2	4.6	5.8	6.7	7.6	8.2	5.1	3.6%
Kuwait	1.3	3.1	2.5	2.7	2.9	3.1	3.4	0.3	0.4%
Qatar	0.4	2.1	2.0	2.2	2.5	2.8	2.9	0.8	1.2%
Saudi Arabia	7.1	11.6	10.8	11.5	12.4	13.0	13.4	1.9	0.6%
United Arab Emirates	2.4	3.5	3.6	3.6	3.8	4.0	4.2	0.7	0.6%
Non-Middle East	7.5	10.0	10.0	10.6	11.1	11.9	12.6	2.6	0.9%
Algeria	1.3	1.6	1.5	1.5	1.5	1.7	1.8	0.2	0.4%
Angola	0.5	1.8	2.0	1.8	1.6	1.5	1.4	-0.4	-1.0%
Ecuador	0.3	0.5	0.4	0.4	0.3	0.3	0.3	-0.2	-2.1%
Libya	1.4	1.0	1.0	1.6	1.9	2.0	2.2	1.2	3.1%
Nigeria	1.8	2.5	2.2	2.3	2.5	2.8	3.1	0.6	0.8%
Venezuela	2.3	2.7	2.9	3.0	3.3	3.6	3.9	1.2	1.4%
Total OPEC	23.9	36.8	37.3	40.4	43.6	46.8	49.5	12.7	1.1%
OPEC share	36%	42%	40%	42%	44%	47%	49%	7%	n.a.
Conventional	23.9	36.1	35.9	38.5	41.3	43.9	46.3	10.2	0.9%
Crude oil	21.9	30.0	29.1	31.1	32.9	34.7	36.4	6.4	0.7%
Natural gas liquids	2.0	6.0	6.7	7.4	8.4	9.2	9.9	3.9	1.9%
Unconventional	0.0	0.7	1.5	1.9	2.3	2.8	3.2	2.5	5.7%
Venezuela extra-heavy	0.0	0.4	1.1	1.4	1.7	2.1	2.4	2.0	6.6%
Gas-to-liquids	-	0.2	0.2	0.2	0.3	0.3	0.4	0.3	3.8%

* Compound average annual growth rate. Note: Data for Saudi Arabia and Kuwait include 50% each of production from the Neutral Zone.

Saudi Arabia has projects underway which are designed to keep the country's production capacity around the official target level of 12.5 mb/d. The offshore Manifa field, which started production in 2013, is expected to reach full production capacity of 900 kb/d already by the end of 2014; upgrades to the Shaybah and Khurais onshore fields are expected to follow. These developments will allow for some easing of reliance on Ghawar, allowing for additional efforts to improve extraction and recovery rates at the world's largest field. Looking further ahead, there is room for further onshore expansion at the Zuluf and Berri fields, as well as more heavy oil offshore at Safaniyah. Possible difficulties in achieving Iraqi production growth underline the importance of a timely second wave of expansion projects in Saudi Arabia. Although the complexity of Saudi developments is anticipated to increase – a trend, along with the search for gas, that is already reflected in its increased rig count – average costs are, nonetheless, expected to remain among the lowest in the world. We project Saudi production to reach 13.4 mb/d in 2040, of which 2.8 mb/d will be NGLs, preserving 2 mb/d of spare crude capacity, even if the latter is not raised from the current official target of 12.5 mb/d.

Uncertainty over the outlook for Iraq has risen again with the turmoil in large parts of the north of the country. The confrontation thus far has had only limited direct impact on the country's oil sector: although it has disrupted the northern export route as well as the operation of the country's largest refinery, the conflict has been far away from the main centres of Iraqi oil production in the south, around Basrah. But events have underlined the political hazards facing Iraq and the grave weakness of national institutions, factors that are likely to hold back large-scale investment in production growth in the years to come. Our expectation for Iraqi production is revised downwards this year to 4.6 mb/d by 2020 and 7.6 mb/d by 2035. Iraq remains the largest source of global oil production growth over the entire period to 2040, even though our outlook is progressively getting closer to the "Delayed Case" examined in *WEO-2012*, in which institutional and political obstacles were assumed to hold back upstream investment in Iraq. Any further shortfall in anticipated Iraqi output would bring new threats to oil markets, particularly in the period after 2020 when the global market starts to rely on a smaller number of producers for additional production.

The outlook for production in Iran, a country with similar resource potential to Iraq, is also shrouded by the political uncertainties relating to the international sanctions imposed on the country in response to its nuclear programme. A resolution that would allow for a normalisation of Iran's place in the international energy system still seems some way off, so much remains to be done to open up the longer term possibility of a level of production commensurate with Iran's huge remaining resource base (Box 3.5).

In the United Arab Emirates, there is a short-term risk of under-investment in Abu Dhabi's mature onshore fields because of continued uncertainty over the renewal of the concession contracts that expired in 2014 (other offshore contracts are due to expire in 2018). These ageing fields require the application of sophisticated technology to maximise recovery. Nonetheless, overall production is expected to rise in the medium term with the expansion of the production capacity of the Upper Zakum fields to 750 kb/d and the start-up of other smaller fields. In our *Outlook*, United Arab Emirates total oil production, including NGLs, is projected to climb from 3.5 mb/d in 2013 to 4.2 mb/d in 2040.

Box 3.5 ▷ **What would it take for Iran to bounce back?**

With reported proven reserves of 157 billion barrels of crude and natural gas liquids and 34 trillion cubic metres of gas, Iran is one of the richest oil and gas resource-holders on the planet. Yet sanctions and under-investment reduced crude oil output to just 2.8 mb/d in the first half of 2014, the lowest level since 1989, although this was slightly offset by a large rise in the production of NGLs, to more than 600 kb/d, most of the volume coming from the development of the world's largest gas field, South Pars (the field straddles the Qatari border where it is called the North field).[13]

Figure 3.14 ▷ **Conventional oil production in Iran in the New Policies Scenario**

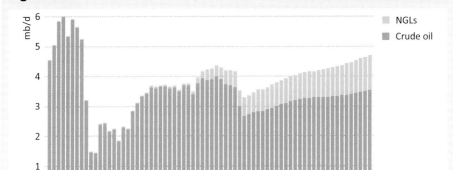

Most of the reduction in oil output from Iran has been a direct result of customers cutting their purchases because of sanctions, but the lack of access to new technologies and under-investment has also meant a reduction in effective capacity. This will take time to replace. Iran's large fields, such as Gachsaran and Marun, have been in production for over 50 years and are in sore need of rehabilitation to stem decline rates of nearly 8% per year. Our projections allow for a positive outcome of negotiations over sanctions stemming from Iran's nuclear programme, but, even in that event, there will still be major uncertainties over the pace at which Iran's oil industry can bounce back: in our projections, production rises above 4 mb/d only in the early 2020s, reaching 4.7 mb/d (of which 1.2 mb/d are NGLs) by 2040. This modest increase reflects the numerous questions that remain, not least how investment will be affected by institutional inefficiencies and domestic competition for influence across the oil industry; what terms might be available for upstream investors if, as seems likely, the unfavourable "buy-back" contract terms in place since 1979 are replaced; and whether Iran will be successful in raising domestic energy prices and holding back rapidly increasing domestic demand.

---

13. Export of NGLs has fared better in Iran than export of crude since international sanctions came into force; a continued focus on wet gas leads to NGLs output growing faster than gas output over the coming years.

Kuwait's oil production prospects continue to depend on the country's ability to access the necessary expertise for heavy oil and EOR projects, requiring, in turn, a resolution of the longstanding political debate over the participation of international companies in the upstream. The official target is to reach 4 mb/d of capacity by 2020. We are more cautious at this point, in the absence of greater clarity on how new development projects will move ahead. Our projections for Kuwait production see smaller projects not quite offsetting declines at mature fields, with output dropping to around 2.7 mb/d until 2025 before edging higher to 3.4 mb/d by 2040. In Qatar, all of the projected 800 kb/d growth in oil production to 2.9 mb/d in 2040 comes from NGLs and gas-to-liquids projects, the former bolstered by an eventual post-moratorium expansion of gas production and LNG exports. This more than offsets the declining production at the country's mature fields, including the offshore Al-Shaheen field, which, 20 years after first production, still delivers more than 40% of the country's daily output.

The Middle East accounts for by far the largest share of OPEC projected output over the period to 2040 (Figure 3.15). The next largest contribution comes from the African OPEC members. The two sub-Saharan African countries, Nigeria and Angola, are discussed in the focus on Africa in Part C. In North Africa, oil output in Libya has rebounded since mid-2014, but the prospects remain very uncertain in the light of continued violence, political fragmentation and rows over control of key oil infrastructure. An improvement in the security situation is vital if Libya is to see a sustained increase in output; but prolonged shut-in of fields or damage to infrastructure could lead to significantly lower operational capacity. In our projections, Libya's oil production recovers by the mid-2020s, but the prospects for further growth are limited by weak institutions and by political and regulatory risks. Assuming longer term improvements in these areas, Libyan oil production rises to 2.2 mb/d by 2040.

Figure 3.15 ▷ **OPEC oil production by region and type in the New Policies Scenario**

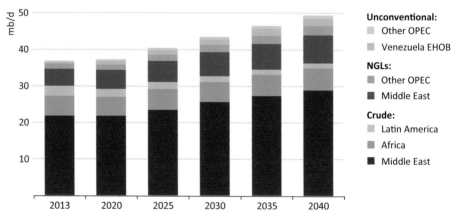

Notes: Other OPEC unconventional includes gas-to-liquids and production of additives. Venezuela extra-heavy oil and bitumen (EHOB) is from the Orinoco Belt.

Algeria is likewise facing political and technical uncertainties, with a fall in discoveries and a decline in production since 2007 to around 1.6 mb/d in 2013. Despite the absence of new security alerts this year, the country is still feeling the consequences of the attacks on the In Amenas gas facilities in 2013. Only 4 blocks out of 31 on offer in a new bidding round, held in 2014, were awarded, indicating that concerns about security and hesitations about the attractiveness of the updated upstream terms on offer are still having an impact on the level of interest from companies, despite the large size of Algeria's remaining resource base. This affects our anticipated outlook into the 2020s (when output falls below 1.5 mb/d) although production does pick up again towards the end of the projection period, reaching 1.8 mb/d by 2040.

The production prospects for Venezuela are affected in the immediate future by the legacy of under-investment by the national company, PDVSA, ongoing political tensions (albeit generally far from oil production areas) and state politics that have deterred or cut international involvement in upstream opportunities. Conventional oil production is set to decline by 0.8 mb/d by 2040, but over the projection period as a whole, this is more than outweighed by a stronger increase in extra-heavy oil production in the Orinoco Belt (even though, here too, current projects have been persistently delayed). Total production is set to increase from 2.7 mb/d in 2013 to 3.9 mb/d in 2040. Ecuador, the smallest OPEC producer, is projected to raise production as new fields come online following the controversial government approval of developments in the Amazon region, but these projects do not stem the long-term decline in output, which falls from 0.52 mb/d in 2013, to 0.45 mb/d in 2020, and 0.29 mb/d in 2040.

Refining and trade

The composition of oil supply is changing. An increasing share of products is finding its way to market without passing through the refining sector at all. Products derived from NGLs at fractionation facilities, fuels (usually diesel and gasoline) produced via coal-to-liquids (CTL) or gas-to-liquids (GTL) technologies, and additives that go into gasoline volumes all decrease the market share of the refining industry.[14] As a result, while total liquids demand (including biofuels) grows by 17 mb/d between 2013 and 2040, demand for refined products grows only by 10 mb/d (Table 3.9)

Refining capacity (including condensate splitters) increases by 16 mb/d between 2013 and 2040. This is a net number, around 19 mb/d of new-built capacity being offset by about 3 mb/d of shutdowns (either already planned or considered likely) affecting mostly old excess capacity that is already in poor condition. China accounts for one-third of the net capacity growth, with the Middle East and India following closely. Africa, Brazil and Southeast Asia also see significant net capacity additions. With global refining capacity

---

14. We estimate that, in 2013, about 60% of global NGLs were fractionated into products, such as ethane, LPG and light naphtha, with condensate accounting for the remainder. This changes very little over the projection period: by 2040: the share of condensate increases by some 6 percentage points. Condensate is then refined in condensate splitters or refineries, yielding mostly light and middle distillate products.

exceeding 108 mb/d, while refinery runs go up to only to 87 mb/d, the excess of refining capacity over refinery runs continues to rise, implying continued pressure on refining margins and the likelihood of additional decisions to cut capacity, most notably in Europe.

Table 3.9 ▷ **Global total demand for liquids, products and crude throughput in the New Policies Scenario** (mb/d)

	2013	2020	2040
Total liquids demand	91.4	98.1	108.5
of which biofuels	1.3	2.2	4.6
Total oil demand	90.1	96.0	103.9
of which CTL/GTL and additives	0.9	1.1	3.1
of which direct use of crude oil	1.4	1.0	0.4
Total oil product demand	87.8	93.8	100.4
of which fractionation products (from NGLs)	7.7	9.1	10.2
Refinery products demand	80.1	84.8	90.2

Table 3.10 ▷ **World refining capacity and refinery runs in the New Policies Scenario** (mb/d)

	2013 capacity	Net capacity additions to 2040	Refinery runs			Capacity at risk	
			2013	2020	2040	2020	2040
Europe	16.8	-0.6	13.3	12.0	10.0	2.3	4.6
North America	20.8	0.9	18.3	18.8	16.5	0.1	2.7
China	11.6	5.6	9.4	12.1	14.6	0.4	0.2
India	4.4	3.2	4.3	4.9	7.4	-	-
OECD Asia	8.0	-1.4	6.6	5.7	4.7	0.5	1.1
Southeast Asia	4.8	1.8	3.9	4.2	6.0	0.2	0.1
Russia	6.2	0.3	6.0	6.1	5.2	-	0.4
Middle East	7.7	4.0	6.6	8.5	10.6	-	-
Brazil	2.0	1.3	2.0	2.4	3.1	-	-
Africa	3.5	0.8	1.9	2.4	3.4	0.6	0.4
Other	6.8	0.2	5.0	5.3	5.5	0.6	0.7
Total	92.6	16.1	77.3	82.4	86.9	4.7	10.1

Notes: "Capacity at risk" is defined for each region as the difference between refinery capacity, on one hand, and refinery runs, on the other, with the latter including a 14% allowance for downtime. This is always smaller than the spare capacity, which is the difference between total capacity and refinery runs.

As with refinery capacity development, the net changes in refinery runs involve significant reductions in some regions and large-scale increases in others. Refinery runs decrease by more than 7.8 mb/d in Europe, North America, OECD Asia and Russia, but rise by about 17.4 mb/d elsewhere, especially in China, India and the Middle East (Table 3.10). The main driver for these changes is the trajectory of local demand. European refiners are poorly placed to compete in a world where oil demand shifts to Asian markets. Local European consumption is in structural decline, while Russian and US refiners are set to export products in ever greater volumes, their margins supported by local crude oil. European refiners are thus competing with other refiners, both at home and in their main export markets, such as North and West Africa. At the same time, China and India, whose local crude production is projected to stay well below their demand levels, are able to increase refining capacity and runs, supported by their growing inland markets and the cost of long-distance transport of refined product.

Trade in crude oil and oil products

We estimate that the crude oil import requirements of Asia have recently caught up with the volume of crude available from the Middle East, so that the East of Suez region (comprising the Middle East and Asia-Pacific regions) is already a net importer of crude oil, reversing the historical situation. More and more crude oil and condensate is flowing to Asia to feed increasing refinery runs there and also to replace lower levels of local crude production. By 2020, the East of Suez region requires almost 5 mb/d of imports from the rest of the world, and by 2040 this number grows to 7.7 mb/d (Figure 3.16). The required additional volumes come from Russia (which reduces supplies to Europe), from Brazil and from other countries in Latin America. Canada likewise emerges as a significant exporter to Asia: both Korea and India have recently shown high-level interest in the possibility of importing Canadian crude, with the Korean government offering to cover part of the transportation costs from Canada to encourage its refiners to decrease their reliance on the Middle East. Exports from West Africa, another key oil producing region, are expected to decline, as local output declines and local demand increases, with higher projections of refinery runs (see Part C).

Figure 3.16 ▷ **Asian imports versus Middle Eastern exports of crude oil in the New Policies Scenario**

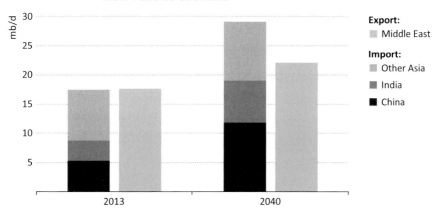

For different reasons, the requirement for crude oil imports from some of today's large importers tails off. North America reduces its reliance on international oil markets, thanks to output in the United States, rising Canadian and Mexican production, and, lower refinery runs due to lower demand. The North American net requirement for imported crude oil, 5 mb/d in 2013, disappears by 2040. However, since some Canadian exports are anticipated to go to Asian markets, there will be corresponding imports into the United States from other regions. Overall, the United States is still expected to import 6 mb/d to feed its refining system by 2040. Against this backdrop, if the export ban for crude is lifted it may result in episodic or even regular exports of condensate but not, in our projections, of medium or heavy US crudes.[15] At the same time, Alaskan crude is losing its main market, the US west coast refineries, to tight oil and – because it is not subject to the export ban – it may become profitable to move Alaskan crude to Asian markets instead. In Europe, local production of crude oil and condensate decreases by 40% from the current 3 mb/d, but anticipated refinery runs decrease even more, and this has the effect of reducing crude oil imports from over 10 mb/d in 2013 to 8 mb/d in 2040.

Overall, the volume of global interregional trade in crude oil grows by some 7 mb/d, reaching just over 44 mb/d in 2040 of which two-thirds, around 29 mb/d, will be flowing to Asian ports (compared with less than half today). This is likely to result in changes to the global crude pricing system, regional markers and trading hubs. Global product trade volumes also grow, by over 4 mb/d to close to 18 mb/d in 2040, with imports to Asian countries again an important destination. Despite significant increases in refinery runs, the region is still not able to meet its oil product demand in full. Product imports into Europe at first increase, into the 2020s, as a result of local refinery shutdowns, but they drop to close to current levels by 2040 as demand falls back. The Middle East and the United States emerge as large product exporters, the former thanks to higher refinery runs, the latter thanks to a combination of lower internal demand and a robust refining system. Russian product exports increase in the first half of our projection period, but fall back below current levels in 2040 (although Russia remains a larger product exporter than the United States). Unsurprisingly, gasoline and diesel are expected to be the most traded products, with the United States expected to become a net exporter of gasoline by the 2020s.[16]

---

15. Some cargoes of condensate were exported from the United States to Asian markets in the summer of 2014. However, this seems to have resulted from a very specific interpretation of condensate stabilisation as a manufacturing process, enabling shippers to avoid being subject to the export ban on crude. Usually, condensate stabilisation is regarded as an integral part of upstream operations.

16. As detailed in the discussion on petrochemicals, the United States is also set to start a steady flow of ethane exports to Europe and India, a first in long-distance seaborne transportation of ethane.

Chapter 4

Natural gas market outlook
LNG to the rescue?

Highlights

- Global gas use continues to grow in all scenarios compared with today's levels, although consumption trajectories diverge strongly, especially post-2020, depending on the way that government policies evolve. In the New Policies Scenario, gas demand of 5.4 tcm in 2040 means that gas draws level with coal as the second-largest fuel in the global energy mix, after oil.

- The main regions pushing global gas demand higher are China, which becomes a larger gas consumer than the European Union around 2035, and the Middle East. Gas plays an important role in mitigating coal use and related air pollution in China's cities, and in limiting oil use for power generation in the Middle East.

- Within the OECD, US gas demand grows to 900 bcm by 2040 and becomes the largest fuel in the US energy mix, while in Japan consumption falls back to pre-Fukushima levels, in both cases influenced by new policy announcements affecting the outlook for power generation. Gas consumption in Europe returns to 2010 levels only in the early 2030s, with the outlook likewise heavily contingent on policy action, notably on CO_2 pricing.

- On the supply side, production increases in every major region except Europe. Unconventional gas accounts for almost 60% of the growth in global production, helping China to register the fastest gas output growth among the major producers. The United States remains the largest global gas producer, although production levels off in the late 2030s as shale gas output starts to fall back.

- The way that gas will be priced on domestic and international markets is a key uncertainty. Within many non-OECD countries, including India and across the Middle East, and in some international negotiations (albeit not for US LNG export), finding a price level and pricing mechanisms acceptable to consumers but nonetheless sufficient to incentivise large new investments in gas supply is proving challenging. 2014 did, though, see the long-awaited agreement between China and Russia on gas pipeline deliveries, unlocking the development of Russia's East Siberian resources.

- Conflict between Russia and Ukraine has moved concerns about gas security back up the agenda in Europe. The long-term outlook sees rising import needs in Europe and across many parts of Asia, but also a growing cast of international suppliers and a growing share of LNG in international trade. LNG becomes an important tool for gas security, as trade flows can be re-directed in response to price signals coming from increasingly interconnected regional markets. But the capital intensity of gas infrastructure still represents a barrier to the globalisation of gas markets.

Global overview

Growth in global gas demand was subdued in 2013, held back in part by developments in the OECD.[1] Natural gas prices in the United States continued their gradual rise from the low point reached in early 2012, triggering a partial switch back to coal for electricity generation. European Union (EU) natural gas consumption fell to 476 billion cubic metres (bcm), a level not seen since the turn of the century, because of a sluggish economy and the continued inroads made by renewables and coal as power generation fuels. In Japan, after the big increase in domestic gas consumption in recent years due to the shutdown of nuclear plants, natural gas demand flattened – held back, in part, by efficiency measures that reduced electricity consumption.

The levelling off of OECD gas demand in 2013 was accompanied by slightly higher consumption growth in non-OECD countries. Estimates for 2013 show China's gas demand expanded at the fastest pace, with a growth of 18% year-on-year, pushed higher by policies aimed at reducing the share of coal in the domestic energy mix and curbing local pollution. Other faster-growing regions included Latin America, mainly Brazil, due to poor conditions for hydropower. Subsidised prices helped to sustain the momentum behind rising gas demand in the Middle East.

Under all of our scenarios, natural gas demand is expected to continue its expansion throughout the projection period (Figure 4.1). In line with projections in previous *Outlooks*, natural gas confirms its status as the fastest growing fossil fuel, although the pace of expansion differs markedly between the 450 Scenario and the New and Current Policies Scenarios (see Chapter 1). In the New Policies Scenario, demand for natural gas increases from 3.4 trillion cubic metres (tcm) in 2012 to 5.4 tcm in 2040. In this scenario, the share of natural gas in the global energy mix increases from 21% in 2012 to 24% in 2040, drawing level with coal in the process. China, which in 2013 became the third-largest global gas consumer behind the United States and Russia, accounts alone for about one-third of the increase in non-OECD gas demand to 2040, bringing the non-OECD share of global demand to 62% by 2040.

Demand rises more quickly in the Current Policies Scenario, at 1.9% per year, as the lack of new government policies aimed at curbing energy consumption drives up demand for all fuels. Natural gas demand in the 450 Scenario is held back as a consequence of reduced electricity demand and the introduction of additional policies to reach the goal of limiting the long-term global temperature increase to two degrees Celsius (increased deployment of carbon capture and storage technology does though allow for a slight increase in consumption in the 2030s). Whichever scenario is considered, non-OECD countries are set to account for the largest part of the growth in natural gas consumption.

---

1. Gas in this chapter refers to fossil gas. Biogas is covered in Chapter 7 on renewables. All demand and supply numbers in this chapter refer to "marketed production", i.e. they do not include gas re-injected in oil fields or gas flared at oil producing sites.

Figure 4.1 ▷ **World natural gas demand by scenario**

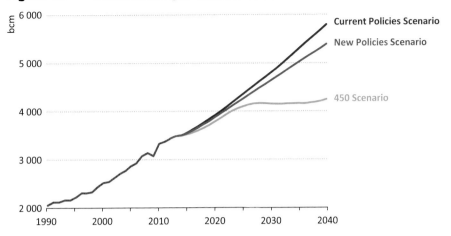

In line with the variations in projections of global demand, gas production increases at different rates across the scenarios, rising from 3.4 tcm in 2012 to between 4.2 tcm and 5.8 tcm in 2040 (Table 4.1). Unconventional gas production continues to expand its share in total gas supply, rising from 17% to more than 30% in all three scenarios and helping China to register the fastest gas production growth among the major producers. Gas supply expands significantly also in the Middle East and in Eurasia. Thanks to Mozambique and, to a lesser degree, Tanzania, the east coast of Africa emerges as an important gas-exporting region from the mid-2020s (see Part C). Among the OECD regions, supply continues to grow from North America and Australia, both of which cement their positions as significant exporters, while production in Europe continues its steady decline.

Table 4.1 ▷ **Natural gas production by major region and scenario** (bcm)

			New Policies		Current Policies		450 Scenario	
	1990	2012	2020	2040	2020	2040	2020	2040
OECD	881	1 228	1 423	1 634	1 421	1 785	1 387	1 242
Non-OECD	1 181	2 210	2 448	3 744	2 492	4 009	2 393	2 990
World	2 063	3 438	3 872	5 378	3 913	5 795	3 779	4 232

Demand

Regional trends

In the New Policies Scenario, the central scenario of this *Outlook*, non-OECD countries continue to dominate natural gas demand growth: all of the fastest growing gas markets are outside the OECD (Figure 4.2). As a whole, non-OECD natural gas demand grows on average at 2.2% per year, accounting for almost 80% of the overall increase in global natural gas demand. The main geographical centres of this growth are China and the Middle East.

These are quite distinct cases (discussed below), with China relying in part on imported gas and the Middle East benefiting more from an ample domestic resource: but the common attraction of gas is the way that it reduces reliance on other fuels in the power sector, mitigating the environmental cost of coal combustion in China and the financial cost of burning oil for power in the Middle East. In these two markets alone, the projected rise in gas demand in absolute terms is more than twice that of the rise in the whole of the OECD.

Figure 4.2 ▷ **Natural gas demand by selected region in the New Policies Scenario**

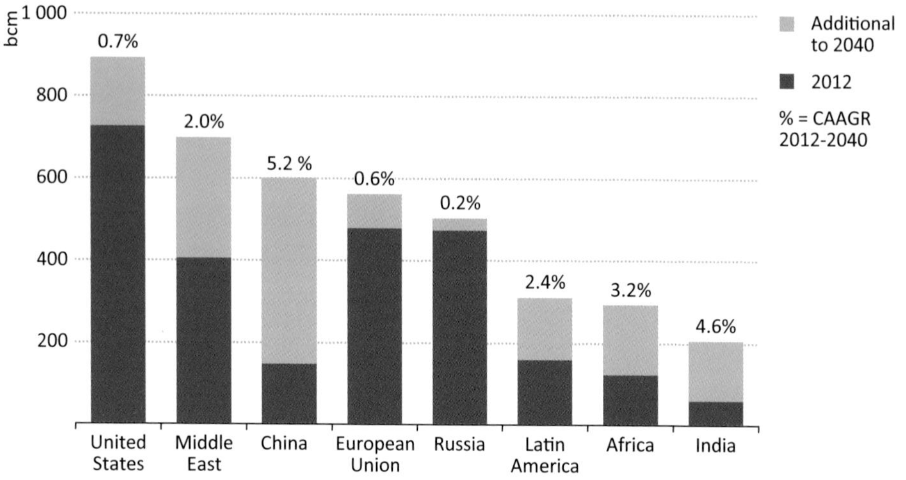

Note: CAAGR = compound average annual growth rate.

The steady increase in the domestic gas price in the United States in recent years, from an average around $2.75 per million British thermal units (MBtu) in 2012 to one higher than $4.50 in the first eight months of 2014, has shifted the balance between gas and coal in the power generation sector back slightly towards coal, but our long-term outlook for US natural gas consumption is, nonetheless, slightly higher than in *WEO-2013* (IEA, 2013a). This is based on ample supply availability (albeit at steadily increasing prices) and new policies, notably the Clean Power Plan put forward by the US Environmental Protection Agency, which tend to favour gas utilisation over other fossil fuels in power generation and in end-use sectors. Overall, demand is expected to grow by 0.7% per year on average, reaching 900 bcm by 2040, with power generation accounting for more than one-third of gas demand growth and the transport sector for more than 20%. These trends make natural gas the only fossil fuel for which demand increases in the United States over the *Outlook* period. Before 2030, natural gas is expected to overtake oil as the most utilised fuel in the US energy mix.

In Europe, natural gas demand is expected to rebound to 2010 levels only by around 2030 (in the case of OECD Europe) or 2035 (for the European Union), before increasing gradually thereafter (Table 4.2). Power generation accounts for most of the incremental gas demand between 2012 and 2040, given the expected rise in carbon prices to $30/tonne in 2025 and $50/tonne by the end of projection period and the need to replace retiring coal-fired and nuclear capacity. Europe's gas use also grows in the buildings sector, mainly in space heating with fuel switching from oil and coal, and in road transport. Substantial uncertainties exist, as full implementation of the proposed 2030 energy and climate package[2] and potential measures to reduce reliance on Russian gas imports could curb the outlook for gas in Europe. In the New Policies Scenario, gas consumption in the European Union is set to fall behind that of the Middle East by the mid-2020s.

Table 4.2 ▷ **Natural gas demand by region in New Policies Scenario** (bcm)

	1990	2012	2020	2025	2030	2035	2040	2012-2040	
								Delta	CAAGR*
OECD	1 036	1 626	1 724	1 809	1 888	1 952	2 004	378	0.7%
Americas	628	901	994	1 048	1 109	1 146	1 184	283	1.0%
United States	533	727	791	827	869	881	895	168	0.7%
Europe	325	507	531	558	572	595	610	103	0.7%
Asia Oceania	83	218	199	203	207	211	210	- 7	-0.1%
Japan	57	127	99	99	101	103	102	-25	-0.8%
Non-OECD	1 004	1 806	2 142	2 431	2 724	3 035	3 343	1 537	2.2%
E.Europe/Eurasia	738	692	693	714	740	775	807	115	0.5%
Caspian	100	117	134	146	155	166	177	60	1.5%
Russia	447	471	455	459	471	488	504	33	0.2%
Asia	85	433	645	793	934	1 086	1 240	807	3.8%
China	16	148	295	387	471	545	603	455	5.2%
India	13	57	82	109	136	167	202	145	4.6%
Middle East	86	404	469	531	598	650	696	292	2.0%
Africa	35	120	156	185	215	250	294	174	3.2%
Latin America	60	156	178	208	237	273	306	150	2.4%
Brazil	4	32	38	54	66	81	96	64	4.0%
World	2 040	3 432	3 872	4 249	4 626	5 007	5 378	1 946	1.6%
European Union	371	478	491	515	528	546	559	81	0.6%

* Compound average annual growth rate.

In Japan, after the steep rise in natural gas consumption in 2011 and 2012 (22% higher than in 2010), dictated by the need to compensate for the shutdown of the country's nuclear capacity, gas demand levelled off in 2013 due to the effect of conservation measures

---

2. The European Commission climate and energy package, tabled in early 2014, proposes a reduction in greenhouse-gas emissions of 40% below 1990 levels and a renewable energy target of at least 27% (see Chapter 1).

triggered by high liquefied natural gas (LNG) import prices and the fact that gas-fired power plants were already operating at high load factors. In April 2014, the government approved a new Strategic Energy Plan which provides for a step-by-step reintroduction of nuclear power into the domestic energy mix (see Chapter 10). The assumed implementation of the Strategic Energy Plan means a downward revision of the gas consumption outlook, compared with *WEO-2013*, due to its major emphasis on energy conservation measures and the expansion of renewables, alongside the anticipated gradual return of nuclear. As a result, Japan's natural gas demand is expected to return to pre-Fukushima levels (around 100 bcm) by the end of the current decade and then to increase at a very moderate pace throughout the rest of the projection period.

Box 4.1 ▷ A gas thirsty Middle East

Natural gas demand in the Middle East rose by almost two-and-half-times between 2000 and 2012 to exceed 400 bcm. In 2011, gas overtook oil to become the largest contributor to regional consumption, accounting for more than 50% of energy use.[3] This rapid expansion rests on growing demand for electricity (where end-user prices are subsidised), for use in energy-intensive desalination plants, upstream and downstream energy sector projects, and in industry, particularly for petrochemicals, in each case supported by low prices for gas. Natural gas prices in the region – around $0.75/MBtu in Saudi Arabia, $0.8/MBtu in Kuwait and $1/MBtu in Qatar and the UAE – are well below the international market value of the gas. These low price levels undercut the economic attraction of other power generation technologies, such as renewables, that governments in the region are trying to promote, as well as slowing the uptake of more efficient technologies in end-use sectors (see Chapter 9).

The logic of using more gas at home, in order to free up more valuable oil for export, is strong, but prices at such low levels mean that investment in non-associated gas has been sluggish and supply has often struggled to keep up with demand. The region's natural gas resources are concentrated in three countries, Iran, Qatar and Saudi Arabia. Excluding Qatar, a major exporter but a relatively small consumer, the region has only a small net surplus of gas (in fact, the Middle East – excluding Qatar – was for a time in 2008-2009 a net gas importer). Iran's gas exports by pipeline to Turkey and the South Caucasus are broadly balanced by imports from Turkmenistan. Oman, Yemen and Abu Dhabi are LNG exporters, while Jordan and Bahrain are expected soon to join Kuwait and Dubai as LNG importers.

Natural gas use expands in the Middle East energy mix to reach 700 bcm by 2040, continuing to account for more than half of the region's total primary energy demand (Figure 4.3). This makes the region the second-largest source of additional global gas demand, after China. Reflecting announced intentions to reform domestic natural gas

---

3. In addition, around 80 bcm of gross natural gas production is re-injected into oil fields to maintain reservoir pressure: this is the equivalent of around 15% of the region's marketed production (re-injected volumes are not included in IEA production data).

pricing, notably in Iran and Saudi Arabia, but also the political challenge to implement price increases in practice, end-user prices are assumed to rise only gradually in real terms, but this is nonetheless enough to provide incentive for upstream activity and greater efficiency. Power generation accounts for 40% of the growth in gas demand: gas-fired generation more than doubles to 1 220 terawatt-hours (TWh). Industry is the second-biggest source of incremental gas demand, but the rate of growth, at 2.2% on average per year, is expected to be significantly lower than the rate experienced over the last decades. Thanks mainly to Qatar, the region continues to be a net contributor to global gas supply.

Figure 4.3 ▷ **Natural gas demand in the Middle East by sector in the New Policies Scenario**

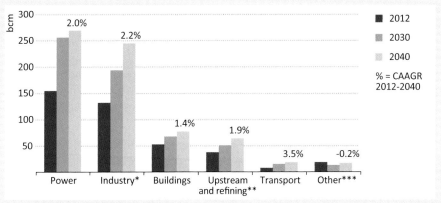

* Industry includes gas used as petrochemical feedstocks and energy consumption in coke ovens and blast furnaces. ** Upstream and refining includes own-use in oil and gas extraction, petroleum refineries and gas-to-liquids transformation. *** Other includes agriculture and any other energy and non-energy uses.

Note: CAAGR = compound average annual growth rate.

China is the country expected to see the largest growth in natural gas demand between 2012 and 2040. Over the last few years, the Chinese government has targeted an expansion of natural gas consumption as a way to diversify the energy mix, particularly in and around large urban areas, where air quality and pollutants have become paramount issues of social and political concern. This expansion will require the continuation of gas reform initiatives that China has launched in recent years, bringing domestic prices to levels that provide sufficient incentive to develop domestic resources as well as covering the average costs of imported gas. Policies are assumed to be put in place to develop the domestic gas infrastructure for transmission and distribution as well as for storage, with various upstream players and shippers having reliable access to this infrastructure. China has already tested the ground in many of these areas, including pilot programmes for gas price reforms: in September 2014, the Chinese government raised the wholesale price of natural gas for non-residential use by over 20% to about $10/MBtu, following a similar 15% increase for non-residential gas consumers in July 2013.

The result is that, in the New Policies Scenario, gas demand in China increases from 148 bcm in 2012 to 390 bcm in 2025 and more than 600 bcm in 2040, accounting for 11% of the country's primary energy demand by the end of the projection period, compared with 4% today. The largest increase by volume comes in electricity generation, where gas use reaches 185 bcm by 2040 – producing almost 900 TWh of power. Gas use grows by more than four-times in industry (including feedstocks) and more than triples in the buildings sector. Gas demand rises rapidly in the transport sector as China expands its natural gas vehicle (NGV) fleet, which helps to mitigate urban air pollution problems and oil import levels.

The share of natural gas in India's energy mix, 6% in 2012, was modest by international standards, due to the combination of limited domestic supply, competition from low-cost coal and the difficulty of accommodating relatively expensive LNG imports.[4] As in many gas markets, pricing reform is key: domestic prices have been too low to stimulate domestic investment or to bring new gas supplies profitably into the market. A long-awaited price rise and simplified pricing scheme was announced in October 2014, with an average price set at $5.6/MBtu, subject to revision every six months. Whether this pricing mechanism will be acceptable to the key gas-consuming sectors (power generation, fertiliser and other industry, and transport), while still ensuring adequate supply is a critical uncertainty. Even with reforms in place, our expectation is that India's natural gas market remains restrained over the next few years, after which rising LNG imports and higher domestic production sustain demand growth. India's gas consumption increases from 57 bcm in 2012 to 82 bcm in 2020 and about 200 bcm in 2040, pushed higher by demand from the power sector (although the share of gas there reaches only 12% by 2040) and for road transport.

In Russia, natural gas consumption of around 470 bcm in 2012 already accounted for more than half of the primary energy mix (the highest proportion among the world's major economies), leaving limited scope for further growth, particularly given the huge efficiency savings that are available throughout its gas infrastructure. Compared with last year's *Outlook*, we have revised downwards our projections for Russian gas demand, reflecting slightly reduced expectations for economic growth, although this also implies a slower renewal or replacement of inefficient capital stock, limiting the extent to which available efficiency savings are exploited. Gas consumption in Russia is expected to fall back slightly over the current decade and then rise at a relatively slow place, to reach 500 bcm in 2040.

In Africa, gas demand is expected to increase almost two-and-half-times, from 120 bcm in 2012 to 290 bcm in 2040. As discussed in more detail in Part C, there is potential to expand gas use in sub-Saharan Africa further, particularly in the power sector, but this prospect is constrained by limited gas infrastructure and the difficulty of finding viable business models for new gas projects.

---

4. Preliminary 2013 data for India show a steep decline of natural gas consumption (11%) and production (13%) compared with 2012, mainly due to the fall in production at the KG-D6 offshore block.

In Latin America, natural gas continues to make inroads, with the largest increase by volume seen in the industry and power sectors, but the most rapid growth is in road transport: Brazil and Argentina already have almost 4 million NGVs on the road (equal to about one-quarter of the world NGV stock). Gas demand for power is also expected to increase in Central America, as countries (including Panama, which is set to play an increasing role in LNG trade with the widening of the Panama Canal) take advantage of their proximity to US Gulf Coast export projects to substitute gas for expensive oil in the power sector. Overall, gas demand in Latin America reaches 305 bcm by 2040, an average annual growth of 2.4%.

Sectoral trends

The power sector remains the single largest source of incremental gas demand over 2012-2040. Gas use for electricity (and heat) generation rises to more than 2.1 tcm by 2040, at an annual rate of 1.5% (Figure 4.4). Gas is the only fossil fuel whose share in power generation increases (from 22% today to 24% in 2040), while that of coal declines and oil use becomes marginal. Of the more than 700 bcm rise in gas consumption for electricity generation over 2012-2040, about 80% is in non-OECD countries, where gas-fired capacity more than doubles to 1 440 gigawatts (GW) by 2040. Gas is well placed to enjoy a competitive advantage over many other fuels for power generation, given its higher efficiency, greater flexibility, lower capital costs and shorter plant construction times. However, the trend in gas use in the power sector remains very sensitive to its cost competitiveness versus other fuels (a calculation in which carbon pricing can play an important role), as well as to government policies aimed at diversifying the fuel mix or reducing the environmental footprint of electricity generation. Gas overtakes coal in electricity generation in OECD countries around the mid-2020s, but coal remains by far the most favoured power generation fuel in non-OECD countries throughout the projection period, due to less stringent environmental standards and cheaper supplies.

Figure 4.4 ▷ **World natural gas demand by sector in the New Policies Scenario**

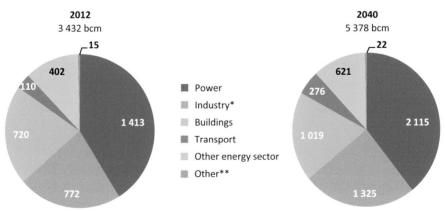

*Industry includes gas used as petrochemical feedstocks and energy consumption in coke ovens and blast furnaces.
**Other includes agriculture and any other non-energy use.

The second-largest sector for gas demand today is industry. In our *Outlook*, non-OECD countries account for almost the entire net increase in gas demand for industry to 2040. China, the Middle East and countries in Southeast Asia account for more than 60% of this growth (Figure 4.5), although the United States also contributes because of the increased competitiveness of the petrochemicals sector and the anticipated revival of production of fertilisers. Use of natural gas in the energy sector increases by more than half to reach 625 bcm, or 12% of global gas demand by 2040, due to more upstream oil and gas activities, larger volumes of natural gas used in the liquefaction and regasification processes for LNG, and the conversion of gas-to-liquid fuels (GTL). Thanks to technological developments and a favourable differential between oil and gas prices, GTL production is expected to rise in the second-half of the *Outlook* period to almost 1 million barrels per day (mb/d) by 2040, requiring some 90 bcm in gas feedstock.

Figure 4.5 ▷ **Change in natural gas demand by sector in selected regions in the New Policies Scenario, 2012-2040**

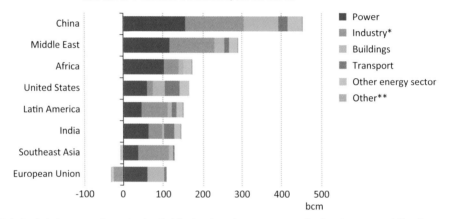

*Industry includes gas used as petrochemical feedstocks and energy consumption in coke ovens and blast furnaces.
**Other includes agriculture and any other non-energy use.

The buildings sector (residential and services) currently accounts for one-fifth of total gas consumption, mainly for space and water heating. Demand growth in this sector is concentrated in non-OECD countries, as urban populations rise and residential gas distribution networks expand. The share of non-OECD countries in total buildings sector gas demand rises from 34% in 2012 to 44% by 2040, largely because of rising demand in China.

Although use in volumetric terms is small at present, the transport sector is set to expand its gas demand at the fastest pace (3.4% on average). High oil prices, environmental impacts and, in many countries, concerns about oil import dependence have spurred the interest of many governments in alternatives for mobility. The latest data available show that, at the end of 2012, there were 16.7 million NGVs on the road (a 10% increase on a yearly basis), of which about 80% are found in Iran, Pakistan, Argentina, Brazil, China, India and Italy.[5] The expansion of the NGV fleet worldwide has been accompanied by growth in the number of natural gas refuelling stations, which increased from less than 15 000 in 2008 to more than 21 000 by the end of 2012. Although the majority of NGVs are cars, there is increasing interest in gas-powered buses and trucks (mainly fuelled by LNG), as the economic logic for fuelling high-mileage vehicles with natural gas appears to be favourable, despite higher upfront costs for the vehicle itself and the need to expand refuelling infrastructure (see *WEO-2013*). In our projections, natural gas use in the road transport is set to expand at 5.1% per year, from 40 bcm in 2012 to 160 bcm in 2040.

About 40% of the growth in natural gas use in road transport occurs in the United States and China. China is advancing fast in the deployment of NGVs with almost 3 million NGVs on the road at the end of 2013, a large increase from 2012. Of these, 169 000, mainly trucks and buses, are fuelled by LNG. Furthermore, China is rapidly expanding its refuelling infrastructure, having added 1 700 natural gas stations in 2013 for a total of 4 500 (of which 1 900 are for LNG-powered vehicles). The picture is similar in the United States, where the expansion of natural gas in the transport sector is expected to be led by the use of LNG for long-haul trucks. There is strong upside potential in these and other transport markets for natural gas to make further gains, at the expense of oil product use; but in our projections stronger penetration of natural gas in transport is constrained by a number of barriers, including the need for strong and sustained policy support, the major investment required in gas infrastructure and the need for incentives to encourage customers to switch to NGVs. The recent increase in China's domestic gas prices and the projected rise in US natural gas prices also play a role in limiting the uptake of natural gas in the road transport sector. By 2040, the share of natural gas in total road transport demand reaches 5% on an energy-equivalent basis, up from 2% in 2012.

The prospect of stricter emissions controls on the sulphur content of bunker fuels is opening up new avenues for LNG use in the international maritime sector (see Chapter 3, Box 3.2). Alongside LNG, options for compliance with new regulatory measures include a switch to lower-sulphur oil products or the introduction of "scrubber" technologies that clean up bunker fuel gases before they are released to the atmosphere. The prospects for LNG in this sector are tempered by the high upfront capital costs of LNG-powered vessels (or retrofits) and the need to build refuelling infrastructure. LNG bunkering for ships is currently available only in a limited number of ports.[6] And, in a typical "chicken-and-egg" situation, investment in infrastructure will depend on anticipated deployment of LNG-fuelled ships, whose construction, in turn, hinges on confidence that LNG infrastructure and supplies will be widely available. While these considerations slow the growth of LNG

---

5. Detailed statistics on NGV fleets are available at *www.iangv.org*.

6. The ports of Antwerp and Rotterdam in Europe already have facilities to supply LNG to inland barges and trucks, and are aiming to start providing this service soon to sea-going vessels (in July 2014, GDF SUEZ, Mitsubishi and NYK signed a framework agreement aiming to provide LNG bunkering supply service in Zeebrugge port from 2016). Rotterdam has its own LNG import terminal while Antwerp uses LNG imported through Zeebrugge. Some German and Scandinavian ports, and international shipping hubs such as Singapore, are also expressing interest in LNG bunkering.

use in marine transport, it gains ground over the longer term, increasing gradually towards 15 bcm by 2030 and then doubling to 2040, by when it accounts for more than 10% of total bunker fuel use (replacing the equivalent of about 0.5 mb/d of oil products).

Production

Resources and reserves

The remaining resources of natural gas are abundant and can comfortably meet the projections of global demand growth included in all three scenarios of this *Outlook* to 2040 and well beyond. Proven reserves stood at 216 tcm at the end of 2013, equal to more than 60 years of production at current rates. However, proven reserves are only a fraction of total remaining technically recoverable resources, which provide a better indication of the available resource base and are the key parameter used in our modelling of future gas production. We estimate that, at the end of 2012, total remaining technically recoverable resources amounted to more than 800 tcm, almost four-times larger than proven reserves (Table 4.3).

Table 4.3 ▷ **Remaining technically recoverable natural gas resources by type and region, end-2013** (tcm)

	Conventional	Unconventional				Total	
		Tight gas	Shale gas	Coalbed methane	Sub-total	Resources	Proven reserves
E. Europe/Eurasia	143	11	15	20	46	189	73
Middle East	124	9	4	-	13	137	81
Asia-Pacific	43	21	53	21	95	138	19
OECD Americas	46	11	48	7	65	111	13
Africa	52	10	39	0	49	101	17
Latin America	31	15	40	-	55	86	8
OECD Europe	25	4	13	2	19	45	5
World	465	81	211	50	342	806	216

Notes: Shale gas resources are taken in large part from the US EIA/ARI study. Though this has broad coverage, it leaves out many regions. The Middle East, in particular, is likely to have significantly larger shale gas resources than indicated, but there is no assessment available. Resources of methane hydrates are not included in the table: they are vast, in all likelihood significantly larger than all other types combined, but are not expected to play a major role during the projection period.

Sources: BGR (2013); BP (2014); Cedigaz (2013); O&GJ (2014); US EIA/ARI (2013); USGS (2000); USGS (2012a, 2012b); IEA databases and analysis.

Gas production trends

More than 40% of the gas required to meet rising projected levels of consumption comes from conventional sources, but unconventional gas plays an increasingly important role in the overall supply picture to 2040. Unconventional gas – primarily shale gas, but also coalbed methane (CBM), tight gas and, to a much lesser extent, coal-to-gas and methane hydrates[7] – accounts for close to 60% of the growth in production, meaning that its share in total gas output rises from 17% today to 31% by the end of our projection period (Figure 4.6 and Table 4.4). North America continues to be the largest single source of unconventional output, even though signs of the impact of resource depletion appear in the trajectory of US shale gas production in the second-half of the 2030s. But unconventional gas becomes a much more widespread global phenomenon over the coming decades, as Australia and China, then other countries such as India and Argentina pick up the baton. The motivation for developing unconventional gas varies: even though production costs are higher outside the United States and Canada, for importing countries such as China or India the incentive is to reduce the need for costly LNG imports, while for some exporting countries, such as Algeria, it is to replace declining conventional production. By 2040, half of the total unconventional gas is produced outside the United States and Canada.

Figure 4.6 ▷ **World natural gas production by type in the New Policies Scenario**

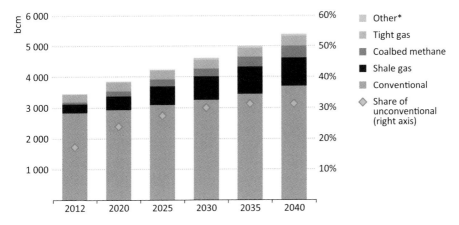

* Includes coal-to-gas and methane hydrates.

In the New Policies Scenario, gas production increases in all major countries and regions of the world, with the exception of Europe, where the downward trend that started around the mid-2000s is set to continue throughout the projection period (Table 4.5). Among Europe's major gas producers, Norway sees only a slight decline in output between 2012 and 2040, while Netherlands gas production plunges steeply to around 20 bcm by 2040, due to the decline of the giant Groningen field after 2020 (output is also capped by government-mandated restrictions following recent seismic events). The decline in European gas supply

---

7. This edition of the *World Energy Outlook* for the first time takes into account coal-to-gas, a process in which mined coal is first turned into syngas (a mixture of hydrogen and carbon monoxide) and then into "synthetic" methane, as well as production from methane hydrate deposits. The former is planned to experience rapid growth in China with more than 20 plants on the drawing board (IEA, 2014a). For methane hydrates we project only a modest contribution in Japan.

would be even more pronounced if it were not for some unconventional output, mainly in Poland and the United Kingdom. However, the contribution of unconventional supply to domestic European production remains modest: in the EU, unconventional gas contributes 17 bcm to the outlook by 2040, some 15% of total production and only 3% of total demand. The resource base would support significantly higher levels of output, but we expect the industry to face an uphill struggle to gain public and political acceptance in many countries.

Table 4.4 ▷ **Global production of unconventional gas in the New Policies Scenario** (bcm)

	2012	2020	2025	2030	2035	2040	2012-2040	
							Delta	CAAGR*
Shale gas	279	454	610	772	895	954	675	4.5%
Coalbed methane	76	148	216	274	314	356	280	5.7%
Tight gas	237	294	292	291	308	327	90	1.2%
Coal-to-gas	0.3	32	42	47	49	51	51	20.4%
Methane hydrates	-	-	0.1	0.3	0.7	0.9	0.9	n.a.
Total	592	928	1 160	1 385	1 567	1 689	1 097	3.8%

* Compound average annual growth rate.

The picture is completely different in North America, where unconventional gas production pushes overall supply to more than 1 250 bcm by 2040. The United States is expected to remain the largest global gas producer throughout the *Outlook* period, its production expanding from 681 bcm in 2012 to a high point of around 930 bcm in the mid-2030s, before a decline in shale gas output brings the total down slightly by 2040 (Box 4.2). Some of this production is exported as LNG and by pipeline to Mexico, although in the New Policies Scenario these volumes remain fairly modest (see concluding section).

In Canada, the increase in US gas production, by driving down prices and limiting demand for Canadian exports, has created numerous challenges for upstream projects. As in the case of oil, the task facing the gas industry in Canada is to open access to alternative markets, with the obvious choice (at least for resource-holders in the Western Canada Sedimentary Basin) to look to Asia. Canada does not have any LNG export facilities at present, nor does it have infrastructure linking the production areas in Alberta and eastern British Columbia to the coast, but a number of LNG and natural gas pipeline project proposals are looking to fill these gaps. We assume that concerns from environmental groups and First Nations about the construction of gas pipelines can be assuaged, and, as these outlets to international markets start to become available, so Canada's gas production increases gradually, climbing to 235 bcm by 2040.

Table 4.5 ▷ Natural gas production by region in the New Policies Scenario (bcm)

	1990	2012	2020	2025	2030	2035	2040	2012-2040 Delta	2012-2040 CAAGR*
OECD	881	1 228	1 423	1 495	1 554	1 597	1 634	406	1.0%
Americas	643	885	1 036	1 105	1 168	1 223	1 254	369	1.3%
Canada	109	156	168	184	192	204	233	77	1.4%
Mexico	26	47	51	60	78	90	96	50	2.6%
United States	507	681	817	859	897	928	923	242	1.1%
Europe	211	278	253	234	225	218	210	-68	-1.0%
Israel	0	2	8	15	18	20	20	17	7.7%
Norway	28	115	111	105	103	103	101	-14	-0.5%
Asia Oceania	28	64	134	157	160	157	170	106	3.5%
Australia	20	56	128	152	157	154	167	111	4.0%
Non-OECD	1 181	2 210	2 448	2 753	3 072	3 409	3 744	1 534	1.9%
E. Europe/Eurasia	831	873	918	971	1 029	1 107	1 198	325	1.1%
Azerbaijan	10	18	25	35	46	47	49	31	3.7%
Russia	629	658	667	669	680	736	788	130	0.6%
Turkmenistan	85	69	95	118	139	158	190	120	3.7%
Asia	132	423	527	600	682	763	841	418	2.5%
China	15	107	171	217	266	318	368	261	4.5%
India	13	40	50	64	83	98	112	72	3.8%
Indonesia	48	77	100	114	130	144	157	80	2.6%
Middle East	91	529	572	660	746	831	903	374	1.9%
Iran	23	156	153	170	195	232	272	115	2.0%
Qatar	6	159	164	183	207	224	237	78	1.4%
Saudi Arabia	24	81	92	103	118	130	139	58	1.9%
Africa	67	213	236	296	348	406	470	258	2.9%
Algeria	46	85	99	108	119	131	145	60	1.9%
Mozambique	-	4	3	24	36	50	61	57	10.3%
Nigeria	4	41	45	52	60	72	85	44	2.6%
Latin America	60	172	196	227	267	302	331	158	2.4%
Argentina	20	41	42	54	76	94	109	68	3.6%
Brazil	4	19	30	52	74	89	102	83	6.2%
World	2 063	3 438	3 872	4 249	4 626	5 007	5 378	1 940	1.6%
European Union	213	174	144	129	123	114	106	-68	-1.7%
Unconventional									
OECD	*8%*	*45%*	*55%*	*60%*	*64%*	*66%*	*65%*	*20%*	*n.a.*
Non-OECD	*0%*	*2%*	*6%*	*10%*	*13%*	*15%*	*17%*	*15%*	*n.a.*
World	*3%*	*17%*	*24%*	*27%*	*30%*	*31%*	*31%*	*14%*	*n.a.*

* Compound average annual growth rate.

Box 4.2 ▷ **Does depletion bring the end of the US shale boom into view?**

In a similar way to tight oil, discussed in Chapter 3, the future production of shale gas in the United States (or elsewhere for that matter) is driven by simple economics: the value of the recovered gas per well needs to exceed the cost of drilling and completing the well. As more production takes place, operators need to start drilling outside the "sweet spots", the zones yielding the best recovered gas volumes per well. As activity moves to zones of the shale formation giving less gas per well, the economics deteriorate (assuming no technology breakthroughs that cut costs or increase recovery per well), eventually reaching the point at which the commercial economics fail. This is what drives the peak and then the decline that we project for tight oil production in the United States. So will the same happen for shale gas?

Yes, but this process will take some time. Because North America largely operates as a closed gas market (currently there is very little import and no export; even after LNG export starts, the exported volume will remain small compared with domestic demand), the move to more expensive production does not result in a decline of production, but rather an increase in price. This is the driver for our projected increase in the US natural gas price (from $3.65/MBtu in 2013 to $8.20/MBtu in 2040). It is only after the price becomes high enough for US shale gas to become uncompetitive, either in international markets against other sources of LNG or in the domestic market against other sources of gas, such as deepwater Gulf Coast, that production peaks and starts declining. In our projections, this peak just comes into view before 2040. Its exact timing will vary with different domestic and international gas prices and could easily be pushed beyond 2040.[8] But this serves as a reminder that, unlike diamonds, shale gas is not forever.

With about 20 tcm of remaining technically recoverable resources, about 80% of which are unconventional gas, Mexico has the potential to expand its gas production significantly. The energy reforms introduced in December 2013 are opening up new prospects for the Mexican gas sector, through the possibility of an influx of private investment and capital (see Chapter 3, Box 3.4). In terms of unconventional production, Pemex, the national oil company, has large-scale plans and has already invested about $300 million in shale gas exploration and drilled several wells, but greater involvement of private companies would accelerate the process of developing these resources. Production prospects are affected by the need to build transportation infrastructure, as well as by the stiff competition provided by relatively cheap gas imports from the United States. In the New Policies Scenario, total gas production in Mexico increases to 60 bcm by 2025 and accelerates slightly in the second-half of the projection period to reach 96 bcm by 2040. Unconventional gas output rises to 42 bcm by 2040, accounting for more than 80% of production growth.

---

8. Our modelling outcome assumes technology learning but no technology breakthroughs and no significant increase above the current estimates of recoverable resources.

Australia's gas production is set to expand quickly over the period to 2020, due to the start of seven LNG liquefaction plants before the end of the current decade. However, the longer-term outlook is for slower growth, as the simultaneous construction of these plants – three alone on Queensland's Curtis Island – has put huge strain on labour and other resources, pushing up costs and pushing back deadlines.[9] Together with the expectation of increasing competition from North American LNG supplies and supplies from East Africa after 2020, this has slowed final investment decisions for further expansion of Australia's LNG liquefaction capacity. Overall, Australia's natural gas production rises from 56 bcm in 2012 to 130 bcm in 2020, then to almost 170 bcm by 2040.

Chinese production in 2012 of 107 bcm was enough to make it the sixth-largest gas producer in the world, just ahead of Norway. Currently, the four largest production centres in China are the Ordos Basin, in the northwest, the Tarim Basin in the west, the Sichuan Basin in the southwest and the South China Sea.[10] Given the large gas resource base (4.4 tcm of proven reserves and almost 50 tcm of remaining technically recoverable gas resources) and the strong political willingness to expand the role of gas in its energy mix, China's output is set to expand significantly over the next years. The main elements of the increase are shale gas and coalbed methane, supplemented by coal-to-gas. Of the major Chinese companies involved in unconventional gas development, Sinopec put itself in a leading position with its announcement in March 2014 that the Fuling shale gas play would be producing 10 bcm per year by 2017. This implies a reasonable likelihood of China meeting its 2015 production target for shale gas of 6.5 bcm. The target for 2020, previously given as a range of 60-100 bcm, however, is under revision, and may – according to a recent announcement by the Chinese National Energy Administration – be cut in half, i.e. to a low of 30 bcm. In our projections, shale gas production rises towards 25 bcm in 2020, before growing steadily thereafter to reach almost 110 bcm in 2040. Among the issues that may hold back China's production over the longer term are the relative scarcity of water resources in the arid Tarim Basin (Box 4.3), constraints arising from population density, and production and transport costs. Overall, China's gas production expands by more than 260 bcm during the period to reach 370 bcm by 2040, with almost 80% from unconventional sources.

India follows a path similar to China, albeit on a smaller scale. Its domestic gas production more than doubles, from 40 bcm to over 110 bcm, due mainly to rising production from shale gas and coalbed methane after 2020. In October 2013, India inaugurated a new policy on shale gas, granting licenses to its state-owned companies (ONGC and Oil India) to explore shale gas resources in 190 blocks. Following the drilling of the first shale gas wells in the Cambay basin, ONGC has announced plans to drill an additional 30 shale gas wells in 2014 and 2015. However, some of the initial enthusiasm for India's shale gas and coalbed methane has cooled because of delays in introducing gas pricing reform.

---

9. For detailed analysis of LNG investment trends, see the *World Energy Investment Outlook* (IEA, 2014b).

10. Prospects for South China Sea gas production remain uncertain because of the disputed status of certain territorial and maritime boundaries.

Box 4.3 ▷ Is water a constraint on shale gas production?

Water use and the risk of water contamination are key issues for unconventional gas development; they are at the forefront of public concern about hydraulic fracturing. Each well for hydraulic fracturing needs between a few thousand and 20 000 cubic metres of water. This has fed the public perception that unconventional gas uses a disproportionate amount of water compared with other forms of energy production although, in practice, this is not the case. Shale gas or tight gas developments use more water per produced volume than conventional gas production, but often less than that used for conventional oil production on an equivalent energy basis (IEA, 2012).

Yet the issue of water nonetheless looms large for shale gas production, for four main reasons. Transportation of water from its source to the well site – and away for disposal – is a large-scale activity often carried out by truck, which can be disruptive for local communities. In areas of water scarcity, the extraction of water for drilling and hydraulic fracturing can have serious environmental consequences, as well as affecting the water available for other users, for example in agriculture. The treatment and disposal of the waste water that flows back to the surface in the days and weeks following the hydraulic fracturing can give rise to concerns about environmental damage. There is also the risk of contamination of local water supplies, whether from accidental spills at the surface, leakage underground or poor management of waste water. Public concern has focused on the risk of leakage of hydrocarbons or chemicals from the producing zone, where the fracturing takes place, up into shallow aquifers, although there are typically many hundreds of metres of intervening rock. In practice, as shown by recent groundwater studies, in the limited number of cases where water contamination has occurred, the most likely cause has been poor sealing of the cement column around the casing of a well, indicating a need for rigorous construction standards and enforcement (Darrah et al, 2014).

Dealing with the various water-related issues requires a multi-pronged approach, starting with the measurement of key environmental indicators, including groundwater quality, prior to commencing activity. During operations, there are many ways to increase the efficiency of water use, notably through increased re-use and recycling of waste water, and to ensure the safe storage, treatment and disposal of any water that cannot be reused. To avoid competition with other water uses, operators are reducing their water consumption and getting water from alternative sources like deep saline aquifers. Pipeline networks for water can obviate the need for many thousands of truck movements. And regulators have a critical role to play in gaining and retaining public confidence in the rigour of their supervision and the quality of the underlying analysis of the regional or basin-wide impacts of water use: a good example comes from Queensland, Australia, where the authorities have pioneered an approach assessing cumulative groundwater impacts, from coalbed methane production across the Surat basin. In some cases waterless technologies, such as hydraulic fracturing using propane as a fluid, can be used, though they have their own safety and environmental issues.

The possible hazards associated with water use in unconventional gas production – and the ways to address them by industry and by regulators – were the focus of the 2014 IEA *Unconventional Gas Forum*, organised in Calgary. The next in the series of these meetings will take place in April 2015, hosted by China – another pivotal country for the future of unconventional gas.[11]

With around 140 tcm of remaining technically recoverable natural gas resources, the Middle East has the potential to greatly expand its gas supply; but above-ground factors, such as heavily subsidised domestic gas prices and geopolitical tensions, are expected to limit gas production in many countries. Regional production is nonetheless projected to rise from 530 bcm today to more than 900 bcm by 2040. Qatar, Iran, Saudi Arabia and Iraq are the main contributors to long-term production growth, accounting for almost 90% of gas output growth in the region to 2040. All face significant constraints on the pace of growth.

In the case of Qatar, the main limitation is by choice, in that the moratorium on new projects tapping the huge North Field is set to remain in place, at least until the end of 2015. For Iran, the prospects are clouded by international sanctions, which have largely closed access to foreign investment and technology, affecting not only the development of the South Pars field (part of the same deposit as the Qatari North Field) but also many other giant and super-giant reservoirs, such as North Pars, Kish and Golshan. Over the longer term, assuming that current political constraints can be lifted, the production profile is expected to be driven by the size of Iran's huge resource base, bringing overall production above 270 bcm by 2040.

The multiple challenges facing Iraq include greater utilisation of associated gas from the huge oil fields in the south around Basrah, much of which continues to be flared, and significant uncertainties over whether the security and political environment will allow for production of non-associated gas and export from the northern Kurdistan region. In 2012, Saudi Arabia completed its first offshore non-associated gas project, Karan, and it is also proceeding with development work on the Wasit Gas Plant, which – together with Karan – will increase the Kingdom's gas processing capacity by around 40%. As with other countries in the region, recovering the costs associated with the development of non-associated gas is incompatible with present pricing and marketing arrangements based on associated gas, which is available at very low cost as a by-product of investment in upstream oil projects. The region's massive production infrastructure also makes it the major source of leakage of methane – a very potent greenhouse gas – into the atmosphere (Spotlight).

---

11. More information on the IEA Unconventional Gas Forum is available at *www.iea.org/ugforum*.

What is the contribution of oil and gas production to methane emissions?

Methane, the primary component of natural gas, accounts for 16% of all greenhouse-gas (GHG) emissions resulting from human activities. Because methane is a powerful GHG (though a relatively short-lived one compared with carbon dioxide), achieving significant reductions would have a rapid effect on atmospheric warming. About 10% of the anthropogenic methane emissions are associated with upstream oil and gas output (IEA, 2013b). The main pathways through which methane could escape into the atmosphere are leaks (in wellheads, pipelines, pumps), vents (of well casings, pneumatic devices, storage tanks, dehydrators), incomplete combustion and operational upsets. With sizeable oil and gas operations and an ageing and widespread stock of wells, pipes and equipment, Russia (and Caspian countries) and the Middle East are the regions with the highest estimated emissions of methane related to oil and gas extraction (Figure 4.7). But with the large increase in the number of wells that are hydraulically fractured in North America, emissions from this type of operations have also become a source of controversy and a subject of regulatory focus in recent years.

Figure 4.7 ▷ **Estimated methane emissions associated with oil and natural gas production, 2012**

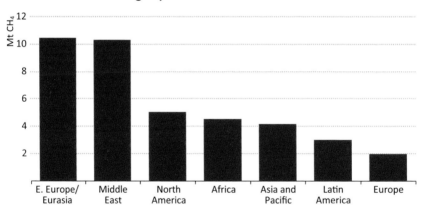

Minimising methane emissions from upstream oil and gas operations is one of four measures identified in the *World Energy Outlook* special report, *Redrawing the Energy-Climate Map* (IEA, 2013b) as a means of keeping the door open to the 2 °C climate target while negotiations continue on an international climate agreement. The United States has announced that curbing methane emissions will be critical to the overall effort to address global climate change and it is expected that the oil and gas sector will contribute to that endeavour both through voluntary programmes (because methane is in the end a valuable commodity) and as a result of targeted regulation.

Better measurements of methane emissions along the entire energy chain, from reservoir to power socket (or wheel) are indispensable to assess the environmental impact of gas production and consumption and to test the widely held proposition that gas brings greenhouse-gas emissions reductions compared with the other fossil fuels. The need for sound data is underlined by studies that find a large discrepancy between top-down (airborne measurement of atmospheric concentrations) and bottom-up (equipment and activity inventories, multiplied by emission factors per activity) study protocols. The University of Texas is leading a programme that collects data during completion operations for hydraulically fractured wells and the Environmental Defense Fund (EDF) is co-ordinating a programme to do the same in other parts of the value chain. These studies will help to locate where the methane escapes and to assess what the most cost-effective measures are to reduce the emissions.

Some measures to reduce methane emissions can produce quick returns: improving operating practices through increased inspection and repairs; minimising emissions during completion operations and work-overs; and reducing the frequency of start-ups and blow-downs. A study prepared for the EDF suggests that 40% of methane emissions in the United States can be eliminated by spending just $0.01 per thousand cubic feet of natural gas (or per 28 cubic metres) (ICF International, 2014). The Gas Star Program of the US Environmental Protection Agency (EPA) proposes specific cost-effective improvements for equipment and practices. Our calculations, using these suggestions, show that by spending an additional 1% of the total investments in oil and gas production, methane emissions from the upstream sector could be reduced by 40% worldwide before 2020.

Gas production in Eastern Europe and Eurasia, including Russia and the Caspian region, expands by more than 320 bcm in the New Policies Scenario, to reach almost 1.2 tcm by 2040. Russia accounts for 40% of this growth, as it speeds up the development of its large gas resources in eastern Siberia and the Russian Far East to feed new supply commitments to Asia-Pacific markets, notably the agreement for Gazprom to supply up to 38 bcm/year to China by pipeline, starting from the latter part of this decade (see next section). Russian production is not limited by resources or production capacity but by markets: domestic demand is not projected to grow significantly, nor the demand of its traditional European customers (although Europe's import needs grow more quickly); so growth comes mainly from accessing Asian markets by pipeline and LNG.

Within Russia, an important trend over recent years has been the declining share of Gazprom in total production; from more than 85% in 2005, Gazprom's production fell to less than three-quarters by 2013. The main contributing factor has been increased competition on the domestic market, with Novatek and the major Russian oil companies, led by Rosneft, increasing their sales to the wholesale market and to major gas consumers, offering gas at prices below Gazprom's regulated domestic sales price. In the future, competitive pressures are set to extend in part to Russian export markets, where Gazprom's grip has been loosened by the decision to allow selected Russian companies to participate in LNG export projects. Novatek is set to be the first to take advantage of this partial liberalisation, as it made the final investment decision on its Yamal LNG project in late 2013. Rosneft may soon follow suit with its participation alongside ExxonMobil in a new LNG export project from Sakhalin (although the timing of both of these may well be pushed back by the US and EU sanctions imposed in 2014 that limit Russia's access to long-term financing and to certain technologies). We project Russian output to increase by 130 bcm over the period to 2040, reaching 790 bcm (Figure 4.8). Adding together their announced plans, Gazprom, Novatek and Rosneft anticipate that their production will grow by around 100 bcm already by 2020, implying continued political and commercial competition between them for markets both at home and abroad.

Figure 4.8 ▷ **Change in natural gas production in selected countries in the New Policies Scenario**

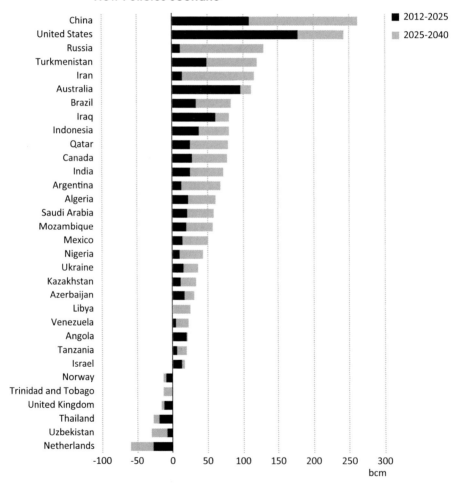

Gas production in Turkmenistan increases to 95 bcm by 2020 and then doubles in the second-half of the *Outlook* to reach 190 bcm in 2040. Production in Turkmenistan, until well into the 2020s, is contingent on the implementation of upstream projects linked to gas exports east to China, as neither Russia or Iran, Turkmenistan's other current export markets, are likely to increase purchases. A milestone in 2013 was the start of production from the huge Galkynysh field, the world's second-largest, which is expected to account for a major share of output growth. To accommodate increased exports, a third eastward export line is due for completion by the end of 2015, boosting total export capacity to China to 55 bcm/year. Construction work on a fourth line, expected to follow a different route via northern Afghanistan, Tajikistan and Kyrgyzstan (thus by-passing Uzbekistan), is scheduled for completion later in the decade. Further long-term expansion of exports from Turkmenistan depends on the opening of new export routes to the south and/or west; proposals for pipelines to Pakistan and India, as well as a trans-Caspian gas link, remain on the table, but both need to overcome serious political and commercial obstacles if they are to be realised. Our projections are consistent with a route to South Asia being opened in the 2020s.

On the other side of the Caspian, in Azerbaijan, the long-awaited final investment decision on phase II of the Shah Deniz development was taken in late 2013, a decision that will prompt the expansion of pipeline links across Georgia, Turkey, Greece, Albania and Italy. Together with cross-border links into Bulgaria, this will make the much-discussed southern gas corridor a reality, with additional gas starting to arrive in European markets towards 2020. With enhanced access to Europe, Azerbaijan's production is expected to reach 50 bcm by 2040, with further development of Shah Deniz, deep gas layers at the ACG complex and other fields, such as Absheron, all contributing to the growth.

Africa has significant potential as a gas producer: the prospects for sub-Saharan producers in West Africa and the promise of new supply from Mozambique and Tanzania in the east are covered in detail in Part C. The main established producers in North Africa – despite ample resources – are all facing substantial medium-term difficulties in attracting investment in order to raise output. Algeria is seeking to double its natural gas production over the next decade, from around 85 bcm in 2012, partly by boosting unconventional gas production. The resource base could undoubtedly support higher output and this eventually materialises in our projections, which reach 145 bcm by 2040, but there are significant obstacles. Algerian gas production has been declining over the past seven years and new investment will have to compensate for the decline of mature gas fields, such as Hassi R'Mel, while Sonatrach needs to develop the many discoveries made over the past years. In early 2014, the Algeria government invited companies to bid for oil and gas exploration rights in its fourth competitive exploration round, a test of investor appetite following the attack on the In Amenas plant in 2013 and the adoption of new, more attractive contract terms. However, only 4 of the 31 blocks on offer (and none of the several blocks with unconventional gas potential) were awarded.

Egyptian production fell back to 54 bcm in 2012 and political uncertainty has since added to other structural problems facing the country's gas market. Since late 2012, the Damietta liquefaction plant, run by Union Fenosa, a Spanish company, has been idle, while

BG's Idku plant has been running at around one-third of its capacity. Low domestic gas prices are the key issue, encouraging wasteful consumption of natural gas, notably in the power and industrial sectors, and deterring investment decisions where the gas is to be sold on the domestic market. The gas price reform announced in July 2014 as part of a broader reduction in energy subsidies could unlock substantial production in the longer term. There is strong potential in Egypt's Nile Delta area, where BP and Eni have made recent discoveries. In our projections, current uncertainties drive gas production lower, to around 45 bcm by 2025, before it recovers to about 55 bcm by 2040. Current turmoil likewise affects the outlook for Libya, but – if political conditions allow – a large resource base underpins longer term production of around 35 bcm.

Offshore discoveries made in the eastern Mediterranean make this an area of rich promise but, with the exception of Israel's Tamar field (that is already supplying the Israeli domestic market), the timelines and volumes of gas development remain quite uncertain. Energy has the potential to act as a stimulus towards greater co-operation. However, regional politics complicate the various options for pipeline and LNG development and are likely to result in prolonged delays to project execution. We anticipate that most of the gas produced in the eastern Mediterranean will be sent to markets within the region. Turkey and Egypt are the largest regional consumers, although there are also smaller markets across the Middle East, such as Jordan, that are looking to import gas. Egypt's difficulties in supplying gas to its LNG export facilities are opening up a ready-made outlet for eastern Mediterranean projects.

In Latin America, natural gas production almost doubles, to reach 330 bcm by 2040. Most of the growth occurs after 2020, thanks mainly to shale gas supply in Argentina and associated gas from offshore fields in Brazil. Argentina holds the second-largest shale gas resources in the world, and the 2014 settlement with Repsol, following the expropriation of its share in YPF, has played a part in restoring investor confidence. Drawing on tax and pricing reforms, shale gas production from Argentina is projected to rise in the 2020s to reach 65 bcm by 2040, more than half of total gas output. In Brazil, the prospects for natural gas production are linked mainly to the development of offshore associated gas; Brazil's gas output expands to 30 bcm by 2020 and reaches 100 bcm in 2040.

Outlook for gas supply security

The 2014 conflict between Russia and Ukraine has once again brought into focus the issue of the security of gas supply. As during any period of heightened risk, an immediate concern has been whether the system has the resilience to cope with any interruption to supply. This has two main aspects: an external dimension, related to the availability of gas from alternative international sources (or from existing suppliers via different routes); and a domestic one, related to the functioning of markets and the adequacy of the infrastructure, including gas storage, to deliver this gas to the consumers that may be affected by a disruption. The projections for supply, demand and trade in the *World Energy Outlook* can shed light on how one of these dimensions – external supply – might evolve over the coming decades. Which countries or regions remain, or become, heavily dependent on imported gas? To what extent can these importers rely on a diverse mix of imported supplies, including pipelines and LNG, or might they be, in some cases, heavily dependent on a single source? Will markets and contractual mechanisms for internationally traded gas, particularly for LNG, evolve so that more gas is potentially available on a short-term basis? And are there risks to the adequacy of investment in the gas value chain that could call into question the reliability and affordability of longer-term supply?

Rising gas import needs

There are two large current destinations for internationally traded gas (Table 4.6). The European market is by far the largest; despite the travails of the continent's gas market in recent years, OECD Europe nonetheless imported some 230 bcm of gas in 2012, mostly by pipeline.[12] In the Asia-Pacific region, imports are dominated by Japan and Korea, whose combined imports of 174 bcm in 2012 accounted for more than 50% of global LNG trade. Imports to China are though rising rapidly, reaching 41 bcm in 2012, split between pipeline deliveries and imports of LNG.

Looking at the evolution of these flows in recent years, in Europe since 2010 there has been a trend towards proportionally greater reliance on pipeline supply from Russia, i.e. higher dependence on a single external supplier, and lower supplies in the form of LNG (Figure 4.9).[13] This is partly a function of adjustments to pricing mechanisms that made Russian gas more competitive with other sources, as well as problems that have restricted imports from North Africa. There has also been a greater diversity of routes bringing Russian gas to Europe, i.e. both Russia and Europe as a whole became less dependent on transit through Ukraine.

Over the same period, gas imports to Asia have increased substantially, because of higher Japanese demand following the closure of its nuclear plants post-Fukushima Daiichi, combined with the emergence of China as an LNG importer. These developments underpinned a continued price premium in Asian markets that attracted most of the supply available on a short-term basis. The rise in Asian LNG imports, alongside the reduction in LNG import flows to Europe, could be seen as a sign that international LNG markets are functioning well, responding flexibly to shifts in global consumption. But this is only partly the case: the availability of "spare" gas in practice had a lot to do with sluggish European gas demand and the collapse in North American LNG import needs: it was not necessarily an indication of any broader flexibility in global LNG supply. The idea that LNG markets already function as a significant gas security buffer should not be overstated.

---

12. This section discusses European imports primarily in terms of OECD Europe, rather than the European Union; the countries covered in each category are defined in Annex C. Gas import data for the two differ in important ways, not least because OECD Europe includes Norway, a significant gas exporter, and Turkey, a significant gas importer, both of which are outside the European Union.

13. Europe had a large amount of under-utilised LNG import capacity in 2013, with actual LNG imports of 50 bcm, compared with import regasification capacity of close to 200 bcm in 2013.

Figure 4.9 ▷ **European natural gas imports by source**

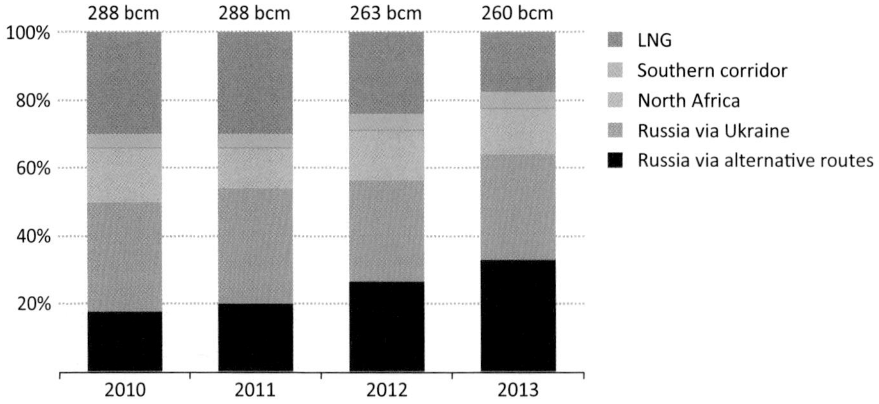

Note: This figure is for imports for Europe as a whole (OECD and non-OECD) from external sources and so differs from the net trade figures in Table 4.6.

The structure and pricing of internationally traded gas remains relatively rigid. In many parts of the world, destination clauses and take-or-pay obligations limit the ability of either buyer or seller to re-route cargoes, while oil indexation in long-term contracts, which remains the prevalent pricing mechanism across the Asia-Pacific region and in many parts of southern Europe, means that the prices of imported gas do not respond promptly to shifts in the supply/demand balance for gas. The relatively low price elasticity of demand in Japan and Korea (where there are few alternatives to imported gas and limited storage capacity) similarly narrows the scope to free up gas for other parts of the world, if needed. For the moment, there is also a concentration of market power on the supply side: Qatar accounts for almost one-third of global LNG supply, a similar share to that of the next four largest LNG exporters put together (Malaysia, Australia, Indonesia and Nigeria). The current picture of relative lack of diversity plus structural rigidities indicates vulnerabilities.

The New Policies Scenario sees growing reliance on imports in major regions of the world: OECD Europe's gas imports reach 400 bcm by 2040, the combination of a slight growth in demand together with declining indigenous production. Imports to Japan and Korea tail off in volume terms (although dependence on imports remains close to 100%), but the more dramatic shift takes place elsewhere in Asia, where rising gas use pushes imports to China up to 235 bcm and to India up to 90 bcm by 2040. Moreover, increasing consumption within Southeast Asia means that the net exportable surplus from this region (which includes two major current LNG suppliers in Malaysia and Indonesia) disappears.[14] Does this spell risks for the global gas system in terms of the security and reliability of supply?

---

14. An example of the way that Southeast Asian production is increasingly directed to meet the region's own needs was the start of LNG deliveries in 2014 from Indonesia's Tangguh field in West Papua to Indonesian domestic customers in Sumatra and West Java.

Table 4.6 ▷ **Natural gas net trade by region in the New Policies Scenario**

Net importing regions	Imports (bcm)			Imports as a share of demand		
	2012	2025	2040	2012	2025	2040
OECD Europe	-229	-324	-400	45%	58%	66%
China	-40	-171	-234	27%	44%	39%
Japan & Korea	-174	-151	-154	98%	99%	99%
India	-18	-44	-91	31%	41%	45%
Other Asia	-10	-20	-65	12%	20%	40%
Other Europe	-70	-57	-52	67%	52%	41%
Southeast Asia[15]	58	42	-8	n.a	n.a	3%
European Union	-304	-386	-453	64%	75%	81%

Net exporting regions	Exports (bcm)			Exports as a share of production		
	2012	2025	2040	2012	2025	2040
Russia	187	210	285	28%	31%	36%
Middle East	125	128	208	24%	19%	23%
Caspian	64	104	159	35%	41%	47%
Australia	20	106	114	34%	68%	68%
Sub-Saharan Africa	31	65	95	54%	54%	43%
North Africa	61	45	81	39%	27%	34%
North America	-12	62	77	n.a	6%	6%
Latin America	16	20	24	9%	9%	7%

Notes: Positive numbers denote exports; negative numbers imports. The table shows inter-regional trade, i.e. trade between the countries and regions given in this table. Trade within a region shown here is not included (so, for example, trade between the United States, Canada and Mexico, or between Latin American countries is not counted as part of inter-regional trade). Trade is ranked by volumes in 2040.

A growing cast of gas suppliers

Considering how growing gas needs are to be met, a first, broad issue is the extent of future concentration in global gas supply, i.e. the degree to which global supply relies on a small number of producers. The trends on this point are generally positive and quite distinct from those in the oil sector (Figure 4.10). The share of the top-five global gas producers in global supply drops below 50% by the end of the period to 2040 (a period over which total gas production rises substantially) and there is also a tendency towards a less skewed distribution of production among them, whereas, on the oil side, there are signs of increasing reliance on a smaller number of producers, the share of the top-five producers in total output rises from 44% to about 50%.

---

15. Southeast Asia refers to the countries of ASEAN: Brunei Darussalam, Cambodia, Indonesia, Lao PDR, Malaysia, Myanmar, Philippines, Singapore, Thailand and Vietnam.

Figure 4.10 ▷ Share of top-five producers of oil and gas in total production in the New Policies Scenario

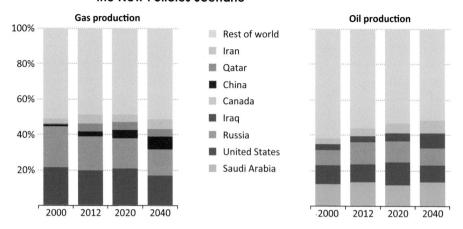

Gas production

Oil production

Rest of world
Iran
Qatar
China
Canada
Iraq
Russia
United States
Saudi Arabia

But a more pertinent consideration, particular in the case of gas, is diversity of sources of internationally traded gas, i.e. the number of exporters (or even the number of liquefaction sites).[16] Because of its low energy density compared with other fossil fuels, gas is expensive and difficult to transport. As a result, the majority of gas is consumed within its region of origin. At present, only around 20% of the gas consumed globally is traded between the regions shown in Table 4.6. This share increases very slightly over the projection period, reaching 21% by 2040. But, within this share of internationally traded gas, there is a more significant shift, away from gas traded by pipeline and towards gas traded by LNG. By 2040, almost half of inter-regional trade in gas is in the form of LNG (Figure 4.11).

Figure 4.11 ▷ Inter-regional natural gas trade by pipeline and LNG in the New Policies Scenario

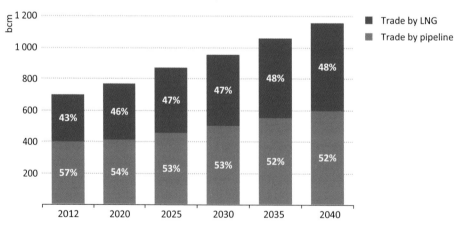

Trade by LNG
Trade by pipeline

---

16. The number of liquefaction sites operating worldwide (each of which can contain multiple projects or trains) has doubled since 2000, reaching 26 in 2013. In the New Policies Scenario, the anticipated number of sites increases to more than 70 by 2040.

Inter-regional trade by pipeline is largely a Eurasian phenomenon. Considering the huge resource base in Turkmenistan and inland Siberia, there are simply no other viable options to move resources from the centre of the Eurasian landmass to the large consuming markets. Over the projection period, we anticipate that pipeline capacities are strengthened from the Caspian Sea and Middle East to Southeast and Southern European markets, and from Turkmenistan to China, and that new infrastructure is put in place to bring gas from Russia to China as a result of the agreement reached in 2014 and, eventually (and more speculatively), from Turkmenistan southwards towards the expanding markets of South Asia. Between them, Russia and the Caspian exporters account for almost 70% of inter-regional pipeline gas trade in 2040.

A much greater degree of flexibility comes from international supplies of LNG, where there is a much more visible shift in the cast of suppliers (Figure 4.12). Some existing LNG exporters fade from prominence, in Southeast Asia but also in Africa (Egypt) and in the Middle East (Abu Dhabi, Oman, Yemen); but this is more than compensated by the range of major new exporters arriving on the scene or strengthening their existing presence. The first of these is Australia, which steps up exports over the course of this decade and, by early 2020s, is expected to export more than 100 bcm to international markets, up from 30 bcm exported in 2012. Australia is joined by North America from 2016.

Figure 4.12 ▷ **Inter-regional LNG exports by source in the New Policies Scenario**

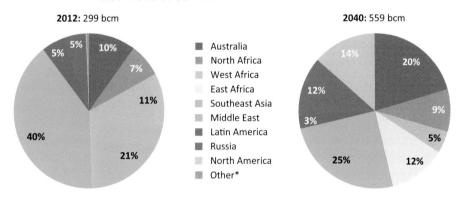

* Other includes OECD Europe and Other Developing Asia; anticipated exports from this region are less than 1% of the total in both 2012 and 2040.

The initial North American export projects are concentrated in the US Gulf of Mexico, but into the 2020s they are joined by western Canada, taking advantage of its relative proximity to Asian markets. Total LNG exports from North America rise to 60 bcm by 2025, reach a peak above 80 bcm in 2035 and then slightly decline in the last part of the projection period. The outlook for LNG exports from the United States is somewhat tighter than in *WEO-2013*, as US policy and domestic wholesale prices push larger volumes of gas into domestic power generation and other end-use sectors, while the extension of our *Outlook* to 2040 also brings into view a flattening of domestic gas production (based on our current estimates of recoverable resources and assumptions about the pace of technology learning, discussed above) as well as a continued rise in US wholesale gas prices, which reach \$8/MBtu by 2040.[17]

There is also the prospect of an expansion in Russian LNG supply from the Yamal peninsula and from the Pacific coast, as well as the emergence of East Africa as a major global LNG player, based on the huge discoveries offshore Mozambique and Tanzania (see Part C). Judging by the announcements from project developers, the start-up of many of these LNG export projects is planned for around the end of this decade and into the early 2020s – a period during which new pipeline supply from Russia to China is also scheduled to begin. In practice, this means that some projects will be pushed back into a later period, as they will not find the critical mass of committed buyers necessary to justify an early final investment decision.

This more diverse picture, and the emergence of new business models for gas supply that comes with it, will entail changes in the nature and allocation of risks along the gas value chain. One aspect is that three of the enlarged cast of suppliers are OECD countries, a consideration that may shift, in some cases, the perception of risks associated with reliance on imported gas. Another, more fundamental change is in the way that gas is set to be traded internationally, a transformation that is being led by LNG. In the past, LNG trade was typically structured in a way that emulated point-to-point pipeline projects, as part of an integrated project linking development of a specific resource to its use by a defined set of buyers (who would often in turn have monopolistic franchise areas). Over time, the system of international trade is set to become more open, with more of the characteristics of a standard commodity market.

One catalyst for this is the process of market liberalisation, entailing the removal of restrictions on trade, such as clauses limiting the re-sale of the gas. In Europe, against a backdrop of growing competition and uncertainty over long-term market share, many buyers have preferred more flexible contracts, often with shorter time horizons. A related shift, notably in northern Europe, has been towards prices set by the interplay of gas supply and demand, rather than prices indexed exclusively to oil or oil products. On the supply side, a small but growing share of international trade is taken by LNG marketers (often called aggregators), that sell gas from a global portfolio and look for arbitrage opportunities between the various regional import prices. Over the projection period, we anticipate a continued trend towards hub-based pricing and shorter term or spot sales in Europe. In the Asia-Pacific region, contracting structures are also expected to become less rigid, albeit at a slower pace, including greater availability of LNG with shorter contract terms and diminishing reliance on oil indexation.

---

17. The relatively low numbers, compared to the volumes from proposed projects, is linked to the level of global demand in the New Policies Scenario and the competition from other exporters (Australia, East Africa, Russia and others). In the Current Policies Scenario, with its higher global demand, LNG exports from North America reach 160 bcm in 2040.

The move towards a more interconnected and flexible global gas market does not mean the end of long-term contracting, which remains an important way to improve the bankability of new, capital-intensive gas infrastructure projects by guarding against the risk of their under-utilisation (this long-term contracting can either be of the gas itself, as per the traditional model of risk reduction, or of access to liquefaction capacity, as in the United States). However, at the margin, it means that buyers and sellers are able to react more readily to short-term circumstances. Buyers limit the risk of having to pay, under take-or-pay provisions, for unwanted volumes, although face the possibility that prices may be high if and when they need additional gas.[18] Sellers tend to have fewer guaranteed clients for all of their gas, but have the opportunity to seek the highest bidder and the most favourable price for some portion of their sales.

A fundamental question for gas security is whether more competitive markets, including those in which prices are set by gas-to-gas competition, can provide sufficient security for new large-scale investments in the upstream and in gas transportation infrastructure. Evidence from North America and liberalised parts of the European market suggests that they can, and this message has been reinforced by the decision, taken in late 2013, to proceed with Azerbaijan's multi-billion dollar Shah Deniz project (which triggered, in turn, plans to expand infrastructure along the route to Italy). The Shah Deniz project is underpinned by multiple long-term contracts with different offtakers, with prices tied to European hubs, mainly the TTF in the Netherlands.

A more challenging environment arises in the Asia-Pacific region, where delivered costs for gas have been higher but buyers are determinedly seeking lower purchase prices. The credibility of the traditional JCC pricing mechanism underpinning long-term import contracts (linked to the average price of crude oil imports to Japan, or Japan Crude Cocktail) is being called in question by the unwillingness of buyers to commit on this basis, even though there are, for the moment, no obvious alternative reference prices that would reflect supply and demand for gas in the region.[19] Until there is greater certainty about the direction and speed of this commercial transition, there is a risk that both buyers and sellers will adopt a "wait-and-see" approach. US export projects, priced off the US wholesale gas price, are largely insulated from this debate (Box 4.4). But the uncertainty moderates our expectation of the timing of new LNG liquefaction projects and could even contribute to a tightening of LNG markets in the medium term.

---

18. One way for buyers to balance out these risks is to take equity positions in upstream projects, an increasingly common aspect of the modern gas business.

19. Incorporating partial or full indexation to Henry Hub is a possibility, but North American indices by definition reflect their own market dynamics. As mentioned below, China is a prime candidate to take on a role as a price-setter in the region, but there is, for the moment, no suitable Chinese benchmark price.

Box 4.4 ▷ It tolls for thee: implications of the US LNG business model

LNG export projects in the United States have a distinctive business model, which has potentially significant implications for the operation of global LNG markets. Instead of the standard approach of concluding supply contracts with various purchasers, those investing in the LNG plant seek long-term take-or-pay commitments for the use of the plant's liquefaction capacity. These are known as tolling arrangements. Gas is not sourced from a specific upstream project, but is bought on the US wholesale market. Once the contracts are in place for use of the liquefaction capacity, there are no restrictions on the marketing of the LNG, the owners of which are free to seek the most favourable international destination and price. The risks and rewards for the owner of the liquefaction plant are largely set: they receive no share in any extra profit if there is a large margin between US wholesale prices and prices in the destination markets; their downside risk exposure is likewise limited.

The key risk for the offtakers arise if the price premium for sale into the non-US markets narrows to the extent that it no longer covers the liquefaction (tolling) fee and the costs of transportation. There might even come a point where the offtakers choose to pay the tolling fee without actually taking delivery of any LNG (or, alternatively, that they sell any contracted gas back on the North American market), rather than continuing to export at a higher loss. This responsiveness to fluctuations in different regional prices makes the business model fundamentally different from that of the standard integrated project, where costs are locked in to a much larger degree and there is always an incentive to keep export flows going.

Implications for the main importing regions

Gas imports into Europe (figures below are for OECD Europe) are set to become somewhat more diverse over the projection period (Figure 4.13). After a contraction in the medium term, there is a recovery in the volumes anticipated to come from North African suppliers. The southern gas corridor permits both the Caspian and the Middle East to become significant exporters to OECD Europe by pipeline. The share of LNG in total European imports is expected to rise from 27% in 2013 to 32% in 2025 and then fall back to around 30% by 2040, coming from a reasonably diverse range of sources. Regasification capacity is already at a level that could accommodate this level of LNG imports. The security of European gas supply is likely to be improved over this period by the construction of new interconnections (including provisions for reverse flows) that facilitate cross-border trade across an increasingly integrated market.

Our projections do not anticipate large-scale delivery of gas from North America to European markets, as the netbacks for these flows are not as attractive as those on offer from Asian importing markets.[20] Export volumes from Russia rise in absolute terms, but Russia's share in supply to OECD Europe declines to around 40% in 2040, from above 50% in 2012. Over the same period, Russian reliance on revenues from export to Europe also falls back, as deliveries to China and other Asian markets grow. We estimate that OECD Europe accounted for some 90% of total Russian gas export revenue in 2012; by 2040 this figure falls to 60%.[21] Nonetheless, at the projected levels of European imports from all sources (400 bcm in 2040), Russia could still (if it so chooses) out-compete on price most other sources of gas supply to Europe, giving it market power over large parts of the continent, even if Europe succeeded in creating a completely well-functioning and interconnected gas market.[22]

Figure 4.13 ▷ **Natural gas imports by source to OECD Europe in the New Policies Scenario**

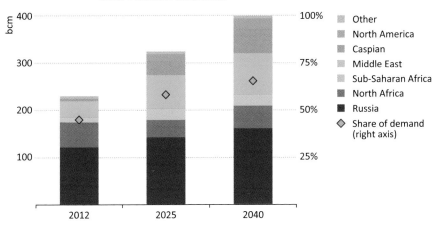

The Asia-Pacific market becomes the main destination for internationally traded gas over the period to 2040. The main existing importers, Japan and Korea, are joined by two emerging gas-consuming powers, China and India, and a host of other smaller consumers (Figure 4.14). As net exports from Southeast Asia tail off, so Asian importers rely even more, in the aggregate, on more distant supplies, as well as focusing – wherever possible – on developing indigenous gas output. But, despite the large increase in import needs,

---

20. A note of caution for those expecting large volumes of US export to arrive in Europe (once the projects start operating from 2015) was struck in the early months of 2014, when lower-than-expected demand for LNG in Europe and in some of the main Asia-Pacific markets pushed the price in Europe well below the level required to make US LNG exports to Europe economic.

21. In 2013, revenue from gas export accounted for around 15% of Russia's total export sales; exports of crude oil and oil products provide a much larger share of export revenue, more than half of the total.

22. Some of the structural changes in the European market have the potential to enhance Russia's influence: prices set by gas-to-gas competition have benefits in terms of efficiency and transparency, but they also open up the possibility of Russian strategic behaviour on pricing (an option that is not open with oil-indexed deliveries).

the overall outlook in terms of diversity of supply is relatively reassuring, in part through the possibility of new pipeline links across Eurasia, but more pertinently from the array of potential LNG suppliers from different regions.

Figure 4.14 ▷ Gas imports by source to selected Asian markets in the New Policies Scenario

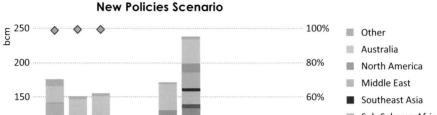

China becomes the cornerstone of Asian gas markets, not only because of the volume of its consumption but also due to the diversity of its pipeline and LNG supply, as well as its potential for sizeable domestic production. The gas agreement reached with Russia in 2014 (Box 4.5) confirmed that China appears to have a range of import options around the $10-13/MBtu range. This opens up the possibility – if regulation and physical infrastructure are in place – for domestic gas trading and transparent wholesale pricing, with the potential to set a new gas pricing benchmark for the broader region. With the rise of China and other emerging gas importers, the nature of Asia-Pacific import demand also has the potential to change over time, becoming more market and price-responsive than at present (assuming that contracting and pricing structures for LNG become less rigid). China's large stock of coal-fired power plants gives it greater scope, compared with Japan or Korea, to switch away from gas, and it also has an expanding upstream sector of its own. This makes it more probable that signals from a more integrated global gas market would elicit some kind of market response, whether on the demand side or on the supply side.

Grounds for confidence in the adequacy and reliability of future gas supply do come with some important qualifications. The various infrastructure and regulatory barriers that hinder the efficient allocation of gas supplies across regions will not disappear overnight. And, even if existing traded volumes can be re-directed efficiently in response to short-term market signals, the extent and speed with which prices would then drive a broader adjustment in supply and demand in the various regions is open to question. On the supply side, the high cost of putting gas infrastructure in place means that there are few commercial incentives to build slack into the system. Under-utilised liquefaction facilities and pipelines increase the resilience of a gas supply system and bring benefits in terms of security of supply, but they are anathema to investors (which is precisely why such infrastructure tends to be built only with long-term contractual guarantees underpinning its use). So the expectation that a significant shortfall in a gas-importing region can quickly or economically be compensated for by calling upon additional international supply may be misplaced.[23] On the demand side, it cannot be taken for granted that fuel switching capability away from gas will increase over time; the opposite may well be the case in some markets, notably in the OECD, as coal plants (the main source of substitution capability today) are decommissioned.

Box 4.5 ▷ What are the implications of the Russia-China gas agreement?

China and Russia have been negotiating a gas pipeline deal for more than ten years and an agreement, including the long-standing missing link on price, was finally reached in May 2014.[24] It envisages that, once upstream and transportation infrastructure is in place, pipeline deliveries will start towards the end of the current decade and rise to 38 bcm/year by the mid-2020s. The project is a hugely expensive undertaking, with estimated capital costs in excess of $70 billion. The main sources of gas supply are anticipated to be the Chayanda and Kovytka fields, both situated in very remote parts of eastern Siberia. The new "Power of Siberia" pipeline to China would run along the ESPO oil pipeline for part of its 4 000 km route; It nonetheless traverses some very challenging terrain. Price provisions have not been reported, but are believed to be for a delivered price of around $10/MBtu at the Chinese border.

The Russia-China gas agreement adds to the competition facing exporters to the Asia-Pacific market, affecting the prospects and timing of some of the more marginal gas export projects looking to supply the same market in the early to mid-2020s (and, potentially, beyond if a mooted follow-on deal is concluded for additional volumes; we project that pipeline supply from Russia to China expands to reach 55 bcm by 2040). Some European commentary has viewed this development as a zero-sum game, in which gas exported to Asia is not available to Europe: this is misleading. The opening of this new conduit for gas trade is encouraging not just for China but also for other gas-importing countries. The huge distances involved mean that there is no possibility of eastern Siberian gas being developed with the European market in mind: it will either be developed for Asia or remain in the ground. There is some competition for investment capital within Russia, particularly while US and EU sanctions remain in place. But Russia has, for the moment, ample production capacity to serve its westward export routes. And in a world where markets are increasingly inter-linked, any investment in gas supply – wherever it takes place, and particularly if the gas ends up on internationally traded markets – should be welcome news for importing countries.

---

23. In practice, one of the very few current global supply routes with significant current redundancy in both gas production and transport capacity is that from Russia to Europe.

24. Alongside the pipeline deal, CNPC and Novatek signed a 4.1 bcm per year 20-year contract for LNG supply.

Nonetheless, the greater diversity and flexibility of gas trade flows, particularly of LNG, do represent important gains for gas security in this evolving landscape. There are reasons to believe that key gas-consuming markets will become generally more sensitive to shifts in regional prices (that, in turn, are increasingly likely to be driven by the dynamics of gas-to-gas competition rather than the price of oil). On the supply side, there is likewise a picture of greater choice; not so much from the expansion of pipelines, which are by their nature inflexible, but rather from a diverse range of LNG suppliers increasingly looking for opportunities for arbitrage, rather than relying solely on fixed-term relationships with a defined group of customers. There will be bumps along the road, but a more diverse, flexible and more integrated system of international gas trade is set to provide a more reliable mechanism for the world to respond to shortfalls or disruptions to supply.

Chapter 5

Coal market outlook
India the leaping tiger, China a pausing dragon?

Highlights

- In the decade to 2013, coal demand grew by over 50%, meeting almost half of the increase in the world's total primary energy needs. China was the principal source of the surge in coal demand; OECD coal demand dropped by 8%. Today, coal demand is approaching that of oil, while back in 2003 demand for oil was 45% higher. In the New Policies Scenario, at 24% of the global energy mix in 2040, coal remains just ahead of natural gas and behind oil. Renewables (including hydro) overtake coal around 2035 as the leading source of electricity generation: coal's share shrinks from 41% today to 31%.

- Global coal demand in the New Policies Scenario grows on average by 0.5% per year between 2012 and 2040. This compares with growth of 2.5% per year over the past 30 years. Almost two-thirds of the projected increase in world coal demand occurs in the next ten years. Coal demand to 2040 is projected to decline in all major OECD regions, including the United States, where coal use for power plunges by more than a third between 2012 and 2040. China's coal demand growth also slows sharply, peaking around 2030. India, where demand continues to rise briskly, overtakes the United States as the world's second-biggest coal consumer before 2020.

- In absolute terms, global coal trade grows by 40% to 2040; from 18% today to 23% of global coal demand, driven by strong Asian demand. China surpassed the EU as the world's largest net coal importer in 2012 and it maintains this status over the current decade. By 2025, when imports level off, China is overtaken by India, where imports triple to 430 Mtce by 2040. Australia and Indonesia account for 70% of the global increase in coal trade.

- China, India, Indonesia and Australia alone account for over 70% of global coal output by 2040, underscoring Asia's importance in global coal trade and pricing. Coal prices have fallen by one-third from their 2008-2010 peaks, dropping to $86/tonne in 2013. Low coal prices, caused by overcapacity, have put pressure on coal mine owners worldwide to cut costs and close high-cost capacity. Coal prices in real terms are projected to recover to over $100/tonne in 2020, but will still be lower than international gas prices, on an energy-equivalent basis, especially in the key Asian power sector. Prices increase further to over $110/tonne in 2040 as trade increases and supply becomes more costly.

- In the absence of rapid and widespread adoption of high-efficiency coal-fired generation technologies and, in the longer term, of CCS, the increased use of coal will be incompatible with climate goals. Since deployment of CCS remains slow, in part due to high costs, continued policy support is needed. New high-efficiency coal-fired plants, with scope for later CCS retrofit, can form part of a shrewd asset management strategy.

Overview

Coal's share in the global primary fuel mix has increased by five percentage points over the past decade to reach 29% in 2013, reinforcing its role as the second most important fuel behind oil.[1] Today, coal demand is approaching that of oil, while back in 2003 the difference was 45%. China's economic and industrial development has been the driving force behind this surge in global coal use (Box 5.2). In contrast, coal demand in the OECD has been falling: in 2013, it was 8% lower than in 2003 as a result of several factors, including the global financial crisis, the surge of unconventional gas production in the United States and energy policies promoting energy efficiency and the decarbonisation of the power sector.

As the most carbon-intensive fossil fuel, coal is the leading source of carbon-dioxide (CO_2) emissions, as well as a major contributor to local air pollution. These problems are aggravated where coal is consumed in inefficient power plants and industrial plants that lack pollution control systems. But coal has positive attributes that translate to important advantages for industrial competitiveness and affordability: it is an abundant, low-cost and secure energy resource. The interplay of market signals, energy and climate policies, and the development and deployment of low-carbon technology will determine the future role of coal in the global energy system. Energy-related developments in non-OECD countries will weigh most heavily on the outlook for coal, as these countries already account for three-quarters of global demand.

In the New Policies Scenario, the central scenario in this *World Energy Outlook* (*WEO*), global primary coal demand grows on average by 0.5% per year between 2012 and 2040, reaching over 6 350 million tonnes of coal equivalent (Mtce).[2] This growth rate compares with average annual growth of 2.5% over the past 30 years. The significantly slower pace of growth in demand reflects the impact of government measures already adopted or announced to improve energy efficiency, support low-carbon fuels and, in some cases, put a price on CO_2 emissions (see Chapter 1).[3] Almost two-thirds of the projected increase in coal demand occurs in the next ten years, with the pace of growth slowing thereafter, in large part because Chinese coal demand peaks by around 2030. China, together with other developing Asian economies, accounts for nearly all the growth in coal demand in non-OECD countries, while coal demand in the OECD is more than one-third lower by 2040, as decarbonisation policies in the United States, Europe, Korea and Japan take effect. At 24% of the global energy mix in 2040, coal remains just ahead of natural gas and behind oil (Figure 5.1). Renewables including hydro, overtake coal around 2035 as the leading source

---

1. For 2013, preliminary data for aggregate coal demand, production and trade by country are available; while the sectoral breakdown for coal demand is estimated (complete data are available to 2012).

2. A tonne of coal equivalent equals 7 million kilocalories (kcal) or 0.7 tonnes of oil equivalent.

3. Despite these policy measures, global energy-related CO_2 emissions still rise in the New Policies Scenario by 20% to 2040, leaving the world on a trajectory consistent with a long-term average temperature increase of 3.6 °C (see Chapter 2).

of electricity generation worldwide, with coal's share of that market shrinking from 41% in 2012 to 31% by 2040 (although coal-fired power still grows by a third in absolute terms). Global coal trade grows by 40% over the period 2012-2040 – a bigger increase than the 15% increase in coal demand, as many Asian countries require higher imports to cover mounting domestic demand (Table 5.1). By 2040, 40% of global coking coal production and 21% of steam coal production is traded internationally, compared with 30% and 17% respectively in 2012.

Figure 5.1 ▷ **Share of world energy demand and electricity generation by fuel and scenario**

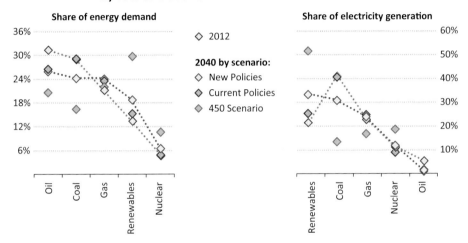

The outlook for coal is very different in the other two scenarios. In the Current Policies Scenario, which measures where we are going if governments implement no additional policies beyond those already formally enacted as of mid-2014, world coal demand grows on average at 1.5% per year over 2012-2040, three times faster than in the New Policies Scenario, with coal overtaking oil as the world's leading fuel by around 2025. With a share of 40%, a level similar to today, coal remains the leading source of global electricity generation in 2040. Virtually all of the growth in coal demand is in non-OECD countries, coal use in the OECD remaining essentially flat over the projection period. Relative to growth in demand for coking coal in the New Policies Scenario, the increase in steam coal demand by 2040 in the Current Policies Scenario is stronger, since fuel switching and substitution is more readily available in the power generation sector compared with the iron and steel industry. Inter-regional coal trade nearly doubles to over 1 850 Mtce by 2040, representing 22% of global coal production.

The outlook for coal use is weak in the 450 Scenario, which assumes that policies are adopted to set the energy system on track to have a 50% chance of keeping the long-term increase in average global temperature to 2 °C. Global coal demand is one-third lower in 2040 relative to 2012, returning to the level of use in the early 2000s. Demand peaks in the current decade and then falls rapidly. 45% of the reduction relative to today's level occurs in

OECD countries. The share of coal in the global fuel mix and in electricity generation declines by 12 and 27 percentage points respectively over the projection period, reaching 17% and 13% by 2040. Demand for, and trade in, steam coal, 70% of which is consumed in the power sector today, is the coal type most affected by policies to promote decarbonisation of the energy system (see Annex B). Global steam coal trade effectively halves by 2040, while coking coal trade sees only an 8% decline, relative to 2012 levels, since there are fewer alternatives to this type of coal in industrial applications.

Table 5.1 ▷ **Coal demand, production and trade by scenario** (Mtce)

				New Policies		Current Policies		450 Scenario	
		1990	2012	2020	2040	2020	2040	2020	2040
OECD	Demand	1 543	1 457	1 378	931	1 475	1 486	1 224	608
	Production	1 533	1 361	1 344	1 172	1 458	1 697	1 195	696
Non-OECD	Demand	1 643	4 084	4 637	5 424	4 892	6 885	4 376	3 092
	Production	1 661	4 306	4 671	5 182	4 909	6 674	4 405	3 004
World	Demand	3 186	5 541	6 015	6 354	6 367	8 371	5 600	3 700
	Steam coal	2 244	4 347	4 757	5 280	5 076	7 098	4 413	2 907
	Coking coal	542	885	950	850	979	965	924	705
	Lignite	400	309	309	225	312	308	263	88
	Production	3 194	5 667	6 015	6 354	6 367	8 371	5 600	3 700
	Inter-regional trade*	309	1 022	1 187	1 432	1 279	1 856	1 062	594
	Steam coal	162	759	899	1 101	966	1 472	792	354
	Coking coal	186	268	296	336	321	390	279	247

* Total net exports for all *WEO* regions, not including trade within regions. Notes: Historical data for world demand differ from world production due to stock changes. Lignite also includes peat.

The extent to which carbon capture and storage (CCS) technology is deployed varies enormously across the three scenarios. In the Current Policies Scenario, CCS makes only limited in-roads by 2040, with nearly 40 gigawatts (GW) of coal-fired power generation capacity equipped with CCS, as the supportive government policies needed to drive its deployment are notably absent. In the New Policies Scenario, about 70 GW of coal-fired power generation – accounting for about 3% of total coal-fired power – is equipped with CCS by the end of the projection period. China and the United States, which have a lot of coal-fired plants and good access to CO_2 storage, account for over 60% of these installations. Unsurprisingly, it is in the 450 Scenario that CCS plays the largest role in reducing emissions from coal-fired generation. In this scenario, around 80 GW of CCS equipped coal and gas capacity is projected to be operating by 2025, with a massive expansion then occurring between 2030 and 2040. By 2040, globally, 580 GW of coal-fired power generation is equipped with the technology – 40% of total coal-fired capacity, and this accounts for 80% of coal-fired electricity generation (compared with just 4% in the New Policies Scenario). In addition, 22% of gas-fired generation comes from plants fitted with CCS.

The current rate of CCS demonstration and deployment needs to be stepped up sharply if these projections are to be realised. At the same time, understanding of the role for CCS in achieving climate goals – and the implications of its absence – is increasing. As an illustration of the importance of CCS, in the 450 scenario, if CCS were not to be available and the emission savings that are attributed to CCS had to be met by increased wind power, wind generation would need to increase twenty-fold between 2012 and 2040, compared with ten-fold if CCS were available.

To achieve high rates of CCS deployment in the power sector, more than 60% of power plants would need to be retrofitted. Given the large energy losses involved in using CCS, higher efficiency plants are likely to be retrofitted in preference to lower efficiency plants (Box 5.1). This is another reason for building only coal plants of the highest possible efficiency in the next decade or two (notably in non-OECD countries, where most new builds are to be found). To do so will be to keep open the option of CCS retrofits later in the projection period if the evidence justifying this becomes compelling (Spotlight). It also highlights the importance of careful design of fossil-fuelled plants to facilitate the future use of CCS and of taking this consideration into account in decisions on plant siting. Providing today for possible later installation of CCS is an important asset management strategy, not just for the coal mining sector, but also for those using coal-fired equipment, notably power generators.

Box 5.1 ▷ **First steps in using CCS technology with coal**

CO_2 emissions from coal-fired power plants can be reduced through the use of a group of technologies known as carbon capture and storage. The first step in CCS is the capture of CO_2, which can be achieved by separating out the gas from the fuel or flue gas or by altering the operation of the boiler so that combustion takes place in pure oxygen rather than air. The captured CO_2 must then be transported to a suitable storage site, where it is injected and the site monitored to ensure that the gas does not escape into the atmosphere. While pipeline transport of CO_2 (and similar fluids) is already widely practised, particularly in the United States, identification and development of storage sites can be costly and time consuming. Installation of CO_2 capture technologies is expected to increase the capital cost of a coal-fired power plant by around 45% for pre-combustion capture from an integrated gasification combined-cycle (IGCC) plant and 75% for post- and oxy-combustion capture from a conventional pulverised coal plant. In addition to increasing the capital cost, capture systems need heat to regenerate solvents and electricity for operation of pumps and compressors. These additional energy use requirements are expected to reduce the efficiency of the plant by 15-20%, and may also result in increased water consumption. Costs for CO_2 storage depend on the geology of the storage site and, thus, are highly variable: they are expected to be in the order of a few dollars per tonne of CO_2. The net result is an increase in the levelised cost of electricity[4] of 40-75%. The costs of building and operating the handful of demonstration plants that have so far been built have been relatively high, but costs are expected to fall through learning-by-doing and technological innovation. Even with these reductions, the effect of CCS on the cost of the ultimate product is clearly a formidable barrier to its widespread adoption.

The first commercial-scale coal-fired power plant with CO_2 capture was commissioned in October 2014 in Saskatchewan in Canada. The Saskpower Boundary Dam project involves the addition of post-combustion capture to an existing pulverised coal unit generating 110 megawatts (MW). The captured CO_2 is to be sold to the operator of nearby oilfields to be used for enhanced oil recovery (EOR), a technique that involves injecting the gas to increase pressure in an oilfield, raising oil output while utilising and storing the gas. The total capital cost of the project is approximately $1.3 billion, of which about two-thirds can be attributed to the capture and storage system and the remainder to refurbishment of the 45 year-old unit. A second plant is expected to begin operation in the state of Mississippi in the United States in early-2015. The Mississippi Power Kemper County Plant is a new 582 MW IGCC unit. This plant will demonstrate a new gasification technology developed specifically for low-grade coal, with pre-combustion capture of 65% of the produced CO_2. The developers envisage that emissions will be comparable to those from an equivalent gas-fired combined-cycle gas turbine (CCGT) plant. As with the Boundary Dam plant, the captured CO_2 will be sold for use in EOR. The estimated capital cost of the plant has nearly doubled since the start of construction, reaching $4.7 billion; it is due to be commissioned in early-2015. The successful operation of these two CCS-equipped power plants will be an important step in building confidence in the use of CCS for power generation (and in industry) and accelerating CCS deployment. These projects are generating important lessons that are expected to allow future plants to be developed at lower, albeit still substantial, cost.

Demand

Regional trends

In the New Policies Scenario, OECD coal demand is projected to fall substantially, pushing down the OECD's share in the global coal market from around one-quarter in 2012 to less than 15% by 2040 (Table 5.2). More than four-fifths of the decline occurs after 2020 as use of renewables, nuclear and natural gas for power expands, resulting in a 40% drop in the use of coal in the OECD power generation fuel mix (a sector that today accounts for four-fifths of OECD coal demand). By 2040 only 16% of OECD electricity generation comes from coal, compared with almost a third today. The United States remains the largest coal user in the OECD, despite a post 2020 decline in demand resulting from the assumed

---

4. The levelised cost of electricity represents the average cost of producing electricity from a given technology, including all fixed and variable costs, expressed in terms of the present value equivalent.

imposition of standards requiring limits on CO_2 emission from both new and existing coal-fired power plants (see Chapter 2). Within the OECD, Europe sees the largest absolute drop in coal use, with demand nearly halving over the projection period in response to policy measures related to renewables, energy efficiency and CO_2 emissions. Korea and Japan also see a significant decline in coal use by 2040, in response to policy support for renewables and nuclear power aimed at improving their energy security and meeting climate goals.

Table 5.2 ▷ **Coal demand by region in the New Policies Scenario** (Mtce)

	1990	2012	2020	2025	2030	2035	2040	2012-2040 Delta	2012-2040 CAAGR*
OECD	1 543	1 457	1 378	1 264	1 105	992	931	- 526	-1.6%
Americas	701	656	647	588	505	468	450	- 206	-1.3%
United States	658	607	591	534	458	427	411	- 196	-1.4%
Europe	645	462	404	362	306	253	234	- 228	-2.4%
Asia Oceania	198	340	327	314	294	271	247	- 93	-1.1%
Japan	109	160	153	147	142	130	120	- 41	-1.0%
Non-OECD	1 643	4 084	4 637	4 869	5 098	5 283	5 424	1 340	1.0%
E. Europe/Eurasia	525	355	332	336	341	346	345	- 10	-0.1%
Russia	273	191	167	169	171	168	162	- 28	-0.6%
Asia	991	3 543	4 090	4 293	4 494	4 651	4 767	1 224	1.1%
China	762	2 824	3 134	3 174	3 191	3 149	3 033	209	0.3%
India	148	506	647	748	863	975	1 092	586	2.8%
Southeast Asia	18	127	210	258	310	381	474	347	4.8%
Middle East	1	4	6	6	7	7	7	3	1.8%
Africa	106	150	167	184	197	214	235	84	1.6%
South Africa	95	139	142	146	146	145	145	6	0.2%
Latin America	21	31	43	51	59	65	70	39	2.9%
Brazil	14	22	30	33	36	40	42	20	2.4%
World	3 186	5 541	6 015	6 133	6 203	6 275	6 354	813	0.5%
European Union	651	420	356	312	257	206	187	- 233	-2.9%

* Compound average annual growth rate.

Non-OECD coal use grows by one-third to 2040, as a result of robust economic and electricity demand growth in Asian economies; but the relative importance of the leading consuming countries changes markedly over the course of the projection period. China remains the leading source of coal demand growth in the current decade, but growth slows sharply thereafter, as policy action to limit the share of coal in the domestic energy mix takes effect. China's coal demand peaks by around 2030, at which stage India becomes the largest source of incremental non-OECD coal demand through to the end of the projection period. India becomes the world's second-largest consumer of coal during the current decade, overtaking the United States.

In the Southeast Asian countries, taken as a whole, coal demand almost quadruples by 2040, to overtake the United States. Indonesia, today the world's largest steam coal exporter, emerges as a key demand centre: its coal use reaches that of the European Union by 2040. In addition to Indonesia, coal is the fuel of choice in the expansion of the power sectors of Vietnam, Thailand and Malaysia. Coal demand also expands in Eastern Europe/Eurasia countries (except Russia), Latin America and Africa. South Africa, which today accounts for over 90% of Africa's coal demand, sees its share decline to 62% by 2040, as installed coal-fired power capacity in sub-Saharan Africa grows (see Chapter 14). Brazil is the largest Latin American coal user, but although its coal use nearly doubles, coal continues to have only a small share of demand, at 6%, in 2040.

Box 5.2 ▷ Coal demand in the roaring 2000s

In the decade to 2013, coal demand grew by over 50%, meeting almost half of the increase in the world's total primary energy needs (Figure 5.2). China was the principal source of this surge in coal demand, together with India and other emerging Asian economies. OECD coal demand dropped by 8%. Today, China accounts for over half of global coal demand (compared with 34% in 2003), while non-OECD Asia as a whole accounts for two-thirds (up from 45%).

Figure 5.2 ▷ Annual change in coal demand by key region

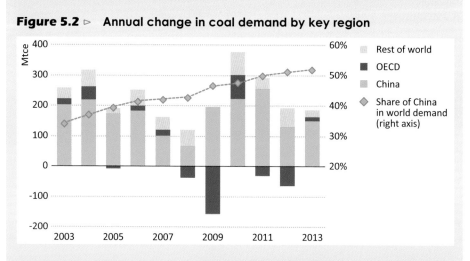

Just over half of the increase in coal demand over 2003-2013 came from the power sector, with the remainder coming mainly from industry, especially steel and cement production. China again was dominant, as its crude steel production more than tripled, and its cement production and coal-fired generation nearly tripled. However, Chinese economic growth is slowing and the economy is rebalancing towards less energy-intensive industries, leading to a slowdown in coal demand. Over the period 2007-2013, Chinese coal demand grew on average by 7.2% per year, compared with 11.6% over 2001-2007. In 2013 and 2012, demand grew at the comparatively leisurely rate of around 5% per year. There is little doubt that the growth in Chinese coal demand will continue to taper off in the coming decades, though China will continue to play a leading role in coal markets over the projection period.

Sectoral trends

The power sector, which today accounts for more than 60% of global coal demand, is projected to remain the leading sector, both in terms of its share of the coal market and of incremental demand, in the New Policies Scenario. As in the past decade, coal use in the OECD power sector declines over the projection period; the decline accelerating as electricity end-use efficiency improves and ageing coal-fired plants are replaced (to a large degree by natural gas and low-carbon sources). China remains the principal non-OECD user of coal for power generation to 2030, with India and Southeast Asian countries gaining in importance over the projection period.

The rise in industrial coal consumption (including its use in blast furnaces and coke ovens, as a petrochemical feedstock and in other conversion processes) slows, and flattens out after 2030, largely due to China's industrial demand peaking around 2020 (Figure 5.3). The decline in industrial coal use in China after 2020 results from improved efficiency, fuel substitution and a shift towards less energy-intensive industrial activity. This is observed, in part, in a projected decrease in Chinese crude steel and cement production after 2020, although output of these commodities still remains high with, for example, steel output above 600 million tonnes (Mt) in 2040. Increased use of coal in China as a feedstock for the petrochemicals industry and in coal-to-gas and coal-to-liquids plants largely offsets the declining trend observed in heavy industry subsectors. Elsewhere in the world, growth in industrial coal use is limited by efficiency gains and switching to electricity and natural gas.

Figure 5.3 ▷ **Incremental coal demand by key sector, region and decade in the New Policies Scenario**

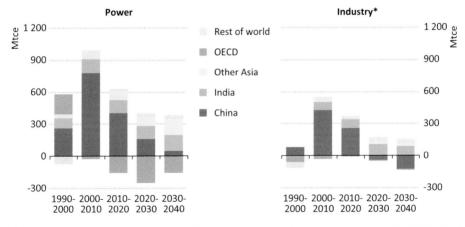

* Industry coal use also includes own-use and transformation in blast furnaces and coke ovens, petrochemical feedstocks, coal-to-liquids and coal-to-gas plants.

The importance of efficiency in coal-fired power plants

Improved efficiency in power generation, the main coal-consuming sector, is a key and readily available way of reducing coal's environmental impact. The thermal efficiency of both existing coal-fired power plants and those being commercialised today, i.e. the share of the energy content of the coal inputs that is converted to electrical energy, varies considerably. The most efficient new German and Japanese plants, using technology termed ultra-supercritical, can operate with efficiencies as high as 45%, emitting some 25% less CO_2 per megawatt-hour (MWh) than a plant operating at average worldwide efficiency. In other words, these plants can produce one-third more power with the same amount of coal. If all coal-fired plants globally achieved ultra-supercritical efficiency levels (43-47%) by the end of the projection period, coal-fired CO_2 emissions in 2040 would be 17% lower than in the New Policies Scenario. CO_2 emissions would be reduced by almost 0.8 gigatonnes (Gt) per year on average or cumulatively by 17 Gt over the projection period.

Where a decision to add coal-fired capacity is being taken, investors do not always opt for the most efficient plant, even though more efficient plant technologies often have lower lifetime costs. This is especially the case where capital is constrained, because more efficient plants are generally more expensive to build. Despite the lower operating efficiency, it can be more attractive to build a less efficient plant where there is no carbon price (nor likely to be one soon) or where coal is cheap (as is the case with lignite). Around half of the coal-fired stations being built today around the world use less efficient subcritical technology.

There are big differences in the attractiveness of investing in more efficient plants across the regions where coal-fired capacity is expanding at a fast pace. In China, where coal-fired capacity has expanded substantially in the last 15 years or so, coal-fired capacity is projected to further increase by around 420 GW by 2040, although the pace of expansion slows sharply in the last decade of the projection period. Around one-third of the new plant capacity being brought online at present in China is subcritical. But this share has been falling, as more supercritical and ultra-supercritical plants are being built. China's policy of retiring old inefficient units saw some 80 GW of capacity retired between 2005 and 2010, helping to boost the average efficiency of the country's coal-fired plants by more than 3.5 percentage points over that period. These two factors resulted in savings of 140 Mtce per year of coal by 2012, compared to what would have been consumed had average efficiency stayed at the level of 2005 and old plants remained online (roughly equal to the total annual coal consumption of Germany and Italy combined). More efficiency gains are on their way: by 2020, annual savings are projected to amount to around 250 Mtce per year, equivalent to about half of Indian coal use in 2012.

In India, most new plants being built today are still subcritical, despite their first supercritical plant having come online a few years ago. As part of a programme to increase energy efficiency, supercritical technology is to be made mandatory for all plants starting construction after 2017 (IEA, 2012). In Southeast Asian countries, where coal is set to remain the leading fuel for new power stations, subcritical technology continues to be widely deployed in our New Policies Scenario as the fleet expands over the projection period.

The gains from higher energy efficiency potential available over the lifetime of plant place an onus of responsibility on decision-makers not to be seduced by lower initial capital cost solutions which bring higher total lifetime costs. This policy option is discussed further in *Redrawing the Energy-Climate Map* (IEA, 2013a).

Supply

Reserves and resources

World proven coal reserves (volumes that are known to exist and are thought to be economically and technically exploitable at today's prices) amounted to over 1 000 billion tonnes at the end of 2012 (BGR, 2013).[5] At today's production levels, this coal would last for 135 years. 30% of global coal reserves are located in non-OECD Asia, the main demand centre, while significant reserves are also found in the two leading OECD producers, the United States and Australia. Coal resources are 20 times larger than reserves; many of these resources could be exploited with relatively modest price increases or technical innovations. Subject to the evolution of global coal demand, supply costs for newly developed coal mines are expected to increase modestly in real terms, due to rising input costs, higher labour costs and the infrastructure costs related to the development of coal resources in remote or undeveloped areas.

Production

In the New Policies Scenario, 90% of world coal production during the projection period comes from just eight countries (Figure 5.4). China, India, Indonesia and Australia alone account for about 70% of global coal output by 2040. Consequently, developments in Asian markets will be of increasing importance for global coal trade and pricing. World coal production increases by around 700 Mtce over the period 2012-2040, a volume similar to the total production of the United States in 2012. In line with demand trends, the bulk of incremental world coal supply comes from non-OECD countries. The increase is concentrated in the period to 2025.

In line with the historical pace of decline between 1990 and 2012, OECD coal production continues to fall at an average annual rate of 0.5% per year between 2012 and 2040 (Table 5.3). The United States, which today accounts for over half of total OECD coal

---

5. Classifications of coal types (coking, steam and lignite) can differ between BGR and IEA due to statistical allocation methodologies.

output, sees the largest decrease in production by 2040 in absolute terms. This fall is mostly a reaction by US producers to dwindling domestic coal demand, in the face of strict environmental standards for coal-fired power plants and competition from low-carbon generation and unconventional gas. But a decline in opportunities for coal exports also contributes to lower output, as high-cost mines in the eastern United States find it difficult to compete in a saturated Atlantic coal market, with coal use in Europe projected to nearly halve by 2040. With the projected slump in coal demand and high costs of production, European coal output declines twice as fast as the decline in the United States, with production falling over the *Outlook* period to barely 40% of current levels. Australia, the world's second-largest coal exporter today, becomes the largest OECD coal producer by 2035, with continued strong growth in exports.

Figure 5.4 ▷ **Share of world coal production by key country in the New Policies Scenario**

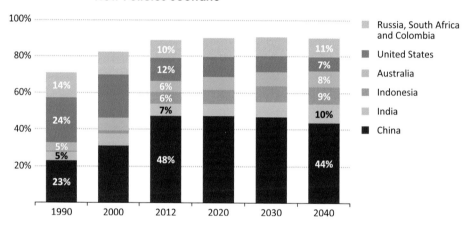

Non-OECD coal production increases by almost 900 Mtce, or 20%, over the projection period, with India and Indonesia together accounting for 60% of the growth. With a near doubling of coal production, both India and Indonesia overtake the United States around 2030, to become the world's second- and third-largest coal producers. Despite the increase in India's coal production, imports more than triple to satisfy strong domestic demand. Indonesian coal exports grow to 2040, but 60% of the projected rise in production goes to satisfy rampant domestic demand. China sees the third-largest production increase among non-OECD countries, with most of the increase coming before 2020 and production peaking around 2030, in line with domestic demand. Nonetheless, China remains by far the world's largest coal producer in 2040 and requires imports to meet only 8% of its domestic demand. Colombia, South Africa, Mozambique and Mongolia also increase production, in large part to serve export markets, while Russian output remains fairly flat over the projection period, as an increase in exports is offset by a decline in domestic demand.

Table 5.3 ▷ **Coal production by region in the New Policies Scenario** (Mtce)

	1990	2012	2020	2025	2030	2035	2040	2012-2040 Delta	2012-2040 CAAGR*
OECD	1 533	1 361	1 344	1 278	1 201	1 168	1 172	- 188	-0.5%
Americas	836	767	732	663	584	539	526	- 240	-1.3%
United States	775	708	671	600	525	484	472	- 236	-1.4%
Europe	526	246	194	155	131	115	103	- 143	-3.1%
Asia Oceania	171	348	418	459	486	515	543	195	1.6%
Australia	152	343	413	454	481	510	539	196	1.6%
Non-OECD	1 661	4 306	4 671	4 856	5 002	5 107	5 182	876	0.7%
E. Europe/Eurasia	533	461	463	468	470	470	471	10	0.1%
Russia	275	287	287	290	290	290	289	2	0.0%
Asia	952	3 538	3 850	4 000	4 115	4 187	4 225	687	0.6%
China	741	2 695	2 853	2 911	2 925	2 884	2 779	84	0.1%
India	150	372	417	452	510	575	664	292	2.1%
Indonesia	8	365	454	498	529	563	600	235	1.8%
Middle East	1	1	1	1	1	1	1	0	0.9%
Africa	150	218	241	262	280	301	326	108	1.4%
South Africa	143	209	222	230	234	238	241	33	0.5%
Latin America	25	88	115	125	135	148	159	71	2.1%
Colombia	20	83	108	117	126	136	145	63	2.0%
World	3 194	5 667	6 015	6 133	6 203	6 275	6 354	688	0.4%
European Union	528	239	177	136	110	95	85	- 154	-3.6%

* Compound average annual growth rate.

Note: Historical data and the world CAAGR differ from world demand in Table 5.2 due to stock changes.

Trade

Coal net trade between *WEO* regions in the New Policies Scenario increases by 40%, to reach 1 430 Mtce by 2040 (Table 5.4). Steam coal accounts for more than four-fifths of the increase in trade, due to strong growth in demand from coal-fired power plants in Asia. By 2040, 21% of global steam coal production is traded inter-regionally, compared with 17% in 2012. Steam coal trade is sensitive to power sector developments globally, for example the impact on steam coal trade of a low nuclear case is discussed in Chapter 12. The growth in coking coal trade is more subdued, since global crude steel output reaches a plateau after 2025. Still, the share of global coking coal production that is traded increases from around 30% today to 40% by 2040, reflecting the fact that many demand centres are insufficiently endowed with this fundamental input in iron and steel production. Soon after 2020, the OECD as a whole becomes a coal net exporter, as buoyant volumes of coal are exported from Australia and, to a lesser extent from North America, exceeding imports into Europe, Japan and Korea.

Table 5.4 ▷ **Inter-regional coal trade in the New Policies Scenario**

	2012		2020		2040		2012-2040
	Trade (Mtce)	Share of demand*	Trade (Mtce)	Share of demand*	Trade (Mtce)	Share of demand*	Delta (Mtce)
OECD	- 97	7%	- 34	2%	242	21%	339
Americas	104	14%	85	12%	77	15%	- 27
United States	97	14%	79	12%	61	13%	- 36
Europe	- 213	46%	- 210	52%	- 132	56%	- 81
Asia Oceania	11	3%	91	22%	296	55%	285
Australia	278	81%	346	84%	479	89%	201
Japan	- 160	100%	- 153	100%	- 120	100%	- 41
Non-OECD	134	3%	34	1%	- 242	4%	- 375
E. Europe/Eurasia	99	22%	131	28%	126	27%	27
Russia	96	33%	120	42%	126	44%	30
Asia	- 85	2%	- 240	6%	- 542	11%	457
China	- 218	8%	- 280	9%	- 253	8%	35
India	- 126	25%	- 231	36%	- 429	39%	302
Indonesia	323	88%	379	83%	412	69%	89
Middle East	- 3	77%	- 5	81%	- 6	82%	2
Africa	66	30%	75	31%	92	28%	26
South Africa	70	34%	80	36%	97	40%	27
Latin America	57	66%	72	62%	88	56%	31
Colombia	79	95%	103	95%	138	95%	59
World**	1 022	18%	1 187	20%	1 432	23%	410
European Union	- 178	42%	- 179	50%	- 101	54%	- 76

* Production in net-exporting regions. ** Total net exports for all *WEO* regions, not including intra-regional trade.

Notes: Positive numbers denote net exports and negative numbers denote net imports of coking and steam coal. OECD and non-OECD trade should sum to zero; the difference in 2012 is due to stock changes.

The Pacific market consolidates its leading role in worldwide coal trade, accounting for 80% of the global market by 2040 – up from 65% today. China overtook the European Union as the world's largest net coal importer in 2012 and it maintains this position over the current decade. By 2025, China's imports level off and China is overtaken by India. Even so, at over 250 Mtce in 2040, of which 80% is steam coal, China's imports in 2040 remain above current levels and China remains an important market for exporters, representing 18% of global trade in 2040. India's imports more than triple over 2012-2040 to 430 Mtce, or 30% of global coal trade. Despite registering the largest global increase over that period, Indian coal output fails to keep pace with consistently strong growth in demand, most of which comes from power plants located at the coast in order to use imported coal. By 2040, India's coal import dependency reaches nearly 40% compared with 25% in 2012. Coal imports into other Asian non-OECD countries (including Malaysia, Thailand, Chinese Taipei, Bangladesh and Pakistan) nearly triple collectively by 2040, to over 290 Mtce, a larger figure than projected Chinese imports. On the other hand, imports into Japan and

Korea drop by 30% by 2040, as end-use electricity efficiency improves and the share of low-carbon fuels in the power generation fuel mix rises. Europe's imports also fall heavily over the projection period, despite expensive domestic mines being shut due to competition from international suppliers. The region's import dependency nonetheless continues to rise, more slowly towards the end of the projection period, to 56% by 2040, compared with 46% in 2012.

Among the coal-exporting countries, Australia and Indonesia see the largest increases in absolute terms and remain the leading exporters over the *Outlook* period (Figure 5.5). Before 2030, Australia regains from Indonesia the position as the world's leading coal exporter, in part due to a slowdown in Indonesian exports stemming from robust domestic demand. However, Indonesia remains the world's largest exporter of steam coal, with under 40% of the global trade, while Australia continues to command nearly 60% of global coking coal trade. Colombia, Russia and South Africa also increase exports, while increasing volumes from new suppliers, including Mongolia and Mozambique, help to diversify the global coal market. By 2040, coking coal exports from Mozambique reach 20 Mtce, or 6% of the global market (see Chapter 16). The United States sees a fall in exports, resuming its role as a high-cost swing supplier. Steam coal exports remain fairly flat over the projection period, at around 25 Mtce, while coking coal exports drop. US coking coal exports today come exclusively from the Appalachian Basin, a relatively high cost and mature producing region facing depletion and stiff competition from other exporters over the projection period.

Figure 5.5 ▷ Share of world coal trade by type and key country in the New Policies Scenario

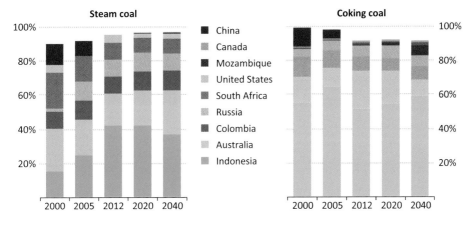

Pricing of internationally traded coal

Although only 18% of global coal consumption is at present traded internationally, the prices prevailing on international markets are a key indicator of the state of coal markets generally, since the international coal market connects the various regional markets through arbitrage opportunities. Indeed, in those coal markets that are well connected to international trade, domestic prices generally fluctuate in line with international prices, while domestic prices in regions that are remote and without access to export or import infrastructure are usually hardly affected by international price movements. Another factor that explains price differences is coal quality. Lignite, for example, has such low energy content per tonne that trade over long distance is uneconomic; as a result, it is usually burned in power plants close to the mines. Coking coal, on the other hand, has a much higher value, due to its steel-making properties and relative scarcity, allowing it to be traded over long distances: for example, Australia exports coking coal to Europe. Since coal has a relatively low value-to-weight ratio, transportation costs between mines, ports and demand centres are relatively high, resulting in big differences in prices across regional markets. A lack of access to export infrastructure or supply bottlenecks can also affect coal prices. Since global coal reserves are abundant and the capital cost of developing mines is relatively low, variable costs are the biggest component of total coal supply costs and, therefore, prices (IEA, 2014). The evolution of demand and capacity investments determines the utilisation rate of the supply chain. With increasing demand, more costly production is needed to balance supply and demand, resulting in increasing prices and vice versa.

Rapidly increasing demand for coal in the Pacific Basin between 2007 and 2011 resulted in sharp price spikes in the international coal market and a hike in seaborne freight rates. This triggered a substantial expansion of mining, infrastructure and shipping capacity, notably in China, Indonesia and Australia. During this period, China switched from being a net exporter to a net importer of coal, with imports reaching nearly 220 Mtce in 2012. Since then, global coal demand growth has slowed, although global and Chinese imports are still rising. Meanwhile, export capacity has continued to expand rapidly across the world as a result of investment decisions taken earlier, when demand was expected to continue to grow strongly. This has resulted in over-capacity and put downward pressure on the prices of internationally traded coal. Indonesian mining companies increased their exports by 20% and Australian companies by 18% between 2011 and 2013; exports from Russia have also grown strongly.

Other factors have contributed to the recent weakening of international prices. In China, consolidation and restructuring of the mining industry has boosted productivity and cut costs, helping to lower domestic prices. In the United States, a mild winter in 2012, together with increasing domestic gas production (see Chapter 4) and, to a lesser extent, coal plant retirements, reduced domestic coal demand by around 80 Mtce between 2011 and 2012. Some of the displaced US coal was offered in the export market (Europe is the natural destination due to geography), driving an increase of US steam coal exports to Europe and a drop in US imports from Colombia. Net US steam coal exports rose from 6 Mtce in 2010 to nearly 40 Mtce in 2012, and these developments have further depressed prices in the Atlantic Basin, which has diverted South African coal to Asia. The average price of imported steam coal across the OECD in 2013, at $86 per tonne, was one-third lower than the peak level reached in 2008. Prices remained weak in 2014.

With China's rapid assumption of the role of the world's largest importer of coal, it has become a key player in global price setting of internationally traded coal (Figure 5.6). Qinhuangdao is a hub for domestic Chinese coal shipments along the coast from the mines in the north to consuming regions further south (Figure 5.11). Those mines, whose costs (including transportation to the customer) are relatively high, set the market price there and determine arbitrage opportunities between domestic and international coal along the coast. Inland, especially near the mines, where transport costs are minimal, coal prices can be much lower than on the coast. In the United States, regional variations in coal prices are even bigger. Coal from the Appalachian fields – today still the main exporting region – while higher quality, also has a higher cost. Prices in the Powder River Basin in the west and in the Illinois Basin in the centre are much lower and despite the comparatively long transport distances, US coal consumers benefit from some of the lowest prices in the world, well below the average in Europe or coastal China.

Figure 5.6 ▷ **Steam coal prices in coastal China, Europe and the United States in the New Policies Scenario**

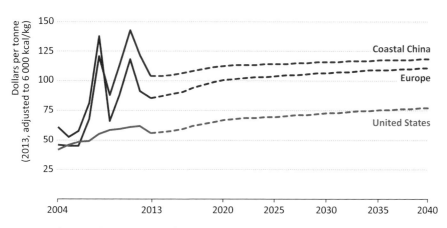

Note: Coastal China and Europe prices are for imports, while US price is an average.

Recent low coal prices have squeezed the margins of coal producers and production at many mines has been stopped or cut back and the workforce reduced over the last two years. Some producers may sell below production cost. In Australia, for example, take-or-pay rail freight contracts incentivise producers to export at prices below total cost, as long as the revenues recover part of the rail tariff. Furthermore, many producers have sought to lower their unit costs by increasing output, thereby increasing supply on the international market. Further shedding of high-cost capacity, industry consolidation and increasing demand are expected to bring supply and demand back into balance over the medium term. In the New Policies Scenario, the OECD steam coal import price increases to over $100/tonne (in year-2013 dollars) by 2020, emphasising the cyclical nature of resource markets. In the long term, the average OECD steam coal import price increases with rising demand, reaching over $110/tonne in 2040. The price evolution is driven mainly by increases in the underlying supply costs and increasing demand (Figure 5.7). In mature mining regions, depletion and a deterioration of mining conditions are expected to increase costs, while, in newly developed mining regions, costs can rise because mines are often located further from the demand centres, driving up transportation costs and the need for additional investment in railway lines and ports. Another factor is higher oil prices: oil products are a key cost component in open-cast mining and coal transportation.

Figure 5.7 ▷ **FOB cash costs and market volume for global seaborne steam coal trade in the New Policies Scenario**

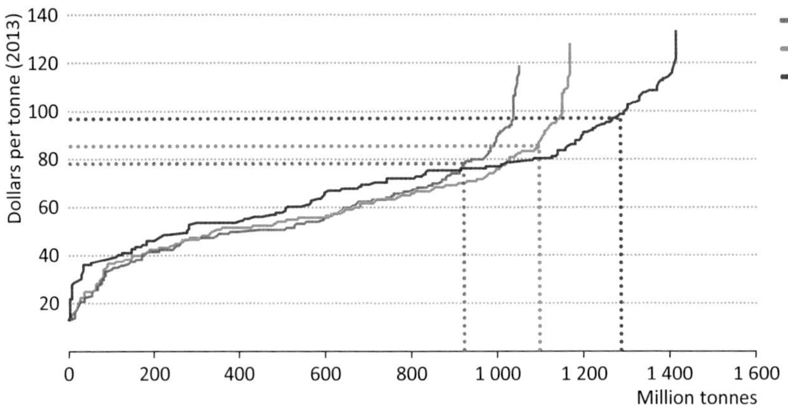

Notes: FOB cash costs includes mining costs, costs of coal washing and preparation, inland transport, mine overhead and port charges. While standard definitions of cash costs often exclude royalties and taxes they are included in this graph. Seaborne shipping costs are excluded. Dotted lines represent seaborne steam coal trade volume and corresponding FOB cash costs. Sources: IEA analysis and Wood Mackenzie databases.

The variable costs of coal exports (often termed free on board [FOB] cash costs) tend to drive international coal prices, as trade volumes vary. Marginal FOB costs in the seaborne market rise from the current upper-$70/tonne range to the upper-$80/tonne range by 2020 and approach $100/tonne level by 2040. The cost curve for internationally traded coal shifts upwards over time, due to cost increases at existing mines. The variable supply costs of new mines are spread across the range of the curve, but large greenfield projects are typically on the low-cost side, since they need a sufficient margin to justify capital investment (and so be approved for development). Older mines typically move up the curve over time as their reserves deplete and mining conditions deteriorate. Seaborne freight costs, which are projected to remain moderate, link the supply cost curves with delivered coal prices. Current differences between prices in the Atlantic Basin (Europe) and coastal China are expected to narrow, but they remain significant throughout the *Outlook* period. Average coal prices in the United States remain relatively low, but they, too, rise due to higher mining costs, longer transport distances and a stronger link between western and international coal prices. There is a modest increase in exports from the Powder River Basin.

Costs and investment

For a given coal price, the variable costs of production and transport determine whether production is economically viable or not. The capital costs of coal supply infrastructure are low, compared with those of conventional oil and gas production. So a margin of a few dollars per tonne is often sufficient for a coal mine to generate an acceptable return on investment. If the price falls below variable costs, a mine must seek to increase productivity. If economic conditions are not expected to improve, closing or idling a mine can avoid variable costs altogether. In the current low-price environment, with coal prices below $75/tonne at all major exporting ports, many coal mining operations are struggling. Coal mines have been closed or mothballed in all high-cost countries. For example, central Appalachia in the United States has seen several mine closures, while some Canadian and Australian operations have also been idled. Higher cost producers in Indonesia are currently also under pressure.

In Australia, mining costs soared during the high-price years of 2007 to 2011. With lower prices since then, Australian producers have had to cut their costs to remain competitive in the international market. Many miners boosted production in order to benefit from economies of scale and the resultant lower unit costs. These efforts, combined with a weakening exchange rate, have borne fruit, with cash costs dropping by almost 20% between 2012 and mid-2014 (Figure 5.8). Indonesia has also managed to cut costs slightly, despite the heavy fuel-price exposure of its truck-and-shovel surface mines – a clear sign that the low-price environment is also affecting low-cost producing countries. As in Australia, Indonesian companies increased output despite falling prices to try to lower unit costs. The Indonesian government is considering an export cap at 400 Mt to counter over-supply in the international market, with the stated aim of stabilising international prices, and to ensure adequate domestic supply. Indonesian authorities have taken steps to constrain illegal coal exports, which are estimated at around 70 Mt in 2013 (equivalent to total South African exports).

Figure 5.8 ▷ **Average FOB cash costs for key steam coal exporters**

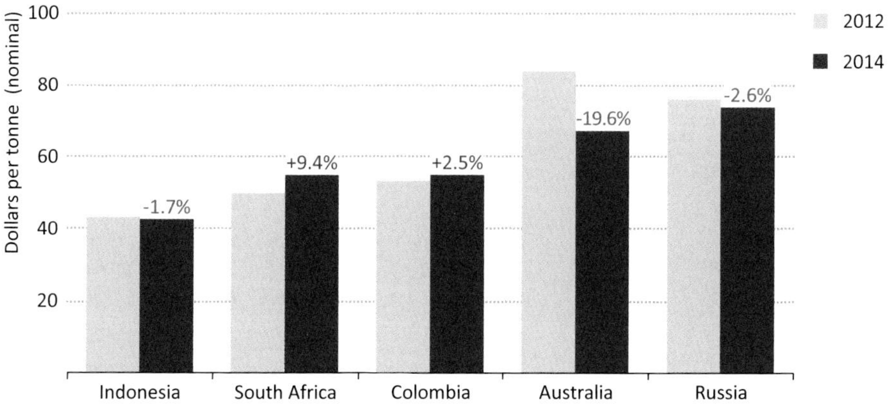

Sources: IEA analysis and Wood Mackenzie databases.

There is less pressure for low-cost producers in Colombia and South Africa to cut costs, since most of their mines are still competitive at current prices. Both countries have experienced fierce industrial action by unions in pursuit of increased wages and better working conditions, resulting in lost output and higher labour costs. Russia has seen a small fall in total costs with lower mining costs and exchange rates that favour exporters; but rail tariffs are a major cost of delivered Russian coal. Due to the huge transport distances, railway tariffs are often the largest cost component for Russian exporters and therefore rising tariffs can have a marked impact on FOB costs. Indeed, transport costs can account for up to half of FOB costs in Russia.[6]

Figure 5.9 ▷ **World coking and steam coal production by type of mine in the New Policies Scenario**

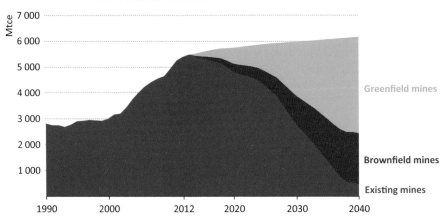

In the New Policies Scenario, cumulative investments of $1.4 trillion (in year-2013 dollars) are needed in the global coal supply chain over the period 2014-2040, a relatively small amount compared with oil and gas investment of $28.5 trillion. Of this, mining is the largest component, accounting for $1 trillion, followed by transport infrastructure ($314 billion) and ports ($54 billion). Almost half of the mining expenditure is needed to sustain production levels of operating mines (including the replacement of ageing equipment), while the rest is for developing new mines. Roughly two-thirds of new mining capacity involves greenfield projects (Figure 5.9). In 2030, slightly more than half of the currently operating coking and steam coal capacity is still in production; this share will drop to under 10% by the end of the *Outlook* period. Brownfield projects, involving the expansion of an existing mine, provide the remaining one-third of new capacity.

---

6. IEA (2013b) provides a detailed analysis of the Russian coal transportation sector.

Regional insights

China

China is the world's largest consumer, producer and importer of coal. Today, more than half of all the coal produced worldwide is consumed in China (Figure 5.10). Chinese economic prosperity has been underpinned mainly by coal, which provides over two-thirds of China's primary energy supply today. The country is set to consume more coal than the rest of the world combined for the next two decades, with China's share in global coal demand dipping below 50% only after 2035 in the New Policies Scenario. Chinese coal demand growth slows before 2025, reaches a plateau by around 2030 and starts to decline slowly after 2035. This trend is driven by a slowdown in economic growth and a rebalancing of the economy away from heavy industry, as well as policies to diversify the fuel mix in the power sector, reduce CO_2 emissions, improve air quality and increase energy efficiency. China has also become the dominant force in coal trade, with one out of five tonnes traded internationally being shipped to the Chinese coast – a trend that continues over the medium term. After 2020, China's share in international trade declines as demand growth slows and other key importers emerge in Asia. As the largest emitter of energy-related greenhouse gases, China and its coal use are pivotal to global efforts to combat climate change.

Figure 5.10 ▷ **Share of China in global coal markets and China's coal import dependence in the New Policies Scenario**

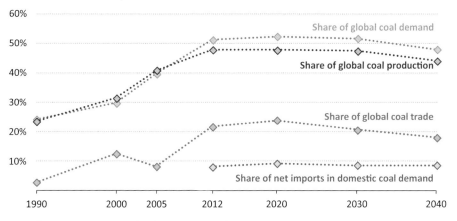

Note: China was a net exporter of coal in 1990, 2000 and 2005.

With GDP growing nearly 10% per year on average over the last two decades, China's coal consumption has grown exceptionally fast (Table 5.5). In the period 2000-2006, coal demand grew by 11% per year on average, slowing to over 7% per year between 2006 and 2012. Preliminary estimates suggest that GDP growth dropped to 7.5% and coal consumption growth to 5.3% in 2013 – still high, but a marked slowdown compared to previous years. In 2011, Chinese authorities adopted the 12th Five-Year Plan, covering the period to 2015, which sets targets for cutting energy and CO_2 intensity. Diversification of the fuel mix away from coal in the power sector is central to meeting these goals: 60 GW of renewable energy capacity was added in 2013, almost half of which was wind and solar photovoltaic (PV). Continued political support for renewables, nuclear energy and gas, combined with measures to reduce air pollution are set to curb growth in coal-fired power generation over the projection period. Hence, the growth rate of coal-fired power drops from over 11% per year in the decade to 2012 to just 0.6% per year between 2030 and 2040; but coal-fired power generation continues to grow right through the projection period, increasing by almost half. Combined with the progressive deployment of more efficient coal-fired technology, coal use in the power sector plateaus after 2030, but still increases by more than a quarter to 2040.

Table 5.5 ▷ **Coal-related indicators for China in the New Policies Scenario**

	Compound average annual growth rate (%)					
	1990-2000	2000-2006	2006-2012	2012-2020	2020-2030	2030-2040
Gross domestic product	9.9	9.9	9.8	6.9	5.3	3.2
Electricity generation	7.9	13.1	9.5	4.6	2.6	1.4
Coal-fired generation	8.7	13.6	8.6	2.2	1.4	0.6
Crude steel production	6.7	22.1	9.5	1.6	- 1.2	- 1.7
Cement production	10.9	12.9	10.2	0.6	- 1.9	- 2.0
Coal demand	2.7	11.0	7.3	1.3	0.2	- 0.5
Steam coal	2.8	9.7	6.8	1.4	0.5	- 0.3
Coking coal	1.4	20.3	9.7	0.8	- 1.3	- 2.0

China has been undertaking an extensive infrastructure development programme since the early 2000s, constructing and expanding a large network of roads, motorways, bridges and railway lines. Together with urbanisation, this has resulted in a surge in demand for building materials, such as cement and steel. Much of the infrastructure development programme has been completed and urbanisation is now slowing down. In addition, the government is seeking to rebalance the economy away from energy-intensive industries. Crude steel output growth is already in decline, having grown by 9.5% per year in the period 2006-2012, compared with over 22% per year between 2000 and 2006. It peaks before 2020 and then declines (although remaining above current levels until 2030), dragging down coking coal demand. Cement production follows a similar declining trend, falling by 1.3% per year on average over the *Outlook* period, compared with growth rates 10% per year over the last six years. Total industrial coal demand peaks around 2020 and then declines to today's levels by 2040, despite increasing coal use in the chemical industry (growing 2% per year) and rising coal consumption in coal-to-liquids and coal-to-gas transformation processes (15% per year).

Chinese coal production is projected to grow by 0.7% per year between 2012 and 2020. As a result of sluggish demand growth and rising costs in the mature mining regions, production stays fairly flat throughout the 2020s and then goes into slow decline after

2030. Although small coal mines are spread across China, the main production centres are concentrated in the northern and north-eastern provinces of Shanxi, Shaanxi and Inner Mongolia. Together, these three provinces account for roughly 60% of the country's total coal output. Power plants and industrial hubs, however, are primarily located in the coastal provinces, requiring large amounts of coal to be transported over long distances, either directly by railway or by a combination of railway and coastal shipping through the ports in the gulf of Bohai (including Qinhuangdao, Huanghua and Jingtang). Chinese production costs increased on average by 11% (in nominal terms) between 2012 and 2014, though production costs vary widely. More than 80% of the country's output can be produced at less than $65/tonne, but some older and deeper mines, particularly in Shanxi, have production costs closer to $80/tonne. Transportation can add up to $35/tonne to the cost of supply to Chinese consumers, depending on where they are located. The relatively high cost of some domestic coal has created arbitrage opportunities between domestic and imported coal in China's southern coastal provinces, leading to a surge in imports over the last four years (Figure 5.11). Coal imports increased by over 15% in 2013 to reach around 255 Mtce.

Figure 5.11 ▷ **Major coal mines and coal-fired power plants in China, 2013**

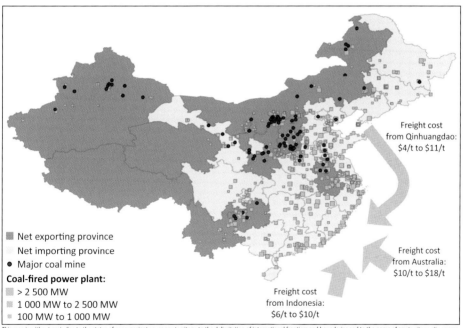

This map is without prejudice to the status of or sovereignty over any territory, to the delimitation of international frontiers and boundaries and to the name of any territory, city or area.

Sources: IEA analysis and Wood Mackenzie databases.

Along the southern coast, imported coal is competitive with domestic Chinese coal throughout the projection period (Figure 5.12). Imports peak before 2020 at around 285 Mtce and go into slow decline thereafter, though they remain around today's levels by 2040. Much of the imported coal comes from Indonesia, which is only a short distance from southern China. Shipping costs from Indonesia to Guangdong are in much the same range as the costs of transporting coal southward along the coast from Qinhuangdao. Despite higher freight rates, Australian companies can still export to China profitably throughout the projection period, thanks to high quality coal. Given the wide range of import costs, the projected slowdown in coastal Chinese coal demand is expected to affect high-cost domestic producers before significant amounts of imports are displaced. Import regulations governing coal quality (which are being discussed), and import taxes for coal (which were announced in mid-October) may limit procurement from the international market and affect the source of imports as well.

Figure 5.12 ▷ **Cash costs of steam coal to southern coastal China*, 2020**

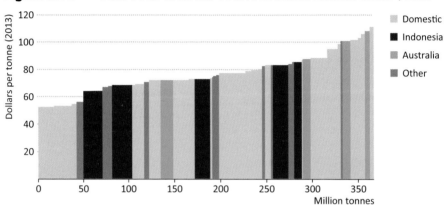

* In this graph, southern coastal China comprises the provinces of Guangxi, Hainan, Guangdong, Fujian and Zhejiang. It is in these provinces that competition between imports and domestic supply is most pronounced. Total Chinese coastal coal trade is larger, amounting to about 900 Mt in 2012.

Sources: IEA analysis and Wood Mackenzie databases.

United States

One of the biggest changes in the projections in the New Policies Scenario in this year's *WEO* is seen in the United States, where new proposals to lower greenhouse-gas emissions in the power sector have been made by the administration and are taken into consideration in our figures (see Chapter 2). While the proposals are flexible, they are expected to have a significant impact on older coal plants, which seem likely to close, given their inability to meet new pollutant standards and the difficulty of attracting capital for refurbishments. As a result, while coal regains in the next few years some of the power market share that it lost to gas in 2010-2013, coal use begins to drop again from around 2017. The impact of these measures is felt mainly after 2020, with coal use falling by a third over the projection period, as gas-fired electricity production overtakes coal-fired production around 2025 (Figure 5.13).

Figure 5.13 ▷ United States power generation fuel mix in the New Policies Scenario

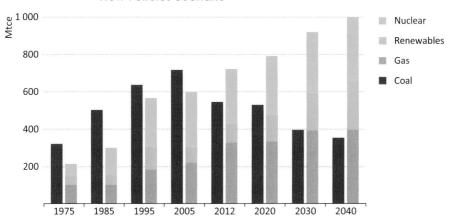

Note: Oil is not shown due to its minor contribution.

As the power sector absorbs almost 90% of United States coal demand, developments in this sector, and particularly competition with gas, are fundamental to future trends in coal demand. Natural gas spot market prices started dropping in 2011 and fell below $2 per million British thermal units (MBtu) in April 2012. This resulted in an unprecedented degree of switching by US power generators from coal-to-gas, with output from gas-fired plants almost matching that from coal plants in the first quarter of 2012 (see Chapter 4). Since then, spot prices for natural gas have increased, allowing coal to regain some market share in the power sector. However, gas remains the key rival for coal and whether a coal plant can compete against a CCGT depends primarily on whether it is able to procure low-cost coal. For power plants close to the Powder River and Illinois basins, coal typically has a cost advantage over gas. But in the eastern United States, where coal prices are typically higher, old coal plants run less and less in the face of competition from gas.

The large-scale fuel switching in recent years would not have been possible without flexible markets: almost 60% of the gas used in power generation is procured from the spot market. Despite nearly 90% of the power sector's annual coal burn being purchased through term contracts, the typical duration of a coal contract is rather short in the United States: some 40% of the coal volumes contracted in 2013 expired within the same year (Figure 5.14). Over the medium term, only a fraction of the power sector's projected coal consumption is currently locked-in under contract (much of this is lignite and low-cost Powder River Basin coal). This allows power generators to react rapidly to changing market conditions. Even in the short term, power plant operators can react to price movements by stockpiling contracted coal (which resulted in coal stockpiles being above average throughout 2012, US DOE/EIA, 2012). In short, the terms of coal contracts have done little to protect coal producers against developments in natural gas markets.

Figure 5.14 ▷ Coal deliveries to the power sector under contract in the United States by source as of 2013

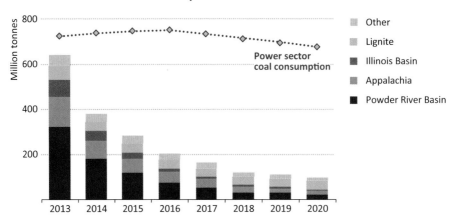

Sources: IEA analysis and US Energy Information Administration.

The duration of the recent modest recovery in coal use for power generation in the United States will also depend on federal government environmental policy, as described in Chapter 2. The standards for new power plants proposed by the US Environmental Protection Agency (EPA) in 2013 would effectively mean that any new coal-fired plant would need to employ carbon capture and storage within a few years of entering service, since even best practice coal plants cannot meet this standard.

The EPA proposed additional regulation on standards for the power plant fleet in June 2014 (Clean Power Plan). The guidance sets a target of reducing carbon emissions from the power sector by 30% by 2030, compared with 2005 levels, as well as reducing pollution that leads to soot and smog by more than 25%. States have the flexibility to propose their own plans or develop multi-state plans to meet the targets for power plants by June 2016, which are subject to EPA approval within one year. Four identified "building blocks" are to be used to reduce emissions, including: improved efficiency in coal-fired plant performance; emphasis on combined-cycle gas-fired power; more nuclear and renewables; and improved end-use energy efficiency. We assume in the New Policies Scenario that the proposals are implemented as proposed. The impact on coal demand is profound. While coal-fired power is projected to increase moderately in the next few years as coal recovers market share from gas, it begins to fall after 2017 as the new measures – especially the new standards for existing plants – take effect. Many US coal-fired power stations are old (most capacity additions since the mid-1990s have been gas and renewables) and they are more likely to be closed than be refurbished to meet the new standards. By the end of the projection period, coal demand in the power sector is projected to fall to half the peak it reached in 2005. Gas overtakes coal as the number one source of US power generation before 2025, mainly through greater utilisation of existing gas-fired capacity.

US coal production, which has been in decline in recent years, fell by a further 8% in 2012, to around 710 Mtce. After a slight recovery over the medium term, with higher demand, production is projected to enter a long-term decline, dropping by 1.4% per year on average over the *Outlook* period. Many high-cost mines in Appalachia – where substantial amounts of mining capacity have been shut over the last two years – are slowly pushed out of the market, since there is little scope to cut costs further. Coking coal mines, in particular, face higher costs as their reserves are depleted over the long term. Producers in the Powder River Basin and the Illinois Basin, where production costs are lower, face better prospects, but they will have to continue to cope with rising costs and long transport distances.

These production trends also affect the role of the United States as a coal exporter. Coal exports reached a recent high of nearly 100 Mtce in 2012 (with steam coal exports rising to 40 Mtce), but have fallen back since then. They are projected to drop to 60 Mtce in 2040, although as a share of production, exports stay at a similar level as in 2012. Strong coal exports from the east coast in recent years have resulted from producers, often selling below cost, striving for survival in a fiercely competitive, shrinking market. Although industry consolidation has advanced and over-capacity has been reduced, a trend that is set to continue over the medium term, Australian and Indonesian producers have increased output in recent years, to an extent which is expected to keep prices at levels over the next couple of years which will prove unsustainably low for some high-cost Appalachian mines. Consequently, steam coal exports from the east coast are expected to continue their recent fall, with the Appalachian mines reverting to their role as swing suppliers in the Atlantic Basin, while exports from the Illinois Basin increase moderately. In total, US steam coal exports are projected to drop to around 20 Mtce in 2020. After 2020, steam coal exports from the Powder River Basin into the Pacific market rise gradually, compensating for declining exports into the Atlantic market. As a result, total US steam coal exports increase slowly towards 30 Mtce in 2040. With increasing exports from the Powder River Basin the calorific value of US exports is set to drop, so the volumetric fall relative to today's levels is smaller than the energy-based data suggests.

Coking coal exports remain fairly flat over the medium term, standing at nearly 60 Mtce in 2020. However, after 2020, depletion of existing mines in Appalachia reduces output. Moreover, with the advent of exports from Mozambique, much of which goes to Brazil, US producers face increasing competition in the Atlantic Basin – their key market. Coking coal exports drop to around 40 Mtce in 2030 and then to 30 Mtce in 2040.

India

India, China and the United States, account for 70% of global coal use today. India's coal demand doubled over the ten years to 2012, India overtaking the European Union to become the world's third-largest coal market. Most of the increase in coal use in India was for power generation: coal provided three-quarters of the increase in electricity output over 2002-2012, with nearly 60% of India's power generation capacity at the end of the period coal-fired. Annual per-capita power use remains very low at just 700 kilowatt-hours, or around one-eighth that in the European Union.[7] With economic and population growth remaining strong, continued growth in coal needs for power generation is expected, driving a steady increase in coal demand and imports through to 2040. In the New Policies Scenario, Indian coal demand is projected to more than double over the period 2012-2040 and, globally, India is the largest source of incremental coal demand. Within the current decade Indian coal use overtakes flagging demand in the United States, and India remains the world's second-largest coal market over the rest of the projection period, behind China.

Coal production in India increased rapidly over the period 2003-2009, but has since grown relatively slowly, by between 1% and 3% per year. While India's coal resources are substantial, their quality is declining and it has proven difficult to invest in new mining capacity for various reasons, including planning difficulties and environmental concerns. The new government in 2014 has identified the coal sector as an important focus for reform, and has merged the coal and power portfolios. Additional measures announced by the new government, including more incentives for regional governments, smooth and timely environmental clearances and the participation of foreign companies in certain coal mining operations may lower some obstacles, but a surge in production is unlikely in the short term. In August 2014, the Indian Supreme Court ruled invalid more than 200 coal leases granted since 1993 to mines whose output is destined to an adjoining industrial facility on the basis of a lack of clear and transparent procedures for awarding the leases. This will complicate rapid development of domestic coal resources, but may have longer term beneficial effects.

Most of the projected near doubling of India's coal production in the New Policies Scenario occurs after 2025. The mismatch between the pace of expansion in domestic production and domestic demand results in India's coal import volumes continuing their rising trend; they more than triple, to 430 Mtce by 2040. Before 2025, India overtakes China, to become the world's largest importer of coal (Figure 5.15). By the end of the projection period India is the destination for 30% of all the coal traded inter-regionally and its import dependency increases from 25% in 2012 to nearly 40% by 2040. Conscious of the shortfall in domestic coal supply and the rising exposure to international price variations and supply disruptions, Indian power generators and steel mills are increasingly investing in the development of their own sources of coal supply in Indonesia, Australia and Mozambique.

The power sector currently accounts for 70% of total Indian coal use (see Chapter 6) and industry (primarily steel and cement) for most of the rest. India currently has nearly 160 GW of coal-fired power generation capacity, more than half of which was built in the last decade. Although this capacity is quite new, its thermal efficiency is relatively low, at around 30%. More than 90% of the coal-fired fleet uses subcritical technology: India commissioned its first supercritical plant, with an efficiency of around 40%, only a few years ago. Moreover, many stations are small, face ambient conditions of generally high temperatures and high humidity and, have to burn poor quality domestic coal, which has a relatively high ash content and therefore low energy value.

---

7. A quarter of the population in India still does not have access to electricity (see Chapter 2).

Figure 5.15 ▷ Global coal trade by major importing regions in the
New Policies Scenario

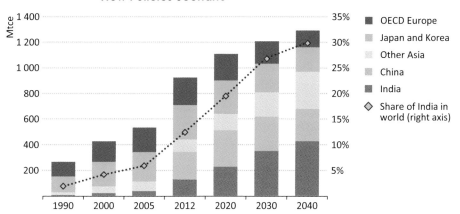

India's fleet of coal-fired generating plants is projected to expand rapidly, despite efforts to diversify the power mix through greater use of nuclear power and renewables. Wind and solar generation capacity are projected to expand by 90 GW and 125 GW respectively, while coal capacity increases by 340 GW to 500 GW by 2040. This expansion of coal-fired generation is an opportunity to improve efficiency; but presently it is not being exploited as most new plants still adopt less efficient subcritical technology (Spotlight). India accounts for well over half of the subcritical units currently being built around the world, whereas the share of this technology in the coal fleet under construction globally is around 30%. India's 12th Five-Year Plan, which ends in 2017, sets a target of about 60% for new coal plants using supercritical technology. Future plans may require all new units to use this technology. Before 2030, Indian coal-fired power output overtakes that in the United States, India becoming the second-largest coal-fired power producer globally, behind China. In the projections of the New Policies Scenario, although coal-fired power increases by almost 150% over the *Outlook* period, coal consumption in the sector increases by about 95%, as more efficient plants are built.

Europe

Having been in decline for much of previous two decades as a result of increased reliance on natural gas and renewables in the power sector (the principal user of coal), European coal use has seen a resurgence in recent years. In the New Policies Scenario, coal use continues to decline, particularly after 2020. In the medium term, although coal-fired power plants are older and less efficient than gas-fired units, coal-fired generation remains fairly robust in a number of countries because of low international coal prices relative to gas prices; but as the current over-supply in coal markets diminishes in the current decade, international coal prices are set to rise and, at the same time, CO_2 prices in the EU Emission Trading Scheme rise from $6/tonne in 2013 to $22/tonne in 2020 and $50/tonne in 2040. These developments, coupled with retirements of ageing coal-fired plants, and policy support for low-carbon fuels, result in a fall of more than half in steam coal use in the European power sector by 2040. European coal production also continues to decline over the projection period, as a result of the shutdown of ageing mines and the phase-out of mining subsidies in some countries, notably Germany (Figure 5.16). By 2040, 70% of European coal production consists of lignite.

Figure 5.16 ▷ **OECD Europe coal production, net imports and import dependency in the New Policies Scenario**

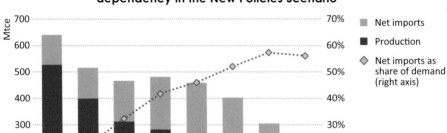

Coal imports into OECD Europe grew substantially over the two decades to 2006, reaching a peak of nearly 220 Mtce in that year. They then declined, especially in 2009 in the aftermath of the global financial crisis, before resuming their upward trend in 2010. In 2012, they were close to their historic peak. Although coal demand declined, import dependency increased, from 22% in 1995 to 46% in 2012, due to a slump in indigenous coal production. Robust European coal imports are seen by some critics as a sign of the ineffectiveness of European climate policy. However they are, for the most part, the result of low international coal prices relative to more expensive gas. In the New Policies Scenario, European coal imports oscillate slightly above or below their historical peak over the coming decade and then enter a decline, ending up nearly 40% lower by 2040, compared with 2012. Coal import dependency remains below 60%. The projected long-term decline of European imports to some 130 Mtce by 2040 weakens further the importance of this region in global coal trade, its share dropping from 21% in 2012 to 9% by 2040. Most of the projected decline in European coal imports is in the form of steam coal: coking coal imports remain fairly robust over the projection period, since indigenous production declines at an even faster pace than demand. Steam coal imports, on the other hand, remain fairly flat till 2025, and then go into a sharp decline, to nearly halve by 2040. Late in the projection period they stabilise at around 90 Mtce – a level last seen in the late 1990s.

Chapter 6

Power sector outlook
Towards more efficient and sustainable electricity

Highlights

- Electricity is set to remain the fastest-growing final form of energy worldwide. In the New Policies Scenario, world electricity demand grows by 2.1% per year on average over 2012-2040, its share in total energy use rising in all sectors and regions.

- Global installed generation capacity increases from about 5 950 GW in 2013 to just over 10 700 GW in 2040. Cumulative capacity additions total 7 200 GW over 2014-2040, of which 2 450 GW are needed to replace retired plants. Almost 40% of existing capacity and about 200 GW of renewables capacity that is built during the projection period are replaced by 2040. The need to replace the capacity existing today is particularly large in the European Union, as close to 60% of it is retired by 2040. The comparable need is lowest in China, at 16%.

- The global power mix sees a significant transformation over 2013-2040, as the share of fossil fuels in electricity generation declines from its peak in 2013, pulled down by falling shares of coal and oil. Gas and nuclear see their share in the power mix increase. Renewables-based electricity generation, including hydropower, nearly triples over 2013-2040, increasing more than coal and gas combined. With this growth, renewables overtake coal to become the largest source of electricity.

- Trends in the electricity generation mix vary markedly across regions. In the US, new regulations help to stimulate a large increase in the use of gas for power over 2012-2040 (40%) and contribute to the growth in renewables (165%). In the EU, the share of renewables in total generation almost doubles, reaching 46% in 2040, while maintaining the reliability of the electricity supply depends on being able to secure investment for new thermal plants. In China, coal-fired generation grows more than anywhere else, but its share still declines sharply. The share of coal also drops in India, despite coal-fired output increasing more than that from any other source.

- Globally, the total costs of power generation rise from $1.6 trillion in 2012 to about $2.9 trillion in 2040 (in year-2013 dollars) and are recovered through regulated or competitive wholesale electricity prices, and, to a lesser extent, support measures for renewables. The average cost of power generation increases in most regions over time, with rising fuel and carbon prices. The US and EU power sectors become more capital-intensive due in part to more renewables, while China remains heavily reliant on fossil fuels, leading to carbon costs over $170 billion in 2040.

- Large regional differences in prices and in the share of electricity in industrial production costs remain throughout the projection period, impacting international industrial competitiveness. In 2040, Chinese industrial electricity prices are 75% higher than those in the United States, while EU prices are almost twice as high.

Context

The power sector is undergoing one of the most profound transformations since its birth in the late 19th century. With the increasing digitisation of the world economy and continuously growing demand for electrical services, the need for reliable and affordable power supplies has never been greater. At the same time, the power sector – the single largest source of greenhouse-gas emissions – is the principal focus of efforts to tackle climate change, which call for a reduction in its heavy reliance on fossil fuels and the adoption of new, low-carbon generation and demand-side technologies. The need to integrate into the network variable renewable sources, the proportion of which is growing briskly in most regional systems, is posing new technical and economic challenges for electricity systems and for regulators.

While change – and the need for change – is universal, the precise nature of these challenges, how the industry and public authorities are addressing them, and recent market trends vary considerably across countries and regions. This reflects the limited connectivity currently existing between (and, sometimes, within) national power systems, the diversity of utility ownership, policy approaches, big differences in market design, resource endowment and other local market characteristics. The rate of growth in electricity demand also differs widely across the world. Electricity load in more mature, industrialised economies is barely growing now due to the combined effects of saturation in some sectors, the implementation of energy efficiency policies, more moderate economic and population growth, the fall-out from the 2007-2008 financial crisis and shifts away from intensive uses. By contrast, industrialisation, rising incomes and expanding populations are pushing up electricity use rapidly in the emerging economies.

The electricity generation mix is also changing in different ways around the world. Renewables are growing particularly rapidly in many OECD countries, thanks to generous government support, while most emerging economies continue to remain heavily reliant on fossil fuels; in the case of China, India and some other countries, coal remains the dominant fuel, though renewables are starting to play a significant role in some of them. Nuclear power is growing in some countries (especially in Asia), is being phased out in some others and plays no role at all in others (see Part B).

The last year has seen divergent trends in the choice of fuel for generation, but several common developments in policy. In North America, a rebound in gas prices has driven some generators to switch back to coal from gas, though this trend is expected to be short-lived: the US Environmental Protection Agency issued a proposed regulation in June 2014 to limit greenhouse-gas emissions in the power sector, which is expected to have a major impact on coal use in the longer term. Solar photovoltaics (PV) had a record year in the United States in 2013 – their capacity additions being second only to gas – while wind deployment was less than 10% of the previous year due to uncertainties on the extension of the production tax credits and to a change in the qualifying criteria. Europe, in 2013 saw a further strong expansion in renewables capacity (mainly wind and solar PV) and experienced a period of weak demand, which together further depressed wholesale electricity prices, further undermining the financial health of the sector. In January 2014, the European Commission announced a proposed climate policy framework to drive progress towards a low-carbon energy system, including new targets for greenhouse-gas emissions and renewables and reform of the EU Emissions Trading Scheme. In Japan, all nuclear reactors remain shut; as of September 2014 only one plant had received regulatory approval to restart and it had not yet gone back into service. The country remains heavily dependent on imported gas, oil and coal to generate power, though the contribution of solar PV is growing rapidly (sustained by a very generous subsidy scheme); wind is struggling to make inroads.

Among the emerging economies, in absolute terms, China saw the sharpest rise in demand and highest additions of generation capacity in 2013. The year marked a turning point for the country. Record additions of renewables capacity overtook those of coal, which, though still substantial, were at their lowest level since 2004. Nuclear construction starts in China have slowed, with work starting on just three reactors in 2013 and none in the first nine months of 2014, compared with nine and ten, respectively, in 2009 and 2010, before the accident at Fukushima (though some new starts are expected towards the end of 2014). The start of construction of new hydropower plants has also slowed, mainly due to dwindling opportunities for new large-scale dams, though the Xiluodu hydropower plant – the third-largest in the world – is due for completion in 2014. China's government has signalled that it plans to introduce a cap on CO_2 emissions, which is expected to be accompanied by new measures to accelerate the decarbonisation of power generation.

Despite the rapid expansion of generation capacity in India, 9% of the country's power demand could not be met in 2012, with negative repercussions on the economy; but recent data suggest that in 2013 the power shortage decreased markedly, as demand growth was lower than expected. Often thermal power plants were running at much lower levels than in previous years due to bottlenecks in coal and gas supply. Indian utilities often cannot recover their full cost, due to low regulated tariffs and high network losses, which exceed 25%. As a result, Indian utilities incurred financial losses of $14 billion in the financial year 2011-2012 (IEA, 2014a). In response to this situation, the Indian government has launched a debt restructuring scheme, which includes increases to power tariffs; but it is likely that the financial health of the utilities will need to be further improved to allow for adequate investment in new generation capacity, including renewables, for which ambitious targets have been set. South Africa is moving forward with a programme to deploy onshore wind power and solar PV, with three licensing rounds already completed for a total of around 4 gigawatts (GW) of capacity. A decision on the expansion of nuclear power capacity in South Africa has yet to be announced. In the Middle East, gas and oil remain the dominant sources of generation, with more than 95% of electricity generated from gas- and oil-fired plants. Nuclear power is due to make a greater contribution later this decade, when the new reactors under construction in Abu Dhabi are completed.

Electricity demand

The outlook for electricity demand[1] worldwide differs to some degree across the three scenarios presented in this *World Energy Outlook* (*WEO*), though less so than demand for most other final forms of energy. It is more consistent because there is limited scope for substitution in many uses of electricity and there is a close relationship between gross domestic product (GDP) growth (incomes are assumed to be the same across scenarios) and power demand growth (unless energy efficiency is rolled-out large scale). Moreover, there is a general switch towards electricity use in several sectors. In the New Policies Scenario, demand increases from 19 560 terawatt-hours (TWh) in 2012 to almost 34 900 TWh in 2040 – an average rate of growth of 2.1% per year (Figure 6.1). Demand grows even faster in the Current Policies Scenario, by 2.4% per year, but slows to 1.6% per year in the 450 Scenario, owing to higher prices and strong government measures to promote energy efficiency and conservation (though the effect of these is partially offset by switching to electricity in some end-use applications, such as in transport, or to heat pumps for space heating).

Figure 6.1 ▷ **Electricity demand by region in the New Policies Scenario**

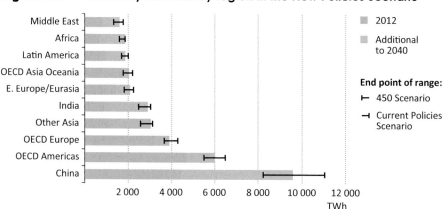

Electricity remains among the fastest growing forms of energy in final uses in all scenarios and regions. In the New Policies Scenario, electricity meets 23% of the world's final energy needs in 2040, up from 18% in 2012. Several factors explain the attractiveness of electricity to consumers. It offers a variety of services from mechanical power to light, often in a more practical, convenient, effective and cleaner way than alternative forms of energy. For some applications, such as electronic appliances, electricity is the only option. In addition, electricity produces no waste or emissions at the point of use and is available to consumers immediately on demand (where service is reliable) without any need for storage.

Income is the principal driver of electricity demand, though other factors – notably price – can have an impact. Globally, electricity consumption rose almost as fast as GDP

---

1. Electricity demand is defined as total gross electricity generated less own-use in generation, plus net trade (imports less exports), less transmission and distribution losses.

in purchasing power parity (PPP) terms between 2000 and 2012, largely due to booming demand in non-OECD countries. In the New Policies Scenario, electricity intensity – electricity use per dollar of GDP – declines slowly, mainly because of energy efficiency improvements. The decline is less than that in the intensity of final energy as a whole, as the share of electricity in energy use for heating, cooling and transport expands (Figure 6.2).

Figure 6.2 ▷ **World electricity and total final energy intensity in the New Policies Scenario**

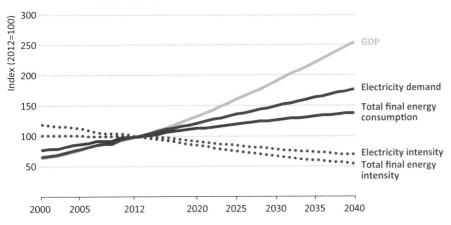

Note: Intensity is calculated as electricity or final energy consumption per dollar of real GDP in PPP terms.

Differences in the prospects for economic growth play a large part in the divergences in projected trends in electricity consumption across regions. In the more mature economies, demand growth is expected to continue to slow: demand for electrical services will still grow with economic activity (though saturation effects limit the potential for further increases), but the rate of growth will be diminished in most countries by incremental improvements in the energy efficiency of electrical equipment and appliances, the net result being modest growth rates. In the New Policies Scenario, OECD demand grows by 0.8% per year on average over 2012-2040, while its population expands by 0.4% per year and GDP grows by 1.9% per year over the same period (Table 6.1).

Electricity demand continues to grow much more rapidly in the emerging economies, where the market for electrical services is still far from satisfied and economic and population growth is much faster. Rising electrification rates will boost demand: in Africa alone, over 1 billion people gain access to electricity between 2012 and 2040, the share of the population with access to electricity services rising from 42% to 73%.[2] Over four-fifths of projected growth in world electricity consumption occurs outside the OECD,

---

2. Although progress is made on improving energy access, this projection implies that the UN goal of universal electricity access by 2030 will not be achieved. Detailed information on access to electricity and other forms of modern energy can be found at www.worldenergyoutlook.org/resources/energydevelopment/. See Part C for an analysis of the prospects for electricity access in sub-Saharan Africa.

over half of which is in China and India. Non-OECD demand in total expands, on average, by 3% per year, underpinned by GDP growth of 4.2% per year. As in the OECD, consumption rises most, in absolute terms, in the buildings sector (residential and services), reflecting growth in the stock of heating and cooling equipment, computers, electronic devices and electrical appliances. China registers the biggest increase in demand of any country or region – demand doubling between 2012 and 2040 – an increase equal to the combined demand of Canada, the United States and Japan today. Nonetheless, India sees a much faster rate of increase, averaging 4.4% per year, resulting in demand more than tripling, though its demand remains well below that of Europe.

Table 6.1 ▷ **Electricity demand* by region in the New Policies Scenario** (TWh)

	1990	2012	2020	2025	2030	2035	2040	CAAGR** 2012-40
OECD	6 591	9 523	10 393	10 788	11 136	11 505	11 922	0.8%
Americas	3 255	4 645	5 133	5 335	5 523	5 722	5 983	0.9%
United States	2 713	3 818	4 172	4 308	4 430	4 548	4 721	0.8%
Europe	2 320	3 188	3 406	3 529	3 635	3 758	3 881	0.7%
Asia Oceania	1 016	1 690	1 855	1 925	1 978	2 026	2 058	0.7%
Japan	758	937	993	1 010	1 026	1 043	1 051	0.4%
Non-OECD	3 501	10 039	13 675	15 973	18 305	20 645	22 965	3.0%
E. Europe/Eurasia	1 584	1 400	1 554	1 687	1 820	1 959	2 086	1.4%
Russia	909	858	935	1 014	1 095	1 176	1 248	1.3%
Asia	1 052	6 317	9 081	10 733	12 382	13 982	15 525	3.3%
China	558	4 370	6 359	7 383	8 269	9 016	9 560	2.8%
India	215	869	1 254	1 590	2 007	2 441	2 915	4.4%
Southeast Asia	131	682	960	1 157	1 387	1 665	2 018	3.9%
Middle East	195	753	989	1 142	1 303	1 442	1 590	2.7%
Africa	263	620	852	1 035	1 258	1 540	1 868	4.0%
Latin America	407	948	1 199	1 376	1 542	1 722	1 895	2.5%
Brazil	214	487	618	722	815	911	999	2.6%
World	10 092	19 562	24 068	26 761	29 442	32 151	34 887	2.1%
European Union	2 241	2 862	3 028	3 121	3 197	3 286	3 374	0.6%

* Electricity demand is defined as total gross electricity generated less own-use in generation, plus net trade (imports less exports), less transmission and distribution losses. ** Compound average annual growth rate.

A consequence of the faster projected rates of growth in electricity use in the emerging economies is some convergence between regions in the share of electricity in total final energy use. In 2012, that share ranged from 7% in sub-Saharan Africa to 26% in Japan; in 2040 the range is 15-33%. Differences in per-capita electricity consumption across countries and regions also narrow, but to a lesser extent, these differences remaining very large in 2040, reflecting differences in per-capita income and economic structure. In 2040, sub-Saharan African per-capita consumption amounts to 730 kilowatt-hours (kWh) on average, while US per-capita consumption at the other extreme, amounts to 12 300 kWh – much more than in most other countries (Figure 6.3).

Figure 6.3 ▷ Annual electricity consumption per capita and share of electricity in total final energy consumption by selected region in the New Policies Scenario

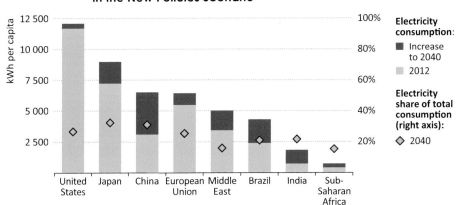

At a global level, the share of electricity use in each sector increases over the projection period. Industry remains the single largest end-use sector, its share of total electricity use edging up from 27% in 2012 to 32% in 2040 (Figure 6.4). Demand in the residential sector grows the most in percentage terms, its share of total energy use in the sector surging from 21% in 2012 to 34% in 2040. In the services sector electricity reinforces its position as the main fuel, its share of total energy use reaching 55% in 2040. The fastest rate of expansion in percentage terms is in the transport sector, primarily due to the increasing take-up of electric vehicles (plug-in hybrids and battery-electric vehicles), but electricity's share of total transport energy demand still reaches only 2.4%, compared with 1% at present (see Chapter 3 for a discussion of transport fuel demand).

Figure 6.4 ▷ World electricity consumption by sector in the New Policies Scenario

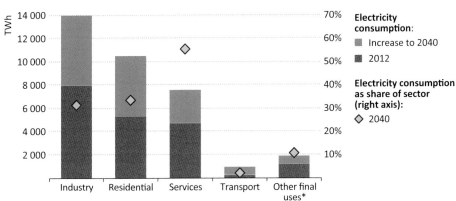

* Includes other energy sector and agriculture.

Electricity supply

Overview

The evolution of the fuel mix in power generation differs markedly across regions and across the three scenarios in this *WEO*, according to the strength of policies to decarbonise energy use and limit greenhouse-gas emissions.[3] The use of coal, the most carbon-intensive fuel, and reliance on non-hydro renewables, which emit no CO_2, are particularly sensitive to policy action: the share of coal in power supply in 2040 varies from 13% to 40% and that of non-hydro renewables from 12% to 31% across the scenarios (Table 6.2).

Table 6.2 ▷ World electricity generation by source and scenario (TWh)

	1990	2012	New Policies		Current Policies		450 Scenario	
			2020	2040	2020	2040	2020	2040
Total	11 825	22 721	27 771	40 104	28 489	44 003	26 760	35 043
Fossil fuels	7 495	15 452	17 265	22 232	18 264	29 101	16 138	10 635
Coal	4 425	9 204	10 377	12 239	11 271	17 734	9 428	4 606
Natural gas	1 760	5 104	6 056	9 499	6 124	10 806	5 929	5 777
Oil	1 310	1 144	832	494	869	561	781	251
Nuclear	2 013	2 461	3 243	4 644	3 215	3 856	3 293	6 435
Hydro	2 144	3 672	4 553	6 222	4 458	5 862	4 561	6 943
Other renewables	173	1 135	2 709	7 007	2 553	5 184	2 768	11 030
Fossil fuels	63%	68%	62%	55%	64%	66%	60%	30%
Coal	37%	41%	37%	31%	40%	40%	35%	13%
Natural gas	15%	22%	22%	24%	21%	25%	22%	16%
Oil	11%	5%	3%	1%	3%	1%	3%	1%
Nuclear	17%	11%	12%	12%	11%	9%	12%	18%
Hydro	18%	16%	16%	16%	16%	13%	17%	20%
Other renewables	1%	5%	10%	17%	9%	12%	10%	31%

Power generation capacity

A major shift in the types of generation capacity used occurs over the projection period, as some old plants are closed and new capacity is added to replace those plants and meet rising demand. In the New Policies Scenario, installed capacity worldwide rises by 80%, from 5 952 GW in 2013 to just above 10 700 GW in 2040.[4] This increase is 10% larger than the projected rise in total generation, because the level of availability of capacity is expected to fall as the share of variable renewables expands: wind turbines generate power only when the wind blows and solar plants when the sun shines, so additional capacity is required to ensure system adequacy (Box 6.1).

---

3. In each scenario, the rate of growth of power generation worldwide is slightly lower than that of demand, because of a reduction in both the shares of transmission and distribution losses and own-use of energy in power stations.

4. Historical data on installed capacity are available to 2013, while data on generation are available only to 2012 (preliminary data are available for some countries).

Box 6.1 ▷ **Keeping the lights on**

Electricity security – basically, a matter of keeping the lights on at all times – is a question of the ability of the power sector to deliver electricity to all connected users, within acceptable standards and in the amounts desired at any given time (IEA, 2014b). It comprises three distinct, but interrelated, elements:

- ▪ *Fuel security*: maintaining reliable fuel supplies to power stations, so they are able to respond in real time to demand.

- ▪ *System adequacy*: the capability of the power system to meet changes in aggregate power requirements in the present and future, using existing and new resources, and in future with new resources as required.

- ▪ *System security*: the capability of the power system, using existing resources, to maintain reliable supplies in the face of unexpected surges in demand or sudden disruptions to supply.

Maintaining system adequacy and security requires efficient, timely and well-located investment. Governments play a key role in shaping investment decisions, whether through direct ownership of electric utilities or through the design of markets and the incentives that are provided by the regulatory and policy framework (IEA, 2014a). They can also act to enhance the security of fuel supplies, including through emergency-response mechanisms, such as those established by the IEA for oil, and policy co-operation.

Rapidly increasing deployment of variable renewables-based generation – notably wind and solar power – significantly changes the way electricity systems function from day-to-day, as sudden changes in weather conditions can lead to abrupt swings in the availability of supply from certain types of capacity. This complicates the task of maintaining system adequacy and system security. Other types of flexible capacity need to be instantly at hand to cope with these sudden and, sometimes, unpredictable changes in supply. Increased grid connections across regions, demand-side response and storage can help to alleviate the problem.

In addition, the growing share of renewables in total power capacity, when this is pushed through support measures beyond the level demanded by normal capacity turnover, can lower the value of existing generation assets, both because they are called upon less to meet system load and the price of the power they do supply may be depressed at certain times. While this does not pose a significant short-term threat to generation adequacy in systems that have adequate overall capacity, it can undermine the attractiveness of new investments in dispatchable capacity. To cope with this, the regulatory frameworks concerning energy security need strong co-ordination and standardisation over the relevant geographic area of an integrated market (IEA, 2014c). Moreover regulatory frameworks need to ensure that adequate incentives exist to attract investment in the assets needed to maintain system adequacy and security, including smart-grid technology. Recent examples include market reforms in the United Kingdom and the PJM Interconnection, the largest regional transmission organisation in the United States, in both cases involving the introduction of a capacity mechanism.

Around 2 250 GW, or 38%, of the power capacity currently in operation around the world is expected to be retired before 2040, in addition to about 200 GW of the capacity – mostly renewables – that is commissioned during the projection period and needs to be replaced by 2040. Consequently, total capacity retirements over 2014-2040 are 2 450 GW, or about one-third of the 7 200 GW of global gross capacity additions over the period. Retirements of oil-fired capacity exceed gross additions by a factor of about three, while retirements of coal-fired capacity amount to almost half of gross additions. A bigger share of existing capacity is replaced in OECD countries, where the average age of power stations is highest: over 40% of all fossil fuel-fired capacity is more than 30 years old, as is nearly half of the installed nuclear capacity.[5] Over 45% of existing OECD capacity is retired by 2040, compared with only 16% of Chinese capacity (60% of which is renewables-based capacity) and 40% in other non-OECD countries, on average.

Figure 6.5 ▷ **Power generation capacity flows by source in the New Policies Scenario, 2014-2040**

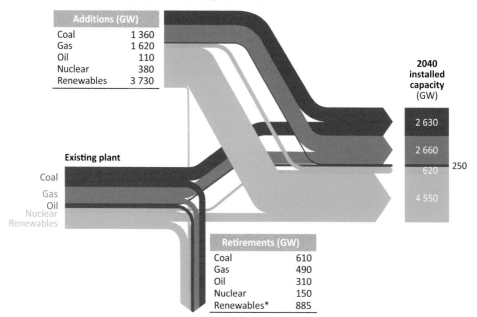

*Note: Over the projection period, a portion of renewable additions is retired, consistent with the average lifetime assumption for wind and solar PV of 25 years.

---

5. The technical lifetimes of thermal plant vary, but average around 40-50 years for fossil fuel-fired plants, 40-60 years for nuclear, 70 years for hydropower. The normal lifetime for solar and wind is around 25 years.

Global additions to renewables-based power capacity exceed those of fossil fuels and nuclear together over the projection period, both in terms of net additions (incremental installed capacity) and in terms of gross additions (including the capacity needed to offset retirements). Over the last few years of the projection period, coal-fired capacity ceases to be the single most important type of capacity, as natural gas exceeds it, although by a marginal amount, both coal and gas accounting for almost one-quarter of total global installed capacity by 2040 (Figure 6.6). After gas and coal, the largest installed capacities in 2040 are hydro, wind, solar PV and nuclear power. Globally, net and gross additions to capacity rise over the projection period, despite the slowdown in demand, as ageing plants are retired and growing volumes of wind and solar are added (Table 6.3 and Table 6.4).

Figure 6.6 ▷ **Net change in world power generation capacity by fuel type and region in the New Policies Scenario, 2013-2040**

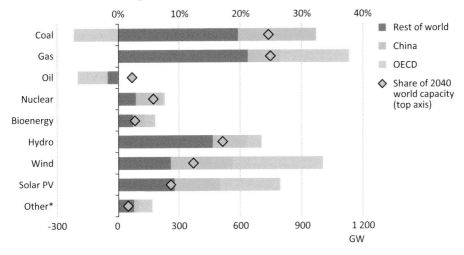

* Includes geothermal, concentrating solar power and marine.

In the OECD, about 60% of gross capacity additions between 2013 and 2040 result from the retirement of existing and new capacity, with the remainder due to increasing demand and to policies to decarbonise the power sector. The biggest additions to capacity come from renewables, which account for almost two-thirds of all the new capacity brought online, the bulk of it wind and solar PV; gas accounts for roughly one-quarter. Gross capacity additions are particularly large in the European Union (second only to China and about the same as India), as almost 60% of existing capacity (in addition to some capacity that is due to be commissioned in the next few years) is due to be retired before the end of the projections period. In OECD countries as a whole, 870 GW of thermal capacity (fossil fuels and nuclear) are retired over the projection period; virtually an equal amount is added.

Table 6.3 ▷ Cumulative power plant capacity retirements by region and source in the New Policies Scenario (GW)

	2014-2025						2026-2040						2014-2040
	Coal	Gas	Oil	Nuclear	Renewables	Total	Coal	Gas	Oil	Nuclear	Renewables	Total	Total
OECD	149	114	131	51	86	530	188	133	47	56	473	898	1 428
Americas	59	68	57	5	30	219	86	70	18	19	146	339	558
United States	56	61	47	4	23	192	76	67	9	17	119	287	479
Europe	77	21	37	31	47	212	72	32	15	34	267	420	632
Asia Oceania	13	26	37	15	8	98	30	32	14	3	60	139	238
Japan	6	21	34	14	6	81	10	22	12	3	44	91	172
Non-OECD	101	106	52	10	25	294	171	135	81	32	301	720	1 014
E. Europe/Eurasia	57	75	13	9	8	162	45	44	8	25	23	145	307
Russia	25	53	3	8	5	94	21	36	2	12	8	79	172
Asia	34	6	11	1	10	62	99	36	24	3	242	404	466
China	22	0	2	-	3	28	55	1	4	-	193	253	281
India	8	0	0	0	3	12	35	7	3	1	34	79	91
Southeast Asia	0	2	5	-	3	11	5	20	12	-	11	47	58
Middle East	0	15	13	-	0	27	0	32	28	-	2	62	89
Africa	8	4	7	-	1	20	25	15	12	2	12	67	86
Latin America	2	7	9	0	6	24	3	7	9	1	21	42	66
Brazil	1	1	1	-	4	8	2	0	1	1	16	19	26
World	250	220	183	61	111	824	360	268	128	88	774	1 618	2 442
European Union	81	23	39	29	42	214	72	30	15	34	262	413	627

Note: A breakdown of renewables capacity retirements by technology type can be found in Chapter 7, Table 7.3.

Table 6.4 ▷ Cumulative power plant capacity additions by region and source in the New Policies Scenario (GW)

	2014-2025						2026-2040						2014-2040
	Coal	Gas	Oil	Nuclear	Renewables	Total	Coal	Gas	Oil	Nuclear	Renewables	Total	Total
OECD	63	333	20	39	548	1 004	56	253	12	79	940	1 340	2 343
Americas	9	162	15	9	207	402	16	147	2	28	367	560	962
United States	5	126	14	9	155	309	14	102	0	25	286	427	736
Europe	36	107	1	12	249	404	28	80	2	35	436	582	986
Asia Oceania	18	65	4	19	93	197	12	25	9	16	137	198	395
Japan	5	51	4	3	64	126	3	13	7	3	86	112	238
Non-OECD	554	454	37	118	885	2 048	690	580	41	144	1 360	2 815	4 863
E. Europe/Eurasia	47	105	1	20	36	210	36	84	3	36	73	232	442
Russia	17	64	0	17	18	116	12	56	1	22	36	127	244
Asia	471	174	4	89	666	1 404	597	264	8	87	921	1 877	3 281
China	257	81	0	75	467	881	202	78	2	57	496	835	1 716
India	135	43	1	10	112	302	250	71	0	24	258	603	905
Southeast Asia	58	36	2	1	42	138	112	71	5	4	83	274	412
Middle East	1	78	15	6	23	122	0	73	14	9	109	206	328
Africa	31	60	8	-	63	162	50	100	14	7	140	312	473
Latin America	4	37	8	3	97	150	6	59	3	4	118	189	339
Brazil	2	10	4	1	59	77	3	23	0	3	69	97	174
World	617	788	57	157	1 433	3 052	746	833	53	222	2 301	4 155	7 207
European Union	33	92	1	12	229	366	25	62	2	33	408	531	897

Note: A breakdown of renewables capacity additions by technology type can be found in Chapter 7, Table 7.4.

6

What could revolutionise electricity supply?

In most parts of the world, the basic model of electricity supply has changed little since the dawn of the industry: power is still produced mainly by large, centralised, hydro plants and by thermal power plants, in which fossil fuels are burned or uranium engaged in nuclear reaction to create steam to turn turbines, and is transmitted over high-tension cables to centres of demand, where it is distributed through local distribution networks at lower voltage to final customers. But things are changing: technical advances, including the application of information and communication technology, have greatly improved the efficiency of generation, reduced transmission and distribution losses, encouraged distributed generation, facilitated demand-side management and the creation of markets in wholesale and retail power supply. In addition, government incentives have boosted the development and deployment of new generating technologies, based on non-hydro renewable energy sources, opening up the long-term prospect of a decarbonisation of power supply. More technological change is on its way. How quickly it happens will determine what the industry looks like in 2040 and beyond.

The *Outlook* does not assume technological breakthroughs, the nature of which cannot be foreseen. The further development of existing technologies is, however taken into account, based on our assumptions about learning and an assessment of the technical potential for further advances and their impact on costs. But breakthroughs are of course possible. And they could revolutionise the provision of electricity. Picking winners is always a risky undertaking, but there are several promising candidates. Among existing generating technologies, there is expectation that advances in solar and wind power will enable them to compete with little or no subsidy in regions with favourable conditions. Carbon capture and storage (CCS) technologies also hold promise, with ongoing research and development activities in many countries seeking to prove their viability and affordability. The widespread deployment of CCS technologies would enable the world to carry on burning large quantities of fossil fuels while keeping CO_2 emissions to an acceptable level (see Chapter 5). Generation IV nuclear reactors with enhanced safety characteristics and less waste could put nuclear energy on the path to greater expansion (see Chapter 10). Other sources of generation could also prove commercially viable on a large scale at some point. For example, research into marine energy has already overcome some technical barriers and lowered costs; further advances could make it competitive with conventional technologies in certain locations.

Beyond power generation technologies themselves, there are several technologies that could change the complexion of the power sector. A breakthrough substantially reducing the cost of energy storage technologies could drastically reduce the need for power generation to be dispatchable, possibly opening new opportunities for variable renewables, including solar PV, to meet a much larger share of the world's electricity needs than in the New Policies Scenario. High-voltage direct current circuit breakers could make direct current grids (with lower losses) more practical, opening up opportunities for long-distance transmission. Roll out of smart-grid technology – a suite of information, communication and other advanced technologies to monitor and manage the distribution of electricity from all generation sources – and micro-grids could be central to the efficient integration of decentralised power supplies.

In non-OECD countries, four-fifths of the projected gross capacity additions are needed to meet rising demand. Compared with the OECD, a smaller share (30%) of existing capacity needs to be retired before 2040. This share differs widely across countries and regions, according to the history of the industry: in some countries, much of the existing capacity was built only in the last decade or two, so the average age is much lower. In Eastern Europe and Eurasia, where plants are generally much older, around two-thirds of existing capacity needs to be replaced. In total, non-OECD countries add almost 50% more renewables capacity than OECD countries, but the share of renewables capacity additions in total additions is smaller, at about 45%.

Power generation

Despite the large projected increase in renewables-based power capacity in all major countries and regions, the contribution of renewables to total generation remains more limited, because in most cases their utilisation rates are much lower than those for thermal plant. Nonetheless, renewables-based electricity generation almost triples over the projection period in the New Policies Scenario, renewables output increasing more than coal and gas combined through to 2040 (Figure 6.7). They account for 48% of incremental generation from 2012 to 2040, resulting in the electricity output of all renewables technologies combined exceeding that of gas in 2014 and that of coal towards the mid-2030s.

Figure 6.7 ▷ **World electricity generation by source in the New Policies Scenario**

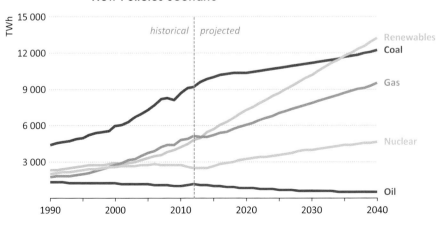

At the global level, generation increases by just over three-quarters between 2012 and 2040, to 40 100 TWh (Figure 6.8). Coal's share of the global power mix falls constantly over the period, from 41% to 31%. This decline is particularly pronounced in the OECD countries – where the share halves – but the trend is similar in the non-OECD countries, where coal's share drops from 48% today to 38% in 2040. The share of oil in global generation drops too, from 5% to 1%, while gas is the only fossil fuel that sees its share increase over the projection period, from 22% today to 24% in 2040. Overall, the share of fossil fuels drops from 68% today to 55% in 2040, while that of nuclear power increases marginally, from 11% to 12%. The share of all renewables combined jumps by more than half, reaching one-third of global generation in 2040. All of the increase in the share of renewables comes from non-hydro resources; wind power alone accounts for half of the increase.

Figure 6.8 ▷ **World electricity generation by source in the New Policies Scenario**

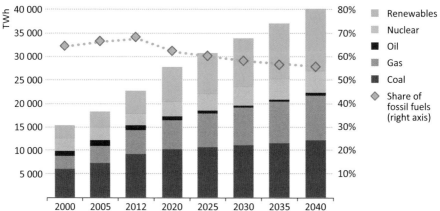

These trends hide significant differences across countries and regions, corresponding broadly to the degree of economic maturity the vigour of the policy push, and the local resource endowment. Reflecting the power capacity changes discussed earlier, the share of renewables in total output grows more in OECD countries, jumping from 21% in 2012 to 37% in 2040. In the European Union, the level reaches 46%, almost double the current level (Figure 6.9). In non-OECD countries, despite the much larger deployment in volume terms, the increase in the share of output is less marked, rising by nine percentage points to 31%. Coal-fired generation rises by over three-quarters over the *Outlook* period, but its share of total generation drops from 48% to 38%. China, which currently accounts for two-thirds of non-OECD coal use in the power sector, is the main driver of this trend: the share of coal in Chinese electricity generation drops from 76% to 52%. The share of nuclear power in total non-OECD generation doubles to 8%, again primarily due to China, where its share increases five-fold to 10% (see Chapter 11).

Figure 6.9 ▷ **Share of electricity generation by source and selected region in the New Policies Scenario**

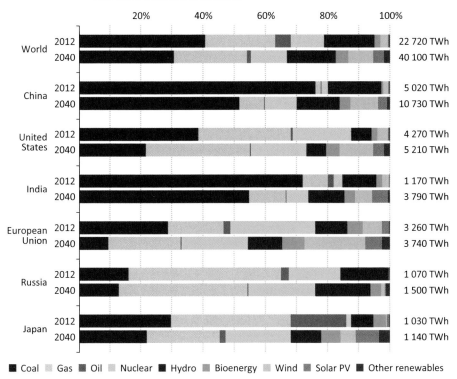

■ Coal ▨ Gas ■ Oil ▨ Nuclear ■ Hydro ▨ Bioenergy ▨ Wind ▨ Solar PV ■ Other renewables

Investment[6]

Worldwide investment in the power sector increased sharply during the 2000s, reaching an estimated $663 billion in 2013 – roughly two-and-a-half times more in real terms than in 2000 and equal to about 40% of total investment in energy supply infrastructure (Figure 6.10).[7] The bulk of this investment (and an even larger share of the increase over 2000-2013) went to building power generation capacity: capital spending on generation capacity amounted to almost $415 billion in 2013, compared with $250 billion of spending on transmission and distribution networks. Investment in generation capacity peaked at around $445 billion (in real 2013 prices) in 2011, combined spending on wind and solar falling back in 2012 by around 9% and by another 10% in 2013, because of sharp falls in unit costs and the discontinuation of support policies in some countries. Investment in solar PV accounted for 24% of total investment in generation, followed by hydro (20%),

---

6. Global power sector investment prospects were analysed in detail in the special report *World Energy Investment Outlook 2014* (IEA, 2014), and is available at *www.worldenergyoutlook.org/investment/* as a free download.

7. Investments for power generation and T&D capacity are allocated to the year in which the capacity is first in operation, i.e. they reflect "overnight investment costs". In reality, investment in new capacity will be spread over the years preceding the completion of projects.

coal (19%), wind (15%) and gas (12%). The breakdown of investment between OECD and non-OECD regions did not change radically over 2000-2013: though overall capacity additions were much greater in non-OECD countries, more non-hydro renewables capacity – which is much more expensive per unit of capacity – was built in OECD countries. In 2013, around 70% of all the money spent in the OECD on new capacity went to non-hydro renewables; the share in non-OECD countries was much lower, at 27%.

Figure 6.10 ▷ **World investment in the power sector* by region in the New Policies Scenario**

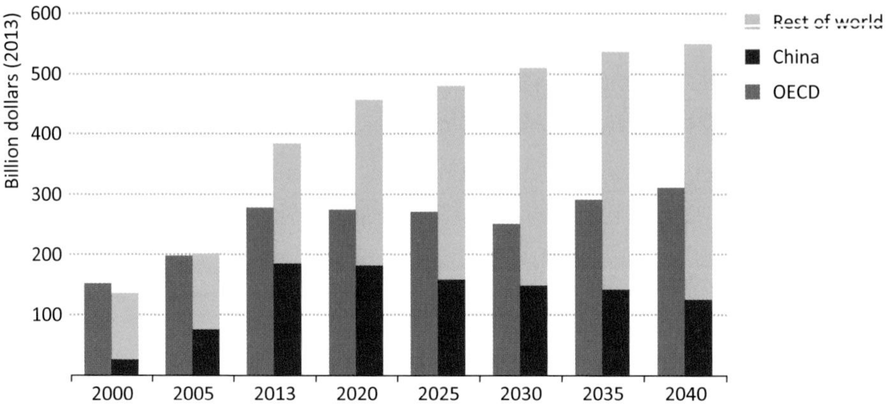

* Includes investment in power capacity as well as transmission and distribution.

In the New Policies Scenario, cumulative global investment in the power sector amounts to $20.8 trillion (in 2013 dollars) over 2014-2040, an average of around $770 billion per year (Table 6.5). Investment rises over the period, from an average of some $740 billion in 2014-2020 to almost $850 billion in 2036-2040, mainly because the level of capacity additions increases over time. Building new power plants and refurbishing existing ones make up 58% of cumulative investment, with the rest going to networks. Wind accounts for the largest share (one-fifth) of power generation investment, followed by investment in hydropower and coal-fired power plants (16% each), solar PV (13%) and natural gas (11%). Combined investment in wind and solar PV rises from just over $170 billion in 2013 to $200 billion in 2040, with rising deployment largely offset by a continuing decline in unit costs, thanks to technology learning and technical improvements (Figure 6.11). The share of investments in new gas plants over the projection period remains at about 10-11% of the total, this share having peaked in the early 2000s, mainly driven by a significant expansion of these plants in OECD countries, where gas installed capacity almost doubled from 2000 to 2013. Investment in nuclear power increases significantly, compared with the period 2000 to 2013, its projected share more than tripling to 11%, mainly to meet increasing demand from non-OECD countries (see Chapter 11).

Table 6.5 ▷ **Cumulative investment in the power sector by region and type in the New Policies Scenario** ($2013 billion)

| | 2014-2025 | | | | | | 2026-2040 | | | | | | 2014-2040 |
	Fossil fuels	Nuclear	Renewables	Total Plant	T&D	Total	Fossil fuels	Nuclear	Renewables	Total Plant	T&D	Total	Total
OECD	476	261	1 381	2 119	1 282	3 401	468	450	1 908	2 827	1 404	4 231	7 632
Americas	196	90	503	789	569	1 359	246	178	739	1 163	646	1 809	3 168
United States	158	87	387	632	460	1 093	197	159	571	927	495	1 422	2 515
Europe	174	102	605	881	468	1 348	162	202	863	1 228	502	1 730	3 078
Asia Oceania	106	70	273	449	245	694	60	70	306	436	256	691	1 385
Japan	70	14	196	280	130	410	26	22	191	239	143	382	793
Non-OECD	1 002	354	1 570	2 925	2 479	5 405	1 294	468	2 517	4 279	3 521	7 799	13 204
E. Europe/Eurasia	202	83	80	364	234	598	164	143	164	471	292	763	1 361
Russia	100	71	41	212	101	313	87	84	90	260	127	387	700
Asia	586	239	1 080	1 905	1 606	3 511	843	249	1 525	2 617	2 217	4 834	8 345
China	255	193	700	1 148	982	2 129	218	152	726	1 096	1 034	2 130	4 260
India	176	29	194	400	289	688	321	67	440	827	499	1 326	2 015
Southeast Asia	112	2	89	203	247	449	220	16	178	414	502	915	1 365
Middle East	83	21	52	156	117	273	74	32	216	323	156	479	751
Africa	93	-	151	245	282	527	160	27	344	531	566	1 097	1 624
Latin America	37	12	207	256	240	496	53	16	268	337	290	627	1 123
Brazil	11	5	126	143	145	288	21	11	155	186	172	359	646
World	1 478	615	2 951	5 044	3 761	8 805	1 762	918	4 426	7 106	4 925	12 030	20 836
European Union	155	104	557	815	413	1 228	139	198	802	1 139	439	1 578	2 806

Note: T&D = transmission and distribution.

6

Investment in transmission and distribution (T&D) infrastructure totals $8.7 trillion over 2014-2040, or an average of $320 billion per year. More than two-thirds of this investment is in non-OECD countries, reflecting the need to expand the networks to meet the higher electricity demand growth. Globally, 56% of T&D investment is needed to expand capacity to meet the projected increase in demand, while refurbishment and replacement of existing assets accounts for 40% and network integration of renewables for the remaining 4%. Network capacity expansion accounts for a higher share of the total in all non-OECD countries (with the exception of Russia and other Eastern European/Eurasian countries), because demand there grows much more rapidly and because networks were built more recently. Three-quarters of global T&D Investment is in distribution lines, which represent more than 90% of the total length of current networks worldwide.

Figure 6.11 ▷ **Cumulative world investment in the power sector by generating type, 2014-2040**

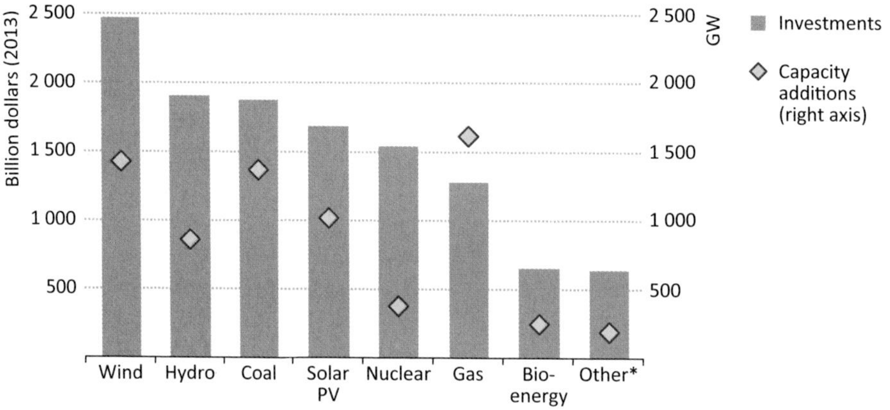

*Includes oil, geothermal, concentrating solar power and marine.

Non-OECD countries account for 63% of cumulative global power sector investment over 2014-2040. Investment is highest in China, averaging around $160 billion per year over the projection period; half of it is for power capacity (Figure 6.12). Annual investment in China remains broadly flat until 2020 and then declines over time because demand growth (and so the need for new generating and T&D capacity) slows. Investment in the European Union as a whole is the second-highest and about a third lower; although demand is sluggish, a large share of existing capacity is retired and replaced. Investment is further boosted by the fact that the bulk of this new capacity is non-hydro renewables, the investment cost of which is more costly per kilowatt (kW) than that of fossil-fuelled plants.

Success in financing all the investment needed in the New Policies Scenario depends largely on government policy and the regulatory framework. Private sector participation is essential, but mobilising this capital will require a concerted effort to reduce political and regulatory uncertainties. Financing low-carbon power generation projects, which are generally very capital intensive, can be difficult in competitive markets as they are designed today, because of the risk that wholesale prices may prove too low to cover upfront costs. In many countries, governments have a direct influence over investment decisions, as nearly half of the world's power generation capacity is in the hands of state-owned companies. Some governments, notably in the OECD, which stepped back from direct influence over electricity markets when opening them to competition, have now stepped back in, typically to promote deployment of low-carbon sources of electricity (IEA, 2014a).

Figure 6.12 ▷ Cumulative global power sector investment by type and selected region in the New Policies Scenario, 2014-2040

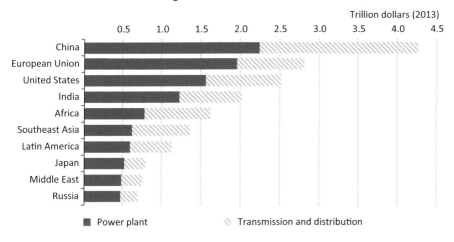

■ Power plant   ░ Transmission and distribution

Power generation costs

The total costs of global power generation increase from an estimated $1.6 trillion in 2012 (in year-2013 dollars) to about $2.9 trillion in 2040 in the New Policies Scenario as the supply of power increases by nearly 80% and the average cost of generation remains fairly stable at just above $70 per megawatt-hour (MWh). Covering the entire fleet, these costs include the costs associated with both old and new power plants, of all fuel types. Power generation costs can be broken down into investment costs (the payments needed to recover past capital investments [including the cost of capital]), fuel costs, operation and maintenance (O&M) costs and carbon penalties. Separating out each component provides a snapshot of the cost structure of power supply, which reflects a host of region-specific factors, including government policies and measures, technology developments, public opinion, the pace of electricity demand growth and resource availability. These factors affect generation costs through the mix of technologies deployed, the capital costs of each technology, the timing of capacity additions and payments to recover the capital expenditures, fuel consumption and prices, plus carbon costs. Power generation costs provide the basis for wholesale electricity prices, contributing to the formation of prices in competitive and price regulated wholesale electricity markets in different ways. Some costs are also covered through support measures for renewables in power, which increase from $85 billion today to about $170 billion in 2040 and may or may not be recovered in prices to end-users (see Chapter 7).

Figure 6.13 ▷ **Total power generation costs by selected region in the New Policies Scenario, 2020**

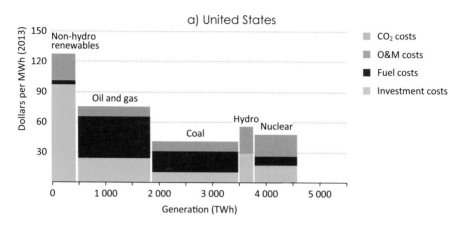

a) United States

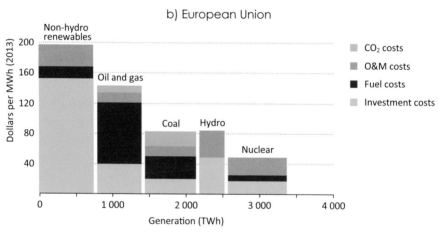

b) European Union

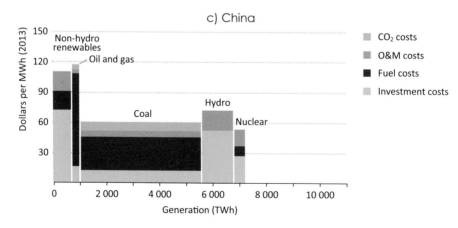

c) China

Note: Investment costs are calculated as the annuity payments required to recover past capital investments.

World Energy Outlook 2014 | Global Energy Trends

Figure 6.14 ▷ Total power generation costs by selected region in the New Policies Scenario, 2040

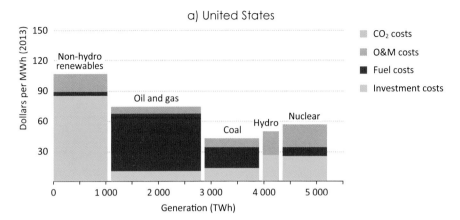

a) United States

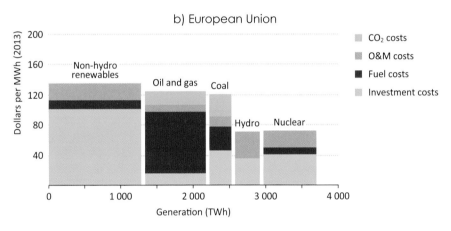

b) European Union

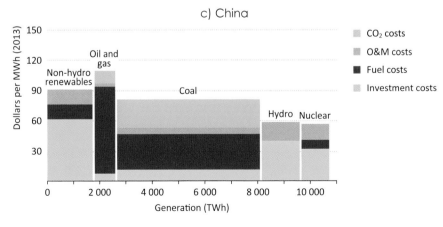

c) China

Note: Investment costs are calculated as the annuity payments required to recover past capital investments.

In the United States, total power generation costs reach $280 billion in 2020 and $350 billion in 2040, up from an estimated $240 billion in 2012 (Figure 6.13). This equates to the average costs of generation rising from around $55/MWh today to close to $70/MWh in 2040. Renewable energy subsidies recover 7% of the total costs in 2012, falling to 6% in 2040, as the capital costs of renewables decline and the average wholesale electricity price increases.[8] The US power sector becomes more capital intensive, and this is reflected in a rise in the share of investment recovery in total costs, from 37% in 2012 to 42% in 2040. The share of fuel in total costs increases by five percentage points from 2012-2040, as fossil fuel prices increase, even with improved efficiency in coal- and gas-fired generation. O&M costs make up lesser shares of total costs over time, as gas-fired power plants and non-hydro renewables, with relatively low O&M costs, makes up a larger share of the power mix. In terms of technologies, non-hydro renewables account for one-third of power generation costs by 2040, up from about one-sixth in 2012, while the share for fossil-fuelled power plants falls from over 60% to less than half.

In the European Union, total power generation costs rise from an estimated $325 billion in 2012 to about $410 billion by 2030, then remain broadly at the same level through 2040. This equates to a much higher average total costs of generation than in the United States, increasing from about $100/MWh in 2012 to over $115/MWh by 2030, before falling back to $110/MWh by 2040. The decline at the end of the projection period is largely due to the expiration of support measures that were committed to renewables capacity that is already in place today. In line with this, renewable subsidies fall to 7% of total costs in 2040, compared with an estimated 16% in 2012 and 18% in 2020. Investment costs represent about half of EU power generation costs over 2012-2040, even with continued deployment of non-hydro renewables. Despite higher fuel prices, fuel costs continue to make up about one-quarter of power generation costs over the projection period. The strong decarbonisation of the EU power sector also slows the increase in the cost of CO_2 penalties, these holding steady at around 6% of total costs from 2020-2040 (Figure 6.14). Overall, non-hydro renewables account for over 40% of EU power generation costs by 2040, just surpassing the share for fossil-fuelled power plants.

In China, the power sector continues to grow at a rapid pace, giving rise to nearly $500 billion in total power generation costs in 2020 and over $800 billion in 2040, compared with $325 billion in 2012. The average costs per MWh are similar to those in the United States, but much lower than in the European Union: they steadily increase from $65/MWh in 2012 to near $70/MWh in 2020 and over $75/MWh in 2040. By contrast with the European Union, renewables support remains a small share of total costs throughout the projection period, remaining below 5%. Contrary to both the US and EU power sectors, payments to recover capital costs in China fall from 37% of total generation costs in 2012 to less than 30% in 2040,

---

8. In Figures 6.13 and 6.14, costs and support levels for non-hydro renewables are weighted averages for several technologies, though some technologies, such as wind onshore are often close to competitiveness, while others, including solar PV, require more support per unit of electricity.

in large part due to the increasing carbon price (from \$10/tonne in 2020, when it is introduced, to \$35/tonne in 2040). Total CO_2 costs for electricity generation increase over time in China, reaching \$170 billion in 2040 as coal-fired power plants (with CCS technologies) continue to generate more than half of total power generation. In turn, CO_2 costs rise to 8% of costs in 2020 and over 20% in 2040. Total fuel costs double to over \$300 billion, from 2012 to 2040, but they account for a smaller share of total costs over time. Non-hydro renewables and nuclear power account for increasing shares of total generation costs over time, reaching 19% and 8% respectively in 2040. By 2040, hydropower accounts for only 10% of generation costs, down 11 percentage points from today, partly because projects completed before 2005 are fully paid for by that date. Fossil-fuelled power plants continue to make up the greater part of power generation costs, accounting for more than 60% of costs through to 2040.

Electricity-related carbon-dioxide emissions

Global emissions of carbon dioxide (CO_2) from the production of electricity using fossil fuels have been growing strongly in recent years, mainly as a result of the surge in coal-fired generation in China, India and other emerging economies, but the pace of the rise in emissions is expected to moderate in the coming years as the share in generation of renewables expand, power stations become more efficient and electricity demand growth slows in many regions (global climate policy, however, requires a reduction in emissions). In the New Policies Scenario emissions from electricity generation and centralised heat production grow from 13.2 gigatonnes (Gt) in 2012 to 15.4 Gt in 2040, at an average rate of 0.5%, in the New Policies Scenario. Emissions diverge across regions: in OECD countries as a whole, they decline sharply from 4.8 Gt in 2013 to 3.2 Gt in 2040, as the carbon intensity of power generation almost halves.[9] By contrast, emissions in non-OECD countries jump from 8.5 Gt in 2013 to 12.2 Gt in 2040, as a 34% reduction in the carbon intensity is not enough to compensate for a more than doubling of electricity demand.

China's emissions grow from 4.1 Gt in 2012 to 5.4 Gt in 2040 (Figure 6.15), when they are almost 70% larger than emissions from all OECD countries combined. But emissions could be higher, at 7.6 Gt in 2040, if the Chinese government's ambitions to diversify and decarbonise the power sector were not fully met (as we assume in the Current Policies Scenario). Emissions from the Indian power sector in the New Policies Scenario are the second-largest globally by 2040, exceeding those of the United States. This occurs despite strong deployment of low-carbon technologies, reliance on coal remains high and electricity demand growth remains strong.

---

9. In 2040, on average the power sector in OECD countries emits 220 grammes of CO_2 per kWh (g CO_2/kWh) generated, the equivalent of two-thirds of the emissions of a high-efficiency combined-cycle gas turbine (CCGT) gas plant, and down from 420 g CO_2/kWh in 2012.

Figure 6.15 ▷ **Electricity-related CO$_2$ emissions and carbon intensity of electricity generation in the New Policies Scenario**

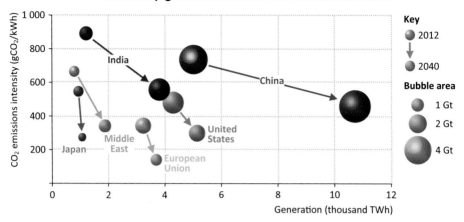

Note: The steep fall in intensity in Japan also reflects the fact that 2012 (the base year) was an exceptional year, due to the closure of all of the country's nuclear plants and temporarily heavy reliance on fossil fuels.

Electricity prices

The outlook for electricity prices differs substantially according to the scenario and by region, primarily because of differences in the price of fuel inputs to power generation and the strength of climate policy action.[10] Wholesale prices in the United States remain among the lowest in the world. In the New Policies Scenario, they increase from around $50/MWh today to around $75/MWh in 2040. This is largely due to abundant and low-cost reserves of coal and gas combined with the absence of CO$_2$ pricing. Low gas prices allow CCGTs, which have low capital costs, to operate as baseload plants, so encouraging investment in these plants and thereby reducing overall investment expenditure in the system. Chinese wholesale prices are today close to the levels prevailing in the United States, but they are projected to increase more, by 65%, over the projection period, reaching in excess of $80/MWh by 2040. This trend results from higher coal prices, a larger share of high-cost gas in the mix, the introduction of carbon penalties (on the assumption that these costs are passed on to consumers) and a relaxation of price controls, allowing generators to increase prices in order fully to recover their costs.

Wholesale prices and future trends vary across the European Union; on average, they are projected to increase by almost 50% over the *Outlook* period in the New Policies Scenario. Current wholesale price levels, of around $70/MWh, are not sufficient fully to cover the fixed costs of all power plants in the system. Reform of wholesale markets will be necessary if prices are to rise to $100/MWh in 2030 and to around $110/MWh in 2040 – the price levels that would allow for full recovery of fixed and variable costs. Such an increase would result in higher end-user prices in Europe, compared to some other countries.

---

10. See Chapter 1 for the outlook for fuel prices.

Despite Japanese wholesale prices having decreased slightly from their peak in 2012, they remained at very high levels during 2013. For the present, high-cost oil and gas-fired plants still have to run at untypically high load factors to compensate for the reduction in nuclear output since the nuclear fleet went offline in the aftermath of the Fukushima Daiichi accident. Japanese wholesale prices fall back over the period as the country's nuclear reactors come back online. However, in 2040 Japanese wholesale prices are projected to be more than 60% higher than US prices and more than 40% higher than those in China.

Box 6.2 ▷   What makes up the electricity price

The price a consumer pays for electricity has several components: the wholesale price (covering the generation cost, plus a margin), the cost of transmitting and distributing electricity through the network, retail costs and any taxes or subsidies applied by governments to electricity sales. The formation of wholesale electricity prices is system-specific and depends on the individual market design (liberalised or regulated), the power mix, the cost of fuels (domestic or international), the extent of environmental levies (e.g. CO_2 prices, NO_x or SO_x penalties) and the extent of interconnectivity with other power systems. Wholesale electricity prices, which are a key component of end-user prices, can accordingly differ widely between countries and regions.

Although wholesale prices are the main driver of differences in end-user prices, subsidies, taxes, grid costs and support mechanisms can also have a substantial impact. The relationship between wholesale and end-user prices is not always straightforward, as recent developments in some European countries show: the expansion of renewables-based capacity, which is typically remunerated outside the wholesale market, together with weaker than expected demand growth, has created over-capacity in the system and so depressed wholesale prices. However, since most renewables cannot cover their total costs from prices received on the wholesale market, this has increased the end-user price, as consumers are called upon to cover the extra cost of renewables for example through a renewable energy levy (where this is passed through in the electricity tariffs).

Combined with increasing consumption, higher prices are set to drive up electricity bills for both households and industrial consumers in absolute terms. However, improvements in energy efficiency will substantially moderate the impact of rising prices on electricity bills substantially over the *Outlook* period. Households in advanced economies can look forward to their expenditure on electricity falling as a proportion of total household expenditure.

Industry

Large differences between countries and regions in the weight of electricity in industrial production costs and in electricity prices remain throughout the projection period, affecting international industrial competitiveness (see Chapter 8). In the New Policies Scenario, in 2040, although industrial electricity prices in the United States increase by 30% between 2013 and 2040, more than in other economies, Chinese industrial electricity prices in 2040 are 75% higher than those in the United States, while EU prices are almost double the US prices. Despite this competitive advantage US industry spends 50% more on power in 2040 than in 2013 (Figure 6.16), primarily due to the rise in domestic prices. Electricity prices for industrial consumers in the European Union are already among the highest in the world today and increase by another 10% by the end of the *Outlook* period. As a result, industrial electricity spending in the EU increases by 16%, from $156 billion in 2013 to $180 billion 2040 – despite savings of around $45 billion in 2040 from energy efficiency improvements. Japanese industry spends 20% less on electricity in 2040, compared to today, due both to lower prices (as a result of reduced reliance on high-cost oil and gas-fired generation) and lower consumption. Chinese industrial expenditure on electricity increases by almost 2.5 times, reaching over $900 billion in 2040. Efficiency improvements counter rising bills to the tune of $145 billion.

Figure 6.16 ▷ Industrial electricity spending including taxes and savings due to energy efficiency improvements by selected region in the New Policies Scenario

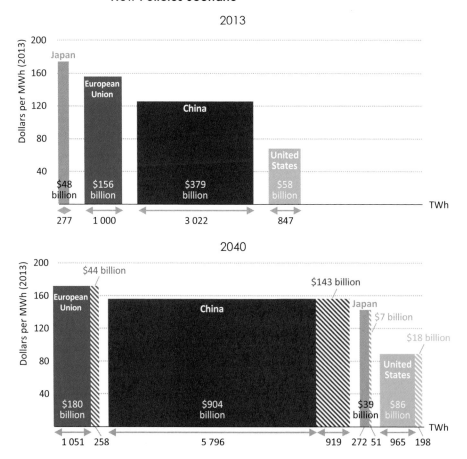

Note: Hatched areas represent savings on electricity spending due to improved energy efficiency.

Residential

Residential electricity prices are projected to increase in nearly all regions through 2040 as fuel prices rise worldwide and support to renewable energies continues. In the New Policies Scenario, total household spending on electricity rises by 25% in the United States. This increase is primarily driven by increasing prices. More efficient household appliances save US consumers about $40 billion in 2040.

Figure 6.17 ▷ **Residential electricity spending including taxes and savings due to energy efficiency improvements by selected region in the New Policies Scenario**

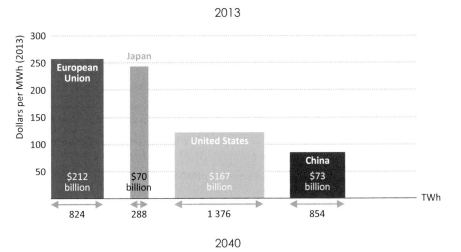

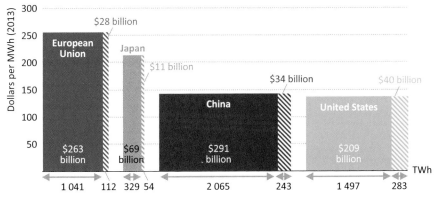

Note: Hatched areas represent savings on electricity spending due to improved energy efficiency.

In the European Union, residential consumers' expenditure on electricity increases by 25% between 2013 and 2040. Residential power prices in the European Union decline in the long-run, after peaking in the late 2020s. The price evolution is driven by support for renewables, which first increases, with rapid expansion of renewables, and then drops in the long-run, with ongoing cost reductions for renewable technologies – the trend is similar but more pronounced, in absolute terms, to that in industry. As in the United States, consumer bills increase in real terms, though less rapidly than household incomes. Japan sees its consumer bills remain flat over the *Outlook* period, due to falling retail prices, which counter a 14% increase in household power consumption. Chinese household spending on electricity quadruples, as residential electricity consumption doubles between 2013 and 2040. Despite savings of $35 billion due to improved efficiency the share of total household income spent on electricity is increasing in China. Residential power prices remain well below industrial end-user prices in China, due to continued cross-subsidisation.

Regional focus

United States

In the New Policies Scenario, electricity demand in the United States increases by about one-quarter over 2012-2040. Averaging 0.8% per year, the rate of electricity demand growth is only around a third that of economic growth, thanks mainly to end-use efficiency gains (Figure 6.18). State and federal government policies, together with the low natural gas prices from the shale gas boom, continue to drive a transformation of the US power sector. A new regulation proposed by the US Environmental Protection Agency (EPA) to cut carbon pollution from power plants, the Clean Power Plan, is expected to speed up decarbonisation. The proposal – included in the New Policies Scenario – sets an overall target to cut CO_2 emissions from power plants by 30% over 2005 levels by 2030 (and a continuation of efforts thereafter), with different targets for each state. It allows for flexibility in how states and utilities implement the reductions, which are expected to be achieved by making electricity generation more efficient, switching from coal to gas, increasing the contributions from nuclear and renewables, and curbing demand growth through more efficient end-use.

Figure 6.18 ▷ United States electricity generation by source and CO_2 intensity in the New Policies Scenario

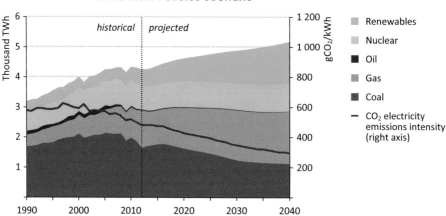

It is mainly because of these measures that coal-fired generation in the United States falls in the New Policies Scenario by a third during the projection period, while gas-fired generation increases by almost 40%. The proposed new EPA regulations constrain the use of coal, effectively limiting the construction of new coal-fired plants and the refurbishment and use of old plants (insofar as CCS remains uncompetitive). This leads to the retirement of 40% of the existing fleet of coal-fired plants by 2040. Gas-fired installed capacity increases by more than 20% during the projection period, after nearly doubling over 2000-2013. Nuclear capacity increases by around 10% as new capacity and uprates more than offset the retirement of around one-fifth of today's fleet.

Renewables continue to be deployed rapidly, led by wind and solar PV. Though it remains uncertain whether electricity production tax credits for certain renewables technologies will be renewed, state-level renewable portfolio standards and the national emissions reduction goal underpin steadily increasing additions of renewables-based capacity. Renewables-based generation increases by more than two-and-a-half times, exceeding coal-fired generation in the early 2030s and reaching a level 10% higher than gas-fired generation today. The increase of renewables-based generation in the period to 2040 is equivalent to 90% of incremental demand.

Total capacity additions in the United States amount to 740 GW over the projection period, requiring a cumulative $1.6 trillion investment, plus almost a further $1 trillion in T&D expansion and replacement. Around three-quarters of investment in new plants goes to low-carbon (renewables and nuclear) technologies. Despite gas-fired capacity additions being largest (over 30% of total additions), their share of investment is much lower (13%), as they are among the least capital-intensive plants.

European Union

In the New Policies Scenario, the projected pace of growth in electricity demand in the European Union is among the lowest in the world – averaging 0.6% during the projection period – because of the maturity of the economy, relatively weak economic prospects and a stable level of population. Despite this, capacity additions in the EU are similar in scale to those in India, but lower than those in China, due to the age of the existing fleet and the expected continuation of policies aimed at decarbonising the power sector. As a result, the European Union retires some 630 GW of capacity in the period to 2040, while it adds more than 900 GW. With the help of government support, over 70% of capacity additions are renewables-based, led by wind and solar PV, resulting in renewable technologies (including hydropower) almost doubling their share of generation to 46% in 2040 (Figure 6.19).

The recent rebound in coal use for power generation in the EU, which has driven down gas use, is reversed in the coming years, with relative fuel prices projected to improve for gas and higher CO_2 prices under the EU Emissions Trading Scheme (ETS) (see Chapter 1). Coal-fired generation falls by more than 60% in the period to 2040 as more coal-fired plants are retired than added and CO_2 prices rise, lowering the load factor of coal plants. Gas-fired generation, which fell further in 2013, remains relatively low until the end of the current decade when higher CO_2 prices, declining generation from coal-fired plants and the need for system flexibility (due to growth of variable renewables) push it back up. Nuclear power output falls 10% as half of existing capacity is retired (in line with phase-out plans and because of the age of the fleet) and only about 70% of it is replaced.

Figure 6.19 ▷ **European Union electricity generation by source and CO_2 intensity in the New Policies Scenario**

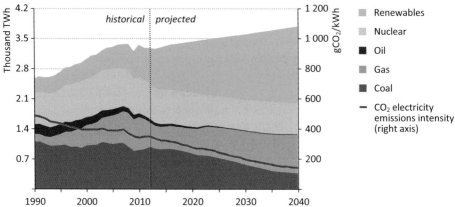

Renewables have attracted around four-fifths of investment in new capacity in the European Union over the past decade. In the New Policies Scenario, total investment in Europe in new plants reaches a cumulative total of $2 trillion by 2040: 69% for renewables, 16% for nuclear, 8% for coal and 7% for gas. In the decade to 2025, about 150 GW of thermal (fossil fuel and nuclear) capacity is expected to be retired, requiring additions of about 120 GW of new thermal plants to ensure system reliability. These additions are lower than retirements because of the current over-capacity, but are still essential to the reliability of the power system as the growing amounts of variable renewables cannot generally be relied upon to the same extent as thermal capacity at times of peak demand, therefore requiring traditional dispatchable capacity to be in the mix. Increased transmission across regions and countries, demand-side management and storage can also help.

Some of this investment, in particular that which relies on competitive wholesale prices to recover costs, might not take place under current market rules.[11] Especially financing over 40 GW of new nuclear plants (beyond those already under construction) can prove to be very challenging, unless changes are made in the market design, including rewarding under-utilised capacity for contributing to the reliability and adequacy of the system or providing some other form of government support. Several countries are envisaging or putting in place such reforms, and the consistency of country-level measures with EU-wide approaches, including instruments to ensure market participation of all technologies

---

11. An in-depth analysis of the current and future situation of the European power market was presented in the *World Energy Investment Outlook Special Report* available at: *www.worldenergyoutlook.org/investment*.

(including renewables and nuclear) and providing appropriate long-term signals for investment, will be critical to achieving decarbonisation goals for the EU power sector. Prices in recent years have been lower than the level required for new conventional plants to recover their investments (especially for CCGT plants) by an estimated $20/MWh (IEA, 2014a). Low prices have been the result of several factors, but mainly over-capacity following the 2008-2009 economic crisis and a continued push to deploy renewables beyond the natural turnover of capacity. Higher wholesale prices could increase end-user bills, adding to the strain on households and on the competitiveness of European industry, and attention will need to be given so these costs do not create hardship for end-users and national economies.

Japan

In the New Policies Scenario, Japan sees the world's slowest growth in electricity demand (just 0.4% per year) over 2012-2040 because of its mature economy, a falling population, continued energy efficiency improvements and saturation effects in end-uses. The new Strategic Energy Plan, released by Japan's government in April 2014, outlines a prominent role for renewables in meeting the country's future electricity needs, but also envisages the retention of a significant nuclear share in generation.

Renewables-based capacity additions account for almost two-thirds of total capacity additions during the projection period. Solar PV, in particular, grows strongly, underpinned by the recent approval of a feed-in-tariff for 69 GW of new capacity (as of July 2014), while additions in 2013 were already the second-largest in the world. Japan's fleet of nuclear plants, which were taken offline following the accident at Fukushima, is expected gradually to restart operations, following stringent plant-by-plant regulatory approval.[12] As of September 2014, the Sendai plant was the only one that had received such approval, though it had not yet restarted. In the New Policies Scenario, two new nuclear plants currently under construction are assumed to be completed by 2020 and another two units come online by 2040. Almost all the nuclear plants built after the mid-1980s have their lifetimes extended from 40 years to 60 years.

In the medium term, the restart of operations at Japan's reactors notably reduces the share of generation from gas and oil, which surged after Fukushima, as well as from coal. This eases reliance on imports of liquefied natural gas and fuel oil, lowering associated import bills (see Chapter 2). The surge in renewables capacity underpins steady growth in their share of generation, which was just 13% in 2012. By 2040, Japan's electricity mix becomes much more diversified: 32% of generation comes from renewables, 23% from gas, 22% from coal and 21% from nuclear (Figure 6.20). The investment required in Japan's power sector totals almost $800 billion cumulatively over 2014-2040 in the New Policies Scenario, with around $520 billion going to build new plants and the remainder to T&D. Three-quarters of capacity additions are renewables-based plants.

---

12. Some of the older units are likely to be shut permanently.

Figure 6.20 ▷ Japan electricity generation by source and CO$_2$ intensity in the New Policies Scenario

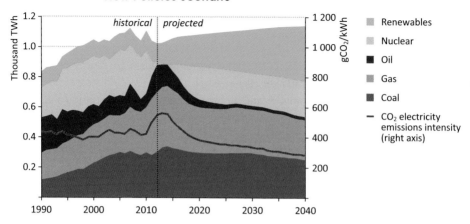

China

Electricity demand in China grew more rapidly than anywhere else in the world during the last decade, the growth rate averaging almost 12% per year. But the pace of expansion is slowing as the economy matures and the pace of industrialisation decelerates. In the New Policies Scenario, this trend continues during the projection period, with the average rate of electricity demand growth dropping to 4.8% per year in 2012-2020 and to 2% per year in 2021-2040. The electricity mix that evolves to meet these needs is driven by government targets (including those set out in the 12th Five-Year Plan for 2011-15) and strategic priorities, including diversifying generation away from the current heavy reliance on coal, mitigating local air pollution, tempering fuel imports and establishing national industries to deploy low-carbon energy technologies.

Figure 6.21 ▷ China electricity generation by source and CO$_2$ intensity in the New Policies Scenario

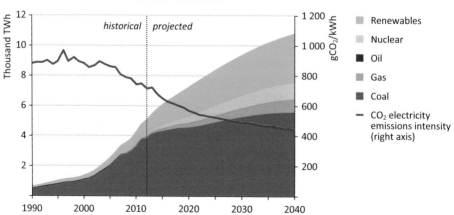

China deploys all sources of generation in large increments during the projection period, but renewable energy generation (including hydropower) increases more than coal, gas or nuclear. The year 2013 marked the first time that combined capacity additions of renewables in China outpaced those of fossil fuels collectively. China achieved the largest annual solar PV deployment in history (13 GW). Over the *Outlook* period, China installs over 960 GW of renewables-based capacity – led by wind, solar PV, and hydropower – accounting for 55% of total national additions and a quarter of renewables-based additions worldwide. China has decided to adopt more stringent technology and safety standards in the aftermath of the Fukushima Daiichi accident for new nuclear power plants, opting for generation III reactor technology for their new builds (see Chapter 10). This has caused the average rate of construction starts to slow, from the 11 GW achieved annually over 2009-2010 to 3 GW over 2012-2013. China remains the world leader in nuclear capacity additions during the projection period, averaging nearly 5 GW per year.

Coal-fired generation in China is projected to grow more than in any other region, but the share of coal in the country's electricity mix nonetheless declines substantially, from 76% in 2012 to 52% in 2040. Around 45% of the coal-fired generation capacity additions in the period 2014-2040 are highly efficient ultra-supercritical or integrated gasification combined-cycle (IGCC) plants. Consistent policy support pushes up the shares of generation from non-hydro renewables (3% to 16%), nuclear (2% to 10%) and gas (2% to 8%). The share of hydropower falls by four percentage points, as opportunities to build large-scale dams diminish, though hydro generation still increases by 70% over the *Outlook* period, accounting for almost one-fourth of incremental hydro generation worldwide. Increased deployment of low-carbon sources means the carbon intensity of China's electricity mix falls by more than a third (Figure 6.21). These trends imply cumulative power sector investment needs of $4.3 trillion (in 2013 dollars) during the projection period. Annual investment requirements decline sharply through to 2040, to around $125 billion, after increasing sharply during the 2000s (about seven times from 2000 to 2010) and averaging around $180 billion over the decade to 2020.

India

India's rate of electricity demand growth in the New Policies Scenario is among the fastest globally, averaging 4.4% per year, driven by an expanding population and rising incomes. Nonetheless, there remains a need for further growth: some 300 million people lack access to electricity today (see Chapter 2) and per-capita electricity use at the end of the projection period remains low, reaching just 22% of the average in OECD countries (from 9% in 2012).

Keeping up with India's booming electricity demand requires large capacity additions. Coal-fired plants continue to play a central role in the mix despite their share of generation falling from 72% to 55% (Figure 6.22). Increasing additions of supercritical coal plants and the expected introduction of ultra-supercritical plants, combined with higher volumes of imported (higher quality) coal and the expansion of coal washing capacity, raise the average efficiency of India's coal-fired fleet from 29% in 2012 to 36% in 2040. Gas supply problems prevent gas-fired plants from achieving higher utilisation rates at present, but that situation is resolved after 2020, pushing the share of gas in the electricity mix from 8% to 12%. India plans to give nuclear power a key role, with the rate of additions doubling after 2020 (from 0.6 GW to 1.5 GW per year, on average). Renewables benefit from strong policy support. Led by solar PV, wind and hydropower, they account for over 40% of India's capacity additions in the period to 2040, taking their share of generation from 15% to 26%.

Figure 6.22 ▷ **India electricity generation by source and CO_2 intensity in the New Policies Scenario**

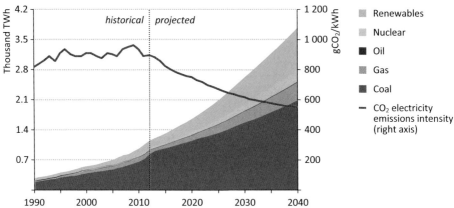

Maintaining adequate electricity supply will represent a significant investment challenge for India. Around $2 trillion (in 2013 dollars) needs to be invested in the period to 2040, with about 40% going to expand and improve T&D networks and 21% for new coal-fired plants. However, incentives to invest in new power plants are presently diminished by high T&D losses and low end-user tariffs, which mean that many utilities struggle to make a commercial return on capital or even recover their costs. If network losses were brought down to 15% (the current levels exceed 25%), this would allow generators to become financially solvent while limiting the real rise in end-user bills to just 5% (IEA, 2014a). The situation improves during the projection period, but losses are still high compared with other regions. Although power demand in India is almost 15% below EU-levels in 2040, the country's power output exceeds that of the European Union by the end of the *Outlook* period because of the persistently high rate of losses.

Middle East

Middle East electricity demand growth to 2040 averages 2.7% per year in the New Policies Scenario, underpinned by strong economic and population growth across the region and subsidised electricity prices to end-users in many countries (see Chapter 9). Contrasting sharply with other regions, the electricity mix today is dominated by gas and oil, which account for 61% and 36% of generation, respectively.

Oil-fired generation plays a marginal role in nearly all other regions, mainly because of its very high cost. Prices for oil inputs to electricity generators in the Middle East are often subsidised to a level that covers the cost of producing the oil but does not reflect its value in international markets (see Chapter 9). It is assumed in the New Policies Scenario that subsidies to end-user prices for oil and gas in the region remain in place. This causes oil-fired generation in the Middle East to shrink by nearly a third during the projection period, though the region still accounts for 45% of global oil-fired generation in 2040 (Figure 6.23).

Figure 6.23 ▷ **Middle East electricity generation by source and CO$_2$ intensity in the New Policies Scenario**

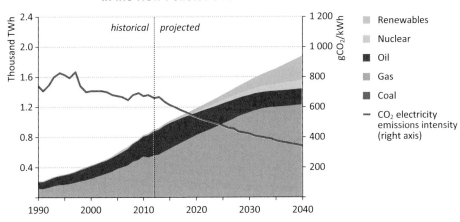

Incremental demand and the loss of oil-fired generation in the Middle East during the projection period are covered by gas, renewables and nuclear. Gas-fired plants make up nearly half of capacity additions in the period to 2040. The increase in gas-fired generation is equivalent to 80% of incremental electricity demand. Growth in gas-fired generation begins to slow down around 2030, as generation from renewables and nuclear increases more rapidly to meet new demand. Combined water and power plants, which produce both freshwater and electricity, win an increasing role in the region, accounting for some 23% of total capacity additions during the projection period. These trends necessitate cumulative power sector investment of $750 billion in the New Policies Scenario, about 65% for new plants and the rest for T&D.

Chapter 7

Renewable energy outlook
Empowering the future?

Highlights

- Rapidly increasing use of modern renewables to produce power, heat and biofuels drives up their share of the primary energy mix in the New Policies Scenario from 13% to 19% over 2012-2040. Renewables-based electricity generation increases by around 8 420 TWh over this period, nearly half of the increase in total generation. Gross capacity additions of renewables far outweigh retirements, increasing installed capacity by some 2 850 GW to about 4 550 GW in 2040.

- Capacity additions of wind power are the second–largest of all power technologies, behind gas-fired capacity, wind power capacity reaching 1 320 GW in 2040. The size of the global wind power market reaches almost 75 GW (net additions plus replacements) per year towards 2040. The share of renewables in the global power mix gains 12 percentage points through to 2040, half of which is due to wind. Wind reaches 20% of total EU power generation, the highest penetration level in the world.

- After wind, solar PV sees the second-largest increase of installed capacity among renewables. Global capacity reaches 930 GW in 2040, its maximum output equivalent to 15% of estimated peak demand. The share reaches more than 35% in Japan and even higher in parts of Europe, levels at which it would increasingly displace conventional technologies with low operating costs.

- Cumulative investment of $7.8 trillion is needed for renewable energy supply in the period to 2040, around 95% of which is spent on power generation technologies. Wind power attracts the largest amount of capital expenditure ($2.5 trillion), followed by hydropower ($1.9 trillion) and solar PV ($1.7 trillion). Annual average investment in renewables for power is around $270 billion over 2014-2040, 75% higher than the average over 2000-2013. In OECD countries, two-thirds of the overall investment in new power plants goes to renewable technologies.

- Renewables are increasingly competitive, but continued subsidies are needed to facilitate their deployment and drive down their costs. Global subsidies to renewables were $121 billion in 2013, 15% higher than in 2012. They increase to 2030, nearing $230 billion before declining to $205 billion in 2040 due to the retirement of supported capacity. The EU remains the largest financial supporter of renewables through to 2040, though the US is a close second after 2035 and developing countries collectively account for the bulk of global subsidies in 2040.

- The use of renewable energy in power generation, heat production and transport helps reduce the consumption of fossil fuels, avoiding energy-related CO_2 emissions of 7.2 Gt in 2040, in the New Policies Scenario, up from 3 Gt of avoided emissions estimated for 2012.

Recent trends and policies

The role of renewables in the global energy mix continues to expand, especially in the power sector and in regions where policies are in place to support their use. Several renewable energy technologies experienced very rapid growth in 2013. Solar photovoltaic (PV), for example, saw the largest capacity additions ever in a single year. The renewable energy industry employed approximately 6.5 million people in 2013, an increase of 800 000 over 2012 (IRENA, 2014).

In the United States, uncertainties on the extension of the Production Tax Credit and a change in the qualifying criteria for these credits substantially slowed wind deployment in 2013: capacity additions dipped to 1 gigawatt (GW), compared with 13 GW in 2012. The result was a fall in wind activity globally, to the lowest level of deployment in five years (35 GW versus a range of 40-45 GW in the preceding four years). Wind capacity additions are, however, expected to rebound in 2014 with the completion of a large number of projects under construction. US solar PV installations continued apace in 2013, reaching almost 5 GW, supported by a federal investment tax credit and state-level incentives.

In Europe, the boom-and-bust cycle that has characterised growth in the solar PV market saw capacity additions fall for a second consecutive year (from 17 GW in 2012 to 10 GW in 2013). This was partly attributable to a slowdown of installations in Germany, which had deployed much more capacity in the two previous years. Wind deployment in the European Union as a whole (11 GW) was stable at approximately the average level of the past five years, though a higher share of the projects that came online were located offshore.

Last year was a milestone for China: it was the first time more renewables capacity was added (61 GW) than coal (38 GW). Coal-fired capacity additions fell, in accordance with broad efforts to diversify the sector, while additions of renewables – notably hydropower and solar PV – continued to boom. China commissioned a record 31 GW of hydropower capacity in 2013. Operations began at the Xiluodu project which, at 14 GW, will rank as the third-largest hydropower plant in the world when it reaches full capacity later this year. More solar PV capacity was added in China in 2013 than ever before (13 GW). This was partly the result of developers' rush to complete projects ahead of an early 2014 deadline to qualify for an electricity production subsidy. Recent developments in Japan, along with those in China, underscore the shift in the balance of solar PV installations to Asia. Japan has a considerable volume of approved solar PV projects in the pipeline (69 GW), under a generous feed-in tariff scheme, 6 GW of which were completed in 2013.

In sub-Saharan Africa, many large hydropower projects continue to be developed, with several major projects having started construction or reached the final phases of planning in the last year, including Grand Ethiopian Renaissance (6 GW) and Gilgel Gibe III (1.9 GW) in Ethiopia, Inga III (4.8 GW) in Democratic Republic of Congo (DR Congo), Mambilla (3.1 GW) in Nigeria and Laúca (2.1 GW) in Angola (see Part C). Wind and solar PV projects in the region are growing in number. These are generally on a very small scale, but, by contrast in

South Africa, a recently introduced auctioning system has resulted in commitments from private investors to almost 4 GW of grid-connected renewables capacity. Geothermal is being actively developed in Kenya and Ethiopia.

Biofuels production saw only modest growth in 2013, relative to the large increases over 2006-2010. Several recent policy developments are worth noting. In the United States, an attempt retroactively to restore and extend a federal production tax credit to biodiesel failed. The US Environmental Protection Agency (EPA) is proposing to reduce the supply requirements for advanced biofuels and total biofuels under the Renewable Fuels Standard, in recognition of lower than expected vehicle fuel demand (so lower biofuel volumes needed under mandated shares) and limited progress in the production of advanced biofuels. In the European Union (EU), the proposed 2030 energy and climate package does not foresee binding targets for biofuels for the period after 2020. Biofuels based on food crops have come under increasing scrutiny and the European Commission has proposed that such fuels should not receive public support after 2020. India, which currently has a requirement to blend ethanol at 5%, is considering raising the mandated level to 10% in the short term and potentially higher later.

Outlook by scenario

Renewable energy use increases substantially in all three scenarios presented in this *Outlook* (Table 7.1). This reflects policy and market conditions that facilitate continuous reductions in the cost of renewable energy technologies, thereby improving their competitiveness with other energy sources.

The use of renewable energy grows at varying rates, according to the strength of government support, in each scenario. In the New Policies Scenario, in which planned policies and current energy and climate commitments are implemented, their share of total primary energy demand jumps from 13% in 2012 to 19% in 2040. In the 450 Scenario, in which policies required to achieve the internationally agreed goal of limiting the average global temperature increase to two degrees Celsius are fully implemented, the share of renewables increases much more, to 30%. It rises much more slowly, to 15%, in the Current Policies Scenario, in which no additional policies, beyond those already enacted, are assumed. The range of projections varies the most for the use of biofuels, which increases seven-fold in the 450 Scenario but by less than three-fold in the Current Policies Scenario.

The projections for total renewable energy in all three scenarios depend upon two opposing trends. On one hand, there is strong growth in the use of modern renewable energy technologies – notably bioenergy for power, heat and transport, wind power, hydropower, solar PV, geothermal and concentrating solar power (CSP). On the other hand, there is a steady decline in the traditional use of solid biomass[1] – including fuel wood, charcoal, animal waste and agricultural residues – as poor households gain access

---

1. Traditional use of solid biomass in this chapter refers to use in households only, as data is limited for use in services and industry. Solid biomass refers to the raw feedstock. See Annex C for further definitions.

to modern energy services and move to urban areas. In all scenarios, renewables are used mainly in buildings (because of the sheer volume of traditional use of solid biomass in the developing world) and for generating electricity. Traditional use of solid biomass accounts for between 3% and 4% of world total primary energy demand in 2040, depending on the scenario, compared with close to 6% in 2012. Among the different sectors, the share of modern renewables in energy consumption is highest in all scenarios in the power sector (Figure 7.1). Hydropower remains the dominant source of renewables-based electricity, but it grows less rapidly than the emerging technologies.

Table 7.1 ▷ **World renewables consumption by scenario**

		New Policies		Current Policies		450 Scenario	
	2012	2020	2040	2020	2040	2020	2040
Primary demand (Mtoe)	1 802	2 254	3 455	2 223	3 095	2 276	4 658
United States	136	186	346	181	290	188	555
European Union	198	263	390	255	351	267	504
China	316	410	589	397	501	414	842
Share of global TPED	*13%*	*15%*	*19%*	*15%*	*15%*	*16%*	*30%*
Electricity generation (TWh)	4 807	7 263	13 229	7 010	11 046	7 329	17 973
Bioenergy	442	764	1 569	740	1 299	768	2 261
Hydro	3 672	4 553	6 222	4 458	5 862	4 561	6 943
Wind	521	1 333	3 345	1 254	2 552	1 376	4 953
Geothermal	70	120	378	113	287	121	557
Solar PV	97	449	1 291	408	832	459	1 982
Concentrating solar power	5	41	357	34	173	42	1 158
Marine	1	3	66	3	41	3	119
Share of total generation	*21%*	*26%*	*33%*	*25%*	*25%*	*27%*	*51%*
Heat (Mtoe)*	345	431	716	431	670	450	932
Industry	198	242	367	246	381	249	447
Buildings* and agriculture	147	189	348	185	289	201	485
*Share of total final demand**	*10%*	*11%*	*16%*	*11%*	*14%*	*12%*	*23%*
Biofuels (mboe/d)**	1.3	2.2	4.6	1.8	3.6	2.1	8.7
Road transport	1.3	2.2	4.5	1.8	3.6	2.1	7.2
Aviation***	-	-	0.0	-	0.0	-	1.5
Share of total transport fuels	*2%*	*4%*	*6%*	*3%*	*5%*	*4%*	*20%*
Traditional use of solid biomass (Mtoe)	758	755	648	760	671	750	633
Share of total bioenergy	*56%*	*49%*	*32%*	*49%*	*35%*	*48%*	*25%*
Share of renewable energy use	*42%*	*34%*	*19%*	*34%*	*22%*	*33%*	*14%*

* Excludes traditional use of solid biomass in households. ** Expressed in energy-equivalent volumes of gasoline and diesel. *** Excludes international bunkers. Notes: Mtoe = million tonnes of oil equivalent; TPED = total primary energy demand; TWh = terawatt-hour; mboe/d = million barrels of oil equivalent per day.

Figure 7.1 ▷ **Share of global renewables consumption by sector in the New Policies Scenario**

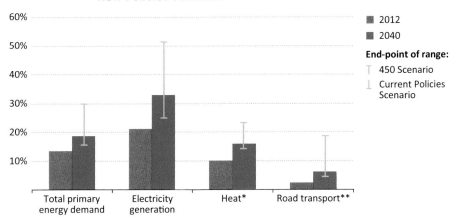

* Excludes traditional use of solid biomass in households ** Refers to biofuels only.

Note: The end-points of the ranges shown in green illustrate the span between the 450 Scenario (upper bound) and the Current Policies Scenario (lower bound), relative to the New Policies Scenario.

Renewables outlook by sector in the New Policies Scenario

Global and regional trends

In the New Policies Scenario, the central scenario in this *Outlook*, the global use of all types of renewables (including hydropower and traditional use of solid biomass) almost doubles between 2012 and 2040. Modern use of renewable energy sources, i.e. excluding traditional use of solid biomass, but including hydropower, nearly triples, their share of primary demand reaching 15% (up from 8% today).[2] Supportive government policies, including carbon pricing and direct subsidies (such as feed-in tariffs), help to drive this growth, but technological advances (which drive down costs) and higher fossil-fuel prices, also contribute. In contrast, the traditional use of solid biomass falls over the course of the projection period, though it remains an important household fuel in some low-income countries, notably in sub-Saharan Africa, where it still meets 29% of total primary energy demand in 2040, compared with 46% today (see Part C).

The share of renewables in energy supply expands substantially in all regions and sectors (Figure 7.2). The biggest gains in share occur in Europe, where policies for modern renewables are particularly strong, and North America, which has large wind, solar and bioenergy resources, as well as a supportive policy environment. Japan's use of renewables – mainly solar PV and wind– grows more rapidly, but from a lower base. Among non-OECD countries, China sees the largest expansion, led by the rise in wind power. India also sees

---

2. Modern use of renewable energy sources comprise bioenergy (with the exception of the traditional use of solid biomass), geothermal, hydropower, solar photovoltaics (PV), concentrating solar power (CSP), wind and marine (tide and wave) energy.

a significant expansion, with a continuing expansion in hydropower and, to a lesser extent, wind and solar PV which, together, more than offset the drop in the traditional use of solid biomass after 2020.

Figure 7.2 ▷ **Share of global renewables consumption by sector and region in the New Policies Scenario**

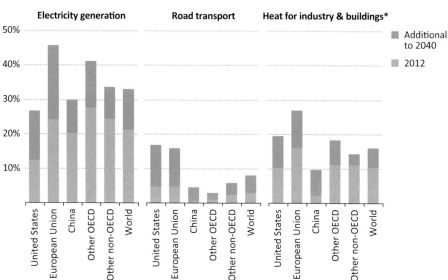

* Excludes traditional use of solid biomass in households.

Sectoral trends

The bulk of renewable energy development will be for power generation, though some non-electricity uses, most notably biofuels in transport, increase slightly faster. Renewable energy consumed in the power sector accounts for 32% of total renewable energy supply in 2012, rising to 51% in 2040 (Figure 7.3). In absolute terms, renewable energy in the power sector more than triples, with large increases coming from bioenergy, geothermal, wind and hydropower (though electricity generation from marine, solar PV and CSP all increase at faster rates). The uses of bioenergy shift markedly: at present, over 70% is used in traditional ways for cooking and heating in poor households in developing countries; but this share drops to below 45% in 2040, as these uses decline in absolute terms over the projection period. By contrast, the use of bioenergy for the production of biofuels used in transport (mostly road transport) increases more than three-and-a-half-fold, its share of total bioenergy use increasing from 4% to 11% and its share of total renewables supply doubling from 3% to 6%. The rest is used directly as a source of heat in the residential, commercial and industrial sectors.

Figure 7.3 △ **World renewable energy balances in the New Policies Scenario, 2040** (Mtoe)

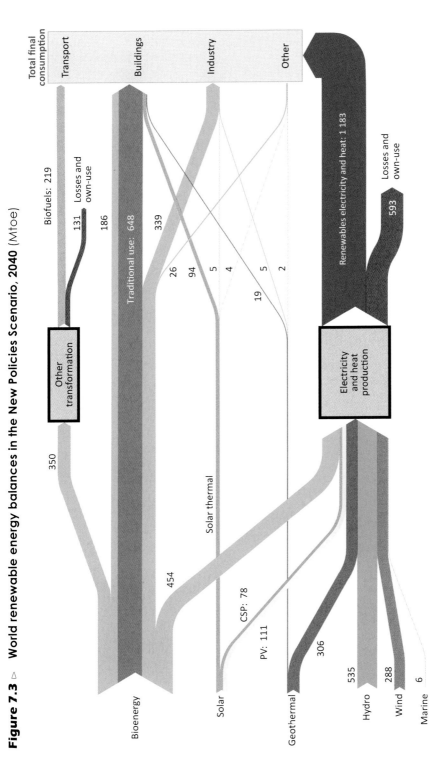

Notes: Other transformation includes bio-refining (processing of bioenergy to make biofuels). CSP = concentrating solar power; PV = photovoltaics.

Power generation

Renewables-based power generation worldwide continues to expand very rapidly over the projection period in the New Policies Scenario, almost tripling to 13 230 terawatt-hours (TWh) in 2040 (Table 7.2). Renewables provide close to half of the total increase in power generation, their combined share in overall generation rising from 21% in 2012 to 33% in 2040. Collectively, renewables overtake coal as the primary source of power generation by around 2035. Each renewable energy technology expands substantially: wind power increases the most in absolute terms, ahead of hydropower, which remains the single largest source (Figure 7.4). The rate of expansion of hydropower slows over time as opportunities to install new large-scale dams diminish. As a result, the share of hydropower in total renewables-based output decreases from more than 75% today to less than 50% in 2040.

Table 7.2 ▷ **Renewables-based electricity generation by region in the New Policies Scenario**

	Renewables electricity generation (TWh)				Share of total generation		Share of variable renewables* in total generation	
	2012	2020	2030	2040	2012	2040	2012	2040
OECD	2 219	3 039	3 996	4 893	21%	37%	4%	17%
Americas	998	1 329	1 770	2 200	19%	33%	3%	14%
United States	527	766	1 081	1 397	12%	27%	4%	15%
Europe	1 026	1 376	1 739	2 056	28%	47%	8%	23%
Asia Oceania	195	334	487	637	11%	28%	1%	13%
Japan	128	212	288	364	13%	32%	1%	13%
Non-OECD	2 588	4 224	6 221	8 336	22%	31%	1%	9%
E. Europe/Eurasia	294	366	466	602	17%	24%	0.4%	3%
Russia	169	209	272	361	16%	24%	0.0%	1%
Asia	1 395	2 565	3 863	5 081	19%	28%	2%	10%
China	1 010	1 933	2 646	3 209	20%	30%	2%	12%
India	177	315	620	993	15%	26%	3%	11%
Middle East	22	42	123	317	2%	17%	0.0%	10%
Africa	118	232	463	780	16%	35%	0.4%	7%
Latin America	759	1 019	1 306	1 556	66%	69%	0.6%	7%
Brazil	456	616	779	904	83%	78%	0.9%	9%
World	4 807	7 263	10 217	13 229	21%	33%	3%	12%
European Union	788	1 136	1 447	1 712	24%	46%	8%	25%

* Variable renewables here include solar PV and wind power.

Power generation from wind turbines increases rapidly over the next few years and during the 2020s, but slows thereafter, as other sources of renewables expand more rapidly, notably solar PV. Generation from wind turbines increases more than six-fold, from 520 TWh in 2012 to almost 3 350 TWh in 2040. Onshore wind farms in 2040 account for 79% of the wind power output, even though the output of offshore wind expands rapidly, especially after 2020. The share of wind power in renewables-based generation increases from just over 10% in 2012 to one-quarter in 2040.

Figure 7.4 ▷ **Incremental global electricity generation from renewables by type in the New Policies Scenario**

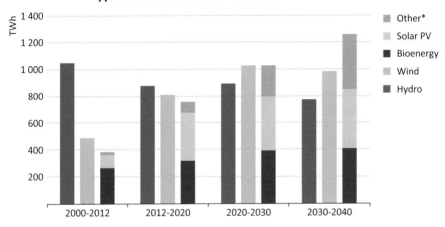

* Other includes geothermal, concentrating solar power and marine.

The worldwide use of bioenergy – wood, agricultural residues, municipal waste and biogas – to generate power is relatively modest at present, but is projected to grow strongly. This evolution is driven by a combination of government policies, technological advances (particularly in co-generation) which are expected to lower production costs, and higher prices of fossil fuels and rising carbon prices, which make bioenergy a more competitive alternative in power generation. Output rises from 442 TWh in 2012 to almost 1 600 TWh in 2040, driving up the share in total renewables generation from 9% to 12%. With continued policy support, the output of solar PV increases by an order of magnitude over the projection period. However, reaching 1 290 TWh in 2040, it still generates less electricity than hydropower, wind or bioenergy. The share of solar PV in renewables power generation reaches 10% in 2040. However, the share in total power generation remains small, at 3%, despite the rapid expansion.

Non-OECD countries lead the growth in generation from renewables, accounting for over two-thirds of the additional output over the *Outlook* period (Figure 7.5). In 2040, 63% of the power from renewable energy sources is generated in developing countries, compared with 54% today. China alone accounts for more than one-quarter of the global expansion in renewables-based power generation. Today, hydropower provides 17% of China's power supply, making up 85% of the country's renewables-based electricity. Hydropower continues to play a key role in the Chinese renewables mix, accounting for 27% of the additional renewables-based generation over the *Outlook* period. Wind power accounts for an even larger share at 39% of additional power generation from renewables. In 2040, more than one of every four megawatt-hours (MWh) generated from wind turbines is in China. In India, the share of renewables in total power generation increases from 15% today to 26% in 2040, based largely on a mixture of hydropower, wind and solar PV. In Latin America, where two-thirds of today's power generation is based on renewables (largely hydropower), the renewables share approaches 70% by the end of the projection period, with the major contribution still provided by hydropower.

Figure 7.5 ▷ Incremental electricity generation from renewables by region in the New Policies Scenario, 2012-2040

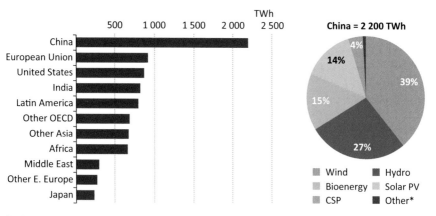

* Other includes geothermal and marine and represents only 1% of incremental generation in China between 2012 and 2040.

Among the OECD regions, the use of renewables grows particularly strongly in the European Union, where its share in total generation jumps from 24% in 2012 to 46% in 2040, thanks to both strong policy push and growing competitiveness. Almost 60% of the growth in renewables in the EU comes from wind power, which overtakes hydropower around 2020 to become the primary source of renewables generation, and contributes 20% to total power generation by 2040. In the United States, 27% of total power generation comes from renewable energy technologies in 2040, up from 12% today. This expansion is clearly driven by the deployment of wind power, which accounts for almost 50% of the additional renewable generation to 2040, followed by solar PV, which accounts for over 20% of the growth. In Japan, recently introduced policies to accelerate the commissioning of renewables capacity, partly to compensate for the temporary loss of nuclear capacity and to support the long-term goal of reducing dependence on nuclear and fossil-fuelled generation, drive very rapid growth in renewables, mainly solar PV and wind.

Table 7.3 ⊳ Cumulative renewable capacity retirements by region and source in the New Policies Scenario (GW)

	2014-2025						2026-2040						2014-2040
	Hydro	Bioenergy	Wind	Solar PV	Other*	Total	Hydro	Bioenergy	Wind	Solar PV	Other*	Total	Total
OECD	48	14	20	1	2	86	54	30	224	156	8	473	559
Americas	19	5	4	0	2	30	22	9	86	24	4	146	176
United States	13	5	3	0	1	23	15	7	71	22	3	119	142
Europe	23	7	16	0	0	47	25	18	127	93	3	267	314
Asia Oceania	6	1	0	1	0	8	7	3	10	39	1	60	68
Japan	4	1	0	1	0	6	5	2	4	32	0	44	50
Non-OECD	19	3	2	0	1	25	30	18	179	69	4	301	327
E. Europe/Eurasia	7	1	0	-	0	8	11	2	6	3	0	23	31
Russia	4	1	0	-	0	5	6	2	0	0	0	8	13
Asia	7	1	2	0	1	10	10	10	161	58	3	242	253
China	3	-	0	0	0	3	5	6	133	49	0	193	196
India	2	-	1	0	-	3	2	0	25	6	0	34	37
Southeast Asia	1	1	-	-	1	3	1	4	1	2	3	11	13
Middle East	0	-	0	0	-	0	0	0	0	1	0	2	2
Africa	1	0	0	0	0	1	3	1	4	5	0	12	13
Latin America	5	1	0	0	0	6	6	5	8	2	0	21	27
Brazil	3	1	0	-	-	4	4	4	7	1	-	16	20
World	67	17	22	1	4	111	84	49	403	226	13	774	885
European Union	18	7	16	0	0	42	21	18	126	94	3	262	304

* Other includes geothermal, concentrating solar power and marine.

7

Table 7.4 ⊳ Cumulative renewable capacity additions by region and source in the New Policies Scenario (GW)

	2014-2025						2026-2040						2014-2040
	Hydro	Bioenergy	Wind	Solar PV	Other*	Total	Hydro	Bioenergy	Wind	Solar PV	Other*	Total	Total
OECD	84	39	237	167	21	548	90	59	450	285	57	940	1 488
Americas	34	18	87	55	12	207	36	26	189	98	18	367	574
United States	19	14	64	49	9	155	20	20	148	85	12	286	441
Europe	40	16	129	59	4	249	40	25	223	123	26	436	685
Asia Oceania	10	5	21	52	5	93	14	8	39	63	13	137	230
Japan	7	3	7	44	2	64	10	5	16	49	6	86	150
Non-OECD	338	59	266	203	19	885	341	92	476	366	86	1 360	2 245
E. Europe/Eurasia	21	3	8	3	1	36	32	11	20	8	2	73	109
Russia	12	2	3	1	1	18	19	8	6	1	2	36	54
Asia	212	46	231	170	7	666	188	59	371	269	35	921	1 587
China	123	32	184	126	3	467	51	29	251	143	22	496	964
India	36	6	37	32	1	112	69	12	78	93	6	258	370
Southeast Asia	22	5	4	8	3	42	34	9	14	18	6	83	124
Middle East	7	1	4	8	3	23	5	3	45	36	19	109	131
Africa	30	4	8	15	6	63	52	7	18	39	25	140	203
Latin America	68	5	15	7	1	97	64	11	22	15	5	118	214
Brazil	38	4	13	5	-	59	36	8	16	7	2	69	128
World	422	98	503	370	40	1 433	431	151	926	650	143	2 301	3 734
European Union	31	15	120	58	4	229	29	24	209	121	25	408	637

* Other includes geothermal, concentrating solar power and marine.

Worldwide, over 3 700 GW of renewables generation capacity are built between 2013 and 2040, equal to about three-times the current total installed capacity of China. Taking into account the retirement of almost 890 GW of older installations that need to be replaced, total renewables capacity increases by 2 850 GW to about 4 550 GW in 2040. Installed wind power capacity expands more than that of any other type of renewables-based generation technology between 2013 and 2040, with over 1 400 GW of capacity being added and 425 GW retired (Table 7.3 and Table 7.4). Solar PV sees the second-largest capacity additions, with more than 1 000 GW of new installations and some 225 GW of retirements. Hydropower capacity increases less than wind power and solar PV to 2040, though output from hydropower increases more than solar PV because its average capacity factor (the ratio of output to capacity) is higher. Renewable energy technologies account for 60% of the growth in total installed power generation capacity. The average share of renewables in total global capacity reaches 42% in 2040, up from 29% today: it is slightly higher in the OECD at 46%, and slightly lower at 40% in non-OECD countries.

Transport

The annual global consumption of biofuels in transport has more than tripled since 2005, increasing from 1.1% to 3.2% of total road-transport energy consumption in 2012, under the impetus, primarily, of expanding supportive policies in the United States, European Union and Brazil, and high oil prices (Figure 7.6). However, the rate of growth has slowed in the past few years, partly due to several extraneous factors. The global financial crisis and the associated reductions in gross domestic product (GDP) growth, together with implementation of policies to reduce the average fuel consumption of road vehicles, have suppressed the growth in demand for liquid transport fuels. As biofuels policies typically support the blending of specified volumes of ethanol into gasoline and of biodiesel into conventional oil-based diesel, this has reduced the amount of biofuels required to meet the blending mandates and lowered the growth of biofuels use. The effect has been widespread, as over 60 countries around the world have introduced this type of measure (though not all are mandatory). In addition, poor harvests in some key countries and policies which have adversely affected the competitiveness of biofuels have slowed growth in recent years. As a result of lower than expected demand, investment in biofuel refineries has slowed dramatically in all major markets, falling from $6.5 billion globally in 2010 to $2.9 billion in 2012, having peaked in 2007 at $28 billion. However, biofuels continue to command some policy support, even though concerns about the sustainability of biofuels, particularly in Europe, have held back growth to some degree – a constraint compounded by a lack of progress in the commercialisation of advanced biofuels. But as the global economy recovers, harvests improve and advanced biofuels are commercialised at scale from around 2020 (as is assumed in the New Policies Scenario), growth in the consumption of biofuels resumes to some degree.

In the New Policies Scenario, global consumption of biofuels increases from 1.3 million barrels of oil equivalent per day (mboe/d) in 2012 to 2.2 mboe/d in 2020 and 4.6 mboe/d in 2040 (Table 7.5). Biofuels account for 8% of road-transport energy consumption by the end of the projection period, drawing on continued support measures and technological advances, which reduce costs and improve competitiveness as the cost of fossil fuels rise. Biofuels continue to be used mainly for road transport, but their use as aviation fuel begins to take off during the *Outlook* period. Ethanol remains the leading biofuel, enjoying widespread policy support and increasing its share of total biofuels consumption from 66% in 2012 to 72% in 2040. Biodiesel production also increases, but at a less rapid pace.

Figure 7.6 ▷ Biofuels consumption in road transport by region in the New Policies Scenario

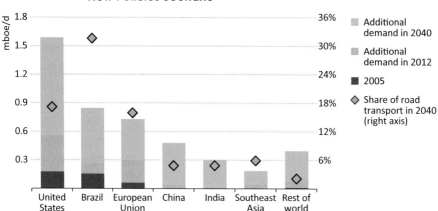

In the New Policies Scenario, the consumption of biofuels remains concentrated in the United States, European Union and Brazil, though their combined share of global consumption drops, from nearly 90% in 2012 to 70% in 2040, largely as a result of growing consumption in China and other Asian countries. The prospects for biofuels remain sensitive to changes in blending mandates and other forms of market support, which occurs regularly. For example, India is considering doubling its ethanol blending mandate to 10% (though this policy change is not included in the New Policies Scenario).

In the United States, the main driver of biofuels use is the Renewable Fuel Standard programme, which was introduced in 2005 and expanded in 2007. Now known as RFS2, it requires minimum volumes of renewable fuels to be blended into gasoline and diesel each year, rising (though this is under review) to a total of 36 billion gallons (136 billion litres) by 2022. In the New Policies Scenario, the assumed continuation of policy support leads to a rise in total biofuels consumption in the United States from 0.6 mboe/d in 2012 to 0.9 mboe/d in 2025 and 1.6 mboe/d in 2040. However, reaching the volumes set out under the fuel standard faces two challenges. The first is that gasoline demand is lower than projected when the RFS2 was adopted, lowering the maximum volume of ethanol to be blended into gasoline that can be consumed by the fleet of vehicles – the so-called "blend wall". At present E10 (gasoline with 10% ethanol) has been approved by the EPA for sales to all vehicles and E15 for all vehicles built after 2001. Higher ethanol blends, such as E85, can only be used by specially designed flex-fuel vehicles. Unless sales of the higher ethanol blends can be expanded, the fleet of vehicles in operation may not be able to consume the amount of biofuels required by the EPA rule. In recognition of this constraint, the EPA has proposed a downward adjustment in the renewable fuel mandate for 2014. The second constraint is the availability of advanced biofuels, the amount of which has fallen short of the mandated volumes to date, forcing the EPA to lower the volumes required, including lowering the 2013 requirement from 6 million ethanol-equivalent gallons (22.7 million litres) to 800 000 (3.0 million litres). Rapid expansion of the capacity of advanced biofuel refineries is needed to catch up and keep pace with the original productiontargets.

Table 7.5 ▷ **Biofuels consumption in road transport by type of fuel and region in the New Policies Scenario** (mboe/d)

	Ethanol		Biodiesel		Total		Share of road-transport	
	2012	2040	2012	2040	2012	2040	2012	2040
OECD	0.6	1.6	0.3	0.8	0.9	2.4	4%	13%
Americas	0.5	1.4	0.0	0.3	0.6	1.7	4%	15%
United States	0.5	1.3	0.0	0.3	0.6	1.6	5%	17%
Europe	0.1	0.2	0.2	0.5	0.3	0.7	5%	14%
Non-OECD	0.2	1.7	0.1	0.4	0.4	2.1	2%	6%
E. Europe/Eurasia	0.0	0.0	0.0	0.0	0.0	0.0	0%	2%
Asia	0.0	0.8	0.0	0.1	0.1	1.0	1%	5%
China	0.0	0.5	0.0	0.0	0.0	0.5	1%	5%
India	0.0	0.3	0.0	0.0	0.0	0.3	0%	5%
Latin America	0.2	0.8	0.1	0.2	0.3	1.0	9%	22%
Brazil	0.2	0.7	0.1	0.1	0.3	0.8	17%	32%
World	0.8	3.3	0.4	1.2	1.3	4.5	3%	8%
European Union	0.1	0.2	0.2	0.5	0.3	0.7	5%	16%

In the European Union, biofuels have made up an increasing share of total liquid fuel demand for transport since 2005, reaching 5% in 2012. In the New Policies Scenario, this share continues to increase, driven by the Renewable Energy Directive that sets a target of 10% for renewable energy in transport by 2020. The contribution of biofuels derived from food crops has been controversial and in June 2014, the European Union Energy Council agreed, in principle, to limit to 7% the amount of these biofuels that may be counted towards meeting the 2020 target. This decision is subject to final approval by the European Parliament. The Energy Council also set a non-binding target for advanced biofuels, which can be made from a variety of feedstocks, of 0.5%. For the longer term, the European Commission in January 2014 proposed a framework for energy and climate policy to 2030 that sets a target that at least 27% of EU energy demand should be obtained from renewables, though it would be up to member states to determine the precise contribution of biofuels and other types of renewables. Though the proposal reinforced that food-based biofuels should not receive public support after 2020, a decision on the 2030 package is due to be taken by the Council of Ministers in October 2014. In the New

Policies Scenario, total EU biofuels consumption is projected to rise from 0.3 mboe/d in 2012 to 0.7 mboe/d in 2040, advanced biofuels increasingly making inroads as their economics improve.

In Brazil, biofuels have been an important part of liquid fuel supply for many years, making up a larger share of liquid fuels for transport than in any other country in the world. Since 2010, growth in biofuels consumption has stopped, due to depressed levels of consumption of hydrous ethanol compared to previous years. The under-pricing of gasoline has reduced the competitiveness of hydrous ethanol, which made up more than two-thirds of ethanol consumption in 2010, but only just above half in 2012 (IEA, 2013). Below-average harvests in recent years have limited the availability of sugarcane – the main feedstock for ethanol production in Brazil. This resulted in a reduction of the ethanol blending mandate, reducing the consumption of anhydrous ethanol (ethanol with low water content appropriate for blending). An improved harvest in 2013 allowed a return to a blending mandate of 25%, though the under-pricing of gasoline persisted. In the medium and long term, consumption continues to increase, supported by policy and growth in the number of flex-fuel cars on Brazil's roads that are able to use fuels with a wide range of ethanol content. Since almost all new cars in Brazil are now flex-fuel; they will make up a large share of the cars on the road in 2020. In the New Policies Scenario, consumption of biofuels in Brazil increases from 0.3 mboe/d in 2012 to 0.5 mboe/d in 2020 and 0.8 mboe/d in 2040.

A principal factor in the long-term prospects for biofuels is the likelihood of commercialisation of advanced technologies that offer higher yields and have better environmental credentials (including lower life-cycle carbon emissions, lower water requirements and avoid causing indirect land-use change). Cellulosic ethanol is a promising advanced biofuel that can be produced from many feedstocks, including agricultural and forestry residues, dedicated energy crops or forestry products. A few commercial plants and a number of demonstration plants are in operation around the world, but a significant increase in capacity hinges on reducing costs. Algae-based advanced biofuels are also promising, with many research efforts under way to improve the efficiency of the process and reduce the costs of production. We assume that, as technologies advance, some forms of advanced biofuels will become commercial on a large scale around the start of the next decade. The share of advanced biofuels in total biofuels climbs from less than 1% today to around 20% by 2040 in the New Policies Scenario.

Industry and buildings

Renewables produce a significant amount of process heat in industry and are used for space heating, water heating and cooking in the buildings sector. Heat in buildings from renewables is currently derived primarily from the traditional use of solid biomass for heating and cooking in developing countries. If traditional use of solid biomass is counted, heat produced from renewables worldwide was 1 102 Mtoe in 2012, equivalent to about one-quarter of the total heat produced globally. However, because of its harmful effects on human health and its poor fuel conversion efficiency, the traditional use of solid biomass is evolving, in favour of cleaner fuels and modern renewables. Excluding traditional use of solid biomass (as in our projections), heat produced from modern renewables globally amounted to 345 Mtoe in 2012, or 10% of the heat mix.

In the New Policies Scenario, heat produced from modern renewables expands at 2.6% per year over 2012-2040, to reach about 715 Mtoe. Growth is quicker in the buildings sector than in industry, with each sector consuming about half of the heat produced by modern renewables in 2040. In buildings, the European Union continues to lead the world in heat from modern renewables, principally in the form of bioenergy use in space heating (Figure 7.7). These technologies, along with increasing deployment of solar water heaters, also underpin significant growth in the buildings sector in the United States and China. In industry, bioenergy accounts for 90% of the global growth in heat production from modern renewables in the period to 2040. China, India and Africa see the largest incremental growth.

Figure 7.7 ▷ **Heat demand provided by renewable sources in the buildings and industry sectors by region in the New Policies Scenario**

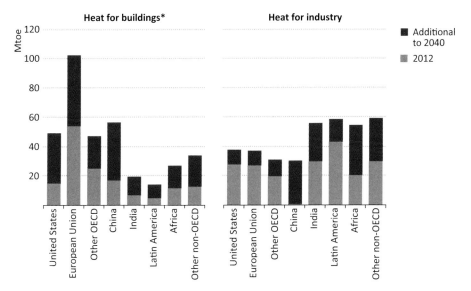

*Excludes traditional use of solid biomass in households.

Avoided CO₂ emissions

Renewable energy technologies emit no greenhouse gases as they generate electricity, making them an essential component of any strategy to mitigate climate change. The carbon dioxide (CO_2) emissions avoided annually, thanks to the deployment of these power generation technologies, can be estimated by calculating the additional CO_2 emissions that would have arisen if the amount of electricity generated by renewables was, instead, generated by the mix of other generation technologies in use in the year when the renewable energy technologies were built. Using this approach, in 2012, hydropower is estimated to have avoided 2.4 gigatonnes (Gt) of CO_2 emissions from fossil-fuel generation. Other renewables (mainly wind and bioenergy, but also solar PV and geothermal) avoided a further 0.5 Gt CO_2. The total of almost 3 Gt CO_2 avoided corresponds to 22% of global energy-related CO_2 emissions in the power sector in 2012 and is equivalent to the 2012 emissions of the power sector of the United States, Japan and Korea combined.

There is wide scope for renewables-based generation to further offset fossil-fuelled generation, thereby avoiding emissions in the power sector – currently the largest-emitting sector. As renewables power generation almost triples over 2012-2040 in the New Policies Scenario, annual CO_2 emissions avoided reach 6.6 Gt in 2040 (equivalent to about 40% of the total emissions in the power sector), with almost three-quarters of these savings coming from new power plants (Figure 7.8). The largest share of CO_2 emissions avoided in 2040 is attributable to increased output from hydropower (51%), followed by wind (24%), bioenergy (11%) and solar PV (9%). As the power mix in most regions becomes less dominated by coal over time, renewables displace fewer CO_2 emissions per unit of electricity generated. While in 1971, an additional kilowatt-hour (kWh) of electricity from hydropower avoided an average 848 grammes of CO_2 per kWh globally, it avoids 658 g CO_2/kWh today and is projected to avoid only 535 g CO_2/kWh in 2040.

Figure 7.8 ▷ Global CO_2 emissions avoided from greater use of renewables in the New Policies Scenario

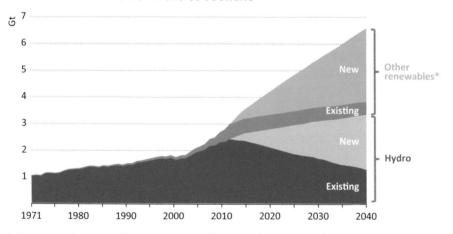

*Other renewables includes bioenergy, wind, solar PV, CSP, geothermal and marine. Note: Estimates of avoided CO_2 emissions are calculated by assuming that renewables generation would be replaced by generation from all other sources, which are scaled-up based on their mix as in the given year.

In addition to the CO_2 emissions avoided by renewables-based power generation technologies, the displacement of fossil fuels for heat production avoids almost 230 million tonnes (Mt) in 2040. Moreover, the use of biofuels in the transport sector reduces emissions by some 450 Mt in 2040 – provided that biofuels production does not lead to increased emissions from direct or indirect land-use changes. Altogether, the total emissions avoided by renewables amount to 7.2 Gt in 2040.

Renewables outlook by source in the New Policies Scenario

Bioenergy

Demand

Global demand for bioenergy was 1 344 Mtoe in 2012, accounting for 10% of total global primary energy demand. Bioenergy is unique among renewable energy technologies in being used in all sectors, including transport, where it can directly displace oil-product consumption (Figure 7.9). Traditional use of solid biomass in the buildings sector, mainly used in low-efficiency applications in residential settings, accounted for more than half of the global demand for bioenergy in 2012. Modern bioenergy is also consumed in buildings, for example in wood pellet-fuelled water heaters or space heaters. Bioenergy is also well-suited for power generation, as it is a combustible fuel (allowing the power output to be controlled more readily than variable resources like wind and solar). As a source of process heat and steam, bioenergy accounts for 7% of final energy consumption in industry. Bioenergy also makes a contribution to the energy transformation, including as a source of heat and power in refineries producing liquid biofuels. From 1990 to 2012, the increase in the absolute level of demand for modern bioenergy was more than double that of other non-hydro renewables, even though the growth rate was much lower.

Figure 7.9 ▷ **Global bioenergy use by sector in the New Policies Scenario**

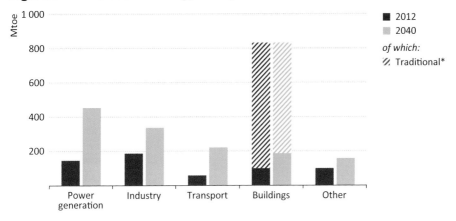

* Refers to traditional use of solid biomass in households.

In the New Policies Scenario, global demand for bioenergy increases to 2 000 Mtoe in 2040. In this total, the share of modern bioenergy rises to over two-thirds, as consumption in power generation and transport more than triple and use in industry increases by 80%. Growth also occurs in modern bioenergy use in the buildings sector, in both OECD and non-OECD countries, though efficiency gains over time help to temper the rate of growth. For example in industry, cumulative technology improvements from 2012 save 60 Mtoe of final consumption of bioenergy by 2040, nearly one-third of the amount consumed in 2012.

Consumption of traditional use of solid biomass in non-OECD countries declines over time due to greater penetration of improved cookstoves, increased urbanisation and improved availability of fuels that allow households to switch to modern forms of energy that are more energy efficient and have better health characteristics (see Chapter 15).

Production and trade

Matching demand growth, global supply of bioenergy increases substantially in the New Policies Scenario. Domestic resources are able to meet the vast majority of rising demand in all regions over the *Outlook* period, as policies supporting the increased use of bioenergy, including biofuel targets and mandates, tend to be adopted in regions with available biomass resources. Local resources tend to be the least-cost supply option, due to the relatively high cost of transporting biomass feedstocks. Aside from traditional use of solid biomass, all biomass feedstocks are called upon to contribute to the increasing supply, including non-food crops grown specifically for use in the energy sector, forestry and agricultural residues, forestry products (restricted to those that are available without reducing forested land area) and new feedstocks, such as algae. The total potential for production of bioenergy is enormous; more than ten-times the total demand levels reached in the New Policies Scenario, and, generally, well above demand levels in each region.

In the New Policies Scenario, the share of international trade in modern bioenergy remains small, less than 4%, through to 2040 due to the relatively high transport cost and the abundance of potential domestic supply. However, in volume terms, this means that net trade in bioenergy between regions is set to increase by several times from 2012 to 2040. Aggressive government policies and measures supporting the consumption of biofuels and use of bioenergy to generate power and produce heat do result in domestic supply being insufficient in some regions. Both trade in biofuels for transport and in solid biomass for power generation and heat production increase over time, each making up about half of net trade in bioenergy throughout the projection period. Raw biomass feedstocks are processed, dried and compressed into biomass pellets in order to increase the energy density and uniformity of the product, ultimately lowering transportation costs and improving the competitiveness of imported products in relation to domestic resources. Trade of most other forms of bioenergy is not commercially viable because of their low energy content per tonne and correspondingly high transport costs.

Inter-regional trade in biofuels for transport grows steadily until the early 2030s, eventually reaching a plateau as increasing domestic production of advanced biofuels tempers the demand for imports. Over the projection period, Brazil establishes itself as the main supplier to the world market, with vast resources available to produce low-cost sugarcane-based ethanol (Figure 7.10). This sugarcane production remains within the geographical areas set aside for biofuels, so it does not displace food crops or other agricultural products (IEA, 2013). In addition, the development of processes to produce ethanol from lignocellulosic feedstocks over the projection period releases more ethanol for export. Over time, the European Union continues to expand the demand it makes on the international market, remaining the largest net importer of biofuels through to 2040, as it strives to increase the share of renewable energy in its energy mix. The United States imports large amounts of sugarcane-based ethanol from Brazil today, as it is one of the few biofuels available at scale that qualifies as an advanced biofuel under the Renewable Fuel Standard. US exports of total biofuels have fallen sharply since 2011, pulled down by exports of fuel ethanol falling nearly 50%, despite strong growth in biodiesel exports. Over the projection period, demand for biofuels outstrips production in the United States, making the country more reliant on biofuel imports from Brazil. Other players emerge over the projection period, as countries in Southeast Asia contribute supply to the world market, in part taken up to meet growing demand in China, India and Korea.

Figure 7.10 ▷ **Production of biofuels by type and total biofuels demand by region in the New Policies Scenario, 2020 and 2040**

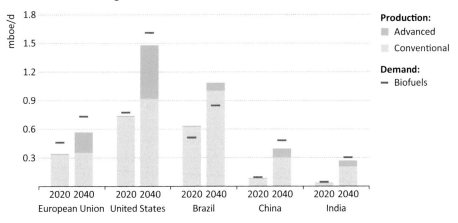

Hydropower

Hydropower is one of the oldest and most important renewable energy technologies. In 2012, it accounted for 16% of global electricity generation and its level of output was more than three-times that of all other renewables combined. Offering one of few economically viable forms of energy storage available, large dams with reservoirs or pumped storage provide flexibility to meet fluctuations in electricity load, which are becoming more frequent and more acute with the rapid growth in generation from wind and solar PV.

In the New Policies Scenario, some 850 GW of hydropower capacity is added worldwide in the period to 2040, with retirements of about 150 GW. About 80% of additions occur in non-OECD countries, where electricity demand growth is strong and considerable large-scale potential remains untapped. The scope to add further hydropower capacity in OECD countries is, by contrast, limited, as the best resources have already been tapped. China alone accounts for one-fifth of global capacity additions, though the rate of additions slows after 2020, as opportunities for large-scale projects diminish (Figure 7.11). Elsewhere, capacity expansion is biggest in other parts of Asia, namely India and Southeast Asia, and in Latin America, which still has large untapped resources in the Amazon region (IEA, 2013). Sub-Saharan Africa, where hydropower is fundamental to meeting incremental electricity needs, also sees significant growth in capacity (Box 7.1).

Figure 7.11 ▷ **Hydropower capacity additions by region in the New Policies Scenario**

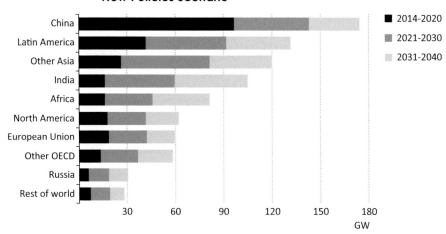

Hydropower generation increases by 2 550 TWh (70%) in the New Policies Scenario, the second-largest increase in renewables-based generation after wind. Its share of the global electricity mix remains flat at 16% in 2040, meaning it remains the third-biggest source of generation behind coal and gas. In most regions, hydropower accounts for less than 20% of electricity generation at the end of the projection period (Figure 7.12). Hydropower plays a much larger role in Latin America, where it accounts for about 55% of the power mix in 2040. This is largely due to an even higher share in Brazil.

Figure 7.12 ▷ **Hydropower generation and share of total generation in the New Policies Scenario**

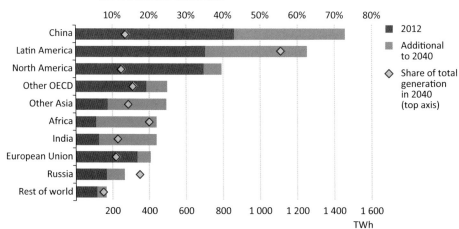

Box 7.1 ▷ **Hydropower in sub-Saharan Africa**

In sub-Saharan Africa, hydropower has long been an important source of power for several countries (see Part C). At the end of 2012, sub-Saharan Africa had 20 GW of installed hydropower capacity (about 5% of the world total), providing more than one-fifth of the region's total electricity supply. The largest hydropower projects, including Cahora Bassa in Mozambique, Inga I and II in DR Congo, Merowe in Sudan and Akosombo in Ghana, make up most of the hydropower capacity, though there is also widespread potential for small hydropower that could help millions of people in the region gain access to electricity.

Significant hydropower resources remain untapped, concentrated in a few countries, notably DR Congo and Ethiopia, as well as Angola, Madagascar, Cameroon, Nigeria and Gabon. In total, over 280 GW is technically feasible in sub-Saharan Africa. There is great interest in exploiting this potential in order to meet rapidly growing demand, increase access to electricity and improve the quality of the power supply. Some large hydropower projects could involve exports to neighbouring countries. International development agencies are generally supportive of these projects, as they are often economically attractive and compatible with climate policy objectives, though there can be environmental and social reservations. The development of regional power pools, including new transmission lines, increases the size of the potential electricity market, thereby making development of large hydropower projects more viable.

There are several large hydropower projects under construction or in the final planning phases, including Grand Ethiopian Renaissance and Gilgel Gibe III in Ethiopia, Inga III in DR Congo, Mambilla in Nigeria and Laúca in Angola. Combined, these projects account for about 18 GW and make up nearly half of the increase in total hydropower capacity in sub-Saharan Africa to 2030 in the New Policies Scenario. By 2040, installed hydropower capacity reaches 94 GW in the region.

Wind power

Installed wind power capacity increased from 17 GW in 2000 to 317 GW in 2013, an average growth rate of 25% per year. This increase corresponded to about 13% of the increase of total installed power capacity globally. The expansion was led by the European Union (104 GW), China (91 GW), the United States (58 GW) and India (19 GW). Together, they accounted for over 90% of the additions, mainly thanks to support policies. The share of wind generation in total generation worldwide rose from 0.2% in 2000 to 2.3% in 2012.

More countries have introduced policies to support wind power in recent years, thereby boosting capacity additions. About 40 GW of new wind power capacity was added in 2009, 46 GW in 2012 and 35 GW in 2013. The lower level in 2013 was particularly due to a decline of capacity additions in the United States, where regulatory uncertainties led capacity additions of wind power to drop from 13 GW in 2012 to 1 GW in 2013.

Both the record year in 2012 and the drop in 2013 in the United States were due to issues over qualification for the Production Tax Credit (PTC) – the main support system in place in the United States. In the first case, uncertainty about possible renewal of the PTC led to a rush to complete projects before the end of the year (more than 8 GW in the final quarter) in order to qualify for support before it expired (AWEA, 2014). By compressing the construction period, this provided a boost to the capacity additions in 2012, but also helps to explain why virtually no wind projects were completed in the first half of 2013. Also in 2013, there was a change in the regulation that allowed projects to qualify for the PTC if they had started construction by the end of the year. With this change, the incentive for developers was to start more projects by the end of the year instead of rushing to finish projects already in progress. By the end of 2013, there were more than 12 GW of wind power projects under construction in the United States, which will help global capacity additions rebound in the next few years.

In the New Policies Scenario, wind continues to grow strongly over the projection period, reaching 1 320 GW of installed capacity in 2040 and accounting for over 8% of the global generation mix. This strong deployment of wind power is a result of ongoing support measures in many countries, including renewable energy targets, of the continued fall of production costs and of increasing wholesale prices. These factors make onshore wind power competitive in several countries, compared with average wholesale prices. However, in most cases, offshore wind still requires support through the *Outlook* period, even with a strong reduction of costs per unit of production (about 40% over the projection period). The rate of deployment of offshore wind power in the New Policies Scenario depends on the wind power industry being able to achieve significant cost reductions.

Onshore wind exceeds 1 130 GW in 2040, almost quadrupling the current level and still accounting for the majority (about 85%) of the total installed wind capacity in 2040. Offshore wind deployment grows at a much faster rate – 13% per year, but starts from a much lower base. Installed capacity of offshore wind power reaches almost 190 GW in 2040, with a growing share of annual additions over the projection period, reaching about 15% of annual wind power additions in the 2030s. About one-fifth of the increase in total wind capacity from 2013 to 2040 is located in the European Union and a further 30% in China (Figure 7.13).

In capacity terms, wind power achieves the second-largest increase over 2013-2040 among all power technologies, second only to gas-fired power plants. Wind power capacity increases by around 40 GW per year until 2020 – mainly driven by targets and support measures in Europe, China, the United States and India – and then gradually slows to an average of 34 GW in the 2030s (Figure 7.14). With an assumed lifetime of 25 years[3], all existing capacity and a

---

3. The technical lifetime for both onshore and offshore wind was assumed at 20 years in previous WEOs. It has been changed to a distribution centred around 25 years, ranging from 20 to 30 years. This change is based on growing evidence of the greater durability of turbines than originally expected.

further 108 GW yet to be added (for a total of 425 GW) will need to be replaced[4] over the projection period, amounting to annual replacements of around 40 GW per year in the late 2030s. The size of the global market (net additions plus replacements) of wind capacity remains fairly stable at just above 40 GW for the first-half of the projection period; it then gradually increases to almost 75 GW per year towards 2040.

Figure 7.13 ▷ **Installed wind power capacity by type and region in the New Policies Scenario, 2040**

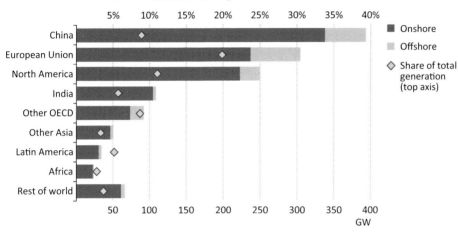

The increase in installed wind power capacity over the *Outlook* period is highest in China (302 GW), followed by the European Union (187 GW), the United States (137 GW) and India (89 GW). As in the past, these four regions account for the bulk of the increase in global wind capacity over the projection period, but they account for a declining share of annual wind additions over time. Additions slowdown, in particular, in the European Union and China, as the quality of potential sites diminishes, electricity demand slows and other low-carbon sources are deployed.

Through the strong deployment of new capacity, wind achieves the largest increase in power generation among all renewables sources, including hydropower. The share of wind in total power generation increases more than that of any other source, though remaining below 10% globally, and wind contributes half of the increase in the share of renewables in the global mix. At low shares (5-10%) of annual generation, the integration of generation from variable renewables, including wind power, does not present major technical challenges (IEA, 2014a). The share of wind generation alone exceeds this range in some regions, particularly the European Union (reaching 20% in 2040), indicating that some technical challenges will need to addressed in order to achieve this level of generation.

---

4. All renewable capacities are assumed to be replaced at the end of their technical lifetime by the latest version of the technology, but typically at 80% of the investment cost for a new plant.

Figure 7.14 ▷ **Wind power capacity additions and replacements, and share of total generation by selected region in the New Policies Scenario**

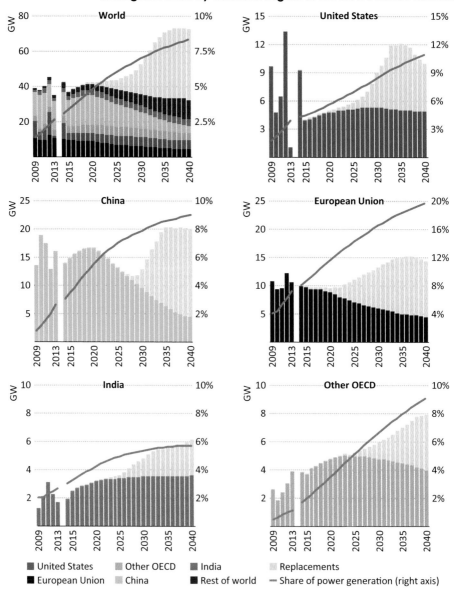

United States   ■ Other OECD   ■ India   ▨ Replacements
■ European Union   ▨ China   ■ Rest of world   — Share of power generation (right axis)

Solar photovoltaics (PV)

The last few years have seen an unprecedented boom in the deployment of solar PV in several countries, as a result of policy incentives and a steep decline in the price of PV technology. European countries accounted for the majority of this increase until 2012. In 2013, additions were largest in China and Japan, after new support measures were put in place and they accounted for half of the new capacity installed in 2013, setting a new record for annual global solar PV deployment. Global installed capacity of solar PV reached 136 GW in 2013, almost all of it built in the last decade and over 70% in the last three years. In 2013, only five countries had more than 10 GW installed: Germany (36 GW), China (20 GW), Italy (18 GW), Japan (13 GW) and the United States (13 GW). Combined, these countries account for almost three-quarters of the global total. Other European countries account for a further 25 GW in aggregate and India for 2 GW.

The fall in the unit costs of solar panels in recent years was the result of several factors. A growing number of countries put in place support policies for solar PV, pushing up the demand for new panels and the expectation for demand for more panels in the future. Rapid expansion of panel manufacturing capacity led to improvements in technology, economies of scale, and, eventually, the emergence of over-capacity in PV panel production as some countries scaled back their deployment of solar PV. The growing production of low-cost panels from China also contributed to falling unit costs.

The European Union accounted for about 60% of global solar PV installed capacity in 2013. Within the EU, Germany accounts for some 45% of the solar PV capacity, with nine other countries having over 1 GW installed and together accounting for a further 50% – Italy (23%), Spain (6%), France (6%), United Kingdom (4%), Belgium (4%), Greece (3%), Czech Republic (3%), Romania (1%) and Bulgaria (1%). Many of these countries experienced short-lived spikes of deployment, focused in one or two years, followed by sharp reductions as support measures for new installations were reduced or removed. This boom-and-bust phenomenon often reflected inability to adjust support policies quickly enough to match changing market conditions and falling costs, resulting in total deployment and support costs that went beyond expectations. Japan is currently making a very strong push for solar PV, with a feed-in-tariff put in place in July 2012 that has resulted in the approval of 69 GW of projects over less than two years, 37 GW of this having been approved during the first three months of 2014. As of October 2014, it is not clear whether all the approved projects will be developed or how long strong support for further additions will continue.

In the New Policies Scenario, overall solar PV capacity continues to grow strongly, at 7.4% per year, to reach some 930 GW in 2040 and account for 3% of global electricity generation – more than seven-times the share in 2012. This deployment is underpinned by ongoing government support as, despite the continuous falling costs of production, solar PV becomes competitive only in a few locations on a cost parity basis (when it is compared against the wholesale electricity price [IEA, 2013]).[5] Households with PV systems and connections to the grid should pay their full share of the costs to maintain and reinforce the power grid, to avoid a free-rider effect that unfairly shifts the burden of these costs onto those households without PV systems. To address this concern, regulators in the two leading states in the United States in terms of solar PV deployment, California and Arizona, have recently provided for fixed charges to be levied on the power bills of households with solar PV systems. Some EU countries are considering similar measures. Changes could be made in the rate structure to make tariffs reflective of the fixed costs incurred.

---

5. The analysis was presented in the Renewable Energy Outlook in the World Energy Outlook 2013, available at www.worldenergyoutlook.org/media/weowebsite/2013/WEO2013_Ch06_Renewables.pdf.

Figure 7.15 ▷ **Solar PV capacity by type and region in the New Policies Scenario, 2040**

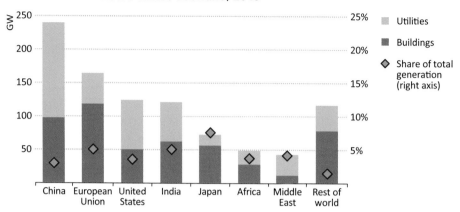

Almost 50 GW, or 36%, of the currently installed capacity of solar PV is in large, utility-scale, installations. In the New Policies Scenario, the capacity of utility-scale solar PV increases at a faster rate than solar PV in buildings, reaching about 425 GW in 2040, nine-times the level today. Deployment is led by China, the United States and India (Figure 7.15). Solar PV installed capacity in buildings grows from 87 GW in 2013 to over 500 GW, though installations in buildings account for a shrinking share of total solar PV over time, falling from more than two-thirds today to just over half in 2040.

Over the *Outlook* period, the annual increase of total global installed solar PV capacity slows from the peak of 38 GW in 2013 to 29 GW in 2020, then levels off at just above 28 GW through to 2040. With an assumed lifetime of 25 years, all capacity in place today and a further 90 GW added in the coming years (for a total of 227 GW) will need to be replaced by 2040.[6] Annual replacements reach about 33 GW per year in the late 2030s (Figure 7.17). The size of the global solar PV market (new installations plus replacements) decreases in line with the rate of new installations initially and then increases in the late 2020s as more replacements are required, reaching about 60 GW towards 2040.

Solar PV capacity is set to increase strongly in many regions in the New Policies Scenario, driven mainly by government policies reflecting environmental goals, the solar resource potential and economic considerations (including subsidies). The level of deployment of solar PV should be taken into consideration when designing support measures, as there is a threshold at which additional solar PV will be difficult to accommodate while maintaining the reliability of electricity supply, unless coupled with additional investment in energy storage technologies, expansion of demand-side management programmes and transmission grid interconnections, or curtailment of solar PV output. The mid-day summer peak demand (the highest level of

---

6. The technical lifetime for PV in buildings was assumed to be 20 years in previous *WEOs*, while that of large-scale PV was 25 years. In this edition, they are both set to a distribution centred around 25 years, ranging from 20 to 30 years. This change is based on growing expectations of the durability of PV panels.

demand in the middle of the day during summer months) provides an approximation of this threshold, representing the maximum level of solar PV output that could be accommodated under certain conditions.[7] Mid-day summer peak demand typically occurs on sunny days (in particular in countries with significant electricity demand due to air conditioning), when solar PV is producing the most – typically 80-90% of total installed capacity, as some panels may be sub-optimally oriented, shaded or in need of maintenance. Therefore, the share of maximum solar PV output in mid-day summer peak demand provides a useful indicator of the scale of the impact of solar PV deployment on the power system. It also provides an indicator of the value of solar PV in the system at different levels of deployment (see Spotlight). By contrast, the share of solar PV generation in total generation on an annual basis, a commonly used measure of solar PV deployment, fails to provide an indication of when the level of solar PV deployment is approaching the threshold at which additional changes to the power system are required.

The increase of solar PV capacity over the *Outlook* period is highest in China (220 GW), followed by India (118 GW), the United States (111 GW), the European Union (85 GW) and Japan (60 GW). These five regions account for three-quarters of the total increase in solar PV capacity, though the share they represent declines over time as the decreasing costs of new capacity lead to more widespread deployment throughout the world. The slowdown of annual net capacity additions is mainly due to a slowdown in additions in Japan, China and the EU that is only partially offset by an increase in other countries.

In Japan, the annual increase of installed solar PV capacity peaks in the next couple of years at around 8 GW and then fall back quickly to around 1 GW after 2020, as the share of PV output in mid-day summer peak demand approaches 30%, and reaches 37% in 2040. In China, additions remain similar to the record year in 2013 in the first years of the projections, with a slight slowdown to 2020, in line with the government ambition of reaching 100 GW by 2020. As electricity demand growth slows over the projection period and other low-carbon technologies continue to be added to the power mix, the pace of capacity additions of solar PV slows. The share of PV output in mid-day summer peak demand reaches 10% soon after 2020 and over 14% by 2040.

In the European Union, the annual growth in solar PV capacity drops substantially from the peak of over 22 GW in 2011, averaging 5-6 GW per year in the period 2015-2020 and slowing thereafter because of saturation in major markets and limited additional support measures. Nonetheless, the solar PV market (new installations plus replacements) reaches almost 15 GW per year around 2035. In the United States, the annual increase of installed capacity is steadier (about 4 GW) through to 2040, as the share of solar PV in mid-day summer peak demand rises from only 2% at present to around 15% by 2040, mainly driven by state-level renewable portfolio standards and by the new EPA regulations (the Clean Power Plan). With very ambitious solar PV targets, India keeps increasing annual additions to a plateau of 6 GW per year, reaching more than 23% of summer peak demand by 2040.

---

7. Mid-day summer peak demand represents the maximum solar PV output that can be accommodated assuming three conditions: (1) a perfect grid able to deliver output from solar PV to all demand without any losses; (2) perfect flexibility of all other power plants (including other renewables), able to compensate for solar PV output and meet electricity demand; and (3) zero availability of energy storage or demand-side management.

Solar PV: declining costs and value with increasing deployment

To determine the competitiveness of any technology, including solar PV, both the cost and the value must be considered. While the economics of solar PV from the household perspective could be an important driver of the deployment, the system perspective is appropriate for policy-makers, concerned with the overall reliability and economic efficiency of the system in line with environmental goals, energy security concerns and other considerations. The falling costs of solar PV in recent years (due in part to increasing deployment) have lead to discussions concerning its competitiveness, suggesting that, once below a specific cost level, solar PV will dominate the market. However, this simplification fails to consider the value of solar PV at different levels of deployment. From the electricity system perspective, the value of deployed solar PV is closely tied to the avoided costs in the entire system. The larger portion of this value is generally represented by the avoided operating costs (fuel, CO_2 and variable O&M) and fixed costs (investment and fixed O&M) of the other power plants (RMI, 2013). With increasing levels of solar PV deployment, the avoided operating and fixed costs tend to fall for two main reasons: (1) solar PV increasingly displaces generation from technologies with lower operating costs and (2) it can displace the need for other capacity, but only a limited amount (unless energy storage is available).

Figure 7.16 ▷ **Illustrative electricity load curve for high-demand summer day**

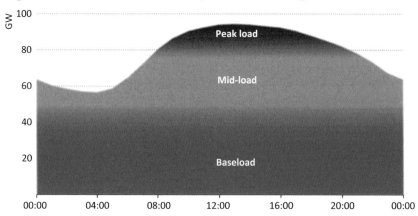

To illustrate these points, consider an example daily load curve that has a maximum demand of 95 GW around mid-day (Figure 7.16).[8] The output from the first 15 GW of solar PV deployed in the example (the maximum output is equal to about 14% of the peak level of demand) displaces generation from high-cost peakload power plants,

---

8. The shape of this demand is similar to observed data for high-demand summer days in important solar PV markets, such as Germany, Italy, Japan and California (US).

typically oil-fired power plants with operating costs often above $200/MWh, or open-cycle gas turbine plants with operating costs between $50-$150/MWh (depending on the gas price and plant efficiency). A carbon price of $20/tonne of CO_2 would add $10-20/MWh to these operating costs. Solar PV output consumed on-site also avoids transmission and distribution (T&D) losses, so that 1 unit of solar PV output displaces 1.1 units of output from on-grid generators (at the world average T&D loss rate of 9%). For deployment of solar PV from 15 GW to 40 GW, the output displaces generation from mid-load plants with moderate operating costs, in the range of $30-100/MWh. The deployment of solar PV beyond 40 GW (when its maximum output approaches 40% of the mid-day peak demand) displaces generation from baseload plants that have the lowest operating costs, often below $50/MWh. When this baseload generation comes from nuclear, hydropower or other renewables, the additional solar PV does not reduce CO_2 emissions, nor gain an advantage based on a carbon price.

In addition to avoiding operating costs, the deployment of solar PV can reduce the need for other types of generation capacity in summer-peaking systems, displacing the associated fixed costs. However, the addition of solar PV capacity does not reduce the need for other capacity by an equal amount, as its capacity credit[9] is always lower than for dispatchable plants. In summer-peaking systems, the capacity credit of solar PV is highest for the first capacity deployed, upwards of 40% (PJM, 2014), and could avoid levelised fixed costs as high as $40-70/MWh (based on peakload plants operating for only 5-6% of the hours in a year). However, the capacity credit falls to zero when the highest level of residual demand[10] occurs at sunset (after the first 15 GW in the example) and solar PV can no longer help to meet this demand. Therefore, only the need for peakload power plants can be directly displaced by the deployment of solar PV. In winter-peaking or in evening-peaking systems, the capacity credit of solar PV is generally close to zero, so even the first GW of solar PV deployed does not displace any fixed costs.

Combining the avoided operating and fixed costs, the output from the first solar PV deployed could have a value to the system of over $300/MWh when it displaces oil-fired power plants and has a relatively high capacity credit. Where solar PV displaces open-cycle gas turbines, the avoided costs are closer to $200/MWh. With deployment of solar PV beyond 15 GW in the example (when maximum output is about 14% of mid-day peak demand), the avoided operating and fixed costs fall significantly – to the range of $30-100/MWh (before including avoided T&D losses or a carbon price). The avoided costs continue to fall with further deployment of solar PV, just as the costs are driven down. In the end, both the declining cost and value to the system must be considered in determining the competitiveness of solar PV from the power system perspective.

9. Capacity credit refers to the portion of installed capacity that can be confidently relied on during periods of peak demand, and is a measure of the contribution of the capacity to system adequacy.

10. Residual demand here refers to the load curve that remains after subtracting the output of solar PV. (See *World Energy Outlook 2013* for examples).

Figure 7.17 ▷ Solar PV capacity additions and share of maximum PV output in peak demand* by selected region in the New Policies Scenario

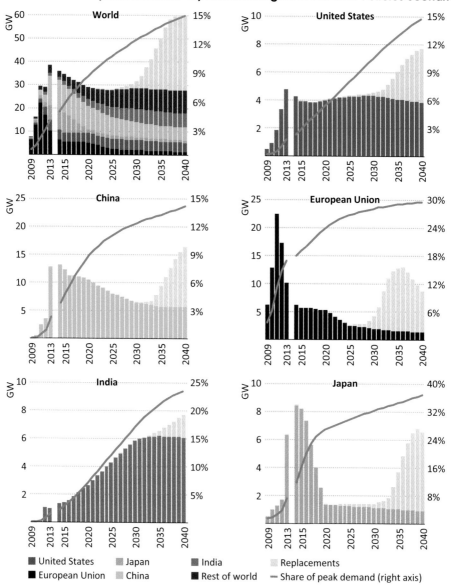

United States	Japan	India	Replacements
European Union	China	Rest of world	— Share of peak demand (right axis)

*Peak demand in these graphs refers to mid-day summer peak demand.

Other renewables

Geothermal electricity generation in the New Policies Scenario increases from 70 TWh in 2012 to almost 380 TWh in 2040. Capacity additions during the projection period are spread relatively evenly around the world, though the largest amounts are installed in Africa, the United States, Japan and Southeast Asia. Geothermal power can be very attractive because it provides reliable baseload power, though its development in any region hinges strongly on the availability of economically viable resources.

Electricity output from CSP grows very quickly in the New Policies Scenario, at an average annual rate of 16.7%, to reach around 360 TWh in 2040. This is just less than 30% of the level of generation from solar PV at the end of the projection period, partly as a result of weaker policy support and the additional costs incurred to build transmission lines to reach CSP installations located far from load centres. CSP capacity additions in the next few years occur primarily in the United States, though China, the Middle East and Africa lead additions after 2020. Average capacity factors for CSP plants improve during the projection period, because of increasing use of technologies with thermal storage.

Marine energy makes a small but growing contribution to meeting global energy needs in the New Policies Scenario, with generation increasing from 0.5 TWh in 2012 to 66 TWh in 2040. Capacity additions occur mainly in the EU. The viability of technologies that convert the kinetic energy of tides to power depends on a large tidal range and the proximity of the installation to existing transmission infrastructure. Wave power has significant potential, but related technologies require further improvement to drive down costs.

Economics of renewables

Investment

Investment in renewable energy technologies totalled $2.3 trillion over 2000-2013, of which over 90% went into power generation technologies, with the remainder spent on biofuel refineries. Over the period, investment in renewables in the power sector surged almost five-fold from $57 billion in 2000 to over $290 billion in 2011, and then fell to about $270 billion in 2012 and 2013. The decline was largely caused by significant reductions in the cost of solar PV, while the level of deployment remained constant in 2011 and 2012. Less wind power deployment also contributed to the decline in 2013.

Investment in renewables-based power plants accounted for 58% of global power generation investment between 2000 and 2013. Regional differences in this spending are marked: in OECD countries renewables accounted for 65% of the investment in new power plants in that period, about 70% for wind and solar PV and much of it installed outside the traditional utility sector (Box 7.2). In non-OECD countries, renewables accounted for half of investment in power plants over the same period, but only 37% of the expenditure went to non-hydro technologies, highlighting the dominant role of hydropower in developing countries.

Over the *Outlook* period to 2040, investments amounting to $7.8 trillion are needed for renewable energy supply globally, $0.4 trillion in biofuels and the remainder in power generation technologies. These projected investments do not include the additional $337 billion needed to extend and upgrade electricity T&D networks in order to integrate renewables (4% of the total T&D investment over the *Outlook* period). The bulk of the investment in renewables ($7.4 trillion) is to power generation technologies, roughly 60% of the total power plant investment in that period (Table 7.6). Most of this capital expenditure goes into wind power ($2.5 trillion) followed by hydropower ($1.9 trillion) and solar PV ($1.7 trillion) (Figure 7.18). Non-OECD countries account for 55% of worldwide investment in renewable power generation. In developing countries, investments in renewables are 57% of total investment in power plants, compared with 66% in OECD countries.

Figure 7.18 ▷ **Global investment in renewables-based power capacity by source in the New Policies Scenario**

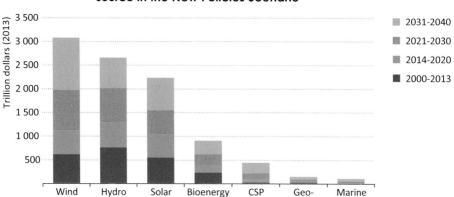

The European Union steps up investment in wind and solar PV over time, accounting for almost one-quarter of worldwide investment in the New Policies Scenario in renewables for power over the course of the *Outlook* period – more than any other region. Renewables make up around 70% of EU power capacity investment. The investment pattern in China makes a remarkable shift: in the period 2000-2013, 32% of the investment in renewables was for wind and solar PV, while 63% was invested in hydropower projects. From 2014-2040, 65% of the investment in renewables goes to wind and solar PV, while the share into hydropower drops to 21%. US investment in renewables for power is almost $960 billion over the *Outlook* period, accounting for more than 60% of total power capacity investments in the country. Wind power accounts for the bulk of the expenditure (24%), followed by solar PV (18%) and bioenergy (9%).

The rapid deployment of non-hydro renewables, such as wind and solar, will require careful attention both to the design of electricity markets and the nature of support schemes. The expansion of non-hydro renewables has so far been underpinned by widespread government support. Further deployment hinges on continuity of this support over most of the *Outlook* period. While providing this support, governments should ensure as much competition as possible between different renewable energy technologies. They should also aim to withdraw from fostering renewables as soon as they can compete on their own, though giving sufficient notice to safeguard continuing financial flows into the sector. With the right conditions, the risk of investment in renewables can be lowered, helping to boost their expansion. Of equal importance, during the period of continued financial support of renewables, is close attention to the adequacy of incentives in the competitive market for the necessary complementary investment in other generation technologies.

Table 7.6 △ Cumulative renewable investments by region and type in the New Policies Scenario ($2013, billion)

	2014-2025						2026-2040						2014-2040
	Hydro	Bioenergy	Wind	Solar PV	Other*	Total	Hydro	Bioenergy	Wind	Solar PV	Other*	Total	Total
OECD	215	139	521	421	85	1 381	227	190	846	438	207	1 908	3 289
Americas	88	69	166	136	44	503	91	86	329	174	59	739	1 243
United States	48	60	120	122	36	387	49	73	256	151	42	571	958
Europe	104	54	302	121	23	605	103	82	429	143	106	863	1 468
Asia Oceania	23	16	53	164	17	273	33	23	87	120	43	306	579
Japan	16	10	19	146	5	196	24	12	39	96	21	191	387
Non-OECD	666	117	396	323	69	1 570	798	214	712	510	284	2 517	4 087
E. Europe/Eurasia	42	11	16	7	2	80	69	39	38	12	5	164	243
Russia	24	8	5	1	2	41	41	30	13	2	4	90	131
Asia	397	77	331	248	26	1 080	439	120	522	325	120	1 525	2 605
China	211	46	264	167	12	700	90	61	348	146	80	726	1 425
India	73	13	51	53	5	194	172	19	103	124	22	440	634
Southeast Asia	45	10	7	19	8	89	88	16	26	34	14	178	266
Middle East	15	2	7	15	13	52	11	8	80	57	60	216	268
Africa	64	13	14	36	24	151	123	21	30	90	79	344	496
Latin America	147	13	27	17	3	207	156	26	41	26	20	268	475
Brazil	83	10	23	10	-	126	86	18	29	13	9	155	281
World	881	256	917	744	153	2 951	1 024	404	1 558	949	491	4 426	7 377
European Union	80	51	285	118	23	557	73	79	403	141	105	802	1 359

* Other includes geothermal, concentrating solar power and marine.

Box 7.2 ▷ **Sources of investment in non-hydro renewables for electricity**

The ownership of non-hydro renewables-based generating assets in some parts of the world is unlike that of large-scale fossil-fuelled, nuclear and hydropower plants. The traditional generating assets are typically owned by large public utilities or well-established independent power producers, often operating in several countries, who are well-positioned to fund investment out of their own cash flows or externally, through borrowing or bonds. By contrast, non-hydro renewables projects, such as roof-top solar PV, small hydro, small onshore wind farms and agricultural biogas projects, involve a variety of players, including households, municipalities, small businesses, specialised project developers and small power companies, all of whom rely on external financing more than utilities. This is because of the generally smaller scale of the projects and the fact that investment conditions are site specific, requiring knowledge of the local market, policies and regulations (IEA, 2014b).

In the European Union, which leads the world in non-hydro renewables generation, ownership by municipalities, small businesses and households is particularly high, especially in the case of wind power and solar PV. By contrast, ownership of such assets in China and the United States is dominated by established electric utilities. Based on data from Bloomberg New Energy Finance, we calculate that retained earnings and equity cover only about 45% of total finance for non-hydro renewables – much lower than for conventional power generation assets – with most of the rest coming from short- and long-term borrowing. Renewables projects can permit higher leveraging (debt financing) where revenues are guaranteed by fixed feed-in tariffs under long-term purchase agreements, so reducing the risk of shortfalls in cash flow and providing security to lenders.

Subsidies

Various forms of subsidies are used in a growing number of countries around the world to encourage the development and deployment of renewables. The rationale for these subsidies rests on the benefits their use brings – to energy security, the environment, economy and energy access – benefits that are not adequately reflected in market prices. By early 2014, at least 138 countries had renewable energy support policies in place, up from 127 a year before (REN21, 2014). Most measures concern renewables for power, the most common and important being tax credits, feed-in tariffs, price premiums and portfolio obligations (Table 7.7). The leading form of support for biofuels remains blending mandates, complemented by tax incentives and direct public financing. The cost of these subsidies may be borne by taxpayers or passed through to end-users.

Although significant technology cost reductions have been achieved during recent years, in particular for solar PV, the average cost of generating electricity is still higher for several renewable energy technologies compared with conventional technologies. Further reductions in production costs are required to boost the role of renewables in the future energy mix. The principal exceptions are hydropower and geothermal, which are already mature and fully competitive in many countries, although new projects may incur higher costs as the best sites have already been exploited in some parts of the world. The cost of electricity from bioenergy-based power plants is unlikely to fall significantly, as the technology is mature and the costs are largely driven by the price of the feedstock, which is not expected to fall. Similarly, the scope for lowering the production costs of conventional biofuels is constrained by feedstock prices. Cost reductions for conventional biofuels are expected to be modest in the New Policies Scenario, due to incremental technological improvements that lead to lower capital costs and marginal efficiency gains. Despite rising oil prices over the projection period, which improve the competitiveness of biofuels, subsidies are still needed in most cases to attract large-scale investment in biofuels.

Table 7.7 ▷ **Government support schemes for renewables-based electricity generation and quantification method**

Support scheme	Description	How support is quantified
Feed-in tariffs (FITs)	FITs are granted to operators for the renewables-based electricity fed into the grid. They are usually technology-specific, have a duration of 20 years and take the form of a fixed price per MWh.	(FIT minus wholesale electricity price) multiplied by renewable energy generated.
Production tax credit (PTC)	Direct reduction in tax liability.	PTC multiplied by renewable energy generated.
Investment tax credit (ITC)	Direct reduction in tax liability.	ITC multiplied by renewables capacity added in the year.
Grant programmes	Direct cash payments to reduce upfront capital costs.	Grant multiplied by renewables capacity added in the year.
Tenders and auctions	A process to generate offers from multiple bidders to fulfil specific energy needs, such as a target for renewables capacity, at the most competitive price.	Additional cost per unit of energy compared with least-cost alternative multiplied by renewable energy generated.
Green certificates (GC)	A green certificate is a tradeable commodity which provides evidence of the production and the use of a certain amount of renewable energy.	Annual average price of GC multiplied by amount of GC released.
Price premiums	Premiums are an additional payment to producers on top of the electricity price received by the producer (market-driven or regulated).	Premium multiplied by renewable energy generated.

Based on an update of our survey of established national policies and of deployment of new capacity, we estimate that the total value of subsidies to renewables of all types worldwide totalled $121 billion in 2013, $16 billion, or 15%, higher than in 2012 (Figure 7.19). Biofuels accounted for about 20% of the total and renewables for power for the remaining 80%. Subsidies to biofuels increased by around one-fifth compared to the previous year, from $20 billion to $24 billion, mainly due to higher consumption in most countries and a larger price gap between ethanol and gasoline in the United States. Support to renewables-based power technologies increased by $11 billion compared to 2012, mainly due to increased deployment of solar PV and wind.

Figure 7.19 ▷ Change in global renewables power subsidies, 2012 to 2013

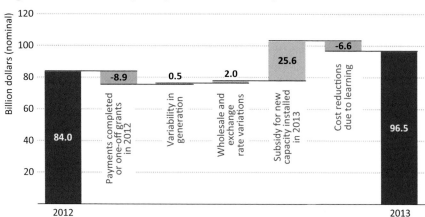

Notes: Variability in generation includes changes in generation from variable sources and also the additional generation for those plants that started operation part-way through 2012. Cost reductions due to learning capture the learning effects from 2012 deployment on the investment costs for new installations in 2013.

The amount of subsidies from year-to-year changes for a variety of reasons, the most important of which are: one-time payment programmes (typically grants or investment tax credits); changes in wholesale prices or exchange rates; payments for capacity that came online the previous year but did not fully operate in that year; and new capacity. The increase in subsidies related to the deployment of new installed capacity is tempered by the reduction of investment costs achieved through learning, when this reduction is factored in through a reduction of the support schemes for new installations. In 2013, this reduction accounted for $6.6 billion, or about 25% of the additional cost that would otherwise have been incurred.

Subsidies to renewables for power are concentrated in just a handful of countries: in 2013, the five leading countries – Germany, the United States, Italy, Spain and China – accounted for almost 70% of the global total and the top-fifteen countries accounted for 90% of total support (Figure 7.20). In these countries, the bulk of the renewable power subsidies went to solar PV (47%) and most of the rest to wind power (28%) and bioenergy (21%).

In the New Policies Scenario, the global expansion of renewable energy use drives an increase in the total level of subsidies through to 2030, which peaks at around $230 billion (in 2013 dollars), before declining over the last decade of the *Outlook*, due to the expiry of subsidies granted in the 2010s (as support measures generally last 20 years). The estimated total in 2040 is around $205 billion. Falling unit costs and increased competitiveness as wholesale prices rise in most regions contribute to limiting the increase in subsidy costs.

Figure 7.20 ⊳ Renewables power subsidies by source in the top-15 countries, 2013

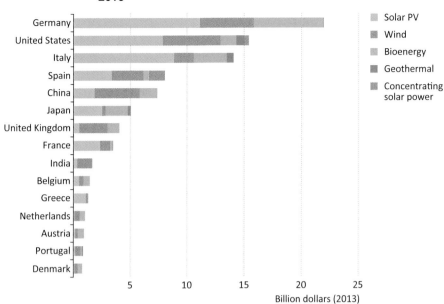

Over the projection period, close to 20% of the cumulative renewable energy subsidies go to biofuels, $1.0 trillion out of the total $5.4 trillion. By 2040, they increase over 40% from current levels, reaching $35 billion per year. By then, annual subsidies for renewables-based power generation amount to almost $170 billion, having peaked at $186 billion in 2030. Solar PV remains the leading recipient of subsidies over much of the projection period, eventually being overtaken by bioenergy for power (Figure 7.21). Subsidies to onshore wind reach a peak just before 2020 and then decline steadily as onshore wind becomes competitive with conventional power plants in many locations. In contrast, subsidies to CSP and offshore wind power increase dramatically to make up more than 30% of total subsidies to renewables in the power sector in 2040 (currently they account for 4%).

There are marked differences between regions in the pattern of support for renewables. The European Union is currently the leading region, accounting for $69 billion or 57% of the total renewables subsidy. EU subsidies continue to grow, as a consequence of the continuing expansion of the deployment of renewables, until they reach a plateau, at around $80 billion, just before 2020 (though this increase is moderated by the increasing wholesale prices for electricity). Renewable subsidies in the European Union fall to about half the current level by 2040, mainly as the subsidies granted to the large amount of solar PV capacity commissioned in the recent years come to an end (Figure 7.22). In the United States, government support grew steadily over the last five years, reaching $27 billion in 2013. This is expected to increase by some 50%, to about $40 billion, in the early 2030s and then decline to $36 billion by 2040.

Figure 7.21 ▷ Global renewables subsidies by source in the New Policies Scenario

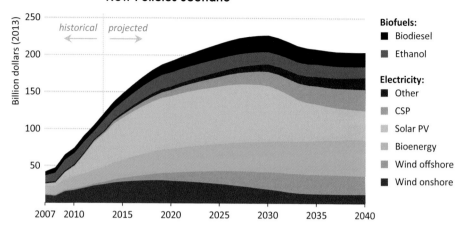

Notes: Subsidies to renewables for power are calculated as the difference between the levelised cost of electricity and the wholesale price in each region, multiplied by the amount of generation for each renewable energy technology. For biofuels, subsidies are calculated by multiplying the consumption by the difference between their production cost and the regional reference price of the comparable oil-based product in each region.

The European Union remains the largest financial supporter of renewables over the projection period, though the United States is a close second after 2035, with the rapid decline of EU subsidies to power generation technologies and larger subsidies to biofuels in the United States. Subsidies to renewables in China and Japan show a similar pattern to those in the United States, peaking respectively at $30 billion and $19 billion in the around 2030. By 2040, the Unites States, European Union, Japan and China combined account for just over half of global subsidies, as subsidies to renewable energy in India and many other countries continue to grow.

Figure 7.22 ▷ Global renewables subsidies by region in the New Policies Scenario

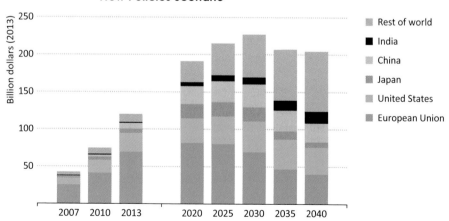

Chapter 8

Energy efficiency outlook
Can efficiency help countries to compete?

Highlights

- Global energy intensity fell by 1% per year on average over 2010-2013, reverting to the long-term trend after a brief period (the global economic crisis) during which it increased. Several notable energy efficiency policies have been announced or implemented in the past year, including China's efforts to phase out inefficient coal use in industry, the US Clean Power Plan, the EU Energy Efficiency Directive and India's passenger vehicle fuel-economy standard.

- In the New Policies Scenario, the efficiency policies that have been adopted (albeit not yet fully implemented) reduce energy demand by 1 200 Mtoe (compared with the Current Policies Scenario) in 2040. This slows fossil-fuel demand growth, diminishes required supply-side investment and reduces international energy prices. If those energy efficiency measures were not implemented over time, oil demand in 2040 would be 23 mb/d higher (or 22%), gas demand 940 bcm (or 17%) higher and coal demand 920 Mtce (or 15%) higher.

- Adopting energy efficient technologies in energy-intensive industries, such as steel, aluminium or plastics, can partly alleviate concerns about declining competitiveness because of disparities in energy prices between high- and low-cost regions. By exploiting the full energy efficiency potential of these sectors, the European Union could close the energy cost gap with the United States by 10-35%. A move towards higher-value products, greater innovation, and more recycling and re-use could complement energy efficiency measures and enhance competitiveness.

- Cross-sectoral energy efficiency policies, notably in transport and buildings, stimulate overall economic competitiveness by increasing demand for domestically produced goods and increasing disposable household income. Implementing economically viable energy efficiency measures across the economy would lead to an increase of up to 5% in industrial value added and 2% higher household consumption in the major economies by 2030. Tighter fuel-economy standards for cars, requiring cumulative spending of $5.3 trillion to 2040, would boost economic activity by $4.8 trillion in industry and $0.5 trillion in the services sector.

- Beyond cutting energy use, gains from energy efficiency include: lower energy bills, better trade balances and reduced CO_2 emissions. Efficiency measures over the projection period reduce oil- and gas-import bills in 2040 by $230 billion in China and oil-import bills in the United States by $320 billion. In terms of CO_2 emissions, energy efficiency delivers about half of the cumulative savings in the New Policies Scenario (compared with the Current Policies Scenario).

Introduction

Every day, global energy production, distribution and use is becoming more efficient as a result of countless routine actions, such as households replacing light bulbs with more efficient ones or using internet-enabled devices, motorists upgrading to more fuel-efficient vehicles, businesses replacing old boilers and municipalities insulating public buildings. Backed by a reinvigorated policy focus on energy efficiency and driven by relatively high energy prices, these actions are helping to lower the growth in global energy demand. Energy efficiency offers an effective way to reduce the need for additional capital expenditure on energy supply, tackle environmental concerns and sustain economic growth. However, as highlighted by the *World Energy Investment Outlook*, the level of spending on energy efficiency is difficult to track not only due to definitional challenges but also because about 60% of it is self-financed as part of more general expenditures (IEA, 2014a).

This chapter highlights recent trends in energy efficiency and key policy developments, and analyses the role energy efficiency plays in curbing energy demand in the period to 2040. Building on the in-depth focus on energy competitiveness in the *World Energy Outlook 2013* (*WEO*), the link between energy efficiency and economic and industrial competitiveness is explored (IEA, 2013). In addition, this chapter briefly discusses the benefits of energy efficiency in reducing energy imports, cutting household energy expenditure and curbing carbon-dioxide (CO_2) emissions.

Current status of energy efficiency

Recent progress

Global energy intensity – measured as the amount of energy required to produce a unit of gross domestic product (GDP) (at market exchange rates for 2013) – fell by 0.6% in 2013, compared with the averages of 0.9% from 1992-2012, 1.0% in 2012 and 1.3% in 2011.[1] The only major energy-consuming region in which energy intensity increased from 2012 to 2013 was the United States, which strongly influenced the modest improvement in energy intensity at the global level compared with the long-term trend. The trend in the United States can be explained mainly by two factors: first, the temporary cold weather in 2013, wherein heating degrees days (a measure of heating requirements) were 23% higher than in 2012, leading to much higher energy demand for space heating; second, a structural factor, whereby energy-intensive sectors (such as oil extraction and refining) expanded more than the rest of the economy, reflecting the surge in unconventional oil and gas production.

---

1. Energy intensity is often used as a proxy for energy efficiency, but it is not a perfect indicator as it is influenced by a range of other factors, such as changes in economic structure and climatic conditions. For more details on the relationship between energy intensity and energy efficiency refer to IEA (2014b).

In the period from 2005 to 2008, global energy intensity improved at a faster rate than the historic average, driven to some extent by increasing oil and gas prices (Figure 8.1). Subsequently, the financial and economic crisis contributed to a reversal of this trend in 2009 and 2010. There were three main contributing factors. First, energy consumption in industry increased more quickly than value added because industrial facilities ran below full capacity, a situation which *raises* energy intensity as some energy needs persist whatever the level of production. Second, global energy consumption in households (particularly for appliances and consumer electronics) and in road transport in developing countries was less affected by the economic downturn and grew faster than economic activity. Third, developing countries, which are generally more energy intensive than the world average, accounted for a larger share of the global economy, particularly as their growth did not slow as much as developed countries during the financial and economic crises over 2009 and 2010. Russia, Japan and the European Union, which were hit hardest by the recession, saw energy intensity increase most visibly. The effect of the economic downturn on energy intensity was less pronounced in India and Africa, though their rate of improvement fell.

Figure 8.1 ▷ **Annual change in primary energy intensity**

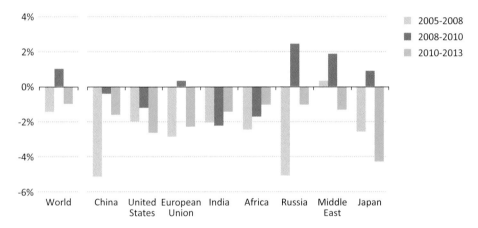

Note: Primary energy intensity is measured using GDP in year-2013 dollars at market exchange rates.

Energy supply needs can be diminished by increasing the efficiency of energy conversion, distribution and use. In 2012, global transmission and distribution (T&D) losses of 1 880 terawatt-hours (TWh), equivalent to 8.8% of total generation (or the annual output of about 250 one-gigawatt [GW] nuclear power plants) were incurred in getting electricity from power plants to households and businesses. T&D losses are affected by the efficiency of the grid and its operation, climatic conditions, distances and non-technical matters. Today such losses average less than 5% in Japan but more than 10% in Russia, partly because of longer distances to cover and lower population density, but also ageing infrastructure. In India, non-technical losses, such as power theft, significantly add to overall T&D losses. In most countries, T&D losses as a share of generation have declined over the last decade (Figure 8.2).

Figure 8.2 ▷ **Transmission and distribution loss rates**

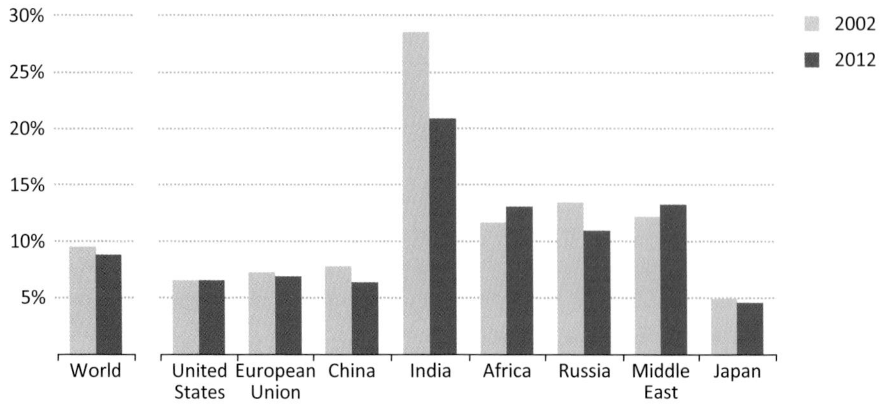

Note: T&D loss rates are calculated as a share of total supply (net generation plus imports less exports).

The reduction of global T&D losses by 0.7 percentage points achieved from 2002 to 2012 saved about 160 TWh per year, equivalent to Poland's current electricity generation. T&D grids in many parts of the world are increasingly more actively managed than in the past, in part, to accommodate decentralised supply and variable generation profiles. Good maintenance of the infrastructure is the first requirement. Energy efficient transformers, high-voltage transmission grids, smart distribution grids and a higher share of decentralised power generation are options to decrease losses further in the future.

Recent policy developments

New energy efficiency policies have been announced or introduced in many countries over the past year (Table 8.1). China, the world's largest energy consumer, is putting more emphasis on energy efficiency measures, in part to help cut air pollution, a major concern in many cities. New measures in industry include accelerating boiler renovation, phasing out small and inefficient coal-fired boilers and reducing outdated production practices in energy-intensive industries. In China's transport sector, "yellow label" vehicles (i.e. cars that fail to meet the Euro 1 emissions standard[2]) produced before the end of 2005 are to be phased out from 2015. At least half of all new buildings are to comply with the "green" building standard by 2015, which imposes design, construction and operational requirements that reduce energy consumption (MOHURD, 2013).

In June 2014, the US Environmental Protection Agency (EPA) proposed the Clean Power Plan, which aims to reduce CO_2 emissions from existing power plants to 30% below 2005 levels by 2030 (see Chapters 1 and 6). The plan identifies four building blocks – including the more efficient use of electricity – as central to reaching the goal. The United States has also

---

2. Euro 1 is a European Union emissions standard for light-duty vehicles that covers carbon monoxide (CO), oxides of nitrogen (NO_X) and particulate matter.

introduced stricter building codes and announced tighter standards for electric motors, and commercial refrigerators and freezers. In 2013, Mexico introduced CO_2 emission standards for cars. The Chilean government presented the 2014-2018 energy agenda in May 2014, which includes additional energy efficiency labels for household appliances and support measures to improve efficiency in industry.

Throughout 2014, European Union member states continued to implement the provisions of the Energy Efficiency Directive through national laws. The Directive sets an obligation to deliver 1.5% cumulative annual energy end-use savings between 2014 and 2020 through utility or alternative schemes and requires development of building renovation strategies. The EU's Ecodesign Directive was extended to include standards for space and water heaters, and cooking appliances. In July 2014, the European Commission proposed a 30% savings target for 2030 as part of the wider 2030 policy framework for climate and energy, which might lead to several EU directives on energy efficiency being reviewed.[3]

In early 2014, India became the latest major car market to introduce fuel-economy standards for passenger vehicles. More than 75% of all passenger vehicle sales in the world are now subject to either fuel or CO_2 emissions standards. In the buildings sector, the Energy Conservation Building code is to be mandatory by 2017 and stricter efficiency standards have been announced for air conditioners and refrigerators.

In the Middle East, several countries have implemented policies to slow the rapid growth in energy demand. Measures adopted focus on improving thermal insulation of buildings and increasing the efficiency of air conditioners (air conditioners are responsible for the bulk of residential electricity demand across the region – 70% in the case of Saudi Arabia). Additionally, Saudi Arabia introduced fuel-economy labels for all passenger vehicles sold from 2015 and set fuel-economy standards for imported vehicles at up to 18.5 kilometres per litre (km/l) (equivalent to 5.4 l/100 km) by 2019-2020 depending on the size of the car. Unless subsidies on transport fuels are sharply reduced, however, energy savings from these measures may be limited.

The past year also brought some set-backs in efficiency policy at national levels. In the United States, some energy efficiency legislation (Energy Savings and Industrial Competitiveness Act of 2013) failed to win congressional approval. In the European Union, some member states are behind schedule in implementing provisions of the Energy Efficiency Directive. Australia repealed its CO_2 emissions cap-and-trade scheme and closed the successful Energy Efficiency Opportunities programme, which required large energy-using companies to undertake energy efficiency assessments (though under Australia's Direct Action Plan, the government also set up the Emissions Reduction Fund, which should start in 2015 and fund, among others, efficiency projects in buildings and industry).

3. As of September 2014, the target is still subject to approval by the European Council and the European Parliament. See *http://ec.europa.eu/clima/policies/2030*.

Table 8.1 ▷ Selected energy efficiency policies announced or introduced in 2013 and 2014

Region	Sector	New policy measure
China	General	Acceleration of the efficient use of coal in support of the goal to reduce coal use in several provinces, e.g. by phasing out small, inefficient coal-fired boilers.
	Industry	Implementation of the phase-out of outdated production capacity in the steel, cement and glass industries, including closing or upgrading coal-fired boilers.
	Buildings	More than 50% of new buildings to comply with "green" building standards from 2015. 400 million m² of buildings in Northern China are to be retrofitted.
	Transport	Phase out (from 2015) low-efficient "yellow label" vehicles produced prior to 2005.
United States	General	Clean Power Plan proposed, which includes improving end-use energy efficiency as a central element of reducing CO_2 emissions from power plants.
	Buildings	Announcement of stricter building codes and tighter standards for electric motors and commercial coolers and freezers, plus certain types of light bulbs.
	Industry	Announcement of stricter standards for electric motors.
European Union	Buildings	Implementation of regulations for cooking appliances, space and water heaters, and power transformers within the framework of the Ecodesign Directive. Revision of energy labelling for domestic ovens.
India	Transport	Introduction of vehicle fuel-economy standards requiring 5.5 l/100 km by 2016-2017 and 4.8 l/100km by 2021-2022, and subsidies for hybrid/electric cars.
	Buildings	Energy Conservation Building Code mandatory nationwide by 2017 covering building envelope, lighting, heating, ventilation and air conditioning. New energy efficiency norms announced for 2015 for air conditioners and refrigerators.
Japan	Buildings and industry	Extension of the Top Runner Programme among others to commercial electric refrigerators and freezers, heat pump water heaters, self-ballasted light-emitting diodes (LED) lamps and three-phase induction motors. Announced targets for newly constructed buildings to be net-zero energy on average by 2030.
Middle East	Transport	Saudi Arabia: Announcement of a fuel-economy labelling for cars in 2015 and standards for imported vehicles up to 18.5 km/l (5.4 l/100 km).
	Buildings	Saudi Arabia: Introduction of mandatory thermal insulation standards for new buildings and tightening of minimum energy performance standards (MEPs) for air conditioners. Public awareness campaign to cut electricity use.
		United Arab Emirates (Dubai): Introduction of compulsory building codes.
		Qatar: Introduction of efficiency standards for air conditioners.
Africa	Industry	South Africa: Introduction of tax incentives for energy efficiency savings.
	Buildings	Nigeria: Announced the implementation of MEPs for household appliances.
Southeast Asia	General	Malaysia: Published the National Energy Efficiency Action Plan to cut electricity demand by 6% in ten years via appliance labelling, MEPs, energy audits and grants.
	Buildings	Singapore: Introduced MEPs for clothes dryers and a television labelling scheme.
	Industry	Singapore: Launched the Energy Efficiency Initiative using grants to carry out audits and implement energy efficiency measures.
Mexico	General	Goal to increase energy efficiency regulation from 46% of final energy consumption in 2012 to 51% in 2018 (PRONASE).
	Transport	Adoption of CO_2 emission standards for cars in 2016, equivalent to 6.7 l/100 km.
Chile	General	Announcement of additional energy efficiency labels for household appliances and introduction of energy management systems and energy audits for large industrial consumers as part of the new energy agenda (Agenda de Energía).

Outlook for energy efficiency

In the New Policies Scenario, primary energy demand expands by 37% between 2012 and 2040, an average annual growth rate of 1.1%. This growth rate is much slower than in past decades (it was 1.9% between 1980 and 2011) as energy consumption and economic growth continue to decouple because of energy efficiency improvements, structural changes and saturation effects, particularly in terms of vehicle use. In 2040, energy demand in the New Policies Scenario is 9% lower than in the Current Policies Scenario, with two-thirds of the savings arising from energy efficiency (Figure 8.3).[4] Energy intensity decreases by 1.8% annually to 2040, a rate about twice as high as that achieved over the last two decades. To limit the long-term increase in the global mean temperature to 2 °C, as modelled in the 450 Scenario, requires average improvements of 2.4% per year in energy intensity, which, if achieved, would result in energy demand being 15% lower than in the New Policies Scenario in 2040.

Figure 8.3 ▷ **Factors contributing to global savings in primary energy demand in the New Policies Scenario relative to Current Policies Scenario**

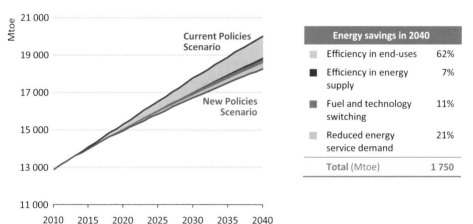

Energy savings in 2040	
Efficiency in end-uses	62%
Efficiency in energy supply	7%
Fuel and technology switching	11%
Reduced energy service demand	21%
Total (Mtoe)	1 750

In contrast to the Current Policies Scenario, the New Policies Scenario takes into account not only those policies and measures already adopted but also those that have been proposed, but yet to be put into effect (more information on assumed policies in both scenarios can be found in Annex B and Chapter 1). Around 60% of the energy savings in the New Policies Scenario arise from end-use energy efficiency improvements. Energy efficiency in energy supply, mainly power generation and refineries, is more limited as less

---

4. This *Outlook* uses a decomposition technique on a sub-sectoral level to distinguish three effects: efficiency effect (both in end-uses and supply), fuel and technology switching effects, and the effect from changes in the demand for useful energy or energy service demand. Note that while both the *World Energy Outlook* and the IEA's energy efficiency indicators use the same decomposition technique, differences arise due to different definitions of activity and structure variables. For more detail on the methods used, see IEA (2014b) and *www.worldenergyoutlook.org/weomodel/documentation*.

new supply infrastructure (which is generally more efficient than the existing stock) is built in the New Policies Scenario than in the Current Policies Scenario.

Next to energy efficiency, other factors contribute to the energy savings in the New Policies Scenario, including a reduction in the demand for energy services *vis-à-vis* the Current Policies Scenario. As energy efficiency leads to lower international energy prices in the New Policies Scenario, the rebound effect might be expected to increase demand for energy services. However, as end-user prices do not always follow international prices (because of fossil-fuel subsidy removal, increasing CO_2 prices and changes in the fuel mix), end-user prices increase in some countries, despite lower international prices. The result is a lower level of demand for energy services on a global level. Additionally, the New Policies Scenario integrates a faster transition to a service economy in China, which also reduces demand for energy services. Fuel and technology switching, particularly towards gas-fired generation and renewables in the power sector, account for the remaining savings.

Figure 8.4 ▷ **Global primary energy savings from energy efficiency by fuel and sector in the New Policies Scenario relative to the Current Policies Scenario, 2040**

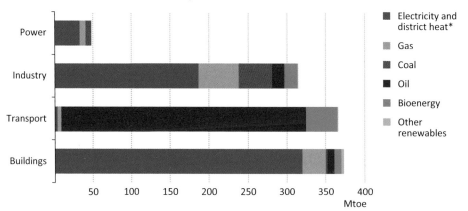

* Electricity and district heat demand savings in end-use sectors are converted into equivalent primary energy savings and attributed to each end-use. The savings allocated to the power sector arise from the increased efficiency of the plant and of grid and system management (efficiency improvements in transmission and distribution are labelled as "electricity and heat" in power).

Note: Energy savings of 90 Mtoe in agriculture, oil and gas extraction, refineries, gas and coal processing, and biofuel refineries are not depicted, while non-energy use does not have any efficiency-related savings between the two scenarios.

Looking at the primary energy savings by sector that stem from improved energy efficiency in the New Policies Scenario relative to the Current Policies Scenario, the power sector accounts for less than 5% of total savings, as most of the primary energy savings are due to reduced electricity consumption in industry and buildings (Figure 8.4). The buildings and transport sectors save the most (31% each), followed by industry (26%).[5] Most of the energy efficiency savings in transport reduce the consumption of oil and biofuels, while in buildings and industry the savings are primarily electricity.

Trends by fuel

In the New Policies Scenario, energy efficiency measures play an important role in mitigating the growth in demand for fossil fuels. Cumulative efforts to increase energy efficiency from 2012 reduce demand for coal, oil and gas by almost one-fifth. While most oil savings arise from efficiency improvements in transport, industry and power generation are responsible for the bulk of efficiency savings related to coal and gas. Efficiency measures generate savings in oil demand in 2040 of 23 million barrels per day (mb/d), or more than the current combined production of Saudi Arabia and Russia (Figure 8.5). The gas savings in 2040, 940 billion cubic metres (bcm), are more than the current output of North America. The coal savings in 2040, 920 million tonnes of coal equivalent (Mtce), are equal to about one-third of China's current coal production.

Figure 8.5 ▷ **Global fossil-fuel demand and cumulative energy efficiency savings by fuel in the New Policies Scenario**

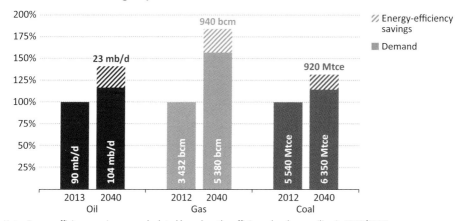

Note: Energy efficiency savings are calculated based on the efficiency levels prevailing in 2012/2013.

Without energy efficiency improvements, total final energy consumption in the New Policies Scenario would increase by 66% rather than the projected 38%, a savings of 2 640 Mtoe in 2040. The largest share of the savings can be attributed to the consumption of oil (1 210 Mtoe), followed by electricity (540 Mtoe), natural gas (380 Mtoe), coal (230 Mtoe), bioenergy (180 Mtoe), heat (80 Mtoe) and other renewables (15 Mtoe).[6]

---

5. Unlike in the IEA energy balances and Annex A, here the industry sector includes energy consumption in coke ovens, blast furnaces and petrochemical feedstocks as these are integral parts of the steel and chemical industries.

6. Other renewables include solar and geothermal heat.

Figure 8.6 ▷ **Change in global final energy consumption by selected fuel, sector and contributing factor in the New Policies Scenario**

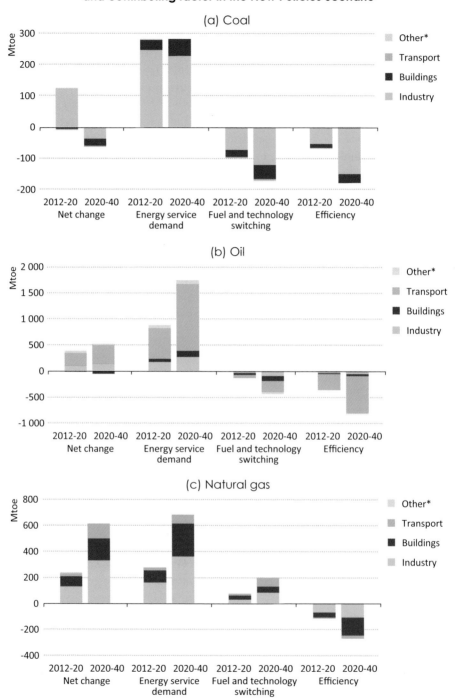

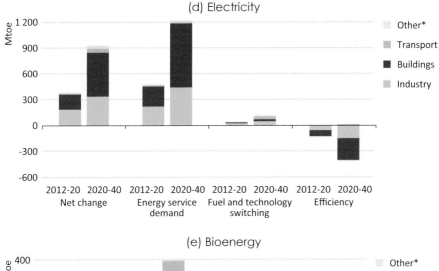

(d) Electricity

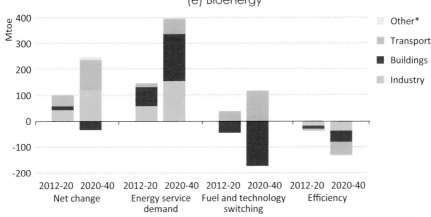

(e) Bioenergy

*Other includes agriculture and non-energy use (except petrochemical feedstock).

Notes: "Energy service demand" represents changes in energy consumption related to changes in demand for energy services, such as mobility, heating or lighting, while "fuel and technology switching" reflects changes due to fuel switching (e.g. the uptake of electric heat pumps instead of gas-fired boilers) and industrial process changes (e.g. from primary to secondary steel-making). "Efficiency" represents energy changes as a consequence of the adoption of efficiency measures (e.g. replacing a conventional with a condensing water boiler).

Decomposition analysis can provide insights into the relative contributions which different factors – higher demand, structural factors and energy efficiency – make to the overall growth in final energy consumption (Figure 8.6).[7] Within final energy consumption, industry currently accounts for 88% of coal consumption, with almost 50% of coal consumed in the iron and steel industry and 15% in cement production, and the bulk of the remainder is consumed in buildings for heating. Despite an increase in industrial activity of 120% to 2040,

7. The remainder of this section "Trends by fuel" discusses trends in final energy consumption, i.e. it excludes energy transformation, such as power generation.

coal consumption is projected to increase by only 5% from 2012 to 2040 in the New Policies Scenario. This slow growth primarily reflects a slowdown from 2020 in demand for steel and cement in China. But there are also other contributing factors. Improvements in industrial energy efficiency over the projection period, particularly in China and India, reduce growth in coal consumption by approximately 190 Mtoe in 2040. Fuel switching in industry, mainly towards gas, and the uptake of less energy-intensive industrial processes save 180 Mtoe. Higher scrap metal use (mainly in electric arc furnaces) saves 70 Mtoe of coal consumption in blast furnaces in the iron and steel industry in 2040. Coal consumption for heating in buildings is phased out over time, while coal gains in importance as a feedstock for methanol production.

The transport sector currently accounts for about two-thirds of oil demand, followed by industry (mainly petrochemical feedstocks), with 19%, and buildings, with 9%. In the New Policies Scenario, demand for mobility services (not only for passenger vehicles, but also rail, navigation and aircraft) would increase transport oil demand by more than 80% between 2012 and 2040, were it not for energy efficiency improvements, particularly in passenger light-duty vehicles (PLDVs), resulting from fuel-economy standards that are applied in all the large markets. Growth in oil demand is also mitigated by the increasing use of biofuels and electric vehicles in transport, as well as fuel switching from oil to gas in transport, buildings and industry. Oil consumption in the petrochemical industry increases by 50%, reflecting rapid growth in the use of oil as a raw material.

In 2012, the industry sector accounted for 48% of natural gas demand, followed by buildings (44%) and transport (7%). In the New Policies Scenario, natural gas demand rises by 64% between 2012 and 2040, the largest increase of all the fossil fuels. The increase would be 92% without the assumed energy efficiency savings. Efficiency gains in buildings through the widespread adoption of condensing boilers for space and water heating, particularly in Organisation for Economic Development and Co-operation (OECD) countries, as well as efficiency improvements in industrial furnaces and boilers, particularly in non-OECD countries, reduce gas consumption by 380 Mtoe. However, since natural gas is a less polluting alternative to coal and oil, and in some cases also cheaper, there is an increase in gas consumption of 270 Mtoe. This is the result of fuel switching to gas from coal and oil in buildings and industry, and from oil in transport.

Among all energy carriers, electricity consumption increases the most in the New Policies Scenario, rising by 80% from 2012 to 2040. Higher demand from electric motors, process heat, cooling and lighting in industry, as well as from household appliances, air conditioning and lighting in buildings are the key drivers. The purely demand driven increase for electricity amounts to almost 1 700 Mtoe, higher than today's global consumption. Energy efficiency in the form of more efficient appliances, lighting and motor systems reduces the growth by 540 Mtoe in 2040. A factor that increases electricity consumption is the higher penetration of electricity in industry and buildings, replacing fossil fuels (mainly in the form of electric heat pumps), and in transport, through the introduction of plug-in and electric vehicles, which are much more efficient than cars using internal combustion engines.

Currently three-quarters of bioenergy is used in the residential sector, 90% of which is traditional, mainly for cooking, in developing Asia, Africa and Latin America. While in non-OECD countries traditional use of solid biomass is increasingly being substituted by liquefied petroleum gas (LPG), electricity and natural gas, in OECD countries there is a trend towards increasing the modern use of biomass for space and water heating. In the New Policies Scenario, use of bioenergy increases most in transport, in the form of biofuels, whereas in industry the bioenergy share increases in OECD countries and China, but decreases in most other countries. Efficiency savings are highest in transport and industry and somewhat lower in buildings, as a substantial amount of the reduction in the residential use of bioenergy is achieved through switching from solid biomass to modern fuels (Chapter 15).

Trends by sector

Buildings

The buildings sector accounts for one-third of today's final energy consumption, with households accounting for about three-quarters and the services sector for about one-quarter.[8] Driven by higher population, economic growth, more people gaining access to electricity and greater use of electrical appliances as a consequence of increasing living standards, energy consumption in buildings rises from 2 937 Mtoe in 2012 to 3 870 Mtoe in 2040, an average annual growth rate of 1.0%. Among all types of energy, electricity sees the largest increase, driven by a growing demand for appliances, lighting and cooling, while coal and oil become less important, as consumers switch to other fuels for space heating. The share of fuelwood and charcoal is reduced from 26% in 2012 to 17% in 2040, as households in developing countries, including Africa, gradually adopt improved cookstoves and modern fuels for cooking (including LPG, natural gas and electricity) driven by policy support and wider availability of alternative fuels (see Chapter 15).

Energy consumption in buildings in the New Policies Scenario in 2040 is 280 Mtoe (7%) lower than in the Current Policies Scenario (Table 8.2). More than half of the reduction can be attributed to end-use efficiency. The rest is due to a reduction in the demand for energy services, particularly for space heating, e.g. by lowering the thermostat setting. This occurs mainly in countries where end-user prices increase as a consequence of the phase-out of fossil-fuel subsidies, including in China, Russia and the Middle East. A further factor is fuel switching, especially in space heating towards electric heat pumps.

In the New Policies Scenario, the services sector is responsible for more than half of the efficiency-related savings in 2040, despite the fact that it accounts for only 30% of energy consumption. This high contribution is primarily due to ambitious policy measures being adopted in public and commercial buildings, more so than those taken in residential buildings. Among the end-uses, the highest cumulative efficiency savings are related to space and water heating (43% of total savings) as a consequence of improved buildings insulation, retrofits, increased uptake of more efficient boilers and more use of automation

8. The services sector includes commercial activities and public services, such as hospitals, schools and public administration.

and control systems. Efficiency improvements in appliances – including refrigerators, washing machines, dishwashers and air conditioners – account for another 39% of overall savings. Most of these savings stem from policies aimed at introducing or tightening the efficiency standards of appliances, such as the Ecodesign Directive in the European Union, and the Energy Star programme and Clean Power Plan in the United States. However, an increasing share of electricity consumption is attributable to new equipment which, in most cases, is not yet covered by standards or labels, such as smartphones, tablets, small electronics and kitchen gadgets. In 2013, such devices consumed more than 600 TWh of electricity, or 3% of global demand. Adopting more efficient technologies could reduce the energy demand of network-enabled devices by up to 65% (IEA, 2014c).

Table 8.2 ▷ Savings in energy demand and CO_2 emissions in buildings from energy efficiency in the New Policies Scenario (Mtoe)

| | Demand | | | Change versus Current Policies Scenario | | | |
| | | | | Total | | Due to efficiency | |
	2012	2020	2040	2020	2040	2020	2040
Coal	125	119	96	-5	-20	-2	-3
Oil	321	307	258	-11	-42	-3	-8
Gas	596	676	843	-13	-69	-5	-25
Electricity	863	1 038	1 551	-31	-169	-18	-114
Heat	150	157	171	-4	-13	-1	-6
Other renewables*	124	159	299	3	54	0	-3
Fuelwood, charcoal**	758	755	648	-5	-23	-2	-7
Total	2 937	3 211	3 867	-65	-283	-31	-166
CO_2 emissions (Gt)***	8.3	8.6	9.6	-0.5	-2.8	-0.2	-1.1

* Other renewables include wind, solar, geothermal energy and modern use of biomass. ** This also includes the use of animal dung and agricultural residues in stoves with very low efficiency. *** CO_2 emissions include indirect emissions from electricity generation and energy use for heat.

Without the deployment of energy efficiency over time, energy consumption in buildings in the New Policies Scenario would be 690 Mtoe (or 18%) higher in 2040. Three markets account for more than half of all the expected efficiency improvements: the United States, China and the European Union. This is a reflection of the high level of their current energy consumption and their respective national policies, aimed at improved efficiency for appliances and a better building envelope (including mandatory energy requirements in buildings codes in some US states, the Civil Construction Energy Conservation Design Standard in China, and the EU's Energy Performance of Buildings Directive and Ecodesign and Energy Labelling Directive).

Lighting, which is an end-use that has received a lot of attention by policy-makers in the past, currently accounts for 18% (or 150 Mtoe) of total electricity demand in buildings. Driven by higher demand, electricity consumption for lighting is projected to increase to 260 Mtoe. Without increased energy efficiency, this number would have been 350 Mtoe (Figure 8.7).

Currently, the global lighting stock in households is dominated by incandescent light bulbs (51%), compact fluorescent lamps (CFL) (26%) and linear fluorescent lamps (17%), while in the services sector linear fluorescent lamps account for two-thirds of all lamps, followed by CFLs (20%). Switching from an incandescent light bulb to a CFL can reduce energy use by 75%, while switching to LEDs can reduce energy use by around 80%. In the commercial sector, the replacement of linear fluorescent lamps by more efficient types can cut energy consumption by 25%. Combining more efficient lighting technology with more active control can achieve substantially larger savings.

Figure 8.7 ▷ **Electricity demand for lighting in buildings by contributing factor**

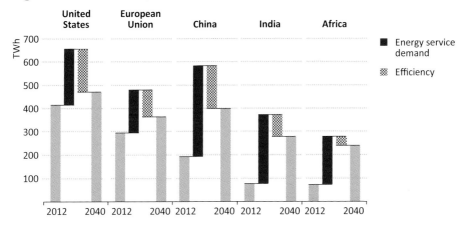

In view of the increasing demand for energy use for lighting, many countries have introduced relevant efficiency policies in the form of a phase-out of incandescent light bulbs, standards and/or labelling. Due to energy standards in the United States and the European Union, energy demand growth for lighting in the New Policies Scenario is significantly less than in the past. Next to China, the largest absolute increase in the demand for lighting is observed in India and Africa, where more people gain access to electricity and where the scope for efficiency policies is limited and standards are not always strictly enforced.

Transport

The transport sector currently accounts for almost 30% of global final energy consumption and for almost two-thirds of oil consumption. In the New Policies Scenario, energy consumption increases by 1.2% annually from 2012 to 2040, with demand growth higher in the period to 2025 (1.4% annually) than thereafter (0.9%). Biofuels see the second-largest increase among all fuels as an increasing number of regions utilise them, among others, to reduce dependence on oil and to cut CO_2 emissions. Natural gas consumption gains in importance and increases its share from 4% in 2012 to 7% in 2040, with higher consumption in road vehicles and in ships (in the form of liquefied natural gas). Compared with the Current Policies Scenario, transport CO_2 emissions in 2040 are 12% lower in the New Policies Scenario, mainly as a result of stricter energy efficiency policies (Table 8.3).

Table 8.3 ▷ Savings in energy demand and CO_2 emissions in transport from energy efficiency in the New Policies Scenario (Mtoe)

				Change versus Current Policies Scenario			
	Demand			Total		Due to efficiency	
	2012	2020	2040	2020	2040	2020	2040
Coal	3	3	1	0	0	0	0
Oil	2 325	2 563	2 937	-62	-474	-33	-333
Gas	91	116	229	10	62	-1	-10
Electricity	26	34	82	1	20	0	-2
Biofuels	60	101	218	14	44	-1	-25
Total	2 504	2 816	3 467	-37	-347	-35	-369
CO_2 emissions (Gt)	7.2	7.9	9.3	-0.2	-1.3	-0.1	-0.9

The transport energy efficiency savings in the New Policies Scenario, relative to the Current Policies Scenario, total 370 Mtoe in 2040. About 70% of the savings are attributable to PLDVs, with stricter fuel-economy standards in several regions in the New Policies Scenario. In early 2014, India became the last major car market to adopt mandatory fuel-economy standards for PLDVs. The Indian Corporate Average Fuel Consumption standard specifies 4.8 l/100 km by 2021-2022. This corresponds to about a 15% increase in fuel efficiency compared with today's average.

All major car markets – China, the European Union, North America, Japan, Brazil, India and Korea – have now established fuel-economy standards. Together, these markets cover more than three-quarters of global PLDV sales and about 70% of PLDV oil consumption in road transport (Figure 8.8). Their lower share of oil consumption reflects higher vehicle efficiency compared with other markets. In 2040, regions with fuel-economy standards in place cover a larger share of vehicle sales (80%) as a consequence of the rapidly growing markets in China and India. However, the share in global oil consumption of PLDVs from these regions declines as a direct consequence of their higher fuel-economy standards. On-road vehicle fuel efficiency can be significantly less than what is achieved in a test cycle, which is the basis for most standards. Making test cycles more representative of real life conditions would be an important step in attaining higher fuel efficiency levels in transport.

Since nearly all PLDV sales today are covered by fuel-economy standards, there may be a question as to whether similar regulations are needed in the remaining regions (or whether they will naturally benefit from regulations elsewhere). While there are some spill-over effects (most manufacturers supply global markets), there are reasons why the geographic scope of regulations needs to be extended. For example, in order to improve their competitiveness, manufacturers tend to adapt vehicles to local conditions, which can mean dispensing with costly, more energy-efficient components unless they are mandated. Compulsory retirement standards, based on the age or mileage of a vehicle, or restrictions on imported cars (already implemented in several African countries, including Angola, Botswana, Ivory Coast and Mozambique [see Chapter 13]) can be an important means of improving the fuel economy of the overall fleet.

Figure 8.8 △ Market share in global passenger light-duty vehicle sales in the New Policies Scenario

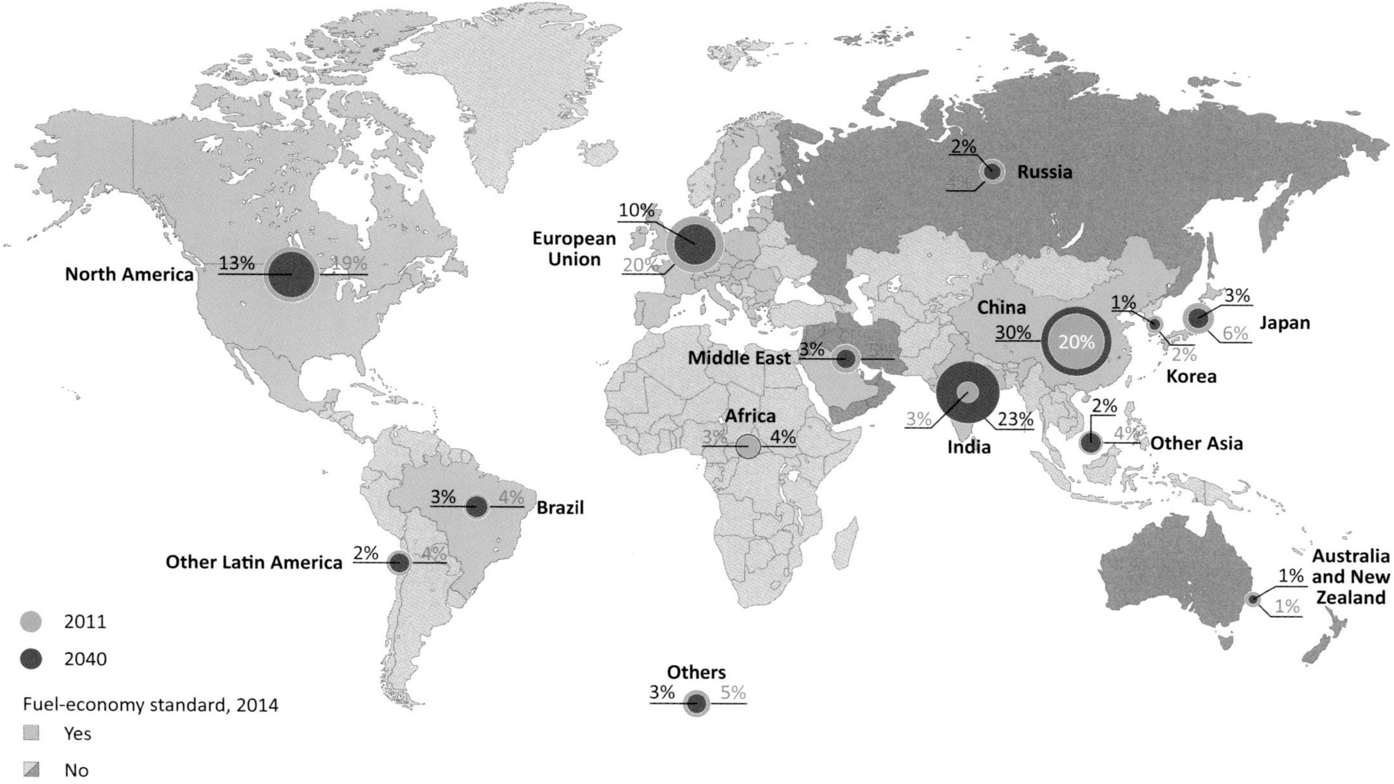

Russia
2%

Japan
3%
6%

Korea
1%
2%

China
30%
20%

India
23%
3%

Other Asia
2%
4%

Australia
and New
Zealand
1%
1%

European
Union
10%
20%

Middle East 3%

Africa
3%
4%

North America
13%
19%

Brazil
3%
4%

Other Latin America
2%
4%

Others
3%
5%

2011
2040

Fuel-economy standard, 2014
Yes
No

This map is without prejudice to the status of or sovereignty over any territory, to the delimitation of international frontiers and boundaries, and to the name of any territory, city or area.

8

Road freight accounts for the second-highest energy efficiency savings (50 Mtoe or 14%) in transport in 2040 in the New Policies Scenario compared with the Current Policies Scenario. Policy-makers have so far concentrated on standards for PLDVs, and today only the United States, Canada and Japan have fuel efficiency or emissions standards for freight vehicles. As a consequence of rapid growth in road freight and the absence of fuel-economy standards, the share in oil consumption of total road transport increases from 40% in 2012 to 43% in 2040. The implementation of efficiency standards for trucks and commercial vehicles is not only important from an energy efficiency perspective but it can also improve local air quality, though it is complicated by the wide range of chassis and engines that are in use. Several regions are currently involved in capacity building, measurement and stakeholder consultation aimed at the implementation of road freight fuel-economy standards. The European Union and China have concrete plans to introduce regulations in 2015.

Non-road transport, i.e. rail, aviation, navigation and pipeline transport, currently represents less than one-quarter of total energy consumption in transport, but its energy use is projected to grow at an annual rate of 1.2% in the New Policies Scenario (compared with 1.1% for road transport). Currently, there are no national policies explicitly aimed at improving fuel efficiency in this sub-sector, although efficiency guidelines have been adopted by the International Maritime Organisation and the International Civil Aviation Organisation is in the process of developing a market-based emissions scheme. Due to rapidly increasing air passenger and freight traffic and moderate energy efficiency improvements, energy consumption in aviation expands by 1.6% annually over the projection period. While we assume only moderate energy efficiency improvements in aviation, fuel efficiency improvements of 30% or more in use by aircraft could be achieved after 2020 through operational optimisation, infrastructure improvement and changes to engines and airframes (IATA, 2013).

Industry

Industry accounts for almost 40% of final energy consumption today. Industrial energy consumption grows annually by 1.3% between 2012 and 2040 in the New Policies Scenario, a rate of growth lower than that seen over the past thirty years (1.7%). While energy-intensive industries (steel, cement, chemicals and paper) currently account for more than 60% of total energy consumption in industry, their share declines to 55% in 2040. This is a result of fast growth in non-energy-intensive industries and the relatively slower production growth in the steel and cement industries, particularly as production levels off in China as demand for buildings and infrastructure construction passes its peak.

In 2040, energy consumption in industry reaches 4 860 Mtoe in the New Policies Scenario, which is 320 Mtoe (6%) lower than in the Current Policies Scenario (Table 8.4). Almost 60% of the savings can be attributed to improved energy efficiency, particularly in non-energy-intensive industries. Most of the energy efficiency gains in energy-intensive industries realised in the New Policies Scenario are already incorporated in the Current Policies

Scenario and most of the policies under consideration aim to reduce energy consumption in non-energy-intensive industries. These policies include incentives to adopt energy management systems and to undergo energy audits, the phase-out of fossil-fuel subsidies, the enhanced use of energy service companies and fiscal incentives. Energy efficiency improves fastest in motor-driven systems, steam systems and furnaces for the provision of heat. The second most important driver for reducing energy consumption between the two scenarios is the reduction in the demand for energy services. Other drivers, including fuel switching and changes in industrial processes, play a lesser role.

Table 8.4 ▷ **Savings in energy demand and CO_2 emissions in industry from energy efficiency in the New Policies Scenario** (Mtoe)

| | Demand | | | Change versus Current Policies Scenario | | | |
| | | | | Total | | Due to efficiency | |
	2012	2020	2040	2020	2040	2020	2040
Coal	1 047	1 171	1 133	-31	-92	-12	-37
Oil	681	785	911	-7	-24	-4	-14
Gas	641	771	1 103	-14	-69	-9	-44
Electricity	689	872	1202	-20	-116	-14	-71
Heat	131	143	153	-2	-3	-2	-7
Bioenergy*	187	231	356	-4	-18	-4	-17
Total	3 377	3 972	4 859	-78	-322	-45	-190
CO_2 emissions (Gt)**	10.6	11.7	12.7	-0.3	-2.3	-0.2	-0.8

*Includes other renewables. ** CO_2 emissions include indirect emissions from electricity and heat.

From a regional perspective, more than three-quarters of all energy efficiency savings in the industry sector in the New Policies Scenario are realised outside of the OECD. China makes the biggest contribution globally (31%), primarily because of the sheer scale of the remaining opportunities, coupled with the recently initiated and planned measures to phase out small, inefficient coal-fired boilers and to lift industrial energy performance standards. The European Union has the second-highest savings, at 9%, driven by several elements of the Energy Efficiency Directive: mandatory and regular energy audits for large enterprises, encouragement for small and medium enterprises (SMEs) to undergo energy audits and incentives for the use of energy management systems. India accounts for 8% of the savings, mainly based on the assumed extension of the tradeable energy efficiency certificate scheme. Despite its significant potential to improve energy efficiency, Africa contributes only 5% of cumulative efficiency-related energy savings during the projection period because of the barriers hindering the uptake of energy efficiency (Box. 8.1).

Box 8.1 ▷ **Obstacles to industrial energy efficiency in Africa**

Despite its many benefits, energy efficiency is still an underutilised resource: about 60% of the global potential in industry is not realised (IEA, 2012). In a supply-constrained continent, like Africa, energy efficiency has a part to play in making energy more accessible. Though energy efficiency investments in industry are almost always profitable, with payback periods of less than three years, a wide array of barriers prevents their uptake. Some barriers in Africa are the same as those in developed countries; some are not:

■ Widening access to a reliable supply of energy is a principal objective for many in Africa (see Chapter 13). One obstacle is that the supply of electricity and other forms of energy tends to be irregular, leading to interruptions of production and to the use of inefficient standby power systems, e.g. diesel generators. Concerns over the reliability of supply tend to outweigh considerations about how to use energy more efficiently, as the potential losses from power outages are much higher than the possible gains from efficiency savings.

■ Lack of information about energy efficient technologies is another problem in Africa. Energy efficiency labels are in place in only a few countries, energy consumption is often not adequately measured, due to a lack of metering equipment, and the public dissemination of information about energy efficiency is limited. These circumstances make any search for information about energy efficiency costly, leaving many companies with old and outdated technology.

■ Artificially low energy prices are another barrier to energy efficiency in Africa. In some cases, fossil-fuel subsidies increase the payback period for energy efficiency investments to a point where the investment can become uneconomic (IEA, 2013). Fossil-fuel subsidies in Africa amounted to $67 billion in 2013, 12% of the global total.

■ A lack of financing is another major impediment to energy efficiency investments in Africa. Energy efficiency projects sometimes require a substantial upfront investment, which is later recovered through energy savings. Investments in new technologies are perceived as particularly risky and the technical capacity to evaluate the opportunities associated with such investments is limited. Moreover, the cost of capital in Africa is much higher than that in most developed countries, which leads to a requirement for unrealistically short payback periods.

Cement production is the world's third-largest energy-consuming industry (after chemicals and iron and steel). Worldwide cement production consumes more energy each year than Brazil. Given a projected peak in cement demand in China in the coming decade, global cement production in the New Policies Scenario increases by just 14% from 2012, to reach 4.3 billion tonnes in 2040. Global energy consumption in this industrial sector in 2040 is slightly lower than in 2012, as the energy consumption per tonne of cement declines, compared with today. The energy intensity of cement production can be reduced by improving the energy efficiency of clinker production (either through adopting more efficient technologies or systems optimisation) or by modifying the production process by substituting energy-intensive clinker for other materials. However, the use of alternative raw materials[9] is limited by their availability and price, a perception of high risk and the required technical specifications of the final product.[10]

In the New Policies Scenario, the energy intensity of cement production is reduced by 0.5% per year on average, a fairly modest rate that reflects the limited remaining energy savings potential. A reduction of the clinker-to-cement ratio is responsible for 30% of total energy savings, while technical energy efficiency and systems optimisation account for the rest (Figure 8.9). Energy consumption for clinker production is dependent on the kiln technology used, which differs according to the water content of the raw material. While dry rotary kilns with preheaters and precalciners are the state-of-the-art technology, dry long kilns, semi-dry and wet rotary kilns, which can consume up to twice as much energy per tonne of cement, still exist (EC, 2010). The energy intensity reduction achieved by 2040 is significant in the European Union as the outdated production techniques still used there (including semi-dry and wet kilns) are phased-out over the next 25 years.

Figure 8.9 ▷ **Reduction in energy intensity in cement production by contributing factor in the New Policies Scenario, 2012-2040**

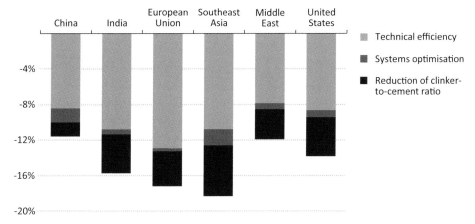

Note: These regions accounted for more than 80% of global cement production in 2012.

Next to the replacement or retrofit of older technologies by dry kilns with preheaters and precalciners and the installation of additional preheater cyclone stages, most of the savings in the New Policies Scenario result from more efficient clinker cooler technologies,

9. The most energy-consuming step in cement production is the production of clinker, the primary material in cement. The main substitutes for clinker are coal fly ash, granulated blast furnace slag, pozzolans and limestone powder.

10. In addition to making the cement production process more energy efficient, energy can be saved by reducing the demand for cement through improved concrete construction techniques.

waste heat recovery for power generation and kiln shell heat loss reduction. The more than 700 waste heat recovery power systems adopted in China recently have led to substantial electricity savings, and strong potential remains in Asia and Latin America (IIP and IFC, 2014). The uptake of energy efficiency is limited in the Middle East and the United States partially because of their comparatively low energy prices, which make the adoption of more efficient equipment more difficult to justify and in some cases even uneconomic. In China and India, the energy intensity savings achieved in the New Policies Scenario are comparatively low because a significant share of current capacity has been added over the last decade, using, in most cases, the latest technology.

Energy efficiency and competitiveness

The role of energy in international competitiveness and economic growth has come to prominence in political, economic and environmental debate in recent years with the emergence of large disparities in energy prices across countries and regions at a time when many advanced economies are struggling to combat recession and deflation. Energy represents a significant share of production costs for certain industries, so regional price differences, particularly for electricity and natural gas, can have a significant impact on industrial competitiveness and overall economic competitiveness.[11] Concerns about a loss of competitiveness have been growing in energy-importing countries facing relatively high prices; conversely, those countries enjoying relatively low energy prices are hopeful of being able to exploit this advantage by boosting the production and export of energy-intensive goods. Our analysis shows that pursuing energy efficiency in energy-intensive industries has only limited remaining potential to mitigate the consequence of current price differentials and thus improve industrial competitiveness. However, overall economic competitiveness, including that of energy-intensive industries, can be stimulated through cross-sectoral efficiency policies that lead to increasing economic activity.

In a globalised world, while energy prices play a particular role in the choice of the location of energy-intensive industries, location close to local demand may be more important for other businesses, particularly those selling into dynamic economies, where domestic requirements develop the fastest, such as China, India, or Southeast Asia. The strategic location of energy-intensive industries is influenced also by their place in global value chains, which have become a dominant feature of world trade and investment (OECD, WTO and UNCTAD, 2013; European Commission, 2013). Government action to stimulate spending on energy efficiency can form part of a comprehensive industrial policy aimed at promoting the supply of intermediate products with high value-added content that can be produced domestically. In the case of high energy price regions, like Europe or Japan, the overall loss of competitiveness can be contained, if local manufacturers can exploit

---

11. The term "economic competitiveness" refers to the productivity of an entire economy – industry, agriculture and services – relative to that of others. Industrial competitiveness refers to the relative productivity of industry (particularly its energy-intensive segments) and thus its ability to compete internationally. Higher productivity allows national economies to grow faster over the longer term, sustain higher wage levels and boost public welfare (IEA, 2013).

the changes in demand for goods and services that result from high energy prices. For example, an EU policy push for the adoption of efficient cars may create opportunities for European auto suppliers.

The fraction of domestically created value added, as opposed to the value added embedded in imported goods, is a key indicator of competitiveness, notably in highly integrated industries, such as the chemical industry (UNCTAD, 2013). The content of domestic value added in chemicals rises with the size of the domestic energy resource endowment and the size of the economy: large and energy-rich economies feature more diversified industrial activities, including a variety of chemicals production and rely more heavily on domestically produced intermediate goods (Figure 8.10). Such countries, including the United States or Russia, generate 80% or more of their value added in chemicals domestically and are therefore less sensitive to price swings, for example in the price of gas, on international markets. The proportion of value added in EU products is equivalent to, if not higher than, that of products in the United States. As most trading partners of EU member countries are other member countries, chemical value chains often develop locally, so that higher energy costs in Europe are not only an impediment to local businesses but may eventually spread through the whole European Union.

Figure 8.10 ▷ Composition of value added in chemicals exports by country of origin, 2009

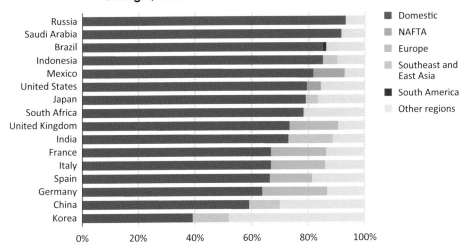

Note: NAFTA = North American Free Trade Agreement.

Sources: OECD-WTO Trade in Value Added (TiVA) database (OECD and WTO, 2012); IEA analysis.

How energy efficiency affects international competitiveness

Analysis in the 2013 and 2012 editions of the *World Energy Outlook* identified energy efficiency as an attractive option for countries facing relatively high energy prices to control the impact on their overall costs. Policies to stimulate improvements in the efficiency of energy use offer several benefits: not only can they reduce production costs, they can also improve the stability and reliability of production systems, lower maintenance needs, improve product quality, reduce waste streams, boost disposable household incomes, raise economic growth and prosperity and cut airborne emissions of pollutants and greenhouse gases (IEA, 2014d).

The scope for doing so is undoubtedly large. Only one-third of the potential for improving the efficiency of energy use globally (around 40% in industry) is exploited in the New Policies Scenario (IEA, 2012). The remaining potential for efficiency gains in industry, particularly in the most energy-intensive sectors, is lower as they already use relatively efficient technologies because of the strong financial incentive to save energy as a means to boost profitability. The remaining global economic potential for improving efficiency, which involves a whole range of actions to make smaller absolute gains, will not be fully realised without action by governments to encourage households and businesses to alter their spending and investments. This intervention is necessary in order to overcome the manifold and divergent barriers to energy efficiency, including the lack of visibility, low awareness, limited know-how and fragmentation of energy consumption.

Scope for energy efficiency to cut costs in energy-intensive industries

Energy accounts for a larger share of total supply costs in industry than in other sectors of the economy, so energy costs are of particular importance to industrial competitiveness. In recent years, regional price differentials have tended to grow. Notable examples are the fall in natural gas and electricity prices in North America, thanks to booming shale gas production and the rise in coal, gas and electricity prices in China and other Asian countries, with surging demand and growing import dependence. These relative price movements, alongside a host of other non-energy-related factors, have contributed to shifts in regional industrial and economic competitiveness. A more competitive domestic industry is not only favourable in its own right but benefits the entire economy as across-the-board intermediate and final consumption goods can be produced at lower cost. Packaging materials, such as plastic bottles, are one illustrative example of a product group that incorporates intermediary energy-intensive products (Spotlight).

Often, profitable investment opportunities to improve energy efficiency as a way of reducing energy costs are available; but they may not be taken up for a variety of reasons, including information gaps or a lack of access to capital. The most energy-intensive industries have long recognised the importance of minimising energy costs to profitability and have over time invested heavily in more efficient processes and technologies, especially where energy prices are relatively high, such as in Europe. But that is not to say that there are no remaining opportunities for improving efficiency: progressive advances in production technology and changing market conditions mean that there is always potential for using energy more efficiently. Even in low-cost regions, improving energy efficiency in the long-term makes sense as long as they are economically viable driven by the need to improve productivity. The potential exists even in steel-making using electric arc furnaces and chemicals – two of the most energy-intensive industries.

Can energy efficiency make the production of bottles and cans competitive in high-cost regions?

Some everyday consumer goods require a lot of energy to make, so regional differences in energy prices can have a big impact on production costs. But this may not lead to migration of production to low energy price regions if the end products are expensive to transport. Two examples are plastic bottles made from polyethylene terephthalate (PET) and aluminium beverage cans.

The PET for plastic bottles is produced from two intermediary products: para-xylenes, made from naphtha, and ethylene, that can be made using different oil-based feedstocks, including ethane in the United States and Middle East and mainly naphtha in China, the European Union and Japan. Since naphtha is a globally traded commodity, prices are fairly similar across regions. But feedstock prices for ethylene production vary significantly. Thanks to the boom in shale-gas production, the United States enjoys the lowest ethane prices in the world after the Middle East, while European, Chinese and Japan rely mostly on expensive naphtha. Mainly as a result of these price differences, the cost of producing a bottle (assuming the entire production chain is domestic) ranges from just 1.7 US cents in the Middle East to 3.7 US cents in Japan (Figure 8.11).

It is a similar story for cans made from primary aluminium, due to differences in the cost of electricity – the main energy input: its share of total production costs ranges from 27% to 46% in the countries/regions assessed here. These differences largely explain the wide range in total production costs, from 1.8 US cents in the Middle East (thanks to cheap natural gas) to 3 US cents in the European Union (where electricity is most expensive).

Figure 8.11 ▷ **Estimated unit production cost of a plastic bottle and an aluminium beverage can in selected regions, 2013** (US cents)

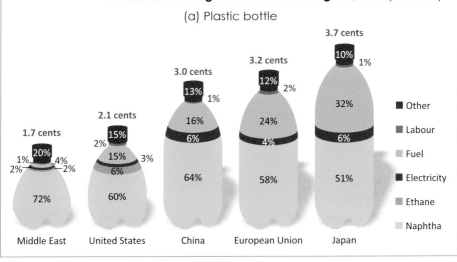

(a) Plastic bottle

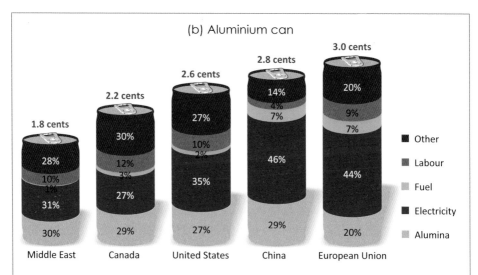

(b) Aluminium can

				Other
				Labour
				Fuel
				Electricity
				Alumina

Note: It is assumed that the aluminium can is made entirely from primary aluminium.

Sources: Argus (2014), AT Kearney (2013), CEPS (2013), IEA (2009), IEA (2014e), IHS (2013), PE Americas (2010), Platts (2013a and 2013b), World Aluminium (2014); IEA analysis.

Energy efficiency can help to reduce these cost differences even though it cannot eliminate them entirely. Europe is currently one of the regions where aluminium smelters require the highest electricity input per tonne of aluminium produced. Adopting the latest smelting technology could reduce the cost of making a can in Europe by around 0.1 US cents. Similarly, the adoption of best-practice technologies could reduce the production costs of a plastic bottle in Japan and the European Union by 0.1-0.2 US cents (after providing for recovery of the capital cost of the initial efficiency investment). Due to the relatively high cost of transporting these bulky goods, they are likely to continue to be produced domestically. However, production of the intermediary goods – aluminium and plastic – is gravitating to low energy price regions.

Recycling represents another way to address high production costs. Today about 70% of aluminium cans are recycled worldwide (IAI, 2009). Producing a can from recycled material can reduce electricity consumption by up to 95%. Producing plastic bottles from recycled material, however, is currently not possible, due to the different types of plastic in use, contamination and colour differences.

Steel-making with electric arc furnaces

Electricity is a key production cost factor in secondary steel production in electric arc furnaces (EAFs), which smelt scrap metal or direct reduced iron (the production of which involves the use of a mixture of hydrogen and carbon monoxide as a reducing agent). Today 29% of global steel production is produced in EAFs, accounting for about 3% of total industrial electricity consumption. The largest producers of EAF steel are China, the United

States and India.[12] Scrap metal typically makes up about 80% of the total cost of producing steel in EAFs, while electricity – the main operating expense – represents on average close to 10% (depending on the local price and the efficiency of the plant) and labour, alloys and other additives the rest (Grimmond, 2011). The price of scrap metal is broadly the same for all EAF steel producers, as it is a globally traded commodity, though differences can arise due to contractual arrangements and freight costs.

Among the leading EAF producing countries, with the exception of the United States, average electricity prices fall within a fairly narrow range of $75-90 per megawatt-hour (MWh) (Figure 8.12). In Indiana, the US state that produces the most (14% of total US secondary steel production in 2013), electricity prices are around $50/MWh – lower than in any other major steel-producing country, thanks to cheap domestic coal (which keeps the cost of generation down) and exemptions from network costs and taxes. Electricity prices for Chinese steel producers are comparable to those in Europe, Japan and Korea; although electricity generation costs in China are lower, cross-subsidisation from industrial to household consumers and penalty tariffs for energy-intensive plants that cannot reach national targets boost the price in China. In India, power from captive generation, which is mostly smaller in size and thus less efficient (though some plants benefit from domestic low-cost resources), plays a significant role in the steel industry. EAFs in Germany enjoy exemptions from the renewable levy and taxes. In Italy, producers benefit from lower prices by accepting interruptible load contracts and from the virtual import service (an incentive towards European market integration).

Figure 8.12 ▷ **Average estimated electricity prices for electric arc furnaces in selected countries, 2013**

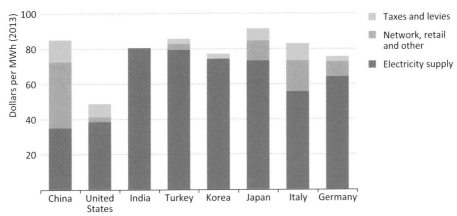

Notes: Prices for China are for Hebei (the largest steel-producing province). Indiana was chosen to reflect US prices as it is the largest producing US state. Prices for India are based on captive coal-fired generation.
Sources: BDEW (2014), US DOE/EIA (2014), Eurostat (2014), Grave and Breitschopf (2014), Mizuho (2014), NDRC of China (2013), PFC (2013), SteelConsult International (2013); IEA analysis.

12. In China, almost half of the input to EAFs is pig iron due to lack of scrap metal (Hasanbeigi, Jiang and Price, 2013). In India, EAFs mostly rely on direct reduced iron (DRI) as input; about half of the steel from DRI is produced in induction furnaces (Ministry of Steel, 2013).

Improving energy efficiency is one way for countries producing EAF steel to reduce the competitiveness gap arising from electricity price differentials. It is estimated that EAFs in Europe are around 8% less energy efficient than those in the United States (Pardo et al., 2012; Worrell et al., 2010). Taking account of differences in both efficiency and prices, energy costs per tonne of steel produced are currently around $15 higher in Europe than in the United States; by adopting latest technologies, operators of EAFs in Europe could improve their efficiency by around 20%, compared with the current industry average, reducing the gap between their energy costs and those paid by their US competitors to $10/tonne of steel (after accounting for the capital cost in improving energy efficiency).

Over the projection period, US producers see the largest increase in electricity tariffs (more than 25%) in the New Policies Scenario, mainly due to rising gas prices that drive up electricity wholesale prices. The increase in Chinese tariffs is as big as in the United States as a result of the assumed introduction of a CO_2 price. Prices in Japan decline, with lower gas import prices and the gradual reintroduction of nuclear power. Electricity prices for European producers increase by around 15%, mainly as a result of increasing CO_2 prices and the greater reflection in wholesale prices of new investment needs (IEA, 2014a). Although electricity prices are expected to rise less than in the United States, fully exploiting the energy efficiency potential would not be enough for European operators to close the price gap with US competitors, though it could improve the position significantly vis-à-vis competitors in other world regions. Since Europe is likely to remain a relatively high-cost energy region, the steel industry there is likely to remain focused on producing innovative, high-value products.

Chemicals

The chemicals industry is the largest energy-consuming sector and the largest industrial sub-sector by value added, with global output totalling around $5 trillion in 2012 – almost equal to Japan's entire GDP. It is highly fragmented and diverse, including basic petrochemicals, industrial gases, fertilisers, primary plastics and synthetic rubber, agrochemical products, paints, pharmaceuticals, soap and detergents. The industry has changed profoundly since 2000 with the combination of a sharp rise in energy bills and, consequently, an overall reduction in value added in total output (Figure 8.13).

On average, the proportion of energy in total costs in the global chemical industry (including both energy-intensive sectors and less intensive ones, such as pharmaceuticals) increased by a third between 2000 and 2011 to 14% of total expenditure. By contrast, the United States, where cheap natural gas has helped the industry to limit the share of energy costs to 11% (marginally above the level of 2000), reinforced its competitive position *vis-à-vis* other major chemical producing regions. Indian chemical producers have also seen an improvement in their competitive position, as a result of large investments in improving energy intensity and greater use of recycling (India Planning Commission, 2012). China has broadly managed to keep the share of energy in total costs down by regulating prices, but non-energy-related factors (including more expensive intermediary goods, more stringent environmental regulation and increasing labour cost [European Climate Foundation, 2014]) have led to a fall in relative value added: it dropped by around seven percentage points to 21% of the value of output.

Figure 8.13 ▷ **Change in energy spending and value added in the chemicals industry, 2000-2011**

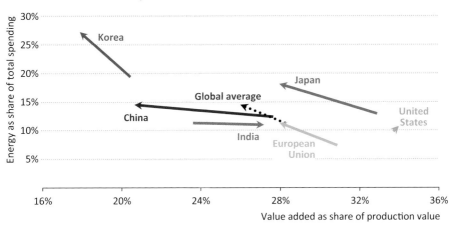

Sources: World Input-Output Database (WIOD); IEA analysis.

However, the sharp rise in fuel prices after 2007 was particularly harmful to the competitiveness of chemical companies located in large energy-importing regions, such as Europe, where plants tend to be less energy efficient than the much larger and more recent plants in the Middle East or Asia (Broeren et al., 2014). The burden of energy expenditures for European chemical firms increased on average by more than half over 2000-2011, though trends differed appreciably across countries. In France, energy as a share of total spending increased by a staggering 85%. In Japan and Korea, the share of energy in total expenditures rose by 40% over 2000-2011. One-sixth of the ageing naphtha-based steam cracker capacity in Japan is expected to close within a decade in the face of falling domestic demand, the global capacity surplus and intense competition from the Middle East.

Improving energy efficiency is one obvious response to the high price of energy inputs to chemicals production. But the potential for further efficiency improvements, especially in bulk petrochemicals, is diminishing as most opportunities have already been exploited. Over the projection period to 2040, global energy intensity in the bulk chemical industry increases by a mere 0.4% annually. While the European Union, Japan and Korea (all of which face high energy prices) accounted for 42% of basic petrochemical production in 1990, they only account for 27% today and we project this share will decline further to 12% in 2040.[13] As a result, chemical companies facing high energy prices are moving towards less energy-intensive chemicals, higher value derivatives (such as specialty products or pharmaceuticals) and smaller production scales, resulting in greater market segmentation. As in other sectors, other external factors, including the overall business and investment climate and access to skilled labour, will also play a role in determining the international competitiveness of chemicals producers around the world (ECEEE, 2013). Technological breakthroughs in production processes and products could always transform the situation.

---

13. The shares refer to global ethylene production, the most widely produced petrochemical product.

Impact of improved energy efficiency on economic competitiveness

In the New Policies Scenario, cumulative spending by businesses and households on energy efficiency (i.e. on energy-using equipment that is more efficient than the average in 2012) amounts to $14.5 trillion over 2014-2040, with two-thirds going to the transport sector. Efficiency spending in transport leads to lower vehicle fuel consumption, boosting economic competitiveness directly as a result of reduced imports of oil (see next section), which improves the trade balance and boosts GDP. There are also indirect benefits to households and businesses, as lower business costs are passed on in the form of lower consumer prices. Similar impacts occur as a result of efficiency measures in other sectors. For example, in the buildings sector, reduced energy needs stimulate all kinds of manufacturing activities, such as cement, aluminium, construction and chemicals, particularly the production of insulation material.

Figure 8.14 ▷ **Diffusion of cumulative energy efficiency spending on cars worldwide through the manufacturing and services sectors in the New Policies Scenario, 2014-2040** ($2013 trillion)

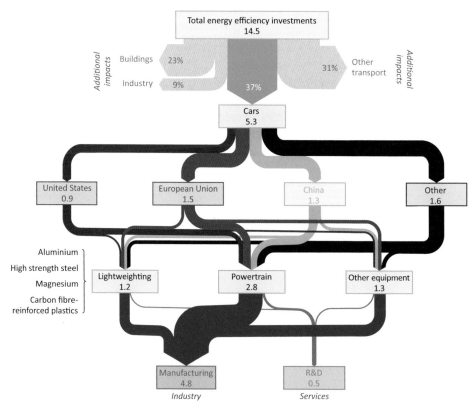

Note: R&D spending is only directed towards upgrading the components of existing vehicle types but excludes fundamental research. R&D requirements are based on European data.

Source: European Commission (2011); IEA analysis.

The effect of measures to boost efficiency in transport on economic activity and competitiveness are particularly large because of the sectors' importance in all economic activities and because of the sizeable scope for efficiency gains. The purchase of more efficient cars alone accounts for 37% of overall efficiency spending. Fully 70% of the fuel efficiency spending on passenger vehicles occurs in the United State, the European Union and China, and is driven by national fuel-economy measures or emissions standards. The manufacturing of efficient vehicles mobilises a number of other manufacturing and services sectors as it requires a wide range of intermediate inputs and engineering to make them lighter, to improve on-board energy management systems and to integrate new manufactured equipment, such as efficient engines, hybrid systems, start-stop systems, direct injection for gasoline cars and improved aerodynamics (Figure 8.14). The $5.3 trillion of spending on efficient passenger vehicles leads to cumulative indirect spending of $1.2 trillion on lightweight materials (largely aluminium-based) and $2.8 trillion on powertrains, including optimised engines. Similarly, efficiency measures implemented in buildings, another key recipient of efficiency investments, and industry lead to additional economic stimulation, and eventually value creation, in all manufacturing sectors and services.

8

Figure 8.15 ▷ Change in energy intensity and value added by sector in the Efficient World Scenario relative to the New Policies Scenario, 2030

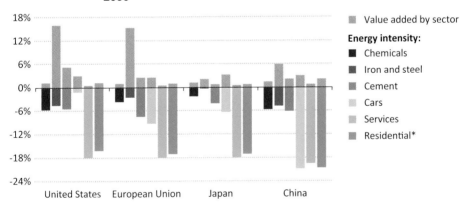

* In the case of the residential sector, value added is replaced by real household consumption.

Source: IEA analysis based on Chateau et al. (2014).

The economy-wide impacts, measured in value-added terms, of across-the-board measures to tap into the full economic potential to improve energy efficiency are described in the *WEO* Efficient World Scenario (IEA, 2012). In that scenario, government measures that lead to spending on and investment in more efficient equipment and appliances in all cases where it is economically viable (i.e. where they pay for themselves) are assumed to be adopted. The overall economic gains are significant: global GDP rises by an estimated 1% by 2030 – a cumulative economic gain of over $11 trillion – as production and consumption of less energy-intensive goods and services free up resources to be allocated more efficiently elsewhere. In the major economies, value added in industry, transport and services rises with increased economic activity by 3% on average; household consumption also rises by between 1% and 2% (Figure 8.15). As economic activity increases, there is a gradual reorientation of the global economy towards more efficient economic structures, encouraging production and consumption of less energy-intensive goods and services (Chateau et al., 2014).

Broader benefits

Household spending on energy

The share of energy in total household expenditure has increased over the past decade in most regions as a result of higher energy prices, particularly for gasoline and diesel. The current share varies significantly from one region to another (Figure 8.16). It is currently highest for the European Union (8%) as a result of both higher energy prices and taxes. With lower price and tax levels as well as higher income levels, it is only 5% in the United States. In China, the share is lower today than in Europe or the United States, because fewer people own cars and there are fewer household appliances.

Figure 8.16 ▷ Share of energy expenditures in household income in selected regions in the New Policies Scenario

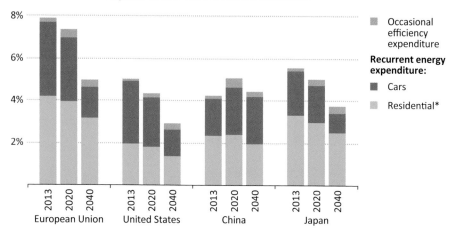

* Residential energy expenditures represent spending for heating, cooling, cooking, lighting and appliances.

While in OECD countries the share of energy expenditures in household income decreases over the projection period in the New Policies Scenario as a result of higher incomes, increasingly efficient cars, equipment and appliances and stable energy prices, it increases in the medium term in China, where energy efficiency gains are outweighed by higher end-user prices, as a result of an assumed subsidy phase out, and increasing demand for energy-consuming goods. Household spending on energy efficiency, defined as the additional spending on devices and vehicles to raise their efficiency above the average level in 2012, currently accounts for 0.1-0.2% of household income. In the future, this share increases in all countries to up to 0.3%, but remains a small fraction of both income and total energy expenditures. Thus, financial constraints do not generally pose a problem for energy efficiency spending by households but, especially for larger amounts (e.g. for buildings insulation) financing mechanisms are needed that address the issues related to high upfront cost. Some policies to facilitate spending on energy efficiency are already in place and include public loan programmes and utility on-bill financing (IEA, 2014a). The advantage of residential energy efficiency measures is not only the reduction in energy costs, but also the warmer, drier and cleaner environment and the associated health benefits (IEA, 2014d).

Fossil-fuel import bills

Reducing energy demand through energy efficiency offers net-importing regions a way to both enhance energy security and reduce import bills. In the New Policies Scenario, thanks to improved energy efficiency compared with 2012 levels, the five-largest energy-importing regions save almost $1 trillion in 2040, which corresponds to two-thirds of their current import bills (Figure 8.17). The United States sees the largest benefits, mainly through reduced oil-import costs as a direct consequence of fuel-economy standards for cars and trucks. Energy efficiency improvements from 2012 to 2040 cut fuel-import bills in the European Union in 2040 by almost a third, as a result of more efficient vehicles and lower natural gas consumption in better insulated buildings. In China, efficiency improvements in industry and energy transformation make up 58% of all natural gas savings and 24% of the oil savings (most of the remaining oil savings come from more efficient vehicles).

Figure 8.17 ▷ **Oil and natural gas import bills and avoided import bills due to energy efficiency by region in the New Policies Scenario**

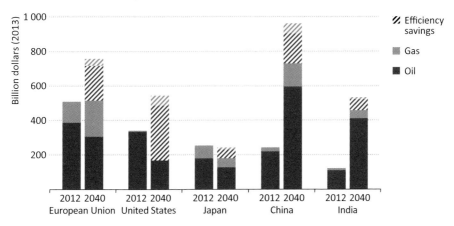

Notes: In the New Policies Scenario, the United States is a net-exporter of natural gas in 2040. The efficiency savings are calculated based on the efficiency levels prevailing in 2012.

CO₂ emissions

In the New Policies Scenario, energy-related CO_2 emissions increase from 31.6 Gt in 2012 to 38 Gt in 2040, or about 7.9 Gt (17%) less than in the Current Policies Scenario (Figure 8.18). Energy efficiency measures account for about half of cumulative CO_2 emissions savings, with the share being even higher in the short term. The largest efficiency savings in 2040 come from end-use sectors, with buildings accounting for most (37%), followed by transport (32%) and industry (28%). Efficiency gains in energy supply, including power plants, transmission and distribution, refineries, and oil and gas extraction, are responsible for 9% of cumulative savings throughout the projection period. In order to reduce emissions to a level compatible with limiting the long-term temperature increase to 2 °C, as projected in the 450 Scenario, energy efficiency needs to be complemented by a higher penetration of renewables, nuclear power and carbon capture and storage (CCS).

Figure 8.18 ▷ **World energy-related CO₂ emissions abatement in the New Policies Scenario relative to the Current Policies Scenario**

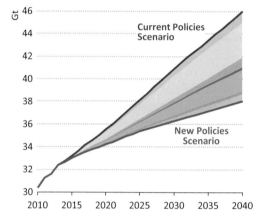

CO₂ abatement	2020	2040
Energy service demand	19%	11%
End-use efficiency	46%	39%
Supply efficiency	9%	11%
Fuel and technology switching in end-uses	2%	3%
Renewables	17%	24%
Biofuels	3%	3%
Nuclear	3%	7%
CCS	1%	2%
Total (Gt CO₂)	1.3	7.9

Chapter 9

Fossil-fuel subsidies
A roadmap for rational pricing

Highlights

- Subsidies to fossil fuels, which encourage wasteful consumption, remain a big problem, despite major efforts on the part of many countries around the world to reduce or eliminate them – primarily where they have become too much of a burden on the public purse. In 2013, the global value of subsidies that artificially lower end-user prices for all forms of fossil energy totalled $548 billion – a $25 billion cut from the previous year. Oil products accounted for over half of the total value of subsidies to fossil fuels in 2013.

- Ten countries account for almost three-quarters of the world total for fossil-fuel subsidies; five of them – all oil and gas exporters – are in the Middle East or North Africa. Most of the other leading subsidisers are also important hydrocarbon producers. They generally set domestic prices above the cost of production, but well below the prices those fuels could reach on the international market, net of transport costs.

- Globally, 40 countries have been identified as subsidising fossil-fuel consumption. In total, they account for over half of world energy consumption. The value of subsidies as a share of total GDP of these countries averages 5%. The rate of subsidisation (the ratio of the subsidy to the international reference price) averages 23%, with the highest in Venezuela at 93%.

- One of the most damaging effects of subsidising fossil fuels is on clean energy investment. In the Middle East, more than one-third of electricity is generated using subsidised oil, absorbing nearly 2 mb/d. In the absence of subsidies, all of the main renewable energy technologies, as well as nuclear power, would generally be competitive with oil-fired plants in the Middle East. Gasoline prices in Saudi Arabia are currently less than one-tenth of the average price in Europe, so it takes around 16 years to recoup the cost of upgrading from a vehicle with average fuel economy to one that uses half as much fuel per kilometre. The removal of Saudi gasoline subsidies would cut the payback period to just three years.

- Most countries with large fossil-fuel subsidies recognise the need to eliminate or, at least, reduce them, but often run into difficulties – usually because of strong resistance from those consumers and producers that stand to lose the most. Experience points to the need to follow some basic principles in reforming subsidies: the starting point must be to get pricing right, i.e. ensure that energy prices reflect their full economic value by introducing market pricing and removing price controls. The reform process must also build broad-based support for change, selectively managing the adverse effects on different economic actors.

Overview[1]

Subsidies to fossil fuels remain a big problem globally – imposing enormous economic, social and environmental costs – despite commitments on the part of many countries to reform them. In 2013, the global value of subsidies that artificially lower end-user prices for all forms of fossil energy totalled $548 billion – $25 billion down on the previous year, in part due to the drop in international energy prices (Figure 9.1). Those subsidies were over four-times the value of subsidies to renewable energy and more than four-times the amount invested globally in improving energy efficiency (IEA, 2014). Oil products account for over half of the total, with oil subsidies concentrated in the oil- and gas-exporting countries.

Figure 9.1 ▷ **Economic value of global fossil-fuel subsidies by fuel**

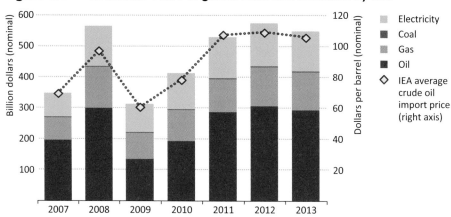

Several countries, including members of the G-20, Asia-Pacific Economic Cooperation (APEC) and Organisation for Economic Co-operation and Development (OECD), have already taken action to phase out or reduce their fossil-fuel subsidies (including some important measures during the past year – see Table 9.1), primarily where they have become too much of a burden on the public purse. But much remains to be done, as our latest estimates show. An update of developments in fossil-fuel subsidies, together with an assessment of the lessons learned for policy-making and guidelines for reform, is provided in the last

---

1. The analysis and information presented in this chapter forms part of the ongoing input to the G-20 in support of their 2009 commitment to "rationalise and phase out over the medium term inefficient fossil-fuel subsidies that encourage wasteful consumption" (G-20, 2009). A similar commitment was made by leaders of the Asia-Pacific Economic Cooperation (APEC) forum in November 2009. The IEA has established an online database to increase the availability and transparency of energy subsidy data – an essential step in building momentum for global fossil-fuel subsidy reform (available at: www.iea.org/subsidy/index.html). Improved access to data on fossil-fuel subsidies is raising awareness about their magnitude and incidence and is encouraging informed debate on whether those subsidies represent an economically efficient allocation of resources or whether it would be possible to achieve the same objectives by alternative means. The IEA continues to work with other international organisations to analyse the effects of fossil-fuel subsidies and encourage countries around the world to reform them.

section. The rest of the chapter sets out in detail the updated results of our quantitative analysis of global fossil-fuel subsidies, their impact on clean energy investment and the potential gains from removing them.

Identifying the problem

Defining fossil-fuel subsidies

The IEA defines an energy subsidy as any government action directed primarily at the energy sector that lowers the cost of energy production, raises the price received by energy producers or lowers the price paid by energy consumers. It can be applied to fossil and non-fossil energy in the same way. Several other definitions are also in use (Box 9.1). In addition to the fossil-fuel subsidies that are easily recognised, for example when gasoline is sold at prices well below international-parity levels, or when a coal producer is guaranteed a premium payment for coal produced from high-cost mines, this broad definition also captures many of the other diverse and obscure types of energy subsidy that commonly exist, such as mandates requiring utilities to buy a certain volume of coal or renewables-based energy, which normally increase the market price for those sources, or publicly funded research and development that helps to lower the cost of energy supply.

Energy subsidies are frequently differentiated according to whether the benefit goes directly to consumers or producers. Consumer subsidies are those that benefit consumers by lowering the prices they pay for energy. These are now rare in most OECD countries, but are still present in many other countries. Producer subsidies, by contrast, benefit producers by raising the revenue they receive or by lowering their cost of production in order to encourage domestic supply. They remain an important form of subsidy in developed and developing countries alike, though they are directed mainly at non-fossil energy in the former.

Forms of subsidy and why they exist

Fossil fuels receive many types of subsidy, provided through various direct and indirect channels. The most common types that fall within our definition of energy subsidy are price controls that result in end-users paying prices below market levels; direct financial transfers (such as grants) to artificially lower the effective price to end-users or reduce the costs paid by producers; transfers of risk from the private sector to the government (such as through soft loans or loan guarantees); tax concessions (for both consumption and production); purchase mandates and other market guarantees; public funding of research and development; and trade instruments to protect domestic producers.[2]

The stated objective of subsidising fossil energy through these measures is usually one or more of the following: holding down the cost of energy to poor households for social reasons; redistributing national resource wealth; reducing dependence on imported

---

2. For more detail on the types of government intervention that can constitute a subsidy, see OECD (2013) and Global Subsidies Initiative (GSI) (2010).

energy for energy security reasons; promoting national or regional economic development by conferring an advantage to domestic energy-consuming industries and protecting employment in a domestic industry against international competition. Subsidies are often seen as an administratively convenient way of pursuing one or more of these objectives.

Box 9.1 ▷ **Towards agreement on defining "subsidy"**

The World Trade Organization (WTO) adopted a legal definition of subsidy in 1994 within the Agreement on Subsidies and Countervailing Measures (ASCM) – one of the agreements that were reached during the Uruguay Round of multilateral trade negotiations. It lists four transfer mechanisms through which a subsidy confers a benefit: the direct transfer of funds or liabilities; revenue foregone or not collected; the provision of below-cost goods or services; and the provision of income or price support. The International Monetary Fund (IMF) and the United Nations Statistics Division have come up with other definitions, while the European Commission produced its own legal definition of "state aid" in the European Commission Treaty, Article 87 in 1998. The OECD defines a subsidy in general terms as any measure that keeps prices for consumers below market levels, or for producers above market levels or that reduces costs for consumers and producers. This is in line with the IEA's definition of an energy subsidy.

While the accepted general definitions of subsidies should be applicable to energy products, in practice several definitions are used for various reasons. The G-20 initiative on fossil-energy subsidy reform that was launched in 2009 has revived attempts to seek a definition of "subsidy" acceptable to all. Achieving that goal will be tricky: subsidies are closely linked to sensitive political issues such as the sovereignty of governments to use natural resources as they see fit, trade competition and poverty alleviation. Even if it proves possible to agree on a common definition, using it to identify and measure subsidies in the real world is fraught with difficulties, not least because of potential arguments about what baseline to use. For example, should the basis for determining the market price of a fuel be that which would prevail in the absence of any government intervention or should it reflect externalities, such as environmental effects? The IMF has argued, for example, that if baseline costs and prices are assumed to take account of external costs and benefits (i.e., they are economically optimal), a failure by the government to address a market failure involving an external cost could be considered a subsidy.

While differences in definitions persist, the leading international bodies working on energy subsidies – including the IEA – measure them in similar ways, typically involving a comparison between national prices and international benchmarks (GSI, 2014a) (Box 9.3). By contrast, several oil- and gas-exporting countries consider that selling domestically produced fuel in their home market at a price that is below the international price level (allowing for transport costs), but equal to or above the cost of production, does not constitute a subsidy.

How governments choose to go about subsidising energy depends on a number of factors including: the overall cost of the programme; the transaction and administration costs it involves; how the cost of the subsidy affects different social groups and how transparent the subsidy is. In many cases, governments prefer to keep subsidies "off-budget" for political and financial reasons: the true financial cost is less apparent, no explicit government spending or higher taxes are involved, and accountability is, accordingly, reduced. For example, in oil-producing countries, subsidies to oil products take the form of price controls that set prices below full market value but still typically above production costs, avoiding the need to pay compensation to domestic producers.

Why reform is needed

A subsidy, by its very nature, involves a complex set of changes in economic resource allocation through its impact on costs or prices, or both. These shifts inevitably have wide-ranging economic, social and environmental effects. One thing is certain: the cost of fossil fuels to an economy is not reduced by subsidies; it is just redistributed. Consumers as a whole usually still have to pay the full cost of the energy – through higher taxes and lower spending elsewhere in the economy – though some consumers effectively end up paying less than others (UNEP, 2003). In the case of countries that are large exporters of energy, while domestic costs may be reduced in the short run, the exhaustibility of the resource means that higher consumption now reduces sales in the future.

Critically, the market distortions created by fossil-fuel subsidies lead to a misallocation of resources, which results in a longer term economic cost.[3] Subsidies, where they involve grants or tax benefits, aggravate fiscal imbalances, crowd-out more productive and meritorious government spending, and depress private investment, including in the energy sector itself. Where energy suppliers suffer financial losses because of under-pricing, subsidies can create a vicious cycle of under-investment, poor maintenance and under-supply, particularly in the oil-refining and electricity sectors. Subsidies also encourage excessive fossil-fuel consumption, which can aggravate pollution, boost greenhouse-gas emissions, artificially promote energy-intensive industries, accelerate the depletion of natural resources and reduce incentives for investment in renewables and improving energy efficiency. They may also encourage black marketeering, smuggling and fuel adulteration, in the case of oil products, which are easy to transport and store. Fuel shortages and flourishing black markets with high prices are common in countries where low official prices constrain supply. In exporting countries, subsidies reduce the availability of fuels for export by driving up domestic demand.

To make matters worse, subsidies often fail to bring much benefit to the people for whom they are intended. In practice, a large share – if not the bulk – of the subsidies aimed at helping the poor often ends up going to higher income households, as they can afford to consume more of the subsidised fuels, aggravating the very inequality they are meant to

---

3. See, for example, Burniaux et al., (2009), Plante (2013) and Clements et al., 2013.

reduce. Even schemes designed to limit the price of a basic first tranche of energy can have the same affect, for example, where a wealthy person's second home generates a separate entitlement. IEA analysis indicates that only 8% of the money spent on fossil-fuel subsidies reaches the poorest 20% of the population and that other direct forms of welfare support would cost much less (IEA, 2011).

Measuring their size

Methodology

Measuring the exact worth of fossil-fuel subsidies worldwide is hard, whatever the definition or estimation method used. The IEA uses a price-gap approach.[4] The price gap is the amount by which the average final consumer price for a given fuel falls short of its reference price, which corresponds to the full cost of supply or, where appropriate, the international market price, adjusted for the costs of transportation and distribution and value-added tax (VAT). For a given country, the total value of fossil-fuel subsidies is the aggregated size of the price gap for each fuel in each sector, multiplied by the volume consumed. The IEA estimates cover subsidies to fossil fuels consumed by end-users (households and businesses) and subsidies to fossil-fuel inputs to electric power generation. The principal advantage of the price-gap approach is that it avoids the need to compile detailed information on different types of government intervention by focusing on the combined net effects on prices. The principal drawback is that it captures only interventions that collectively result in lower final prices than those that would prevail in a competitive market (Koplow, 2009). Others, such as under-collection of bills, tax concessions, fuel vouchers or other payments made directly to low-income households and many producer subsidies, are not captured by the analysis of price gaps. However, the approach has proved to be the most practical one available for estimating the general magnitude of subsidies across a number of countries; more detailed analysis of subsidies at the national level may also warrant the use of other approaches, such as a bottom-up inventory of government interventions (ADB, 2014).

For countries that import a given product, subsidy estimates derived through the price-gap approach are explicit. In other words, they represent net expenditures resulting from the domestic sale of imported energy (purchased at world prices in hard currency), at lower, regulated prices. In contrast, for countries that export a given product – and therefore do not pay world prices – subsidy estimates are implicit and have no direct budgetary impact. Rather, they represent the opportunity cost of pricing domestic energy below market levels, i.e. the rent that could be recovered by the supplier if domestic consumers paid world prices. For countries that produce a portion of their consumption themselves and import the rest, the estimates presented represent a combination of opportunity costs and direct government expenditures.

---

4. The other main approach involves compiling an inventory of quantitative estimates of direct budgetary support and tax expenditures supporting the production or consumption of fossil fuels. This is the approach used by the OECD (see OECD, 2013 for the latest estimates for OECD countries) and the Global Subsidies Initiative (GSI, 2010).

A large amount of data is required to calculate the price gaps for each fuel in each sector and in each country. End-user price and consumption data are drawn from IEA databases and, where necessary, other secondary sources. For oil products, natural gas and coal, reference prices are calculated on the basis of international prices. Electricity reference prices are estimated on the basis of annual average costs (Box 9.2). Some governments and analysts regard this method of determining reference prices as inappropriate. In particular, as mentioned above, a number of energy-resource-rich economies are of the opinion that the reference price in their markets should be based on their costs of production, rather than prices on international markets as applied within this analysis. The basis for their view, typically, is that natural resources are being used to promote the nation's general economic development and that the resultant economic gain more than offsets the notional loss of value by selling the resource domestically at a price below the international price. Our counter-argument is that there is an opportunity cost associated with not pricing on the basis of what the fuel would fetch in the international market, which results in an economically inefficient allocation of domestic economic resources and reduces economic growth in the longer term.

Box 9.2 ▷ How we calculate the reference, or "right", price of a fossil fuel

For net importers, reference prices are based on the import-parity price – i.e., the price of a product at the nearest international hub, adjusted for quality differences if necessary, plus the cost of freight and insurance to the net importer, plus the cost of internal distribution and marketing and any VAT that is applied. VAT is added to the reference price where the tax is levied on final energy sales as a proxy for the general rate of tax on all economic activities needed to fund public services. If a lower or zero rate of VAT is applied to a particular fuel, it would represent a subsidy. Other taxes, including excise duties, are not included in the reference price. This means that there is no net subsidy where excise duties are larger than the gap between the reference price and the *pre-tax* retail price. As an illustration, the breakdown of 2013 reference prices for oil products in Indonesia, a net importer, is shown in Figure 9.2.

For net exporters, reference prices are based on the export-parity price; that is, the price of a product at the nearest international hub, adjusted for any quality differences, *minus* the cost of freight and insurance from the exporting country, *plus* the cost of internal distribution and marketing and any VAT. All calculations are carried out using local prices and the results are converted to US dollars at market exchange rates.

Assumed costs for transporting oil products vary according to the distance of the country from its nearest hub; they are taken from average costs, as reported in industry data. Average internal distribution and marketing costs for oil products are estimated based on available data. For natural gas and coal, transport and internal distribution costs are estimated on the basis of available shipping data. Reference prices are adjusted for quality differences, which affect the market value of a fuel. As a result, reference prices are below observed import prices in some cases, such as in countries that rely on low-quality domestic coal but import small volumes of higher quality coal.

Unlike oil, gas and coal, electricity is not extensively traded over national borders, so no international price, upon which the reference price can be based, exists in most cases. Therefore, reference prices for electricity generated from fossil fuels are based on annual average cost pricing for electricity in each country, which depends on the makeup of generating capacity, the unsubsidised cost of fossil-fuel inputs, and estimates of transmission and distribution costs. No other costs, such as allowances for building new capacity, are taken into account in our electricity reference prices.

Figure 9.2 ▷ **Example of the calculation of subsidies for oil products in Indonesia, 2013**

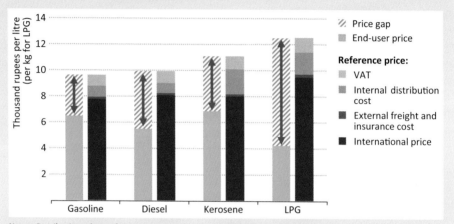

Notes: Retail prices shown for Premium gasoline and Automotive Diesel Oil (Solar) are those in place following the reforms in mid-2013, which reduced the level of subsidy (and price gap). Liquefied petroleum gas (LPG) and kerosene represent prices for households.

Estimates of fossil-fuel subsidies in 2013

The value of fossil-fuel subsidies worldwide totalled $548 billion in 2013, some $25 billion lower than in 2012.[5] For 2013, our global survey identified a total of 40 countries where at least one fossil fuel was found to be subsidised. Those countries account for well over half of world fossil-energy consumption. While there are additional countries that are known to subsidise fossil-fuel consumption, we have included in our estimate only those for which adequate energy pricing and consumption data are available. Energy use in the countries that have been excluded is relatively small, so their subsidies would not make a sizeable difference to our global total, but may still represent a significant financial burden for the countries themselves.

Iran remains the single biggest subsidising country, with total consumption subsidies topping $84 billion – around 50% of them going to oil products (Figure 9.3). The total subsidy figure is very close to last year's: reforms resulted in end-user prices being increased sharply for

---

5. The IEA first measured subsidies in the *World Energy Outlook* in 1999 and has been measuring them systematically on an annual basis since 2007.

some products, but this was offset by a sharp depreciation of the local currency against the US dollar. Saudi Arabia and India are next on the list, their energy consumption subsidies being worth about $62 billion and $47 billion respectively. The only other country whose fossil-energy subsidies exceed $40 billion is Russia, the result of under-pricing natural gas both to end-users (industry and households) and to electric power generators.

Figure 9.3 ▷ **Economic value of fossil-fuel consumption subsidies by fuel for the top 25 countries, 2013**

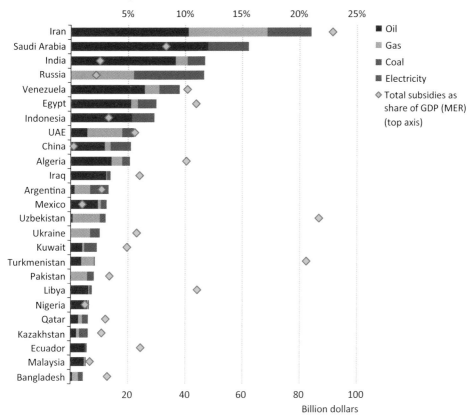

Note: MER = market exchange rate.

For the 40 countries identified as subsidising fossil-fuel consumption, the value of subsidies as a share of total gross domestic product (GDP) measured at market exchange rate (MER) averages 5% – a larger share than that of public spending on education or health in many countries. However, some smaller countries with relatively small subsidies in absolute terms have much higher subsidies as a share of GDP. Similarly, the average rate of subsidisation, i.e. the ratio of the subsidy to the international reference price, also varies significantly from country to country. Among all countries it averages 23%, with the highest being in Venezuela at 93%.

Fossil-fuel subsidies in ten countries account for $401 billion or around three-quarters of the world total (Figure 9.4). Of the 25 countries with the highest value of subsidies, nine are in the Middle East or North Africa – all of them oil and gas exporters. Most of the other major subsidisers are also important oil and gas producers. The rate of subsidisation is also generally highest among oil and gas producers. The main exceptions are India, Indonesia and Pakistan, all of which are net importers of oil products and gas, and which continue to subsidise certain household fuels for social reasons, despite recent moves to scale them back.

Globally, fossil-fuel subsidies fell slightly in 2013, after rising marginally in 2012 and more sharply in 2011, in line with international energy prices and policy reforms in a number of countries, which offset higher consumption of subsidised fuels. Subsidies remain strongly correlated with oil prices, as many countries – especially the oil exporters – set domestic oil, gas and electricity prices without regard to international market levels; as a result, a rise in international prices automatically increases the amount of subsidy, unless regulated domestic prices are increased by at least the same amount. Subsidy estimates also fluctuate from year-to-year in line with changes in exchange rates and demand.

Box 9.3 ▷ **How do *IEA* subsidy estimates compare with those of other organisations?**

Two other international organisations measure subsidies and other types of government support for fossil fuels worldwide.[6] Estimates of fossil-fuel subsidies differ because they cover various types of support (which, due to their distinctive effects and nature, need to be measured using specific techniques), a variety of countries and fuels and dissimilar time periods.

The OECD, which uses an inventory approach, estimates that producer and consumer subsidies combined fluctuated between $55 billion and $90 billion per year between 2005 and 2011 for all OECD countries (OECD, 2013). Preferential tax treatment makes up two-thirds of the subsidy mechanisms identified. The IMF, which, like the IEA, measures price gaps, estimates that its "post-tax subsidies", which factor in the negative environmental externalities from energy consumption and road traffic, amounted to $2.0 trillion in 2011, based on an assumed carbon-dioxide price of $36 per tonne (Clements et al., 2013). The advanced economies account for about 40% of the global total; oil exporters account for about one-third. What the IMF defines as "pre-tax subsidies", which exclude externalities and incorporate IEA estimates for several countries, stood at $492 billion, compared with our estimate for that same year 2011 of $527 billion. The IEA figure is higher because it includes a broader range of oil products.

---

6. The Global Subsidies Initiative estimates the value of fossil-fuel subsidies for individual countries but has not prepared a global aggregate. The World Bank also monitors subsidies to oil products worldwide (Kojima, 2013).

Figure 9.4 △ Value of fossil-fuel subsidies in selected countries and rate of subsidisation of fossil fuels, 2013

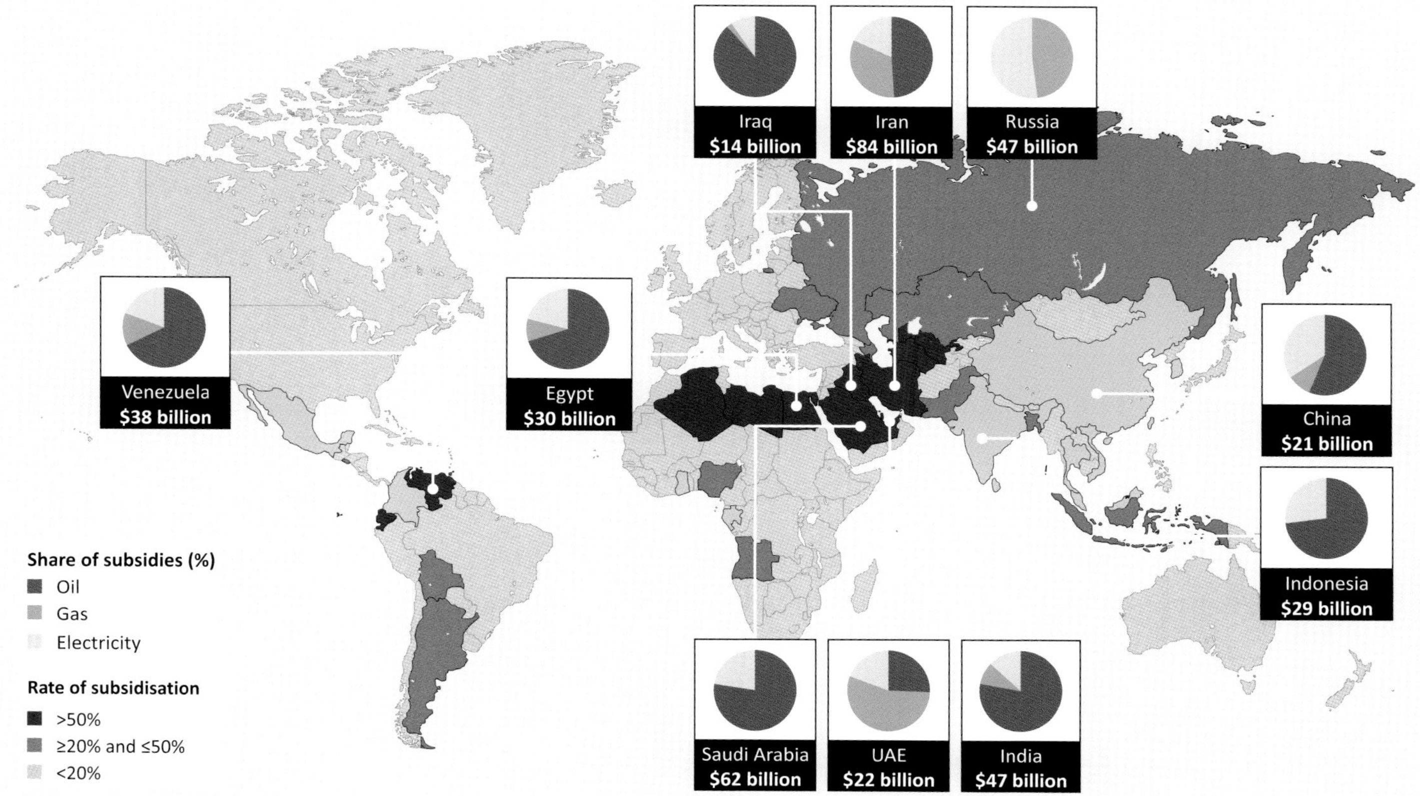

Share of subsidies (%)
- Oil
- Gas
- Electricity

Rate of subsidisation
- >50%
- ≥20% and ≤50%
- <20%

China $21 billion

Indonesia $29 billion

Russia $47 billion

Iran $84 billion

Iraq $14 billion

India $47 billion

UAE $22 billion

Saudi Arabia $62 billion

Egypt $30 billion

Venezuela $38 billion

This map is without prejudice to the status of or sovereignty over any territory, to the delimitation of international frontiers and boundaries, and to the name of any territory, city or area.

9

Impacts of fossil-fuel subsidies on clean energy technologies

Low-carbon power generation

One of the most damaging effects of subsidising fossil fuels is that low-carbon technologies, and in particular emerging renewable energy technologies, are less able to compete. This hinders investment in renewables, leading to stronger reliance on fossil fuels and higher greenhouse-gas emissions than would otherwise be the case. In addition, slower deployment of renewables, in turn, reduces learning rates and slows the pace of cost reduction as the technologies mature. In other words, the more a government subsidises fossil fuels, the more it has to subsidise renewables if it wants to keep a level playing field. Fossil-fuel subsidies rig the game against renewables and act as a drag on the transition to a more sustainable energy system. On the other hand, subsidies to renewables can, if well-designed, aid the deployment of sustainable technologies in support of energy security and environmental goals.

The extent to which low-carbon electricity generation technologies suffer a competitive disadvantage as a result of fossil-fuel subsidies differs markedly across countries and regions. The competitive gap is biggest on average for the Middle East where more than one-third of the region's electricity is generated using oil (absorbing nearly 2 million barrels per day [mb/d]), with almost all of the rest coming from gas-fired plants. In some countries in the region, subsidies to natural gas are also a major impediment to switching from oil- to gas-fired generation, which would bring economic and environmental benefits, as gas supplies are limited due to the fact that low-market pricing means the private sector has very little incentive to expand production.

Both oil and natural gas are heavily subsidised in many countries in the Middle East. In our estimates, oil subsidies reduce electricity generating costs for new oil-fired plants starting operations in 2020 to around 30% of the level they would be if full reference prices were paid, while gas subsidies reduce costs to around 45% of the unsubsidised level (Figure 9.5).[7] As a result, low-carbon power technologies are unable to compete against either existing or new capacity. Were oil not subsidised in the Middle East, new oil-fired plants would not be able to compete with any of the main renewable energy technologies or with nuclear power. In the absence of subsidies to natural gas, nuclear and onshore wind power would still be more expensive options than gas-fired power plants, but the gap would be significantly reduced.[8] Subsidies to natural gas have a significant effect on

---

7. Levelised cost is a convenient measure of the overall competiveness of different generating technologies. Actual plant investment decisions are affected by the specific technological and regional characteristics of a project, which involve numerous other factors including projected utilisation rates, the existing generation mix, and capacity value (the contribution that a given type of capacity makes to overall system adequacy), which depends on the ease with which capacity can be used to match load variations in real time. All these factors can vary dramatically across countries and regions. As a result, comparing costs can only provide a general guide to the economic competitiveness of various power generation options.

8. Regional averages mask big differences across countries and locations within each country. Consequently, renewables or nuclear power may not always be the lowest cost source of new generating capacity.

the cost competitiveness of renewables in Russia too, though less so than in the Middle East. Even without gas subsidies, most non-hydro renewables in Russia would struggle to compete, though onshore wind might rival both existing single-cycle and new combined-cycle gas turbine plants.

Figure 9.5 ▷ Electricity generating costs in the Middle East, 2020

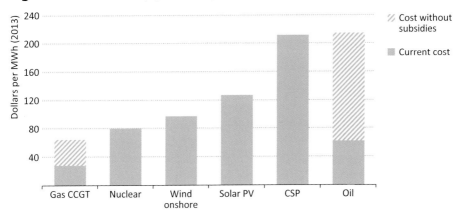

Notes: MWh = megawatt-hour; CCGT = combined-cycle gas turbine; PV = photovoltaic (utility-scale); CSP = concentrating solar power. Generating costs are for new plants coming online in 2020; assumptions are available at *www.worldenergyoutlook.org/weomodel/investmentcosts*.

It is difficult to judge just how much impact these cost distortions have on actual investment in generating technology. In practice, the governments of countries that heavily subsidise fuel inputs to generation are conscious of the competitive disadvantage to other technologies that are not subsidised or, at least, are subsidised to a lesser degree. In some cases, they seek to redress this imbalance, often by directing public investment to non-fossil-fuel technologies or raising subsidies to them. For example, they may subsidise renewables to counteract subsidies to fossil fuels. In the Middle East, several oil- or gas-exporting countries – for example, the United Arab Emirates (UAE) (an oil exporter) – are looking to boost the role of non-fossil-based power generation in order to free up hydrocarbons for export (an implicit acknowledgement of the opportunity cost of subsidising domestic oil and gas) and to reduce greenhouse-gas emissions – even if gas is often the most economic source of new generation. The UAE government has authorised the construction of four nuclear reactors at Barakah, three of which are being built, and is investing in renewables; the country is already among the world leaders in CSP capacity and investment.

Saudi Arabia, which has among the fastest rates of growth in electricity demand in the region, is also seeking to diversify away from oil-fired generation to natural gas, nuclear and renewables. It has announced measures to boost the deployment of renewables to compensate for their lack of competitiveness against both oil- and gas-fired power generation: oil supplied to domestic power stations is priced at just $4.40 per barrel (around 5% of its current international market value) and gas is just $0.75 per million British thermal unit (MBtu) (7% of current European prices). In 2012, the Saudi government announced plans to build 41 gigawatts (GW) of solar PV and CSP capacity by 2032 – enough to meet one-third of the country's electricity needs (based on its official forecast) – as well as to develop wind, geothermal and waste-to-energy capacity. It has also announced plans to build 16 nuclear reactors over the next two decades.

S P O T L I G H T

How do subsidies to fossil fuels compare with those to renewables and nuclear power?

Subsidies to renewable sources of energy are generally much smaller than those to fossil fuels in absolute terms, though the rate of subsidy per unit of energy is often higher. They are predominately found in countries that do not subsidise the consumption of fossil fuels. Subsidies to renewables are intended to support environmental and economic objectives by boosting their competitiveness *vis-à-vis* conventional fuels. We estimate that the value of renewable subsidies worldwide totalled $121 billion in 2013. This was $16 billion, or 15%, higher than in 2012 (see Chapter 7). The increase in subsidies to renewables in 2013 reflects their continuously growing level of deployment. The falling cost of production of the main technologies, particularly onshore wind and PV, is helping them to get closer to competitiveness with fossil-fuel technologies, while reducing the need for additional subsidies for new facilities. Solar PV attracts the largest subsidies ($45 billion), followed by wind power ($28 billion) and liquid biofuels ($24 billion). These subsidies take a variety of forms, the most common of which are quotas and portfolio standards, feed-in tariffs, tax credits and blending mandates (for biofuels). The United States has the biggest renewables subsidies of any country, totalling $27 billion in 2013, most of which go to biofuels, solar PV and wind power. The European Union as a whole subsidised renewables to the tune of $69 billion in 2013, the bulk of which went to solar PV power.

The degree to which nuclear power is subsidised is difficult to assess. There are no authoritative global estimates, as much of the spending was made in the 1960s and 1970s by government and research centres and is now hard to track. Nuclear projects have often benefited from guaranteed prices and other risk-sharing devices. Today, nuclear industries in some countries are supported by means of state ownership of key companies, however, few countries subsidise nuclear power in an overt manner.

Energy efficiency

Subsidies to fossil fuels and to other forms of energy that lower prices to end-users mask the real cost of energy and undermine the financial attractiveness of investment by businesses and by households on more energy-efficient equipment and appliances: a lower price for a fuel reduces the amount of money that can be saved by buying a more energy-efficient device. Assessing the payback period for a project aimed at improving energy efficiency or spending on more efficient equipment is a simple, common method to gauge the financial viability of the expenditure. The payback period is the amount of time needed to recover an initial expenditure through reduced energy bills. Energy subsidies lengthen the effective payback periods for investments in energy efficiency, by reducing the savings on energy bills. The higher the rate of fuel or electricity subsidy, the longer the payback period and the less likely consumers will be to commit to the initial spending on improved efficiency. To motivate consumers, payback periods often need to be very short, especially where relatively modest amounts of spending are involved and financing is by private individuals, who may struggle to afford the more costly efficient equipment and appliances.

In the transport sector, fuel economy is just one of several factors that consumers take into account when buying a new or used car. But it carries more weight when fuel prices are high. So higher pump prices as a result of the removal of subsidies to gasoline and diesel would be expected to lead to a shift in demand towards more fuel efficient vehicles, with knock-on effects on overall oil consumption, import needs (or availability of oil for export), air pollution and carbon-dioxide (CO_2) emissions.

The Middle East provides a striking example of the effect of subsidies on energy efficiency. With the exception of a few countries in the region, the prevalence of energy subsidies has slowed the uptake of modern, energy-efficient technologies in most end-use sectors. In the transport sector, the average passenger car uses 60% more fuel per kilometre than the average car in the OECD (though this is partly because cars are generally larger). For example, in Saudi Arabia, gasoline prices at the pump are currently around $0.15 per litre (compared with $0.97 in the United States and $2.10 in Europe on average in 2013). It would take around 16 years for a Saudi motorist to recover the cost of upgrading from a vehicle with the current average fuel economy to one that uses half as much fuel per kilometre – a payback period that most motorists would consider highly unattractive (Figure 9.6). Removing gasoline subsidies would cut the payback period to just three years. Saudi Arabia has recently taken steps to improve vehicle efficiency by introducing fuel-economy labelling for new cars and fuel-economy standards requiring up to 18.5 kilometres per litre for imported vehicles (by 2019-2020).

A similar case applies to lighting, which accounts for more than 15% of electricity demand in the buildings sector in the Middle East. Light-emitting diodes (LED) consume much less electricity than incandescent bulbs. But given the large subsidies to electricity, the payback period for installing LEDs is almost 10 years on average across the region, compared with about 1.5 years if electricity tariffs were to cover the full cost of supply.

Subsidies to fossil fuels can also distort consumer awareness of the potential gains from energy efficiency. In some cases, even with subsidised prices, the payback periods associated with the purchase of more efficient equipment are shorter than levels typically required to shift purchasing habits, but are not having the expected effect. For example, in the UAE, air conditioners are available that use half as much electricity as the current average and their additional upfront expense could be recovered in less than two years; but they have yet to become the market leader. If subsidies to electricity were removed, the payback period for the same air conditioner would drop to just eight months. In both cases, these particularly short payback periods are linked to the very high rates of utilisation of air conditioners.

Figure 9.6 ▷ **Payback periods to invest in more efficient energy-consuming equipment in selected Middle East countries**

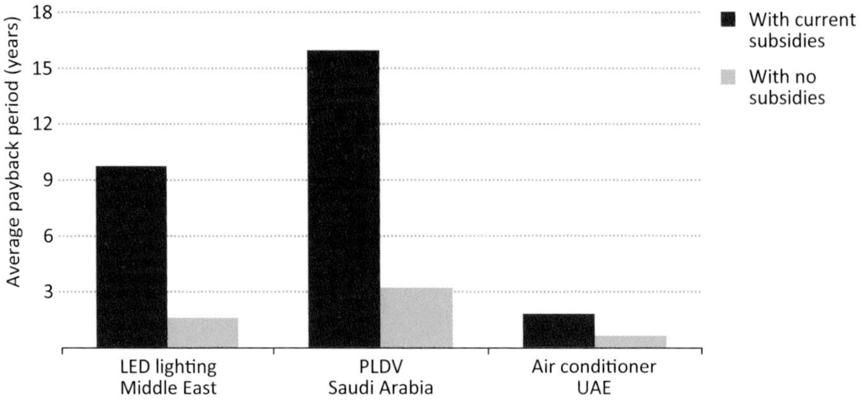

Notes: LED = light-emitting diodes; PLDV = passenger light-duty vehicle.

As with other countries in the region, heavily subsidised electricity prices in Saudi Arabia – which are currently at around 10% of the European average – represent the main barrier to the adoption of more energy-efficient technologies. The potential savings from improved energy efficiency are substantial. In the case of air conditioning, which is responsible for a remarkable 70% of the country's total residential electricity consumption, the reduction in electricity demand available by increasing efficiency to current best practice levels would free up about 120 thousand barrels per day (kb/d) of oil and almost 5 billion cubic metres (bcm) of natural gas that is currently being used to generate electricity.[9] At current international prices, this amounts to a saving of almost $7 billion per year. In addition, subsidy removal would encourage investment in building insulation, which could yield large additional energy savings in the longer term. The Saudi government has introduced minimum energy-performance standards in recent years for a range of electrical devices, including air conditioners, which is a start to tap some of this potential.

Implementing reforms

Reducing or phasing out fossil-fuel subsidies would bring major benefits, not just to the countries that currently subsidise, but also to the rest of the world. Fossil-fuel subsidy reform, by raising prices to power generators and end-users, would encourage more rational use of energy, more efficient investment in energy supply and less waste, leading to less pollution and lower emissions of greenhouse gases. It would also bring economic gains to the countries with subsidies though a better allocation of economic resources, reduced

---

9. This split is based on the current fuel mix and average efficiency of power generation in Saudi Arabia.

fiscal burdens and improved trade balances. Most countries recognise the benefits of such reforms and are seeking to implement them, though political factors and public resistance continue to retard progress.

Recent policy developments

There have been some important steps towards reducing or phasing out fossil-fuel subsidies in a number of countries during the last few years, with continued significant progress in some of them – including several that have some of the largest subsidies. These reforms, largely driven by fiscal pressures, have had a material impact on the total amount of subsidy worldwide, and more is to come. Notable advances include hikes in road-fuel prices in India, Indonesia, Mexico and Morocco, a rise in natural gas prices in Russia, a general rise in energy prices in Egypt, and hikes in electricity tariffs in Bangladesh, Ecuador, Indonesia and Malaysia (Table 9.1). In some cases, reforms are being driven by the conditions placed on loans for energy projects by international lending agencies and sovereign lending by the IMF (e.g. in Egypt). In Iran, a hike in the price of gasoline – its most heavily subsidised form of energy and involving the first price increase since 2011 – came into effect in April 2014: the price for a monthly ration of 60 litres rose from Iranian rials (IRR) 4 000 ($0.16) to IRR 7 000 per litre ($0.28), while the price for additional fuel rose from IRR 7 000 to IRR 10 000 per litre ($0.40). However, the effect of these increases on the extent of the subsidy has been largely offset by the sharp drop in the local currency, which has increased the gap between domestic prices and the international value of the fuel. The government plans further price rises.

Case studies of reform

Most countries with large fossil-fuel subsidies recognise the need to eliminate or, at least, reduce them, but often run into difficulties – usually because of strong resistance from those consumers that stand to lose the most and their political supporters. Lessons from reviewing the successes and failures of past attempts to rein in subsidies can be instructive. Understanding the objectives and the particular circumstances, approaches and outcomes is of particular value for other such countries. Experiences from three of them – Egypt, Indonesia and Nigeria – are described below. The lessons that may be drawn from these experiences are developed in the guidelines on best practice section.

Egypt

Egypt is a relatively poor country with a large and rapidly growing population (82 million) – the third-largest population in Africa. Egypt's energy use has soared in recent years, partly as a result of large subsidies: energy demand expanded at an average annual rate of 5.6% over 2000-2012. Egypt has recently become a net importer of oil and its natural gas exports have been declining due to rising domestic demand, with one of its two liquefied natural gas (LNG) facilities remaining idle since 2013; indeed, there are plans to import LNG in the near future to cover a shortfall in domestic supply. Power generation capacity has failed to keep pace with rapid demand growth, leading to frequent brownouts and blackouts.

Table 9.1 ▷ **Recent developments in fossil-fuel subsidy reform around the world**

Country	Recent developments
Angola	In September 2014, increased gasoline and diesel prices by 25% each, from $0.61 to $0.76 per litre for gasoline and from $0.41 to $0.51 per litre for diesel.
Argentina	In April 2014, a 20% reduction in natural gas subsidies for commercial and residential users was announced in a bid to cut a large fiscal deficit, with price increases following in April, June and August. Government estimates savings of up to ARS 13 billion ($1.6 billion), earmarked to cover utility costs and finance social spending.
Bahrain	The government is considering doubling the price of diesel by 2017 to reduce the heavy subsidy burden on state finances.
Bangladesh	The fiscal budget 2014-2015 for fuel subsidies was slashed by 67% to BDT 24 billion ($309 million) to meet IMF loan conditions. The government is committed to keep refined oil product prices within BDT 10 ($0.13) per litre of international prices. Retail electricity prices were raised by 64% to BDT 6.15 ($0.08) per kWh on average between March 2010 and March 2014.
China	In March 2014, a new tiered pricing mechanism for natural gas was announced and is to be introduced by the end of 2015. There are three pricing bands: the first covers 80% of the average monthly consumption volumes for household users, the second the next 15% and the third above 95%.
Ecuador	In May 2014, the electricity tariff for commercial and industrial sectors was increased by $0.02 as part of a plan to reduce electricity subsidies.
Egypt	In July 2014, the price of 92-octane gasoline was increased by 41% to EGP 2.60 ($0.37) and that of 80-octane gasoline went up 78% to EGP 1.60 ($0.22) per litre. The price of automotive diesel was raised by 63% to EGP 1.80 ($0.25) per litre and that of natural gas for vehicles to EGP 1.10 ($0.15) per litre. Electricity prices were raised by EGP 0.23 ($0.03) per kWh on average, as the first step towards doubling prices and eliminating subsidies within five years. Natural gas prices for a range of industries increased by 30% to 70%.
Ghana	In July 2014, subsidies for gasoline and diesel were abolished, leading to an increase of at least 22% in pump prices.
India	Since January 2013, regulated diesel prices have increased by INR 0.5 ($0.01) per litre each month and may be deregulated in December 2014. It proposed to almost double the natural gas price (from $4.2/MBtu) in April 2014, but implementation has been deferred.
Indonesia	In January 2014, Pertamina announced a 68% price hike for LPG sold in 12 kg canisters. The price increase met with significant public opposition, resulting in a final price increase of only 17%. In September 2014, Pertamina announced a new 23% price hike for 12 kg LPG canisters, from IDR 7 733 ($0.65) to IDR 9 525 ($0.81) per kg. Electricity tariffs for selected user categories were increased in July 2014. Tariff increases are due to be extended to other categories before the end of 2014.
Iran	In April 2014, gasoline prices were increased by 75% to IRR 7 000 ($0.28) per litre for a ration up to 60 litres, above which the price is IRR 10 000 ($0.40). Diesel and compressed natural gas increased by 40% and 32% respectively. Cash payments to low-income families were increased to compensate.
Kuwait	In September 2014, subsidies to diesel were reduced and plans announced to cut subsidies to kerosene and electricity.
Malaysia	In October 2014, increased gasoline and diesel prices by MYR 0.20 ($0.06) each. In January 2014, electricity tariffs were increased on average by 15% to MYR 0.38 ($0.12) per kWh. Fuel cost pass-through, based on international gas price movements, was resumed in the same month. In May 2014, increased natural gas prices by up to 26% for certain categories of users.
Mexico	The government has been raising the prices of gasoline and diesel each month in 2014 to bring them closer to international levels.

Morocco	Gasoline and fuel-oil subsidies have been eliminated and diesel subsidies cut significantly as part of plans to improve public finances. In July 2014, the cost of diesel was MAD 10 ($1.20) per litre.
Myanmar	In 2014, a new block electricity tariff scheme for households and industry was approved, though tariffs are still among the lowest in Asia.
Nepal	In March 2014, gasoline, diesel, kerosene and aviation fuel prices were raised, but the move was subsequently reversed following protests. Adopted a new fuel pricing mechanism in September 2014 that is based on international prices trends.
Nigeria	In June 2014, the National Conference held discussions on the complete removal of fuel subsidies. Natural gas prices for power generation and industry were raised in August 2014.
Oman	In May 2014, plans were announced to gradually reduce fuel subsidies, especially for gasoline.
Russia	In 2014, the government postponed planned increases in natural gas prices for industry until July 2015 (4.8%) and July 2016 (4.9%).
Sudan	In September 2013, the price of gasoline was increased by 68% to SDG 4.6 ($1.04) per litre, price of diesel by 75% to SDG 3.08 ($0.70) per litre and price of LPG by 66% to SDG 2 ($0.45) per kg.
Thailand	In August 2014, modified its system of cross subsidies by increasing diesel prices by THB 0.14 ($0.01) per litre and decreasing gasoline prices by THB 1.1-3.9 ($0.03-0.12) per litre. In October 2014, increased the price of compressed natural gas for vehicles by THB 1 ($0.03) per kilogramme.
Tunisia	In May 2014, subsidised gasoline prices were increased by 6.3%, from TD 1.57 ($0.89) to TD 1.67 ($0.95) per litre.
Turkmenistan	In February 2014, the price of natural gas for households was raised in line with the objective of phasing out some energy subsidies.
Ukraine	In April 2014, the IMF lent the country $17 billion (with an overall $27 billion pledged over the next two years) in exchange for cuts in government spending and natural gas subsidies. Natural gas prices for industrial consumers were subsequently raised by 29% to $366 per 1 000 cubic metres, while the price charged to government agencies was increased by 64% to $354 per 1 000 cubic metres.
Uzbekistan	In July 2014, diesel prices were increased by 11.7% to UZS 1 910 ($0.84) per litre.
Yemen	In July 2014, the price of gasoline was increased by 60% to YER 200 ($0.93) per litre and that of diesel by 95% to YER 195 ($0.91) per litre. Subsides were partially restored in September 2014 following massive protests.

Until this year, Egypt had made little headway in reducing its large and long-standing energy (and food) subsidies. In 2013, fossil-fuel subsidies totalled $30 billion, making up 11% of GDP and, according to the official budget statements, absorbing around one-fifth of total public spending – an amount seven-times larger than that spent on healthcare (and comparable to country's fiscal deficit). Oil products have been the most heavily subsidised, with most of the rest going to electricity – mainly through subsidised natural gas inputs to power plants (Figure 9.7). Subsidies result from the government directly setting fuel prices, in most cases well below the full cost of supply. In 2013, the rate of subsidisation averaged 68% for oil products and 61% for fossil energy as a whole. The government made whole the losses incurred by state companies (which hold exclusive marketing rights in Egypt) in selling at the regulated prices. Overall, subsidies in 2013 were marginally higher than in 2012 (as the depreciation of the Egyptian pound (EGP) against the dollar and the increase in consumption outweighed lower international prices), and well up on the 2000s.

Figure 9.7 ▷ **Fossil-fuel subsidies by fuel in Egypt**

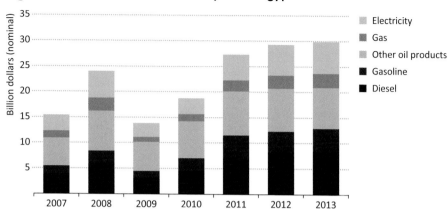

Fossil-fuel subsidies have placed a heavy burden on the economy, diverting resources away from other sectors, encouraging waste and exacerbating pollution. Fuel smuggling, black marketeering and diversion to unauthorised uses have occurred on a large scale: in early 2014 the Energy Minister announced that 15-20% of oil products sold in the country are smuggled out because of higher prices in neighbouring countries. In addition, unlike food subsidies, only a small share of fuel subsidies benefits the poor, as richer people are better able to take advantage of cheap gasoline and LPG (Rohac, 2013).

In recognition of these problems, Egyptian governments have repeatedly announced plans to scale back energy subsidies, but have then tended to backtrack, in the face of public opposition. Between 2005 and 2008, electricity and diesel prices were raised and a mechanism for gradually increasing electricity prices towards market levels introduced; but the 2008-2009 financial crisis and subsequent political turmoil put the implementation of further reforms on hold. In 2012, the government sharply raised the price of 95 Research Octane Number (RON) gasoline, but this led motorists to switch to still subsidised 92 RON fuel, resulting in shortages. In early 2013, the former government announced plans to limit subsidised gasoline and diesel supplies by introducing a smart-card scheme so as to restrict the use of subsidised fuel to the needy and curb smuggling, but nothing more has been heard of these measures since the change of government in July 2013.

A renewed effort to rein in energy subsidies has been launched by the new government. In July 2014, cuts were announced in the 2014/2015 budget allocation to fuel subsidies with the aim of reducing the budget deficit from 12% of GDP at present to 10%. The prices of all grades of gasoline, as well as diesel, kerosene, heavy fuel oil and natural gas were increased sharply (Table 9.2) with the aim of saving EGP 50 billion in the fiscal year. In addition, electricity tariffs for all end-users were increased, as part of a plan to reach cost-recovery levels over a five-year period.

Table 9.2 ▷ **Increases for selected products in Egypt, July 2014**
(per litre for oil products; per m³ for CNG)

Product	Old price		New price		Increase
	EGP	US $	EGP	US $	
80 RON gasoline	0.90	0.13	1.60	0.23	78%
92 RON gasoline	1.85	0.27	2.60	0.37	41%
95 RON gasoline	5.85	0.84	6.25	0.90	7%
Diesel	1.10	0.16	1.80	0.26	64%
Compressed natural gas	0.45	0.06	1.10	0.16	144%

Note: Prices in US dollars are calculated using an average exchange rate for 2014 of EGP 6.97 per dollar.

An important new feature of the approach to the recent reforms was the attention paid by the government to communicating the benefits to the public, immediately before and after the changes were announced (GSI, 2014b). Although the energy price increases came at the same time as announcements about a new property tax and higher levies on other commodities, causing unrest among taxi, mini-bus drivers and farmers, whose earnings are directly connected to the price of fuels, a series of measures were also announced aimed at mitigating the impact of the new austerity measures on the poorer segments of the population. These measures included the introduction of a minimum wage for public servants, an increase in pensions and bigger subsidies on food products available at state-run stores.

The initial announcement was made by the President. Since then, with the support of the Prime Minister and senior Ministers, the president has conducted an intensive public information campaign, speaking almost daily on the matter and meeting with aggrieved stakeholders. Although the announcement of the reform was immediately followed by demonstrations, organised mainly by transport sector workers, the public outcry has not been as pronounced as that provoked by past attempts to rein in subsidies. The government appears to be resolute in its intention of holding firm in resisting pressure to reverse the price increases.

Indonesia

Indonesia is the world's fourth most populous country and is spread over a large archipelago. It is by far the largest energy consumer in Southeast Asia, accounting for 37% of the region's total primary consumption in 2012. Indonesia's energy demand increased by 29% between 2002 and 2012 and continues to experience rapid demand growth over the projection period, almost doubling between 2012 and 2040 in the New Policies Scenario. With the exception of oil, Indonesia is self-sufficient in all types of energy. The country became a net oil importer in 2004 and suspended its membership in the Organization of Petroleum Exporting Countries (OPEC) in 2008. Major energy challenges include a need to boost investment in power generation capacity to meet shortfalls in supply and raising the electrification rate: supply currently reaches only 76% of the population.

Table 9.3 ▷ Summary of experience with fossil-fuel subsidy reform in Egypt, Indonesia and Nigeria

Country	Status of reforms	Lessons learned
Egypt	The government is seeking to reduce the budget deficit from 12% to 10% of GDP in 2014 by, among others, taking measures to reduce subsidies for fossil fuels.	Adequate compensation to the poor is essential for reform to win public support.
Indonesia	Important steps have been taken to rein in oil, gas and electricity subsidies in recent years, but they continue to impose a huge burden on the central government budget. There are plans to reduce subsidies further, by raising prices and encouraging a shift to LPG and compressed natural gas in transport.	Price increases are more acceptable to the public if they are accompanied by complementary social welfare programmes and well-designed information campaigns. Pricing is best left to the market.
Nigeria	Subsidies to diesel were eliminated and those to gasoline reduced in 2012. Moves to abolish kerosene subsidies are on hold pending a senate inquiry. Some progress has been made in cutting natural gas subsidies to power generators but the end-user price of electricity is still heavily subsidised.	Oil subsidies can fall victim to fraud. Compensation packages are difficult to implement where there is limited administrative capacity. Deregulation and functioning markets are key to efficient pricing.

Energy subsidies are a major and long-standing problem in Indonesia, despite successive efforts to rein them in. Subsidies greatly increased at the end of the 1990s; direct spending on fuel subsidies absorbed between 7% and 25% of total annual public spending between 2005 and 2013. According to our latest estimates, subsidies amounted to $29 billion in 2013, with over half of the total on gasoline and diesel. Yet steps have been taken to reduce the level of these subsidies in order to relieve pressure on the state budget, improve the efficiency of social welfare policies, enhance energy security and combat climate change. Fossil-fuel subsidies are down from $34 billion in 2012, largely thanks to increases in gasoline prices and a successful programme to get poor households to switch from heavily subsidised kerosene to LPG.

The main form of subsidy to fossil fuels in Indonesia is below market pricing of oil products (for which marketers are compensated through a volume-related payment) and electricity. The rate of subsidy is highest for transport fuels. The prices of two low-grade fuels – Premium (88 RON gasoline) and Solar (diesel) – are set by the government on an ad hoc basis at irregular intervals. Even after sharp increases in June 2013, prices for these products (which are unchanged since then) remain well below the spot prices at the closest international trading hub (Singapore), which is the basis of our reference price calculations for Indonesia (Figure 9.8). By contrast, the prices of the higher grades of gasoline, Pertamax and Pertamax Plus (and of industrial diesel oil) are updated regularly, in line with international oil prices, but the much higher prices discourage most motorists from using these fuels. Kerosene and LPG are also subsidised.

Figure 9.8 ▷ Gasoline and diesel prices in Indonesia compared to spot prices in Singapore

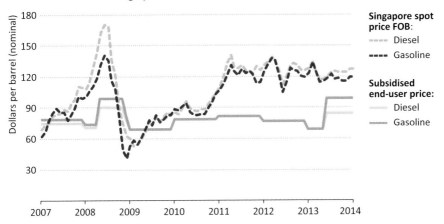

Notes: FOB = free on board. Monthly prices are shown for the period from January 2007 to December 2013.

Sources: CEIC Indonesia; IEA analysis.

Electricity consumption is subsidised through under-pricing, while generation is also subsidised through the under-pricing of fuels, low-interest loans, loan guarantees and obligations to supply indigenous fuel to power stations. Perusahaan Listrik Negara (PLN), the state-owned electricity company, has a monopoly on electricity distribution throughout Indonesia and dominates power generation. The government sets electricity tariffs at levels that are far below supply costs, so that PLN and private independent producers are unable to recover their investment costs. This has led to under-investment and power shortages. Failure to pay electricity bills exacerbates these problems. We estimate that the cost of subsidies to electricity from under-pricing of fossil energy inputs to generation alone amounted to $7.9 billion in 2013.

A major attempt was made to tackle the energy subsidy problem in 2003, in the wake of rising international oil prices. It failed in the face of public protest, with a big cut in subsidies quickly being reversed. A further attempt to raise energy prices in 2007 met with greater success, partly because the government placed more emphasis on explaining the need for subsidy reform in order to free up resources for health, education and public infrastructure (Box 9.4). In addition, the government sought to secure support for its reforms by adopting a range of social welfare measures to help the population adjust to the higher energy prices, under the umbrella of the Fuel Subsidy Reduction Compensation Program and the Unconditional Cash Transfer Program. A major component of these reforms was a programme, started in 2007, to encourage households to switch from kerosene, which absorbed the bulk of fuel subsidies at that time, to LPG. As the subsidy to LPG was considerably smaller than that to kerosene, the overall cost was sharply reduced. Consumers were happy to switch fuels because LPG is a more efficient, cleaner and safer cooking fuel. However, rising international prices between 2007 and 2009, together with rapidly rising demand and a partial reversal of price rises in 2008 and 2009, caused the LPG subsidy bill to rebound sharply. In 2012, the government considered imposing restrictions on access to subsidised gasoline, but the measure was not implemented. However, it did launch the "fuel-to-gas" programme – an initiative to promote the use of natural gas and LPG as transport fuels – though a lack of refuelling and conversion infrastructure has held back the development of this new market.

Box 9.4 ▷ **Indonesia's information campaigns to win support for subsidy reform**

An effort to reduce the consumption of fossil fuels, reduce CO_2 emissions and cut fossil-fuel subsidies launched at the end of 2007 was accompanied by a campaign to inform the public about the aims of the policy, designed to avert public resistance (Indriyanto et al., 2013; Chung, 2013). This involved advertisements in print and electronic media (including dissemination of telephone text messages), the distribution of pins, stickers, pamphlets and brochures, appearances by public officials on television talk shows, communication via village notice boards and efforts to seek support from non-governmental organisations and students.

Associated features of this policy were promoting the use of bicycles (for example, a "car-free day" campaign that involved the closure of several main streets in central areas of Jakarta) and free public transportation. To avoid controversy, the government sought to avoid categorising its action as the removal or phasing out of subsidies, calling instead on the public to join its "fuel-efficiency movement". More recently, the government's communication efforts on energy subsidy reforms have been extended to include public seminars and cultural performances to drive home messages about the rationale for reform and the public benefits.

New steps have been taken over the last couple of years, as part of a new subsidy reform action plan that resulted from a process of research and public consultation. To try to overcome public resistance, the authorities have been taking more care in communicating the need for price increases and their timing. In June 2013, the price of Premium gasoline (the grade that is subsidised) was increased by 44% and that of Solar diesel by 22%. The same year, electricity tariffs were increased by around 15%. As a result, total government spending on subsidies fell for the first time since 2009. Parliament adopted new energy regulations in January 2014, which included plans to gradually phase out direct fuel and electricity subsidies and measures to increase the supply of renewables. In the same month, Pertamina, the national oil company, raised the price of a 12 kg cylinder of LPG by 68%, a move that was not accompanied by an extensive communication campaign like the ones that accompanied the hikes in the gasoline and diesel prices in 2007. There was a strong public outcry, causing the government to rein back the price increase to just 17%. However in September 2014, Pertamina increased the price of 12kg LPG cylinders by almost 25%. Electricity tariffs for certain users were increased in July 2014; the government plans to increase tariffs for other user groups too before the end of the year.

The government has also been trying to curb gasoline and diesel consumption, including by reducing the number of pumps at service stations in Jakarta (GSI, 2014c) and is investigating the possibility of building gas distribution pipelines to conventional service stations to incentivise station owners to invest in refuelling facilities. Pertamina has estimated that the maximum quotas set by the government for annual sales of subsidised gasoline and diesel are likely to be breached before the end of 2014 (a measure aimed at limiting the total amount of subsidised gasoline and diesel that Pertamina could sell was dropped shortly after it was introduced in August 2014 due to panic buying).

Packages of compensatory measures have played an important role in mitigating the impact of past efforts to reform fossil-energy subsidies in Indonesia. Indeed, a reform package in 2005 provided the means for setting up the country's first-ever welfare payment programme, which involved the creation of a nationwide registry of poor households (Perdana, 2014). Other measures have included rice subsidies, health insurance, public works projects, educational grants and cash transfers with conditions (for example, school attendance).

Despite efforts to cut fossil-energy subsidies, they continue to pose a heavy burden on the state budget. The June revision of the 2014 budget provides for IDR 350.3 trillion ($29.4 billion) of fuel and electricity subsidies – 24% more than in the initial budget (Indonesian Government, 2014) – mainly driven by depreciation of the rupiah against the dollar. The government has indicated that the subsidy budget will be cut to IDR 344.7 trillion ($28.8 billion) in 2015. The new President, who is due to take office in October 2014, has indicated that the new government's top priority will be to tackle energy subsidies, though political opposition to cuts in subsidies is expected to remain strong.

Nigeria

Nigeria, with the largest population in sub-Saharan Africa, is the region's leading oil and gas producer. There is strong potential for oil and gas production to grow, but political and social instability are holding back investment. Although Nigeria is an exporter of LNG, gas use within Nigeria remains minimal, due to a lack of supply and distribution infrastructure. Nigeria has one of the lowest per-capita rates of electricity consumption in the world and more than half of its population has no access to electricity, with generation and network capacity falling far short of demand. The government has given priority to attracting investment in the power sector and improving Nigeria's electrification rate (see Chapter 14).

As a major oil- and gas-exporting country, Nigeria has traditionally set fossil-fuel prices well below the cost of supply. Although these subsidies have well-intentioned objectives, the results provide a graphic illustration of their harmful effects: *inter alia* a heavy fiscal burden on the state, lack of finance for investment in domestic supply infrastructure, corruption, pollution and smuggling. Subsidies on oil products spur unofficial exports to neighbouring Togo, Ghana, Burkina Faso and Benin. Benin estimates that more than three-quarters of the gasoline consumed in the country is illegally imported from Nigeria (see Chapter 13).

Nigeria is forced to import the bulk of its gasoline and kerosene needs as its refineries are unable to process sufficient volumes of crude oil to meet rising domestic demand. As in many other developing countries, reducing subsidies has proved extremely difficult in the face of strong public resistance. Yet Nigeria has had some successes: it eliminated subsidies to diesel a few years ago and reduced gasoline subsidies in 2012. The government is currently trying to remove kerosene subsidies and reduce natural gas subsidies.

The Nigerian government sets the domestic prices of premium gasoline, household kerosene, natural gas[10] and electricity directly. In each case, the retail price is below the cost of supply. In 2013, based on our estimates, the total cost of fossil-fuel subsidies amounted to $6.5 billion, of which oil is the biggest component (Figure 9.9). In the case of gasoline and kerosene, the state pays to marketers the difference between the retail price and the "Expected Open Market price" – a price that is calculated on the basis of international prices allowing for import/export costs. As retail prices are changed irregularly and do not follow international price fluctuations, the financial cost of the subsidy inevitably rises when world oil prices increase. The Petroleum Products Pricing Regulatory Agency is tasked with administering the system. All other oil products, including LPG (the use of which is very small) are deregulated and marketed at free market prices.

Figure 9.9 ▷ **Fossil-fuel subsidies by fuel in Nigeria, 2013**

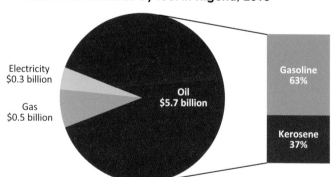

Regulated gasoline and kerosene prices in Nigeria are among the lowest in sub-Saharan Africa. The price of gasoline averaged $0.62 per litre in 2013, equal to 70% of the international market-based reference price. The official price of kerosene in 2013 was $0.32 per litre, or 30% of the reference price, but in reality the fuel is often sold at much higher prices. The majority of the kerosene distributed in Nigeria is sold by private retailers, who are able to sell at well above official prices (ranging from $0.95 to $1.95 per litre) because of strong demand and scarce supply. Only the petrol stations owned by the national oil company and a few retailers in big cities sell at the official price.

10. The majority of natural gas in Nigeria is sold at a regulated price under the Domestic Gas Obligation, a scheme under which gas producers have to dedicate a specific portion of their gas reserves and production for supply to the domestic market.

Unlike its approach to subsidising gasoline and kerosene, the government does not provide specific payments to power utilities to compensate for low electricity tariffs. Instead, electricity suppliers are provided with lump sums each year to carry out all activities. According to the Nigerian Electricity Regulatory Commission, the government's failure to make adequate payments has starved utilities of revenue. In addition, the low rate of bills collected – estimated at just one-quarter – represents another source of "subsidy" (not included in our estimates) (World Bank, 2009). Electricity is also subsidised through the under-pricing of natural gas, which fuels around 60% of the country's power generation mix. Until August 2014, gas was priced at around $1/MBtu for power stations and industry, well below our estimate of the average cost of supply of $3/MBtu (and much lower than export prices), though the price has recently been raised to around $2.50/MBtu in order to encourage investment in gas supply infrastructure. Non-payment by consumers effectively makes prices much lower in some cases.

The most recent attempt by the government to rein in oil subsidies was made in January 2012, when it decided to all but eliminate the subsidy to gasoline by raising the pump price from Nigerian naira (NGN) 50 ($0.32) per litre to what it considered to be the international market level of NGN 141 ($0.91) per litre – an effective overnight increase of 117%. This move was accompanied by the setting up of the Subsidy Reinvestment and Empowerment Programme to utilise the funds saved by the reduction in subsidies for social safety net programmes and infrastructure projects. However, there was a lack of public confidence in the programme and huge demonstrations and a general strike, which paralysed the country, ensued. After a week of protest, the reform was suspended and the gasoline subsidy partially reinstated, with the price of gasoline reduced to NGN 97 ($0.62) per litre. In January 2014, the government announced it had no plans for further price increases.

The future of the subsidy to kerosene is unclear. It appears that the national oil company continues to supply independent marketers with the product at the subsidised price, claiming funds from the government to recoup the under-recovery on the price it has to pay to import the fuel. As of mid-2014, no announcement had been made about whether to abolish or reduce the subsidy, despite widespread recognition that it largely benefits marketers, who often make large profits, rather than consumers, most of whom pay prices well above the official price (GSI, 2012b).

Some progress has been made in raising natural gas and electricity tariffs, with a recent hike in the gas prices and the phased transition to cost-reflective electricity pricing that is being implemented over 2008-2022 as part of a broader programme of power sector restructuring. However, the intention is to maintain subsidised tariffs for household electricity, on social grounds, with the cost being covered by higher tariffs to other consumers. For the time being, the federal government continues to allocate funds to the electricity companies to bridge the gap between prices and costs and put forward a bailout package of more than NGN 210 billion ($1.3 billion) in September 2014.

Guidelines on best practice

The experiences summarised for Egypt, Indonesia and Nigeria as well as that in other countries demonstrate that energy subsidies, once in place, can be very difficult – but not impossible – to remove. There is no single formula for success, and national circumstances and changing market conditions have to be taken into account when preparing reforms. The prospects for success can, however, be enhanced by adherence to some basic principles. As with any economic or social reform, the steps must involve clearly determining the objective, setting the timetable, assessing the effects on different economic actors and how those effects can be mitigated and managed, selecting the preferred course for implementation and, at all stages, consulting and communicating in order to win broad-based support for the decisions that are required. Experience has shown that an effective approach to reform needs to integrate all these elements and be backed up by resolute political will (Figure 9.10).

Figure 9.10 ▷ **Critical steps of a process to reform fossil-energy subsidies**

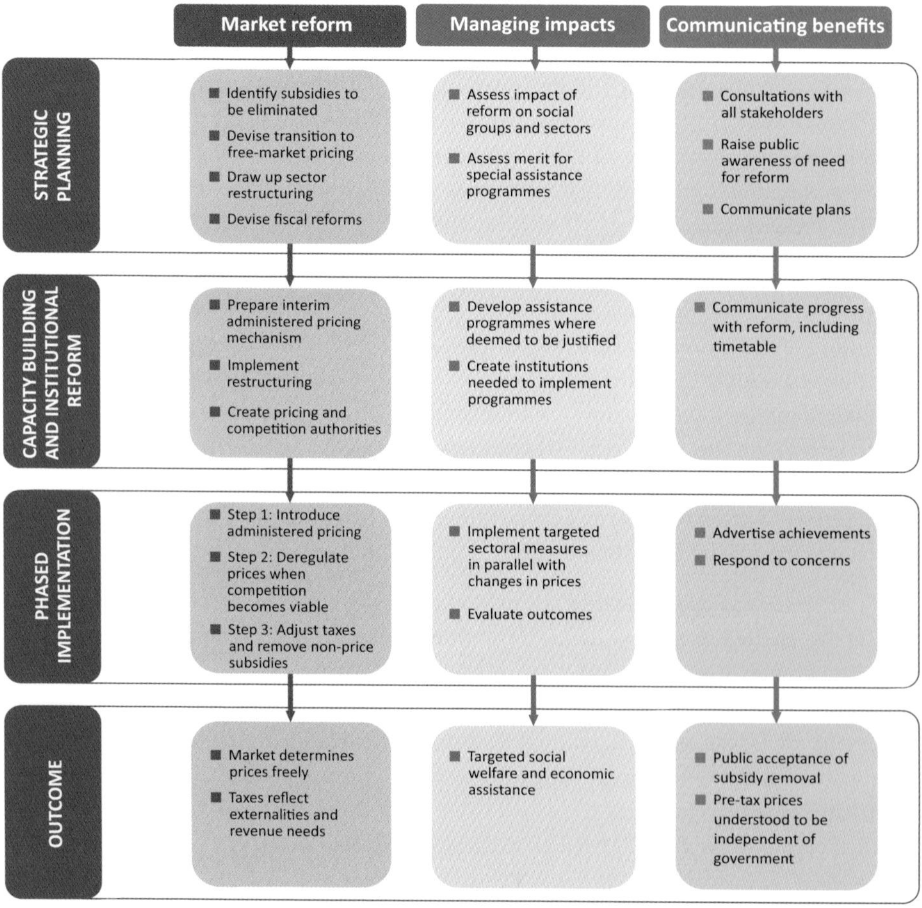

Sources: IEA based on Beaton, et al. (2013); IEA, OPEC, OECD and World Bank (2010a).

Establishing the goal of reform

The essential objective of government policies to reform fossil-fuel subsidies is to get prices right, i.e. ensure that energy prices reflect their true economic value. This must involve letting the market determine pre-tax prices freely, ensuring that a competitive market, once created, works efficiently; and identifying and unravelling all other forms of government intervention that cannot be economically justified, where they have the effect of lowering fuel prices to consumers or the cost of production, or raising the price received by producers. Competition, by incentivising investment in new supply infrastructure and encouraging efficiency, is a far more cost-effective way of lowering energy costs than fuel subsidies. As part of the overall process, the government has to consider the appropriate level of tax that should be applied to the fuel to reflect economic, social and environmental externalities, taking account of the need to raise tax revenues.

There are rarely good economic or social grounds for subsidising any fossil fuel directly, whether to consumers or producers. There may be legitimate concerns about the burden of energy costs on the poorest portions of the community, but, in general, social goals are best served by direct welfare payments to households and the provision of public services, such as health, education and social protection schemes, rather than fuel subsidies. Nonetheless, in certain circumstances, there will be a case for direct intervention in energy markets, for example to make energy available and more affordable for poor households. Where this is the case, it may make sense to apply the subsidy to the purchase of related equipment or services, such as an LPG cookstove, energy-efficient equipment or building insulation. Electricity may be seen as a special case, as access to it is essential to alleviate dire poverty and improve living standards; there may well be justification for subsidising access by applying a social, or lifeline, tariff for the an initial small tranche of consumption – a common and widely accepted form of subsidy – though it may be difficult to limit this subsidy to poor households (see Chapter 15 for a discussion of electricity access in sub-Saharan Africa).[11]

Steps in implementing market reforms

In most cases, it is inadvisable to introduce market pricing of fossil fuels too abruptly, given that this would typically lead to a sudden and possibly sharp rise in prices, as well as short-term price volatility. A practical approach, which can assist in the transition to full market pricing, is to introduce a formula-based automatic pricing mechanism that ensures that retail prices reflect movements in international prices. Such a mechanism can be applied progressively, such that prices rise in a step-fashion towards full market levels. This is particularly sensible where prices need to be raised several-fold to reach

---

11. Connection subsidies that are designed to reach a majority of the electricity deprived population living in areas connected to a grid are superior to consumption subsidies, and in most cases are also progressive. Where consumption is subsidised, volume-differentiated tariff structures, whereby the lowest price for the smallest block is only available to the poor, are generally a better way of targeting subsidies to the poor than the more commonly used inverted block tariffs, whereby the price of a kWh rises with consumption (IEA/OPEC/OECD/World Bank, 2010b).

market levels: one-off, very big hikes in prices generally prove too disruptive and provoke a public outcry. As prices rise towards market levels, the frequency of price adjustments can be increased so that consumers gradually get used to the frequent small price movements likely to be experienced in a competitive market. This approach has the advantage of being fully transparent and, eventually, distancing the government from individual changes in prices, helping to depoliticise energy price-setting.

The process of subsidy reform has to go hand-in-hand with proactive measures to restructure the energy sector to enable competition to take hold. This may require breaking up dominant companies (usually state-owned), mandating third-party access to infrastructure and other steps to facilitate the entry into the sector of new players. Clear regulations on competition need to be drawn up and enforced. Once retail prices have risen to international levels and the domestic market has been restructured in a way that allows for effective competition in wholesale and retail supply, the government can abandon the administered pricing mechanism and allow the market to determine prices freely. It is easier to gauge the degree of price competition if the government is setting price ceilings rather than fixing price levels; prices that fall below price ceilings and that vary between companies are signs of emerging competition (Kojima, 2013). Once competition is established and prices are deregulated, the government's only role in price-setting is to monitor how the market is operating to ensure that competition is effective. In parallel with the move towards market pricing, all other sources of subsidy to fossil fuels need to be identified and removed, alongside fiscal reform aimed at achieving a rational structure of taxes.

Managing the effects of subsidy reform

It is evident that it can be very difficult to reform subsidies in the face of hostility from those who benefit from them. By its very nature, the costs of an energy subsidy are spread broadly throughout the economy, while most of its benefits are often enjoyed by only a small segment of the population. The beneficiaries will always have an interest in defending that subsidy when their gains exceed their share of the economic and environmental costs. The resistance to cutting subsidies can be very strong: moves to ration heavily subsidised gasoline have led to serious civil unrest in several countries in recent years, including in Egypt, Indonesia and Nigeria. The longer the subsidies have existed, the more entrenched the opposition to reduce them tends to be – especially if they have led consumers to adopt energy-intensive technologies and practices over a prolonged period.

Resistance to subsidy reform is understandable where the beneficiaries of the subsidies stand to suffer real hardship. That is why reforms need to be managed in such a way as to reduce or offset the negative consequences for those groups of consumers that stand to lose out, especially the poor. The first step is to identify and measure the likely effects of reform. Only then can the need to compensate affected groups be assessed and appropriate measures devised. It is generally advisable to involve representatives of the affected groups in this work in order to benefit from their knowledge and experience, to ensure that the compensatory measures respond adequately to their concerns, and to raise awareness and gain support for the reform and the accompanying measures. The partial success of energy price reforms in Iran in 2010-2011 owes much to the decision to accompany huge increases in oil, gas and electricity prices with compensatory monthly cash payments to households. Putting cash in the hands of consumers through conditional payments as an alternative to blanket subsidies can offer major benefits: (i) it allows for better targeting to those that need it the most, making sure the benefits are not skewed towards the richest; (ii) it puts the decision-making in the hands of the consumer, and can thereby encourage more efficient energy use; (iii) with extra money (not being spent on energy because this is consumed more efficiently), consumer spending or saving will be boosted, which in either case, will be a boon to the economy

In some cases, the need for social and economic support, such as conditional cash transfers, might only be temporary, to help consumers or producers get over the initial shock of subsidy removal. Where more permanent support is justified, measures are likely to involve strengthening social safety nets, improved provision of health and education, and direct welfare payments to the poor and vulnerable – a generally much more efficient and cost-effective way of providing assistance to those groups than fossil-fuel subsidies. The precise mix of measures adopted will usually reflect a mixture of what is practical, consumer or producer preferences and what is politically feasible (Beaton et al., 2013). Once in place, the effectiveness of those measures needs to be carefully monitored and evaluated.

Communicating the benefits of reform

Effective communication of the benefits of reforming fossil-fuel subsidies is critical to building broad support and countering resistance from vested interests. This can be difficult in practice. Politicians often struggle to explain in a comprehensible way the economic costs of a subsidy and the gains that can be had from eliminating it. In oil-exporting countries, the task of persuading the public that oil products should be sold at their opportunity cost and not their cost of production can be particularly hard – all the more so when the spoils from exploiting oil resources are not otherwise shared by the population at large. In many resource-rich countries, cheap fuels are often considered an integral part of the social contract between the government and its citizens. In some cases, the public is likely to be unconvinced by government promises to redirect spending to other public goods and services.

Subsidy reform can have far-reaching effects and so a consultation and communication strategy needs to be co-ordinated across all relevant government agencies. Planning careful communication strategies including media and public campaigns in order to reach out to the poor and those who will be most affected by the subsidy reform can help minimise public opposition (IEA, OPEC, OECD and World Bank, 2010a and 2010b; Beaton et al., 2013). Good communication must be based on listening, so consultation with all interested parties – through public inquiries, discussion groups, surveys and workshops – is vital. Communication needs to take the form of simple messages, targeted at specific groups of energy users and using appropriate media, including radio, television, public speeches and announcements, debates, advertisements and web-based communications (Beaton et al., 2013). Honesty and openness are critical to a successful communications strategy (Clements et al., 2013): the messages must be honest and clear, focusing on central aspects of the need for reform. They need to include the magnitude of the cost under-recoveries by energy companies and the compensatory financial payments by the government; how the subsidies are captured by different income groups and the effects of reform on them; the non-fiscal costs of subsidies such as smuggling, fuel diversion, fuel shortages and deteriorating infrastructure; and an exposition of how social and economic goals can be better met using alternatives to subsidies.

There are several examples of how good communication has helped to build support for reform. In Nigeria, the government used the fact that fuel subsidies exceeded capital expenditure to call for reform, though implementation has proved difficult as highlighted in the case study. In Ghana, the government undertook an independent poverty and social impact analysis in 2004 and made the findings public to make the costs and incidence of subsidies, along with the impact on different groups of their removal, well understood (IMF, 2013). The success of Iran's energy subsidy reforms in 2010-2011 was aided by a public relations campaign to get the message across that subsidies cause waste and are socially unjust because they benefit the rich the most. By contrast, a failure by the Bolivian government to warn the public of a sudden hike in gasoline and diesel prices in 2010 and explain its need led to transport and teachers unions going on strike, large-scale demonstrations in major cities and, eventually, reinstatement of the subsidies by the government.

OUTLOOK FOR NUCLEAR POWER

PREFACE

Part B of this *WEO* (Chapters 10-12) assesses the outlook for nuclear power, an energy source that has become a significant feature of the global energy landscape and that currently faces a suite of economic, technical and political challenges.

Chapter 10 traces the history of nuclear power and puts it in a current energy context. It outlines government policies towards nuclear power in key markets and discusses several of the other main factors that will shape its future prospects, including the economics and financing of nuclear power plants and public attitudes to the technology.

Chapter 11 provides detailed projections of nuclear power's place in the market to the year 2040 in various scenarios and cases and for different countries and regions, including an assessment of prospects for nuclear fuel supply. It also analyses related issues, namely the associated investment requirements and the challenge that will be presented by the large number of nuclear power plants that are set to be retired.

Chapter 12 discusses the implications of the outlook for nuclear power for energy security, the balance of trade and the environment. It concludes by outlining a set of policy issues relevant to most countries, whether they are using, pursuing or phasing out nuclear power.

Chapter 10

Nuclear power today and decisions to come
Influences on the choices of policy-makers and the public

Highlights

- In 2013, the world's 392 GW of installed nuclear capacity accounted for 11% of electricity generation. This share has declined gradually since 1996, when it reached almost 18%, as the rate of new nuclear additions (and generation) has been outpaced by the expansion of other technologies. After hydropower, nuclear is the world's second-largest source of low-carbon electricity generation.

- Some 80% of nuclear capacity is in OECD countries. Of that, more than three-quarters is over 25 years old, raising important questions in the medium term about the schedule for retirements. By contrast, around half of the capacity in non-OECD countries (excluding Russia) is less than 15 years old.

- Of the 76 GW of nuclear capacity under construction, three-quarters is in non-OECD countries (40% in China), which have been adding large increments of capacity to meet fast-growing electricity demand and to reduce air pollution. In most OECD countries, construction starts on new reactors have been very slow in the last several decades; activity in their nuclear sectors has centred on improving capacity factors, achieving power uprates and extending the lifetime of existing plants.

- Government policy – which reflects the unique energy security, economic and environmental priorities of individual countries – underpins the outlook for nuclear power. Nearly all new builds in recent years have taken place in markets in which electricity prices are regulated or in markets where government-owned entities build, own and operate plants. In competitive markets, the risks in constructing and operating new plants have been too significant to attract investment, though some governments have offered subsidies to mitigate these risks.

- Influenced by a combination of local, national and global factors, public attitudes to nuclear power are critical to its future development. Public concerns typically include safety, radioactive waste management, nuclear weapons proliferation, transparency in the approach to public consultation, climate change and energy security. Confidence in regulatory frameworks and institutional capacity is also a key factor, especially in countries planning to introduce their first reactors.

- The commercial economics of nuclear power depend on many factors that vary according to market, regulatory and policy conditions in particular regions. Like other technologies, it has external costs as well as external benefits, such as avoided CO_2 emissions and local pollution, and its contribution to energy security. Nuclear generating costs are most sensitive to changes in the cost of capital and the overnight cost of plant construction. Future overnight costs depend on whether construction can be repeated by experienced entities in a stable and efficient regulatory framework, utilising standardised practice and equipment supplied through well-developed industrial pipelines.

Context

Nuclear power has become a significant feature of the global energy landscape during the past half century. Today, fast-growing electricity demand in some regions, coupled with goals to improve energy security and avoid emissions of greenhouse gases and other air pollutants, suggest that nuclear power could continue to play an important role in future energy systems. Yet some governments and their citizens have rejected the use of nuclear power; and even where this is not the case, there is often uncertainty about the pace and scale at which new reactors will be built and how long existing ones will operate.

Nuclear power faces big challenges with respect to the economics and financing of new builds. With high upfront investment costs and long construction times for new reactors, this is especially true in competitive markets where utilities face significant market and regulatory risk. Nuclear power also faces intense public concern about a wide range of issues that may limit its prospects if they are not adequately addressed. Safety is the dominant concern – in operating plants, managing radioactive waste and preventing the spread of nuclear weapons. The scale of these issues is such that, ultimately, only governments can determine the future of nuclear power. Individual countries, taking into account their own situation and priorities, will assess its relative costs and benefits and intervene with appropriate policy action. Policies may be more or less stringent: they may set an explicit course either to support nuclear power or to phase it out, or they may affect nuclear power more generally by determining the structure of electricity markets.

This chapter traces the history of nuclear power and puts it in a current energy context. It covers key national policies, whether the countries concerned have long-established programmes, have opted to phase out nuclear power or are potential newcomers to the technology. The chapter discusses the key issues of nuclear economics and financing, and also of public acceptance. It builds towards Chapter 11, which gives detailed projections of nuclear power's place in the market to the year 2040, in various scenarios and cases. Chapter 12 follows with a discussion of the implications of the outlook for nuclear power for energy security, the economy and the environment, identifies issues which most governments must face, whatever their basic disposition towards nuclear power.

Historical and current developments

Nuclear power for commercial use emerged from scientific work in the first half of the 20th century to investigate and harness energy at the nuclear level. This work was originally driven by the development of nuclear energy for military applications, notably weapons and naval propulsion. The 1950s saw intensive research, development and demonstration in reactor design and operation.[1] During that time, several countries led separate but parallel efforts that brought the first nuclear power plants online.[2]

---

1. *WEO-2014* discusses only nuclear reactors used for commercial power generation. Other uses of nuclear reactors include military applications and research.

2. In 1951, electricity was produced from a nuclear reactor for the first time in Idaho in the United States. In 1954, a 5-megawatt reactor at Obninsk in the Soviet Union was connected to the grid.

Nuclear plant construction starts accelerated during the 1960s and peaked after the oil price shock of 1973-1974 (Figure 10.1). During that time, Europe and the United States accounted for the majority of new nuclear builds. The nuclear industry entered a downturn in the late 1970s because of slowing electricity demand growth and, in the United States, regulatory changes (motivated by safety concerns) that led to project delays and higher construction costs. The accident at Three Mile Island in the United States in 1979 heightened public opposition to nuclear power and further slowed licence approvals around the world, reinforcing this trend. Construction starts fell sharply and many projects were suspended or cancelled, though installed nuclear capacity and output continued to increase as completed plants came into operation. The accident at Chernobyl in Ukraine in 1986 further depressed activity, especially in Europe.

Figure 10.1 ▷ **Reactor construction starts and timeline of events**

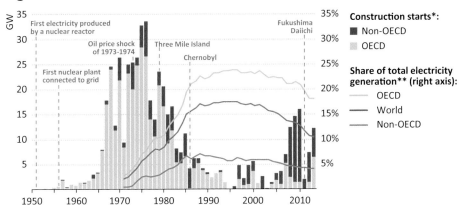

* The data do not include construction starts for units that were later cancelled. Some reactors that are currently under construction, however, may yet be cancelled. ** Data are available from 1971.

Sources: International Atomic Energy Agency (IAEA) Power Reactor Information System; IEA databases.

The 1990s and early 2000s saw very little new nuclear construction outside of Japan, Korea and China. Gas and electricity markets in many OECD countries were deregulated and gas prices were low and were expected to remain so. In many countries, investment in new nuclear plants became less attractive than investment in alternatives, particularly combined-cycle gas turbines (CCGTs). Moreover, slow electricity demand growth and over-build in the previous decade meant that many countries had excess capacity in many countries. A large number of projects in transition economies that had been planning significant nuclear additions were suspended or cancelled.

There was a resurgence in new nuclear builds in the late 2000s, driven by non-OECD countries – mainly China – seeking to meet fast-growing electricity demand and to reduce air pollution. Construction starts on new reactors in most OECD countries remained very limited. Activity there focused on existing plants: raising capacity factors, increasing capacity through power uprates and extending lifetimes (Box 10.1). Strong public concern about safety re-emerged following the accident at Fukushima Daiichi in Japan in 2011, causing a slowdown in new

Box 10.1 ▷ Getting the most out of existing nuclear plants

It is generally more economic, and less demanding in terms of regulatory effort and winning public acceptance, to maximise the use of existing nuclear plants rather than build new power generation capacity (of all types). This explains the focus by utilities over the past several decades – particularly in OECD countries, where demand growth has been slow – on improving capacity factors, achieving power uprates and extending operating lifetimes at existing nuclear plants.

Increasing the hours of operation has been the most important way to increase generation from existing units. Between 1980 and 2010, the average global capacity factor for reactors increased from 56% to 79%. This has been a result of better management, which has significantly shortened outage periods for planned maintenance and refuelling. The best-performing reactors achieve capacity factors of around 95%. As plants age, however, such high levels may be difficult to reach, as more frequent inspection and testing of components is required.

Utilities have increasingly sought uprates for existing reactors – the process by which a plant raises its electricity generation capacity by capturing more of the heat produced by the reactor (mainly as a result of incorporating components made of materials that can withstand greater heat flows). Depending on the reactor type, the uprate potential for nuclear plants can be between 2% and 30% of the original licensed capacity; for pressurised water reactors, the most common reactor type, the maximum is around 20%. Small uprates can be achieved relatively easily and inexpensively by using more accurate measurement methods. Extended uprates involve major plant modifications that may take several years to complete and are much more costly. Between 1977 and 2013, the US Nuclear Regulatory Commission (NRC) approved 149 uprates in the United States, collectively totalling around 7 GW – roughly the same as building 5-7 new large-scale reactors. The potential for further uprates in the United States and in several other countries is now limited, though opportunities remain in Europe and in Russia.

Lifetime extensions for ageing nuclear plants have been another focal point of activity. Such extensions allow units that meet required safety standards to continue to operate beyond their original design life; they typically require capital investment in the replacement and refurbishment of key components (see later section on capital investment in refurbishments). Lifetime extensions can ease the need to build new plants, which could be important given the significant number of reactors (those built in the 1970s and 1980s) that might otherwise retire in a relatively short period of time. Regulatory processes to extend operating licences vary, but essentially take one of two forms: extension subject to periodic safety reviews (for instance every ten years), or licence renewal for a defined period. At end-2013, 73 out of 100 reactors in the United States had been granted a licence renewal allowing them to operate for up to 60 years, and applications for another 18 reactors were under review (US NRC, 2014a).

construction and prompting authorities worldwide to re-assess nuclear safety. Some countries accelerated or adopted plans to phase out nuclear power, though most did not change their views on its long-term role in their energy systems.

Table 10.1 ▷ **Key nuclear power statistics by region, end-2013**

	Operational reactors	Installed capacity (GW)	Electricity generation (TWh)*	Share of electricity generation*	Under construction (GW)**
OECD	324	315	1 961	18%	20
United States	100	105	822	19%	6.2
France	58	66	424	74%	1.7
Japan***	48	44	9	1%	2.8
Korea	23	22	139	26%	6.6
Canada	19	14	103	16%	0
Germany	9	13	97	15%	0
United Kingdom	16	11	71	20%	0
Other	51	41	297	11%	2.7
Non-OECD	110	78	517	4%	56
Russia	33	25	171	16%	9.1
China	20	17	117	2%	32
Ukraine	15	14	83	44%	2.0
India	21	5.8	32	3%	4.3
Other	21	16	113	2%	9.5
World	434	392	2 478	11%	76

* Electricity generation data are the latest available estimates for 2013. ** Differences in the definition of the start of construction may lead to discrepancies between the figures here and those in other sources. The *World Energy Outlook* uses the IAEA definition, which specifies the start of construction as the date of the first major placing of concrete, usually for the base mat of the reactor building. *** While Japan's nuclear reactors are operable, they have largely been idled since the accident at Fukushima Daiichi in March 2011. Notes: GW = gigawatts; TWh = terawatt-hours.

Sources: IAEA Power Reactor Information System (PRIS); IEA databases.

In 2013, the world's 392 gigawatts (GW)[3,4] of installed nuclear capacity accounted for 11% of total electricity generation. This share has declined gradually since 1996, when it reached almost 18%, as the rate of new nuclear additions (and output growth) has been outpaced by the expansion of other technologies. After hydropower, nuclear is the second-largest source of low-carbon electricity generation worldwide and the largest in OECD countries. Globally, its output is estimated to be nearly four-times greater than that of wind power and 18 times that of solar photovoltaics (PV) (though these ratios are declining quickly

---

3. All electrical capacities and generation are expressed in gross (as opposed to net) terms, therefore accounting for own-use by power plants.

4. As of September 2014, additional reactors had entered operation – two in China (2.2 GW total) and one in Argentina (745 MW) – and had began construction – one each in the United Arab Emirates (1.4 GW), Belarus (1.2 GW) and Argentina (29 MW).

because of the fast growth of renewables). Some 80% of operational capacity is in OECD countries; however, it is non-OECD countries that are presently driving new construction. Of the 76 GW of nuclear capacity being built at the end of 2013, three-quarters was in non-OECD countries (and 40% in China). This reflects the need to add large increments of baseload capacity to meet fast-growing electricity demand, and to diversify the power mix, while emitting fewer air pollutants.

The average age of nuclear capacity worldwide is 27 years, while expected technical lifetimes for reactors are 30-60 years, depending on the reactor type and location. More than three-quarters of the fleet in OECD countries is over 25 years old, posing big questions in the medium term about the schedule for retirements and how such a large tranche of capacity might be replaced. By contrast, around half of the capacity in non-OECD countries (excluding Russia) is less than 15 years old (Figure 10.2).

Figure 10.2 ▷ **Age profile of nuclear capacity by selected region** (years)

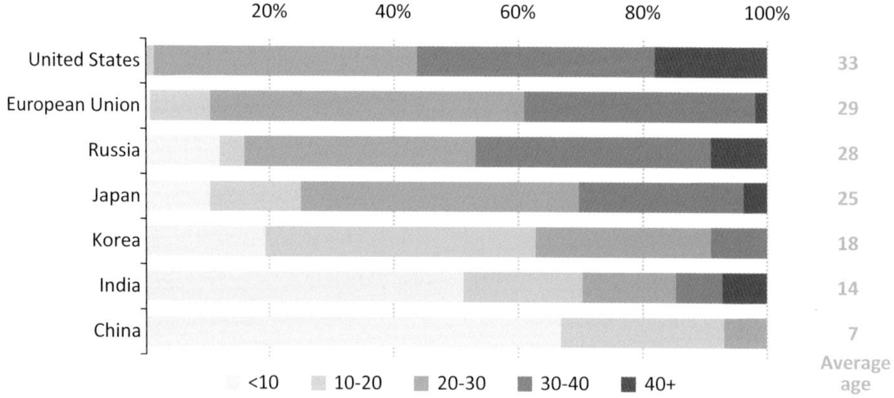

Sources: IAEA PRIS; IEA analysis.

Box 10.2 ▷ **Non-proliferation of nuclear weapons**

The development of nuclear energy for commercial power generation has a shared history with the pursuit of nuclear weapons. Enrichment and reprocessing technologies, which extract fissile material from uranium or spent (used) nuclear fuel to make fuel for nuclear power plants, can also be used for weapons development. The dual-nature of the technology therefore necessitates safeguards to ensure that civilian energy programmes are not used to build weapons.

The Treaty on the Non-Proliferation of Nuclear Weapons (NPT), signed by 190 nations, is the foundation of the international regime to address this relationship. The NPT seeks to prevent the spread of nuclear weapons while at the same time promoting co-operation in the peaceful uses of nuclear energy. It empowers the International Atomic Energy Agency (IAEA) of the United Nations to inspect nuclear facilities to verify the commitments made by non-nuclear weapons states not to divert nuclear materials from peaceful uses to nuclear weapons. Complementing the work of the inter-governmental IAEA, the Nuclear Suppliers Group seeks to contribute to the non-proliferation of nuclear weapons by issuing guidelines for nuclear and nuclear-related exports. While this framework has been in place for more than 40 years, it has not fully eliminated the security concerns associated with nuclear technology. Non-proliferation remains an imperative for international security, though such issues are beyond the scope of this report.

Reactor technology and designs

Just as fossil-fuelled power plants generate electricity by harnessing the thermal energy released when burning coal, gas or oil, nuclear reactors do so by converting the thermal energy released during nuclear fission. Nuclear fission is a process in which the nucleus of an atom splits into smaller parts when struck by a neutron and, when occurring in a controlled sustained chain reaction, releases a large amount of usable energy. Uranium is used in all of the world's commercial reactors – 92% of capacity uses low-enriched uranium (sometimes in association with mixed-oxide [MOX] fuel) and 8% uses natural or slightly-enriched uranium[5] – because of its low cost and abundance.

Figure 10.3 ▷ Overview of basic nuclear reactor technologies and their share of construction starts

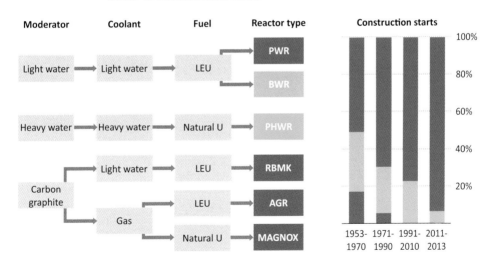

Notes: LEU = low-enriched uranium; Natural U = natural or slightly-enriched uranium; PWR = pressurised-water reactor; BWR = boiling-water reactor; PHWR = pressurised heavy-water reactor; RBMK = high power channel-type reactor; AGR = advanced gas-cooled reactor; MAGNOX = magnesium non-oxidising.

Sources: IAEA PRIS; IEA analysis.

---

5. For use in commercial light-water reactors, uranium is enriched to 3 to 5% ^{235}U (low-enriched uranium). MOX fuel is composed of uranium blended with some plutonium from reprocessing. Slightly-enriched uranium, used in pressurised heavy-water reactors, has a ^{235}U concentration of 0.9% to 1.2%.

Almost 90% of the capacity in operation is both moderated and cooled with ordinary, or "light", water, and these reactors are therefore known as light-water reactors (Figure 10.3). Of these, two major types exist: pressurised-water reactors (PWRs), which make up around two-thirds of installed nuclear capacity, and boiling-water reactors (BWRs), which account for about one-fifth.[6] Most of the other reactors are cooled by either heavy water or gas. Each basic type may include several unique designs built by different entities at different times, in accordance with customer needs and the prevailing state of technological development.

Reactor technologies have continued to evolve based on operational experience. There is no universally shared definition of reactor generations but, in broad terms, so-called "Generation I" reactors were built in the 1950s and 1960s. Generation II reactors, which comprise the majority of the reactors in operation today, were mostly built after 1970. Early models of Generation III reactors first became commercially available in the 1990s. This generation of reactors aims to enhance safety, relative to the preceding generation, by incorporating design changes that lower the risk of a severe accident and, should a severe accident occur, by using appropriate mitigation systems to limit its impact on the population and the environment. Improvements may include more redundancy (back-up systems), greater use of passive systems (which rely on natural forces such as gravity) or fewer components.

Generation III reactors make up more than half of the capacity under construction globally (the rest are Generation II designs); since the accident at Fukushima in March 2011, they have accounted for most construction licence approvals. Generation III reactors encompass a variety of designs, with some still being developed, others under construction and only a handful built (Table 10.2). Construction and operational experience as new designs are scaled up will determine which will be most successful.

Table 10.2 ▷ **Selected Generation III reactor designs***

Design(s)	Vendor(s)	Type	Capacity (MW)**	Status at end-2013 (number of units)
AP1000	Westinghouse Toshiba	PWR	1 200	**Under constr. (8):** China (4), United States (4)
EPR	Areva	PWR	1 700	**Under constr. (4):** China (2), France (1), Finland (1)
AES91/92 AES2006	Rosatom	PWR	1 000- 1 200	**Built (1):** India **Under constr. (9):** Russia (5), Belarus (1), China (2), India (1)
ABWR	GE, Hitachi, Toshiba	BWR	1 380	**Built (4):** Japan **Under constr. (4):** Chinese Taipei (2), Japan (2)
APR1400	Kepco, KHNP	PWR	1 400	**Under constr. (6):** Korea (4), UAE (2)

* There are many Generation III reactor designs. Those shown here were selected because they either are built or are under construction. ** Indicative gross capacity, which may vary from reactor to reactor.

6. The difference is in how they produce steam. BWRs make steam within the reactor core by contact of water with the nuclear fuel assembly. PWRs prevent boiling in the reactor core by keeping the cooling water under high pressure but require an intermediate component called a steam generator to transfer the heat from the core and convert it into steam.

Future reactor technologies and associated fuel cycles will seek continued improvements over the current generation in the areas of safety, economics, fuel use, waste production and non-proliferation of weapons materials. Those being developed tend to be tailored to deliver specific benefits. Generation IV reactors, for example, aim to optimise the nuclear fuel cycle, which means using fuel resources more efficiently and minimising the environmental impacts of waste (Box 10.3). Six types of advanced reactors have been selected by the Generation IV International Forum for further research and development, but none of them is expected to be available commercially before 2030.[7]

Box 10.3 ▷ Looking ahead to Generation IV technologies

Generation IV reactors are design concepts that aim to improve upon the performance of today's reactors by changing the fuel or coolant to produce different effects. From a fuel perspective, Generation IV reactor concepts often vary greatly from current reactors by using different materials to encase the fuel, for example relying on liquid fuels, or even dissolving fuel into the coolant. Their main objectives are to promote more effective fuel utilisation and minimise the amount of nuclear waste produced while delivering advances in safety, reliability and proliferation resistance. But these reactors will first have to demonstrate economic benefits relative to other energy supply technologies and show that they deliver on their promise.

One line of research seeks to increase the temperature at which the reactor operates (from about 300 °C to more than 500 °C, perhaps approaching 1 000 °C) to make electricity generation more efficient or to provide process heat for industrial applications. This requires replacing the water coolant by one that can be used at higher temperatures, such as helium gas, molten lead or molten salts. Each of these choices entails other trade-offs within the design, affecting aspects such as the size of the reactor, the need to contain hazardous materials, and the need to manage long-term maintenance issues associated with some of these materials.

Some advanced reactor concepts seek to make changes to fuel use and spent fuel management. Fast reactors, for example, do not use moderators to slow neutrons to encourage a chain reaction. While this difference usually means that they require fuel that is enriched to higher levels than in today's reactors, it also allows different fuel cycles to be employed. Fast reactors can be designed to "breed" fissile material by producing more new fissile atoms than were destroyed to release energy. Some models are designed to achieve high safety levels by using passive systems and to reduce the lifetime of the radioactive waste produced, thus reducing the burden to manage it over the long term.

10

---

7. These include thermal reactor technologies such as the molten salt reactor (MSR), very-high-temperature reactor (VHTR) and supercritical-water-cooled reactor (SCWR), as well as fast reactor technologies, such as the gas-cooled fast reactor (GFR), sodium-cooled fast reactor (SFR) and lead-cooled fast reactor (LFR).

Small modular reactors (SMRs), which encompass a range of designs generally less than 300 MW in size, could have potential in certain markets because of comparative advantages over large-scale reactors. They could be added incrementally, as required, making them better suited to small grids and markets expecting limited electricity demand growth. With lower upfront costs due to smaller unit sizes, they might be more easily financed (see Spotlight in Chapter 11). The main trade-off, relative to large-scale reactors, is that SMRs would be unable to achieve the same economies of scale in their construction. However, if fully manufactured and assembled in a controlled environment, rather than on-site, they may make costs and construction times more predictable. Demonstration projects are underway to evaluate the merits of SMRs (though these early models will not be factory produced).

Policy framework

Government policy is the most significant determinant of the prospects for nuclear power. It is influenced by the unique energy security, economic and environmental priorities of individual countries and their judgement as to the benefits and costs of its use versus that of alternatives. Where there is opportunity for public involvement in decision-making, government policy can be strongly influenced by public views towards nuclear power, with general acceptance being an enabling condition and sharp opposition being a limiting one (see later section on addressing public concerns).

There is marked variation between national policies in terms of the view towards nuclear power and the degree of direction or intervention undertaken (Table 10.3). The spectrum includes countries that plan to introduce, maintain or expand their nuclear fleets and those that have prohibited the introduction of nuclear power or are committed to phasing it out (Figure 10.4). Some countries have firm targets for nuclear power that are backed by forms of government intervention. Others offer few or no incentives to nuclear power, leaving it to compete in the electricity market, or focus on promoting other forms of electricity generation. Policy approaches also vary according to whether or not countries already have established nuclear power programmes, in view of the added institutional, technical and financial challenges that newcomers must overcome.

The role of governments seeking to support nuclear power has changed as market structures have evolved. In competitive markets, utilities face a high degree of risk in building and operating a new nuclear plant, particularly because of the degree of uncertainty around expected wholesale electricity prices and revenues. This has made it difficult to justify the investment and to secure financing. Nearly all new builds in recent years have taken place in markets in which electricity prices are regulated or in markets where government-owned entities build, own and operate plants. In competitive markets, different forms of subsidies have been offered to attract private investment in new projects.

Figure 10.4 △ **Status of nuclear power programmes, end-2013**

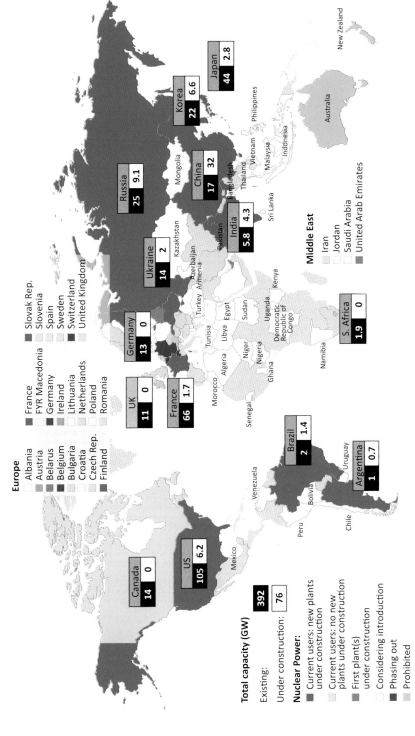

This map is without prejudice to the status of or sovereignty over any territory, to the delimitation of international frontiers and boundaries, and to the name of any territory, city or area.

Countries with existing programmes

In the *United States*, various incentives are in place to support investment in new nuclear plants. These include a loan guarantee fund ($18.5 billion), which is available for up to 80% of the cost of building a new plant and transfers the risk of default to the government; only one guarantee (for $6.5 billion) had been granted as of September 2014. There also is a tax credit of $18 per megawatt-hour (MWh) for the first 6 GW of new capacity that enters service before the end of 2020, limited to the first eight years of operation. The 6.2 GW under construction are all in markets that regulate prices so as to offer utilities some assurance of a reasonable rate of return; investment has not materialised in competitive markets, even with the offering of some incentives to new nuclear construction. The fleet of US reactors is one of the oldest in the world, and plant lifetimes will have a significant impact on the country's need for new power generation capacity. With the majority of reactors having entered service in the 1970s, and most of them licensed to operate for 60 years, a wave of retirements is due to begin in the 2030s. Retirements could be delayed or spread out if approval is sought (and granted) to license some reactors for 80 years.

Japan's new Strategic Energy Plan, approved in April 2014 following a three-year review of energy policy in response to the Fukushima Daiichi accident, identifies nuclear power as an important source of baseload electricity. Since the accident, nuclear has played a very limited role in Japan's power mix and there have been lengthy periods during which all reactors were offline. As of September 2014, none of its 48 reactors was operating. The new plan calls for reactors to be restarted once necessary regulatory approvals have been obtained; at the time of writing, only the Sendai plant had received such approval, though it had not yet restarted. The plan does not specify targets for the future shares of different fuels in the energy mix, although these are expected to be announced later. Major placing of concrete has been completed on two new nuclear units, while advanced preparatory work is underway at the site of a third. In addition, a further six reactors have been earmarked as priority projects by the government. Operating licences are currently granted for 40 years, setting the scene for a surge of retirements from around 2020, though plants can apply for a maximum extension of 20 years.

Korea's new Basic Energy Plan, approved in early 2014, revised downward the target for the nuclear share of installed capacity in 2035 from 41% to 29%. The decision came amid public concern about nuclear safety linked in part to a scandal over fraudulent safety certificates for parts used in nuclear reactors. The new target still implies an expansion of nuclear capacity, given the expectation of robust electricity demand growth. As of September 2014, 6.6 GW were under construction. Sixteen of the existing 23 units are due to retire before 2040, unless operating licences are extended beyond their current limit (30 or 40 years, depending on the type of reactor).

France is preparing a new energy law (expected to be finalised in early 2015) that may cap nuclear capacity at the present level (66 GW) with a view to reducing its share in the electricity mix. One Generation III reactor is under construction at Flamanville, the opening of which may coincide with the closing of another reactor or two if the new law is finalised without major change. Operating licences are provided for ten-year periods, after periodic safety reviews, without any maximum lifetime being set. With the average age of France's nuclear fleet at around 28 years, additional requests to extend licences from 30 to 40 years are expected. A preliminary assessment on extending reactor lifetimes to 50 years is expected in 2015, with a final opinion given by the safety regulator by 2019. If the opinion favours extensions, approvals would be needed on a reactor-by-reactor basis.

Table 10.3 ▷ **Key nuclear power-related policies and targets in selected countries with operable reactors**

	Key policies and targets
Argentina	15-18% share of nuclear in electricity mix.
Belgium	Phase out nuclear by 2025.
Brazil	Increase nuclear capacity to 3.4 GW by 2022.
China	Increase nuclear capacity to 61 GW by 2020 (with further 30 GW under construction); preferential tariffs for electricity generation from new nuclear.
France	A new energy law is anticipated in early 2015; it may cap nuclear capacity at the present level, with a view to reducing its share in the electricity mix.
Germany	Phase out nuclear by the end of 2022.
India	Increase share of nuclear in electricity mix to 5% by 2020, 12% by 2030 and 25% by 2050.
Japan	Reduce reliance on nuclear power, but recognise it as an important source of baseload electricity; potential for operating lifetimes to be extended from 40 to 60 years.
Korea	Increase nuclear capacity to 29% of installed capacity by 2035.
Russia	Increase nuclear capacity to 50 GW by 2035 (22.5% of electricity mix).
Sweden	Construction of new reactors permitted at existing sites, but only to replace current units.
Switzerland	Reactors will not be replaced when they reach the end of their design life, implying a phase-out by 2034.
Ukraine	Maintain the current share of nuclear in electricity mix.
United Kingdom	Agreed to a "contract-for-difference" with EDF that reduces the investment risk for Hinkley Point C (which would be the first new unit built since 1995).
United States	Loan guarantees and production tax credits to support investment in new nuclear; operating license extensions granted to 60 years for most plants.

Germany has committed to phase out nuclear power by the end of 2022 at the latest. The decision was taken in 2011 after the accident at Fukushima Daiichi and accelerated previous plans to phase out nuclear power by the 2030s. Eight of the country's oldest reactors (8.7 GW) were immediately closed following the accident. The nine reactors still operating are scheduled to be retired before they reach the end of their design lifetimes: one plant in each of 2015, 2017 and 2019 and then three in each of 2021 and 2022.[8]

---

8. The operator of the plant to be retired in December 2015 has announced plans to close it seven months ahead of the planned date.

Germany plans to offset the loss of nuclear production, while at the same time meeting climate targets, by an energy sector transition referred to as "Energiewende". Among its cornerstones are increasing renewables-based power generation (it has ambitious plans to further develop solar PV, wind and bioenergy-based technologies) and energy efficiency, as well as improving transmission and distribution networks.

The *United Kingdom* has one of the oldest fleets of nuclear plants in the world. While further lifetime extensions may be possible for some units, more than half of nuclear capacity is currently due to retire by around 2025. Any new reactors in the United Kingdom are to be privately financed, built and operated. A consortium led by EDF has agreed to build the Hinkley Point C nuclear plant (which would be the first new unit constructed since 1995) after the government agreed to a "contract-for-difference" which guarantees a price of GBP 92.5/MWh ($145/MWh) for the electricity the plant produces over a period of 35 years.[9] There are also plans to build reactors at Sizewell, Wylfa and Oldbury. The UK's 2013 Nuclear Industrial Strategy proposes building 16 GW of new capacity by 2030.

Russia's new Energy Strategy to 2035 envisages the nuclear share of electricity generation rising to 22.5% by 2035, with installed capacity increasing to 50 GW. As of September 2014, 9.1 GW were under construction, including 70 MW as part of the world's first floating commercial nuclear power plant (the Akademik Lomonosov). Most of Russia's plants had initial design lifetimes of 30 years, but nearly half have passed that age and have received licences to continue operating for an additional 15-25 years. Rosatom, the state-owned nuclear monopoly is very active constructing reactors not only in Russia but worldwide.

China has the world's most ambitious plans to expand nuclear power, with a target to expand capacity from 17 GW in 2013 to 58 GW by 2020 (with a further 30 GW under construction). Following the accident at Fukushima Daiichi, new plant approvals were suspended for 20 months while tighter safety measures were introduced. Since approvals resumed, construction starts have been much slower than before the accident, when they reached a record level of 11 GW per year in both 2009 and 2010. Plans to build the country's first inland plants were also deferred and remain on hold. As of September 2014, 29 GW were under construction. New nuclear builds are supported by tariffs that favour their output more than that of other forms of generation. China's nuclear capacity is relatively young, so it does not yet face the retirement challenges that confront more mature markets.

India plans to expand the nuclear share in electricity generation from around 3% today to 5% by 2017, 12% by 2030 and 25% by 2050. Development of nuclear power was delayed by an embargo on the trade of nuclear technology and materials between 1974-2008, imposed because of India's refusal to join the Treaty on the Non-Proliferation of Nuclear

---

9. The price is fully indexed to the consumer price index. The plant operator is to receive "top-up" payments if market prices are below the threshold, and has to repay the difference if prices are higher. If a final investment decision on another proposed project (Sizewell C) is taken, the guaranteed price will fall to GBP 89.5/MWh ($140/MWh) on the basis of the projects sharing "first-of-a-kind" costs.

Weapons (Box 10.2). Following the US-India Civil Nuclear Cooperation Initiative and India's commitment to subject all of its civilian nuclear facilities to IAEA safeguards, sanctions were lifted in 2008. Nuclear power was opened to foreign entities, speeding the pace of development. As of September 2014, 4.3 GW were under construction. Some foreign entities have been deterred by India's nuclear liability law, which makes parts suppliers potentially liable for damages in accidents caused by faulty or defective equipment. In the long term it plans to use reactor technologies based on thorium fuel which, unlike uranium, is abundant in India.

In addition to Germany, several other countries have decided either to phase out nuclear power or to rule out its introduction. *Switzerland* has decided not to replace any of its five reactors once they reach the end of their design lifetimes, which means it will be nuclear free in 2034. A referendum in *Italy* in 2011 rejected plans to restart a nuclear programme, which it had abandoned in the late 1980s. *Belgium*, which generates half of its electricity from nuclear power, has announced plans to phase out nuclear power by 2025. *Australia, Austria, Denmark, Ireland* and *New Zealand* also prohibit, directly or indirectly, the introduction of nuclear power. Doubts have increased about the future of nuclear power in Chinese Taipei: in April 2014, due to stiff public opposition, work was suspended on its fourth nuclear plant with construction around 80% complete.

Potential newcomer countries

Almost 40 countries are considering introducing nuclear power. The majority of these are located in Southeast Asia, the Middle East and Africa (Figure 10.4). Though the group is large, caution should be exercised in assessing which might actually build a first nuclear plant and over what timeframe.

There are many hurdles to introducing nuclear power. An adequate regulatory framework, overseen by an entity that is both competent and independent, is imperative. Also critical are a country's underlying economic, political and social conditions. To build a large-scale reactor, adequate financial resources must be available and the grid must be large enough to accommodate it. Of the countries that have at least expressed interest in developing nuclear power, only 15 have economies larger than $50 billion and grids of more than 10 GW in size (Table 10.4).[10] These criteria are not part of the modelling approach adopted in the *World Energy Outlook* (*WEO*), but they may provide a rough indication of which countries may be the strongest candidates to proceed with nuclear development. Financial and grid-related barriers can be mitigated, for example, by arrangements to share output from plants between countries, grid interconnections, or use of small modular reactors.

10

---

10. Based on a standard 1 GW nuclear reactor, good practice dictates that a minimum grid capacity of 10 GW is required before a nuclear reactor can be introduced, to avoid difficulties when it needs to be taken offline. The concept of assessing newcomers using such criteria is based on Goldemberg (2009).

Table 10.4 ▷ **Countries considering introduction of nuclear power**

	GDP < $50 billion and/or grid capacity < 10 GW	GDP > $50 billion and grid capacity > 10 GW
First reactor(s) under construction*	Belarus	UAE
Actively preparing or has expressed interest in starting a nuclear power programme	Albania, Azerbaijan, Bangladesh, Bolivia, Croatia, DR Congo, Ghana, Jordan, Kenya, Libya, Lithuania**, Mongolia, Morocco, Namibia, Niger, Nigeria, Peru, Senegal, Sri Lanka, Sudan, FYR Macedonia, Tunisia, Uganda, Uruguay	Algeria, Chile, Egypt, Indonesia, Kazakhstan, Nigeria, Malaysia, Philippines, Poland, Saudi Arabia, Thailand, Turkey, Venezuela, Vietnam
Total countries	24	15

* The start of construction is the date of the first major placing of concrete, usually for the base mat of the reactor building. Site work on a plant in Turkey (in Akkuyu) is ongoing but has not yet reached this key milestone. ** Lithuania previously had nuclear power, but closed its last unit in 2009 as a condition of joining the European Union.

Additional insights can be gleaned from reviewing the progress individual countries have made towards bringing their first reactors online. In 2012, the United Arab Emirates (UAE) became the first newcomer to start construction of a new plant in almost three decades (China was the last in 1985). The first of four reactors is scheduled to come online in 2017 and the UAE plans to generate up to 25% of its electricity from nuclear in 2020. In 2013 and 2014, first concrete was poured at two separate projects in Belarus. Construction of first nuclear plants is expected by Turkey in 2015-2016 and by Vietnam in 2017-2018.

Economics and financing

Economic considerations are a major determinant of whether a nuclear power plant is built, when it is run and its lifetime. Utilities that plan to build a power plant assess the lifetime costs of generating electricity by nuclear compared with alternative options, taking into account their specific portfolio of power generation capacity and relative risks (Table 10.5). Operators of existing nuclear power plants make decisions about whether a plant will continue to operate, and to what extent, on the basis of the ability to recover variable operating costs.

The commercial economics of nuclear power are influenced by many factors – including the level of investment required, the cost of financing, construction time, the capacity factor, fuel costs, non-fuel operation and maintenance (O&M) costs and decommissioning costs – some of which vary significantly according to the conditions in a particular region or market. Like other generation technologies, nuclear power is also associated with different types of external costs. For nuclear, these include damage not covered by utilities (because of their limited liability) in the event of a severe accident, a potential shortfall in funds for plant decommissioning and the long-term management of radioactive waste, government subsidies to support nuclear deployment and various forms of social or environmental costs. Set against these external costs are external benefits, namely avoided emissions of carbon dioxide (CO_2) and other air pollutants, and enhanced energy security (see Chapter 12).

Table 10.5 ▷ **Relative attributes of power generation technologies**

	Nuclear	Coal steam	Gas CCGT	Wind onshore and solar PV
Investment cost	Very high	Moderate	Low	Moderate-high
Construction time*	4-10 years	4-5 years	2-3 years	0.5-2 years
Operational cost	Low	Low-moderate	Low-high	Very low
Operational characteristics	Baseload, limited flexibility	Baseload, moderate flexibility	Mid-load, high flexibility	Variable output, low load factor
CO_2 emissions	Negligible	High-very high	Moderate	Negligible
Key risks	Regulatory (policy changes), public acceptance, market	Regulatory (CO_2 and pollution), public acceptance, market	Regulatory (CO_2), market	Regulatory (policy changes)

* Construction time is the time between the start of a reactor's construction and its connection to the grid.

The overall investment cost of a new nuclear power plant is generally higher than that of any other power generation technology, due to the high unit investment costs and the typical size of a nuclear plant, usually 1 000-1 500 MW (requiring investment in the range of $2-11 billion, depending on the region). Securing financing for such large-scale projects can be challenging in both regulated and competitive markets, but the greater uncertainty of revenues in competitive wholesale markets adds an additional hurdle to obtaining necessary financing. In some countries, government intervention in the markets (in particular support policies aimed at fostering the deployment of renewable technologies), exacerbate the difficulties faced by conventional power plants in recovering their investment and put in question their ability to raise financing for new plants (IEA, 2014).

Operating costs

For a nuclear plant, operating costs consist of the cost of fuel and non-fuel O&M. The costs of long-term radioactive waste disposal and plant decommissioning are often also considered to be operating costs, as in many countries designated funds to cover these expenses are set aside during plant operation (Figure 10.5). Once built, a nuclear plant is typically cheaper to run than coal- and gas-fired plants, which have higher fuel costs, but it is more expensive than wind and solar PV, which incur no fuel costs. Accordingly, nuclear plants usually generate electricity continuously, operating in a baseload mode: such a mode of operation is necessary for nuclear plants, like other plants with high investment costs and low fuel costs, in order to recover their large upfront expenditure.

Figure 10.5 ▷ **Costs in the lifecycle of a nuclear power plant**

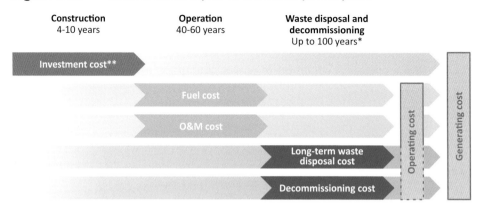

* Timeframe corresponds to the typical period over which a plant is decommissioned and high-level waste is removed from the plant site to a permanent disposal facility. ** The investment cost is comprised of the overnight cost of plant construction and the financing cost.

Notes: The timeframes for different stages in the lifecycle of a nuclear power plant vary by project and by region. A plant can also incur investment costs during its operation, e.g. for refurbishment. Spent nuclear fuel, if not reprocessed, is sent for long-term disposal after a plant is closed, though provision is typically made for this cost during plant operation. The costs of waste disposal and decommissioning may be accounted for in the operating cost.

Nuclear fuel costs – which include the cost of "front-end" activities such as uranium mining (40-50% of the total), conversion (5%), enrichment (25-35%) and fuel fabrication (15-25%)[11] – are lower and less volatile than the cost of fossil-fuel inputs to power generation. On an energy-equivalent basis, nuclear fuel costs ranged from $5-8/MWh in the period 2000-2012, compared with $16-47/MWh for coal inputs and $20-126/MWh for gas inputs.[12] Raw uranium accounts for a much lower share of fuel costs, compared to coal or gas, making nuclear fuel costs less susceptible to fluctuations in the price of the commodity. Enrichment costs are stable: only centrifuge technology is being used at present, capacity for which around the world is ample to meet demand. Enrichment services are typically provided on fixed-term contracts (5-15 years) to ensure recovery of the large amounts of capital that must be invested in the facilities. Non-fuel O&M costs include all other expenses necessary to operate a nuclear power plant. They consist mainly of spending on personnel, routine maintenance and logistics. Routine maintenance involves expenses related to plant upkeep and is distinct from capital investment for refurbishment.

When a plant closes, sufficient funds are needed to cover the costs of long-term disposal of high-level radioactive waste (HLW) and plant decommissioning. HLW, which is comprised of spent fuel and waste streams from reprocessing, must be safely isolated in permanent

---

11. Share of nuclear fuel costs are based on a "once-through" fuel cycle. Some countries pursue a "closed" fuel cycle, in which spent fuel is reprocessed and recycled. There are additional costs for these activities, though they are compensated by the gain in primary fuel supply (NEA, 2013).

12. Nuclear fuel costs over 2000-2012 are based on NEI (2014) and IEEJ (2013). Coal and gas fuel costs are based on the price of OECD steam coal imports and gas prices in major regions (Asia-Pacific, Europe and North America). They have been adjusted to take into account the average thermal efficiency of coal- and gas-fired power generation.

facilities while its radioactivity decreases to acceptable background levels (see Chapter 12). The main costs include the cost of transporting the HLW from the plant site, encapsulation of the waste, and construction and operation of the disposal facility. Funds for these activities are commonly accrued during the operation of a nuclear plant by raising a levy per unit of electricity generated. Alternatively, nuclear operators make lump payments in proportion to the volumes of HLW produced. Different approaches are taken to manage these funds, though in most countries the funds are separated and administered by a third-party (such as a government-designated waste management organisation).

Decommissioning is the final step in the life of any power plant, but is particularly important in the case of a nuclear plant given the need to safely manage radioactive materials. It includes all activities from shutdown and removal of fissile material to environmental restoration of the site. Costs depend on many factors, including the timing and sequencing of the various stages of the particular decommissioning programme chosen, the plant location, the arrangements for nuclear waste storage and disposal, the level of decontamination required (i.e. greenfield or brownfield), legal requirements, any cost escalation and the discount rate assumed. This range of plant-specific cost drivers and the relatively limited experience in completing decommissioning projects for commercial reactors leave some uncertainty about the magnitude of expected nuclear plant decommissioning costs.[13] Most countries legally require utilities to make provisions for adequate funding of decommissioning activities, with regulatory authorities playing a major role in approving the mechanism to assure funding and the amount to be set aside (see section on facing up to public concerns). For a nuclear plant built today, the decommissioning cost is assumed in our analysis to be around 15% of the investment cost for the plant (in real terms). When funds are collected during the operation of a nuclear plant, these costs amount to a small percentage of electricity rates.

Economics of existing capacity

Capital investment in refurbishments

Where policy allows and the economics are favourable, the owner of a nuclear power plant may consider additional capital investment in refurbishment to extend a plant's lifetime or to increase its power output through uprates.[14] Nearly all components of a nuclear plant are replaceable, with the two notable exceptions being the reactor pressure vessel and the

---

13. Decommissioning projects in the United States that were begun in the 1990s estimated costs at around $550-700 million per reactor (in year-2013 dollars). US utilities that have shut down reactors in 2013 expect higher costs, ranging from $0.9-2.2 billion per unit (US NRC, 2013 and 2014b). German utilities estimate individual projects may cost up to $1-1.3 billion (Nicola and Johnson, 2013).

14. An investment to maintain or improve operating performance may also serve to extend the lifetime of the plant. Steam generators, for example, typically have a design lifetime of 30 years. Reactors with a 40-year operating licence often have to replace steam generators to continue operation of the plant through the full licence period, involving expenditure of several hundred million dollars per generator. However, new steam generators may also be required if the operating licence of the plant is to be extended, thus providing an equally important reason for the replacement of the old components.

containment building. Factors that affect the decision by a utility to invest in refurbishment of a nuclear plant are similar to those for other types of investment. The principal concerns are whether future conditions – given market, regulatory and political risks – will allow for recovery of the investment, plus a sufficient return, and whether making such an investment is more economic than building a new plant (of any type) or none at all. In a market in which prices are regulated, the utility has some assurance of the return on their investment as the risks facing it are reduced considerably. In a competitive market, utilities bear a higher level of risk, which causes them to seek a higher return on their investment.

Provided that enabling conditions are in place, the economic case for lifetime extensions at existing nuclear plants can be very strong. For a typical plant to fully recover the cost of a $1 000 per kilowatt (kW) refurbishment, for example, it would need to receive an additional $15/MWh (after covering its operating costs) over a 20-year period. In some markets, however, utilities may judge that the prospective return on such an investment is not worth the risk. In the United States, decisions have recently been made to close several nuclear plants, rather than undertake refurbishments and extend their lifetimes. The policy outlook is also very important in the context of lifetime extension: a national decision to phase out nuclear power, if implemented over a short time horizon, might impose much shorter plant lifetimes than expected.

Economics of new builds

Key drivers

Building a nuclear power plant is a very capital-intensive undertaking involving a large upfront investment cost – by far the largest expense associated with a new nuclear plant over its economic lifetime. It is commonly thought of as comprising an overnight cost[15] of construction, plus the cost of financing. Today, the overnight cost for new nuclear plants varies widely, from around $2 000/kW for the most recently completed Generation II reactors in China to an estimated $6 500-7 000/kW for "first-of-a-kind" Generation III designs in Europe that are still under construction.[16] Several factors, particular to projects in each region and market, explain the diversity in these costs:

- **Reactor model and location.** First-of-a-kind designs, which have had no opportunity to benefit from learning, can take much longer to build and involve much higher costs than designs which are more mature. Advanced reactor models are generally more expensive than their predecessors, due to the inclusion of additional features (mainly to improve safety) and greater technical complexity. The location of a plant can also have a significant impact on costs: the choice of a greenfield site or brownfield development, seismic risk, land value, distance to a cooling source and topography.

---

15. The overnight cost is the cost that would be incurred if a plant could be built "overnight", so it excludes any financing costs.

16. The figure for overnight costs in China is approximate, but is based on reported costs to build units at Hongyanhe, Ningde and Yangjiang. Overnight costs in Europe are public estimates for the reactors being built at Olkiluoto in Finland and Flamanville in France.

- **Standardisation and industrial organisation.** Standardisation around a more limited number of technologies and designs allows for greater familiarity with those models among regulators, builders, buyers and operators. This helps to facilitate licensing, accelerate learning, and reduce construction time. The level of industrial experience in manufacturing nuclear components and managing large infrastructure projects affects risks in the construction phase of a nuclear power plant.

- **The regulatory regime.** Safety requirements influence the number and type of safety-related features at a plant (e.g. system redundancy, containment and control room isolation), which have direct implications for costs. Another major determinant of costs is the way in which the regulatory regime is structured, understood and applied. Requirements that are unclear or regulatory changes that are sudden or frequent generally lead to delays and higher costs.

The contrast between the experiences with new builds of the United States and France in the 1970s and 1980s is illustrative. In the United States, there were several reactor models developed, a diverse group of technology suppliers and many plant owners. While the tightening of regulatory standards improved safety, sudden changes interrupted construction and caused long delays. The result was soaring overnight costs for construction. In France, there was a preference for fewer models, one technology supplier and one plant owner. Safety requirements similarly increased, but the new regulations did not slow ongoing construction to the same degree. Costs in France were largely contained (Figure 10.6). How overnight costs for new nuclear builds will evolve in those countries and elsewhere depends on the extent to which construction can be repeated ("number-of-a-kind") by experienced entities, within a clear and consistent and regulatory framework, utilising standardised practices and equipment supplied along well-developed industrial pipelines. Such conditions exist to some extent today in China, Korea and Russia.

Figure 10.6 ▷ **Historical overnight cost of construction for nuclear power plants in France and the United States**

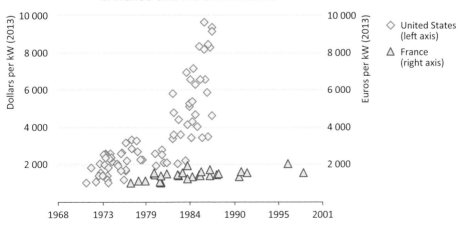

Note: Overnight costs are shown for the year in which plants came online.

Sources: Cour des Comptes (2012), US CBO (2008) and US DOE/EIA (1986).

The cost of financing accounts for a significant share of the investment cost of building a nuclear plant. Investors and lenders determine their willingness to provide capital and on what terms (the cost of capital) based on the risks a project might face, the likelihood that those risks will materialise and the expected consequences if they do. Nuclear power arguably faces higher hurdles to financing than other technologies in some regions because of numerous market, regulatory and political risks: these have in the past led to delays in construction, project abandonment, cost overruns or early plant closure (see later section on financing issues). The cost of capital tends to be lower in countries where plants are built by or with the strong support of public entities and therefore can draw on lower cost government-backed finance.

Countries with well-developed nuclear programmes can expect total lead times (including the planning, licensing and construction phases) on the order of 10-15 years, whereas newcomers might take longer to develop the necessary capacities. Depending on the region, construction times alone range from 4-10 years and sometimes longer if a project experiences delays (as is often the case with first-of-a-kind reactors). Longer construction times affect the economics of nuclear power by delaying the receipt of revenues and result in the accrual of larger interest payments. The capacity factor of a nuclear plant is also important for evaluating the attractiveness of nuclear power. Because investment costs are high, the revenue flow – and hence, reactor operations – should be interrupted as little as possible, the reactor ideally generating at near full capacity year round. Capacity factors have increased substantially in most regions in the last decades, helping to reduce average annual costs (or to maximise revenues) (Box 10.1) (Figure 10.7).

Figure 10.7 ▷ **Historical construction times and capacity factors for nuclear power plants by selected region**

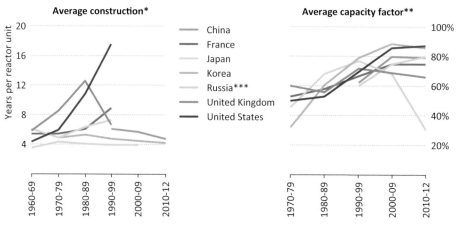

* Construction time is taken as the time between the start of a reactor's construction and its connection to the grid. Data in the figure correspond to the year in which each reactor was connected to the grid. **Average capacity factors are for all plants that were operational in each region shown. *** Data on construction time is not shown for 2000-2013 because projects coming online during that time had been suspended for very long periods following the collapse of the Soviet Union. Sources: IAEA PRIS; IEA databases and analysis.

Electricity generating costs

The levelised cost of electricity generation (referred to hereafter as "generating costs") is a useful – albeit imperfect – indicator of the lifetime economics of a new power plant, including all costs that will be incurred by the plant over its economic lifetime (the period in which the return on investment is sought). This indicator is often used to compare different technologies and measure the competitiveness of one power plant against another. However, competitiveness is better assessed based on the profitability of a power plant, which must include consideration of expected revenues. To be profitable, the average electricity price received by the operator over the power plant's economic lifetime must be greater than its generating costs. If this is not the case, it means that the investment cost will not be fully recovered at the interest rate and desired profit margin over the period.

Comparing generating costs to assess the relative competitiveness of technologies requires considerable care. A broad comparison is worthwhile only where the value of the electricity produced (or the average price received by the generator) is comparable among them. For example, power plants that operate for only a few hours per year (peak-load plants) typically have higher generating costs than baseload plants, limiting their usefulness for comparison. Similarly, comparison of the generating costs of baseload plants with those of renewable energy technologies – in particular, variable sources such as wind and solar PV – produces a misleading result, as they are unlikely to receive similar average annual revenues per unit of generation (even if they were to compete directly in the market).

Nuclear generating costs vary considerably across regions. They are most sensitive to changes in the cost of capital and in the overnight cost of construction. Relative to a "base case" nuclear plant[17] that has generating costs of $90/MWh, varying the cost of capital by plus or minus three percentage points changes generating costs by between -25% and +30%. If the overnight construction cost is $1 000/kW higher or lower than in the base case, generating costs change by between -15% and +15% (Figure 10.8). Such changes are certainly large enough to alter investment decisions, especially in competitive electricity markets. Changes in construction time, fuel cost and capacity factor have lesser but important effects. By contrast, changes to other parameters are much less important: for example, an increase in the decommissioning cost of a nuclear power plant from 15% to 25% of the investment cost, increases generating costs by just 1%.

A decision to build a new nuclear power plant depends on several factors (and the outlook for those factors), including the power mix, the market and regulatory framework, and the economics relative to competing alternatives, namely coal-fired and CCGTs. Generating costs from these sources are, in turn, strongly influenced by fuel prices and the stringency of any CO_2 pricing regime. Fuel prices, like many of the variables used in generating cost calculations, can change over time and across regions, making comparisons of generating costs difficult.

10

---

17. The assumptions for the base case are those shown in Figure 10.8: overnight cost of $4 200/kW; weighted average cost of capital of 7%; construction period of seven years; capacity factor of 85%; fuel cost of $10/MWh; economic lifetime of 35 years and decommissioning costs equal to 15% of the investment cost.

Figure 10.8 ▷ Sensitivity of nuclear generating costs to changes in parameters

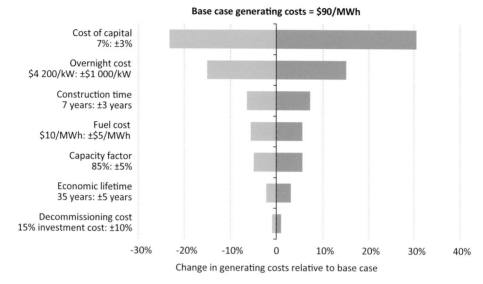

Base case generating costs = $90/MWh

Note: The non-fuel O&M cost is assumed to be $170/kW.

In countries with abundant fossil fuels at relatively cheap prices, new nuclear plants struggle to compete with new coal- or gas-fired plants. In the case of the United States, coal- and gas-fired plants remain more competitive than nuclear power, even at relatively high fuel costs (and assuming a $30/tonne shadow price for CO_2) (Figure 10.9a). Nuclear may be attractive in areas where cheaper fossil fuels are unavailable, or in parts of the country where electricity prices are regulated. Nuclear is more competitive relative to new coal plants equipped with carbon capture and storage (CCS) (which still needs to be demonstrated commercially), a technology which new coal plants will increasingly have to incorporate based on proposed US environmental regulations that aim to cut power sector CO_2 emissions. In general, higher carbon prices would be needed to make nuclear more competitive with coal-fired plants, though nuclear generating costs would still be considerably higher than those of CCGT plants (Figure 10.9b).

In regions where fossil-fuel prices are higher, as in the European Union, nuclear generating costs are more attractive. The competitiveness of nuclear in the European Union is further enhanced by higher CO_2 prices, provided that the cost reductions expected for later units of today's first-of-a-kind reactors currently under construction can be achieved. CCS-equipped coal-fired plants, in addition to being demonstrated commercially, would need to achieve significant cost reductions to approach competitiveness with nuclear. In China, nuclear and coal-fired plants have similar generating costs, while a higher level of gas prices limits the competitiveness of CCGT plants. A higher level of CO_2 prices would enhance the competitiveness of nuclear, particularly with respect to coal-fired plants.

Figure 10.9 ▷ Generating costs for selected new power plants under different fuel price and CO_2 price assumptions

(a) Sensitivity to fuel price assumptions

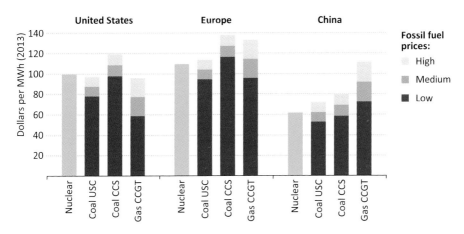

(b) Sensitivity to CO_2 price assumptions

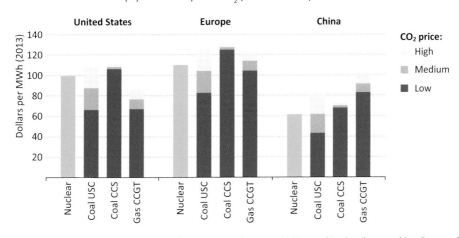

Notes: USC = ultra- supercritical, CCS = carbon capture and storage; CCGT = combined-cycle gas turbine. Data used for the generating cost calculations are shown in Table 10.6. The assumed values are roughly in line with the assumptions for plants coming online in 2030 in the New Policies Scenario. Figure 10.9a assumes CO_2 prices in each region corresponding to "medium" values in Table 10.6. Figure 10.9b assumes fuel prices in each region corresponding to "medium" values in Table 10.6. Comparing generating costs for different technologies is worthwhile only where the value of the electricity produced (or the average price received by the generator) is comparable among them. Comparing generating costs of baseload with those of renewable energy technologies such as wind and solar PV produces a misleading result since they are unlikely to receive similar average annual revenues per unit of generation.

Table 10.6 ▷ Assumptions used to calculate generating costs in Figure 10.9

		Nuclear	Coal USC	Coal CCS	Gas CCGT
United States	**Investment cost ($/kW)**	4 800	2 300	4 000	1 000
	Non-fuel O&M cost ($/kW)	200	69	160	25
	Capacity factor (%)	92	75	80	60
	WACC (%)	8	8	8	8
	Thermal efficiency* (%)	33	48	40	62
	Fuel costs (various)** High	10	90	90	10
	Medium	10	60	60	7
	Low	10	30	30	4
	CO₂ prices ($/tonne)	High = 60, Medium = 30, Low = 0			
Europe	**Investment cost ($/kW)**	5 100	2 200	4 000	1 000
	Non-fuel O&M cost ($/kW)	165	66	160	25
	Capacity factor (%)	85	75	80	50
	WACC (%)	8	8	8	8
	Thermal efficiency* (%)	33	48	40	62
	Fuel costs (various)** High	10	140	140	15
	Medium	10	110	110	12
	Low	10	80	80	9
	CO₂ prices ($/tonne)	High = 65, Medium = 35, Low = 5			
China	**Investment cost ($/kW)**	2 750	800	1 700	550
	Non-fuel O&M cost ($/kW)	120	32	85	18
	Capacity factor (%)	85	75	80	60
	WACC (%)	7	7	7	7
	Thermal efficiency* (%)	33	47	39	60
	Fuel costs (various)** High	10	120	120	14
	Medium	10	90	90	11
	Low	10	60	60	8
	CO₂ prices ($/tonne)	High = 50, Medium = 25, Low = 0			

* Gross, lower heating value. ** Nuclear in $/MWh, coal in $/tonne, gas in $/MBtu.

Notes: USC = ultra-supercritical; CCS = carbon capture and storage; CCGT = combined-cycle gas turbine, WACC = weighted average cost of capital. Investment costs are overnight costs. For coal and nuclear, capacity factors are estimated averages for baseload operation, with mid-load operation for gas CCGT. The assumed values are roughly in line with the assumptions for plants coming online in 2030 in the *WEO-2014* New Policies Scenario.

Financing

Financing a new nuclear plant can be a significant hurdle given the very large amount of capital required and the significant risks to realising an adequate return on the investment. In the construction phase, when capital is committed but a plant has not yet begun to generate revenues, these risks stem principally from the long construction time and the prospect of delays, especially for first-of-a-kind reactors. Advancing through necessary regulatory processes is a potential source of delay prior to reactor operation, particularly in the case of projects that incorporate new technology and require extra scrutiny. Once plant operations have commenced, expected wholesale electricity prices and revenues represent another set of risks (albeit ones that commonly apply to other technologies). In competitive markets, the price of electricity is not set in advance and there are no guarantees that the long-term revenues to a plant will be sufficient to provide the required return on the investment. Policy uncertainties add a further dimension of risk, namely the outlook for electricity markets to capture the value of energy security and of the low-carbon attributes of power generation as well as the potential for the policy environment to oppose nuclear and force plants to close early.

Different approaches have been taken to share or offset the financial risks involved in building new nuclear plants. Some projects include multiple owners, organised as a consortium, who divide the output from a plant while diluting risks that would be too onerous to bear for a smaller number of companies. The Olkiluoto project in Finland, for example, is backed by several industrial firms which seek stable electricity prices (the so-called "Mankala" model). Two ongoing projects in the United States are each owned by multiple utilities that will sell the electricity to their customers. Other consortia have been considered that would include the vendors constructing the plant so as to ensure that all participants in a project share risk and have a stake in its success. Government guarantees to lenders has been another way to address financial risks faced by new nuclear builds in competitive markets (amounting to a transfer of risk). The scale of investment for a nuclear project can be too large for small utilities without some form of support to diminish the risks they face. The United States, for example, has created a federal loan guarantee fund ($18.5 billion) available to new nuclear builds, which transfers the risk of default to the government. Export credit agencies also fulfil this role, in some cases, by providing financing for nuclear projects built in other countries.

Many tools can remove uncertainty in prices and revenues once a plant is operational. The traditional approach in regulated markets has been to authorise the utility to pass along costs to electricity consumers, as long as expenditures are deemed prudent. In competitive markets, other arrangements are possible. Governments or firms can agree from the outset to purchase the electricity at an agreed price (a long-term power purchase agreement). A variant of this approach in the United Kingdom will provide a long-term price guarantee through a "contract-for-difference" that will supplement the market price if it falls below an agreed level, while requiring the utility to repay any revenue received above the agreement. This model caps the total revenue that the plant will generate while providing an incentive to contain costs (see the section on policy framework).

Box 10.4 ▷ **Ownership of nuclear power generation assets**

The ownership structure of power generation assets can have a major impact not only on the cost of financing but also on the ability to raise the necessary capital for the large-scale investments involved. Worldwide the nuclear power plant fleet is primarily owned by governments. They hold 55% of the global installed capacity; but this share is only a slightly higher percentage than that of fossil-fuelled plants and large hydropower, where state ownership is just below 50%. The regional distribution of nuclear plant ownership is significant: in non-OECD countries, virtually all nuclear plants are held by governments, while in OECD countries, state ownership is around 45% (Figure 10.10). Nuclear plants in the United States are typically owned by publicly listed companies, which are privately owned; the same is true, though to a lesser degree, for nuclear plants in Japan and Europe. Due to the large size and high capital cost of nuclear plants, however, ownership by smaller private players is rare.

The current ownership situation of nuclear power in OECD countries reflects the market liberalisation process that has taken place in many OECD countries since the mid-1990s. In this process, many formerly state-owned utilities were privatised, while power markets were re-organised to give greater play to competitive market forces. This has changed not only the ownership structure but also the economics and risk profile of nuclear investments, contributing to a marked slowdown in the number of nuclear projects coming to fruition. Most nuclear power plants in the OECD were built by state-backed companies or under regulated market conditions in the 1970s and 1980s.

Figure 10.10 ▷ **Ownership of nuclear power generation assets, 2012**

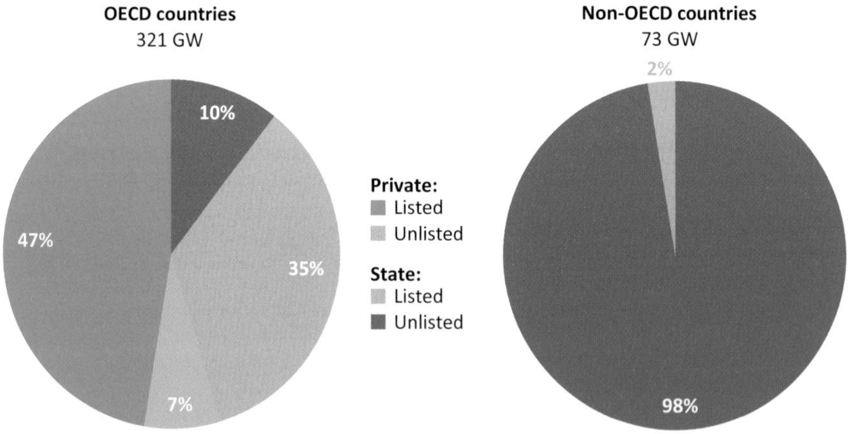

OECD countries
321 GW

Non-OECD countries
73 GW

Private:
■ Listed
■ Unlisted

State:
■ Listed
■ Unlisted

Privately owned companies face several major risks when investing in nuclear power in competitive markets: the risk of strategic changes to energy policy and regulation, e.g. nuclear phase-out decisions or preferential support for competing forms of power generation, and the normal commercial risk that electricity prices or load factors might be affected by changing market conditions. Today's difficulties in competitive markets often stem from government interventions in the market designed to redress perceived imperfections, such as the failure of markets to deal with the external costs attributable to environmental or social damage. But markets in which prices are set both by competition and by regulation are very uncertain sources of financial return to those investors whose plant does not enjoy preferential treatment. There are doubts whether such markets can provide the conditions required for investment in new nuclear power plants. Changes in market design are being considered, including mechanisms to reward generating capacity which contributes significantly to security of supply and to extend schemes that put a price on carbon emissions.

Developing countries have seen a rapid increase in new nuclear builds in the past decade. This has rested not only on direct state funding but also on state intervention in markets to guarantee the purchase of the output of nuclear plants or to reduce the risk stemming from the high capital cost and the long timescale of nuclear investments. Contrary to private companies striving for profit maximisation, state-owned companies are often required to pursue secondary targets not central to their commercial interests. State-owned investors may be able to secure loans below market interest rates to support these activities; but they may also be obliged to re-invest cash-flows in these objectives rather than making provision for future mainstream investment.

Facing public concerns

Public concerns exert a powerful influence on energy policy and particularly with respect to nuclear power. The March 2011 accident at Fukushima Daiichi in Japan is only the most recent example of how public perceptions of nuclear power and safety can quickly change. Moreover, it showed how they can profoundly impact the industry, having resulted in the early retirement of reactors, delays and cancellations of new builds and more stringent regulatory requirements. Countries already using nuclear power and those considering its introduction face serious issues surrounding public awareness and concern with respect to nuclear power-related activities at the local, regional and national level. Those countries closing down nuclear programmes also face challenges in this respect. This section identifies and discusses these public concerns. Chapter 12 highlights how they might be addressed, to ensure that public acceptance is given appropriate consideration as countries try to meet energy and climate change objectives.

In general, the public places nuclear power in a higher category of risk than other forms of electricity generation. It involves the use of hazardous radioactive materials and an accident at a nuclear installation or during the transport or storage of radioactive materials, though the likelihood is very low, can have far-reaching and long-lasting consequences for human health and the environment. Perceptions of nuclear power are also intrinsically connected with the military applications of nuclear technology and concerns over the proliferation of nuclear weapons.

Box 10.5 ▷ The accident at Fukushima Daiichi and lessons learned

In March 2011 a massive earthquake and a subsequent tsunami devastated the eastern region of Japan's main island, Honshu. These events disabled the power supply and the cooling systems for three of the six reactors at the Fukushima Daiichi nuclear power plant, resulting in severe damage to the reactor cores and the release of large amounts of radioactive material into the environment. Approximately 150 000 people within a 30-kilometre radius of the plant were evacuated. No radiation-related fatalities or acute diseases have been observed to date among the workers and general public exposed to radiation from the accident, and no discernable increased incidence of radiation-related health effects are expected among exposed members of the public or their descendants (UNSCEAR, 2014). Nonetheless, a significant part of the evacuated area remains off limits and the toll on the mental and social well-being of residents has been heavy.

Following the accident, all of Japan's reactors progressively went offline. The Japanese government ordered nuclear safety reassessments of all of the country's reactors and authorised two independent committees to investigate the causes. One, reporting to the National Diet, found that the accident was "man-made" and foreseeable, and that the plant could not withstand the earthquake and the tsunami (National Diet, 2012). Another, reporting to the Cabinet, confirmed that the loss of vital functions at the plant was not caused by the earthquake but by the power outage that resulted from the tsunami (Cabinet of Japan, 2012). Safety requirements set by the Nuclear and Industrial Safety Agency (NISA), the regulator, were found to be inadequate and grave questions were raised about the agency's independence. TEPCO, the plant operator, was found to have failed to assess the likelihood of a foreseeable accident and make preparations to contain collateral damage.

The direct costs related to the accident – including decontamination work, the storage of contaminated material, decommissioning, compensation to victims, healthcare and reconstruction – have been estimated to be $110 billion (Cabinet of Japan, 2012). The decision to idle or close reactors necessitated increased thermal power generation, which led to very high costs for fossil-fuel imports (contributing to a record high trade deficit) and higher CO_2 emissions. Moreover, major challenges remain with respect to managing the resultant radioactive waste – the material already stored on-site as well as the large volume of contaminated water, soil and damaged fuel and fuel debris – and preventing the release of contaminated water.

Japan has dissolved the NISA and established a new regulator with independent authority (the Nuclear Regulation Authority). Tougher safety standards, based on international best practice, have been adopted. Internationally, the accident prompted wide efforts to re-evaluate and strengthen nuclear safety and emergency preparedness, particularly in the context of major external events. Safety inspections or "stress tests" were carried out at existing reactors in many countries and certain types of reactors were ordered to make safety modifications.

While there was a high degree of public confidence in nuclear power technology during the early stages of its development, this was gravely shaken by the accidents at Three Mile Island in 1979 and Chernobyl in 1986. These events led to demands for greater public accountability and raised questions about the industry's ability to manage the complex technology safely over an extended period. From the early 2000s, public concern waned in most places and interest in nuclear power by governments, industry and investors increased. The sector began to grow again, especially beyond OECD countries, before the accident at Fukushima Daiichi in 2011 prompted a significant re-evaluation of nuclear power programmes worldwide (Box 10.3).

Public concerns surrounding nuclear power have been expressed most forcefully in OECD countries, but they are of increasing significance elsewhere too. In India, for example, earlier debate about nuclear power plants focused on the displacement of communities; but these concerns have been supplemented by more widespread concerns about plant safety and the risks of nuclear technology. Recent protests over the siting of nuclear facilities in China's interior regions point to increasing public concerns in that country.[18]

Issues across the lifecycle of nuclear power

The lifecycle of nuclear power comprises three main stages: the "front-end" of the nuclear fuel cycle, from uranium mining to the delivery of fuel assemblies to the reactor; the construction and operation of the reactor; and power plant decommissioning and the "back-end" of the nuclear fuel cycle, including the storage and disposal of nuclear waste. Each stage raises important, if somewhat different, public concerns (Table 10.7).

10

Front-end of the nuclear fuel cycle

The concerns relating to the front-end of the nuclear fuel cycle are similar to those for conventional mining and resource extraction, though the radioactive nature of uranium and its use in military applications mean that some are unique to uranium mining. Economic, environmental and social issues (benefits, as well as risks) arise, ranging from the impact on the national and local economy, to water quality affects and the health and safety of workers and the public. Public acceptance has been particularly influenced by lax regulatory oversight over uranium mining worldwide during the Cold War period, often resulting in poorly managed or abandoned pits and tailings dams. Considerable advances in managing the health, safety and environmental risks of uranium mining have been made in recent years, including in tailings management, and financial measures have been taken, including setting aside funds to manage site remediation on completion of mining. Leading operators, mostly in OECD countries, have demonstrated the value of public participation as an integral part of the planning and approval processes for uranium mining, and have endorsed the principle of transparency throughout the project lifecycle, for example by independent monitoring (NEA, 2014).

18. In 2013, protests in Heshan Guangdong forced local authorities to abandon plans for a uranium processing facility.

There are, nevertheless, important concerns regarding the environmental and social impacts of uranium extraction. For example, producers in Canada, the United States and Australia are confronted by issues over access to indigenous peoples' lands. Fear of nuclear weapons proliferation is another persistent concern. Developing countries that are rich in uranium resources – in particular those in Africa – are permitting increased mining activity, even though many governments do not have the experience or trained workforce to regulate this activity effectively. Even where basic environmental and health regulations are in place, their application and enforcement are often inadequate: responsibility for addressing and implementing best practice rests principally with the operator (Dasnois, 2012). The IAEA, in conjunction with partner countries such as Finland, is assisting African countries (Tanzania, for example) to establish strong regulatory frameworks.

Ensuring appropriate management of the environmental and social issues associated with uranium mining is vital if nuclear power is to remain an important part of the global energy mix. Failure to do so will almost certainly give rise to local grievances, resulting in increased social conflict and greater public opposition. As experience from around the world shows, adverse public opinion, once aroused, is difficult to appease and public opposition can delay infrastructure projects, lead to increased costs and result in project abandonment. Any large-scale increase in the use of nuclear power globally, such as that envisaged in our New Policies Scenario (see Chapter 11), with the concomitant increase in uranium mining, will exacerbate these issues.

Construction and operation of nuclear plants

Public concerns during the construction and operation of a nuclear power plant include siting issues, the day-to-day operational safety of reactors, the risk of severe accidents and hazards associated with transporting radioactive materials. These are set against broader public concerns about energy security and climate change, issues which tend to increase support for nuclear power. Nevertheless, it is usually the more local environmental, political and socio-economic issues that dominate debate about new nuclear plants.

Site-specific environmental issues raised by the construction and operation of nuclear plants include water resource impacts, increased traffic, spatial and landscape effects, radioactive contamination in the event of an accident, and on-site storage of radioactive waste. They also encompass impacts on socially valued aspects of the physical environment and on the social structure itself. For example, there may be concerns about sudden, temporary population growth during construction, which might strain the financial, organisational and cultural resources of a host community and create a degree of dependence on the facility. Construction of nuclear plants can also result in resettlement, which is a particular concern in densely populated regions, such as in India. On the other hand, nuclear plants attract highly qualified and well-paid staff, whose presence can have a positive socio-economic impact locally and can increase the local tax base and provide local economic stimuli – points which are true for any large new power plant.

During the design, siting, permitting and construction of nuclear plants, there are numerous points of public concern. During the permitting stage, there is an initial opportunity, and a need, for public involvement in decision-making. In most OECD countries and in a growing number of non-OECD countries, the environmental impact assessment process and requirements for public access to information define the minimum required extent of public involvement. Because of the importance of siting issues, some licensing systems require a prior government decision on siting, which can help to address public concerns prior to permitting. Many countries, such as the United States, France and the United Kingdom, site new plants in areas where the population density does not exceed a specific threshold, and where population growth can be monitored and controlled (e.g. through land-use planning). In addition, most governments give preference to locating new builds on existing plant sites, which greatly facilitates the permitting process.

Table 10.7 ▷ **Key public considerations for nuclear power**

	Potential concerns	Potential benefits
General	• Competence and independence of regulatory regime • Proliferation of nuclear weapons • Long-term disposition of high-level radioactive waste • Adequacy and availability of funds for waste disposal, plant decommissioning	• Reduction of CO_2 emissions and other air pollutants • Boost energy self-sufficiency • Increase balance of payments
Local/regional	• Radioactive contamination • Public/worker health and safety • Environmental impact and site restoration • Restricted land use or loss of land • Visual amenity and noise • Decreased property value • Increased traffic • Impact on local communities, in some places indigenous	• Employment opportunities • Income growth • Public infrastructure availability (roads, lighting, power, health and education) • Increased tax revenue • Economic stimulus

However, public concerns arise during all project phases and can touch on the national energy policy context, operational safety issues, trust in the regulator and the regulatory system and many other country-specific political, economic and environmental issues. As existing nuclear plants age and, in some cases, lifetime extensions are sought, public concerns can come forward once more. It can be difficult to predict when and where public opposition to nuclear plants will arise. Even in areas characterised by high levels of local public acceptance, for example, facilities can attract opposition from outside a region.

Builders and operators of nuclear plants must pay continuing attention to good public communication throughout a project. Meaningful stakeholder engagement and communication by both government and the industry at large are particularly important in the process of building public confidence, as is the degree of transparency surrounding policy decision-making. Countries such as France with good engagement policies and a good operational safety record generally have relatively high popular acceptance of nuclear power. However, public concerns can and do persist. A recent EU-based opinion poll showed that, while the public accepts the value of nuclear power in many respects, particularly as a means of decreasing energy import dependence, a majority believes that the risks outweigh the benefits, and that while use of existing reactors should continue, new builds are unwelcome (Foratom, 2012). Within such polls, there is a high diversity of opinion, between and within countries, and across gender and age groups.

Back-end of the nuclear fuel cycle and plant decommissioning

The storage and disposal of radioactive waste generated at the back-end of the nuclear fuel cycle has long been a focal point of public concern with respect to nuclear power. High-level waste (HLW), which includes spent nuclear fuel and waste streams from reprocessing, accounts for nearly all of the radiotoxicity of waste produced (and significant heat output) and remains more radioactive than its surroundings for thousands of years.[19] It therefore must be handled with extreme care. HLW is stored initially at reactor sites, however, it eventually must be moved to permanent disposal facilities for long-term isolation. Key issues at the back-end of the nuclear fuel cycle include the handling of the radiological hazards of the material in temporary storage or at a permanent disposal facility as well as the risk of groundwater contamination. Additionally, the establishment of permanent waste disposal facilities often leads to land-use restrictions, with related social and economic impacts, though there can also be benefits in terms of employment and income.

Successive opinion polls identify radioactive waste disposal as one of the key factors determining public attitudes to nuclear power. Surveys also show that if this issue were satisfactorily resolved, support for nuclear power would increase substantially (MIT, 2011; NEA, 2010). Surveys also indicate that, while people tend to be worried about nuclear waste, they are not well informed about its management. The expert technical and policy communities generally view deep geologic repositories as a viable solution to safely isolate HLW over the long time periods required (IAEA, 1995; NEA, 2003). Finding suitable sites, however, can be a lengthy process. In the United States, work on the partially developed Yucca Mountain repository, which began some 30 years ago, funded by a levy on nuclear power sales, has been suspended while protracted legal challenges from stakeholders continue. Finland, France and Sweden have selected sites for such facilities, which are planned to be in operation around 2020-2025. However, no country currently has an operational permanent disposal facility for commercial HLW.

The general public perceives nuclear waste disposal as highly risky (NEA, 2010) and hosting disposal sites, like those of nuclear plants themselves, can be subject to economic stigma. New industries may be particularly reluctant to set up near nuclear waste facilities for fear that their products will suffer negative nuclear stereotyping. In the United States, pre-emptive concerns about the effect on the tourist and cattle industries were expressed in the states of Nevada and Texas when sites in these states were proposed for repositories.

---

19. HLW represents only some 2-3% of the total volume of radioactive waste produced in the nuclear fuel cycle, with the balance being lower level waste that is much less hazardous to human health and considerably easier to handle.

Local opposition to the siting of such facilities is unsurprising, as the commitment involved is very long term. Considerations of inter-generational equity arise, since today's decisions regarding nuclear technology impose a burden on future generations. One reason for choosing deep geological waste repositories, as embodied in France's policy, for example, is that such repositories can be designed to enable the retrieval of waste at some point in the future, thus preserving options for future generations. It is worth noting that, despite the perceived risks of hosting HLW facilities, in Finland and Sweden there is strong support at community level for hosting such a repository. Fundamentally a local or regional issue (although transport of waste to a central facility also needs to be carefully managed), the problem of permanent disposal of HLW will persist. Nuclear waste exists, whether in countries with continuing nuclear power programmes or those which have opted to abandon the technology, and that waste needs to be safely treated and stored.

The decommissioning of nuclear power plants has not become a major public issue: there is acceptance that plants must be safely closed at the end of their lifetime. However, with the number of reactors that will need to be decommissioned set to increase substantially in the coming years, two public acceptance issues need careful attention. The first is the large volume of mostly low-level radioactive waste that must be managed during decommissioning, though, as noted, it is far less hazardous to human health and the environment than high-level waste. The second is the adequacy of funds to cover the costs of decommissioning and assurance that they will be available. In most countries, plant owners are responsible for developing a decommissioning strategy, estimating costs (with minimum amounts sometimes prescribed by law) and establishing a funding mechanism prior to beginning operations. Safety regulators must review and approve the approach, and owners are often required to submit periodic updates on the cost estimate and the status of funds during plant operation. Provisions assuring the availability of funds are typically set out by regulation. The most common method is for plant owners to create an external trust that accumulates funds through contributions made during the operating lifetime of a plant. Other approaches include prepayment of decommissioning costs, whereby a deposit is made into a dedicated account before the start of plant operation, or a guarantee from the parent company. Access to funds is typically restricted until the regulator authorises disbursement for decommissioning expenses.

Risk, perception and public opinion

Opinion polls consistently show that the public perceives nuclear power as riskier than alternatives such as renewables or fossil fuels, though as noted earlier, there is a wide variation of views within and among countries, and among various groups. While the nuclear industry may have a cumulative environmental and safety record in operating power plants that is comparable to other energy sources, the essential difference is that risks extend to the public at large, whereas for other energy sources risks are more limited in scope. Nuclear power's negative image is partly a legacy of the 1970s and 1980s, when there was a lack of transparency in decision-making and a top-down approach to stakeholder engagement and public communication. It is also a reflection of the three major accidents in the industry over 40 years.

In most countries there is a consistent divergence between the public perception of the risks associated with nuclear power, and how such risks are perceived by those working in the sector itself. Within the industry, risks are often assessed using probabilistic methodologies, which measure risk as a product of the likelihood of an adverse occurrence multiplied by the consequence of that occurrence. Public perception of nuclear risk, on the other hand, tends to focus more on the worst cases and may be characterised by a lack of confidence in the capability of the industry or its regulators to control the technology.

The level of risk perception and the degree of trust in the regulatory system and the institutions responsible for it are, to some extent, linked. Where the public perceives regulators and actors involved in nuclear power to be strong, independent, effective and trustworthy, risk perception can be lower. Conversely, where public trust has been compromised, either by regulatory failure, a poor industrial track record or an accident, the public can, with reason, perceive nuclear power to be more dangerous. Providing quality information on the risks and benefits associated with nuclear power in a transparent, understandable and unbiased manner to the public is an important means to improve public acceptance of nuclear power. At the same time, the impact of such information on the public perception of risk should not be overstated, as views on nuclear power tend to be robust once adopted and are not easily altered.

Meaningful stakeholder consultation and engagement is essential to public acceptance of nuclear power. There has been a shift in the past 20 years away from the traditional "decide, announce and defend" model towards more open and participatory models of decision-making. Today, the trend in OECD countries and, increasingly, in non-OECD countries, is to focus on consultation, effective dialogue, collaboration and partnership between institutions and affected communities, though how far this extends into public participation in decision-making varies greatly across countries. As in the energy sector more generally, carrying out consultation from the earliest stages of planning a nuclear project and throughout its lifecycle is recognised as best practice. Experience from energy and infrastructure projects around the world demonstrates that early, frequent and ongoing engagement with all key stakeholders, and transparency in relation to project-related information and developments, is critical to keeping projects on schedule and minimising the risk of social conflict. Conversely, failure in these respects considerably increases the risk of local opposition and delays.

Notwithstanding the lessons learned in stakeholder engagement, challenges concerning public trust in the nuclear industry persist. There is often still an implicit assumption by project proponents that when the public is better educated about the benefits versus the relative risks of nuclear energy, its advantages as a secure, low-carbon source of electricity should be sufficient to ensure public acceptance. Difficulties also arise when the general public, through participation in an engagement process, come to believe they will decisively influence the final choice. This experience is, in some countries, shared with other large infrastructure projects and can lead to delays in project development. It is part of the responsibility of governments to specify the scope of stakeholder consultation processes to ensure that citizens have their say and that these processes lead to concrete outcomes.

Chapter 11

Prospects for nuclear power to 2040
Retreat, recovery or renaissance?

Highlights

- Nuclear power capacity increases by almost 60% in the New Policies Scenario, from 392 GW in 2013 to 624 GW in 2040. The share of nuclear power in global electricity generation rises by just one percentage point to 12%. The number of economies operating reactors rises from 31 to 36 as newcomers outnumber those that abandon nuclear power. Investment in nuclear capacity over the period to 2040 amounts to $1.5 trillion.

- Nuclear fares best in markets where electricity is supplied at regulated prices, utilities have state backing or where governments act to facilitate private investment. Given the scale of expansion in China, developments there will have implications for the industry globally. Of the growth in nuclear generation to 2040, China accounts for 46% while India, Korea and Russia collectively make up a further 30%. Nuclear generation increases by 16% in the United States, rebounds in Japan (although not to the levels just before the accident at Fukushima Daiichi) and falls by 10% in the European Union.

- A wave of retirements of ageing nuclear reactors is approaching: almost 200 of the 434 reactors operating at the end of 2013 are retired in the period to 2040, with the vast majority in the European Union, the United States, Russia and Japan. The industry will need to manage this unprecedented rate of decommissioning, while also building substantial new capacity for those reactors that are replaced. Even with assumed lifetime extensions, half of EU nuclear capacity is retired in the period to 2040; if the assumed extensions are not authorised, and there are no new builds, EU nuclear capacity would fall to 5% of current levels by 2040.

- The Low Nuclear Case explores the implications of nuclear power declining due to a combination of plausible events – such as shifts in policy, limited lifetime extensions and deteriorating economics. Capacity falls to 366 GW in 2040 and nuclear's share of generation to 7%. In the High Nuclear Case, by contrast, capacity rises to 767 GW and the share of generation to 14%, as more plants start to be built on schedule and within budget, and greater value is attributed to nuclear power's contribution to carbon abatement and baseload output. Nuclear capacity is even higher in the 450 Scenario, at 862 GW in 2040, highlighting the potential of nuclear power to play a role in meeting ambitious climate targets.

- Uranium resources are more than sufficient to provide fuel to satisfy any of these projections. Identified resources equate to over 120 years of consumption at current rates of use; but new mines will need to be developed as early as the 2020s, as production at existing facilities declines and demand increases.

Introduction

Government policy, public acceptance, economics and financing will fundamentally shape the outlook for nuclear power. Taking assumptions about these factors country-by-country, the main focus of this chapter is on projections for nuclear power in the period to 2040 in the New Policies Scenario – the central scenario in this *World Energy Outlook* (*WEO-2014*). In view of the uncertainties facing nuclear power, however, this chapter also considers how unexpected yet plausible events might alter this course. A Low Nuclear Case is built upon the realisation of the downside risks, while upside potential is explored in a High Nuclear Case; both cases are variants of our central scenario and so share many of the same assumptions for the underlying framework. The 450 Scenario, by contrast, assumes a policy shift involving more stringent action to scale-up deployment of low-carbon energy technologies, showing the role nuclear power could play alongside other options in meeting ambitious climate targets. To conclude, we analyse the prospects for nuclear fuel supply. The projections that follow are not a prediction of what will happen. Rather, they are intended to exhibit different plausible pathways reflecting the uncertainties, thereby allowing quantitative analysis of the associated considerations as a contribution to more informed decision-making (see Chapter 12).

New Policies Scenario

Approach and key assumptions

Projections for nuclear power draw on the International Atomic Energy Agency's (IAEA) Power Reactor Information System (PRIS) database (IAEA, 2014), which includes plant-by-plant information, and an in-house IEA database of planned reactor additions and expected capacity uprates, license renewals and closures. As such information is typically not available or is less reliable over a longer time horizon, the projections beyond 2020 reflect the policies to expand or phase out nuclear power that had been adopted as of mid-2014 and other relevant commitments that have been announced, even when the precise implementation measures have yet to be fully defined (Table 11.1). Judgement has been exercised on the extent to which these commitments will be implemented, allowing for the various institutional, political and economic circumstances that could intervene. A cautious approach has been adopted for potential newcomer countries (its extent depending on the progress they have made) in view of the higher likelihood in such cases of plans being delayed, deferred or abandoned.

The IEA's World Energy Model is the principal tool used for all of the projections presented in this *Outlook*, including those for nuclear power.[1] The projections are made in the context of the policy framework in place and the competitiveness of nuclear power *vis-à-vis* other generating options, drawing on an IEA database of power generation investment costs and how they are assumed to evolve over the projection period. Non-policy assumptions

---

1. An extensive survey of experts from utilities, equipment vendors, governments, universities, international organisations and non-governmental organisations was undertaken in early 2014 to update the IEA power generation investment cost database in preparation for the *World Energy Investment Outlook* (IEA, 2014).

vary across regions and countries and over time and have been derived from extensive consultations with experts in government and industry. Assumptions on the overnight cost of building reactors, the cost of capital, construction times, fuel, operating and maintenance costs, capacity factors and plant economic lifetimes are key to determining the economics of nuclear power, although other costs are also taken into account, such as the cost of decommissioning, waste storage and disposal.[2] Assumptions concerning lifetime extensions are particularly important in mature markets, as many existing reactors will reach the limit of their currently permitted operating lifetimes within the time horizon of our analysis. Like the age of the nuclear fleet and the reactor technologies in use, license periods and practices vary from country to country; a number of countries are expected to soon start considering whether or not to extend current limits.

Table 11.1 ▷ **Key assumptions for nuclear power in the New Policies Scenario***

Parameter	Assumptions
Government policy	Judgement is exercised on the extent to which policies to develop nuclear power are implemented, with more cautious interpretation for newcomer countries. Plans to phase out nuclear power and announced closures of specific plants proceed as planned.
Overnight cost	Varies significantly across countries and through the projection period; ranges from $2 000 per kilowatt (kW) to $6 600 per kW.
Weighted average cost of capital	Varies significantly across countries; averages 7% in non-OECD countries and 8% in OECD countries (real, pre-tax).
Construction time	Varies from an average of 5 years in Korea to 7-8 years in the European Union and the United States.
Capacity factor	Typically varies from 80% to 92%, depending on the power mix, market regulations and demand profile.
Licenced operating lifetimes	
United States	Typically 60 years, with possibility of up to 80 years (around 60% of plants that reach 60 years before 2040 receive extensions).
European Union	Typically 40 years, with possibility of up to 60 years in some countries.
Japan	Typically 40 years, with possibility of extensions up to 60 years.
Russia	Typically 30 years, with possibility of extensions up to 50 years; 60 years for newer units.
Korea	Typically 40 years, with possibility of several 10 year extensions (up to a maximum of 60 years).
Power uprates	Contribute around 5 gigawatts (GW) of capacity globally over the period.
Decommissioning cost	15% of the capital cost of a new nuclear plant.
Fuel cycle cost**	$10/MWh (includes cost of purchasing fuel for reactors and costs associated with the back-end of the fuel cycle [spent fuel transport, storage and reprocessing]).

* See Chapter 1 for assumptions for competing technologies in the power sector and CO_2 pricing. See detailed assumptions by region at www.worldenergyoutlook.org/investment. ** The fuel cycle cost of a "once-through cycle" is assumed to be the same as a "single reprocessing cycle", on the basis that the extra-cost for reprocessing is compensated by the gain in primary fuel supply (NEA, 2013).

2. See definitions, in Annex C.

11

A useful – though imperfect – means of assessing the lifetime economics of new power plants is to consider the costs of electricity generation, compiled on a levelised cost basis (discussed in Chapter 10). In the New Policies Scenario, assumed nuclear generating costs vary significantly across countries and regions and over the projection time horizon, according to the characteristics of each market. For plants coming online in 2030, they range from around $65 per megawatt-hour (MWh) in China and India to around $110/MWh in the European Union (Figure 11.1). Faster than projected rates of deployment, particularly of a limited range of reactor types installed by a limited range of firms, could lower these costs by speeding-up learning effects. The magnitude of the investment cost – the overnight cost of construction plus financing costs – is the main reason for the differences between regions. In China and India, investment costs remain around 40-60% of the level in various OECD countries throughout the *Outlook* period. Decommissioning costs account for less than 1.5% of generating costs in all regions, on the assumption that they are accrued over the entire economic lifetime of plant operation.

Figure 11.1 ▷ **Nuclear power generating costs for new plants in selected regions in the New Policies Scenario, 2030***

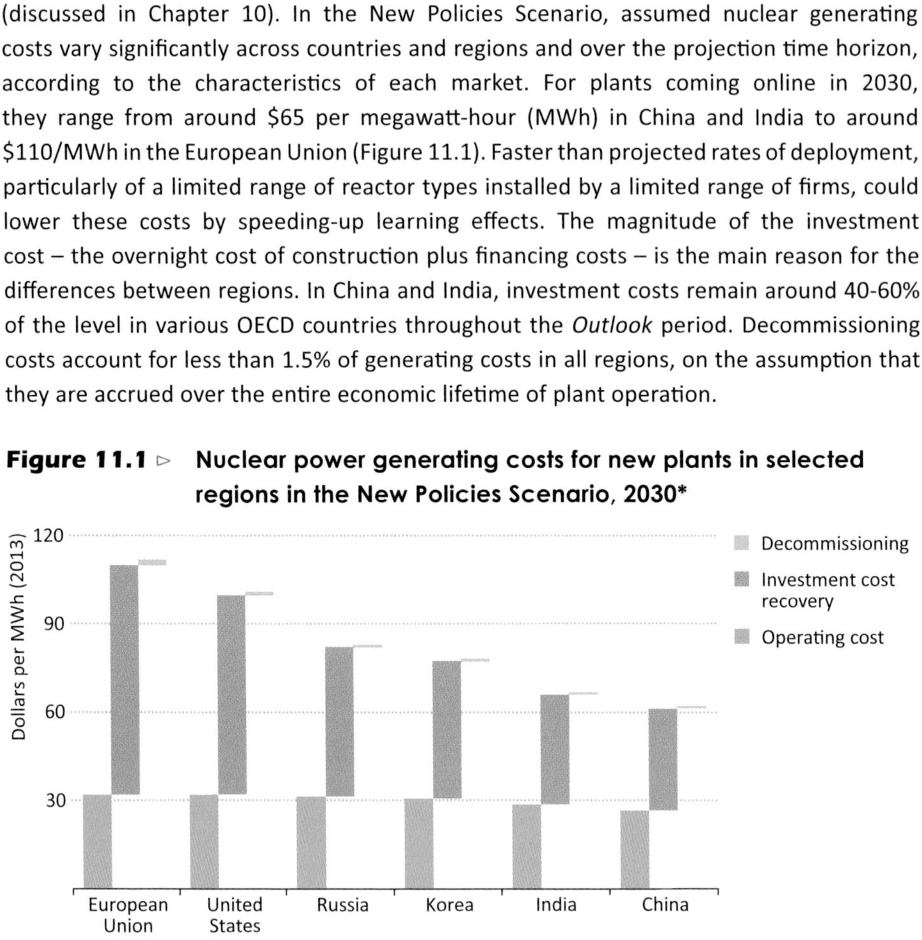

* Plants come online in the year 2030. Note: See Chapter 1 and *www.worldenergyoutlook.org/weomodel/ investmentcosts* for detailed assumptions.

Nuclear power capacity and generation[3]

Capacity additions and retirements

In the New Policies Scenario, nuclear power capacity increases by almost 60%, from 392 gigawatts (GW) in 2013 to 624 GW in 2040 (Figure 11.2).[4] This increase includes 76 GW of capacity that is already under construction. Total capacity additions amount to 380 GW, or 64% higher than net additions due to the need to replace some units which are retired.

---

3. The energy security, environmental and economic implications of the projections for nuclear power are expanded upon in Chapter 12.

4. All nuclear capacities presented in *WEO-2014* are expressed in gross terms (some government targets are in net terms, accounting for own-use by generators, which generally reduces declared capacity by about 6%).

Figure 11.2 ▷ **World installed nuclear power capacity by region in the New Policies Scenario**

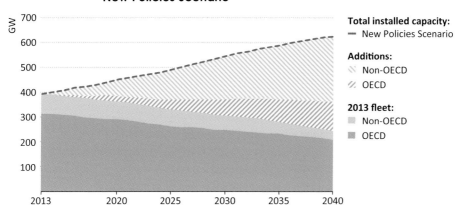

The number of economies worldwide operating nuclear reactors increases from 31 in 2013 to 36 in 2040, as newcomers more than offset countries that phase out nuclear power (Belgium, Germany and Switzerland). Nuclear capacity factors increase over time, with the global average rising from 72% in 2013 (or 81% if Japan's reactors are excluded) to 85% in 2040.

China, India, Korea and Russia see the most significant increases in installed nuclear capacity. The increase in China, of 132 GW, exceeds the current installed capacity of the United States and Russia combined (Figure 11.3). India's and Russia's nuclear power capacity rises by 33 GW and 19 GW, respectively. Despite capacity in Korea more than doubling over the period, to 49 GW, the OECD share of global nuclear capacity falls from 80% in 2013 to 52% in 2040.

Figure 11.3 ▷ **Installed nuclear power capacity by key region in the New Policies Scenario**

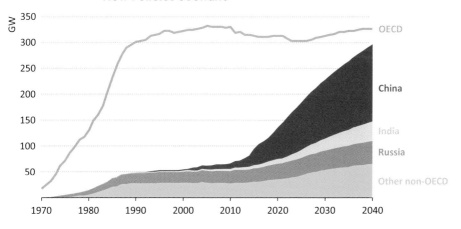

Around 150 GW of nuclear capacity is retired in the period to 2040, equivalent to 38% of the current capacity (or 44% of the fleet). This reflects stated policies and plans to close existing plants and our assumptions for reactor operating lifetimes and licence renewals; it translates into the closure of almost 200 reactors. Reflecting the age profile of their fleets, the bulk of the retirements are in mature markets, particularly the European Union, Russia, Japan and United States (Figure 11.4). The rate of retirements picks up in the first half of the 2020s, in line with already announced plans and as reactors built during the 1970s are taken offline, and then again in the late 2030s. This is set to pose challenges for industry and regulators and possibly strain engineering and project management capabilities. There are generally two approaches to decommissioning: immediate dismantling or deferred dismantling. Although many utilities today are choosing the immediate dismantling strategy (to take advantage, for example, of the expertise of the staff that operated the plants), if there is a high rate of plant closures, deferred dismantling may become the more common option.

Figure 11.4 ▷ **Nuclear power capacity additions and retirements by key region in the New Policies Scenario, 2014-2040**

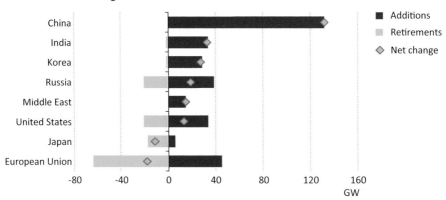

Reaching the projected level of capacity in 2040 implies a construction rate of 14 GW per year on average (Figure 11.5). The average rate of construction increases from 12 GW per year for the remainder of the 2010s – the bulk of which is already under construction, in some cases at advanced stages – to around 15 GW per year thereafter, partly to compensate for the retirement of current capacity. These rates are well below the peak of 34 GW of new capacity brought online in 1984 and include contributions from a greater number of countries than was then the case, including China which is today the global leader in new builds. However, they are significantly faster than the rates realised in the recent past[5] and need to be maintained over a sustained period. Moreover, the reactors being built will be larger and potentially more technologically complex than their predecessors, though efforts are being made to reduce complexity and move to greater modularisation and factory production.

---

5. During the 1990s the rate of construction starts on nuclear plants was slow, resulting in just 3 GW per year coming online on average in the 2000s. However, the rate picked up from the late 2000s (with 76 GW under construction at the end of 2013), leading to a significant amount of capacity scheduled to come online in the near- to mid-term.

Figure 11.5 ▷ Global nuclear power capacity additions and retirements in the New Policies Scenario

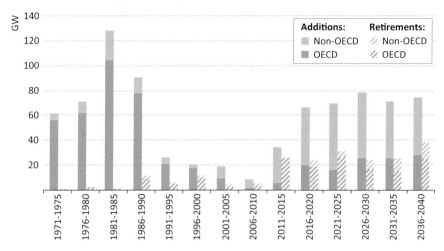

One particular constraint on the rate at which nuclear capacity expands could be the availability of a highly skilled and experienced workforce (Box 11.1). Another could be the availability of heavy forging capacity to manufacture reactor pressure vessels. New forging capacity has been added in recent years and we estimate that it could now support the construction of around 25 nuclear power plants per year; but some of this capacity is likely to be closed in the absence of orders for new reactors over the next decade or so. Most investment in forging capacity in recent years has been made in China and its capacity is consistent with its projected growth in nuclear power.

Box 11.1 ▷ Help wanted

The nuclear industry, more than any other sector of the power industry, requires people specifically trained in specialised engineering, science and technology. As a result, many professionals in the nuclear industry have skill sets that are readily transferrable to other sectors of industry. The nuclear industry also needs to maintain suitable manpower resources over long time horizons. Nuclear power plants are often licensed to operate for up to 60 years, while resources need to be sustained over the much longer-term to regulate and affect the safe shut down and decommissioning of facilities and to address the long-term disposal of nuclear waste. But attracting young professionals to the field and then retaining them could prove especially difficult as few individuals will wish to work in a field for which the future is, in many cases, uncertain. In those countries pursuing a nuclear policy, the need is no less, but the challenge is less severe.

Approximately, 250 000 people are working directly in the nuclear energy sector in the European Union (European Commission, 2012), including around 25 000 people within the UK civil nuclear industry and nearly 125 000 people in France, or around 4%

of its industrial employment (PWC, 2011). The nuclear industry in the United States employs over 120 000 people (Nuclear Energy Institute [NEI]), in Japan over 84 000 people (METI, 2012) and in Russia over 250 000 people. Whether national policy favours nuclear power or not, the impending retirements of a large number of highly specialised individuals in the nuclear industry will be a challenge for those responsible for the operation, regulation and decommissioning of nuclear facilities. According to the European Human Resource Observatory for the Nuclear Energy Sector (EHRO-N, 2012), nearly half of those employed in the European Union in 2010 were over the age of 45. More starkly, according to the latest workforce analysis by the NEI in the United States, 38% of the nuclear workforce is eligible to retire within the next few years. In 2003, the age of the nuclear workforce in the United States was fairly normally distributed; however, according to recent NEI data, the age distribution in 2013 was more skewed towards both ends of the age spectrum. The increase in the number of younger employees can be seen as a prudent response to the pending large number of retirements, but it also indicates a loss of expertise in the industry.

Generation

In the New Policies Scenario, nuclear electricity generation increases from 2 461 terawatt-hours (TWh) in 2012 to just over 3 200 TWh in 2020 and to nearly 4 650 TWh in 2040, an average rate of growth of 2.3% per year (Figure 11.6). Nuclear power expands at a faster rate than electricity supply as a whole (2.1%), resulting in its share of total generation increasing by one percentage point to 12%. The expansion of nuclear power slows after 2020, reflecting slower growth in electricity demand as the emerging economies mature and as policies to improve the efficiency of electricity use increasingly take effect. Nuclear remains the fourth-largest source of power generation globally after coal, natural gas and hydropower, although if all sources of non-hydro renewable generation are combined it slips to fifth-largest around 2025.

Figure 11.6 ▷ **Nuclear power generation by region in the New Policies Scenario**

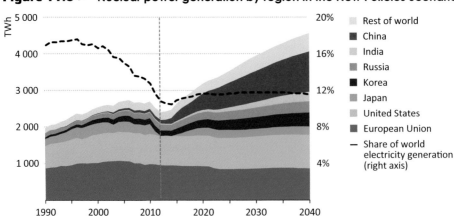

World Energy Outlook 2014 | Outlook for Nuclear Power

Trends in nuclear generation at the global level mask significant differences regionally. Growth is strongest in China, India, Korea and Russia, which each see nuclear power take an increased share of their electricity supply and collectively account for three-quarters of the increase in global nuclear generation (Figure 11.7). In the United States over 60% of new builds are offset by retirements and it is overtaken by China just after 2030 as the world's largest nuclear power producer. In Japan there is a progressive increase in nuclear electricity generation with the gradual restart of the reactors which are now idle and some new builds, although the share of nuclear in total generation does not return to the level prior to the Fukushima Daiichi accident. Although there are increases in nuclear generating capacity in some European Union countries, these are outweighed across the European Union by retirements, leading to a reduction in the region's nuclear generation.

Figure 11.7 ▷ **Change in share of nuclear power generation and capacity by selected region in the New Policies Scenario**

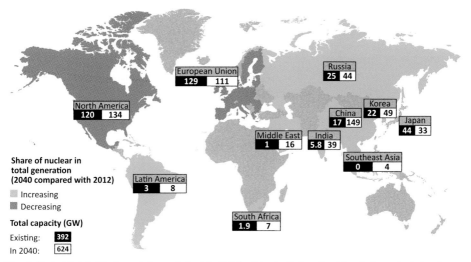

This map is without prejudice to the status of or sovereignty over any territory, to the delimitation of international frontiers and boundaries, and to the name of any territory, city or area.

Investment needs and associated costs

Investment in nuclear power plants amounts to $1.5 trillion over 2014-2040 (in year-2013 dollars) in the New Policies Scenario, or $57 billion per year on average (Table 11.2).[6] This includes investment in new plants and for uprating and refurbishments for life extensions at existing ones. In many cases, such as where reactors operate for 60 years, the plants

---

6. Consistent with the approach for projecting investment in all parts of the energy supply chain used in the *WEO*, the financing cost for new capacity, allowances for cost escalation due to possible delays, and costs related to operation and maintenance are not included in these capital cost numbers. Because of the importance of regulatory, political and public acceptability risks, plus the relatively long-lead times from the final investment decision to income generation, the cost of financing new capacity is typically more significant for nuclear than for other technologies.

built will continue to operate and reap returns well beyond the projection horizon. Investment needs for nuclear power represent around 13% of total projected investment in new power plants to 2040 (or 3% of total energy supply infrastructure investment). The regional breakdown of investment is sensitive to many factors, particularly the rate of plant construction, variations in the costs of construction from country-to-country – which can be significant – and the age profile of the existing fleet. Cumulative investment needs are largest in China, at $345 billion, followed by the European Union ($301 billion), the United States ($247 billion), Russia ($155 billion), Korea ($103 billion) and India ($96 billion). Although installed nuclear capacity in the OECD is broadly flat to 2040, almost one-third of global capacity additions are built in the OECD, primarily offsetting retirements and requiring almost half of global investment. Investment needs in the OECD are disproportionally high as the average cost for building a new plant is about 50% higher than in non-OECD countries and as many plants undergo refurbishments to meet regulatory conditions for lifetime extension.

Table 11.2 ▷ **Cumulative global investment and associated costs in nuclear power in the New Policies Scenario, 2014-2040** ($2013 billion)

| | Investment in nuclear plants* | Associated costs | | Total capacity additions (GW) |
		Fuel cycle	Decommissioning	
China	345	191	-	132
European Union	301	220	51	45
United States	247	236	15	33
Korea	103	78	1	29
India	96	37	1	34
Japan	37	54	10	6
Rest of world	406	161	27	101
Total	1 533	977	104	380

* Investment in new plants and for uprates and refurbishments for life extensions at existing ones.

In addition to investment in capital assets, there are other costs that will need to be incurred along the nuclear supply chain to satisfy the projections. The fuel cycle cost for the global fleet of nuclear reactors (both existing plants and new capacity) is projected to amount to almost $1 trillion over the period, which includes the cost of reactor fuel and spent fuel transport, storage, reprocessing and disposal. The fuel cycle cost equates to $73 million per year on average for a standard 1 GW reactor, or $10/MWh of electricity produced. The cost of decommissioning power plants that are retired is estimated to be $104 billion (based on 15% of the capital cost of a new plant), with costs varying substantially from plant to plant and country to country.

Can SMRs lead to a new view of nuclear economics?

Early in the commercial nuclear era, the desire to drive down costs led to concerted efforts to increase reactor capacity, so as to take advantage of economies of scale. The idea was that the fixed costs of having a nuclear power plant – security, spent fuel handling, and emergency planning, for example – were going to be significant for a facility of any size, and should, ideally, be spread over a large output. The drive towards larger units has had some drawbacks, as these reactors have become increasingly complex, contributing to extended construction times as well as huge investment costs.

Small modular reactor (SMR) designs are being advanced to address these concerns. They take a different approach to reducing costs, eschewing the economies of scale in favour of the economies of replication. Their simplified designs can be made in dedicated factories that would improve quality control for nuclear-grade fabrication while potentially also offering declining costs through improvement in fabrication with experience. Such learning effects have occurred with other energy technologies, such as wind and solar photovoltaic (PV), and modular manufacturing techniques have been successfully used in other industries (aircraft and shipbuilding). By moving complex nuclear construction to a factory environment, SMRs could potentially reduce the capital cost of new nuclear capacity.

SMRs being proposed today are generally less than 300 MW in capacity but may be configured as multiple units operating as a single plant. Designs are actively being developed in the United States, China, Russia, Korea and Argentina. The technologies generating the most attention are pressurised water reactors (PWRs) using low-enriched uranium fuel (the same as most large light-water reactor designs). Their appeal stems from the extensive operating experience already achieved with these types of reactors and the knowledge base that regulators have in assessing their safety. For SMR designs to be commercialised, however, they will need regulatory approval not only on their historically familiar features but also for enhanced safety characteristics, such as reliance on natural circulation in the event of an accident.

For their promise to be realised, the economics of SMRs must be demonstrated – this will take time. Designing, engineering, and licensing new reactors are expensive elements, measured in hundreds of millions of dollars, and take many years. Realising the benefits of building nuclear units in dedicated factories will depend on there being sufficient demand to warrant investment in such a factory. The modular construction techniques that are at the heart of this approach have been attempted with some of the reactors currently being built, with mixed results. Resolving these uncertainties may well necessitate further government investment to test whether SMRs can be a viable option.

11

Regional trends

China

China has been the leader in nuclear new build for more than a decade and had 27 plants under construction as of September 2014, yet nuclear power as yet supplies only 2% of its total power generation. This reflects the starting base and the rapid large-scale deployment of other generation sources in parallel. China's nuclear power programme slowed after the Fukushima Daiichi accident, with approvals for new plants temporarily suspended and additional inspections carried out on plants operating and under construction. However, the accident has not altered the country's long-term commitment to building new capacity. In the New Policies Scenario, active policy support underpins a large expansion of nuclear power, with capacity rising from 17 GW in 2013 to 60 GW in 2020 and almost 150 GW in 2040 (Figure 11.8). The increase, of 132 GW, includes 29 GW of capacity already under construction and accounts for 35% of total worldwide capacity additions (including additions to replace retiring reactors). Nuclear's share of China's power generation rises to 6% in 2020 and 10% in 2040.

Based on these projections, China meets its target of 58 GW of nuclear capacity by 2020 (simply by completing the capacity currently under construction it will achieve 84% of the target). While the challenges to the expansion of nuclear power are not expected to be as severe in China as in some other markets, there are still a number of reasons to be cautious. These include questions about the regulatory and industry capability to deliver an expansion of the extent envisaged (rates of additions comparable to the New Policies Scenario have previously been seen only in the United States and France). There is also a prospect of heightened public concern about building nuclear plants inland, rather than in coastal locations: China had planned to start building the country's first inland plants, by now, but approvals for these have been suspended and are now not expected to be granted until at least 2016.

Given the scale of the expansion that is envisaged in China, developments in the country will have major implications for the nuclear industry worldwide. Total investment in nuclear power plants in China in the period to 2040 is projected at $345 billion (in year-2013 dollars), or almost $13 billion per year on average. Currently a wide variety of indigenous and foreign reactor designs are in use and under construction, with international and local companies competing to maintain or increase their shares of the expanding market. Their aspirations would be affected (one way or the other) if China opts to standardise the fleet by favouring a small number of reactor types in a bid to lower costs, speed up construction times or simplify regulatory controls. Further success in developing and deploying a Chinese nuclear technology in China would also give a boost to its aspirations to export nuclear technologies to other countries. Similarly, success in export markets would help foster the development and performance of the Chinese industry domestically. Despite the scale of China's nuclear expansion, its nuclear capacity in 2040, though the biggest in the world, does not match that of the OECD as a whole.

Figure 11.8 ▷ Nuclear power capacity and share of generation by selected region in the New Policies Scenario

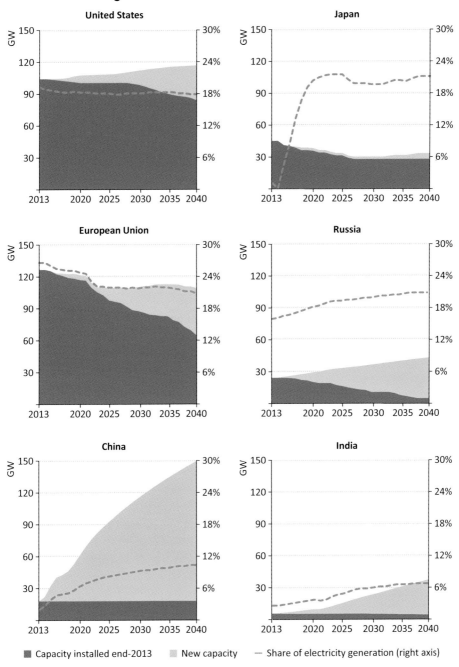

Capacity installed end-2013   New capacity   — Share of electricity generation (right axis)

Note: See Table 11.1 for assumptions on lifetime extensions.

United States

Four nuclear reactors have permanently shut down in the United States since 2013 (Crystal River-3, Kewaunee and San Onofre 2 and 3) and it has been announced that one other (Vermont Yankee) will also close before the end of 2014. The closures, which amount to 4.4 GW of capacity, have been linked to a range of factors, including the high cost of repairs and low wholesale electricity prices. Despite the difficulties seen by some operators, most utilities have applied for lifetime extensions and five new reactors are currently under construction, all in states where electricity is supplied largely at regulated prices (South Carolina, Georgia and Tennessee), highlighting the importance of market structure to the economics of nuclear power.

In the New Policies Scenario, US nuclear power capacity increases by 13 GW, from 105 GW in 2013 to 118 GW in 2040. This includes 6.2 GW of new capacity already under construction and takes account of the capacity that has been earmarked for closure. US nuclear power generation rises from 801 TWh in 2012 to around 930 TWh in 2040, an overall increase of 16% (Figure 11.8). As this is slower than growth in total electricity generation, the contribution of nuclear power to the US power mix drops from 19% to 18% over the period. Nonetheless, rising natural gas prices gradually help improve the competitive position of nuclear *vis-à-vis* other generating options, easing the difficulties it currently faces in parts of the country.

Projected US total capacity additions to 2040, of 33 GW, are significantly higher than the increase in installed capacity due to the effect of retirements. The US nuclear power fleet is one of the oldest in the world, with an average age of 33 years. Based on our assumption that some plants are granted licences to operate for up to 80 years (most currently have licences that allow operation for up to 60 years), 21 GW of capacity is decommissioned over the period to 2040. Total US investment in nuclear power capacity is projected at $247 billion, or $9 billion per year on average. The cost of decommissioning capacity that is retired amounts to $15 billion.

European Union

Nuclear power currently contributes over one-quarter of the electricity produced in the European Union (second only to coal), with 14 out of the 28 EU member states operating nuclear power plants (131 reactors in total). Its role in the EU energy mix is projected to decline over the coming decades, driven by faster growth in other options for power generation and the decisions taken by Germany and Belgium to progressively phase it out (like Switzerland, although it is not an EU member). In the New Policies Scenario, installed nuclear capacity in the European Union declines by around 14%, from 129 GW in 2013 to 111 GW in 2040. EU nuclear generation falls by 10%, with its share of the power mix dropping from 27% to 21% over the *Outlook* period (down from a peak of 33% in 1997) (Figure 11.8). However, these projections mask important differences across the region, with some individual EU member states projected to increase reliance on nuclear power and others to abandon it. The reduction in nuclear power is more than offset by increases in other forms of low-carbon electricity, with the share of renewables in generation rising from 24% to 46%.

Despite the drop in installed nuclear capacity in the EU, total capacity additions amount to 45 GW (including 4.3 GW of capacity currently under construction), predominately reflecting new builds to replace some of the reactors that are retired, but also some capacity expansion at existing plants. The EU nuclear fleet has a current average age of 30 years, and a number of member states are in the process of considering plant lifetime extensions. In the New Policies Scenario, 63 GW of capacity is retired in the period to 2040 (or almost half of the current installed capacity), with the rate of retirements picking-up from the early 2020s. Assumed lifetime extensions make a greater contribution to overall EU capacity than projected additions. However, if these extensions are not authorised, EU nuclear capacity could fall dramatically in the 2020s, in the absence of significant new build. As an illustrative example, if there were no extensions at all to current licences, and no new build, EU capacity would be cut to 70 GW in 2025 and to 6 GW in 2040 (Figure 11.9). Projected investment in nuclear power capacity in the European Union totals $301 billion between 2014 and 2040, or 15% of total investment in generation capacity, while the cost of decommissioning plants that are retired amounts to $51 billion.

Figure 11.9 ▷ **EU nuclear power capacity in the New Policies Scenario and retirement profiles under different lifetime extension assumptions**

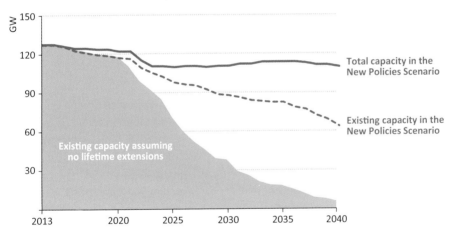

Japan

The projections for Japan in the New Policies Scenario are based on the key assumptions that most of the nuclear power plants that have been in extended shut down since the accident at Fukushima Daiichi in March 2011 steadily return to service after receiving the necessary regulatory approvals and that many have their licenced operating lifetimes extended. Japan's installed nuclear power capacity reaches 33 GW in 2040, compared with 44 GW in 2013. This is the net effect of the completion of a small number of new builds being offset by the gradual retirement of ageing reactors and the more immediate retirement of reactors that do not obtain the approvals necessary to restart. Nuclear power generation increases from 16 TWh in 2012 (when almost all nuclear plants were closed) to 220 TWh in 2020 and nearly 240 TWh in 2040. The share of nuclear in the power mix rises sharply, from 2% in 2012 to 21% in 2040, yet still remains below the level of 26% in 2010. Nuclear power makes an important contribution to boosting the share of Japan's electricity that comes from low-carbon sources, which rises from 14% in 2012 to 54% in 2040.

Japan has recently clarified requirements for lifetime extensions, with operators now having the possibility to apply for a one-time extension, from the current limit of 40 years to a maximum of 60 years (as is the limit in the United States today). In the New Policies Scenario, the majority of plants built since the mid-1980s receive extensions to operate for 60 years. A total of 17 GW of capacity is decommissioned over the *Outlook* period, with most of the retirements concentrated between 2015 and 2025.

While Japan's new Strategic Energy Plan expresses clear intentions, there still remains uncertainty about the role nuclear power will play in the country's future energy mix. In particular, the plan leaves open the possibility of building new plants which, if they materialise on a reasonable scale, would alter the outlook in our projections, in which new builds are limited. Some industry groups have called for the construction of new plants, suggesting private investment would be available. In the New Policies Scenario, projected investment in nuclear power amounts to $37 billion (in year-2013 dollars) between 2013 and 2040, while the cost of decommissioning nuclear power plants that are retired amounts to a further $10 billion.

Russia

In the New Policies Scenario, Russia's installed nuclear power capacity increases from 25 GW in 2013 to 30 GW in 2020 and 44 GW in 2040. Total capacity additions over the period total 39 GW. This includes 9 GW of capacity that Rosatom – the state-controlled nuclear power corporation – currently has under construction, made up of 10 reactors on 6 sites (including a floating nuclear power plant being built to service remote Arctic locations). Nuclear generation in Russia rises by 82%, pushing its share of the electricity mix from 17% to 21% over the *Outlook* period. About 80% of current capacity, or 20 GW, is projected to be retired in the period to 2040. Replacing these ageing units and bringing on new capacity will involve huge costs. Investment in new plants and other forms of capacity addition in the New Policies Scenario is projected at $155 billion (in year-2013 dollars), while the cost of decommissioning plants amounts to $12 billion.

The projections are conservative compared with some government and industry plans, including Russia's new Energy Strategy to 2035. This proposes a target of 22.5% for the share of nuclear power in electricity generation by 2035 (with total capacity doubling to 50 GW in 2035). Our lower trajectory reflects a lower projected level of electricity demand in the New Policies Scenario (compared with various Russian plans) and general caution, as Russian industry is likely to face financial and human resource challenges as it seeks to deliver the scale of expansion it envisages. These include achieving a major increase in domestic installed capacity while also replacing ageing units that are retired, and potentially increasing its share in the global export market by building – and in some cases operating – reactors abroad. Moreover, Russia has excess domestic production capacity of natural gas, significant reserves of coal and a fairly relaxed climate change policy, all of which combine to weaken the economic case for nuclear power in the country.

India

India became the first developing country to use nuclear power when its first commercial reactor came online in 1969. It now ranks as the world's fourteenth-largest economy in terms of generation, although nuclear power represents only 3% of the overall power mix. In the New Policies Scenario, India sees the second-largest growth in nuclear capacity globally after China, with installed capacity rising from 5.8 GW in 2013 to 39 GW in 2040. Nuclear generation increases by a factor of eight and its share of the generation mix rises to 4% in 2020 and 7% in 2040. By the end of the period, India has the world's sixth-largest nuclear output. These developments are driven by active support by policy-makers, focused on meeting rapidly growing energy needs, while managing high reliance on fossil fuel imports, including supplying the over 300 million people currently without access to electricity.

Total capacity additions are slightly higher than net additions, at 34 GW, as one-third of existing reactors are retired and replaced during the period. Some 4.3 GW of projected additions are already under construction, with first concrete expected to be poured on several other plants in the near future. To meet the projections, India requires investment in nuclear capacity of $96 billion (in year-2013 dollars), or $3.5 billion per year on average.

Like many other countries, India has historically faced difficulties in expanding the use of nuclear power and has missed stated targets. Some of the problems it has faced are linked to the high population density in parts of the country, difficult land acquisition and local governance issues, and the country's large fiscal and current account deficit, making it very reliant on foreign capital. However, prospects for nuclear power have brightened since an agreement was reached in 2008 that opened the door for India to trade with foreign suppliers of nuclear fuel and technologies. Nonetheless, our projections still fall short of India's target of boosting capacity to 14.6 GW by 2020 (even if all capacity currently under construction comes online by 2020, a gap of 4.5 GW will remain). Looking further ahead, the expansion of nuclear power in India faces many of the same challenges seen elsewhere, particularly securing finance for high upfront investments. There is a particular risk that India's nuclear liability law could deter foreign suppliers, as there is an unresolved concern that they may be held liable for damages in case of nuclear accidents. There are also concerns that the quality of the power grid may pose problems in integrating supply from large-scale nuclear assets.

11

Low Nuclear Case

The Fukushima Daiichi accident in 2011 ended what some viewed as the start of a global nuclear renaissance. Responses to the accident included the suspension of construction activities (for safety reviews), temporary and permanent plant shut downs and, in a few countries, decisions to phase out nuclear power completely. It also led both governments and utilities to review the long-term generating capacity needs. Close to four years later, many other factors – some independent of the accident – can be seen as supporting the thesis that the nuclear component of future power generation may be low. Some of these are nuclear-specific, including adverse recent experiences with existing nuclear power plants and plants under construction, while others relate to policy and demand uncertainty and a changing understanding of the availability of competing energy resources and technologies. As these mean that our core projections are subject to a range of uncertainties, this section discusses some of these components of risk and the implications of a possible slowdown in the expansion of nuclear power.

Developments that could slow the expansion of nuclear power

Added policy and regulatory uncertainty

As nuclear power involves long lead-times and amortisation periods, it is best suited to markets where there is agreement that it is an integral part of the energy mix over the longer-term. Except for a handful of OECD countries, Russia and the fast industrialising developing countries in Asia, such certainty is now far from a reality. In several countries, government policy on nuclear power is still in flux and some governments in countries which have been contemplating a move to include nuclear power in their power generation mix have become less enthusiastic after wrestling with the complexities and lead times involved. The proposal in France to cap the nuclear capacity at its present level (around 66 GW) with a view to reducing its share in the electricity mix, signals a possible departure from a long-established nuclear course. The situation in Japan remains unresolved. Although the government has come out firmly in favour of restoring the nuclear component of supply and applications to restart many of the reactors have been submitted to the regulatory authority, public anxieties remain and political and regulatory considerations could result in particular proposals being delayed or even abandoned.

Future decisions on lifetime extensions represent another source of uncertainty, as many existing nuclear power plants are approaching the end of their licenced lifetimes. Reluctance and procrastination on the part of authorities over extensions remains a possibility, or political or regulatory barriers could be raised to the point at which operators are discouraged from applying for extensions.

Deterioration of economic factors

Recent experience, including in France, Finland and the United States, has shaken confidence in the ability of the industry to build on schedule and on budget. Many of the delays and cost overruns can be reasonably explained (e.g. first-of-a-kind designs, the effects of an extended period of construction inactivity), and the experience in China (and it appears in the United Arab Emirates [UAE]) illustrates that construction on time and within budget can be achieved. However, these arguments have not fully reassured investors about the degree of risk involved and, if delays and cost overruns continue, nuclear power projects could continue to be seen as requiring high risk premiums on lending and stronger guarantees and government incentives.

The shale gas revolution has contributed to a reduction in the competitiveness of commercial nuclear power in parts of the United States. Although it was licensed to operate until 2033, a decision to close the Kewaunee nuclear power plant in Wisconsin was taken in May 2013, partly because of competition from power produced from inexpensive natural gas. Likewise, the decision to retire the Vermont Yankee plant at the end of its current fuel cycle in late 2014 has been attributed, in part, to low wholesale electricity prices, driven largely by lower natural gas prices. So far the shale gas revolution has been largely a North American phenomenon but, if it is replicated elsewhere, it might contribute to the delay or abandonment of new nuclear build in both existing and newcomer markets.

In competitive markets, a high share of variable renewables generation can have a significant impact on the wholesale electricity prices and on the operating hours of dispatchable plants (in particular mid-merit ones), sometimes to the point that some generators become unprofitable (IEA, 2014). At very high shares of variable renewables, the residual demand profile (actual demand less electricity production from variable renewables) can result in more pronounced peaks and troughs, which can affect the operation of baseload plants, including nuclear plants. As any capital-intensive technology, nuclear plants are aimed at running the maximum amount of hours possible, to reduce their average cost of generation and maximise revenues, in order to recover their investment. As a consequence, high deployment of variable renewables, where not coupled with reforms to market design, can reduce the profitability of nuclear power to the point of making them unattractive for new investment. A deterioration in the economic factors could increasingly concentrate nuclear generation in those markets where suppliers' investment risks are minimised by regulated tariffs which are based on generating costs plus reasonable rates of return.

Assumptions

The Low Nuclear Case explores the implications of less nuclear power in the *Outlook* period than in the New Policies Scenario due to the influence of policy and regulatory uncertainties and deteriorating economic factors. While the assumptions are plausible, they do not represent the expected course of events so the case should not be interpreted as a forecast but as a quantitative basis for decision-making in an uncertain world. The main assumptions are:

- Implementation of plans to reduce the role of nuclear power that have recently been, or are currently being debated, but until now have not been adopted.

- Limits on lifetime extensions, which result in plant operating lifetimes being, on average, ten years shorter than in the New Policies Scenario.

- In the OECD, plants currently under construction are completed, but there are no new builds, except in Korea, and no replacement of retiring reactors.

- In non-OECD regions, plants currently under construction are completed, but there are limited new builds.

- Potential newcomer countries abandon their plans.

- Due to financing and economic difficulties, the weighted average cost of capital for new builds is on average two percentage points higher than in the New Policies Scenario (i.e. 10% instead of 8% in the OECD and 9% instead of 7% in non-OECD countries).

Nuclear power capacity and generation

Global installed nuclear capacity in the Low Nuclear Case contracts from 392 GW today to 366 GW in 2040. This is the net result of a reduction of 146 GW in OECD countries and an increase of 120 GW elsewhere compared to 2013 levels (Figure 11.10). The biggest decreases in installed capacity, relative to today, are in the European Union (71 GW), Japan (44 GW), and the United States (41 GW). The biggest increases are in China (87 GW), India (18 GW), Korea (18 GW) and Russia (12 GW). Global nuclear capacity in 2040 is around 40% lower than the level projected in the New Policies Scenario. The gap between the two trajectories widens from 2030 due to the faster rate of reactor retirements in the Low Nuclear Case and the slower rate of new builds. A total of about 230 GW of capacity is retired globally, with retirements heavily concentrated in OECD countries (where almost 60% of existing capacity is permanently shutdown).

Figure 11.10 ▷ **Nuclear power capacity in the Low Nuclear Case**

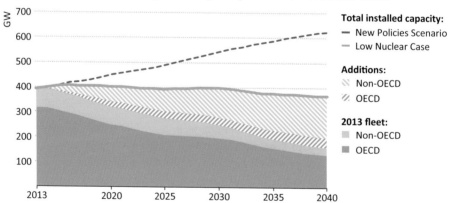

Although generation of nuclear electricity increases by around 250 TWh (10%), in the Low Nuclear Case, the nuclear share of global electricity generation drops from 11% in 2012 to 7% in 2040, its lowest level since 1976. Again, trends differ between regions, with the share of nuclear in generation dropping from 18% to 10% in the OECD and rising from 4% to 5% elsewhere. Notable differences between the Low Nuclear Case and the New Policies Scenario in terms of the share of nuclear in generation in 2040 include Japan (0% versus 21%), the European Union (11% versus 21%), the United States (10% versus 18%) and China (7% versus 10%). Taken at the global level, a substantial shift away from nuclear power, as depicted in the Low Nuclear Case, has adverse implications for energy security, and economic and climate trends, with more severe consequences for import-dependent countries that had been planning to rely relatively heavily on nuclear power. On the other hand, further opportunities are created for the use of renewables in power generation and there is a reduction in the scale of the challenge of nuclear waste disposal (see Chapter 12).

High Nuclear Case

The upside potential to the expansion of nuclear power should not be discounted. Prospects could brighten rapidly, particularly if plants start being built regularly on time and within budget, if public concerns are adequately addressed and if there is greater support for nuclear power in response to energy security, climate and clean air concerns.

A number of factors could drive down costs of nuclear power worldwide, thereby improving its competiveness versus competing power generation technologies. Standardisation around the new first-of-a-kind reactors now entering the market – which have involved a huge amount of investment in design and engineering – could generate significant efficiency gains. Learning effects from the new reactor models currently entering the market could improve construction methods and project management techniques, potentially resulting in major cost reductions and boosting confidence in the technologies. Reinforcement of the efforts already underway to improve the independence and competence of regulatory and safety authorities could increase public support for nuclear power – a prerequisite for faster deployment. Such developments, by improving the prospects for the industry, would also help ease the human resource challenges that currently exist by making nuclear engineering a more attractive career option and encourage industry investment in manufacturing capacity (Box 11.1).

Assumptions

The High Nuclear Case investigates the implications of a sustained nuclear resurgence and, though optimistic in some respects, like the Low Nuclear Case, is based on plausible assumptions that could materialise and are technically feasible. They include:

- All announced targets to expand nuclear power (and to phase it out) are realised.
- Potential newcomer countries implement their plans, except those that have yet to make any firm progress.
- Financing constraints ease, decreasing the weighted average cost of capital for new build (from 8% to 6% in the OECD and 7% to 5% in non-OECD countries).
- A greater share of existing plants receives licence extensions.

Nuclear power capacity and generation

In the High Nuclear Case, installed nuclear capacity reaches 767 GW in 2040 (23% higher than in the New Policies Scenario) (Table 11.3). The share of nuclear power in electricity generation rises from 11% today to 14% in 2040 (compared with 12% in the New Policies Scenario). The gap between the two trajectories widens around 2025, reflecting the lead times involved in building new plants and the different retirement profiles. The rate of capacity additions averages 18 GW per year over the period (compared with the historical peak of 34 GW in 1984). In the High Nuclear Case many countries increase in their energy self-sufficiency rates and energy diversity, spend less on energy imports and make more progress in decarbonising the power sector. On the other hand, the quantity of nuclear waste generated is greater than in the New Policies Scenario (see Chapter 12) and there are heightened concerns regarding nuclear proliferation as the number of countries operating reactors increases.

Table 11.3 ▷ Nuclear power capacity, additions and retirements in the New Policies Scenario and the High and Low Nuclear Cases (GW)

	Installed capacity				Change in capacity* 2014-2040			
	2013	2040			Additions		Retirements	
		NPS	LNC	HNC	LNC	HNC	LNC	HNC
OECD	315	326	169	368	-80	26	77	-16
Americas	120	134	73	151	-30	8	30	-10
United States	105	118	63	132	-26	7	28	-7
Europe	129	111	56	127	-42	11	12	-6
Asia Oceania	66	82	39	90	-8	7	35	-
Japan	44	33	-	36	-3	3	30	-
Non-OECD	78	297	197	399	-95	87	5	-15
E. Europe / Eurasia	43	65	48	84	-16	8	1	-11
Russia	25	44	37	53	-6	6	1	-3
Asia	29	202	133	268	-65	66	4	-1
China	17	149	104	195	-45	46	-	-
India	6	39	24	52	-14	14	1	-
Middle East	1	16	9	24	-7	8	-	-
Africa	2	7	3	12	-3	4	-	-2
Latin America	3	8	4	10	-4	1	-	-1
World	392	624	366	767	-175	113	82	-30
European Union	129	111	58	126	-41	8	12	-7

* Change is relative to the New Policies Scenario. Notes: NPS = New Policies Scenario; LNC = Low Nuclear Case; HNC = High Nuclear Case.

Figure 11.11 ▷ **Nuclear power capacity by region, by scenario and case**

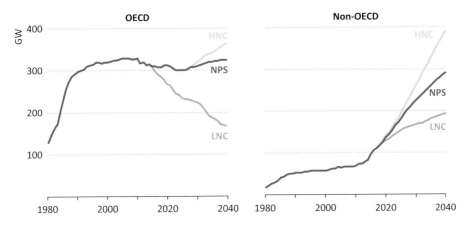

Notes: HNC = High Nuclear Case; NPS = New Policies Scenario; LNC = Low Nuclear Case.

450 Scenario

The High Nuclear Case does not represent an upper limit of the potential nuclear power has to contribute to global energy supply. One of the reasons for this is that many of its underlying assumptions are those of the New Policies Scenario. In the 450 Scenario, by contrast, it is assumed that an international climate agreement is put in place that results in effective action to limit the rise in long-term average global temperature to two degrees Celsius (2 °C) above pre-industrial levels, including actions which are conducive to a greater expansion of nuclear power. While there are different ways to achieve the 2 °C goal, the 450 Scenario represents a cost-effective transition as the emission reductions are primarily realised through the help of firm price signals and supporting low-carbon technologies.

In the 450 Scenario, there is a radical transformation of energy production and use across all sectors and much faster improvements in energy efficiency across the board (see Chapter 2). Carbon abatement in the power sector results from fuel-switching to less carbon-intensive forms of generation, power sector efficiency improvements and reduced electricity demand. Of the portfolio of low-carbon electricity generation technologies that see increased deployment (compared with the New Policies Scenario), coal-fired power stations that are fitted with carbon capture and storage (CCS) and nuclear power make the most important contributions to abatement followed by hydropower, wind power and solar photovoltaics (PV). However, if taken as a group, non-hydro renewables contribute more to abatement than nuclear power. Nuclear power's role in reducing emissions is more significant in certain countries than the global average and grows over time, reflecting the long-lead times required to build new nuclear capacity and the increasing attractiveness of nuclear, as lower-cost and quicker-to-implement options are exhausted.

To achieve the 450 Scenario, global nuclear capacity more than doubles to 862 GW in 2040, 38% higher than in the New Policies Scenario and 12% higher than in the High Nuclear Case (Figure 11.12). Average annual capacity additions accelerate to more than 30 GW in the late 2020s, close to the peak brought online in the early 1980s and far outstripping the rates of capacity additions seen more recently. The 450 Scenario depends on some $81 billion per year in investment in new nuclear plants over 2014-2040. Such a rapid rate of deployment means that some of the current technical challenges to nuclear power development would have to be overcome quickly – such as construction delays, and cost overruns. More important, broad public consent would be needed, for example to identify and reach consent for suitable sites for new plants. There would have to be a major effort to attract and train skilled workers and regulators, both in countries with longstanding nuclear capacity but especially in countries developing nuclear power for the first time. Greater progress would also be required on establishing permanent facilities for the disposal of high-level radioactive waste.

Figure 11.12 ▷ **Global nuclear power capacity by scenario and case**

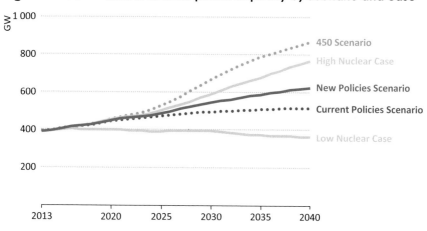

Outlook for nuclear fuel

Uranium supply

As outlined in Chapter 10, nuclear reactors generate electricity by converting the thermal energy released during nuclear fission. Several options for fissile material exist but virtually all reactors today use uranium, due to its low cost and abundance. While the vast majority use low- or slightly-enriched uranium (including some that mix uranium oxide with plutonium [MOX] fuel), the remainder use uranium, as found in nature. The process of fabricating fuel is known as the "front-end cycle" and involves the mining and milling of uranium ore through to the delivery of fabricated fuel assemblies to reactors. As a rule of thumb, a typical 1 GW reactor requires 140-180 tonnes of uranium to operate continuously for one year.[7] By comparison, to produce the same amount of electricity from a typical coal or gas-fired power plant currently requires approximately 2.6 million tonnes of coal or 1.8 billion cubic metres of gas.

Figure 11.13 ▷ **Nuclear fuel cycle and competition from secondary sources options**

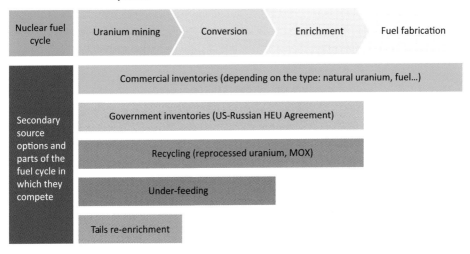

Nuclear plants source uranium from either newly mined primary sources or from secondary sources (Figure 11.13). Primary sources currently account for the largest share of supply, although the proportions have varied fairly significantly from year-to-year. Until recently, the most significant secondary supply came through the US-Russian Highly Enriched Uranium (HEU) Agreement, which came to an end in 2013. It involved down-blending highly-enriched uranium from Russian nuclear warheads with low-enriched uranium fuel for use in commercial nuclear power plants. Currently, the most prominent source of secondary supply is reprocessed spent fuel, followed by the under-feeding of enrichment plants.[8] While uranium that has been mined and held as inventory is the simplest form of secondary supply, it currently accounts for only a small portion of the total supply picture. Another source of secondary supply that could play a growing role in the future (depending on economic conditions and available technologies) is tails re-enrichment.[9]

---

7. Unless otherwise stated, a tonne of uranium refers to uranium metal (U), which is typically used when measuring uranium consumption, production and resources. Natural uranium oxide, or U_3O_8, is typically used for transactions of uranium on the market. To convert from tonnes of U to tonnes of U_3O_8 divide by 0.85.

8. Under-feeding is the process whereby enrichment companies "create" uranium, for subsequent sale, by reducing the percentage of fissile material remaining in depleted uranium to below the level contracted with the customer.

9. Uranium can also be produced by re-enriching depleted uranium tails. A significant amount of tails is currently in storage.

Uranium resources and production

Uranium resources are well-distributed geographically and present on all continents. Total identified resources are sufficient for more than 120 years at current rates of consumption (Table 11.4). If undiscovered resources (those that are thought to exist based on knowledge of discovered deposits and geological mapping) are included, the global resources-to-consumption ratio extends to over 250 years. Australia is the world's largest uranium resource-holder with 29% of the total identified resources that can be produced at relatively low cost (under $130 per kilogramme), followed by Kazakhstan with 12%. No other single country has more than a 10% share of total identified resources.

Table 11.4 ▷ **World uranium resources** (million tonnes as of end-2013)

Resource category*	<40 $/kgU	<80 $/kgU	<130 $/kgU	<260 $/kgU	Total**	R/P ratio
Identified	0.68	1.96	5.90	7.63		128
Undiscovered***	-	0.67	3.86	4.70		79
Total	0.68	2.62	9.77	12.33	15.32	257

* Values are not to be summed: resources below $80/kgU include those below $40/kgU. ** Total across all categories includes 3.0 million tonnes of speculative resources in an unassigned cost range. *** Undiscovered resources may prove higher since the United States did not report data for the last edition of NEA/IAEA (2014).

Global uranium production was estimated at around 60 000 tonnes in 2013. It has been increasing in recent years, as the efficiency of production in new mines increased and they got closer to output near their nameplate capacities. Kazakhstan is the world's largest producer, with 36% of global production, followed by Canada and Australia. The world's top-five producers (Niger and Namibia being the other two) account for approximately four-fifths of global output. Since the accident at Fukushima Daiichi, the uranium market has been over-supplied, with prices declining from around $70 per pound ($182 per kgU) to lows of under $30 per pound ($78 per kgU). Inventories have built up, particularly in Japan as, although most of its reactors have been offline, contracted fuel deliveries have continued more or less as before. The slump in global prices has resulted in some mine development and expansion plans being delayed and some operating mines being mothballed. It is likely that mining activity will start to pick up only when uranium prices rise, which depends very much on how quickly inventories start to be run down and reactors in key growth markets, such as China, come online, and when reactors in Japan are restarted. Current uranium prices are well below the levels that would spur investment in new mines, so prices will need to rise in order for the projections in the New Policies Scenario to be realised.

Uranium demand

In the New Policies Scenario, demand for uranium for nuclear power plants increases from 56 000 tonnes in 2012 to 106 000 tonnes in 2040 (Figure 11.14). The most significant increase comes from China, which becomes the world's largest uranium consumer around 2035, with its share of global demand rising from 4% to 25%. In the OECD, consistent with the projections for generation, demand for uranium increases fairly significantly in Korea and Japan, and moderately in the United States, while it declines in the European Union. Compared with the New Policies Scenario, uranium requirements in 2040 are 41% lower and 23% higher in the Low and High Nuclear Cases respectively.

Figure 11.14 ▷ Uranium demand in the New Policies Scenario by region

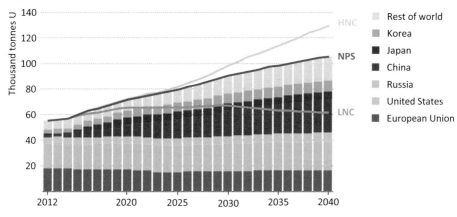

Notes: HNC = High Nuclear Case; NPS = New Policies Scenario; LNC = Low Nuclear Case.

Source: IEA analysis based on WNA 2013.

Uranium resources are more than sufficient to meet requirements to 2040 and well beyond, even if there is a significantly faster rate of deployment of nuclear power than projected. In the New Policies Scenario, cumulative demand for mined uranium amounts to 2.3 million tonnes to 2040 (measured as projected uranium requirements less secondary sources). This equates to around 40% of today's identified resources that can be produced for under $130 per kilogramme. Nonetheless, new mines will be required as production at existing mines declines. Based on demand for uranium in the New Policies Scenario, forecast output from existing and planned mines is approximately 45 000 tonnes lower than the level required in 2040 (Figure 11.15). Mines that are not yet under development will be required to be producing in the early 2020s to avoid a shortfall, implying that investment in new mining capacities needs to commence within the next few years.

Figure 11.15 ▷ Uranium demand in the New Policies Scenario compared with existing and planned production

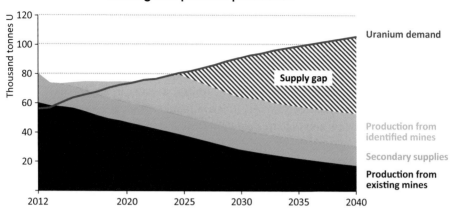

Notes: Identified mines incorporate prospective and planned mines and those under development. Some of those mines are already under construction; others are projects likely to proceed only if adequate price signals are sent by the market. Source: IEA analysis based on WNA 2013.

Exploitation of as yet undiscovered resources could provide uranium supplies much further into the future, subject to significant exploration and development being carried out. Furthermore, unconventional uranium resources (in phosphates and seawater), as well as alternative fuel cycles based on thorium, hold promise as nuclear fuels in the long term, subject to further technological development. A wide range of nuclear technologies is currently under development (e.g. Generation IV reactors), which together with reprocessing, could also contribute to pushing any fuel constraints into the much longer term.

Chapter 12

The implications of nuclear power
Elements in decision-making

Highlights

- Provided waste disposal and safety issues can be satisfactorily addressed, nuclear power's limited exposure to disruptions in international fuel markets and its role as a reliable source of baseload electricity can enhance energy security. The New Policies Scenario illustrates the role it can play in this respect, particularly for some import-dependent countries. By contrast, in the Low Nuclear Case these countries face greater risks to energy security: the biggest drops in self-sufficiency in 2040 compared with the New Policies Scenario are in Japan (13 percentage points), Korea (six) and the European Union (four). In some competitive power systems, concerns are being raised about long-term reliability of supply due to the risks involved in investing in new thermal capacity, including nuclear plants, under current market design.

- No country has yet established permanent facilities for the disposal of high-level radioactive waste from commercial reactors, which continues to build-up in temporary storage. In the New Policies Scenario, the amount of spent nuclear fuel (containing elements that must be safely isolated for thousands of years) more than doubles, reaching 705 000 tonnes. All countries which have ever had nuclear generation facilities have an obligation to develop solutions for long-term storage.

- Nuclear power is one of a limited number of options available at scale to reduce CO_2 emissions. It has avoided the release of an estimated 56 Gt of CO_2 since 1971, or close to two years of emissions at current rates. The average cost of avoiding emissions through new nuclear capacity depends on the mix and the costs of the fuels it displaces, and therefore ranges from very low levels to over $80/tonne. Even with higher deployment of renewables in the Low Nuclear Case, CO_2 emissions in 2040 are higher than in the New Policies Scenario with the sharpest increases in Japan (14%), Korea (11%) and the European Union (5%).

- The upfront costs to build new nuclear plants are high and, often, uncertain, but they can offer economic benefits by adding stability to electricity costs and improving balance of payments. In the Low Nuclear Case, higher import requirements push up global import bills for natural gas and coal by 6% compared with the New Policies Scenario, with sharper increases in certain countries.

- Given that nuclear power inherently works on long timelines, policy-makers have a responsibility to provide long-term guidance and stability. One example, where the approach to nuclear power is supportive, is to provide clarity on lifetime extensions. Public consent to nuclear power requires transparency at all stages and public conviction that their voice will be heard and taken into account. Confidence in the competence and independence of regulatory oversight is essential.

Introduction

Like other forms of electricity generation, nuclear power has characteristics of national value beyond the electricity it produces. It can enhance energy security and contribute to efforts to meet climate targets and improve air quality. It also has adverse characteristics. It carries with it the risk of accidents that could have major consequences to public health and the environment, it results in waste that must be safely isolated for thousands of years and the upfront costs to build new plants are high and, often, uncertain. Nuclear power is also facing growing competition from some renewable power generation technologies that are undergoing rapid cost reductions. This chapter probes further into the considerations which should influence national policy towards nuclear power through to 2040, analysing the implications for energy security, the balance of trade and the environment of the projections in the New Policies Scenario, our central scenario. Comparisons are made, where appropriate, with a Low Nuclear Case, to elicit the implications of a decline in nuclear power due to a combination of plausible events (Table 12.1). Comparisons are also made with a High Nuclear Case, although these are more limited in recognition of the fact that the balance of uncertainties in relation to nuclear power is for the moment, at least, on the downside. Based on the analysis in this special focus on nuclear power, we end with a set of policy priorities relevant to most countries, whether they are using, pursuing or phasing out nuclear power.

Table 12.1 ▷ **Selected projections in the New Policies Scenario and Low Nuclear Case**

	New Policies Scenario (NPS)	Low Nuclear Case (LNC)	% Change (LNC vs NPS)
Net energy self-sufficiency in 2040			
Japan	31%	19%	-40%
Korea	40%	34%	-15%
European Union	50%	46%	-8%
Cumulative spending on natural gas and coal imports (2014-2040) ($2013, billion)			
Japan	2 001	2 389	19%
Korea	1 104	1 160	5%
European Union	5 050	5 282	5%
China	3 446	3 589	4%
Energy-related CO_2 emissions in 2040 (power sector CO_2 emissions in 2040) (Gt)			
United States	4.1 (1.5)	4.2 (1.6)	2% (6%)
Japan	0.8 (0.3)	0.9 (0.4)	14% (35%)
Korea	0.4 (0.2)	0.5 (0.2)	11% (26%)
European Union	2.3 (0.7)	2.5 (0.8)	7% (19%)
Cumulative spent nuclear fuel (1971-2040) (thousand tonnes)	705	624	-12%
Natural gas trade in 2040 (bcm)	1 154	1 224	6%
Steam coal trade in 2040 (Mtce)	1 101	1 196	9%

Notes: Gt = gigatonnes; bcm = billion cubic metres; Mtce = million tonnes of coal equivalent.

Energy security

Energy security, which can be defined in broad terms as the uninterrupted availability of energy at an affordable price, can be enhanced in several ways by nuclear power. Following the oil supply crises of 1973 and 1979, oil-importing countries wanting to reduce their dependency on oil-fired generation saw boosting the construction of nuclear plants as an effective solution. Today, with oil use reduced to very low levels in the power sector, nuclear power's contribution to energy security is measured more in terms of its place alongside other fuels in electricity generation.

When nuclear power displaces fossil-fuelled generation, it can help ease any tightness that might be present in regional markets. For countries that import energy, nuclear power can help manage geopolitical risks to energy security by reducing the dependence of electricity on foreign fuel supplies or muting the effect of increases in fossil fuel prices in international markets (see Spotlight on the treatment of nuclear power as imported or indigenous energy). These considerations can be particularily important in those resource-poor countries which are confronted with large-scale dependence on energy imports from a limited number of suppliers or from suppliers whose chain of supply may be less stable. Nuclear plants contribute to power system resilience by adding diversity to the options available to generate electricity. They also possess attributes that lend long-term reliability to power grids:

■ Fuel and operating costs are relatively low and stable, thereby providing a hedge against volatility in fossil fuel costs and, in some markets, carbon pricing (see Chapter 10).

■ They can generate electricity continuously for extended periods, 24 hours per day, seven days a week, before going offline for refuelling.

■ They have long operating lifetimes, typically 40-60 years.

■ They can provide services important for the functioning of electricity systems, namely maintaining grid frequency.

There is, though, another side to the story. Countries that rely heavily on nuclear power and have limited alternatives, including interconnections (few would have substantial unused generating capacity), face the risk that a major accident (such as that in Japan in 2011) could quickly close a significant portion, or the whole, of their nuclear fleet. In smaller power systems, even the loss of a single unit can pose serious problems as nuclear plants are relatively large. In general, the more sudden the loss of nuclear supply and the more limited (or high cost) the alternatives, the greater the expense or threat to system reliability. Other energy security risks associated with nuclear power include the possibility of disruption to fuel supplies, particularly if they come from foreign suppliers. Nuclear power's susceptibility to abrupt changes in public and political attitudes brings with it a different type of risk to security of supply.

Energy trade, self-sufficiency and diversity

Comparison between the Low Nuclear Case and the New Policies Scenario illustrates the sensitivity of various dimensions of energy security to the level of deployment of nuclear power.[1] While a sudden removal of nuclear capacity can necessitate the use of oil-fired capacity, due to its high cost (and in most cases a lack of capacity) oil does not feature as a long-term option in the Low Nuclear Case. Instead, the reduction in nuclear capacity of 258 gigawatts (GW) in 2040, compared with the New Policies Scenario, is offset by increases in generating capacity using renewables (by 246 GW), natural gas (by 138 GW) and coal (by 64 GW) (Figure 12.1).

Figure 12.1 ▷ **Change in global capacity and generation in the Low Nuclear Case compared with the New Policies Scenario, 2040**

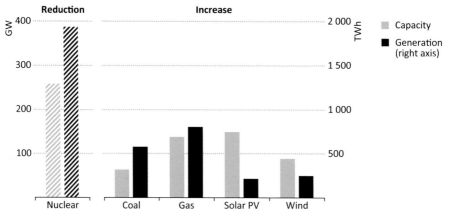

Note: TWh = terawatt-hours.

The shift in the power mix in the Low Nuclear Case increases global primary demand for natural gas by 166 billion cubic metres (bcm) (comparable to the current production of Qatar) and for steam coal by 156 million tonnes of coal equivalent (Mtce) (approaching the current exports of Australia) in 2040. Increased gas demand is primarily covered by higher indigenous production in North America, by liquefied natural gas (LNG) imports in China and Japan and by piped imports in Europe (from Russia). In terms of steam coal, Japan, India, the European Union, Korea and China lead the demand for increased imports, while Indonesia, Australia, Colombia and South Africa are the exporters who benefit most from the increasing demand for their supplies. The overall effect is to push inter-regional trade in natural gas higher by 6% and in steam coal higher by 9% (Figure 12.2).

Energy self-sufficiency is not necessarily a desirable goal: when foreign energy supplies are available, affordable and reliable, they may represent the best option for satisfying demand, based on a constructive relationship of mutual dependence between suppliers and buyers. Moreover, energy self-sufficiency is no substitute for well-functioning and diversified

---

1. See Chapter 11 for details of nuclear capacity and generation in each of the scenarios and cases.

markets. However, the extent of energy import-dependence does provide one indicator of the gravity of any serious interruption in foreign energy supplies. It is useful in the context of the contingency planning of the response – either substitution by other resources or suppliers – to disruptions in international energy markets. Energy self-sufficiency can be increased by the use of nuclear power, although there are other ways of achieving the same result, including boosting indigenous production of fossil fuels, increasing the deployment of renewables and cutting demand by improving energy efficiency.

Figure 12.2 ▷ **World natural gas and steam coal trade in the New Policies Scenario and Low Nuclear Case**

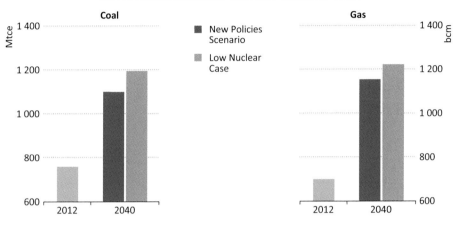

In the New Policies Scenario, changes in the use of nuclear power have implications for net energy self-sufficiency rates. The expansion of nuclear power in Asia plays a particularly important role in energy security in the region as some countries there lack indigenous energy resources and have limited or no power interconnections with neighbours. For example, domestic resources meet 31% of Japan's energy needs in 2040, up from 20% before the Fukushima Daiichi accident (but only 6% in 2012), as the nuclear component of supply is re-established and the deployment of renewable energy sources extended. Although Japan remains heavily dependent on energy imports compared to most other large consumers – the OECD average net self-sufficiency rate increases from 74% to 92% over the period – it realises a meaningful reduction in its vulnerability to disruptions in international energy markets. In Korea, against the backdrop of rising energy demand, nuclear power contributes to rising net self-sufficiency, which reaches 40% in 2040 (from 17% in 2012). While the rapid expansion of nuclear power in China and India is not sufficient to reverse the trend towards increasing dependence on energy imports, it does temper the growth.

Although the European Union has a much greater degree of market integration and interconnections than most parts of Asia, security of electricity supply will remain a key concern during the projection period. The European Union's dependence on energy imports remains high, at around 50% throughout the period, as rapid deployment of renewables is offset by reductions in fossil fuel production and nuclear power generation. Unlike many other major energy consumers, the United States' dependence on imported energy falls over the projection period, with net self-sufficiency rising from 84% to 96%.

Based on the assumptions in the Low Nuclear Case, energy self-sufficiency rates in countries that utilise nuclear power are reduced compared with the New Policies Scenario, leaving them more susceptible to supply disruptions and sudden increases in fossil fuel prices. The biggest reductions in net self-sufficiency rates relative to the New Policies Scenario in 2040 are in Japan (31% to 19%), Korea (40% to 34%) and the European Union (50% to 46%) (Figure 12.3).

Figure 12.3 ▷ **Net energy self-sufficiency in selected regions in the New Policies Scenario and the Low Nuclear Case**

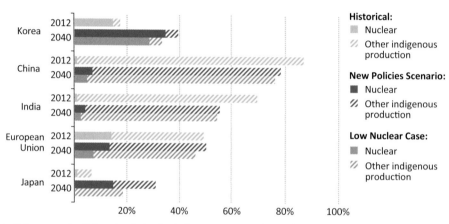

Note: Net energy self-sufficiency is calculated as indigenous energy production (including nuclear power) divided by total primary energy demand (Spotlight).

A country with a diverse energy mix is generally better able to manage the effects of supply disruptions and price volatility, particularly when it is not overly reliant on one supplier or group of suppliers. In the New Policies Scenario, the contribution of nuclear power to energy diversity at the global level rises slightly: it provides 12% of electricity generation in 2040, compared with 11% in 2012. Global numbers, however, mask more significant changes at the regional level. Outside the OECD, the share of nuclear in power generation rises from 4% to 8% over the period, a notable increase as structural shifts in an energy mix are typically slow moving. Countries in which nuclear power plays an important role in increasing diversity in the power mix include China, Japan, Korea and India (Figure 12.4). In the Low Nuclear Case, nuclear provides 7% of global electricity generation in 2040. By contrast in the High Nuclear Case, the nuclear component of supply grows, reaching 14% of total generation.

Should nuclear power be considered imported or indigenous energy?

Most countries with nuclear reactors obtain nuclear fuel from foreign sources, relying on them for the entire fuel supply chain – uranium extraction, conversion, enrichment and fuel fabrication – or at least parts of it. It can therefore be argued that nuclear power is imported energy just as fossil fuels are for those countries dependent on imports. However, there are counterarguments that support the view that it is inherently more secure, in a manner similar to indigenous supply. Indeed, this is how it is treated in energy balances prepared by many institutions, including the United Nations, International Energy Agency, Asia-Pacific Economic Cooperation and Eurostat.

Uranium supplies are well-spread geographically and (like oil, gas, and coal) more than adequate to meet demand, even in the event of a significant scale-up in nuclear power (see Chapter 11). The global supply chain for nuclear fuel has yet to experience a serious disruption and as nuclear power involves long lead times, the industry has ample time to anticipate and respond to changes in demand. The volume of nuclear fuel needed to generate a unit of electricity is much less than for fossil-fuelled plants, making strategic reserves easier and cheaper to build and maintain. This is illustrated by the case of France, which is the second-biggest user of nuclear power and has no indigenous uranium (and almost no oil) production: it currently imports around 8 000 tonnes of uranium per year compared with almost 80 million tonnes of oil. Nuclear plants typically have several months or sometimes even years of fuel stored on site. Moreover, reactors can operate for up to 24 months between refuelling, which would generally allow time to resolve any disruptions that might arise.

The economic impact of fuel price spikes is much less severe for generation from nuclear than fossil fuels. Generating costs for nuclear are much less sensitive to changes in fuel costs, thereby providing stability in wholesale electricity costs: with a 50% increase in the fuel cost, the levelised cost of electricity rises by around 5%. By comparison, a 50% rise in gas prices pushes up the generating cost of a combined-cycle gas turbine (CCGT) plant by around one-third. Moreover, increases in the cost of nuclear fuel imports are unlikely to dent a country's balance of payments, as can be the case with oil and gas, as the volumes and values involved are typically much smaller.

Nevertheless, countries will make their own judgements about the security of outsourcing nuclear fuel supply, and to whom. Just as some nations are concerned about dependence on Middle Eastern oil or Russian natural gas, newcomer countries might be reluctant to become dependent on the world's largest suppliers of nuclear fuel or to rely exclusively on a single supplier to provide all of their nuclear fuel or "cradle to grave" services. To address such concerns and create an incentive for countries not to build their own facilities to produce nuclear fuel, the International Atomic Energy Agency (IAEA) is developing a "nuclear fuel bank" to provide a source of low-enriched uranium supply in the event of politically motivated disruptions (not for technical breakdowns or commercial disputes).

In the Low Nuclear Case, even with higher deployment of renewables there is an increase in reliance on generation from fossil fuels in most countries compared with the New Policies Scenario, with implications for diversity of the energy mix and security of supply depending on where the fossil fuels are produced. Japan sees the biggest increase in the share of fossil fuels in the power sector, with nuclear completely absent compared with it making up 21% of generation in 2040 in the New Policies Scenario. The European Union and the United States converge towards power systems with increasing reliance on natural gas and renewables as the share of nuclear power declines (this trend is already evident in the New Policies Scenario, but is more pronounced in the Low Nuclear Case).

Figure 12.4 ▷ **Power generation mix by selected region in the New Policies Scenario and Low Nuclear Case**

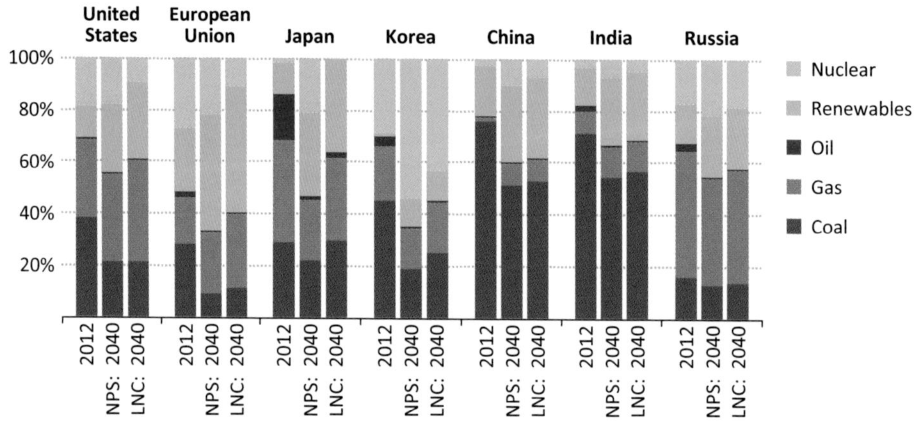

Notes: NPS = New Policies Scenario; LNC = Low Nuclear Case.

National economic considerations

Economic factors, such as cutting spending on fossil fuel imports, reducing exposure to price spikes in international fuel markets and providing stability to the cost of generating electricity, influence many governments in favour of the construction of new nuclear power plants, despite their high upfront costs. In terms of existing nuclear power plants, these same factors provide a strong economic case for their maximum utilisation, provided it can be done safely, as the initial upfront costs are effectively "sunk" and the running costs are in most cases relatively low, stable and predictable, compared with the costs of fossil-fuelled electricity generation. For energy exporters, oil exporters in particular, where rising domestic fossil fuel demand threatens to erode the country's surplus production, nuclear power can preserve the volume and value of exports, which may be important to maintain or grow revenues from trade. These considerations are cited in Russia and the Middle East in discussions about whether or not nuclear power should play a greater role.

In the Low Nuclear Case, higher import requirements push up import bills for countries dependent on foreign supplies of natural gas and coal. Global expenditure on inter-regional trade in these commodities rises from an estimated $413 billion in 2012 to just over $780 billion in 2040 (in year-2013 dollars), around 6% higher than in the New Policies Scenario. Japan is a major contributor to the global increase, its import bill reaching $84 billion in 2040, compared with $73 billion in the New Policies Scenario (Figure 12.5). Spending in 2040 is also higher in China (up 7%), the European Union (up 7%) and India (up 3%). The United States is a net exporter of natural gas and coal in 2040 in the Low Nuclear Case, but its export earnings over the period are slightly lower than in the New Policies Scenario, due to higher domestic needs.

Figure 12.5 ▷ **Natural gas and coal import bills by selected region in the New Policies Scenario and Low Nuclear Case**

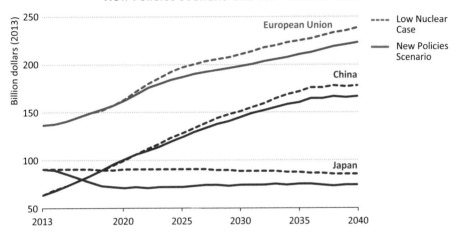

Note: The use of oil-fired power generating capacity does not increase over the longer term in the Low Nuclear Case compared with the New Policies Scenario due to its high cost.

Environment

The full lifecycle of nuclear power entails a mix of environmental benefits and costs, some of which extend over very long time horizons. It is a low-carbon source of electricity generation, and therefore an important option for mitigation of climate change. It does not emit the hazardous air pollutants – sulphur dioxide, nitrogen oxides and particulates – that come from fossil fuel-based electricity generation, thereby avoiding their related adverse impacts on public health and ecosystems. At the same time, however, the nuclear fuel cycle produces radioactive waste that must be safely isolated for centuries to protect human health and the environment. Like other thermal power plants, nuclear power plants also use large amounts of water for cooling, reliance on which can introduce risks to nuclear facilities and stress to local water resources, particularly if plants are located inland. We examine three of these issues, carbon-dioxide (CO_2) emissions, nuclear waste disposal and water needs. All require attention at a national level, without diminishing the importance of full local environmental appraisal.

CO$_2$ emissions

Nuclear power is a low-carbon technology that can provide a significant contribution to the decarbonisation of the power sector, particularly given its availability at scale and role in baseload generation. It produces negligible greenhouse-gas emissions at the point of electricity generation, though some emissions result from the use of fossil fuels at different stages of the nuclear fuel cycle and in cement production for plant construction. On a lifecycle basis, the greenhouse-gas emissions intensity of nuclear power – the amount of CO$_2$-equivalent (CO$_2$-eq) emitted per unit of electricity generated – is currently about 15 grammes of CO$_2$-eq per kilowatt-hour. This figure is comparable to that of wind power and around 1% of the average figure for coal-fired generation at present.

Today, nuclear power is the world's second-largest source of low-carbon electricity (34%), after hydropower (51%); in OECD countries, it is the largest source of low-carbon electricity. In the New Policies Scenario, the share of global electricity generation from low-carbon sources (nuclear, renewables and fossil-fuelled generation with carbon capture and storage) grows from 32% in 2012 to 46% in 2040. Despite an absolute increase in nuclear power output, its share of low-carbon generation drops to 25% in 2040, because of faster growth of renewables.

We estimate that in the absence of nuclear power, global energy-related CO$_2$ emissions would have been around 1.7 Gt higher in 2012,[2] corresponding to around 5% of current global CO$_2$ emissions (or 13% of power sector emissions). In the New Policies Scenario, avoided CO$_2$ emissions increase to 2.2 Gt in 2040, by which time they equate to 6% of global emissions (or 14% of power sector emissions) (Figure 12.6). Avoided CO$_2$ emissions do not increase at the same rate as nuclear power generation, reflecting the falling carbon intensity of the rest of the power mix. This gradual decarbonisation of power supply is due to the introduction of more efficient plants and a shift in the power mix towards renewable sources and – within fossil fuels – towards natural gas rather than coal. The role of nuclear power as a means of limiting CO$_2$ emissions is, naturally, greater in regions that rely more heavily on it in their electricity mix, particularly when it substitutes for fossil fuel alternatives. CO$_2$ emissions avoided due to installed nuclear capacity in 2040 (as a share of the region's total emissions at that time) reach almost 50% in Korea, 12% in Japan, 10% in the United States, 9% in the European Union and 8% in China.

---

2. Estimates of avoided CO$_2$ emissions are derived from analysis of what sources of generation would be most likely to fill the gap if nuclear power was not present. For estimates of historical emissions avoided, in OECD countries, nuclear generation is assumed to be replaced by fossil fuel sources, which are scaled-up based on the historical mix. In non-OECD countries, the same approach is taken, with some allowance for additional hydropower given their large unexploited resources. For estimates of future emissions avoided, nuclear generation is assumed to be replaced by generation from all other sources (including renewables) which are scaled-up based on their additions as projected in the New Policies Scenario.

Figure 12.6 ▷ Global energy-related CO_2 emissions and CO_2 emissions avoided by nuclear in the New Policies Scenario

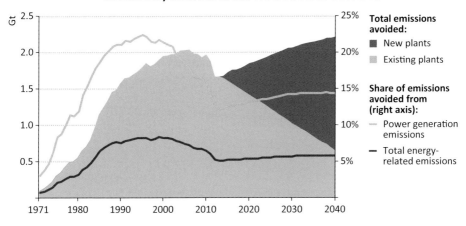

Note: See Footnote 2 for a description of the methodology used to calculate CO_2 emissions avoided.

In cumulative terms, we estimate that nuclear power avoided the release of over 56 Gt of CO_2 globally between 1971 and 2012. This is equivalent to almost two years of global energy-related emissions at current rates. In the New Policies Scenario, cumulative global CO_2 emissions avoided by nuclear power are projected to climb to 111 Gt in the period 1971-2040. Looking at individual markets, cumulative emissions avoided by nuclear power over the period amount to 33 Gt in the United States, 29 Gt in the European Union and 14 Gt in China (Figure 12.7).

Figure 12.7 ▷ Cumulative CO_2 emissions avoided by nuclear power by selected region in the New Policies Scenario, 1971-2040

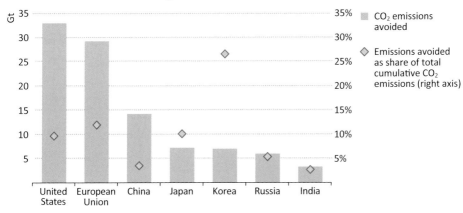

The cost of avoiding CO_2 emissions as a result of the deployment of nuclear power can be calculated as the difference between the generation costs of nuclear power and those of fossil-fuelled generation (excluding CO_2 prices) that would be most likely to fill the

gap if nuclear power was not present divided by the CO_2 emissions avoided.[3] As nuclear generation costs – as well as fossil fuel costs and the mix that could substitute for nuclear power – vary significantly from country to country and over time, the cost of avoiding emissions through the use of nuclear power also varies significantly. In general terms, nuclear power is a more expensive option for reducing emissions in markets where it faces strong competition due to relatively low fossil fuel prices (e.g. natural gas in the United States or oil and gas in countries that subsidise them). Conversely, if nuclear power is fully competitive with fossil fuel options without a carbon price, then there is no additional cost to avoid emissions and potentially a negative cost (where nuclear is less expensive than the alternative fossil fuel options).

In the New Policies Scenario, the average cost of avoiding CO_2 emissions as a result of the deployment of new nuclear power is close to zero in India and China and below zero in Korea, as these countries have the lowest costs for nuclear new builds (Figure 12.8).[4] It is below \$10/tonne in Japan mainly due to the high fuel costs, especially for natural gas, and around \$40/tonne in the European Union and in the United States. In the European Union, it varies from very high values due to the high costs of first-of-a-kind new nuclear plants to lower values as less costly plants are added in the mix and fossil fuel prices increase over the *Outlook* period. In the United States, the cost of avoiding CO_2 emissions is quite high, as the cost of the alternatives, in particular natural gas, is low, but it is moderated by the relative low cost of expanding nuclear capacity through uprates. The cost in Russia and in the Middle East is higher than in other markets, due to subsidised fossil alternatives.

Figure 12.8 ▷ **Average cost of CO_2 emissions avoided by nuclear power by selected region in the New Policies Scenario, 2014-2040***

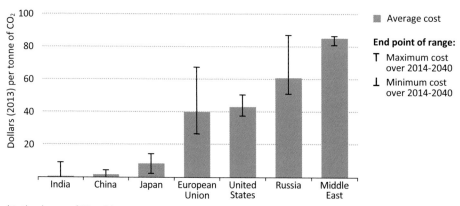

* In the absence of CO_2 pricing.

---

3. These calculations do not include the nuclear power generation replaced by renewables or their associated generation costs (which could be higher or lower than that of nuclear plants depending on the region and technologies in use) as they are also low-carbon technologies.

4. Costs have been calculated as a weighted average through time and deployment, both for new plants and for uprates.

In the Low Nuclear Case, the transition to a low-carbon energy system is slower than in the New Policies Scenario. Renewables fill 26% of the gap in generation left by nuclear power, but increased output from coal and gas plants results in global energy-related CO_2 emissions in 2040 that are higher by 0.8 Gt (2%) (Figure 12.9). The increase is greater if the comparison is confined to the power sector: global power sector CO_2 emissions are 5% higher in 2040 in the Low Nuclear Case than in the New Policies Scenario. The share of low-carbon generation worldwide rises from 32% in 2012 to 43% in 2040, compared with 46% in the New Policies Scenario. Looking at particular markets, the emissions increase depends on the degree to which generation from nuclear power is reduced and which alternatives are available. Countries that see sharper increases in energy-related CO_2 emissions in 2040 compared with the New Policies Scenario include Japan (14%), Korea (11%), and the European Union (5%).

Figure 12.9 ▷ **Change in global CO_2 emission indicators in the Low Nuclear Case relative to the New Policies Scenario**

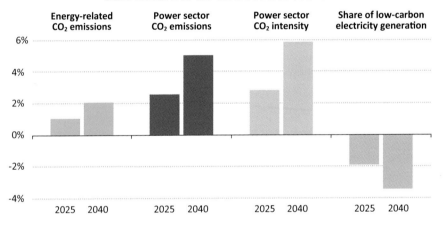

High-level radioactive waste disposal

The commercial nuclear fuel cycle generates radioactive waste that varies in its radioactive content as well as its physical and chemical form.[5] High-level waste (HLW) – which consists of spent (used) nuclear fuel and waste streams from reprocessing – is the longest-lived and the most highly radioactive, making its management and disposal the principal challenge at the back-end of the nuclear fuel cycle. It accounts for nearly all of the radioactive content of the waste produced in the nuclear fuel cycle (as well as significant heat output) despite representing just a small proportion of its volume. Because HLW remains more radioactive than its natural surroundings for thousands of years, it must be safely isolated to protect human health and the environment until the radioactivity has decayed to acceptable background levels.

---

5. Radioactive waste is generally categorised as high-level waste, intermediate-level waste and low-level waste according to the degree of radiological hazards involved and requirements for safe containment (in terms of physical shielding and length of isolation).

No matter which strategy is employed at the back-end of the nuclear fuel cycle – direct disposal (a "once-through" approach) or reprocessing – the result is HLW that eventually requires permanent disposal. Reprocessing does not obviate the need for permanent disposal of HLW, though it can reduce its volume and thermal load.[6] The expert technical and policy communities generally view deep geologic repositories as a viable solution to safely isolate HLW over the very long time periods required (NEA, 1995; IAEA, 2003). The concept relies on surrounding rock, clay or salt to provide natural barriers to the escape of radioactivity and engineered barriers to add further layers of containment and shielding.[7] Consequently, such facilities are commonly being pursued across countries that currently have or are expecting to have inventories of HLW.

National efforts to develop deep geologic repositories are at varying stages (Table 12.2). To date, no country has fully implemented such a facility (for commercial HLW). Finland, France and Sweden have selected disposal sites; Finland has undertaken preliminary site work at the Olkiluoto site and is awaiting approval of the construction licence for the main part of the facility (expected in 2015). These countries expect to have repositories operational and to begin receiving HLW in the 2020-2025 timeframe. Elsewhere, longer time horizons for opening deep geologic repositories are envisaged. Technical and political challenges, particularly during site selection processes, have slowed implementation plans. Aside from the lengthy period of scientific study required to determine site feasibility, site selection has often been met by public concern in local communities (see Chapter 10).

We estimate that reactors worldwide have generated over 349 000 tonnes of spent nuclear fuel since 1971 and that this is currently increasing by around 9 000 tonnes per year.[8] Some of this has been reprocessed – for example, in France, Japan, Russia and the United Kingdom. Today, all HLW is in temporary storage at reactor sites or, in some cases, more centralised facilities. From a technical, safety and economic perspective, this is not necessarily problematic for some time. The US Nuclear Regulatory Commission has, for example, determined that spent nuclear fuel can be stored safely in dry casks[9] for at least 60 years beyond the licenced lifetime of any reactor without significant environmental effects. Furthermore, temporary storage in dry casks is relatively inexpensive, and can

---

6. Reprocessing can thereby reduce capacity requirements for nuclear waste repositories or the number that need to be built. Since reprocessing isolates highly radioactive elements from the fissile elements in spent fuel, it raises proliferation concerns and requires special provisions for safety and security.

7. The feasibility of deep geologic repositories has been demonstrated in the United States with the Waste Isolation Pilot Plant (WIPP) for disposal of HLW from military applications.

8. The estimates rely on the IEA's detailed time-series statistics for nuclear generation, which date back to 1971, hence the choice of base year. Adding in the volume of spent nuclear fuel generated prior to 1971 would not substantially increase the overall estimate.

9. Dry casks refer to thick metal containers that are filled with spent fuel elements (once they have been allowed to cool in pools for several years at the reactor site) and inert gas, and then sealed. The casks are then placed in vaults to provide continuous shielding from radiation leakage, located either at the reactor site or at a centralised waste storage facility. Dry casks are preferred for long-term storage because they involve no moving parts (relying on natural air circulation for heat removal) and require very little maintenance.

reduce the cost of storage in repositories (by allowing the radioactive content and heat output of HLW to diminish). The additional time bought by temporary storage may also allow for the development of better technologies to manage HLW.

Table 12.2 ▷ **Back-end fuel cycle strategy and progress towards repositories for high-level radioactive waste disposal in selected countries**

Country	Strategy	Progress towards disposal
Site selected		
Finland	Direct disposal	• Deep geologic repository (DGR) design selected; application for construction licence submitted; preliminary site work started. • Disposal at Olkiluoto site targeted around 2020.
France	Reprocessing	• DGR approach legally adopted; DGR design studies and site planning underway. • Disposal at Meuse/Haute-Marne site targeted around 2025.
Sweden	Direct disposal	• DGR design selected; application for construction licence submitted; preliminary site work started. • Disposal at Forsmark site targeted around 2025.
Site to be selected		
Canada	Direct disposal	• Waste management organisation (WMO) implementing Adaptive Phased Management, of which end state is DGR; siting phase launched in 2010, ongoing engagement with self-selected interested communities.
Czech Republic	Direct disposal	• WMO established; direct disposal in DGR approach assumed. • Site selection targeted by 2025.
China	Reprocessing	• Atomic Energy Authority responsible for developing disposal plans. • Site selection targeted by 2020.
Germany	Direct disposal	• Commission launched to develop site selection process and criteria. • Site selection targeted by 2031.
Japan	Reprocessing	• WMO established; responsible for site selection, construction, operation, maintenance, closure. • Site selection targeted by around 2030.
Russia	Reprocessing	• WMO established; responsible for site selection, design, construction, operation; assessment of required infrastructure underway.
Korea	Direct disposal (under review)	• Commission launched in 2013 to draw up consent-based national plan. • Joint research with the United States on pyroprocessing technology.
United Kingdom	Reprocessing	• WMO established and is responsible for DGR design and site selection; stakeholder/community engagement for site selection underway.
United States	Direct disposal	• DGR approach legally adopted; site at Yucca Mountain partially developed.

Notes: DGR = deep geologic repository; WMO = waste management organisation.

Sources: NEA (2014), Posiva (2014), Andra (2013) and IAEA (2006).

12

In the New Policies Scenario, the cumulative amount of spent nuclear fuel generated globally since 1971 more than doubles to 705 000 tonnes in 2040 (Figure 12.10). New reactors that achieve improved fuel "burn-up" reduce the cumulative amount of spent fuel produced in the period to 2040 by 21 000 tonnes (or 3%). By 2040, the European Union and United States have produced the most spent fuel, with 29% and 27% of the global total. China's fast-increasing use of nuclear power means it becomes the largest producer on an annual basis (3 600 tonnes per year in 2040). Korea also sees a sharp increase in spent fuel production, which more than triples. The slow progress made to date on deep geologic repositories in many countries, and long lead times to build them, means that there is a distinct possibility either that much of the world's spent fuel will still be in temporary storage at the end of the projection period or that public concern on this point will diminish support for nuclear power.

In the High Nuclear Case, the cumulative amount of spent nuclear fuel produced globally in 2040 is 734 000 tonnes, or 4% higher than in the New Policies Scenario. By contrast, in the Low Nuclear Case, it is 624 000 tonnes, or 12% lower than in the New Policies Scenario. However, the need for deep geologic repositories remains. Whether governments support nuclear power or oppose it, those that have, at some time, adopted nuclear power have HLW which must be disposed of. Permanent facilities will provide safer containment than the present temporary arrangements. Supporters and opponents of nuclear power alike have an interest in advancing the development of such facilities.

Figure 12.10 ▷ **World cumulative spent nuclear fuel discharged since 1971 in the New Policies Scenario**

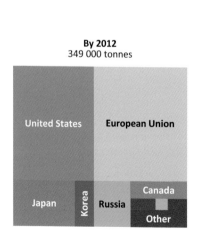
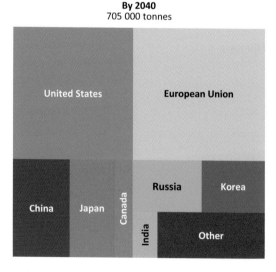

Notes: Spent nuclear fuel includes uranium and fission products, plus the fuel assembly. Estimates assume that 3.7 tonnes of fuel are currently discharged per TWh of electricity generated. Historical figures reflect a 130% improvement in fuel burn-up from 1971 and our projections reflect a further 10% improvement in fuel burn-up in the period to 2040.

Water

Nuclear plants, like most types of thermal power plants, use large quantities of water for cooling. A 1 GW nuclear plant equipped with a "once-through" (or open-loop) cooling system requires approximately 4 million cubic metres of water per day – roughly equivalent to the daily potable water needs of the city of New York. A small part of the volume used (less than 5%) is consumed, while the rest is returned to the source, albeit at a warmer temperature. While nuclear plants are typically sited in locations where ample water is available, unforeseen seasonal variations in climate or extreme weather events, such as droughts or heat waves, can reduce water availability or raise water temperatures to levels that necessitate a curtailment of generation (the latter has occurred in France and the United States).

Water constraints are set to increase during the projection period, particularly for inland nuclear plants with once-through cooling, as demand for water for all purposes continues to grow and as climate change affects the water cycle. Nuclear plants can implement cooling systems that minimise water use. Indeed, nuclear plants with re-circulating cooling systems can cut water requirements by up to 95%. However, such systems consume a higher share of the water volumes and incur higher costs. General policy towards nuclear power must take into account the needs of national and regional water policy, while plans for individual plants must include appraisal of the local impact of water use on the environment and society.

Policy priorities for nuclear power

Government policy is central to the future of nuclear power as the technology has attributes that are not routinely recognised by the market and raises issues of major public concern, both nationally and internationally. Governments can adopt one of three broad approaches. First, they may engender a policy framework that actively supports nuclear power, perhaps allocating significant public or other resources (for example, through levies on power consumers), such as many governments do to aid renewables. Second, they may allow nuclear power to compete in the market with minimal market intervention, but rigorous regulatory control. Alternatively, they may phase out or ban nuclear power outright. Each approach calls for different policies; but measures demand surprisingly similar attention in the three cases.

Market design in competitive electricity markets

In competitive electricity markets, the energy security, climate and system benefits of nuclear power (and other technologies) are not always recognised by a price signal and so may not enter into the commercial decision whether or not to build a new plant or to continue to operate an existing one. In the parts of the United States where wholesale electricity prices are mainly determined by the market, some nuclear plants have been struggling to generate sufficient revenues to recover their costs because of low wholesale prices (mainly due to low gas prices), high repair costs and, in some cases, the increasing shares of renewables-based generation. Moreover, in parts of the United States and Europe, there are doubts about whether current conditions in competitive markets can trigger investment in new thermal plants, including nuclear power. This carries with it the risk that reliability of electricity supply could be compromised by an absence of adequate price signals to invest in new dispatchable capacity.

Though the process to internalise all significant externalities – positive and negative – in competitive electricity markets is fraught with difficulty, some steps have already been taken in this direction. For example, an increasing number of markets are putting a price on carbon emissions and a small number of markets are putting a value on reliability attributes, through mechanisms such as capacity payments. Without such reforms, governments interested in maintaining or expanding the use of any generation technology that provides additional benefits to the system beyond the value of the electricity it produces may need to establish targeted policies to reflect those wider considerations.

Provide long-term policy guidance

Nuclear power inherently works on long timelines. New plants require extensive planning and construction time and, once built, may operate for 60 years or more. Radioactive waste needs to be safely isolated for thousands of years. Policy decisions extending over such timescales make exceptional demands on the decision-takers: changes in the policy or investment framework could entail a radical departure from the conditions in which the original decision was made. It is easy to call for stability in the policy environment in which the costs and benefits of nuclear power are assessed, but not very realistic. Nonetheless, some uncertainties can be reduced:

- **Clarity on lifetime extensions:** Almost half of the existing nuclear fleet is scheduled to retire before 2040, with the rate or retirements picking up in the first half of the 2020s, in line with already announced plans and as reactors built during the 1970s are taken offline, and then once again in the late 2030s. If the lifetime extensions that we assume are not authorised, plants will be taken offline at an even faster rate. Given the lead times and the scale of investment involved, utilities need to start planning either to continue operating existing plants or to develop alternative power generation capacity years in advance of nuclear plants reaching the end of their current licence periods. To facilitate this planning, governments should provide clarity on their approach to license extensions and details of the regulatory steps involved well ahead of possible plant closures.

- **Waste disposal:** Nations which have, or have had, any nuclear component in their power supply need to provide for the very long-term disposal of high-level radioactive waste, whatever policy towards nuclear power prevails today. Deep geologic repositories have been identified by policy-makers and the technical community as the safest option for the long-term disposal of high-level radioactive waste though more remains to be done to prove the concept and to convince the general public.

While several countries are making progress towards establishing such facilities, today – 60 years since the first nuclear reactor started operating – none have been completed and the waste that has been produced in the interim period remains in temporary storage, typically at the plants that produced it. In our central scenario, the amount of spent fuel in 2040 is more than twice as large as it is today. Governments must ensure that adequate funds are securely set aside to pay for the long-term management of this waste and that the funds are appropriately managed, as is already done in a number of countries.

■ **Phase-out strategies:** Countries contemplating or implementing a phase-out of nuclear power have as much of an obligation to set the relevant facts before the public as those disposed to support nuclear power. Reliable analysis is needed from the outset on the sources and mix of fuels that might fill the gap when nuclear plants are taken offline and what this might mean for the cost of electricity, the security of energy supply, network stability and the feasibility of meeting climate targets and minimising emissions of other air pollutants. Independent and transparent audit arrangements are highly desirable. Any transition period needs to be carefully managed to ensure that other energy security, economic and environmental policy goals are not unnecessarily jeopardised. Maintaining a robust nuclear safety culture remains essential: decommissioning will remain a necessity and nuclear waste needs to be managed over a very long timescale as older reactors inevitably reach the end of their operating lifetimes. Attracting young professionals to facilitate the transition away from nuclear power could be challenging, because few individuals will wish to enter a field that is perceived to have a questionable future.

Strengthen governance and the independence of regulatory oversight

An effective regulatory framework and sound, independent regulatory oversight are prerequisites for safe operation of a nuclear fleet and critical to establishing and maintaining public confidence in nuclear power. This was highlighted by official investigations into the Fukushima Daiichi accident in 2011, which concluded that the accident could and should have been foreseen and prevented, and stressed the need to improve the competence and independence of the regulatory body. The message is clear to all countries that have or are planning to introduce a nuclear power programme. For countries planning to introduce nuclear power, it is vital to recognise that operating nuclear plants requires sophisticated technical, industrial, institutional, and legal capacities. Robust and independent oversight regimes are similarly necessary for nuclear waste storage and disposal.

Work together on common issues

By its very nature, nuclear power has implications beyond national boundaries and, in any case, many of the challenges posed by nuclear power can be daunting for an individual nation. Challenges facing all countries with nuclear programmes can be addressed

12

collectively. Institutions have been established to facilitate such co-operation, for example on best practice in regulation, safe operation and managing nuclear waste, bringing together industry, regulators, national and international bodies. Organisations such as the International Atomic Energy Agency, the OECD Nuclear Energy Agency (NEA) and the World Association of Nuclear Operators provide fora for promoting high standards and engaging in joint technology development. These institutions are of particular value to countries with small or new nuclear programmes to enable them to draw upon the broader experience of more established nuclear enterprises. Co-operation should also extend to research and development aimed at advances in safety and cost reduction (IEA, 2015).[10] The safety and security requirements for the technical facilities required and the long timelines required before research investments yield returns are strong reasons for international collaborative endeavours.

Improve public engagement and transparency

Decisions concerning nuclear power need to be taken with the informed consent of the public. Public engagement needs to occur both at the national level during the process of broad policy formation or its revision, and at the local level concerning specific projects. It should include all relevant stakeholders – industry, policy-makers, regulators, civil society and the potential host communities. The commitment to public engagement does not stop after the initial planning decision: it must extend all the way through to decommissioning and waste management. The public must have the opportunity to comment on both plans and operations and needs to be assured that its concerns have been heard and taken into account. Definition of the precise mechanism to achieve this will vary with local circumstances, as will the precise extent of the public role in final decision-making. Governments are ultimately accountable to the public for the effectiveness of these procedures and, accordingly, for their establishment and successful operation. Finland and Sweden have succeeded in gaining public approval of the sites for long-term waste disposal facilities on the basis of best practices in this respect.

---

10. IEA (2015), *Technology Roadmap: Nuclear Energy*, OECD/IEA/NEA, Paris, forthcoming.

PREFACE

Part C of this *WEO* (chapters 13-16) continues the past practice of conducting a detailed study of the energy sector of a particular country or region. This year the IEA presents its most comprehensive analytical study to date of the energy outlook for Africa, specifically sub-Saharan Africa.

Chapter 13 sets the scene by analysing sub-Saharan Africa's energy sector as it is today. It outlines important economic and social trends, and quantifies the number of people without access to modern energy. It details the existing energy architecture, including the power sector and other energy-consuming sectors, the scale of sub-Saharan Africa's energy resources and its energy production trends. Patterns of energy trade are mapped out and, finally, it considers the critical issue of energy affordability.

Chapter 14 looks to the future, assessing the energy demand and supply prospects for sub-Saharan Africa through to 2040. These are analysed by fuel, by sector and by sub-region, to present a comprehensive outlook for the energy sector, including for international energy trade and some of the main environmental implications.

Chapter 15 examines five key features of the sub-Saharan energy outlook in-depth. These include: the role of different solutions in providing access to electricity; how rapidly the region might make the transition to cleaner alternatives for cooking; the extent to which oil can fuel progress in Nigeria; the costs and benefits of South Africa diversifying its electricity system towards renewables and the policies involved; and, the opportunities and obstacles that Mozambique and Tanzania face as they seek to get the best value from their natural gas resources.

Chapter 16 considers how to maximise the gain from sub-Saharan energy, as a means to build a path to prosperity for its citizens. An "African Century Case" shows how progress in three key areas of energy policy could deliver a major boost to economic and social development in the region. These are: increased investment in supply, in particular of electricity, to meet the region's growing energy needs; improved management of natural resources and associated revenues; and deeper regional co-operation. It concludes by setting Africa's energy choices in a global context, as many of the actions that need to be taken in the region cannot be isolated from the prevailing trends in global energy markets.

Chapter 13

Energy in Africa today
Resource-full, but not yet power-full

Highlights

- Africa's energy sector is vital to its development and yet is one of the most poorly understood parts of the global energy system. Since 2000, much of sub-Saharan Africa (the focus of this study) has experienced more rapid economic growth than in the past, raising expectations of a new phase of development. Policies are being put in place in many countries aimed at securing a much-needed expansion in domestic energy provision. However, the current state of the energy system represents a major threat to the realisation of the region's economic hopes.

- Energy demand in sub-Saharan Africa grew by around 45% from 2000 to 2012, but accounts for only 4% of the world total, despite being home to 13% of the global population. Access to modern energy services, though increasing, remains limited: despite many positive efforts, more than 620 million people in sub-Saharan Africa remain without access to electricity and nearly 730 million rely on the traditional use of solid biomass for cooking. Electricity consumption per capita is, on average, less than that needed to power a 50-watt light bulb continuously.

- On-grid power generation capacity was 90 GW in 2012, with around half being in South Africa. 45% of this capacity is coal (mainly South Africa), 22% hydro, 17% oil (both more evenly spread) and 14% gas (mainly Nigeria). Insufficient, unreliable or inaccessible grid supply has resulted in large-scale private ownership of oil-fuelled generators (supplying 16 TWh in 2012) and greater focus on developing mini- and off-grid power systems. Renewables-based capacity is growing rapidly but from a very low base (with the exception of hydropower). Huge renewable resources remain untapped; excellent solar across all of Africa, hydro in many countries, wind mainly in coastal areas and geothermal in the East African Rift Valley.

- Sub-Saharan Africa produced 5.7 mb/d of oil in 2013, primarily in Nigeria and Angola. While 5.2 mb/d of crude oil were exported, around 1.0 mb/d of oil products were imported. Natural gas use of 27 bcm in 2012 is similar both to the volume that was exported and to the volume that was flared. In the last five years, nearly 30% of world oil and gas discoveries were made in sub-Saharan Africa; but the challenge to turn these discoveries into production and the resulting revenue into public benefits is formidable. Coal production (nearly 220 Mtce in 2012) is concentrated in South Africa; and the region accounts for 18% of world uranium supply.

- Low incomes, coupled with inefficient and costly forms of energy supply, make energy affordability a critical issue. Electricity prices are typically very high by world standards, despite often being held below the cost of supply, while oil products are subsidised in many oil-producing countries.

Context

Africa's energy sector is vital to its future development and yet remains one of the most poorly understood regions within the global energy system. The continent is huge in scale – around the size of the United States, China, India and Europe combined – and while it has energy resources more than sufficient to meet domestic needs, more than two-thirds of its population does not have access to modern energy. Those that do have access often face high prices for supply that is poor quality and rely on an under-developed system that is not able to meet their needs. The effective development of Africa's energy resources, and of the energy sector as a whole, could unlock huge gains across the economy. But how quickly can modern energy be brought to the huge population now deprived of it? How can existing and emerging energy-rich countries maximise the value of their resources? What actions in the energy sector can unleash stronger economic and social development?

While this in-depth study presents selected energy data and projections for all of Africa, the focus of the analysis and discussion is on sub-Saharan Africa. There is a wide diversity of sub-Saharan countries from those that are energy-resource rich to many that are among the world's most energy poor. It is a region whose energy sector is not well understood, facing challenges that, in many cases, differ from those of North Africa. For example, gross domestic product (GDP) per capita in North Africa is around two-and-a-half times that of sub-Saharan Africa and less than 1% of the population are without electricity. In this study, sub-regions for which aggregated data are given include West Africa, Central Africa, East Africa and Southern Africa (defined in Annex C and shown in Figure 13.1).

There are positive signs of progress in sub-Saharan Africa, such as economic growth, higher income per capita and longer life expectancy. Areas of potential advantage that have yet to be exploited fully include rich natural resource endowments and a growing working-age population. However, there are also myriad challenges, such as high levels of poverty and inequality, a major shortage of infrastructure, poor governance and corruption, relatively low levels of productivity and skills, and varying levels of political stability. Many of these factors contribute to a business environment in which it is often judged difficult and costly to operate.

Economy

The sub-Saharan economy has more than doubled in size since 2000 to reach $2.7 trillion in 2013 (year-2013 dollars, purchasing power parity [PPP] terms). Yet, even after such strong growth, the economic output of the almost 940 million people in sub-Saharan Africa in 2013 remains significantly below that of the 82 million in Germany (Figure 13.2). Recent sub-Saharan economic growth can be attributed to a variety of factors, including a period of relative stability and security, improved macroeconomic management, strong domestic demand driven by a growing middle class, an increased global appetite for Africa's resources (coupled with the rising price of many of these resources), population growth and urbanisation. However, rapid population growth has meant that GDP per capita has increased more slowly (about 45%).

Figure 13.1 ▷ **Map of Africa and main sub-regions for this study**

This map is without prejudice to the status of or sovereignty over any territory, to the delimitation of international frontiers and boundaries and to the name of any territory, city or area.

Notes: Africa sub-regions are derived from those used by the United Nations (UN) and the existing regional power pools (bodies set up to strengthen regional power sector integration across Africa). For countries that are members of more than one power pool, such as Tanzania, a decision has been taken to assign it to just one sub-region. This is driven primarily by analytical considerations specific to this study, and so may not be consistent with other groupings (such as Africa's regional economic communities).

Nigeria and South Africa are the largest economies by far – together accounting for more than half of the sub-Saharan economy – with Angola, Ethiopia, Sudan and Ghana being the next largest. Agriculture remains a large sector in many economies, accounting for around 20% of regional GDP (compared with a 6% share globally) and around 65% of employment (AfDB, OECD and UNDP, 2014). But it also remains largely unmodernised, with huge scope for productivity gains through the application of modern energy. Mining (energy and non-energy commodities) is an important industry in several sub-Saharan economies, both as an employer and as a source of export revenue, with mining output typically exported in a raw or semi-processed state. In resource-rich countries, energy export revenues are an important source of government income but the sector is not necessarily a large employer, nor does it constitute a large share of the economy overall. Improved macroeconomic stability has been important in underpinning growth, but it has not been achieved uniformly and many countries still struggle to balance their budgets.

Figure 13.2 ▷ **GDP of sub-Saharan Africa and Germany (PPP terms), 2013**

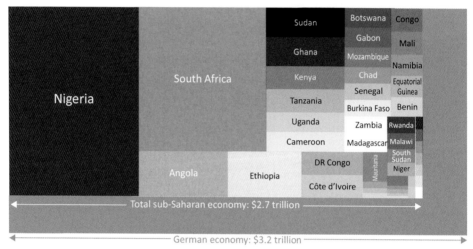

Sources: IMF; IEA analysis.

Rapid economic growth has yet to change the fact that sub-Saharan Africa is home to a large proportion of the world's poorest countries (Figure 13.3). Even though increasing average incomes across much of sub-Saharan Africa have helped to lift a large number of people out of absolute poverty, defined as living on less than $1.25 per day, sub-Saharan Africa accounts for 27 out of 36 low income countries and only one high income country (Equatorial Guinea).[1] While the share of the total population living in absolute poverty has declined (from around 56% in 1990 to below 49% in 2010), rapid population growth means that the *number* of people still living in absolute poverty has actually increased (World Bank, 2014a). Broader measures of human development, such as the Inequality-adjusted Human Development Index (IHDI), also show improvement in many sub-Saharan countries over time while also consistently ranking them very low.[2]

---

1. While average income levels result in Equatorial Guinea being categorised as a high-income country, it suffers from many of the issues seen in low-income sub-Saharan countries.

2. In line with the UN Human Development Index (HDI), IHDI takes account of the achievements of a country on health, education and income measures, and it also reflects how those achievements are distributed among its citizens by "discounting" each dimension's average value according to its level of inequality.

Figure 13.3 ▷ Number of countries by level of national income and number of people in sub-Saharan Africa living on less than $1.25 per day

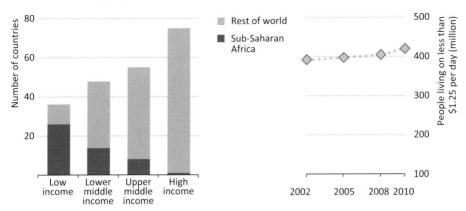

Note: National income categories are based on gross national income per capita and follow those defined in World Development Indicators. Sources: World Bank (2014a); IEA analysis.

From very low levels, sub-Saharan Africa has seen trade and foreign direct investment (FDI) grow rapidly in recent years, with commodities continuing to dominate the export picture for most countries. While the European Union is the largest trade partner, China, India and other emerging markets have been the major drivers of growth, with China's total trade with the sub-Saharan region having increased from around $6 billion in 2000 to $160 billion in 2013 (Figure 13.4). The role of China is notable both for the increase of bilateral trade, which has grown by more than 25% a year since 2000, and its increasing willingness to invest in the region, particularly in oil, gas and other natural resources (Box 13.1), which account for 80% of China's imports from Africa (Sun, 2014).

Figure 13.4 ▷ Growth in sub-Saharan trade by region

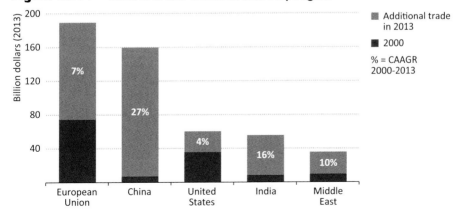

Note: CAAGR is compound average annual growth rate. Sources: IMF (2014); IEA analysis.

Box 13.1 ▷ China's increasing investment in African energy

Chinese engagement in the sub-Saharan energy sector has grown significantly in recent years. In terms of overseas development assistance (just one form of such engagement), nearly $10 billion is estimated to have flowed from China into the sub-Saharan energy sector from 2005-2011. This is nearly double the level of the European Union and several times that of the United States over the same period, although both of these economies also direct significant assistance into North Africa (AidData). FDI in the energy sector is much more difficult to track, but the data available points both to larger overall flows and to a similar picture when comparing across these major economies.

Chinese investment is not spread evenly across the sub-Saharan region, with countries such as Angola, Ethiopia, Zimbabwe, South Africa and Nigeria receiving a greater share, or across projects, with a relatively small number of hydropower projects receiving large sums. China's increasing stake in oil and gas plays across Africa is well-known and takes in both large oil producers, like Angola, and more nascent ones, such as Chad and Uganda. It also includes emerging gas producers, as exemplified by CNPC's purchase of a 20% stake in a consortium developing part of the Rovuma Basin in Mozambique.

China's interest in African energy resources is not restricted to hydrocarbons; Chinese companies are among the largest investors in renewables across the continent, including major hydropower projects, but also solar, wind and biogas. For example, the Export-Import Bank of China has provided financing for transmission lines related to the Gilgel Gibe III hydropower project in Ethiopia and a $500 million project loan to the Transmission Company of Nigeria (TCN).

Demography

The population changes underway in sub-Saharan Africa have major implications for the development of the energy sector. Growth is rapid, having increased by 270 million people since 2000 to around 940 million in 2013, and it is expected to reach one billion well before the end of this decade. This huge increase, concentrated mainly in West and East Africa, brings new opportunities, such as a rising working-age population, but also magnifies many existing challenges, such as the quest to achieve modern energy access. Population growth has been split relatively evenly between urban and rural areas, in contrast to the strong global trend to urbanisation. Only 37% of the sub-Saharan population lives in urban areas – one of the lowest shares of any world region – which has important implications for the approach to solving the energy challenges. Average life expectancy has increased by 5.5 years since 2000, to reach 55 years (UNDP, 2013), and the young, working-age population is increasing, with both factors serving to boost the available labour force. Some elements of the existing energy sector are relatively labour-intensive, such as charcoal production and distribution, while many aspects of a modern energy sector instead are capital-intensive, such as power generation and oil and gas production.

Improving the relatively poor state of the existing energy infrastructure, as a contribution towards a more modern energy system, will require a much expanded skilled and semi-skilled workforce throughout the energy sector, including technical skills, as well as skills related to policy, regulation and project management. The need to invest in building human capacity is increasingly recognised and is reflected in projects such as the EU Energy Initiative – Partnership Dialogue Facility (EUEI PDF) and Barefoot College, which trains solar engineers in rural communities. Nevertheless, the population of sub-Saharan Africa receives less than five years of schooling on average (UNDP, 2013), suggesting that the level of education and skills will remain a key challenge.

Business environment and infrastructure

Businesses in sub-Saharan Africa most frequently cite inadequate electricity supply as a major constraint on their effective operation. It is a widespread problem that affects both countries with large domestic energy resources and those that are resource poor. Insufficient and inferior power supply has a large impact on the productivity of African businesses (Escribano, Guasch, and Pena, 2010). Examples include:

- On average, 4.9% of annual sales are estimated to be lost due to electrical outages, with very high losses reported in the Central African Republic and Nigeria, but much lower levels in South Africa (Figure 13.5) (World Bank, 2014b).

- The use of back-up power generation to mitigate poor grid-based supply increases costs for businesses. In 2012, the cost of fuel for back-up generation (across businesses and households) is estimated to have been at least $5 billion.

- Poor quality grid-based supply reduces utility revenues (non-payment) and makes it more difficult to increase tariffs (of particular importance to utilities with rates below their costs of supply), thereby constraining the availability of finance for investment.

The problem of inadequate electricity supply is multifaceted: it includes a lack of generating capacity, rundown existing stock and limited transmission and distribution infrastructure. Since GDP growth of nearly 6% per year has been achieved despite poor electricity supply, the vision of economic and social development with ample electricity supply should motivate policy-makers everywhere (see Chapter 16).

The scarcity of other infrastructure such as roads also presents a massive barrier to economic activity in sub-Saharan Africa. Only 318 000 km of paved roads exist in the region (equivalent to around two-thirds of Italy's figure) and only 60% of people have access to improved water supplies. The large size and low population density of many sub-Saharan countries increases infrastructure costs and constrains the pace of improvement. The Programme for Infrastructure Development in Africa (PIDA) identifies a need for $360 billion programme of infrastructure investment through to 2040, spread across energy, transport, information and communication technologies (ICT) and trans-boundary

13

water resources.[3] Many countries face difficulties in financing the needed infrastructure, with low domestic savings rates and tax revenues limiting the available pool of domestic finance, and the credit ratings of many countries (often below investment grade) deterring international investors (or at least highlighting the premium required for them to do so). While international oil and gas companies can often finance investments from retained earnings, power generation and transmission projects are typically more reliant on third-party finance (loans or guarantees).[4] In this respect, funding from development banks, bilateral assistance and so-called "south-south" investment have all proved important.

Figure 13.5 ▷ **Duration of electrical outages and impact on business sales in selected countries**

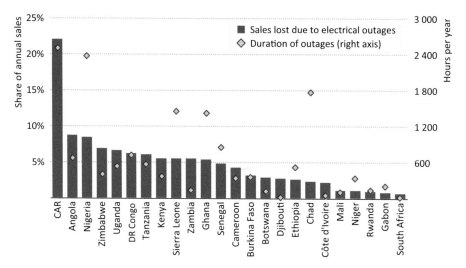

Notes: CAR = Central African Republic. Data is from the latest available business survey for a given country.
Sources: World Bank (2014b); IEA analysis.

Governance

One requirement to enable the countries of sub-Saharan Africa to realise their development ambitions is the establishment of more effective systems of governance. Governance shortcomings in the region are well documented: they relate to corruption, inadequate regulatory and legal frameworks, weak institutions or poor transparency and accountability. But the picture is not uniform across countries. The Mo Ibrahim Foundation produces an index that monitors changes in more than 130 indicators of governance in sub-Saharan countries. The index reveals an improvement across much of Africa since 2000, but also wide disparity. For example, Mauritius and Botswana have performed relatively well, but Somalia and Democratic Republic of Congo (DR Congo) relatively poorly.

---

3. PIDA is led by the African Union Commission (AUC), the New Partnership for Africa's Development (NEPAD) and the African Development Bank (AfDB).

4. For more on energy sector investment see the IEA's *World Energy Investment Outlook Special Report* (IEA, 2014a), download at *www.worldenergyoutlook.org/investment*.

While concerns regarding poor governance are not exclusive to Africa, such failings are often cited by businesses as a constraint to invest in the continent. This is a key issue for the energy sector because it needs to attract vast sums of investment and to manage large financial flows, including energy export revenues (mainly oil, but also gas, coal, uranium and electricity), oil product import bills (all countries import oil products) and energy consumption subsidies. For significant natural resource-holders, failing to tackle these issues will squander available resource-led growth.

Many sub-Saharan countries have made progress in improving energy sector governance but action is, in a number of cases, far from complete. For instance, of the nine countries in sub-Saharan Africa that currently produce around 100 thousand barrels per day (kb/d) of hydrocarbon liquids or more, five (Nigeria, Ghana, Gabon, Congo and South Africa) have new petroleum legislation under consideration (see Chapter 15 for more on Nigeria's efforts to implement regulatory reform and reduce oil theft), and two (Chad and South Sudan) are in the process of implementing petroleum laws already enacted. Power sector reforms are also underway in many sub-Saharan countries, those in Nigeria being one notable example. An increasing number of African countries have also achieved compliance with the requirements of the Extractive Industries Transparency Initiative. In recent years, many international companies have also faced increased pressure from within their home jurisdictions to take further action to ensure that they are not complicit with illegal business practices in Africa. Transparency and accountability will continue to be important features of energy sector decision-making designed to command public acceptance and international respect (See Chapter 16 on the impact of improved governance).

Access to modern energy

Every advanced economy has required secure access to modern energy to underpin its development and growing prosperity. Modern, high quality and reliable energy provides services such as lighting, heating, transport, communication and mechanical power that support education, better health, higher incomes and all-round improvements in the quality of life. Sub-Saharan Africa has yet to conquer the challenge of energy poverty. But the barriers to doing so are surmountable and the benefits of success are immense.

In societies suffering from energy poverty, such as sub-Saharan Africa, the first step in assessing future energy demand is to measure the extent to which the population of the region lacks access to modern energy. This issue is critical to many other aspects of this study, such as electricity supply, solid biomass use and deforestation, and the assessment of the strong positive social and economic impact that broader and better access to modern energy can provide. It is the key to understanding why, in subsequent chapters, projections based simply on an extrapolation of past trends, or even on the basis of declared policy intentions, would fail to capture this crucial potential or, expressed another way, this huge pent-up energy demand. The International Energy Agency's (IEA) effort to collect comprehensive energy sector data, covering all aspects of the sub-Saharan energy system (Box 13.2), includes a full update of its energy access database, which estimates national, urban and rural populations without electricity access.

Box 13.2 ⊳ **Africa's energy sector data**

An extensive programme of data collection and reconciliation has been undertaken for this in-depth study, with the objective of bringing together the best available energy information (see the *Africa Energy Outlook* Special Report [IEA, 2014b] for detailed energy data and projections). In addition to the wide range of existing data sources to which the IEA has access, new energy surveys have been carried out for this study. For energy supply, government sources have been supplemented by data from power utilities, and oil and gas companies. For energy demand, new data has been sourced from many African governments, international organisations, aid agencies (such as the US Agency for International Development and its Power Africa initiative, and Germany's Gesellschaft für Internationale Zusammenarbeit [GIZ]) and, for oil demand and refinery output, from CITAC Africa Ltd. The IEA's energy access database has also been updated. The IEA conducted fact-finding missions to South Africa, Nigeria, Ghana, Mozambique and Ethiopia. It also hosted international workshops in Paris and Abuja which were attended by many African government representatives and experts.

Africa's energy data collection is improving – with efforts such as those by the African Energy Commission (AFREC) and SIE-Afrique proving important – but the situation still varies widely by country and sector. Data on oil and gas production, refinery output and, to a lesser degree, on installed power capacity and electricity generation, are relatively reliable, while data on energy trading are not yet adequate. Robust or recent energy demand data are hard to find, and in many cases the level of detail is not sufficient to give a clear picture of energy consumption.

Two areas which are particularly difficult to measure are bioenergy[5] consumption and the use of back-up power[6] generation. Bioenergy is the largest component of the energy mix, but much of it is not marketed and there are few surveys measuring its use, making it difficult to estimate consumption levels accurately. For this study, IEA data have been cross-checked using the most comprehensive data available. Analysis of collected energy data sources concludes that fuel consumption for back-up power generation is typically included in overall demand data, but that volumes are not then allocated specifically as being consumed for this purpose. This study has attempted to estimate and allocate the volumes of fuel used specifically for back-up power generation.

---

5. Bioenergy is the energy content in solid, liquid and gaseous products derived from biomass feedstocks and biogas. It covers solid biomass (fuelwood, charcoal, agricultural residues, wood waste and other solid waste), biofuels (liquid fuels, including ethanol and biodiesel) and biogas.

6. Households and businesses connected to the main power grid may also have some form of "back-up" power generation capacity that can, in the event of disruption, provide electricity. Back-up generators are typically fuelled with diesel or gasoline and capacity can be from as little as a few kilowatts. Such capacity is distinct from mini- and off-grid systems, without connections to the main power grid.

There is no single internationally accepted and internationally adopted definition of "modern energy access". Yet significant commonality exists across definitions, including:

- Household access to a minimum level of electricity.

- Household access to safer and more sustainable (i.e. minimum harmful effects on health and the environment as possible) cooking and heating fuels and stoves.

- Access to modern energy that enables productive economic activity, e.g. mechanical power for agriculture, textile and other industries.

- Access to modern energy for public services, e.g. electricity for health facilities, schools and street lighting.

All of these elements are crucial to economic and social development, as are a number of related issues that are sometimes referred to collectively as "quality of supply", such as technical availability, adequacy, reliability, convenience, safety and affordability.

At different points, this study examines all of these aspects of modern energy access but its main focus when discussing "access" is on the household level, and specifically on two elements: a household having access to electricity and to a relatively clean, safe means of cooking (Box 13.3). A lack of access to such services often results in households relying on expensive, inefficient and hazardous alternatives. For example, households can typically spend 20-25% of their income on kerosene even though the cost of useful lighting (measured as $/lumen hour of light) can be 150-times higher than that provided by incandescent bulbs and 600-times higher than that from compact fluorescent lights. Each year 4.3 million premature deaths, of which nearly 600 000 are in Africa, can be attributed to household air pollution resulting from the traditional use of solid fuels, such as fuelwood and charcoal (WHO, 2014).

Box 13.3 ▷ Defining modern energy access for this study

In the energy modelling results presented in this study, households gaining access to electricity start from a low base and over time their consumption increases to reach regional average levels. The initial threshold level of electricity consumption for rural households is assumed to be 250 kilowatt-hours (kWh) per year and for urban households it is 500 kWh per year. Both are calculated based on an assumption of five people per household. In rural areas, this level of consumption could, for example, provide for the use of a mobile telephone, a fan and two compact fluorescent light bulbs for about five hours per day. In urban areas, consumption might also include an efficient refrigerator, a second mobile telephone per household and another appliance, such as a small television or a computer. The fact that electricity consumption grows over time to reach the regional average level is intended to recognise that the minimum threshold level is only sufficient to provide limited access to modern energy services. While these assumed threshold levels for electricity consumption are consistent with previous *World Energy Outlook (WEO)* analyses, it is recognised that different levels are sometimes adopted. Sanchez (2010),

13

for example, assumes 120 kWh per person (600 kWh per household, assuming five people per household). While the Energy Sector Management Assistance Program (ESMAP) has led the development of a framework that categorises household electricity access into six tiers based on supply levels (tier 0 being no electricity, tiers 4 and 5 being greater than 2 000 watts) and different attributes of supply.

The traditional use of biomass for cooking, such as on three-stone fires, brings with it several negative health and social outcomes, such as indoor air pollution and the time-consuming and physically demanding task of fuel collection (often suffered disproportionately by women and children). In our definition of modern energy access, households also gain access to cooking facilities that are considered safer, more efficient and more environmentally sustainable than the traditional facilities that make use of solid biomass which is common practice across sub-Saharan Africa.[7] We refer to the progress as having access to "clean cooking facilities", where the means for cooking are typically in the form of either an improved solid biomass cookstove or a stove that uses alternative (cleaner) fuels, such as biogas, liquefied petroleum gas (LPG), ethanol and solar. While improved solid biomass cookstoves are both more efficient than traditional three-stone fires and produce fewer emissions, they have not been shown to deliver health benefits comparable to those achieved by the use of alternative fuels.

Access to electricity

Sub-Saharan Africa has more people living without access to electricity than any other world region – more than 620 million people, and nearly half of the global total (Figure 13.6).[8] It is also the only region in the world where the number of people living without electricity is increasing, as rapid population growth is outpacing the many positive efforts to provide access. In 37 sub-Saharan countries the number of people without electricity has increased since 2000 while the regional total rose by around 100 million people. On a more positive note, about 145 million people gained access to electricity since 2000, led by Nigeria, Ethiopia, South Africa, Ghana, Cameroon and Mozambique. Overall, the electricity access rate for sub-Saharan Africa has improved from 23% in 2000 to 32% in 2012. In North Africa, more than 99% of the total population has access to electricity.

Nearly 80% of those lacking access to electricity across sub-Saharan Africa are in rural areas, an important distinction when considering appropriate energy access strategies and technical solutions. Around the world, increasing urbanisation has often facilitated increasing household access to modern energy. While it can play a similar role in sub-Saharan Africa, the extent to which this will occur is less clear because, unlike many

---

7. The traditional use of solid biomass refers to basic technologies used to cook or heat with solid biomass, such as a three-stone fire, often with no or poorly operating chimneys. Modern use of solid biomass refers to improved cookstoves using solid biomass and modern technologies using processed biomass such as pellets.

8. Full data tables for access to electricity and clean cooking facilities are available in the *Africa Energy Outlook* Special Report (IEA, 2014b).

world regions, sub-Saharan Africa is expected to continue to see significant growth in both its urban and rural populations. In this light, efforts towards universal modern energy access will require effective solutions for rural, as well as urban and peri-urban, communities.[9] Several African countries have dedicated policies, programmes or institutions to provide electricity access in rural areas. While such a tailored approach appears warranted, the success rate has been uneven.

Figure 13.6 ▷ **Number and share of people without access to electricity by country, 2012**

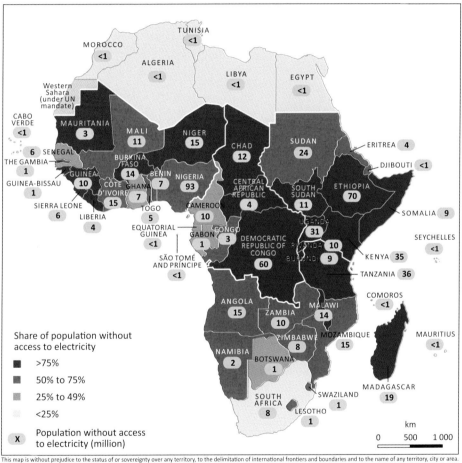

In West Africa, electricity access rates range from below 20% in Liberia, Sierra Leone, Niger and Burkina Faso to more than 50% in Senegal and above 70% in Ghana. More than 90 million people in Nigeria (55% of the population), do not have access to (grid) electricity. However, the widespread use of back-up generators suggests that the population without

---

9. Around 62% of the urban population in sub-Saharan Africa lived in slums in 2012 (UN-Habitat, 2013).

access to any form of electricity is smaller (see power section). Nigeria's own targets are to make reliable electricity available to 75% of the population by 2020 and 100% by 2030 (Energy Commission of Nigeria, 2013). Ghana is among the most successful countries in improving electricity access, having shown long and strong political commitment since the launch of its National Electrification Scheme in 1989. Mali, a large and sparsely-populated country, has seen electricity access reach 27%, with a focus on mini-grid solutions.

Electrification rates in Central Africa show very large variation across the region, from the relatively high levels in Equatorial Guinea (66%), Gabon (60%) and Cameroon (54%) to the very low levels in Central African Republic (less than 3%), Chad (4%) and DR Congo (9%). Chad is one of many countries where low levels of energy access go hand-in-hand with low rates of access to other basic services, such as potable water, basic sanitation and paved roads. This is in spite of the fact that crude oil has become the country's primary source of export earnings. Around 60 million people in DR Congo do not have access to electricity, even though it has very large hydropower potential.

More than 200 million people in East Africa are without electricity, around 80% of its population. Ethiopia, Kenya and Uganda are among the most populous countries in East Africa, and have the largest populations both with and without access to electricity. Kenya established a Rural Electrification Authority in 2006 with the goal of achieving universal access by 2030. As of 2013, 90% of public facilities have access to electricity, but household access remains low. Rwanda's electrification rate has increased rapidly in recent years (from 6% in 2008 to 17% in 2012). Its Electricity Access Rollout Programme offers ready-to-use switchboards that can be paid for in instalments and enable low income households to connect to grid electricity without the need for expensive house wiring.

The picture in the Southern Africa sub-region is skewed by the unique situation of South Africa: at around 85%, South Africa has the highest electrification rate on mainland sub-Saharan Africa. Around 11% of households do not have access to electricity and a further 4% rely on illegal access (non-paying) or obtain access informally (from one household to another but paying) (Statistics South Africa, 2013). More than three-quarters of households use pre-paid meters, which helps overcome the problem of non-payment. Despite positive overall progress to improve access, the most recent National Development Plan in South Africa warns that reliability of supply has deteriorated and prices are rising quickly. In Mozambique, around 40% of people have access to electricity, either through the grid or mini/off-grid systems. The government has promoted solar photovoltaic (PV) and mini-hydropower solutions in rural areas, reporting that 700 schools, 600 health centres and 800 other public buildings in rural areas now have electricity from solar PV (AllAfrica, 2014). Electricity access in Tanzania increased from around 13% in 2008 to 24% in 2012, with a reduction in connection fees (by 40% in urban areas and 60% rural areas) recognised as an important contributory factor.

For those that do have electricity access in sub-Saharan Africa, average residential electricity consumption per capita is 317 kWh per year (225 kWh excluding South Africa), equivalent to around half the average level of China, 20% of Europe and 7% of the

United States.[10] Consumption per capita is significantly lower in rural areas, typically in the range of 50 to 100 kWh per year. For a five person household, annual consumption of 50 kWh per person could, for instance, allow the use of a mobile phone, two compact fluorescent light bulbs and a fan for five hours a day. In urban areas, households generally own more appliances, such as televisions, refrigerators or an electric water heater. There are also disparities in consumption levels across and within sub-regions (Figure 13.7). Levels in Central Africa average 220 kWh per capita per year but vary from less than 100 kWh in Cameroon to around 900 kWh in Gabon. In Southern Africa, average consumption per capita is the highest of all sub-regions, but this is driven principally by very high levels in South Africa and relatively high levels in Zambia, Botswana and Zimbabwe (all above 500 kWh per capita per year). Levels in Mozambique and Tanzania are much lower (below 200 kWh per capita per year).

Figure 13.7 ▷ **Average electricity consumption per household in sub-Saharan Africa, 2012, and indicative consumption levels by appliance**

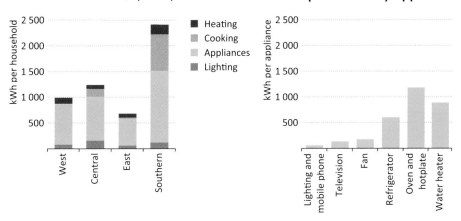

Notes: The "appliances" category includes cooling systems. The indicative electricity consumption levels shown for various appliances are based on: charging a mobile phone three times a week; using three 10-watt compact fluorescent lights for five hours per day (almost half of light bulbs in sub-Saharan Africa are incandescent); and using a television for four hours per day. The number of people per household varies by sub-region from below four to almost six.

Sources: UNEP (2014); USAID (2014); OECD (2014); IEA analysis.

Excluding South Africa, appliances account for around 70% of residential electricity consumption across the other sub-regions, on average. There are an estimated 43 million televisions (equivalent to about one in every four households), 17 million refrigerators (around one in every ten households) and 450 million mobile phones (about one for every two people). Ownership of mobile phones in sub-Saharan Africa has risen at a brisk pace and provides access to multiple services, such as personal and business communications

_____

10. Electricity consumption per-capita levels are estimated taking into account residential electricity consumption and population with electricity access by country.

and online banking, for relatively low electricity consumption. In reality, a small share of households owns a relatively large share of electric appliances. An even smaller share use electricity for water heating or cooking, both of which consume relatively high levels of electricity (mainly households in Southern Africa).

Access to clean cooking facilities

Nearly 730 million people in sub-Saharan Africa rely on the traditional use of solid biomass for cooking typically with inefficient stoves in poorly ventilated space. A transition to cleaner cooking fuels and appliances is not straightforward, as people who have access to modern fuels, such as LPG, natural gas, biogas or electricity, may also continue to use solid biomass for cultural or affordability reasons, a phenomenon known as "fuel stacking" (see Chapter 15).

Five countries – Nigeria, Ethiopia, DR Congo, Tanzania and Kenya – account for around half of the sub-Saharan population using solid biomass for cooking (Figure 13.8). Although this seems to suggest that this situation is concentrated in just a few countries, the reality is very different. In 42 countries, more than half of the population relies on solid biomass for cooking needs and in 23 of these the share is above 90%. Nearly three-quarters of those dependent on solid biomass for cooking live in rural areas and often devote hours of each day to collect fuelwood.

Figure 13.8 ▷ **Largest populations relying on the traditional use of solid biomass for cooking in sub-Saharan Africa by sub-region, 2012**

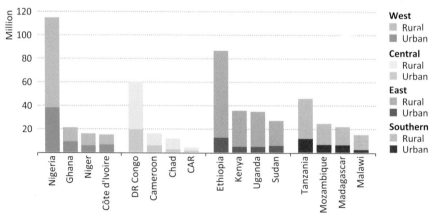

Note: CAR = Central African Republic.

Sources: World Health Organization; IEA databases and analysis.

While this issue is often given less attention than that of electricity access, several countries have implemented programmes to promote clean cooking fuels and stoves. Kenya has plans to eliminate kerosene use in households by 2022 and has a relatively developed market for improved biomass cookstoves in urban and peri-urban areas (but much less so in rural areas). In Senegal, strong policies and incentives have supported LPG use and less than 25% of the urban population now uses solid biomass. Ghana has set the ambitious goal of providing 50% of households with LPG by 2016, compared to less than 20% today. The picture is less positive in Ethiopia, with nearly all rural households and 80% of urban households dependent on solid biomass for cooking.

Around 80% of residential energy demand in sub-Saharan Africa is for cooking, compared with around 5% in Organisation for Economic Co-operation and Development (OECD) countries. This is due, mainly, to households prioritising energy for cooking (and lighting) within very restrictive budgets (when paid for) and the low efficiency of the cookstoves used (typically 10-15% efficiency for a three-stone fire, compared to 55% for an LPG cookstove). Estimates of the amount of fuelwood consumed by households differ markedly, both within and across countries, which has a huge impact on estimates of total solid biomass use (Figure 13.9).

Figure 13.9 ▷ **Fuelwood consumption per capita per day in selected countries**

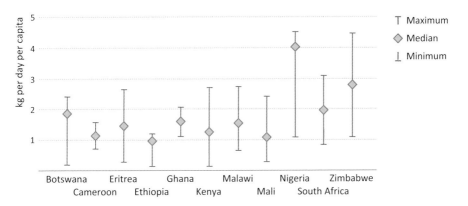

Sources: Department of Energy at the Politecnico di Milano; IEA analysis.

The main factors that help explain differing levels of fuelwood consumption are:

■ Climate/seasonality – consumption can increase in a cold season relative to a hot one, while the moisture content of fuelwood also affects its energy content.

■ Household size – significant variations in household size affect consumption patterns.

■ Ease of access – scarcity of supply tends to reduce waste and overuse; while relatively easy access can increase consumption (deforestation and land degradation is discussed in Chapter 14).

■ Population density – increasing urban populations are a key driver of charcoal use, which feeds through to higher levels of fuelwood depletion (see Chapter 14, Box 14.2 on charcoal production and the size of the market).

■ Availability and price of alternative fuels and stoves – if solid biomass remains cheap or "free" relative to alternatives, then increasing incomes may not be a critical trigger for households to switch to modern cooking fuels.

13

- Alternative uses – Competing uses for solid biomass for other activities (such as brick-making and tobacco curing) can affect whether it is used for cooking.

- Cultural factors and nutritional habits – there is a complex relationship between solid biomass consumption, cultural factors and food choices.

There is almost exclusive use of solid biomass for cooking in rural areas (mainly fuelwood and agricultural waste), but a more diverse use of fuels in urban areas (Figure 13.10). In rural areas, solid biomass use (mainly in the form of fuelwood and agricultural waste) dominates in all regions except South Africa, where electricity is commonly used for cooking. Even in South Africa, traditional use of solid biomass is concentrated heavily in rural areas and among those with the lowest incomes. The choice of fuels for cooking is much more varied in urban areas. Solid biomass is still very common, but there is a greater tendency to use charcoal as it has higher energy content and is easier to transport than fuelwood. Kerosene use is common in urban parts of Nigeria (where it is supported by subsidies), as well as in South Africa and Kenya. While LPG use is less common in Nigeria, it is used by one-fifth of urban households in the rest of West Africa.

Figure 13.10 ▷ **Main fuel used by households for cooking**

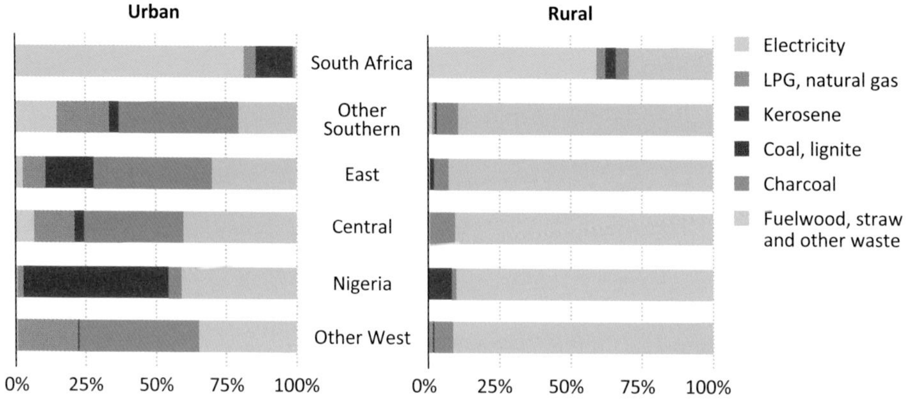

Sources: USAID (2014); Department of Energy, South Africa (2013); WHO (2013); IEA analysis.

Overview of energy demand

Primary energy demand in Africa stood at 739 million tonnes of oil equivalent (Mtoe) in 2012, of which North Africa accounted for 23%. Since 2000, energy demand in sub-Saharan Africa has increased by half – reaching 570 Mtoe in 2012 – but still accounts for only 4% of the world total. While growth in sub-Saharan energy demand has outpaced that in the rest of the world, it has lagged behind economic expansion, as in many countries it was led by sectors with relatively low energy intensity such as tourism and agriculture. The energy intensity of the sub-Saharan economy has decreased by around 2.5% per year since 2000, but remains significantly higher than North Africa and is more than double the world average. The region's largest energy demand centres are Nigeria (141 Mtoe) and

South Africa (141 Mtoe) together accounting for more than 40% of total demand (but only a quarter of the population) (Figure 13.11). Ethiopia, the next largest consumer, is a distant third (45 Mtoe), followed by Tanzania, DR Congo and Kenya.

Energy use per capita is, on average, one-third of the world average (2.1 tonnes of oil equivalent [toe] per capita excluding sub-Saharan Africa) and only half of the level of developing Asia, the world's second most energy-poor region. Only South Africa's per capita energy demand exceeds the world average, while Nigeria's demand per capita is lower than that of Gabon and Mauritius. Ethiopia, DR Congo, Tanzania and Kenya also have relatively large populations but low demand on a per-capita basis. Across sub-Saharan Africa, there are large differences in per-capita consumption between urban and rural areas, with those in cities tending to be wealthier, and often enjoying better access to energy than those in rural areas (either through the grid or the use of back-up generators).

Figure 13.11 ▷ Population and per capita energy demand by country in sub-Saharan Africa, 2012

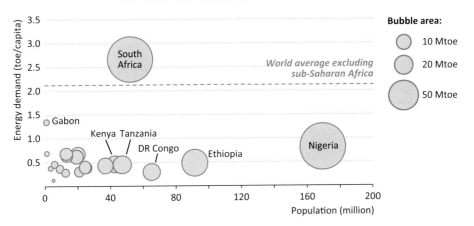

Note: The size of the bubble indicates the relative size of total primary energy demand.

Bioenergy is dominant in the energy mix of sub-Saharan Africa, accounting for more than 60% of total energy use. Despite rising incomes, bioenergy consumption continues to increase in the region and its growth since 2000 has been greater than that of all other fuels combined. This is largely driven by the traditional use of biomass for cooking, which constitutes a large industry in some areas (typically to supply charcoal to urban areas) and a non-traded commodity in others (collected and consumed by individual households, often in rural areas). South Africa and Namibia are the only countries in mainland sub-Saharan Africa where bioenergy does not dominate the energy mix (Figure 13.12).

Oil demand in sub-Saharan Africa stood at 1.8 million barrels per day (mb/d) in 2012 and made up 15% of total energy demand. South Africa accounts for around 30% of oil demand and Nigeria for more than 20%, with the remaining 40-plus countries collectively consuming less oil than the Netherlands (even though their aggregate population is

13

30 times higher than that of the Netherlands). Diesel – a versatile fuel that can be used in many sectors – accounted for 30% of the oil demand growth since 2000, increasing significantly across most parts of sub-Saharan Africa (Figure 13.13). Gasoline accounted for nearly 40% of demand growth over the same period but this growth was concentrated in Nigeria, where the official selling price is around 40% lower than diesel. Demand for LPG rose more strongly than that for kerosene (increasing by around 60% since 2000) but starting from a lower point. While growth has been particularly strong in parts of West and East Africa, LPG is still seen as a premium cooking fuel in many countries compared with solid biomass (see Chapter 15).

Figure 13.12 ▷ **Sub-Saharan Africa primary energy mix by sub-region, 2012**

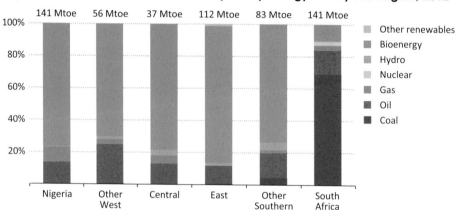

Coal is the second-largest component of the sub-Saharan energy mix after bioenergy, but this is wholly attributable to its large-scale use in South Africa, where it accounts for around 70% of primary demand. Its primary use in South Africa is in the power sector, but South Africa is also one of very few countries in the world where coal-to-liquids accounts for a significant part of transport fuel. Beyond South Africa, coal appears in the mix of just a dozen countries (and in relatively small volumes), although Mozambique plans to make increasing domestic use of its vast resources. Natural gas makes up a very small share of the sub-Saharan energy mix (4% compared with 21% globally), despite existing resources and its significant role in neighbouring North Africa. Natural gas demand has been rising and reached 27 billion cubic metres (bcm) in 2012, with Nigeria accounting for nearly 60% of the total, as gas flaring declined and volumes consumed in the power sector increased. Nigeria is the largest consumer of natural gas and yet it represents just 9% of Nigeria's domestic demand. Gabon and Côte d'Ivoire rely more heavily on gas but consume much smaller volumes.

Overall, modern renewables (hydro, solar, wind, geothermal and bioenergy except the traditional use of solid biomass) account for less than 2% of the sub-Saharan energy mix, but there are countries that have achieved a significantly higher share. Modern renewables have also grown significantly in recent years, supported by policies and declining costs in many cases, but (with the exception of hydropower) this growth has been from a very low base. Hydropower has long been a part of the energy systems of several countries and yet, very little of the potential has so far been tapped. For example, only 2% in DR Congo, 4% in Angola, 5% in Ethiopia, 12% in Congo and 14% in Mozambique. The use of other modern renewables is far more limited, but there are pockets of progress, with South Africa holding auctions for new capacity and Kenya harnessing some of its geothermal resources (7% of its energy mix in 2012).

Figure 13.13 ▷ Oil product demand growth by sub-region, 2000-2012

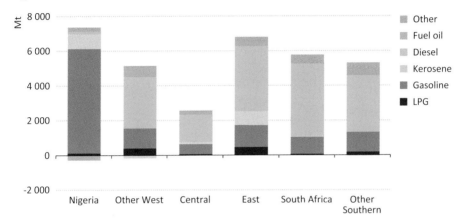

Notes: Mt = million tonnes; kerosene includes jet fuel. Sources: CITAC; IEA analysis.

Power sector

Electricity demand

Electricity demand in much of Africa is constrained by available supply, resulting in people either not having any access or not being able to consume as much as they would like. Such unmet demand is not captured in electricity data and makes it difficult to measure electricity demand in a holistic sense. This section then focuses on electricity demand that is met by grid-based supply or by mini- and off-grid sources. Electricity demand in Africa was 605 terawatt-hours (TWh) in 2012, with North Africa accounting for around 40% of the total. In sub-Saharan Africa, total electricity demand increased by 35% since 2000 to reach 352 TWh in 2012, just 70% of the level of Korea, which has a population 5% of the size. In fact, the electricity demand of only one country in the region (South Africa) exceeded that of London in 2012. On a per capita basis electricity demand in sub-Saharan Africa has remained largely unchanged for the last decade (at close to 400 kWh), with total consumption levels rising in step with the population. This is the lowest rate of per capita consumption of any major world region, 75% below that of developing Asia and less than the electricity needed to power one 50-watt light bulb continuously for a year. For comparison, electricity demand per capita in North Africa increased by more than 80% from 2000 to 2012, reaching 1 500 kWh.

13

In sub-Saharan Africa, electricity constitutes 7% of final energy consumption (4% if South Africa is excluded), compared with 18% globally and 19% in North Africa. In 2012, industry (led by mining and refining activities) accounted for the largest share of electricity consumption in sub-Saharan Africa (50%), but much of it was concentrated in South Africa, Nigeria, Ghana and Mozambique (Figure 13.14). The residential sector represented only 27% of total electricity consumption, as there are relatively few electricity-consuming appliances per household and limited disposable income. Services accounted for 20% of electricity consumption in sub-Saharan Africa, though demand in this sector is burgeoning in some countries such as Nigeria. A boom in communications, particularly for mobile telephones, has helped drive up demand in the services sector rapidly in recent years.

Figure 13.14 ▷ **Electricity consumption in Africa by end-use sector and sub-region, 2012**

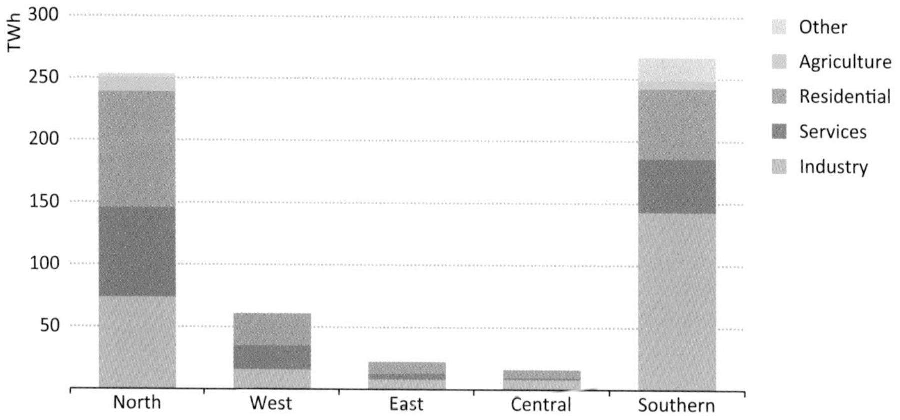

Electricity supply

Installed grid-based power generation capacity in Africa has been steadily increasing in recent years and reached 158 gigawatts (GW) in 2012.[11] Grid-based power generation capacity in sub-Saharan Africa has increased from around 68 GW in 2000 to 90 GW in 2012, with South Africa alone accounting for about half of the total. Coal-fired generation capacity is 45% of the sub-Saharan total, followed by hydropower (22%), oil-fired (17%), gas-fired (14%), nuclear (2%) and other renewables (less than 1%). Until recently, countries developed their power systems largely independently of one another, focusing on domestic resources and markets, but there has been progress towards regional co-operation to permit concentrated resources, such as large hydropower, to serve larger markets. While at varying stages of development, regional power pools aim to strengthen integration through co-operative planning and improved physical linkages, and have been playing a larger role in

---

11. Installed capacity refers to the sum of gross (nameplate) power generation capacity, including both power plants whose main activity is generating electricity for sale and auto-producers that generate power mainly for their own consumption (as is common in industry). The total installed capacity may not be available at all times, due to maintenance, need for repair or other outages.

the recent expansion of generation capacity. In addition to capacity linked to the main grid, there has been increasing emphasis on developing mini-grids (small grid systems linking households and other consumers, but not connected to larger regional grids) and off-grid systems (stand-alone systems for individual households or consumers (see Chapter 15). To further supplement their power supply, many individuals and businesses have access to small diesel or gasoline-fuelled generators (Spotlight).

In sub-Saharan Africa, the amount of power that is available to consumers is substantially less than the level of total installed capacity might suggest. One important reason is that the amount of capacity in operation is usually far less than the total installed capacity, due to poor maintenance which causes power stations to fall into disrepair. Many rehabilitation projects are ongoing, but much of the capacity in disrepair will never restart. Improving the operations of existing power plants is one of the most cost-effective and important ways of improving and expanding the power supply (WEC, 2010). Other factors also reduce the total capacity in operation, including lack of reliable fuel supply, particularly for gas, inefficient grid operations and insufficient transmission capacity.

The effect of fuel supply limitations is made worse by the fact that the fleet of fossil-fuelled power plants in sub-Saharan Africa consists largely of technologies with the lowest efficiencies, often favoured due to their lower upfront capital costs. For example, the average efficiency of the fleet of gas-fired power plants was 38% in 2012, due to the predominance of open-cycle gas turbines (instead of higher efficiency combined-cycle gas turbines) even though the power plants were frequently called upon to operate. Had the average efficiency been equal to that of gas-fired power plants in India (46%), the unused fuel could have generated 8 TWh (21%) more electricity. Similarly, the fleet of coal-fired power plants employs low-efficiency subcritical technologies, with a fleet average efficiency of 34%. While this technology was the most commonly available at the time the plants were built, more efficient supercritical or ultra-supercritical technologies would generate more electricity from the same amount of fuel.

Transmission and distribution (T&D) losses reduce the supply ultimately available to end-use sectors by more than 20% in some countries in sub-Saharan Africa, averaging 18% across the region, when South Africa is excluded (Figure 13.16). T&D losses are noticeably lower in South Africa and North Africa, at 10% and 14% respectively. The loss rate in sub-Saharan Africa (excluding South Africa) is more than double the world average and that of many developing countries in Asia. Similar to the problem with power plants, lack of proper maintenance is a main contributor, along with inefficient system design and operation. Such high loss rates reduce the reliability of the power supply, which is already insufficient to meet demand in most countries. In addition, high losses increase the cost of the power actually delivered. Across sub-Saharan Africa in 2012, the average cost of generating electricity was around $115 per megawatt-hour (MWh). At an 18% loss rate, this translates (for generation costs alone) into around $140 per MWh consumed, still without provision for the other substantial costs related to power supply. These additional costs, including the T&D infrastructure and retail costs, can add $50-$80 per MWh to the average cost to the consumer (as in China).

Falling back on back-up generators

Grid-based electricity supply is insufficient to meet electricity demand in sub-Saharan Africa. It is reported to be unavailable for 540 hours per year on average (6% of the year), but this figure is much higher in some countries, such as Nigeria, Guinea and the Central African Republic. In grid-connected areas, the high frequency of power outages means that demand is either unmet or met by other means (mostly by diesel-fuelled back-up generators). However, relative to grid supply, back-up power generation is expensive and levels of use are generally not recorded in energy statistics.

We estimate that the amount of electricity demand served by back-up generators in sub-Saharan Africa was almost 16 TWh in 2012, more than 80% of which went to services and industry (Figure 13.15).[12] This implies that total electricity supply was around 3% higher than reported and that around 90 kb/d of oil was used to generate the additional electricity, at an estimated cost of over $5 billion. Nigeria accounts for almost three-quarters of electricity supply provided by back-up generators, while levels are relatively low in East and Central Africa, where grid access is more limited.

Figure 13.15 ▷ **Electricity demand met by back-up generators by sub-region, 2012**

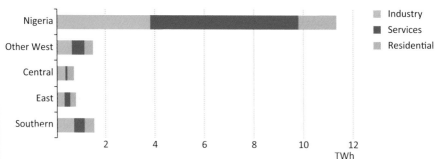

Source: IEA analysis and estimates.

Even after back-up generation has been included, there is still electricity demand that remains unmet. Those without a generator are left without electricity during outages, while those with them face significant costs and often make do with a reduced level of supply. Also, where outages are frequent and long-standing, consumers may have changed their equipment purchases – and, hence, use of energy services – to reflect this. Where reliable grid-based electricity is established, the level of additional demand can be expected to increase well beyond the existing level of back-up power generation. Furthermore, electricity prices in parts of sub-Saharan Africa are among the highest in the world. If end-user prices were to fall following power system improvements, such as reducing transmission and distribution losses, then additional hidden electricity demand could be expected to materialise.

---

12. Estimate is based on fuel consumption data from CITAC and World Bank Enterprise Surveys.

Figure 13.16 ▷ Transmission and distribution losses and loss rates, 2012

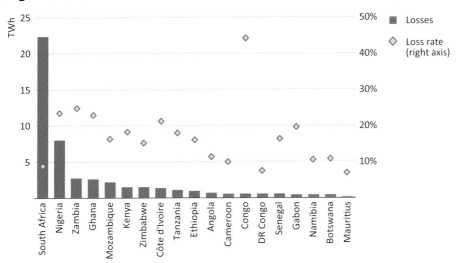

Southern Africa has more installed grid-based capacity than any of the other sub-regions with 58 GW, of which 46 GW is in South Africa (Figure 13.17). By far most of South Africa's capacity is coal-fired at 85% with 6% oil-fired, 5% hydropower and 4% nuclear from the continent's only nuclear power plants (Koeberg I and II [900 MW each]). Since 2000, oil and hydropower have provided the bulk of net capacity additions, while coal capacity remained stable. Excluding South Africa, the remaining three-quarters of the population of Southern Africa rely on some 12 GW, just 21% of the installed generation capacity. Their technology mix has a very different complexion, with hydropower accounting for more than half of capacity, oil for 22%, coal for 16% and gas for 8%. In some cases, such as Angola and Mozambique, a number of sub-national systems serve different parts of the country and there is no integrated national grid. The average cost of grid generation across Southern Africa is relatively low – at around $55 per MWh – due to the reliance on low-cost coal generation in South Africa and hydropower in other countries.

Grid-based capacity in West Africa was 20 GW in 2012. More than half of this capacity is gas-fired, mostly in Nigeria where it is the dominant power generation technology. Oil accounts for almost 30% of total West African capacity and is spread across the region, while hydropower accounts for 20% of capacity (but a larger share of generation). While hydropower had long been the major source of power in the region (led by large projects such as the Akosombo dam in Ghana), oil-fired capacity increased rapidly in the 1990s and gas-fired capacity has done so more recently, as Nigeria boosted efforts to capture and utilise its associated gas production. Despite being rich in oil and gas resources, Nigeria suffers from significant under-capacity in electricity generation, with frequent power outages driving consumers towards large-scale use of expensive back-up generation. Some countries in the region, such as Benin, Burkina Faso and Niger are reliant on electricity imports for a significant share of their supply. The high share of fossil fuels results in a relatively high average cost of generation in West Africa, at around $140 per MWh.

13

Figure 13.17 ▷ **Installed grid-based capacity by type and sub-region**

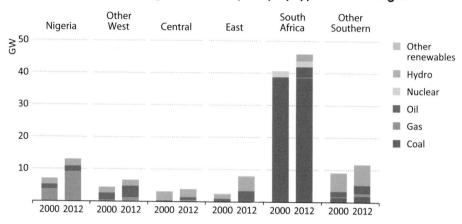

In Central Africa, grid capacity is 4 GW, equivalent to 4% of the sub-Saharan total despite the population being 12% of the whole. The average pace of capacity additions has been very slow since 2000 (less than 60 MW per year), but the pace of gas-fired capacity additions has increased in the last few years. Hydropower accounts for a large share of installed capacity (65%), followed by oil (20%) and gas (15%). At around $95 per MWh, the average cost of generation is relatively low for sub-Saharan Africa, with the high cost of oil-fired generation offset by the low cost of hydropower. Several countries rely heavily on hydropower (such as DR Congo, Cameroon and Congo), although regional capacity is particularly concentrated in DR Congo. A lack of maintenance (Inga I and II, in DR Congo, were built in the 1970s and 1980s) and hydrological variability means that only around half of the capacity of Inga I and II is available to the system. Central Africa nonetheless has the largest hydropower potential of any sub-region (mainly in DR Congo). There are ongoing efforts to add a third dam at Inga of 4.8 GW, and possibly additional phases that collectively make up the Grand Inga project.

Grid-based capacity in East Africa totals 8.1 GW: hydropower is more than half, oil-fired capacity about 45% and the remainder made up of geothermal and gas-fired capacity. Total capacity has more than tripled since 2000, mainly as a result of oil-based additions and hydropower projects coming online in 2009 and 2010. The Merowe hydropower dam in Sudan began operations in 2009 (1.25 GW capacity) and accounts for more than 15% of total power supply in East Africa. Ethiopia's Beles II hydropower project (460 MW) and Gilgel Gibe II (420 MW) began operation in 2010. Gilgel Gibe III (1.87 GW) is nearing completion, while the Grand Renaissance Dam (6 GW) is in progress. Such projects reflect Ethiopia's ambition to become an electricity supplier to east coast neighbours such as Kenya, Burundi, Tanzania, Uganda and Rwanda. More than half of this region's total oil-based capacity is in Sudan, but oil is present in the mix of all countries to some extent. Geothermal is mainly in Kenya, with around 250 MW of capacity in 2012 in the southern part of the Rift Valley, and further developments being undertaken by the state-owned Geothermal Development Company. The existing power mix (and relatively high losses) results in an average cost of generation of around $110 per MWh.

End-use sectors

In many sub-Saharan countries, economic development is at an early stage, a point reflected by the fact that two-thirds of total energy use occurs in the residential sector – mostly for cooking – compared with an average of 25% in other developing countries and just 20% across the OECD. The share of energy consumption in other end-use sectors is much lower than in other world regions, reflecting the very low availability of energy services: transport accounts for only 11% of final energy consumption, and productive uses (including industry, agriculture and services) together account for only 21%. A share of residential energy use is also directed to productive uses, in the form of energy used by cottage industries, but this proportion is, by its nature, difficult to quantify.

Transport

Energy consumption in transport in sub-Saharan Africa has increased by 4% per year since 2000 and was around 50 Mtoe in 2012. The geography of the region is vast, and urbanisation rates are low, implying a high latent demand for transport services. However, the reality is that the transport sector is largely under-developed in most countries and, where it does exist, mass transport infrastructure is often poorly maintained. There is little rail infrastructure in most countries and only around 5% of global airline traffic originates from or goes to Africa (Boeing, 2013). Energy use in transport in sub-Saharan Africa is therefore heavily concentrated on vehicles, but the road infrastructure is also under-developed. Road density is extremely low, at 89 km per 1 000 km^2 of area, it is less than a third of the world average. In addition, less than 20% of African roads are paved (compared with to almost 55% in Middle East, for example), while around 60% of the rural population (400 million people) live more than 2 km from an all-season road (AfDB, 2014).

The affordability of transport services is an important issue in many African countries. This is reflected in very low (albeit increasing) levels of car ownership, with only South Africa, Botswana and Namibia having ownership rates of at least 50 cars per 1 000 people (Figure 13.18). The price of vehicles can be relatively low, but this effect can be offset by high import costs. For example, importing a car from China to Kenya costs around $4 000 and to then transport it to neighbouring Uganda can cost around the same again (UNECA, 2010). Transport fuel is subsidised in several countries (see affordability section), but is still expensive relative to average incomes. The generally poor condition of the roads and the low affordability of fuels also lead to relatively low use of cars and trucks, compared with the global average. As a result, the cost of transporting goods in Africa is among the highest in the world – another barrier to growth. Despite the low level of car ownership, congestion in cities is frequent and public transport by bus and minibus is largely unregulated and informal, which leads to delays in commuting to work in many African cities, creating another obstacle to income generation.

Road transport in sub-Saharan Africa is typically characterised by a high degree of diesel use (almost 0.4 mb/d), with buses and trucks dominating demand. Diesel accounts for 39% of oil consumption in road transport across sub-Saharan Africa, but the figures are heavily

13

influenced by countries with a comparatively high level of vehicle ownership (such as South Africa, with 42% diesel) and those where gasoline prices are relatively low (such as Nigeria, with only 12% diesel). Most of the rest of Africa has diesel shares of around 45% in road transport.

Figure 13.18 ▷ **Car ownership in selected countries, 2012**

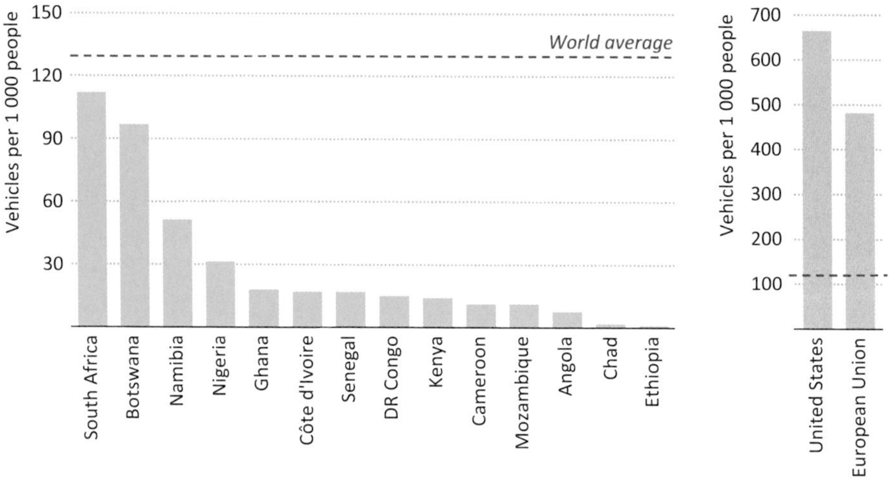

Sources: World Bank (2014a); country communications; IEA databases and analysis.

Improving vehicle efficiency has not been a major focus of policy, in part because only South Africa has domestic manufacturing capacity for passenger cars and other countries rely on imports, often of second-hand vehicles.[13] In 2012, around 2.2 million cars and motorbikes were imported to Africa (UN COMSTAT). Directly or indirectly, Japan and Europe are among the main suppliers of these vehicles, indicating that fuel-economy standards in these regions will progressively impact on energy consumption in Africa, albeit with a significant time lag and depending on proper vehicle maintenance (which is often not the case today). Nevertheless, policy efforts are increasing, with Nigeria and South Africa being among the first countries in the region to adopt Euro 2 emissions standards. Angola, Botswana and Kenya are examples of countries that have introduced import restrictions on vehicle age. Another handful of sub-Saharan countries have introduced fuel quality standards, although poor fuel quality can reduce vehicle efficiency, even where such standards exist. While there is already some limited auto manufacturing and assembly plants (such as Foton, a Chinese producer), several global car manufacturers, such as Renault-Nissan, Kia and Tata are reported to be considering locating assembly plants in Africa. This is an opportunity not only for job creation and growth, but could provide stronger grounds upon which to introduce and enforce stricter fuel-economy standards.

---

13. General Motors leads a joint venture in Kenya that manufactures trucks and buses.

Productive uses

Despite employing far less people than agriculture, and generating less value added than services, industry uses more than two-thirds of the energy used for productive purposes in sub-Saharan Africa. Agriculture accounts for one-quarter of value added (excluding South Africa) and employs most of the working population, but makes very little use of modern energy. Fertilisers are seldom used and subsistence farming still represents a significant portion of total activity. As a result, energy use in agriculture, at 6 Mtoe, is very low by world standards. The services sector – mainly telecommunications and a variety of small businesses – also has limited energy use, but at 22 Mtoe it is still almost four-times larger than agriculture.

While data on energy consumption in specific industries is poor, it is clear that mining is a key energy consumer. Mining is a significant component in a number of economies (e.g. copper in Zambia, copper and cobalt in DR Congo, gold in Ghana, diamonds in Botswana, uranium in Namibia and iron ore in Guinea, Liberia and Sierra Leone), and extraction of these resources requires modern energy. Energy demand for cement production is showing signs of growth, starting in Nigeria with the Dangote plant, the largest in Africa. South Africa and Nigeria are the only countries with a significant petrochemical industry, while other notable energy-intensive large manufacturing activities include aluminium smelting in Mozambique (the Mozal plant near Maputo accounts for more than half of the country's demand) and the automotive, and iron and steel sectors in South Africa. Despite ambitions for manufacturing, to date most economic activity and growth is focused in non energy-intensive sectors, such as agriculture, tourism and textiles.

Overview of energy resources and supply

Energy resources in sub-Saharan Africa as a whole are more than sufficient to meet regional needs, both now and into the foreseeable future. This holds true across the range of energy resources, with remaining recoverable resources of oil sufficient for around 100 years at the current level of production, coal for more than 400 years and gas for more than 600 years (Figure 13.19). Uranium is also present in large quantities in some countries and the region has a range of high quality renewable resources, including solar, hydro, wind and geothermal. Many of these resources are spread unevenly across the huge continent and are at differing stages of development. A significant proportion of them are, as yet, undeveloped (particularly non-hydro renewables). In fact, many of the known resources are not yet fully surveyed or understood, and there remains good reason to believe that sub-Saharan Africa's energy resources will increase as exploration and assessment continue. The opportunity is present to develop a modern energy sector across Africa that draws on these varied resources; but the path from theoretical potential to harnessed supply is likely to be long and complicated.

13

Figure 13.19 ▷ Sub-Saharan Africa natural gas, coal and oil resources, end-2013

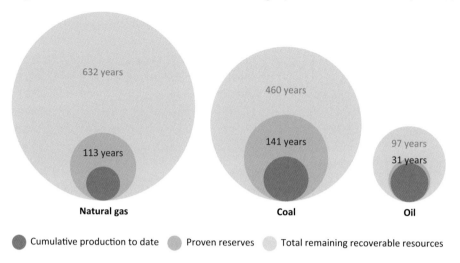

Natural gas — Coal — Oil

632 years / 113 years

460 years / 141 years

97 years / 31 years

● Cumulative production to date ● Proven reserves ○ Total remaining recoverable resources

Notes: All bubbles are expressed as a number of years production based on estimated production levels in 2013. Production numbers for gas include flaring – if flaring were to cease today, there would be sufficient resources for around 960 years of production at 2013 production levels. Remaining recoverable oil and gas resource numbers include conventional and unconventional resources.

Sources: USGS (2000); USGS (2012a); USGS (2012b); Cedigaz (2013); BGR (2013); IEA analysis.

Oil and natural gas

Resources

Recent discoveries are bringing about a transformation in our understanding of sub-Saharan Africa's oil and gas resources, with traditional, mainly West African, sources of supply being joined by new resource-holders, such as Kenya and Uganda in the East African Rift and Mozambique and Tanzania with their offshore gas finds. Overall, sub-Saharan Africa holds around 7% of world conventional oil resources and 6% of world gas resources.[14]

Sub-Saharan Africa accounted for nearly 30% of global oil and gas discoveries made in the last five years (Figure 13.20). In particular, 2012 saw an estimated 14 billion barrels of oil equivalent (boe) discovered, nearly 60% of the world total. While large gas discoveries in Mozambique (mainly in the offshore Rovuma Basin) and in Tanzania dominated the overall picture, these were complemented by pre-salt oil and gas discoveries in the Kwanza Basin in Angola.[15] Sub-Saharan Africa also led global discoveries in 2013, with oil finds in the Keta-Togo-Benin Basin in Nigeria and further natural gas finds in Mozambique. African discoveries this century have been across a range of basins (Box 13.4 and Figure 13.21) and countries: aside from Nigeria, Angola, Mozambique and Tanzania, ten countries have

---

14. Includes unconventional gas volumes.

15. "Pre-salt" oil and gas resources are referred to as such because they predate the formation of a thick salt layer, which overlays the hydrocarbons and traps them in place.

collectively discovered nearly 10 billion barrels of oil equivalent (boe) of resources. Chad, Ghana and Equatorial Guinea have already started production, while discoveries in Kenya and Uganda offer the potential to open up production in the East African Rift Basin before the end of this decade. Improved seismic and drilling technologies, supported by general improvements in the business environment, have meant that a number of African countries with little or no current production have seen higher rates of exploration and exploration success.

Figure 13.20 ▷ **Global discoveries of oil and gas**

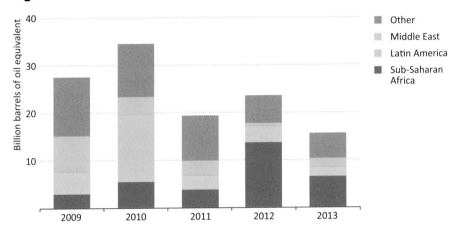

Sources: Rystad Energy AS; IEA analysis.

As of 2013, remaining recoverable oil resources in sub-Saharan Africa are estimated at over 200 billion barrels (Table 13.1), of which around 70% are located offshore. Nigeria holds the largest oil resources by far (63 billion barrels), with a significant share being proven reserves. Further down the west coast, Congo, Gabon and Angola also hold significant resources, with the latter seeing particularly active exploration in the pre-salt Kwanza Basin. East Africa has around 18 billion barrels of oil resources, with South Sudan, Sudan and Uganda holding the majority; most East African countries are at a very early stage of resource development. Sub-Saharan Africa also has unconventional oil potential, particularly heavy oil in Madagascar, with resources estimated to be 2 billion barrels. USGS also estimates that Madagascar has 16 billion barrels of conventional oil yet to be discovered. Overall, the scale of oil resources is not transformative in a global sense, but it has the potential to be important both for meeting domestic needs, which are currently very small, and providing a source of much-needed export revenue.

13

Box 13.4 ▷ Major hydrocarbon basins in sub-Saharan Africa

Exploration and production is underway across many hydrocarbon basins, including:

■ **Niger Delta Basin** – A long-standing source of oil and gas production in Africa, the majority of the basin lies in Nigerian waters and produces high quality sweet crude from its hundreds of small deposits. The eastern edge of the Niger Delta extends into Cameroon and Equatorial Guinea (Rio Del Rey Basin) and accounts for most of their production. The US Geological Survey (USGS) ranks the Niger Delta as the 12th richest basin in undiscovered petroleum resources in the world, with over 30 billion barrels of undiscovered oil resources and 60 billion barrels of total remaining recoverable oil resources.

■ **East African Rift** – The East African Rift Basin has recently brought the prospect of oil production to Uganda, Kenya and several of their neighbours (such as DR Congo, Rwanda, Burundi, Tanzania and Ethiopia). Recent drilling activity has been most intense in Uganda, with the Kingfisher discovery in 2007 and others in the vicinity amounting to 1.7 billion barrels of recoverable oil. Exploration in Kenya has so far discovered 600 million barrels of recoverable resources, principally in the Lokichar Basin. Ethiopia is thought to hold further promise in the Ogaden Basin.

■ **East African Coastal** – Over 5 trillion cubic metres (tcm) of gas resources have been discovered in East African coastal waters off Mozambique and Tanzania in the last five years, predominantly in the Rovuma and Tanzanian coastal basins. USGS estimate that there are 41 billion barrels of oil and 13 tcm of gas to be found in the four geologic provinces off the east coast of Africa (including the Seychelles and Madagascar).

■ **West African Transform Margin** – The discovery of the Jubilee field in Ghana in 2007 has fed expectations of more to come in this relatively under-explored basin stretching from Mauritania to the Niger Delta. The area under license has doubled in the last five years, with technical discoveries being made in Liberia, Sierra Leone and Côte d'Ivoire, but further appraisal is required to ascertain their commerciality.

■ **West Coast Pre-Salt** – Gabon (Diaman discovery), Congo (Marine XII block) and Angola (Lontra and Mavinga) have seen discoveries below salt layers, proving that such pre-salt systems exist in West Africa. Volumes discovered so far have been modest and mainly natural gas, but explorers hope that larger finds await and there is particular interest in Angola's Kwanza and Benguela basins. Pre-salt prospects are also being explored in Cameroon, Equatorial Guinea and Namibia.

Sub-Saharan Africa as a whole has around 65 billion barrels of proven oil reserves, equivalent to around 5% of the world total. Three-quarters of these oil reserves are held in two countries (Nigeria and Angola), with the next largest (South Sudan and Uganda) accounting collectively for only 9% of the total. In the case of Nigeria, proven oil reserves have stagnated at 37 billion barrels since 2008, and will decline unless more exploration takes place. A serious challenge for many African countries is how best to turn resources into reserves and, ultimately, production.

Africa is estimated to have 52 tcm of remaining recoverable conventional natural gas resources, of which 31 tcm are in sub-Saharan Africa (Table 13.2). Proven gas reserves in sub-Saharan Africa have increased by 80% since 2000 and now stand at 9 tcm (5% of the global total), of which around 70% is in deepwater and 18% on land. One-sixth of proven sub-Saharan natural gas reserves are associated with oil. Until recently much of this gas was flared; an estimated total of 1 tcm of gas has been flared to date. Over the past five years, flared volumes have dropped from around 35 bcm per year to 28 bcm. Most of this reduction (6 bcm) is in Nigeria which now flares around 17 bcm per year, slightly more than the country's annual consumption. While gas flaring in other West African producing countries has remained around 12 bcm per year, it has done so while total gas supply (including flared and reinjected) from the same countries has increased significantly, reaching 34 bcm in 2012 (Cedigaz, 2013), meaning that the share of total production that is flared has declined. In lieu of flaring, increased volumes of available gas have been delivered to markets (mainly as liquefied natural gas [LNG] exports from Equatorial Guinea since 2007) or re-injected to sustain oil production (mainly in Congo).

Figure 13.21 ▷ **Major energy infrastructure and main hydrocarbon basins**

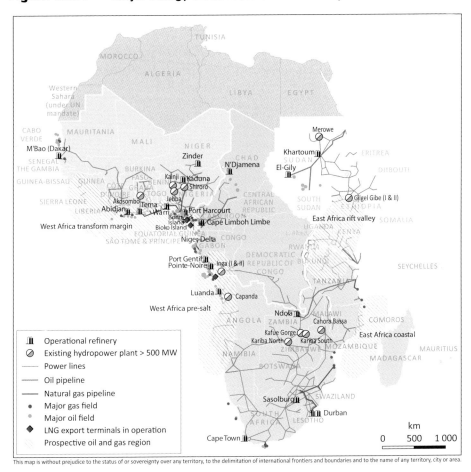

This map is without prejudice to the status of or sovereignty over any territory, to the delimitation of international frontiers and boundaries and to the name of any territory, city or area.

Table 13.1 ▷ **Africa oil resources and reserves** (billion barrels)

	Proven reserves end-2013	Ultimately recoverable resources	Cumulative production end-2013	Remaining recoverable resources	Remaining % of ultimately recoverable resources
Africa	131	454	115	339	75%
North Africa	**65**	**196**	**60**	**136**	**69%**
Sub-Saharan Africa	**65**	**258**	**55**	**203**	**79%**
West Africa	38	107	32	75	70%
Ghana	0.7	1.1	0.1	1.0	88%
Côte d'Ivoire	0.1	3.4	0.3	3.1	92%
Nigeria	37	94	32	63	66%
Central Africa	7	47	10	37	78%
Cameroon	0.2	3.7	1.4	2.3	62%
Chad	1.5	3.4	0.5	2.9	84%
Congo	1.6	14	2.6	12	82%
Equatorial Guinea	1.7	4.0	1.5	2.4	61%
Gabon	2.0	21	3.9	17	81%
East Africa	8	20	1.7	18	92%
Kenya	-	1.5	-	1.5	100%
South Sudan	3.5	9	1.2	8	87%
Sudan	1.5	5.4	0.5	4.9	91%
Uganda	2.5	2.5	-	2.5	100%
Southern Africa	13	84	11	73	87%
Angola	13	36	11	25	70%
Madagascar	-	16	-	16	100%
Tanzania	-	3.5	-	3.5	100%
Unconventional*	-	*40*	*<0.1*	*40*	*100%*

* Unconventional volumes are not included in the regional/country totals.

Sources: USGS (2000), (2012a) and (2012b); O&GJ (2013); IEA databases and analysis.

Nigeria has enormous resources of natural gas but, as in much of the rest of sub-Saharan Africa, gas development has not been a priority until recently. Mozambique and Tanzania have been established as significant natural gas resource-holders within a very short period of time, with the challenge now of proving up the resources by progressing production and export projects through the approval process. Substantial shale gas resources have also been identified in South Africa: three formations in the Karoo Basin have recoverable gas volumes estimated at 11 tcm. Some early exploratory drilling has taken place, but progress was delayed by a moratorium on exploration that was lifted in 2012.

Table 13.2 ▷ **Africa natural gas resources and reserves** (trillion cubic metres)

	Proven reserves end-2013	Ultimately recoverable resources	Cumulative production end-2013*	Remaining recoverable resources	Remaining % of ultimately recoverable resources
Africa	17	56	4.1	52	93%
North Africa	**8**	**24**	**3.3**	**21**	**86%**
Sub-Saharan Africa	**9**	**32**	**0.8**	**31**	**98%**
West Africa	5	10	0.6	10	94%
Ghana	<0.1	0.2	<0.1	0.2	100%
Côte d'Ivoire	<0.1	0.7	<0.1	0.6	96%
Nigeria	5	8	0.6	7	93%
Central Africa	0.4	2.4	0.1	2.3	97%
Cameroon	0.2	0.4	<0.1	0.4	99%
Chad	-	0.3	<0.1	0.3	100%
Congo	0.1	0.6	<0.1	0.6	99%
Equatorial Guinea	0.1	0.3	<0.1	0.2	82%
Gabon	<0.1	0.8	<0.1	0.8	99%
East Africa	0.2	2.8	<0.1	2.8	100%
Ethiopia	<0.1	<0.1	-	<0.1	100%
Kenya	-	0.6	-	0.6	100%
South Sudan	0.1	1.0	<0.1	1.0	100%
Sudan	<0.1	<0.1	<0.1	<0.1	100%
Uganda	<0.1	<0.1	-	<0.1	100%
Southern Africa	3.2	17	0.1	17	99%
Angola	0.3	1.5	<0.1	1.5	98%
Madagascar	<0.1	4.7	-	4.7	100%
Mozambique	2.8	5	<0.1	5	99%
South Africa	<0.1	1.1	<0.1	1.0	96%
Tanzania	<0.1	1.4	<0.1	1.4	100%
*Unconventional**	*0.1*	*49*	*<0.1*	*49*	*100%*

* Figures exclude cumulative gas production that has been flared. Flared volumes include Côte d'Ivoire (1 bcm), Nigeria (745 bcm), Cameroon (42 bcm), Congo (46 bcm), Equatorial Guinea (19 bcm), Gabon (61 bcm) and Angola (131 bcm). ** Unconventional volumes, which are concentrated in South Africa and Nigeria in sub-Saharan Africa, are not included in the regional/country totals.

Sources: USGS (2000), (2012a) and (2012b); Cedigaz (2013); O&GJ (2013); IEA databases and analysis.

Oil production

Oil production in sub-Saharan Africa has doubled since 1990, reaching 6.2 mb/d in 2011, before dropping back to 5.7 mb/d in 2013 (Figure 13.22). Over the years, an increasing share of production has come from offshore fields, with more than 40% of the total now coming from deep or ultra-deep water. Nigeria and Angola alone account for three-quarters of total

13

sub-Saharan oil production, but the evolution of production in the two countries has been very different in recent decades. Nigeria has consistently been the largest oil producer in sub-Saharan Africa and has seen production levels increase gradually and sporadically, to 2.5 mb/d in 2013. Angolan oil production has quadrupled since 1990, reaching 1.8 mb/d in 2013, and accounting for 30% of total sub-Saharan production. Angolan production growth has come exclusively from offshore developments, such as Dalia, Girassol and Greater Plutonio.

Figure 13.22 ▷ **Sub-Saharan Africa oil production by country and total demand**

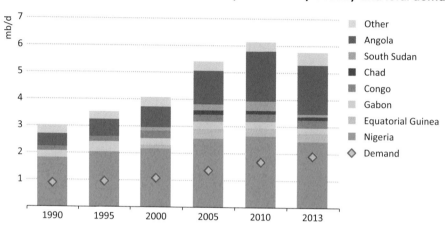

New deepwater discoveries came on-stream in Gabon and Congo to boost production levels to around 240 kb/d and 280 kb/d respectively in 2013. Chad started oil production in 2003, when the Chad-Cameroon pipeline (CCP) was finished, allowing exports to the Atlantic coast. Output peaked at around 170 kb/d in 2004, but stood at 130 kb/d in 2013. In Cameroon, production peaked at 180 kb/d in 1985 and has declined gradually to reach 70 kb/d in 2013. Equatorial Guinea saw oil production take-off in the late 1990s, when the Zafiro complex of fields to the northwest of Bioko Island came on-stream, reaching a plateau of around 350 kb/d for the five-year period from 2004; production in 2013 had dipped to 270 kb/d. Production from Ghana comes almost entirely from the Jubilee field, which came on-stream in late-2010 and produces around 100 kb/d. For the moment, associated gas is being re-injected, limiting oil production to below the 120 kb/d expected from the field, pending completion of the Jubilee gas project (expected later this year). South Africa contributes 100 kb/d to total hydrocarbon liquids production by converting coal-to-liquids, at Sasol's Secunda plant, and gas-to-liquids. Despite fairly modest levels of oil production in most sub-Saharan countries, even lower levels of domestic demand and refining capacity mean that 13 countries in sub-Saharan Africa were exporters of crude oil in 2013 (albeit importers of oil products) (see energy trade section). Apart from Cameroon, Niger and Sudan, all of these countries exported more than 85% of their oil production (namely Angola, Chad, Congo, DR Congo, Equatorial Guinea, Gabon, Ghana, Mauritania, Nigeria, and South Sudan).

Natural gas production

Sub-Saharan gas production increased from around 7 bcm in 1990 to 58 bcm in 2012, making it a small but growing contributor to global gas supply (Figure 13.23). Growth has come largely from associated gas linked to the West African offshore oil boom. Historically, much of the produced gas has been flared, but more stringent regulations have excluded this option for most new developments in the last decade. Production made available to the market is five-times greater than it was in 2000, mainly from Nigeria, which now has six LNG trains, but also from Equatorial Guinea and Angola, which joined the ranks of global LNG exporters in 2007 and 2013 respectively.[16] The only other gas exporting country in sub-Saharan Africa is Mozambique, which exports around 3.5 bcm per year by pipeline to South Africa. The main countries currently making use of their gas resources domestically are Cameroon, Congo, Côte d'Ivoire, Nigeria, South Africa (mainly at the Mossel Bay gas-to-liquids [GTL] plant) and Tanzania. Huge scope remains across many countries to increase natural gas supply, exports and domestic consumption. Putting gas gathering and processing facilities in place, building gas networks and developing effective markets and pricing are major tasks for governments in the region, as local availability of gas for power generation or industrial use is very low in most countries.

Figure 13.23 ▷ **Sub-Saharan Africa natural gas production by country and total demand**

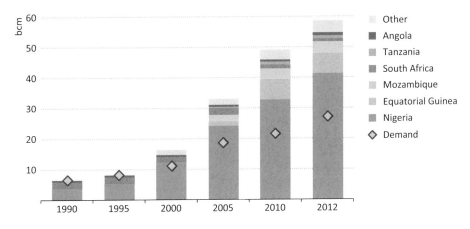

Renewables

Renewable energy technologies (mainly hydropower) make up a large share of total power supply in Africa and there is potential for this to expand as a wider range of technologies is deployed. Many countries are actively developing or considering developing their renewable energy resource potential. Renewables potentially improve energy security by

---

16. The Angola LNG installation that started operation in 2013 is currently shut down for remedial work and is expected to resume operations in 2015.

reducing the reliance on imported fuels and help diversify the power mix. They can be deployed in a decentralised manner, which may enable them to be deployed faster than centralised power plants (although small-scale projects can be costly in terms of scarce administrative skills), and can provide local employment for deployment and maintenance. Renewables are also critical technologies to help provide access to remote communities.

Bioenergy

Bioenergy dominates the sub-Saharan energy mix, mainly accounted for by the traditional use of solid biomass in the residential sector, while the modern use of solid biomass and biogas for power generation and heat make up only a very small share. Around one-third of sub-Saharan Africa is covered by forest, with total forest biomass stock estimated to be 130 billion tonnes in 2010, but the amount available annually without causing deforestation is much smaller (see Chapter 14). In addition to forest products and residues, agricultural residues represent a significant portion of the available biomass resources, though some residues must be left in-field to maintain the agricultural productivity of the land. Biomass is spread throughout much of the African continent, with forested areas most prevalent in Central Africa and parts of Southern Africa, while agricultural activities occur largely in East and West Africa. Tapping into these available resources could provide fuel for a significant share of electricity supply in some countries. For example, sustainably extracted agricultural and forestry residues could supply close to 40% of Cameroon's electricity consumption (Ackom, et al. 2013). There is existing installed capacity of around 325 MW of electricity from bioenergy, mainly spread across East and South Africa. However, large-scale deployment will be challenging, as the levelised costs of power generation from bioenergy are often higher than gas-fired generation and hydropower, due in part to the cost of collecting the biomass feedstocks.

Hydropower

Hydropower has long been an important part of many African power systems and is the most used renewable energy source (excluding bioenergy). Hydropower is attractive because of the large-scale of potential development and the low average costs of electricity generated, lower than any other technology, renewable or otherwise. The technical hydropower potential in Africa is estimated at 283 GW (Figure 13.24), and is able to generate close to 1 200 TWh per year – 8% of the global technical potential. This amount of electricity is more than three-times the currect electricity consumption in sub-Saharan Africa. Less than 10% of the technical potential has so far been tapped. More than half of the remaining potential is in Central and East Africa, particularly in Cameroon, Congo, DR Congo, Ethiopia and Mozambique, but there are also significant opportunities in Southern Africa (Angola, Madagascar, Mozambique and South Africa) and West Africa (Guinea, Nigeria and Senegal). The large hydropower potential in DR Congo has long been a focus of policy-makers, both in terms of the Inga III project (4.8 GW) that is planned and the several phases of the long-discussed Grand Inga project (around 44 GW) which, if constructed, could transform the African power supply picture.

Several barriers exist to exploiting the economic hydropower potential in sub-Saharan Africa. Large hydropower projects require large sums of upfront capital and, often, for power purchase agreements to be in place to raise the necessary financing. Low levels of regional interconnection mean that there are limited opportunities to export large volumes of electricity, while domestic markets can be small. While hydropower is a low-cost source of baseload power generation, it can also be subject to seasonal and annual variations. Environmental concerns, social considerations and competition for water resources also require very careful consideration and public consultation, as hydropower dams may require flooding large land areas, potentially displacing communities and reducing the flow of water available for other uses downstream, such as agriculture. In addition, a lack of required technical expertise is a brake on hydropower development in some countries.

Figure 13.24 ▷ **Existing hydropower capacity and potential in Africa**

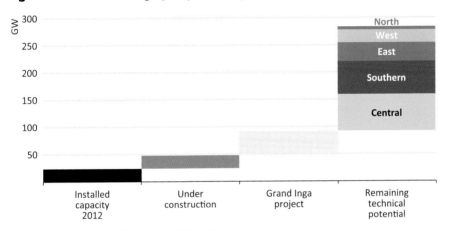

Sources: IPCC (2011); IJHD (2009) and (2010); IEA analysis.

Currently, 20 GW of hydropower capacity is installed in sub-Saharan Africa, with several countries, including Mozambique, DR Congo, Uganda and Kenya, relying on it for a significant share of power generation. Many large projects are planned e.g. further developments at the Inga site in DR Congo and Mphanda Nkuwa in Mozambique. Many smaller projects are also being developed, as perennial rivers cover much of sub-Saharan Africa. Small hydropower may be an economic means of electricity access for communities near these waterways.

Solar power

Solar technologies have played a limited role in the power sector in Africa, but are gaining attention in many countries. Africa is particularly rich in solar energy potential, with most of the continent enjoying an average of more than 320 days per year of bright sunlight and experiencing irradiance levels of almost 2000 kWh per square metre (kWh/m²) annually (twice the average level in Germany) (European Commission JRC, 2011). The best solar resources stretch across the Sahara, North Africa and parts of Southern Africa, with irradiation levels close to 2 500 kWh/m². Central and West Africa generally have lower irradiance levels, particularly near the Gulf of Guinea. Potential solar power generation far exceeds electricity demand today and into the foreseeable future, though vast areas of land or rooftops would be required. For example, to generate the same amount of power as current electricity consumption in sub-Saharan Africa (352 TWh) would require more than 200 GW of solar PV, spanning an area close to 7 000 km².

The average cost to generate electricity from solar PV in sub-Saharan Africa currently exceeds $175 per MWh, which is above the average cost of electricity generated from other grid technologies (Figure 13.25). In some cases, the existence of very high quality solar resources and technology that is readily available can result in lower costs, as recent bids in the Renewable Energy Independent Power Producer Procurement Programme in South Africa have indicated. Despite the apparent cost disadvantage, solar is gaining a foothold in sub-Saharan Africa where installed capacity increased from 40 MW in 2010 (mainly small-scale PV) to around 280 MW in 2013 (including some large PV and concentrating solar power [CSP] plants). There are several grid-connected projects under construction, including the 155 MW Nzema plant in Ghana and 150 MW of projects in South Africa, for example. In addition, other countries are considering projects on the scale of 100 MW or more, including Mozambique, Sudan, Nigeria and Ethiopia.

Figure 13.25 ▷ Indicative levelised costs of electricity for on-grid and off-grid technologies in sub-Saharan Africa, 2012

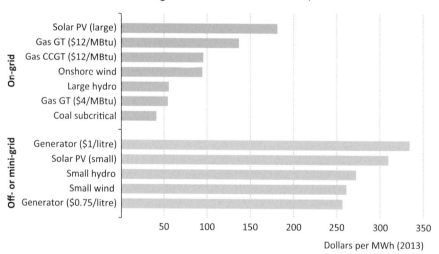

Notes: Costs are indicative and figures for specific projects could vary significantly, depending on their detailed design. GT = gas turbine; CCGT = combined-cycle gas turbine; MBtu = million British thermal units.

Solar PV is much more competitive in off-grid or mini-grid applications, where the main alternative at present is generation fuelled by diesel or gasoline (see Chapter 15). Where adequate resources are available, small hydro and wind projects can compete with solar

PV for off- or mini-grid uses. Solar can also be an effective element in a broader suite of modern energy solutions, such as solar lanterns, ovens and water heaters.

Wind power

Wind power deployment to date has been very limited when compared to hydropower, with only 190 MW in all of sub-Saharan Africa, even though the levelised cost of electricity from onshore wind technologies has declined significantly in recent years. Sub-Saharan Africa's wind potential is estimated at around 1 300 GW (Mandelli, et al, 2014), which would produce several times the current level of total African electricity consumption. Much the same as solar, there are medium to high quality wind resources across most of North Africa (European Commission JRC, 2011), though harsh desert conditions pose a significant challenge to the long-term operation of wind turbines. In sub-Saharan Africa, high quality wind resources are confined to a few areas, mainly the Horn of Africa, eastern Kenya, parts of West and Central Africa bordering on the Sahara and parts of Southern Africa. Somalia has the highest onshore potential of any country, followed by Sudan, Libya, Mauritania, Egypt, Madagascar and Kenya (AfDB, 2013). The offshore wind energy potential is best off the coast of Madagascar, Mozambique, Tanzania, Angola and South Africa. Wind can be cost competitive with other technologies where the resources are good, but other factors could limit its deployment. For instance, in East and West Africa, where the greatest potential lies, domestic markets are small and the power grids are not well developed, meaning that variable generation from wind would introduce additional challenges to an already unstable and intermittent system. With improvements in the operations of power systems in Africa and the increasing size of the systems, the amount of wind power that can be added without creating formidable operational challenges will increase. For those systems with hydropower, the variability of wind power can be accommodated more readily. South Africa and parts of East Africa are leading the way in increasing their wind capacity with, for example, Kenya planning to add over 400 MW of wind capacity by 2020.

Geothermal

Geothermal technologies make up a small fraction of Africa's power supply, but can be an attractive option adequate resources exist. These resources are concentrated in the East African Rift Valley, which is considered one of the most exciting prospects in the world for geothermal development, with total potential estimated at between 10 GW and 15 GW – more than East Africa's total existing power generation capacity, a large share of which is concentrated in Ethiopia and Kenya. The cost of generation is competitive with fossil fuels and geothermal power is not characterised by the variability issues associated with some renewables, so that it can serve as baseload generation. Kenya has around 250 MW of installed geothermal capacity and a further 280 MW is under development. More than 40 wells a year currently are being drilled in Kenya, and the target is to develop more than 5 000 MW by 2030 (about half of the estimated potential). Ethiopia is also actively developing its geothermal resources, led by the Corbetti Power Project that aims to add 1 GW of capacity over the next decade. A number of other countries are exploring their geothermal potential, but projects are challenging and typically have long-lead times. Zambia has a number of sites planned, while Tanzania is carrying out exploration (and has potential of around 650 MW), and Eritrea, Djibouti, Rwanda and Uganda have also carried out geothermal exploration.

Other

Coal

Africa's estimated 120 billion tonnes of coal resources are concentrated in the southern part of the continent. They amount to less than 1% of world coal resources, but this relatively low figure reflects, in part, the lack of exploration in much of the continent. South Africa dominates Africa's coal industry with over 90% of the 36 billion tonnes of proven reserves and virtually all of the continent's production. However, other southern African nations, including Mozambique, Zimbabwe, Botswana, Tanzania, Zambia, Swaziland and Malawi, are endowed with significant coal reserves. In particular, Mozambique is one of the largest undeveloped coal regions in the world (with estimated coal resources of 25 billion tonnes) and international companies have started exports and are announcing expansion plans. The profitability of exports is expected to be high (due to the abundant and shallow coal deposits) once the necessary infrastructure is fully developed. The ports of Beira and Nacala are far from the coal basins and the Zambezi River is environmentally sensitive and so unlikely to carry coal barge traffic. Plans to expand rail and port capacity are advanced and big investments have been announced, but construction will take several years. Zimbabwe holds large hard coal reserves (totalling 500 Mt), and resources of 25 billion tonnes, many of which can be mined using low cost open-cast methods. However, a lack of transportation facilities and an adverse investment climate are substantial barriers to development. Botswana also has limited production but plenty of potential, with estimated resources of 21 billion tonnes. Several projects to develop various coalfields have been proposed, but again it will not be easy to build the infrastructure required for exports to target markets in Asia.

Nuclear

Sub-Saharan Africa includes three of the ten-largest uranium resource-holders in the world (Namibia, Niger and South Africa). While exploration has increased uranium resource estimates over the last decade, prevailing prices dictate when mining commences. At prices lower than $80 per kilogramme of uranium (kgU), $130/kgU and $260/kgU respectively, Africa holds over 6%, 19% and 21% of world uranium resources (IAEA/NEA, 2011). Sub-Saharan African resources are relatively accessible, regulators are flexible and labour costs are low, resulting in it providing a significant share of global production (18%). Namibia provides 8.2% of global production, Niger 7.7%, Malawi 1.2% and South Africa 1.1%. South Africa is the only country with existing nuclear power generation capacity, and has stated its intention of expanding it. Some other countries have stated their interest in introducing nuclear power into their domestic mix (e.g. Kenya and Namibia). However, the introduction of nuclear power brings many challenges, not least of which is the very large upfront capital investment required, the need to develop technical and regulatory capacity, and to have the electricity demand and infrastructure capacity to absorb the resulting baseload supply.

Energy trade

Crude oil and oil products

As a region, sub-Saharan Africa is a significant exporter of crude oil, behind only the Middle East and Russia in global terms. Countries on the west coast account for the bulk of exports (more than 5 mb/d), with around 2.3 mb/d from Nigeria and 1.8 mb/d from Angola. Congo, Equatorial Guinea and Gabon export between 200-270 kb/d each. East African exports are limited, and are currently constrained by political uncertainty in South Sudan. Other small producers (some land-locked) make up the remaining sub-Saharan exports.

The destination of crude oil exports from the west coast of Africa (rather than just West Africa) has undergone a rapid shift as a result of the tight oil boom in the United States (Figure 13.26). Since 2008, when the first significant volumes of tight oil came on-stream, exports to the United States have reduced by two-thirds, to less than 600 kb/d in 2013, as the United States cut the import of light crude oil, mostly at the expense of Nigeria and Angola. At the same time, Europe has increased purchases from sub-Saharan Africa to replace its own decreasing oil production and to compensate for Libyan output disruption. As a result, Nigerian exports to the United States now account for only 10% of the total, compared with around 26% in 2008, with increased flows to Europe and India now accounting for around one-third and one-quarter of Nigerian exports respectively. Chinese refinery expansions have provided additional markets, proving particularly important for Angola, whose exports to China account for almost half of the country's total crude output.

Figure 13.26 ▷ **Crude oil exports from Africa's west coast by destination**

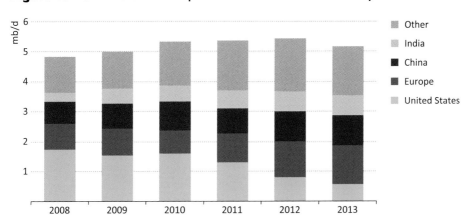

Note: Includes crude oil exports from Angola, Cameroon, Chad, Congo, Côte d'Ivoire, DR Congo, Equatorial Guinea, Gabon, Ghana, Niger and Nigeria.

Sub-Saharan Africa's refining operations are severely constrained by the state its refining assets. These are mostly decades old and in relatively poor condition due to years of under-investment and neglect, making their operation less economic. As a result, despite increasing crude oil output by 2 mb/d from 2000, sub-Saharan Africa's oil product imports doubled (to around 1 mb/d in 2012), with diesel and gasoline each accounting for one-third of the volume. European and, more recently, US refiners have been successful in selling excess or lower-specification gasoline, kerosene and diesel in sub-Saharan Africa, where fuel quality standards tend to be lower. South Africa and countries in East Africa import oil products from the Middle East or India. South Africa has an adequate refining system that runs at around 90% utilisation rates and supplies more than two-thirds of the domestic market (which was just under 0.5 mb/d in 2012). Nigeria has the second-largest refining capacity, at 0.45 mb/d, which if run optimally could meet total demand. However, run rates can be as low as 20%, meaning that over 80% of the oil products consumed in the country are imported. Ghana also imports most of its oil products despite producing sufficient levels of crude oil, as its refinery operates at extremely low rates. Côte d'Ivoire, Cameroon, Niger and Chad cover most of their demand from local refinery supplies, with the latter two having had new (but small) refineries built by Chinese upstream investors. In East Africa, only Sudan and Zambia have active refineries. Rapidly growing oil product imports into sub-Saharan Africa need not be a critical concern, within a well-supplied and functioning global market. However, the energy security risk needs to be watched, particularly when considered together with the growing strain on the energy import and distribution infrastructure, which has struggled to expand.

Two key factors play an important role in sub-Saharan oil product trade flows – geography and subsidies. Land-locked countries are, for the most part, reliant on importing supplies from the nearest port (which can be a thousand kilometres or more away) and the lack of pipeline and rail infrastructure means that much of these supplies are transported by road. This can leave these countries vulnerable to supply disruptions and to very high import prices. Relative pricing can also play an important role in shaping cross-border trade in oil products, particularly in Nigeria, where low domestic prices spur unofficial exports to Togo, Ghana, Burkina Faso and Benin. As well as having a significant impact on Nigerian state revenues through a subsidy cost whose (limited) benefits are not captured locally, smuggled products also deny the government of Benin an important source of tax revenue.

Natural gas

Sub-Saharan Africa exports around half of the natural gas that it produces, but only from a small number of countries (Figure 13.27). In 2012, Nigeria, Equatorial Guinea and Mozambique exported gas, predominantly through LNG shipments, with 26 bcm being exported from Nigeria and 5 bcm from Equatorial Guinea. Mozambique (over 3 bcm to South Africa) and Nigeria (0.6 bcm) are key exporters to other countries on the continent. In the case of Nigeria, gas is exported through the West African Gas Pipeline, which links Nigeria to Benin, Togo and Ghana (see Chapter 16, Box 16.3 on the West African Gas Pipeline). At the end of 2013, Angola started exporting LNG from its first train at Soyo (capacity of 5.2 million tonnes per year [around 7 bcm]), sending cargoes to China, Japan and South Korea, but these exports have since been disrupted by operational problems.

Figure 13.27 ▷ Africa's major international energy trade flows by sub-region, 2012

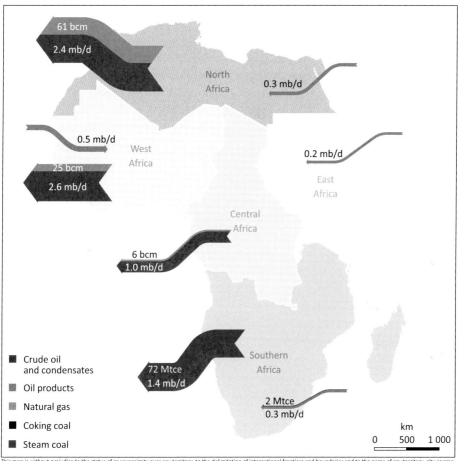

This map is without prejudice to the status of or sovereignty over any territory, to the delimitation of international frontiers and boundaries and to the name of any territory, city or area.

Note: Mtce = million tonnes of coal equivalent. Sources: CITAC; IEA databases and analysis.

Electricity

There are clear ambitions to increase electricity trade across sub-Saharan Africa. While at varying stages of development, regional power pools have been established with the aim of achieving greater efficiency through co-operative planning and improved transmission interconnections. At present electricity trade in sub-Saharan Africa is relatively limited, and is concentrated in the Southern Africa Power Pool, where over 5.3 TWh of electricity were traded in 2012-13 (SAPP, 2013). The bulk of this trade involved supply from South Africa to Botswana (meeting almost all of Botswana's demand) and Namibia (nearly half of its demand). South Africa also imported electricity from Mozambique's Cahorra Bassa project (around 10 TWh in 2012), but much of this was then exported back to Mozambique's southern region to supply Maputo (and particularly the Mozal smelter). Despite being the most developed regional power pool, Southern Africa's electricity trade is heavily constrained by the limitations of the transmission network.

Elsewhere in sub-Saharan Africa, Ghana and Côte d'Ivoire have successfully traded electricity in both directions for many years, with current supplies going from Côte d'Ivoire to Ghana, and some of this then transiting to meet demand in Togo and Benin. Burkina Faso and Niger also import electricity from neighbouring countries. In East Africa, Kenya imports some electricity from Uganda, while Djibouti imports from Ethiopia. Ethiopia has plans to increase electricity exports to other parts of East Africa, based on new hydropower generation, and construction is underway to boost interconnections with Kenya. As well, there are hydropower projects that share output between countries, including the Manantali dam in Mali and the Ruzizi dam on the border between Rwanda and DR Congo.

Coal

Sub-Saharan Africa exported around 71 million tonnes of coal equivalent (Mtce) in 2012, bouncing back from the lower exports seen in 2008-2009 to reach new highs. South Africa is the epicentre of African coal trade (accounting for all but a fraction of the sub-Saharan total). It has been a coal exporter since the late-1970s and has one of the world's largest coal export terminals at Richards Bay. It exports around one-third of its total production and has seen the balance of trade shift more towards Asian markets in recent years. Remaining sub-Saharan exports are made up of coking coal from Mozambique, which, in light of high prices (although these have subsided somewhat) and rapidly growing demand from Asia, has attracted international coal companies to invest in the Tete province. Despite difficult geology, mining costs are on the low side for coking coal in Mozambique and, while the lack of export infrastructure (railway lines and ports) has impeded a rapid increase of exports to date, the intention is to increase exports over time.

Energy affordability

Energy prices

End-user energy prices vary significantly across sub-Saharan Africa (Figure 13.28), with much of the variability reflecting the relative ease of energy supply and the extent to which energy prices are subject to government controls. Consumer oil product prices are regulated in most countries and therefore not responsive to changes in international markets. In most non oil-producing countries, prices are regulated but not subsidised when assessed against a benchmark price, while in several oil-producing countries prices are set lower than such a benchmark. Where subsidies exist, they are often designed to support energy access for the poor, but they are frequently not well targeted to that end. In 2013, the subsidisation rate (relative to the benchmark price) for gasoline in Nigeria was estimated to be around 29% and 32% in Angola. Angola also has a 58% subsidy rate on diesel. Other oil exporters, including Congo, Equatorial Guinea, Gabon and Sudan, also subsidise gasoline, diesel or both. Such subsidies serve to incentivise fuel smuggling into nearby markets with higher prices.

Figure 13.28 ▷ Oil product price differentials between Nigeria, Angola and neighbouring countries, 2013

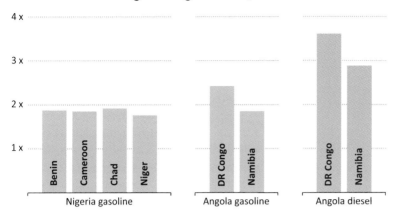

Note: CAR = Central African Republic. Sources: CITAC; IEA analysis.

Kerosene subsidies are relatively common across sub-Saharan Africa, reflecting deliberate policies to promote its use by households. Prices for kerosene intended for domestic use vary from $0.10 per litre in Mauritius and $0.27 per litre in Angola, to $1.36 per litre in the Central African Republic (Figure 13.29). Based on available pricing and demand data, the weighted average subsidisation rate for kerosene is estimated to be around 45% in 2013. LPG prices are also subsidised to encourage fuel switching. Based on analysis of countries accounting for more than three-quarters of consumption, the average subsidisation rate for LPG is estimated to be around 40%. However, not all LPG sales within a country may be subsidised, so this estimate is likely to be high. Total sub-Saharan oil product subsidies are estimated to be $10.2 billion in 2013, with Nigeria and Angola accounting for nearly 75% of this sum.

Figure 13.29 ▷ Kerosene price and subsidy in selected countries, 2013

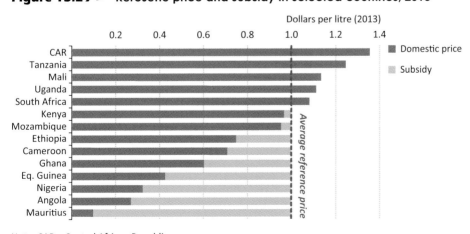

Note: CAR = Central African Republic.

Sources: CITAC; IEA analysis.

End-user electricity tariffs in many parts of sub-Saharan Africa do not fully reflect the cost of electricity supply. While tariffs may be higher than the average cost of generation (Figure 13.30), additional costs such as those relating to T&D losses, T&D investment and retail can add $60-$100 per MWh to the total cost of electricity supply. Poor quality of supply, low household income and high T&D losses are all obstacles to full cost recovery. Such prices serve as a deterrent to greater levels of investment in the power sector. Even so, sub-Saharan electricity tariffs, though varying by country and by type of customer, are in many instances among the highest anywhere in the world. On average, sub-Saharan electricity tariffs are between $130-140/MWh, with those for services and industries being 5% and 8% higher (on average) than those charged to households. In comparison, electricity tariffs in Latin America, Eastern Europe and East Asia are around $80/MWh (Briceño-Garmendia and Shkaratan, 2011). The inability to set electricity tariffs at levels that reflect both costs and a reasonable return on capital is a major obstacle to the long-term sustainability of many utilities in sub-Saharan Africa. According to the International Monetary Fund, state-owned electricity companies across the region were, in 2010, operating with deficits equivalent to 1.4% of sub-Saharan GDP (IMF, 2013).

Figure 13.30 ▷ **Grid electricity prices by end-use sector in selected countries, 2013**

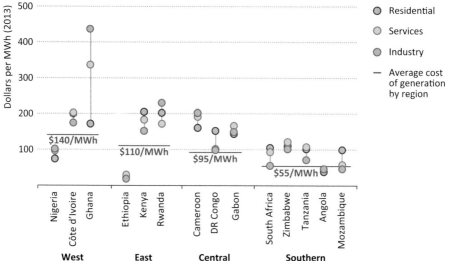

Energy expenditure

In a region where average incomes are low, the importance of the relationship between incomes, energy prices and energy expenditure is starkly evident. Across sub-Saharan Africa, the wealthiest 20% of households account for about half of total residential spending on energy, on average, while the poorest 20% account for around 5%. Around 40% of total energy expenditure is on electricity and 25% is on kerosene, but this picture is distorted by the consumption of unpriced solid biomass.[17] In general, as one would expect, the heavy burden of energy expenditures tends to get lighter as household incomes increase (Figure 13.31). For instance, energy expenditures in South Africa account for around 3.5% of total income, while in Malawi, where income levels are typically much lower, the share is more than double. Large disparities in electricity consumption are also evident: in countries with intermediate levels of income, the wealthiest 20% of households tend to account for around 40% of consumption while, in the extreme case of Malawi, the richest 20% consume more than 80% of the total. Urban and rural households are also very different, with urban households typically having higher incomes and greater access to electricity services. In Rwanda, for example, more than 40% of urban households report electricity spending, while in rural areas the figure is 4% (National Institute of Statistics of Rwanda, 2012).

Figure 13.31 ▷ Household energy spending as share of income

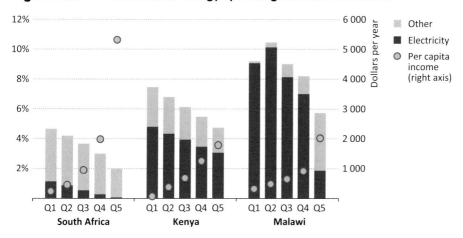

Note: Q1 is the lowest income quintile (20%) in a country, while Q5 is the highest.

Sources: Statistics South Africa (2012); IFC (2012); Barnes, Singh and Shi (2010); IEA analysis.

---

17. Based on World Bank (2012).

Chapter 14

Outlook for African energy to 2040
Energy to grow or a growing need for energy?

Highlights

- The sub-Saharan energy system expands rapidly to 2040, but so do the demands placed upon it. The economy quadruples in size, the population nearly doubles (to 1.75 billion) and energy demand grows by around 80% in the New Policies Scenario. The capacity and efficiency of the system improves, and access to modern energy services grows; but many of the existing energy challenges are only partly overcome.

- Bioenergy demand grows by 40% in absolute terms by 2040, exacerbating stress on the forestry stock. However, the share of bioenergy in the energy mix declines from above 60% to below half and the share of modern fuels edges higher. Oil demand more than doubles to 4 mb/d in 2040 (over 0.5 mb/d is residential use of LPG and kerosene) and becomes the second-largest fuel in the mix, overtaking coal. Natural gas use grows by nearly 6% per year, to reach 135 bcm.

- The sub-Saharan power system expands rapidly, with generation capacity quadrupling to 385 GW. The power mix becomes more diverse, with coal (mainly South Africa) and hydropower (all regions), being joined by greater use of gas (Nigeria, Mozambique, Tanzania), solar (notably in South Africa and Nigeria) and geothermal (East Africa). The share of renewables in total capacity more than doubles to 44%. Total power sector investment averages around $46 billion per year, with just over half of it in transmission and distribution.

- Oil production rises above 6 mb/d by 2020 but then tails off to 5.3 mb/d in 2040. Nigeria and Angola remain the dominant producers, although Uganda and Kenya ramp up oil output in the 2020s. Gas production rises to 230 bcm in 2040, led by Nigeria and the expansion of output from Mozambique (60 bcm in 2040), and Angola and Tanzania (each 20 bcm). Coal supply grows by 50% to reach 325 Mtce, still concentrated in South Africa but joined increasingly by Mozambique and others.

- Sub-Saharan energy exports are drawn increasingly towards Asian markets. Crude oil net exports decline to just over 3.8 mb/d in 2040, partly due to a greater share being refined and consumed domestically. Rising gas output from Mozambique and Tanzania brings sub-Saharan LNG export towards 100 bcm by 2040 (around 17% of inter-regional LNG trade), and Mozambique also joins South Africa as a key coal exporter.

- Sub-Saharan Africa makes only a small contribution to global energy-related CO_2 emissions, accounting for merely 3% of the total in 2040, but is on the front line when it comes to the potential impacts of a changing climate. In particular, hydropower prospects can be affected by changing patterns of rainfall and run-off. The fuelwood and charcoal sectors operate largely outside the formal economy, meaning that policy-makers have few levers to promote more sustainable forestry.

Projecting future developments

The successful development of the energy sector will be a crucial factor in determining the pace of economic and social development in Africa. As noted in Chapter 13, understanding the directions in which Africa's energy sector is set to develop is therefore essential for policy-makers and investors: if the picture which emerges is unacceptable, action can be taken to change it. This chapter accordingly presents energy projections and analysis for the period to 2040 based upon the **New Policies Scenario**, the central scenario of this *Outlook*. This scenario describes the probable pathway for energy markets based on the continuation of existing policies and measures, and the implementation, albeit often cautiously, of the commitments and plans announced as of mid-2014, even if they are yet to be formally adopted. It allows for the existence of a range of institutional, political and economic circumstances that affect the pace and extent of implementation and, in some cases, a lack of detail about new initiatives and how they will be executed. The projections also take into account prospective technology developments in the energy sector and how they might affect supply costs, energy efficiency and fuel choice, without assuming any fundamental technological breakthroughs. Long-term projections are always subject to a range of uncertainties, including extreme events such as war and famine, but projections are not forecasts – they describe trends – and such events are not taken into account. Instead, a level of stability is assumed to prevail that allows for the expectations of economic and population growth which underlie the analysis (both of which are consistent with those of other international organisations) to be realised. Chapter 16 goes beyond the projections of the New Policies Scenario to illustrate, in an **African Century Case**, the energy and economic implications of a more ambitious, yet attainable future.[1]

Economic and population growth

The sub-Saharan economy grows by nearly $8 trillion in the New Policies Scenario (expressed in year-2013 dollars in purchasing power parity [PPP] terms) to reach four-times its current size by 2040 (Figure 14.1). The rate of growth (which averaged 5.7% from 2000 to 2012) slows gradually over time – from 5.5% per year to 2020 to 4.9% per year after 2030 – as a number of economies, having grown fast, start to mature. This economic growth path for sub-Saharan Africa as a whole is higher than those in the *World Energy Outlook 2013* by 1% per year on average, a revision consistent with the medium-term economic outlooks of other international organisations, including the International Monetary Fund and African Development Bank. Over the longer term, it reflects an improved methodology that includes region-by-region analysis of labour, capital, and overall productivity across sub-Saharan Africa. In the period to 2040, sub-Saharan Africa is among the world's most rapidly growing regions and sees its share of global gross domestic product (GDP) rise from 3% to nearly 5%. However, in many cases this rapid growth is from a very low starting level and is nowhere near enough to achieve a significant convergence between sub-Saharan Africa and other major economies on a per-capita basis. In 2040, sub-Saharan GDP per

---

1. See the *Africa Energy Outlook* Special Report (IEA, 2014a) for data and projections tables for the New Policies Scenario and the African Century Case.

capita remains less than one-quarter of the average level of the rest of the world, as strong economic growth is matched by strong population growth.

Figure 14.1 ▷ **Growth in GDP and GDP per capita by region in the New Policies Scenario** (year-2013 dollars, PPP terms)

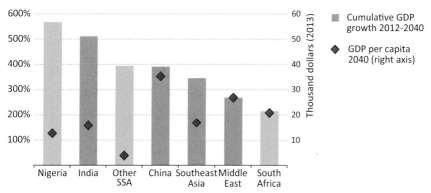

Notes: Other SSA = other sub-Saharan Africa.

West Africa experiences the most rapid economic growth of the sub-Saharan regions, at more than 6% per year on average (Table 14.1).[2] Nigeria grows faster than the region as a whole, based on its expanding services and industrial sectors, and accounts for 42% of the entire sub-Saharan economy by 2040 (up from 30% today). Nigeria's economy is more than three-times the size of the South African economy by 2040 and yet it is still only around 60% of the South African level in per-capita terms. East and Central Africa are smaller economies and grow at slightly slower rates (5.4% and 4.5% respectively), while Southern Africa's average growth rate is moderated by the more mature economy of South Africa. The composition of many of the sub-Saharan economies changes, with the very high share of agriculture gradually being eroded by rapid growth in industrial and services activity. For example, in East Africa, where agriculture is currently a large component of the economy, its share of total GDP falls from around one-third in 2012 to one-quarter in 2040 (still high relative to most other world regions).

Population dynamics are an important driver of energy trends and the assumptions adopted in this study follow the "medium variant" of the latest United Nations projections (UNPD, 2013). The population of sub-Saharan Africa continues to grow very rapidly, expanding by more than 850 million, to exceed 1.75 billion people by 2040, equivalent to one-fifth of the global population (Figure 14.2). The growth rate slows over time, from 2.6%

2. A study by the World Bank finds that beyond the human cost the Ebola epidemic currently afflicting parts of West Africa it is having a measurable economic impact. These impacts include the costs of health care and forgone productivity of those directly affected but, more importantly, from the aversion behaviour of others in response to the disease. The report estimates the short-term (2014) impact on GDP to be around 2.1 percentage points in Guinea; 3.4 percentage points in Liberia and 3.3 percentage points in Sierra Leone. However, the analysis finds that economic costs can be limited if swift national and international responses succeed in containing the epidemic and mitigating aversion behaviour (World Bank, 2014).

Table 14.1 ▷ **GDP growth rates in Africa by sub-region in the New Policies Scenario** (year-2013 dollars, PPP terms)

	GDP ($ billion)	Compound average annual growth rates			
	2012	2012-2020	2020-2030	2030-2040	2012-2040
Africa	3 751	5.1%	4.8%	4.4%	4.7%
North Africa	**1 175**	**4.2%**	**3.8%**	**3.1%**	**3.7%**
Sub-Saharan Africa	**2 577**	**5.5%**	**5.2%**	**4.9%**	**5.1%**
West Africa	1 052	6.6%	6.1%	5.8%	6.1%
Nigeria	785	6.7%	6.4%	6.2%	6.4%
Central Africa	194	5.0%	4.3%	4.4%	4.5%
East Africa	366	6.4%	5.4%	4.6%	5.4%
Southern Africa	965	3.9%	3.8%	3.3%	3.7%
Mozambique and Tanzania	101	7.2%	5.8%	4.1%	5.6%
South Africa	585	2.8%	2.9%	2.6%	2.8%
World	84 938	3.7%	3.6%	3.0%	3.4%

per year on average before 2020 to 2.2% per year after 2030, but it is consistently more than twice the average global rate of population growth. The urban population increases from 340 million in 2012, to 645 million in 2030 and 900 million by 2040 (exceeding the rural population in the late-2030s). The rural population (decreasing in most other parts of the world) also increases, albeit more slowly, from 575 million in 2012 to 780 million in 2030 and 875 million in 2040 – then making up more than one-quarter of the world total. All regions grow significantly, with the highest growth in West Africa (2.6% per year). Nigeria doubles in size, making it the world's fourth most populous country in 2040 (after India, China and the United States).

Figure 14.2 ▷ **Population growth in sub-Saharan Africa by sub-region**

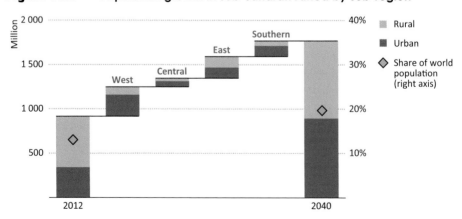

Policy environment

While it is not practical here to present all energy policies for each country in sub-Saharan Africa, an extensive review of national and regional energy policies and plans has been undertaken for this study. As is to be expected, a patchwork of policies exists that are at varying levels of development, revision and implementation (Table 14.2). Many countries, such as Angola, Cameroon, Ethiopia, Ghana, Kenya, Rwanda and South Africa, have national energy strategies, but the time horizon often varies (typically from five to twenty years), as does the extent to which they are regularly updated or systematically implemented. Ethiopia, Ghana and South Africa have a relatively integrated set of energy policy documents. In some cases, energy or sectoral strategies are part of broader strategies designed to boost economic development or reduce poverty, such as in Rwanda. Some other countries are characterised more by strategies or plans for particular sectors, such as Mozambique (natural gas master plan), Nigeria (gas and renewables master plans) and Tanzania (power system master plan). Most countries have electricity access targets and policies in place, but fewer have objectives and approaches related to clean cooking.

Policy development and co-ordination at continental and regional level is undertaken by the African Union (AU) and the New Partnership for Africa's Development (NEPAD), which have formulated the AU/NEPAD African Action Plan, and, with the African Development Bank, the Programme for Infrastructure Development in Africa (PIDA) Priority Action Plan. Relevant efforts are also undertaken by the regional economic communities and the regional power pools and their associated master plans (discussed in Chapter 13). Much of the policy focus at this level is on trans-national infrastructure development. A number of multilateral and bilateral initiatives interplay with national plans, such as: the US Power Africa initiative; Sustainable Energy for All Initiative; Energising Development initiative (European Union); Energy+ (Norway, United Kingdom and others); EnDev programme (Germany, Norway and others). An example of policy co-operation is the Africa-EU Energy Partnership 2020 targets and its related programme to develop renewable energy markets (the Africa-EU Renewable Energy Co-operation Programme). In addition, there is a broad range of civil society-led initiatives that are often in line with national energy objectives while not necessarily linked to them explicitly.

In the New Policies Scenario, the existence of a policy or target is not assumed to be sufficient to achieve complete success. While implementation can be improved, the track record of past policy implementation is an important criterion against which the likelihood of achieving a given policy goal is judged. The level of active commitment by government and other stakeholders is considered, as is the extent to which regulatory and financing issues have been resolved, whether plans have been developed in lock-step with related policy areas and whether the necessary implementation capacity is in place. For this study, the IEA's World Energy Model has undergone several important developments in order to better reflect the situation in sub-Saharan Africa (Box 14.1).

14

Table 14.2 ▷ **Selected energy policies and targets in sub-Saharan Africa**

Country	Sector	Policies and targets
Angola	Power	Implement new power market model with a single power purchaser and equal rights for public and private power producers.
	Access	Increase electrification rate from 30% to 60% by 2025.
	Integration	Establish transmission lines with Namibia and Congo.
DR Congo	Access	Increase electrification rate from 9% to 14% by 2015 and 26% by 2020.
	Power	Announcement of stricter standards for electric motors.
Ethiopia	Renewables	Targets in place for new renewables capacity (geothermal, hydro, wind).
	Access	Disseminate 9 million improved cookstoves by 2015.
Ghana	Oil and gas	Strategy to intensify exploration, utilise revenues to reduce poverty, maximise local participation and develop a petrochemical industry.
	Efficiency	Reduce transmission losses to 18% by 2018. Standards and labels in place for lighting and air conditioners.
	Renewables	Feed-in tariff established by the Renewable Energy Act in 2011.
Kenya	Efficiency	Standards for electrical appliances; energy efficiency obligations for utilities. Energy Bill 2014 provides for the creation of an Energy Efficiency and Conservation Agency to enforce energy efficiency standards.
	Buildings	Eliminate kerosene as a household fuel by 2022. Requirement to install solar water heaters in buildings served by the grid.
Mozambique	Gas	Master plan to maximise the value of gas resources approved in 2014.
	Access	Increase electrification rate from 39% to 85% by 2035.
	Renewables	Install 100 000 solar water heaters, 50 000 lighting systems, 5 000 refrigeration systems and 2 000 televisions powered by solar PV or wind turbine systems in off-grid areas by 2025.
Nigeria	Oil and gas	Draft Petroleum Industry Bill intended to revise several areas of the existing framework.
	Power	As laid out in the Roadmap for Power Sector Reform, continue sector-wide reforms to enable private sector investment, establish a competitive electricity market and achieve stable power supply.
	Access	Make reliable electricity available to 75% of the population by 2020 and 100% by 2030 (45% today). Connect an average of 1.5 million households per year.
	Buildings	Announced the design and implementation of minimum energy performance standards for appliances and industrial equipment.
Rwanda	General	Reduce share of bioenergy in primary energy demand to 50% by 2020. Expand the transmission network by 2 100 km by 2017.
	Access	Increase electrification rate from 17% to at least 60% by 2020 and give access to all schools and hospitals by 2017.
Senegal	Renewables	Target 20% of total energy supply from renewable sources by 2017.
South Africa	Renewables	The 2013 update of the Integrated Resource Plan sets out a strategy to diversify the power mix, moving strongly towards low-carbon sources of electricity supply.
	Energy prices	Electricity prices to be adjusted gradually to better reflect costs. CO_2 tax under consideration.

Energy prices in the New Policies Scenario are determined in the World Energy Model, and vary by region, sector and fuel. These prices are linked to variations in international price movements, but also include assumptions regarding price subsidies and the extent to which these are phased out over time. It is assumed that oil product subsidies are removed in all net oil-importing countries and in those oil exporting countries that have policies in place or have a stated intention to do so. After accounting for subsidy regime changes, average oil product prices increase over the projection period, but by less than international prices (between 15% and 18% depending on the region). Fuelwood and charcoal prices adjust to reflect relative scarcity in each sub-region, but also the different "market" dynamics in rural and urban areas. For example, regions with extensive forestry, like Central Africa, see smaller price increases than Nigeria, while urban areas generally see more pronounced price increases than rural areas (where fuelwood remains untraded and has a zero price in many cases). Average end-user electricity prices also vary by region, but are generally assumed to adjust gradually over time to reflect the average cost of electricity supply, including domestic generation and the cost of electricity imports, network, retail and other costs (see Chapter 1 for more on energy prices).

Box 14.1 ▷ **Modelling energy demand and supply in sub-Saharan Africa**

For this African energy outlook, the IEA's World Energy Model (WEM) has undergone several important developments to represent more closely the specificities of the region.[3] New country and regional level energy models have been developed, providing a much greater level of detail. Consistent with the regional definitions set out in Chapter 13, the following countries and sub-regions are modelled separately for energy demand and the power sector: Nigeria, Other West Africa (West Africa other than Nigeria), Central Africa, East Africa, Mozambique and Tanzania collectively (to examine the impact of new gas resources), South Africa and Other Southern Africa (Southern Africa other than South Africa, Mozambique and Tanzania). Modelling of access to modern energy has undergone significant development to better reflect access to electricity (grid, mini-grid and off-grid) and access to clean cooking facilities (different solutions and fuels). Power generation modelling has been modified to incorporate back-up generation explicitly. For oil and gas supply, the number of sub-Saharan countries modelled separately has increased to 35. Investment cost assumptions have been updated based upon those in the IEA's *World Energy Investment Outlook* (IEA, 2014b), published in June 2014. The economic outlook is derived from an interaction between the WEM and a GDP model developed specifically for this study, which takes account of developments in the labour force, accumulation of capital stock (investment) and total factor productivity. In some cases, data limitations have resulted in the scope being narrowed, such as energy demand in some sub-sectors in some regions.

14

3. Details of the World Energy Model are available at www.worldenergyoutlook.org/weomodel.

Overview of energy demand trends

Energy demand in sub-Saharan Africa is very low – at 570 million tonnes of oil equivalent (Mtoe) – but there are several factors pointing towards potentially rapid and prolonged growth: strong economic expansion, increasing urbanisation, industrialisation and modernisation, a burgeoning middle class in many countries and a legacy of unmet energy demand. In the New Policies Scenario, the sub-Saharan economy quadruples in size, the population almost doubles and primary energy demand increases by around 80% to exceed 1 000 Mtoe in 2040 (Figure 14.3). Average energy demand growth moderates from more than 3% per year since 2000 to around 2% per year over the outlook period, reflecting changes to the mix of fuels demanded and the increased efficiency with which they are consumed. Total energy demand grows in absolute terms by less than half the growth in India and less than 40% that of China, even though the region overtakes them both in terms of population. Relative to other regions, sub-Saharan Africa remains energy poor in 2040, with one-fifth of the global population accounting for only around one-twentieth of world energy demand.

Figure 14.3 ▷ **Total primary energy demand and demand per capita in sub-Saharan Africa in the New Policies Scenario**

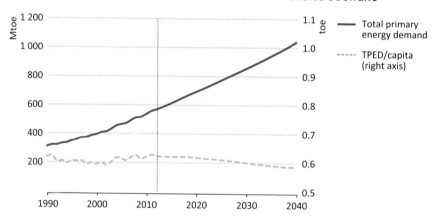

Energy use per capita in sub-Saharan Africa declines slightly over the projection period, dropping just below 0.6 tonnes of oil equivalent (toe) per capita and remaining far below the average of the rest of the world (which increases from 2.1 toe per capita in 2012 to 2.4 toe per capita in 2040). While such a trend may appear surprising for a region that grows so strongly, it masks a number of important interrelated developments. These include: rapid population growth alongside energy demand growth, the move towards much more efficient forms of cooking (a major factor in dampening energy demand growth), gradual efficiency improvements in the power, transport and other sectors, and constraints in supply that translate to a significant level of unmet energy demand in the New Policies Scenario. Considerable disparities remain within sub-Saharan Africa in 2040, with Nigerian energy demand per capita (0.7 toe per capita) being around double that of Central Africa and many other parts of West Africa in 2040, but still only a fraction of that in South Africa (3 toe per capita).

The energy intensity of the sub-Saharan economy falls by 3% per year on average and by 2040 is 55% lower than in 2012. While this drop in energy intensity is encouraging, it is also a signal of how inefficiently energy is used at present: energy intensity levels today in sub-Saharan Africa are double the world average and triple the OECD average. By 2040, sub-Saharan Africa still uses 50% more energy than the world average for each unit of economic output and 40% more than China, though less than India and the Middle East. Across sub-Saharan Africa, the largest reductions occur in Nigeria, where energy intensity falls by 4.1% per year, other West Africa (2.9%) and East Africa (2.6%).

Despite increasing incomes and a move towards other fuels, the primary energy mix of sub-Saharan Africa continues to be dominated by bioenergy, with demand growing by 40%, to reach 490 Mtoe in 2040 (Figure 14.4). However, the share of bioenergy in the primary energy mix declines over time, from 61% in 2012 to 47% in 2040, and the mix between different types of bioenergy shifts, reflecting more modern use (improved cookstoves) and a shift to more modern forms (such as biogas and pellets). Sub-Saharan Africa accounts for around one-quarter of world bioenergy demand today (in primary energy demand terms) and this share declines only a little by 2040. Oil demand experiences strong growth, more than doubling to reach 4 million barrels per day (mb/d) in 2040, with 60% of this growth coming from the transport sector. Oil overtakes coal to become the second-largest fuel in the sub-Saharan Africa energy mix by the mid-2020s and accounts for 17% of total energy demand in 2040. Nigeria alone sees a larger increase in oil use than any other sub-Saharan country or sub-region, followed by East Africa and Southern Africa.

Figure 14.4 ▷ Primary energy demand in sub-Saharan Africa by fuel in the New Policies Scenario

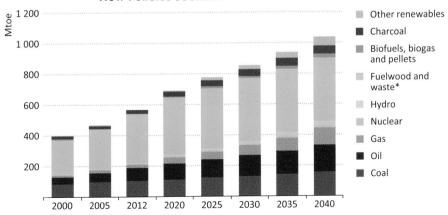

* Waste includes agricultural, animal, municipal and industrial waste.

Coal demand in sub-Saharan Africa increases by around 50% to reach 220 million tonnes of coal equivalent (Mtce) in 2040 (Table 14.3), but the share of coal in the demand mix declines from 18% to 15% (much below the world average). Demand remains concentrated in South Africa though also expands in some other countries, mostly in other parts of Southern Africa, but also in Nigeria and parts of East Africa. Collectively, Southern Africa accounts for more than half of coal demand growth predominantly for use in power generation but also for coal-to-liquids production (in South Africa). Among fossil fuels, demand for natural gas grows the most with an annual average of nearly 6%, to reach 135 billion cubic metres (bcm) by 2040. Half of this growth occurs in resource-rich Nigeria, where gas use reaches 72 bcm, predominantly for use in power generation and industry; but Mozambique and Tanzania also see significant growth, following increased domestic production. Overall, Southern Africa accounts for 30% of gas demand growth, while natural gas use remains relatively small in Central and East Africa.

Table 14.3 ▷ **Primary energy demand in Africa in the New Policies Scenario** (Mtoe)

2012	Oil	Gas	Coal	Nuclear	Bioenergy	Hydro	Other*	Total
Africa	168	100	105	3	352	10	2	739
North Africa	82	78	4	-	4	1	0.2	170
Sub-Saharan Africa	85	22	101	3	348	8	1	570
West Africa	33	14	0.4	-	147	1	<0.1	197
Nigeria	20	13	<0.1	-	108	0.5	-	141
Central Africa	5	2	-	-	29	1	-	37
East Africa	13	<0.1	0.4	-	95	2	1	112
Southern Africa	34	6	101	3	76	4	<0.1	223
Mozambique and Tanzania	3	1	<0.1	-	27	1	<0.1	33
South Africa	21	4	97	3	15	0.2	<0.1	141

2040	Oil	Gas	Coal	Nuclear	Bioenergy	Hydro	Other*	Total
Africa	278	243	164	12	496	38	91	1 322
North Africa	98	133	10	-	8	3	31	284
Sub-Saharan Africa	180	110	154	12	488	35	60	1 039
West Africa	76	69	15	-	180	9	6	355
Nigeria	46	58	12	-	124	5	5	251
Central Africa	10	7	-	-	55	8	1	81
East Africa	37	3	11	-	131	8	42	232
Southern Africa	56	31	127	12	121	11	11	371
Mozambique and Tanzania	8	16	4	-	57	5	1	91
South Africa	27	9	101	12	26	0.4	10	186

* Other includes geothermal, wind, solar PV, concentrating solar power and marine.

Renewables other than bioenergy experience strong growth across sub-Saharan Africa, growing from 2% of energy demand today to 9% in 2040 (95 Mtoe). Hydropower is already part of the mix in many countries, and its role in power supply increases in nearly all regions by 2040. Other renewables, including solar, wind and geothermal grow more rapidly, but from a lower base. South Africa and Nigeria see particularly strong growth in solar, while East Africa sees strong growth in geothermal, and South Africa and East Africa see some (albeit more modest) increase in wind. Despite some stated aspirations to build capacity, nuclear energy remains confined to South Africa in the New Policies Scenario, continuing to account for around 1% of primary energy demand in 2040.

Future energy demand prospects are very diverse across the continent. Nigeria becomes the unrivalled centre of energy demand, almost doubling to more than 250 Mtoe in 2040. Over the projection period, Nigeria continues to account for one-quarter of total sub-Saharan demand, while South Africa sees its share decline from one-quarter to below one-fifth. Other countries in West Africa see their collective demand double by 2040 but, this collective demand is still lower than that of Nigeria today. Central Africa, which is home to 12% of the sub-Saharan population, accounts for only 7% of energy demand today and this share increases only marginally (to 8%), despite annual demand growth of 2.8%. Energy demand in East Africa grows by 2.6% per year, to reach around 230 Mtoe in 2040. Half of this increase is the result of an expansion of electricity supply to meet increasing demand. Southern Africa, led by South Africa, Mozambique and Tanzania, experiences the second-largest energy demand growth of any sub-region (behind West Africa). Across Mozambique and Tanzania, demand growth is particularly strong, increasing by an annual average of 3.7%, driven by strong economic growth that is in part due to new gas and coal production.

Outlook for the power sector

Electricity demand

Despite all sub-Saharan sub-regions seeing a significant increase in the number of people with access to electricity, 530 million people remain without it in 2040 – far short of the progress desired (see Chapter 15 for detailed analysis of the outlook for electricity access). Sub-Saharan electricity demand more than triples by 2040 in the New Policies Scenario, to reach 1 300 terawatt-hours (TWh). Of this expansion, only 20% is attributable to those that gain electricity access over the period (Figure 14.5). Industry is currently the largest end-user of electricity in sub-Saharan Africa and its demand more than doubles by 2040: national economies grow (boosting demand) while, at the same time, industries use energy more efficiently over time (restraining demand growth). Residential demand rises to more than five-times current levels to reach 520 TWh in 2040. At more than 6% per year, this rapid growth rate exceeds that of GDP growth over the period, and yet even this leaves unsatisfied the very large latent electricity demand that could emerge as access to electricity increases and the quality of supply improves.

14

Figure 14.5 ▷ Electricity demand in sub-Saharan Africa and the share from those that gain access in the New Policies Scenario

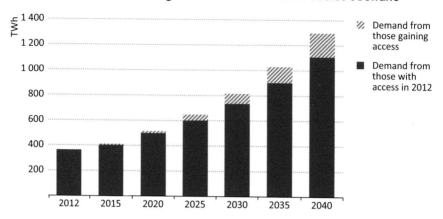

Electricity demand increases fastest in Nigeria and East Africa, each averaging more than 7% per year (Table 14.4); but the rest of West Africa and Central Africa also grow by 6% per year or close to it. South Africa's current high levels of access and of electricity consumption mean that its demand growth rate is slower (2%) but, by 2040, South Africa is still the largest electricity consumer in sub-Saharan Africa by some way (both in aggregate and per-capita terms). At the other end of the spectrum, electricity demand in Central Africa is, and remains, lower than in all other regions.

Table 14.4 ▷ Electricity demand* in Africa in the New Policies Scenario (TWh)

	2000	2012	2020	2030	2040	2012-2040	
						Delta	CAAGR**
Africa	385	621	852	1 258	1 869	1 248	4.0%
North Africa	**116**	**253**	**338**	**447**	**572**	**319**	**3.0%**
Sub-Saharan Africa	**269**	**368**	**514**	**812**	**1 297**	**929**	**4.6%**
West Africa	29	61	107	216	417	356	7.1%
Nigeria	14	37	68	146	291	254	7.7%
Central Africa	9	16	26	45	74	58	5.7%
East Africa	9	23	44	95	177	154	7.6%
Southern Africa	222	268	337	456	630	361	3.1%
Mozambique and Tanzania	4	16	30	60	99	83	6.6%
South Africa	190	212	248	298	364	152	2.0%

* Electricity demand is calculated as the total gross electricity generated, less own-use in the production of electricity, less transmission and distribution losses. ** Compound average annual growth rate.

Electricity supply

In sub-Saharan Africa, total power generation capacity (which includes on-grid, mini- and off-grid and back-up generation capacity) quadruples to reach 385 gigawatts (GW) in 2040. This reflects efforts to improve the quality of electricity supply and to expand supply to meet rapidly growing demand. Capacity additions increase over time, averaging around 7 GW per year this decade, to around 10 GW in the 2020s and over 13 GW per year in the 2030s. This reflects a power sector that is gradually expanding and maturing, but is still far behind some other developing countries (India expands three-times as much, for example). The expansion of the power sector projected in the New Policies Scenario requires a significant increase in investment, relative to historical levels: a cumulative total of $1.25 trillion (2014-2040) is invested – around $46 billion per year – with generating capacity accounting for nearly half of the total and transmission and distribution (T&D) the remainder (see Chapter 16 for more on investment). The relatively high share of investment in T&D is not unusual for emerging economies that are building their grid networks.

The sub-Saharan power generation capacity mix becomes increasingly diverse, with the large shares of coal (South Africa) and hydropower (all regions) supplemented by natural gas and an increasing share of other renewables (including solar, wind, geothermal and biomass). The share of installed capacity that is fossil-fuelled declines from 77% in 2012 to 54% in 2040, and also sees the relative share of gas grow strongly. Installed natural gas capacity increases by around 7.5% per year, on average, its share of installed capacity going from less than 60% of the level of oil in 2012 to overtake it by 2020 and then overtake coal and hydropower (just) before 2040. While coal is overtaken by gas and hydropower in terms of capacity, its role as a source of reliable, baseload electricity means that coal continues (narrowly) to be the largest source of electricity supply. Oil capacity remains stable, with back-up generation capacity declining in grid-connected areas as grid supply becomes more reliable. In contrast, oil-fuelled capacity grows in peri-urban and rural areas as an off-grid electricity access solution or as part of a hybrid solution.

Renewables increase to make up 44% of sub-Saharan Africa's power generation capacity in 2040, more than double the share of today. The expansion of hydropower capacity (reaching 93 GW in 2040) closely matches that of gas, with several major projects (such as Inga III and the Grand Renaissance dam) coming online incrementally over the projection period. Hydropower as a share of electricity supply increases from 22% of the total today to 26% in 2040. From their low base, solar photovoltaics (PV) and concentrating solar power (CSP) both see double-digit growth, collectively growing to account for 12% of total generation capacity and 6% of electricity supply in 2040. While solar PV capacity increases throughout the projection period, deployment of CSP starts around the mid-2020s (following cost reductions) and, by 2040, CSP provides around the same level of capacity as wind (both around 12 GW). Unlike in some other world regions, wind capacity expands relatively modestly, although there is no shortage of potential, as alternatives prove to be more competitive in many cases. Geothermal energy makes an increasing impact, reaching 3% of total electricity generation in 2040, mainly concentrated in East Africa.

14

In the New Policies Scenario, the greater part of electricity supplied to businesses and households in sub-Saharan Africa continues to come from centralised power plants, and is delivered through national and regional power grids (Figure 14.6). This is largely because these grids dominate supply in urban areas, which account for the lion's share of electricity consumption. Electricity access improves in both urban and rural areas in the New Policies Scenario, but urban electrification rates continue to be higher and, on average, business and households in urban areas consume more electricity. Grid-based systems do provide electricity to rural populations when those communities are in close proximity to transmission lines and extending the grid to them is a viable option.

Figure 14.6 ▷ **Electricity generation by fuel in sub-Saharan Africa in the New Policies Scenario, 2012 and 2040**

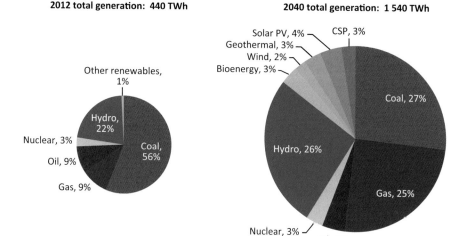

For the large rural population that is distant from power grids, mini-grid or off-grid systems provide the most viable means of access to electricity (see Chapter 15 for a focus on different routes to electricity access). In the New Policies Scenario, 315 million people in rural areas gain access to electricity, with around 80 million of these being through off-grid systems, and around 140 million people through mini-grids requiring the development of between 100 000 and 200 000 mini-grids, depending on the number of households connected to each system. The mix of technologies is quite distinct from the centralised power mix, with solar PV and oil being the dominant sources of supply. Small-scale hydropower, wind and bioenergy also play a more significant role in these small systems, when the resources are available. The systems installed in the New Policies Scenario do not come close to satisfying the full potential demand of a huge and growing rural population. The shortfall reflects the existing impediments to higher levels of adoption – such as the lack of proven business models, of adequate and appropriate forms of financing, of established supply chains and of implementation capacity – all of which deficiencies must be overcome in order to replicate the positive examples at the scale that is required.

West Africa sees its grid-based power generation capacity grow to more than four-times its current size, to around 110 GW in 2040, and generating nearly 475 TWh of electricity (Figure 14.7). Nigeria sees a large increase in installed capacity, reaching 77 GW. The power mix expands, mainly based on domestic resources. Associated gas from domestic oil production fuels strong growth in gas-fired generation, and forms the core of the Nigerian power sector for the foreseeable future. Also drawing on domestic resources, coal-fired generation increases substantially. Large hydropower expands to fully utilise Nigeria's available potential (over 11 GW), starting with the Mambilla dam, as well as significant growth in smaller-scale projects. Taking advantage of impressive resources, solar PV and CSP together reach 12 GW by 2040 – 15% of the total installed capacity. Back-up generation reduces significantly as the reliability and quality of grid-based power improves. As the West African Power Pool develops, Nigeria imports more electricity via the improved interconnections and, in addition, imports electricity from Cameroon. Power sector expansion in Nigeria requires investment in new power plants of $4 billion per year, on average, and $6 billion per year in T&D. The recent move towards power sector privatisation in Nigeria is assumed to help to mobilise investment. More than two-thirds of the investment in generation capacity is for renewables.

Elsewhere in West Africa, installed capacity expands by 5.8% per year, on average, to reach 36 GW in 2040. The generation mix is led by gas (46% in 2040), hydropower (28%) and oil (9%). The completion of the West African Power Transmission Corridor (currently under construction) improves interconnectivity and enables priority hydropower projects in Guinea, Liberia and Côte d'Ivoire to be developed. Gas-fired generation expands, largely in Ghana, where domestic supply grows and liquefied natural gas (LNG) regasification terminals come online to supply power plants. Oil continues to be a significant part of the power mix, though it expands little, with many relatively small power plants spread across the region. Non-hydro renewables account for a growing share of generation, driven by the Economic Community of West African States (ECOWAS) long-term target of 12% of electricity demand by 2030, with deployment of bioenergy, solar PV, CSP and wind.

Installed capacity in Central Africa increases from very low levels to reach 36 GW in 2040. Hydropower remains dominant in terms of capacity and generation, with the development of Inga III (4.8 GW) in Democratic Republic of Congo (DR Congo), early stages of the Grand Inga project and additional projects in Cameroon all reflected in the New Policies Scenario. Much of this capacity is developed to export electricity to other countries, including South Africa and Nigeria. Scale can often reduce the levelised cost of electricity per unit of capacity, provided the market is large enough to absorb the output. The scale of Central Africa's domestic demand and the relative lack of cross-border transmission capacity therefore continue to constrain the full development of the Grand Inga project. Gas-fired capacity accounts for one-third of installed capacity in 2040, serving to back-up and supplement hydropower during dry periods so as to ensure reliable power. During average years, in terms of rainfall and river flows, this capacity would operate at relatively low capacity factors, limiting fuel costs.

14

Figure 14.7 ▷ **Electricity generation by fuel in the New Policies Scenario** (TWh)

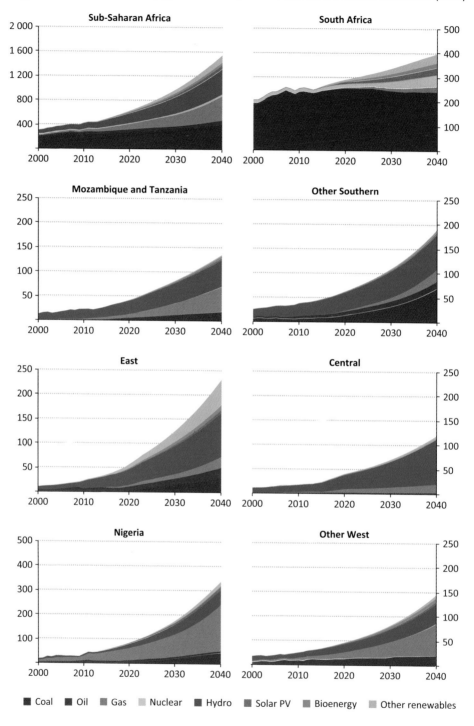

World Energy Outlook 2014 | Africa Energy Outlook

In East Africa, installed capacity grows from over 8 GW to 55 GW in 2040, with hydropower and oil joined increasingly by a range of other fuels resulting in a more diversified power mix. Hydropower remains the largest source of electricity, as Ethiopia develops several large projects, including the Grand Renaissance dam, Gilgel Gibe III and Gilgel Gibe IV, which collectively have a capacity of 9.4 GW. Much of the capacity developed in Ethiopia provides electricity for export to neighbouring countries and regions. Geothermal energy becomes the second-largest source of electricity in East Africa by the mid-2020s, with notable development in Kenya and Ethiopia. Other non-hydro renewables contribute 9% of the total generation in 2040. Coal-fired generation becomes the largest fossil fuel source of power in the second-half of the projection period, overtaking oil.

In Southern Africa, power generation capacity expands to 180 GW, with South Africa seeing its share of the regional total decrease from 78% to around 60% in 2040. Even though the power sector in South Africa is already relatively well-developed, installed capacity more than doubles to nearly 110 GW. Capacity expansion in South Africa requires investment of $7.1 billion per year, with an additional $3.4 billion for T&D infrastructure. Cumulative power sector investment in South Africa over the period tops $285 billion. The power mix becomes very diverse, tapping nearly every available technology. Coal, which accounted for 94% of total generation in 2012, remains the dominant fuel for power generation, but falls to 61% by 2040, despite an increase in coal-fired capacity of 14 GW. Gas-fired capacity increases by 9 GW, though gas continues to play a supporting role in the power mix. With strong emphasis being placed on their deployment, non-hydro renewables emerge as the favoured option to meet rising electricity demand. Installed capacity of non-hydro renewables increases from below 1 GW to over 30 GW, making up 21% of the power mix in 2040. Solar PV capacity increases the most of any technology over the projection period (increasing by 15 GW). CSP, wind and bioenergy all expand substantially, representing close to 5% of the power mix each. South Africa is the only country in sub-Saharan Africa with a nuclear power plant today, and its nuclear capacity expands after 2025, reaching 6.6 GW in 2040, and generating 12% of total electricity (See Chapter 15 for more detailed analysis on the development of South Africa's power generation mix).

In Mozambique and Tanzania collectively, installed capacity increases to 28 GW in 2040, more than six-times the current level. Expansion is focused on hydropower projects and gas-fired capacity, with more than 8 GW of each added over the projection period. Hydropower projects, including Mphanda Nkuwa in Mozambique and Stiegler Gorge in Tanzania, are developed as a source of electricity exports to other countries, mainly South Africa. Gas-fired capacity increases to capitalise on some of the additional domestic supply (see Chapter 15). Coal-fired capacity and generation grows, using domestically produced coal, to reach 12% of total generation in 2040. Non-hydro renewables also increase, though they make up less than 10% of the power mix.

In the remaining parts of Southern Africa, total installed capacity increases five-fold as a result of average annual capacity additions of 1.5 GW, and total installed capacity reaches 44 GW in 2040. Hydropower remains the largest source of electricity over the projection period, with additional capacity of 11 GW, led by the Laúca dam now under construction in

Angola. With domestic coal resources available in several countries in the Southern Africa region, the importance of coal in the power mix increases. There are coal-fired capacity additions in Botswana, Madagascar, Zambia and Zimbabwe. Angola sees new oil-fired and gas-fired capacity come online to serve domestic consumers with indigenous resources. Non-hydro renewables remain very limited in this region.

Electricity transmission and trade

The expansion of generation capacity needs to be matched by a similar step-change in transmission and distribution (T&D) infrastructure. In the New Policies Scenario, annual investments in T&D increase to about nine-times today's level by 2040 and, in total, outpace those for new power generation capacity over the period. Investment is unsurprisingly concentrated in expansion rather than replacement, and distribution networks account for two-thirds of the total T&D investment. The length of sub-Saharan transmission lines increases more than five-fold to reach 0.8 million kilometres (km), while distribution lines increase more than three-fold to reach nearly 5 million km in 2040 – a large expansion, but still short of the ultimate requirements. Grid expansions are supplemented by mini- and off-grid systems in more remote areas.

National grids expand gradually across sub-Saharan Africa, supporting wider electricity access, improving reliability of supply and, in cases such as Mozambique, connecting elements of the sub-national infrastructure. Electricity trade within sub-regions grows (as the power pools support greater regional cooperation), as does trade across sub-regions. DR Congo, Ethiopia and Mozambique are the largest net exporters of electricity by 2040, each developing large hydropower projects for the purpose, while South Africa (net imports meet 5% of demand in 2040), Nigeria (the second-largest importer, after South Africa) and some other parts of Southern Africa are the main net importers. Expansion of cross-border transmission lines broadly follows the plans as outlined by the regional power pools and in the Programme for Infrastructure Development in Africa (PIDA), but are only partially implemented by 2040. The degree to which Central Africa is connected to other sub-regions is an important constraint in the New Policies Scenario when compared to the African Century Case (see Chapter 16). In parallel with expanding the power supply infrastructure, investment will be required to build the necessary human technical capacity.

Outlook for other energy-consuming sectors

Total final energy consumption in sub-Saharan Africa increases by 70% to reach 722 Mtoe in 2040 in the New Policies Scenario (Table 14.5), equivalent to half the level of the United States today. Bioenergy remains, by a big margin, the largest fuel in final consumption (around 380 Mtoe in 2040), but its share of the total declines from around 70% to just over half. At a growth rate of less than 1% per year, growth is slower than that of any fuel and essentially plateaus by 2040 – a major milestone in sub-Saharan energy sector development. The use of bioenergy becomes slightly less concentrated in the residential sector, though it still accounts for more than 80% of household final consumption in 2040, compared with 42% in India, 24% in China and 18% in Europe.

Table 14.5 ▷ **Total final energy consumption in Africa in the New Policies Scenario** (Mtoe)

2012	Residential	Transport	Productive uses*	Total
Africa	307	90	142	538
North Africa	**27**	**42**	**47**	**116**
Sub-Saharan Africa	**280**	**48**	**94**	**422**
West Africa	120	16	26	161
Nigeria	93	10	18	121
Central Africa	24	3	7	33
East Africa	74	6	8	88
Southern Africa	62	24	54	139
Mozambique and Tanzania	19	2	6	26
South Africa	17	17	39	72

2040	Residential	Transport	Productive uses*	Total
Africa	435	161	313	909
North Africa	**51**	**53**	**83**	**187**
Sub-Saharan Africa	**384**	**109**	**230**	**722**
West Africa	152	40	93	286
Nigeria	99	26	73	198
Central Africa	43	6	17	67
East Africa	90	19	23	132
Southern Africa	99	43	96	238
Mozambique and Tanzania	36	5	24	64
South Africa	25	28	50	102

* Productive uses includes industry, services, agriculture and non-energy use.

Oil consumption more than doubles to reach 4 mb/d in 2040. The share of oil in final consumption increases gradually to reach around one-quarter, reflecting its increased use in transport and industry, as well as in the residential sector in the form of liquefied petroleum gas (LPG). The share of electricity in final consumption increases from 7% in 2012 to 15% in 2040, with significant growth in all sub-regions across the residential, services and industrial sectors. Gas consumption overtakes coal in the late-2030s, but remains relatively low in 2040 (around 40 bcm), with little used for heating or cooking and limited distribution networks. Use of coal increases by around 13 Mtce (led by industry), but its share of total final consumption declines slightly. Of the end-use sectors, services and industry grow most quickly (both more than 3% per year), and industry increases its share of final consumption from 14% to 20% in 2040. Nigeria continues to account for nearly 30% of final consumption in sub-Saharan Africa. South Africa sees its share of total sub-Saharan final consumption decline slightly to 14%, as does East Africa to 18%. In contrast, the strong growth in consumption in Mozambique and Tanzania results in their collective share of total final consumption in sub-Saharan Africa increasing to 9% in 2040, even though they account for around 4.5% of the total economy.

14

Residential

The residential sector continues to be a very large energy consumer in sub-Saharan Africa, but demand only increases by just over 1% per year in the New Policies Scenario (despite the population growth), reaching 384 Mtoe in 2040. Energy demand per household drops by almost 40%, from 1.5 toe to 0.9 toe in 2040. This masks an even larger decrease for cooking, which is partially offset by higher consumption for lighting, appliances and cooling. The decline for cooking is driven by changes in the fuels and stoves used: traditional use of solid biomass is gradually reduced on a per household basis, with households switching to more efficient, less polluting cookstoves, such as improved biomass cookstoves, or fuels, such as LPG, biogas or solar (see Chapter 15).

By fuel type, solid biomass, electricity and oil lead the increase in total residential energy consumption (Figure 14.8). Oil use in the residential sector increases from 165 thousand barrels per day (kb/d) to around 510 kb/d in 2040 (around 65% LPG and the rest kerosene). Growth in gas use is much smaller and is focused on cooking and water heating in gas-rich countries, mainly Nigeria, Mozambique and Tanzania. Use of solid biomass declines in some regions, either due to its scarcity or successful policy action to encourage switching; but, overall it increases by 0.6% per year (while the total population grows by 2.4% and the rural population by 1.5% per year).

Figure 14.8 ▷ **Change in residential energy demand by fuel in sub-Saharan Africa in the New Policies Scenario, 2012-2040**

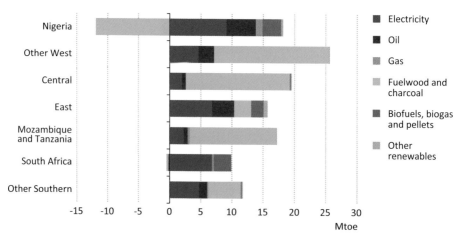

Total residential electricity demand in the sub-Saharan region grows by 6% per year to 2040, with increasing and more reliable supply, and rising incomes funding the purchase of more appliances. Electricity use per electrified household grows by 14%, to just over 1 800 kilowatt-hours (kWh) in 2040; but this relatively modest increase hides efficiency improvements that take place in parallel. Consumption per capita is still only one-third of the world average in 2040. There are disparities in consumption levels across and within sub-regions (Figure 14.9). In South Africa, high levels of electricity access and relatively low prices spur its use for various end-uses, so electricity, which accounts for 20% of residential consumption today, more than doubles its share. Household electricity consumption in Nigeria grows by around 70%, though it still lags South Africa and other Southern African countries in aggregate terms. Growth in other sub-regions is more modest and generally in the range of 1 000-1 500 kWh per electrified household by 2040 (average consumption in electrified households in India today is 1 000 kWh and in China it is 1 700 kWh).

Figure 14.9 ▷ **Electricity demand per electrified household in sub-Saharan Africa in the New Policies Scenario**

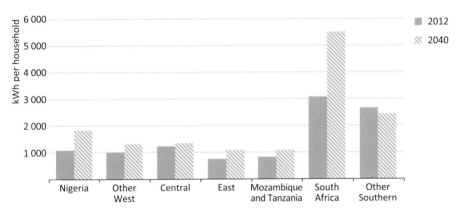

Transport

Today only 2% of the sub-Saharan population owns a passenger light-duty vehicle (PLDV), compared with 70% in the United States, 50% in Europe and 6% in China, indicating huge growth potential. The number of PLDVs in sub-Saharan Africa almost triples to 2040 (to exceed 50 million vehicles), with more than half of the growth in Nigeria and South Africa (Figure 14.10). South Africa is already a rapidly growing vehicle market, while Nigeria's GDP per capita exceeds $5 000 before 2030, a level at which PLDV ownership often accelerates rapidly (Chamon, Mauro and Okawa, 2008). Throughout much of the rest of Africa, GDP per capita remains at much lower levels, impeding vehicle demand growth. This, combined with a growing population, means that only around 3% of the sub-Saharan population owns a PLDV in 2040, with even this low level being overshadowed by the ownership concentration in South Africa (20%) and Nigeria (5%). The number of commercial vehicles and buses grows from around 8 million vehicles in 2012 to 25 million in 2040. East Africa leads the way with average growth of nearly 5% per year, driven by a rapidly growing population and demand from the services and industry sectors. Mozambique and Tanzania see average growth of more than 4% per year, but from lower levels. As urban areas grow significantly in size in sub-Saharan Africa, urban development policies can play an important role in guiding users of transport services towards private or public forms of transportation, and therefore influence future transport energy demand.

14

Figure 14.10 ▷ Vehicle stock in sub-Saharan Africa by type in the
New Policies Scenario

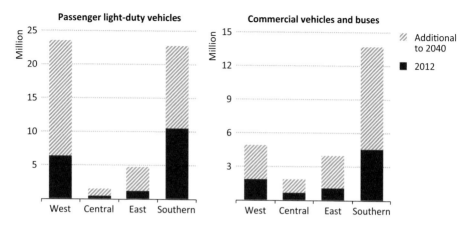

Over the projection period, types of transport other than road and aviation remain relatively under-developed, as the policies and investment of the New Policies Scenario are not sufficient to promote a widespread modal shift. However, some expansion plans do exist, for example the new line that is planned from the Kenyan port of Mombasa to the capital Nairobi and on to neighbouring states in East Africa, to be built with Chinese support. In other cases it is anticipated that an expansion of the rail network will be driven by industrial interests to transport commodities from inland to ports. The transport sector remains almost entirely reliant on oil products, with few policies in place to promote the use of alternative fuels, such as biofuels. Total transport demand for oil more than doubles to reach 2.2 mb/d – 55% of which is gasoline and 40% is diesel (Figure 14.11).

Figure 14.11 ▷ Oil demand in transport in sub-Saharan Africa in the
New Policies Scenario

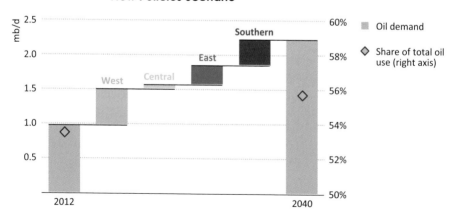

A constraint on fuel demand for road transport is the severe lack of paved roads. This improves over time, but far below the full potential. A second and more positive factor is vehicle fuel efficiency, which for new vehicles improves across sub-Saharan Africa by more than 20%, on average, to reach 7.2 litres per 100 km in 2040. However, this still means that by 2040, average vehicle efficiency in the region falls some way short of the level of the European Union today. Sub-Saharan Africa relies heavily on imports of second-hand vehicles from Japan and Europe, in particular, which both have comprehensive fuel-economy standards in place. To a degree, these standards are progressively imported helping to improve the region's average efficiency. Interest in building vehicle manufacturing or assembly plants in Africa is also expected to be a factor in pushing policy-makers to consider fuel-economy policies more seriously or, where they exist, to impose them more stringently.

Productive uses[4]

Energy consumption by productive sectors in sub-Saharan Africa grows by nearly two-and-a-half times to reach 230 Mtoe in 2040 (Figure 14.12), but this is less than one-third of the energy consumed by industry in China today. In 2012, South Africa accounted for 41% and Nigeria for 19% of total sub-Saharan energy consumption for productive uses. However, by 2040 these positions are reversed, with Nigeria's strong economic growth boosting its share to nearly one-third while South Africa grows more slowly and its share drops to around one-fifth. East and Central Africa see energy consumption in 2040 for productive uses increase to 23 Mtoe and 17 Mtoe respectively, both still very low absolute levels.

Figure 14.12 ▷ **Final energy consumption in productive uses in sub-Saharan Africa in the New Policies Scenario**

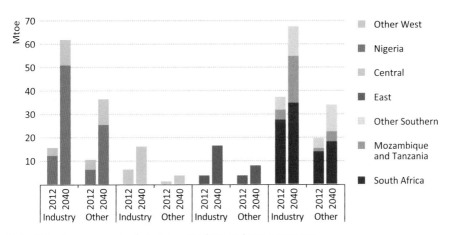

Note: Other is an aggregate of services, agriculture and non-energy use.

4. Industry, services, agriculture and non-energy use. Some energy demand from the transport sector (e.g. freight-related) could also be considered as productive, but is covered separately in this analysis.

Together with power generation, these productive sectors are key sources of economic growth. Their share of sub-Saharan final energy consumption increases from around 20% in 2012 to 30% in 2040. The trend of energy consumption is driven by the energy-intensive industries, including mining, and cement and iron and steel sub-sectors that are, in turn, stimulated by dynamic economic growth. Overall, industry represents 70% of total productive energy use and services another quarter. Agriculture, which benefits from progressive mechanisation and enhanced productivity through wider use of modern means such as fertilisers and irrigation, continues to account for around 5%. Improving agricultural productivity is a priority area in the African Union's "Agenda 2063" and the scope for doing so is far from exhausted within the New Policies Scenario. The progressive modernisation of the agricultural sector will reduce its role as the mainstay of rural employment, requiring a greater focus on policies to develop other rural industries to support local economies.

In the New Policies Scenario, patterns of economic growth and diversification differ across sub-regions, but generally result in the industrial and services sectors growing more quickly than agriculture and, as a consequence the share of agriculture in the overall economy declines by one-third in Nigeria, Mozambique and Tanzania by 2040 (Figure 14.13). In Nigeria, both industry and the services sector act as strong drivers of growth, with services raising its share of GDP to nearly 60% by 2040. In Mozambique and Tanzania, industry plays a relatively greater role in economic growth, boosted by rising energy supply, mainly gas, and related downstream chemical activities, including feedstock production.

Figure 14.13 ▷ **Change in GDP by sector and related energy use in the New Policies Scenario**

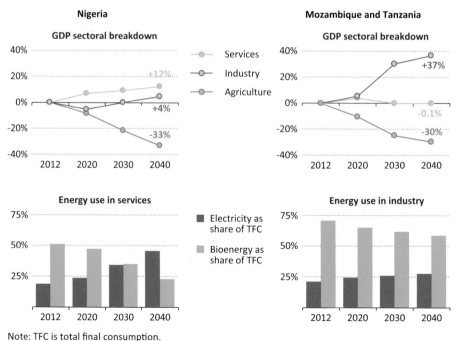

Note: TFC is total final consumption.

The fuel mix in productive energy consumption is largely sector dependant. Moreover, countries tend to specialise in certain industrial sub-sectors and make fuel choices based on their specific requirements and domestic resource availability. More than 85% of coal consumed for productive uses is consumed in South Africa, while almost half of gas consumption for this purpose is in Nigeria. While the causality between energy use and economic growth is difficult to establish, the creation of value in sub-Saharan countries is accompanied by a rise in modern and more efficient energy use. This is evident in the increased use of electricity throughout the economy, often at the expense of less efficient alternatives. One example is Nigeria's services sector, where electricity consumption grows by more than 25 percentage points to meet almost half of the sector's energy needs.

Outlook for energy supply

Oil

Sub-Saharan oil production reaches its historical peak of nearly 6.2 mb/d before 2020 and then sees a gradual decline to reach 5.3 mb/d in 2040 (Figure 14.14). Nearly 75% of the production in 2040 comes from new fields brought online to offset the production declines from existing fields, illustrating that this production profile requires significant new investment and development. Our figures necessarily incorporate judgements on several sources of uncertainty, such as the success of exploration and development in pre-salt deposits off the west coast of Africa and the evolution of the multitude of "above ground" challenges discussed throughout this study (Spotlight). The trends and the drivers vary from place to place in sub-Saharan Africa, but the cumulative effect is that, by the end of the projection period, oil production becomes more heavily concentrated in its two largest producers (Nigeria and Angola, which are Organization of the Petroleum Exporting Countries [OPEC] members) and in Nigeria in particular (increasing from around 40% in 2013 to nearly 60% in 2040). (See Chapter 15 for detailed analysis on Nigeria's oil outlook.)

Figure 14.14 ▷ **Oil production in sub-Saharan Africa in the New Policies Scenario**

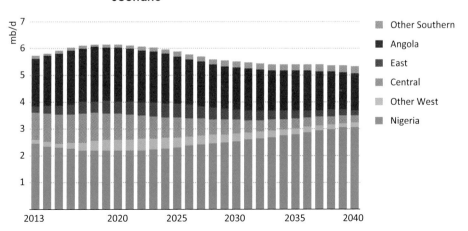

14

Why does oil production not directly reflect resource potential?

At first glance, upstream capital and operating costs in sub-Saharan Africa compare reasonably well with those in many oil and gas provinces worldwide. Over time, these costs tend to be influenced by the fundamentals of the remaining resource size and accessibility which, for sub-Saharan Africa, favour (for example) Nigeria over its West African neighbours or those of the East African Rift. The overall calculation of a project's expected profitability inevitably includes a risk factor, and beyond the medium term (where a pipeline of projects is visible) our modelling prioritises the most profitable projects for development based on their net present value (NPV) after adjusting for risk.

Based on such an analytical process, projects in Central and East Africa would look favourable in the longer term only at low rates of assumed risk in our projections, whereas those in Nigeria look profitable even at a higher residual risk level (Figure 14.15). Compared with developments in other parts of the world, sub-Saharan projects tend to look relatively less attractive. The evaluation of the appropriate risk factor takes into account political and economic risk, the risk of instability in the legal or fiscal environment, and more operational or security-related risks. There is inevitably a significant degree of subjectivity in such an assessment, with different types of companies (national oil companies versus international oil companies) or those with various existing portfolios or expertise judging the same situation very differently. Governments can influence many of the factors that play into such an assessment through actions to improve political, economic, fiscal and legal stability and the physical infrastructure (see the African Century Case in Chapter 16).

Figure 14.15 ▷ **Net present value of oil developments at different risk levels using post-2030 cost assumptions**

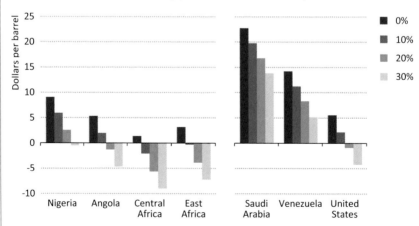

Notes: NPV calculations are made assuming $110 per barrel oil, 7% discount rate and 50% equivalent profit tax in all cases. Risk rates represent a factor multiplying the future cash flow (i.e. if the risk = 10% there is a 10% chance that future earnings do not materialise).

In the period to 2020, total sub-Saharan oil production increases by more than 400 kb/d, breaking through the 6 mb/d level around 2016 and remaining close to that level at end of the decade. Growth in this period is dominated by the region's smaller producers, which collectively increase production from under 1.5 mb/d in 2013 to nearly 2 mb/d in 2020 (Figure 14.16). Overall, increases from South Sudan (over 200 kb/d), Ghana (around 100 kb/d) and, to a lesser extent, Niger, Mauritania and Congo serve to more than offset a dip in Nigerian production (around 250 kb/d). For South Sudan, this represents a return to around the 2011 level of production, following recent disruption. Ghana's oil production is boosted by around 80 kb/d from the Tweneboa Enyenra Ntomme (TEN) fields, which come on-stream later this decade, and from the Jubilee field, which produces close to its 120 kb/d capacity once the related gas project is completed next year.

Figure 14.16 ▷ **Oil production in sub-Saharan countries other than Nigeria and Angola in the New Policies Scenario**

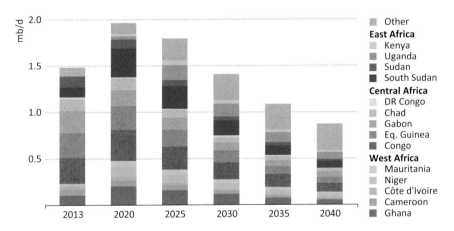

While Congo's oil production has relied heavily on mature offshore fields, there has been a revival in the last decade in new offshore projects, such as N'Kossa, N'Soko and the pre-salt M'Boundi field coming on-stream. In the New Policies Scenario, Congo produces more than 300 kb/d in 2020, with contributions from the Chevron Lianzi deepwater field and Eni's shallow water Nene Marine development. The government is currently considering revision of its fiscal terms to encourage further exploration. Exploration has recently intensified in Niger and its oil production is set to increase to five-times the current level by 2020, reaching more than 100 kb/d. While the China National Petroleum Company-funded Zinder refinery processes the 20 kb/d of crude production from the Agadem Basin, much of the remaining volumes are exported via a new 600 km pipeline linking to the Chad-Cameroon pipeline (allowing export through the port of Kribi in Cameroon).

A different production picture emerges in the 2020s, with Nigerian production starting to bounce back, and Uganda and Kenya emerging, while Angola and several smaller producers show signs of decline (Table 14.6). The size of Nigeria's resource base (nearly

14

one-third of the sub-Saharan total), and permissive investment conditions, underpin Nigeria's production increase to around 2.5 mb/d in 2030 and 3.1 mb/d in 2040. Uganda and Kenya collectively bring about 160 kb/d of new onshore production online by 2030, a significant development for their respective economies. Ugandan oil production ramps up in the early-2020s, exploiting recently discovered volumes in the Albert-Edward rift basins. Production is expected to go to the 60 kb/d refinery planned for the eastern shore of Lake Albert and also to export markets, once the 1 400 km export pipeline to Lamu at the Kenyan coast is completed. Production starting in the early-2020s from the Gregory Rift discoveries in Kenya's Lokichar basin will feed into this pipeline. South African coal is the third-largest source of hydrocarbon liquids in sub-Saharan Africa, with coal-to-liquids output increasing with the assumed construction of long-discussed additional capacity by Sasol.

Table 14.6 ▷ **Oil production in Africa in the New Policies Scenario** (mb/d)

	2013	2020	2030	2040
Africa	9.0	9.2	9.4	9.8
North Africa*	**3.3**	**3.1**	**3.9**	**4.5**
Sub-Saharan Africa	**5.7**	**6.2**	**5.5**	**5.3**
West Africa	2.6	2.6	2.8	3.2
Ghana	0.1	0.2	0.1	<0.1
Nigeria	2.5	2.2	2.5	3.1
Central Africa	1.0	1.0	0.5	0.3
Congo	0.3	0.3	0.2	0.1
Equatorial Guinea	0.3	0.3	0.1	<0.1
East Africa	0.2	0.5	0.4	0.2
South Sudan	<0.1	0.3	0.2	<0.1
Southern Africa	1.9	2.1	1.8	1.6
Angola	1.8	2.0	1.6	1.4

* Much of the growth reflects the assumed gradual return of Libyan output to pre-war levels.

Elsewhere in sub-Saharan Africa, the post-2020 picture is less rosy, with an expectation of gradual decline in production. Angola leads this decline, with production going from 2.0 mb/d in 2020 to 1.4 mb/d in 2040: in the medium term the projected path is only modestly below Angola's stated aim, but the overall outlook is prompted by the fast decline rates typically observed in deepwater fields and a cautious assessment regarding pre-salt oil. In the 2030s, the pattern of slow decline continues for several producers, including Equatorial Guinea, Congo, Côte d'Ivoire, Cameroon, South Sudan and Chad.

Refining outlook

Around half of sub-Saharan oil product demand is met by imports and, even if existing refining capacity was able to be fully utilised, the region would still be reliant on imports. In the New Policies Scenario, sub-Saharan Africa sees consumption of almost all oil products grow significantly, with gasoline and diesel increasing the most in absolute terms (Table 14.7).

LPG sees the largest relative growth over the projection period (from very low levels) and overtakes the level of kerosene by 2040, the use of which increases in both aviation and the buildings sector (residential and services). Residual fuel oil demand has the slowest growth rate, while demand for oil products used exclusively in the petrochemicals sector, such as naphtha and ethane, remains small.

Table 14.7 ▷ **Oil product demand in sub-Saharan Africa in the New Policies Scenario** (mb/d)

	2012	2020	2030	2040	CAAGR* 2012-2040
LPG	<0.1	0.1	0.2	0.4	7.3%
Gasoline	0.6	0.8	1.0	1.3	2.5%
Kerosene	0.2	0.2	0.3	0.4	2.5%
Diesel	0.6	0.7	0.9	1.3	2.7%
Other	0.4	0.4	0.5	0.6	2.1%
Total	1.8	2.3	3.0	4.0	2.8%

* CAAGR = compound average annual growth rate. Sources: CITAC; IEA analysis and projections.

The average utilisation rates of installed refining capacity, outside South Africa, are very low and major investment is required if they are to expand output and switch to higher-quality products. Refineries in Nigeria and Ghana, for example, have been running at under 30% of capacity in recent years because of inefficient management and a lack of regular maintenance. In the New Policies Scenario, we assume that 400 kb/d of current capacity is eventually shut down, sufficient investments are made to upgrade the remaining capacity for higher runs, and another 0.8 mb/d of new refinery capacity comes online between now and 2040. Before 2020, only two mini-refineries are expected to be built, in Uganda and South Sudan. More significant capacity additions start to come online in the second half of the 2020s, with new refineries in Angola, Nigeria and East Africa. Overall, capacity additions are heavily skewed towards West Africa, close to the sources of oil production. Nigeria accounts for the majority of the retired capacity as it eventually shuts down some of its oldest, most inefficient refineries, and this also contributes to an improvement in the overall refinery utilisation rate. When examined together, it is clear that the gap between operational sub-Saharan refining capacity and oil product demand grows significantly in the New Policies Scenario, resulting in an increasing need for oil product imports over the projection period.

The case for building up Africa's local refining capacity would appear to be strong, yet – as in other parts of the world – relatively few projects actually make it off the drawing board. There are a number of reasons why. To realise economies of scale, refineries are now typically built with a minimum of 200 kb/d capacity, with a view to high operating rates. At present, only Nigeria and South Africa have demand higher than this level. By the end of the projection period, some four or five other countries are expected to meet this demand threshold, but the rest will still have smaller national markets.

14

Availability of local crude oil supply is another key constraint. In the New Policies Scenario, almost all the new capacity is projected to be for countries that have local crude production (only one new refinery in East Africa is expected to rely on imported crude). The availability of local production can even justify relatively small-scale refineries in land-locked countries with a growing internal market (as the logistical costs of crude export and product imports justify otherwise uneconomic projects). This has already been the case in Chad and Niger (both with 20 kb/d refineries). Uganda and South Sudan have similar projects that are very likely to materialise. Elsewhere, though, the most efficient solution is to build refineries that are capable of meeting not just domestic product needs, but also those of neighbouring countries: as with other projects looking to realise economies of scale, this implies a strong degree of regional co-operation.

The calculation of the costs and benefits of local refining also depends on which products are being imported. Although it is sometimes assumed that refining locally is cheaper than importing products, it makes a big difference in practice if the product required is a premium product on the market (with strong interest among buyers elsewhere – and high margins for refiners) or a by-product (potentially more readily and cheaply available). Prices for naphtha and residual fuel oil, for example, tend to be lower than the crude oil price. Gasoline in the European market in winter, which is the low driving season in Europe and the United States, can also at times be worth less than crude oil. In the case of LPG, refining crude oil is not the only source of supply, as the yields of LPG are quite low in refining and it can be produced from natural gas liquids at lower cost. In short, if a country is importing mainly gasoline and LPG, then a local refinery in Africa may not be able to produce these products at lower cost.

Another important consideration is the opportunity cost of a new refinery. Refineries require significant upfront investments. In the New Policies Scenario, new refining capacity (including upgrading existing capacity) requires investment of $40 billion, while a further $15 billion is required to cover maintenance costs (assuming an adequate maintenance programme), which contributes to higher availability of refining capacity. There are many competing and deserving possibilities for infrastructure spending and investment in refinery capacity may not be high on the list of priorities. Nor is it clear, in many cases, who will do the investing, whether governments or local or international private investors, particularly in cases where local oil product prices are subsidised. On balance, the projections assume that governments and investors do see some opportunities in the expanding market to realise new refineries. But capacity additions do not keep pace with growing demand, meaning that sub-Saharan Africa remains a net importer of products.

Natural gas

Sub-Saharan Africa makes the fourth-largest contribution globally to incremental gas supply through to 2040, behind the Middle East, China and the United States but ahead of Latin America, the Caspian region, Russia and Australia. In the New Policies Scenario, production increases to four-times existing levels, from 58 bcm in 2012 to around 80 bcm in 2020, 160 bcm in 2030 and 230 bcm in 2040 – average annual growth of 5% (Table 14.8). Production growth derives from the large undeveloped resources of Nigeria, Mozambique, Angola and Tanzania, with the speed of resource development being determined by a range of factors including, but not limited to, the levels of domestic demand and gas liquefaction capacity and the volumes of LNG that can be sold on the global market. While total gas production grows in all four sub-regions, this occurs at very different speeds and reaches very different levels. The current concentration of production in West Africa (mainly Nigeria) is diminished over time, with the Southern Africa region (which includes Mozambique, Angola and Tanzania) overtaking it as the largest producing region around 2025. Overall, Nigeria produces over 40% of all sub-Saharan gas over the projection period, followed by Mozambique (20%) and Angola (13%). The remaining quarter of production is spread across more than 30 producers, led by Tanzania and South Africa, and smaller contributions from Equatorial Guinea, Côte d'Ivoire and Congo.

Table 14.8 ▷ **Natural gas production in Africa in the New Policies Scenario** (bcm)

	2012	2020	2030	2040
Africa	213	235	347	469
North Africa	**154**	**157**	**186**	**240**
Sub-Saharan Africa	**58**	**78**	**161**	**230**
West Africa	43	48	69	98
Nigeria	41	45	60	85
Central Africa	8	9	13	16
Equatorial Guinea	6	5	3	3
East Africa	<1	<1	1	1
Southern Africa	7	21	78	114
Angola	<1	16	22	21
Mozambique	4	3	36	60
Tanzania	<1	<1	10	20
South Africa	1	1	9	12

Nigeria is, and remains, the largest gas producer in sub-Saharan Africa over the period, with production of 85 bcm in 2040. Nigeria's Gas Master Plan details the aim to increase domestic supply and to bring in new pricing and policy regulations, and provides a blueprint for gas infrastructure. The strategy is to anchor gas supply around "gas to power" in the immediate term while also developing a broader agenda for gas to support industrialisation and provide gas for export. One of the clearest examples is the envisaged Ogidigben gas industrial park in Delta State, which is estimated to require $15-20 billion in investment and includes gas processing, petrochemicals, fertiliser production and a gas-fired power plant. Also, Nigeria saw first production of gas-to-liquids at its plant at Escravos this year. Not all of the elements required to underpin the objectives of the master plan are yet in place, such as the necessary gas and electricity pricing mechanisms and appropriate upstream incentives. Within the New Policies Scenario, it is assumed that these will be

14

forthcoming in time and that, in line with the Master Plan, domestic supply commands first priority. Following this approach, all incremental supply between 2020 and 2040 goes to the domestic market, of which 50% is for power generation and 30% goes to supply industry.

A critical uncertainty for Nigeria's gas supply outlook is its ability to stimulate significant production of non-associated gas. Huge resources exist, sufficient to cover both domestic demand and exports. Production of non-associated gas increases in our projection period, but it is gradual. Exploiting this resource requires a change in focus by the upstream sector and, importantly, the government to establish a framework to incentivise the necessary large-scale capital investment. This will require a stable, attractive investment environment generally and the development of a bankable commercial structure in Nigeria's gas sector which includes price reforms, improvements in regulatory arrangements, a redefinition of the role of public companies in the gas sector and an alternative to the current Nigerian National Petroleum Corporation (NNPC) joint venture financing model. Failure to achieve this would lower the supply outlook significantly.

Mozambique joins Nigeria as the other major gas producer in sub-Saharan Africa and, in 2040, these two countries collectively account for nearly two-thirds of regional production (Figure 14.17). Mozambique sees the largest growth in gas production in the sub-Saharan region, starting in the early-2020s, to reach 35 bcm in 2030 and 60 bcm in 2040, and is joined by neighbouring Tanzania (which also grows from the early-2020s to 20 bcm by 2040) to bring online a large source of supply on Africa's east coast. (See Chapter 15 for further analysis on natural gas outlook for Mozambique and Tanzania).

Figure 14.17 ▷ **Natural gas production in sub-Saharan countries in 2012 and change to 2040 in the New Policies Scenario**

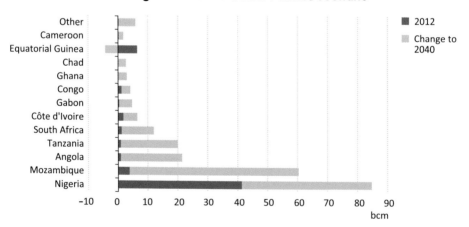

Note: Production in Equatorial Guinea is 3 bcm in 2040, declining by around 3 bcm from 2012.

Angola has the third-largest proven gas reserves in sub-Saharan Africa (behind Nigeria and Mozambique) and yet is currently only a small producer. Like Nigeria, its primary focus has tended to be on oil, gas becoming a concern only recently. In the last decade, Sonangas (a state-owned company) has been established, increased action has been taken to limit flaring and reinjection and a process begun to establish a new regulatory framework. In the New Policies Scenario, production in Angola increases early in the projection period, with the stalled Angola LNG project achieving its expected export volumes in 2016, reaching around 20 bcm in 2025 and maintaining about that level to 2040. While production remains focused on associated gas, non-associated gas production also gradually comes on-stream.

South African supply increases from its current relatively low levels to reach 12 bcm in 2040, with new supply coming in the form of unconventional gas from the Karoo basin. While environmental concerns regarding water usage and hydraulic fracturing led to a moratorium on new exploration licenses being imposed in 2011, this has since been lifted and South Africa's cabinet has proposed new technical regulations to govern petroleum exploration, particularly standards for shale gas exploration and hydraulic fracturing. Implicit in these projections are the assumptions that exploration will provide a much clearer understanding of the geology and economics of the resource base, a commercial basis for production will be put in place and that environmental concerns will be addressed (see analysis on the future of the energy mix in South Africa in Chapter 15).

Gas production in Central Africa grows modestly, staying flat overall for the first decade of the projection period before gradually increasing to reach 16 bcm by 2040. Equatorial Guinea – the second-largest producer in sub-Saharan Africa today – is the only existing producer in the region whose output is lower than today in 2040, holding at around 6 bcm in the early years of the projection period, before gradually declining. The government has stated an ambition to construct more gas-fired power generation capacity and develop a domestic petrochemicals industry, but consideration of a second LNG train is at the feasibility stage, pending greater certainty regarding gas supply. Elsewhere in Central Africa, the outlook is more positive. Cameroon, Gabon, Chad and Congo all produce more gas in 2040 than in 2012, despite a reduction in oil supply. While volumes are insufficient for LNG exports, they are very significant relative to existing levels of domestic demand, pointing strongly towards a domestic-led gas strategy.

Many gas producers have stated that priority should be given to domestic power use and then, where volumes are sufficient, to other domestic sectors, such as industry, or to exports. However, in the New Policies Scenario around 40% of the growth in gas supply goes to exports (mainly Mozambique), while more than one-third goes to power generation and 13% to industry (Figure 14.18). The trade-offs between different uses of gas vary by country. In Mozambique, expected production volumes comfortably exceed domestic needs, even before accounting for the fact that it has other competitive power generation options (hydropower and coal). Tanzania's resources are smaller, meaning that decisions regarding gas use are more of a trade-off rather than a simpler question of balancing large resources across sectors. For a number of the other small producers, the scale of production is typically well in excess of domestic demand, and using gas for power generation would, in many cases, be replacing expensive liquid fuels. This makes it an attractive economic option, although not necessarily an easy option to implement.

14

Figure 14.18 ▷ **Destination of gas production in sub-Saharan Africa in the New Policies Scenario**

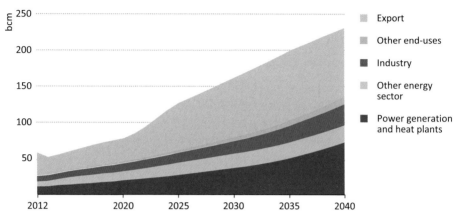

Notes: Other energy includes gas used in oil and gas extraction (largely for on-site power generation) and in refineries. Other end-uses include transport, residential, services, agriculture and other non-energy use.

Coal

Coal production in sub-Saharan Africa is projected to increase by around 50% by 2040, reaching 325 Mtce. South Africa continues to lead the way, seeing its production increase gradually over time (0.5% per year) to 240 Mtce, 75% of the regional total. But South Africa is joined increasingly by other countries in the region, at a low level initially but increasing by more than 7% per year to reach 30 Mtce in 2025 and 85 Mtce in 2040, a level similar to that of Latin American coal production today. Increased production outside of South Africa is led by Mozambique, where coking coal reaches 20 Mtce in 2040 (virtually all of which is exported) and steam coal reaches nearly 15 Mtce (around 65% is consumed domestically and the remainder is exported). Around 55% of sub-Saharan coal production in 2040 comes from greenfield projects, highlighting the importance of infrastructure development. Overall, the share of sub-Saharan coal production retained for domestic consumption remains steady at around two-thirds, albeit at an increasing level of supply.

A key factor in sub-Saharan coal resource development – particularly in Southern Africa – is the remoteness of the coal fields and the present lack of suitable railway and port infrastructure. Future production increases are driven primarily by growing domestic coal demand and (except in the case of Mozambique) to a lesser extent by export considerations. For Zimbabwean coal, transport distances to export ports are 1 400-2 200 km and for Botswana 1 300-1 500 km; but in neither case is there sufficient railway infrastructure in place. The Waterberg, a coal field in South Africa's northern Limpopo province, is considered a key growth centre for South Africa's future coal production and yet shares a similar constraint, as it is 1 300 km away from the port of Richard's Bay. Compared to major coal exporters like Colombia, Indonesia or Australia, these distances are very long, although shorter than those in the United States or Russia (where the transport infrastructure exists).

Investment in export infrastructure has been proposed, but the railway development cost is high and, since coal-rich countries like Botswana and Zimbabwe are land-locked, co-ordination and commitment will be required from both the producing countries and the terminal countries. Such large-scale cross-border infrastructure investments can be secured with long-term take-or-pay contracts but they typically require political stability over many decades as a prerequisite. Moreover, development at such a scale would require modern technology and a skilled workforce.

Low mining costs – in the range of $10-30 per tonne – are a key element in decisions to undertake production, either for domestic consumption or export markets. Much of the coal in Southern African has high ash content and would require upgrading to cut transportation costs and bring it to international quality standards. This poses two additional problems that would need to be overcome: scarcity of water may impede washing (or drive the washing costs up) and the process results in at least two distinct coal fractions of very different value (product for export and low rank coal that would need to find a domestic market or be disposed of). The free on board (FOB) cash-cost of coal from Botswana, Zimbabwe or the South African Waterberg is expected broadly to fall in a range of $60-80 per tonne, which is comparable with other long-term supply options for the international market, like the Galilee Basin in Australia. However, the Galilee Basin benefits from an established and efficient coal mining industry, economies of scale, political stability and cash-rich investors from India and China.

Yet, the outlook for coal production in the Southern Africa region is not as bleak as it may appear. Mozambique has seen rapid development of a coal export industry, driven by large private sector investors, like Vale. Mozambique has good quality coking coal reserves that command a higher price than the steam coal prevalent in neighbouring countries. Furthermore, by Southern African standards, the transport distances are relatively low (600-900 km). That being said, the existing infrastructure has reached its limits and profitability is low at today's coal prices. Sufficient economies of scale and further export growth hinges crucially on the development of a new railway line and deepwater port (e.g. the proposed corridor to Nacala in northern Mozambique). The remote South African Waterberg region, near the border with Botswana, hosts one of the largest coal mines in the world and a project to expand the railway line that links the Waterberg with the main coal fields in the Witbank region (east of Pretoria) is underway. Most of the coal that leaves the Waterberg will be consumed in domestic power plants but, depending on how fast output and shipments increase, this could in turn free-up coal in the Witbank region for export and indirectly boost coal exports. Madagascar also has production coming to fruition in the projection period, with the most promising coal fields located 150-200 km from the Western shoreline. Moreover, there are coal-fired power plant projects in the pipeline in most of Southern Africa's countries. These projects rely on domestic coal or land borne imports from neighbouring countries and support low but steady growth for the regional mining industry.

14

Renewables

Sub-Saharan Africa has untapped renewable resources which could deliver levels of supply in excess of domestic consumption to 2040 and far beyond. In the New Policies Scenario, energy supply from renewables (including bioenergy) increases by nearly 65%, to reach around 585 Mtoe in 2040, but its share of total energy supply decreases to below 60% (the share excluding bioenergy increases from 2% to 9%, reflecting a gradual reorientation of the energy mix). The supply of solid biomass for cooking continues to dominate the overall picture for renewables. However, the power sector sees rapid growth of renewables-based capacity, which grows from around 20 GW to nearly 170 GW. Renewables account for more than 50% of the increase in total capacity over the projection period. The share of renewables-based capacity in the power mix increases from 21% to 44%. This share is higher in 2040 than that of China, the United States or India. Bioenergy finds its way increasingly into industry to produce heat for industrial processes accounting for around one-third of industrial energy consumption in 2040; but, in the absence of supportive policies and supply infrastructure, biofuels play no more than a minor role in transport across the region.

Renewables supply expands across sub-Saharan Africa, with South Africa, Nigeria and East Africa leading the way (Figure 14.19). Nigeria already has plans to expand hydropower and in the New Policies Scenario, accounting for half of its total renewables expansion, and also with a significant increase in solar capacity (PV and CSP), mainly in the second half of the projection period. Elsewhere in West Africa, renewables make up over 40% of electricity generation by 2040, mainly from hydropower, but also from solar PV, wind and bioenergy.

Figure 14.19 ▷ Increase in renewables-based capacity by sub-region and type in sub-Saharan Africa in the New Policies Scenario, 2012-2040

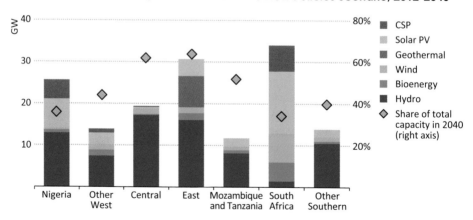

Central and East Africa see a similar increase in hydropower capacity (over 16 GW), despite Central Africa having much the greater overall potential. East Africa leads the way in geothermal capacity, with a significant increase in Kenya, followed by Ethiopia, and, to a much smaller degree, in wind; but solar plays only a small role, despite strong technical potential. South Africa – consistent with its Integrated Resource Plan to 2030 – sees a large increase in solar and wind capacity, with capacity auctions already underway. While South Africa does not significantly increase its hydropower capacity, it does import increasing volumes of hydropower from other parts of Southern Africa and Central Africa.

Bioenergy

Supply grows to meet a 40% increase in bioenergy demand in the New Policies Scenario, reaching 490 Mtoe in 2040 – one-quarter of world demand at that time. The rate of growth slows over the projection period as different factors interact. On one hand, growth is restrained by a shift towards other fuels for cooking and improved cookstoves that consume solid biomass more efficiently (see Chapter 15). On the other, a rising urban population boosts charcoal consumption relative to fuelwood (Box 14.2) and, despite greater use of semi-industrialised kilns over time (improving the conversion efficiency), this also boosts fuelwood demand. Biogas, biofuels and pellets collectively account for just 6% of total supply in 2040. Fuelwood, charcoal and waste dominate the picture, with over one billion tonnes of wood needed to meet demand (including that which is lost in the charcoal conversion process) (Table 14.9).

Table 14.9 ▷ **Forest biomass stock and fuelwood* consumption in sub-Saharan Africa in the New Policies Scenario**

	Forest area per capita (ha/cap)	CAAGR	Biomass forestry stock (Gt)	Fuelwood consumption (Mt)	
	2010	1990-2010	2010	2012	2040
Sub-Saharan Africa	0.7	-2.7%	132	694	1 071
West Africa	0.3	-2.6%	14	247	389
Nigeria	<0.1	-5.6%	2.5	147	253
Central Africa	2.4	-3.1%	75	75	142
East Africa	0.4	-3.5%	6	218	291
Southern Africa	0.9	-2.7%	37	153	250
South Africa	0.3	<0.1%	1.7	36	40

* Includes fuelwood consumed directly by households and fuelwood used to produce charcoal.

Notes: ha/cap = hectare per capita; CAAGR = compound average annual growth rate; Gt = gigatonnes; Mt = million tonnes. Sources: FAO (2010); IEA analysis.

While wood is considered as renewable, it is exhaustible unless used carefully and stocks managed sustainably. In 2010, the total forest biomass stock (including dead wood) in sub-Saharan Africa is estimated to have been around 130 billion tonnes. However, even an annual consumption rate that is equivalent to 1% or less of the existing stock should not be taken to imply that current levels of use are sustainable. Forest biomass stock is not uniformly spread across the region, and so may be relatively abundant in some areas while scarce elsewhere. Current levels of consumption are already reducing the stock of biomass in some regions of sub-Saharan Africa, but the exact extent and the implications vary.

14

Box 14.2 ▷ Charcoal production and the size of the market

The availability of wood in many parts of sub-Saharan Africa at low or no-cash cost relative to alternative energy sources is a crucial factor in its status as the fuel of choice for a large part of the sub-Saharan population. In addition, its supply can be an important source of employment and therefore income for the local population. The charcoal industry, for example, creates jobs for wood producers, charcoal producers, transporters and vendors. In Rwanda, in 2007, the value of transactions at fuelwood and charcoal markets was estimated to be $122 million, amounting to 5% of GDP, 50% of these revenues stayed in the rural areas.

Within urban areas, charcoal is a popular fuel choice as it offers higher energy content per weight than wood, making it easier to transport, store and distribute. Over the projection period, the urban population increases by 560 million people, driving up charcoal demand and thereby diminishing the availability of fuelwood, unless it is produced sustainably. At present the conversion of fuelwood to charcoal is highly inefficient in sub-Saharan Africa, as most of it is produced using traditional earth-mound kilns that have a conversion efficiency of 8% to 12%, compared to industrial kilns, which have an efficiency of above 25%. However, such improved kilns increase the unit costs of charcoal production even though the amount of charcoal produced is higher and negative environmental impacts are reduced. Policies and effective regulation of the charcoal market are needed to increase the share of more efficient kilns as the charcoal market is not expected to diminish in the future. As in the case of improved cookstoves, greater adoption of improved kilns will depend upon the availability of simple, small-scale, fast-cycle and economical charcoal producers.

In the New Policies Scenario, we have assumed a smooth switch from traditional kilns to more efficient ones at varying rates in the sub-Saharan regions. As forest reserves around towns are exhausted, wood for charcoal must be sourced from further away, increasing the transportation costs and the price to the consumer. Charcoal prices have increased in recent year across Africa, but price changes rarely reflect shifts in the availability of the fuel. In 2012, charcoal production in sub-Saharan Africa is estimated to have amounted to 36 million tonnes, with an estimated market value of $11 billion. In the New Policies Scenario, a combination of increasing levels of consumption and higher prices result in the market value growing to almost $70 billion by 2040. The large size and unregulated nature of the charcoal industry can lead to criminal activity. For example, in DR Congo the industry is a lucrative source of illicit income that provides funding to militias (UNEP and INTERPOL, 2014).

Since 1990, Nigeria has experienced a decrease of its forest area in excess of 3% per year, one of the highest deforestation rates observed on a global scale. Loss of almost 50% of its forest area has resulted. Some other countries in West Africa have also seen significant reductions in their forest area, such as Togo, which experienced a decrease of more than

4% per year between 1990 and 2010. In East Africa, there has been a decrease of just 0.6% per year over the same period, though the forest area per capita is lower than in many other parts of Africa. But the situation is not uniform across eastern countries. The deforestation rate in Uganda has been increasing since 1990, reaching almost 3% per year between 2005 and 2010, while the forest area in Rwanda has increased over the same period (see the energy and environment section). Scarcity of fuelwood around cities and villages increases the distance that people must travel to collect it, amplifying the burden that often falls on women and children. Currently, people spend from less than one hour to up to five hours daily collecting wood. Overall, the extent to which the use of solid biomass in sub-Saharan Africa could be considered sustainable is doubtful. Besides contributing to land degradation, the typical partial combustion of fuelwood emits carbon dioxide, methane and black carbon, and is a major cause of indoor air pollution, with damaging health effects.

Hydropower

In the New Policies Scenario, installed hydropower capacity in sub-Saharan Africa increases from around 20 GW in 2012 to nearly 95 GW in 2040, and accounts for one-quarter of the growth in total power generation capacity. Capacity grows by more than 7% per year to 2020, then slows to around 6% per year in the 2020s and below 5% in the 2030s. Sub-Saharan Africa's share of world hydropower capacity increases to 5% and hydropower's share of regional electricity generation increases from 22% to 26%. In West Africa, Nigeria is developing its hydropower potential (Mambilla and Zunguru projects) and is expected to continue to do so to help meet rapidly rising electricity demand. In the New Policies Scenario, its capacity increases to around 15 GW by 2040, utilising by this time, most of its remaining economically viable hydropower potential (Figure 14.20). In the rest of West Africa, expansion occurs across several countries, including Côte d'Ivoire, Ghana, Guinea, Niger, Senegal and Sierra Leone, drawing on resources such as those of the Niger and Senegal river basins (although this is highly seasonal). The highly seasonal river flows in parts of this region lead to relatively low average capacity factors for hydropower. By 2040, capacity in other West Africa countries reaches 9.4 GW, leaving several gigawatts of untapped potential in 2040.

Central Africa has the richest hydropower resources in Africa (concentrated in but not limited to, DR Congo). However, presently it does not have sizeable demand centres and lacks interconnections that would be essential for large hydropower development. The Congo River – the main source of hydropower potential – has strong and relatively stable flows throughout the year, lending itself to power generation. In the New Policies Scenario, Inga III reaches full output by the mid-2020s and early phases of Grand Inga come online before 2040. However, the scale, cost and complexities of Grand Inga give rise to significant uncertainty regarding its development. If it is pushed ahead vigorously, it can be transformational for sub-Saharan electricity supply (see Chapter 16). Smaller scale hydropower comes online elsewhere, for example in Cameroon and Gabon. Overall, Central Africa sees capacity grow from 2.6 GW to 20 GW in 2040.

Figure 14.20 ▷ **Sub-Saharan hydropower capacity and remaining potential in the New Policies Scenario** (GW)

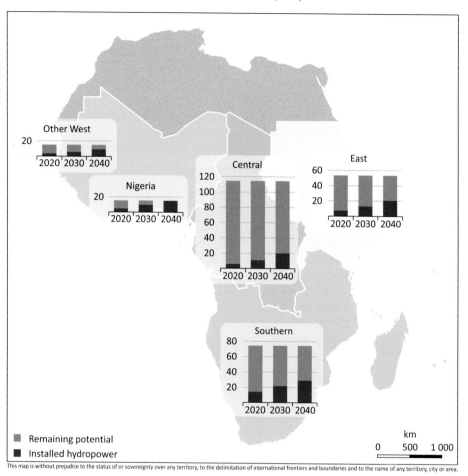

Sources: IPCC (2011); IJHD (2009); IJHD (2010); IEA analysis.

In East Africa, there is already a lot of activity underway to expand hydropower capacity, with Ethiopia dominating the picture. In the New Policies Scenario, Gilgel Gibe III and IV and the Grand Renaissance dam make the largest contributions to the increase in hydropower capacity, which reaches 20 GW by 2040; but capacity is also expected to grow in Sudan and Uganda. Several countries in Southern Africa have significant untapped hydropower potential, especially those in the Zambezi River basin, such as Mozambique, Angola, Zambia and Zimbabwe. The Southern Africa Power Pool has plans for the expansion of hydropower: developments are already underway at Cambambe (Angola) and Kafue Gorge (Zambia) and other major projects are also being taken forward in Tanzania and Mozambique, for example. Overall, hydropower capacity in Southern Africa more than triples to reach 29 GW by 2040, with 11 GW located collectively in Mozambique and Tanzania.

Large hydropower naturally accounts for the bulk of installed capacity, with small hydropower projects playing a growing role in terms of the number of projects. Small hydropower projects are, in a number of circumstances, an attractive option because they take less time to build, require less capital and can often be located near demand centres. Some parts of Africa experience significant seasonal hydropower variability and water stress, including occasional periods of prolonged drought. For dam-based projects, reservoirs can help manage the variability of water flow but entail additional social and environmental concerns that need to be diligently addressed. In some cases, water availability may be limited due to requirements for other uses, such as irrigation.

Two key factors dictating the pace of large-scale hydropower development are the availability of finance and the degree of regional co-operation. The fiscal positions of many sub-Saharan countries puts funding for such projects beyond their own capacity, which often makes access to bilateral, multilateral and international private finance necessary. Effective regional co-operation typically involving inter-state agreements can make large projects viable by aggregating demand to the level necessary for a viable commercial case for investment. It also offers opportunities to share the output and benefits among countries to address electricity supply deficits and support economic development.

Solar power

In the New Policies Scenario, sub-Saharan Africa progressively taps its vast solar potential with South Africa and Nigeria installing most new capacity. Sub-Saharan solar capacity exceeds 6 GW by 2020 and is around 45 GW in 2040, with solar PV then accounting for nearly three-quarters of the total and CSP the remainder. Solar capacity additions rise from around 0.9 GW per year on average to 2020 and then to 2.2 GW per year on average thereafter. By the end of the projection period, solar (PV and CSP) accounts for 12% of total capacity and 6% of electricity supply. South Africa has a clear intention to increase the role of solar power and around half of the total capacity in sub-Saharan Africa in 2040 is located there, taking advantage of excellent solar resources. Solar PV in South Africa grows strongly over the entire projection period (reaching 15 GW by 2040), while CSP capacity comes online from around the mid-2020s (reaching 6 GW in 2040). Nigeria's solar capacity increases to 12 GW in 2040, nearly one-quarter of peak electricity demand at that time. In other parts of sub-Saharan Africa, solar capacity increases steadily, but, despite significant cost reductions over time, its growth is still held back in places by its expense relative to competing fuels and technologies.

Other renewables

Potential supply of energy from geothermal resources is limited to the East African Rift Valley. It is already proving itself to be a valuable element in the generation mix in Kenya and other countries have stated their intention to explore their national potential. In the New Policies Scenario, East Africa's geothermal capacity grows to over 1 GW in 2020, more than 3 GW in 2030 and around 8 GW by 2040 – an average rate of 0.3 GW capacity additions per year, but weighted towards the second-half of the projection period. The costs of geothermal-based electricity are competitive with thermal power generation and it has a high capacity factor, although regular drilling of new wells is often required. By 2040, geothermal sources make up nearly 15% of East Africa's power generation capacity. While development remains centred in Kenya, developments occur also in other countries over time, including in Ethiopia, Rwanda and Tanzania.

Wind power capacity in sub-Saharan Africa increases by around 12 GW by 2040 in the New Policies Scenario, with average annual capacity additions of 0.5 GW. South Africa is most active in developing wind capacity, with average annual capacity additions of 0.3 GW, to reach 2 GW in 2020 and nearly 7 GW in 2040 (more than half of the sub-Saharan total). Most of the wind development is located onshore. All other sub-regions introduce wind capacity, but to a smaller extent and typically later in the projection period. Capacity factors are around 26-27%, on average, which is comparable to that of many other parts of the world. Wind accounts for just over 3% of total power generation capacity and 2% of electricity supply in 2040. Factors holding back a more rapid expansion of wind capacity include the lack of a developed wind power industry in most countries and constraints on the ability (or desire) of many countries to manage a significant volume of variable capacity within their systems.

International energy trade

The growth in sub-Saharan energy demand and supply that is projected in the New Policies Scenario affects not just the region, but also the balance of its energy trade with the rest of the world. This is felt in a gradual decline in crude oil exports, as well as a rise in net oil product imports, although net exports of natural gas and of coal both grow as the increase in production (notably in Mozambique) outpaces that of regional consumption. With all exported commodities, there is a shift in destination markets, away from the Atlantic basin and towards the major import markets of the Asia-Pacific.

Crude oil

There is a shift both in volumes and in destination for crude oil exports from sub-Saharan Africa to other parts of the world. Net crude oil exports, which remain dominated by Nigeria and Angola, decline by 1.7 mb/d to just over 3 mb/d in 2040 (Figure 14.21). This is due to the decline in overall output, and to increased volumes of African refining to meet the increase in regional consumption. Of the major exporters, only Nigeria manages to keep exports at a similar level in 2040 compared with today, as the eventual rise in oil production keeps pace with the increase in refinery runs to 450 kb/d. Angola's crude oil exports decline by a third to just over 1 mb/d, as production declines and refinery runs increase to 200 kb/d.[5] All the other countries that are currently net crude exporters either become net importers by 2040 to feed crude into their refineries (Cameroon and Sudan), or they see exports dropping significantly (Chad, Congo, Equatorial Guinea, Gabon, Ghana

---

5. Nonetheless, our projections suggest that Nigeria remains a net importer of oil products in 2040 while Angola becomes a net oil product exporter.

and South Sudan). In terms of external markets, exporters on Africa's west coast face a rapidly changing picture with the continued growth of production in North and South America over the coming decades.

Figure 14.21 ▷ Sub-Saharan Africa crude oil exports and imports in the New Policies Scenario

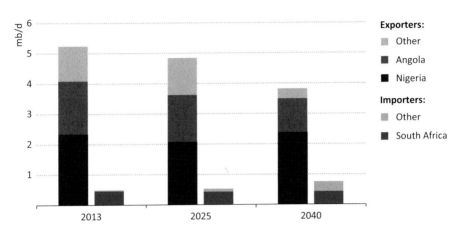

Note: This includes only exports and imports to/from countries outside of sub-Saharan Africa.

As noted in Chapter 13, exports from Nigeria and Angola to the United States have reduced by two-thirds since 2008. We project that westward export volumes continue to shrink in aggregate, although Europe continues to be an important market, but that a larger share of exports are drawn eastwards towards Asia, to India, China and South Asia. Among those buying crude from international markets, Kenya becomes a significant importer (of about 120 kb/d in 2040) as we expect a refinery to be built here for the growing and highly undersupplied East African market, but South Africa remains the largest buyer of international crude. It supplies its refineries mainly with crude imported from the Middle East, a trade flow that is expected to continue, although with a greater share of West African crudes added to the mix.

Oil products

In the New Policies Scenario, we assume that 400 kb/d of current refining capacity in sub-Saharan Africa is eventually shut down, sufficient investments are made to upgrade the remaining capacity for higher runs, and another 0.8 mb/d of new refinery capacity comes online between now and 2040. The net result is that total product imports increase in volume terms to reach 1.8 mb/d in 2040, but overall dependence on imports (as a share of regional demand) for some key oil products edges lower (Figure 14.22). With the exception of a couple of countries with very small local markets and a working refining system, all countries in sub-Saharan Africa are expected to remain net importers of oil products.

14

Figure 14.22 ▷ Import dependence for selected oil products in sub-Saharan Africa (excluding South Africa) in the New Policies Scenario

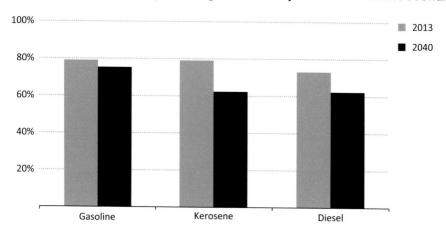

What are the implications of these projections for the security of oil product supply? With domestic demand set to more than double in the projection period, product imports would increase to 2.7 mb/d if no new refining capacity were added and if existing refineries did not ramp up runs. Such high reliance on imports would bring with it some important hazards: oil products imports to Africa come primarily from European and US ports for West Africa, and from the Middle East or India for East Africa, some 5 to 20 sailing days away. The flow of products can be disrupted for a variety of reasons, affecting either the physical availability of the product or its transportation: a refinery going into an unplanned shutdown or an unexpectedly cold winter spell might affect the supply of gasoline, diesel or kerosene. In addition to the shipping distance from major refining hubs, very often an importing country in Africa (and, often, its land-locked neighbour) depends on a single jetty in a sole coastal terminal to unload all imported products: this is the case, for example, in Ghana. Land-locked countries are particularly vulnerable to the risks of long-distance supply lines: inland storage capacity is inadequate and product pipelines largely non-existent. Experience shows that the effects of a supply disruption or of bottlenecks in transportation are felt quickly by end-users, either through higher prices or physical scarcity. Setting up emergency stocks can offer a buffer against this risk, but these are expensive and can be difficult to develop in markets where demand is growing.

Natural gas

In the New Policies Scenario, sub-Saharan Africa's net contribution to inter-regional natural gas exports triples, growing from 31 bcm in 2012 to around 95 bcm in 2040 (Figure 14.23). The focus also changes from the west coast of Africa to the east coast, with the rise of LNG exports from Mozambique and Tanzania (discussed in detail in Chapter 15). Africa's west coast remains a steady source of LNG exports to global markets, but does not see scope for the sort of expansion that is anticipated in Nigeria, where four new LNG projects are under consideration (Brass LNG, OK LNG and trains 7 and 8 at Nigeria LNG). There are sufficient gas resources to satisfy a greater volume of export projects in Nigeria, as well as meeting projected domestic demand (only around one-quarter of ultimately recoverable gas resources have been used in Nigeria by 2040 in our projections). However, the government faces a challenge to mobilise the necessary upstream investment and, even if the netback prices are less attractive, the government is assumed to prioritise domestic supply over export.[6] Overall LNG exports from Nigeria fall to 13 bcm in 2040, a level that could, in principle, be supplied from today's liquefaction capacity.

Figure 14.23 ▷ **LNG exports from sub-Saharan Africa in the New Policies Scenario**

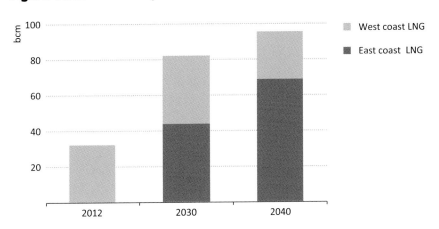

As with oil, the anticipated markets for LNG exports from the west coast have shifted with rising production from North America. Atlantic basin LNG markets have become less attractive and more competitive; Europe is the main remaining importer, although there are smaller opportunities available also in Latin America. Being based mainly on relatively cheap associated gas, these LNG projects can absorb some of the additional costs of seeking more distant export markets. Although more expensive to produce, LNG projects on the east coast of Africa are much more advantageously positioned in relation to the main sources of LNG import growth in Asia, in particular India, although slightly less so for Northeast Asia, because of the additional distance (Figure 14.24).

As a new source of gas, Mozambique and Tanzania are of interest to buyers as a means of diversifying their LNG portfolios. The task of marketing the gas in Mozambique is eased by the presence of large Asian importers in the main producing consortia, including companies from China (CNPC), India (ONGC, Bharat Petroleum and Oil India), Thailand (PTT), Japan (Mitsui) and Korea (KOGAS). Geography also helps, with LNG delivery distances meaning that those exporters on Africa's east coast are well placed to benefit

14

---

6. As a 49% partner in the LNG facilities, the government gains significant benefit from gas exports, sharing in the margin between the domestic supply price and the international LNG price, in addition to receipt of taxes and royalties. However, it is assumed that political factors (including the importance of improved electricity supply) and a gradual increase in domestic gas prices outweigh these factors.

from arbitrage between Asia-Pacific markets and Europe (the position currently enjoyed by Qatar). Indeed, we project that, although most east coast LNG export volumes go to Asian markets, a small share ends up going to meet Europe's gas import needs.

Figure 14.24 ▷ **Indicative delivered costs of LNG from selected sources to Europe and main Asian import markets, 2025**

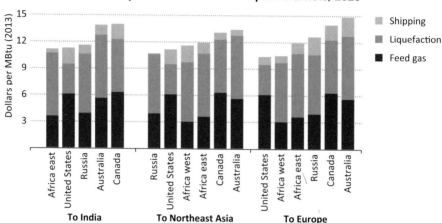

Notes: MBtu = million British thermal units. Africa east is LNG exports from sub-Saharan Africa's east coast. Africa west is LNG exports from the west coast. Cost estimates are indicative and figures for specific projects could vary significantly, depending on their detailed design. The calculation of life-cycle costs is based on generic capital and operating cost assumptions, including a 10% discount rate and 30-year asset lives.

The anticipated evolution of the LNG market does present some challenges to Africa's exporters, particularly around the end of the current decade, when the project developers in both Mozambique and Tanzania plan first LNG deliveries. The competition for LNG buyers looks set to intensify into the early 2020s, as the first wave of Australian LNG is followed by projects in the United States, Canada and Russia, as well as the anticipated start of pipeline deliveries from Russia to China. The 2018-2019 start dates for LNG delivery claimed by the consortia in both Mozambique and Tanzania, if realised, would give the them a head-start against some of these competitors; but the risk of delay is substantial in these remote locations with very little local infrastructure or industrial capacity to support construction. In the New Policies Scenario, it is assumed that the first four trains of Mozambique LNG and a floating LNG facility are fully operational only by the late-2020s, with the first LNG train in Tanzania becoming operational in the same period.

In addition, against a backdrop of high prices for imported LNG, buyers in the Asia-Pacific region are also looking for concessions on pricing from prospective LNG suppliers. Anadarko, operator of Mozambique's Area 1, has already indicated that pricing formulas for Mozambique LNG export may be indexed, in part, to gas prices at Henry Hub, as well as to oil prices. This would make the delivery price for Mozambique's LNG more sensitive to the supply-demand dynamics in gas markets (albeit those in North America) rather than to the average Japanese crude import price, which has been the preferred index for pricing LNG supplies to the Asian market in the past.

Coal

South Africa is the sixth-largest coal exporter in the world, providing (almost exclusively) steam coal to the international market. It has seen its share of international steam coal trade decrease in recent years, going from 14% in 2003 to 8% in 2012. South Africa also used to be the main supplier of coal to Europe but, over the last few years, has seen its exports flow increasingly to the Pacific basin, where demand is growing more quickly and prices are higher. South Africa benefits from a position at the low end of the global cost curve, with FOB costs broadly falling in a range of $40-70 per tonne. It also has a favourable geographical location that allows exporters to supply into both the Atlantic and Pacific basins at a reasonable freight cost. Despite these advantages, the South African coal industry is facing problems that have held back export growth. Production from the major current producing areas, in Mpumalanga province, is set to decline, necessitating a shift towards the abundant but more distant Waterberg fields, near the border with Botswana. This means major new investment in railway transportation, shortage of which is already a constraint on export: throughput capacity at Richard's Bay Coal Terminal, has been lifted to over 90 million tonnes per annum (Mtpa), but the 580 km railway line linking the main existing mining area to the port is constrained at around 72 Mtpa and other ports can handle only small quantities. Assuming that these constraints can gradually be lifted, South African coal exports increase to almost 100 Mtce in the New Policies Scenario in 2040, with the majority destined for India.

Mozambique is the second-most important player when it comes to coal in Africa. However, in contrast to South Africa, its prospects lie mainly in coking coal and therefore follow a different dynamic. For the moment, the lack of export infrastructure has impeded a rapid increase of exports. The idea of barging coal down the Zambezi River has been ruled out by the Mozambican authorities due to environmental concerns, so the main transport option to bring the coal to port is the railway. The existing 590 km Sena railway line that links the Tete coal fields with the port of Beira is currently constrained to around 6 Mtpa. To foster further increases in exports, capacity expansion and additional infrastructure is needed; the preferred route is the so-called Nacala corridor, a 900 km railway line crossing southern Malawi to link the mines with a new deepwater terminal at Nacala. In the New Policies Scenario, exports from Mozambique are projected to increase from around 3 Mtce in 2012 to around 30 Mtce in 2040, the majority being coking coal. As with South Africa, the natural destination for the coal is India, but Brazil is also expected to be a market for Mozambique's coal export.

Coal production in other Southern African countries like Botswana, Zimbabwe or Zambia is also set to increase, but exports remain small scale, mainly involving land borne trade with neighbouring countries. Due to the remoteness of the coal reserves and the land-locked geography of these countries, infrastructure requirements to provide access to the seaborne market would be huge. Madagascar is an exception, with the proposed coal mines being located only 150-200 km from the coast. However, political instability has so far prevented any export-oriented coal operation coming to fruition.

14

Energy and the environment

The energy projections in the New Policies Scenario have a wide range of environmental implications, both in terms of local impacts in Africa and the much broader issue of global climate change. These can include: energy-related greenhouse-gas emissions, such as from power generation and transport; local pollution, particularly in growing urban areas; indoor air pollution, as the widespread traditional use of solid biomass for cooking continues; deforestation and land degradation as the result of unsustainable practices to cater for fuelwood and charcoal consumption; other forms of environmental degradation, such as from open-cast mining or oil spills resulting from oil theft or sabotage; a range of environmental considerations linked to new hydropower projects (especially those with reservoirs); emissions from the venting or flaring of natural gas (Box 14.3); and, handling and storage of potentially harmful waste or by-products from energy-related processes, such as nuclear waste. While all of these are important factors for policy-makers to monitor and tackle, and often require ongoing social engagement, this section concentrates on two, energy-related carbon dioxide (CO_2) emissions and the environmental consequences of sub-Saharan Africa's heavy reliance on solid biomass.

Box 14.3 ▷ Natural gas flaring in sub-Saharan Africa

Around 28 bcm of natural gas (primarily consisting of methane, a potent greenhouse-gas) is estimated to have been flared or vented in sub-Saharan Africa in 2012, a volume that, had it all been consumed in gas-fired (CCGT) power plants could have increased sub-Saharan electricity supply by around 35% (nearly 155 TWh).[7] Nigeria accounted for around 60% of the gas flared in 2012 (around 17 bcm), and Angola, Congo and Gabon for much of the remainder. Flaring reduction (and gas utilisation) has become a greater policy focus in several sub-Saharan countries, as they recognise its wasteful nature in the face of growing domestic energy needs, as well as its potential to generate revenue from the utilised gas and its negative environmental effects. Just one example of the positive action being taken is the membership of Nigeria, Angola, Congo, Gabon and Cameroon in the Global Gas Flaring Reduction Partnership, an initiative that supports national efforts to use currently flared gas by promoting effective regulatory frameworks and tackling the constraints on gas utilisation.

The New Policies Scenario sees volumes of flared and vented gas in sub-Saharan Africa reduce over time, reaching around 15 bcm in 2025 and less than 10 bcm by 2040, as a result of both positive policy efforts (such as pricing and regulatory reforms that incentivise marketing of the gas), declining production in some of the oil fields where flaring takes place today and greater action to avoid or minimise flaring in new fields. While actions taken in Nigeria are the most important (see Chapter 15), other countries also contribute to the declining trend. In aggregate, countries other than Nigeria are expected to reduce flaring to around 5 bcm by the early 2020s and continue to decline

---

7. Assuming plant efficiency of 57%, the CCGT fleet average in sub-Saharan Africa.

gradually thereafter. Central to this trend is Angola's plan to commercialise more of its natural gas reserves through its LNG facility at Soyo (which is due to come back into operation from 2015). When the LNG plant reaches full capacity, it is designed to receive up to 10 bcm per year of mainly associated gas from offshore oil fields, contributing to a significant reduction of gas flaring in the country. Gabon has already introduced penalties to curb gas flaring but these have yet to be enforced. Following government encouragement, the country's largest operators have launched their own gas flaring reduction programmes. In Congo, the government has imposed requirements to reduce gas flaring, which have already decreased volumes by around 40% from their 2005 peak (over 2 bcm). Furthermore, gas that would previously have been flared has been used to fuel two power plants.

Energy-related CO$_2$ emissions

Sub-Saharan Africa accounts for only a very small share of cumulative historical energy-related CO$_2$ emissions: in the 1900 to 2012 period, the region was responsible for 1.8% of the global total (0.6% if South Africa is excluded). In the New Policies Scenario, energy-related CO$_2$ emissions double in sub-Saharan Africa, reaching 1.2 gigatonnes (Gt) in 2040. The region's share of global emissions increase from 2% to 3%, while emissions per capita barely change, remaining below 0.7 tonnes per capita in 2040, around 15% of the global average (Figure 14.25). The economies of sub-Saharan Africa in 2040 are, on average, only half as carbon intensive as they are today, as economic growth encompasses a shift towards less energy-intensive economic activity, including services. Rising levels of access to modern energy have a negligible impact on emissions, with the improvement in electricity access accounting for around 10% of the increase in sub-Saharan emissions (around 70 Mt) or just over 1% of the increase in global emissions from now to 2040.

Figure 14.25 ▷ **Energy-related CO$_2$ emissions by selected country and region in the New Policies Scenario**

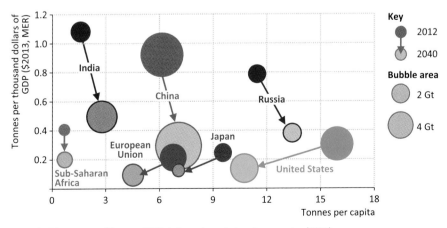

Note: GDP is presented in year-2013 dollars at market exchange rates (MER).

Africa's contribution to global greenhouse-gas emissions may be relatively limited, but its involvement in the issue is pronounced. In particular, temperatures across the continent are projected to rise faster than the global average (James and Washington, 2013). The nature and scale of the challenge is subject to a broad range of uncertainty, but existing climate models suggest that, in scenarios broadly consistent with the outcomes of the New Policies Scenario, annual average temperatures across the continent will rise between 3 °C and 6 °C by 2100, compared to the 1986-2005 average (IPCC, 2014). The African continent, already prone to weather extremes, would be affected in several ways, including droughts in some areas, extreme precipitation in others and rising sea-levels affecting coastal areas (where many large populations are based and substantial components of economic output are concentrated).

One key uncertainty for Africa's power sector is the impact of climate change on hydropower capacity and potential. Climate change could increase run-off and increase output from hydropower in East Africa, but decrease water run-off in parts of West and Southern Africa (Hamududu and Killingtveit, 2012). The Zambezi River system, along which a significant share of hydropower capacity in Southern Africa is expected to be located by 2040, could be one of the worst affected in Africa, suffering reduced run-off as a result of decreased rainfall of between 10% and 15% across the basin (Beilfuss, 2012). Increased evaporation will affect the level of "stored" energy in reservoirs, while increasing temperatures can be expected to boost demand for water resources from other sectors, such as for irrigation, intensifying problems of water scarcity. Such changes emphasise the need for future energy projects, in the hydropower sector as in others, to be tested for their climate resilience as a standard element of assessing their overall feasibility and acquiring societal consent.

Deforestation and forest degradation

As discussed earlier in this chapter, sub-Saharan Africa continues to rely heavily on bioenergy in the New Policies Scenario, consuming nearly 1 100 Mt of fuelwood in 2040. The extent to which this fuelwood can be considered a renewable source of energy depends on how it is produced and consumed. Many sub-Saharan countries already face deforestation (and even desertification) and it is clear that reversing this loss depends on policies all along the value chain. One example of what can be done comes from the Bugasea region in Rwanda, which was completely stripped of available wood in the 1980s, mainly to produce charcoal for Kigali. Government efforts to support replanting and to promote efficient charcoaling techniques, supplemented by other efforts, have resulted in the area once again being covered in eucalyptus trees. Rwanda is one of the few African countries to have seen an increase in its forest area in recent years.

The need for national strategies for bioenergy is gaining recognition among several African governments, including Ethiopia, Mozambique, Liberia, Sierra Leone and others that are engaging with the EU Energy Initiative Partnership Dialogue Facility to develop their own Biomass Energy Strategy Plans. Among others, policies are needed to regulate fuelwood and charcoal markets which, despite being an important source of income and employment in sub-Saharan Africa, are at present almost entirely unregulated. For example, in Tanzania, at least 80% of charcoal is reportedly produced and traded outside the formal economy (World Bank, 2009). An estimated $1.9 billion of government revenue is lost in Africa each year as a result of unregulated charcoal trade (UNEP and INTERPOL, 2014). Furthermore, because the price of charcoal traded on the informal market does not adequately reflect the cost of reforestation, if at all, charcoal produced in a more sustainable way is often priced out of the market. On the demand side, there is a need to boost the uptake of improved biomass cookstoves. The higher efficiency of improved biomass cookstoves can decrease fuelwood consumption by half when used correctly. They can also reduce carbon monoxide and particulate matter emissions during cooking. An essential feature of successful policies in this area, as in all areas of energy production and consumption with important social and environmental implications, is serious engagement of the community in understanding the issues and contributing to their resolution.

14

Chapter 15

African energy issues in focus
Five key features of the sub-Saharan energy outlook

Highlights

- Over the period to 2040, 950 million people are projected to gain access to electricity in sub-Saharan Africa. Urban populations gain access via connections to the grid; in rural areas, mini-grid and off-grid solutions, increasingly powered by renewables, play a much larger role. Against a backdrop of strong population growth, cumulative investment of more than $200 billion lowers the total without access by 15%: a major step forward, but not far enough, as it still leaves 530 million people in the region, primarily in rural communities, without electricity in 2040.

- Solid biomass, much of it used by households for cooking, accounts for 70% of final energy use in sub-Saharan Africa today, with adverse environmental consequences and health effects from household air pollution. Rising incomes over the period to 2040 produce only a gradual shift in the cooking fuels and technologies used. Policy actions and wood scarcity accelerate the switch in some regions to alternative fuels, notably to LPG and to more efficient cookstoves, but 650 million people, again mainly in rural areas, still cook with biomass in an inefficient and hazardous way in 2040.

- Angola is set to temporarily overtake Nigeria as the largest sub-Saharan Africa producer of crude oil, as regulatory uncertainty in Nigeria, militant activity and oil theft in the Niger Delta impact production there. Oil theft is estimated at 150 kb/d today, leads to oil spills and represents lost revenue of more than $5 billion per year, an amount that would be sufficient to fund universal access to electricity for all Nigerians by 2030. Reducing the risks facing investors will also be critical if Nigeria is to make productive domestic use of its abundant gas resources.

- A successful programme for grid-based renewables in South Africa is stimulating private investment and helping to diversify a power mix dominated by coal, a process to which regional hydropower projects, natural gas and, eventually, additional nuclear capacity contribute. Coal faces rising costs with a move to new production areas. Even so, it remains a low-cost option for new capacity, a competitive strength in a society concerned about the affordability of electricity.

- Expectations are high in Mozambique and Tanzania that major recent gas discoveries can spur domestic economic development. Upstream projects depend on large-scale gas export, in the form of LNG, and also produce an estimated $150 billion in fiscal revenue to 2040. But the respective governments are also determined to pursue the challenging and long-term endeavour of promoting gas use in domestic power generation and industry. Developing a local consumer base for gas requires a careful choice and location of projects to anchor the development of a gas grid, but is an appropriate way to get value from gas.

Five features of Africa's energy outlook

Africa presents a very heterogeneous energy landscape, with large country-by-country variations in resource endowments, patterns of consumption and policy challenges. But certain questions recur. In this chapter, we focus on five of them, drawing on the results of our projections in the New Policies Scenario. The aim is to illuminate features that, in our judgement, are critical to the energy future of sub-Saharan Africa:

- Limited access to electricity is a fundamental weakness in sub-Saharan Africa's energy system and a huge barrier to development: which policies, fuels and technologies can improve the situation, and how quickly is the energy access gap being closed?

- Traditional use of solid biomass for cooking accounts for the largest part of household energy consumption, but has significant health and environmental impacts: how rapidly might Africa see a transition to cleaner alternatives?

- Oil has been central to Nigeria's modern history, but for many the large revenues have not been translated into tangible socio-economic benefits: can oil still be part of the way forward for Africa's largest economy?

- South Africa is diversifying a heavily coal-dominated electricity system, with renewable energy playing a much larger role: what are the policies, costs and benefits involved?

- The major natural gas discoveries in the offshore waters of Mozambique and Tanzania are creating high expectations, but what are the avenues – and obstacles – facing these countries as they look to get the best value from natural gas?

Electricity access: what is the path to power?

As highlighted in Chapter 13, lack of access to electricity is a fundamental brake on development in many parts of Africa. As of 2012, almost half of those around the world without access are on the African continent; the vast majority of these are in sub-Saharan Africa. In our projections, 1 billion people gain access to electricity in Africa by 2040, 950 million of them in sub-Saharan Africa; but population growth in sub-Saharan Africa and progress in other parts of the world means that the remaining global population without electricity access becomes increasingly concentrated in sub-Saharan Africa – this figure reaches 75% in 2040, compared with half today (Figure 15.1). This projection indicates that current efforts to tackle this problem are set to fall well short of the goal of achieving universal access by 2030, the target of the Sustainable Energy for All initiative. Instead, some 635 million people in sub-Saharan Africa are set to remain without electricity by this date, leaving a sombre gap in the global energy system.

Why do so many remain without electricity access in sub-Saharan Africa? There are a number of contributing factors, including the current state of electricity infrastructure, the nature and extent of expected flows of investment to different parts of the power sector and the huge size of many countries. Demographic trends also play an important part. Sub-Saharan Africa is distinctive in our global projections in two aspects: a significant rate of population growth, and a large increase in the rural population. By 2040, around 90% of the sub-Saharan population without access to electricity lives in rural areas (accounting for two-thirds of the global population without access), where providing electricity is that much more difficult than in urban areas.

Figure 15.1 ▷ **Population without access to electricity by sub-region in sub-Saharan Africa in the New Policies Scenario**

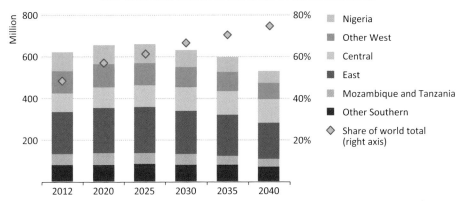

The size of the challenge that remains in our projections should not obscure the progress that is being made, aided by the numerous national and multilateral initiatives focusing on this issue. At present, population growth is outpacing efforts at electrification, but – as Figure 15.1 makes clear – this trend is reversed in the mid-2020s, as the total population without access to electricity in sub-Saharan Africa peaks and then goes into decline. Over the projection period, the number of people without access in sub-Saharan Africa declines by 15% from today's level, to around 530 million. The pace of change is fastest among the urban population, where the number of people without access is reduced by more than half.

Our projections also point to some distinctive regional developments within sub-Saharan Africa (Figure 15.2):

■   Nigeria brings electricity access to more people than any other country in Africa, reducing the absolute number of those without access by around 40% by 2040. The electrification rate goes from 45% today to nearly 85% in 2040, which translates into more than 200 million people gaining access. However, as highlighted later in this section, the rural population without access sees only a small decrease in absolute terms, thereby accounting for around 80% of Nigerians without access in 2040. Other parts of West Africa see continued progress in raising electrification rates, such that, by 2040, West Africa has the highest electrification rate (80%) of all the African sub-regions. Outside Nigeria, around 85% of those remaining without access in West Africa in 2040 are in rural areas.

- The problem of electricity access is more persistent in Central Africa. Although some countries, like Equatorial Guinea and Gabon start from relatively high electrification rates and continue to make progress, others, like Chad and the Central African Republic, start from a very low base. More than half of the total population of this sub-region remains without access in 2040 in our projections. Countries with very low population densities, like Congo, face particularly severe challenges in bringing electricity to their rural communities.

- East Africa is the sub-region which achieves the most rapid pace of growth in providing electricity access, with Ethiopia, Kenya and Rwanda leading the way; but a large part of the rural population here, too, remains without access: one-third of the sub-Saharan African population remaining without access in 2040 consists of rural communities in East Africa. The challenge is particularly acute for Ethiopia, which currently has the world's second-largest rural population without access to electricity (almost 70 million).

- In South Africa, the government aims to reach a 97% electrification rate by 2025 through a combination of on-grid and off-grid technologies (mainly solar home systems). This target is achieved by 2030 in our projections and a 100% electrification rate is reached in the late 2030s, thanks to supportive financing schemes, such as charging poor households without access a minimal fee for the connection and providing 50 kilowatt-hours (kWh) per month free of charge. Progress with electrification in Mozambique and Tanzania is helped by an expansion of gas use in the power sector, but also by a large push for mini-grid and off-grid solutions in rural areas. In other parts of Southern Africa, good progress is made as well, notably in Botswana and Zambia.

Figure 15.2 ▷ Electricity access by region in sub-Saharan Africa in the New Policies Scenario

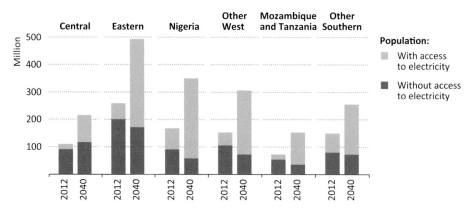

The impact of increased electricity access on overall power demand in sub-Saharan Africa is very limited. The population gaining access throughout the period to 2040 adds around 190 terawatt-hours (TWh) to total power consumption in 2040 (Figure 15.3). This is only around 20% of the overall increase in electricity demand over the projection period, and less than 15% of total sub-Saharan African power demand in 2040, which is projected to reach 1 300 TWh. Of the population gaining access, two-thirds live in urban areas and are connected to a main grid. In rural areas, mini- and off-grid solutions play a much more prominent role, accounting for 70% of new access-related demand over the period to 2040.

Figure 15.3 ▷ **Electricity demand from the population gaining access to electricity in sub-Saharan Africa in the New Policies Scenario**

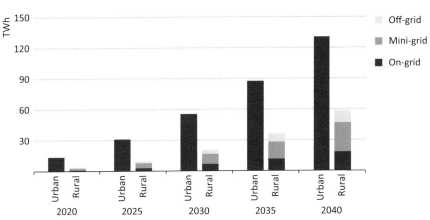

The type of access that is provided is heavily contingent on a range of country-specific factors, including the nature of policies and financing for access-related projects, the current state and coverage of the transmission and distribution systems, the status of plans to extend the grid and the capacity and financing to realise these plans (Spotlight). Alongside policy-related considerations, actual costs are also strongly affected by the density of population in the area without access. For areas with significant concentrations of population, i.e. in urban areas or larger settlements, on-grid supply is typically the most cost-effective solution. Indeed, urban populations gaining access in our projections do so entirely via the grid because of the relatively low cost of additional connections and because the fixed costs of extending the grid are spread over a larger amount of electricity consumed.

On-grid connections can also be cost-effective for more dispersed populations living within a reasonable distance of transmission and distribution lines, even allowing for the additional expense of extending the service. The maximum economic distance for extending the grid tends to reduce over time, as the costs of generation in mini-grids or off-grid systems come down, but the average cost of supplying grid-based electricity remains below the cost of the alternatives in our projections. Moreover, as transmission and distribution systems expand

15

to connect growing demand centres, new power plants and large "anchor" consumers, such as mining operations, this has the effect of bringing the grid closer to other settlements and so reducing the grid costs in comparison with other connection options.

S P O T L I G H T

With grid or without? The varied dynamics of expanding electricity access in Nigeria and Ethiopia

The most cost-effective way to expand electrification varies widely between and within countries in sub-Saharan Africa, as well as changing over time as incomes and consumption patterns change. A detailed spatial analysis for Nigeria and Ethiopia, undertaken for this report, illustrates how a range of factors – including population density, tariffs for grid-based electricity, technology costs for mini-grid and off-grid systems and the final cost of diesel at the point of consumption – affect the optimal mix of grid-connected, mini-grid and off-grid generation options.[1]

In Nigeria, higher population density and more widespread coverage by the transmission grid tends to favour on-grid supply as the most cost-effective route to electricity access (Figure 15.4). In the New Policies Scenario, this is the principal means by which the electricity rate is increased from 45% in 2012 to around 85% in 2040, providing new access to over 200 million people. In areas where grid extensions are not cost-effective, mini-grids tend to provide the preferred solution.

In Ethiopia too, a significant proportion of the population lives in areas that can be best connected through the grid. But the overall population density of Ethiopia is considerably lower – the number of people per square kilometre is half that of Nigeria – meaning that mini- and, especially, off-grid solutions play a much more prominent role. Overall, the electrification rate in Ethiopia increases from 23% in 2012 to around 60% in 2040. The 40% remaining without access to electricity in 2040 tend to be in dispersed rural communities.

The levelised cost of electricity supply for those that gain access to electricity through grid extensions is typically well below the cost of supply from mini-grids or off-grid systems. Within mini-grids and off-grid systems in both Nigeria and Ethiopia, diesel generators and solar photovoltaic provide the largest shares of electricity. Solar technologies are key to setting up a large number of off-grid systems that each supply small amounts of electricity. At higher levels of electricity consumption, there is a tendency to rely more on mini-grids powered by diesel generators and, where available, small hydropower.

---

1. The geographic analysis of the type of access that contributes to increased electrification rates in Nigeria and Ethiopia has been developed in collaboration with the KTH Royal Institute of Technology, division of Energy Systems Analysis (KTH-dESA).

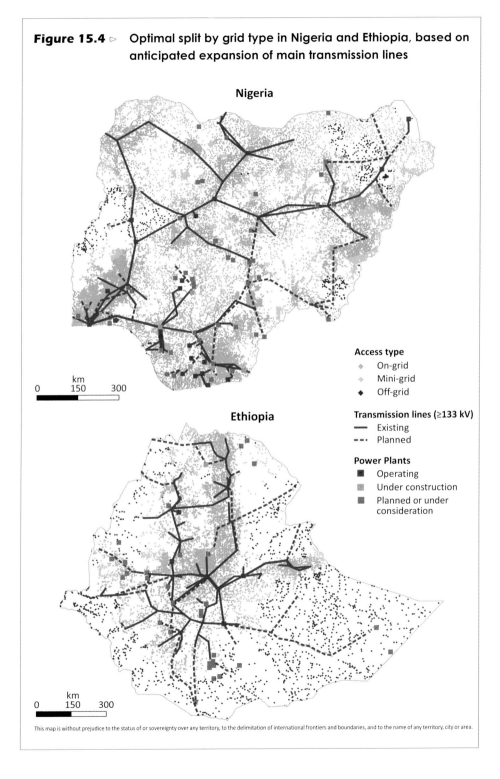

Figure 15.4 ▷ Optimal split by grid type in Nigeria and Ethiopia, based on anticipated expansion of main transmission lines

Nigeria

km
0   150   300

Access type
◆ On-grid
◆ Mini-grid
◆ Off-grid

Ethiopia

Transmission lines (≥133 kV)
—— Existing
---- Planned

Power Plants
■ Operating
■ Under construction
■ Planned or under consideration

km
0   150   300

This map is without prejudice to the status of or sovereignty over any territory, to the delimitation of international frontiers and boundaries, and to the name of any territory, city or area.

Nonetheless, beyond a certain distance, the costs of grid extensions become prohibitive, tipping the balance in favour of mini-grids or off-grid systems (Figure 15.5). The comparison between these two options turns on the density of settlement, with higher density favouring the development of mini-grids. The main technologies available for these types of systems are diesel generators or renewable energy technologies – solar photovoltaic (PV), small hydropower and small wind systems.

Figure 15.5 ▷ **Indicative levelised costs of electricity for on-grid, mini-grid and off-grid technologies in sub-Saharan Africa, 2012**

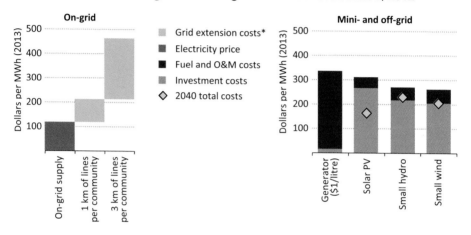

*Costs of grid extension are calculated as the average cost of extending the medium-voltage grid a certain distance (e.g. 1 km) to each community on a levelised cost basis.

Notes: Costs are indicative and could vary significantly depending on local conditions such as electricity tariffs, population density and the delivered cost of diesel. The quality of service for the different technologies also varies: additional investment in batteries or back-up power may be needed to compensate for the variability of renewables or intermittent grid supply. O&M = operation and maintenance.

The choice of generating system for mini-grid or off-grid access depends on multiple variables. The attractiveness of renewable technologies is much higher when costs are considered on a life-cycle basis, but finance must be available to meet the relatively high upfront outlay, which – even as costs come down – remains significantly above that required for a diesel generator. Generators have the advantage of providing power when needed (if fuel is available), but also face the significant downside of ongoing fuel costs, which can vary substantially. Diesel or gasoline is subsidised in some of the major oil-producing and exporting countries, notably Nigeria, Angola and Gabon, which improves the relative attraction of oil-based electricity generation to the final consumer, albeit at a fiscal and environmental cost. But even in countries where fuels are subsidised, bringing oil products to remote communities adds quickly to the final cost of generation.

There are also potential synergies between different technologies. Hybrid systems combining fossil fuel and renewables power generation (e.g. diesel and solar PV) can bring considerable flexibility and higher reliability of supply.[2] The Government of Mali plans to increase hybridisation of its mini-grids by adding PV capacity to diesel power plants. Tanzania's Rural Electrification Agency also favours hybrid diesel-PV systems for remote areas that are expected not to be connected to the main grid before 2020. An important consideration for off-grid or mini-grid systems is the ability to scale-up supply: options that provide electricity for lighting may not be sufficient to run a refrigerator, let alone to start a business. The interactions between these different factors can be complex: some renewables off-grid options can integrate well with grid extensions, but the commercial interests of diesel suppliers are undercut. Uncertainty over the likelihood and pace of grid extensions can hold back investment in other solutions.

Figure 15.6 ▷ **Technology mix for mini-grid and off-grid power generation in sub-Saharan Africa in the New Policies Scenario, 2040**

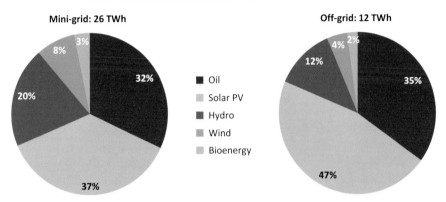

Solar PV is expected to become increasingly competitive with diesel generation, as well as with other renewable technologies. Although solar PV has one of the highest average costs of generation today, it is still an attractive option for remote areas when the transport costs for diesel are high. The solar resource is very good across many parts of sub-Saharan Africa, providing generally reliable power during the day. Renewables options alone cost less over time, benefiting from technological advances and a larger scale of production; by 2040, the delivered cost of diesel would have to be less than $0.50 per litre to be competitive with the anticipated cost of generation from solar PV. For the poorest communities, smaller solar technologies, such as solar lamps, can provide an invaluable initial step towards electricity access. Very small-scale hydro (also known as pico hydro) can generate electricity at very low average costs, where suitable waterways are close. The attraction of small-scale wind generation also depends on local conditions, but provides limited reliability on its own. A snapshot of mini-grid and off-grid power generation in 2040 (Figure 15.6) shows that solar PV provides the largest share in both mini-grid and off-grid systems, followed by diesel generators, then small hydro and wind, with smaller amounts of bioenergy.

15

<hr>

2. The speed at which battery technologies improve will also be an important variable in determining the reliability of systems powered solely by renewable energy; in the New Policies Scenario, we anticipate incremental technology improvements and learning, but no technology breakthroughs.

Bringing the electrification rate in sub-Saharan Africa up from 32% today to 70% in 2040 is estimated to cost around $205 billion in capital investment, less than one-fifth of total power sector investment in the region. Projected investment flows largely mirror the split by the type of access. Most of the investments go towards providing on-grid access, with more than half of the total required for new transmission and distribution lines. Mini-grids and off-grid solutions that are less capital-intensive and require less investment in infrastructure account for around 30% of the total. By sub-region, the largest share goes to West Africa, with $75 billion over the projection period (60% of which in Nigeria). Southern Africa follows with around $65 billion, East Africa with $50 billion and Central Africa with $15 billion.

Averaged over the projection period, this amounts to capital investment in energy access of around $7.5 billion per year, a figure not far from our current estimate of total annual power sector investment in sub-Saharan Africa (see Chapter 16). It accordingly represents a significant increase in spending for this purpose over the coming decades, reflecting declared government intentions. Achieving this level of investment will require not only steady improvements in the investment conditions for electricity access-related projects, but also rapidly improving capacity and effective co-ordination among the various actors involved. Realism, clarity and consultation over the pace of grid extension allows the stakeholders, including local communities, to make an informed assessment about the best options for expanding access, whether through co-ordinated development of the grid, mini-grids or off-grid systems. Donor programmes likewise need to be managed carefully, both to ensure that the beneficiaries are fully involved from the outset, not least to guarantee adequate and on going maintenance, and to avoid undercutting fledgling commercial energy providers.

Grid extensions are set to remain largely within the domain of the public authorities and utilities, relying on a combination of self-financing from within the power sector (if the tariff structure allows for a degree of cross-subsidisation), government budgetary allocations and funding from international donors. The spread of decentralised access also involves other public entities, such as rural electrification agencies, and a range of non-government organisations and private entities, as well as local communities. Private capital is proving to be increasingly important in rural areas: in Senegal for instance, the structuring of rural electrification concessions with private sector participation helped raise the rural electrification rate from 8% in 2000 to 26% in 2012. Small-scale options, commercialised by the private sector, may be the only way forward where there are shortcomings in public policies or institutions. New business models, often involving pre-payment or pay-as-you-go for a certain level of service, underpin some of these commercial efforts, but expensive finance, regulatory barriers in some countries and limited capacity among the poorest to pay for energy remain major constraints on scaling-up the provision of rural energy services.

Biomass: here to stay?

Solid biomass is the largest energy source in sub-Saharan Africa, accounting (in IEA data) for 70% of the region's current total final energy consumption. If South Africa is excluded, this share rises to 80%.[3] Of the estimated 280 million tonnes of oil equivalent (Mtoe) of solid biomass currently used in sub-Saharan Africa (outside South Africa), 90% is used by households, almost all being fuelwood, straw, charcoal or dried animal and human waste, mostly used as cooking fuel. Overall, cooking accounts for more than 80% of household energy usage, compared with less than 5% in Europe. Of the population of around 915 million in sub-Saharan Africa in 2012, an estimated 730 million people do not have access to clean cooking facilities (see definition in Chapter 13). Especially for those cooking indoors in poorly ventilated spaces, this means daily exposure to noxious fumes, with adverse health impacts – and the burden of collecting fuelwood – falling heavily on women and children.

The correlation between high levels of solid biomass use for cooking and high levels of poverty in much of sub-Saharan Africa can give rise to a perception that an increase in average incomes will lead to a fall in the traditional use of solid biomass, as use of other fuels increases. However, this is not borne out by historical trends: in sub-Saharan Africa, outside South Africa, GDP per capita has increased by 3% on an annual average basis since 1995 and population by 2.7% per year, but the number of people without access to clean cooking facilities has still increased by 2.4% per year, i.e. the population relying on traditional use of solid biomass has tracked population growth fairly closely, despite increasing incomes.

In our projections to 2040, demand for energy services by households across sub-Saharan Africa continues to rise along with incomes, but the mix of fuels used is relatively slow to change. Solid biomass still accounts for half of total final consumption in sub-Saharan Africa in 2040, this figure rising to almost 60% if South Africa is excluded. Looking only at fuels used for cooking (Figure 15.7), the position of fuelwood is undercut to a degree by alternative fuels in urban areas, but hardly at all among the rural population (where consumption is much larger).[4] As explored in more detail below, the way in which preferences for cooking fuels evolve is a complex question – and certainly more complex with the idea of a fixed "energy ladder", whereby choice of fuel graduates from solid to non-solid fuels as households get richer.

---

3. South Africa relies less on traditional use of solid biomass than any other country in mainland sub-Saharan Africa. Only 15% of its final energy consumption comes from bioenergy, in large part because only 13% of the population still relies on solid biomass for cooking: at the other extreme, up to 93% of total final consumption in DR Congo consists of bioenergy.

4. As the efficiency of alternative cookstoves is higher compared with traditional ones – and cooking times are generally shorter – the move away from traditional cookstoves results in significantly lower energy consumption for the same service provided.

Figure 15.7 ▷ Household energy consumption for cooking by fuel in sub-Saharan Africa* in the New Policies Scenario

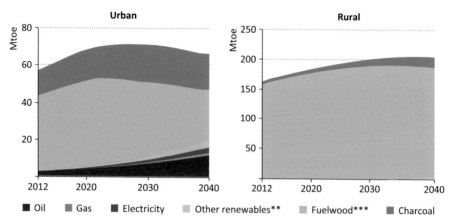

* Excluding South Africa. ** Other renewables include solar, biogas, biofuels and pellets.
*** Fuelwood includes agriculture and animal wastes.

One of the major changes in our projections is not captured in Figure 15.7, because it involves not a fuel switch but a change in the way that solid biomass is used. Gaining access to clean cooking facilities encompasses not only switching to alternative fuels, but also access to improved biomass cookstoves (fired with fuelwood, charcoal or pellets) that are more efficient and reduce household air pollution. Together, fuel switching and the spread of improved cookstoves lead to a decrease in the number of people in sub-Saharan Africa without access to clean cooking to 650 million in 2040 – a 10% decline in relation to the figure for 2012. Within the overall context of a rising population, this means, more positively, that around 1.1 billion people do have access to clean cooking facilities in 2040, two-thirds of them living in urban areas (Figure 15.8).

Figure 15.8 ▷ Population with and without clean cooking access in sub-Saharan Africa in the New Policies Scenario

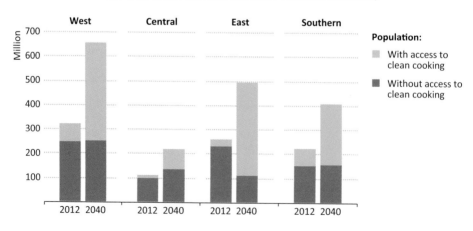

Examining the trends by sub-region, the area in which the largest decrease in the number of people without access occurs is East Africa, where currently around 70% of the urban population and 95% of the rural population rely on solid biomass. More than 350 million people gain access to clean cooking facilities in the region. Without the shift to more efficient use of biomass, the risks to an already depleting forest biomass stock would be significantly higher in East Africa (see Chapter 14), especially around urban areas where high demand for solid biomass and lack of regulation of the charcoal industry are blamed for 10-20% of the deforestation occurring in these areas (GIZ, 2014). Another notable shift is in Nigeria, where around 230 million people gain access to clean cooking facilities over the period to 2040. By contrast, in Central Africa, where forest biomass is more plentiful (and therefore relatively cheap), the population without access actually increases by 40%.

The options for access to clean cooking facilities

If economic development and income growth do not automatically lead to a decrease in the traditional use of solid biomass, then what are the factors that can lead to an improvement in access to clean cooking facilities? In practice, there are numerous considerations, besides income, that are in play, particularly the relative prices and availability of the various alternatives and scarcity of forest biomass – felt in the availability and price of fuelwood, or the time required to collect it. In some cases, an increase in solid biomass prices makes alternative fuels competitive. This is particularly likely in urban areas, where charcoal can lose out to more accessible alternative fuels.

There is also some evidence that households attach a fairly low priority to cleaner cooking facilities when deciding how to spend incremental income (compared with other options, such as food, lighting, education or communications). Policies and programmes play a major role in changing the picture, for example, through provision of finance to cover the upfront investment costs associated with more efficient cookstoves (Table 15.1), raising public awareness of the issues involved or promotion of the distribution of an alternative fuel. Programmes aimed at promoting access to clean cooking are much less prevalent than those promoting access to electricity, but they can make a major difference – as many countries in Asia and in some parts of West Africa are demonstrating.[5]

An additional complication is that, where new sources of energy for household use are adopted, this often does not mean that the use of the older one is discarded, a phenomenon known as "fuel stacking". As explored below, choices are influenced by fluctuations in relative prices, but also by confidence in the physical availability of the alternatives to solid biomass. Until distribution networks are sufficiently well established to ensure reliable supply of alternative energy carriers at reasonably predictable prices, consumers typically (and rationally) prefer to retain the option to switch.

15

---

5. Among the regional initiatives in place, ECOWAS (the Economic Community of West Africa States) initiated a programme in 2012 called the West African Clean Cooking Alliance which aims to ensure that by 2030 the entire ECOWAS population has access to efficient, sustainable and modern cooking fuels and devices.

Table 15.1 ▷ Technology characteristics of different cooking options

	Investment cost ($)	Efficiency	Daily hours for cooking	Consumption per household (toe/year)
Traditional cookstoves				
Charcoal	3 - 6	20%	2 - 4	0.5 - 1.9
Fuelwood, straw	0 - 2	11%	2 - 4	1.0 - 3.7
Alternative cookstoves				
Kerosene	30	45%	1 - 3	0.1 - 0.2
LPG	60	55%	1 - 3	0.08 - 0.15
Electricity	300	75%	1.2 - 2.4	0.07 - 0.13
Biogas digester	600 - 1 500	65%	1 - 3	0.07 - 0.14
Improved cookstoves:				
Charcoal	14	26%	1.5 - 3	0.4 - 1.5
Fuelwood	15	25%	1.9 - 3.8	0.5 - 1.6

Note: toe = tonnes of oil equivalent.
Sources: Jeuland and Pattanaya, (2012); Department of Energy at the Politecnico di Milano; IEA analysis.

Improved biomass cookstoves

More efficient cookstoves provide a very cost-effective way to reduce household air pollution as well as the environmental and other risks associated with solid biomass use. In many rural areas, where alternative fuels are either unavailable or unaffordable, they are often the only practicable way forward. There are various models and technologies available, but common features are that they reduce the amount of smoke that is released, compared with the classic three-stone open fire, and achieve a much more complete combustion of the fuel if they are correctly used and maintained. They typically operate either with fuelwood (or with biomass that is processed into pellets) or with charcoal.

Among the factors pushing the uptake of improved cookstoves in our projections, consumer preference can be important, particularly where public information campaigns have helped to make indoor pollution or economic benefits a factor in household decision making. Economic arguments in favour of improved cookstoves are strongest in areas where wood depletion or competition for wood between household and other final uses pushes up the price of charcoal (notably for urban users) and of fuelwood.[6] This is the case in East Africa, which has the lowest forest biomass stock and, in our projections, accounts for more than half of the 390 million people taking up improved biomass cookstoves in sub-Saharan Africa over the projection period. The availability of an affordable local commercial manufacturer of cookstoves can also make a major difference, as with the Kenyan Ceramic Jiko, the first models of which came into production in the 1980s. The further penetration of cookstoves is being pushed up by government and donor programmes, such as the initiative, supported

---

6. Biomass is also used for other economic activities such as brick-making, fish/meat smoking, food processing and tobacco curing.

by the Swedish Energy Agency, to distribute more than half a million improved cookstoves in both urban and rural areas in sub-Saharan Africa and GIZ's Energising Development (EnDev) programme, which aims to encourage the commercial development of improved cookstoves and expand their use.

Oil products (LPG, kerosene)

The two oil products that can provide alternatives to solid biomass, liquefied petroleum gas (LPG) and kerosene present a very different balance of risks and opportunities.[7] In addition to refinery supply, LPG is also produced from natural gas liquids, a by-product of gas production, and its market price is typically well below that of kerosene, which is a premium middle distillate fuel. However, subsidising kerosene is a decades-old tradition in some African countries, creating the misleading perception that it is the lower cost fuel. LPG is not hazard-free, but using kerosene as a household fuel involves significant risks of ingestion (often by children) or fire, as well as household air pollution. Yet kerosene has a key practical advantage, in that it can be transported and delivered with relative ease.

Even though LPG does not need a pipeline or distribution grid like natural gas, it requires dedicated infrastructure. In regions where LPG is potentially available at competitive prices, overcoming the infrastructure constraints is the key to its expanded use. Due to its volatile nature, LPG has to be transported in special pressurised trucks and stored in pressurised facilities. While using LPG has health advantages in terms of indoor air pollution, it can be dangerous if safety precautions are not followed. LPG cylinders, trucks and refuelling facilities need regular check-ups and maintenance. Trust in LPG is consequently contingent on well-functioning institutions and regulation. There is anecdotal evidence that, in Nigeria, some landlords specifically ban the use of LPG on their premises for fear of the risks arising from old, uncontrolled, sometimes damaged LPG cylinders. This is an area where government financing could usefully be deployed – facilitating upfront investments in safe LPG stoves and cylinders, rather than subsidising fuel prices, although in some situations initial fuel price subsidies may also be necessary (Box 15.1).

Another requirement for wider LPG use is the development of the supply chain from the production site or import terminal to the consumer. Strained import infrastructure, bad road conditions, vehicle breakdowns, the absence of stocks in inland storage facilities and low density of retail outlets mean that sometimes even consumers who are able and willing to pay to refuel their cylinders face a long wait for supply. This can drive many back to solid biomass, with LPG used only when it is readily available. In our projections we assume that both the infrastructure and regulatory issues of LPG supply and distribution

15

---

7. Some governments are making specific policy efforts to move residential consumers away from kerosene and towards LPG. In Nigeria, around 45 million people in urban areas currently rely on kerosene as a cooking fuel, which is both hazardous for residential use and represents a significant fiscal burden because the price is subsidised. The government has a national target to help 10 million households make the switch to LPG by 2021.

are effectively addressed. With residential oil demand expected to triple by the end of the projection period, residential LPG consumption increases rapidly to 320 thousand barrels per day (kb/d), while kerosene rises more modestly to 190 kb/d.

Box 15.1 ▷ **Bottled gas: half-full or half-empty?**

Some countries in sub-Saharan Africa have improved their clean cooking access rates by deploying government programmes promoting LPG use by households, often with the aim of reducing fuelwood collection from the country's forests. Notable examples are Senegal, Ghana and Côte d'Ivoire: Senegal and Ghana rely almost entirely on imported LPG, while Côte d'Ivoire meets about 70% of its demand through local refinery output. In Nigeria, which is the leading LPG producer in sub-Saharan Africa with around 3 million tonnes annual output, only around 0.2 million tonnes are used locally.

However, further analysis of the countries that have been lauded for their LPG access rates shows the challenges involved in establishing and maintaining a viable LPG supply chain. Senegal started its programme in the 1970s, with the promotion of a small LPG cylinder-stove, the elimination of taxes and duties on LPG equipment and the introduction of a subsidy covering smaller-volume cylinders for household use. By the 2000s, 70% of urban households had access to LPG, (though it may not have been the only fuel used for cooking). The subsidy was removed in 2010, to alleviate the financial burden on the government. Within a year, consumption dropped significantly. The government later removed value-added tax from the LPG price, which helped to restore demand. Currently, even with the highest rates of per-capita consumption of LPG in the region, the share of this fuel in household energy consumption in Senegal is only 7%.

Electricity and natural gas

Electricity does not emerge as a major alternative cooking fuel in our projections. Despite its increasing availability (see electricity access section above), it accounts – outside South Africa – for less than 10% of cooking fuel in urban areas and less than 1% in rural areas in 2040. It is already the case globally that those with access to electricity still often use solid fuels for cooking, meaning that cooking is often not seen as a priority for incremental electricity use compared with lighting and appliances.

Natural gas contributes to access to clean cooking facilities only in countries where there is significant projected production. Even in such cases, building a residential gas distribution network is justified only where income levels and population density are sufficiently high, or there are baseload customers in the vicinity, such as power plants or large industrial facilities. In our projections, we assume that some of the largest cities in gas-rich countries, notably Lagos, Dar es Salaam, Accra and parts of Mozambique develop distribution networks, starting on a relatively small scale in the 2020s and expanding steadily thereafter. More than 40 million people rely on gas for cooking purposes by the end of the projection period in 2040.

Renewable alternatives

The main renewables-based alternatives to solid biomass for cooking are biogas and solar cookers.[8] Domestic biogas digesters enable more efficient use of animal manure and human waste, converting it into methane that can be used as a cooking fuel. The size of digesters (and their costs) can vary widely, from those used by a single household to community-based systems. The technology is mature and proven, but its broad application is held back by a number of technical and non-technical constraints, including the type and availability of feedstock to determine the optimal digester size, availability of water and of local construction and maintenance services, and access to finance to cover the relatively high upfront costs. The existence and design of state support can play a critical role: Ethiopia has had a National Biogas Programme since 2008, resulting in more than 7 000 digesters being installed by the end of 2013, primarily in rural communities; but the implementation of similar programmes in Uganda and Tanzania has been slower. In our projections, more than 6 million rural households in sub-Saharan Africa rely on biogas in 2040, more than half of which are in East Africa.

There are various technologies already available to capture the sun's heat for cooking. Given the solar resource available in many parts of sub-Saharan Africa, this is an attractive option especially for those with limited access to other options, e.g. in rural areas, especially those where biomass is scarce, or in conjunction with a biomass cookstove, to ensure reliable cooking at all times of day and evening. Take-up of solar cookers depends both on their capacity to match the performance of conventional options and the existence of sufficient distribution channels. Almost 4 million households are projected to rely in full or in part on solar for cooking by 2040.

The cost of cleaner cooking

There are important distinctions between the urban and rural populations to be made in the type of access gained over the projection period, and also between different regions. Within urban areas, most of those gaining access do so by switching to other fuels, with LPG being the best placed of the alternatives. The share of urban households outside South Africa relying on traditional cookstoves decreases from 65% to 20% over the projection period. In rural areas, where household energy use continues to be dominated by solid fuels, those gaining access do so almost entirely via improved biomass cookstoves (Figure 15.9).

The investments in access to clean cooking in sub-Saharan Africa reach a cumulative $9.5 billion over the period to 2040. The main component of this sum is the cost of the improved or alternative cookstoves (the cost of infrastructure related to LPG, electricity or natural gas distribution is not included). Cookstoves require replacement, but only the cost of the first stove and half of the cost of a second stove is included, reflecting an assumed

15

---

8. There are also a number of projects, such as project Gaia in Ethiopia, that promote biofuel-based cookstoves; Ethiopia's National Biofuels Policy plan promotes ethanol both for stoves and for blending with gasoline as a transport fuel.

path towards such investment becoming self-financing.[9] Around 45% of the total is related to LPG cookstoves, 30% is for biogas digesters and 25% for solar cookers and improved biomass cookstoves.

Figure 15.9 ▷ **Primary fuel/technology used by households for cooking in sub-Saharan Africa in the New Policies Scenario**

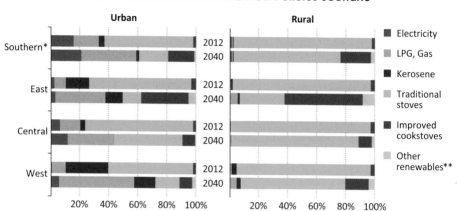

* Excludes South Africa. ** Other renewables includes biogas, biofuels and solar cookers.

Is oil the way forward for Nigeria?

Oil is a major feature of the modern history of Nigeria. The start of production in the Niger Delta in the late 1950s, quickly followed by independence from the United Kingdom, brought great aspirations of economic development, which have yet to be completely fulfilled. Since 1980, oil export has brought in more than $1 trillion in cumulative revenue (in year-2013 dollars). But, even with the re-basing of the country's GDP in 2014, which made Nigeria the largest economy in sub-Saharan Africa, on a per-capita basis the country performs no better on several key human development indicators, ranging from the level of education to life expectancy, than the sub-Saharan Africa average. This reflects the failure of successive governments to translate sizeable natural resource revenues into tangible socio-economic benefits.

The part oil will play in Nigeria's future is less easy to discern. On one hand, the revised categorisation of GDP makes it clear that the non-oil sectors of the economy, services in particular, are in practice a greater source of dynamism and national wealth than had previously been thought. On the other, the oil sector, for the moment, remains an indispensable pillar of fiscal revenue, accounting for more than half of the anticipated total in 2014. It is arguable – and our projections tend to support this view – that, insofar as Nigeria's future depends on its resource base, natural gas is as important as oil, as a means

---

9. An improved biomass cookstove typically requires replacement every 2-4 years, stoves using LPG every 5-15 years, those using kerosene every 4-6 years.

of generating power and of powering industrial development. But, if gas is indeed the way forward for Nigeria, then many of the constraints affecting the oil sector will have, in any case, to be overcome.

Nigeria has, by a distance, the largest oil resource base in sub-Saharan Africa. Yet a sobering indicator of the state of the oil sector is that, from around 2016 until the early 2020s in our projections, Nigeria is overtaken as Africa's largest producer of crude oil by Angola (Figure 15.10). During this period, Angola is also likely to be Africa's largest crude oil exporter.[10] This situation is reversed later in our projection period, as Nigerian crude output edges higher to 2.2 million barrels per day (mb/d) by 2040 and total liquids production, buoyed by natural gas liquids, reaches 3 mb/d.

Figure 15.10 ▷ Nigeria and Angola conventional oil production in the New Policies Scenario (crude and natural gas liquids)

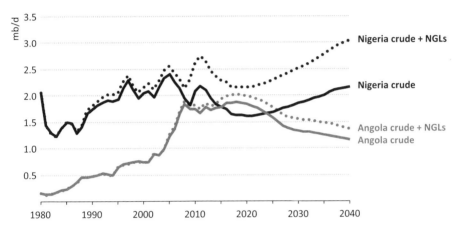

Note: NGLs = natural gas liquids.

Signs of this role reversal between Nigeria and Angola have been present for a while. Upstream investments have been flowing more readily to Angola in recent years.[11] A telling comparison is between the extent of the "pipeline" of major offshore projects in the two countries (Figure 15.11). Although Angola has seen some slowing of commitments to new projects since a tightening of fiscal terms in 2006, more than 1.3 mb/d of nameplate capacity is due to come into operation between 2014 and 2020, compared with 0.9 mb/d in Nigeria. More telling still is that only 40% of the planned capacity in Nigeria has passed the final investment decision (FID), whereas 70% of the planned capacity in Angola has already passed this milestone. In the last year, only Total has taken a final investment decision in

15

---

10. Angola had a taste of this position in May 2014, when monthly exports from Nigeria dipped below those of Angola, largely due to theft and sabotage-related outages.

11. Nigeria has not held a licensing round for new exploration acreage since 2007 (a promised round of marginal fields has not materialised so far in 2014), whereas Angola has held pre-salt rounds, offshore in 2011 and onshore in 2013. In the ten years to 2013, Angola drilled 166 exploration and appraisal wells in deep water while Nigeria drilled 144.

Nigeria (Egina project). A key obstacle in Nigeria is uncertainty over regulatory provisions, with the much-delayed passage of the Petroleum Industry Bill (Box 15.2). A Nigerian Senate Committee has estimated that $28 billion of upstream investment is dependent on the passage of this legislation: until commercial decision-makers are in a position to evaluate their projects against a more-or-less well-defined set of fiscal and regulatory conditions, continued project delays are inevitable.

Figure 15.11 ▷ **Comparison of planned projects in Nigeria and Angola**

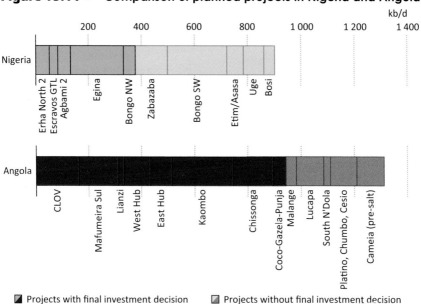

☑ Projects with final investment decision   ☑ Projects without final investment decision

Notes: Figure includes projects of more than 20 kb/d that are beyond the design phase and planned for delivery between end-2013 and 2020. Capacities are name-plate production capacities. Dark shading represents projects for which the final investment decision has been taken. Total's CLOV project saw first oil in June 2014.

Sources: Company reports; IEA analysis.

Box 15.2 ▷ **Will Nigeria's Petroleum Industry Bill see the light of day?**

The wide-ranging Petroleum Industry Bill (PIB), which was first drafted in 2008, aims to resolve two key – and intensely political – questions for the oil and gas sector:

■ How the government can maximise its benefits from hydrocarbon resource development, while still encouraging efficient private investment.

■ How revenue from the sector will be distributed and used among the various layers of government and administration.

It has a particular focus on measures necessary to increase domestic gas supply. All stakeholders agree that sweeping fiscal and non-fiscal reforms are sorely needed, but finding the right balance in a comprehensive and detailed piece of legislation has made its progress into law very slow and difficult. The provisions for revenue distribution between the 36 states and 774 local governments in Nigeria are particularly contentious.

From the perspective of future investment flows, two issues stand out. The first is the detailed provision on licensing, concessions, fiscal terms and cost allocation that will have a strong impact on investors' assessment of risk and return. The contractual system for deepwater projects is particularly sensitive. The deepwater production sharing contracts, which have been awarded since 1993 with a view to encourage frontier exploration, are now seen by many as too generous to the companies: technology advances have meant that the sliding-scale provision, whereby royalties decrease with increasing water depth, is more favourable than anticipated. The government would also like to gain more benefit from oil prices which are higher than were estimated in 1993, when oil was at $20/barrel. Analysis of the PIB, as currently drafted, suggests that it would increase government accruals slightly for onshore and shallow water operations (to more than 90%), but have a much more significant impact (from 50% towards 80%) on deepwater projects. Detractors argue that any revenue windfall from this will be short-lived if further investment and future production do not materialise. The PIB would also have strong implications for the institutional set-up of the oil sector, introducing both a crucial separation of duties between policymaking, regulatory compliance and commercial operations, and the unbundling of the NNPC to form a commercially viable, partially privatised entity that can be a stronger player in its own right and in dealing with international companies.[12]

There is a growing realisation that, although all stakeholders are aligned on the overall aims, the PIB may be too ambitious to survive as a single, comprehensive piece of legislation. Consultations in 2014 have suggested that it be broken into its constituent parts, which could then be considered as separate pieces of legislation – a pragmatic approach but one that could come at the cost of overall coherence and consistency. For the moment, uncertainty persists, but our projections assume that a more stable regulatory and fiscal environment, reflecting the key aims of the PIB, is achieved by 2020, providing a stimulus for upstream investment and a particular boost to the gas sector.

Oil theft and sabotage

Uncertainty over the regulatory environment is only one of the challenges facing Nigeria's oil sector. A more pressing immediate concern is the impact of unrest and militant activity in the Niger Delta region, which results both in oil theft and sabotage to the energy infrastructure. This has been a problem in Nigeria for many years, but the scale has increased. No hard numbers are available on the volume of crude that is stolen, but we estimate it to be just over 150 kb/d, when pilfering from crude trunk lines and product

---

12. The draft PIB, though, would give significant discretionary power to the Ministry of Petroleum, including the right to set royalty levels which are not specified in the bill.

theft have been added to theft between wellheads and the fiscal metering points in the Niger Delta (Figure 15.12). Additional losses come from deferred production due to damage to pipelines and other infrastructure. Together these losses add up to an annual average total of about 335 kb/d, or around 14% of total output. A distinction can be made between small-scale oil theft, which typically feeds local artisanal refineries that illegally supply the domestic market, and theft on an industrial scale by well-organised criminal groups using sophisticated techniques and with both the financial strength and international reach to support their operations.[13]

Oil theft brings with it a range of severe consequences. The most visible is that the environment in the Niger Delta has been severely compromised by the tapping and sabotage to pipelines that are always accompanied by some degree of oil spillage. The primitive technologies used in illegal bush refineries produce only limited amounts of refined product; it is estimated that more than 70% of crude is wasted in this type of operation. The environmental damage resulting from dumping the residues is widespread and affects agriculture, fisheries and the quality of water sources.

The way that oil theft sustains militant groups, and the concurrent weakness of administration in parts of the Delta region, also constrains adequate provision in the region of basic services, including piped water, electricity, health and education (Box 15.3). The revenues from selling 150 kb/d could amount to more than $5 billion per year, equivalent to the total sum budgeted in 2013 for federal spending on education and health together. This is also the annual amount that would be required, in our estimation, to fund universal access to electricity to all Nigerians by 2030.

The leaks in the Nigerian oil system are not confined to the upstream. Nigeria has four main refineries, two in Port Harcourt and one each in Kaduna and Warri, with a combined installed capacity of 445 kb/d. A history of poor maintenance and lack of investment in these refineries, particularly during the periods of military rule, resulted in the effective capacity in 2013 being only one-fifth of this figure. NNPC is responsible for keeping the domestic market adequately supplied with oil products; product demand is around 400 kb/d and NNPC in 2013 was allocated 435 kb/d of crude for this purpose. The nominal capacity of Nigeria's refineries is sufficient to meet this level of demand, but effective refining capacity of less than 100 kb/d means that other, often opaque arrangements are made, including sending crude to neighbouring countries to be refined, swapping crude for products through traders and selling crude to buy products.

---

13. It is difficult to track the destination of oil stolen in Nigeria but, given its limited refinery capacity the vast majority of this oil is thought to be exported illegally to international markets. This often involves the use of barges and small tankers that transport oil through the dense network of swamps and estuaries to larger vessels positioned offshore.

Box 15.3 ▷ **Tackling oil theft**

Oil theft is a multi-faceted issue, symptomatic of problems that stretch well beyond the energy sector. Potential solutions involve remedies that go well beyond the immediate issue of criminal activity. A lasting resolution must involve a consistent effort to tackle the main societal problems in the Delta region, including high unemployment, poverty and a lack of infrastructure and public services, in order to demonstrate that development of this national resource can bring tangible benefits to the local population. Weak institutions and corruption not only allow the theft to take place, but stifle efforts to address it.

In concert with a broader approach to address these points, more targeted measures in the following areas could also be effective in limiting oil theft and related activities:

- **Enhance pipeline protection, measurement and monitoring:** preventative measures cannot work in the absence of effective Nigerian law enforcement, but are essential to reduce access to pipelines, detect leaks and intrusions, improve response times and to pin down the nature and extent of the theft. Technology can contribute, but cannot provide a complete answer. Bringing local communities on-board is much more challenging, but essential.

- **Prevent stolen oil from getting to market:** a key measure to deter theft is to make stolen oil difficult to monetise. In the Delta, this includes marine patrolling of the main estuaries through which oil is transported to international waters. Other measures include improved control of documentation (bills of lading) for cargoes and increased oversight of purchases by refineries.

- **Follow the money:** intelligence on the financial flows associated with stolen oil is essential if those responsible beyond the immediate low-level participants are to face prosecution. This means identifying suspicious financial transactions and repositories, and cracking down on money-laundering.

The Nigerian experience underlines the problems that arise when there is little or no local gain from the development of a national resource. Early consultation and investment in local infrastructure and services is essential if public consent to resource development is to be obtained and maintained. Good measurement and transparency are essential to prevent flows of oil or money from being stolen. But perhaps the most important lesson from Nigeria is that theft must not be allowed to grow unchecked. Nigeria's difficulties at times seem intractable because the problem has been allowed to grow to a scale where the techniques can be very sophisticated, the groups involved very well-financed, and the vested interests well-entrenched.

15

Figure 15.12 ⊳ **Average daily oil production and distribution in Nigeria, 2013**

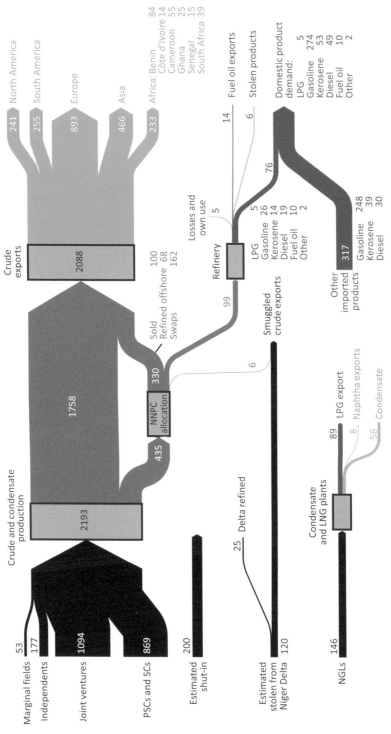

Notes: Numbers shown on diagram are in kb/d. Changes in storage levels account for flow imbalances. PSC = Production-Sharing Contract; SC = Service Contract

Sources: Based on NNPC annual statistical bulletin 2013; CITAC data; company reports; IEA analysis.

The outlook for oil

The development of the large and relatively accessible resources of the Delta region is constrained in our projections by considerations of cost. Costs are pushed higher by the existence of a large number of small oil fields and the difficulty of producing from swampy terrain. But a major additional barrier is the risk premium associated with operating in the Delta, due to security needs and expenditure on repair and maintenance of damaged infrastructure. The decision of some large international oil companies to divest their onshore Nigerian assets is symptomatic of their doubts over the outlook in this area, even though these divestitures also create opportunities for other players, typically local independent companies. Already in 2013, independent operators were producing nearly 100 kb/d, alongside a further 100 kb/d from the Nigerian Petroleum Development Company (NPDC), the operating arm of NNPC. The production outlook is heavily contingent on the evolution of the political and security situation in the Delta: in our projections, onshore production edges higher, to around 1 mb/d by 2040.

The production outlook for offshore areas, particularly in deep water, depends to a larger degree on the way that fiscal and regulatory issues evolve. As is the case with most deepwater projects, costs are relatively high and there are also particular pressures and bottlenecks in Nigeria arising from local content requirements (although investments are being made to bring local capacity up to the required levels). Our longer term outlook is predicated on the assumption of greater regulatory clarity being achieved by the end of this decade; with this in place, investments planned for the deepwater continue and additional resources are developed. By 2040, half of Nigeria's 2 mb/d of offshore output comes from deepwater projects (at a water depth greater than 400 metres).

With production of 3 mb/d in 2040, Nigeria remains a significant player in global oil markets: the second-largest OPEC producer outside the Middle East (after Venezuela), the largest African oil producer by a distance (well ahead of Libya and Algeria, and producing more than double the projected output of Angola). Cumulative estimated fiscal revenues from oil in the period to 2040 amount to more than $1.5 trillion. Yet, even if Nigeria were to be more successful in developing its huge resource base and managing its revenues, it is difficult to argue that oil will shape the way forward for the country. In many ways, Nigeria's prosperity depends on how quickly it can reduce its dependence on oil, by building up the non-oil sectors of the economy and broadening the tax base, so lessening the importance of petroleum fiscal revenue.

And yet the oil sector is nonetheless an important barometer of Nigeria's prospects. If investment in oil is not forthcoming, then investment in Nigeria's abundant gas resources is unlikely to materialise. In our projections, gas output – buoyed by a gradual reduction in the amounts that are wastefully flared – plays an increasingly important role in the domestic energy mix: gas more than doubles its share in the domestic energy mix by 2040 (from 9% to 23%), overtaking oil along the way and so playing a critical role in the country's

15

development.[14] All incremental natural gas production post-2020 is needed to underpin domestic economic growth, with 28 billion cubic metres (bcm) of additional supply to power generation by 2040 and 16 bcm of additional supply to industry (Figure 15.13). The list of policy conditions associated with a thriving domestic gas sector is considerably longer and more challenging than those for oil: not only a supportive framework for the upstream, but a host of pricing and regulatory reforms to govern its transportation and use on the Nigerian market.[15] Managing oil wealth has proved a stern test for Nigeria: successfully creating and nurturing a vibrant natural gas industry will be an even more imposing task.

Figure 15.13 ▷ **Gas production in Nigeria in the New Policies Scenario**

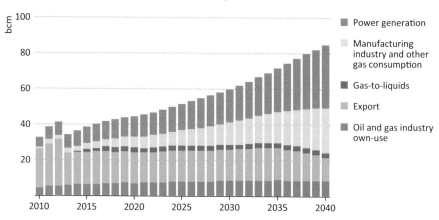

Notes: The drop in 2013 gas production was caused by an industrial dispute that interrupted operation of the LNG export terminal and also by the need during the year to repair theft-related damage to pipelines. It also reflects in part an underlying shortage of recent investment in gas field developments.

South Africa: will energy diversity deliver?

Coal is the mainstay of the South African energy system, meeting around 70% of primary energy demand and accounting for more than 90% of domestic electricity output, but its position in the energy mix is not quite as secure as such a dominant position might suggest. Most South African coal comes from the mature Witbank coal fields in the north-eastern Mpumalanga province, where coal has been produced for many decades and as a result,

---

14. Nigeria's efforts to reduce gas flaring have met with some success, but an estimated 17 bcm was still flared in 2012, the second-largest volume globally after Russia. Our assumption of further reductions in gas flaring over the projection period is underpinned by several factors, including: the completion of new gas gathering projects now underway (by Shell, Total, Eni and others); the declining share of production from oil fields not equipped with the appropriate infrastructure (new fields should by law be zero-flaring); and greater incentives to market the gas because of pricing and other regulatory reforms. The increased availability of gas previously flared accounts for almost half of incremental gas supply in the period to 2025.

15. The Nigerian Gas Master Plan, published in 2011, identifies policy actions for the sector and provides a blueprint for gas infrastructure development. Producers are required to sell gas to the Gas Aggregation Company of Nigeria at a wholesale price which is set by the government. The government has been taking steps to increase this price as part of measures to ensure the availability of gas to power plants.

coal qualities and geological conditions are deteriorating; expanding coal supply from the more distant deposits, such as the Waterberg, located near the border with Botswana, brings a requirement for new infrastructure and the likelihood of upward pressure on costs. Other clouds on the horizon arise from a broader debate around the future of the South African power system. Low fuel input costs and ample reserve margins (resulting from over-building of capacity in the 1970s and 1980s) mean that South Africa's electricity prices have been among the lowest in the world. But the balance has tightened dramatically over the last ten years. Delays in bringing on new generation capacity – including two huge 4.8 gigawatts (GW) coal-fired plants at Medupi and Kusile being built by the state-owned utility Eskom – mean that the system is now supply constrained, causing load-shedding. The average price of Eskom electricity has tripled in real terms since 2005. Expensive oil-fired peaking plants are being called upon on a regular basis to meet demand, setting an implicit benchmark against which almost all alternative sources of power provide good value. And these alternatives are starting to appear, notably a well-designed programme to support renewable power projects, which has held three bidding rounds since 2011. These three rounds resulted in commitments from private investors to almost 4 GW of grid-connected renewables capacity: the first projects started operation in late 2013.

This new context for South African energy policy is reflected in a late 2013 update to the Integrated Resource Plan (IRP) for Electricity, the main long-term planning document for generation capacity. The existing IRP, promulgated in 2011, set out a vision of long-term diversification of the power mix and moves towards lightening the carbon footprint of the sector.[16] The update responds to a new set of circumstances and uncertainties; the likely pace of demand growth, falling technology costs for renewables, the costs of nuclear (see Chapter 10) and of future coal supply, the possible rise of shale gas (a resource that South Africa is estimated to have in abundance) and natural gas discoveries in Mozambique and Tanzania. The 2013 IRP provides a starting point for our assessment of the prospective diversity of the South African power sector, how the fuel mix and costs of generation play out in the future, the questions that remain and the potential implications for the affordability of power and the environmental performance of the South African power sector.

What can displace coal?

Electricity demand in South Africa in 2012 was 212 TWh, the same level as in 2006, even though the economy had expanded by almost 3% per year in the meantime.[17] Recent circumstances in the power sector are quite atypical, including not only load-shedding but also a power buy-back programme, instigated by Eskom in late 2012, in which large industrial consumers were paid to switch off production capacity, thereby avoiding broader shortages. Nonetheless, the flattening of power consumption in recent years is

15

---

16. South Africa's president pledged at the Copenhagen climate meeting in 2009 that the country would reduce its carbon-dioxide emissions 34% below a business-as-usual case by 2020 and 42% below by 2025, provided the international community supported South Africa with financial aid and appropriate technology.

17. Net of own-use in power generation and transmission and distribution losses.

symptomatic of broader questions that arise over the trajectory of future demand. As the economy shifts away from an energy-intensive phase of development, growth in GDP should de-link from growth in power consumption. A further dampening effect on demand comes from the rapid rise in end-user prices, which have created powerful incentives for efficiency improvements, spurred on by new efficiency programmes from the national government and municipalities. Our projections of demand growth (Figure 15.14) come in at the bottom end of the range foreseen in the updated IRP.[18]

Figure 15.14 ▷ **Electricity demand growth by sector in South Africa in the New Policies Scenario**

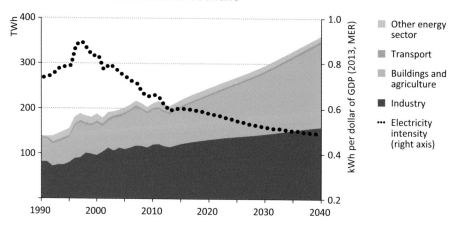

Policy-makers, concerned about over-building generation capacity, have changed the emphasis of power sector development planning. Whereas the previous approach prized large-scale capital-intensive projects (including new nuclear plants) to meet high expectations of consumption growth, the updated IRP is wary of the risks of locking in capital and technology in a fast-changing energy environment. While large-scale regional projects are still part of the picture, a more flexible approach is advocated towards the domestic market, aimed to bring production closer to demand and to reduce transmission and integration costs.[19]

The implications of this strategy are poor for nuclear power; and additional nuclear capacity is postponed in our projections until the latter part of the 2020s. They are, though, positive for non-hydro renewables, which by their nature are smaller scale and can often be situated closer to demand centres. In our projections, the share of renewables in the

18. Electricity demand for 2030 in the 2013 IRP is projected to be in the range of 345-416 TWh (this definition of demand includes own-use in the power sector and transmission and distribution losses). This already represents a lowering of the demand outlook, compared with the original IRP. The equivalent demand figure for 2030 in the *WEO* New Policies Scenario is 347 TWh. GDP growth assumptions in the New Policies Scenario are lower than those in South Africa's National Development Plan, upon which the IRP is based.

19. The current South African power system relies on a series of large power stations clustered inland near the country's mining and industrial heartland, with long transmission lines to the coast.

power mix rises from 1% today to 22% in 2040, with solar power (PV and concentrating solar power [CSP]) making up more than half of this expansion (Table 15.2). By 2040, the share of CSP in the South African generation mix is among the highest in the world. One important implication is a significant drop in the carbon dioxide (CO_2) emissions intensity of the power sector, as average emissions per kWh (which are currently among the highest in the world) are reduced by around half in 2040.

Table 15.2 ▷ **Electricity balance for South Africa in the New Policies Scenario** (TWh)

	2000	2012	2020	2030	2040
Coal	193	239	257	247	243
Oil	-	0.2	0.2	0.2	0.2
Gas	-	-	4	12	22
Hydro	1	2	4	4	4
Nuclear	13	13	13	25	47
Other renewables	0.3	0.4	16	51	84
Wind	-	0.1	5	11	17
Solar PV	-	0.1	5	17	27
CSP	-	-	2	11	20
Total generation	208	255	293	339	401
(+) Net imports	12	-5	-2	8	20
(-) Distribution losses and own-use	30	38	43	49	58
Total demand	190	212	248	298	364

The envisaged expansion in renewables is delivered mainly through continued bidding rounds for renewables capacity, of the sort currently undertaken by the Renewable Energy Independent Power Producer Procurement Programme. This programme, which has attracted a range of domestic and international project developers, sponsors and equity shareholders, has so far accounted for the lion's share of private capital attracted to the power sector, not just in South Africa but in sub-Saharan Africa as a whole.[20] As with Brazil's pioneering auction system for new capacity, it uses competitive bidding to establish the price at which participants are ready to supply power to the market; this bid price then underpins a long-term power purchase agreement. The three bidding rounds thus far have delivered a large reduction in average prices for the various renewable technologies, mainly because of increased competitive pressure as more companies became interested in participation (the total amount of power to be procured was also restricted after Round 1, with this in mind), but also because of declining unit costs. As well as large scale renewable projects, the government also plans to encourage distributed generation, predominantly rooftop solar PV.

---

20. Of the 22 power sector projects in sub-Saharan Africa registered in the World Bank's Private Infrastructure Projects database as reaching financial closure in 2012, 18 of them are renewables-based projects in South Africa.

The scale of the South African market also makes it a major player in all discussions about regional renewable energy projects. South Africa is already a major customer for the Cahora Bassa hydropower facility in Mozambique and there are other projects being considered with the South African market in mind, including an expansion of Cahora Bassa and the new Mphanda Nkuwa project in Mozambique, as well as the huge Grand Inga project in DR Congo (see Chapter 14).

Another diversification option for South Africa is natural gas. The country is a minor producer from maturing offshore fields in the south, which feed the 45 kb/d gas-to-liquids plant in Mossel Bay, but a larger importer by pipeline from Sasol-operated fields in Mozambique (see next section), used primarily by industrial consumers. The new discoveries in the north of Mozambique have stimulated interest in the expansion of regional gas trade but, given the distances involved, this is more likely to be in the form of liquefied natural gas (LNG). The main potential for increasing the role of natural gas in the South African energy mix comes from indigenous shale gas (Box 15.4).

Box 15.4 ▷ **Karoo Basin shale – a domestic gas source for South Africa?**

The large Karoo Basin in central South Africa holds significant shale gas resources, estimated at 11 trillion cubic metres (tcm) (US EIA, 2013). However, while discussion of exploiting the shale gas resource started at least six years ago, no exploration drilling or even modern seismic surveying has occurred, so figures for resources and development costs remain provisional.

Shell, Australian-based Challenger Energy and a number of other companies have been awarded exploration licenses. But in 2011 the government imposed a moratorium on hydraulic fracturing, effectively stopping activity, citing the need to develop an appropriate regulatory framework. The Karoo Basin is arid, and although sparsely populated, many communities rely on groundwater supplies. As elsewhere (see Chapter 4) concern over the possible impact of hydraulic fracturing on scarce water supplies dominates environmental concerns. Although the moratorium was lifted late in 2012, environmental opposition continues to be strong, focusing not only on water impacts, but also vehicle movements and other aspects of unconventional gas production.

The government is taking a supportive but measured approach to the development of its nascent gas industry, with significant work still to be done on the regulatory framework before any commercial shale gas activity begins in earnest. In our projections, development of shale gas in South Africa is assumed to start in the 2020s, with output rising steadily to reach 11 bcm by 2040. The absence of gas distribution infrastructure is expected to slow the uptake, so that over the projection period, South African gas use expands only slightly, from the current 3% in the primary energy mix (more than half of which is used for transformation into liquid fuels) to around 5% by 2040. The contribution to power generation rises to around 20 TWh, or 6% of total power output.

But coal remains at the centre of South Africa's energy outlook, and a critical question for the sector in a new competitive landscape is the extent of prospective upward pressures on coal costs and domestic prices. Eskom accounts for over 60% of coal consumption and is by far the main buyer of domestic coal. As things stand, most of Eskom's coal-fired generating stations are grouped around the mines in the Mpumalanga region, with relatively short transport distances. The utility procures most of its coal needs through long-term contracts that are typically priced at production cost, plus a rate of return. The main alternative market for coal producers is export: the coal fields in Mpumalanga are connected by railway to Richard's Bay Coal Terminal – the country's main export hub.[21] Coal mines that produce export-quality coal have an incentive to export any surplus that is not contracted domestically (moreover, the export options have broadened with Indian power companies willing to buy coal with high-ash content). The cost-plus coal prices paid by Eskom are typically much lower than the international coal price at Richard's Bay, even if theoretical transport cost to the export terminal plus washing and handling cost ($20-28 per tonne) are included (Figure 15.15).

Figure 15.15 ▷ **South Africa mine-by-mine coal supply curve and the average coal export price, 2013**

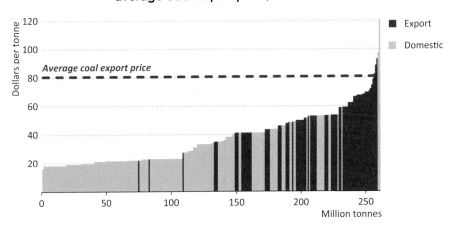

Notes: The graph shows the cash costs of South African coal mines at the point of sale. For domestic mines the point of sale is typically the mine-mouth while export mines sell on a free-on-board (ocean-going vessel) basis.

Sources: IEA analysis; Wood Mackenzie databases.

Many of the mines supplying power plants in Mpumalanga and providing exports are nearing exhaustion. New mines and expansion of existing capacity in Mpumalanga will only partially compensate for the long-term decline in production from this region. To increase

21. While throughput capacity at Richard's Bay Coal Terminal has been lifted to over 90 million tonnes per annum (Mtpa), the 580 km-railway line linking the mines to the port is currently constrained to around 72 Mtpa and other ports can handle only small quantities. Thus infrastructure bottlenecks are essentially impeding growth in South African coal exports.

production from today's 210 million tonnes of coal equivalent (Mtce) to 240 Mtce by 2040, as projected in the New Policies Scenario, South African coal producers have to move further north to greenfield projects in the Waterberg fields in Limpopo province. However, these coal fields are far from the export terminals, the existing coal-fired generation fleet and the electricity load centres.[22] The distance from the Waterberg to the coal plants in Mpumalanga is about 700 km and the distance to Richard's Bay is around 1 300 km.

Although Eskom has secured most of its coal needs for the coming years through long-term contracts, it will occasionally need to buy additional quantities on a spot basis, and then re-negotiate supply contracts over the medium term as they expire. This will take place against a backdrop of the gradual move to new coal production areas, an expansion of transport capacity to Richard's Bay, and increasing demand for lower quality coal from the international market. We assume that these pressures will bring domestic prices for coal in South Africa closer to export prices, at least for the share of the production that is of export quality.[23]

This shift in prices has an impact on our calculation of the costs of coal-fired power relative to other fuels (Figure 15.16). Yet, due to the relatively low transport distances to power stations and the high share of low quality material, coal is expected to remain on average significantly cheaper in South Africa than in most other countries.[24] Another factor affecting coal's competitive position is an envisaged gradual increase in the efficiency of coal-fired power plants. All coal-fired plants currently in operation are using subcritical technology and are hence operating at relatively low efficiencies of around 34% on average. With over 75% of current installed coal capacity built before 1990, and a typical technical lifetime of 50 years, many existing plants will need to be replaced before the end of the projection period. In our outlook, the first supercritical coal plants (the huge Medupi and Kusile plants) enter service by the end of this decade. After 2020, additional supercritical and, later, also ultra-supercritical plants are added, which push the average efficiency of the coal fleet close to 40% by 2040.[25]

---

22. New coal-fired power plants are also planned in the Waterberg region to reduce coal transportation requirements in the longer term. Since the power demand hubs in Gauteng and along the east coast are located far away from these plants, this would require an expansion of long-distance transmission lines.

23. This confluence of circumstances has nourished fears that Eskom might not be able to secure sufficient amounts of low-cost coal to satisfy power demand. This has led to a debate on whether partial nationalisation of the coal industry or the introduction of a domestic supply obligation could increase national welfare. Were this to happen, it would affect the domestic price outlook but also the likelihood of investment in new mines and transport capacity.

24. The government proposal to introduce a modest CO_2 price, envisaged for 2016, would not make a material difference to the relative costs shown in Figure 15.16. However, stricter environmental standards on other emissions could have more far-reaching implications for both coal power generation and coal-to-liquids production.

25. Part of the new fleet will be designed to use high-ash coal and discard material from coal washing combining fluidised-bed combustion with latest steam-cycle technology.

Figure 15.16 ▷ Levelised costs of power generation by fuel and technology in South Africa

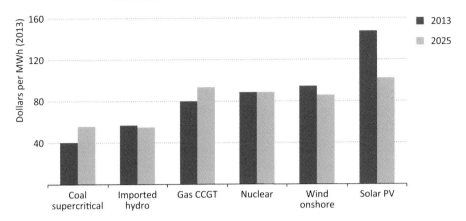

Note: Levelised costs are calculated based on an assumed weighted average cost of capital of 7%, though this may vary under certain market conditions.

The net result is that, even though rising coal prices narrow the gap between the cost of advanced coal-fired plants and alternative sources of power generation, coal remains a low-cost option for South Africa, with only imported hydro offering comparable value (demonstrating how regional integration can reduce the cost of energy). Renewables, in our estimates, become increasingly competitive and the bid system is well placed to track and take advantage of any reductions in unit costs. But the analysis suggests that commercial considerations alone will not deliver diversification of the power mix. Other considerations, such as local air pollution, reduction of CO_2 emissions, the lead times to build new capacity, and locational and grid issues need to be taken into account.

While the options appear diverse, the affordability of electricity supply looms as a key concern and, potentially, a constraint on the diversification agenda. The structure of consumption and of spending on electricity is skewed towards higher income groups, with the richest 20% of the population accounting for more than half of the total. In recent polling conducted by the Department of Energy, three-quarters of South Africans stated that the priority for government energy policy should be to keep electricity prices low: economic considerations outweighed other priorities by a considerable margin (Department of Energy, 2013). Regarding the future fuel mix, nearly a third of respondents agreed with the statement: "it does not matter which source, as long as it is the cheapest". But a quarter of respondents explicitly supported renewable energy sources, with a further 14% placing emphasis on sources that are not damaging to the environment. As elsewhere, the government will face complex choices as it pursues its energy policy objectives and needs to pursue an active policy of public engagement in the debate. But South Africa's combination of integrated policymaking, strong regulation, well-designed incentives for low carbon investment (including private investment), greater efficiency and regional integration gives it enviable strength for the task.

15

Mozambique and Tanzania: how to get best value from gas?

Major offshore gas discoveries in Mozambique and Tanzania (Figure 15.17) have created high expectations, both within the countries concerned and internationally, about the opportunities that might open up both for the domestic economy and for supply to more distant markets. In our projections, Mozambique and Tanzania are among the main sources of sub-Saharan gas supply growth, contributing 44% of the 170 bcm increase in the region's gas output. But, even as the extent of East Africa's energy resource wealth becomes clearer, so the focus shifts to questions above the ground: how can gas, considered a premium fuel in many parts of the world, foster local industrial and economic development in fast-growing but still very poor countries? And what are the options and risks facing national policy-makers as they attempt to maximise the value of their gas resources?

Gas is more challenging to develop than other fossil fuels. In particular, its low energy density means that the end-product is more difficult and costly to transport. With oil discoveries, project developers can proceed safe in the knowledge that they can expect readily to find a buyer. By contrast, in the absence of a large and proximate market, gas tends to stay in the ground until there are clear and specific commitments as to its use, as well as clarity on how it will reach the relevant end-user. Achieving these is a delicate and complicated process, requiring co-ordination along the value chain, anchor volumes of demand at sufficient scale and adequate regulation of markets and networks.

Developing gas resources is also a hugely capital-intensive process, with cost estimates for the first phase of upstream and LNG development in Mozambique being well above the country's entire annual GDP. In addition, the gas resource is very dry, i.e. with a very low share of the natural gas liquids that can often considerably boost project economics. Although favourably located in international terms, in relative proximity to the fast-growing markets of Asia, local gas consumption and infrastructure – particularly in Mozambique – are at a very early stage of development.

Options for gas utilisation

Appraisal of the gas discoveries made since 2010 off the coast of northern Mozambique and southern Tanzania is still underway but, based on the information available, the amount of gas recoverable from the new discoveries could be in excess of 5 trillion cubic metres (tcm), most of which is in Mozambique. Both countries only used a combined 1 bcm in 2012 in their domestic markets (0.02% of the estimated resource), most of this in Tanzania. Against this backdrop, it is clear that the main market for gas is export, bringing revenues to the national budget which can be used to fund domestic infrastructure and other spending priorities.

Figure 15.17 ▷ **Main gas fields and infrastructure in Mozambique and Tanzania**

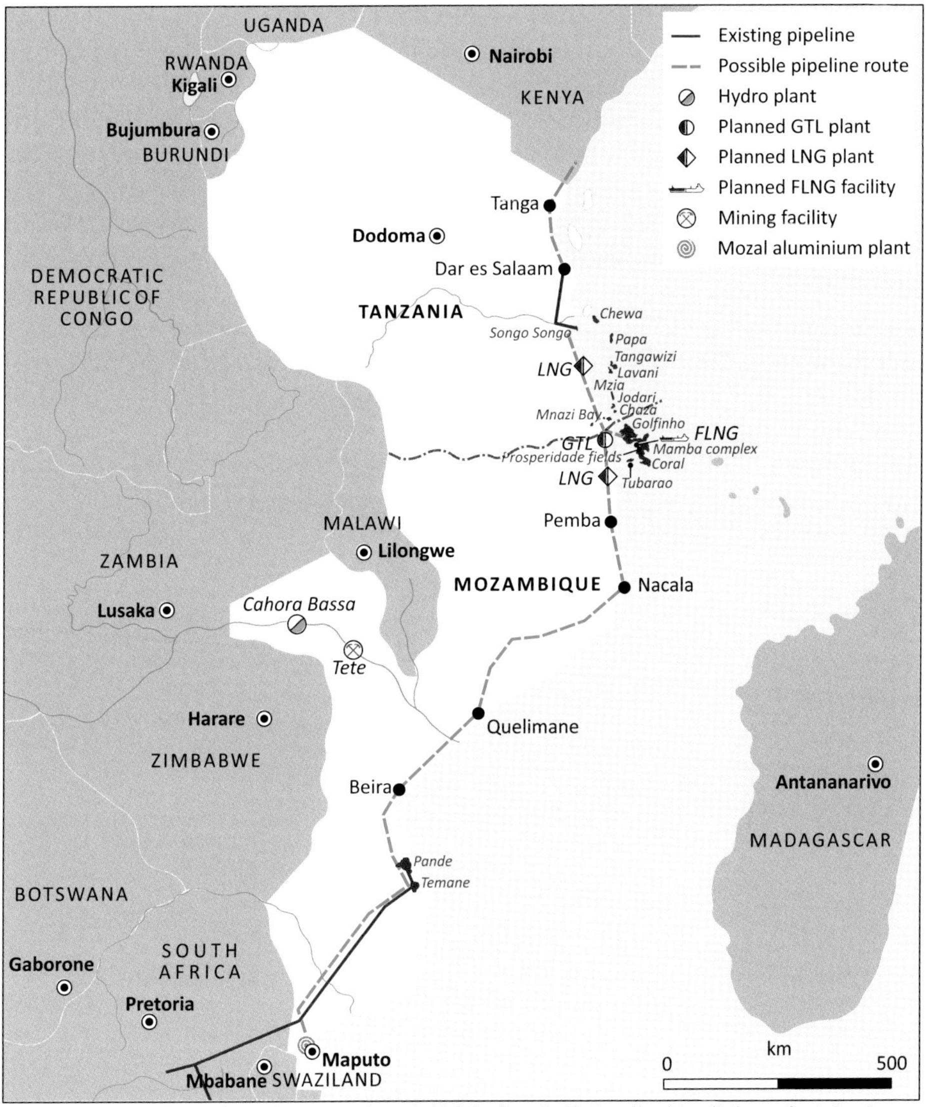

Legend:
- ─── Existing pipeline
- --- Possible pipeline route
- ⊘ Hydro plant
- ◑ Planned GTL plant
- ◈ Planned LNG plant
- ⌐ Planned FLNG facility
- ⊗ Mining facility
- ◎ Mozal aluminium plant

This map is without prejudice to the status of or sovereignty over any territory, to the delimitation of international frontiers and boundaries and to the name of any territory, city or area.

In our projections, LNG facilities start operating in Mozambique in the early 2020s, with four LNG trains and a floating LNG (FLNG) facility on stream by the latter part of the decade. By 2040, further expansion brings total projected gross export capacity in Mozambique to 60 bcm per year (43 million tonnes of LNG). LNG export from Tanzania is anticipated on a smaller scale and to start somewhat later than in its southern neighbour, with one train fully operational in the 2020s and a second following in the 2030s. These expectations for the timing of the start of new LNG facilities are later than those envisaged by the companies involved. The reason is not related to the size or quality of the resource base, but rather to multiple factors that could contribute to delays in project implementation. The region in which the LNG facilities are planned – particularly on the Mozambique side – is remote with very limited infrastructure, complicating all aspects of the construction phase.[26] There are arguments in favour of co-operation between different consortia on either side of the border: in Mozambique to develop the parts of the Prosperidade and Mamba prospects that straddle Areas 1 and 4, and in Tanzania to combine the resource bases of smaller fields in different license areas (Table 15.3). But resolving whether and how this co-operation might work in practice is likely to be a complex and lengthy business. There is also residual uncertainty over the legal and regulatory frameworks, notably in Tanzania, where a constitutional review is underway that could affect natural resource ownership. Last but not least, there are questions about the marketing of the LNG to prospective buyers, given that strong competition between suppliers is expected in the early 2020s (see Chapters 4 and 16).

Table 15.3 ▷ **Main new upstream gas projects in Mozambique and Tanzania**

Block / main fields	Partners	Status
Mozambique		
Area 1: Golfinho, Tubarao, Prosperidade	**Anadarko** (26.5%), Mitsui (20%), ONGC (16%), ENH (15%), Bharat (10%), PTT (8.5%), Oil India (4%)	Area 1 is closest to the Mozambique coastline. Discoveries in 2010-2012; part of the Mamba field (Area 4) straddles the border with Area 1
Area 4: Coral, Mamba	**Eni** (50%), CNPC (20%), Galp Energia (10%), KOGAS (10%), ENH (10%)	Discoveries in 2011-2013, part of the Prosperidade field (Area 1) straddles the border with Area 4
Tanzania		
Blocks 1,3,4: Chaza, Jodari, Mzia, Papa, Chewa	**BG** (60%), Ophir (20%) Pavilion (20%)	Nine discoveries in total in 2010-2014, although considerably smaller than those in Mozambique
Block 2: Lavani, Tangawizi, Piri,	**Statoil** (65%), ExxonMobil (35%)	Six discoveries in 2012-2014

Notes: Existing production in Mozambique comes from the Sasol-operated Pande and Temane fields (connected by pipeline with South Africa) and in Tanzania mainly from the Songo Songo field. These were discovered in the 1960-1970s, but only started operation in the 2000s. No final investment decision has yet been taken on any of the projects in the table above.

New gas developments are a major potential source of fiscal revenue to the host governments. Our projections envisage a cumulative $115 billion over the period to 2040 in Mozambique and about $35 billion in Tanzania. This income flow provides an opportunity to step up the pace of investment in power generation, water supply and sanitation, transport, education and health. Prudent borrowing against future income would allow

---

26. Construction risk and onshore environmental impacts are limited with floating LNG facilities, which can be manufactured at a distance and towed into place; but the downside is the absence of economies of scale if facilities need to be expanded. There are also fewer benefits in terms of onshore development, which can be a barrier for acceptance by host governments.

this investment to start well in advance of first gas being produced.[27] However, LNG projects and their associated revenue streams do not satisfy the desire of the countries concerned to see gas become a direct driver for national development, whereas there is a widely shared determination among governments – and a strong expectation from the public – that the benefits of these gas developments should be felt more directly. Two issues dominate this debate: that there should be the maximum amount of local sourcing during the construction phase of the upstream and LNG projects, i.e. requirements for local content; and that every effort should be made to build up domestic gas-consuming sectors.

The issue of local content is rising in prominence in both countries. Tanzania is in the process of adopting legislation providing that training and procurement opportunities open up for local firms. Mozambique is not far behind, although on this issue as on others, they may take a less prescriptive stance. In both countries there is an acute shortage of capacity to provide goods and services for the gas industry and, for now, this limits the potential impact in terms of employment and value added. Capacity will take time to develop, and will tend to start in areas such as logistics and catering, before progressing to more skilled areas like equipment maintenance, welding, fabrication and component manufacturing. Local content provisions that run too far ahead of capacity can quickly lead to bottlenecks in the supply chain.

Domestic gas-consuming sectors also have to be built from a very low base (Figure 15.18), although, in Tanzania, gas from the Songo Songo field already feeds power stations and provides process heat to local industrial facilities. Compressed natural gas (CNG) is also used as a transport fuel in Dar es Salaam. The ambition to expand domestic consumption is clearly expressed in Tanzania's Natural Gas Policy, adopted in 2013, which states that the government shall "ensure that the domestic market is given first priority over the export market in gas supply" and this is reflected in an obligation on gas producers to sell a portion of their output to the domestic market. Larger resources and anticipated production volumes means that a greater share of Mozambique's gas is destined for export as LNG, but here too – as expressed in a Gas Master Plan and a new Petroleum Law adopted in 2014 – Mozambique is determined to create new outlets for domestic gas supply. [28]

The dilemma facing both countries, and particularly Mozambique, is that building up a sizeable domestic gas-consuming sector is a challenging and expensive undertaking. Tanzania is in a slightly easier position, because of the relative proximity of the gas discoveries to the major consumption centre of Dar es Salaam: there is already a pipeline link from Songo Songo and a major Chinese-built coastal pipeline, with 8 bcm/year capacity,

15

---

27. In the case of Mozambique (and many other African jurisdictions), capital gains tax applied to the sales of stakes in the various blocks – irrespective of the locations of the companies concerned – has already been a major source of early income from the gas discoveries.

28. Of the total gas currently produced and exported to South Africa from the Sasol-operated Pande and Temane fields, around 5% is consumed in Mozambique in industry, transport (as CNG) and the residential sector.

is due to start operation in 2015 (well in advance of the start of production from the major offshore discoveries). In Mozambique, by contrast, the gas discoveries are more than 2 000 km from the capital, Maputo, and there is very limited access to major population or industrial centres. International experience offers little guidance for countries seeking to expand gas consumption from this starting position (Box 15.5).

Figure 15.18 ▷ **Gas consumption and export in Mozambique and Tanzania in the New Policies Scenario**

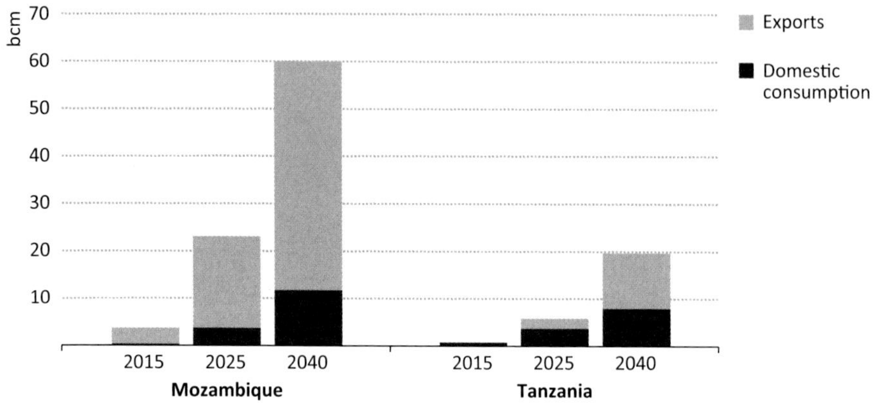

Notes: Mozambique exports in 2015 are from the Pande and Temane fields to South Africa. Domestic consumption includes the gas used in the liquefaction process for LNG.

Both Tanzania and Mozambique are looking for sizeable projects (so-called mega-projects) that can buttress the development of the domestic gas sector. The power sector seems an obvious place to start. A high share of the population in both countries is without access to electricity. This is combined with an urgent need in Tanzania to reduce its use of high cost emergency power plants that burn oil products. But putting in place sizeable power projects requires a high degree of assurance about the adequacy of future revenue streams, both for power generators and gas suppliers. The record here has been mixed in Tanzania, with Tanesco, the state power utility, running up large debts to the operators of the Songo Songo field.

In Mozambique, the nearest existing consumption centres to the gas discoveries are the port cities of Pemba and Nacala, but these are not now major industrial centres. Moreover, the further south that gas penetrates into Mozambique, the higher the infrastructure cost and the greater the challenge of competition from other indigenous energy sources (coal, large hydro and other renewables), a consideration that holds back the growth of gas-fired power in our projections. In the New Policies Scenario, gas use for power generation in Mozambique and Tanzania rises from 0.8 bcm in 2012 to 3 bcm in 2025 and 9 bcm in 2040, with Tanzania accounting for 40% of the eventual total. By 2040, gas provides more than one-third of combined electricity production from the two countries.

Box 15.5 ▷ Building up a customer base for natural gas

Historical data for natural gas use suggest that a rapid expansion in domestic gas use has, by and large, occurred only in countries which already have a large and diversified base of power generation and industrial assets, parts of which can switch to gas and other parts of which can use gas to fuel their expansion. With investment in distribution systems, gas can also make quick in-roads as a fuel for residential use where population density is high. A notable example was in West Germany in the 1970s, following the start of large-scale gas imports from the Soviet Union: domestic gas use increased by almost 50 bcm in the space of ten years. The United Kingdom and the Netherlands also achieved large increases in domestic demand to accommodate the rise in their gas production.

For countries without a large existing base of potential consumers, the speed at which gas consumption can be developed is much more constrained. Large "anchor" projects are essential to underpin the economics of pipelines and other gas infrastructure, with investment co-ordinated with the upstream to ensure that gas output finds a ready market. These projects come in two categories: those using process heat from gas combustion (mainly gas-for-power, but also industrial plants for steel or cement manufacture, or refineries) and those using gas primarily as a feedstock (as for gas-to-liquids technology, or the production or ammonia, urea and methanol).

Trinidad and Tobago provides an interesting case of a gas-producing country that, with limited potential for growth in gas demand from the residential and power sectors, chose to stimulate gas demand in domestic industry. With ample and relatively cheap gas supply, the country became the world's largest exporter of ammonia and the second-largest exporter of methanol. However, these are both capital-intensive export-oriented sectors, that have generated revenue but have had only a relatively limited impact on domestic employment. Other initiatives in Trinidad and Tobago have been less successful: a gas-to-liquids plant approved in 2005 was never finished and was eventually dismantled and sold for scrap. Much depends on the availability of markets, Trinidad and Tobago is fortunate because of its proximity to the large North American market. Landlocked Turkmenistan, by contrast, has many fewer options to monetise its gas which is why petrochemical and other initiatives to use the gas domestically (outside the power sector) have enjoyed only limited success.

Outside the power sector, the most promising avenues for industrial gas consumption, apart from the LNG facilities themselves, would be the manufacture of various chemicals, notably fertilisers (ammonia, urea) and methanol, as well as gas-to-liquids projects. All of these are under consideration and involve different degrees of capital intensity and commercial risk (Figure 15.19). The chemicals projects would rely to varying degrees on exports: local and regional demand for fertiliser is higher than for methanol, but a reasonable-sized plant of either type would need to target international markets. While

15

capturing additional value, compared with gas export, and diversifying commodity price risk away from gas, these projects would still be subject to significant hazards from fluctuating international prices. A gas-to-liquids project would use a much larger volume of gas, with the attractions related more to import substitution and the possibility of selling a gas-based product into a market that has different dynamics; but this option has the highest (and least certain) capital costs.

Figure 15.19 ▷ **Indicative capital intensity and gas utilisation for different large-scale uses of gas**

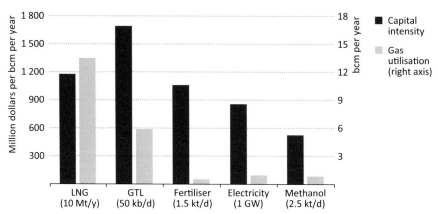

The relative virtues of the various mega-project proposals will require careful and transparent assessment by the respective national authorities, based on a clear vision of how gas will be priced on the domestic market. What is already evident though, is that such mega-projects are unlikely to spread the benefits of gas more widely through society by themselves. They are highly capital-intensive, with low direct impacts in terms of employment.[29] To ensure a broader impact, these projects need to act as catalysts for developing pipelines and other infrastructure, facilitating gas distribution to smaller commercial and residential consumers along the way. This effect is already visible in Dar es Salaam, where the delivery of piped gas to the Ubungo power plant on the outskirts of the city has allowed businesses, ranging from bottling plants and food processing to textile and glass manufacturers, to tap into this source of gas supply, some switching from more expensive oil products. While typically accounting for a relatively small share of pipeline throughput, these end-users can play a much larger role in job creation. Distributing fiscal revenues from exports to the community is a relatively simple task: reaching them with reliable gas supply is much more difficult, but potentially represents a much longer-lasting source of value to the economy.

---

29. These characteristics are shared with some of the main mega-projects implemented thus far in Mozambique. Mozal (a major aluminium plant) and the Cahorra Bassa hydropower plant were multi-billion dollar capital investments; (they account for around 10% of GDP and 60-70% of Mozambique's exports by value), but employ less than 0.05% of the labour force (IMF, 2014).

Chapter 16

Building a path to prosperity
How can sub-Saharan Africa make the most of energy?

Highlights

- Securing a more prosperous future for sub-Saharan Africa depends on progress in three areas of energy policy: increased investment in supply, in particular of electricity, to meet the region's growing energy needs; improved management of natural resources and associated revenues; and deeper regional co-operation. The pace of change will be set by the quality and integrity of the public institutions concerned, as well as the transparency and accountability of their operations.

- Since 2000, two out of every three dollars invested in sub-Saharan energy has gone to produce energy for export. Some of the policy and regulatory constraints holding back a much-needed expansion in domestic power supply are eased in the New Policies Scenario, bringing in a new cast of investors including more private companies. Over the period to 2040, two-thirds of investment in the energy sector goes towards providing energy to be consumed within sub-Saharan Africa itself.

- Projected oil and gas output to 2040 generates more than $3.5 trillion in cumulative fiscal revenues, an amount higher than the $3 trillion invested in the sub-Saharan energy sector over the same period. These revenues are though concentrated in a much smaller group of countries, first among them Nigeria followed by Angola, that face a stern challenge to manage them efficiently. Despite the large anticipated increase in gas output, around 90% of hydrocarbon fiscal revenues come from oil.

- Regional co-operation is a major element of Africa's vision for its future, providing a cost-effective way to increase the availability and security of energy supply. Energy trade rises, but some major projects, notably for hydropower, still face technical, political and social hurdles that increase reliance on expensive alternatives.

- The New Policies Scenario sets a demanding agenda for Africa's policy-makers, but hardly reflects the full potential of energy to act as an engine for prosperity. Opportunities are missed, or not captured in full. Power supply remains unreliable and more than half a billion are left without access to electricity and clean cooking facilities. In an African Century Case, more rapid energy development, set against a backdrop of improved governance, gives a 30% boost to GDP by 2040.

- An extra $450 billion in power sector investment in the African Century Case, accompanied by deeper regional integration, accelerates progress with energy access, especially in rural areas. More reliable and affordable power supply removes a major obstacle to business development: every $1 invested in power supply generates more than $15 in incremental GDP. Oil and gas production is higher and a larger share of the resulting revenue is invested productively in reversing deficiencies in essential infrastructure.

Towards a better-functioning sub-Saharan energy sector

The two faces of energy, its positive and negative aspects, are more clearly visible in sub-Saharan Africa than in any other part of the world. As underlined in earlier chapters, energy is a critically important enabler of social and economic development and a source of revenue for much-needed investment in infrastructure and other purposes. But – particularly where electricity is lacking or resources are poorly managed – it can also become a source of division, conflict, environmental degradation, poverty and under-performance.

What conditions will need to be met for the positive contribution of energy to predominate? In this chapter, we focus on three areas that are critical, in our judgement, to a better-performing sub-Saharan African energy sector.

- **A step-change in investment in domestic energy supply:** since 2000, we estimate that two out of every three dollars invested in sub-Saharan Africa went to produce energy for exports, with only one dollar in three going towards providing energy to be consumed within the region. Increasing investment in the sub-Saharan power sector is essential to bring this equation into line with the region's energy needs.

- **Better management of the region's resources:** sub-Saharan Africa has ample energy resources, both fossil fuel and renewable, but the opportunities that these offer to support sustained economic growth are often missed. A glaring example is the way that deficiencies in essential infrastructure in many countries are perpetuated by ineffective or corrupt misuse of revenues from fossil fuel extraction.

- **Deeper regional energy co-operation:** expanding cross-border trade can be a very cost-effective way to increase the reliability and affordability of energy supply, but this is often hindered in practice by a range of technical and political barriers. The lack of regional scale is a particular obstacle for the development of sub-Saharan Africa's large remaining hydropower potential.

These conditions are inter-linked, not least because their achievement depends in large part on the broader standards of governance that countries succeed in maintaining, both inside and outside the energy sector.[1] Governance indicators are generally weak in sub-Saharan Africa, compared with other parts of the world (although stronger in some southern parts of the region, notably Botswana, Namibia and South Africa), implying substantial risks arising from policy and regulatory uncertainty, inadequate protection of contracts and property rights, poor-quality administration and the actions of governments that are only weakly accountable to their citizens. Tackling these weaknesses will require

---

1. Governance is defined as "the traditions and institutions by which authority in a country is exercised" and encompasses such factors as the process by which governments are selected, monitored and replaced; the capacity of the government to effectively formulate and implement sound policies; and the respect of citizens and the state for the institutions that govern economic and social interactions among them (Worldwide Governance Indicators Project, 2014).

actions across a broad front; particularly important elements from an energy perspective are investment in the skills and knowledge required for a modernising energy economy and the transparency and consultation on energy policies that is essential to winning public consent.

In this chapter, the discussion is viewed initially through the lens of the projections in the New Policies Scenario. This scenario sets a demanding agenda by taking into account the energy policy ambitions and targets of African countries, but accompanied by a careful assessment of the prospects for realising them in full, bearing in mind the difficulties that often arise with securing the necessary budgetary and financial support and, crucially, in ensuring adequate performance of the relevant institutions and administrative mechanisms that formulate and implement policies. This means that official targets are often not met in our projections, or their achievement is postponed.

The energy path outlined in the New Policies Scenario therefore represents a realistic, but not a fully satisfactory outcome for sub-Saharan Africa. This scenario does not reflect the full potential of the energy sector to act as an engine for economic transformation and growth. Some opportunities are missed, or not captured in full. Progress remains uneven and constrained. Constraints on the availability or reliability of energy supply continue to act as a brake on economic activity and welfare. Power generation steps up, but the problem of unreliable supply could be expected to persist in many countries; moreover, over half a billion people are left in 2040 without access to electricity.

Much more could be done. What might be achievable in sub-Saharan Africa is illustrated in an African Century Case, in which more rapid development of the energy sector, set against a broader backdrop of improved governance, plays a significant part in bringing about a faster improvement in living conditions and prospects (Figure 16.1). Although still not achieving universal access to modern energy for all of Africa's citizens by 2040, this outlook is one in which uninterrupted and reliable energy supply increasingly becomes the rule, rather than the exception, thereby reducing the economic losses and inconveniences to businesses and households caused by brown-outs and disruptions.

The actions that underpin the African Century Case (described in more detail later in this chapter) target the same three critical areas identified above, but go beyond what is achieved in the New Policies Scenario: an additional $450 billion in power sector investment; higher revenue from the oil and gas sectors, a larger share of which is invested in improving infrastructure; and deeper regional co-operation, which allows for more efficient use of the continent's resources. These actions take time to feed back into greater economic activity, but we estimate that, by 2040, they generate a very substantial return, sufficient to boost the combined GDP (at market exchange rates) of sub-Saharan Africa by 30% above the levels anticipated in the New Policies Scenario, an increase in regional output of almost $2 trillion. Over the projection period as a whole, the annual average growth rate for sub-Saharan Africa is raised by one percentage point, from 5.1% to 6.1%. The level of per-capita income reached in 2040 ($4 500 per capita, calculated at market

16

exchange rates) would be reached only after 2050 in the New Policies Scenario, suggesting that the impact of the African Century Case is to generate an additional decade's worth of growth.

Figure 16.1 ▷ **Policy actions and outcomes in the African Century Case**

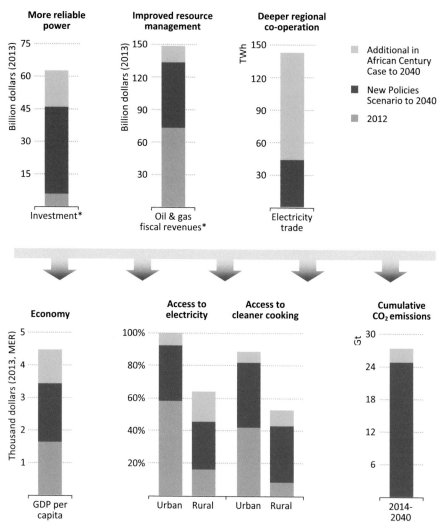

*Data are annual averages. Historical annual average data are shown for the period 2000-2013. Projections show the additional annual average for the period 2014-2040.

Note: MER = market exchange rate.

Three keys to Africa's energy future

Investment in the region's energy supply

An improved energy outlook for sub-Saharan Africa will require sustained investment, at higher levels than have been seen in the past, as well as a significant re-balancing of overall investment flows towards the provision of energy to domestic consumers within Africa. We estimate that, since 2000, investment in sub-Saharan African energy supply has more than doubled in real terms, from around $30 billion per year in the early 2000s to an annual average of around $65 billion since 2006 (Figure 16.2). Africa is a growing destination for international investment flows, from both developed and emerging economies. However, the bulk of this increase is attributable to a rise in spending on projects in the oil sector, which reached an average of $50 billion, almost 15% of total oil investment outside the OECD. For the period 2000-2013 as a whole, oil accounted for almost three-quarters of total investment in sub-Saharan African energy supply, a higher percentage even than in the Middle East (where oil spending accounted for around 60% of total energy supply investment) and a much higher share than in the rest of the world (where oil made up around one-third of the total).

Figure 16.2 ▷ **Investment in energy supply in sub-Saharan Africa**

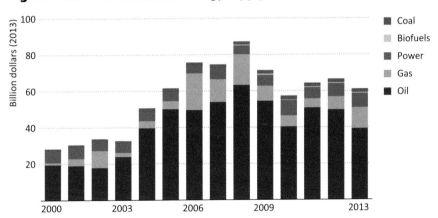

The mismatch between the direction of current investment flows and the continent's energy needs becomes even clearer when looking at the power sector. Although spending has increased over the last decade, annual investment in the sub-Saharan African power system is currently estimated at around $8 billion per year, or 0.5% of GDP. This compares very unfavourably with the non-OECD average of 1.3% of GDP invested in the power sector, and remains well below what is needed to improve the reliability and coverage of the electricity system. This has led to the present situation – as detailed in Chapter 13 – where the power sector more often limits economic growth rather than boosting it. To accelerate capital flows to projects in electricity generation, transmission and distribution is a critical

16

challenge – recognised both in Africa's own policy ambitions and in international efforts, such as the Sustainable Energy for All and US Power Africa initiatives.[2]

In the New Policies Scenario, investment in all areas of the sub-Saharan energy sector increases substantially, averaging more than $110 billion per year, with a steadily growing share of this investment directed towards meeting the region's own energy demand. Over the period 2000-2013, two-thirds of the total invested in sub-Saharan Africa went to produce energy for exports, with only one-third going towards providing energy to be consumed within the region. In the New Policies Scenario, this situation is gradually reversed, so that two-thirds of energy investment in sub-Saharan Africa to 2040 goes towards meeting the region's own energy needs. This is reflected in the large increase in the share of the power sector in total energy investment (Figure 16.3).

Figure 16.3 ▷ **Shares of investment by sector in sub-Saharan Africa in the New Policies Scenario**

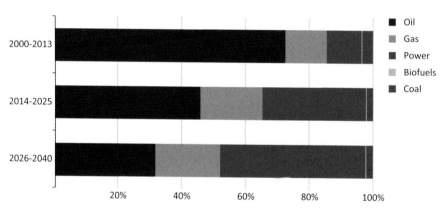

Over the period to 2040, there remains a steady stream of investment aimed in full or in part at bringing sub-Saharan energy resources to international markets. Indeed, this remains the driver for many upstream oil and gas projects, as well as for some Southern African coal investments (see section on international energy trade in Chapter 14). Such projects produce an invaluable flow of national income for application to other projects commanding national priority. However, this changing balance of investment in the energy sector does imply a large increase, to an average of $75 million per year, in the amount invested in projects supplying sub-Saharan African consumers with fuels and electricity.

2. For consistency with our projections of future trends, our historical investment numbers reflect "overnight investment", i.e. the capital spent is assigned to the year that production is started, rather than to the year when it was actually incurred. In the case of the African power sector, the figures for current investment do not therefore include the significant number of projects in which capital investment is ongoing, but which have not yet started operation.

A necessary condition for achieving this step-change in capital flows is government action to create sufficient opportunities for investment. This challenge extends well beyond the energy sector, involving a reduction of the risks arising from macroeconomic or political instability and from weak protection of contract and property rights (Spotlight). But it also means consistent attention to reform of the way the power sector operates, in order to realise the policy ambitions of governments across sub-Saharan Africa to improve the reliability and coverage of their electricity systems. Reform programmes, including plans for electrification, have been put in place in countries including Nigeria, Angola, Uganda, Rwanda, Ethiopia, Ghana, Mozambique, Tanzania, the Democratic Republic of Congo (DR Congo) and Benin. Some early movers, such as Kenya, have implemented measures that increase access to electricity and reduce electricity losses, while maintaining affordable tariffs. As discussed in Chapter 15, South Africa has put in place a model for procurement of low-carbon generation in the power sector that could find much broader application. In our projections, these and related initiatives provide the foundation for a large increase in annual average investment in the power sector of sub-Saharan Africa, where spending is projected to rise over the next ten years to more than $30 billion per year and increase again to more than $60 billion per year in the 2030s (Table 16.1).

Table 16.1 ▷ **Investment in energy supply in sub-Saharan Africa in the New Policies Scenario, 2014-2040** ($2013 billion)

	Sub-Saharan Africa (excluding South Africa)		South Africa	
	Cumulative	Annual average	Cumulative	Annual average
Oil	**1 119**	**41**	**26**	**1**
Upstream	1 038	38	16	1
Transport	32	1	4	0.1
Refining	50	2	6	0.2
Gas	**544**	**20**	**21**	**1**
Upstream	394	15	17	1
Transport	150	6	4	0.1
Coal	**17**	**0.6**	**49**	**2**
Mining	9	0.3	46	2
Transport	9	0.3	2	0.1
Power generation	**415**	**15**	**193**	**7**
Oil	9	0.3	0.2	0.0
Coal	42	2	81	3
Gas	51	2	6	0.2
Nuclear	-	-	27	1
Hydro	172	6	3	0.1
Other renewables	143	5	76	3
Power transmission & distribution	**549**	**20**	**92**	**3**
Total energy supply*	2 644	98	380	14

* Includes biofuels.

The nexus of governance and energy sector reforms: a key to poverty reduction and economic growth?

Not all of the factors holding back the expansion of energy provision in sub-Saharan Africa are to be found within the energy sector itself. Comparing the shares of investment in GDP in different sub-Saharan countries with a composite indicator for standards of governance, there is a clear coincidence in many countries between low levels of capital formation, i.e. low investment, and weak governance (Figure 16.4).[3] Very few sub-Saharan countries have shares of investment in GDP comparable to those seen in some major emerging economies: in India and Indonesia, this figure is around 35%, in China close to 50%. The capital stock created in this way provides the means – together with labour – to expand future output of goods and services.

Improvements in the indicators for governance have tended to be correlated with increased levels of investment, a relationship that is backed up by studies looking specifically at flows of foreign direct investment to sub-Saharan Africa (Wernick, Haar and Sharma, 2014) (Naudé and Krugell, 2007). A cautionary note is that this link is weaker or absent in countries that possess abundant oil and gas, where the pull of natural resources is sufficiently strong that substantial foreign investment is forthcoming even without efforts to improve the quality of institutions. However, in the absence of attention to this issue, these resource-rich countries risk losing out on investment in the non-resource sectors of the economy, including the power sector.

Improvements in governance also show a strong association with the reliability of electricity supply, implying that a reduction in political risk plays through into a higher level of power sector investment (Figure 16.5). Beyond this, there are strong signs that reliable electricity supply is among the most important factors underpinning economic development and poverty reduction. International Monetary Fund (IMF) analysis shows how poverty levels in sub-Saharan Africa are higher in countries with low quality electricity infrastructure; the correlation is higher than for other types of infrastructure or for general structural variables, such as levels of health or education (IMF, 2014a). Poor electricity infrastructure and unreliable supply is also widely understood as a key factor holding back business development. World Bank Enterprise Survey data shows that African enterprises identified problems with power supply as the most pressing obstacle to the growth of their business, ahead of access to finance, red tape and corruption (AfDB, OECD, UNDP, ECA, 2012). This nexus of power sector and governance indicators suggests high priority should be given to strengthening the capacity and accountability of institutions in and around the energy sector, as well as the quality of regulation, as a means to reduce poverty and stimulate economic growth.

---

3. Gross capital formation refers to the net additions to a country's capital stock in a given year, e.g. investment in new equipment, buildings and other intermediate goods.

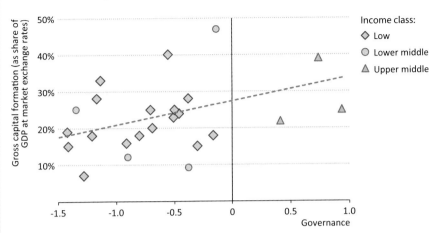

Figure 16.4 ▷ **Relationship between indicators for governance and for gross capital formation in sub-Saharan Africa**

Notes: The score for governance is an average of six indicators (with possible scores from a low of -2.5 to a high of +2.5) prepared by the Worldwide Governance Indicators project, which combines the views of a large number of enterprise, citizen and expert survey respondents on country performance in the following areas: voice and accountability; political stability and absence of violence; government effectiveness; regulatory quality; the rule of law; and control of corruption.

Sources: (for governance) Worldwide Governance Indicators, *www.govindicators.org*; (for investment) World Bank World Development Indicators, *http://wdi.worldbank.org/tables*. Country income classifications are from the World Bank.

Figure 16.5 ▷ **Relationship between indicators for governance and for quality of electricity supply in sub-Saharan Africa**

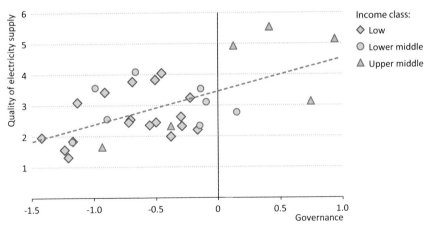

Notes: The scores and sources for governance indicators are above in Figure 16.4. The indicator for quality of power supply is based on survey responses to the question: "In your country, how would you assess the reliability of the electricity supply (lack of interruptions and lack of voltage fluctuations) on a scale from 1 (not reliable at all) to 7 (extremely reliable)".

Source: World Economic Forum, Global Competitiveness Report 2013-2014 *www.weforum.org/reports/global-competitiveness-report-2013-2014* (for quality of electricity supply).

16

Successful power sector reform will require a sustained effort to harness and develop the expertise required to formulate and implement energy policies, to plan the development of the sector (i.e. identify the least-cost options to meet anticipated demand) and to manage and operate the power system efficiently. Capacity in many of these areas has been understandably weak, given the stage of development of many countries. An improvement in power supply will also require an expanded cast of investors. Up until now, investment by private companies and international players has been heavily concentrated in the oil and gas sectors (Figure 16.6) and investment in these areas is likely to continue to have a strong private and international appeal, albeit with increasing involvement of African independents (a process that has already started in Nigeria) and more internationally-minded national oil companies (NOCs), particularly from Asian importing nations. The power sector is a different case. Ownership of today's generation fleet is dominated by state-owned utilities. It is difficult to see how the rise in power sector investment foreseen in the New Policies Scenario – much less, investment beyond that – can fully be achieved without serious efforts to improve the commercial discipline and circumstances of these utilities, along with a concerted attempt to harness the capital and expertise of the private sector.[4]

Figure 16.6 ▷ **Ownership structure of oil and gas output, and power generation capacity in sub-Saharan Africa**

2013 oil and gas output: 6.6 Mboe/d

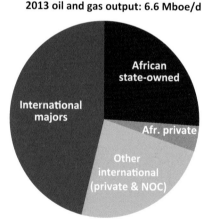

2012 power generation capacity*: 90 GW

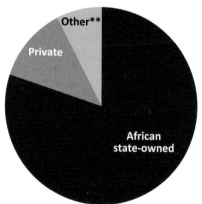

* Includes only grid-based power generation capacity. ** Other includes auto-producers, i.e. an industrial plant that has generating capacity that primarily serves its own needs (but is also grid-connected).

Notes: Mboe/d = million barrels of oil equivalent per day. NOC is national oil company. The seven international majors are BP, Chevron, ConocoPhillips, Eni, ExxonMobil, Shell and Total.

---

4. Private sector investment in the power sector, while small in relation to sub-Saharan Africa's needs, nonetheless already represents a significant share of the estimated investment actually going into the sector. According to the World Bank Private Participation in Infrastructure database, 22 new energy projects with private participation reached financial closure in 2012; these represent some $5 billion in investment (www.ppi.worldbank.org).

There is no uniform set of conditions in the power sector that can accelerate capital flows and bring new private investors on board: there are, however, some recurring policy and regulatory themes that need to be addressed:

- **Integrated and realistic strategic planning:** well-designed, comprehensive strategies covering efficient generation capacity, grid expansion and access are essential to avoid generation projects being held back by a lack of transmission capacity, or off-grid initiatives being deterred by the promise of a grid extension that never arrives. With Africa's large and growing rural population, governments need to lay out clear plans as to how electricity is to get to populations that will be hard-to-reach with the grid, albeit with scope for pragmatic and flexible variations to the details. There are also major gains to be had from regional co-operation and co-ordination, without which large-scale generation projects, notably for hydropower, struggle to make headway (see section on regional co-operation below).

- **Project development, procurement and contracting:** amid a host of more general concerns about governance, a key issue is the ability to get projects off the ground with integrity, using a transparent set of procedures and approvals, extending to social and environmental aspects. South Africa's Renewable Energy Independent Power Producer Procurement Programme (described in Chapter 15) provides a good example of what can be achieved in a well-run process, attracting $14 billion of investment commitments, from a wide range of international project developers, sponsors and equity shareholders, within three years of inception. Much investment is required in human capacity building within public institutions, to assist in distinguishing between legitimate demands from a potential investor and unwarranted demands for guarantees, government undertakings and so on.

- **Risk of non-payment:** private investment in power generation in sub-Saharan Africa typically takes place on the basis of power purchase agreements with a national utility, which then distributes and sells the power to customers: a major concern for investors is non-payment for the electricity produced. A tariff structure that secures overall cost recovery is vital to the financial health of the counterparty transaction and the security of the investor, though other financial mechanisms can be put in place to enhance the creditworthiness of the institutional buyer. An example comes from Nigeria, where the World Bank is providing credit enhancement and debt mobilisation guarantees to the Nigeria Bulk Electricity Trading company to facilitate private investment in Nigeria's reforming power sector.

- **Gas pricing and allocation:** in our projections, the share of natural gas in sub-Saharan Africa's power mix rises from less than 10% today to one-quarter in 2040, meaning that, from around 10 billion cubic metres (bcm), the amount of gas used in power generation exceeds 70 bcm by the end of the period. This will not happen without a sophisticated regulatory framework for gas transmission and distribution infrastructure, as well as contracting and pricing arrangements that guarantee both reliable supply and a reasonably predictable return to those producing the gas.

16

- **Pricing and tariff structures:** getting these right is clearly challenging where there is limited ability to pay and consumers have low expectations of the quality of service. Nonetheless, subsidised tariff structures that consistently fail to reach cost-recovery levels are a recipe for low investment (Box 16.1).

The development of large-scale power projects, in hydro as elsewhere, will continue to be heavily contingent on governments and international financing. The ambition to bring in new private investors, by contrast, implies a different (parallel) path towards the transformation of the power sector, involving multiple, smaller scale projects rather than a limited number of high-impact initiatives. Although this might grow over time, the typical power generation project attracting the attention of private investors (even in South Africa) is small-to-medium size with capacity of around 10 megawatts (MW) to 100 MW, i.e. a scale at which commitments of capital and risks by private investors are deemed manageable. These are largely grid-based projects, although there is growing awareness of the potential for private initiatives to contribute to improving access to electricity.[5] Bringing a sufficient quantity of these ideas to fruition requires a serious effort to reduce transaction costs and ensure adequate access to finance, but more projects, greater project diversity and more private sector participation can be instrumental in meeting African consumers' needs for reliable power – as well as to help bridge the energy access gap.

Financing energy projects

If improvements in the energy policy and regulatory framework are successful in generating a steady stream of bankable projects, the next hurdle relates to sources of capital: will financing be available to cover the envisaged scale of investment in sub-Saharan Africa? Capital comes to the energy sector from a variety of sources, as self-financing (via the revenue from existing operations), through an allocation from the state budget or from external financing (via lending institutions or capital markets). Access to capital is easiest for international companies, especially those with significant revenue streams from existing assets. The situation can be very different for African state-owned companies, which, whether involved in the extractive sector or in power supply, are often drained of resources because of subsidised fuel prices and competition from other spending priorities, as in Nigeria, or which, as in Mozambique, face the challenge of financial participation in huge capital-intensive projects.[6] For power utilities, the extent to which they generate any revenue in excess of costs depends on the way that tariffs (and subsidies) are structured in relation to the income levels of their customers (Box 16.1).

---

5. Electrification programmes are largely supported by public and donor funds, but the money already spent by those without access on poor-quality energy supply (kerosene lamps, candles, batteries) can also open up some commercial opportunities for provision of household-level devices such as solar lamps and improved biomass cookstoves as well as for some community-level mini-grids (IFC, 2012).

6. Nigeria's NNPC is a good example: it does not have control over the revenue that it generates but passes it on to the government, which in turn allocates an annual budget to the organisation. In recent years, the NNPC budget allocation has been in the region of $10 billion, meant to cover capital and operating costs for all of its joint projects with international companies. However, high operating costs in Nigeria have meant that very little budget is left for capital investments.

Box 16.1 ▷ Power tariffs: trapped between affordability and cost recovery?

End-user electricity tariffs are subject to two primary, and typically competing, considerations: the importance of recovering the costs of supply, as a step towards earning the necessary return on investment and to fund future capital spending; and the social imperative to keep prices at levels that allow consumers to benefit from affordable energy services. In many parts of sub-Saharan Africa, utilities can appear trapped between these two objectives: tariffs are either too high for consumers, or too low in relation to the costs of supplying them with power.[7] The risk is that this locks the power sector into a cycle of low revenues, high debts, inadequate maintenance, under-investment and poor quality of service.

There are ways out. Although there are options to improve tariff design, the amounts charged for electricity in many parts of sub-Saharan Africa are already high – as noted in Chapter 13, residential tariffs are among the highest in the world. The underlying problem is rather the elevated costs of generation, caused by reliance on expensive oil products rather than deployment of cheaper fuels and technologies. Reducing the share of oil-based generation plants in the power mix is a sure way to bring down the average cost of generation, often entailing readiness to challenge the vested interests that profit from expensive diesel supply. An important route to least-cost generation planning for many countries can be regional interconnections and cross-border electricity trade. In the New Policies Scenario, the expansion of lower cost sources of power supply is the main factor easing the burden of energy costs on household budgets: even as consumption rises, household energy expenditure as a share of household disposable income declines in this scenario, from 3.8% today down towards 3% by 2040.

A second priority is to reduce losses and improve efficiency. This applies both to the operation of the utility itself and the way that electricity is used (e.g. through the introduction of efficiency standards for lighting and appliances), but in particular to the transmission and distribution infrastructure. We estimate that, on average, around 18% of grid-based electricity generated in sub-Saharan Africa (outside South Africa, where losses are lower) is lost in transmission and distribution, a very high figure by international standards. These losses are reduced to 14% by 2040 in the New Policies Scenario, thanks to investment in upgrading the grid and improving its maintenance and operation. If losses were to remain at today's levels, more than 40 terawatt-hours (TWh) of additional electricity output would be needed in 2040, requiring around 10 gigawatts (GW) of generation capacity, which would cost in the order of $7 billion.

---

7. Research for the World Bank shows how tariffs in countries such as Chad, Mozambique, Rwanda and Uganda have fared well for cost recovery, but poorly for affordability: whereas in South Africa, DR Congo, Tanzania and Zambia tariffs are more affordable relative to incomes, but are well below the average costs of supply (Briceño-Garmendia and Shkataran, 2011).

16

In addition, there are the measures that utilities can take to optimise their tariff structures. In an environment where a large share of the population remains without access to electricity, any subsidy on the electricity tariff reaches only a small group, typically those with higher incomes. In Rwanda, for example, where the electrification rate is under 20%, we estimate that more than 90% of household electricity is consumed by those in the top 20% income bracket. Under these circumstances, it can make more sense for governments to direct their support to the cost of new connections, rather than lowering tariffs that are paid by relatively few. In any case, as the electrification rate rises and incomes increase, a typical tariff structure would see consumers facing higher unit prices as their consumption goes up, with lifeline tariffs or other schemes protecting, where possible, the poorest consumers.[8]

A major constraint in many parts of sub-Saharan African is a lack of domestic sources of capital, due to low savings rates and an undeveloped financial sector. Improving access to basic financial services is a key way to encourage domestic savings and to channel them efficiently into investment. There are some signs of improvement: the number of people with a commercial bank account has risen sharply in recent years, from 70 per 1 000 adults in 2004 to 295 per 1 000 adults in 2012 (IMF, 2014b), and this may understate actual levels because of the rise of mobile phone-based accounts. However, this is still well below the levels reached in other parts of the world, and the positive signs are very unevenly distributed. Local financing is starting to play a role in the larger economies, notably in Nigeria as a source of support for the emerging independent oil and power producers. There are also growing pension fund resources seeking productive long-term investment. But it remains the case that, in most countries, financing from local institutions is either unavailable or prohibitively expensive.

Most capital flows come, instead, from abroad, through foreign direct investment and multilateral and bilateral development assistance, with a small but growing share of international bank lending. As we have seen, much of the foreign direct investment has been directed to the hydrocarbons sector, driven in part by rising consumption in the emerging economies of Asia, matched by rising outward investment from these countries, notably China. Chinese companies and development banks are also becoming active investors in infrastructure projects. Cross-border bank lending to sub-Saharan Africa dropped during the financial crisis of 2008-2009, but has since shown some signs of a rebound: banks from South Africa are also increasingly active across other parts of sub-Saharan Africa.

---

8. Effective tariff design and implementation requires progress with metering as well as data on consumption patterns, typically obtained via household surveys. Rwanda is distinctive in this respect because of its regular surveys of household living conditions, which are a key source of data for government and for development policies.

For the moment, the bottlenecks holding back an increase in investment appear to arise more from considerations of policy and project preparation, rather than financing. But if policy and capacity constraints are eased and investment projects are proposed at the rate projected in the New Policies Scenario, then the limitations of the region's financial systems may become much more pertinent. The way that capital has been mobilised quickly and at scale for South African renewables projects since 2011 indicates what is possible; but domestic financial intermediation will take time to mature in other parts of sub-Saharan Africa, particularly for large-scale projects. More restrictive capital adequacy requirements, the focus of the Basel III Accord reached in the aftermath of the financial crisis, may also take their toll on the availability and cost of long-term funding from commercial banks. In practice, there is likely to be a heavy dependence on development bank funding, perhaps with a greater emphasis on enabling private sector investment through guarantee schemes, complemented by emerging south-south financial flows from China, India and Brazil, before more sustainable private and/or indigenous sources of financing are ready to take on a larger share of the burden.

Making the most of Africa's resources

A second critical variable that will shape the energy outlook for sub-Saharan Africa is the way that its resource wealth is managed. Considerations vary widely, depending on the type of resource: the extractive energy industries – oil, gas and coal – present a very different set of challenges and opportunities compared with renewable resources and, among the latter, the challenge of developing a large hydro project is quite distinct from that of a smaller scale wind or solar project. But a common thread is that the realisation of social and economic benefits is dependent on high quality and integrity in the public institutions concerned.

For renewable resources, a principal need is for effective policies for land use, forest management and sustainable wood production and measures to bring markets for charcoal and fuelwood into the formal economy. A sound policy and regulatory environment is also essential to foster the large-scale development of other modern renewable resources, particularly in the electricity sector where the projected share of power produced from renewables rises from 23% today (the overwhelming share of which is from large hydro) to more than 40% by 2040, with solar, wind and geothermal accounting for one-third of the growth. Among the investments in renewable energy, the challenge of large hydropower developments stands out because of the range of environmental and social impacts involved and the need, in an African context, for interconnected markets, involving regional accords. The attraction of other, non-hydro developments increases steadily over time, as technologies become more widely and cheaply available.[9]

16

---

9. Grid-connected renewable projects require a more robust governance framework to succeed, but some smaller-scale and off-grid projects have greater potential to sidestep institutional weaknesses (though other hurdles can include poor access to finance and to replacement / maintenance services).

Adequate investment in extractive industries is likewise dependent on a clear policy framework and high-quality regulation, but the hazards are different – notably that projects move ahead without producing tangible benefits to society. The deterministic view that resource development is necessarily detrimental to the chances for prosperity no longer prevails, but governments and societies face a difficult task to ensure that the systems governing the exploitation of natural resources maximise the chances of sustained economic benefits.[10] If not, then the example of Nigeria examined in Chapter 15 is illustrative of the perils.

Three main avenues exist for a state to secure a positive return on natural resource development: tax revenue, use of the commodity produced, and participation by local companies in the investment and supply chain. Using these channels productively requires comprehensive, long-term strategies and a coherent set of rules, along with competent institutions to design, administer and enforce them. Participation from civil society in the formulation of these resource strategies – and an ability to hold governments to account for their implementation – is instrumental to their chances of success.

In industries such as oil and gas, where foreign investment is high and much equipment and labour is necessarily foreign-sourced (especially for offshore developments), the task of maximising local benefits falls heavily on the tax regime. The way that tax regimes and contractual terms evolve is particularly relevant to our *Outlook,* because so many of the major resource-holding countries are in the process of revising or rewriting legislation in these areas (a process which, as in Nigeria, is itself holding companies back from committing capital). In the New Policies Scenario to 2040, we estimate that hydrocarbon extraction generates more than $3.5 trillion in cumulative fiscal revenue for resource-owning governments across sub-Saharan Africa (Figure 16.7). The overwhelming majority of this revenue comes from oil, only 11% from gas. Revenues are concentrated in a few countries, first among them Nigeria, followed by Angola, Ghana, Mozambique and Congo.

Generating these revenues requires a well-designed fiscal system, combining some standard elements with some that are adapted to the specific circumstances of extractive industries. Among the standard features, simplicity and transparency are especially valuable where tax assessment and collection capabilities are poorly developed; the stability of the tax regime is likewise important, especially for highly capital-intensive industries. But, precisely because of this capital intensity, there needs to be a balanced trade-off between the government's desire for early revenue and the need for companies to recover large upfront costs as quickly as possible. Crucially, the system needs to provide for variations in commodity prices; capturing a fair share of these resource rents is not only desirable, but essential if public support for extractive investment by non-national companies is to be earned or maintained. While any tax system needs to be tailored to a country's circumstances and the nature of its resources, a combination of a royalty system

---

10. The Natural Resource Charter is a global initiative that provides useful guidance, in the form of twelve principles, on how to manage opportunities created by natural resources (*www.resourcegovernance.org*).

(normally at a modest level, but at least ensuring a revenue flow as soon as production starts), a normal corporate income tax (to ensure neutrality versus other sectors of the economy) and a resource rent tax (to capture economic rents) is a typical way to balance the various objectives. The levels at which these taxes are set is critical, as the state risks either losing out on revenue or losing out on investment if it misjudges this part of the equation.

Figure 16.7 ▷ **Estimated fiscal revenue from hydrocarbon extraction in sub-Saharan Africa in the New Policies Scenario**

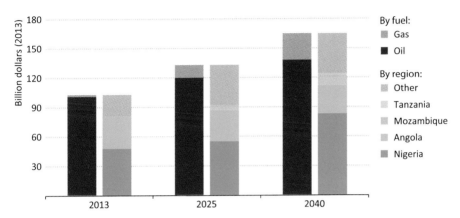

For the countries concerned, deciding how to allocate revenues of the magnitude shown in Figure 16.7 is not a simple process: there are urgent requirements for present-day spending, but also a strong case that revenues should be invested (or saved) in a way that benefits future generations. For many countries in sub-Saharan Africa, spending heavily on reversing deficiencies in essential infrastructure would seem to be an obvious solution: by funding power generation needs, investing in education and health, and building water and sanitation systems and transport infrastructure. Set against this, however, are questions over the administrative capacity to select projects well and to spend funds efficiently, and doubts in many countries over whether the domestic economy can absorb large increases in public spending. Strong oversight and public, multi-year spending plans, and disclosure of realised mineral revenues, costs incurred, and taxes actually paid (as advocated by the Extractive Industries Transparency Initiative) all have a major role to play. The creation of mechanisms to smooth revenue flows and expenditure – normally stand-alone funds, insulated from political interference – help to avoid macroeconomic pitfalls and inefficient spending.

The task of securing a positive return on natural resource development is made harder if a country is reliant on a single extractive industry or commodity; this increases the likelihood that revenues are strongly affected by fluctuations in commodity prices, exacerbating the risk of an (inefficient) expansion of spending in boom times and sharp contractions when prices fall. The risk of macroeconomic instability is particularly important in many African countries, where resource-related revenues account for high shares of total government revenue: in Nigeria and Angola, petroleum revenues accounted for some 75% of total government revenues on average over the period 2001-2010; the figure was even higher, almost 90%, in Equatorial Guinea and above 50% in both Chad and Sudan (IMF, 2012). At the same time, the example of Botswana suggests that the risks associated with high dependence on a single resource can be mitigated (Box 16.2).

Box 16.2 ▷ Botswana – a model for resource governance?

Since gaining independence in 1966, when it was classified among the world's ten poorest countries, Botswana has become an upper-middle income country, its per-capita income increasing 100-fold to reach $7 300 in 2013, the sixth-highest in Africa. Much of this growth is attributed to the development of the diamond extraction industry, and the successful management of the revenue that this has brought in.[11] Over the last two decades, the number of Batswana living below the poverty line has fallen from a third to under a fifth; the proportion of households with access to electricity has increased from 13% to over 65%; and literacy rates have increased from under 70% to more than 85%.

Botswana's success rests on several interwoven factors: the country has maintained a multi-party democratic political system since independence, with an established culture of accountability and transparency that is anchored in the Tswana traditions of consultation, participation and consensus. It has consistently been rated among the least corrupt African countries for over a decade. Public spending is planned over multi-year cycles to iron out the effect of the boom years that are a feature of commodity cycles. The accumulation of international reserves has allowed the government to manage the exchange rate in a way that stopped the currency from appreciating, facilitating the government's drive for development of the non-mineral sectors of the economy. Apart from monetary and fiscal prudence, the care with which Botswana's domestic infrastructure investments was handled has also proven to be high: public projects need to be ratified by parliament, while the government takes into careful consideration the absorptive capacity of the domestic economy to guard against investments that generate poor returns.

Fiscal considerations are part of a broader calculation of risk and reward affecting the prospects for investment. As argued in the Spotlight in Chapter 14, the political, economic

---

11. In Botswana, revenues from mining accounted for more than 40% of total government revenue on average over the period 2001-2010. Royalties are levied at between 3 and 10% of the gross market value at the mine gate of the mineral concerned, the high rate being for precious stones, the lower rate for other minerals. For the last 15 years, the mining tax has been levied at a variable rate, whichever is the greater of the normal corporate tax rate of 22% or that determined by a formula based on the ratio between net and gross income (a proxy of the existence of super-profits). The tax formula includes the three elements discussed in the text: royalty system, corporate income tax and resource rent tax.

and institutional context, outside the energy sector, has a direct impact on the risk calculation for prospective upstream investors, discouraging – or encouraging – investment in marginal projects (a factor that underpins higher production in the African Century Case). The broader context also determines the extent of spin-offs from extractive projects to other sectors and their contribution to industrialisation, employment and welfare. These co-benefits can be realised via end-users which use the commodity produced, e.g. power plants or gas-related industrial projects. Potentially larger gains, in terms of value added, employment and skills, typically come from domestic sourcing of the goods and services used by major extractive projects. This can be a boon for firms in areas such as construction, machine maintenance and repair, and services such as catering and industrial clothing, but over time also in the supply of equipment and more specialised engineering, technical and advisory services. Governments tend to reach quickly for local content provisions in an attempt to realise these benefits, but often then fail to provide sufficient investments in training and capacity or a supportive and low-risk environment for local business development.

In addition, the need of major extractive projects for infrastructure can also be a source of value. Coal extraction creates demand for new railways: upstream and mining operations all need large amounts of electricity. Investing companies often, in practice, build their own facilities (because of the unreliability or scarcity of local supply), but this can have knock-on effects, particularly if there are incentives to "over-build" generation capacity and become power suppliers to the grid. Alternatively, such companies can act as anchor customers that ensure the viability of other generation or transmission projects. There are opportunities, in any case, for the co-ordinated growth of project infrastructure through national or regional plans, for example, building gas transmission pipelines along routes that encourage other smaller consumers to take advantage of gas availability.

Regional energy co-operation and integration

Regional co-operation is a major component of Africa's vision for its future. A number of initiatives are underway, with the most comprehensive being the Programme for Infrastructure Development in Africa (PIDA), launched in 2010 and led by the African Union, the New Partnership for Africa's Development and the African Development Bank. PIDA defines a series of goals to be achieved by 2020, 2030 and 2040, focusing on transport, energy and information and telecommunications technologies. If implemented as planned, this would be a major step towards relieving some of the trans-border constraints on energy sector development and facilitate a major expansion of energy trade.

Yet, as in many parts of the world, there is in practice a large and persistent gap between the potential gains from regional co-operation in sub-Saharan Africa and the actual record of achievement. Examples of successful cross-border co-operation and cross-border infrastructure are relatively few and far between. The regional power pools are something of an exception (see Chapter 14), but they are still often poorly interconnected in practice, with most cross-border flows regulated by long-term bilateral agreements: they do not yet

16

operate as integrated regional power markets. Of the two cross-border gas pipelines, one has functioned as intended (from Mozambique to South Africa); the other, the West Africa Gas Pipeline (WAGP), stands as an example of the pitfalls as well as the potential for such projects (Box 16.3).

Box 16.3 ▷ **The West Africa Gas Pipeline: partial delivery of its promise**

The West Africa Gas Pipeline was first proposed in 1982 as a way to enhance regional economic growth, linking resource-rich regions in western Nigeria to centres of potentially burgeoning demand in Benin, Togo and Ghana. The pipeline, which stretches 680 km and has a capacity of around 5 bcm/year, was seen as a way to monetise a portion of the gas flared in Nigeria (over 20 bcm/year at the time), enabling the region to expand electricity supply and reduce its reliance on expensive liquid fuels for power generation. A final investment decision on the WAGP was taken 23 years later, in 2005, delayed by the complexity of reaching agreement among multiple countries and companies[12], the challenge of securing adequate financing and loan guarantees, and opposition from local communities troubled by the social and environmental footprint of the project. The project itself was also delayed in the construction phase, with first gas reaching Ghana only at the end of 2008.

Since the pipeline became operational, supply has been intermittent, halted at times by acts of vandalism in the Niger Delta, damage in offshore Togo and, most seriously, by an incident in 2012 during the re-commissioning of the Takoradi metering station in Ghana. When it has been in operation, the pipeline has supplied far less than envisaged, due to a shortage of gas that has been exacerbated by increasing consumption in Lagos (situated on the pipeline route and which itself has an economy of comparable size to that of Ghana). Some benefits of cross-border flows have, nonetheless, been realised. By end-2013, even the limited gas supplied through WAGP has been estimated to bring down the weighted average generation cost of electricity in Ghana by more than 10%, reflecting the cheaper cost of gas-fired generation compared to the oil-fired alternative. But the lack of reliable supply has also forced Ghana to ration its power, and to explore options for liquefied natural gas (LNG) imports. The prospect of Nigerian domestic gas demand and LNG plants absorbing much of any gas surplus and Ghana's access to new supply sources along the coast, notably the Jubilee development, diminishes further the prospects of the WAGP achieving the lofty ambitions initially set out for it.

Lack of infrastructure is one of the main barriers to regional energy co-operation, but far from the only one. The dominant position of state utilities in most countries means that national investment plans tend to take priority and are often not aligned with regional initiatives. At the root of the problem is that, while many countries and dominant state utility companies are happy to see themselves in the role of energy exporter, few are ready

---

12. The consortium includes Chevron as operator as well as NNPC, Shell, GhanaNPC, Societe Beninoise de Gaz S.A. and Societe Togolaise de Gaz S.A.

to rely on imports for more than a small share of their domestic needs, because of doubts about the reliability of supply or the political consequences of import dependence. Given the patchy record of implementing regional projects in practice, we envisage partial, but not full implementation of PIDA projects in the New Policies Scenario. The lack of regional scale is a particular constraint on the development of Africa's hydropower: the domestic markets of the countries with large hydropower potential (DR Congo, Ethiopia, Ghana, Guinea, Cameroon) are not of sufficient size to justify major project development. Without the regional market dimension, countries can be locked into less efficient – and more expensive – generation options.

Low levels of cross-border co-operation do not afflict only the power sector or trade in fossil fuels. They are also a vexed question for companies operating in different parts of the energy sector that may be looking to expand beyond their home markets. Barriers to trade include weak transport links, a variety of technical and non-technical barriers to trade and rules on local content, and mean that it is very difficult to move skilled labour, parts and supplies across borders from one African country to another. The difficulty of optimising supply chains on a regional basis pushes up costs for many energy projects.

An African Century Case

By easing some of the key constraints that hold back the development of the energy sector in the New Policies Scenario, the African Century Case offers a brighter vision of how energy can contribute to inclusive economic growth in sub-Saharan Africa. In this case, three targeted actions in the energy sector, set against a backdrop of improved standards of governance, deliver a major boost to economic activity. The sub-Saharan African economy in 2040 is 30% larger in the African Century Case than in the New Policies Scenario, an increase larger than the current GDP of sub-Saharan Africa today (Figure 16.8).

Figure 16.8 ▷ GDP growth in sub-Saharan Africa in the African Century Case and the New Policies Scenario

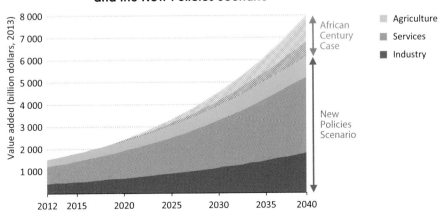

Note: Measured at market exchange rates (MER) in year-2013 dollars.

The actions that underpin the African Century Case are:

■ An additional $450 billion in power sector investment, compared with the New Policies Scenario, with a consequent improvement in the reliability of electricity supply, reducing the incidence of power outages by half, and in access to electricity.

■ A larger share of the revenue from the oil and gas sectors reinvested in infrastructure, accompanied by a rise in oil and gas production to keep pace with higher demand.

■ Increased regional co-operation and integration, facilitating new large-scale generation and infrastructure projects, faster development of the regional power pools and the interconnections between them.

A $450 billion boost to power sector investment

Although the New Policies Scenario sees a large step up in power sector investment compared with current trends, the investment level runs at an average of only around 1.3% of GDP over the projection period. By way of comparison, China has invested the equivalent of around 1.9% of GDP in its power sector since 2000 and India 2.6%. The persistently high number living without access to electricity in the New Policies Scenario provides additional evidence of a continued shortfall in power sector investment relative to sub-Saharan Africa's needs.

The increase in power sector investment in the African Century Case, by more than one-third relative to the New Policies Scenario, brings annual average spending up to 1.5% of GDP. Of these additional investments, 30% are directed at providing access to electricity. This means that, by the end of our projection period, full access is achieved in urban areas in all countries of sub-Saharan Africa and the proportion of the rural population with access rises to two-thirds. Of the additional 230 million that gain access to electricity in the African Century Case, more than 70% are in rural areas, the growth in supply coming predominantly from mini-grid or off-grid solutions. By 2040, around 300 million people remain without access to electricity in sub-Saharan Africa. This figure is still very high; but it is a reduction of more than 40% compared with the New Policies Scenario. An additional 150 million people also gain access to cleaner cooking facilities in the African Century Case, again with the majority being in rural areas. The implication is that this Case contributes significantly to a closing of the rural / urban divide and a reduction in extreme rural poverty in many countries.

The African Century Case is accompanied by improved maintenance and management of the power system, reducing the incidence of assumed power outages by half.[13] Total electricity consumption increases by more than 30%, compared with the New Policies Scenario, reaching 1 700 TWh by 2040. The contribution of expanded electricity access to this increase is modest, at only 110 TWh, representing about one-quarter of the total

---

13. Our modelling of the relationship between the energy sector and GDP in sub-Saharan Africa includes a constraint representing the impact of unreliable power supply on economic activity. This constraint is cut in half in the African Century Case.

incremental electricity consumption; the remainder is a product of higher household consumption, driven by rising incomes, and increased demand from the industrial and service sectors. The improved reliability of power supply has the effect of raising the productivity of African companies, i.e. the efficiency with which they are able to turn inputs of capital and labour into outputs, providing a significant boost to the economy. Every additional $1 invested in the power sector in the African Century Case generates more than $15 in incremental GDP.

A larger share of (higher) petroleum revenue invested in infrastructure

Higher economic growth pushes up domestic demand for all energy carriers, although the traditional use of solid biomass is replaced more rapidly by modern fuels, compared with the New Policies Scenario, relieving to an extent the pressure on the forestry biomass stock. The incremental demand for fossil fuels is largely met by increased production from within sub-Saharan Africa. Improved governance and transparency in the management of the oil and gas sectors reduce the risks facing investors, making African oil and gas developments more competitive with production from other sources. This facilitates higher investment (also in exploration) that allows production to edge higher from the 2020s onwards. Fiscal revenues reach $200 billion by 2040, 20% higher than the figure in the New Policies Scenario. The additional funds available to governments (a cumulative $410 billion over the projection period) are assumed to finance a faster pace of infrastructure investment, making an additional contribution to overall economic growth.

Oil production is 1.2 mb/d higher in 2040, with the additional output coming in part from Nigeria, but also from faster growth of oil production in East Africa and from investment that allows other mature producers in Central Africa, such as Cameroon and Congo, to slow the pace at which their oil production declines. Contributions to incremental output also come from the new frontiers where today's estimates of resources are high, such as Madagascar and deep offshore resources in Angola, Congo and Gabon. In the case of natural gas, production of which rises to 270 bcm in 2040 (17% higher than in New Policies Scenario), major contributions to the increase in output come from Nigeria, largely in the form of associated gas, and also from Mozambique and Tanzania, where the resource base is sufficient to support higher levels of production. Higher levels of oil and gas production are a consequence of a system in which risks to economic activity and investment are reduced. The larger narrative though lies outside the extractive industries, in the opportunities for human development and prosperity that a well-functioning energy system can create across sub-Saharan Africa.

Deeper regional co-operation

In the African Century Case, improved regional energy co-operation allows countries to take better advantage of opportunities for trade within and between their respective power systems, moving towards a more integrated African power grid, based on the existing power pools. It also means that some large regional projects, notably the expansion of

16

hydropower capacity from the Grand Inga project in the DR Congo, move ahead more quickly. Even with the increase in electricity demand, this brings the average cost of Africa's power generation down to levels slightly below those seen in the New Policies Scenario. The share of hydropower, a relatively cheap source of power, rises in the overall electricity mix to 31% in 2040 (from 22% today), five percentage points higher than in the New Policies Scenario, with the effect of displacing more expensive power generation options, notably oil-fired generation. Even though electricity use is higher in the African Century Case, the share of energy in household expenditures is slightly lower.

Figure 16.9 ▷ **Increase in regional electricity generation and trade in sub-Saharan Africa in the African Century Case versus the New Policies Scenario, 2040**

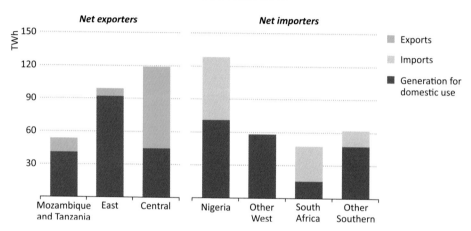

Enhanced power connections across Central Africa are a main differentiating feature of the African Century Case (Figure 16.9). On the back of an extra $130 billion of investment (30% of the total additional power sector investment in the African Century Case), Central Africa becomes a hub for regional energy trade by harnessing 25 GW of additional hydropower capacity, in effect more than doubling its hydro capacity compared with the New Policies Scenario. Similar dynamics are at play in East Africa, mostly in Ethiopia, and Mozambique, where a proliferation of hydropower projects is made financially viable by the prospect of increased trade. The African Century Case sees a much greater expansion of trade than suggested by the sum of import or export numbers. Kenya, for example, simultaneously imports electricity from Ethiopia in the north and exports to Tanzania in the south.

Africa's energy choices in a global context

The choices facing sub-Saharan Africa's policy-makers cannot be seen outside the context of international prices and patterns of energy trade, global competition for investment capital, and shifts in the efficiency and cost of the competing energy technologies available on the African and international markets. The interactions extend also to the environmental sphere. Although the South African energy economy is relatively carbon-intensive, sub-Saharan Africa as a whole continues to contribute very little to energy-related carbon dioxide (CO_2) emissions (even in the African Century Case, sub-Saharan Africa's share in global emissions in 2040 rises to 4%, compared with 3% in the New Policies Scenario). It is, though, in the front line among the regions most likely to face impacts from a changing global climate.[14]

Overall, our projections suggest a significant improvement in the energy situation of many people in sub-Saharan Africa, but also that the difficulty of providing energy services to a rapidly growing population will leave a significant gap in 2040 in most countries, relative to global average levels of energy use. Taking electricity as an example, there are 16 countries in sub-Saharan Africa where average per-capita electricity consumption in 2012 was below 100 kilowatt-hours (kWh), compared with a global per-capita average in 2012 of close to 2 800 kWh. This number of countries falls to six in the New Policies Scenario – and only one in the African Century Case (Figure 16.10). There is likewise an increase in the number of countries where average per-capita consumption levels rise above 1 000 kWh by 2040, with a larger number passing this threshold in the African Century Case. But, even in this more optimistic outlook, in only three sub-Saharan African countries (South Africa, Botswana and Namibia) does this indicator surpass the projected 2040 global average of 3 900 kWh per capita. Increasing the provision of energy services in large urban and peri-urban areas is eased by high population density, but our *Outlook* points to some persistent and formidable challenges in extending this coverage to all rural communities.

Figure 16.10 ▷ **Country-by-country growth in electricity consumption per capita in sub-Saharan Africa by scenario**

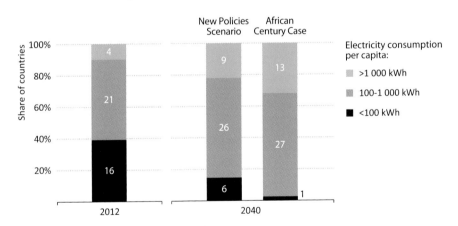

Source: IEA analysis in collaboration with KTH Royal Institute of Technology.

A projected oil price that rises to more than $130 per barrel in real terms by 2040 affects the outlook in numerous ways. It means high import bills for many countries that lack indigenous resources as well as the possibility of oil shocks in case of volatile price

16

---

14. The improvement in energy access in both scenarios has only negligible implications for energy-related CO_2 emissions and no discernible impact on the price or availability of fuels on the world market.

movements, with land-locked importers particularly vulnerable to the risk of interruptions to physical supply. It means a continued windfall for resource-owners, amplifying the potential benefits from improvements in infrastructure, as well as the risks associated with resource and revenue mismanagement. It also increases pressure for change: the opportunity cost, and, in some cases, the actual fiscal cost, of subsidising oil products is unsustainably high, as is the cost of generating electricity from oil products. This means rising momentum, already visible in some countries, behind a shift towards cheaper and often cleaner alternative fuels and technologies for all stationary uses. Natural gas answers this call in some countries in our projections, but economic drivers and falling costs for some technologies create widespread opportunities for modern renewable energy to play a much larger role in Africa's energy future.

How far these opportunities are taken up will depend on the policies adopted by sub-Saharan Africa's governments. The solutions to their energy dilemmas vary widely across the region: in some areas, the most effective actions are local and small scale; in others, national or regional initiatives are essential. But an increasing number of governments are seriously tackling the barriers that have held back investment, both domestic and foreign, from meeting African consumers' needs: if these constraints are effectively tackled, Africa's energy and economic future can look very different from its past.

ANNEXES

World Energy Outlook links

General information: www.worldenergyoutlook.org

Tables for Scenario Projections (Annex A)
www.worldenergyoutlook.org/annexa/
User ID: WEO2014AnnexA
Password: 85_phLLygls

Factsheets
www.worldenergyoutlook.org/media/weowebsite/2014/factsheets.pdf

Model

Documentation and methodology
www.worldenergyoutlook.org/weomodel/documentation/

Investment costs
www.worldenergyoutlook.org/weomodel/investmentcosts/

Policy databases
www.worldenergyoutlook.org/weomodel/policydatabases/

Topics

Energy access
www.worldenergyoutlook.org/resources/energydevelopment/

Energy subsidies
www.worldenergyoutlook.org/resources/energysubsidies/

Water-energy nexus
www.worldenergyoutlook.org/resources/water-energynexus/

Unconventional gas forum
www.iea.org/ugforum/

Recent special reports

World Energy Investment Outlook
www.worldenergyoutlook.org/investment/

Africa Energy Outlook
www.worldenergyoutlook.org/africa/

Redrawing the Energy-Climate Map
www.worldenergyoutlook.org/energyclimatemap/

Southeast Asia Energy Outlook
www.worldenergyoutlook.org/southeastasiaenergyoutlook/

Tables for Scenario Projections

General note to the tables

The tables detail projections for *fossil-fuel production, energy demand, gross electricity generation* and *electrical capacity*, and *carbon-dioxide (CO$_2$) emissions* from fossil-fuel combustion in the New Policies, Current Policies and 450 Scenarios. The following regions are covered: World, OECD, OECD Americas, the United States, OECD Europe, the European Union, OECD Asia Oceania, Japan, non-OECD, Eastern Europe/Eurasia, Russia, non-OECD Asia, China, India, the Middle East, Africa, sub-Saharan Africa, South Africa, Latin America and Brazil. The definitions for regions, fuels and sectors can be found in Annex C. By convention, in the table headings CPS and 450 refers to the Current Policies and 450 Scenarios respectively.

Data for *fossil-fuel production, energy demand, gross electricity generation* and *CO$_2$ emissions* from fossil-fuel combustion up to 2012 are based on IEA statistics, published in *Energy Balances of OECD Countries, Energy Balances of non-OECD Countries, CO$_2$ Emissions from Fuel Combustion* and the *IEA Monthly Oil Data Service*. Historical data for *gross electrical capacity* are drawn from the Platts World Electric Power Plants Database (December 2013 version) and the International Atomic Energy Agency PRIS database.

Both in the text of this book and in the tables, rounding may lead to minor differences between totals and the sum of their individual components. Growth rates are calculated on a compound average annual basis and are marked "n.a." when the base year is zero or the value exceeds 200%. Nil values are marked "-".

Definitional note to the tables

Total primary energy demand (TPED) is equivalent to power generation plus other energy sector excluding electricity and heat, plus total final consumption (TFC) excluding electricity and heat. TPED does not include ambient heat from heat pumps or electricity trade. Sectors comprising TFC include industry, transport, buildings (residential, services and non-specified other) and other (agriculture and non-energy use). Projected gross electrical capacity is the sum of existing capacity and additions, less retirements. Total CO$_2$ includes emissions from other energy sector in addition to the power generation and TFC sectors shown in the tables. CO$_2$ emissions and energy demand from international marine and aviation bunkers are included only at the world transport level. Gas use in international bunkers is not itemised separately. CO$_2$ emissions do not include emissions from industrial waste and non-renewable municipal waste.

New Policies Scenario

				Production				Shares (%)		CAAGR (%)
	1990	2012	2020	2025	2030	2035	2040	2012	2040	2012-40
Oil production and supply (mb/d)										
OECD	18.9	19.7	24.5	24.5	24.3	24.0	23.7	23	23	0.7
Americas	13.9	15.6	20.6	21.2	21.3	21.0	20.7	18	21	1.0
Europe	4.3	3.4	3.1	2.5	2.2	2.2	2.2	4	2	-1.6
Asia Oceania	0.7	0.6	0.8	0.8	0.8	0.8	0.8	1	1	1.1
Non-OECD	46.7	67.2	68.9	71.9	74.1	75.8	77.0	77	77	0.5
E. Europe/Eurasia	11.7	13.9	14.2	14.2	13.6	12.8	12.1	16	12	-0.5
Asia	6.0	8.0	7.6	6.9	6.4	6.1	5.8	9	6	-1.1
Middle East	17.7	28.1	28.6	31.1	33.9	36.1	37.9	32	38	1.1
Africa	6.7	9.8	9.2	9.5	9.4	9.5	9.8	11	10	-0.0
Latin America	4.5	7.5	9.3	10.2	10.9	11.3	11.4	9	11	1.5
World oil production	65.6	86.8	93.4	96.4	98.4	99.8	100.7	100	100	0.5
Crude oil	59.6	69.7	68.0	68.4	67.8	67.0	66.4	78	64	-0.2
Natural gas liquids	5.6	12.2	14.6	15.4	16.4	17.2	18.2	14	17	1.4
Unconventional oil	0.4	5.0	10.8	12.6	14.3	15.6	16.2	6	16	4.3
Processing gains	1.3	2.1	2.5	2.8	2.9	3.0	3.2	2	3	1.5
World oil supply	66.9	89.0	96.0	99.2	101.3	102.8	103.9	99	96	0.6
World biofuels supply	0.1	1.3	2.2	2.8	3.4	4.1	4.6	1	4	4.7
World liquids supply	67.0	90.2	98.1	102.0	104.8	107.0	108.5	100	100	0.7
Natural gas production (bcm)										
OECD	881	1 228	1 423	1 495	1 554	1 597	1 634	36	30	1.0
Americas	643	885	1 036	1 105	1 168	1 223	1 254	26	23	1.3
Europe	211	278	253	234	225	218	210	8	4	-1.0
Asia Oceania	28	64	134	157	160	157	170	2	3	3.5
Non-OECD	1 181	2 210	2 448	2 753	3 072	3 409	3 744	64	70	1.9
E. Europe/Eurasia	831	873	918	971	1 029	1 107	1 198	25	22	1.1
Asia	132	423	527	600	682	763	841	12	16	2.5
Middle East	91	529	572	660	746	831	903	15	17	1.9
Africa	67	213	236	296	348	406	470	6	9	2.9
Latin America	60	172	196	227	267	302	331	5	6	2.4
World	2 063	3 438	3 872	4 249	4 626	5 007	5 378	100	100	1.6
Unconventional gas	*70*	*592*	*928*	*1 160*	*1 385*	*1 567*	*1 689*	*17*	*31*	*3.8*
Coal production (Mtce)										
OECD	1 533	1 361	1 344	1 278	1 201	1 168	1 172	24	18	-0.5
Americas	836	767	732	663	584	539	526	14	8	-1.3
Europe	526	246	194	155	131	115	103	4	2	-3.1
Asia Oceania	171	348	418	459	486	515	543	6	9	1.6
Non-OECD	1 661	4 306	4 671	4 856	5 002	5 107	5 182	76	82	0.7
E. Europe/Eurasia	533	461	463	468	470	470	471	8	7	0.1
Asia	952	3 538	3 850	4 000	4 115	4 187	4 225	62	66	0.6
Middle East	1	1	1	1	1	1	1	0	0	0.9
Africa	150	218	241	262	280	301	326	4	5	1.4
Latin America	25	88	115	125	135	148	159	2	2	2.1
World	3 194	5 667	6 015	6 133	6 203	6 275	6 354	100	100	0.4
Steam coal	*2 227*	*4 443*	*4 757*	*4 907*	*5 019*	*5 144*	*5 280*	*78*	*83*	*0.6*
Coking coal	*571*	*914*	*950*	*942*	*917*	*889*	*850*	*16*	*13*	*-0.3*

Current Policies and 450 Scenarios

	Production						Shares (%) 2040		CAAGR (%) 2012-40	
	2020	2030	2040	2020	2030	2040	CPS	450	CPS	450
	Current Policies Scenario			450 Scenario						
Oil production and supply (mb/d)										
OECD	25.2	26.2	27.3	23.8	20.3	16.5	24	24	1.2	-0.6
Americas	21.2	23.0	24.0	20.0	17.7	14.5	21	21	1.5	-0.3
Europe	3.2	2.4	2.4	3.0	1.9	1.5	2	2	-1.3	-2.9
Asia Oceania	0.8	0.9	1.0	0.8	0.7	0.6	1	1	1.8	-0.1
Non-OECD	70.2	79.2	85.7	67.1	63.2	52.8	76	76	0.9	-0.9
E. Europe/Eurasia	14.5	14.5	13.5	13.8	11.8	8.7	12	13	-0.1	-1.6
Asia	7.8	7.0	6.6	7.4	5.5	4.2	6	6	-0.7	-2.3
Middle East	29.3	35.9	42.2	27.5	28.7	25.6	37	37	1.5	-0.3
Africa	9.1	10.0	10.5	9.3	8.2	6.7	9	10	0.3	-1.4
Latin America	9.5	11.9	12.9	9.2	9.1	7.7	11	11	2.0	0.1
World oil production	95.4	105.5	113.0	90.9	83.5	69.4	100	100	0.9	-0.8
Crude oil	69.3	72.3	73.9	66.6	58.0	45.4	63	63	0.2	-1.5
Natural gas liquids	14.9	17.0	19.5	13.8	14.0	13.3	17	18	1.7	0.3
Unconventional oil	11.2	16.2	19.6	10.4	11.4	10.7	17	15	5.0	2.8
Processing gains	2.6	3.2	3.5	2.5	2.6	2.6	3	4	1.8	0.6
World oil supply	98.0	108.7	116.6	93.4	86.1	71.9	97	89	1.0	-0.8
World biofuels supply	1.8	2.7	3.6	2.1	5.5	8.7	3	11	3.9	7.2
World liquids supply	99.8	111.4	120.2	95.5	91.5	80.7	100	100	1.0	-0.4
Natural gas production (bcm)										
OECD	1 421	1 549	1 785	1 387	1 378	1 242	31	29	1.3	0.0
Americas	1 028	1 133	1 361	1 023	1 022	911	23	22	1.5	0.1
Europe	257	239	223	233	203	190	4	4	-0.8	-1.4
Asia Oceania	137	177	201	131	153	141	3	3	4.2	2.9
Non-OECD	2 492	3 244	4 009	2 393	2 763	2 990	69	71	2.1	1.1
E. Europe/Eurasia	944	1 124	1 331	911	927	931	23	22	1.5	0.2
Asia	530	700	867	527	675	828	15	20	2.6	2.4
Middle East	576	783	963	545	608	607	17	14	2.2	0.5
Africa	237	346	488	228	333	391	8	9	3.0	2.2
Latin America	205	291	361	181	220	232	6	5	2.7	1.1
World	3 913	4 793	5 795	3 779	4 142	4 232	100	100	1.9	0.7
Unconventional gas	924	1 412	1 840	922	1 240	1 341	32	32	4.1	3.0
Coal production (Mtce)										
OECD	1 458	1 567	1 697	1 195	749	696	20	19	0.8	-2.4
Americas	817	841	882	654	351	359	11	10	0.5	-2.7
Europe	192	145	144	176	85	58	2	2	-1.9	-5.0
Asia Oceania	449	580	671	366	313	279	8	8	2.4	-0.8
Non-OECD	4 909	5 849	6 674	4 405	3 471	3 004	80	81	1.6	-1.3
E. Europe/Eurasia	490	550	588	450	285	236	7	6	0.9	-2.4
Asia	4 035	4 795	5 482	3 644	2 876	2 530	65	68	1.6	-1.2
Middle East	1	1	1	1	1	1	0	0	1.0	0.6
Africa	251	318	388	226	227	185	5	5	2.1	-0.6
Latin America	131	185	215	83	82	51	3	1	3.3	-1.9
World	6 367	7 416	8 371	5 600	4 221	3 700	100	100	1.4	-1.5
Steam coal	5 076	6 123	7 098	4 413	3 273	2 907	85	79	1.7	-1.5
Coking coal	979	984	965	924	823	705	12	19	0.2	-0.9

World: New Policies Scenario

	Energy demand (Mtoe)						Shares (%)		CAAGR (%)
	1990	2012	2020	2025	2030	2035	2040	2012	2040	2012-40
TPED	8 782	13 361	14 978	15 871	16 720	17 529	18 293	100	100	1.1
Coal	2 231	3 879	4 211	4 293	4 342	4 392	4 448	29	24	0.5
Oil	3 232	4 194	4 487	4 612	4 689	4 730	4 761	31	26	0.5
Gas	1 668	2 844	3 182	3 487	3 797	4 112	4 418	21	24	1.6
Nuclear	526	642	845	937	1 047	1 137	1 210	5	7	2.3
Hydro	184	316	392	430	469	503	535	2	3	1.9
Bioenergy	905	1 344	1 554	1 675	1 796	1 911	2 002	10	11	1.4
Other renewables	36	142	308	435	581	744	918	1	5	6.9
Power generation	2 987	5 091	5 800	6 239	6 708	7 204	7 719	100	100	1.5
Coal	1 225	2 400	2 586	2 639	2 686	2 753	2 849	47	37	0.6
Oil	377	304	229	191	158	142	132	6	2	-2.9
Gas	583	1 169	1 253	1 383	1 508	1 631	1 751	23	23	1.5
Nuclear	526	642	845	937	1 047	1 137	1 210	13	16	2.3
Hydro	184	316	392	430	469	503	535	6	7	1.9
Bioenergy	60	147	236	288	342	400	454	3	6	4.1
Other renewables	32	114	259	371	498	639	788	2	10	7.2
Other energy sector	901	1 632	1 761	1 821	1 869	1 902	1 918	100	100	0.6
Electricity	*183*	*327*	*380*	*412*	*447*	*483*	*519*	*20*	*27*	*1.7*
TFC	6 290	8 943	10 174	10 836	11 437	11 986	12 487	100	100	1.2
Coal	768	909	1 016	1 034	1 038	1 032	1 014	10	8	0.4
Oil	2 607	3 642	4 009	4 193	4 329	4 416	4 477	41	36	0.7
Gas	947	1 339	1 575	1 723	1 875	2 033	2 191	15	18	1.8
Electricity	834	1 628	2 008	2 238	2 466	2 697	2 930	18	23	2.1
Heat	335	287	305	314	321	326	327	3	3	0.5
Bioenergy	796	1 110	1 212	1 270	1 325	1 378	1 418	12	11	0.9
Other renewables	4	28	49	64	83	104	130	0	1	5.6
Industry	1 806	2 595	3 050	3 268	3 454	3 643	3 809	100	100	1.4
Coal	475	728	821	834	835	833	823	28	22	0.4
Oil	327	312	332	337	338	339	338	12	9	0.3
Gas	357	550	655	727	796	870	945	21	25	2.0
Electricity	381	688	871	964	1 047	1 129	1 201	27	32	2.0
Heat	153	130	143	148	151	153	152	5	4	0.6
Bioenergy	113	187	227	255	282	312	339	7	9	2.2
Other renewables	0	1	2	3	5	7	10	0	0	9.5
Transport	1 575	2 504	2 816	3 017	3 194	3 340	3 467	100	100	1.2
Oil	1 479	2 325	2 563	2 708	2 822	2 892	2 937	93	85	0.8
Of which: Bunkers	*201*	*350*	*386*	*410*	*433*	*457*	*482*	*14*	*14*	*1.2*
Electricity	21	26	34	41	51	64	82	1	2	4.2
Biofuels	6	60	101	132	162	195	218	2	6	4.7
Other fuels	69	94	119	136	159	189	229	4	7	3.2
Buildings	2 243	2 937	3 211	3 368	3 537	3 699	3 867	100	100	1.0
Coal	238	125	119	115	111	104	96	4	2	-0.9
Oil	324	321	307	289	272	262	258	11	7	-0.8
Gas	431	596	676	721	768	810	843	20	22	1.2
Electricity	402	863	1 038	1 158	1 287	1 415	1 551	29	40	2.1
Heat	173	150	157	160	164	168	171	5	4	0.5
Bioenergy	671	855	871	867	861	849	835	29	22	-0.1
Other renewables	4	26	44	57	73	91	113	1	3	5.4
Other	666	907	1 096	1 183	1 252	1 304	1 345	100	100	1.4

World: Current Policies and 450 Scenarios

	Energy demand (Mtoe)						Shares (%)		CAAGR (%)	
	2020	2030	2040	2020	2030	2040	2040		2012-40	
	Current Policies Scenario			450 Scenario			CPS	450	CPS	450
TPED	15 317	17 768	20 039	14 521	14 934	15 629	100	100	1.5	0.6
Coal	4 457	5 191	5 860	3 920	2 955	2 590	29	17	1.5	-1.4
Oil	4 584	5 028	5 337	4 363	3 961	3 242	27	21	0.9	-0.9
Gas	3 215	3 921	4 742	3 104	3 387	3 462	24	22	1.8	0.7
Nuclear	838	957	1 005	859	1 280	1 677	5	11	1.6	3.5
Hydro	383	448	504	392	511	597	3	4	1.7	2.3
Bioenergy	1 551	1 761	1 933	1 565	2 022	2 535	10	16	1.3	2.3
Other renewables	289	462	658	319	819	1 526	3	10	5.6	8.9
Power generation	5 988	7 277	8 637	5 522	5 708	6 602	100	100	1.9	0.9
Coal	2 791	3 415	4 067	2 326	1 399	1 157	47	18	1.9	-2.6
Oil	239	175	146	217	111	73	2	1	-2.6	-5.0
Gas	1 265	1 580	1 969	1 227	1 286	1 148	23	17	1.9	-0.1
Nuclear	838	957	1 005	859	1 280	1 677	12	25	1.6	3.5
Hydro	383	448	504	392	511	597	6	9	1.7	2.3
Bioenergy	229	310	382	236	419	644	4	10	3.5	5.4
Other renewables	242	392	563	265	702	1 305	7	20	5.9	9.1
Other energy sector	1 803	1 992	2 146	1 722	1 702	1 628	100	100	1.0	-0.0
Electricity	390	484	581	365	386	424	27	26	2.1	0.9
TFC	10 352	12 011	13 444	9 941	10 482	10 748	100	100	1.5	0.7
Coal	1 042	1 095	1 102	993	963	898	8	8	0.7	-0.0
Oil	4 094	4 648	5 037	3 908	3 677	3 067	37	29	1.2	-0.6
Gas	1 592	1 925	2 268	1 529	1 725	1 914	17	18	1.9	1.3
Electricity	2 061	2 635	3 203	1 937	2 220	2 590	24	24	2.4	1.7
Heat	311	333	344	300	298	288	3	3	0.7	0.0
Bioenergy	1 205	1 306	1 394	1 220	1 483	1 768	10	16	0.8	1.7
Other renewables	46	70	95	54	116	221	1	2	4.5	7.7
Industry	3 119	3 635	4 093	2 990	3 208	3 375	100	100	1.6	0.9
Coal	842	877	883	805	784	738	22	22	0.7	0.0
Oil	339	354	358	324	309	286	9	8	0.5	-0.3
Gas	669	837	1 013	637	718	762	25	23	2.2	1.2
Electricity	891	1 115	1 317	847	941	1 040	32	31	2.3	1.5
Heat	145	155	155	140	139	129	4	4	0.6	-0.0
Bioenergy	231	294	359	233	300	373	9	11	2.4	2.5
Other renewables	2	4	7	3	16	47	0	1	8.2	15.7
Transport	2 853	3 382	3 814	2 741	2 801	2 641	100	100	1.5	0.2
Oil	2 624	3 078	3 411	2 487	2 256	1 660	89	63	1.4	-1.2
Of which: Bunkers	392	455	529	370	347	331	14	13	1.5	-0.2
Electricity	33	46	61	34	72	196	2	7	3.2	7.5
Biofuels	87	129	174	99	278	469	5	18	3.9	7.6
Other fuels	109	130	167	121	196	316	4	12	2.1	4.4
Buildings	3 276	3 722	4 150	3 117	3 249	3 431	100	100	1.2	0.6
Coal	123	122	116	113	92	72	3	2	-0.3	-1.9
Oil	319	307	300	293	240	217	7	6	-0.2	-1.4
Gas	689	806	913	646	662	669	22	20	1.5	0.4
Electricity	1 069	1 387	1 720	992	1 129	1 266	41	37	2.5	1.4
Heat	160	173	184	153	154	154	4	4	0.7	0.1
Bioenergy	874	865	835	873	880	888	20	26	-0.1	0.1
Other renewables	42	61	82	47	93	163	2	5	4.2	6.8
Other	1 104	1 272	1 386	1 092	1 224	1 301	100	100	1.5	1.3

World: New Policies Scenario

Electricity generation (TWh)	1990	2012	2020	2025	2030	2035	2040	Shares (%) 2012	Shares (%) 2040	CAAGR (%) 2012-40
Total generation	11 825	22 721	27 771	30 817	33 881	36 977	40 104	100	100	2.1
Coal	4 425	9 204	10 377	10 800	11 191	11 658	12 239	41	31	1.0
Oil	1 310	1 144	832	695	582	531	494	5	1	-3.0
Gas	1 760	5 104	6 056	7 010	7 875	8 690	9 499	22	24	2.2
Nuclear	2 013	2 461	3 243	3 594	4 016	4 361	4 644	11	12	2.3
Hydro	2 144	3 672	4 553	5 004	5 449	5 847	6 222	16	16	1.9
Bioenergy	132	442	764	961	1 161	1 373	1 569	2	4	4.6
Wind	4	521	1 333	1 853	2 362	2 870	3 345	2	8	6.9
Geothermal	36	70	120	173	237	305	378	0	1	6.2
Solar PV	0	97	449	643	851	1 068	1 291	0	3	9.7
CSP	1	5	41	77	140	240	357	0	1	16.7
Marine	1	1	3	7	17	36	66	0	0	19.1

Electrical capacity (GW)	2012	2020	2025	2030	2035	2040	Shares (%) 2012	Shares (%) 2040	CAAGR (%) 2012-40
Total capacity	5 683	7 301	8 179	9 045	9 887	10 716	100	100	2.3
Coal	1 805	2 096	2 245	2 394	2 504	2 631	32	25	1.4
Oil	442	371	325	285	267	251	8	2	-2.0
Gas	1 462	1 883	2 095	2 278	2 475	2 659	26	25	2.2
Nuclear	394	451	489	543	588	624	7	6	1.7
Hydro	1 085	1 351	1 483	1 612	1 724	1 829	19	17	1.9
Bioenergy	101	154	187	220	255	289	2	3	3.8
Wind	282	598	798	982	1 154	1 321	5	12	5.7
Geothermal	11	18	26	35	45	56	0	1	5.9
Solar PV	98	364	505	647	790	930	2	9	8.4
CSP	3	13	24	42	70	102	0	1	14.0
Marine	1	1	2	6	13	25	0	0	14.6

CO_2 emissions (Mt)	1990	2012	2020	2025	2030	2035	2040	Shares (%) 2012	Shares (%) 2040	CAAGR (%) 2012-40
Total CO_2	20 938	31 615	34 203	35 370	36 291	37 163	38 037	100	100	0.7
Coal	8 316	13 926	15 081	15 270	15 325	15 396	15 523	44	41	0.4
Oil	8 815	11 229	11 811	12 101	12 294	12 417	12 489	36	33	0.4
Gas	3 807	6 460	7 311	7 999	8 672	9 351	10 024	20	26	1.6
Power generation	7 476	13 238	13 932	14 270	14 540	14 913	15 400	100	100	0.5
Coal	4 915	9 547	10 278	10 436	10 527	10 671	10 918	72	71	0.5
Oil	1 199	948	720	600	495	446	412	7	3	-2.9
Gas	1 362	2 742	2 934	3 235	3 518	3 797	4 070	21	26	1.4
TFC	12 461	16 797	18 545	19 328	19 944	20 414	20 777	100	100	0.8
Coal	3 262	4 068	4 501	4 533	4 501	4 435	4 325	24	21	0.2
Oil	7 061	9 673	10 469	10 889	11 198	11 380	11 496	58	55	0.6
Transport	*4 383*	*6 941*	*7 648*	*8 084*	*8 429*	*8 641*	*8 780*	*41*	*42*	*0.8*
Of which: Bunkers	*620*	*1 081*	*1 191*	*1 261*	*1 333*	*1 403*	*1 479*	*6*	*7*	*1.1*
Gas	2 139	3 056	3 576	3 906	4 245	4 599	4 956	18	24	1.7

World: Current Policies and 450 Scenarios

	Electricity generation (TWh)						Shares (%)		CAAGR (%)	
	2020	2030	2040	2020	2030	2040	2040		2012-40	
	Current Policies Scenario			450 Scenario			CPS	450	CPS	450
Total generation	28 489	36 253	44 003	26 760	30 296	35 043	100	100	2.4	1.6
Coal	11 271	14 445	17 734	9 428	5 977	4 606	40	13	2.4	-2.4
Oil	869	656	561	781	391	251	1	1	-2.5	-5.3
Gas	6 124	8 360	10 806	5 929	6 649	5 777	25	16	2.7	0.4
Nuclear	3 215	3 670	3 856	3 293	4 912	6 435	9	18	1.6	3.5
Hydro	4 458	5 207	5 862	4 561	5 936	6 943	13	20	1.7	2.3
Bioenergy	740	1 039	1 299	768	1 434	2 261	3	6	3.9	6.0
Wind	1 254	1 962	2 552	1 376	3 186	4 953	6	14	5.8	8.4
Geothermal	113	188	287	121	324	557	1	2	5.2	7.7
Solar PV	408	630	832	459	1 156	1 982	2	6	8.0	11.4
CSP	34	85	173	42	310	1 158	0	3	13.7	21.7
Marine	3	10	41	3	22	119	0	0	17.0	21.6

	Electrical capacity (GW)						Shares (%)		CAAGR (%)	
	2020	2030	2040	2020	2030	2040	2040		2012-40	
	Current Policies Scenario			450 Scenario			CPS	450	CPS	450
Total capacity	7 345	9 148	10 794	7 169	9 031	11 073	100	100	2.3	2.4
Coal	2 207	2 794	3 341	1 999	1 614	1 439	31	13	2.2	-0.8
Oil	374	299	262	359	258	212	2	2	-1.8	-2.6
Gas	1 918	2 439	2 930	1 826	2 178	2 382	27	22	2.5	1.8
Nuclear	447	496	517	458	661	862	5	8	1.0	2.8
Hydro	1 321	1 534	1 715	1 352	1 768	2 050	16	19	1.6	2.3
Bioenergy	150	199	243	154	266	403	2	4	3.2	5.0
Wind	565	834	1 043	617	1 288	1 873	10	17	4.8	7.0
Geothermal	17	28	42	18	48	81	0	1	4.8	7.3
Solar PV	333	495	636	371	856	1 396	6	13	6.9	10.0
CSP	11	26	49	13	86	330	0	3	11.0	18.8
Marine	1	4	15	1	8	45	0	0	12.7	17.2

	CO_2 emissions (Mt)						Shares (%)		CAAGR (%)	
	2020	2030	2040	2020	2030	2040	2040		2012-40	
	Current Policies Scenario			450 Scenario			CPS	450	CPS	450
Total CO_2	35 523	40 848	45 950	32 479	25 424	19 300	100	100	1.3	-1.7
Coal	16 035	18 552	20 929	13 915	8 049	4 582	46	24	1.5	-3.9
Oil	12 098	13 313	14 229	11 441	10 052	7 814	31	40	0.8	-1.3
Gas	7 390	8 984	10 793	7 123	7 323	6 903	23	36	1.8	0.2
Power generation	14 812	17 717	20 944	12 793	7 262	3 989	100	100	1.7	-4.2
Coal	11 099	13 478	15 898	9 238	4 081	1 504	76	38	1.8	-6.4
Oil	748	548	457	680	350	228	2	6	-2.6	-5.0
Gas	2 964	3 690	4 589	2 875	2 831	2 257	22	57	1.9	-0.7
TFC	18 960	21 253	22 984	18 020	16 749	14 134	100	100	1.1	-0.6
Coal	4 623	4 749	4 704	4 387	3 739	2 896	20	20	0.5	-1.2
Oil	10 721	12 143	13 145	10 166	9 249	7 246	57	51	1.1	-1.0
Transport	7 833	9 194	10 197	7 421	6 742	4 974	44	35	1.4	-1.2
Of which: Bunkers	1 209	1 402	1 626	1 141	1 073	1 026	7	7	1.5	-0.2
Gas	3 617	4 361	5 135	3 466	3 760	3 992	22	28	1.9	1.0

A

OECD: New Policies Scenario

	Energy demand (Mtoe)							Shares (%)		CAAGR (%)
	1990	2012	2020	2025	2030	2035	2040	2012	2040	2012-40
TPED	4 522	5 251	5 436	5 423	5 392	5 399	5 413	100	100	0.1
Coal	1 080	1 020	964	885	773	694	651	19	12	-1.6
Oil	1 870	1 901	1 827	1 719	1 596	1 495	1 396	36	26	-1.1
Gas	843	1 345	1 424	1 494	1 559	1 612	1 655	26	31	0.7
Nuclear	451	509	589	585	609	631	640	10	12	0.8
Hydro	102	119	127	132	136	139	143	2	3	0.6
Bioenergy	147	277	346	391	438	485	525	5	10	2.3
Other renewables	29	80	159	218	282	343	403	2	7	6.0
Power generation	1 718	2 198	2 281	2 301	2 327	2 363	2 414	100	100	0.3
Coal	759	810	760	683	580	505	470	37	19	-1.9
Oil	154	88	40	27	22	19	16	4	1	-5.9
Gas	176	506	500	540	575	597	614	23	25	0.7
Nuclear	451	509	589	585	609	631	640	23	27	0.8
Hydro	102	119	127	132	136	139	143	5	6	0.6
Bioenergy	53	95	123	139	155	170	184	4	8	2.4
Other renewables	25	70	143	196	251	301	346	3	14	5.8
Other energy sector	403	480	500	503	503	506	508	100	100	0.2
Electricity	105	127	130	132	133	135	137	26	27	0.3
TFC	3 107	3 574	3 735	3 735	3 711	3 712	3 712	100	100	0.1
Coal	234	121	117	111	105	99	94	3	3	-0.9
Oil	1 592	1 705	1 685	1 602	1 498	1 410	1 322	48	36	-0.9
Gas	589	699	762	779	796	814	830	20	22	0.6
Electricity	552	799	873	907	937	968	1 003	22	27	0.8
Heat	43	59	62	64	65	66	67	2	2	0.5
Bioenergy	94	181	221	250	280	313	338	5	9	2.3
Other renewables	4	9	16	22	30	42	57	0	2	6.7
Industry	827	798	838	840	830	826	825	100	100	0.1
Coal	160	96	93	88	83	78	74	12	9	-0.9
Oil	168	102	96	90	85	80	76	13	9	-1.1
Gas	226	253	266	265	261	259	258	32	31	0.1
Electricity	222	256	281	287	289	293	298	32	36	0.5
Heat	15	24	24	24	23	22	22	3	3	-0.3
Bioenergy	37	67	78	84	88	92	95	8	12	1.3
Other renewables	0	1	1	1	2	2	2	0	0	4.8
Transport	940	1 184	1 187	1 153	1 112	1 091	1 066	100	100	-0.4
Oil	914	1 108	1 084	1 027	957	901	842	94	79	-1.0
Electricity	8	9	11	14	19	26	36	1	3	5.1
Biofuels	0	43	61	75	91	110	121	4	11	3.8
Other fuels	19	25	30	36	45	54	66	2	6	3.6
Buildings	985	1 206	1 289	1 321	1 356	1 394	1 434	100	100	0.6
Coal	69	21	20	19	19	18	17	2	1	-0.8
Oil	209	156	136	117	98	83	72	13	5	-2.7
Gas	304	394	434	446	459	470	476	33	33	0.7
Electricity	316	524	570	594	618	638	658	43	46	0.8
Heat	27	35	38	40	42	43	45	3	3	0.9
Bioenergy	56	68	78	86	95	105	115	6	8	1.9
Other renewables	4	8	13	19	26	37	51	1	4	6.8
Other	354	385	421	421	412	400	387	100	100	0.0

OECD: Current Policies and 450 Scenarios

	Energy demand (Mtoe)						Shares (%)		CAAGR (%)	
	2020	2030	2040	2020	2030	2040	2040		2012-40	
	Current Policies Scenario			450 Scenario			CPS	450	CPS	450
TPED	5 523	5 696	5 895	5 284	4 920	4 808	100	100	0.4	-0.3
Coal	1 033	1 033	1 040	857	470	425	18	9	0.1	-3.1
Oil	1 857	1 734	1 597	1 792	1 368	945	27	20	-0.6	-2.5
Gas	1 432	1 603	1 793	1 400	1 357	1 176	30	24	1.0	-0.5
Nuclear	586	559	548	593	669	764	9	16	0.3	1.5
Hydro	127	134	140	127	141	150	2	3	0.6	0.8
Bioenergy	335	403	473	350	539	721	8	15	1.9	3.5
Other renewables	153	230	303	164	377	627	5	13	4.9	7.6
Power generation	2 334	2 488	2 672	2 192	2 095	2 246	100	100	0.7	0.1
Coal	824	830	844	658	293	272	32	12	0.1	-3.8
Oil	42	24	18	39	16	10	1	0	-5.6	-7.6
Gas	499	593	691	507	475	306	26	14	1.1	-1.8
Nuclear	586	559	548	593	669	764	21	34	0.3	1.5
Hydro	127	134	140	127	141	150	5	7	0.6	0.8
Bioenergy	119	144	166	123	172	222	6	10	2.0	3.1
Other renewables	138	205	266	145	330	523	10	23	4.9	7.4
Other energy sector	505	521	563	485	451	423	100	100	0.6	-0.5
Electricity	132	142	154	126	119	119	27	28	0.7	-0.2
TFC	3 783	3 900	3 994	3 655	3 432	3 252	100	100	0.4	-0.3
Coal	119	110	100	113	96	80	3	2	-0.7	-1.4
Oil	1 714	1 634	1 521	1 655	1 288	896	38	28	-0.4	-2.3
Gas	771	818	865	734	709	693	22	21	0.8	-0.0
Electricity	888	989	1 095	848	868	925	27	28	1.1	0.5
Heat	63	68	72	60	59	58	2	2	0.7	-0.0
Bioenergy	214	257	304	226	365	497	8	15	1.9	3.7
Other renewables	15	25	37	18	47	103	1	3	5.1	9.0
Industry	853	865	867	824	785	756	100	100	0.3	-0.2
Coal	94	86	77	90	77	64	9	8	-0.8	-1.4
Oil	97	87	78	94	80	68	9	9	-0.9	-1.4
Gas	271	271	268	261	241	218	31	29	0.2	-0.5
Electricity	286	304	318	275	267	267	37	35	0.8	0.2
Heat	25	23	22	24	21	19	2	3	-0.4	-0.8
Bioenergy	79	93	103	78	92	105	12	14	1.6	1.6
Other renewables	1	1	2	2	7	14	0	2	4.0	12.0
Transport	1 200	1 196	1 191	1 168	1 009	853	100	100	0.0	-1.2
Oil	1 106	1 072	1 019	1 066	777	454	86	53	-0.3	-3.1
Electricity	11	14	19	11	33	103	2	12	2.8	9.1
Biofuels	55	74	99	60	153	223	8	26	3.1	6.1
Other fuels	29	36	53	30	46	73	4	9	2.8	3.9
Buildings	1 309	1 426	1 547	1 243	1 234	1 264	100	100	0.9	0.2
Coal	21	20	20	19	16	14	1	1	-0.2	-1.6
Oil	141	116	89	128	81	52	6	4	-2.0	-3.8
Gas	440	480	513	412	392	372	33	29	0.9	-0.2
Electricity	580	660	746	551	557	545	48	43	1.3	0.1
Heat	38	44	50	36	37	39	3	3	1.3	0.4
Bioenergy	76	85	96	82	113	158	6	13	1.2	3.0
Other renewables	13	21	33	15	37	84	2	7	5.1	8.8
Other	422	412	389	420	405	379	100	100	0.0	-0.1

OECD: New Policies Scenario

	Electricity generation (TWh)							Shares (%)		CAAGR (%)
	1990	2012	2020	2025	2030	2035	2040	2012	2040	2012-40
Total generation	7 628	10 779	11 681	12 094	12 456	12 843	13 286	100	100	0.7
Coal	3 092	3 478	3 332	3 028	2 598	2 291	2 140	32	16	-1.7
Oil	686	386	168	110	88	77	62	4	0	-6.3
Gas	782	2 744	2 883	3 195	3 437	3 597	3 733	25	28	1.1
Nuclear	1 729	1 952	2 258	2 243	2 338	2 420	2 458	18	18	0.8
Hydro	1 181	1 389	1 481	1 532	1 577	1 619	1 660	13	12	0.6
Bioenergy	124	315	414	481	548	608	660	3	5	2.7
Wind	4	379	781	1 025	1 267	1 496	1 706	4	13	5.5
Geothermal	29	45	71	101	134	158	177	0	1	5.1
Solar PV	0	86	262	332	396	460	522	1	4	6.6
CSP	1	5	27	42	59	82	105	0	1	11.7
Marine	1	0	3	7	16	34	63	0	0	19.0

	Electrical capacity (GW)						Shares (%)		CAAGR (%)
	2012	2020	2025	2030	2035	2040	2012	2040	2012-40
Total capacity	2 844	3 221	3 391	3 543	3 686	3 833	100	100	1.1
Coal	651	607	575	535	473	442	23	12	-1.4
Oil	208	127	99	82	73	65	7	2	-4.1
Gas	856	1 034	1 099	1 135	1 183	1 218	30	32	1.3
Nuclear	321	314	304	313	323	326	11	9	0.1
Hydro	466	490	505	519	530	542	16	14	0.5
Bioenergy	66	82	93	103	113	122	2	3	2.2
Wind	179	323	411	493	568	637	6	17	4.6
Geothermal	7	10	15	19	23	25	0	1	4.7
Solar PV	87	223	275	321	364	404	3	11	5.6
CSP	3	9	13	17	23	29	0	1	9.1
Marine	1	1	2	6	13	24	0	1	14.5

	CO$_2$ emissions (Mt)							Shares (%)		CAAGR (%)
	1990	2012	2020	2025	2030	2035	2040	2012	2040	2012-40
Total CO$_2$	11 099	12 027	11 652	11 153	10 474	9 940	9 528	100	100	-0.8
Coal	4 142	3 904	3 659	3 313	2 825	2 438	2 195	32	23	-2.0
Oil	5 030	5 002	4 693	4 388	4 065	3 812	3 556	42	37	-1.2
Gas	1 928	3 121	3 301	3 453	3 584	3 690	3 776	26	40	0.7
Power generation	3 961	4 755	4 363	4 091	3 695	3 376	3 184	100	100	-1.4
Coal	3 063	3 288	3 062	2 740	2 283	1 925	1 711	69	54	-2.3
Oil	487	276	128	86	69	62	50	6	2	-5.9
Gas	411	1 191	1 173	1 266	1 342	1 389	1 423	25	45	0.6
TFC	6 545	6 576	6 545	6 317	6 039	5 820	5 598	100	100	-0.6
Coal	1 015	526	507	485	458	433	409	8	7	-0.9
Oil	4 180	4 418	4 280	4 033	3 743	3 507	3 270	67	58	-1.1
Transport	*2 681*	*3 271*	*3 198*	*3 029*	*2 824*	*2 658*	*2 484*	*50*	*44*	*-1.0*
Gas	1 349	1 632	1 758	1 799	1 838	1 880	1 918	25	34	0.6

OECD: Current Policies and 450 Scenarios

	Electricity generation (TWh)						Shares (%) 2040		CAAGR (%) 2012-40	
	Current Policies Scenario			450 Scenario			CPS	450	CPS	450
	2020	2030	2040	2020	2030	2040				
Total generation	11 883	13 181	14 541	11 341	11 496	12 156	100	100	1.1	0.4
Coal	3 610	3 735	3 933	2 907	1 334	1 160	27	10	0.4	-3.8
Oil	174	98	70	164	59	33	0	0	-5.9	-8.4
Gas	2 873	3 557	4 208	2 932	2 831	1 670	29	14	1.5	-1.8
Nuclear	2 248	2 144	2 103	2 276	2 567	2 932	14	24	0.3	1.5
Hydro	1 477	1 557	1 623	1 483	1 639	1 747	11	14	0.6	0.8
Bioenergy	398	499	581	414	614	815	4	7	2.2	3.5
Wind	755	1 094	1 366	796	1 640	2 358	9	19	4.7	6.7
Geothermal	69	105	136	71	162	239	1	2	4.1	6.2
Solar PV	249	333	406	267	482	715	3	6	5.7	7.9
CSP	26	50	77	27	149	377	1	3	10.5	16.9
Marine	3	10	38	3	20	110	0	1	16.8	21.3

	Electrical capacity (GW)						Shares (%) 2040		CAAGR (%) 2012-40	
	Current Policies Scenario			450 Scenario			CPS	450	CPS	450
	2020	2030	2040	2020	2030	2040				
Total capacity	3 245	3 587	3 891	3 167	3 588	4 079	100	100	1.1	1.3
Coal	640	643	656	592	365	264	17	6	0.0	-3.2
Oil	127	83	66	120	66	45	2	1	-4.0	-5.3
Gas	1 051	1 222	1 342	990	1 082	1 093	34	27	1.6	0.9
Nuclear	313	287	278	316	346	392	7	10	-0.5	0.7
Hydro	488	512	529	491	541	573	14	14	0.5	0.7
Bioenergy	79	95	108	82	114	147	3	4	1.8	2.9
Wind	313	435	529	328	622	846	14	21	3.9	5.7
Geothermal	10	15	19	10	23	34	1	1	3.7	5.8
Solar PV	213	276	327	227	382	534	8	13	4.8	6.7
CSP	8	15	22	9	41	110	1	3	8.1	14.4
Marine	1	3	14	1	7	42	0	1	12.5	16.9

	CO$_2$ emissions (Mt)						Shares (%) 2040		CAAGR (%) 2012-40	
	Current Policies Scenario			450 Scenario			CPS	450	CPS	450
	2020	2030	2040	2020	2030	2040				
Total CO$_2$	12 045	12 029	12 027	11 060	7 449	4 925	100	100	0.0	-3.1
Coal	3 940	3 863	3 762	3 226	1 170	524	31	11	-0.1	-6.9
Oil	4 785	4 484	4 171	4 591	3 372	2 170	35	44	-0.6	-2.9
Gas	3 320	3 683	4 094	3 242	2 907	2 232	34	45	1.0	-1.2
Power generation	4 635	4 763	4 915	3 962	1 769	697	100	100	0.1	-6.6
Coal	3 331	3 299	3 246	2 647	724	205	66	29	-0.0	-9.4
Oil	132	77	56	125	50	30	1	4	-5.5	-7.6
Gas	1 172	1 387	1 612	1 190	994	463	33	66	1.1	-3.3
TFC	6 663	6 515	6 300	6 379	5 106	3 771	100	100	-0.2	-2.0
Coal	517	478	437	492	380	272	7	7	-0.7	-2.3
Oil	4 367	4 148	3 863	4 194	3 130	2 003	61	53	-0.5	-2.8
Transport	3 261	3 162	3 006	3 144	2 292	1 337	48	35	-0.3	-3.1
Gas	1 779	1 889	2 000	1 693	1 596	1 496	32	40	0.7	-0.3

OECD Americas: New Policies Scenario

	Energy demand (Mtoe)							Shares (%)		CAAGR (%)
	1990	2012	2020	2025	2030	2035	2040	2012	2040	2012-40
TPED	2 260	2 618	2 781	2 782	2 771	2 793	2 821	100	100	0.3
Coal	491	459	453	412	353	328	315	18	11	-1.3
Oil	920	971	985	931	862	812	763	37	27	-0.9
Gas	517	742	816	861	911	942	973	28	34	1.0
Nuclear	180	236	250	251	261	267	272	9	10	0.5
Hydro	52	61	65	67	69	70	72	2	3	0.6
Bioenergy	82	119	149	173	200	231	255	5	9	2.8
Other renewables	19	30	62	87	115	143	171	1	6	6.4
Power generation	852	1 058	1 114	1 125	1 135	1 155	1 188	100	100	0.4
Coal	419	411	404	362	304	278	266	39	22	-1.5
Oil	47	23	14	10	8	6	5	2	0	-5.6
Gas	95	270	282	307	334	342	354	26	30	1.0
Nuclear	180	236	250	251	261	267	272	22	23	0.5
Hydro	52	61	65	67	69	70	72	6	6	0.6
Bioenergy	41	29	40	47	55	63	71	3	6	3.2
Other renewables	19	28	59	81	106	128	149	3	13	6.1
Other energy sector	192	250	270	278	285	291	296	100	100	0.6
Electricity	*56*	*64*	*67*	*69*	*70*	*71*	*73*	*26*	*24*	*0.5*
TFC	1 548	1 774	1 907	1 907	1 894	1 907	1 920	100	100	0.3
Coal	61	27	29	28	26	25	24	2	1	-0.4
Oil	809	901	926	882	822	781	739	51	39	-0.7
Gas	361	360	403	412	422	432	443	20	23	0.7
Electricity	272	389	430	447	464	481	503	22	26	0.9
Heat	3	7	7	7	6	5	5	0	0	-1.4
Bioenergy	41	89	109	126	145	167	183	5	10	2.6
Other renewables	0	2	4	6	9	15	23	0	1	9.3
Industry	361	348	383	387	387	390	396	100	100	0.5
Coal	51	26	28	27	26	25	24	7	6	-0.3
Oil	60	37	37	35	34	34	33	11	8	-0.3
Gas	138	140	155	155	154	154	154	40	39	0.4
Electricity	94	104	117	120	121	124	128	30	32	0.8
Heat	1	6	6	6	5	5	5	2	1	-0.8
Bioenergy	17	36	40	43	46	49	52	10	13	1.3
Other renewables	0	0	0	0	1	1	1	0	0	7.9
Transport	562	718	729	706	680	676	666	100	100	-0.3
Oil	543	669	665	626	576	544	510	93	77	-1.0
Electricity	1	1	2	3	6	12	19	0	3	10.8
Biofuels	-	28	39	48	61	77	85	4	13	4.1
Other fuels	18	20	24	29	36	43	52	3	8	3.5
Buildings	461	551	597	611	626	641	658	100	100	0.6
Coal	10	1	1	1	0	0	0	0	0	-7.9
Oil	64	56	49	41	34	28	23	10	4	-3.0
Gas	184	187	208	212	216	219	220	34	33	0.6
Electricity	176	280	307	319	331	340	351	51	53	0.8
Heat	2	1	1	1	1	0	0	0	0	-6.0
Bioenergy	24	25	29	32	35	39	43	4	6	2.0
Other renewables	0	2	3	5	8	13	21	0	3	9.2
Other	164	157	198	202	201	200	198	100	100	0.8

OECD Americas: Current Policies and 450 Scenarios

	Energy demand (Mtoe)						Shares (%)		CAAGR (%)	
	2020	2030	2040	2020	2030	2040	2040		2012-40	
	Current Policies Scenario			450 Scenario			CPS	450	CPS	450
TPED	2 833	2 963	3 120	2 703	2 509	2 494	100	100	0.6	-0.2
Coal	508	536	565	394	205	224	18	9	0.7	-2.5
Oil	1 002	957	902	967	738	506	29	20	-0.3	-2.3
Gas	806	881	996	810	792	693	32	28	1.1	-0.2
Nuclear	248	249	244	253	283	325	8	13	0.1	1.1
Hydro	65	68	71	65	69	73	2	3	0.5	0.6
Bioenergy	145	181	223	150	258	374	7	15	2.3	4.2
Other renewables	59	91	117	64	165	300	4	12	5.0	8.6
Power generation	1 149	1 241	1 344	1 064	1 004	1 116	100	100	0.9	0.2
Coal	458	484	512	346	161	185	38	17	0.8	-2.8
Oil	15	9	6	13	5	2	0	0	-4.6	-7.8
Gas	270	298	345	288	274	183	26	16	0.9	-1.4
Nuclear	248	249	244	253	283	325	18	29	0.1	1.1
Hydro	65	68	71	65	69	73	5	7	0.5	0.6
Bioenergy	38	48	60	40	64	91	4	8	2.6	4.1
Other renewables	56	83	105	59	148	256	8	23	4.8	8.2
Other energy sector	271	293	330	262	255	242	100	100	1.0	-0.1
Electricity	69	75	81	65	62	64	25	26	0.9	-0.0
TFC	1 932	2 003	2 080	1 869	1 748	1 673	100	100	0.6	-0.2
Coal	29	27	25	28	24	20	1	1	-0.2	-1.1
Oil	941	916	877	911	706	492	42	29	-0.1	-2.1
Gas	406	426	452	392	377	365	22	22	0.8	0.1
Electricity	437	488	545	416	427	466	26	28	1.2	0.7
Heat	7	6	5	7	6	4	0	0	-1.2	-1.7
Bioenergy	106	133	163	110	193	282	8	17	2.2	4.2
Other renewables	3	7	12	5	17	43	1	3	6.9	11.9
Industry	391	404	416	375	362	357	100	100	0.6	0.1
Coal	28	26	25	27	23	20	6	5	-0.2	-1.0
Oil	37	36	34	36	32	30	8	8	-0.3	-0.7
Gas	158	159	160	152	140	127	38	36	0.5	-0.3
Electricity	119	128	136	113	108	110	33	31	1.0	0.2
Heat	6	5	5	6	5	4	1	1	-0.7	-1.1
Bioenergy	41	49	56	40	49	57	13	16	1.6	1.7
Other renewables	0	1	1	1	4	9	0	3	6.5	16.9
Transport	737	741	755	719	623	547	100	100	0.2	-1.0
Oil	677	661	639	655	473	278	85	51	-0.2	-3.1
Electricity	1	2	5	2	16	62	1	11	5.3	15.6
Biofuels	36	50	68	38	99	154	9	28	3.3	6.3
Other fuels	23	28	43	24	36	53	6	10	2.7	3.5
Buildings	606	657	711	578	567	575	100	100	0.9	0.1
Coal	1	1	0	1	0	0	0	0	-2.3	-13.4
Oil	51	42	32	46	29	18	4	3	-2.0	-4.0
Gas	210	222	233	200	185	169	33	29	0.8	-0.4
Electricity	312	353	399	297	298	289	56	50	1.3	0.1
Heat	1	1	0	1	1	0	0	0	-5.7	-6.9
Bioenergy	28	32	36	29	42	66	5	12	1.3	3.6
Other renewables	3	6	11	3	12	32	2	6	6.8	11.0
Other	198	201	198	197	197	193	100	100	0.8	0.7

OECD Americas: New Policies Scenario

	Electricity generation (TWh)							Shares (%)		CAAGR (%)
	1990	2012	2020	2025	2030	2035	2040	2012	2040	2012-40
Total generation	3 819	5 268	5 790	6 007	6 203	6 415	6 697	100	100	0.9
Coal	1 796	1 767	1 768	1 594	1 351	1 251	1 207	34	18	-1.4
Oil	211	102	63	44	35	29	20	2	0	-5.7
Gas	406	1 496	1 670	1 859	2 046	2 119	2 227	28	33	1.4
Nuclear	687	905	961	964	1 000	1 025	1 043	17	16	0.5
Hydro	602	711	756	779	800	820	837	13	12	0.6
Bioenergy	91	96	138	173	207	240	272	2	4	3.8
Wind	3	157	319	420	527	634	734	3	11	5.7
Geothermal	21	24	38	50	63	73	82	0	1	4.5
Solar PV	0	9	63	99	137	176	214	0	3	11.8
CSP	1	1	15	24	32	43	53	0	1	15.4
Marine	0	0	0	0	3	5	7	0	0	22.1

	Electrical capacity (GW)						Shares (%)		CAAGR (%)
	2012	2020	2025	2030	2035	2040	2012	2040	2012-40
Total capacity	1 356	1 476	1 556	1 629	1 698	1 777	100	100	1.0
Coal	353	314	304	281	254	234	26	13	-1.5
Oil	88	59	47	41	36	30	7	2	-3.7
Gas	496	574	599	619	643	676	37	38	1.1
Nuclear	124	124	124	129	132	134	9	8	0.3
Hydro	194	204	210	216	220	224	14	13	0.5
Bioenergy	20	27	33	39	44	49	1	3	3.3
Wind	67	119	154	190	224	257	5	14	4.9
Geothermal	4	6	7	9	10	12	0	1	3.7
Solar PV	9	45	69	94	119	143	1	8	10.5
CSP	1	5	7	10	12	15	0	1	12.9
Marine	0	0	0	1	2	2	0	0	18.6

	CO_2 emissions (Mt)							Shares (%)		CAAGR (%)
	1990	2012	2020	2025	2030	2035	2040	2012	2040	2012-40
Total CO_2	5 574	6 090	6 167	5 935	5 608	5 406	5 249	100	100	-0.5
Coal	1 916	1 749	1 709	1 539	1 294	1 161	1 072	29	20	-1.7
Oil	2 469	2 626	2 569	2 412	2 230	2 102	1 971	43	38	-1.0
Gas	1 189	1 714	1 889	1 984	2 084	2 143	2 205	28	42	0.9
Power generation	2 015	2 328	2 279	2 155	1 971	1 854	1 788	100	100	-0.9
Coal	1 643	1 620	1 572	1 406	1 167	1 039	954	70	53	-1.9
Oil	150	76	47	33	26	22	15	3	1	-5.6
Gas	222	632	660	717	777	794	819	27	46	0.9
TFC	3 213	3 360	3 431	3 311	3 158	3 061	2 964	100	100	-0.4
Coal	270	118	124	119	114	109	106	3	4	-0.4
Oil	2 115	2 396	2 378	2 241	2 071	1 954	1 837	71	62	-0.9
Transport	*1 585*	*1 963*	*1 948*	*1 834*	*1 689*	*1 594*	*1 495*	*58*	*50*	*-1.0*
Gas	829	846	929	950	973	998	1 022	25	34	0.7

OECD Americas: Current Policies and 450 Scenarios

	Electricity generation (TWh)						Shares (%) 2040		CAAGR (%) 2012-40	
	2020	2030	2040	2020	2030	2040	CPS	450	CPS	450
	Current Policies Scenario			450 Scenario						
Total generation	5 890	6 550	7 293	5 595	5 688	6 165	100	100	1.2	0.6
Coal	1 998	2 153	2 339	1 529	765	835	32	14	1.0	-2.6
Oil	66	42	27	57	24	11	0	0	-4.7	-7.8
Gas	1 580	1 820	2 164	1 702	1 689	1 078	30	17	1.3	-1.2
Nuclear	951	957	937	970	1 087	1 246	13	20	0.1	1.1
Hydro	753	793	828	754	804	848	11	14	0.5	0.6
Bioenergy	132	176	216	139	247	363	3	6	3.0	4.9
Wind	302	423	528	328	707	1 050	7	17	4.4	7.0
Geothermal	37	52	63	38	76	120	1	2	3.5	5.9
Solar PV	57	104	148	65	183	321	2	5	10.3	13.4
CSP	14	29	38	15	104	280	1	5	14.0	22.5
Marine	0	2	6	0	3	14	0	0	21.3	25.1

	Electrical capacity (GW)						Shares (%) 2040		CAAGR (%) 2012-40	
	2020	2030	2040	2020	2030	2040	CPS	450	CPS	450
	Current Policies Scenario			450 Scenario						
Total capacity	1 486	1 639	1 783	1 443	1 634	1 900	100	100	1.0	1.2
Coal	338	355	374	308	183	142	21	7	0.2	-3.2
Oil	59	41	30	51	29	18	2	1	-3.7	-5.4
Gas	574	629	685	550	602	613	38	32	1.2	0.8
Nuclear	123	123	120	125	140	160	7	8	-0.1	0.9
Hydro	203	213	221	204	217	229	12	12	0.5	0.6
Bioenergy	26	33	40	27	45	64	2	3	2.5	4.2
Wind	112	154	188	122	254	359	11	19	3.8	6.2
Geothermal	6	8	9	6	11	17	1	1	2.8	5.1
Solar PV	41	73	103	46	124	212	6	11	9.2	12.1
CSP	5	9	12	5	28	82	1	4	11.9	20.0
Marine	0	1	2	0	1	5	0	0	17.6	21.7

	CO_2 emissions (Mt)						Shares (%) 2040		CAAGR (%) 2012-40	
	2020	2030	2040	2020	2030	2040	CPS	450	CPS	450
	Current Policies Scenario			450 Scenario						
Total CO_2	6 422	6 546	6 728	5 867	3 853	2 544	100	100	0.4	-3.1
Coal	1 937	2 022	2 083	1 478	369	147	31	6	0.6	-8.5
Oil	2 619	2 514	2 392	2 518	1 851	1 184	36	47	-0.3	-2.8
Gas	1 866	2 010	2 253	1 872	1 633	1 213	33	48	1.0	-1.2
Power generation	2 477	2 617	2 784	2 061	833	327	100	100	0.6	-6.8
Coal	1 797	1 891	1 959	1 345	276	91	70	28	0.7	-9.8
Oil	49	31	20	43	18	8	1	2	-4.6	-7.7
Gas	630	696	804	674	540	228	29	70	0.9	-3.6
TFC	3 489	3 448	3 399	3 363	2 658	1 935	100	100	0.0	-2.0
Coal	126	118	110	120	84	51	3	3	-0.2	-2.9
Oil	2 426	2 347	2 244	2 338	1 736	1 112	66	57	-0.2	-2.7
Transport	1 985	1 937	1 873	1 918	1 385	814	55	42	-0.2	-3.1
Gas	937	983	1 045	905	838	773	31	40	0.8	-0.3

A

United States: New Policies Scenario

	Energy demand (Mtoe)							Shares (%)		CAAGR (%)
	1990	2012	2020	2025	2030	2035	2040	2012	2040	2012-40
TPED	1 915	2 136	2 256	2 233	2 197	2 192	2 190	100	100	0.1
Coal	460	425	414	374	320	299	288	20	13	-1.4
Oil	757	771	787	738	673	627	581	36	27	-1.0
Gas	438	596	647	676	711	721	732	28	33	0.7
Nuclear	159	209	222	224	232	239	243	10	11	0.5
Hydro	23	24	25	26	27	28	28	1	1	0.6
Bioenergy	62	88	113	132	153	179	198	4	9	2.9
Other renewables	15	23	47	63	81	100	120	1	5	6.0
Power generation	750	894	929	930	927	932	949	100	100	0.2
Coal	396	382	371	331	278	257	247	43	26	-1.5
Oil	27	7	5	5	4	3	2	1	0	-4.5
Gas	90	227	231	251	274	273	277	25	29	0.7
Nuclear	159	209	222	224	232	239	243	23	26	0.5
Hydro	23	24	25	26	27	28	28	3	3	0.6
Bioenergy	40	22	30	35	40	46	52	2	6	3.1
Other renewables	14	22	44	58	72	86	100	2	11	5.6
Other energy sector	150	200	211	210	210	207	202	100	100	0.0
Electricity	49	51	53	53	53	53	54	25	26	0.2
TFC	1 294	1 426	1 530	1 518	1 495	1 497	1 498	100	100	0.2
Coal	56	22	23	22	20	19	18	2	1	-0.7
Oil	683	720	738	694	635	596	555	51	37	-0.9
Gas	303	289	326	333	340	348	356	20	24	0.8
Electricity	226	321	351	362	373	383	398	22	27	0.8
Heat	2	7	6	6	5	5	4	0	0	-1.6
Bioenergy	23	66	83	97	113	133	145	5	10	2.8
Other renewables	0	2	3	5	8	13	21	0	1	9.3
Industry	284	248	273	273	269	267	268	100	100	0.3
Coal	46	21	22	21	20	19	18	8	7	-0.5
Oil	44	20	20	19	18	17	17	8	6	-0.6
Gas	110	102	115	114	111	110	109	41	41	0.2
Electricity	75	73	81	82	81	82	83	29	31	0.5
Heat	-	5	5	5	5	4	4	2	1	-1.0
Bioenergy	9	27	30	32	33	35	36	11	14	1.0
Other renewables	-	0	0	0	0	0	1	0	0	6.1
Transport	488	597	607	583	557	554	544	100	100	-0.3
Oil	472	553	547	509	460	430	396	93	73	-1.2
Electricity	0	1	1	3	6	11	18	0	3	13.1
Biofuels	-	26	36	46	58	73	80	4	15	4.1
Other fuels	15	18	22	26	33	40	49	3	9	3.7
Buildings	389	464	500	510	520	528	540	100	100	0.5
Coal	10	1	1	1	0	0	0	0	0	-8.6
Oil	48	41	34	27	20	15	10	9	2	-5.0
Gas	164	162	180	183	186	188	188	35	35	0.5
Electricity	152	245	266	276	284	289	295	53	55	0.7
Heat	2	1	1	1	1	0	0	0	0	-6.0
Bioenergy	14	12	15	18	20	23	27	3	5	2.8
Other renewables	0	2	3	4	7	12	20	0	4	9.4
Other	133	117	150	153	150	148	146	100	100	0.8

United States: Current Policies and 450 Scenarios

	Energy demand (Mtoe)						Shares (%)		CAAGR (%)	
	2020	2030	2040	2020	2030	2040	2040		2012-40	
	Current Policies Scenario			450 Scenario			CPS	450	CPS	450
TPED	2 300	2 370	2 451	2 191	1 987	1 957	100	100	0.5	-0.3
Coal	468	492	517	360	188	210	21	11	0.7	-2.5
Oil	799	753	696	773	575	386	28	20	-0.4	-2.4
Gas	634	671	727	646	620	522	30	27	0.7	-0.5
Nuclear	219	220	221	224	249	285	9	15	0.2	1.1
Hydro	25	27	28	25	28	30	1	2	0.5	0.8
Bioenergy	110	138	173	113	202	289	7	15	2.4	4.3
Other renewables	46	69	89	49	125	236	4	12	4.9	8.6
Power generation	961	1 028	1 103	887	821	912	100	100	0.8	0.1
Coal	425	447	473	318	150	178	43	20	0.8	-2.7
Oil	6	5	3	4	2	1	0	0	-3.4	-7.1
Gas	215	231	254	240	231	148	23	16	0.4	-1.5
Nuclear	219	220	221	224	249	285	20	31	0.2	1.1
Hydro	25	27	28	25	28	30	3	3	0.5	0.8
Bioenergy	29	36	45	30	49	71	4	8	2.6	4.3
Other renewables	43	63	79	45	111	199	7	22	4.7	8.2
Other energy sector	212	217	225	206	190	174	100	100	0.4	-0.5
Electricity	*54*	*57*	*61*	*51*	*47*	*48*	*27*	*28*	*0.7*	*-0.2*
TFC	1 549	1 585	1 628	1 500	1 378	1 303	100	100	0.5	-0.3
Coal	24	21	19	23	18	15	1	1	-0.5	-1.4
Oil	749	714	669	727	542	365	41	28	-0.3	-2.4
Gas	329	342	361	318	300	288	22	22	0.8	-0.0
Electricity	357	394	436	339	345	377	27	29	1.1	0.6
Heat	7	5	4	6	5	4	0	0	-1.4	-2.0
Bioenergy	81	102	127	84	153	218	8	17	2.4	4.3
Other renewables	3	6	11	4	14	37	1	3	6.8	11.6
Industry	278	280	281	267	251	242	100	100	0.4	-0.1
Coal	23	20	18	22	18	15	7	6	-0.5	-1.3
Oil	20	19	17	19	17	15	6	6	-0.6	-0.9
Gas	117	115	113	112	101	88	40	37	0.4	-0.5
Electricity	82	86	88	78	72	72	31	30	0.7	-0.0
Heat	5	5	4	5	4	4	1	1	-0.8	-1.3
Bioenergy	31	35	39	30	35	40	14	17	1.3	1.4
Other renewables	0	0	0	1	3	7	0	3	5.2	16.3
Transport	612	608	615	599	512	450	100	100	0.1	-1.0
Oil	556	533	506	540	376	216	82	48	-0.3	-3.3
Electricity	1	2	4	1	15	57	1	13	6.9	17.7
Biofuels	34	47	65	36	89	128	11	29	3.3	5.9
Other fuels	20	25	40	22	32	49	6	11	3.0	3.7
Buildings	509	547	587	485	469	469	100	100	0.8	0.0
Coal	1	1	0	1	0	-	0	-	-2.3	-100.0
Oil	36	27	15	33	17	7	3	1	-3.6	-6.3
Gas	182	191	199	174	158	141	34	30	0.7	-0.5
Electricity	271	304	342	258	256	246	58	53	1.2	0.0
Heat	1	1	0	1	1	0	0	0	-5.7	-6.9
Bioenergy	15	18	21	16	27	46	4	10	1.9	4.8
Other renewables	3	6	10	3	10	29	2	6	6.9	10.9
Other	150	150	145	149	147	142	100	100	0.8	0.7

United States: New Policies Scenario

Electricity generation (TWh)	1990	2012	2020	2025	2030	2035	2040	Shares (%) 2012	Shares (%) 2040	CAAGR (%) 2012-40
Total generation	3 203	4 270	4 641	4 781	4 904	5 025	5 209	100	100	0.7
Coal	1 700	1 643	1 627	1 459	1 238	1 157	1 122	38	22	-1.4
Oil	131	33	24	22	19	15	10	1	0	-4.4
Gas	382	1 265	1 372	1 520	1 677	1 694	1 750	30	34	1.2
Nuclear	612	801	852	860	889	917	931	19	18	0.5
Hydro	273	279	296	306	315	323	330	7	6	0.6
Bioenergy	86	79	112	138	164	190	215	2	4	3.6
Wind	3	142	259	331	411	493	569	3	11	5.1
Geothermal	16	18	28	34	39	43	47	0	1	3.5
Solar PV	0	9	57	89	122	156	188	0	4	11.4
CSP	1	1	14	22	28	36	44	0	1	14.6
Marine	-	-	0	0	1	3	4	-	0	n.a.

Electrical capacity (GW)	2012	2020	2025	2030	2035	2040	Shares (%) 2012	Shares (%) 2040	CAAGR (%) 2012-40
Total capacity	1 137	1 212	1 265	1 312	1 354	1 405	100	100	0.8
Coal	330	290	281	262	237	219	29	16	-1.5
Oil	64	37	31	28	25	23	6	2	-3.7
Gas	446	506	517	525	535	552	39	39	0.8
Nuclear	108	108	109	113	116	118	10	8	0.3
Hydro	101	105	108	110	112	113	9	8	0.4
Bioenergy	16	21	26	30	34	39	1	3	3.2
Wind	59	95	120	147	173	197	5	14	4.4
Geothermal	3	4	5	6	6	7	0	0	2.5
Solar PV	8	40	61	83	104	124	1	9	10.4
CSP	1	4	6	9	11	13	0	1	12.2
Marine	-	0	0	1	1	1	-	0	n.a.

CO$_2$ emissions (Mt)	1990	2012	2020	2025	2030	2035	2040	Shares (%) 2012	Shares (%) 2040	CAAGR (%) 2012-40
Total CO$_2$	4 850	5 043	5 075	4 834	4 513	4 300	4 119	100	100	-0.7
Coal	1 797	1 613	1 557	1 391	1 169	1 056	977	32	24	-1.8
Oil	2 042	2 056	2 018	1 877	1 708	1 590	1 466	41	36	-1.2
Gas	1 011	1 375	1 500	1 565	1 636	1 654	1 677	27	41	0.7
Power generation	1 848	2 064	2 005	1 888	1 722	1 609	1 538	100	100	-1.0
Coal	1 550	1 507	1 447	1 286	1 070	962	886	73	58	-1.9
Oil	88	25	18	16	13	11	7	1	0	-4.5
Gas	210	531	540	587	639	637	645	26	42	0.7
TFC	2 730	2 696	2 747	2 623	2 469	2 373	2 272	100	100	-0.6
Coal	245	95	98	93	88	83	79	4	3	-0.7
Oil	1 788	1 919	1 895	1 760	1 595	1 485	1 369	71	60	-1.2
Transport	*1 376*	*1 622*	*1 602*	*1 489*	*1 349*	*1 259*	*1 161*	*60*	*51*	*-1.2*
Gas	697	682	754	770	787	806	824	25	36	0.7

United States: Current Policies and 450 Scenarios

	Electricity generation (TWh)						Shares (%)		CAAGR (%)	
	2020	2030	2040	2020	2030	2040	2040		2012-40	
	Current Policies Scenario			450 Scenario			CPS	450	CPS	450
Total generation	4 722	5 195	5 730	4 484	4 520	4 897	100	100	1.1	0.5
Coal	1 851	1 981	2 153	1 408	718	802	38	16	1.0	-2.5
Oil	26	24	14	18	10	4	0	0	-3.1	-7.1
Gas	1 262	1 404	1 598	1 421	1 428	870	28	18	0.8	-1.3
Nuclear	841	845	849	861	956	1 095	15	22	0.2	1.1
Hydro	293	308	324	296	324	349	6	7	0.5	0.8
Bioenergy	107	142	173	112	203	301	3	6	2.8	4.9
Wind	247	330	399	267	567	836	7	17	3.8	6.5
Geothermal	28	39	47	28	51	83	1	2	3.4	5.6
Solar PV	53	95	136	59	164	281	2	6	10.2	13.1
CSP	14	27	35	14	99	264	1	5	13.7	22.2
Marine	0	1	3	0	2	10	0	0	n.a.	n.a.

	Electrical capacity (GW)						Shares (%)		CAAGR (%)	
	2020	2030	2040	2020	2030	2040	2040		2012-40	
	Current Policies Scenario			450 Scenario			CPS	450	CPS	450
Total capacity	1 222	1 325	1 420	1 186	1 328	1 537	100	100	0.8	1.1
Coal	314	327	344	285	167	132	24	9	0.1	-3.2
Oil	37	28	22	29	17	12	2	1	-3.7	-5.8
Gas	503	529	550	487	528	525	39	34	0.7	0.6
Nuclear	107	107	107	109	121	138	8	9	-0.0	0.9
Hydro	104	108	111	105	113	118	8	8	0.3	0.6
Bioenergy	20	26	32	21	37	53	2	3	2.5	4.4
Wind	91	119	142	99	202	283	10	18	3.2	5.8
Geothermal	4	6	7	4	7	12	0	1	2.5	4.6
Solar PV	37	66	93	42	110	182	7	12	9.3	11.9
CSP	4	8	11	4	27	78	1	5	11.5	19.8
Marine	0	0	1	0	1	4	0	0	n.a.	n.a.

	CO_2 emissions (Mt)						Shares (%)		CAAGR (%)	
	2020	2030	2040	2020	2030	2040	2040		2012-40	
	Current Policies Scenario			450 Scenario			CPS	450	CPS	450
Total CO_2	5 300	5 336	5 390	4 819	3 001	1 902	100	100	0.2	-3.4
Coal	1 777	1 850	1 923	1 343	316	127	36	7	0.6	-8.7
Oil	2 054	1 946	1 812	1 979	1 408	869	34	46	-0.4	-3.0
Gas	1 469	1 539	1 655	1 496	1 277	907	31	48	0.7	-1.5
Power generation	2 187	2 301	2 430	1 812	699	253	100	100	0.6	-7.2
Coal	1 666	1 748	1 829	1 237	245	86	75	34	0.7	-9.7
Oil	19	17	10	14	8	3	0	1	-3.3	-7.1
Gas	502	537	591	561	445	163	24	65	0.4	-4.1
TFC	2 790	2 709	2 625	2 694	2 057	1 456	100	100	-0.1	-2.2
Coal	100	91	82	95	63	36	3	2	-0.5	-3.4
Oil	1 930	1 828	1 707	1 865	1 327	816	65	56	-0.4	-3.0
Transport	1 629	1 561	1 482	1 580	1 100	632	56	43	-0.3	-3.3
Gas	761	791	836	734	668	605	32	42	0.7	-0.4

A

OECD Europe: New Policies Scenario

	Energy demand (Mtoe)							Shares (%)		CAAGR (%)
	1990	2012	2020	2025	2030	2035	2040	2012	2040	2012-40
TPED	1 630	1 769	1 762	1 738	1 717	1 704	1 697	100	100	-0.1
Coal	452	323	283	254	214	177	164	18	10	-2.4
Oil	616	572	527	494	457	423	388	32	23	-1.4
Gas	260	419	438	460	472	490	503	24	30	0.7
Nuclear	205	230	222	199	206	211	206	13	12	-0.4
Hydro	38	48	51	53	54	56	57	3	3	0.6
Bioenergy	54	136	169	186	202	216	229	8	13	1.9
Other renewables	5	41	73	92	111	131	150	2	9	4.7
Power generation	626	757	755	746	749	757	769	100	100	0.1
Coal	279	239	206	180	145	112	103	32	13	-3.0
Oil	51	21	11	7	6	5	4	3	0	-6.1
Gas	41	130	135	154	164	178	188	17	24	1.3
Nuclear	205	230	222	199	206	211	206	30	27	-0.4
Hydro	38	48	51	53	54	56	57	6	7	0.6
Bioenergy	9	55	68	74	80	85	88	7	11	1.7
Other renewables	3	35	62	78	94	110	124	5	16	4.7
Other energy sector	152	148	138	132	125	124	123	100	100	-0.7
Electricity	*39*	*46*	*44*	*44*	*44*	*45*	*45*	*31*	*37*	*-0.1*
TFC	1 130	1 234	1 259	1 262	1 255	1 248	1 242	100	100	0.0
Coal	124	53	50	48	45	43	41	4	3	-0.9
Oil	524	512	482	456	425	392	359	41	29	-1.3
Gas	201	268	282	286	288	292	294	22	24	0.3
Electricity	193	268	287	298	307	317	328	22	26	0.7
Heat	40	46	49	51	53	54	56	4	4	0.7
Bioenergy	46	80	99	110	120	129	139	7	11	2.0
Other renewables	2	6	10	13	17	21	26	1	2	5.2
Industry	324	291	291	288	280	274	269	100	100	-0.3
Coal	71	32	29	28	26	24	23	11	8	-1.2
Oil	59	33	30	27	25	22	20	11	8	-1.7
Gas	78	88	83	80	76	73	71	30	26	-0.8
Electricity	88	99	104	105	105	106	106	34	40	0.3
Heat	14	16	16	16	16	16	15	6	6	-0.2
Bioenergy	14	23	28	30	31	32	33	8	12	1.3
Other renewables	0	0	0	0	1	1	1	0	0	3.8
Transport	268	326	324	320	311	298	286	100	100	-0.5
Oil	262	303	292	281	267	248	228	93	80	-1.0
Electricity	5	6	7	8	9	10	12	2	4	2.7
Biofuels	0	14	22	26	29	32	35	4	12	3.2
Other fuels	1	3	4	5	6	8	10	1	4	4.7
Buildings	405	481	512	525	540	559	577	100	100	0.7
Coal	49	19	18	18	17	17	16	4	3	-0.5
Oil	97	63	52	43	34	28	23	13	4	-3.5
Gas	105	164	182	188	193	198	201	34	35	0.7
Electricity	97	159	171	179	188	197	204	33	35	0.9
Heat	24	30	33	35	37	38	40	6	7	1.0
Bioenergy	30	41	47	51	56	62	68	9	12	1.8
Other renewables	2	5	9	12	15	19	24	1	4	5.4
Other	133	136	132	129	123	117	110	100	100	-0.7

OECD Europe: Current Policies and 450 Scenarios

	Energy demand (Mtoe)						Shares (%)		CAAGR (%)	
	2020	2030	2040	2020	2030	2040	2040		2012-40	
	Current Policies Scenario			450 Scenario			CPS	450	CPS	450
TPED	1 788	1 810	1 844	1 714	1 590	1 530	100	100	0.1	-0.5
Coal	289	268	254	251	131	108	14	7	-0.9	-3.9
Oil	538	495	443	516	386	253	24	17	-0.9	-2.9
Gas	455	527	587	425	407	356	32	23	1.2	-0.6
Nuclear	222	180	169	224	229	248	9	16	-1.1	0.3
Hydro	51	54	56	51	57	60	3	4	0.5	0.8
Bioenergy	163	188	211	172	239	288	11	19	1.6	2.7
Other renewables	71	98	125	74	141	217	7	14	4.1	6.1
Power generation	767	796	852	730	692	723	100	100	0.4	-0.2
Coal	209	194	186	176	67	54	22	8	-0.9	-5.1
Oil	11	6	4	11	5	2	0	0	-5.8	-7.4
Gas	147	202	248	137	132	86	29	12	2.3	-1.5
Nuclear	222	180	169	224	229	248	20	34	-1.1	0.3
Hydro	51	54	56	51	57	60	7	8	0.5	0.8
Bioenergy	67	77	84	68	85	101	10	14	1.5	2.2
Other renewables	61	83	105	63	117	172	12	24	4.0	5.9
Other energy sector	140	132	135	133	113	106	100	100	-0.3	-1.2
Electricity	45	47	51	43	40	40	38	37	0.4	-0.5
TFC	1 277	1 320	1 341	1 230	1 170	1 105	100	100	0.3	-0.4
Coal	51	48	45	48	42	35	3	3	-0.6	-1.5
Oil	493	462	411	472	359	233	31	21	-0.8	-2.8
Gas	287	304	317	268	257	251	24	23	0.6	-0.2
Electricity	292	327	362	280	290	309	27	28	1.1	0.5
Heat	50	55	61	47	47	48	5	4	0.9	0.1
Bioenergy	94	109	125	102	152	186	9	17	1.6	3.0
Other renewables	10	15	20	11	24	45	2	4	4.3	7.3
Industry	296	293	287	286	267	252	100	100	-0.0	-0.5
Coal	30	27	24	28	24	20	8	8	-1.0	-1.6
Oil	30	26	21	29	23	19	7	7	-1.5	-2.0
Gas	85	80	75	81	71	62	26	24	-0.5	-1.3
Electricity	106	111	115	103	100	98	40	39	0.5	-0.0
Heat	16	16	15	16	14	13	5	5	-0.3	-0.8
Bioenergy	29	33	35	28	32	36	12	14	1.6	1.7
Other renewables	0	1	1	1	2	4	0	2	3.2	9.8
Transport	328	331	317	318	280	219	100	100	-0.1	-1.4
Oil	300	294	270	286	209	112	85	51	-0.4	-3.5
Electricity	7	8	11	7	13	31	3	14	2.2	6.3
Biofuels	18	24	30	21	50	59	10	27	2.7	5.1
Other fuels	4	5	6	4	8	16	2	7	3.0	6.5
Buildings	521	572	625	494	502	526	100	100	0.9	0.3
Coal	18	19	19	17	15	13	3	2	-0.0	-1.4
Oil	55	43	32	50	29	17	5	3	-2.4	-4.5
Gas	185	207	223	170	165	161	36	31	1.1	-0.0
Electricity	175	203	232	166	173	175	37	33	1.4	0.3
Heat	33	39	45	31	32	35	7	7	1.5	0.5
Bioenergy	45	50	56	50	66	86	9	16	1.1	2.6
Other renewables	8	13	18	10	20	39	3	7	4.4	7.3
Other	133	124	112	132	121	108	100	100	-0.7	-0.8

A

OECD Europe: New Policies Scenario

Electricity generation (TWh)	1990	2012	2020	2025	2030	2035	2040	Shares (%) 2012	Shares (%) 2040	CAAGR (%) 2012-40
Total generation	2 682	3 661	3 861	3 984	4 094	4 221	4 350	100	100	0.6
Coal	1 040	994	870	771	623	480	429	27	10	-3.0
Oil	216	79	38	25	19	17	12	2	0	-6.6
Gas	168	682	726	860	920	1 008	1 062	19	24	1.6
Nuclear	787	881	852	763	792	811	791	24	18	-0.4
Hydro	446	562	592	614	631	647	662	15	15	0.6
Bioenergy	21	173	214	237	258	274	286	5	7	1.8
Wind	1	208	414	528	632	725	807	6	19	5.0
Geothermal	4	12	16	20	24	28	32	0	1	3.6
Solar PV	0	67	129	151	165	179	192	2	4	3.8
CSP	-	4	10	14	21	30	38	0	1	8.6
Marine	1	0	1	3	8	20	39	0	1	17.2

Electrical capacity (GW)	2012	2020	2025	2030	2035	2040	Shares (%) 2012	Shares (%) 2040	CAAGR (%) 2012-40
Total capacity	1 034	1 200	1 267	1 324	1 380	1 429	100	100	1.2
Coal	193	180	159	144	119	115	19	8	-1.8
Oil	62	37	27	20	18	14	6	1	-5.1
Gas	232	290	327	343	367	375	22	26	1.7
Nuclear	129	123	110	112	114	111	12	8	-0.6
Hydro	202	215	222	227	232	237	20	17	0.6
Bioenergy	38	45	48	51	53	55	4	4	1.3
Wind	106	187	229	266	297	325	10	23	4.1
Geothermal	2	2	3	3	4	4	0	0	3.5
Solar PV	69	118	137	149	159	167	7	12	3.2
CSP	2	3	4	6	9	11	0	1	6.2
Marine	0	0	1	3	8	15	0	1	15.8

CO_2 emissions (Mt)	1990	2012	2020	2025	2030	2035	2040	Shares (%) 2012	Shares (%) 2040	CAAGR (%) 2012-40
Total CO_2	3 959	3 723	3 480	3 316	3 060	2 843	2 702	100	100	-1.1
Coal	1 708	1 249	1 091	967	788	622	546	34	20	-2.9
Oil	1 674	1 509	1 380	1 289	1 188	1 097	1 006	41	37	-1.4
Gas	578	965	1 009	1 060	1 084	1 124	1 151	26	43	0.6
Power generation	1 399	1 358	1 200	1 118	967	842	793	100	100	-1.9
Coal	1 140	987	848	734	567	413	348	73	44	-3.7
Oil	164	67	35	24	18	16	12	5	1	-6.1
Gas	95	303	317	361	381	413	434	22	55	1.3
TFC	2 382	2 184	2 118	2 046	1 956	1 865	1 774	100	100	-0.7
Coal	528	228	212	204	193	184	174	10	10	-1.0
Oil	1 394	1 337	1 255	1 183	1 097	1 007	921	61	52	-1.3
Transport	*775*	*909*	*874*	*843*	*799*	*743*	*683*	*42*	*39*	*-1.0*
Gas	460	619	651	660	666	674	680	28	38	0.3

OECD Europe: Current Policies and 450 Scenarios

	Electricity generation (TWh)						Shares (%)		CAAGR (%)	
	2020	2030	2040	2020	2030	2040	2040		2012-40	
	Current Policies Scenario			450 Scenario			CPS	450	CPS	450
Total generation	3 935	4 366	4 822	3 770	3 850	4 064	100	100	1.0	0.4
Coal	888	853	860	744	252	191	18	5	-0.5	-5.7
Oil	39	20	13	38	13	6	0	0	-6.2	-8.7
Gas	800	1 162	1 428	744	720	376	30	9	2.7	-2.1
Nuclear	852	692	649	860	877	950	13	23	-1.1	0.3
Hydro	591	624	646	592	664	700	13	17	0.5	0.8
Bioenergy	209	248	275	214	275	331	6	8	1.7	2.3
Wind	407	580	704	419	780	1 079	15	27	4.4	6.0
Geothermal	15	19	25	16	30	42	1	1	2.6	4.6
Solar PV	124	146	163	131	190	248	3	6	3.2	4.8
CSP	10	18	32	10	37	79	1	2	8.0	11.5
Marine	1	5	26	1	10	64	1	2	15.5	19.2

	Electrical capacity (GW)						Shares (%)		CAAGR (%)	
	2020	2030	2040	2020	2030	2040	2040		2012-40	
	Current Policies Scenario			450 Scenario			CPS	450	CPS	450
Total capacity	1 210	1 350	1 477	1 186	1 356	1 532	100	100	1.3	1.4
Coal	183	163	156	174	93	62	11	4	-0.8	-4.0
Oil	37	20	15	37	19	13	1	1	-4.9	-5.4
Gas	305	402	466	277	323	337	32	22	2.5	1.3
Nuclear	123	99	91	124	126	134	6	9	-1.3	0.1
Hydro	214	225	232	215	238	250	16	16	0.5	0.8
Bioenergy	44	49	53	45	54	63	4	4	1.2	1.8
Wind	185	251	296	189	317	413	20	27	3.7	5.0
Geothermal	2	3	3	2	4	6	0	0	2.6	4.6
Solar PV	113	132	145	120	168	205	10	13	2.7	4.0
CSP	3	5	9	3	11	23	1	2	5.6	9.2
Marine	0	2	11	0	4	26	1	2	14.2	17.9

	CO_2 emissions (Mt)						Shares (%)		CAAGR (%)	
	2020	2030	2040	2020	2030	2040	2040		2012-40	
	Current Policies Scenario			450 Scenario			CPS	450	CPS	450
Total CO_2	3 578	3 522	3 431	3 285	2 281	1 566	100	100	-0.3	-3.0
Coal	1 115	1 006	913	960	395	220	27	14	-1.1	-6.0
Oil	1 414	1 304	1 170	1 347	970	584	34	37	-0.9	-3.3
Gas	1 048	1 213	1 349	978	917	762	39	49	1.2	-0.8
Power generation	1 245	1 262	1 284	1 080	523	268	100	100	-0.2	-5.6
Coal	867	772	696	724	207	84	54	31	-1.2	-8.4
Oil	35	19	13	35	15	8	1	3	-5.8	-7.4
Gas	343	471	576	321	301	176	45	66	2.3	-1.9
TFC	2 169	2 118	2 002	2 051	1 650	1 207	100	100	-0.3	-2.1
Coal	217	205	191	206	165	121	10	10	-0.6	-2.2
Oil	1 288	1 209	1 077	1 226	900	534	54	44	-0.8	-3.2
Transport	898	880	808	856	627	336	40	28	-0.4	-3.5
Gas	663	704	733	619	585	552	37	46	0.6	-0.4

European Union: New Policies Scenario

	Energy demand (Mtoe)							Shares (%)		CAAGR (%)
	1990	2012	2020	2025	2030	2035	2040	2012	2040	2012-40
TPED	1 642	1 641	1 615	1 582	1 552	1 534	1 523	100	100	-0.3
Coal	456	294	249	218	180	144	131	18	9	-2.9
Oil	607	526	476	441	403	369	336	32	22	-1.6
Gas	297	392	403	423	434	448	459	24	30	0.6
Nuclear	207	230	223	202	206	211	207	14	14	-0.4
Hydro	25	29	33	34	34	35	35	2	2	0.7
Bioenergy	47	137	169	186	201	214	226	8	15	1.8
Other renewables	3	33	61	78	95	112	129	2	9	5.1
Power generation	646	706	695	681	678	682	691	100	100	-0.1
Coal	287	227	189	162	128	96	87	32	13	-3.4
Oil	62	20	11	7	6	5	4	3	1	-6.0
Gas	55	116	116	134	143	156	164	16	24	1.3
Nuclear	207	230	223	202	206	211	207	33	30	-0.4
Hydro	25	29	33	34	34	35	35	4	5	0.7
Bioenergy	8	54	66	71	77	81	83	8	12	1.6
Other renewables	3	30	56	71	85	98	111	4	16	4.8
Other energy sector	152	136	125	120	113	112	111	100	100	-0.7
Electricity	*39*	*42*	*39*	*38*	*38*	*38*	*39*	*31*	*35*	*-0.3*
TFC	1 130	1 141	1 150	1 146	1 132	1 121	1 111	100	100	-0.1
Coal	122	38	35	32	30	28	25	3	2	-1.5
Oil	504	471	434	405	372	338	306	41	28	-1.5
Gas	226	258	270	273	275	278	279	23	25	0.3
Electricity	186	241	255	263	270	277	284	21	26	0.6
Heat	54	48	51	52	54	55	56	4	5	0.5
Bioenergy	38	82	101	112	122	132	141	7	13	2.0
Other renewables	1	2	5	7	10	14	18	0	2	7.6
Industry	343	265	263	259	251	244	238	100	100	-0.4
Coal	69	25	23	22	20	18	17	10	7	-1.4
Oil	58	31	28	26	23	21	19	12	8	-1.7
Gas	97	83	77	75	71	68	65	31	27	-0.9
Electricity	85	87	91	91	90	90	90	33	38	0.2
Heat	19	16	16	16	15	15	14	6	6	-0.4
Bioenergy	14	23	28	30	31	32	32	9	14	1.2
Other renewables	-	0	0	0	0	0	1	0	0	13.6
Transport	259	307	298	290	277	262	248	100	100	-0.8
Oil	253	284	265	251	233	213	192	92	77	-1.4
Electricity	5	6	7	7	8	10	11	2	5	2.6
Biofuels	0	15	22	27	30	33	36	5	14	3.2
Other fuels	1	3	4	5	6	7	9	1	4	4.2
Buildings	395	445	471	483	496	512	528	100	100	0.6
Coal	49	10	9	8	7	7	6	2	1	-1.7
Oil	90	56	47	40	32	26	22	13	4	-3.2
Gas	108	157	173	179	183	188	191	35	36	0.7
Electricity	91	145	154	160	167	174	179	32	34	0.8
Heat	34	32	35	37	38	40	42	7	8	0.9
Bioenergy	24	42	48	53	58	63	70	10	13	1.8
Other renewables	1	2	5	7	10	13	17	0	3	7.7
Other	133	124	118	114	109	103	97	100	100	-0.9

European Union: Current Policies and 450 Scenarios

	Energy demand (Mtoe)						Shares (%)		CAAGR (%)	
	2020	2030	2040	2020	2030	2040	2040		2012-40	
	Current Policies Scenario			450 Scenario			CPS	450	CPS	450
TPED	1 638	1 636	1 652	1 571	1 451	1 395	100	100	0.0	-0.6
Coal	255	224	200	221	112	93	12	7	-1.4	-4.0
Oil	487	439	387	466	340	219	23	16	-1.1	-3.1
Gas	418	484	539	391	377	334	33	24	1.1	-0.6
Nuclear	223	184	174	225	231	244	11	18	-1.0	0.2
Hydro	32	34	35	33	35	37	2	3	0.7	0.9
Bioenergy	162	187	209	172	236	282	13	20	1.5	2.6
Other renewables	60	83	107	63	120	186	7	13	4.4	6.4
Power generation	705	720	760	672	636	661	100	100	0.3	-0.2
Coal	193	169	152	162	63	53	20	8	-1.4	-5.1
Oil	11	6	4	11	5	3	0	0	-5.8	-6.6
Gas	126	178	221	118	117	79	29	12	2.3	-1.4
Nuclear	223	184	174	225	231	244	23	37	-1.0	0.2
Hydro	32	34	35	33	35	37	5	6	0.7	0.9
Bioenergy	65	74	80	66	81	94	11	14	1.4	2.0
Other renewables	55	75	95	57	104	151	12	23	4.2	5.9
Other energy sector	127	119	122	121	102	96	100	100	-0.4	-1.3
Electricity	40	41	44	38	35	34	36	36	0.2	-0.7
TFC	1 167	1 192	1 200	1 124	1 061	1 002	100	100	0.2	-0.5
Coal	35	31	28	34	28	24	2	2	-1.1	-1.7
Oil	445	407	354	426	314	196	30	20	-1.0	-3.1
Gas	275	291	302	257	245	241	25	24	0.6	-0.2
Electricity	259	287	315	249	256	271	26	27	1.0	0.4
Heat	51	56	61	49	48	49	5	5	0.8	0.0
Bioenergy	96	111	127	104	153	186	11	19	1.6	3.0
Other renewables	5	8	13	6	16	35	1	3	6.3	10.2
Industry	267	262	253	259	240	225	100	100	-0.2	-0.6
Coal	23	21	18	22	19	16	7	7	-1.2	-1.7
Oil	28	24	20	27	22	17	8	8	-1.6	-2.1
Gas	79	74	69	76	66	57	27	25	-0.6	-1.3
Electricity	92	95	97	90	86	84	38	37	0.4	-0.1
Heat	16	15	14	16	14	12	5	5	-0.5	-0.9
Bioenergy	29	33	35	28	32	36	14	16	1.5	1.6
Other renewables	0	0	0	0	1	3	0	1	12.8	20.1
Transport	302	296	277	293	253	196	100	100	-0.4	-1.6
Oil	273	259	231	260	183	92	83	47	-0.7	-3.9
Electricity	6	8	10	7	12	28	4	14	2.2	6.0
Biofuels	18	23	30	22	50	60	11	31	2.5	5.1
Other fuels	3	5	6	4	8	15	2	8	2.7	6.3
Buildings	480	525	572	455	462	486	100	100	0.9	0.3
Coal	9	8	8	9	7	6	1	1	-1.1	-1.9
Oil	50	40	30	45	27	17	5	3	-2.3	-4.2
Gas	177	197	213	162	157	154	37	32	1.1	-0.1
Electricity	157	180	204	149	155	156	36	32	1.2	0.3
Heat	35	41	47	33	34	36	8	7	1.4	0.4
Bioenergy	47	52	59	51	66	85	10	18	1.2	2.5
Other renewables	4	8	12	5	15	32	2	7	6.3	10.0
Other	118	109	97	118	107	95	100	100	-0.9	-1.0

A

European Union: New Policies Scenario

Electricity generation (TWh)	1990	2012	2020	2025	2030	2035	2040	Shares (%) 2012	Shares (%) 2040	CAAGR (%) 2012-40
Total generation	2 576	3 260	3 400	3 488	3 563	3 652	3 742	100	100	0.5
Coal	1 050	935	788	682	540	402	346	29	9	-3.5
Oil	224	73	37	23	17	16	11	2	0	-6.6
Gas	193	582	583	707	768	838	881	18	24	1.5
Nuclear	795	882	856	776	790	811	793	27	21	-0.4
Hydro	289	335	379	391	399	405	410	10	11	0.7
Bioenergy	20	170	209	229	248	262	272	5	7	1.7
Wind	1	206	398	500	592	672	742	6	20	4.7
Geothermal	3	6	9	12	15	19	22	0	1	4.9
Solar PV	0	67	130	150	164	177	189	2	5	3.8
CSP	-	4	10	14	21	30	38	0	1	8.6
Marine	1	0	1	3	8	20	39	0	1	17.2

Electrical capacity (GW)	2012	2020	2025	2030	2035	2040	Shares (%) 2012	Shares (%) 2040	CAAGR (%) 2012-40
Total capacity	960	1 096	1 148	1 190	1 232	1 267	100	100	1.0
Coal	189	168	145	127	103	98	20	8	-2.3
Oil	62	36	25	18	16	12	6	1	-5.6
Gas	215	260	291	304	321	324	22	26	1.5
Nuclear	129	123	111	112	114	111	13	9	-0.5
Hydro	149	159	163	167	169	171	16	14	0.5
Bioenergy	37	44	47	49	51	53	4	4	1.2
Wind	106	183	221	254	281	304	11	24	3.8
Geothermal	1	1	2	2	2	3	0	0	4.7
Solar PV	69	119	137	148	157	164	7	13	3.1
CSP	2	3	4	6	9	11	0	1	6.2
Marine	0	0	1	3	8	16	0	1	15.8

CO_2 emissions (Mt)	1990	2012	2020	2025	2030	2035	2040	Shares (%) 2012	Shares (%) 2040	CAAGR (%) 2012-40
Total CO_2	4 051	3 442	3 147	2 961	2 701	2 481	2 336	100	100	-1.4
Coal	1 732	1 137	960	829	653	493	415	33	18	-3.5
Oil	1 656	1 408	1 263	1 162	1 055	963	873	41	37	-1.7
Gas	663	898	924	970	993	1 026	1 048	26	45	0.6
Power generation	1 497	1 273	1 089	997	848	725	672	100	100	-2.3
Coal	1 172	940	782	662	498	349	282	74	42	-4.2
Oil	197	62	35	23	17	16	11	5	2	-5.9
Gas	128	271	272	313	333	360	378	21	56	1.2
TFC	2 379	2 003	1 913	1 830	1 731	1 636	1 545	100	100	-0.9
Coal	523	168	153	143	132	122	112	8	7	-1.4
Oil	1 340	1 241	1 139	1 058	966	875	789	62	51	-1.6
Transport	748	852	796	753	698	638	576	43	37	-1.4
Gas	515	594	621	628	633	639	643	30	42	0.3

European Union: Current Policies and 450 Scenarios

	Electricity generation (TWh)						Shares (%)		CAAGR (%)	
	2020	2030	2040	2020	2030	2040	2040		2012-40	
	Current Policies Scenario			450 Scenario			CPS	450	CPS	450
Total generation	3 462	3 798	4 156	3 320	3 362	3 541	100	100	0.9	0.3
Coal	805	728	681	675	228	181	16	5	-1.1	-5.7
Oil	38	18	11	36	13	7	0	0	-6.4	-8.0
Gas	645	987	1 237	602	606	320	30	9	2.7	-2.1
Nuclear	856	706	666	865	886	938	16	26	-1.0	0.2
Hydro	378	395	406	379	412	432	10	12	0.7	0.9
Bioenergy	204	239	263	209	262	307	6	9	1.6	2.1
Wind	392	545	654	401	703	951	16	27	4.2	5.6
Geothermal	8	12	16	9	21	31	0	1	3.8	6.1
Solar PV	124	146	163	131	186	238	4	7	3.2	4.6
CSP	10	18	32	10	35	73	1	2	8.0	11.1
Marine	1	5	26	1	11	64	1	2	15.6	19.2

	Electrical capacity (GW)						Shares (%)		CAAGR (%)	
	2020	2030	2040	2020	2030	2040	2040		2012-40	
	Current Policies Scenario			450 Scenario			CPS	450	CPS	450
Total capacity	1 106	1 215	1 316	1 083	1 214	1 361	100	100	1.1	1.3
Coal	171	143	127	162	87	60	10	4	-1.4	-4.0
Oil	36	17	13	36	17	11	1	1	-5.5	-6.0
Gas	275	360	416	249	286	296	32	22	2.4	1.1
Nuclear	123	100	93	125	126	133	7	10	-1.2	0.1
Hydro	158	165	169	159	172	180	13	13	0.5	0.7
Bioenergy	43	48	51	44	52	59	4	4	1.1	1.6
Wind	181	240	280	184	292	372	21	27	3.5	4.6
Geothermal	1	2	2	1	3	4	0	0	3.6	6.0
Solar PV	114	132	145	120	165	199	11	15	2.7	3.8
CSP	3	5	9	3	10	22	1	2	5.6	8.9
Marine	0	2	11	0	4	26	1	2	14.3	18.0

	CO_2 emissions (Mt)						Shares (%)		CAAGR (%)	
	2020	2030	2040	2020	2030	2040	2040		2012-40	
	Current Policies Scenario			450 Scenario			CPS	450	CPS	450
Total CO_2	3 238	3 108	2 961	2 972	2 035	1 396	100	100	-0.5	-3.2
Coal	984	832	699	845	328	179	24	13	-1.7	-6.4
Oil	1 296	1 165	1 024	1 232	862	502	35	36	-1.1	-3.6
Gas	959	1 112	1 238	895	845	715	42	51	1.2	-0.8
Power generation	1 131	1 100	1 079	982	478	262	100	100	-0.6	-5.5
Coal	801	668	554	671	197	90	51	34	-1.9	-8.0
Oil	36	18	12	35	15	9	1	4	-5.8	-6.6
Gas	294	414	513	276	266	163	48	62	2.3	-1.8
TFC	1 961	1 882	1 754	1 852	1 462	1 054	100	100	-0.5	-2.3
Coal	156	139	123	149	113	77	7	7	-1.1	-2.7
Oil	1 172	1 073	934	1 113	793	451	53	43	-1.0	-3.5
Transport	820	778	694	781	549	276	40	26	-0.7	-3.9
Gas	633	670	696	590	555	526	40	50	0.6	-0.4

A

OECD Asia Oceania: New Policies Scenario

	Energy demand (Mtoe)							Shares (%)		CAAGR (%)
	1990	2012	2020	2025	2030	2035	2040	2012	2040	2012-40
TPED	631	864	893	903	905	903	895	100	100	0.1
Coal	138	238	229	219	206	189	173	28	19	-1.1
Oil	335	358	315	294	277	260	244	41	27	-1.4
Gas	66	184	170	173	176	180	179	21	20	-0.1
Nuclear	66	43	116	134	142	152	162	5	18	4.8
Hydro	11	10	12	12	13	13	14	1	2	1.1
Bioenergy	10	22	28	31	35	39	42	3	5	2.3
Other renewables	4	9	25	39	56	69	81	1	9	8.2
Power generation	241	382	412	430	443	451	456	100	100	0.6
Coal	60	160	151	142	131	116	102	42	22	-1.6
Oil	56	43	15	10	8	8	8	11	2	-6.0
Gas	40	107	82	79	77	77	72	28	16	-1.4
Nuclear	66	43	116	134	142	152	162	11	36	4.8
Hydro	11	10	12	12	13	13	14	3	3	1.1
Bioenergy	3	11	15	17	20	23	25	3	5	3.1
Other renewables	3	8	22	36	52	63	73	2	16	8.3
Other energy sector	59	81	92	94	92	91	89	100	100	0.3
Electricity	*11*	*17*	*19*	*19*	*19*	*19*	*19*	*21*	*22*	*0.5*
TFC	429	565	569	567	562	557	550	100	100	-0.1
Coal	49	40	38	36	33	31	29	7	5	-1.2
Oil	259	293	278	264	251	238	224	52	41	-1.0
Gas	27	72	77	81	86	90	93	13	17	0.9
Electricity	86	142	156	162	166	170	173	25	31	0.7
Heat	0	6	6	6	6	6	7	1	1	0.6
Bioenergy	7	11	13	14	15	16	16	2	3	1.4
Other renewables	2	1	2	3	4	6	8	0	1	7.4
Industry	143	160	164	165	163	162	159	100	100	-0.0
Coal	38	38	36	34	31	29	27	24	17	-1.2
Oil	49	32	29	28	26	24	22	20	14	-1.3
Gas	11	26	28	30	31	32	33	16	21	0.9
Electricity	40	53	60	62	62	63	64	33	40	0.6
Heat	-	2	2	2	2	2	2	1	1	-0.5
Bioenergy	5	8	9	10	10	11	11	5	7	1.1
Other renewables	0	0	0	0	0	0	0	0	0	3.1
Transport	110	140	133	126	121	117	114	100	100	-0.8
Oil	109	136	128	120	114	109	104	97	92	-1.0
Electricity	2	2	3	3	3	4	5	2	4	2.7
Biofuels	-	1	1	1	1	1	1	0	1	1.4
Other fuels	0	2	2	3	3	3	4	1	4	3.1
Buildings	120	174	181	185	190	195	198	100	100	0.5
Coal	10	1	1	1	1	1	1	1	0	-2.0
Oil	47	37	35	32	30	27	25	22	12	-1.5
Gas	15	43	45	47	50	52	54	25	27	0.8
Electricity	44	85	92	95	99	101	103	49	52	0.7
Heat	0	3	4	4	4	5	5	2	2	1.2
Bioenergy	2	2	3	3	4	4	4	1	2	2.2
Other renewables	1	1	2	2	3	4	7	0	3	7.5
Other	56	92	91	90	87	83	79	100	100	-0.5

OECD Asia Oceania: Current Policies and 450 Scenarios

	Energy demand (Mtoe)						Shares (%)		CAAGR (%)	
	2020	2030	2040	2020	2030	2040	2040		2012-40	
	Current Policies Scenario			450 Scenario			CPS	450	CPS	450
TPED	902	923	931	867	821	784	100	100	0.3	-0.3
Coal	236	229	222	212	134	94	24	12	-0.2	-3.2
Oil	318	283	253	309	244	185	27	24	-1.2	-2.3
Gas	171	195	210	166	158	127	23	16	0.5	-1.3
Nuclear	116	129	135	116	157	192	14	24	4.1	5.5
Hydro	11	12	13	12	15	17	1	2	0.9	1.9
Bioenergy	27	33	39	28	43	59	4	8	2.1	3.6
Other renewables	23	42	60	25	71	110	7	14	7.0	9.3
Power generation	418	451	476	398	398	407	100	100	0.8	0.2
Coal	156	152	145	136	65	32	31	8	-0.3	-5.6
Oil	16	9	8	16	6	5	2	1	-6.0	-7.7
Gas	83	92	97	81	69	37	20	9	-0.3	-3.7
Nuclear	116	129	135	116	157	192	28	47	4.1	5.5
Hydro	11	12	13	12	15	17	3	4	0.9	1.9
Bioenergy	14	18	22	15	22	30	5	7	2.6	3.7
Other renewables	21	38	56	23	65	95	12	23	7.2	9.3
Other energy sector	94	97	97	89	83	74	100	100	0.6	-0.3
Electricity	19	20	22	18	17	16	22	21	0.9	-0.3
TFC	574	577	573	556	514	474	100	100	0.0	-0.6
Coal	39	34	30	37	31	25	5	5	-1.1	-1.7
Oil	280	256	233	272	223	171	41	36	-0.8	-1.9
Gas	77	87	96	73	76	77	17	16	1.0	0.2
Electricity	158	174	187	152	151	150	33	32	1.0	0.2
Heat	6	6	7	6	6	6	1	1	0.7	0.4
Bioenergy	13	15	17	13	20	30	3	6	1.4	3.5
Other renewables	2	3	5	3	7	15	1	3	5.3	9.7
Industry	166	168	165	163	156	146	100	100	0.1	-0.3
Coal	36	32	28	35	29	24	17	16	-1.1	-1.7
Oil	30	26	23	29	24	20	14	13	-1.3	-1.8
Gas	28	32	33	28	30	30	20	20	0.9	0.6
Electricity	60	64	66	59	59	58	40	40	0.8	0.3
Heat	2	2	2	2	2	2	1	1	-0.5	-0.7
Bioenergy	10	11	12	10	11	12	7	8	1.4	1.3
Other renewables	0	0	0	0	1	1	0	1	2.6	6.1
Transport	134	124	119	131	106	87	100	100	-0.6	-1.7
Oil	129	117	111	126	95	64	93	73	-0.7	-2.7
Electricity	3	3	4	3	5	9	3	11	2.3	5.3
Biofuels	1	1	1	1	4	11	1	12	0.6	10.6
Other fuels	2	3	4	2	2	3	3	4	2.8	2.3
Buildings	183	198	211	172	165	163	100	100	0.7	-0.2
Coal	1	1	1	1	1	1	0	0	-1.1	-2.3
Oil	35	31	26	32	24	17	12	10	-1.2	-2.8
Gas	45	51	57	42	42	41	27	25	1.0	-0.1
Electricity	94	105	115	88	86	81	54	50	1.1	-0.2
Heat	4	4	5	4	4	4	2	3	1.2	0.9
Bioenergy	3	3	4	3	4	6	2	4	1.8	3.5
Other renewables	1	2	3	2	5	13	2	8	4.9	10.1
Other	91	87	79	91	86	77	100	100	-0.5	-0.6

OECD Asia Oceania: New Policies Scenario

Electricity generation (TWh)	1990	2012	2020	2025	2030	2035	2040	Shares (%) 2012	Shares (%) 2040	CAAGR (%) 2012-40
Total generation	1 127	1 850	2 029	2 103	2 159	2 207	2 239	100	100	0.7
Coal	256	717	695	662	624	560	504	39	23	-1.3
Oil	259	205	67	41	33	31	30	11	1	-6.6
Gas	208	566	487	476	470	470	443	31	20	-0.9
Nuclear	255	166	445	516	545	583	623	9	28	4.8
Hydro	133	116	134	139	145	152	160	6	7	1.1
Bioenergy	12	46	61	72	83	93	102	2	5	2.9
Wind	-	14	48	77	108	137	165	1	7	9.2
Geothermal	4	9	18	31	46	57	64	0	3	7.3
Solar PV	0	10	70	82	93	104	116	1	5	9.3
CSP	-	0	2	3	6	10	14	0	1	35.3
Marine	-	-	2	3	5	9	17	-	1	n.a.

Electrical capacity (GW)	2012	2020	2025	2030	2035	2040	Shares (%) 2012	Shares (%) 2040	CAAGR (%) 2012-40
Total capacity	454	545	568	590	609	626	100	100	1.2
Coal	106	114	112	110	100	94	23	15	-0.4
Oil	58	32	25	21	19	20	13	3	-3.8
Gas	127	171	173	173	173	166	28	27	1.0
Nuclear	68	67	70	72	77	82	15	13	0.7
Hydro	69	71	73	76	78	80	15	13	0.5
Bioenergy	8	10	12	14	16	17	2	3	2.8
Wind	6	18	27	37	47	55	1	9	8.1
Geothermal	1	2	5	7	8	9	0	2	7.5
Solar PV	10	59	69	78	86	94	2	15	8.3
CSP	0	0	1	1	2	3	0	1	28.1
Marine	0	1	1	2	3	6	0	1	11.7

CO_2 emissions (Mt)	1990	2012	2020	2025	2030	2035	2040	Shares (%) 2012	Shares (%) 2040	CAAGR (%) 2012-40
Total CO_2	1 566	2 214	2 005	1 903	1 805	1 691	1 577	100	100	-1.2
Coal	518	906	859	807	742	655	577	41	37	-1.6
Oil	887	866	744	687	647	613	579	39	37	-1.4
Gas	161	443	403	409	416	423	420	20	27	-0.2
Power generation	548	1 069	884	817	757	679	603	100	100	-2.0
Coal	280	680	642	600	549	474	409	64	68	-1.8
Oil	174	132	46	29	25	23	23	12	4	-6.0
Gas	94	256	196	188	183	182	170	24	28	-1.4
TFC	950	1 032	995	960	926	894	860	100	100	-0.6
Coal	217	181	171	162	151	141	130	17	15	-1.2
Oil	672	684	647	609	576	545	513	66	60	-1.0
Transport	*321*	*400*	*376*	*353*	*336*	*321*	*306*	*39*	*36*	*-1.0*
Gas	61	167	178	189	199	208	217	16	25	0.9

OECD Asia Oceania: Current Policies and 450 Scenarios

	Electricity generation (TWh)						Shares (%)		CAAGR (%)	
	2020	2030	2040	2020	2030	2040	2040		2012-40	
	Current Policies Scenario			450 Scenario			CPS	450	CPS	450
Total generation	2 058	2 264	2 426	1 975	1 958	1 927	100	100	1.0	0.1
Coal	724	729	734	634	317	133	30	7	0.1	-5.8
Oil	70	36	30	70	22	16	1	1	-6.6	-8.7
Gas	493	575	616	486	422	216	25	11	0.3	-3.4
Nuclear	446	496	517	445	603	737	21	38	4.1	5.5
Hydro	133	141	149	136	170	199	6	10	0.9	1.9
Bioenergy	58	75	89	61	92	120	4	6	2.4	3.5
Wind	46	91	135	50	153	230	6	12	8.4	10.5
Geothermal	16	33	49	18	56	77	2	4	6.3	8.1
Solar PV	68	83	94	71	109	146	4	8	8.5	10.2
CSP	1	4	7	2	8	18	0	1	31.8	36.5
Marine	2	3	6	2	6	32	0	2	n.a.	n.a.

	Electrical capacity (GW)						Shares (%)		CAAGR (%)	
	2020	2030	2040	2020	2030	2040	2040		2012-40	
	Current Policies Scenario			450 Scenario			CPS	450	CPS	450
Total capacity	548	598	631	537	598	647	100	100	1.2	1.3
Coal	118	125	127	110	90	61	20	9	0.7	-1.9
Oil	32	22	20	32	18	13	3	2	-3.7	-5.1
Gas	172	191	191	163	157	143	30	22	1.5	0.4
Nuclear	67	65	68	67	80	98	11	15	-0.0	1.3
Hydro	71	74	76	72	85	94	12	15	0.3	1.1
Bioenergy	10	12	15	10	15	20	2	3	2.3	3.4
Wind	16	31	45	18	51	74	7	11	7.3	9.2
Geothermal	2	5	7	2	8	12	1	2	6.5	8.3
Solar PV	59	71	79	61	90	117	13	18	7.6	9.2
CSP	0	1	2	1	2	4	0	1	24.8	29.2
Marine	1	1	2	1	2	11	0	2	7.1	14.5

	CO_2 emissions (Mt)						Shares (%)		CAAGR (%)	
	2020	2030	2040	2020	2030	2040	2040		2012-40	
	Current Policies Scenario			450 Scenario			CPS	450	CPS	450
Total CO_2	2 046	1 961	1 868	1 907	1 315	816	100	100	-0.6	-3.5
Coal	888	835	766	789	407	157	41	19	-0.6	-6.1
Oil	752	666	610	726	551	403	33	49	-1.2	-2.7
Gas	406	460	493	392	357	256	26	31	0.4	-1.9
Power generation	913	883	847	820	413	102	100	100	-0.8	-8.0
Coal	667	636	591	578	241	30	70	30	-0.5	-10.5
Oil	48	27	23	47	18	14	3	14	-6.0	-7.6
Gas	199	221	233	195	154	58	27	56	-0.3	-5.2
TFC	1 006	949	899	965	798	629	100	100	-0.5	-1.8
Coal	174	155	135	166	131	100	15	16	-1.0	-2.1
Oil	653	592	541	630	494	358	60	57	-0.8	-2.3
Transport	379	345	325	370	280	187	36	30	-0.7	-2.7
Gas	179	202	222	169	173	171	25	27	1.0	0.1

A

Japan: New Policies Scenario

	Energy demand (Mtoe)							Shares (%)		CAAGR (%)
	1990	2012	2020	2025	2030	2035	2040	2012	2040	2012-40
TPED	439	452	447	440	434	429	422	100	100	-0.2
Coal	77	112	107	103	99	91	84	25	20	-1.0
Oil	250	210	169	152	140	131	122	46	29	-1.9
Gas	44	105	82	83	84	86	84	23	20	-0.8
Nuclear	53	4	57	61	57	59	62	1	15	10.2
Hydro	8	6	8	8	8	9	9	1	2	1.3
Bioenergy	5	10	13	15	16	18	19	2	4	2.2
Other renewables	3	4	12	20	29	36	42	1	10	9.0
Power generation	174	192	203	208	212	215	217	100	100	0.4
Coal	25	63	60	59	58	53	48	33	22	-0.9
Oil	51	37	11	6	5	5	5	19	2	-7.1
Gas	33	72	47	44	43	42	39	37	18	-2.2
Nuclear	53	4	57	61	57	59	62	2	29	10.2
Hydro	8	6	8	8	8	9	9	3	4	1.3
Bioenergy	2	7	10	11	13	14	15	4	7	2.6
Other renewables	1	3	11	18	27	33	38	2	17	9.1
Other energy sector	40	40	39	37	35	33	31	100	100	-0.9
Electricity	*7*	*9*	*9*	*9*	*9*	*9*	*9*	*22*	*29*	*0.1*
TFC	298	309	299	291	284	279	273	100	100	-0.4
Coal	32	27	24	23	21	20	18	9	7	-1.4
Oil	182	164	150	138	128	120	112	53	41	-1.4
Gas	15	35	36	39	41	44	46	11	17	1.0
Electricity	64	79	84	86	87	88	89	26	33	0.4
Heat	0	1	1	1	1	1	1	0	0	1.5
Bioenergy	3	3	3	4	4	4	4	1	1	1.0
Other renewables	1	1	1	1	2	3	4	0	1	7.5
Industry	101	83	82	80	77	74	72	100	100	-0.5
Coal	30	26	24	22	20	19	17	31	24	-1.4
Oil	35	22	20	18	17	16	14	26	20	-1.5
Gas	4	8	10	11	11	12	13	10	18	1.5
Electricity	29	24	25	25	24	24	23	29	33	-0.0
Heat	-	-	-	-	-	-	-	-	-	n.a.
Bioenergy	3	3	3	4	4	4	4	3	5	1.0
Other renewables	-	-	0	0	0	0	0	-	0	n.a.
Transport	72	75	67	60	56	53	50	100	100	-1.4
Oil	70	73	65	58	53	50	47	98	93	-1.6
Electricity	1	2	2	2	3	3	3	2	6	2.5
Biofuels	-	-	-	-	-	-	-	-	-	n.a.
Other fuels	-	-	0	0	0	0	0	-	0	n.a.
Buildings	84	111	113	115	117	120	122	100	100	0.3
Coal	1	0	0	1	1	1	1	0	0	0.4
Oil	36	29	28	26	25	23	22	27	18	-1.1
Gas	11	26	26	28	30	31	33	24	27	0.8
Electricity	34	54	57	58	60	62	62	49	51	0.5
Heat	0	1	1	1	1	1	1	0	1	1.5
Bioenergy	0	0	0	0	0	0	0	0	0	-0.8
Other renewables	1	0	1	1	1	2	4	0	3	7.8
Other	41	40	38	36	34	32	30	100	100	-1.1

Japan: Current Policies and 450 Scenarios

	Energy demand (Mtoe)						Shares (%)		CAAGR (%)	
	2020	2030	2040	2020	2030	2040	2040		2012-40	
	Current Policies Scenario			450 Scenario			CPS	450	CPS	450
TPED	452	438	435	430	387	357	100	100	-0.1	-0.8
Coal	112	111	102	96	62	40	23	11	-0.3	-3.6
Oil	170	143	126	165	119	86	29	24	-1.8	-3.1
Gas	82	96	104	79	72	51	24	14	-0.0	-2.5
Nuclear	57	45	45	57	67	81	10	23	8.9	11.7
Hydro	8	8	9	8	10	12	2	3	1.1	2.1
Bioenergy	12	15	18	13	19	24	4	7	2.0	3.1
Other renewables	11	20	31	12	39	63	7	18	7.8	10.6
Power generation	205	212	224	193	189	188	100	100	0.6	-0.1
Coal	64	69	65	50	24	9	29	5	0.2	-6.7
Oil	11	5	5	11	3	2	2	1	-7.0	-9.6
Gas	46	54	57	46	37	16	25	8	-0.8	-5.3
Nuclear	57	45	45	57	67	81	20	43	8.9	11.2
Hydro	8	8	9	8	10	12	4	6	1.1	2.1
Bioenergy	9	12	14	10	13	16	6	9	2.3	2.9
Other renewables	10	19	29	11	35	53	13	28	8.1	10.5
Other energy sector	40	37	33	38	31	25	100	100	-0.6	-1.7
Electricity	9	10	10	9	8	7	30	27	0.5	-0.9
TFC	302	291	285	290	253	225	100	100	-0.3	-1.1
Coal	25	22	19	24	19	16	7	7	-1.3	-1.9
Oil	151	131	116	146	110	81	41	36	-1.2	-2.5
Gas	37	42	47	34	36	37	16	16	1.1	0.2
Electricity	85	91	97	81	78	73	34	33	0.7	-0.3
Heat	1	1	1	1	1	1	0	0	1.6	0.6
Bioenergy	3	4	4	4	5	8	1	4	1.4	3.8
Other renewables	1	1	2	1	4	10	1	5	4.4	11.2
Industry	83	79	74	81	73	66	100	100	-0.4	-0.8
Coal	24	21	18	23	19	15	24	23	-1.3	-2.0
Oil	20	17	15	20	16	13	20	19	-1.4	-1.9
Gas	10	12	13	10	11	12	17	18	1.6	1.3
Electricity	25	25	24	25	23	22	33	33	0.1	-0.3
Heat	-	-	-	-	-	-	-	-	n.a.	n.a.
Bioenergy	3	4	4	3	4	4	6	6	1.4	1.4
Other renewables	0	0	0	0	0	0	0	1	n.a.	n.a.
Transport	67	57	52	66	46	35	100	100	-1.3	-2.7
Oil	65	54	49	64	42	26	94	74	-1.4	-3.7
Electricity	2	2	3	2	3	5	6	15	2.1	4.4
Biofuels	-	-	-	-	1	3	-	9	n.a.	n.a.
Other fuels	0	0	0	0	0	1	0	2	n.a.	n.a.
Buildings	114	122	129	105	99	95	100	100	0.5	-0.6
Coal	0	1	1	0	0	0	0	0	0.6	-0.2
Oil	28	25	23	25	19	14	18	14	-0.9	-2.7
Gas	26	30	34	24	24	24	26	25	0.9	-0.3
Electricity	58	64	69	54	51	46	54	49	0.9	-0.5
Heat	1	1	1	1	1	1	1	1	1.6	0.6
Bioenergy	0	0	0	0	0	1	0	1	-0.5	12.3
Other renewables	1	1	2	1	3	9	1	10	4.5	11.5
Other	38	34	30	38	34	29	100	100	-1.1	-1.2

A

Japan: New Policies Scenario

Electricity generation (TWh)	1990	2012	2020	2025	2030	2035	2040	Shares (%) 2012	Shares (%) 2040	CAAGR (%) 2012-40
Total generation	836	1 026	1 085	1 103	1 119	1 135	1 142	100	100	0.4
Coal	116	303	299	295	296	272	251	30	22	-0.7
Oil	237	181	53	31	25	23	23	18	2	-7.2
Gas	179	397	302	295	293	287	265	39	23	-1.4
Nuclear	202	16	220	234	218	228	239	2	21	10.2
Hydro	89	75	89	93	98	103	109	7	10	1.3
Bioenergy	11	39	48	55	61	66	71	4	6	2.2
Wind	-	5	13	23	36	48	59	0	5	9.4
Geothermal	2	3	5	13	21	25	28	0	2	8.9
Solar PV	0	7	57	64	72	79	86	1	8	9.4
CSP	-	-	-	-	-	-	-	-	-	n.a.
Marine	-	-	-	0	1	3	9	-	1	n.a.

Electrical capacity (GW)	2012	2020	2025	2030	2035	2040	Shares (%) 2012	Shares (%) 2040	CAAGR (%) 2012-40
Total capacity	288	336	342	349	356	363	100	100	0.8
Coal	47	48	48	48	44	40	16	11	-0.6
Oil	50	25	20	16	14	15	18	4	-4.2
Gas	79	109	112	111	108	102	27	28	0.9
Nuclear	46	38	33	30	31	33	16	9	-1.2
Hydro	49	50	52	53	55	57	17	16	0.5
Bioenergy	6	8	9	10	11	12	2	3	2.2
Wind	3	6	10	14	18	22	1	6	8.0
Geothermal	1	1	2	4	4	5	0	1	8.4
Solar PV	7	50	57	63	68	73	2	20	8.9
CSP	-	-	-	-	-	-	-	-	n.a.
Marine	-	-	0	0	1	3	-	1	n.a.

CO_2 emissions (Mt)	1990	2012	2020	2025	2030	2035	2040	Shares (%) 2012	Shares (%) 2040	CAAGR (%) 2012-40
Total CO_2	1 056	1 215	1 020	956	915	864	810	100	100	-1.4
Coal	291	420	401	384	370	338	309	35	38	-1.1
Oil	651	536	418	370	340	318	297	44	37	-2.1
Gas	115	260	201	202	205	208	205	21	25	-0.9
Power generation	363	562	414	385	374	345	316	100	100	-2.0
Coal	128	276	268	259	254	229	207	49	66	-1.0
Oil	157	111	32	19	15	14	14	20	4	-7.1
Gas	78	175	114	108	105	103	95	31	30	-2.2
TFC	648	611	568	536	508	488	465	100	100	-1.0
Coal	147	127	116	109	101	94	88	21	19	-1.3
Oil	466	403	367	335	310	291	271	66	58	-1.4
Transport	*208*	*215*	*191*	*169*	*156*	*147*	*137*	*35*	*29*	*-1.6*
Gas	35	81	84	91	97	102	107	13	23	1.0

Japan: Current Policies and 450 Scenarios

	Electricity generation (TWh)						Shares (%)		CAAGR (%)	
	2020	2030	2040	2020	2030	2040	2040		2012-40	
	Current Policies Scenario			450 Scenario			CPS	450	CPS	450
Total generation	1 100	1 173	1 242	1 045	994	933	100	100	0.7	-0.3
Coal	319	350	341	254	129	41	27	4	0.4	-6.9
Oil	53	26	23	56	15	10	2	1	-7.1	-9.7
Gas	302	367	392	300	244	100	32	11	-0.0	-4.8
Nuclear	220	174	174	220	259	312	14	33	8.9	11.2
Hydro	88	94	101	91	113	135	8	14	1.1	2.1
Bioenergy	45	55	64	48	63	76	5	8	1.8	2.4
Wind	12	30	53	13	62	100	4	11	8.9	11.4
Geothermal	5	12	21	5	26	39	2	4	7.8	10.2
Solar PV	56	65	72	58	81	102	6	11	8.7	10.1
CSP	-	-	-	-	-	-	-	-	n.a.	n.a.
Marine	-	-	1	-	1	19	0	2	n.a.	n.a.

	Electrical capacity (GW)						Shares (%)		CAAGR (%)	
	2020	2030	2040	2020	2030	2040	2040		2012-40	
	Current Policies Scenario			450 Scenario			CPS	450	CPS	450
Total capacity	338	354	362	331	349	377	100	100	0.8	1.0
Coal	51	55	53	47	37	28	15	7	0.4	-1.8
Oil	25	18	17	25	13	9	5	2	-3.9	-6.0
Gas	111	124	118	103	96	84	33	22	1.5	0.3
Nuclear	38	24	24	38	36	43	7	11	-2.3	-0.2
Hydro	50	52	54	51	59	65	15	17	0.4	1.0
Bioenergy	7	9	11	8	10	12	3	3	1.9	2.4
Wind	5	11	18	6	22	34	5	9	7.3	9.7
Geothermal	1	2	4	1	5	7	1	2	7.3	9.6
Solar PV	50	58	63	52	71	86	17	23	8.4	9.6
CSP	-	-	-	-	-	-	-	-	n.a.	n.a.
Marine	-	-	0	-	0	7	0	2	n.a.	n.a.

	CO_2 emissions (Mt)						Shares (%)		CAAGR (%)	
	2020	2030	2040	2020	2030	2040	2040		2012-40	
	Current Policies Scenario			450 Scenario			CPS	450	CPS	450
Total CO_2	1 043	1 004	950	953	655	397	100	100	-0.9	-3.9
Coal	421	422	388	352	205	92	41	23	-0.3	-5.3
Oil	422	349	311	405	279	195	33	49	-1.9	-3.5
Gas	201	233	251	196	171	110	26	28	-0.1	-3.0
Power generation	430	450	436	369	191	32	100	100	-0.9	-9.7
Coal	286	302	283	223	98	4	65	12	0.1	-14.1
Oil	32	16	14	33	9	6	3	20	-7.1	-9.7
Gas	112	131	139	113	84	22	32	68	-0.8	-7.2
TFC	575	521	484	547	434	341	100	100	-0.8	-2.1
Coal	118	104	90	113	92	75	19	22	-1.2	-1.8
Oil	371	318	284	354	257	180	59	53	-1.2	-2.8
Transport	192	160	145	187	123	75	30	22	-1.4	-3.7
Gas	85	99	109	80	84	85	23	25	1.1	0.2

A

Non-OECD: New Policies Scenario

	Energy demand (Mtoe)							Shares (%)		CAAGR (%)
	1990	2012	2020	2025	2030	2035	2040	2012	2040	2012-40
TPED	4 059	7 760	9 151	10 031	10 883	11 656	12 371	100	100	1.7
Coal	1 150	2 859	3 246	3 409	3 569	3 698	3 796	37	31	1.0
Oil	1 161	1 943	2 274	2 484	2 659	2 779	2 884	25	23	1.4
Gas	825	1 500	1 753	1 987	2 227	2 484	2 738	19	22	2.2
Nuclear	74	133	257	352	438	506	570	2	5	5.3
Hydro	83	196	264	299	333	364	392	3	3	2.5
Bioenergy	758	1 067	1 208	1 284	1 358	1 425	1 476	14	12	1.2
Other renewables	8	62	149	217	300	401	515	1	4	7.9
Power generation	1 268	2 893	3 518	3 938	4 381	4 842	5 305	100	100	2.2
Coal	466	1 589	1 827	1 956	2 107	2 248	2 379	55	45	1.5
Oil	223	216	189	164	136	123	116	7	2	-2.2
Gas	407	663	753	843	933	1 034	1 137	23	21	1.9
Nuclear	74	133	257	352	438	506	570	5	11	5.3
Hydro	83	196	264	299	333	364	392	7	7	2.5
Bioenergy	7	52	113	149	187	230	270	2	5	6.1
Other renewables	8	43	116	175	247	338	442	1	8	8.7
Other energy sector	498	1 152	1 262	1 318	1 367	1 396	1 410	100	100	0.7
Electricity	*78*	*200*	*250*	*281*	*314*	*348*	*382*	*17*	*27*	*2.3*
TFC	2 982	5 020	6 047	6 683	7 281	7 800	8 267	100	100	1.8
Coal	535	789	899	923	933	933	920	16	11	0.6
Oil	814	1 587	1 938	2 181	2 397	2 549	2 673	32	32	1.9
Gas	357	639	808	937	1 069	1 202	1 336	13	16	2.7
Electricity	282	829	1 136	1 331	1 529	1 729	1 926	17	23	3.1
Heat	293	228	243	250	256	260	260	5	3	0.5
Bioenergy	702	930	991	1 019	1 045	1 065	1 079	19	13	0.5
Other renewables	0	19	33	42	52	63	73	0	1	5.0
Industry	979	1 797	2 212	2 428	2 623	2 817	2 984	100	100	1.8
Coal	315	632	728	746	752	755	750	35	25	0.6
Oil	159	210	236	246	253	259	262	12	9	0.8
Gas	132	297	389	461	535	611	687	17	23	3.0
Electricity	159	432	590	677	758	836	903	24	30	2.7
Heat	138	106	118	124	128	131	130	6	4	0.7
Bioenergy	76	120	149	171	194	220	243	7	8	2.6
Other renewables	0	0	1	2	3	5	8	0	0	13.9
Transport	434	970	1 238	1 447	1 638	1 775	1 893	100	100	2.4
Oil	364	867	1 092	1 271	1 431	1 534	1 613	89	85	2.2
Electricity	13	17	23	27	32	38	46	2	2	3.7
Biofuels	6	17	40	56	70	84	96	2	5	6.4
Other fuels	50	69	83	93	104	118	138	7	7	2.5
Buildings	1 258	1 730	1 922	2 046	2 180	2 305	2 433	100	100	1.2
Coal	169	103	99	96	93	86	79	6	3	-1.0
Oil	116	166	172	172	174	178	186	10	8	0.4
Gas	126	202	242	275	309	340	368	12	15	2.2
Electricity	85	339	468	564	669	776	893	20	37	3.5
Heat	146	116	119	120	123	124	126	7	5	0.3
Bioenergy	615	787	792	781	766	744	720	45	30	-0.3
Other renewables	0	18	30	39	47	55	62	1	3	4.5
Other	312	522	675	762	840	903	957	100	100	2.2

Non-OECD: Current Policies and 450 Scenarios

	Energy demand (Mtoe)						Shares (%)		CAAGR (%)	
	2020	2030	2040	2020	2030	2040	2040		2012-40	
	Current Policies Scenario			450 Scenario			CPS	450	CPS	450
TPED	9 401	11 616	13 614	8 863	9 621	10 386	100	100	2.0	1.0
Coal	3 424	4 159	4 819	3 063	2 485	2 164	35	21	1.9	-1.0
Oil	2 334	2 839	3 211	2 201	2 246	1 966	24	19	1.8	0.0
Gas	1 782	2 318	2 948	1 699	2 005	2 240	22	22	2.4	1.4
Nuclear	252	398	457	266	611	913	3	9	4.5	7.1
Hydro	256	314	365	265	370	447	3	4	2.2	3.0
Bioenergy	1 216	1 357	1 459	1 214	1 463	1 756	11	17	1.1	1.8
Other renewables	136	232	355	155	442	900	3	9	6.4	10.0
Power generation	3 654	4 789	5 965	3 330	3 613	4 356	100	100	2.6	1.5
Coal	1 967	2 586	3 223	1 668	1 106	886	54	20	2.6	-2.1
Oil	197	151	129	178	96	63	2	1	-1.8	-4.3
Gas	766	988	1 278	721	812	843	21	19	2.4	0.9
Nuclear	252	398	457	266	611	913	8	21	4.5	7.1
Hydro	256	314	365	265	370	447	6	10	2.2	3.0
Bioenergy	110	166	216	114	247	423	4	10	5.2	7.8
Other renewables	105	187	297	120	372	782	5	18	7.1	10.9
Other energy sector	1 298	1 471	1 583	1 237	1 251	1 206	100	100	1.1	0.2
Electricity	257	341	427	239	268	305	27	25	2.7	1.5
TFC	6 177	7 656	8 919	5 911	6 657	7 060	100	100	2.1	1.2
Coal	923	985	1 002	880	866	818	11	12	0.9	0.1
Oil	1 988	2 559	2 988	1 883	2 043	1 840	33	26	2.3	0.5
Gas	822	1 108	1 403	790	990	1 175	16	17	2.8	2.2
Electricity	1 173	1 645	2 109	1 089	1 352	1 666	24	24	3.4	2.5
Heat	248	266	272	239	239	229	3	3	0.6	0.0
Bioenergy	991	1 049	1 088	995	1 098	1 213	12	17	0.6	1.0
Other renewables	32	45	58	36	69	118	1	2	4.1	6.8
Industry	2 266	2 771	3 226	2 166	2 423	2 619	100	100	2.1	1.4
Coal	747	791	806	715	707	674	25	26	0.9	0.2
Oil	242	267	280	230	229	218	9	8	1.0	0.1
Gas	398	566	745	377	477	543	23	21	3.3	2.2
Electricity	605	812	1 000	572	674	773	31	30	3.0	2.1
Heat	120	131	134	116	118	110	4	4	0.8	0.1
Bioenergy	152	201	256	155	208	268	8	10	2.8	2.9
Other renewables	1	3	6	2	9	33	0	1	12.5	19.9
Transport	1 262	1 730	2 094	1 198	1 399	1 352	100	100	2.8	1.2
Oil	1 126	1 550	1 863	1 051	1 132	875	89	65	2.8	0.0
Electricity	23	31	42	23	39	93	2	7	3.4	6.3
Biofuels	32	54	74	39	105	188	4	14	5.4	9.0
Other fuels	80	94	114	86	124	196	5	15	1.8	3.8
Buildings	1 967	2 296	2 603	1 874	2 015	2 167	100	100	1.5	0.8
Coal	103	102	96	93	75	58	4	3	-0.3	-2.0
Oil	178	192	211	165	158	165	8	8	0.9	-0.0
Gas	249	326	399	234	270	297	15	14	2.5	1.4
Electricity	489	727	975	441	572	722	37	33	3.8	2.7
Heat	122	129	134	117	117	115	5	5	0.5	-0.0
Bioenergy	798	780	739	791	767	730	28	34	-0.2	-0.3
Other renewables	29	40	49	32	56	79	2	4	3.7	5.5
Other	682	860	998	672	819	922	100	100	2.3	2.1

Non-OECD: New Policies Scenario

	Electricity generation (TWh)							Shares (%)		CAAGR (%)
	1990	2012	2020	2025	2030	2035	2040	2012	2040	2012-40
Total generation	4 197	11 942	16 090	18 723	21 425	24 135	26 818	100	100	2.9
Coal	1 333	5 726	7 045	7 772	8 593	9 367	10 098	48	38	2.0
Oil	624	758	664	585	495	453	432	6	2	-2.0
Gas	979	2 360	3 173	3 816	4 438	5 093	5 766	20	22	3.2
Nuclear	283	510	984	1 351	1 678	1 941	2 186	4	8	5.3
Hydro	963	2 283	3 072	3 472	3 873	4 228	4 563	19	17	2.5
Bioenergy	8	127	351	480	613	765	909	1	3	7.3
Wind	0	141	552	828	1 095	1 373	1 640	1	6	9.2
Geothermal	8	26	49	72	104	147	201	0	1	7.6
Solar PV	0	11	187	311	455	608	768	0	3	16.3
CSP	-	0	14	36	81	157	252	0	1	39.9
Marine	-	0	0	0	1	2	3	0	0	21.9

	Electrical capacity (GW)						Shares (%)		CAAGR (%)
	2012	2020	2025	2030	2035	2040	2012	2040	2012-40
Total capacity	2 839	4 080	4 788	5 502	6 200	6 884	100	100	3.2
Coal	1 153	1 489	1 670	1 859	2 031	2 189	41	32	2.3
Oil	234	244	226	204	194	186	8	3	-0.8
Gas	607	849	996	1 143	1 293	1 441	21	21	3.1
Nuclear	73	137	186	230	265	297	3	4	5.1
Hydro	619	861	977	1 093	1 194	1 288	22	19	2.7
Bioenergy	35	72	94	117	142	168	1	2	5.7
Wind	103	276	387	489	586	684	4	10	7.0
Geothermal	4	8	11	16	23	31	0	0	7.3
Solar PV	10	141	230	326	426	526	0	8	15.0
CSP	0	5	11	25	47	73	0	1	26.3
Marine	0	0	0	0	1	1	0	0	20.6

	CO_2 emissions (Mt)							Shares (%)		CAAGR (%)
	1990	2012	2020	2025	2030	2035	2040	2012	2040	2012-40
Total CO_2	9 218	18 506	21 348	22 939	24 458	25 783	26 971	100	100	1.4
Coal	4 175	10 022	11 422	11 958	12 500	12 958	13 328	54	49	1.0
Oil	3 165	5 145	5 927	6 452	6 895	7 202	7 454	28	28	1.3
Gas	1 879	3 339	3 999	4 529	5 063	5 622	6 189	18	23	2.2
Power generation	3 514	8 483	9 569	10 179	10 845	11 537	12 216	100	100	1.3
Coal	1 852	6 260	7 216	7 696	8 244	8 746	9 207	74	75	1.4
Oil	711	672	592	514	426	384	362	8	3	-2.2
Gas	951	1 551	1 761	1 969	2 175	2 408	2 647	18	22	1.9
TFC	5 296	9 140	10 798	11 733	12 546	13 153	13 641	100	100	1.4
Coal	2 247	3 542	3 994	4 049	4 043	4 002	3 916	39	29	0.4
Oil	2 260	4 174	4 998	5 595	6 121	6 471	6 746	46	49	1.7
Transport	*1 082*	*2 588*	*3 259*	*3 793*	*4 272*	*4 580*	*4 817*	*28*	*35*	*2.2*
Gas	790	1 424	1 806	2 090	2 382	2 680	2 979	16	22	2.7

Non-OECD: Current Policies and 450 Scenarios

	Electricity generation (TWh)						Shares (%)		CAAGR (%)	
	2020	2030	2040	2020	2030	2040	2040		2012-40	
	Current Policies Scenario			450 Scenario			CPS	450	CPS	450
Total generation	16 607	23 072	29 462	15 420	18 800	22 887	100	100	3.3	2.4
Coal	7 661	10 711	13 802	6 521	4 643	3 447	47	15	3.2	-1.8
Oil	694	558	491	617	332	218	2	1	-1.5	-4.4
Gas	3 251	4 803	6 598	2 997	3 818	4 107	22	18	3.7	2.0
Nuclear	967	1 526	1 753	1 018	2 345	3 503	6	15	4.5	7.1
Hydro	2 981	3 650	4 239	3 078	4 298	5 196	14	23	2.2	3.0
Bioenergy	342	540	718	354	819	1 446	2	6	6.4	9.1
Wind	499	868	1 186	580	1 546	2 595	4	11	7.9	11.0
Geothermal	45	84	151	49	162	318	1	1	6.5	9.4
Solar PV	159	297	426	192	674	1 267	1	6	13.9	18.4
CSP	8	35	96	15	161	781	0	3	35.1	45.6
Marine	0	0	2	0	2	9	0	0	21.3	27.1

	Electrical capacity (GW)						Shares (%)		CAAGR (%)	
	2020	2030	2040	2020	2030	2040	2040		2012-40	
	Current Policies Scenario			450 Scenario			CPS	450	CPS	450
Total capacity	4 101	5 561	6 903	4 002	5 443	6 994	100	100	3.2	3.3
Coal	1 567	2 151	2 685	1 407	1 250	1 175	39	17	3.1	0.1
Oil	247	216	197	240	193	167	3	2	-0.6	-1.2
Gas	867	1 216	1 588	836	1 096	1 289	23	18	3.5	2.7
Nuclear	134	209	239	141	315	470	3	7	4.3	6.9
Hydro	833	1 022	1 186	861	1 227	1 477	17	21	2.3	3.2
Bioenergy	70	104	134	72	152	256	2	4	4.9	7.3
Wind	252	399	514	288	666	1 027	7	15	5.9	8.6
Geothermal	7	13	23	8	25	47	0	1	6.2	9.0
Solar PV	119	219	309	145	475	862	4	12	12.9	17.1
CSP	3	11	27	5	45	221	0	3	21.8	31.3
Marine	0	0	1	0	1	3	0	0	20.0	26.0

	CO_2 emissions (Mt)						Shares (%)		CAAGR (%)	
	2020	2030	2040	2020	2030	2040	2040		2012-40	
	Current Policies Scenario			450 Scenario			CPS	450	CPS	450
Total CO_2	22 268	27 417	32 297	20 266	16 842	13 240	100	100	2.0	-1.2
Coal	12 095	14 690	17 167	10 688	6 879	4 058	53	31	1.9	-3.2
Oil	6 104	7 426	8 432	5 708	5 607	4 618	26	35	1.8	-0.4
Gas	4 070	5 301	6 698	3 869	4 356	4 563	21	34	2.5	1.1
Power generation	10 177	12 954	16 030	8 832	5 494	3 292	100	100	2.3	-3.3
Coal	7 768	10 180	12 652	6 590	3 358	1 300	79	39	2.5	-5.5
Oil	616	472	401	556	299	198	3	6	-1.8	-4.3
Gas	1 793	2 302	2 977	1 686	1 837	1 794	19	55	2.4	0.5
TFC	11 088	13 336	15 058	10 488	10 510	9 229	100	100	1.8	0.0
Coal	4 105	4 271	4 267	3 895	3 359	2 624	28	28	0.7	-1.1
Oil	5 145	6 593	7 657	4 831	5 047	4 218	51	46	2.2	0.0
Transport	*3 362*	*4 630*	*5 565*	*3 136*	*3 378*	*2 611*	*37*	*28*	*2.8*	*0.0*
Gas	1 838	2 472	3 135	1 762	2 104	2 387	21	26	2.9	1.9

A

E. Europe/Eurasia: New Policies Scenario

	Energy demand (Mtoe)							Shares (%)		CAAGR (%)
	1990	2012	2020	2025	2030	2035	2040	2012	2040	2012-40
TPED	1 538	1 178	1 194	1 238	1 286	1 340	1 384	100	100	0.6
Coal	367	248	233	235	239	242	242	21	17	-0.1
Oil	469	235	242	244	244	239	236	20	17	0.0
Gas	603	570	570	588	609	638	664	48	48	0.5
Nuclear	59	78	87	99	109	117	123	7	9	1.6
Hydro	23	24	28	30	32	35	37	2	3	1.5
Bioenergy	17	21	27	31	37	46	54	2	4	3.3
Other renewables	0	1	6	10	16	22	29	0	2	12.1
Power generation	742	582	580	597	619	650	679	100	100	0.6
Coal	197	145	136	136	138	138	137	25	20	-0.2
Oil	125	21	17	13	10	9	8	4	1	-3.3
Gas	333	307	298	297	301	310	321	53	47	0.2
Nuclear	59	78	87	99	109	117	123	13	18	1.6
Hydro	23	24	28	30	32	35	37	4	5	1.5
Bioenergy	4	6	9	11	14	21	26	1	4	5.2
Other renewables	0	1	5	10	15	21	28	0	4	12.7
Other energy sector	199	215	203	204	203	206	208	100	100	-0.1
Electricity	*35*	*41*	*43*	*45*	*47*	*50*	*53*	*19*	*26*	*0.9*
TFC	1 073	723	765	808	851	889	917	100	100	0.9
Coal	114	57	58	62	64	67	69	8	7	0.6
Oil	280	169	185	195	203	207	207	23	23	0.7
Gas	261	219	227	241	254	267	278	30	30	0.9
Electricity	126	108	120	131	141	152	161	15	18	1.4
Heat	279	156	156	160	165	170	173	22	19	0.4
Bioenergy	13	15	18	20	22	25	27	2	3	2.3
Other renewables	-	0	0	1	1	1	1	0	0	6.7
Industry	396	244	257	275	290	306	318	100	100	0.9
Coal	56	45	47	50	53	55	57	19	18	0.8
Oil	52	19	20	21	21	21	21	8	7	0.4
Gas	86	73	75	81	85	89	91	30	29	0.8
Electricity	75	48	54	59	64	68	73	20	23	1.5
Heat	127	57	57	61	64	67	70	23	22	0.7
Bioenergy	0	2	3	3	4	5	6	1	2	4.6
Other renewables	-	0	0	0	0	0	0	0	0	10.6
Transport	172	144	154	164	173	179	182	100	100	0.8
Oil	123	100	109	116	122	125	125	70	69	0.8
Electricity	12	10	11	12	13	15	16	7	9	1.8
Biofuels	0	0	1	1	2	2	2	0	1	5.9
Other fuels	37	33	34	35	36	38	39	23	21	0.6
Buildings	383	271	278	288	300	312	323	100	100	0.6
Coal	56	11	10	10	10	10	10	4	3	-0.3
Oil	35	17	16	16	15	14	13	6	4	-0.9
Gas	111	92	95	99	106	112	118	34	36	0.9
Electricity	26	46	50	53	56	60	63	17	19	1.1
Heat	143	93	93	95	97	98	100	34	31	0.3
Bioenergy	12	12	13	14	16	17	19	5	6	1.5
Other renewables	-	0	0	0	1	1	1	0	0	6.2
Other	122	64	76	82	87	91	94	100	100	1.4

E. Europe/Eurasia: Current Policies and 450 Scenarios

	Energy demand (Mtoe)						Shares (%)		CAAGR (%)	
	2020	2030	2040	2020	2030	2040	2040		2012-40	
	Current Policies Scenario			450 Scenario			CPS	450	CPS	450
TPED	1 213	1 341	1 467	1 170	1 178	1 210	100	100	0.8	0.1
Coal	236	252	270	220	165	132	18	11	0.3	-2.2
Oil	245	251	249	235	218	185	17	15	0.2	-0.9
Gas	586	657	744	558	545	529	51	44	1.0	-0.3
Nuclear	87	106	109	95	137	167	7	14	1.2	2.8
Hydro	28	32	35	28	36	45	2	4	1.4	2.2
Bioenergy	26	33	43	28	52	100	3	8	2.5	5.7
Other renewables	5	10	17	6	26	52	1	4	10.0	14.5
Power generation	589	642	707	571	572	617	100	100	0.7	0.2
Coal	137	148	161	126	73	45	23	7	0.4	-4.1
Oil	17	10	8	17	9	7	1	1	-3.4	-3.6
Gas	306	325	360	291	265	239	51	39	0.6	-0.9
Nuclear	87	106	109	95	137	167	15	27	1.2	2.8
Hydro	28	32	35	28	36	45	5	7	1.4	2.2
Bioenergy	9	12	18	9	26	64	3	10	3.9	8.6
Other renewables	5	10	16	5	25	50	2	8	10.5	15.1
Other energy sector	205	212	221	199	187	177	100	100	0.1	-0.7
Electricity	44	50	57	42	43	46	26	26	1.2	0.4
TFC	782	894	986	748	778	784	100	100	1.1	0.3
Coal	60	67	71	57	58	57	7	7	0.8	-0.0
Oil	187	210	222	179	180	160	23	20	1.0	-0.2
Gas	235	275	312	223	229	234	32	30	1.3	0.2
Electricity	123	151	177	117	129	141	18	18	1.8	1.0
Heat	159	171	178	154	155	153	18	20	0.5	-0.1
Bioenergy	17	21	25	18	26	36	2	5	1.9	3.3
Other renewables	0	0	1	0	1	2	0	0	4.4	8.7
Industry	262	304	336	252	265	274	100	100	1.1	0.4
Coal	48	54	58	46	47	47	17	17	0.9	0.1
Oil	21	21	21	20	21	21	6	8	0.3	0.4
Gas	78	94	107	74	76	76	32	28	1.4	0.2
Electricity	55	67	78	53	57	63	23	23	1.7	1.0
Heat	58	63	66	57	59	59	20	21	0.5	0.1
Bioenergy	3	4	6	3	5	8	2	3	4.9	5.7
Other renewables	0	0	0	0	0	0	0	0	8.9	13.1
Transport	155	176	193	150	156	146	100	100	1.1	0.0
Oil	109	127	138	104	104	84	71	57	1.1	-0.7
Electricity	10	13	15	10	13	17	8	12	1.7	2.1
Biofuels	1	1	0	1	2	3	0	2	0.4	7.6
Other fuels	34	37	39	34	37	41	20	28	0.6	0.8
Buildings	288	324	359	271	272	274	100	100	1.0	0.0
Coal	11	11	12	10	9	9	3	3	0.2	-0.8
Oil	17	16	16	16	12	10	4	4	-0.4	-1.8
Gas	99	117	135	92	90	87	37	32	1.4	-0.2
Electricity	52	62	73	48	51	53	20	19	1.6	0.5
Heat	96	102	107	92	92	91	30	33	0.5	-0.1
Bioenergy	13	15	17	14	18	24	5	9	1.2	2.4
Other renewables	0	0	0	0	1	2	0	1	3.3	8.3
Other	76	89	97	75	84	89	100	100	1.5	1.2

A

E. Europe/Eurasia: New Policies Scenario

Electricity generation (TWh)	1990	2012	2020	2025	2030	2035	2040	Shares (%) 2012	Shares (%) 2040	CAAGR (%) 2012-40
Total generation	1 894	1 742	1 904	2 047	2 194	2 355	2 502	100	100	1.3
Coal	429	418	409	420	437	448	453	24	18	0.3
Oil	256	40	24	15	8	6	6	2	0	-6.8
Gas	715	693	771	821	866	916	972	40	39	1.2
Nuclear	226	297	333	380	417	449	471	17	19	1.7
Hydro	267	283	326	350	376	403	428	16	17	1.5
Bioenergy	0	4	13	20	33	56	76	0	3	10.8
Wind	-	5	17	26	37	48	61	0	2	9.1
Geothermal	0	0	4	8	13	19	25	0	1	15.2
Solar PV	-	1	5	7	9	10	12	0	0	8.7
CSP	-	-	-	-	-	-	-	-	-	n.a.
Marine	-	-	-	-	0	0	0	-	0	n.a.

Electrical capacity (GW)	2012	2020	2025	2030	2035	2040	Shares (%) 2012	Shares (%) 2040	CAAGR (%) 2012-40
Total capacity	432	465	491	515	547	577	100	100	1.0
Coal	110	105	101	96	95	93	25	16	-0.6
Oil	23	17	11	7	6	6	5	1	-4.5
Gas	156	176	191	206	218	231	36	40	1.4
Nuclear	43	47	54	58	62	65	10	11	1.5
Hydro	93	103	110	117	124	130	22	23	1.2
Bioenergy	2	3	4	6	10	13	0	2	7.5
Wind	4	9	12	17	21	26	1	4	7.4
Geothermal	0	1	1	2	3	3	0	1	13.7
Solar PV	1	5	6	8	9	10	0	2	7.3
CSP	-	-	-	-	-	-	-	-	n.a.
Marine	-	-	-	0	0	0	-	0	n.a.

CO_2 emissions (Mt)	1990	2012	2020	2025	2030	2035	2040	Shares (%) 2012	Shares (%) 2040	CAAGR (%) 2012-40
Total CO_2	3 986	2 714	2 748	2 801	2 861	2 923	2 975	100	100	0.3
Coal	1 336	860	858	874	891	902	905	32	30	0.2
Oil	1 245	583	601	609	614	615	609	21	20	0.2
Gas	1 405	1 271	1 289	1 318	1 356	1 406	1 460	47	49	0.5
Power generation	1 976	1 374	1 315	1 300	1 301	1 315	1 336	100	100	-0.1
Coal	799	586	560	562	567	567	563	43	42	-0.1
Oil	399	67	55	42	32	28	26	5	2	-3.3
Gas	778	721	700	697	701	720	747	52	56	0.1
TFC	1 897	1 206	1 290	1 355	1 413	1 460	1 489	100	100	0.8
Coal	526	265	288	303	314	325	332	22	22	0.8
Oil	780	464	487	509	526	533	531	38	36	0.5
Transport	*365*	*296*	*320*	*341*	*359*	*367*	*367*	*25*	*25*	*0.8*
Gas	591	478	514	543	573	602	626	40	42	1.0

E. Europe/Eurasia: Current Policies and 450 Scenarios

	Electricity generation (TWh)						Shares (%)		CAAGR (%)	
	2020	2030	2040	2020	2030	2040	2040		2012-40	
	Current Policies Scenario			450 Scenario			CPS	450	CPS	450
Total generation	1 949	2 343	2 737	1 851	2 000	2 183	100	100	1.6	0.8
Coal	415	465	534	378	209	107	20	5	0.9	-4.7
Oil	25	8	5	24	7	4	0	0	-7.5	-8.2
Gas	813	1 027	1 249	718	649	478	46	22	2.1	-1.3
Nuclear	333	405	417	364	524	640	15	29	1.2	2.8
Hydro	326	367	413	326	424	523	15	24	1.4	2.2
Bioenergy	13	26	49	13	73	207	2	9	9.2	14.9
Wind	16	29	48	17	80	159	2	7	8.2	12.9
Geothermal	3	8	13	4	20	40	0	2	12.6	17.1
Solar PV	5	7	8	5	13	25	0	1	7.2	11.4
CSP	-	-	-	-	-	-	-	-	n.a.	n.a.
Marine	-	-	0	-	0	1	0	0	n.a.	n.a.

	Electrical capacity (GW)						Shares (%)		CAAGR (%)	
	2020	2030	2040	2020	2030	2040	2040		2012-40	
	Current Policies Scenario			450 Scenario			CPS	450	CPS	450
Total capacity	476	540	613	450	492	576	100	100	1.3	1.0
Coal	108	109	110	96	61	41	18	7	-0.0	-3.4
Oil	17	6	5	17	5	3	1	0	-5.7	-7.2
Gas	185	229	277	166	162	162	45	28	2.1	0.1
Nuclear	47	56	57	52	73	89	9	15	1.0	2.6
Hydro	103	114	125	103	130	157	20	27	1.1	1.9
Bioenergy	3	5	9	3	13	35	1	6	5.9	11.3
Wind	8	14	21	9	34	62	3	11	6.6	10.8
Geothermal	0	1	2	1	3	5	0	1	11.1	15.6
Solar PV	4	6	7	5	11	21	1	4	6.0	10.2
CSP	-	-	-	-	-	-	-	-	n.a.	n.a.
Marine	-	-	0	-	0	0	0	0	n.a.	n.a.

	CO$_2$ emissions (Mt)						Shares (%)		CAAGR (%)	
	2020	2030	2040	2020	2030	2040	2040		2012-40	
	Current Policies Scenario			450 Scenario			CPS	450	CPS	450
Total CO$_2$	2 803	3 040	3 298	2 649	2 253	1 910	100	100	0.7	-1.2
Coal	870	942	1 014	808	548	386	31	20	0.6	-2.8
Oil	608	636	656	581	532	441	20	23	0.4	-1.0
Gas	1 326	1 462	1 629	1 260	1 173	1 083	49	57	0.9	-0.6
Power generation	1 340	1 396	1 519	1 255	917	719	100	100	0.4	-2.3
Coal	566	607	660	518	285	164	43	23	0.4	-4.4
Oil	55	32	25	54	31	24	2	3	-3.4	-3.6
Gas	719	757	833	683	602	531	55	74	0.5	-1.1
TFC	1 320	1 492	1 622	1 255	1 215	1 086	100	100	1.1	-0.4
Coal	295	325	343	281	256	215	21	20	0.9	-0.7
Oil	493	547	575	471	457	382	35	35	0.8	-0.7
Transport	322	373	405	307	305	246	25	23	1.1	-0.7
Gas	532	620	704	503	502	489	43	45	1.4	0.1

A

Russia: New Policies Scenario

	Energy demand (Mtoe)							Shares (%)		CAAGR (%)
	1990	2012	2020	2025	2030	2035	2040	2012	2040	2012-40
TPED	880	741	730	748	770	798	819	100	100	0.4
Coal	191	133	117	119	120	118	114	18	14	-0.6
Oil	264	152	153	151	149	145	141	21	17	-0.3
Gas	367	387	374	377	387	401	414	52	51	0.2
Nuclear	31	47	56	64	71	78	84	6	10	2.1
Hydro	14	14	17	18	20	21	23	2	3	1.7
Bioenergy	12	7	10	11	14	20	24	1	3	4.3
Other renewables	0	0	3	7	10	15	20	0	2	14.8
Power generation	444	397	394	404	419	440	460	100	100	0.5
Coal	105	73	69	73	75	75	74	18	16	0.1
Oil	62	17	15	11	9	7	7	4	1	-3.1
Gas	228	241	227	224	225	228	234	61	51	-0.1
Nuclear	31	47	56	64	71	78	84	12	18	2.1
Hydro	14	14	17	18	20	21	23	4	5	1.7
Bioenergy	4	4	6	7	10	15	18	1	4	5.2
Other renewables	0	0	3	7	10	15	20	0	4	14.8
Other energy sector	127	147	130	126	123	122	120	100	100	-0.7
Electricity	*21*	*27*	*28*	*29*	*31*	*33*	*35*	*18*	*29*	*1.0*
TFC	625	442	454	475	496	515	527	100	100	0.6
Coal	55	26	23	24	24	24	24	6	5	-0.3
Oil	145	97	105	110	114	117	116	22	22	0.6
Gas	143	128	130	136	142	148	153	29	29	0.6
Electricity	71	64	69	76	82	88	93	14	18	1.3
Heat	203	124	123	126	130	133	136	28	26	0.3
Bioenergy	8	3	3	4	4	5	6	1	1	2.7
Other renewables	-	-	0	0	0	0	0	-	0	n.a.
Industry	209	160	160	169	177	184	187	100	100	0.6
Coal	15	22	20	20	21	21	21	14	11	-0.1
Oil	25	11	12	12	12	13	13	7	7	0.4
Gas	30	50	49	51	52	52	52	31	28	0.2
Electricity	41	29	32	35	37	39	41	18	22	1.2
Heat	98	47	47	50	53	56	58	30	31	0.7
Bioenergy	-	0	1	1	1	2	2	0	1	5.8
Other renewables	-	-	-	-	-	-	-	-	-	n.a.
Transport	116	94	99	105	110	114	115	100	100	0.8
Oil	73	59	63	66	69	71	70	63	61	0.7
Electricity	9	8	9	10	11	12	13	8	11	1.8
Biofuels	-	-	-	-	-	-	-	-	-	n.a.
Other fuels	34	27	28	29	30	31	32	29	28	0.6
Buildings	228	153	152	156	162	167	173	100	100	0.4
Coal	40	4	3	3	3	2	2	3	1	-2.4
Oil	12	8	8	7	6	6	5	6	3	-1.6
Gas	57	42	42	44	48	51	54	27	31	0.9
Electricity	15	25	27	29	31	32	34	17	20	1.1
Heat	98	71	70	71	72	73	74	47	43	0.1
Bioenergy	7	2	2	2	3	3	3	1	2	1.5
Other renewables	-	-	0	0	0	0	0	-	0	n.a.
Other	72	35	41	45	48	50	52	100	100	1.4

Russia: Current Policies and 450 Scenarios

	Energy demand (Mtoe)						Shares (%)		CAAGR (%)	
	2020	2030	2040	2020	2030	2040	2040		2012-40	
	Current Policies Scenario			450 Scenario			CPS	450	CPS	450
TPED	745	810	877	720	704	716	100	100	0.6	-0.1
Coal	120	128	129	109	76	58	15	8	-0.1	-2.9
Oil	154	152	147	149	135	112	17	16	-0.1	-1.1
Gas	386	423	475	368	338	314	54	44	0.7	-0.7
Nuclear	56	68	74	64	89	107	8	15	1.7	3.0
Hydro	17	19	22	17	22	28	3	4	1.6	2.4
Bioenergy	10	13	18	10	26	59	2	8	3.2	7.7
Other renewables	3	7	11	3	18	38	1	5	12.5	17.5
Power generation	401	436	478	390	386	417	100	100	0.7	0.2
Coal	71	82	89	62	38	28	19	7	0.7	-3.4
Oil	15	9	7	14	8	7	1	2	-3.2	-3.3
Gas	233	242	262	223	191	161	55	39	0.3	-1.4
Nuclear	56	68	74	64	89	107	15	26	1.7	3.0
Hydro	17	19	22	17	22	28	5	7	1.6	2.4
Bioenergy	6	8	13	6	20	50	3	12	3.9	9.0
Other renewables	3	7	11	3	18	38	2	9	12.5	17.5
Other energy sector	132	129	129	127	110	98	100	100	-0.4	-1.4
Electricity	28	33	38	27	28	30	30	31	1.3	0.4
TFC	466	528	576	446	455	451	100	100	1.0	0.1
Coal	24	25	25	23	21	20	4	4	-0.2	-1.0
Oil	106	117	123	102	103	91	21	20	0.8	-0.3
Gas	136	159	181	128	130	132	31	29	1.2	0.1
Electricity	72	88	103	68	74	81	18	18	1.7	0.8
Heat	126	134	139	121	121	119	24	26	0.4	-0.1
Bioenergy	3	4	5	4	6	9	1	2	2.3	4.4
Other renewables	0	0	0	0	0	0	0	0	n.a.	n.a.
Industry	164	187	201	157	160	161	100	100	0.8	0.0
Coal	20	21	21	19	18	17	11	11	-0.1	-0.9
Oil	12	12	12	12	12	13	6	8	0.2	0.5
Gas	51	60	66	48	46	44	33	28	1.0	-0.4
Electricity	33	40	45	31	33	35	22	22	1.6	0.7
Heat	48	53	55	47	48	48	27	30	0.5	0.1
Bioenergy	1	1	2	1	2	3	1	2	5.7	6.9
Other renewables	-	-	-	-	-	-	-	-	n.a.	n.a.
Transport	99	111	121	97	102	97	100	100	0.9	0.1
Oil	63	71	76	60	61	48	63	50	0.9	-0.7
Electricity	9	11	13	9	11	14	11	15	1.8	2.1
Biofuels	-	-	-	-	-	-	-	-	n.a.	n.a.
Other fuels	28	30	32	28	30	34	26	35	0.6	0.8
Buildings	161	180	200	150	147	144	100	100	1.0	-0.2
Coal	3	3	3	3	3	2	1	1	-1.3	-2.4
Oil	8	7	7	7	5	4	3	3	-0.7	-3.0
Gas	46	56	68	42	41	39	34	27	1.8	-0.2
Electricity	28	34	40	26	27	27	20	18	1.7	0.2
Heat	73	77	80	69	68	67	40	47	0.4	-0.2
Bioenergy	2	2	3	2	3	5	1	4	0.7	3.5
Other renewables	0	0	0	0	0	0	0	0	n.a.	n.a.
Other	42	50	54	41	47	49	100	100	1.5	1.2

A

Russia: New Policies Scenario

Electricity generation (TWh)	1990	2012	2020	2025	2030	2035	2040	Shares (%) 2012	Shares (%) 2040	CAAGR (%) 2012-40
Total generation	1 082	1 069	1 148	1 234	1 324	1 419	1 503	100	100	1.2
Coal	157	169	163	177	190	194	192	16	13	0.5
Oil	129	28	19	11	5	3	3	3	0	-7.9
Gas	512	525	542	564	586	603	624	49	42	0.6
Nuclear	118	178	215	246	271	299	322	17	21	2.2
Hydro	166	166	194	210	228	248	265	16	18	1.7
Bioenergy	0	3	9	13	21	40	54	0	4	10.8
Wind	-	0	3	6	11	15	21	0	1	34.6
Geothermal	0	0	3	7	11	16	21	0	1	14.4
Solar PV	-	-	0	0	1	1	1	-	0	n.a.
CSP	-	-	-	-	-	-	-	-	-	n.a.
Marine	-	-	-	-	-	-	-	-	-	n.a.

Electrical capacity (GW)	2012	2020	2025	2030	2035	2040	Shares (%) 2012	Shares (%) 2040	CAAGR (%) 2012-40
Total capacity	243	257	272	287	304	320	100	100	1.0
Coal	51	46	44	39	37	35	21	11	-1.3
Oil	6	5	3	2	1	1	2	0	-4.7
Gas	111	117	126	136	141	146	46	46	1.0
Nuclear	25	30	34	37	41	44	10	14	2.0
Hydro	49	54	58	63	68	72	20	22	1.4
Bioenergy	1	2	3	4	7	9	1	3	6.7
Wind	0	1	3	4	6	8	0	2	25.1
Geothermal	0	0	1	1	2	3	0	1	13.3
Solar PV	-	0	1	1	1	1	-	0	n.a.
CSP	-	-	-	-	-	-	-	-	n.a.
Marine	-	-	-	-	-	-	-	-	n.a.

CO_2 emissions (Mt)	1990	2012	2020	2025	2030	2035	2040	Shares (%) 2012	Shares (%) 2040	CAAGR (%) 2012-40
Total CO_2	2 179	1 640	1 640	1 657	1 682	1 703	1 715	100	100	0.2
Coal	687	425	428	445	459	461	454	26	26	0.2
Oil	625	350	360	357	356	354	348	21	20	-0.0
Gas	866	865	853	855	867	888	913	53	53	0.2
Power generation	1 162	916	873	865	867	871	876	100	100	-0.2
Coal	432	296	291	305	317	318	312	32	36	0.2
Oil	198	54	47	36	28	24	22	6	3	-3.1
Gas	532	567	534	524	522	529	542	62	62	-0.2
TFC	960	662	698	723	748	765	771	100	100	0.5
Coal	253	125	133	135	137	139	137	19	18	0.3
Oil	389	262	271	281	289	292	289	40	38	0.4
Transport	*217*	*172*	*184*	*194*	*204*	*208*	*207*	*26*	*27*	*0.7*
Gas	318	275	295	307	321	334	345	42	45	0.8

Russia: Current Policies and 450 Scenarios

	Electricity generation (TWh)						Shares (%)		CAAGR (%)	
	2020	2030	2040	2020	2030	2040	2040		2012-40	
	Current Policies Scenario			450 Scenario			CPS	450	CPS	450
Total generation	1 179	1 424	1 662	1 122	1 202	1 305	100	100	1.6	0.7
Coal	168	204	228	145	77	46	14	4	1.1	-4.5
Oil	19	5	2	19	5	2	0	0	-8.7	-8.7
Gas	568	696	829	504	399	219	50	17	1.6	-3.1
Nuclear	215	261	282	245	339	409	17	31	1.7	3.0
Hydro	194	226	260	194	261	325	16	25	1.6	2.4
Bioenergy	9	16	34	9	57	163	2	12	9.0	15.3
Wind	3	8	16	3	47	102	1	8	33.4	42.6
Geothermal	3	7	11	3	17	33	1	3	11.9	16.4
Solar PV	0	0	0	0	1	5	0	0	n.a.	n.a.
CSP	-	-	-	-	-	-	-	-	n.a.	n.a.
Marine	-	-	-	-	-	0	-	0	n.a.	n.a.

	Electrical capacity (GW)						Shares (%)		CAAGR (%)	
	2020	2030	2040	2020	2030	2040	2040		2012-40	
	Current Policies Scenario			450 Scenario			CPS	450	CPS	450
Total capacity	265	305	350	248	262	310	100	100	1.3	0.9
Coal	48	45	44	42	21	11	13	4	-0.5	-5.2
Oil	5	1	1	5	2	1	0	0	-6.7	-6.5
Gas	124	152	182	108	89	78	52	25	1.8	-1.3
Nuclear	30	36	39	35	47	56	11	18	1.5	2.9
Hydro	54	62	70	54	71	88	20	28	1.3	2.1
Bioenergy	2	3	6	2	10	28	2	9	5.1	11.1
Wind	1	4	7	1	19	38	2	12	24.3	32.3
Geothermal	0	1	1	0	2	4	0	1	10.8	15.2
Solar PV	0	0	1	0	2	6	0	2	n.a.	n.a.
CSP	-	-	-	-	-	-	-	-	n.a.	n.a.
Marine	-	-	-	-	-	0	-	0	n.a.	n.a.

	CO_2 emissions (Mt)						Shares (%)		CAAGR (%)	
	2020	2030	2040	2020	2030	2040	2040		2012-40	
	Current Policies Scenario			450 Scenario			CPS	450	CPS	450
Total CO_2	1 681	1 807	1 932	1 582	1 289	1 054	100	100	0.6	-1.6
Coal	439	492	519	395	245	164	27	16	0.7	-3.3
Oil	362	366	370	348	312	253	19	24	0.2	-1.2
Gas	880	949	1 043	839	731	637	54	60	0.7	-1.1
Power generation	893	935	1 000	832	597	465	100	100	0.3	-2.4
Coal	298	345	375	262	142	96	37	21	0.8	-4.0
Oil	47	28	22	46	27	21	2	5	-3.2	-3.3
Gas	547	562	604	524	428	348	60	75	0.2	-1.7
TFC	718	800	858	683	638	544	100	100	0.9	-0.7
Coal	136	142	140	129	101	67	16	12	0.4	-2.2
Oil	273	298	309	262	254	207	36	38	0.6	-0.8
Transport	*185*	*209*	*224*	*177*	*178*	*142*	*26*	*26*	*0.9*	*-0.7*
Gas	309	360	409	292	284	270	48	50	1.4	-0.1

Non-OECD Asia: New Policies Scenario

	Energy demand (Mtoe)							Shares (%)		CAAGR (%)
	1990	2012	2020	2025	2030	2035	2040	2012	2040	2012-40
TPED	1 588	4 551	5 551	6 115	6 653	7 118	7 527	100	100	1.8
Coal	694	2 480	2 863	3 005	3 146	3 256	3 337	54	44	1.1
Oil	318	934	1 144	1 290	1 418	1 500	1 563	21	21	1.9
Gas	69	357	508	623	736	861	986	8	13	3.7
Nuclear	10	46	152	226	290	342	387	1	5	7.9
Hydro	24	100	141	159	177	192	206	2	3	2.6
Bioenergy	466	579	624	647	673	700	723	13	10	0.8
Other renewables	7	54	120	165	214	268	325	1	4	6.6
Power generation	330	1 765	2 289	2 606	2 933	3 251	3 559	100	100	2.5
Coal	226	1 373	1 607	1 728	1 871	2 002	2 124	78	60	1.6
Oil	46	43	34	27	23	17	12	2	0	-4.3
Gas	16	133	183	227	267	317	372	8	10	3.7
Nuclear	10	46	152	226	290	342	387	3	11	7.9
Hydro	24	100	141	159	177	192	206	6	6	2.6
Bioenergy	0	33	82	110	137	164	191	2	5	6.4
Other renewables	7	37	90	128	169	216	267	2	8	7.3
Other energy sector	167	668	743	762	776	780	778	100	100	0.5
Electricity	26	112	148	169	192	214	236	17	30	2.7
TFC	1 216	2 839	3 526	3 919	4 280	4 580	4 833	100	100	1.9
Coal	395	699	801	818	822	816	797	25	16	0.5
Oil	238	824	1 041	1 197	1 334	1 428	1 502	29	31	2.2
Gas	32	166	278	352	424	494	560	6	12	4.4
Electricity	83	526	760	901	1 041	1 178	1 310	19	27	3.3
Heat	14	72	87	90	91	90	87	3	2	0.7
Bioenergy	455	535	530	525	523	522	519	19	11	-0.1
Other renewables	0	18	30	37	45	52	58	1	1	4.3
Industry	401	1 163	1 491	1 633	1 754	1 863	1 944	100	100	1.9
Coal	239	563	651	662	662	658	647	48	33	0.5
Oil	52	106	123	127	130	131	129	9	7	0.7
Gas	9	76	136	176	216	256	293	7	15	5.0
Electricity	51	315	448	519	583	642	690	27	35	2.8
Heat	11	49	61	64	65	64	61	4	3	0.8
Bioenergy	39	55	71	83	96	109	119	5	6	2.8
Other renewables	0	0	1	1	2	4	5	0	0	12.4
Transport	104	454	623	760	885	979	1 065	100	100	3.1
Oil	91	423	568	690	798	870	929	93	87	2.8
Electricity	1	6	11	14	18	22	28	1	3	5.6
Biofuels	-	3	12	20	27	35	44	1	4	9.7
Other fuels	12	21	32	37	42	51	64	5	6	4.0
Buildings	590	914	1 007	1 066	1 133	1 195	1 256	100	100	1.1
Coal	111	86	82	79	76	70	62	9	5	-1.1
Oil	34	89	89	86	84	83	84	10	7	-0.2
Gas	5	46	75	97	117	134	146	5	12	4.3
Electricity	22	176	262	324	392	461	536	19	43	4.0
Heat	3	23	26	26	26	26	26	3	2	0.5
Bioenergy	415	477	446	420	397	374	351	52	28	-1.1
Other renewables	0	17	28	35	41	46	51	2	4	4.0
Other	121	308	405	459	508	543	567	100	100	2.2

Non-OECD Asia: Current Policies and 450 Scenarios

	Energy demand (Mtoe)						Shares (%)		CAAGR (%)	
	2020	2030	2040	2020	2030	2040	2040		2012-40	
	Current Policies Scenario			450 Scenario			CPS	450	CPS	450
TPED	5 742	7 212	8 435	5 370	5 815	6 279	100	100	2.2	1.2
Coal	3 033	3 706	4 299	2 699	2 175	1 888	51	30	2.0	-1.0
Oil	1 183	1 528	1 744	1 116	1 212	1 045	21	17	2.3	0.4
Gas	514	741	1 014	508	734	943	12	15	3.8	3.5
Nuclear	148	259	305	152	425	652	4	10	7.0	10.0
Hydro	134	162	183	141	204	233	2	4	2.2	3.1
Bioenergy	621	650	669	629	755	925	8	15	0.5	1.7
Other renewables	109	166	221	125	309	592	3	9	5.1	8.9
Power generation	2 405	3 287	4 134	2 156	2 335	2 845	100	100	3.1	1.7
Coal	1 743	2 330	2 925	1 465	968	785	71	28	2.7	-2.0
Oil	34	22	13	32	16	7	0	0	-4.3	-6.2
Gas	185	268	387	190	290	379	9	13	3.9	3.8
Nuclear	148	259	305	152	425	652	7	23	7.0	10.0
Hydro	134	162	183	141	204	233	4	8	2.2	3.1
Bioenergy	80	119	148	83	179	287	4	10	5.5	8.0
Other renewables	81	127	174	93	252	500	4	18	5.7	9.8
Other energy sector	761	840	886	728	715	673	100	100	1.0	0.0
Electricity	154	213	272	142	160	183	31	27	3.2	1.8
TFC	3 622	4 540	5 251	3 458	3 934	4 153	100	100	2.2	1.4
Coal	823	869	870	784	765	713	17	17	0.8	0.1
Oil	1 079	1 444	1 682	1 017	1 144	1 005	32	24	2.6	0.7
Gas	283	440	591	273	407	518	11	12	4.6	4.2
Electricity	791	1 135	1 459	732	914	1 125	28	27	3.7	2.7
Heat	88	95	94	85	84	76	2	2	1.0	0.2
Bioenergy	529	518	508	535	563	625	10	15	-0.2	0.6
Other renewables	29	39	47	32	57	91	1	2	3.6	6.1
Industry	1 533	1 868	2 134	1 459	1 628	1 735	100	100	2.2	1.4
Coal	668	697	697	639	625	586	33	34	0.8	0.1
Oil	127	139	143	119	117	104	7	6	1.1	-0.1
Gas	141	234	329	132	203	253	15	15	5.4	4.4
Electricity	461	629	773	434	517	588	36	34	3.3	2.3
Heat	62	68	68	60	59	52	3	3	1.2	0.2
Bioenergy	73	98	121	74	101	127	6	7	2.8	3.0
Other renewables	1	2	4	1	6	25	0	1	11.2	18.7
Transport	645	949	1 166	607	761	752	100	100	3.4	1.8
Oil	596	878	1 063	552	636	481	91	64	3.3	0.5
Electricity	11	17	25	11	24	67	2	9	5.1	8.9
Biofuels	9	18	30	12	50	116	3	15	8.1	13.5
Other fuels	29	36	48	33	52	88	4	12	2.9	5.2
Buildings	1 033	1 198	1 349	987	1 045	1 111	100	100	1.4	0.7
Coal	86	84	77	78	60	44	6	4	-0.4	-2.3
Oil	93	94	96	86	75	72	7	6	0.3	-0.8
Gas	77	121	155	73	102	120	11	11	4.5	3.5
Electricity	279	438	601	248	327	416	45	37	4.5	3.1
Heat	26	26	27	25	25	25	2	2	0.5	0.2
Bioenergy	446	399	353	448	407	370	26	33	-1.1	-0.9
Other renewables	27	36	42	29	49	64	3	6	3.3	4.9
Other	411	525	603	404	500	555	100	100	2.4	2.1

A

Non-OECD Asia: New Policies Scenario

Electricity generation (TWh)	1990	2012	2020	2025	2030	2035	2040	Shares (%) 2012	Shares (%) 2040	CAAGR (%) 2012-40
Total generation	1 274	7 402	10 533	12 413	14 323	16 171	17 954	100	100	3.2
Coal	729	5 023	6 288	6 965	7 735	8 450	9 123	68	51	2.2
Oil	165	151	113	90	73	55	38	2	0	-4.8
Gas	59	658	982	1 272	1 539	1 870	2 225	9	12	4.4
Nuclear	39	175	584	868	1 112	1 312	1 487	2	8	7.9
Hydro	274	1 164	1 637	1 850	2 060	2 229	2 392	16	13	2.6
Bioenergy	1	76	255	354	448	543	636	1	4	7.9
Wind	0	126	475	706	917	1 120	1 289	2	7	8.7
Geothermal	7	20	31	41	54	69	89	0	0	5.5
Solar PV	0	10	161	256	357	460	564	0	3	15.7
CSP	-	0	6	12	27	60	109	0	1	51.3
Marine	-	0	0	0	1	2	3	0	0	21.7

Electrical capacity (GW)	2012	2020	2025	2030	2035	2040	Shares (%) 2012	Shares (%) 2040	CAAGR (%) 2012-40
Total capacity	1 728	2 675	3 216	3 741	4 224	4 688	100	100	3.6
Coal	995	1 319	1 494	1 680	1 843	1 992	58	42	2.5
Oil	64	62	58	54	48	42	4	1	-1.5
Gas	175	279	354	420	496	581	10	12	4.4
Nuclear	25	79	117	151	178	202	1	4	7.8
Hydro	343	511	581	650	705	758	20	16	2.9
Bioenergy	21	50	67	83	99	116	1	2	6.3
Wind	95	246	342	424	493	552	5	12	6.5
Geothermal	3	5	6	8	11	13	0	0	5.2
Solar PV	9	123	194	264	335	404	1	9	14.6
CSP	0	2	3	7	16	28	0	1	27.7
Marine	0	0	0	0	1	1	0	0	20.4

CO_2 emissions (Mt)	1990	2012	2020	2025	2030	2035	2040	Shares (%) 2012	Shares (%) 2040	CAAGR (%) 2012-40
Total CO_2	3 555	11 922	14 151	15 277	16 367	17 268	18 042	100	100	1.5
Coal	2 558	8 737	10 059	10 534	11 026	11 428	11 745	73	65	1.1
Oil	862	2 395	2 899	3 271	3 602	3 814	3 979	20	22	1.8
Gas	135	791	1 193	1 472	1 738	2 027	2 318	7	13	3.9
Power generation	1 072	5 834	6 855	7 386	7 988	8 562	9 107	100	100	1.6
Coal	886	5 387	6 321	6 770	7 294	7 766	8 200	92	90	1.5
Oil	149	137	107	87	71	55	39	2	0	-4.3
Gas	38	310	427	529	622	741	868	5	10	3.7
TFC	2 326	5 629	6 784	7 363	7 833	8 151	8 370	100	100	1.4
Coal	1 612	3 143	3 542	3 568	3 537	3 469	3 360	56	40	0.2
Oil	654	2 112	2 628	3 016	3 356	3 582	3 760	38	45	2.1
Transport	271	1 265	1 697	2 061	2 386	2 602	2 778	22	33	2.8
Gas	60	374	615	779	941	1 100	1 250	7	15	4.4

Non-OECD Asia: Current Policies and 450 Scenarios

	Electricity generation (TWh)						Shares (%)		CAAGR (%)	
	2020	2030	2040	2020	2030	2040	2040		2012-40	
	Current Policies Scenario			450 Scenario			CPS	450	CPS	450
Total generation	10 964	15 651	20 103	10 142	12 472	15 187	100	100	3.6	2.6
Coal	6 886	9 780	12 661	5 820	4 158	3 101	63	20	3.4	-1.7
Oil	114	70	37	108	50	22	0	0	-4.9	-6.6
Gas	996	1 543	2 295	1 031	1 748	2 379	11	16	4.6	4.7
Nuclear	567	995	1 170	584	1 632	2 504	6	16	7.0	10.0
Hydro	1 562	1 879	2 127	1 637	2 377	2 715	11	18	2.2	3.1
Bioenergy	249	387	486	258	593	980	2	6	6.9	9.6
Wind	426	719	939	500	1 231	1 926	5	13	7.4	10.2
Geothermal	29	43	64	31	92	173	0	1	4.3	8.1
Solar PV	135	229	300	166	522	923	1	6	13.1	17.8
CSP	1	5	22	6	66	458	0	3	43.0	59.3
Marine	0	0	2	0	2	5	0	0	21.1	24.5

	Electrical capacity (GW)						Shares (%)		CAAGR (%)	
	2020	2030	2040	2020	2030	2040	2040		2012-40	
	Current Policies Scenario			450 Scenario			CPS	450	CPS	450
Total capacity	2 684	3 763	4 690	2 628	3 679	4 674	100	100	3.6	3.6
Coal	1 392	1 953	2 458	1 249	1 124	1 077	52	23	3.3	0.3
Oil	62	54	41	61	53	40	1	1	-1.5	-1.6
Gas	285	432	604	286	462	605	13	13	4.5	4.5
Nuclear	77	135	159	79	215	331	3	7	6.9	9.7
Hydro	488	589	670	511	756	867	14	19	2.4	3.4
Bioenergy	49	72	89	50	107	172	2	4	5.4	7.9
Wind	224	345	424	258	546	776	9	17	5.5	7.8
Geothermal	5	7	10	5	14	26	0	1	4.0	7.8
Solar PV	103	174	228	126	381	657	5	14	12.3	16.6
CSP	0	1	5	2	18	121	0	3	20.5	34.6
Marine	0	0	1	0	1	2	0	0	19.8	23.2

	CO_2 emissions (Mt)						Shares (%)		CAAGR (%)	
	2020	2030	2040	2020	2030	2040	2040		2012-40	
	Current Policies Scenario			450 Scenario			CPS	450	CPS	450
Total CO_2	14 922	18 803	22 268	13 411	10 587	7 760	100	100	2.3	-1.5
Coal	10 703	13 104	15 345	9 405	5 960	3 412	69	44	2.0	-3.3
Oil	3 010	3 917	4 495	2 813	2 963	2 389	20	31	2.3	-0.0
Gas	1 209	1 782	2 428	1 193	1 663	1 958	11	25	4.1	3.3
Power generation	7 394	9 837	12 388	6 306	3 562	1 800	100	100	2.7	-4.1
Coal	6 856	9 143	11 446	5 762	2 864	1 024	92	57	2.7	-5.8
Oil	108	71	40	102	51	23	0	1	-4.3	-6.2
Gas	430	623	902	442	647	754	7	42	3.9	3.2
TFC	7 006	8 385	9 253	6 613	6 596	5 587	100	100	1.8	-0.0
Coal	3 641	3 741	3 673	3 454	2 947	2 264	40	41	0.6	-1.2
Oil	2 738	3 667	4 262	2 555	2 783	2 264	46	41	2.5	0.2
Transport	*1 781*	*2 626*	*3 183*	*1 650*	*1 901*	*1 438*	*34*	*26*	*3.3*	*0.5*
Gas	626	978	1 318	603	866	1 059	14	19	4.6	3.8

A

China: New Policies Scenario

	Energy demand (Mtoe)							Shares (%)		CAAGR (%)
	1990	2012	2020	2025	2030	2035	2040	2012	2040	2012-40
TPED	879	2 909	3 512	3 802	4 019	4 145	4 185	100	100	1.3
Coal	533	1 977	2 193	2 222	2 234	2 204	2 123	68	51	0.3
Oil	122	468	572	658	712	723	725	16	17	1.6
Gas	13	123	220	288	353	414	460	4	11	4.8
Nuclear	-	25	117	178	221	257	288	1	7	9.1
Hydro	11	74	106	113	118	122	126	3	3	1.9
Bioenergy	200	216	229	239	249	262	272	7	6	0.8
Other renewables	0	26	75	104	132	162	191	1	5	7.4
Power generation	181	1 182	1 542	1 728	1 894	2 030	2 123	100	100	2.1
Coal	153	1 027	1 158	1 212	1 271	1 304	1 301	87	61	0.8
Oil	16	5	5	5	4	4	4	0	0	-1.4
Gas	1	24	58	83	106	130	153	2	7	6.9
Nuclear	-	25	117	178	221	257	288	2	14	9.1
Hydro	11	74	106	113	118	122	126	6	6	1.9
Bioenergy	-	17	51	68	82	96	108	1	5	6.9
Other renewables	0	9	47	70	92	117	142	1	7	10.4
Other energy sector	100	527	572	568	558	541	518	100	100	-0.1
Electricity	15	73	94	103	113	121	126	14	24	1.9
TFC	669	1 714	2 116	2 321	2 468	2 545	2 564	100	100	1.4
Coal	318	559	611	592	562	519	465	33	18	-0.7
Oil	87	428	533	623	680	699	706	25	28	1.8
Gas	9	81	155	202	244	277	298	5	12	4.8
Electricity	41	359	526	612	688	751	797	21	31	2.9
Heat	13	71	86	88	89	88	85	4	3	0.7
Bioenergy	200	199	178	170	166	166	163	12	6	-0.7
Other renewables	0	17	28	34	40	45	49	1	2	3.8
Industry	245	813	1 018	1 077	1 113	1 128	1 113	100	100	1.1
Coal	181	439	477	453	419	380	334	54	30	-1.0
Oil	21	57	62	62	61	58	54	7	5	-0.2
Gas	3	29	64	88	110	129	142	4	13	5.9
Electricity	30	241	347	398	442	477	498	30	45	2.6
Heat	11	48	61	63	64	63	60	6	5	0.8
Bioenergy	-	-	6	11	15	19	21	-	2	n.a.
Other renewables	-	0	1	1	1	3	4	0	0	11.5
Transport	35	240	335	420	479	505	523	100	100	2.8
Oil	25	221	300	375	423	438	448	92	86	2.6
Electricity	1	4	9	12	15	19	24	2	5	6.2
Biofuels	-	1	4	9	15	20	21	1	4	10.8
Other fuels	10	14	22	24	26	28	30	6	6	2.8
Buildings	314	480	525	550	574	590	596	100	100	0.8
Coal	95	71	66	62	58	52	43	15	7	-1.7
Oil	7	41	34	27	21	15	10	9	2	-5.0
Gas	2	32	56	73	88	99	105	7	18	4.4
Electricity	6	100	151	182	210	234	253	21	42	3.4
Heat	2	22	25	25	25	25	25	5	4	0.4
Bioenergy	200	198	167	149	134	124	116	41	19	-1.9
Other renewables	0	16	26	32	37	42	44	3	7	3.6
Other	75	180	238	274	303	322	332	100	100	2.2

China: Current Policies and 450 Scenarios

	Energy demand (Mtoe)						Shares (%)		CAAGR (%)	
	2020	2030	2040	2020	2030	2040	2040		2012-40	
	Current Policies Scenario			450 Scenario			CPS	450	CPS	450
TPED	3 658	4 426	4 834	3 388	3 485	3 524	100	100	1.8	0.7
Coal	2 334	2 662	2 852	2 080	1 609	1 332	59	38	1.3	-1.4
Oil	597	777	811	558	597	456	17	13	2.0	-0.1
Gas	218	329	434	220	364	420	9	12	4.6	4.5
Nuclear	112	204	237	117	329	474	5	13	8.3	11.0
Hydro	102	115	122	106	124	133	3	4	1.8	2.1
Bioenergy	228	237	246	230	292	392	5	11	0.5	2.1
Other renewables	67	102	132	78	170	317	3	9	6.0	9.4
Power generation	1 635	2 163	2 550	1 452	1 512	1 729	100	100	2.8	1.4
Coal	1 267	1 600	1 866	1 062	694	571	73	33	2.2	-2.1
Oil	5	5	4	5	4	2	0	0	-0.9	-2.8
Gas	57	95	137	62	134	147	5	8	6.5	6.7
Nuclear	112	204	237	117	329	474	9	27	8.3	11.0
Hydro	102	115	122	106	124	133	5	8	1.8	2.1
Bioenergy	51	77	92	52	106	153	4	9	6.3	8.2
Other renewables	41	68	92	49	123	249	4	14	8.7	12.6
Other energy sector	587	611	605	561	516	451	100	100	0.5	-0.6
Electricity	*98*	*126*	*148*	*90*	*94*	*99*	*24*	*22*	*2.5*	*1.1*
TFC	2 185	2 650	2 857	2 069	2 245	2 211	100	100	1.8	0.9
Coal	631	608	545	598	523	425	19	19	-0.1	-1.0
Oil	558	745	793	520	570	444	28	20	2.2	0.1
Gas	155	243	307	153	236	275	11	12	4.9	4.5
Electricity	550	766	926	507	600	686	32	31	3.4	2.3
Heat	87	93	92	84	83	75	3	3	0.9	0.2
Bioenergy	177	160	153	178	186	238	5	11	-0.9	0.6
Other renewables	27	35	41	29	47	69	1	3	3.1	5.1
Industry	1 047	1 197	1 265	991	1 023	993	100	100	1.6	0.7
Coal	493	455	393	469	398	314	31	32	-0.4	-1.2
Oil	64	66	60	59	52	37	5	4	0.2	-1.5
Gas	65	111	147	62	107	126	12	13	6.0	5.4
Electricity	357	481	572	335	387	422	45	43	3.1	2.0
Heat	62	68	67	59	59	51	5	5	1.2	0.2
Bioenergy	6	15	22	6	16	26	2	3	n.a.	n.a.
Other renewables	0	1	3	1	4	16	0	2	10.0	17.5
Transport	350	515	567	328	413	391	100	100	3.1	1.8
Oil	318	471	507	292	333	215	89	55	3.0	-0.1
Electricity	9	14	21	9	20	53	4	13	5.7	9.2
Biofuels	3	9	14	4	27	80	2	21	9.1	16.2
Other fuels	20	21	25	23	33	43	4	11	2.2	4.1
Buildings	546	622	666	512	516	512	100	100	1.2	0.2
Coal	69	65	56	62	45	29	8	6	-0.8	-3.1
Oil	36	26	14	32	17	8	2	2	-3.7	-5.7
Gas	58	92	111	55	77	85	17	17	4.6	3.6
Electricity	166	249	310	145	172	191	47	37	4.1	2.4
Heat	25	25	25	25	24	23	4	5	0.4	0.2
Bioenergy	166	133	112	167	139	124	17	24	-2.0	-1.7
Other renewables	25	33	37	27	42	51	6	10	3.0	4.2
Other	242	315	360	237	293	315	100	100	2.5	2.0

China: New Policies Scenario

Electricity generation (TWh)								Shares (%)		CAAGR (%)
	1990	2012	2020	2025	2030	2035	2040	2012	2040	2012-40
Total generation	650	5 024	7 204	8 322	9 310	10 138	10 734	100	100	2.7
Coal	471	3 812	4 528	4 869	5 222	5 461	5 545	76	52	1.3
Oil	49	8	5	4	4	3	3	0	0	-3.2
Gas	3	96	291	442	589	739	871	2	8	8.2
Nuclear	-	97	448	683	849	988	1 107	2	10	9.1
Hydro	127	863	1 231	1 312	1 372	1 421	1 461	17	14	1.9
Bioenergy	-	45	174	237	286	332	374	1	3	7.9
Wind	0	96	394	577	728	862	956	2	9	8.6
Geothermal	-	0	1	3	6	11	17	0	0	18.3
Solar PV	0	6	130	188	234	274	313	0	3	14.9
CSP	-	0	4	8	20	46	86	0	1	50.0
Marine	-	0	0	0	1	1	2	0	0	20.5

Electrical capacity (GW)							Shares (%)		CAAGR (%)
	2012	2020	2025	2030	2035	2040	2012	2040	2012-40
Total capacity	1 198	1 851	2 159	2 408	2 601	2 741	100	100	3.0
Coal	791	975	1 064	1 144	1 197	1 210	66	44	1.5
Oil	11	10	9	9	8	7	1	0	-1.4
Gas	43	97	130	156	180	207	4	8	5.8
Nuclear	14	60	92	114	133	149	1	5	8.9
Hydro	249	375	400	418	433	446	21	16	2.1
Bioenergy	8	30	41	49	57	64	1	2	7.7
Wind	75	202	275	330	368	394	6	14	6.1
Geothermal	0	0	0	1	2	2	0	0	17.3
Solar PV	7	100	145	181	211	240	1	9	13.6
CSP	0	1	2	5	12	21	0	1	39.1
Marine	0	0	0	0	0	1	0	0	19.2

CO_2 emissions (Mt)								Shares (%)		CAAGR (%)
	1990	2012	2020	2025	2030	2035	2040	2012	2040	2012-40
Total CO_2	2 278	8 229	9 459	9 902	10 200	10 225	10 018	100	100	0.7
Coal	1 942	6 794	7 499	7 555	7 570	7 435	7 123	83	71	0.2
Oil	308	1 163	1 410	1 622	1 745	1 762	1 755	14	18	1.5
Gas	28	272	549	725	885	1 028	1 140	3	11	5.2
Power generation	651	4 112	4 723	4 965	5 214	5 357	5 359	100	100	1.0
Coal	597	4 039	4 570	4 756	4 951	5 039	4 988	98	93	0.8
Oil	52	17	17	16	15	13	12	0	0	-1.4
Gas	2	56	135	194	249	305	360	1	7	6.9
TFC	1 541	3 817	4 418	4 610	4 652	4 532	4 323	100	100	0.4
Coal	1 294	2 559	2 745	2 617	2 438	2 221	1 966	67	45	-0.9
Oil	229	1 078	1 324	1 538	1 663	1 684	1 682	28	39	1.6
Transport	*73*	*660*	*896*	*1 121*	*1 265*	*1 309*	*1 337*	*17*	*31*	*2.5*
Gas	18	180	349	455	550	627	675	5	16	4.8

China: Current Policies and 450 Scenarios

	Electricity generation (TWh)						Shares (%)		CAAGR (%)	
	2020	2030	2040	2020	2030	2040	2040		2012-40	
	Current Policies Scenario			450 Scenario			CPS	450	CPS	450
Total generation	7 543	10 372	12 496	6 944	8 069	9 120	100	100	3.3	2.2
Coal	5 004	6 713	8 115	4 208	2 884	2 126	65	23	2.7	-2.1
Oil	5	4	4	4	3	2	0	0	-2.7	-4.4
Gas	285	520	763	327	822	901	6	10	7.7	8.3
Nuclear	431	783	908	448	1 261	1 820	7	20	8.3	11.0
Hydro	1 181	1 333	1 423	1 231	1 438	1 550	11	17	1.8	2.1
Bioenergy	174	267	321	176	360	514	3	6	7.3	9.1
Wind	355	585	733	411	935	1 349	6	15	7.5	9.9
Geothermal	1	3	8	1	6	21	0	0	15.2	19.3
Solar PV	106	160	200	134	311	505	2	6	13.1	16.9
CSP	1	4	20	4	48	330	0	4	42.5	57.4
Marine	0	0	2	0	1	2	0	0	19.9	21.2

	Electrical capacity (GW)						Shares (%)		CAAGR (%)	
	2020	2030	2040	2020	2030	2040	2040		2012-40	
	Current Policies Scenario			450 Scenario			CPS	450	CPS	450
Total capacity	1 861	2 476	2 878	1 818	2 295	2 682	100	100	3.2	2.9
Coal	1 035	1 346	1 563	929	762	647	54	24	2.5	-0.7
Oil	10	9	7	10	9	6	0	0	-1.5	-2.3
Gas	100	160	208	98	200	230	7	9	5.8	6.2
Nuclear	58	105	122	60	164	236	4	9	8.1	10.7
Hydro	360	406	434	375	439	473	15	18	2.0	2.3
Bioenergy	30	46	55	30	61	86	2	3	7.1	8.9
Wind	186	278	326	210	407	537	11	20	5.4	7.3
Geothermal	0	0	1	0	1	3	0	0	14.4	18.2
Solar PV	81	124	155	103	240	384	5	14	11.8	15.5
CSP	0	1	5	1	12	78	0	3	32.1	45.9
Marine	0	0	1	0	0	1	0	0	18.6	20.0

	CO_2 emissions (Mt)						Shares (%)		CAAGR (%)	
	2020	2030	2040	2020	2030	2040	2040		2012-40	
	Current Policies Scenario			450 Scenario			CPS	450	CPS	450
Total CO_2	10 058	11 927	12 938	8 962	6 290	3 630	100	100	1.6	-2.9
Coal	8 029	9 141	9 832	7 042	4 014	1 826	76	50	1.3	-4.6
Oil	1 481	1 927	1 981	1 368	1 408	958	15	26	1.9	-0.7
Gas	548	860	1 125	552	868	846	9	23	5.2	4.1
Power generation	5 151	6 533	7 647	4 350	2 183	729	100	100	2.2	-6.0
Coal	5 001	6 294	7 312	4 189	1 884	496	96	68	2.1	-7.2
Oil	17	16	13	16	12	8	0	1	-0.9	-2.8
Gas	133	223	322	146	287	225	4	31	6.5	5.1
TFC	4 579	5 031	4 905	4 306	3 853	2 689	100	100	0.9	-1.2
Coal	2 835	2 642	2 309	2 677	1 995	1 219	47	45	-0.4	-2.6
Oil	1 395	1 842	1 902	1 286	1 346	916	39	34	2.0	-0.6
Transport	*953*	*1 408*	*1 514*	*875*	*995*	*644*	*31*	*24*	*3.0*	*-0.1*
Gas	349	548	693	343	512	554	14	21	4.9	4.1

A

India: New Policies Scenario

	Energy demand (Mtoe)							Shares (%)		CAAGR (%)
	1990	2012	2020	2025	2030	2035	2040	2012	2040	2012-40
TPED	317	788	1 004	1 170	1 364	1 559	1 757	100	100	2.9
Coal	103	354	453	524	604	682	765	45	44	2.8
Oil	61	177	237	278	332	387	435	22	25	3.3
Gas	11	49	70	92	116	142	172	6	10	4.6
Nuclear	2	9	17	28	43	57	70	1	4	7.8
Hydro	6	11	15	20	26	31	38	1	2	4.6
Bioenergy	133	185	203	211	217	223	230	23	13	0.8
Other renewables	0	3	10	17	25	36	47	0	3	10.2
Power generation	72	311	392	465	557	653	758	100	100	3.2
Coal	56	252	303	338	386	437	494	81	65	2.4
Oil	5	8	6	5	4	3	2	3	0	-4.4
Gas	3	18	24	36	47	59	71	6	9	5.1
Nuclear	2	9	17	28	43	57	70	3	9	7.8
Hydro	6	11	15	20	26	31	38	3	5	4.6
Bioenergy	-	11	18	23	28	34	41	4	5	4.7
Other renewables	0	3	9	15	22	32	41	1	5	10.4
Other energy sector	20	67	94	112	131	147	161	100	100	3.2
Electricity	*7*	*26*	*36*	*45*	*55*	*65*	*75*	*39*	*47*	*3.9*
TFC	250	510	663	775	903	1 034	1 164	100	100	3.0
Coal	42	88	124	151	178	204	229	17	20	3.5
Oil	50	150	211	253	307	362	410	29	35	3.7
Gas	6	24	35	44	54	65	81	5	7	4.5
Electricity	18	75	108	137	173	210	251	15	22	4.4
Heat	-	-	-	-	-	-	-	-	-	n.a.
Bioenergy	133	173	184	188	189	189	188	34	16	0.3
Other renewables	0	0	1	2	3	4	6	0	0	9.3
Industry	69	172	243	294	346	401	452	100	100	3.5
Coal	29	77	113	140	167	194	219	45	49	3.8
Oil	8	19	27	31	35	38	42	11	9	2.9
Gas	1	13	21	25	29	33	37	8	8	3.7
Electricity	9	33	47	58	70	84	98	19	22	4.0
Heat	-	-	-	-	-	-	-	-	-	n.a.
Bioenergy	23	30	36	40	45	51	55	17	12	2.2
Other renewables	0	0	0	0	1	1	1	0	0	14.4
Transport	21	74	112	146	192	244	297	100	100	5.1
Oil	18	70	105	135	177	220	258	96	87	4.7
Electricity	0	1	2	2	2	2	2	2	1	2.3
Biofuels	-	0	1	3	4	8	14	0	5	16.1
Other fuels	2	2	3	6	9	14	23	2	8	9.9
Buildings	138	211	235	252	271	288	307	100	100	1.3
Coal	11	11	11	11	11	10	9	5	3	-0.6
Oil	11	27	31	35	38	43	48	13	16	2.1
Gas	0	2	3	4	5	6	8	1	3	4.1
Electricity	5	27	41	56	76	96	119	13	39	5.4
Heat	-	-	-	-	-	-	-	-	-	n.a.
Bioenergy	111	143	147	145	139	130	119	68	39	-0.7
Other renewables	0	0	1	2	2	3	4	0	1	8.3
Other	22	53	73	83	93	101	108	100	100	2.6

India: Current Policies and 450 Scenarios

	Energy demand (Mtoe)						Shares (%)		CAAGR (%)	
	2020	2030	2040	2020	2030	2040	2040		2012-40	
	Current Policies Scenario			450 Scenario			CPS	450	CPS	450
TPED	1 033	1 469	1 946	975	1 154	1 369	100	100	3.3	2.0
Coal	472	696	936	424	371	354	48	26	3.5	-0.0
Oil	246	363	505	230	280	271	26	20	3.8	1.5
Gas	73	125	185	73	128	208	10	15	4.9	5.3
Nuclear	17	35	54	17	61	119	3	9	6.8	9.8
Hydro	14	20	26	15	39	51	1	4	3.2	5.7
Bioenergy	203	214	218	205	235	270	11	20	0.6	1.4
Other renewables	8	16	22	11	40	96	1	7	7.2	13.1
Power generation	407	622	879	368	397	536	100	100	3.8	2.0
Coal	321	480	673	276	167	117	77	22	3.6	-2.7
Oil	6	5	3	6	3	1	0	0	-3.9	-6.9
Gas	25	47	78	27	55	97	9	18	5.5	6.3
Nuclear	17	35	54	17	61	119	6	22	6.8	9.8
Hydro	14	20	26	15	39	51	3	9	3.2	5.7
Bioenergy	17	22	28	19	35	68	3	13	3.2	6.5
Other renewables	7	13	17	9	36	83	2	16	7.0	13.2
Other energy sector	96	139	176	92	119	136	100	100	3.5	2.6
Electricity	38	61	87	35	46	58	50	43	4.4	2.9
TFC	680	952	1 242	655	838	970	100	100	3.2	2.3
Coal	125	176	221	121	166	197	18	20	3.3	2.9
Oil	219	336	478	205	258	255	38	26	4.2	1.9
Gas	38	63	86	36	57	89	7	9	4.7	4.9
Electricity	112	182	262	105	154	215	21	22	4.6	3.8
Heat	-	-	-	-	-	-	-	-	n.a.	n.a.
Bioenergy	185	192	190	186	199	201	15	21	0.3	0.5
Other renewables	1	3	4	2	4	13	0	1	8.3	12.6
Industry	249	363	472	241	330	407	100	100	3.7	3.1
Coal	113	165	210	111	156	189	45	47	3.6	3.3
Oil	28	38	47	27	32	35	10	9	3.3	2.2
Gas	23	39	54	21	28	33	12	8	5.2	3.3
Electricity	48	73	101	46	66	86	21	21	4.1	3.5
Heat	-	-	-	-	-	-	-	-	n.a.	n.a.
Bioenergy	36	48	58	37	47	57	12	14	2.4	2.3
Other renewables	0	1	1	0	1	7	0	2	13.6	21.5
Transport	117	209	332	108	160	184	100	100	5.5	3.3
Oil	111	197	312	101	135	116	94	63	5.5	1.8
Electricity	2	2	3	2	2	12	1	7	2.5	8.2
Biofuels	1	3	7	1	12	22	2	12	13.2	18.1
Other fuels	4	8	11	4	12	34	3	18	7.0	11.4
Buildings	239	282	324	233	255	271	100	100	1.5	0.9
Coal	12	12	11	11	10	8	3	3	-0.2	-1.4
Oil	33	42	52	31	34	40	16	15	2.4	1.4
Gas	3	4	7	3	6	10	2	4	4.0	4.9
Electricity	43	81	126	39	62	87	39	32	5.6	4.2
Heat	-	-	-	-	-	-	-	-	n.a.	n.a.
Bioenergy	148	141	125	148	140	122	39	45	-0.5	-0.6
Other renewables	1	2	3	1	3	6	1	2	7.3	9.7
Other	75	97	114	73	93	108	100	100	2.8	2.6

India: New Policies Scenario

Electricity generation (TWh)	1990	2012	2020	2025	2030	2035	2040	Shares (%) 2012	Shares (%) 2040	CAAGR (%) 2012-40
Total generation	293	1 166	1 673	2 106	2 640	3 190	3 787	100	100	4.3
Coal	192	838	1 142	1 321	1 563	1 807	2 077	72	55	3.3
Oil	13	25	19	17	14	11	8	2	0	-4.0
Gas	10	94	134	208	278	359	441	8	12	5.7
Nuclear	6	33	64	109	165	218	269	3	7	7.8
Hydro	72	126	174	233	303	363	438	11	12	4.6
Bioenergy	-	21	46	61	78	99	123	2	3	6.6
Wind	0	28	71	105	141	179	217	2	6	7.6
Geothermal	-	-	0	1	1	2	2	-	0	n.a.
Solar PV	-	2	22	49	91	140	190	0	5	17.5
CSP	-	-	2	3	6	13	21	-	1	n.a.
Marine	-	-	-	-	0	0	1	-	0	n.a.

Electrical capacity (GW)	2012	2020	2025	2030	2035	2040	Shares (%) 2012	Shares (%) 2040	CAAGR (%) 2012-40
Total capacity	241	414	556	726	896	1 079	100	100	5.5
Coal	138	228	284	356	424	499	57	46	4.7
Oil	8	9	9	8	7	6	3	1	-0.8
Gas	23	45	67	87	109	131	10	12	6.4
Nuclear	5	10	16	24	31	39	2	4	7.7
Hydro	42	58	77	100	119	144	18	13	4.5
Bioenergy	6	10	13	16	20	24	2	2	5.2
Wind	18	39	56	73	91	109	8	10	6.5
Geothermal	-	0	0	0	0	0		0	n.a.
Solar PV	1	16	34	60	90	121	1	11	17.6
CSP	0	1	1	2	4	6	0	1	28.6
Marine	-	-	-	0	0	0	-	0	n.a.

CO_2 emissions (Mt)	1990	2012	2020	2025	2030	2035	2040	Shares (%) 2012	Shares (%) 2040	CAAGR (%) 2012-40
Total CO_2	580	1 953	2 515	2 943	3 454	3 982	4 518	100	100	3.0
Coal	396	1 359	1 713	1 971	2 274	2 583	2 907	70	64	2.8
Oil	164	489	646	763	919	1 078	1 221	25	27	3.3
Gas	21	104	156	208	261	321	390	5	9	4.8
Power generation	239	1 043	1 248	1 409	1 620	1 842	2 088	100	100	2.5
Coal	215	977	1 174	1 310	1 498	1 694	1 915	94	92	2.4
Oil	16	25	18	16	13	10	7	2	0	-4.4
Gas	8	41	56	83	109	138	166	4	8	5.1
TFC	323	843	1 177	1 434	1 721	2 016	2 294	100	100	3.6
Coal	175	380	534	656	770	882	985	45	43	3.5
Oil	139	412	567	683	835	993	1 134	49	49	3.7
Transport	*55*	*212*	*318*	*408*	*533*	*663*	*778*	*25*	*34*	*4.7*
Gas	9	51	76	95	116	141	176	6	8	4.5

India: Current Policies and 450 Scenarios

	Electricity generation (TWh)						Shares (%)		CAAGR (%)	
	2020	2030	2040	2020	2030	2040	2040		2012-40	
	Current Policies Scenario			450 Scenario			CPS	450	CPS	450
Total generation	1 734	2 826	4 063	1 630	2 323	3 172	100	100	4.6	3.6
Coal	1 221	1 954	2 789	1 072	807	556	69	18	4.4	-1.5
Oil	19	15	9	18	10	5	0	0	-3.5	-5.6
Gas	145	287	484	154	341	611	12	19	6.0	6.9
Nuclear	64	134	205	64	235	455	5	14	6.8	9.8
Hydro	162	231	307	174	457	590	8	19	3.2	5.7
Bioenergy	42	59	75	46	103	223	2	7	4.7	8.9
Wind	60	96	124	77	198	328	3	10	5.4	9.2
Geothermal	0	1	1	0	3	5	0	0	n.a.	n.a.
Solar PV	21	49	68	22	151	273	2	9	13.2	19.0
CSP	0	0	1	2	18	125	0	4	n.a.	n.a.
Marine	-	-	1	-	0	1	0	0	n.a.	n.a.

	Electrical capacity (GW)						Shares (%)		CAAGR (%)	
	2020	2030	2040	2020	2030	2040	2040		2012-40	
	Current Policies Scenario			450 Scenario			CPS	450	CPS	450
Total capacity	413	696	986	411	767	1 113	100	100	5.2	5.6
Coal	237	409	596	215	250	307	60	28	5.4	2.9
Oil	9	8	6	9	9	8	1	1	-0.8	-0.0
Gas	46	85	127	52	104	144	13	13	6.3	6.7
Nuclear	10	19	29	10	34	65	3	6	6.7	9.8
Hydro	54	76	101	58	150	194	10	17	3.2	5.6
Bioenergy	9	12	15	10	20	40	2	4	3.5	7.1
Wind	34	50	63	43	98	141	6	13	4.5	7.5
Geothermal	0	0	0	0	0	1	0	0	n.a.	n.a.
Solar PV	15	35	47	16	97	171	5	15	13.8	19.1
CSP	0	0	0	1	5	42	0	4	14.2	37.7
Marine	-	-	0	-	0	0	0	0	n.a.	n.a.

	CO_2 emissions (Mt)						Shares (%)		CAAGR (%)	
	2020	2030	2040	2020	2030	2040	2040		2012-40	
	Current Policies Scenario			450 Scenario			CPS	450	CPS	450
Total CO_2	2 620	3 918	5 415	2 385	2 288	2 216	100	100	3.7	0.5
Coal	1 786	2 629	3 566	1 598	1 270	1 065	66	48	3.5	-0.9
Oil	671	1 009	1 431	623	745	702	26	32	3.9	1.3
Gas	163	280	419	163	274	449	8	20	5.1	5.3
Power generation	1 319	1 982	2 797	1 151	739	559	100	100	3.6	-2.2
Coal	1 242	1 859	2 607	1 071	601	328	93	59	3.6	-3.8
Oil	19	14	8	17	9	3	0	1	-3.9	-6.9
Gas	58	109	182	62	129	228	6	41	5.4	6.3
TFC	1 212	1 821	2 475	1 149	1 461	1 567	100	100	3.9	2.2
Coal	538	763	951	523	663	732	38	47	3.3	2.4
Oil	593	922	1 336	549	684	653	54	42	4.3	1.7
Transport	334	593	940	304	406	351	38	22	5.5	1.8
Gas	81	135	188	77	113	182	8	12	4.8	4.6

A

Middle East: New Policies Scenario

	Energy demand (Mtoe)							Shares (%)		CAAGR (%)
	1990	2012	2020	2025	2030	2035	2040	2012	2040	2012-40
TPED	211	680	800	899	992	1 070	1 153	100	100	1.9
Coal	1	3	4	4	5	5	5	0	0	1.8
Oil	137	336	390	424	445	459	480	49	42	1.3
Gas	72	338	393	445	500	544	582	50	50	2.0
Nuclear	-	0	5	13	18	24	31	0	3	16.0
Hydro	1	2	2	3	3	4	4	0	0	2.5
Bioenergy	0	1	3	6	9	13	17	0	1	11.4
Other renewables	0	0	2	5	12	22	35	0	3	20.7
Power generation	62	228	261	289	313	333	355	100	100	1.6
Coal	0	0	1	1	1	2	2	0	0	9.0
Oil	27	97	87	78	64	57	57	42	16	-1.9
Gas	34	129	164	189	214	224	226	57	64	2.0
Nuclear	-	0	5	13	18	24	31	0	9	16.0
Hydro	1	2	2	3	3	4	4	1	1	2.5
Bioenergy	-	0	1	2	3	5	8	0	2	27.6
Other renewables	0	0	1	4	9	17	28	0	8	30.0
Other energy sector	18	73	84	91	99	105	111	100	100	1.5
Electricity	4	15	20	22	24	26	28	20	25	2.3
TFC	150	456	558	637	715	779	849	100	100	2.2
Coal	0	2	2	2	2	2	2	0	0	0.1
Oil	103	228	285	326	361	384	408	50	48	2.1
Gas	31	162	184	207	233	259	289	36	34	2.1
Electricity	16	63	83	96	109	121	134	14	16	2.7
Heat	-	-	-	-	-	-	-	-	-	n.a.
Bioenergy	0	1	3	4	6	8	10	0	1	9.5
Other renewables	0	0	1	2	3	4	6	0	1	14.0
Industry	40	148	167	189	212	237	264	100	100	2.1
Coal	0	2	2	2	2	2	2	1	1	0.2
Oil	19	35	37	39	42	44	46	23	17	1.0
Gas	17	98	110	125	143	161	182	66	69	2.2
Electricity	4	14	17	19	21	23	26	9	10	2.3
Heat	-	-	-	-	-	-	-	-	-	n.a.
Bioenergy	-	-	1	3	4	6	8	-	3	n.a.
Other renewables	-	0	0	0	0	0	0	0	0	23.6
Transport	48	126	165	196	222	236	246	100	100	2.4
Oil	48	120	157	186	210	221	230	95	93	2.3
Electricity	-	0	0	0	0	0	0	0	0	0.7
Biofuels	-	-	-	-	-	-	-	-	-	n.a.
Other fuels	-	6	8	10	13	15	16	5	7	3.5
Buildings	33	110	131	146	162	175	191	100	100	2.0
Coal	-	0	0	0	0	0	0	0	0	-1.4
Oil	18	18	19	19	18	17	17	17	9	-0.3
Gas	3	44	49	52	56	60	65	40	34	1.4
Electricity	11	46	61	72	83	92	102	42	53	2.9
Heat	-	-	-	-	-	-	-	-	-	n.a.
Bioenergy	0	1	1	1	1	2	2	1	1	3.4
Other renewables	0	0	1	1	2	4	5	0	3	13.0
Other	29	72	94	106	119	131	147	100	100	2.6

Middle East: Current Policies and 450 Scenarios

	Energy demand (Mtoe)						Shares (%)		CAAGR (%)	
	2020	2030	2040	2020	2030	2040	2040		2012-40	
	Current Policies Scenario			450 Scenario			CPS	450	CPS	450
TPED	810	1 027	1 254	763	847	902	100	100	2.2	1.0
Coal	4	5	5	4	5	4	0	0	2.0	1.4
Oil	399	472	536	376	364	320	43	35	1.7	-0.2
Gas	393	517	661	369	416	435	53	48	2.4	0.9
Nuclear	5	14	17	5	24	45	1	5	13.6	17.6
Hydro	2	3	4	2	4	5	0	1	2.4	3.5
Bioenergy	3	9	17	4	12	26	1	3	11.3	13.1
Other renewables	2	7	15	3	23	66	1	7	17.0	23.5
Power generation	268	329	402	240	256	295	100	100	2.0	0.9
Coal	1	1	2	1	1	1	0	0	9.4	7.4
Oil	94	77	70	83	46	35	17	12	-1.1	-3.6
Gas	164	226	292	146	158	138	73	47	2.9	0.2
Nuclear	5	14	17	5	24	45	4	15	13.6	17.6
Hydro	2	3	4	2	4	5	1	2	2.4	3.5
Bioenergy	1	2	6	1	5	15	2	5	26.6	30.8
Other renewables	1	5	11	1	17	55	3	19	25.8	33.1
Other energy sector	85	105	119	81	85	79	100	100	1.7	0.3
Electricity	20	26	31	18	20	23	26	28	2.7	1.5
TFC	560	736	914	535	620	665	100	100	2.5	1.4
Coal	2	2	2	2	2	2	0	0	0.3	0.3
Oil	286	373	449	275	302	278	49	42	2.5	0.7
Gas	184	235	299	179	211	247	33	37	2.2	1.5
Electricity	84	117	150	75	93	115	16	17	3.1	2.2
Heat	-	-	-	-	-	-	-	-	n.a.	n.a.
Bioenergy	3	6	11	3	7	11	1	2	9.9	10.0
Other renewables	1	2	3	1	5	11	0	2	11.3	16.3
Industry	169	217	276	163	186	202	100	100	2.2	1.1
Coal	2	2	2	2	2	2	1	1	0.4	0.3
Oil	37	43	48	37	39	42	17	21	1.2	0.7
Gas	110	145	189	106	120	125	68	62	2.4	0.9
Electricity	18	22	28	16	18	22	10	11	2.6	1.6
Heat	-	-	-	-	-	-	-	-	n.a.	n.a.
Bioenergy	2	5	9	2	5	9	3	4	n.a.	n.a.
Other renewables	0	0	0	0	1	3	0	1	20.0	32.4
Transport	165	231	282	157	181	166	100	100	2.9	1.0
Oil	158	221	269	148	161	119	95	71	2.9	-0.0
Electricity	0	0	0	0	0	4	0	3	0.3	19.2
Biofuels	-	-	-	-	-	-	-	-	n.a.	n.a.
Other fuels	7	10	13	9	20	43	5	26	2.6	7.1
Buildings	132	170	210	122	142	164	100	100	2.3	1.4
Coal	0	0	0	0	0	0	0	0	-1.4	-1.5
Oil	20	20	19	18	16	15	9	9	0.1	-0.8
Gas	49	59	72	47	51	56	34	34	1.8	0.9
Electricity	62	89	115	55	70	83	55	51	3.3	2.1
Heat	-	-	-	-	-	-	-	-	n.a.	n.a.
Bioenergy	1	1	2	1	2	2	1	1	3.6	3.9
Other renewables	1	1	2	1	4	7	1	4	9.6	14.5
Other	94	118	146	93	111	133	100	100	2.6	2.2

Middle East: New Policies Scenario

Electricity generation (TWh)	1990	2012	2020	2025	2030	2035	2040	Shares (%) 2012	Shares (%) 2040	CAAGR (%) 2012-40
Total generation	224	905	1 187	1 367	1 554	1 713	1 882	100	100	2.6
Coal	0	0	3	4	6	7	7	0	0	10.5
Oil	98	328	305	280	239	222	223	36	12	-1.4
Gas	114	552	816	964	1 116	1 188	1 218	61	65	2.9
Nuclear	-	2	20	48	71	90	117	0	6	16.0
Hydro	12	22	28	34	39	43	45	2	2	2.5
Bioenergy	-	0	3	5	10	18	26	0	1	27.5
Wind	0	0	3	9	24	56	112	0	6	25.2
Geothermal	-	-	-	-	-	-	-	-	-	n.a.
Solar PV	-	0	5	13	30	52	77	0	4	49.4
CSP	-	-	3	9	19	37	57	-	3	n.a.
Marine	-	-	-	-	-	-	-	-	-	n.a.

Electrical capacity (GW)	2012	2020	2025	2030	2035	2040	Shares (%) 2012	Shares (%) 2040	CAAGR (%) 2012-40
Total capacity	256	341	372	415	463	516	100	100	2.5
Coal	0	1	1	1	1	1	0	0	6.1
Oil	74	86	81	71	66	67	29	13	-0.4
Gas	166	227	246	272	286	287	65	56	2.0
Nuclear	1	3	7	10	13	16	0	3	10.5
Hydro	14	18	22	24	26	27	6	5	2.2
Bioenergy	0	0	1	2	3	4	0	1	30.7
Wind	0	1	4	10	24	49	0	9	24.5
Geothermal	0	0	0	0	0	0	0	0	0.0
Solar PV	0	3	8	17	29	43	0	8	27.2
CSP	0	1	3	7	14	22	0	4	29.0
Marine	-	-	-	-	-	-	-	-	n.a.

CO_2 emissions (Mt)	1990	2012	2020	2025	2030	2035	2040	Shares (%) 2012	Shares (%) 2040	CAAGR (%) 2012-40
Total CO_2	554	1 671	1 917	2 105	2 264	2 376	2 486	100	100	1.4
Coal	1	11	14	15	16	17	17	1	1	1.6
Oil	393	900	1 010	1 080	1 115	1 134	1 165	54	47	0.9
Gas	161	760	894	1 011	1 133	1 225	1 304	45	52	1.9
Power generation	165	597	653	685	699	704	706	100	100	0.6
Coal	0	1	3	4	5	6	6	0	1	5.6
Oil	86	293	268	240	196	177	176	49	25	-1.8
Gas	79	303	382	441	498	521	524	51	74	2.0
TFC	349	929	1 111	1 258	1 394	1 493	1 593	100	100	1.9
Coal	1	8	10	9	9	9	9	1	1	0.2
Oil	282	561	685	781	859	899	931	60	58	1.8
Transport	*142*	*362*	*472*	*559*	*630*	*665*	*691*	*39*	*43*	*2.3*
Gas	66	360	416	468	526	586	652	39	41	2.1

Middle East: Current Policies and 450 Scenarios

Electricity generation (TWh)							Shares (%)		CAAGR (%)	
	2020	2030	2040	2020	2030	2040	2040		2012-40	
	Current Policies Scenario			450 Scenario			CPS	450	CPS	450
Total generation	1 205	1 660	2 103	1 082	1 318	1 595	100	100	3.1	2.0
Coal	3	6	7	3	5	4	0	0	10.9	8.8
Oil	332	296	277	291	174	134	13	8	-0.6	-3.2
Gas	809	1 218	1 590	725	832	729	76	46	3.8	1.0
Nuclear	20	53	66	20	93	175	3	11	13.6	17.6
Hydro	28	37	43	28	43	58	2	4	2.4	3.5
Bioenergy	3	8	21	3	17	54	1	3	26.5	30.8
Wind	2	12	44	4	72	175	2	11	21.0	27.2
Geothermal	-	-	-	-	-	-	-	-	n.a.	n.a.
Solar PV	4	15	31	5	49	134	1	8	44.7	52.4
CSP	4	13	23	3	32	133	1	8	n.a.	n.a.
Marine	-	-	-	-	-	0	-	0	n.a.	n.a.

Electrical capacity (GW)							Shares (%)		CAAGR (%)	
	2020	2030	2040	2020	2030	2040	2040		2012-40	
	Current Policies Scenario			450 Scenario			CPS	450	CPS	450
Total capacity	343	431	509	337	435	586	100	100	2.5	3.0
Coal	1	1	1	1	1	1	0	0	6.5	4.7
Oil	88	82	79	84	63	52	15	9	0.2	-1.3
Gas	226	296	344	224	261	273	68	47	2.6	1.8
Nuclear	3	8	9	3	13	24	2	4	8.3	12.1
Hydro	18	23	26	18	26	33	5	6	2.1	3.0
Bioenergy	0	1	3	0	3	9	1	1	29.5	34.0
Wind	1	5	19	2	32	75	4	13	20.4	26.4
Geothermal	0	0	0	0	0	0	0	0	0.0	0.0
Solar PV	3	9	19	3	27	74	4	13	23.6	29.7
CSP	2	5	8	1	10	45	1	8	24.2	32.4
Marine	-	-	-	-	-	0	-	0	n.a.	n.a.

CO$_2$ emissions (Mt)							Shares (%)		CAAGR (%)	
	2020	2030	2040	2020	2030	2040	2040		2012-40	
	Current Policies Scenario			450 Scenario			CPS	450	CPS	450
Total CO$_2$	1 947	2 393	2 844	1 819	1 762	1 568	100	100	1.9	-0.2
Coal	14	16	18	14	15	12	1	1	1.8	0.4
Oil	1 036	1 201	1 341	966	867	686	47	44	1.4	-1.0
Gas	897	1 176	1 485	839	880	870	52	55	2.4	0.5
Power generation	676	772	905	601	508	419	100	100	1.5	-1.3
Coal	3	6	7	3	5	4	1	1	5.9	4.0
Oil	290	239	216	258	143	107	24	26	-1.1	-3.5
Gas	383	528	682	341	360	308	75	73	2.9	0.1
TFC	1 116	1 441	1 748	1 066	1 126	1 048	100	100	2.3	0.4
Coal	10	9	9	10	8	7	1	1	0.4	-0.8
Oil	689	901	1 063	654	681	547	61	52	2.3	-0.1
Transport	474	664	810	446	484	357	46	34	2.9	-0.1
Gas	417	531	676	403	437	495	39	47	2.3	1.1

Africa: New Policies Scenario

	Energy demand (Mtoe)							Shares (%)		CAAGR (%)
	1990	2012	2020	2025	2030	2035	2040	2012	2040	2012-40
TPED	391	739	897	994	1 095	1 203	1 322	100	100	2.1
Coal	74	105	117	128	138	150	164	14	12	1.6
Oil	87	168	203	218	234	255	278	23	21	1.8
Gas	30	100	129	153	178	207	243	14	18	3.2
Nuclear	2	3	3	3	6	10	12	0	1	4.7
Hydro	5	10	16	20	26	32	38	1	3	5.0
Bioenergy	194	352	417	449	475	489	496	48	38	1.2
Other renewables	0	2	11	21	38	61	91	0	7	15.2
Power generation	68	156	199	234	278	340	413	100	100	3.5
Coal	39	65	73	80	84	93	103	42	25	1.7
Oil	11	24	25	23	21	21	22	15	5	-0.3
Gas	11	51	68	81	96	113	136	33	33	3.6
Nuclear	2	3	3	3	6	10	12	2	3	4.7
Hydro	5	10	16	20	26	32	38	6	9	5.0
Bioenergy	0	1	3	6	9	12	15	1	4	10.4
Other renewables	0	2	11	20	36	59	87	1	21	15.3
Other energy sector	58	110	137	157	175	186	191	100	100	2.0
Electricity	*5*	*12*	*16*	*19*	*22*	*27*	*31*	*11*	*16*	*3.4*
TFC	292	538	649	709	771	836	909	100	100	1.9
Coal	20	20	22	24	25	27	29	4	3	1.5
Oil	71	144	178	196	215	236	260	27	29	2.1
Gas	9	29	36	42	49	58	69	5	8	3.2
Electricity	22	52	72	88	107	131	159	10	18	4.1
Heat	-	-	-	-	-	-	-	-	-	n.a.
Bioenergy	171	294	340	358	372	380	387	55	43	1.0
Other renewables	0	0	1	1	2	3	4	0	0	13.4
Industry	55	83	107	122	140	163	189	100	100	3.0
Coal	14	11	14	16	17	19	21	13	11	2.4
Oil	15	15	18	19	21	22	24	18	13	1.7
Gas	5	16	20	24	27	32	39	19	20	3.1
Electricity	12	21	28	32	38	44	50	26	27	3.1
Heat	-	-	-	-	-	-	-	-	-	n.a.
Bioenergy	10	20	26	31	37	45	53	24	28	3.6
Other renewables	-	-	0	0	0	1	1	-	1	n.a.
Transport	38	90	111	123	134	147	161	100	100	2.1
Oil	37	88	108	120	131	143	157	98	97	2.1
Electricity	0	0	1	1	1	1	1	1	1	2.7
Biofuels	-	0	1	1	1	1	1	0	1	23.6
Other fuels	0	1	1	2	2	2	3	1	2	2.4
Buildings	184	337	395	424	452	478	507	100	100	1.5
Coal	3	6	6	6	6	6	6	2	1	-0.2
Oil	11	24	29	33	38	44	51	7	10	2.8
Gas	1	7	8	10	12	14	16	2	3	3.0
Electricity	9	28	41	52	65	82	104	8	20	4.7
Heat	-	-	-	-	-	-	-	-	-	n.a.
Bioenergy	160	272	310	323	330	330	328	81	65	0.7
Other renewables	0	0	0	1	1	2	2	0	0	11.3
Other	15	28	37	40	44	48	51	100	100	2.2

Africa: Current Policies and 450 Scenarios

| | Energy demand (Mtoe) | | | | | | Shares (%) | | CAAGR (%) | |
| | 2020 | 2030 | 2040 | 2020 | 2030 | 2040 | 2040 | | 2012-40 | |
	Current Policies Scenario			450 Scenario			CPS	450	CPS	450
TPED	918	1 146	1 411	873	1 010	1 171	100	100	2.3	1.7
Coal	121	151	189	111	108	105	13	9	2.1	-0.0
Oil	208	253	324	195	199	206	23	18	2.4	0.7
Gas	129	180	241	120	143	158	17	14	3.2	1.7
Nuclear	3	6	11	3	10	27	1	2	4.2	7.7
Hydro	14	22	32	16	29	52	2	4	4.3	6.2
Bioenergy	432	503	543	416	463	487	38	42	1.6	1.2
Other renewables	10	30	72	12	58	136	5	12	14.2	16.9
Power generation	198	277	397	186	243	345	100	100	3.4	2.9
Coal	76	93	117	68	57	48	30	14	2.1	-1.1
Oil	25	20	19	24	16	11	5	3	-0.8	-2.7
Gas	68	98	136	60	64	60	34	17	3.5	0.6
Nuclear	3	6	11	3	10	27	3	8	4.2	7.7
Hydro	14	22	32	16	29	52	8	15	4.3	6.2
Bioenergy	3	8	13	4	12	21	3	6	9.9	11.7
Other renewables	9	29	69	11	54	127	17	37	14.3	16.8
Other energy sector	150	195	226	137	161	171	100	100	2.6	1.6
Electricity	16	22	30	15	19	24	13	14	3.2	2.4
TFC	658	802	969	635	721	818	100	100	2.1	1.5
Coal	23	28	34	22	24	27	4	3	2.0	1.1
Oil	181	235	310	170	185	199	32	24	2.8	1.2
Gas	37	48	62	36	46	61	6	7	2.8	2.8
Electricity	72	105	151	69	96	139	16	17	3.9	3.6
Heat	-	-	-	-	-	-	-	-	n.a.	n.a.
Bioenergy	344	385	408	337	366	382	42	47	1.2	0.9
Other renewables	1	2	3	1	4	9	0	1	12.7	17.0
Industry	109	145	197	105	133	175	100	100	3.1	2.7
Coal	15	19	26	14	16	20	13	11	3.0	2.1
Oil	19	22	25	17	18	17	13	10	2.0	0.6
Gas	21	27	34	20	24	29	17	17	2.7	2.1
Electricity	28	39	54	27	33	44	27	25	3.4	2.6
Heat	-	-	-	-	-	-	-	-	n.a.	n.a.
Bioenergy	26	38	58	27	40	60	29	34	3.8	4.0
Other renewables	0	0	1	0	1	4	0	2	n.a.	n.a.
Transport	111	145	197	105	111	118	100	100	2.8	1.0
Oil	109	143	194	102	104	104	99	88	2.9	0.6
Electricity	1	1	1	1	1	2	0	2	2.5	5.3
Biofuels	-	-	-	1	3	5	-	5	n.a.	30.5
Other fuels	1	2	2	2	3	6	1	5	1.4	5.7
Buildings	401	466	521	388	433	473	100	100	1.6	1.2
Coal	6	6	7	6	6	5	1	1	0.2	-0.6
Oil	30	42	60	29	37	49	11	10	3.4	2.6
Gas	8	11	16	8	11	15	3	3	2.8	2.6
Electricity	41	61	90	39	58	88	17	19	4.2	4.1
Heat	-	-	-	-	-	-	-	-	n.a.	n.a.
Bioenergy	315	344	347	305	320	313	67	66	0.9	0.5
Other renewables	0	1	2	1	2	3	0	1	10.3	12.7
Other	37	46	55	36	44	52	100	100	2.5	2.3

Africa: New Policies Scenario

	Electricity generation (TWh)						Shares (%)		CAAGR (%)
	1990	2012	2020	2025	2030	2035	2040	2012	2040	2012-40
Total generation	316	741	1 023	1 241	1 504	1 835	2 217	100	100	4.0
Coal	165	259	303	336	361	402	451	35	20	2.0
Oil	41	89	93	88	81	83	85	12	4	-0.1
Gas	45	262	383	472	573	694	853	35	38	4.3
Nuclear	8	13	13	13	25	37	47	2	2	4.7
Hydro	56	112	182	235	300	372	442	15	20	5.0
Bioenergy	0	2	11	21	31	42	53	0	2	12.9
Wind	-	2	14	23	35	48	62	0	3	12.4
Geothermal	0	2	9	15	27	45	69	0	3	14.4
Solar PV	-	0	11	24	42	61	83	0	4	22.1
CSP	-	-	5	14	29	50	71	-	3	n.a.
Marine	-	-	-	-	-	-	-	-	-	n.a.

	Electrical capacity (GW)						Shares (%)		CAAGR (%)
	2012	2020	2025	2030	2035	2040	2012	2040	2012-40
Total capacity	165	253	313	384	469	558	100	100	4.5
Coal	42	56	65	72	80	90	26	16	2.7
Oil	34	36	36	36	37	38	20	7	0.4
Gas	60	100	122	146	174	207	37	37	4.5
Nuclear	2	2	2	4	5	7	1	1	4.5
Hydro	25	41	54	70	87	104	15	19	5.3
Bioenergy	0	2	4	6	8	11	0	2	15.5
Wind	1	6	9	14	18	23	1	4	11.6
Geothermal	0	1	3	4	7	11	0	2	15.2
Solar PV	0	7	15	25	36	48	0	9	26.0
CSP	0	2	4	9	14	20	0	4	23.0
Marine	-	-	-	-	-	-	-	-	n.a.

	CO$_2$ emissions (Mt)						Shares (%)		CAAGR (%)
	1990	2012	2020	2025	2030	2035	2040	2012	2040	2012-40
Total CO$_2$	545	1 052	1 260	1 388	1 504	1 660	1 844	100	100	2.0
Coal	234	331	374	404	420	453	491	32	27	1.4
Oil	249	502	604	651	698	758	826	48	45	1.8
Gas	62	218	283	332	385	448	527	21	29	3.2
Power generation	212	447	520	570	608	676	760	100	100	1.9
Coal	152	252	283	308	319	344	373	57	49	1.4
Oil	35	75	77	72	66	67	68	17	9	-0.3
Gas	25	120	159	190	224	265	318	27	42	3.6
TFC	302	556	677	746	819	903	1 001	100	100	2.1
Coal	82	79	91	96	101	108	117	14	12	1.4
Oil	202	409	509	561	614	673	741	74	74	2.1
Transport	109	261	321	356	389	425	465	47	46	2.1
Gas	18	68	78	89	104	121	143	12	14	2.7

Africa: Current Policies and 450 Scenarios

	Electricity generation (TWh)						Shares (%)		CAAGR (%)	
	2020	2030	2040	2020	2030	2040	2040		2012-40	
	Current Policies Scenario			450 Scenario			CPS	450	CPS	450
Total generation	1 017	1 473	2 097	968	1 325	1 892	100	100	3.8	3.4
Coal	316	396	513	282	243	205	24	11	2.5	-0.8
Oil	93	82	79	90	64	44	4	2	-0.4	-2.5
Gas	385	584	833	343	391	358	40	19	4.2	1.1
Nuclear	13	25	41	13	40	105	2	6	4.2	7.7
Hydro	167	258	368	188	338	600	18	32	4.3	6.2
Bioenergy	9	27	45	11	41	72	2	4	12.3	14.2
Wind	13	30	51	15	55	138	2	7	11.6	15.7
Geothermal	8	23	58	9	37	79	3	4	13.6	14.9
Solar PV	10	34	65	11	61	121	3	6	21.0	23.7
CSP	3	14	41	5	55	168	2	9	n.a.	n.a.
Marine	-	-	-	-	0	1	-	0	n.a.	n.a.

	Electrical capacity (GW)						Shares (%)		CAAGR (%)	
	2020	2030	2040	2020	2030	2040	2040		2012-40	
	Current Policies Scenario			450 Scenario			CPS	450	CPS	450
Total capacity	249	367	522	249	403	607	100	100	4.2	4.8
Coal	58	77	101	53	57	49	19	8	3.1	0.5
Oil	36	35	35	36	38	41	7	7	0.2	0.7
Gas	100	145	205	98	137	163	39	27	4.5	3.6
Nuclear	2	4	6	2	6	15	1	2	4.0	7.5
Hydro	38	60	86	41	78	141	16	23	4.6	6.4
Bioenergy	2	6	9	2	8	14	2	2	14.8	16.5
Wind	5	12	19	6	21	53	4	9	10.8	14.8
Geothermal	1	4	9	1	6	12	2	2	14.2	15.5
Solar PV	6	21	40	7	36	71	8	12	25.1	27.7
CSP	1	4	11	2	15	49	2	8	20.6	27.1
Marine	-	-	-	-	0	0	-	0	n.a.	n.a.

	CO$_2$ emissions (Mt)						Shares (%)		CAAGR (%)	
	2020	2030	2040	2020	2030	2040	2040		2012-40	
	Current Policies Scenario			450 Scenario			CPS	450	CPS	450
Total CO$_2$	1 290	1 616	2 082	1 189	1 146	1 084	100	100	2.5	0.1
Coal	390	470	593	353	268	182	29	17	2.1	-2.1
Oil	618	757	968	577	584	592	47	55	2.4	0.6
Gas	282	389	520	260	294	310	25	29	3.2	1.3
Power generation	530	651	828	478	381	271	100	100	2.2	-1.8
Coal	295	358	452	263	180	96	55	36	2.1	-3.4
Oil	77	64	59	74	51	35	7	13	-0.8	-2.7
Gas	158	230	317	141	150	140	38	52	3.5	0.6
TFC	692	883	1 156	652	698	746	100	100	2.6	1.1
Coal	94	112	139	89	88	86	12	12	2.1	0.3
Oil	519	670	887	486	518	545	77	73	2.8	1.0
Transport	324	424	575	303	310	310	50	42	2.9	0.6
Gas	78	101	130	76	92	115	11	15	2.3	1.9

A

Sub-Saharan Africa: New Policies Scenario

	Energy demand (Mtoe)							Shares (%)		CAAGR (%)
	1990	2012	2020	2025	2030	2035	2040	2012	2040	2012-40
TPED	313	570	694	773	855	941	1 039	100	100	2.2
Coal	71	101	111	122	130	141	154	18	15	1.5
Oil	39	85	107	121	136	155	180	15	17	2.7
Gas	5	22	38	50	64	83	110	4	11	5.9
Nuclear	2	3	3	3	6	10	12	1	1	4.7
Hydro	4	8	14	18	23	29	35	1	3	5.3
Bioenergy	191	348	412	443	469	482	488	61	47	1.2
Other renewables	0	1	9	16	27	41	60	0	6	14.1
Power generation	49	96	124	150	184	230	289	100	100	4.0
Coal	39	62	68	74	78	85	94	65	33	1.5
Oil	2	11	11	11	12	14	16	11	6	1.4
Gas	2	9	16	22	30	41	59	9	20	6.9
Nuclear	2	3	3	3	6	10	12	4	4	4.7
Hydro	4	8	14	18	23	29	35	9	12	5.3
Bioenergy	0	1	3	6	9	12	14	1	5	10.2
Other renewables	0	1	8	15	26	40	57	1	20	14.1
Other energy sector	43	90	114	133	149	157	160	100	100	2.1
Electricity	3	8	10	12	15	18	22	9	14	3.7
TFC	241	422	508	557	606	659	722	100	100	1.9
Coal	19	19	22	23	24	26	28	5	4	1.4
Oil	37	75	97	112	127	146	168	18	23	2.9
Gas	1	7	11	14	18	24	32	2	4	5.8
Electricity	16	30	43	54	69	87	111	7	15	4.7
Heat	-	-	-	-	-	-	-	-	-	n.a.
Bioenergy	168	290	335	353	366	374	380	69	53	1.0
Other renewables	0	0	0	1	1	2	2	0	0	13.1
Industry	39	59	76	89	104	124	148	100	100	3.4
Coal	13	11	14	15	16	18	20	19	14	2.3
Oil	6	7	9	10	11	12	13	12	9	2.5
Gas	1	6	9	11	14	18	24	10	16	5.1
Electricity	9	15	19	23	27	32	37	26	25	3.3
Heat	-	-	-	-	-	-	-	-	-	n.a.
Bioenergy	10	20	26	31	36	44	52	34	35	3.5
Other renewables	-	-	0	0	0	0	0	-	0	n.a.
Transport	23	48	62	72	82	94	109	100	100	3.0
Oil	22	47	60	71	81	92	107	99	98	2.9
Electricity	0	0	0	0	0	1	1	1	1	2.1
Biofuels	-	0	1	1	1	1	1	0	1	23.6
Other fuels	0	0	0	0	0	0	0	0	0	2.1
Buildings	171	302	352	376	398	417	440	100	100	1.4
Coal	3	6	6	6	6	6	6	2	1	-0.2
Oil	5	13	17	20	24	29	35	4	8	3.4
Gas	-	0	0	1	2	3	4	0	1	35.0
Electricity	6	14	22	30	40	53	71	5	16	5.9
Heat	-	-	-	-	-	-	-	-	-	n.a.
Bioenergy	157	268	305	318	325	325	323	89	73	0.7
Other renewables	0	0	0	1	1	1	2	0	0	12.3
Other	8	14	18	20	22	23	26	100	100	2.3

Sub-Saharan Africa: Current Policies and 450 Scenarios

	Energy demand (Mtoe)						Shares (%)		CAAGR (%)	
	2020	2030	2040	2020	2030	2040	2040		2012-40	
	Current Policies Scenario			450 Scenario			CPS	450	CPS	450
TPED	712	900	1 120	680	802	931	100	100	2.4	1.8
Coal	115	143	178	106	103	100	16	11	2.0	-0.1
Oil	111	151	218	103	117	134	19	14	3.4	1.6
Gas	36	61	99	33	53	76	9	8	5.5	4.5
Nuclear	3	6	11	3	10	19	1	2	4.2	6.3
Hydro	12	20	29	14	26	48	3	5	4.5	6.5
Bioenergy	427	497	535	411	456	477	48	51	1.6	1.1
Other renewables	8	23	50	9	38	78	4	8	13.3	15.2
Power generation	123	180	272	117	164	239	100	100	3.8	3.3
Coal	71	86	109	64	53	45	40	19	2.0	-1.2
Oil	11	11	14	10	7	6	5	3	0.8	-2.1
Gas	14	28	51	13	21	31	19	13	6.3	4.5
Nuclear	3	6	11	3	10	19	4	8	4.2	6.3
Hydro	12	20	29	14	26	48	11	20	4.5	6.5
Bioenergy	3	8	13	4	11	18	5	7	9.8	11.0
Other renewables	7	21	47	9	36	73	17	30	13.4	15.1
Other energy sector	127	168	194	115	137	147	100	100	2.8	1.8
Electricity	10	14	20	10	13	19	10	13	3.5	3.2
TFC	516	633	775	499	577	663	100	100	2.2	1.6
Coal	23	27	33	22	23	26	4	4	2.0	1.1
Oil	99	142	210	93	114	133	27	20	3.7	2.0
Gas	11	16	26	10	15	24	3	4	5.0	4.7
Electricity	43	66	101	42	63	100	13	15	4.4	4.4
Heat	-	-	-	-	-	-	-	-	n.a.	n.a.
Bioenergy	340	379	402	332	360	375	52	57	1.2	0.9
Other renewables	0	1	3	1	2	5	0	1	13.2	16.3
Industry	78	108	156	76	98	137	100	100	3.6	3.1
Coal	14	18	25	13	15	19	16	14	3.0	2.0
Oil	9	12	15	8	8	9	9	6	2.8	1.0
Gas	9	13	20	8	11	16	13	12	4.4	3.6
Electricity	20	28	40	19	24	33	26	24	3.6	2.9
Heat	-	-	-	-	-	-	-	-	n.a.	n.a.
Bioenergy	26	37	56	27	39	59	36	43	3.8	3.9
Other renewables	0	0	0	0	0	2	0	1	n.a.	n.a.
Transport	62	92	141	59	73	85	100	100	3.9	2.1
Oil	61	91	140	58	69	77	99	90	3.9	1.7
Electricity	0	0	1	0	1	2	0	2	2.0	5.6
Biofuels	-	-	-	1	3	5	-	6	n.a.	30.5
Other fuels	0	0	0	0	0	2	0	2	8.9	16.9
Buildings	357	410	450	346	383	414	100	100	1.4	1.1
Coal	6	6	7	6	6	5	1	1	0.2	-0.6
Oil	18	27	40	17	24	33	9	8	4.0	3.3
Gas	0	1	3	0	1	3	1	1	33.5	34.1
Electricity	21	36	57	21	37	62	13	15	5.1	5.4
Heat	-	-	-	-	-	-	-	-	n.a.	n.a.
Bioenergy	311	339	342	301	315	308	76	74	0.9	0.5
Other renewables	0	1	2	0	1	2	0	1	11.6	13.0
Other	19	23	27	18	22	27	100	100	2.5	2.4

Sub-Saharan Africa: New Policies Scenario

	Electricity generation (TWh)							Shares (%)		CAAGR (%)
	1990	2012	2020	2025	2030	2035	2040	2012	2040	2012-40
Total generation	232	440	621	777	974	1 228	1 541	100	100	4.6
Coal	163	247	283	312	332	368	412	56	27	1.8
Oil	8	40	41	42	45	52	63	9	4	1.7
Gas	7	40	87	130	186	263	385	9	25	8.4
Nuclear	8	13	13	13	25	37	47	3	3	4.7
Hydro	45	96	159	207	269	339	408	22	26	5.3
Bioenergy	0	2	11	20	30	40	50	0	3	12.7
Wind	-	0	7	13	18	24	30	0	2	20.3
Geothermal	0	2	7	12	20	32	48	0	3	12.9
Solar PV	-	0	9	19	31	44	58	0	4	27.1
CSP	-	-	3	8	18	28	39	-	3	n.a.
Marine	-	-	-	-	-	-	-	-	-	n.a.

	Electrical capacity (GW)						Shares (%)		CAAGR (%)
	2012	2020	2025	2030	2035	2040	2012	2040	2012-40
Total capacity	97	154	198	251	315	385	100	100	5.0
Coal	41	53	61	67	75	84	42	22	2.6
Oil	22	24	25	26	29	31	23	8	1.2
Gas	13	28	39	52	70	94	13	24	7.4
Nuclear	2	2	2	4	5	7	2	2	4.5
Hydro	20	34	46	60	77	93	20	24	5.7
Bioenergy	0	2	4	6	8	10	0	3	15.2
Wind	0	3	5	8	10	12	0	3	28.9
Geothermal	0	1	2	3	5	8	0	2	13.8
Solar PV	0	6	11	19	26	34	0	9	27.1
CSP	-	1	3	5	9	12	-	3	n.a.
Marine	-	-	-	-	-	-	-	-	n.a.

	CO_2 emissions (Mt)							Shares (%)		CAAGR (%)
	1990	2012	2020	2025	2030	2035	2040	2012	2040	2012-40
Total CO_2	354	619	753	853	943	1 071	1 238	100	100	2.5
Coal	226	315	352	379	390	418	452	51	37	1.3
Oil	120	262	322	366	414	472	546	42	44	2.7
Gas	8	42	79	108	139	181	241	7	19	6.4
Power generation	160	296	338	375	402	454	529	100	100	2.1
Coal	150	241	265	287	293	315	340	81	64	1.2
Oil	6	34	35	35	37	43	51	11	10	1.5
Gas	4	21	38	52	71	97	138	7	26	7.0
TFC	187	305	388	442	501	573	663	100	100	2.8
Coal	76	75	87	92	97	103	112	24	17	1.5
Oil	108	216	278	320	365	419	483	71	73	2.9
Transport	*66*	*140*	*179*	*209*	*239*	*274*	*316*	*46*	*48*	*2.9*
Gas	3	14	23	30	39	51	68	5	10	5.8

Sub-Saharan Africa: Current Policies and 450 Scenarios

	Electricity generation (TWh)						Shares (%)		CAAGR (%)	
	2020	2030	2040	2020	2030	2040	2040		2012-40	
	Current Policies Scenario			450 Scenario			CPS	450	CPS	450
Total generation	611	933	1 410	591	880	1 369	100	100	4.2	4.1
Coal	296	367	474	265	226	190	34	14	2.4	-0.9
Oil	42	45	57	38	28	23	4	2	1.3	-1.9
Gas	82	174	328	71	135	207	23	15	7.8	6.1
Nuclear	13	25	41	13	37	72	3	5	4.2	6.3
Hydro	145	228	335	165	301	560	24	41	4.5	6.5
Bioenergy	9	26	43	11	36	59	3	4	12.1	13.3
Wind	7	15	24	9	28	70	2	5	19.4	23.9
Geothermal	6	18	43	8	30	56	3	4	12.4	13.5
Solar PV	9	26	45	10	41	77	3	6	25.9	28.3
CSP	2	9	19	3	19	55	1	4	n.a.	n.a.
Marine	-	-	-	-	0	0	-	0	n.a.	n.a.

	Electrical capacity (GW)						Shares (%)		CAAGR (%)	
	2020	2030	2040	2020	2030	2040	2040		2012-40	
	Current Policies Scenario			450 Scenario			CPS	450	CPS	450
Total capacity	151	235	351	151	249	385	100	100	4.7	5.0
Coal	55	73	95	50	53	46	27	12	3.1	0.4
Oil	24	26	30	23	20	19	8	5	1.1	-0.6
Gas	27	48	87	27	51	73	25	19	7.1	6.5
Nuclear	2	4	6	2	5	10	2	3	4.0	6.1
Hydro	31	51	76	35	67	128	22	33	4.9	6.9
Bioenergy	2	5	9	2	7	11	3	3	14.7	15.7
Wind	3	6	10	4	12	28	3	7	27.9	32.7
Geothermal	1	3	6	1	4	8	2	2	12.9	14.0
Solar PV	5	16	27	6	24	45	8	12	26.2	28.4
CSP	1	3	6	1	6	16	2	4	n.a.	n.a.
Marine	-	-	-	-	0	0	-	0	n.a.	n.a.

	CO_2 emissions (Mt)						Shares (%)		CAAGR (%)	
	2020	2030	2040	2020	2030	2040	2040		2012-40	
	Current Policies Scenario			450 Scenario			CPS	450	CPS	450
Total CO_2	776	1 030	1 431	709	710	721	100	100	3.0	0.5
Coal	368	440	554	333	248	166	39	23	2.0	-2.3
Oil	334	459	662	309	354	400	46	56	3.4	1.5
Gas	74	131	215	68	108	154	15	21	6.0	4.7
Power generation	345	432	579	309	236	175	100	100	2.4	-1.8
Coal	277	332	418	247	164	83	72	47	2.0	-3.7
Oil	35	34	42	32	23	19	7	11	0.8	-2.1
Gas	34	65	118	30	50	74	20	42	6.4	4.6
TFC	399	552	795	375	437	504	100	100	3.5	1.8
Coal	91	107	134	86	84	82	17	16	2.1	0.4
Oil	285	409	605	267	323	373	76	74	3.7	2.0
Transport	*181*	*269*	*414*	*171*	*205*	*228*	*52*	*45*	*3.9*	*1.7*
Gas	23	36	56	22	31	48	7	9	5.1	4.5

A

South Africa: New Policies Scenario

	Energy demand (Mtoe)							Shares (%)		CAAGR (%)
	1990	2012	2020	2025	2030	2035	2040	2012	2040	2012-40
TPED	91	141	153	161	169	178	186	100	100	1.0
Coal	67	97	100	102	102	102	101	69	55	0.2
Oil	10	21	25	26	26	27	27	15	14	0.9
Gas	2	4	5	6	7	8	9	3	5	3.1
Nuclear	2	3	3	3	6	10	12	2	7	4.7
Hydro	0	0	0	0	0	0	0	0	0	2.8
Bioenergy	10	15	18	20	22	24	26	11	14	1.9
Other renewables	-	0	2	3	5	8	10	0	5	18.2
Power generation	39	64	68	71	74	79	83	100	100	1.0
Coal	36	60	62	61	57	55	53	94	64	-0.4
Oil	-	0	0	0	0	0	0	0	0	-0.3
Gas	-	-	1	1	2	3	4	-	4	n.a.
Nuclear	2	3	3	3	6	10	12	5	15	4.7
Hydro	0	0	0	0	0	0	0	0	0	2.8
Bioenergy	-	0	1	2	3	4	5	0	6	15.0
Other renewables	-	0	1	3	5	7	8	0	10	26.0
Other energy sector	16	26	29	31	34	35	37	100	100	1.2
Electricity	*2*	*5*	*5*	*5*	*5*	*6*	*6*	*17*	*16*	*0.9*
TFC	51	72	81	87	92	97	102	100	100	1.2
Coal	16	17	17	17	17	17	17	23	17	0.0
Oil	15	25	28	31	33	34	35	35	34	1.1
Gas	-	2	2	2	3	3	3	2	3	2.3
Electricity	12	17	20	22	25	27	30	23	30	2.1
Heat	-	-	-	-	-	-	-	-	-	n.a.
Bioenergy	8	11	13	13	14	14	15	15	15	1.2
Other renewables	-	0	0	0	1	1	1	0	1	10.4
Industry	22	25	27	28	29	30	31	100	100	0.8
Coal	11	9	10	10	10	10	10	38	32	0.3
Oil	2	2	2	2	2	2	2	7	5	-0.6
Gas	-	2	2	2	2	3	3	7	9	2.0
Electricity	7	10	11	12	12	13	14	40	44	1.1
Heat	-	-	-	-	-	-	-	-	-	n.a.
Bioenergy	1	2	2	2	2	2	3	8	8	1.1
Other renewables	-	-	0	0	0	0	0	-	1	n.a.
Transport	10	17	20	23	25	26	28	100	100	1.8
Oil	10	16	19	22	24	25	26	98	94	1.7
Electricity	0	0	0	0	0	1	1	2	2	2.1
Biofuels	-	-	1	1	1	1	1	-	4	n.a.
Other fuels	0	0	0	0	0	0	0	0	0	15.0
Buildings	14	23	25	27	29	32	34	100	100	1.5
Coal	2	6	6	5	5	5	5	26	14	-0.6
Oil	1	2	2	2	2	2	2	8	6	0.3
Gas	-	0	0	0	0	0	0	0	1	23.4
Electricity	4	6	8	9	11	13	15	26	44	3.3
Heat	-	-	-	-	-	-	-	-	-	n.a.
Bioenergy	6	9	10	10	11	11	11	40	33	0.8
Other renewables	-	0	0	0	0	1	1	0	2	8.6
Other	6	8	8	8	8	8	8	100	100	0.3

South Africa: Current Policies and 450 Scenarios

	Energy demand (Mtoe)						Shares (%)		CAAGR (%)	
	2020	2030	2040	2020	2030	2040	2040		2012-40	
	Current Policies Scenario			450 Scenario			CPS	450	CPS	450
TPED	155	180	208	150	156	162	100	100	1.4	0.5
Coal	102	114	126	97	85	73	61	45	0.9	-1.0
Oil	26	28	32	24	22	17	15	10	1.5	-0.8
Gas	5	7	10	5	7	9	5	6	3.1	3.0
Nuclear	3	6	11	3	10	19	5	12	4.2	6.3
Hydro	0	0	0	0	0	0	0	0	2.7	3.6
Bioenergy	17	20	23	19	25	29	11	18	1.5	2.4
Other renewables	1	4	6	2	7	14	3	9	15.9	19.8
Power generation	70	82	98	66	65	70	100	100	1.6	0.3
Coal	64	67	74	59	43	29	75	42	0.7	-2.5
Oil	0	0	0	0	0	0	0	0	-0.4	-0.2
Gas	1	2	4	1	2	3	4	4	n.a.	n.a.
Nuclear	3	6	11	3	10	19	11	27	4.2	6.3
Hydro	0	0	0	0	0	0	0	1	2.7	3.6
Bioenergy	1	3	5	1	4	6	5	9	14.6	15.8
Other renewables	1	3	5	1	6	12	5	18	23.4	27.7
Other energy sector	29	34	38	29	33	35	100	100	1.3	1.0
Electricity	5	6	7	5	4	4	17	13	1.4	-0.1
TFC	82	96	111	79	85	87	100	100	1.6	0.7
Coal	18	18	19	17	16	15	17	17	0.4	-0.5
Oil	29	35	41	28	28	24	37	28	1.7	-0.2
Gas	2	3	3	2	3	4	3	4	2.2	2.6
Electricity	21	27	34	19	22	26	30	30	2.5	1.5
Heat	-	-	-	-	-	-	-	-	n.a.	n.a.
Bioenergy	12	13	14	13	15	17	12	20	0.7	1.6
Other renewables	0	0	1	0	1	2	1	2	9.0	12.1
Industry	28	31	34	27	27	28	100	100	1.1	0.4
Coal	10	11	12	10	9	8	34	29	0.8	-0.5
Oil	2	2	2	2	2	1	5	5	-0.6	-0.9
Gas	2	2	3	2	3	3	8	10	1.8	2.0
Electricity	12	13	15	11	11	12	45	41	1.5	0.5
Heat	-	-	-	-	-	-	-	-	n.a.	n.a.
Bioenergy	2	2	3	2	3	3	8	11	1.2	1.9
Other renewables	0	0	0	0	0	1	1	3	n.a.	n.a.
Transport	20	26	32	20	22	20	100	100	2.3	0.6
Oil	20	26	31	19	20	16	98	81	2.3	-0.1
Electricity	0	0	1	0	1	1	2	8	1.9	5.5
Biofuels	-	-	-	1	1	2	-	10	n.a.	n.a.
Other fuels	0	0	0	-	0	0	0	2	11.9	30.9
Buildings	25	30	36	25	28	31	100	100	1.7	1.2
Coal	6	6	5	5	5	5	15	15	-0.2	-0.8
Oil	2	2	2	2	2	2	7	5	1.1	-0.1
Gas	0	0	0	0	0	0	1	1	23.8	21.9
Electricity	8	12	17	7	9	12	46	38	3.7	2.4
Heat	-	-	-	-	-	-	-	-	n.a.	n.a.
Bioenergy	10	10	11	10	11	12	30	38	0.6	1.0
Other renewables	0	0	1	0	0	1	2	3	7.6	9.9
Other	8	9	9	8	8	8	100	100	0.7	0.1

South Africa: New Policies Scenario

Electricity generation (TWh)	1990	2012	2020	2025	2030	2035	2040	Shares (%) 2012	Shares (%) 2040	CAAGR (%) 2012-40
Total generation	165	255	293	315	339	370	401	100	100	1.6
Coal	156	239	257	257	247	244	243	94	61	0.1
Oil	-	0	0	0	0	0	0	0	0	-0.1
Gas	-	-	4	8	12	17	22	-	6	n.a.
Nuclear	8	13	13	13	25	37	47	5	12	4.7
Hydro	1	2	4	4	4	4	4	1	1	2.8
Bioenergy	-	0	4	8	12	15	19	0	5	16.0
Wind	-	0	5	8	11	14	17	0	4	20.1
Geothermal	-	-	0	0	0	0	0	-	0	n.a.
Solar PV	-	0	5	11	17	22	27	0	7	25.2
CSP	-	-	2	6	11	16	20	-	5	n.a.
Marine	-	-	-	-	-	-	-	-	-	n.a.

Electrical capacity (GW)	2012	2020	2025	2030	2035	2040	Shares (%) 2012	Shares (%) 2040	CAAGR (%) 2012-40
Total capacity	46	65	75	87	98	108	100	100	3.1
Coal	38	47	49	50	51	53	83	49	1.1
Oil	3	3	3	3	3	3	6	2	-0.4
Gas	0	3	4	6	8	10	1	9	12.0
Nuclear	2	2	2	4	5	7	4	6	4.5
Hydro	2	3	4	4	4	4	5	3	1.8
Bioenergy	0	1	2	3	4	5	0	4	12.0
Wind	0	2	3	4	6	7	0	6	26.1
Geothermal	-	0	0	0	0	0	-	0	n.a.
Solar PV	0	3	6	10	13	15	0	14	23.5
CSP	-	1	2	3	5	6	-	6	n.a.
Marine	-	-	-	-	-	-	-	-	n.a.

CO_2 emissions (Mt)	1990	2012	2020	2025	2030	2035	2040	Shares (%) 2012	Shares (%) 2040	CAAGR (%) 2012-40
Total CO_2	254	376	400	404	387	376	363	100	100	-0.1
Coal	207	298	309	303	280	262	243	79	67	-0.7
Oil	46	74	84	93	97	101	104	20	29	1.2
Gas	-	4	6	8	11	14	16	1	4	5.2
Power generation	141	233	241	235	215	200	185	100	100	-0.8
Coal	141	233	239	232	210	193	176	100	95	-1.0
Oil	-	0	0	0	0	0	0	0	0	-0.3
Gas	-	-	1	3	5	7	9	-	5	n.a.
TFC	111	140	155	165	169	173	176	100	100	0.8
Coal	67	66	70	70	70	69	68	47	38	0.1
Oil	44	70	80	89	94	97	101	50	57	1.3
Transport	29	48	56	65	70	74	77	35	44	1.7
Gas	-	4	5	6	6	7	8	3	4	2.3

South Africa: Current Policies and 450 Scenarios

	Electricity generation (TWh)						Shares (%)		CAAGR (%)	
	2020	2030	2040	2020	2030	2040	2040		2012-40	
	Current Policies Scenario			450 Scenario			CPS	450	CPS	450
Total generation	301	371	459	282	299	333	100	100	2.1	1.0
Coal	266	289	331	245	181	117	72	35	1.2	-2.5
Oil	0	0	0	0	0	0	0	0	-0.1	-0.0
Gas	4	13	23	4	13	18	5	5	n.a.	n.a.
Nuclear	13	25	41	13	37	72	9	22	4.2	6.3
Hydro	4	4	4	4	5	5	1	2	2.7	3.6
Bioenergy	3	10	16	4	14	23	4	7	15.4	16.8
Wind	5	10	13	5	16	33	3	10	19.0	22.9
Geothermal	0	0	0	0	0	1	0	0	n.a.	n.a.
Solar PV	5	14	21	5	20	36	5	11	24.1	26.5
CSP	2	5	8	2	12	28	2	8	n.a.	n.a.
Marine	-	-	-	-	0	0	-	0	n.a.	n.a.

	Electrical capacity (GW)						Shares (%)		CAAGR (%)	
	2020	2030	2040	2020	2030	2040	2040		2012-40	
	Current Policies Scenario			450 Scenario			CPS	450	CPS	450
Total capacity	66	91	114	62	85	100	100	100	3.3	2.8
Coal	49	58	68	44	42	30	59	30	2.0	-0.9
Oil	3	3	3	3	3	3	2	3	-0.5	-0.4
Gas	3	7	10	2	6	7	9	7	12.3	10.4
Nuclear	2	4	6	2	5	10	5	10	4.0	6.1
Hydro	3	4	4	3	4	4	3	4	1.8	2.3
Bioenergy	1	3	4	1	3	5	4	5	11.5	12.6
Wind	2	4	5	2	7	12	5	12	25.1	28.9
Geothermal	0	0	0	0	0	0	0	0	n.a.	n.a.
Solar PV	3	8	12	3	12	21	11	20	22.6	24.9
CSP	1	1	2	1	4	8	2	8	n.a.	n.a.
Marine	-	-	-	-	0	0	-	0	n.a.	n.a.

	CO_2 emissions (Mt)						Shares (%)		CAAGR (%)	
	2020	2030	2040	2020	2030	2040	2040		2012-40	
	Current Policies Scenario			450 Scenario			CPS	450	CPS	450
Total CO_2	413	448	498	386	276	151	100	100	1.0	-3.2
Coal	319	331	359	297	181	67	72	44	0.7	-5.2
Oil	87	106	123	82	84	70	25	46	1.8	-0.2
Gas	7	11	17	6	11	14	3	9	5.2	4.6
Power generation	249	263	293	230	130	31	100	100	0.8	-7.0
Coal	247	257	283	229	124	23	97	76	0.7	-7.9
Oil	0	0	0	0	0	0	0	0	-0.4	-0.2
Gas	2	5	9	1	5	7	3	23	n.a.	n.a.
TFC	160	182	202	152	143	118	100	100	1.3	-0.6
Coal	72	74	76	68	57	44	37	37	0.5	-1.4
Oil	84	102	119	79	81	68	59	58	1.9	-0.1
Transport	59	76	93	56	59	47	46	40	2.3	-0.1
Gas	5	6	7	5	5	6	4	5	2.2	1.5

Latin America: New Policies Scenario

	Energy demand (Mtoe)							Shares (%)		CAAGR (%)
	1990	2012	2020	2025	2030	2035	2040	2012	2040	2012-40
TPED	331	611	709	784	857	926	985	100	100	1.7
Coal	15	22	30	36	41	46	49	4	5	2.9
Oil	151	270	294	308	319	326	327	44	33	0.7
Gas	52	134	153	178	204	234	263	22	27	2.4
Nuclear	2	6	9	11	14	14	17	1	2	3.8
Hydro	30	60	77	86	94	102	108	10	11	2.1
Bioenergy	80	114	136	151	165	177	186	19	19	1.8
Other renewables	1	4	10	15	21	28	35	1	4	7.8
Power generation	66	162	189	213	238	268	298	100	100	2.2
Coal	3	7	10	11	12	13	14	4	5	2.6
Oil	14	32	27	24	19	18	17	20	6	-2.3
Gas	14	42	40	48	56	69	81	26	27	2.4
Nuclear	2	6	9	11	14	14	17	4	6	3.8
Hydro	30	60	77	86	94	102	108	37	36	2.1
Bioenergy	2	11	18	21	24	28	31	7	10	3.6
Other renewables	1	4	9	13	19	25	32	2	11	7.9
Other energy sector	57	85	95	104	114	119	123	100	100	1.3
Electricity	8	20	23	26	29	31	34	23	27	1.9
TFC	250	463	550	610	665	716	759	100	100	1.8
Coal	6	11	15	17	19	21	23	2	3	2.6
Oil	122	223	250	267	283	293	296	48	39	1.0
Gas	24	64	82	95	108	123	140	14	18	2.9
Electricity	35	80	101	116	131	146	161	17	21	2.6
Heat	-	-	-	-	-	-	-	-	-	n.a.
Bioenergy	63	85	101	112	121	130	136	18	18	1.7
Other renewables	-	1	1	2	2	3	4	0	0	7.4
Industry	86	158	190	209	228	248	269	100	100	1.9
Coal	6	11	15	17	19	21	22	7	8	2.6
Oil	22	36	38	39	40	41	41	23	15	0.5
Gas	15	34	47	55	64	73	82	22	31	3.2
Electricity	17	34	42	47	52	58	64	21	24	2.3
Heat	-	-	-	-	-	-	-	-	-	n.a.
Bioenergy	27	43	47	50	53	56	58	27	22	1.1
Other renewables	-	-	0	0	0	1	1	-	0	n.a.
Transport	72	156	185	204	222	234	238	100	100	1.5
Oil	65	135	150	160	170	175	173	87	73	0.9
Electricity	0	0	0	1	1	1	1	0	0	2.9
Biofuels	6	13	26	34	40	45	48	9	20	4.7
Other fuels	0	7	8	9	11	13	16	5	7	3.0
Buildings	67	99	111	122	133	144	155	100	100	1.6
Coal	0	0	0	0	0	0	0	0	0	3.3
Oil	17	17	18	18	19	20	20	17	13	0.6
Gas	6	13	15	17	18	20	22	13	14	1.9
Electricity	17	43	55	64	72	81	89	43	57	2.7
Heat	-	-	-	-	-	-	-	-	-	n.a.
Bioenergy	27	26	23	22	21	21	20	26	13	-0.8
Other renewables	-	1	1	1	2	2	3	1	2	6.6
Other	26	50	64	74	82	90	97	100	100	2.4

Latin America: Current Policies and 450 Scenarios

	Energy demand (Mtoe)						Shares (%)		CAAGR (%)	
	2020	2030	2040	2020	2030	2040	2040		2012-40	
	Current Policies Scenario			450 Scenario			CPS	450	CPS	450
TPED	719	890	1 046	686	771	824	100	100	1.9	1.1
Coal	31	45	57	28	32	35	5	4	3.5	1.7
Oil	300	335	358	280	253	211	34	26	1.0	-0.9
Gas	160	222	288	143	166	176	28	21	2.8	1.0
Nuclear	9	12	15	10	15	21	1	3	3.5	4.6
Hydro	77	95	111	77	96	112	11	14	2.2	2.2
Bioenergy	133	162	187	138	182	216	18	26	1.8	2.3
Other renewables	10	18	30	10	27	54	3	7	7.2	9.5
Power generation	194	254	324	177	208	253	100	100	2.5	1.6
Coal	10	14	18	9	6	6	6	3	3.7	-0.2
Oil	28	21	19	22	7	3	6	1	-1.8	-8.1
Gas	44	70	103	34	34	27	32	11	3.3	-1.6
Nuclear	9	12	15	10	15	21	5	8	3.5	4.6
Hydro	77	95	111	77	96	112	34	44	2.2	2.2
Bioenergy	17	24	30	18	25	35	9	14	3.6	4.2
Other renewables	8	16	27	9	24	49	8	19	7.3	9.6
Other energy sector	97	119	131	92	103	105	100	100	1.6	0.8
Electricity	24	30	36	22	26	29	27	28	2.2	1.4
TFC	555	685	799	535	605	640	100	100	2.0	1.2
Coal	15	20	24	14	17	18	3	3	2.8	1.8
Oil	254	297	323	241	232	198	40	31	1.3	-0.4
Gas	83	109	139	80	98	114	17	18	2.8	2.1
Electricity	103	137	173	96	120	146	22	23	2.8	2.2
Heat	-	-	-	-	-	-	-	-	n.a.	n.a.
Bioenergy	98	119	136	102	136	159	17	25	1.7	2.3
Other renewables	1	2	3	1	3	4	0	1	7.0	8.0
Industry	193	237	283	186	211	232	100	100	2.1	1.4
Coal	15	19	24	14	17	18	8	8	2.8	1.8
Oil	39	41	42	37	35	33	15	14	0.6	-0.3
Gas	48	65	85	45	54	60	30	26	3.3	2.0
Electricity	43	55	68	41	48	56	24	24	2.5	1.8
Heat	-	-	-	-	-	-	-	-	n.a.	n.a.
Bioenergy	49	56	63	49	57	64	22	27	1.4	1.4
Other renewables	0	0	1	0	1	1	0	0	n.a.	n.a.
Transport	185	228	256	179	191	170	100	100	1.8	0.3
Oil	154	182	199	144	127	88	78	51	1.4	-1.5
Electricity	0	1	1	0	1	2	0	1	2.9	5.3
Biofuels	23	35	44	26	51	64	17	37	4.3	5.8
Other fuels	8	10	12	8	12	17	5	10	2.0	3.3
Buildings	112	137	163	106	124	144	100	100	1.8	1.4
Coal	0	0	0	0	0	0	0	0	3.8	1.8
Oil	18	19	21	17	18	19	13	13	0.7	0.4
Gas	15	19	23	14	16	19	14	13	2.0	1.3
Electricity	56	77	97	51	66	82	59	57	3.0	2.4
Heat	-	-	-	-	-	-	-	-	n.a.	n.a.
Bioenergy	22	21	20	23	21	21	12	15	-0.8	-0.7
Other renewables	1	2	3	1	2	3	2	2	6.1	6.8
Other	64	82	97	64	80	94	100	100	2.4	2.2

Latin America: New Policies Scenario

Electricity generation (TWh)								Shares (%)		CAAGR (%)
	1990	2012	2020	2025	2030	2035	2040	2012	2040	2012-40
Total generation	489	1 152	1 444	1 654	1 850	2 061	2 263	100	100	2.4
Coal	9	26	42	47	55	60	65	2	3	3.3
Oil	64	150	128	112	93	88	80	13	4	-2.2
Gas	45	195	221	287	344	425	498	17	22	3.4
Nuclear	10	22	34	41	53	53	64	2	3	3.8
Hydro	354	702	898	1 003	1 098	1 181	1 256	61	56	2.1
Bioenergy	7	45	68	79	92	106	118	4	5	3.5
Wind	-	7	43	64	82	100	116	1	5	10.5
Geothermal	1	4	5	7	10	14	18	0	1	5.9
Solar PV	-	0	5	11	17	25	32	0	1	23.8
CSP	-	0	-	1	6	10	15	0	1	26.8
Marine	-	-	-	-	-	-	-	-	-	n.a.

Electrical capacity (GW)							Shares (%)		CAAGR (%)
	2012	2020	2025	2030	2035	2040	2012	2040	2012-40
Total capacity	258	346	397	446	497	544	100	100	2.7
Coal	6	9	9	10	11	13	2	2	2.9
Oil	39	43	40	36	35	33	15	6	-0.5
Gas	50	68	84	100	119	135	19	25	3.6
Nuclear	3	5	6	7	7	8	1	2	3.8
Hydro	143	187	211	233	252	269	56	49	2.3
Bioenergy	13	16	18	20	22	24	5	4	2.3
Wind	3	14	19	25	29	34	1	6	8.6
Geothermal	1	1	1	2	2	3	0	0	5.3
Solar PV	0	4	8	12	16	21	0	4	21.8
CSP	-	-	0	1	3	4	-	1	n.a.
Marine	-	-	-	-	-	-	-	-	n.a.

CO_2 emissions (Mt)								Shares (%)		CAAGR (%)
	1990	2012	2020	2025	2030	2035	2040	2012	2040	2012-40
Total CO_2	577	1 148	1 272	1 367	1 462	1 555	1 623	100	100	1.2
Coal	45	84	117	131	146	159	170	7	10	2.6
Oil	416	765	814	840	866	880	874	67	54	0.5
Gas	116	299	341	396	450	517	579	26	36	2.4
Power generation	90	231	226	238	249	280	306	100	100	1.0
Coal	15	33	49	52	58	62	65	14	21	2.5
Oil	44	101	85	74	61	57	52	44	17	-2.3
Gas	32	98	92	112	130	161	189	42	62	2.4
TFC	423	819	936	1 012	1 086	1 147	1 189	100	100	1.3
Coal	26	47	64	73	82	90	98	6	8	2.6
Oil	342	628	689	728	765	784	783	77	66	0.8
Transport	194	403	448	477	508	521	516	49	43	0.9
Gas	54	144	183	211	239	272	308	18	26	2.7

Latin America: Current Policies and 450 Scenarios

	Electricity generation (TWh)						Shares (%) 2040		CAAGR (%) 2012-40	
	2020	2030	2040	2020	2030	2040	CPS	450	CPS	450
	Current Policies Scenario			450 Scenario						
Total generation	1 472	1 945	2 424	1 377	1 686	2 030	100	100	2.7	2.0
Coal	41	63	86	37	27	29	4	1	4.3	0.3
Oil	131	102	93	104	36	14	4	1	-1.7	-8.0
Gas	249	430	631	179	198	162	26	8	4.3	-0.6
Nuclear	34	48	58	37	57	80	2	4	3.5	4.6
Hydro	898	1 109	1 289	898	1 115	1 300	53	64	2.2	2.2
Bioenergy	68	92	116	68	96	134	5	7	3.4	3.9
Wind	41	77	104	43	107	196	4	10	10.0	12.6
Geothermal	5	9	16	5	13	26	1	1	5.4	7.1
Solar PV	4	12	20	5	29	64	1	3	21.8	26.9
CSP	-	3	10	-	8	23	0	1	24.7	28.6
Marine	-	-	-	-	0	3	-	0	n.a.	n.a.

	Electrical capacity (GW)						Shares (%) 2040		CAAGR (%) 2012-40	
	2020	2030	2040	2020	2030	2040	CPS	450	CPS	450
	Current Policies Scenario			450 Scenario						
Total capacity	349	460	569	339	434	550	100	100	2.9	2.7
Coal	9	11	14	8	7	7	2	1	3.3	0.6
Oil	44	39	37	42	33	32	6	6	-0.2	-0.8
Gas	71	113	158	62	73	86	28	16	4.2	2.0
Nuclear	5	6	8	5	8	11	1	2	3.4	4.7
Hydro	187	236	278	187	237	279	49	51	2.4	2.4
Bioenergy	16	20	24	16	21	26	4	5	2.3	2.6
Wind	13	23	31	14	33	60	5	11	8.2	10.9
Geothermal	1	1	2	1	2	4	0	1	4.9	6.5
Solar PV	3	9	15	4	19	40	3	7	20.3	24.6
CSP	-	1	2	-	2	6	0	1	n.a.	n.a.
Marine	-	-	-	-	0	1	-	0	n.a.	n.a.

	CO_2 emissions (Mt)						Shares (%) 2040		CAAGR (%) 2012-40	
	2020	2030	2040	2020	2030	2040	CPS	450	CPS	450
	Current Policies Scenario			450 Scenario						
Total CO_2	1 306	1 565	1 806	1 198	1 094	918	100	100	1.6	-0.8
Coal	119	158	197	109	88	66	11	7	3.1	-0.8
Oil	831	915	971	771	660	510	54	56	0.9	-1.4
Gas	356	492	637	318	346	342	35	37	2.7	0.5
Power generation	238	297	389	191	126	82	100	100	1.9	-3.6
Coal	48	66	87	44	24	11	22	14	3.5	-3.7
Oil	87	66	61	69	23	10	16	12	-1.8	-8.1
Gas	103	165	242	78	79	61	62	74	3.3	-1.7
TFC	955	1 135	1 279	902	874	761	100	100	1.6	-0.3
Coal	65	85	103	61	60	52	8	7	2.8	0.3
Oil	705	808	869	664	608	480	68	63	1.2	-1.0
Transport	460	543	592	430	378	261	46	34	1.4	-1.5
Gas	185	242	307	177	206	229	24	30	2.7	1.7

A

Brazil: New Policies Scenario

	Energy demand (Mtoe)						Shares (%)		CAAGR (%)
	1990	2012	2020	2025	2030	2035	2040	2012	2040	2012-40
TPED	138	278	337	384	427	465	494	100	100	2.1
Coal	10	15	21	23	25	28	29	5	6	2.4
Oil	59	117	132	144	156	165	167	42	34	1.3
Gas	3	27	33	45	56	69	81	10	16	4.0
Nuclear	1	4	6	6	8	8	11	2	2	3.5
Hydro	18	36	45	50	54	58	60	13	12	1.9
Bioenergy	48	78	96	109	119	128	132	28	27	1.9
Other renewables	-	1	4	6	9	11	13	0	3	9.8
Power generation	22	64	79	93	107	121	136	100	100	2.8
Coal	2	4	5	5	5	6	6	6	4	1.8
Oil	1	5	2	2	2	2	2	7	2	-2.7
Gas	0	9	5	11	15	21	26	13	19	4.1
Nuclear	1	4	6	6	8	8	11	7	8	3.5
Hydro	18	36	45	50	54	58	60	56	44	1.9
Bioenergy	1	6	11	13	15	18	19	10	14	4.0
Other renewables	-	0	3	5	7	9	11	1	8	12.2
Other energy sector	26	40	49	55	60	62	63	100	100	1.6
Electricity	*3*	*10*	*12*	*14*	*16*	*17*	*18*	*25*	*29*	*2.1*
TFC	111	225	273	311	345	376	398	100	100	2.0
Coal	4	8	11	12	14	15	16	4	4	2.6
Oil	53	107	123	135	147	156	159	47	40	1.4
Gas	2	13	18	23	28	34	41	6	10	4.3
Electricity	18	41	52	61	69	77	85	18	21	2.6
Heat	-	-	-	-	-	-	-	-	-	n.a.
Bioenergy	34	57	69	79	86	92	95	25	24	1.9
Other renewables	-	0	1	1	1	2	2	0	0	4.7
Industry	40	83	100	113	124	136	147	100	100	2.1
Coal	4	8	10	12	14	15	16	9	11	2.6
Oil	8	12	14	15	16	16	17	15	11	1.0
Gas	1	9	14	17	21	24	28	11	19	4.0
Electricity	10	18	23	27	30	34	37	22	26	2.6
Heat	-	-	-	-	-	-	-	-	-	n.a.
Bioenergy	17	35	39	42	44	46	48	42	33	1.1
Other renewables	-	-	-	-	-	-	-	-	-	n.a.
Transport	33	79	99	111	125	133	135	100	100	1.9
Oil	27	65	73	78	86	90	90	82	67	1.1
Electricity	0	0	0	0	0	0	1	0	0	3.1
Biofuels	6	12	23	30	35	38	38	15	28	4.3
Other fuels	0	2	2	3	3	4	6	3	5	4.0
Buildings	23	36	39	44	49	55	60	100	100	1.8
Coal	-	-	-	-	-	-	-	-	-	n.a.
Oil	6	7	8	8	9	10	11	20	18	1.5
Gas	0	1	1	1	2	2	3	1	4	6.0
Electricity	8	20	26	31	36	40	44	57	73	2.7
Heat	-	-	-	-	-	-	-	-	-	n.a.
Bioenergy	9	7	4	2	2	1	1	20	1	-7.4
Other renewables	-	0	1	1	1	2	2	1	3	4.7
Other	15	28	36	42	47	52	57	100	100	2.6

Brazil: Current Policies and 450 Scenarios

	Energy demand (Mtoe)						Shares (%)		CAAGR (%)	
	2020	2030	2040	2020	2030	2040	2040		2012-40	
	Current Policies Scenario			450 Scenario			CPS	450	CPS	450
TPED	341	442	524	328	390	417	100	100	2.3	1.5
Coal	21	27	33	20	19	18	6	4	2.8	0.6
Oil	135	163	181	128	123	103	34	25	1.6	-0.5
Gas	36	64	91	28	40	48	17	11	4.4	2.0
Nuclear	6	8	11	6	9	12	2	3	3.5	3.8
Hydro	45	55	65	45	55	62	12	15	2.1	2.0
Bioenergy	94	117	133	98	134	158	25	38	1.9	2.6
Other renewables	4	8	11	4	10	16	2	4	9.4	10.6
Power generation	82	116	151	75	94	116	100	100	3.1	2.2
Coal	5	6	8	5	2	0	5	0	2.8	-6.9
Oil	2	2	2	2	1	1	2	1	-2.5	-5.7
Gas	8	21	36	2	3	6	24	5	5.3	-1.3
Nuclear	6	8	11	6	9	12	7	10	3.5	3.8
Hydro	45	55	65	45	55	62	43	54	2.1	2.0
Bioenergy	11	16	19	11	16	21	13	18	4.0	4.3
Other renewables	3	7	10	3	8	14	6	12	11.7	13.2
Other energy sector	49	62	67	47	56	58	100	100	1.8	1.3
Electricity	13	17	20	12	14	17	30	29	2.4	1.7
TFC	276	354	418	268	318	338	100	100	2.2	1.5
Coal	11	14	17	10	12	12	4	4	2.8	1.5
Oil	126	154	172	119	116	98	41	29	1.7	-0.3
Gas	18	28	39	17	24	30	9	9	4.1	3.2
Electricity	53	73	92	50	64	78	22	23	3.0	2.3
Heat	-	-	-	-	-	-	-	-	n.a.	n.a.
Bioenergy	67	84	96	70	100	118	23	35	1.9	2.7
Other renewables	1	1	2	1	1	2	0	1	4.5	4.8
Industry	102	129	154	98	117	130	100	100	2.3	1.6
Coal	11	14	17	10	12	12	11	9	2.8	1.5
Oil	14	16	17	13	13	13	11	10	1.1	0.1
Gas	14	21	28	13	17	20	18	15	4.1	2.7
Electricity	23	31	39	23	28	33	25	26	2.8	2.2
Heat	-	-	-	-	-	-	-	-	n.a.	n.a.
Bioenergy	40	47	53	40	47	52	34	40	1.5	1.4
Other renewables	-	-	-	-	-	-	-	-	n.a.	n.a.
Transport	98	126	141	96	108	96	100	100	2.1	0.7
Oil	76	92	102	71	58	34	73	35	1.6	-2.3
Electricity	0	0	1	0	0	1	0	1	3.2	6.1
Biofuels	20	31	35	23	46	56	25	58	3.9	5.7
Other fuels	2	2	3	2	3	5	2	5	1.6	3.0
Buildings	40	53	66	38	46	56	100	100	2.2	1.6
Coal	-	-	-	-	-	-	-	-	n.a.	n.a.
Oil	8	9	11	8	9	10	17	18	1.5	1.3
Gas	1	2	3	1	2	2	5	4	6.6	5.7
Electricity	27	39	49	24	33	41	75	72	3.2	2.5
Heat	-	-	-	-	-	-	-	-	n.a.	n.a.
Bioenergy	4	2	1	4	2	1	1	2	-7.4	-6.6
Other renewables	1	1	2	1	1	2	3	3	4.5	4.8
Other	36	47	56	36	47	56	100	100	2.6	2.5

Brazil: New Policies Scenario

	Electricity generation (TWh)						Shares (%)		CAAGR (%)
	1990	2012	2020	2025	2030	2035	2040	2012	2040	2012-40
Total generation	223	552	705	830	940	1 052	1 156	100	100	2.7
Coal	5	14	22	22	24	26	28	3	2	2.4
Oil	5	19	10	10	10	9	9	4	1	-2.6
Gas	0	47	34	74	98	137	173	8	15	4.8
Nuclear	2	16	23	25	31	31	42	3	4	3.5
Hydro	207	415	521	576	627	669	702	75	61	1.9
Bioenergy	4	35	54	61	70	79	86	6	7	3.2
Wind	-	5	37	55	70	82	93	1	8	11.0
Geothermal	-	-	-	-	-	-	-	-	-	n.a.
Solar PV	-	-	3	6	9	13	16	-	1	n.a.
CSP	-	-	-	-	2	5	7	-	1	n.a.
Marine	-	-	-	-	-	-	-	-	-	n.a.

	Electrical capacity (GW)						Shares (%)		CAAGR (%)
	2012	2020	2025	2030	2035	2040	2012	2040	2012-40
Total capacity	120	169	198	226	253	276	100	100	3.0
Coal	3	4	4	5	5	5	3	2	1.7
Oil	7	12	11	11	11	11	6	4	1.4
Gas	10	13	20	26	35	43	8	15	5.3
Nuclear	2	3	3	4	4	5	2	2	3.6
Hydro	84	110	124	137	147	156	70	56	2.2
Bioenergy	11	13	15	16	17	18	9	7	1.9
Wind	3	11	16	20	23	26	2	9	8.7
Geothermal	-	-	-	-	-	-	-	-	n.a.
Solar PV	0	3	5	7	9	11	0	4	23.6
CSP	-	-	-	1	1	2	-	1	n.a.
Marine	-	-	-	-	-	-	-	-	n.a.

	CO$_2$ emissions (Mt)						Shares (%)		CAAGR (%)
	1990	2012	2020	2025	2030	2035	2040	2012	2040	2012-40
Total CO$_2$	192	440	505	566	627	683	717	100	100	1.8
Coal	27	58	81	87	96	105	111	13	16	2.4
Oil	159	323	353	379	408	427	429	73	60	1.0
Gas	7	60	71	100	123	150	177	14	25	4.0
Power generation	12	54	49	61	70	87	101	100	100	2.2
Coal	8	20	29	28	29	32	33	37	33	1.8
Oil	4	14	7	7	7	7	7	26	7	-2.7
Gas	0	20	13	26	34	48	61	37	61	4.1
TFC	165	359	418	461	507	546	568	100	100	1.7
Coal	16	34	46	54	60	66	71	10	13	2.7
Oil	144	295	330	355	384	403	406	82	71	1.1
Transport	*81*	*195*	*218*	*234*	*256*	*270*	*269*	*54*	*47*	*1.2*
Gas	5	29	42	52	63	76	91	8	16	4.1

Brazil: Current Policies and 450 Scenarios

	Electricity generation (TWh)						Shares (%)		CAAGR (%)	
	2020	2030	2040	2020	2030	2040	2040		2012-40	
	Current Policies Scenario			450 Scenario			CPS	450	CPS	450
Total generation	723	1 002	1 267	679	872	1 058	100	100	3.0	2.3
Coal	22	27	36	20	6	2	3	0	3.4	-6.6
Oil	10	10	10	8	4	4	1	0	-2.4	-5.6
Gas	54	144	238	11	24	41	19	4	6.0	-0.4
Nuclear	23	31	42	23	34	45	3	4	3.5	3.8
Hydro	522	645	752	521	639	725	59	69	2.1	2.0
Bioenergy	54	70	85	54	72	91	7	9	3.2	3.4
Wind	36	66	85	37	78	116	7	11	10.6	11.9
Geothermal	-	-	-	-	-	-	-	-	n.a.	n.a.
Solar PV	3	7	12	3	11	24	1	2	n.a.	n.a.
CSP	-	1	6	-	3	8	1	1	n.a.	n.a.
Marine	-	-	-	-	0	1	-	0	n.a.	n.a.

	Electrical capacity (GW)						Shares (%)		CAAGR (%)	
	2020	2030	2040	2020	2030	2040	2040		2012-40	
	Current Policies Scenario			450 Scenario			CPS	450	CPS	450
Total capacity	170	237	298	169	220	273	100	100	3.3	3.0
Coal	4	5	6	4	3	2	2	1	2.2	-2.5
Oil	12	11	11	12	11	11	4	4	1.5	1.3
Gas	15	35	55	13	15	25	18	9	6.2	3.3
Nuclear	3	4	5	3	5	6	2	2	3.6	4.1
Hydro	110	141	168	110	140	162	56	59	2.5	2.3
Bioenergy	13	16	18	13	16	19	6	7	1.9	2.0
Wind	11	19	24	11	22	31	8	12	8.3	9.4
Geothermal	-	-	-	-	-	-	-	-	n.a.	n.a.
Solar PV	2	5	9	3	8	16	3	6	22.8	25.3
CSP	-	0	2	-	1	2	1	1	n.a.	n.a.
Marine	-	-	-	-	0	0	-	0	n.a.	n.a.

	CO_2 emissions (Mt)						Shares (%)		CAAGR (%)	
	2020	2030	2040	2020	2030	2040	2040		2012-40	
	Current Policies Scenario			450 Scenario			CPS	450	CPS	450
Total CO_2	523	673	796	476	434	345	100	100	2.1	-0.9
Coal	82	103	126	75	52	35	16	10	2.8	-1.8
Oil	362	430	472	340	304	224	59	65	1.4	-1.3
Gas	79	140	198	60	78	86	25	25	4.4	1.3
Power generation	57	91	135	37	19	19	100	100	3.3	-3.6
Coal	30	34	43	27	8	3	32	14	2.8	-7.0
Oil	7	7	7	6	3	3	5	14	-2.5	-5.8
Gas	19	50	85	4	8	14	63	72	5.3	-1.3
TFC	428	530	608	402	379	300	100	100	1.9	-0.6
Coal	47	63	76	44	40	30	12	10	2.9	-0.5
Oil	339	405	447	319	289	213	73	71	1.5	-1.2
Transport	226	275	307	211	175	102	50	34	1.6	-2.3
Gas	42	62	86	39	50	57	14	19	3.9	2.4

Policies and measures by scenario

The *World Energy Outlook 2014* (*WEO-2014*) presents projections for three scenarios, which are differentiated primarily by their underlying assumptions about government policies.

The **Current Policies Scenario** is based on those government policies and implementing measures that had been formally adopted as of mid-2014.

The **New Policies Scenario** – our central scenario – takes into account the policies and implementing measures affecting energy markets that had been adopted as of mid-2014, together with relevant policy proposals, even if specific measures needed to put them into effect have yet to be fully developed. It assumes only cautious implementation of such commitments and plans.

The **450 Scenario** sets out an energy pathway that is consistent with a 50% chance of meeting the goal of limiting the long-term increase in average global temperature to 2 °C compared with pre-industrial levels. For the period to 2020, the 450 Scenario assumes more vigorous policy action to implement fully the Cancun Agreements than is assumed in the New Policies Scenario. The 450 Scenario in this report differs in important ways from *WEO-2013*, and is similar to that in the *WEO Special Report*: *Redrawing the Energy-Climate Map*. Recognising that truly concerted global action before 2020 is unlikely, as this is the earliest date by which any agreement reached at COP-21 is expected to come into effect, for the period to 2020 we assume the four measures proposed in the report will be taken up at no net economic cost. After 2020, OECD countries and other major economies are assumed to adopt CO_2 pricing in power generation and industry, while all fossil-fuel subsidies are removed in all regions except the Middle East. Energy consumption in transport and buildings is reduced through an extension and strengthening of minimum performance standards. The set of policies collectively ensures an emissions trajectory consistent with stabilisation of the greenhouse-gas concentration at 450 parts per million.

The key policies that are assumed to be adopted in each of the main scenarios of *WEO-2014* are presented below, by sector and region. The policies are cumulative: measures listed under the New Policies Scenario supplement those under the Current Policies Scenario, and measures listed under the 450 Scenario supplement those under the New Policies Scenario. The following tables start with broad cross-cutting policy frameworks and are followed by more detailed policy assumptions by sector as they have been adopted in this year's *Outlook*.

Table B.1 ▷ **Cross-cutting policy assumptions by scenario for selected regions**

	Current Policies Scenario	New Policies Scenario	450 Scenario
OECD			• Staggered introduction of CO_2 prices in all countries. • $100 billion annual financing provided to non-OECD countries by 2020.

United States	• State-level renewable portfolio standards (RPS) that include the option of using energy efficiency as a means of compliance.
	• Regional Greenhouse Gas Initiative (RGGI): mandatory cap-and-trade scheme covering fossil-fuel power plants in nine northeast states including recycling of revenues for energy efficiency and renewable energy investments.
	• State-wide cap-and-trade scheme in California with binding commitments.
		• Clean Power Plan: CO_2 emissions reduction from the power sector of 30% by 2030 compared with 2005 levels, including the following building blocks:
		  o Make fossil fuel power plants more efficient.
		  o Use low-emitting power sources (natural gas) more.
		  o Use more zero- and low-emitting power sources.
		  o Use electricity more efficiently.
			• 17% reduction in greenhouse-gas (GHG) emissions by 2020 compared with 2005.
			• CO_2 pricing implemented from 2020.

Japan		• 3.8% reduction in GHG emissions by 2020 compared with 2005 according to recent announcements.	• CO_2 pricing implemented from 2020.

European Union	• EU-level target to reduce GHG emissions by 20% in 2020, relative to 1990.
	• EU Emissions Trading System.
	• Renewables to reach a share of 20% in energy demand in 2020.
		• Partial implementation of the EU-level target to reduce primary energy consumption by 20% in 2020:
		  o Partial implementation of the EU Energy Efficiency Directive.
		  o National Energy Efficiency Action Plans.
		• Cautious consideration of the proposed climate and energy policy framework for 2030.
			• 30% reduction in GHG emissions by 2020 compared with 1990.
			• Emissions Trading System strengthened in line with the 2050 roadmap.
			• Full implementation of the 2030 framework for climate and energy policies, as well as the EU Energy Efficiency Directive.

Australia and New Zealand	• New Zealand: emissions trading scheme from 2010.	• Australia: Direct Action Plan including the Emissions Reduction Fund. • New Zealand: 10% cut in GHG emissions by 2020 compared with 1990.	• Australia: 25% reduction in GHG emissions by 2020 compared with 2000. • New Zealand: 20% reduction in GHG emissions by 2020 compared with 1990.
Korea	• Cap-and-trade scheme from 2015 (CO_2 emissions reductions of 4% by 2020 compared with 2005).	• 30% reduction in GHG emissions by 2020 compared with business-as-usual.	• 30% reduction in GHG emissions by 2020 compared with business-as-usual. • Higher CO_2 prices.

Table B.1 ⊳ **Cross-cutting policy assumptions by scenario for selected regions** (continued)

	Current Policies Scenario	New Policies Scenario	450 Scenario
Non-OECD	• Fossil-fuel subsidies are phased out in countries that already have policies in place to do so.	• Fossil-fuel subsidies are phased out within the next ten years in all net-importing countries and in net-exporting countries where specific policies have already been announced.	• Finance for domestic mitigation. • Fossil-fuel subsidies are phased out within the next ten years in net-importing countries and by 2035 in net-exporting countries.*
Russia	• Gradual real increases in residential gas and electricity prices (1% per year) and in gas prices in industry (1.5% per year). • Implementation of the federal law on energy conservation and energy efficiency.	• 15-25% reduction in GHG emissions by 2020 compared with 1990. • 2% per year real rise in residential gas and electricity prices. • Industrial gas prices reach export prices (minus taxes and transport) in 2020.	• 25% reduction in GHG emissions by 2020, compared with 1990. • Quicker rise in residential gas and electricity prices. • CO_2 pricing from 2020. • More support for nuclear and renewables. • Partial implementation of the "Energy saving and increase of energy efficiency for the period till 2020" programme.
China	• Implementation of measures in the 12th Five-Year Plan, including 17% cut in CO_2 intensity by 2015 and 16% reduction in energy intensity by 2015 compared with 2010.	• 45% reduction in CO_2 intensity by 2020 compared with 2005. • CO_2 pricing from 2020. • Share of 15% of non-fossil fuel in total supply by 2020. • Energy price reform including more frequent adjustments in oil product prices and increase in natural gas price by 15% for non-residential users. • Action Plan for Prevention and Control of Air Pollution.	• Exceed 45% reduction in CO_2 intensity by 2020 compared with 2005; higher CO_2 pricing. • Reduction of local air pollutants between 2010 and 2015 (reduction of 8% for sulphur dioxide, 10% for nitrogen oxides).
India	• Trading of renewable energy certificates. • National solar mission and national mission on enhanced energy efficiency.	• 20% reduction in CO_2 intensity by 2020 compared with 2005.	• 25% reduction in CO_2 intensity by 2020 compared with 2005.
Brazil		• 36% reduction in GHG emissions by 2020 compared with business-as-usual. • Implementation of National Energy Efficiency Plan.	• 39% reduction in GHG emissions by 2020 compared with business-as-usual. • CO_2 pricing from 2020.

* Except the Middle East where subsidisation rates are assumed to decline to an average of 8% by 2035.

Note: Pricing of CO_2 emissions is either by an emissions trading scheme (ETS) or taxes.

B

Table B.2 ▷ **Power sector policies and measures as modelled by scenario in selected regions**

	Current Policies Scenario	New Policies Scenario	450 Scenario
OECD			
United States	• State-level renewable portfolio standards (RPS) and support for renewables prolonged over the projection period. • Mercury and Air Toxics Standard. • Clean Air Interstate Rule regulating sulphur dioxide and nitrogen oxides. • Lifetimes of some US nuclear plants extended beyond 60 years. • Funding for CCS (demonstration-scale).	• Implementation of Clean Power Plan (CO_2 emissions reduction from the power sector of 30% by 2030 compared with 2005 levels). • Cautious implementation of carbon pollution standards on new power plants. • Extension and strengthening of support for renewables and nuclear, including loan guarantees. • Shadow price of carbon assumed from 2015, affecting investment decisions in power generation capacity.	• CO_2 pricing implemented from 2020. • Extended support to renewables, nuclear and CCS. • Efficiency and emission standards preventing refurbishment of old inefficient plants.
Japan	• Support for renewables generation. • Decommissioning of units 1-6 of Fukushima Daiichi nuclear power plant.	• Shadow price of carbon assumed from 2015, affecting investment decisions in power generation. • Lifetime of nuclear plants typically amounting to 40 years, with the possibility of extensions up to 60 years. • Harmonisation of support for renewables generation.	• CO_2 pricing implemented from 2020. • Share of low-carbon electricity generation to increase by 2020 and expand further by 2030. • Expansion of renewables support. • Introduction of CCS to coal-fired power generation.
European Union	• Climate and Energy Package: ○ Emissions Trading System. ○ Support for renewables sufficient to reach 20% share of energy demand in 2020. ○ Financial support for CCS. • Early retirement of all nuclear plants in Germany by the end of 2022. • Removal of some barriers to combined heat and power (CHP) plants resulting from the Cogeneration Directive 2004. • Industrial Emissions Directive.	• Extended and strengthened support to renewables-based electricity generation technologies. • Further removal of barriers to CHP through partial implementation of the Energy Efficiency Directive.	• Emissions Trading System strengthened in line with the 2050 roadmap. • Reinforcement of government support in favour of renewables. • Expanded support measures for CCS.

Note: CCS = carbon capture and storage.

Table B.2 ▷ **Power sector policies and measures as modelled by scenario in selected regions** (continued)

	Current Policies Scenario	New Policies Scenario	450 Scenario
Non-OECD			
Russia	• Competitive wholesale electricity market.	• State support to the nuclear and hydropower sectors; strengthening and broadening of the existing support mechanism for non-hydro renewables.	• CO_2 pricing implemented from 2020. • Stronger support for nuclear power and renewables.
China	• Implementation of measures in 12th Five-Year Plan. • Start construction of 40 GW of new nuclear plants by 2015. • Reach 290 GW of installed hydro capacity by 2015. • Reach 100 GW of installed wind capacity by 2015. • 35 GW of solar capacity by 2015. • Priority given to gas use to 2015.	• 12th Five-Year Plan renewables targets for 2015 are exceeded. • 58 GW of nuclear capacity by 2020. • 200 GW of wind capacity by 2020. • 100 GW of solar PV by 2020. • 30 GW of bioenergy-based power capacity by 2020. • CO_2 pricing implemented from 2020.	• Higher CO_2 pricing. • Enhanced support for renewables. • Continued support to nuclear capacity additions post 2020. • Deployment of CCS from around 2020.
India	• Renewable Energy Certificate trade for all eligible grid-connected renewable-based electricity generation technologies. • National solar mission target of 20 GW of solar PV capacity by 2022. • Increased use of supercritical coal technology.	• Renewable energy support policies and targets, including small hydro. • Coal-fired power stations energy efficiency mandates.	• Renewables (excluding large hydro) to reach 15% of installed capacity by 2020. • Expanded support to renewables, nuclear and efficient coal. • Deployment of CCS from around 2020.
Brazil	• Power auctions for all fuel types. • Guidance on the fuel mix from the Ten-Year Plan for Energy Expansion.	• Enhanced deployment of renewables technologies through power auctions.	• CO_2 pricing implemented from 2020. • Further increases of generation from renewable sources.

Notes: Pricing of CO_2 emissions is either by an emissions trading scheme (ETS) or taxes; CCS = carbon capture and storage.

Table B.3 △ Transport sector policies and measures as modelled by scenario in selected regions

OECD	Current Policies Scenario	New Policies Scenario	450 Scenario
			All OECD
United States	• CAFE standards: 35.5 miles per gallon for PLDVs by 2016, and further strengthening thereafter. • Renewables Fuel Standard. • Truck standards for each model year from 2014 to 2018 reduce average on-road fuel consumption by up to 18% in 2018.	• CAFE standards: 54.5 miles per gallon for PLDVs by 2025. • Truck standards for each model year from 2014 to 2018 reduce average on-road fuel consumption by up to 20% in 2018, and further strengthening thereafter. • Support to natural gas in road freight. • Increase of ethanol blending mandates.	• On-road emission targets for PLDVs in 2040: 45 g CO_2/km. • Light-commercial vehicles: full technology spill-over from PLDVs. • Medium- and heavy-freight vehicles: 33% more efficient by 2040 than in New Policies Scenario. • Aviation: 55% efficiency improvements by 2040 (compared with 2010) and support for the use of biofuels. • Other sectors (e.g. maritime and rail): national policies and measures. • Fuels: retail fuel prices kept at a level similar to New Policies Scenario. • Alternative clean fuels: enhanced support to alternative fuels.
Japan	• Fuel-economy target for PLDVs: 16.8 kilometres per litre (km/l) by 2015 and 20.3 km/l by 2020. • Average fuel-economy target for road freight vehicles: 7.09 km/l by 2015. • Fiscal incentives for hybrid and electric vehicles; subsidies for electric vehicles.	• Target share of next generation vehicles (clean diesel vehicles, hybrid vehicles, plug-in hybrid vehicles, electric vehicles and fuel cell vehicles) 50% by 2020.	
European Union	• CO_2 emission standards for PLDVs by 2015 (130 g CO_2/km through efficiency measures, additional 10 g CO_2/km by alternative fuels). • Support to biofuels.	• Climate and Energy Package: Target to reach 10% of transport energy demand in 2020 by renewable fuels. • Fuel Quality Directive: Target to reduce the greenhouse-gas intensity of road transport fuels by 6% in 2020. • More stringent emission target for PLDVs (95 g CO_2/km by 2020), and further strengthening after 2020. • Emission target for LCVs (147 g CO_2/km by 2020), and further strengthening post 2020. • Enhanced support to alternative fuels.	

Notes: CAFE = Corporate Average Fuel Economy; PLDVs = passenger light-duty vehicles; LCV = light-commercial vehicles.

World Energy Outlook 2014 | Annexes

Table B.3 ▷ **Transport sector policies and measures as modelled by scenario in selected regions** (continued)

	Current Policies Scenario	New Policies Scenario	450 Scenario
Non-OECD			**All Non-OECD**
China	• Subsidies for hybrid and electric vehicles and consolidation of vehicle charging standards. • Promotion of fuel-efficient cars. • Ethanol blending mandates 10% in selected provinces. • Cap on PLDV sales in some cities to reduce air pollution and traffic jams. • Enhance infrastructure for electric vehicles in selected cities.	• Fuel economy target for PLDVs: 6.9 l/100 km by 2015, 5.0 l/100 km by 2020. • Extended subsidies for purchase of alternative-fuel vehicles. • Complete fossil-fuel subsidy phase out within the next ten years.	• On-road emission targets for PLDVs in 2040: 65 g CO_2/km. • Light-commercial vehicles: full technology spill-over from PLDVs. • Medium- and heavy-freight vehicles: 43% more efficient by 2040 than in New Policies Scenario. • Aviation: 55% efficiency improvements by 2040 (compared with 2010) and support for the use of biofuels. • Other sectors (e.g. maritime and rail): national policies and measures. • Fuels: retail fuel prices kept at a level similar to New Policies Scenario. • Alternative clean fuels: enhanced support to alternative fuels.
India	• Support for alternative-fuel vehicles.	• Extended support for alternative-fuel vehicles. • Fuel economy standard for PLDVs: 5.5 litres/100km of fuel on average by 2015/2016, and 4.8 litres/100km by 2021/2022. • Increased utilisation of natural gas in road transport. • National Electric Mobility Mission Plan 2020. • All fossil-fuel subsidies are phased out within the next ten years.	
Brazil	• Ethanol blending mandates in road transport between 18% and 25%. • Biodiesel blending mandate of 5%.	• Inovar-Auto initiative targeting fuel efficiency improvement for PLDVs of at least 12% in 2017, compared with 2012/2013). • Increase of ethanol and biodiesel blending mandates. • Local renewable fuel targets for urban transport. • Concessions to improve port, road, rail and air infrastructure, as per the Accelerated Growth Programme 2011-2014. • Long-term plan for freight transport (PNLT), developed by the Ministry of Transport. • National urban mobility plan (PNMU), developed by the Ministry of Cities.	

Note: PLDVs = passenger light-duty vehicles.

Table B.4 ▷ **Industry sector policies and measures as modelled by scenario in selected regions**

	Current Policies Scenario	New Policies Scenario	450 Scenario
OECD			**All OECD**
United States	• Better Buildings, Better Plants programme. • Energy Star Program for Industry. • Climate Voluntary Innovative Sector Initiatives: Opportunities Now. • Boiler maximum achievable control technology rule to impose stricter emissions limits on industrial and commercial boilers and process heaters.	• Tax reduction and funding for efficient technologies. • R&D in low-carbon technologies.	• CO_2 pricing introduced from 2025 at the latest in all countries. • International sectoral agreements with energy intensity targets for iron and steel, and cement industries. • Enhanced energy efficiency standards. • Policies to support the introduction of CCS in industry.
Japan	• Mandatory energy efficiency benchmarking. • Tax credit for investments in energy efficiency. • Mandatory energy management for large business operators. • Top Runner Programme setting minimum energy standards, including for lighting, space heating, and transformers.	• Maintenance and strengthening of top-end/low carbon efficiency standards by: ○ Higher efficiency CHP systems. ○ Promotion of state-of-the-art technology and faster replacement of aging equipment.	
European Union	• Emissions Trading System. • Voluntary energy efficiency agreements in the following countries: Denmark, Finland, Germany, Ireland, Netherlands, Sweden and United Kingdom. • EcoDesign Directive (including minimum standards for electric motors, pumps, fans, compressors and insulation). • Industrial Emissions Directive: ○ Application of best available techniques. ○ Maximisation of energy efficiency. ○ Preventive measures taken against pollution.	• Partial implementation of Energy Efficiency Directive: ○ Mandatory and regular energy audits for large enterprises. ○ Incentives for the use of energy management systems. ○ Encouragement for SMEs to undergo energy audits. ○ Technical assistance and targeted information for SMEs. ○ Training programmes for auditors.	

Notes: R&D = research and development; CHP = combined heat and power; CCS = carbon capture and storage.

Table B.4 ▷ Industry sector policies and measures as modelled by scenario in selected regions (continued)

	Current Policies Scenario	New Policies Scenario	450 Scenario
Non-OECD			**All Non-OECD**
Russia	• Competitive wholesale electricity market price. • Federal law on energy conservation and energy efficiency, including mandatory energy audits and energy management systems for energy-intensive industries and various economic instruments. • Complete phase out of open hearth furnaces in the iron and steel industry.	• Industrial gas prices reach the equivalent of export prices (minus taxes and transportation) in 2020. • Limited phase out of natural gas subsidy.	• CO_2 pricing introduced as of 2020 in Russia, China, Brazil and South Africa. • Wider hosting of international offset projects.
China	• Top 10 000 energy-consuming enterprises programme. • Small plant closures and phasing out of outdated production capacity, including the comprehensive control of small coal-fired boilers. • Partial implementation of Industrial Energy Performance Standards. • Ten Key Projects. • Mandatory adoption of coke dry quenching and top-pressure turbines in new iron and steel plants / Support non-blast furnace iron making. • Priority given to gas use to 2015 (12th Five-Year Plan).	• Contain the expansion of energy-intensive industries. • CO_2 pricing implemented from 2020. Partial implementation of reduction in industrial energy intensity by 21% during the 12th Five-Year Plan period (2011-2015). • Full implementation of Industrial Energy Performance Standards. • Enhanced use of energy service companies and energy performance contracting. • All fossil-fuel subsidies are phased out within the next ten years.	• International sectoral agreements with targets for iron and steel, and cement industries. • Enhanced energy efficiency standards. • Policies to support the introduction of CCS in industry.
India	• Perform, Achieve and Trade (PAT) mechanism, targeting a 5% reduction in energy use by 2015 compared with 2010 through a trade system with plant-based efficiency levels. • Energy Conservation Act. • Mandatory energy audits, appointment of an energy manager in seven energy-intensive industries.	• Further implementation of National Mission for Enhanced Energy Efficiency recommendations including: ○ Enhancement of cost-effective improvements in energy efficiency in energy-intensive large industries and facilities through tradable certificates (extension of PAT). ○ Financing mechanism for demand-side management programmes. ○ Development of fiscal instruments to promote energy efficiency. • All fossil-fuel subsidies are phased out within the next ten years.	
Brazil	• PROCEL (National Program for Energy Conversation). • PROESCO (Support for Energy Efficiency Projects).	• Partial implementation of the National Energy Efficiency Plan: ○ Fiscal and tax incentives for industrial upgrading. ○ Invest in training efficiency. ○ Encourage the use of industrial waste. • Extension of PROESCO.	

Note: CCS = carbon capture and storage.

Table B.5 ▷ **Buildings sector policies and measures as modelled by scenario in selected regions**

	Current Policies Scenario	New Policies Scenario	450 Scenario
OECD			
United States	• AHAM-ACEEE Multi-Product Standards Agreement. • Energy Star: federal tax credits for consumer energy efficiency; new appliance efficiency standards. • Energy Improvement and Extension Act of 2008. • Budget proposals 2011 - institute programmes to make commercial buildings 20% more efficient by 2020; tax credit for renewable energy deployment. • Weatherisation programme: provision of funding for refurbishments of residential buildings.	• Extensions to 2025 of tax credit for energy-efficient equipment (including furnaces, boilers, air conditioners, air and ground source heat pumps, water heaters and windows), and for solar PV and solar thermal water heaters. • Mandatory energy requirements in building codes in some states. • Tightening of efficiency standards for appliances.	• Mandatory energy requirements in building codes in all states by 2020. • Extension of energy efficiency grants to end of projection period. • Zero-energy buildings initiative.
Japan	• Top-Runner Programme. • Energy reduction efforts of 1% per year and annual reports to the governments by large operators. • Energy efficiency standards for buildings and houses (300m² or more).	• Extension of the Top Runner Programme. • Voluntary buildings labelling; national voluntary equipment labelling programmes. • Net zero-energy buildings by 2030 for all new construction. • Increased introduction of gas and renewable energy. • High-efficiency lighting: 100% in public facilities by 2020; 100% of all lighting by 2030.	• Rigorous and mandatory building energy codes for all new and existing buildings. • Net zero-energy buildings by 2025 for all new construction. • Strengthening of high-efficiency lighting for non-public buildings.
European Union	• Energy Performance of Buildings Directive. • EcoDesign and Energy Labelling Directive. • EU-US Energy Star Agreement: energy labelling of appliances. • Phase out of incandescent light bulbs.	• Partial implementation of the Energy Efficiency Directive. • Building energy performance requirements for new buildings (zero-energy buildings by 2021) and for existing buildings when extensively renovated. 3% renovation rate of central government buildings. • Mandatory energy labelling for sale or rental of all buildings and some appliances, lighting and equipment. • Further product groups in EcoDesign Directive.	• Zero-carbon footprint for all new buildings as of 2015; enhanced energy efficiency in all existing buildings. • Full implementation of the Energy Efficiency Directive. • Mandatory energy conservation standards and labelling requirements for all equipment and appliances, space and water heating and cooling systems by 2020.

Notes: AHAM = Association of Home Appliance Manufacturers; ACEEE = American Council for an Energy-Efficient Economy.

Table B.5 ▷ **Buildings sector policies and measures as modelled by scenario in selected regions** (continued)

	Current Policies Scenario	New Policies Scenario	450 Scenario
Non-OECD			
Russia	• Implementation of the federal law on energy conservation and energy efficiency. • Voluntary labelling program for electrical products. • Restriction on sale of incandescent light bulbs.	• Gradual above-inflation increase in residential electricity and gas prices. • New building codes, meter installations and refurbishment programmes. Information and awareness on energy efficiency classes for appliances. • Phase-out of incandescent >100 watt light bulbs. • Limited phase-out of natural gas and electricity subsidies.	• Faster liberalisation of gas and electricity prices. • Extension and reinforcement of all measures included in the 2010 energy efficiency state programme; mandatory building codes by 2030 and phase-out of inefficient equipment and appliances by 2030.
China	• Civil Construction Energy Conservation Design Standards. • Appliance standards and labelling programme.	• Energy efficient buildings to account for 30% of all new construction projects by 2020. • Civil Construction Energy Conservation Design Standard: heating energy consumption per unit area of existing buildings to be reduced by 65% in cold regions; 50% in hot-in-summer and cold-in-winter regions compared to 1980-1981 levels. New buildings: 65% improvement in all regions. • Building energy codes for all buildings to improve building envelope and HVAC system efficiencies in place (applies to cold climate zones); mandatory codes for all new large residential buildings in big cities. • Energy Price Policy (reform heating price to be based on actual consumption, rather than on living area supplied). • Mandatory energy efficiency labels for appliances and equipment. • Labelling mandatory for new, large commercial and governmental buildings in big cities. • Introduction of energy standards for new buildings & refurbishment of existing dwellings. • Phase-out production of incandescent light bulbs over the next ten years. • All fossil-fuel subsidies are phased out within the next ten years.	• More stringent implementation of Civil Construction Energy Conservation Design Standard. • Mandatory energy efficiency labels for all appliances and also for building shell. • Faster Energy Price Policy reform to set stronger incentives for energy savings. • Partial Implementation of the Building Conservation Plan, which foresees that 95% of new buildings achieve savings of 55%- 65% in space heating compared to 1980, depending on the climate zone.

B

Table B.5 ▷ **Buildings sector policies and measures as modelled by scenario in selected regions** (continued)

	Current Policies Scenario	New Policies Scenario	450 Scenario
India	• Measures under national solar mission. • Energy Conservation Building Code 2007, with voluntary requirements for commercial and residential buildings.	• Mandatory standards and labels for room air conditioners and refrigerators, voluntary for five other products. (More stringent minimum energy performance standards for air conditioners). • Phase-out of incandescent light bulbs by 2020. • Voluntary Star Ratings for the services sector. • National Action Plan in Climate Change: Measures concerning building sector in the National Mission on Enhanced Energy Efficiency. • Energy Conservation in building codes made mandatory in eight states and applies among others to building envelope, lighting and hot water. • All fossil-fuel subsidies are phased out within the next ten years.	• Mandatory energy conservation standards and labelling requirements for all equipment and appliances by 2025. • Increased penetration of energy efficient lighting.
Brazil	• Labelling programme for household goods and equipment in public buildings.	• Partial implementation of National Energy Efficiency Plan.	• Full implementation of National Energy Efficiency Plan.

Definitions

This annex provides general information on terminology used throughout *WEO-2014* including: units and general conversion factors; definitions on fuels, processes and sectors; regional and country groupings; and, abbreviations and acronyms.

Units

Area	ha	hectare
	km²	square kilometre
Coal	Mtce	million tonnes of coal equivalent (equals 0.7 Mtoe)
Emissions	ppm	parts per million (by volume)
	Gt CO₂-eq	gigatonnes of carbon-dioxide equivalent (using 100-year global warming potentials for different greenhouse gases)
	kg CO₂-eq	kilogrammes of carbon-dioxide equivalent
	g CO₂/km	grammes of carbon dioxide per kilometre
	g CO₂/kWh	grammes of carbon dioxide per kilowatt-hour
Energy	boe	barrel of oil equivalent
	toe	tonne of oil equivalent
	ktoe	thousand tonnes of oil equivalent
	Mtoe	million tonnes of oil equivalent
	MBtu	million British thermal units
	kcal	kilocalorie (1 calorie x 10³)
	Gcal	gigacalorie (1 calorie x 10⁹)
	MJ	megajoule (1 joule x 10⁶)
	GJ	gigajoule (1 joule x 10⁹)
	TJ	terajoule (1 joule x 10¹²)
	PJ	petajoule (1 joule x 10¹⁵)
	EJ	exajoule (1 joule x 10¹⁸)
	kWh	kilowatt-hour
	MWh	megawatt-hour
	GWh	gigawatt-hour
	TWh	terawatt-hour
Gas	mcm	million cubic metres
	bcm	billion cubic metres
	tcm	trillion cubic metres
	scf	standard cubic foot

Mass	kg	kilogramme (1 000 kg = 1 tonne)
	kt	kilotonnes (1 tonne x 10^3)
	Mt	million tonnes (1 tonne x 10^6)
	Gt	gigatonnes (1 tonne x 10^9)
Monetary	$ million	1 US dollar x 10^6
	$ billion	1 US dollar x 10^9
	$ trillion	1 US dollar x 10^{12}
Oil	b/d	barrel per day
	kb/d	thousand barrels per day
	mb/d	million barrels per day
	mboe/d	million barrels of oil equivalent per day
Power	W	watt (1 joule per second)
	kW	kilowatt (1 watt x 10^3)
	MW	megawatt (1 watt x 10^6)
	GW	gigawatt (1 watt x 10^9)
	TW	terawatt (1 watt x 10^{12})

General conversion factors for energy

Convert to:	TJ	Gcal	Mtoe	MBtu	GWh
From:	multiply by:				
TJ	1	238.8	2.388×10^{-5}	947.8	0.2778
Gcal	4.1868×10^{-3}	1	10^{-7}	3.968	1.163×10^{-3}
Mtoe	4.1868×10^4	10^7	1	3.968×10^7	11 630
MBtu	1.0551×10^{-3}	0.252	2.52×10^{-8}	1	2.931×10^{-4}
GWh	3.6	860	1.6×10^{-5}	3 412	1

Note: There is no generally accepted definition of boe; typically the conversion factors used vary from 7.15 to 7.35 boe per toe.

Currency conversions

Exchange rates (2013 annual average)	1 US Dollar equals:
British Pound	0.64
Chinese Yuan	6.20
Euro	0.75
Indian Rupee	60.52
Japanese Yen	97.60
Nigerian Naira	155.25
Russian Ruble	31.76
South African Rand	9.65

Definitions

Advanced biofuels: Comprise different emerging and novel conversion technologies to produce biofuels that are currently in the research and development, pilot or demonstration phase. This definition differs from the one used for "advanced biofuels" in US legislation, which is based on a minimum 50% lifecycle greenhouse-gas reduction and which, therefore, includes sugarcane ethanol.

Agriculture: Includes all energy used on farms, in forestry and for fishing.

Back-up generation capacity: Households and businesses connected to the main power grid may also have some form of "back-up" power generation capacity that can, in the event of disruption, provide electricity. Back-up generators are typically fuelled with diesel or gasoline and capacity can be from as little as a few kilowatts. Such capacity is distinct from mini- and off-grid systems that are not connected to the main power grid.

Biodiesel: Diesel-equivalent, processed fuel made from the transesterification (a chemical process that converts triglycerides in oils) of vegetable oils and animal fats.

Bioenergy: Energy content in solid, liquid and gaseous products derived from biomass feedstocks and biogas. It includes solid biomass, biofuels and biogas.

Biofuels: Liquid fuels derived from biomass or waste feedstocks and include ethanol and biodiesel. They can be classified as conventional and advanced biofuels according to the technologies used to produce them and their respective maturity.

Biogas: A mixture of methane and carbon dioxide produced by bacterial degradation of organic matter and used as a fuel.

Buildings: The buildings sector includes energy used in residential, commercial and institutional buildings, and non-specified other. Building energy use includes space heating and cooling, water heating, lighting, appliances and cooking equipment.

Bunkers: Includes both international marine bunkers and international aviation bunkers.

Capacity credit: Proportion of the capacity that can be reliably expected to generate electricity during times of peak demand in the grid to which it is connected.

Clean cooking facilities: Cooking facilities that are considered safer, more efficient and more environmentally sustainable than the traditional facilities that make use of solid biomass (such as a three-stone fire). This refers primarily to improved solid biomass cookstoves, biogas systems, liquefied petroleum gas stoves, ethanol and solar stoves.

Coal: Includes both primary coal (including lignite, coking and steam coal) and derived fuels (including patent fuel, brown-coal briquettes, coke-oven coke, gas coke, gas-works gas, coke-oven gas, blast-furnace gas and oxygen steel furnace gas). Peat is also included.

Coalbed methane (CBM)**:** Category of unconventional natural gas, which refers to methane found in coal seams.

Coal-to-gas (CTG): Process in which mined coal is first turned into syngas (a mixture of hydrogen and carbon monoxide) and then into "synthetic" methane.

Coal-to-liquids (CTL): Transformation of coal into liquid hydrocarbons. It can be achieved through either coal gasification into syngas (a mixture of hydrogen and carbon monoxide), combined using the Fischer-Tropsch or methanol-to-gasoline synthesis process to produce liquid fuels, or through the less developed direct-coal liquefaction technologies in which coal is directly reacted with hydrogen.

Coking coal: Type of coal that can be used for steel making (as a chemical reductant and source heat), where it produces coke capable of supporting a blast furnace charge. Coal of this quality is also commonly known as metallurgical coal.

Conventional biofuels: Include well-established technologies that are producing biofuels on a commercial scale today. These biofuels are commonly referred to as first generation and include sugarcane ethanol, starchbased ethanol, biodiesel, Fatty Acid Methyl Esther (FAME) and Straight Vegetable Oil (SVO). Typical feedstocks used in these mature processes include sugarcane and sugar beet, starch bearing grains, like corn and wheat, and oil crops, like canola and palm, and in some cases, animal fats.

Decommissioning (nuclear): The process of dismantling and decontaminating a nuclear power plant at the end of its operational lifetime and restoring the site for other uses.

Decomposition analysis: Statistical approach that decomposes an aggregate indicator to quantify the relative contribution of a set of pre-defined factors leading to a change in the aggregate indicator. The *World Energy Outlook* uses an additive index decomposition of the type Logarithmic Mean Divisia Index (LMDI) I.

Electricity generation: Defined as the total amount of electricity generated by power only or combined heat and power plants including generation required for own-use. This is also referred to as gross generation.

Energy services: Energy that is at disposal for end-users to satisfy their needs. This is also sometimes referred to as "useful energy". Due to transformation losses the amount of useful energy is lower than the corresponding final energy. Forms of energy services include transportation, machine drive, lighting or heat for space heating.

Ethanol: Refers to bio-ethanol only. Ethanol is produced from fermenting any biomass high in carbohydrates. Today, ethanol is made from starches and sugars, but second-generation technologies will allow it to be made from cellulose and hemicellulose, the fibrous material that makes up the bulk of most plant matter.

Gas: Includes natural gas, both associated and non-associated with petroleum deposits, but excludes natural gas liquids. (Also referred to as natural gas.)

Gas-to-liquids (GTL): Process featuring reaction of methane with oxygen or steam to produce syngas (a mixture of hydrogen and carbon monoxide) followed by synthesis of liquid products (such as diesel and naphtha) from the syngas using Fischer-Tropsch catalytic synthesis. The process is similar to those used in coal-to-liquids.

High-level waste (HLW): The highly radioactive and long-lived waste materials generated during the course of the nuclear fuel cycle, including spent nuclear fuel (if it is declared as waste) and some waste streams from reprocessing.

Heat energy: Obtained from the combustion of fuels, nuclear reactors, geothermal reservoirs, capture of sunlight, exothermic chemical processes and heat pumps which can extract it from ambient air and liquids. It may be used for heating or cooling, or converted into mechanical energy for transport vehicles or electricity generation. Commercial heat sold is reported under total final consumption with the fuel inputs allocated under power generation.

Hydropower: The energy content of the electricity produced in hydropower projects, assuming 100% efficiency. It excludes output from pumped storage and marine (tide and wave) plants.

Industry: Includes fuel used within the manufacturing and construction industries. Key industry sectors include iron and steel, chemical and petrochemical, cement, and pulp and paper. Use by industries for the transformation of energy into another form or for the production of fuels is excluded and reported separately under other energy sector. Consumption of fuels for the transport of goods is reported as part of the transport sector, while consumption by off-road vehicles is reported under industry.

International aviation bunkers: Includes the deliveries of aviation fuels to aircraft for international aviation. Fuels used by airlines for their road vehicles are excluded. The domestic/international split is determined on the basis of departure and landing locations and not by the nationality of the airline. For many countries this incorrectly excludes fuels used by domestically owned carriers for their international departures.

International marine bunkers: Covers those quantities delivered to ships of all flags that are engaged in international navigation. The international navigation may take place at sea, on inland lakes and waterways, and in coastal waters. Consumption by ships engaged in domestic navigation is excluded. The domestic/international split is determined on the basis of port of departure and port of arrival, and not by the flag or nationality of the ship. Consumption by fishing vessels and by military forces is also excluded and included in residential, services and agriculture.

Investment: All investment data and projections reflect "overnight investment", i.e. the capital spent is generally assigned to the year production (or trade) is started, rather than the year when it actually incurs. Investments for oil, gas, and coal include production, transformation and transportation; those for the power sector include refurbishments, uprates, new builds and replacements for all fuels and technologies for on-grid, mini-grid and off-grid capacity, as well as investment in transmission and distribution. Investment data are presented in real terms in year-2013 US dollars.

Lignite: Type of coal that is used in the power sector mostly in regions near lignite mines due to its low energy content and typically high moisture levels, which generally makes long-distance transport uneconomic. Data on lignite in the *WEO* includes peat, a solid formed from the partial decomposition of dead vegetation under conditions of high humidity and limited air access.

Lignocellulosic feedstock: Crops cultivated to produce biofuels from their cellulosic or hemicellulosic components, which include switchgrass, poplar and miscanthus.

Liquid fuels: The classification of liquid fuels used in our analysis is presented in Figure C1. Natural gas liquids accompanying tight oil or shale gas production are accounted together with other NGLs under conventional oil.

Figure C.1 ▷ **Classification of liquid fuels**

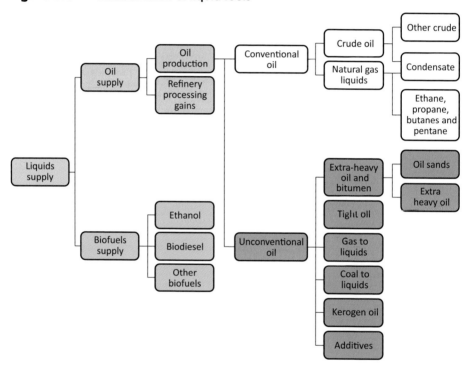

Lower heating value: Heat liberated by the complete combustion of a unit of fuel when the water produced is assumed to remain as a vapour and the heat is not recovered.

Middle distillates: Include jet fuel, diesel and heating oil.

Mini-grids: Small grid systems linking a number of households or other consumers.

Modern energy access: Includes household access to a minimum level of electricity; household access to safer and more sustainable cooking and heating fuels and stoves; access that enables productive economic activity; and access for public services.

Modern renewables: Includes all uses of renewable energy with the exception of traditional use of solid biomass.

Modern use of solid biomass: Refers to the use of solid biomass in improved cookstoves and modern technologies using processed biomass such as pellets.

Natural gas liquids (NGLs): Liquid or liquefied hydrocarbons produced in the manufacture, purification and stabilisation of natural gas. These are those portions of natural gas which are recovered as liquids in separators, field facilities, or gas processing plants. NGLs include but are not limited to ethane (when it is removed from the natural gas stream), propane, butane, pentane, natural gasoline and condensates.

Non-energy use: Fuels used for chemical feedstocks and non-energy products. Examples of non-energy products include lubricants, paraffin waxes, asphalt, bitumen, coal tars and oils as timber preservatives.

Nuclear: Refers to the primary energy equivalent of the electricity produced by a nuclear plant, assuming an average conversion efficiency of 33%.

Off-grid systems: Stand-alone systems for individual households or groups of consumers.

Oil: Oil production includes both conventional and unconventional oil (Figure C.1). Petroleum products include refinery gas, ethane, LPG, aviation gasoline, motor gasoline, jet fuels, kerosene, gas/diesel oil, heavy fuel oil, naphtha, white spirit, lubricants, bitumen, paraffin, waxes and petroleum coke.

Other energy sector: Covers the use of energy by transformation industries and the energy losses in converting primary energy into a form that can be used in the final consuming sectors. It includes losses by gas works, petroleum refineries, blast furnaces, coke ovens, coal and gas transformation and liquefaction. It also includes energy used in coal mines, in oil and gas extraction and in electricity and heat production. Transfers and statistical differences are also included in this category.

Power generation: Refers to fuel use in electricity plants, heat plants and combined heat and power (CHP) plants. Both main activity producer plants and small plants that produce fuel for their own use (autoproducers) are included.

Pre-salt oil and gas: These resources are referred to as such because they predate the formation of a thick salt layer, which overlays the hydrocarbons and traps them in place.

Productive uses: Energy used towards an economic purpose: agriculture, industry, services, and non-energy use. Some energy demand from the transport sector (e.g. freight-related) could also be considered as productive, but is treated separately.

Renewables: Includes bioenergy, geothermal, hydropower, solar photovoltaic (PV), concentrating solar power (CSP), wind and marine (tide and wave) energy for electricity and heat generation.

Residential: Energy used by households including space heating and cooling, water heating, lighting, appliances, electronic devices and cooking equipment.

Self-sufficiency: Corresponds to indigenous production divided by total primary energy demand.

Services: Energy used in commercial (e.g. hotels, catering, shops) and institutional buildings (e.g. schools, hospitals, offices). Services energy use includes space heating and cooling, water heating, lighting, equipment, appliances and cooking equipment.

Shale gas: Natural gas contained within a commonly occurring rock classified as shale. Shale formations are characterised by low permeability, with more limited ability of gas to flow through the rock than is the case with a conventional reservoir. Shale gas is generally produced using hydraulic fracturing.

Solid biomass: Includes charcoal, fuelwood, dung, agricultural residues, wood waste and other solid wastes.

Steam coal: Type of coal that is mainly used for heat production or steam-raising in power plants and, to a lesser extent, in industry. Typically, steam coal is not of sufficient quality for steel making. Coal of this quality is also commonly known as thermal coal.

Tight oil: Oil produced from shales or other very low permeability formations, using hydraulic fracturing. This is also sometimes referred to as light tight oil.

Total final consumption (TFC): Is the sum of consumption by the different end-use sectors. TFC is broken down into energy demand in the following sectors: industry (including manufacturing and mining), transport, buildings (including residential and services) and other (including agriculture and non-energy use). It excludes international marine and aviation bunkers, except at world level where it is included in the transport sector.

Total primary energy demand (TPED): Represents domestic demand only and is broken down into power generation, other energy sector and total final consumption.

Traditional use of solid biomass: Refers to the use of solid biomass with basic technologies, such as a three-stone fire, often with no or poorly operating chimneys.

Transport: Fuels and electricity used in the transport of goods or persons within the national territory irrespective of the economic sector within which the activity occurs. This includes fuel and electricity delivered to vehicles using public roads or for use in rail vehicles; fuel delivered to vessels for domestic navigation; fuel delivered to aircraft for domestic aviation; and energy consumed in the delivery of fuels through pipelines. Fuel delivered to international marine and aviation bunkers is presented only at the world level and is excluded from the transport sector at the domestic level.

Waste storage and disposal: Activities related to the management of radioactive nuclear waste. Storage refers to temporary facilities at the nuclear power plant site or a centralised site. Disposal refers to permanent facilities for the long-term isolation of high-level waste, such as deep geologic repositories.

Regional and country groupings

Africa: Includes Central Africa, East Africa, North Africa, Southern Africa and West Africa.

Caspian: Armenia, Azerbaijan, Georgia, Kazakhstan, Kyrgyz Republic, Tajikistan, Turkmenistan and Uzbekistan.

Central Africa: Cameroon, Central African Republic (CAR), Chad, Congo, Democratic Republic of Congo (DR Congo), Equatorial Guinea and Gabon.

China: Refers to the People's Republic of China, including Hong Kong.

Developing countries: Non-OECD Asia, Middle East, Africa and Latin America regional groupings.

East Africa: Burundi, Djibouti, Eritrea, Ethiopia, Kenya, Rwanda, Somalia, South Sudan, Sudan and Uganda.

Eastern Europe/Eurasia: Albania, Armenia, Azerbaijan, Belarus, Bosnia and Herzegovina, Bulgaria, Croatia, Georgia, Kazakhstan, Kosovo, Kyrgyz Republic, Latvia, Lithuania, the former Yugoslav Republic of Macedonia, the Republic of Moldova, Montenegro, Romania, Russian Federation, Serbia, Tajikistan, Turkmenistan, Ukraine and Uzbekistan. For statistical reasons, this region also includes Cyprus[1,2], Gibraltar and Malta.

European Union: Austria, Belgium, Bulgaria, Croatia, Cyprus[1,2], Czech Republic, Denmark, Estonia, Finland, France, Germany, Greece, Hungary, Ireland, Italy, Latvia, Lithuania, Luxembourg, Malta, Netherlands, Poland, Portugal, Romania, Slovak Republic, Slovenia, Spain, Sweden and United Kingdom.

G-20: Argentina, Australia, Brazil, Canada, China, France, Germany, India, Indonesia, Italy, Japan, Mexico, Russian Federation, Saudi Arabia, South Africa, Korea, Turkey, United Kingdom, United States and the European Union.

Latin America: Argentina, Bolivia, Brazil, Colombia, Costa Rica, Cuba, Dominican Republic, Ecuador, El Salvador, Guatemala, Haiti, Honduras, Jamaica, Netherlands Antilles, Nicaragua, Panama, Paraguay, Peru, Trinidad and Tobago, Uruguay, Venezuela and other non-OECD Americas countries and territories.[3]

---

1. Note by Turkey: The information in this document with reference to "Cyprus" relates to the southern part of the Island. There is no single authority representing both Turkish and Greek Cypriot people on the Island. Turkey recognises the Turkish Republic of Northern Cyprus (TRNC). Until a lasting and equitable solution is found within the context of United Nations, Turkey shall preserve its position concerning the "Cyprus issue".

2. Note by all the European Union Member States of the OECD and the European Union: The Republic of Cyprus is recognised by all members of the United Nations with the exception of Turkey. The information in this document relates to the area under the effective control of the Government of the Republic of Cyprus.

3. Individual data are not available and are estimated in aggregate for: Antigua and Barbuda, Aruba, Bahamas, Barbados, Belize, Bermuda, British Virgin Islands, Cayman Islands, Dominica, Falkland Islands (Malvinas), French Guyana, Grenada, Guadeloupe, Guyana, Martinique, Montserrat, St. Kitts and Nevis, St. Lucia, St. Pierre et Miquelon, St. Vincent and the Grenadines, Suriname and Turks and Caicos Islands.

C

Middle East: Bahrain, the Islamic Republic of Iran, Iraq, Jordan, Kuwait, Lebanon, Oman, Qatar, Saudi Arabia, Syrian Arab Republic, United Arab Emirates and Yemen.

Non-OECD Asia: Bangladesh, Brunei Darussalam, Cambodia, China, Chinese Taipei, India, Indonesia, the Democratic People's Republic of Korea, Malaysia, Mongolia, Myanmar, Nepal, Pakistan, the Philippines, Singapore, Sri Lanka, Thailand, Vietnam and other Asian countries and territories.[4]

North Africa: Algeria, Egypt, Libya, Morocco, Tunisia and Western Sahara (under UN mandate).

OECD: Includes OECD Americas, OECD Asia Oceania and OECD Europe regional groupings.

OECD Americas: Canada, Chile, Mexico and the United States.

OECD Asia Oceania: Australia, Japan, Korea and New Zealand.

OECD Europe: Austria, Belgium, Czech Republic, Denmark, Estonia, Finland, France, Germany, Greece, Hungary, Iceland, Ireland, Italy, Luxembourg, Netherlands, Norway, Poland, Portugal, Slovak Republic, Slovenia, Spain, Sweden, Switzerland, Turkey and United Kingdom. For statistical reasons, this region also includes Israel.[5]

OPEC (Organization of Petroleum Exporting Countries): Algeria, Angola, Ecuador, the Islamic Republic of Iran, Iraq, Kuwait, Libya, Nigeria, Qatar, Saudi Arabia, United Arab Emirates and Venezuela.

Other Asia: Non-OECD Asia regional grouping excluding China and India.

Southeast Asia: Brunei Darussalam, Cambodia, Indonesia, Lao PDR, Malaysia, Myanmar, Philippines, Singapore, Thailand and Vietnam. These countries are all members of the Association of Southeast Asian Nations (ASEAN).

Southern Africa: Angola, Botswana, Comoros, Lesotho, Madagascar, Malawi, Mauritius, Mozambique, Namibia, Seychelles, South Africa, Swaziland, United Republic of Tanzania, Zambia and Zimbabwe.

Sub-Saharan Africa: Africa regional grouping excluding the North Africa regional grouping.

West Africa: Benin, Burkina Faso, Cabo Verde, Côte d'Ivoire, Gambia, Ghana, Guinea, Guinea-Bissau, Liberia, Mali, Mauritania, Niger, Nigeria, São Tomé and Príncipe, Senegal, Sierra Leone and Togo.

---

4. Individual data are not available and are estimated in aggregate for: Afghanistan, Bhutan, Cook Islands, East Timor, Fiji, French Polynesia, Kiribati, Lao PDR, Macau (China), Maldives, New Caledonia, Palau, Papua New Guinea, Samoa, Solomon Islands, Tonga and Vanuatu.

5. The statistical data for Israel are supplied by and under the responsibility of the relevant Israeli authorities. The use of such data by the OECD and/or the IEA is without prejudice to the status of the Golan Heights, East Jerusalem and Israeli settlements in the West Bank under the terms of international law.

Abbreviations and Acronyms

ACC	African Century Case
AU	African Union
APEC	Asia-Pacific Economic Cooperation
ASEAN	Association of Southeast Asian Nations
CAAGR	compound average annual growth rate
CAFE	corporate average fuel-economy standards (United States)
CBM	coalbed methane
CCGT	combined-cycle gas turbine
CCS	carbon capture and storage
CFL	compact fluorescent lamp
CH$_4$	methane
CHP	combined heat and power; the term co-generation is sometimes used
CNG	compressed natural gas
CO	carbon monoxide
CO$_2$	carbon dioxide
CO$_2$-eq	carbon-dioxide equivalent
COP	Conference of the Parties (UNFCCC)
CPS	Current Policies Scenario
CSP	concentrating solar power
CTG	coal-to-gas
CTL	coal-to-liquids
EOR	enhanced oil recovery
EPA	Environmental Protection Agency (United States)
EU	European Union
EU ETS	European Union Emissions Trading System
EV	electric vehicle
FAO	Food and Agriculture Organization of the United Nations
FDI	foreign direct investment
FOB	free on board
GDP	gross domestic product
GHG	greenhouse gases
GTL	gas-to-liquids
HDI	human development index
HFO	heavy fuel oil
IAEA	International Atomic Energy Agency
ICT	information and communication technologies
IGCC	integrated gasification combined-cycle
IMF	International Monetary Fund
IOC	international oil company
IPCC	Intergovernmental Panel on Climate Change
IRP	Integrated Resource Plan for Electricity
LCOE	levelised cost of electricity

LCV	light-commercial vehicle
LED	light-emitting diode
LNG	liquefied natural gas
LPG	liquefied petroleum gas
MER	market exchange rate
MEPS	minimum energy performance standards
NEA	Nuclear Energy Agency (an agency within the OECD)
NGL	natural gas liquids
NGV	natural gas vehicle
NPV	net present value
NOC	national oil company
NO$_x$	oxides of nitrogen
NPS	New Policies Scenario
OECD	Organisation for Economic Co-operation and Development
OPEC	Organization of Petroleum Exporting Countries
PHEV	plug-in hybrid
PIB	Petroleum Industry Bill
PIDA	Programme for Infrastructure Development in Africa
PLDV	passenger light-duty vehicle
PM	particulate matter
PPP	purchasing power parity
PV	photovoltaic
R&D	research and development
RD&D	research, development and demonstration
RRR	remaining recoverable resource
SME	small and medium enterprises
SO$_2$	sulphur dioxide
T&D	transmission and distribution
TFC	total final consumption
TPED	total primary energy demand
UAE	United Arab Emirates
UN	United Nations
UNDP	United Nations Development Programme
UNEP	United Nations Environment Programme
UNFCCC	United Nations Framework Convention on Climate Change
URR	ultimately recoverable resource
US	United States
USC	ultra-supercritical
USGS	United States Geological Survey
WEO	World Energy Outlook
WEM	World Energy Model
WHO	World Health Organization
WTW	well-to-wheel

Part A: Global Trends

Chapter 1: A framework for our energy future

IEA (International Energy Agency) (2013a), *Redrawing the Climate-Energy Map: World Energy Outlook Special Report*, OECD/IEA, Paris.

– (2013b), *World Energy Outlook 2013*, OECD/IEA, Paris.

– (2014a), *World Energy Investment Outlook: World Energy Outlook Special Report*, OECD/IEA, Paris.

– (2014b), *Tracking Clean Energy Progress 2014*, OECD/IEA, Paris.

IMF (International Monetary Fund) (2014), *World Economic Outlook*, IMF, Washington, DC, October.

OECD (Organisation for Economic Co-operation and Development) (2014), *OECD Economic Outlook*, OECD, Paris.

United Nations Population Division (UNPD) (2013), *World Population Prospects: The 2012 Revision*, United Nations, New York.

Chapter 2: Global energy trends to 2040

BGR (German Federal Institute for Geosciences and Natural Resources) (2013), *Energierohstoffe 2013, Reserven, Ressourcen, Verfügbarkeit, Tabellen* (Energy Resources 2013, Reserves, Resources, Availability, Tables), BGR, Hannover, Germany.

BP (2014), *BP Statistical Review of World Energy 2014*, BP, London.

IEA (International Energy Agency) (2013), *Redrawing the Climate-Energy Map: World Energy Outlook Special Report*, OECD/IEA, Paris.

– (2014), *World Energy Investment Outlook: World Energy Outlook Special Report*, OECD/IEA, Paris.

IPCC (Intergovernmental Panel on Climate Change) (2014), *Summary for Policymakers, Climate Change 2013: The Physical Science Basis*, Contribution of Working Group I to the Fifth Assessment Report of the IPCC, Cambridge University Press, Cambridge, United Kingdom and New York, United States.

NEA/IAEA (Nuclear Energy Agency/International Atomic Energy Agency) (2014), *Uranium 2014: Resources, Production and Demand*, OECD/NEA, Paris.

O&GJ (Oil and Gas Journal) (2013), "Worldwide Look at Reserves and Production", *O&GJ*, Pennwell Corporation, Oklahoma City, United States.

USGS (United States Geological Survey) (2012a), "An Estimate of Undiscovered Oil and Gas Resources of the World", *Fact Sheet FS2012-3042*, Boulder, United States.

– (2012b), "Assessment of Potential Additions to Conventional Oil and Gas Resources of the World (Outside the United States) from Reserves Growth 2012", *Fact Sheet 2012-3052*, USGS, Boulder, United States.

Chapter 3: Oil market outlook

BGR (German Federal Institute for Geosciences and Natural Resources) (2013), *Energierohstoffe 2013, Reserven, Ressourcen, Verfügbarkeit, Tabellen (Energy Resources 2013, Reserves, Resources, Availability, Tables)*, BGR, Hannover, Germany.

BP (2014), *BP Statistical Review of World Energy 2014*, BP, London.

IEA (International Energy Agency) (2011), *World Energy Outlook 2011*, OECD/IEA, Paris.

– (2012), *World Energy Outlook 2012*, OECD/IEA, Paris.

– (2013a), *World Energy Outlook 2013*, OECD/IEA, Paris.

– (2013b), *Resources to Reserves 2013 – Oil, Gas and Coal Technologies for the Energy Markets of the Future,* OECD/IEA, Paris.

– (2014a), *World Energy Investment Outlook: World Energy Outlook Special Report*, OECD/IEA, Paris.

– (2014b), *Medium-Term Oil Market Report 2014*, OECD/IEA, Paris.

NEA/IAEA (Nuclear Energy Agency/International Atomic Energy Agency) (2012), *Uranium 2011: Resources, Production and Demand,* OECD/NEA, Paris.

O&GJ (Oil and Gas Journal) (2013), "Worldwide Look at Reserves and Production", *O&GJ*, Pennwell Corporation, Oklahoma City, United States.

US Department of Transportation (2009), *Summary of Travel Trends – 2009 National Household Travel Survey*, US Department of Transportation Federal Highway Administration, Washington, DC.

USGS (United States Geological Survey) (2000), *World Petroleum Assessment,* USGS, Boulder, United States.

– (2012a), "An Estimate of Undiscovered Oil and Gas Resources of the World", *Fact Sheet FS2012-3042*, Boulder, United States.

– (2012b), "Assessment of Potential Additions to Conventional Oil and Gas Resources of the World (Outside the United States) from Reserves Growth, 2012", *Fact Sheet 2012-3052*, USGS, Boulder, United States.

Chapter 4: Natural gas market outlook

BGR (German Federal Institute for Geosciences and Natural Resources) (2013), *Energiestudie 2013, Reserven, Ressourcen und Verfügbarkeit von Energierohstoffen,* (Energy Study 2013, Reserves, Resources and Availability of Energy Resources), BGR, Hannover, Germany.

BP (2014), *BP Statistical Review of World Energy 2014*, BP, London.

Cedigaz (2013), *Natural Gas in the World, 2013 Edition*, Cedigaz, Rueil-Malmaison, France.

Darrah, T., et al. (2014), "Noble Gases Identify the Mechanisms of Fugitive Gas Contamination in Drinking-Water Wells Overlying the Marcellus and Barnett Shales", *Proceedings of the National Academy of Sciences of the United States of America*, Vol. 111, No. 39, Washington, DC.

ICF International (2014), *Economic Analysis of Methane Emission Reduction Opportunities in the U.S. Onshore Oil and Natural Gas Industries*, Environmental Defense Fund, New York.

IEA (International Energy Agency) (2012), *Golden Rules for a Golden Age of Gas: World Energy Outlook Special Report*, OECD/IEA, Paris.

– (2013a), *World Energy Outlook 2013*, OECD/IEA, Paris.

– (2013b), *Redrawing the Energy-Climate Map: World Energy Outlook Special Report*, OECD/IEA, Paris.

– (2014a), *Medium-Term Natural Gas Market Report*, OECD/IEA, Paris.

– (2014b), *World Energy Investment Outlook*, OECD/IEA, Paris.

O&GJ (Oil and Gas Journal) (2014), "Worldwide Look at Reserves and Production", *O&GJ*, Pennwell Corporation, Oklahoma City, United States.

USGS (United States Geological Survey) (2000), *World Petroleum Assessment*, USGS, Boulder, United States.

– (2012a), "An Estimate of Undiscovered Conventional Oil and Gas Resources of the World", *Fact Sheet FS2012-3042*, Boulder, United States.

– (2012b), "Assessment of Potential Additions to Conventional Oil and Gas Resources of the World (Outside the United States) from Reserve Growth", *Fact Sheet FS2012-3052*, USGS, Boulder, United States.

US DOE/EIA (US Department of Energy/Energy Information Administration) / ARI (Advanced Resources International) (2013), *Technically Recoverable Shale Oil and Shale Gas Resources: An Assessment of 137 Shale Formations in 41 Countries Outside the United States*, US DOE/EIA, Washington, DC.

Chapter 5: Coal market outlook

BGR (German Federal Institute for Geosciences and Natural Resources) (2013), *Energiestudie 2013, Reserven, Ressourcen und Verfügbarkeit von Energierohstoffen* (Energy Resources 2013, Reserves, Resources and Availability of Energy Resources), BGR, Hannover, Germany.

IEA (International Energy Agency) (2012), *"Understanding Energy Challenges in India: Policies, Players and Issues"*, Partner Country Series, OECD/IEA, Paris.

– (2013a), *Redrawing the Climate-Energy Map: World Energy Outlook Special Report*, OECD/IEA, Paris.

– (2013b), *Medium-Term Coal Market Report 2013*, OECD/IEA, Paris.

– (2014), *World Energy Investment Outlook: World Energy Outlook Special Report*, IEA/OECD, Paris.

US DOE/EIA (US Department of Energy/Energy Information Administration) (2013), "Coal Stockpiles at Electric Power Plants Were Above Average throughout 2012", *Energy Today*, US DOE/EIA, *www.eia.gov/todayinenergy/detail.cfm?id=9711*, accessed 15 September 2014.

Chapter 6: Power sector outlook

IEA (International Energy Agency) (2014a), *World Energy Investment Outlook Special Report*, IEA/OECD, Paris.

– (2014b), *Energy Technology Perspectives*, IEA/OECD, Paris.

– (2014c), *Seamless Power Markets – Regional Integration of Electricity Markets in IEA Member Countries*, IEA/OECD, Paris.

Chapter 7: Renewable energy outlook

AWEA (American Wind Energy Association) (2014), *U.S. Wind Industry Fourth Quarter Market Report 2013,* AWEA, Washington, DC.

IEA (International Energy Agency) (2013), *World Energy Outlook 2013*, OECD/IEA, Paris.

– (2014a), *The Power of Transformation: Wind, Sun and the Economics of Flexible Power Systems,* IEA/OECD, Paris.

– (2014b), *World Energy Investment Outlook Special Report*, IEA/OECD, Paris.

IRENA (International Renewable Energy Agency) (2014), *Renewable Energy and Jobs – Annual Review 2014*, IRENA, Abu Dhabi.

REN21 (Renewable Energy Policy Network for the 21st Century) (2014), *Renewables 2014 Global Status Report*, REN21 Secretariat, Paris.

RMI (Rocky Mountain Institute) (2013), *A Review of Solar PV Benefit & Cost Studies*, RMI, Boulder, US.

PJM (2014), *Rules and Procedures for Determination of Generating Capability, PJM Manual 21, Revision 11,* PJM, Valley Forge, United States.

Chapter 8: Energy efficiency outlook

Argus (2014), *Weekly Oil Price Reporting, Derivatives and Analysis*, Argusmedia, London.

AT Kearney (2013), *How GCC Smelters Can Continue Growing Profitably*, AT Kearney, Chicago.

BDEW (Bundesverband der Energie- und Wasserwirtschaft e.V.) (2014), *Industriestrompreise – Ausnahmeregelungen bei Energiepreisbestandteilen* (Industrial Electricity Prices – Exemptions for Energy Price Components), BDEW, Berlin.

Broeren, M., D. Saygin and M. Patel (2014), "Forecasting Global Developments in the Basic Chemical Industry for Environmental Policy Analysis", *Energy Policy*, Vol. 64, pp. 273-287.

CEPS (Centre for European Studies) (2013), *Assessment of Cumulative Cost Impact for the Steel and Aluminium Industry*, CEPS, Brussels.

Chateau, J., B. Magné and L. Cozzi (2014), "Economic Implications of the IEA Efficient World Scenario", *OECD Environment Working Papers*, No. 64, OECD, Paris.

EC (European Commission) (2010), *Reference Document on Best Available Techniques in the Cement, Lime and Magnesium Oxide Manufacturing Industries*, EC, Brussels.

– (2011), *Mapping Innovation in the European Transport Sector: An Assessment of R&D Efforts and Priorities, Institutional Capacities, Drivers and Barriers to Innovation*, JRC EUR-24771, EC, Joint Research Center, Seville, Spain.

– (2013), *Competing in Global Value Chains: EU Industrial Structure Report*, DG for Enterprise and Industry, EC, Brussels.

ECEEE (European Council for an Energy Efficient Economy) (2013), "European Competitiveness and Energy Efficiency: Focusing on the Real Issue", *ECEEE Discussion Paper*, Stockholm.

European Climate Foundation (2014), *Europe's Low-Carbon Transition: Understanding the Challenges and Opportunities for the Chemical Sector*, European Climate Foundation.

Eurostat (2014), Gas and Electricity Prices: New Methodology from 2007, Eurostat, *www.epp.eurostat.ec.europa.eu/portal/page/portal/energy/data/database*, accessed 8 July 2014.

Grave, K., and B. Breitschopf (2014), Strompreise und ihre Komponenten – *Ein internationaler Vergleich* (Electricity Prices and their Components – An International Comparison), Ecofys and Fraunhofer ISI, Berlin.

Grimmond, A. (2011), *Energy Subsidies in the Steel Industry*, McLellean and Partners, Paris.

Hasanbeigi, A., Jiang and L. Price (2013), *Analysis of the Past and Future Trends of Energy Use in Key Medium- and Large-Size Chinese Steel Enterprises, 2000-2030*, Lawrence Berkeley National Laboratory, Berkeley, United States.

D

IAI (International Aluminium Institute) (2009), *Global Aluminium Recycling: A Cornerstone of Sustainable Development*, IAI, London.

IATA (International Air Transport Association) (2013), *IATA Technology Roadmap*, IATA, Montréal.

IEA (International Energy Agency) (2009), *Energy Technology Transitions for Industry*, OECD/IEA, Paris.

– (2012), *World Energy Outlook 2012*, OECD/IEA, Paris.

– (2013), *World Energy Outlook 2013*, OECD/IEA, Paris.

– (2014a), *World Energy Investment Outlook: World Energy Outlook Special Report*, OECD/IEA, Paris.

– (2014b), *Energy Efficiency Indicators: Essentials for Policy Making*, OECD/IEA, Paris.

– (2014c), *More Data, Less Energy*, OECD/IEA, Paris.

– (2014d), *The Multiple Benefits of Energy Efficiency*, OECD/IEA, Paris.

– (2014e), Technology Roadmap – Energy and GHG Reduction in the Chemical Industry via Catalytic Processes, OECD/IEA, Paris.

IHS (2013), *2013 World Analysis – Ethylene*, IHS, Englewood, United States.

IIP and IFC (Institute for Industrial Productivity and International Finance Corporation) (2014), *Waste Heat Recovery for the Cement Sector: Market and Supplier Analysis*, IIP and IFC, Washington, DC.

India Planning Commission (2012), *Indian Chemical Industry Five-Year Plan 2012-2017*, Government of India, New Delhi.

Ministry of Steel (2013), *Annual Report 2012-13*, Government of India, New Delhi.

Mizuho (Mizuho Information and Research Institute) (2014), "Energy Conservation Measures and Competitiveness of Japan's Electric Furnace Industry", *Research Note*, Mizuho, Tokyo.

MOHURD (Ministry of Housing and Urban-Rural Development of the People's Republic of China) (2013), Green Building and Green Eco-City Development Plan in the 12th Five-Year Plan, *www.mohurd.gov.cn/zcfg/jsbwj_0/jsbwjjskj/201304/t20130412_213405.html*, accessed 30 September 2014.

NDRC (National Development and Reform Commission of China) (2013), *The Electricity Tariff Document for End-Use Sectors in the North Hebei Grid*, NRDC, *www.zjkyx.gov.cn/km60193/um22o/tmcty?id=597*, accessed 30 September 2014.

OECD and WTO (Organisation for Economic Co-operation and Development and World Trade Organization) (2012), Trade in Value-Added: Concepts, Methodologies and Challenges, Joint OECD-WTO Note.

OECD, WTO, UNCTAD (United Nations Conference on Trade and Development) (2013), *Implications of Global Value Chains for Trade, Investment, Development and Jobs*, Prepared for the G-20 Leaders Summit Saint Petersburg (Russian Federation), September 2013.

Pardo, N., J. Moya and K. Vatopoulos (2012), *Prospective Scenarios on Energy Efficiency and CO_2 Emissions in the EU Iron and Steel Industry*, European Commission, Brussels.

PE Americas (2010), *Life-Cycle Impact Assessment of Aluminium Beverage Cans*, PE Americas, Boston.

PFC (Power Finance Corporation) (2013), *The Performance of State Power Utilities for the years 2009-10 to 2011-12*, PFC, New Delhi.

Platts (2013a), "Asian PET Production Margin Turns Negative Wed", Platts, *www.platts. com/latest-news/petrochemicals/tokyo/asian-pet-production-margin-turns-negative-wed-27092433*, accessed 30 September 2014.

– (2013b), "End of PX's Golden Years as Surplus Exceed 7 million Mt in 2017", Platts, *www.platts. com/news-feature/2013/petrochemicals/asia-paraxylene/index*, accessed 30 September 2014.

SteelConsult International (2013), *Strategies & Realities for Turkish Steel Long Products*, SteelConsult International, Istanbul.

UNCTAD (United Nations Conference on Trade and Development) (2013), *Global Value Chains and Development, Investment and Value Added Trade in the Global Economy*, UNCTAD, Geneva.

US DOE/EIA (US Department of Energy/Energy Information Administration) (2014), *Electric Power Projections by Electricity Market Module Region*, US DOE/EIA, Washington, DC.

World Aluminium (2014), "Primary Aluminium Smelting Energy Intensity", International Aluminium Institute, *www.world-aluminium.org/statistics/primary-aluminium-smelting-energy-intensity*, accessed 30 September 2014.

Worrell, E., et al. (2010), *Energy Efficiency Improvement and Cost Saving Opportunities for the US Iron and Steel Industry*, Lawrence Berkeley National Laboratory, Berkeley, California, United States.

Chapter 9: Fossil-fuel subsidies

ADB (Asian Development Bank) (2014), *Fossil-Fuel Subsidies in Asia – Trends, Impacts and Reforms*, Policy Report, ADB, Manila, forthcoming.

Beaton, C., et al. (2013), *A Guidebook to Fossil-Fuel Subsidy Reform for Policy Makers in Southeast Asia*, IISD/GSI, Geneva.

Burniaux, J., et al. (2009), *The Economics of Climate Change Mitigation: How to Build the Necessary Global Action in a Cost-effective Manner*, OECD Economics Department Working Papers, OECD, Paris.

Chung, R. (2013), *Fuel Subsidy Reform in Indonesia*, Proceedings of the workshop on Innovative Development Case Studies, KDI School/World Bank Institute, Seoul/Washington, DC.

Clements, B., et al. (eds.) (2013), *Energy Subsidy Reform: Lessons and Implications*, International Monetary Fund, Washington, DC.

GSI (Global Subsidies Initiative) (2010), *Measuring Energy Subsidies,* International Institute for Sustainable Development (IISD)/GSI, Geneva.

– (2012a), *Reforming Fossil-Fuel Subsidies to Reduce Waste and Limit CO_2 Emissions while Protecting the Poor*, APEC Energy Working Group Paper, IISD/GSI, Manila.

– (2012b), *A Citizens' Guide to Energy Subsidies in Nigeria,* IISD/GSI, Geneva.

– (2014a), *Comparison of Fossil-fuel Subsidy and Support Estimates,* IISD/GSI, Geneva.

– (2014b), *Energy Subsidy Country Update: Assessing Egypt's Energy Subsidy Reforms*, IISD/GSI, Geneva.

– (2014c), *Indonesia Energy Briefing*, IISD/GSI, Geneva.

IEA (International Energy Agency) (2011), *World Energy Outlook 2011*, OECD/IEA, Paris.

– (2014), *World Energy Investment Outlook: World Energy Outlook Special Report*, OECD/IEA, Paris.

IEA, OPEC, OECD, and World Bank (2010a), *Analysis of the Scope of Energy Subsidies and Suggestions for the G-20 initiative,* prepared for submission to the G-20 Summit Meeting Toronto, Canada, 26-27 June 2010, OECD/IEA, Paris.

– (2010b), *Joint Report by IEA, OPEC, OECD and World Bank on Fossil-Fuel and Other Energy Subsidies: An Update of the G20 Pittsburgh and Toronto Commitments*, OECD/IEA, Paris.

Indonesian Government (2014), *Law Number 12 of 2014 on Amendment to Law Number 23 of 2013 on State Budget of 2014,*Ministry of Finance, Jakarta.

IMF (International Monetary Fund) (2013), *Energy Subsidy Reform in Sub-Saharan Africa: Experiences and Lessons*, IMF, Washington, DC.

Indriyanto, A., et al. (2013), *Fossil-Fuel Subsidy Reform in Indonesia: A Review of Government Communications in 2012*, Indonesian Institute for Energy Economics and IISD/GSI, Geneva.

Kojima, M. (2013), *Petroleum Product Pricing and Complementary Policies: Experience of 65 Developing Countries Since 2009*, Policy Research Working Paper 6396, World Bank, Washington, DC.

Koplow, D. (2009), *Measuring Energy Subsidies Using the Price-Gap Approach: What Does It Leave Out?*, IISD/GSI, Geneva.

OECD (Organisation for Economic Co-operation and Development) (2013), *Inventory of Estimated Budgetary Support and Tax Expenditures for Fossil Fuels*, OECD, Paris.

Perdana, A. (2014), *The Future of Social Welfare Programs in Indonesia: from Fossil-Fuel Subsidies to Better Social Protection,* Briefing Note, IISD/GSI, Geneva.

Plante, M. (2013), *The Long-run Macroeconomic Impacts of Fuel Subsidies*, Federal Reserve Bank of Dallas, Texas, United States.

Rohac, D. (2013), *Solving Egypt's Subsidy Problem*, Cato Institute, Washington, DC.

UNEP (United Nations Environment Programme) (2003), *Energy Subsidies: Lessons Learned in Assessing their Impact and Designing Reforms,* UNEP, Geneva.

– (2008) *Reforming Energy Subsidies: Opportunities to the Climate Change Agenda*, UNEP, Geneva.

World Bank (2009), *Reducing Technical and Non-Technical Losses in the Power Sector*, Background Paper for the World Bank Group Energy Sector Strategy, World Bank, Washington, DC.

Part B: Outlook for Nuclear Power

Chapter 10: Nuclear power today and decisions to come

Cabinet of Japan (2012), *Final Report of the Investigation Committee on the Accident at Fukushima Nuclear Power Station of Tokyo Electric Power Company*, Tokyo.

Cour des Comptes (2012), *The Costs of the Nuclear Power Sector*, Cour des Comptes, Paris.

Dasnois, Nicolas (2012), "Uranium Mining in Africa: A Continent at the Centre of the Global Nuclear Renaissance", *South African Institute of International Affairs*, Occasional Paper No. 122, Johannesburg.

IAEA (International Atomic Energy Agency) (2003), "Scientific and Technical Basis for the Geologic Disposal of Radioactive Wastes", *Technical Reports Series*, No. 413, IAEA, Vienna.

IEA (International Energy Agency) (2014), *World Energy Investment Outlook: World Energy Outlook Special Report*, OECD/IEA, Paris.

IEEJ (Institute for Energy Economics Japan) (2013), *Historical Trends in Japan's Long-Term Power Generation Costs by Source*, IEEJ, Tokyo.

Foratom (European Atomic Forum) (2012), "What People Really Think about Nuclear Energy", January.

Goldemberg, J. (2009), "Nuclear Energy in Developing Countries", *American Academy of Arts and Sciences*, Vol. 1, Cambridge, United States.

MIT (Massachusetts Institute of Technology) (2011), "The Future of Nuclear Power", MIT Study on the Future of the Nuclear Fuel Cycle.

National Diet of Japan (2012), "The Official Report of the Fukushima Nuclear Accident" Independent Investigation Commission, National Diet of Japan, Tokyo.

NEA (Nuclear Energy Agency) (1995), *The Environmental and Ethical Basis of Geological Disposal of Long-Lived Radioactive Wastes*, OECD/NEA, Paris.

– (2010), "Pubic Attitudes to Nuclear Power", *Report No. 6859*, OECD/NEA, Paris.

– (2013), *The Economics of the Back-End of the Nuclear Fuel Cycle*, OECD/NEA, Paris.

NEI (Nuclear Energy Institute) (2014), *Monthly Fuel Cost to US Electric Utilities*, NEI, Washington, DC.

Nicola, S. and J. Johnson (2013), "Nuclear Decommissioning Surge is an Investor Guessing Game", *Bloomberg*, June 17.

UNSCEAR (United Nations Scientific Committee on the Effects of Atomic Radiation) (2014), *UNSCEAR 2013 Report: Sources, Effects and Risks of Ionizing Radiation*, Vol. I (Report to the General Assembly) Scientific Annex A (Levels and Effects of Radiation Exposure due to the Nuclear Accident after the 2011 Great East-Japan Earthquake and Tsunami), United Nations, New York.

US CBO (US Congressional Budget Office) (2008), *Nuclear Power's Role in Generating Electricity*, CBO, Washington, DC.

US DOE/FIA (Department of Energy/Energy Information Administration) (1986), "An Analysis of Nuclear Power Plant Construction Costs", *DOE/EIA-0845*, US DOE/EIA, Washington, DC.

US NRC (Nuclear Regulatory Commission) (2013), *Kewaunee Power Station Post-Shutdown Decommissioning Activities Report*, No. 13-064, US NRC, Washington, DC.

– (2014a), "Status of License Renewal Applications and Industry Activities, *www.nrc.gov/reactors/operating/licensing/renewal/applications.html*, US NRC, accessed 16 September 2014.

– (2014b), *Decommissioning Cost Analysis of the San Onofre Nuclear Generating Station Units 2&3*, No. 164001-DCE-001, US NRC, Washington, DC.

Chapter 11: Prospects for nuclear power to 2040

EC (European Commission) (2012), *Socio-Economic Role of Nuclear Energy to Growth and Jobs in the EU for Time Horizon 2020-2050*, EC, Brussels.

EHRO-N (European Human Resources Observatory for the Nuclear Energy Sector) (2012), *Putting Into Perspective the Supply of and Demand for Nuclear Experts by 2020 within the EU-27 Nuclear Energy Sector*, EC, Brussels.

IEA (International Energy Agency) (2014), *World Energy Investment Outlook Special Report*, OECD/IEA, Paris.

METI (Ministry of Economy, Trade and Industry, Japan) (2012), *Measures to Maintain and Strengthen Nuclear Human Resources,* METI, Tokyo.

NEA (Nuclear Energy Agency) (2013), *The Economics of the Back-End of the Nuclear Fuel Cycle,* OECD/NEA, Paris.

NEA/IAEA (Nuclear Energy Agency/International Atomic Energy Agency) (2014), *Uranium 2014: Resources, Production and Demand,* OECD/NEA, Paris.

PWC (PricewaterhouseCoopers) (2011), *Le Poids Socio-économique de l'Electronucléaire en France,* PWC, Paris.

WNA (World Nuclear Association) (2013), *The Global Nuclear Fuel Market: Supply and Demand 2013-2030,* WNA, London.

Chapter 12: The implications of nuclear power

Andra (2013), *The Cigeo Project – Meuse/Haute-Marne Reversible Geological Disposal Facility for Radioactive Waste,* Andra, Chatenay-Malabry, France.

IAEA (International Atomic Energy Agency) (2003), "Scientific and Technical Basis for the Geologic Disposal of Radioactive Wastes", *Technical Reports Series*, No. 413, IAEA, Vienna.

– (2006), "Storage and Disposal of Spent Fuel and High-Level Radioactive Waste", 50th IAEA General Conference, IAEA, Vienna.

IEA (International Energy Agency) (2015), *Technology Roadmap: Nuclear Energy*, OECD/IEA, Paris, (Forthcoming).

NEA (Nuclear Energy Agency) (1995), *The Environmental and Ethical Basis of Geological Disposal of Long-Lived Radioactive Wastes*, OECD/NEA, Paris.

– (2014), *Radioactive Waste Management Programmes in OECD/NEA Member Countries: Country Profiles and Reports*, OECD/NEA, Paris.

Posiva (2014), "Final Disposal", *www.posiva.fi/en/final_disposal#.VDwCC2eSwa*, accessed 16 September 2014.

Part C: Africa Energy Outlook

Chapter 13: Energy in Africa today

Ackom, E., et al. (2013), "Modern Bioenergy from Agricultural and Forestry Residues in Cameroon: Potential, Challenges and the Way Forward", *Energy Policy*, Vol. 63, Elsevier, pp. 101-113.

AfDB (African Development Bank) (2013), *Development of Wind Energy in Africa*, AfDB, Tunis, Tunisia.

– (2014), *Tracking Africa's Progress in Figures*, www.afdb.org/fileadmin/uploads/afdb/ Documents/Publications/Tracking_Africa%E2%80%99s_Progress_in_Figures.pdf, accessed 19 September 2014.

AfDB, OECD (Organisation for Economic Co-operation and Development) and UNDP (United Nations Development Program) (2014), *African Economic Outlook*, OECD, Paris.

AidData (n.d.), http://aiddata.org/dashboard, accessed 1 September 2014.

AllAfrica (2014), *Mozambique: US $530 million Invested in Rural Electrification*, AllAfrica, 23 April 2014, http://allafrica.com/stories/201404240243.html, accessed 21 July 2014.

Barnes, D., B. Singh and X. Shi (2010), *Modernizing Energy Services for the Poor: A World Bank Investment Review – Fiscal 2000-08*, World Bank Energy Sector Management Assistance Program (ESMAP), Washington, DC.

BGR (German Federal Institute for Geosciences and Natural Resources) (2013), *Energierohstoffe 2013, Reserven, Ressourcen, Verfügbarkeit, Tabellen* (Energy Resources 2013, Reserves, Resources, Availability, Tables), BGR, Hannover, Germany.

Boeing (2013), *Current Market Outlook 2013-2032*, www.boeing.com/assets/pdf/ commercial/cmo/pdf/Boeing_Current_Market_Outlook_2013.pdf, accessed 1 September 2014.

Briceño-Garmendia, C. and M. Shkaratan (2011), *Power Tariffs: Caught between Cost Recovery and Affordability*, World Bank Policy Research Working Paper: 5904, Washington, DC.

Cedigaz (2013), *The 2013 Natural Gas Year in Review*, Institut Francais du Petrole, Rueil-Malmaison, France.

CITAC Africa Ltd. (n.d.), CITAC ADD+ Oil and Gas Database, London.

Department of Energy, Republic of South Africa (2013), *Survey of Energy-Related Behaviour and Perceptions in South Africa, The Residential Sector, 2013*, Department of Energy, Republic of South Africa, Pretoria.

Energy Commission of Nigeria (2013), *National Energy Policy*, Federal Republic of Nigeria.

Escribano, A., J. Guasch and J.Pena (2010), *Assessing the Impact of Infrastructure Quality on Firm Productivity in Africa: Cross-Country Comparisons Based on Investment Climate Surveys from 1999 to 2005*, World Bank Working Paper Series: 5191, Washington, DC.

European Commission Joint Research Centre (2011), *Renewable Energies in Africa*, European Union, Luxembourg.

NEA/IAEA (Nuclear Energy Agency and International Atomic Energy Agency) (2012), *Uranium 2011: Resources, Production and Demand*, OECD/NEA, Paris.

IEA (International Energy Agency) (2014a), *World Energy Investment Outlook: World Energy Outlook Special Report*, OECD/IEA, Paris.

– (2014b), *Africa Energy Outlook: World Energy Outlook Special Report*, OECD/IEA, Paris.

IFC (International Finance Corporation) (2012), *Household Lighting Fuel Costs in Kenya*, Market Intelligence Note, Issue 2, IFC, Washington, DC.

IJHD (International Journal on Hydropower and Dams) (2009), *World Atlas and Industry Guide*, IJHD, Wallington, United Kingdom.

– (2010), *World Atlas and Industry Guide*, IJHD, Wallington, United Kingdom.

IMF (International Monetary Fund) (2013), *Energy Subsidy Reform in Sub-Saharan Africa: Experiences and Lessons*, IMF, Washington, DC.

– (2014), Direction of Trade Statistics, IMF, *http://elibrary-data.imf.org/ finddatareports. aspx?d=33061&e=170921*, accessed 30 July 2014.

IPCC (Intergovernmental Panel on Climate Change) (2011), *Special Report on Renewable Energy Sources and Climate Change Mitigation*, IPCC, Geneva.

Mandelli, S., et al. (2014), "Sustainable Energy in Africa: A Comprehensive Data and Policies Review", *Renewable and Sustainable Energy Reviews* , Vol. 37, Elsevier 37, pp. 656-686.

National Institute of Statistics of Rwanda (2012), *EICV3 Thematic Report – Utilities and Amenities*, National Institute of Statistics of Rwanda.

O&GJ (Oil and Gas Journal) (2013), "Worldwide Look at Reserves and Production", *O&GJ*, Pennwell Corporation, Oklahoma City, United States.

OECD (Organisation for Economic Co-operation and Development) (2014), *African Economic Outlook*, OECD, Paris.

Sanchez, T. (2010), *The Hidden Energy Crisis: How Policies Are Failing the World's Poor*, Practical Action Publishing, London.

SAPP (2013), *Southern African Power Pool Annual Report 2013*, SAPP, Harare, Zimbabwe.

Statistics South Africa (2012), *Income and Expenditure of Households 2010/2011*, Statistics South Africa, Pretoria.

– (2013), *GHS Series Volume V, Energy 2002-2012*, Statistics South Africa, Pretoria.

Sun, Y. (2014), *Africa in China's Foreign Policy*, Brookings, *www.brookings.edu/~/media/ Research/Files/Papers/2014/04/africa%20china%20policy%20sun/Africa%20in%20China %20web_CMG7.pdf*, accessed 30 July 2014.

UN COMSTAT (United Nations Commodity Trade Statistics) (n.d.), UNcomtrade, *www.comtrade.un.org/db/dqBasicQuery.aspx*, accessed 30 July 2014.

UNDP (United Nations Development Programme) (2013), *Human Development Report 2013 the Rise of the South: Human Progress in a Diverse World*, UNDP, New York.

UNECA (United Nations Economic Commission for Africa) (2010), The Case of Transport and Trade Facilitation in Eastern Africa: Challenges and the Way Forward, UNECA, *www.mcli.co.za/mcli-web/events/2010/28apr2010/003b.pdf*, accessed 4 June 2014.

UNEP (United Nations Environment Programne) (2014), Enlighten Initiative, UNEP, *www.enlighten-initiative.org*, accessed 15 July 2014.

UN-Habitat (2013), *Planning and Design for Sustainable Urban Mobility: Global Report on Human Settlements 2013*, UN-Habitat, Nairobi.

USAID (United States Agency for International Development) (2014), USAID Database, STATcompiler, *www.statcompiler.com*, accessed 4 June 2014.

USGS (United States Geological Survey) (2000), *World Petroleum Assessment*, USGS Boulder, United States.

– (2012a), "An Estimate of Undiscovered Oil and Gas Resources of the World", *Fact Sheet FS2012-3042*, USGS, Boulder, United States.

– (2012b), "Assessment of Potential Additions to Conventional Oil and Gas Resources of the World (Outside the United States) from Reserves Growth", *Fact Sheet 2012-3052*, USGS, Boulder, United States.

WEC (World Energy Council) (2010), *Performance of Generating Plant: New Metrics for Industry in Transition*, WEC, London.

WHO (World Health Organization)(2013), Database on use of solid fuels, WHO, *www.who.int/gho/data/node.main.135*, accessed 30 July 2014.

– (2014), *Burden of Disease from Household Air Pollution for 2012*, WHO, *www.who.int/phe/health_topics/outdoorair/databases*, accessed 30 July 2014.

World Bank (2012), Fuel Price Subsidies in Sub-Saharan Africa, *Africa's Pulse*, Vol. 7, World Bank, Washington, DC.

– (2014a), *World Development Indicators*, World Bank, *www.data.worldbank.org/products/wdi*, accessed 30 July 2014.

– (2014b), *Enterprise Surveys*, World Bank: *www.data.worldbank.org/indicator*, accessed 15 June 2014.

Chapter 14: Outlook for African energy to 2040

Beilfuss, R. (2012), *A Risky Climate for Southern African Hydro: Assessing Hydrological Risks and Consequences for Zambesi River Basin Dams*, International Rivers, Berkeley, California, United States.

Chamon, M., P. Mauro and Y. Okawa (2008), "Mass Car Ownership in the Emerging Market Giants", *Economic Policy*, Vol. 23, Issue 54, pp. 243-296.

FAO (United Nations Food and Agriculture Organisation) (2010), *Global Forest Resources Assessment*, FAO, Rome.

Hamududu, B. and A. Killingtveit (2012), "Assessing Climate Change Impacts on Global Hydropower", *Energies*, Vol. 5, Issue 2, pp. 305-322.

IEA (International Energy Agency) (2014a), *Africa Energy Outlook: World Energy Outlook Special Report,* OECD/IEA, Paris.

– (2014b), *World Energy Investment Outlook: World Energy Outlook Special Report*, OECD/IEA, Paris.

IJHD (International Journal on Hydropower and Dams) (2009), *World Atlas and Industry Guide*, IJHD, Wallington, United Kingdom.

– (2010), *World Atlas and Industry Guide*, IJHD, Wallington, United Kingdom.

IPCC (Intergovernmental Panel on Climate Change) (2011), *Special Report on Renewable Energy Sources and Climate Change Mitigation*, IPCC, Geneva.

– (2014), *www.ipcc-wg2.gov/AR5/images/uploads/WGIIAR5-Chap22_FGDall.pdf*, accessed 10 September 2014.

James, R., and R. Washington (2013), "Changes in African Temperature and Precipitation Associated with Degrees of Global Warming", *Climate Change*, Springer, pp. 859-872.

UNEP (United Nations Environment Programme) and INTERPOL (2014), *The Environmental Crime Crisis – Threats to Sustainable Development from Illegal Exploitation and Trade in Wildlife and Forest Resources,*UNEP, *www.unep.org/unea/docs/rracrimecrisis.pdf*, accessed 25 July 2014.

UNPD (United Nations Population Division) (2013), *World Population Prospects: The 2012 Revision*, United Nations, New York.

World Bank (2009), *Environmental Crisis or Sustainable Development Opportunity? Transforming the Charcoal Sector in Tanzania*, World Bank, Washington, DC.

– (2014), *The Economic Impact of the 2014 Ebola Epidemic: Short and Medium Term Estimates for Guinea, Liberia, and Sierra Leone*, World Bank, Washington, DC.

Chapter 15: African energy issues in focus

Department of Energy, Republic of South Africa (2013), *Survey of Energy-Related Behaviour and Perceptions in South Africa, The Residential Sector, 2013*, Department of Energy, Republic of South Africa, Pretoria.

GIZ (Gesellschaft für Internationale Zusammenarbeit) (2014), *Wood Energy: Renewable, Profitable and Modern*, GIZ, Eschborn, Germany.

IMF (International Monetary Fund) (2014), *Mozambique Rising : Building a New Tomorrow*, IMF, Washington, DC.

Jeuland, M. and S. Pattanayak (2012), "Benefits and Costs of Improved Cookstoves: Assessing the Implications of Variability in Health, Forest and Climate Impacts", *PLoS ONE* Vol.7.

Statistics South Africa (2012), *Income and Expenditure of Households 2010/2011*, Statistics South Africa, Pretoria.

US DOE/EIA (US Department of Energy/Energy Information Administration) (2013), *Technically Recoverable Shale Oil and Shale Gas Resources: An Assessment of 137 Shale Formations in 41 Countries Outside the United States*, US DOE/EIA, Washington, DC.

Chapter 16: Building a path to prosperity

AfDB (African Development Bank), OECD (Organisation for Economic Co-operation and Development), UNDP (United Nations Development Programme), ECA (UN Economic Commission for Africa) (2012), *African Economic Outlook 2012, Promoting Youth Employment*, OECD, Paris.

Briceño-Garmendia, C. and M. Shkataran (2011), *Power Tariffs: Caught between Cost Recovery and Affordability*, World Bank, Washington, DC.

IFC (International Finance Corporation) (2012), *From Gap to Opportunity: Business Models for Scaling Up Energy Access*, IMF, Washington, DC.

IMF (International Monetary Fund) (2012), *Fiscal Regimes for Extractive Industries: Design and Implementation*, IMF, Washington, DC.

– (2014a), *World Economic and Financial Surveys, Regional Economic Outlook: Sub-Saharan Africa – Fostering Durable and Inclusive Growth*, IMF, Washington, DC.

– (2014b), *Financial Access Survey*, IMF, *http://fas.imf.org,* accessed 20 September 2014.

Naudé, W. and W. Krugell (2007), "Investigating Geography and Institutions as Determinants of Foreign Direct Investment in Africa using Panel Data", *Applied Economics*, Vol. 39, pp. 1 223-1 233.

Wernick, D., J. Haar and L. Sharma (2014), "The Impact of Governing Institutions on Foreign Direct Investment Flows: Evidence from African Nations", *International Journal of Business Administration*, Vol. 5, No. 2.

World Economic Forum (2014), *The Global Competitiveness Report 2013 – 2014, www. weforum.org/reports/global-competitiveness-report-2013-2014*, accessed 28 August 2014.

World Governance Indicators project (2014),*www.govindicators.org*, accessed 18 September 2014.

The paper used for this document has received certification from the Programme
for the Endorsement of Forest Certification (PEFC)
for being produced respecting PEFC's ecological, social and ethical standards.
PEFC is an international non-profit, non-governmental organization
dedicated to promoting Sustainable Forest Management (SFM) through independent third-party certification.

IEA PUBLICATIONS, 9 rue de la Fédération, 75739 PARIS CEDEX 15
Layout in France by DESK - Printed in France by Corlet, November 2014
(61 2014 03 1P1) ISBN: 978 92 64 20804 9
Photo credits: GraphicObsession